THE
WEEKDAY MISSAL

THE WEEKDAY MISSAL

A NEW EDITION

Weekday Masses for
The Proper of Seasons · Ordinary Time · The Proper of Saints
Occasional Masses · Masses for the Dead
Complete with Readings in One Volume

Illustrations by Mark and Anne Primavesi

Texts approved for use in
England & Wales, Scotland,
Ireland, South Africa

CollinsLiturgical

A Division of HarperCollinsPublishers

HarperCollins*Religious*
77–85 Fulham Palace Road, London W6 8JB

First published in 1982
Reprinted 1998, 2000, 2001
ISBN
Standard, *blue* 0 00 599725 9
  red 0 00 599726 7
  brown 0 00 599730 5
Superior, *blue* 0 00 599727 5
  red 0 00 599728 3
  brown 0 00 599731 3

© copyright compilation and editorial matter, 1975 and 1982,
Wm Collins Sons & Co Ltd

© illustrations 1982 Wm Collins Sons & Co Ltd

Concordat cum originali: John P. Dewis
Nihil obstat: Anton Cowan
Imprimatur: ✠ Philip Harvey, Rt. Rev., V.G., OBE
  Bishop in North London
Westminster, 25 May 1982

Typographical design by Colin Reed
Data capture and manipulation by
Morton Word Processing Ltd, Scarborough, England
Printed in China by Amity

CONTENTS

Acknowledgements — vii
Principal Celebrations of the Liturgical Year — ix
General Instruction on the Roman Missal, ch 1 — xi
Introduction to the Lectionary, extracts — xxvii
Table I: Order for the Readings for the Weekdays in Ordinary Time: Year I — xxxi
Table II: Order for the Readings for the Weekdays in Ordinary Time: Year II — xxxii
General Roman Calendar — xxxiii
A Note on the Illustrations — xlv

WEEKDAY MASSES FOR THE PROPER OF SEASONS
Advent — 3
Christmas Season — 81
Lent — 133
Easter — 263

ORDINARY TIME
Mass Formularies — 400
Readings for Weekdays in Ordinary Time,
    Year I — 437
    Year II — 861

THE CELEBRATION OF MASS
Prayers: Preparation for Mass — 1285
THE ORDER OF MASS — 1288
Prefaces — 1338
Prayers: Thanksgiving after Mass — 1365

THE PROPER OF SAINTS: GENERAL ROMAN CALENDAR — 1369

COMMON MASSES
Dedication of a Church — 1855
The Blessed Virgin Mary — 1858
Martyrs — 1865
Pastors — 1876
Doctors of the Church — 1887
Virgins — 1889
Holy Men and Women — 1894

MASSES FOR VARIOUS OCCASIONS

For the Unity of Christians	1907
Readings for the Unity of Christians	1910
For Peace and Justice	1926
Readings for Peace and Justice	1927
After the Harvest	1936
Readings for After the Harvest	1937
In Time of Famine, Those who Work to Alleviate Famine	1942
Readings for In Time of Famine	1943
For the Sick	1953
For the Dying	1954
Readings for the Sick or Dying	1955
In Thanksgiving	1963
Readings for In Thanksgiving	1964

MASS FOR THE DEAD

Funeral Mass	1977
Anniversary Mass for the Dead	1980
Readings for Mass for the Dead	1982
Readings for Burial Baptised Children	2019
Readings for Non-baptised Children	2029

PROPER OF SAINTS: NATIONAL CALENDARS   2034

Index of Celebrations for the Proper of Saints   2101

ACKNOWLEDGEMENTS

English translation of the Roman Missal, the Roman Calendar, original texts of the Alternative Opening Prayers, music from the Roman Missal © 1973, International Committee on English in the Liturgy Inc (ICEL). All rights reserved.

Extracts from scripture (excepting psalm texts) from the *Jerusalem Bible* version of scripture, © 1966, 1967 and 1968 Darton, Longman & Todd, and Doubleday & Co Inc.

Psalm texts, from *The Psalms, A New Translation*, © copyright 1963 The Grail (England), published by Collins.

The volume follows the editio typica of the Lectionary, revised edition 1981, approved for use in England, Wales, Scotland, Ireland and South Africa.

PRINCIPAL CELEBRATIONS OF THE LITURGICAL YEAR

Year	Sunday Cycle	Weekday Cycle	Ash Wednesday	Easter	Ascension	Pentecost	Corpus Christi	Ordinary Weeks of the Year — Before Lent Until	Week	After Pentecost From	Week	First Sunday of Advent	Year
1997	B	I	12 Feb	30 Mar	8 May	18 May	29 May	11 Feb	5	19 May	7	30 Nov	1997
1998	C	II	25 Feb	12 Apr	21 May	31 May	11 June	24 Feb	7	1 June	9	29 Nov	1998
1999	A	I	17 Feb	4 Apr	13 May	23 May	3 June	16 Feb	6	24 May	8	28 Nov	1999
2000	B	II	8 Mar	23 Apr	1 June	11 June	22 June	7 Mar	9	12 June	10	3 Dec	2000
2001	C	I	28 Feb	15 Apr	24 May	3 June	14 June	27 Feb	7	4 June	9	2 Dec	2001
2002	A	II	13 Feb	31 Mar	9 May	19 May	30 May	12 Feb	5	20 May	7	1 Dec	2002
2003	B	I	5 Mar	20 Apr	29 May	8 June	19 June	4 Mar	8	9 June	10	30 Nov	2003
2004	C	II	25 Feb	11 Apr	20 May	30 May	10 June	24 Feb	7	31 May	9	28 Nov	2004
2005	A	I	9 Feb	27 Mar	5 May	15 May	26 May	8 Feb	5	16 May	7	27 Nov	2005
2006	B	II	1 Mar	16 Apr	25 May	4 June	15 June	28 Feb	8	5 June	9	3 Dec	2006
2007	C	I	21 Feb	8 Apr	17 May	27 May	7 June	20 Feb	7	28 May	8	2 Dec	2007
2008	A	II	6 Feb	23 Mar	1 May	11 May	22 May	5 Feb	4	12 May	6	30 Nov	2008
2009	B	I	25 Feb	12 Apr	21 May	31 May	11 June	24 Feb	7	1 June	9	29 Nov	2009
2010	C	II	17 Feb	4 Apr	13 May	23 May	3 June	16 Feb	6	24 May	8	28 Nov	2010
2011	A	I	9 Mar	24 Apr	2 June	12 June	23 June	8 Mar	9	13 June	11	27 Nov	2011
2012	B	II	22 Feb	8 Apr	17 May	27 May	7 June	21 Feb	7	28 May	8	2 Dec	2012
2013	C	I	13 Feb	31 Mar	9 May	19 May	30 May	12 Feb	5	20 May	7	1 Dec	2013
2014	A	II	5 Mar	20 Apr	29 May	8 June	19 June	4 Mar	8	9 June	10	30 Nov	2014
2015	B	I	18 Feb	5 Apr	14 May	24 May	4 June	17 Feb	6	25 May	8	29 Nov	2015
2016	C	II	10 Feb	27 Mar	5 May	15 May	26 May	9 Feb	5	16 May	7	27 Nov	2016
2017	A	I	1 Mar	16 Apr	25 May	4 June	15 June	28 Feb	8	5 June	9	3 Dec	2017
2018	B	II	14 Feb	1 Apr	10 May	20 May	31 May	13 Feb	6	21 May	7	2 Dec	2018
2019	C	I	6 Mar	21 Apr	30 May	9 June	20 June	5 Mar	8	10 June	10	1 Dec	2019
2020	A	II	26 Feb	12 Apr	21 May	31 May	11 June	25 Feb	7	1 June	9	29 Nov	2020
2021	B	I	17 Feb	4 Apr	13 May	23 May	3 June	16 Feb	6	24 May	8	28 Nov	2021
2022	C	II	2 Mar	17 Apr	26 May	5 June	16 June	1 Mar	8	6 June	10	27 Nov	2022
2023	A	I	22 Feb	9 Apr	18 May	28 May	8 June	21 Feb	7	29 May	8	3 Dec	2023
2024	B	II	14 Feb	31 Mar	9 May	19 May	30 May	13 Feb	6	20 May	7	1 Dec	2024
2025	C	I	5 Mar	20 Apr	29 May	8 June	19 June	4 Mar	8	9 June	10	30 Nov	2025
2026	A	II	18 Feb	5 Apr	14 May	24 May	4 June	17 Feb	6	25 May	8	29 Nov	2026
2027	C	I	10 Feb	28 Mar	6 May	16 May	27 May	9 Feb	5	17 May	7	28 Nov	2027
2028	A	II	1 Mar	16 Apr	25 May	4 June	15 June	29 Feb	8	5 June	9	3 Dec	2028
2029	B	I	14 Feb	1 Apr	10 May	20 May	31 May	13 Feb	6	21 May	7	2 Dec	2029
2030	C	II	6 Mar	21 Apr	30 May	9 June	20 June	5 Mar	8	10 June	10	1 Dec	2030

INTRODUCTION
FROM THE GENERAL INSTRUCTION ON THE ROMAN MISSAL

CHAPTER I

IMPORTANCE AND DIGNITY OF THE EUCHARISTIC CELEBRATION

1. The celebration of Mass is the action of Christ and the people of God hierarchically assembled. For both the universal and the local Church, and for each person, it is the centre of the whole Christian life.[1] The Mass reaches the high point of the action by which God in Christ sanctifies the world and the high point of men's worship of the Father, as they adore him through Christ, his Son.[2] During the course of the year the mysteries of redemption are recalled at Mass so that they are in some way made present.[3] All other actions and works of the Christian life are related to the eucharistic celebration, leading up to it and flowing from it.[4]

2. It is of the greatest importance that the celebration of the Mass, the Lord's Supper, be so arranged that the ministers and the faithful may take their own proper part in it and thus gain its fruits more fully.[5] For this Christ the Lord instituted the eucharistic sacrifice of his body and blood and entrusted it to his bride, the Church, as a memorial of his passion and resurrection.[6]

3. The purpose will be accomplished if the celebration takes into account the nature and circumstances of each assembly and is planned to bring about conscious, active, and full participation of the people, motivated by faith, hope, and charity. Such participation of mind and body is desired by the Church, is demanded by the nature of the celebration, and is the right and duty of Christians by reason of their baptism.[7]

4. The presence and active participation of the people show plainly the ecclesial nature of the celebration.[8] Although at times this participation may be lacking, the eucharistic celebration, in which the priest always acts for the salvation of the people, retains its efficacy and dignity as the action of Christ and the Church.[9]

5. The celebration of the eucharist, and the entire liturgy, is carried out by the use of outward signs. By these signs faith is nourished, strengthened, and expressed.[10] It is thus very impor-

tant to select and arrange the forms and elements proposed by the Church, which, taking into account individual and local circumstances, will best foster active and full participation and promote the spiritual welfare of the faithful.

6. This instruction is intended to give general guidelines for celebrating the eucharist and also norms for each form of celebration. In accord with the Constitution on the Liturgy, each conference of bishops may establish additional norms for its territory to suit the traditions and character of the people, regions, and various communities.[11]

CHAPTER II
STRUCTURE, ELEMENTS AND PARTS OF THE MASS

I. General Structure of the Mass

7. The Lord's Supper or Mass gathers together the people of God, with a priest presiding in the person of Christ, to celebrate the memorial of the Lord or eucharistic sacrifice.[12] For this reason the promise of Christ is particularly true of such a local congregation of the church: 'Where two or three are gathered in my name, there am I in their midst' (Matthew 18:20). In the celebration of Mass, which perpetuates the sacrifice of the cross,[13] Christ is really present in the assembly itself, which is gathered in his name, in the person of the minister, in his word, and indeed substantially and unceasingly under the eucharistic species.[14]

8. Although the Mass is made up of the liturgy of the word and the liturgy of the eucharist, the two parts are so closely connected as to form one act of worship.[15] The table of God's word and of Christ's body is prepared and from it the faithful are instructed and nourished.[16] In addition, the Mass has introductory and concluding rites.

II. Different Elements of the Mass

Reading and Explaining the Word of God

9. When the scriptures are read in the Church, God himself speaks to his people, and it is Christ, present in his word, who proclaims the Gospel.

The readings should be listened to with respect; they are a principal element of the liturgy. In the biblical readings God's word is addressed to all men of every era and is understandable

Introduction xiii

in itself, but a homily, as a living explanation of the word, increases its effectiveness and is an integral part of the service.[17]

Prayers and Other Parts Assigned to the Priest

10. Among the parts assigned to the priest, the eucharistic prayer has precedence; it is the high point of the whole celebration. Next are the prayers: the opening prayer or collect, the prayer over the gifts, and the prayer after communion. The priest, presiding in the person of Christ, addresses the prayers to God in the name of the entire assembly of God's people and of all present,[18] and thus they are called presidential prayers.

11. As president of the congregation, the priest gives instructions and words of introduction and conclusion that are indicated within the rite, proclaims the word of God, and gives the final blessing. He may also very briefly introduce the Mass of the day (before the celebration begins), the liturgy of the word (before the readings), and the eucharistic prayer (before the preface); he may make concluding comments before the dismissal.

12. The nature of the presidential prayers demands that they be spoken in a loud and clear voice so that everyone present may hear and pay attention.[19] While the priest is speaking, there should be no other prayer or song, and the organ and other musical instruments should be silent.

13. As president the priest prays in the name of the whole community. Besides this, he prays at times in his own name so that he may exercise his ministry with attention and devotion. These prayers are said quietly.

Other Texts in the Celebration

14. Since the celebration of Mass is a communal action,[20] the dialogue between the celebrant and the congregation and the acclamations are of special value.[21] These are not only the external signs of the communal celebration but are also the means of greater communication between priest and people.

15. In every form of Mass the acclamations and the responses to the greetings of the priest and the prayers should be made by the faithful. This extent of participation is needed to express clearly and to develop the action of the entire community.[22]

16. Other parts, important in manifesting and stimulating the people's active participation, are also assigned to the whole congregation, especially the penitential rite, the profession of faith, the general intercessions, and the Lord's Prayer.

17. Finally, there are other texts:
   (a) those which constitute an independent rite, such as the

Gloria, the responsorial psalm, the *Sanctus*, the memorial acclamation, and the song after communion;
(b) those which accompany a rite, such as the songs at the entrance, offertory, breaking of the bread (*Agnus Dei*), and communion.

Texts Said Aloud or Sung

18. In texts which are to be said in a clear, loud voice, whether by the priest or by the ministers or by everyone, the tone of voice should correspond to the nature of the text, which may be a reading, a prayer, an instruction, an acclamation, or a song; the tone also depends on the form of celebration and the solemnity of the assembly. The characteristics of different languages and peoples should be considered.

In the rubrics and in the norms of this instruction, the words 'say' or 'proclaim' are used for both singing and speaking and should be understood in the light of these principles.

Importance of Singing

19. The faithful who gather to await the Lord's coming are urged by the Apostle Paul to sing psalms, hymns, and inspired songs (see Colossians 3:16). Song is the sign of the heart's joy (see Acts 2:46), and Saint Augustine said: 'To sing belongs to lovers.'[23] Even in antiquity it was proverbial to say, 'He prays twice who sings well.'

Singing should be widely used at Mass, depending on the type of people and the capability of each congregation, but it is not always necessary to sing all the texts which were composed for singing.

Preference should be given to the more significant parts, especially those to be sung by the priest or ministers with the people responding or those to be sung by the priest and people together.[24] Since people frequently come together from different countries, it is desirable that they know how to sing at least some parts of the Ordinary of Mass in Latin, especially the profession of faith and the Lord's Prayer, set to simple melodies.[25]

Actions and Postures

20. A common posture, observed by all, is a sign of the unity of the assembly and its sense of community. It both expresses and fosters the inner spirit and purpose of those who take part in it.[26]

21. For the sake of uniformity in actions and postures, the

people should follow the directions given by the deacon, priest, or other minister during the celebration. Unless other provision is made, at every Mass they should stand from the beginning of the entrance song or when the priest enters until the opening prayer or collect inclusive; for the singing of the alleluia before the gospel; while the gospel is proclaimed; during the profession of faith and the general intercessions; from the prayer over the gifts to the end of the Mass, with the exceptions below. They should sit during the readings before the gospel and during the responsorial psalm; for the homily and the preparation of the gifts at the offertory; and after communion if there is a period of silence. They should kneel at the consecration unless prevented by lack of space, large numbers, or other reasonable cause.

The conference of bishops may adapt the actions and postures described in the Order of the Roman Mass to the usage of the people,[27] but these adaptations must correspond to the character and meaning of each part of the celebration.

22. The actions include the procession at the entrance of the priest, the bringing forward of the gifts, and the communion. These actions should be carried out with dignity, and the accompanying songs should follow the respective norms.

Silence

23. Silence should be observed at designated times as part of the celebration.[28] Its character will depend on the time it occurs in the particular celebration. At the penitential rite and again after the invitation to pray, each one should become recollected; at the conclusion of a reading or the homily, each one meditates briefly on what he has heard; after communion, he praises God in his heart and prays.

III. Individual Parts of the Mass

a Introductory Rites

24. The parts preceding the liturgy of the word, namely, the entrance song, greeting, penitential rite, *Kyrie, Gloria,* and opening prayer or collect, have the character of beginning, introduction, and preparation.

The purpose of these rites is to make the assembled people a unified community and to prepare them properly to listen to God's word and celebrate the eucharist.

Entrance Song

25. After the people have assembled, the entrance song begins,

and the priest and ministers come in. The purpose of this song is to open the celebration, deepen the unity of the people, introduce them to the mystery of the season or feast, and accompany the procession.

26. The entrance song is sung alternately by the choir and people or by the cantor and the people; or it is sung entirely by the people or the choir alone. The antiphon and psalm of the Roman Gradual or the Simple Gradual may be used, or another song appropriate for this part of the Mass, the day, or the season. The text of such a song is to be approved by the conference of bishops.

If there is no singing at the entrance, the antiphon in the missal is recited either by the people, by some of them, or by a reader. Otherwise it is said by the priest after the greeting.

Veneration of the Altar and Greeting of the People
27. When the priest and the ministers come to the presbyterium, they greet the altar. As a sign of veneration, the priest and ordained ministers kiss the altar; the priest may also incense it.

28. After the entrance song, the priest and congregation make the sign of the cross. Then through a greeting the priest expresses the presence of the Lord to the assembled community. This greeting and the people's response manifest the mystery of the Church that is gathered together.

Penitential Rite
29. After greeting the people, the priest or other suitable minister may very briefly introduce the Mass of the day. Then the priest invites the congregation to take part in the penitential rite, which is a general confession made by the entire assembly and is concluded by the priest's absolution.

Lord, Have Mercy
30. After the penitential rite, the *Kyrie* is begun, unless it has already been included as a part of the penitential rite. This acclamation, which praises the Lord and implores his mercy, is ordinarily made by all, that is, with parts for the people and for the choir or cantor.

Each acclamation is normally made twice, but, because of the nature of the language, the music, or other circumstances, the number may by greater or a short verse (trope) may be inserted. If the *Kyrie* is not sung, it is to be recited.

Gloria
31. The *Gloria* is an ancient hymn in which the Church, assem-

bled in the Spirit, praises and prays to the Father and the Lamb. It is sung by the congregation, by the people alternately with the choir, or by the choir alone. If not sung, it is to be recited by all together or in alternation.

The *Gloria* is sung or said on Sundays outside Advent and Lent, on solemnities and feasts, and at solemn local celebrations.

Opening Prayer or Collect

32. Next the priest invites the people to pray, and together they spend some moments in silence so they may realise that they are in God's presence and may make their petitions. The priest then says the prayer which is called the opening prayer or collect. This expresses the theme of the celebration and by the words of the priest, a petition is addressed to God the Father through the mediation of Christ in the Holy Spirit.

The people make the prayer their own and give their assent by the acclamation, *Amen*

At Mass only one opening prayer is said; this rule applies also to the prayer over the gifts and the prayer after communion.

The opening prayer ends with the longer conclusion:

—if the prayer is directed to the Father:
We ask this (We make our prayer) (Grant this)
through our Lord Jesus Christ, your Son,
who lives and reigns with you and the Holy Spirit,
one God, for ever and ever;

—if it is directed to the Father, but the Son is mentioned at the end:
Who lives and reigns with you and the Holy Spirit,
one God, for ever and ever;

—if it is directed to the Son:
You live and reign with the Father and the Holy Spirit,
one God, for ever and ever.

The prayer over the gifts and the prayer after communion end with the shorter conclusion:

—if the prayer is directed to the Father:
We ask this (Grant this) through Christ our Lord, or
We ask this (Grant this) in the name of Jesus the Lord;

—if it is directed to the Father, but the Son is mentioned at the end:
Who lives and reigns with you for ever and ever, or

You are Lord for ever and ever.

—if it is directed to the Son:
You live and reign for ever.

b Liturgy of the Word

33. Readings from scripture and the chants between the readings form the main part of the liturgy of the word. The homily, profession of faith, and general intercessions or prayer of the faithful develop and complete it. In the readings, explained by the homily, God speaks to his people[29] of redemption and salvation and nourishes their spirit; Christ is present among the faithful through his word.[30] Through the chants the people make God's word their own and express their adherence to it through the profession of faith. Finally, moved by this word, they pray in the general intercessions for the needs of the Church and for the world's salvation.

Scripture Readings

34. In the readings the treasures of the Bible are opened to the people; this is the table of God's word.[31] Reading the scriptures is traditionally considered a ministerial, not a presidential, function. It is desirable that the gospel be read by a deacon or, in his absence, by a priest other than the one presiding; the other readings are proclaimed by a reader. In the absence of a deacon or another priest, the celebrant reads the gospel.[32]

35. The liturgy teaches that the reading of the gospel should be done with great reverence; it is distinguished from the other readings by special marks of honour. A special minister is appointed to proclaim it, preparing himself by a blessing or prayer. By standing to hear the reading and by their acclamations, the people recognise and acknowledge that Christ is present and speaking to them. Marks of reverence are also given to the book of gospels itself.

Chants between the Readings

36. The responsorial psalm or gradual comes after the first reading. The psalm is an integral part of the liturgy of the word and is ordinarily taken from the lectionary, since these texts are directly related to and depend upon the respective readings. To make the people's response easier, however, some texts of psalms and responses have also been selected for the several seasons of the year or for the different groups of saints. These

may be used, whenever the psalm is sung, instead of the text corresponding to the reading.

The cantor of the psalm sings the verse at the lectern or other suitable place, while the people remain seated and listen. Ordinarily the congregation takes part by singing the response, unless the psalm is sung straight through without response.

If sung, the following texts may be chosen: the psalm in the lectionary, the gradual in the Roman Gradual, or the responsorial or alleluia psalm in the Simple Gradual, as these books indicate.

37. According to the season, the second reading is followed by the alleluia or other chant.

(a) The alleluia is sung outside Lent. It is begun by all present or by the choir or cantor; it may then be repeated. The verses are taken from the lectionary or the Gradual.

(b) The other chant consists of the verse before the gospel or another psalm or tract, as found in the lectionary or the Gradual.

38. When there is only one reading before the gospel:

(a) during the time when the alleluia is sung, either the alleluia psalm, or the psalm and alleluia with its verse, or only the psalm or alleluia may be used;

(b) during the time when the alleluia is not sung, either the psalm or the verse before the gospel may be used.

39. If the psalm after the reading is not sung, it is to be recited. The alleluia or the verse before the gospel may be omitted if not sung.

40. Except on Easter Sunday and Pentecost the sequences are optional.

Homily

41. The homily is strongly recommended as an integral part of the liturgy[33] and as a necessary source of nourishment of the Christian life. It should develop some point of the readings or of another text from the Ordinary or the Mass of the day. The homilist should keep in mind the mystery that is being celebrated and the needs of the particular community.[34]

42. The homily is to be given on Sundays and holydays of obligation at all Masses which are celebrated with a congregation. It is recommended on other days, especially on the weekdays of Advent, Lent, and the Easter season, as well as on other feasts and occasions when the people come to church in large numbers.[35]

The homily should ordinarily be given by the celebrant.

Profession of Faith

43. In the profession of faith or creed the people have the opportunity to respond and give assent to the word of God which they have heard in the readings and the homily. It is also a time for the people to recall the teachings of the faith before they begin to celebrate the eucharist.

44. On Sundays and solemnities the profession of faith is to be said by the priest and the people. It may also be said at solemn local celebrations.

If it is sung, this is ordinarily done by the people together or in alternation.

General Intercessions

45. In the general intercessions or prayer of the faithful, the people exercise their priestly function by interceding for all mankind. It is appropriate that this prayer be included in all Masses celebrated with a congregation, so that intercessions may be made for the Church, for civil authorities, for those oppressed by various needs, for all mankind, and for the salvation of the world.[36]

46. As a rule the sequence of intentions is:(a) for the needs of the Church,
(b) for public authorities and the salvation of the world,
(c) for those oppressed by any need,
(d) for the local community.

In particular celebrations, such as confirmations, marriages, funerals, etc., the list of intentions may be more closely concerned with the special occasion.

47. The priest directs the prayer: with a brief introduction he invites the people to pray; after the intentions he says the concluding prayer. It is desirable that the intentions be announced by the deacon, cantor, or other person.[37] The congregation makes its petition either by a common response after each intention or by silent prayer.

c Liturgy of the Eucharist

48. At the Last Supper, Christ instituted the paschal sacrifice and meal. In this meal the sacrifice of the cross is continually made present in the Church when the priest, representing Christ, carries out what the Lord did and handed over to this disciples to do in his memory.[38]

Christ took bread and the cup, gave thanks, broke, and gave to his disciples, saying: 'Take and eat, this is my body. Take and drink, this is the cup of my blood. Do this in memory of me.' The

Church has arranged the celebration of the eucharistic liturgy to correspond to these words and actions of Christ:

(1) In the preparation of the gifts, bread, wine, and water are brought to the altar, the same elements which Christ used.

(2) The eucharistic prayer is the hymn of thanksgiving to God for the whole work of salvation; the offerings become the body and blood of Christ.

(3) The breaking of the one bread is a sign of the unity of the faithful, and in communion they receive the body and blood of Christ as the Apostles did from his hands.

Preparation of the Gifts

49. At the beginning of the liturgy of the eucharist, the gifts which will become the Lord's body and blood are brought to the altar.

First the altar, the Lord's table, is prepared as the centre of the eucharistic liturgy.[39] The corporal, purificator, chalice, and missal are placed on it.

The offerings are then brought forward: it is desirable for the faithful to present the bread and wine which are accepted by the priest or deacon at a suitable place. These are placed on the altar with the accompanying prayers. The rite of carrying up the gifts continues the spiritual value and meaning of the ancient custom when the people brought bread and wine for the liturgy from their homes.

This is also the time to bring forward or to collect money or gifts for the poor and the Church. These are to be laid in a suitable place but not on the altar.

50. The procession with the gifts is accompanied by the offertory song, which continues at least until the gifts are placed on the altar. The rules for the offertory song are the same as those for the entrance song (No. 26). If the antiphon is not sung, it is omitted.

51. The gifts on the altar and the altar itself may be incensed. This is a symbol of the Church's offering and prayer going up to God. Afterwards the deacon or other minister may incense the priest and the people.

52. The priest washes his hands as an expression of his desire for inward purification.

53. The preparation of the gifts concludes with the invitation to pray with the priest and the prayer over the gifts, followed by the eucharistic prayer.

Eucharistic Prayer

54. The eucharistic prayer, a prayer of thanksgiving and sanctification, is the centre and high point of the entire celebration. In an introductory dialogue the priest invites the people to lift their hearts to God in prayer and thanks; he unites them with himself in the prayer he addresses in their name to the Father through Jesus Christ. The meaning of the prayer is that the whole congregation joins Christ in acknowledging the works of God and in offering the sacrifice.

55. The chief elements of the eucharistic prayer are these:

(a) Thanksgiving (expressed especially in the preface): in the name of the entire people of God, the priest praises the Father and gives him thanks for the work of salvation or for some special aspect of it in keeping with the day, feast, or season.

(b) Acclamation: united with the angels, the congregation sings or recites the *Sanctus*. This acclamation forms part of the eucharistic prayer, and all the people join with the priest in singing or reciting it.

(c) Epiclesis: in special invocations the Church calls on God's power and asks that the gifts offered by men may be consecrated, that is, become the body and blood of Christ and that the victim may become a source of salvation for those who are to share in communion.

(d) Narrative of the institution and consecration: in the words and actions of Christ, the sacrifice he instituted at the Last Supper is celebrated, when under the appearance of bread and wine he offered his body and blood, gave them to his Apoostles to eat and drink, and commanded them to carry on this mystery.

(e) Anamnesis: in fulfilment of the command received from Christ through the Apostles, the Church keeps his memorial by recalling especially his passion, resurrection, and ascension.

(f) Offering: in this memorial, the Church – and in particular the Church here and now assembled – offers the victim to the Father in the Holy Spirit. The Church's intention is that the faithful not only offer the spotless victim but also learn to offer themselves and daily to be drawn into ever more perfect union, through Christ the Mediator, with the Father and with each other, so that at last God may be all in all.[40]

(g) Intercessions: the intercessions make it clear that the eucharist is celebrated in communion with the whole Church of heaven and earth, and that the offering is made for the Church and all its members, living and dead, who are called to share in the salvation and redemption acquired by the body and blood of Christ.

(h) Final doxology: the praise of God is expressed in the doxology which is confirmed and concluded by the acclamation of the people.

All should listen to the eucharistic prayer in silent reverence and share in it by making the acclamations.

Communion Rite

56. Since the eucharistic celebration is the paschal meal, in accord with his command, the body and blood of the Lord should be received as spiritual food by the faithful who are properly disposed.[41] This is the purpose of the breaking of the bread and the other preparatory rites which lead directly to the communion of the people:

(a) Lord's Prayer: this is a petition both for daily food, which for Christians means also the eucharistic bread, and for forgiveness from sin, so that what is holy may be given to those who are holy. The priest invites all the faithful to sing or say the Lord's Prayer with him. He alone adds the embolism, *Deliver us;* and the people conclude this with the doxology. The addition to the Lord's Prayer develops the last petition and begs in the name of the community deliverance from the power of evil. The invitation, the prayer itself, the embolism, and the people's doxology are sung or spoken aloud.

(b) Rite of peace: before they share in the same bread, the people express their love for one another and beg for peace and unity in the Church and with all mankind.

The form of this rite is left to the conference of bishops to decide in accord with the customs and mentality of the people.

(c) Breaking of bread: this gesture of Christ at the Last Supper gave the entire eucharistic action its name in apostolic times. In addition to its practical aspect, it signifies that in communion we who are many are made one body in the one bread of life which is Christ (see I Corinthians 10:17).

(d) Commingling: the celebrant drops a part of the host into the chalice.

(e) *Agnus Dei*: during the breaking of the bread and the commingling the *Agnus Dei* is ordinarily sung by the choir or cantor with the people responding; or it may be said aloud.

This invocation may be repeated as often as necessary to accompany the breaking of the bread, and is brought to a close by the words, *grant us peace*.

(f) Private preparation of the prest: the priest prepares himself to receive the body and blood of Christ by praying quietly. The faithful also do this by praying in silence.

(g) The priest then shows the eucharistic bread to the faithful. He invites them to participate in the meal and leads them in an act of humility, using words from the gospel.

(h) It is most desirable that the faithful should receive the body of the Lord in hosts consecrated at the same Mass and should share the cup when it is permitted. Communion is thus a clearer sign of sharing in the sacrifice that is actually being celebrated.[42]

(i) The song during the communion of the priest and people expresses the spiritual union of the communicants who join their voices in a single song, shows the joy of all, and makes the communion procession an act of brotherhood. This song begins when the priest receives communion and continues as long as convenient. The communion song should be concluded in time if there is to be an additional hymn after communion.

An antiphon from the Roman Gradual, with or without the psalm, an antiphon with a psalm from the Simple Gradual, or another suitable song approved by the conference of bishops may be used. It is sung by the choir alone or by the choir or cantor with the people.

If there is no singing, the antiphon in the Missal is recited either by the people, by some of them, or by a reader. Otherwise the priest himself says it after he receives communion and before he gives communion to the congregation.

(j) After communion, the priest and people may spend some time in silent prayer. If desired, a hymn, psalm, or other song of praise may be sung by the entire congregation.

(k) In the prayer after communion the priest petitions for the effects of the mystery just celebrated, and by their acclamation, *Amen*, the people make the prayer their own.

d Concluding Rite

57. The concluding rite consists of:

(a) the priest's greeting and blessing which is on certain days and occasions expanded by the prayer over the people or other solemn form.

(b) the dismissal which sends each member of the congregation to do good works, praising and blessing the Lord.

1. See L 41; E 11; P 2, 5, 6; Decree on the Pastoral Office of Bishops in the Church. *Christus Dominus*, no. 30; Decree on Ecumenism, *Unitatis redintegratio*, no. 15; SRC, EM 3e, 6; *AAS* 59 (1967) 542, 544-545.
2. See L 10. 3. See L 102. 4. See P 5; L 10.
5. See L 14, 19, 26, 28, 30.
6. See L 47. 7. See L 14. 8. See L 41.
9. See P 13. 10. See L 59. 11. See L 37-40.
12. See P 5; L 33.
13. Council of Trent, Session XXII, chapter 1; see Paul VI, Solemn Profession of Faith, June 30, 1968, no. 24: *AAS* 60 (1968) 442.
14. See L 7; Paul VI, encyclical letter *Mysterium Fidei*, September 3, 1965: *AAS* 57 (1965) 764; SRC, EM 9: *AAS* 59 (1967) 547.
15. See L 56; SRC, EM 10: *AAS* 59 (1967) 547.
16. See L 48, 51; Dogmatic Constitution on Divine Revelation, *Dei Verbum*, no. 21; P 4.
17. See L 7, 33, 52.
18. See L 33.
19. See SRC, instruction *Musicam sacram* [=MS], March 5, 1967, no. 14: *AAS* 59 (1967) 304.20. See L 26, 27; SRC, EM 3d: *AAS* 59 (1967) 542.
21. See L 30.
22. See SRC, MS 16a: *AAS* 59 (1967) 305.
23. Sermon 336, 1:PL 38, 1472.
24. See SRC, MS 7, 16: *AAS* 59 (1967) 302, 305.
25. See L 54: SRC, instruction *Inter Oecumenici* [=IOe], September 26, 1964, no. 59: *AAS* 56 (1964) 891; SRC, MS 47: *AAS* 59 (1967) 314.26. See L 30.
27. See L 39.
28. See L 30; SRC, MS 17: *AAS* 59 (1967) 305.
29. See L 33.
30. See L 7.
31. See L 51.
32. See SRC, IOe 50: *AAS* 56 (1964) 889.
33. See L 52.
34. See SRC, IOe 54: *AAS* 56 (1964) 890.
35. See SRC, IOe 53: *AAS* 56 (1964) 890.
36. See L 53.
37. See SRC, IOe 56: *AAS* 56 (1964) 890.
38. See L 47; SRC, EM 3, a, b: *AAS* 59 (1967) 540-541.
39. See SRC, IOe 91: *AAS* 56 (1964) 898; EM 24: *AAS* 59 (1967) 554.
40. See L 48; P 5; SRC, EM 12: *AAS* 59 (1967) 548-549.
41. See SRC, EM 12, 33a: *AAS* 59 (1967) 549, 559.
42. *Ibid.*, 31, 32.

Extracts from
GENERAL INTRODUCTION TO THE LECTIONARY

WEEKDAY READINGS

69. The weekday readings have been arranged in the following way:

1. Each Mass has two readings: the first is from the Old Testament or from an apostle (from a letter or Apocalypse) and during the Easter season from Acts; the second, from the gospels.

2. For the thirty-four weeks of Ordinary Time, the gospel readings are arranged in a single cycle, repeated each year. But the first reading is arranged in a two-year cycle and is thus read every other year. Year I is used during odd-numbered years; Year II, during even-numbered years.

Like the Order for Sundays and the solemnities of the Lord, then, the weekday Order of Readings is governed by similar application of the principles of harmony and of semicontinuous reading, especially in the case of seasons with their own distinctive character.

82. The arrangement of weekday readings provides texts for every day of the week throughout the year. In most cases, therefore, these readings are to be used on their assigned days, unless a solemnity, feast, or memorial with proper readings occurs.[107]

The one using the Order of Readings for weekdays must check to see whether one reading or another from the same biblical book will have to be omitted because of some celebration occuring during the week. With the plan of readings for the entire week in mind, the priest in that case arranges to omit the less significant selections or suitably combines them with other readings, if they contribute to an integral view of a particular theme.

109. 1) The *gospels* are so arranged that Mark is read first (First to Ninth Week), then Matthew (Tenth to Twenty-first Week), then Luke (Twenty-second to Thirty-fourth Week). Mark 1-12 are read in their entirety, with the exception only of the two passages of Mark 6 that are read on weekdays in other seasons. From Matthew and Luke the readings comprise all the matters not contained in Mark. From all three Synoptics or from two of them, as the case may be, all those passages are read that either are

distinctively presented in each Gospel or are needed for a proper understanding of its progression. Jesus' eschatological discourse as contained in its entirety in Luke is read at the end of the liturgical year.

110. 2) The *first reading* is taken in periods of weeks from the Old then from the New Testament; the number of weeks depends on the length of the biblical books read.

Rather large sections are read from the New Testament books in order to give the substance, as it were, of each of the letters of the apostles.

From the Old Testament there is room only for select passages that, as far as possible, bring out the character of the individual books. The historical texts have been chosen in such a way as to provide an overall view of the history of salvation before the Lord's incarnation. But lengthy narratives could hardly be presented; sometimes verses have been selected that make for a reading of moderate length. In addition, the religious significance of the historical events is sometimes brought out by means of certain texts from the wisdom books that are placed as prologues or conclusions to a series of historical readings.

[. . .]

Tables are given to list the way the books of the Old and the New Testament are distributed over the weekdays in Ordinary Time in the course of two years.

At the end of the liturgical year the readings are from Daniel and Apocalypse, the books that correspond to the eschatological character of this period.

CELEBRATIONS OF THE SAINTS

70. Two groups of readings are provided for celebrations of the saints:

1. The proper of Saints provides the first group, for solemnities, feasts, or memorials and particularly when there are proper texts for such celebrations. Sometimes in the Proper, however, there is a reference to the most appropriate among the texts in the Commons as the one to be given preference.

2. The Common of Saints provide the second, more extensive group of readings. There are, first, appropriate texts for the different classes of saints (martyrs, pastors, virgins, etc.), then a great many texts that deal with holiness in general. These are for alternative use wherever the Commons are

indicated as the source for the choice of readings.

83. When they exist, proper readings are given for celebrations of the saints, that is, biblical passages about the saint or the event in the saint's life that the Mass is celebrating. Even in the case of a memorial these readings must take the place of the weekday readings for the same day. This Order of Readings makes explicit note of every case of proper readings on a memorial.

In some cases there are accommodated readings, those, namely, that bring out some particular aspect of a saint's spiritual life or apostolate. Use of such readings does not seem binding, except for compelling pastoral reasons. For the most part references are given to readings in the Commons in order to facilitate choice. But these are merely suggestions: in place of an accommodated reading or the particular reading proposed from a Common, any other reading from the Commons referred to may be selected.

The first concern of a priest celebrating with a congregation is the spiritual benefit of the faithful and he will be careful not to impose his personal preference on them. Above all he will make sure not to omit too often or needlessly the readings assigned for each day in the weekday Lectionary: the Church's desire is to provide the faithful with a richer share at the table of God's word.[108]

There are also general readings, that is, those placed in the Commons either for some determined class of saints (martyrs, virgins, pastors, etc.) or for the saints in general. Because in these cases several texts are listed for the same reading, it will be up to the priest to choose the one best suited to the congregation.

In all celebrations of saints the readings may be taken not only from the Commons to which the references are given in each case, but also from the Common of Holy Men and Women, whenever there is special reason for doing so.

84. For celebrations of the saints:
   a. On solemnities and feasts the readings must be those that are given in the Proper of the Commons. For solemnities and feasts of the General Roman Calendar proper readings are always assigned.
   b. On solemnities belonging to particular calendars, three readings are to be assigned, unless the conference of bishops has decreed that there are to be only two readings.[109] The first reading is from the Old Testament (but during the Easter season, from Acts or Revelation); the second, from an apostle;

the third, from the gospels.

c. On feasts and memorials, which have only two readings, the first can be chosen from either the Old Testament or from an apostle; the second is from the gospels. Following the Church's traditional practice, however, the first reading in the Easter season is to be taken from an apostle, the second, as far as possible, from the Gospel of John.

---

107 See General Introduction of the Roman Missal, no. 319.
108 See ibid., no. 316c. Vatican Council II, Constitution on the Liturgy, no. 51.
109 See General Introduction of the Roman Missal, no. 318.

Table I
ORDER FOR THE READINGS FOR THE WEEKDAYS IN ORDINARY TIME: YEAR I

Week	First Reading	Gospel Reading
1	Hebrews	Mark 1:14–2:17
2	"	Mark 2:18–3:19
3	"	Mark 3:22–4:34
4	"	Mark 5:1–6:30
5	Genesis 1–11	Mark 6:53–8:10
6	"	Mark 8:11–9:13
7	Ecclesiasticus	Mark 9:14–10:16
8	"	Mark 10:17–11:33
9	Tobit	Mark 12:1–12:44
10	2 Corinthians	Matthew 5:1-37
11	"	Matthew 5:38–6:34
12	Genesis 12–50	Matthew 7:1–8:17
13	"	Matthew 8:18–9:17
14	"	Matthew 9:18–10:33
15	Exodus	Matthew 10:34–12:21
16	"	Matthew 12:38–13:30
17	Exodus; Leviticus	Matthew 13:31–14:12
18	Numbers; Deuteronomy	Matthew 14:13–17:20
19	Deuteronomy; Joshua	Matthew 17:22–19:15
20	Judges; Ruth	Matthew 19:16–23:12
21	1 Thessalonians	Matthew 23:13–25:30
22	1 Thessalonians; Colossians	Luke 4:16–6:5
23	Colossians; 1 Timothy	Luke 6:6-49
24	1 Timothy	Luke 7:1–8:15
25	Ezra; Haggai; Zechariah	Luke 8:16–9:45
26	Zecheriah; Nehemiah; Baruch	Luke 9:46–10:24
27	Jonah; Malachi; Joel	Luke 10:25–11:28
28	Romans	Luke 11:29–12:12
29	"	Luke 12:13–13:9
30	"	Luke 13:10–14:11
31	"	Luke 14:12–16:15
32	Wisdom	Luke 17:1–18:8
33	1 and 2 Maccabees	Luke 18:35–20:40
34	Daniel	Luke 21:1-36

Table II
ORDER FOR THE READINGS FOR THE WEEKDAYS IN ORDINARY TIME: YEAR II

Week	First Reading	Gospel Reading
1	1 Samuel	Mark 1:14–2:17
2	"	Mark 2:18–3:19
3	2 Samuel	Mark 3:22–4:34
4	2 Samuel; 1 Kings 1–16	Mark 5:1–6:30
5	1 Kings 1–16	Mark 6:53–8:10
6	James	Mark 8:11–9:13
7	"	Mark 9:14–10:16
8	1 Peter; Jude	Mark 10:17–11:33
0	2 Peter; 2 Timothy	Mark 12:1–12:44
10	1 Kings 17–22	Matthew 5:1-37
11	1 Kings 17–22; 2 Kings	Matthew 5:38–6:34
12	2 Kings; Lamentations	Matthew 7:1–8:17
13	Amos	Matthew 8:18–9:17
14	Hosea; Isaiah	Matthew 9:18–10:33
15	Isaiah; Micah	Matthew 10:34–12:21
16	Micah; Jeremiah	Matthew 12:38–13:30
17	Jeremiah	Matthew 13:31–14:12
18	Numbers; Deuteronomy	Matthew 14:13–17:20
19	Ezekiel	Matthew 17:22–19:15
20	"	Matthew 19:16–23:12
21	2 Thessalonians; 1 Corinthians	Matthew 23:13–25:30
22	1 Corinthians	Luke 4:16–6:5
23	"	Luke 6:6-49
24	"	Luke 7:1–8:15
25	Proverbs; Ecclesiastes	Luke 8:16–9:45
26	Job	Luke 9:46–10:24
27	Galatians	Luke 10:25–11:28
28	Galatians; Ephesians	Luke 11:29–12:12
29	Ephesians	Luke 12:13–13:9
30	"	Luke 13:10–14:11
31	Ephesians; Philippians	Luke 14:12–16:15
32	Titus; Philemon; 2 and 3 John	Luke 17:1–18:8
33	Apocalypse	Luke 18:35–20:40
34	"	Luke 21:1-36

xxxiii

GENERAL ROMAN CALENDAR

JANUARY

1	Octave of Christmas	
	SOLEMNITY OF MARY, MOTHER OF GOD	Solemnity
2	Ss Basil the Great and Gregory Nazianzen,	Memorial
	bishops and doctors of the Church	
3		
4		
5		
6	THE EPIPHANY	Solemnity
7	*St Raymond of Penyafort, priest**	
8		
9		
10		
11		
12		
13	*St Hilary, bishop and doctor of the Church*	
14		
15		
16		
17	St Anthony, abbot	Memorial
18		
19		
20	*St Fabian, pope and martyr*	
	St Sebastian, martyr	
21	St Agnes, virgin and martyr	Memorial
22	*St Vincent, deacon and martyr*	
23		
24	St Francis de Sales, bishop and doctor of the Church	Memorial
25	THE CONVERSION OF ST PAUL, APOSTLE	Feast
26	Ss Timothy and Titus, bishops	Memorial
27	*St Angela Merici, virgin*	
28	St Thomas Aquinas, priest and doctor of the Church	Memorial
29		
30		
31	St John Bosco, priest	Memorial
Sunday after 6 January: BAPTISM OF THE LORD		Feast

*When no rank is given, it is an optional memorial.

February

1		
2	THE PRESENTATION OF THE LORD	Feast
3	*St Blaise, bishop and martyr*	
	St Ansgar, bishop	
4		
5	**St Agatha, virgin and martyr**	Memorial
6	**Ss Paul Miki and companions, martyrs**	Memorial
7		
8	*St Jerome Emiliani*	
9		
10	**St Scholastica, virgin**	Memorial
11	*Our Lady of Lourdes*	
12		
13		
14	**Ss Cyril, monk, and Methodius, bishop**	Memorial
15		
16		
17	*The Seven Founders of the Order of Servites*	
18		
19		
20		
21	*St Peter Damian, bishop and doctor of the Church*	
22	THE CHAIR OF ST PETER, APOSTLE	Feast
23	**St Polycarp, bishop and martyr**	Memorial
24		
25		
26		
27		
28		

MARCH

1		
2		
3		
4	*St Casimir*	
5		
6		
7	**Ss Perpetua and Felicity, martyrs**	Memorial
8	*St John of God, religious*	
9	*St Frances of Rome, religious*	
10		
11		
12		
13		
14		
15		
16		
17	*St Patrick, bishop*	
18	*St Cyril of Jerusalem, bishop and doctor of the Church*	
19	**ST JOSEPH, HUSBAND OF THE BLESSED VIRGIN MARY**	Solemnity
20		
21		
22		
23	*St Turibius de Mongrovejo, bishop*	
24		
25	**THE ANNUNCIATION OF THE LORD**	Solemnity
26		
27		
28		
29		
30		
31		

APRIL

1		
2	*St Francis of Paola, hermit*	
3		
4	*St Isidore, bishop and doctor of the Church*	
5	*St Vincent Ferrer, priest*	
6		
7	St John Baptist de la Salle, priest	Memorial
8		
9		
10		
11	St Stanislaus, bishop and martyr	Memorial
12		
13	*St Martin I, pope and martyr*	
14		
15		
16		
17		
18		
19		
20		
21	*St Anselm, bishop and doctor of the Church*	
22		
23	*St George, martyr*	
24	*St Fidelis of Sigmaringen, priest and martyr*	
25	ST MARK, EVANGELIST	Feast
26		
27		
28	*St Peter Chanel, priest and martyr*	
29	St Catherine of Siena, virgin and doctor of the Church	Memorial
30	*St Pius V, pope*	

General Roman Calendar

MAY

1	*St Joseph the Worker*	
2	**St Athanasius, bishop and doctor of the Church**	Memorial
3	SS PHILIP AND JAMES, APOSTLES	Feast
4		
5		
6		
7		
8		
9		
10		
11		
12	*Ss Nereus and Achilleus, martyrs. St Pancras, martyr*	
13		
14	ST MATTHIAS, APOSTLE	Feast
15		
16		
17		
18	*St John I, pope and martyr*	
19		
20	*St Bernardine of Siena, priest*	
21		
22		
23		
24		
25	*St Bede the Venerable, priest and doctor of the Church* *St Gregory VII, pope. St Mary Magdalene de Pazzi, virgin*	
26	**St Philip Neri, priest**	Memorial
27	*St Augustine of Canterbury, bishop*	
28		
29		
30		
31	THE VISITATION OF THE BLESSED VIRGIN MARY	Feast
	First Sunday after Pentecost: **HOLY TRINITY**	Solemnity
	Thursday after Holy Trinity: **THE BODY AND BLOOD OF CHRIST (CORPUS CHRISTI)**	Solemnity
	Friday following Second Sunday after Pentecost: **THE SACRED HEART OF JESUS**	Solemnity
	Saturday following Second Sunday after Pentecost: *The Immaculate Heart of Mary*	

General Roman Calendar

JUNE

1	St Justin, martyr	Memorial
2	*Ss Marcellinus and Peter, martyrs*	
3	Ss Charles Lwanga and companions, martyrs	Memorial
4		
5	St Boniface, bishop and martyr	Memorial
6	*St Norbert, bishop*	
7		
8		
9	*St Ephrem, deacon and doctor of the Church*	
10		
11	St Barnabas, apostle	Memorial
12		
13	St Anthony of Padua, priest and doctor of the Church	Memorial
14		
15		
16		
17		
18		
19	*St Romuald, abbot*	
20		
21	St Aloysius Gonzaga, religious	Memorial
22	*St Paulinus of Nola, bishop*	
	Ss John Fisher, bishop, and Thomas More, martyrs	
23		
24	THE BIRTH OF ST JOHN THE BAPTIST	Solemnity
25		
26		
27	*St Cyril of Alexandria, bishop and doctor of the Church*	
28	St Irenaeus, bishop and martyr	Memorial
29	SS PETER AND PAUL, APOSTLES	Solemnity
30	*The First Martyrs of the Church of Rome*	

JULY

1.
2.
3. ST THOMAS, APOSTLE — Feast
4. *St Elizabeth of Portugal*
5. *St Anthony Zaccaria, priest*
6. *St Maria Goretti, virgin and martyr*
7.
8.
9.
10.
11. St Benedict, abbot — Memorial
12.
13. *St Henry*
14. *St Camillus de Lellis, priest*
15. St Bonaventure, bishop and doctor of the Church — Memorial
16. *Our Lady of Mount Carmel*
17.
18.
19.
20.
21. *St Lawrence of Brindisi, priest and doctor of the Church*
22. St Mary Magdalene — Memorial
23. *St Bridget, religious*
24.
25. ST JAMES, APOSTLE — Feast
26. SS Joachim and Anne, parents of Mary — Memorial
27.
28.
29. St Martha — Memorial
30. *St Peter Chrysologus, bishop and doctor of the Church*
31. St Ignatius of Loyola, priest — Memorial

General Roman Calendar

AUGUST

1	St Alphonsus Liguori, bishop and doctor of the Church	Memorial
2	*St Eusebius of Vercelli, bishop*	
3		
4	St John Vianney, priest	Memorial
5	*The Dedication of the Basilica of St Mary Major*	
6	THE TRANSFIGURATION OF THE LORD	Feast
7	*Ss Sixtus II, pope and martyr, and companions, martyrs*	
	St Cajetan, priest	
8	St Dominic, priest	Memorial
9		
10	ST LAWRENCE, DEACON AND MARTYR	Feast
11	St Clare, virgin	Memorial
12		
13	*Ss Pontian, pope, and Hippolytus, priest, martyrs*	
14		
15	THE ASSUMPTION OF THE BLESSED VIRGIN MARY	Solemnity
16	*St Stephen of Hungary*	
17		
18		
19	*St John Eudes, priest*	
20	St Bernard, abbot and doctor of the Church	Memorial
21	St Pius X, pope	Memorial
22	The Queenship of Mary	Memorial
23	*St Rose of Lima, virgin*	
24	ST BARTHOLOMEW, APOSTLE	Feast
25	*St Louis*	
	St Joseph Calasanz, priest	
26		
27	St Monica	Memorial
28	St Augustine, bishop and doctor of the Church	Memorial
29	The Beheading of St John the Baptist, martyr	Memorial
30		
31		

SEPTEMBER

1		
2		
3	**St Gregory the Great, pope and doctor of the Church**	Memorial
4		
5		
6		
7		
8	THE BIRTHDAY OF THE BLESSED VIRGIN MARY	Feast
9		
10		
11		
12		
13	**St John Chrysostom, bishop and doctor of the Church**	Memorial
14	THE TRIUMPH OF THE CROSS	Feast
15	**Our Lady of Sorrows**	Memorial
16	**Ss Cornelius, pope, and Cyprian, bishop, martyrs**	Memorial
17	*St Robert Bellarmine, bishop and doctor of the Church*	
18		
19	*St Januarius, bishop and martyr*	
20		
21	ST MATTHEW, APOSTLE AND EVANGELIST	Feast
22		
23		
24		
25		
26	*Ss Cosmas and Damian, martyrs*	
27	**St Vincent de Paul, priest**	Memorial
28	*St Wenceslaus, martyr*	
29	SS MICHAEL, GABRIEL, AND RAPHAEL, ARCHANGELS	Feast
30	**St Jerome, priest and doctor of the Church**	Memorial

General Roman Calendar

OCTOBER

1	St Teresa of the child Jesus, virgin	Memorial
2	The Guardian Angels	Memorial
3		
4	St Francis of Assisi	Memorial
5		
6	*St Bruno, priest*	
7	Our Lady of the Rosary	Memorial
8		
9	*Ss Denis, bishop and martyr, and companions, martyrs*	
	St John Leonardi, priest	
10		
11		
12		
13		
14	*St Callistus I, pope and martyr*	
15	St Teresa of Avila, virgin and doctor of the Church	Memorial
16	*St Hedwig, religious*	
	St Margaret Mary Alacoque, virgin	
17	St Ignatius of Antioch, bishop and martyr	Memorial
18	ST LUKE, EVANGELIST	Feast
19	*Ss John de Brébeuf and Isaac Jogues, priest, and companions, martyrs*	
	St Paul of the Cross, priest	
20		
21		
22		
23	*St John of Capistrano, priest*	
24	*St Anthony Claret, bishop*	
25		
26		
27		
28	SS SIMON AND JUDE, APOSTLES	Feast
29		
30		
31		

NOVEMBER

1	ALL SAINTS	Solemnity
2	THE COMMEMORATION OF ALL THE FAITHFUL DEPARTED (ALL SOULS)	
3	*St Martin de Porres, Religious*	
4	St Charles Borromeo, bishop	Memorial
5		
6		
7		
8		
9	THE DEDICATION OF THE LATERAN BASILICA	Feast
10	St Leo the Great, pope and doctor of the Church	Memorial
11	St Martin of Tours, bishop	Memorial
12	St Josaphat, bishop and martyr	Memorial
13		
14		
15	*St Albert the Great, bishop and doctor of the Church*	
16	*St Margaret of Scotland*	
	St Gertrude, virgin	
17	St Elizabeth of Hungary, religious	Memorial
18	*The Dedication of the Basilicas of Ss Peter and Paul, apostles*	
19		
20		
21	The Presentation of the blessed Virgin Mary	Memorial
22	St Cecilia, virgin and martyr	Memorial
23	*St Clement I, pope and martyr*	
	St Columban, abbot	
24		
25		
26		
27		
28		
29		
30	ST ANDREW, APOSTLE	Feast
	Last Sunday in Ordinary Time: **CHRIST THE KING**	Solemnity

DECEMBER

1		
2		
3	St Francis Xavier, priest	Memorial
4	*St John Damascene, priest and doctor of the Church*	
5		
6	*St Nicholas, bishop*	
7	St Ambrose, bishop and doctor of the Church	Memorial
8	THE IMMACULATE CONCEPTION OF THE BLESSED VIRGIN MARY	Solemnity
9		
10		
11	*St Damasus I, pope*	
12	*St Jane Frances de Chantal, religious*	
13	St Lucy, virgin and martyr	Memorial
14	St John of the Cross, priest and doctor of the Church	Memorial
15		
16		
17		
18		
19		
20		
21	*St Peter Canisius, priest and doctor of the Church*	
22		
23	*St John of Kanty, priest*	
24		
25	THE NATIVITY OF OUR LORD	Solemnity
26	ST STEPHEN, FIRST MARTYR	Feast
27	ST JOHN, APOSTLE AND EVANGELIST	Feast
28	THE HOLY INNOCENTS, MARTYRS	Feast
29	*St Thomas à Becket, bishop and martyr*	
30		
31	*St Sylvester I, pope*	

Sunday within the octave of Chrismas
or if there is no Sunday within the octave, 30 December:

    THE HOLY FAMILY OF JESUS, MARY AND JOSEPH   Feast

xlv

A Note on the Illustrations

The Word is liturgy and scripture contains imagery which is part of its message. Some images are obvious, others are hidden. Even obvious images have many levels of meaning. By using images accessible to human perception, we seek to evoke the divine.

The illustrations in this edition of *The Weekday Missal* seek to explore different visual aspects of the words used, in order to enhance their meaning and reveal the images. The words address us; the images provoke thought; the heart is led to prayer.

The textual sources used for the illustrations are as follows:

page
2   O antiphon for 24 December
80   The lamplighting psalms for Vespers of Christmas Day in the Byzantine liturgy
132   Hosea 6:1-3
262   Mark 16:6
436   Luke 18:17; 17:20-21
586   Matthew 6:26. 28. 30. 33
860   Genesis 1:3; Ephesians 5:8; John 8:12
1186   Luke 10:30-33
1284   Mark 6:41; Matthew 26:26; 6:11
1296   Opening Prayer and Prayer over the Gifts, 19th Sunday in Ordinary Time
1306   Prayer over the Gifts, 20th Sunday in Ordinary Time
1312   Eucharistic Prayer II, invocation of the Holy Spirit
1332   Luke 11:2
1370   John 10:9
1403   Psalm 46:10
1434   Psalm 19:2
1458   John 20:26
1487   Luke 1:28
1524   Galatians 5:16
1574   John 6:48
1616   Acclamation after the Gospel
1679   John 14:27
1719   Acclamation to welcome the Gospel
1761   1 Thessalonians 5:17
1811   Psalm 113:3
1854   John 13:34
1893   Luke 11:28
1906   John 15:5

THE PROPER OF SEASONS
THE SEASON OF ADVENT

RADIANT STAR OF MORNING
SUN OF JUSTICE
ETERNAL LIGHT
COME ENLIGHTEN
THOSE IN DARKNESS & DEATH'S SHADOW

FIRST WEEK OF ADVENT

MONDAY

Entrance Antiphon: Nations, hear the message of the Lord, and make it known to the ends of the earth: Our Saviour is coming. Have no more fear.

Opening Prayer
Lord our God,
help us to prepare
for the coming of Christ your Son.
May he find us waiting,
eager in joyful prayer.

FIRST READING

A reading from the prophet Isaiah 2:1-5
The Lord draws all nations together into the eternal peace of God's kingdom.

The vision of Isaiah son of Amoz, concerning Judah and Jerusalem.

In the days to come
the mountain of the Temple of the Lord
shall tower above the mountains
and be lifted higher than the hills.
All the nations will stream to it,
peoples without number will come to it; and they will say:

'Come, let us go up to the mountain of the Lord,
to the Temple of the God of Jacob
that he may teach us his ways
so that we may walk in his paths;
since the Law will go out from Zion,
and the oracle of the Lord from Jerusalem.'

He will wield authority over the nations
and adjudicate between many peoples;
these will hammer their swords into ploughshares,
their spears into sickles.
Nation will not lift sword against nation,
there will be no more training for war.

O House of Jacob, come,
let us walk in the light of the Lord.

> This is the word of the Lord.

Alternative Reading, for use in Year A when Isaiah 2:1-5 has been read on the First Sunday of Advent.

A reading from the prophet Isaiah   4:2-6
The fruit of the earth shall be the pride and adornment of Israel's survivors.

That day, the branch of the Lord
shall be beauty and glory,
and the fruit of the earth
shall be the pride and adornment
of Israel's survivors.
Those who are left of Zion
and remain of Jerusalem
shall be called holy
and those left in Jerusalem, noted down for survival.
When the Lord has washed away
the filth of the daughter of Zion
and cleansed Jerusalem of the blood shed in her
with the blast of judgement and the blast of destruction,
the Lord will come and rest
on the whole stretch of Mount Zion
and on those who are gathered there,
a cloud by day, and smoke,
and by night the brightness of a flaring fire.
For, over all, the glory of the Lord
will be a canopy and a tent
to give shade by day from the heat,
refuge and shelter from the storm and the rain.

> This is the word of the Lord.

Responsorial Psalm   Ps 121:1-2. 4-5. 6-9. ℟ cf. v.1

> ℟ **I rejoiced when I heard them say:**
> **'Let us go to God's house.'**

1. I rejoiced when I heard them say:
   'Let us go to God's house'.
   And now our feet are standing
   within your gates, O Jerusalem. ℟

2 It is there that the tribes go up,
   the tribes of the Lord.
   For Israel's law it is,
   there to praise the Lord's name.
   There were set the thrones of judgement
   of the house of David. ℟

3 For the peace of Jerusalem pray:
   'Peace be to your homes!
   May peace reign in your walls,
   in your palaces, peace!' ℟

4 For love of my brethren and friends
   I say: 'Peace upon you!'
   For love of the house of the Lord
   I will ask for your good. ℟

Gospel Acclamation cf. Ps 79:4
Alleluia, alleluia!
God of hosts, bring us back:
let your face shine on us and we shall be saved.
Alleluia!

Alternative Acclamations pp.51ff.

GOSPEL

A reading from the holy Gospel according to Matthew 8:5-11
Many will come from east and west to take their places in the kingdom of heaven.

When Jesus went into Capernaum a centurion came up and pleaded with him. 'Sir,' he said 'my servant is lying at home paralysed, and in great pain.' 'I will come myself and cure him' said Jesus. The centurion replied, 'Sir, I am not worthy to have you under my roof; just give the word and my servant will be cured. For I am under authority myself, and have soldiers under me; and I say to one man: Go, and he goes; to another: Come here, and he comes; to my servant: Do this, and he does it.' When Jesus heard this he was astonished and said to those following him, 'I tell you solemnly, nowhere in Israel have I found faith like this. And I tell you that many will come from east and west to take their places with Abraham and Isaac and Jacob at the feast in the kingdom of heaven.'

This is the Gospel of the Lord.

Prayer over the Gifts
Father,
from all you give us
we present this bread and wine.
As we serve you now,
accept our offering
and sustain us with your promise of eternal life.

Preface of Advent I, P1.

Communion Antiphon: Come to us, Lord, and bring us peace. We will rejoice in your presence and serve you with all our heart.

Prayer after Communion
Father,
may our communion
teach us to love heaven.
May its promise and hope
guide our way on earth.

TUESDAY

Entrance Antiphon: See, the Lord is coming and with him all his saints. Then there will be endless day.

Opening Prayer
God of mercy and consolation,
help us in our weakness and free us from sin.
Hear our prayers
that we may rejoice at the coming of your Son,
who lives and reigns . . .

FIRST READING

A reading from the prophet Isaiah 11:1-10
On him the spirit of the Lord rests.

A shoot springs from the stock of Jesse,
a scion thrusts from his roots:
on him the spirit of the Lord rests,
a spirit of wisdom and insight,
a spirit of counsel and power,

a spirit of knowledge and of the fear of the Lord.
(The fear of the Lord is his breath.)
He does not judge by appearances,
he gives no verdict on hearsay,
but judges the wretched with integrity,
and with equity gives a verdict for the poor of the land.
His word is a rod that strikes the ruthless,
his sentences bring death to the wicked.

Integrity is the loincloth round his waist,
faithfulness the belt about his hips.

The wolf lives with the lamb,
the panther lies down with the kid,
calf and lion cub feed together
with a little boy to lead them.
The cow and the bear make friends,
their young lie down together.
The lion eats straw like the ox.
The infant plays over the cobra's hole;
into the viper's lair
the young child puts his hand.
They do no hurt, no harm,
on all my holy mountain,
for the country is filled with the knowledge of the Lord
as the waters swell the sea.

That day, the root of Jesse
shall stand as a signal to the peoples.
It will be sought out by the nations
and its home will be glorious.

This is the word of the Lord.

Responsorial Psalm   Ps 71:1-2. 7-8. 12-13. 17. R/ cf. v.7
> R/ **In his days justice shall flourish
> and peace till the moon fails.**

1 O God, give your judgement to the king,
to a king's son your justice,
that he may judge your people in justice
and your poor in right judgement.   R/

2 In his days justice shall flourish
and peace till the moon fails.

He shall rule from sea to sea,
from the Great River to earth's bounds.

℟ **In his days justice shall flourish
and peace till the morn fails.**

3 For he shall save the poor when they cry
and the needy who are helpless.
He will have pity on the weak
and save the lives of the poor.   ℟

4 May his name be blessed for ever
and endure like the sun.
Every tribe shall be blessed in him,
all nations bless his name.   ℟

Gospel Acclamation   Ps 84:8
Alleluia, alleluia!
Let us see, O Lord, your mercy
and give us your saving help.
Alleluia!

or

Alleluia, alleluia!
Behold, our Lord will come with power
and will enlighten the eyes of his servants.
Alleluia!

GOSPEL

A reading from the holy Gospel according to Luke   10:21-24
Jesus is filled with joy by the Holy Spirit.

Filled with joy by the Holy Spirit, Jesus said, 'I bless you, Father, Lord of heaven and of earth, for hiding these things from the learned and the clever and revealing them to mere children. Yes, Father, for that is what it pleased you to do. Everything has been entrusted to me by my Father; and no one knows who the Son is except the Father, and who the Father is except the Son and those to whom the Son chooses to reveal him.

Then turning to his disciples he spoke to them in private, 'Happy the eyes that see what you see, for I tell you that many prophets and kings wanted to see what you see, and never saw it; to hear what you hear, and never heard it.'

This is the Gospel of the Lord.

Prayer over the Gifts
Lord,
we are nothing without you.
As you sustain us with your mercy,
receive our prayers and offerings.

Preface of Advent I, P1.

Communion Antiphon: The Lord is just; he will award the crown of justice to all who have longed for his coming.

Prayer after Communion
Father,
you give us food from heaven.
By our sharing in this mystery,
teach us to judge wisely the things of earth
and to love the things of heaven.

WEDNESDAY

Entrance Antiphon: The Lord is coming and will not delay; he will bring every hidden thing to light and reveal himself to every nation.

Opening Prayer
Lord our God,
grant that we may be ready
to receive Christ when he comes in glory
and to share in the banquet of heaven,
where he lives and reigns . . .

FIRST READING

A reading from the prophet Isaiah   25:6-10
The Lord invites us to his banquet and wipes away the tears from every cheek.

On this mountain,
the Lord of hosts will prepare for all peoples
a banquet of rich food, a banquet of fine wines,
of food rich and juicy, of fine strained wines.
On this mountain he will remove
the mourning veil covering all peoples,

and the shroud enwrapping all nations,
he will destroy Death for ever.
The Lord God will wipe away
the tears from every cheek;
he will take away his people's shame
everywhere on earth,
for the Lord has said so.
That day, it will be said: See, this is our God
in whom we hoped for salvation;
the Lord is the one in whom we hoped.
We exult and we rejoice
that he has saved us;
for the hand of the Lord
rests on this mountain.

This is the word of the Lord.

Responsional Psalm Ps 22. ℟ v.6

℟ **In the Lord's own house shall I dwell for ever and ever.**

1 The Lord is my shepherd;
there is nothing I shall want.
Fresh and green are the pastures
where he gives me repose.
Near restful waters he leads me
to revive my drooping spirit. ℟

2 He guides me along the right path;
he is true to his name.
If I should walk in the valley of darkness
no evil would I fear.
You are there with your crook and your staff;
with these you give me comfort. ℟

3 You have prepared a banquet for me
in the sight of my foes.
My head you have anointed with oil;
my cup is overflowing. ℟

4 Surely goodness and kindness shall follow me
all the days of my life.
In the Lord's own house shall I dwell
for ever and ever. ℟

Gospel Acclamation
Is 33:22
Alleluia, alleluia!
The Lord is our judge, the Lord our lawgiver,
the Lord our king and our saviour.
Alleluia!

or

Alleluia, alleluia!
Look, the Lord will come to save his people.
Blessed those who are ready to meet him.
Alleluia!

GOSPEL

A reading from the holy Gospel according to Matthew 15:29-37
Jesus cures many and multiplies the loaves.

Jesus reached the shores of the Sea of Galilee, and he went up into the hills. He sat there, and large crowds came to him bringing the lame, the crippled, the blind, the dumb and many others; these they put down at his feet, and he cured them. The crowds were astonished to see the dumb speaking, the cripples whole again, the lame walking and the blind with their sight, and they praised the God of Israel.

But Jesus called his disciples to him and said, 'I feel sorry for all these people; they have been with me for three days now and have nothing to eat. I do not want to send them off hungry, they might collapse on the way.' The disciples said to him, 'Where could we get enough bread in this deserted place to feed such a crowd?' Jesus said to them, 'How many loaves have you?' 'Seven' they said 'and a few small fish.' Then he instructed the crowd to sit down on the ground, and he took the seven loaves and the fish, and he gave thanks and broke them and handed them to the disciples who gave them to the crowds. They all ate as much as they wanted, and they collected what was left of the scraps, seven baskets full.

This is the Gospel of the Lord.

Prayer over the Gifts
Lord,
may the gift we offer in faith and love
be a continual sacrifice in your honour
and truly become our eucharist and our salvation.

Preface of Advent I, P1.

Communion Antiphon: The Lord our God comes in strength and will fill his servants with joy.

Prayer after Communion
God of mercy,
may this eucharist bring us your divine help,
free us from our sins,
and prepare us for the birthday of our Saviour,
who is Lord for ever and ever.

THURSDAY

Entrance Antiphon: Lord, you are near, and all your commandments are just; long have I known that you decreed them for ever.

Opening Prayer
Father,
we need your help.
Free us from sin and bring us to life.
Support us by your power.

FIRST READING

A reading from the prophet Isaiah　　　　　　　　　　26:1-6
Let the upright nation come in, she, the faithful one.

That day, this song will be sung in the land of Judah:
We have a strong city;
to guard us he has set
wall and rampart about us.
Open the gates! Let the upright nation come in,
she, the faithful one
whose mind is steadfast, who keeps the peace,
because she trusts in you.
Trust in the Lord for ever,
for the Lord is the everlasting Rock;
he has brought low those who lived high up
in the steep citadel;
he brings it down, brings it down to the ground,

flings it down in the dust:
the feet of the lowly, the footsteps of the poor
trample on it.

   This is the word of the Lord.

Responsorial Psalm   Ps 117:1. 8-9. 19-21. 25-27. R̸ v.26
   R̸ **Blessed in the name of the Lord
   is he who comes.**

or

   R̸ **Alleluia!**

1 Give thanks to the Lord for he is good,
   for his love has no end.
   It is better to take refuge in the Lord
   than to trust in men:
   it is better to take refuge in the Lord
   than to trust in princes.   R̸

2 Open to me the gates of holiness:
   I will enter and give thanks.
   This is the Lord's own gate
   where the just may enter
   I will thank you for you have given answer
   and you are my saviour.   R̸

3 O Lord, grant us salvation;
   O Lord, grant success.
   Blessed in the name of the Lord
   is he who comes.
   We bless you from the house of the Lord;
   the Lord God is our light.   R̸

Gospel Acclamation   Is 40:9-10
   Alleluia, alleluia!
   Shout with a loud voice, joyful messenger to Jerusalem.
   Here is the Lord God coming with power.
   Alleluia!

or   Is 55:6

   Alleluia, alleluia!
   Seek the Lord while he is still to be found,
   call to him while he is still near.
   Alleluia!

First Week of Advent: Thursday

GOSPEL

A reading from the holy Gospel according to Matthew 7:21. 24-27

The person who does the will of my Father will enter the kingdom of heaven.

Jesus said to his disciples: 'It is not those who say to me, "Lord, Lord", who will enter the kingdom of heaven, but the person who does the will of my Father in heaven.

'Therefore, everyone who listens to these words of mine and acts on them will be like a sensible man who built his house on rock. Rain came down, floods rose, gales blew and hurled themselves against that house, and it did not fall: it was founded on rock. But everyone who listens to these words of mine and does not act on them will be like a stupid man who built his house on sand. Rain came down, floods rose, gales blew and struck that house, and it fell; and what a fall it had!'

This is the Gospel of the Lord.

Prayer over the Gifts
Father,
from all you give us
we present this bread and wine.
As we serve you now,
accept our offering
and sustain us with your promise of eternal life.

Preface of Advent I, P1.

Communion Antiphon: Let our lives be honest and holy in this present age, as we wait for the happiness to come when our great God reveals himself in glory.

Prayer after Communion
Father,
may our communion
teach us to love heaven.
May its promise and hope
guide our way on earth.

FRIDAY

Entrance Antiphon: The Lord is coming from heaven in splendour to visit his people, and bring them peace and eternal life.

Opening Prayer
Jesus, our Lord,
save us from our sins.
Come, protect us from all dangers
and lead us to salvation,
for you live and reign . . .

FIRST READING

A reading from the prophet Isaiah 29:17-24
That day the eyes of the blind will see.

The Lord says this:

In a short time, a very short time,
shall not Lebanon become fertile land
and fertile land turn into forest?
The deaf, that day,
will hear the words of a book
and, after shadow and darkness,
the eyes of the blind will see.

But the lowly will rejoice in the Lord even more
and the poorest exult in the Holy One of Israel;
for tyrants shall be no more, and scoffers vanish,
and all be destroyed who are disposed to do evil:

those who gossip to incriminate others,
those who try at the gate to trip the arbitrator
and get the upright man's case dismissed for groundless
    reasons.

Therefore the Lord speaks,
the God of the House of Jacob,
Abraham's redeemer:
No longer shall Jacob be ashamed,
no more shall his face grow pale,
for he shall see what my hands have done in his midst,
he shall hold my name holy.
They will hallow the Holy One of Jacob,
stand in awe of the God of Israel.

First Week of Advent: Friday

Erring spirits will learn wisdom
and murmurers accept instruction.

This is the word of the Lord.

Responsional Psalm
Ps 26:1. 4. 13-14. ℟ v.1

℟ **The Lord is my light and my help.**

1. The Lord is my light and my help;
   whom shall I fear?
   The Lord is the stronghold of my life;
   before whom shall I shrink? ℟

2. There is one thing I ask of the Lord,
   for this I long,
   to live in the house of the Lord,
   all the days of my life,
   to savour the sweetness of the Lord,
   to behold his temple. ℟

3. I am sure I shall see the Lord's goodness
   in the land of the living.
   Hope in him, hold firm and take heart.
   Hope in the Lord! ℟

Gospel Acclamation
cf. Is 45:8

Alleluia, alleluia!
Send victory like a dew, you heavens,
and let the clouds rain it down.
Let the earth open and bring forth the saviour.
Alleluia!

or

Alleluia, alleluia!
Behold, our Lord will come with power
and will enlighten the eyes of his servants.
Alleluia!

GOSPEL

A reading from the holy Gospel according to Matthew 9:27-31
Two blind men who believe in Jesus are cured.

As Jesus went on his way two blind men followed him shouting, 'Take pity on us, Son of David.' And when Jesus reached the house the blind men came up with him and he said to them, 'Do you believe I can do this?' They said, 'Sir, we do.' Then he touched their eyes saying, 'Your faith deserves it, so let this be done for you.' And their sight returned. Then Jesus sternly warned them, 'Take care that no one learns about this.' But when they had gone, they talked about him all over the countryside.

This is the Gospel of the Lord.

Prayer over the Gifts
Lord,
we are nothing without you.
As you sustain us with your mercy,
receive our prayers and offerings.

Preface of Advent I, P1.

Communion Antiphon: We are waiting for our Saviour, the Lord Jesus Christ; he will transfigure our lowly bodies into copies of his own glorious body.

Prayer after Communion
Father,
you give us food from heaven.
By our sharing in this mystery
teach us to judge wisely the things of earth
and to love the things of heaven.

SATURDAY

Entrance Antiphon: Come, Lord, from your cherubim throne; let us see your face, and we shall be saved.

Opening Prayer
God our Father,
you loved the world so much
you gave your only Son to free us
from the ancient power of sin and death.
Help us who wait for his coming,
and lead us to true liberty.

First Week of Advent: Saturday

FIRST READING

A reading from the prophet Isaiah   30:19-21. 23-26
He will be gracious to you when he hears your cry.

Thus says the Lord God, the Holy One of Israel:
People of Zion, you will live in Jerusalem and weep no more. He will be gracious to you when he hears your cry; when he hears he will answer. When the Lord has given you the bread of suffering and the water of distress, he who is your teacher will hide no longer, and you will see your teacher with your own eyes. Whether you turn to right or left, your ears will hear these words behind you, 'This is the way, follow it.' He will send rain for the seed you sow in the ground, and the bread that the ground provides will be rich and nourishing. Your cattle will graze, that day, in wide pastures. Oxen and donkeys that till the ground will eat a salted fodder, winnowed with shovel and fork. On every lofty mountain, on every high hill there will be streams and watercourses, on the day of the great slaughter when the strongholds fall. Then moonlight will be bright as sunlight and sunlight itself be seven times brighter – like the light of seven days in one – on the day the Lord dresses the wound of his people and heals the bruises his blows have left.

This is the word of the Lord.

Responsorial Psalm   Ps 146:1-6. ℟ Is 30:18

  ℟ **Happy are all who hope in the Lord.**

or

  ℟ **Alleluia!**

1. Praise the Lord for he is good;
   sing to our God for he is loving:
   to him our praise is due.
   The Lord builds up Jerusalem
   and brings back Israel's exiles. ℟

2. He heals the broken-hearted,
   he binds up all their wounds.
   He fixes the number of the stars;
   he calls each one by its name. ℟

3. Our Lord is great and almighty;
   his wisdom can never be measured.
   The Lord raises the lowly;
   he humbles the wicked in the dust. ℟

First Week of Advent: Saturday

Gospel Acclamation   Is 55:6
Alleluia, alleluia!
Seek the Lord while he is still to be found,
call to him while he is still near.
Alleluia!

or   Is 33:22
Alleluia, alleluia!
The Lord is our judge, the Lord our lawgiver,
the Lord our king and our saviour.
Alleluia!

GOSPEL

A reading from the holy Gospel according to Matthew

9:35 – 10:1. 6-8

When he saw the crowds he felt sorry for them.

Jesus made a tour through all the towns and villages, teaching in their synagogues, proclaiming the Good News of the kingdom and curing all kinds of diseases and sickness.

And when he saw the crowds he felt sorry for them because they were harassed and dejected, like sheep without a shepherd. Then he said to his disciples, 'The harvest is rich but the labourers are few, so ask the Lord of the harvest to send labourers to his harvest.'

He summoned his twelve disciples, and gave them authority over unclean spirits with power to cast them out and to cure all kinds of diseases and sickness. These twelve Jesus sent out, instructing them as follows: 'Go rather to the lost sheep of the House of Israel. And as you go, proclaim that the kingdom of heaven is close at hand. Cure the sick, raise the dead, cleanse the lepers, cast out devils. You received without charge, give without charge.'

This is the Gospel of the Lord.

Prayer over the Gifts
Lord,
may the gift we offer in faith and love
be a continual sacrifice in your honour
and truly become our eucharist and our salvation.

Preface of Advent I, P1.

Communion Antiphon: I am coming quickly, says the Lord, and will repay each man according to his deeds.

Prayer after Communion
God of mercy,
may this eucharist bring us your divine help,
free us from our sins,
and prepare us for the birthday of our Saviour,
who is Lord for ever and ever.

SECOND WEEK OF ADVENT

MONDAY

Entrance Antiphon: Nations, hear the message of the Lord, and make it known to the ends of the earth: Our Saviour is coming. Have no more fear.

Opening Prayer
Lord,
free us from our sins and make us whole.
Hear our prayer,
and prepare us to celebrate the incarnation of your Son,
who lives and reigns . . .

FIRST READING

A reading from the prophet Isaiah 35:1-10

God himself is coming to save you.

Let the wilderness and the dry-lands exult,
let the wasteland rejoice and bloom,
let it bring forth flowers like the jonquil,
let it rejoice and sing for joy.

The glory of Lebanon is bestowed on it,
the splendour of Carmel and Sharon;
they shall see the glory of the Lord,
the splendour of our God.

Strengthen all weary hands,
steady all trembling knees
and say to all faint hearts,

Second Week of Advent: Monday

'Courage! Do not be afraid.

'Look, your God is coming,
vengeance is coming,
the retribution of God;
he is coming to save you.'

Then the eyes of the blind shall be opened,
the ears of the deaf unsealed,
then the lame shall leap like a deer
and the tongues of the dumb sing for joy;

for water gushes in the desert,
streams in the wasteland,
the scorched earth becomes a lake,
the parched land springs of water.

The lairs where the jackals used to live
become thickets of reed and papyrus.

And through it will run a highway undefiled
which shall be called the Sacred Way;
the unclean may not travel by it,
nor fools stray along it.

No lion will be there
nor any fierce beast roam about it,
but the redeemed will walk there,
for those the Lord has ransomed shall return.

They will come to Zion shouting for joy,
everlasting joy on their faces;
joy and gladness will go with them
and sorrow and lament be ended.

    This is the word of the Lord.

Responsorial Psalm   Ps 84:9-14. R̷ Is 35:4

  R̷ **Look, our God is coming to save us.**

1 I will hear what the Lord God has to say,
   a voice that speaks of peace,
   peace for his people.
   His help is near for those who fear him
   and his glory will dwell in our land.   R̷

2 Mercy and faithfulness have met;
   justice and peace have embraced.

Faithfulness shall spring from the earth
and justice look down from heaven.

℟ **Look, our God is coming to save us.**

3 The Lord will make us prosper
and our earth shall yield its fruit.
Justice shall march before him
and peace shall follow his steps. ℟

Gospel Acclamation   Lk 3:4. 6

Alleluia, alleluia!
Prepare a way for the Lord,
make his paths straight.
And all mankind shall see the salvation of God.
Alleluia!

or

Alleluia, alleluia!
See, the king, the Lord of the world, will come.
He will free us from the yoke of our bondage.
Alleluia!

GOSPEL

A reading from the holy Gospel according to Luke   5:17-26
We have seen strange things today.

Jesus was teaching one day, and among the audience there were Pharisees and doctors of the Law who had come from every village in Galilee, from Judaea and from Jerusalem. And the Power of the Lord was behind his works of healing. Then some men appeared, carrying on a bed a paralysed man whom they were trying to bring in and lay down in front of him. But as the crowd made it impossible to find a way of getting him in, they went up on to the flat roof and lowered him and his stretcher down through the tiles into the middle of the gathering, in front of Jesus. Seeing their faith he said, 'My friend, your sins are forgiven you.' The scribes and the Pharisees began to think this over. 'Who is this man talking blasphemy? Who can forgive sins but God alone?' But Jesus, aware of their thoughts, made them this reply, 'What are these thoughts you have in your hearts? Which of these is easier: to say, "Your sins are forgiven you" or to say "Get up and walk"? But to prove to you that the Son of Man has authority on earth to forgive sins', – he said to the paralysed man – 'I order you: get up, and pick up your stretcher and go home.' And immediately before their very eyes he got up, picked up what he had been lying on and went home praising God.

They were all astounded and praised God, and were filled with awe, saying, 'We have seen strange things today.'

This is the Gospel of the Lord.

Prayer over the Gifts
Father,
from all you give us
we present this bread and wine.
As we serve you now,
accept our offering
and sustain us with your promise of eternal life.

Preface of Advent I, P1.

Communion Antiphon: Come to us, Lord, and bring us peace. We will rejoice in your presence and serve you with all our heart.

Prayer after Communion
Father,
may our communion
teach us to love heaven.
May its promise and hope
guide our way on earth.

TUESDAY

Entrance Antiphon: See, the Lord is coming and with him all his saints. Then there will be endless day.

Opening Prayer
Almighty God,
help us to look forward
to the glory of the birth of Christ our saviour:
his coming is proclaimed joyfully
to the ends of the earth,
for he lives and reigns . . .

FIRST READING

A reading from the prophet Isaiah 40:1-11
God consoles his people.

'Console my people, console them'
says your God.
'Speak to the heart of Jerusalem
and call to her
that her time of service is ended,
that her sin is atoned for,
that she has received from the hand of the Lord
double punishment for all her crimes.'

A voice cries, 'Prepare in the wilderness
a way for the Lord.
Make a straight highway for our God
across the desert.
Let every valley be filled in,
every mountain and hill be laid low,
let every cliff become a plain,
and the ridges a valley;
then the glory of the Lord shall be revealed
and all mankind shall see it;
for the mouth of the Lord has spoken.'

A voice commands: 'Cry!'
and I answered, 'What shall I cry?'
–'All flesh is grass
and its beauty like the wild flower's.
The grass withers, the flower fades
when the breath of the Lord blows on them.
(The grass is without doubt the people.)
The grass withers, the flower fades,
but the word of our God remains for ever.'

Go up on a high mountain,
joyful messenger to Zion.
Shout with a loud voice,
joyful messenger to Jerusalem.
Shout without fear,
say to the towns of Judah,
'Here is your God.'

Here is the Lord coming with power,
his arm subduing all things to him.

Second Week of Advent: Tuesday

The prize of his victory is with him,
his trophies all go before him.
He is like a shepherd feeding his flock,
gathering lambs in his arms,
holding them against his breast
and leading to their rest the mother ewes.

This is the word of the Lord.

Responsorial Psalm   Ps 95:1-3. 10-13. ℟ cf. Is 40:9-10
  ℟ **Here is our God coming with power.**

1 O sing a new song to the Lord,
   sing to the Lord all the earth.
   O sing to the Lord, bless his name.
   Proclaim his help day by day.   ℟

2 Tell among the nations his glory
   and his wonders among all the peoples.
   Proclaim to the nations: 'God is king.'
   He will judge the peoples in fairness.   ℟

3 Let the heavens rejoice and earth be glad,
   let the sea and all within it thunder praise,
   let the land and all it bears rejoice,
   all the trees of the wood shout for joy
   at the presence of the Lord for he comes,
   he comes to rule the earth.   ℟

4 With justice he will rule the world,
   he will judge the peoples with his truth.   ℟

Gospel Acclamation
   Alleluia, alleluia!
   Come Lord! Do not delay.
   Forgive the sins of your people.
   Alleluia!

or

   Alleluia, alleluia!
   The day of the Lord is near;
   Look, he comes to save us.
   Alleluia!

GOSPEL

A reading from the holy Gospel according to Matthew 18:12-14

God does not wish the little ones to be lost.

Jesus said to his disciples: 'Tell me. Suppose a man has a hundred sheep and one of them strays; will he not leave the ninety-nine on the hillside and go in search of the stray? I tell you solemnly, if he finds it, it gives him more joy than do the ninety-nine that did not stray at all. Similarly, it is never the will of your Father in heaven that one of these little ones should be lost.'

This is the Gospel of the Lord.

Prayer over the Gifts

Lord,
we are nothing without you.
As you sustain us with your mercy,
receive our prayers and offerings.

Preface of Advent I, P1.

Communion Antiphon: The Lord is just; he will award the crown of justice to all who have longed for his coming.

Prayer after Communion

Father,
you give us food from heaven.
By our sharing in this mystery,
teach us to judge wisely the things of earth
and to love the things of heaven.

WEDNESDAY

Entrance Antiphon: The Lord is coming and will not delay; he will bring every hidden thing to light and reveal himself to every nation.

Opening Prayer

All-powerful Father,
we await the healing power of Christ your Son.
Let us not be discouraged by our weaknesses
as we prepare for his coming.
Keep us steadfast in your love.

Second Week of Advent: Wednesday

FIRST READING

A reading from the prophet Isaiah
40:25-31

The Lord almighty gives strength to the wearied.

'To whom could you liken me
and who could be my equal?' says the Holy One.
Lift your eyes and look.
Who made these stars
if not he who drills them like an army,
calling each one by name?
So mighty is his power, so great his strength,
that not one fails to answer.

How can you say, Jacob,
how can you insist, Israel,
'My destiny is hidden from the Lord,
my rights are ignored by my God'?
Did you not know?
Had you not heard?

The Lord is an everlasting God,
he created the boundaries of the earth.
He does not grow tired or weary,
his understanding is beyond fathoming.
He gives strength to the wearied,
he strengthens the powerless.
Young men may grow tired and weary,
youths may stumble,
but those who hope in the Lord renew their strength,
they put out wings like eagles.
They run and do not grow weary,
walk and never tire.

    This is the word of the Lord.

Responsorial Psalm
Ps 102:1-4. 8. 10. ℟ v.1

  ℟ **My soul, give thanks to the Lord.**

1 My soul, give thanks to the Lord,
   all my being, bless his holy name.
   My soul, give thanks to the Lord
   and never forget all his blessings. ℟

2 It is he who forgives all your guilt,
   who heals every one of your ills,

who redeems your life from the grave,
who crowns you with love and compassion.

℟ **My soul, give thanks to the Lord.**

3 The Lord is compassion and love,
slow to anger and rich in mercy.
He does not treat us according to our sins
nor repay us according to our faults. ℟

Gospel Acclamation

Alleluia, alleluia!
Behold, our Lord will come with power
and will enlighten the eyes of his servants.
Alleluia!

or

Alleluia, alleluia!
Look, the Lord will come to save his people.
Blessed those who are ready to meet him.
Alleluia!

GOSPEL

A reading from the holy Gospel according to Matthew 11:28-30
Come to me, all you who labour.

Jesus exclaimed, 'Come to me, all you who labour and are overburdened, and I will give you rest. Shoulder my yoke and learn from me, for I am gentle and humble in heart, and you will find rest for your souls. Yes, my yoke is easy and my burden light.'

This is the Gospel of the Lord.

Prayer over the Gifts

Lord,
may the gift we offer in faith and love
be a continual sacrifice in your honour
and truly become our eucharist and our salvation.

Preface of Advent I, P1.

Communion Antiphon: The Lord our God comes in strength and will fill his servants with joy.

Prayer after Communion
God of mercy,
may this eucharist bring us your divine help,
free us from our sins,
and prepare us for the birthday of our Saviour,
who is Lord for ever and ever.

THURSDAY

Entrance Antiphon: Lord, you are near, and all your commandments are just; long have I known that you decreed them for ever.

Opening Prayer
Almighty Father,
give us the joy of your love
to prepare the way for Christ our Lord.
Help us to serve you and one another.

FIRST READING

A reading from the prophet Isaiah 41:13-20
I, the Holy One of Israel, am your redeemer.

I, the Lord, your God,
I am holding you by the right hand;
I tell you, 'Do not be afraid,
I will help you.'

Do not be afraid, Jacob, poor worm,
Israel, puny mite.
I will help you – it is the Lord who speaks –
the Holy One of Israel is your redeemer.

See, I turn you into a threshing-sled,
new, with doubled teeth;
you shall thresh and crush the mountains,
and turn the hills to chaff.

You shall winnow them and the wind will blow them away,
the gale will scatter them.
But you yourself will rejoice in the Lord,
and glory in the Holy One of Israel.

The poor and the needy ask for water, and there is none,

their tongue is parched with thirst.
I, the Lord, will answer them,
I, the God of Israel, will not abandon them.

I will make rivers well up on barren heights,
and fountains in the midst of valleys;
turn the wilderness into a lake,
and dry ground into waterspring.

In the wilderness, I will put cedar trees,
acacias, myrtles, olives.
In the desert I will plant juniper,
plane tree and cypress side by side;

so that men may see and know,
may all observe and understand
that the hand of the Lord has done this,
that the Holy One of Israel has created it.

This is the word of the Lord.

Responsorial Psalm   Ps 144:1. 9-13. ℟ v.8

℟ **The Lord is kind and full of compassion,
slow to anger, abounding in love.**

1 I will give you glory, O God my King,
   I will bless your name for ever.
   How good is the Lord to all,
   compassionate to all his creatures.   ℟

2 All your creatures shall thank you, O Lord,
   and your friends shall repeat their blessing.
   They shall speak of the glory of your reign
   and declare your might, O God,
   to make known to men your mighty deeds
   and the glorious splendour of your reign.   ℟

3 Yours is an everlasting kingdom;
   your rule lasts from age to age.   ℟

Gospel Acclamation
Alleluia, alleluia!
Come to us, Lord, with your peace
that we may rejoice in your presence with sincerity of heart.
Alleluia!

Second Week of Advent: Thursday

or   cf. Is 45:8

> Alleluia, alleluia!
> Send victory like a dew, you heavens,
> and let the clouds rain it down.
> Let the earth open
> and bring forth the saviour.
> Alleluia!

GOSPEL

A reading from the holy Gospel according to Matthew   11:11-15
A greater than John the Baptist has never been seen.

Jesus spoke to the crowds: 'I tell you solemnly, of all the children born of women, a greater than John the Baptist has never been seen; yet the least in the kingdom of heaven is greater than he is. Since John the Baptist came, up to this present time, the kingdom of heaven has been subjected to violence and the violent are taking it by storm. Because it was towards John that all the prophecies of the prophets and of the Law were leading; and he, if you will believe me, is the Elijah who was to return. If anyone has ears to hear, let him listen!'

This is the Gospel of the Lord.

Prayer over the Gifts
Father,
from all you give us
we present this bread and wine.
As we serve you now,
accept our offering
and sustain us with your promise of eternal life.

Preface of Advent I, P1.

Communion Antiphon: Let our lives be honest and holy in this present age, as we wait for the happiness to come when our great God reveals himself in glory.

Prayer after Communion
Father,
may our communion
teach us to love heaven.
May its promise and hope
guide our way on earth.

FRIDAY

Entrance Antiphon: The Lord is coming from heaven in splendour to visit his people, and bring them peace and eternal life.

Opening Prayer
All-powerful God,
help us to look forward in hope
to the coming of our Saviour.
May we live as he has taught,
ready to welcome him with burning love and faith.

FIRST READING

A reading from the prophet Isaiah 48:17-19
If only you had been alert to my commandments.

Thus says the Lord, your redeemer, the Holy One of Israel:

I, the Lord, your God, teach you what is good for you,
I lead you in the way that you must go.
If only you had been alert to my commandments,
your happiness would have been like a river,
your integrity like the waves of the sea.
Your children would have been numbered like the sand,
your descendants as many as its grains.
Never would your name have been cut off or blotted out
 before me.

This is the word of the Lord.

Responsorial Psalm Ps 1:1-4. 6. ℟ cf. Jn 8:12
 ℟ **Anyone who follows you, Lord,
 will have the light of life.**

1 Happy indeed is the man
 who follows not the counsel of the wicked;
 nor lingers in the way of sinners
 nor sits in the company of scorners,
 but whose delight is the law of the Lord
 and who ponders his law day and night.   ℟

2 He is like a tree that is planted
 beside the flowing waters,
 that yields its fruit in due season
 and whose leaves shall never fade;

Second Week of Advent: Friday

and all that he does shall prosper. ℟

3 Not so are the wicked, not so!
For they like winnowed chaff
shall be driven away by the wind.
For the Lord guards the way of the just
but the way of the wicked leads to doom. ℟

Gospel Acclamation

Alleluia, alleluia!
See, the king, the Lord of the world, will come.
He will free us from the yoke of our bondage.
Alleluia!

or

Alleluia, alleluia!
The Lord will come, go out to meet him.
Great is his beginning and his reign will have no end.
Alleluia!

GOSPEL

A reading from the holy Gospel according to Matthew 11:16-19

They need neither John nor the Son of Man.

Jesus spoke to the crowds: 'What description can I find for this generation? It is like children shouting to each other as they sit in the market place:

"We played the pipes for you,
and you wouldn't dance;
we sang dirges,
and you wouldn't be mourners."

'For John came, neither eating nor drinking, and they say, "He is possessed." The Son of Man came, eating and drinking, and they say, "Look, a glutton and a drunkard, a friend of tax collectors and sinners." Yet wisdom has been proved right by her actions.'

This is the Gospel of the Lord.

Prayer over the Gifts

Lord,
we are nothing without you.
As you sustain us with your mercy,
receive our prayers and offerings.

Preface of Advent I, P1.

Communion Antiphon: We are waiting for our Saviour, the Lord Jesus Christ; he will transfigure our lowly bodies into copies of his own glorious body.

Prayer after Communion

Father,
you give us food from heaven.
Teach us to live by your wisdom
and to love the things of heaven
by our sharing in this mystery.

SATURDAY

Entrance Antiphon: Come, Lord, from your cherubim throne; let us see your face, and we shall be saved.

Opening Prayer

Lord,
let your glory dawn to take away our darkness.
May we be revealed as the children of light
at the coming of your Son,
who lives and reigns . . .

FIRST READING

A reading from the book of Ecclesiasticus 48:1-4. 9-11
Elijah will come again.

The prophet Elijah arose like a fire,
his word flaring like a torch.
It was he who brought famine on them,
and who decimated them in his zeal.
By the word of the Lord, he shut up the heavens,
he also, three times, brought down fire.
How glorious you were in your miracles, Elijah!
Has anyone reason to boast as you have? –
taken up in the whirlwind of fire,
in a chariot with fiery horses;
designated in the prophecies of doom
to allay God's wrath before the fury breaks,
to turn the hearts of fathers towards their children,

Second Week of Advent: Saturday 35

and to restore the tribes of Jacob.
Happy shall they be who see you,
and those who have fallen asleep in love.

This is the word of the Lord.

Responsorial Psalm Ps 79:2-3. 15-16. 18-19. ℟ v.4

℟ **God of hosts, bring us back;**
let your face shine on us and we shall be saved.

1 O shepherd of Israel, hear us,
  shine forth from your cherubim throne.
  O Lord, rouse up your might,
  O Lord, come to our help. ℟

2 God of hosts, turn again, we implore,
  look down from heaven and see.
  Visit this vine and protect it,
  the vine your right hand has planted. ℟

3 May your hand be on the man you have chosen,
  the man you have given your strength.
  And we shall never forsake you again:
  give us life that we may call upon your name. ℟

Gospel Acclamation

Alleluia, alleluia!
The day of the Lord is near;
Look, he comes to save us.
Alleluia!

or Lk 3:4.6

Alleluia, alleluia!
Prepare a way for the Lord,
make his paths straight.
And all mankind shall see the salvation of God.
Alleluia!

GOSPEL

A reading from the holy Gospel according to Matthew 17:10-13

Elijah has come already and they did not recognise him.

As they came down from the mountain the disciples put this question to Jesus, 'Why do the scribes say that Elijah has to come first?' 'True' he replied; 'Elijah is to come to see that everything is once more as it should be; however, I tell you that Elijah has come already and they did not recognise him but treated him as they pleased; and the Son of Man will suffer similarly at their hands.' The disciples understood then that he had been speaking of John the Baptist.

This is the Gospel of the Lord.

Prayer over the Gifts

Lord,
may the gift we offer in faith and love
be a continual sacrifice in your honour
and truly become our eucharist and our salvation.

Preface of Advent I, P1.

Communion Antiphon: I am coming quickly, says the Lord, and will repay each man according to his deeds.

Prayer after Communion

God of mercy,
may this eucharist bring us your divine help,
free us from our sins,
and prepare us for the birthday of our Saviour,
who is Lord for ever and ever.

THIRD WEEK OF ADVENT

MONDAY

Special Masses are given for weekdays from 17-24 December. See pp.54ff.

Entrance Antiphon: Nations, hear the message of the Lord, and make it known to the ends of the earth: Our Saviour is coming. Have no more fear.

Opening Prayer

Lord,
hear our voices raised in prayer.
Let the light of the coming of your Son
free us from the darkness of sin.

Third Week of Advent: Monday 37

FIRST READING

A reading from the book of Numbers 24:2-7. 15-17
A star from Jacob takes the leadership.

Raising his eyes Balaam saw Israel, encamped by tribes; the spirit of God came on him and he declaimed his poem. He said:

'The oracle of Balaam son of Beor,
the oracle of the man with far-seeing eyes,
the oracle of one who hears the word of God.
He sees what Shaddai makes him see,
receives the divine answer, and his eyes are opened.
How fair are your tents, O Jacob!
How fair your dwellings, Israel!
Like valleys that stretch afar,
like gardens by the banks of a river,
like aloes planted by the Lord,
like cedars beside the waters!
A hero arises from their stock,
he reigns over countless peoples.
His king is greater than Agag,
his majesty is exalted.'

Then Balaam declaimed his poem again. He said:

'The oracle of Balaam son of Beor,
the oracle of the man with far-seeing eyes,
the oracle of the one who hears the word of God,
of one who knows the knowledge of the Most High.
He sees what Shaddai makes him see,
receives the divine answer, and his eyes are opened.
I see him – but not in the present,
I behold him – but not close at hand:
a star from Jacob takes the leadership,
a sceptre arises from Israel.'

This is the word of the Lord.

Responsorial Psalm Ps 24:4-9. ℟ v.4

℟ **Lord, make me know your ways.**

1 Lord, make me know your ways.
   Lord, teach me your paths.
   Make me walk in your truth, and teach me:
   for you are God my saviour.   ℟

2　Remember your mercy, Lord,
and the love you have shown from of old.
In your love remember me,
because of your goodness, O Lord.

℟ **Lord, make me know your ways.**

3　The Lord is good and upright.
He shows the path to those who stray,
he guides the humble in the right path;
he teaches his way to the poor.　℟

Gospel Acclamation

Alleluia, alleluia!
The Lord will come, go out to meet him.
Great is his beginning and his reign will have no end.
Alleluia!

or   Ps 84:8

Alleluia, alleluia!
Let us see, O Lord, your mercy
and give us your saving help.
Alleluia!

GOSPEL

A reading from the holy Gospel according to Matthew　　21:23-27
John's baptism: where did it come from?

Jesus had gone into the Temple and was teaching, when the chief priests and the elders of the people came to him and said, 'What authority have you for acting like this? And who gave you this authority?' 'And I' replied Jesus 'will ask you a question, only one; if you tell me the answer to it, I will then tell you my authority for acting like this. John's baptism: where did it come from: heaven or man?' And they argued it out this way among themselves, 'If we say from heaven, he will retort, "Then why did you refuse to believe him?"; but if we say from man, we have the people to fear, for they all hold that John was a prophet.' So their reply to Jesus was, 'We do not know.' And he retorted, 'Nor will I tell you my authority for acting like this.'

This is the Gospel of the Lord.

Prayer over the Gifts
Father,
from all you give us
we present this bread and wine.
As we serve you now,
accept our offering
and sustain us with your promise of eternal life.

Preface of Advent I, P1.

Communion Antiphon: Come to us, Lord, and bring us peace. We will rejoice in your presence and serve you with all our heart.

Prayer after Communion
Father,
may our communion
teach us to love heaven.
May its promise and hope
guide our way on earth.

TUESDAY

Special Masses are given for weekdays from 17-24 December. See pp.54ff.

Entrance Antiphon: See, the Lord is coming and with him all his saints. Then there will be endless day.

Opening Prayer
Father of love,
you made a new creation
through Jesus Christ your Son.
May his coming free us from sin
and renew his life within us,
for he lives and reigns . . .

FIRST READING

A reading from the prophet Zephaniah 3:1-2. 9-13
Messianic salvation is promised to all the poor in spirit.

Trouble is coming to the rebellious, the defiled,
the tyrannical city!

She would never listen to the call,
would never learn the lesson;
she has never trusted in the Lord,
never drawn near to her God.
Yes, I will then give the peoples
lips that are clean,
so that all may invoke the name of the Lord
and serve him under the same yoke.
From beyond the banks of the rivers of Ethiopia my suppliants
will bring me offerings.
When that day comes
you need feel no shame for all the misdeeds
you have committed against me,
for I will remove your proud boasters
from your midst;
and you will cease to strut
on my holy mountain.
In your midst I will leave
a humble and lowly people,
and those who are left in Israel will seek refuge in the name of the
    Lord.
They will do no wrong,
will tell no lies;
and the perjured tongue will no longer
be found in their mouths.
But they will be able to graze and rest
with no one to disturb them.

This is the word of the Lord.

Responsorial Psalm　　　　　　Ps 33:2-3. 6-7. 16. 18-19. 23. ℟ v.7
　℟ **This poor man called; the Lord heard him.**

1 I will bless the Lord at all times,
his praise always on my lips;
in the Lord my soul shall make its boast.
The humble shall hear and be glad.　℟

2 Look towards him and be radiant;
let your faces not be abashed.
This poor man called; the Lord heard him
and rescued him from all his distress.　℟

3 The Lord turns his face against the wicked
to destroy their remembrance from the earth.

Third Week of Advent: Tuesday

The just call and the Lord hears
and rescues them in all their distress.   ℟

4   The Lord is close to the broken-hearted;
those whose spirit is crushed he will save.
The Lord ransoms the souls of his servants.
Those who hide in him shall not be condemned.   ℟

Gospel Acclamation

Alleluia, alleluia!
Look, the Lord will come to save his people.
Blessed those who are ready to meet him.
Alleluia!

or

Alleluia, alleluia!
Come Lord! Do not delay.
Forgive the sins of your people.
Alleluia!

GOSPEL

A reading from the holy Gospel according to Matthew   21:28-32
John came, but it was the sinners who believed in him.

Jesus said to the chief priests and the elders of the people, 'What is your opinion? A man had two sons. He went and said to the first, "My boy, you go and work in the vineyard today." He answered, "I will not go," but afterwards thought better of it and went. The man then went and said the same thing to the second who answered, "Certainly, sir," but did not go. Which of the two did the father's will?' 'The first' they said. Jesus said to them, 'I tell you solemnly, tax collectors and prostitutes are making their way into the kingdom of God before you. For John came to you, a pattern of true righteousness, but you did not believe him, and yet the tax collectors and prostitutes did. Even after seeing that, you refused to think better of it and believe in him.'

This is the Gospel of the Lord.

Prayer over the Gifts
Lord,
we are nothing without you.
As you sustain us with your mercy,
receive our prayers and offerings.

Preface of Advent I, P1.

Communion Antiphon: The Lord is just; he will award the crown of justice to all who have longed for his coming.

Prayer after Communion

Father,
you give us food from heaven.
By our sharing in this mystery,
teach us to judge wisely the things of earth
and to love the things of heaven.

WEDNESDAY

Special Masses are given for weekdays from 17-24 December. See pp. 54ff.

Entrance Antiphon: The Lord is coming and will not delay; he will bring every hidden thing to light and reveal himself to every nation.

Opening Prayer

Father,
may the coming celebration of the birth of your Son
bring us your saving help
and prepare us for eternal life.

FIRST READING

A reading from the prophet Isaiah 45:6-8. 18. 21-26
Send victory like a dew, you heavens!

Apart from me, all is nothing.
I am the Lord, unrivalled,
I form the light and create the dark.
I make good fortune and create calamity,
it is I, the Lord, who do all this.

Send victory like a dew, you heavens,
and let the clouds rain it down.
Let the earth open
for salvation to spring up.
Let deliverance, too, bud forth
which I, the Lord, shall create.

Yes, thus says the Lord,
creator of the heavens,
who is God,
who formed the earth and made it,
who set it firm,
created it no chaos,
but a place to be lived in:

> 'I am the Lord, unrivalled,
> There is no other god besides me,
> a God of integrity and a saviour;
> there is none apart from me.
> Turn to me and be saved,
> all the ends of the earth,
> for I am God unrivalled.
>
> 'By my own self I swear it;
> what comes from my mouth is truth,
> a word irrevocable;
> before me every knee shall bend,
> by me every tongue shall swear,
> saying, "From the Lord alone
> come victory and strength."
> To him shall come, ashamed,
> all who raged against him.
> Victorious and glorious through the Lord shall be
> all the descendants of Israel.'

This is the word of the Lord.

Responsorial Psalm   Ps 84:9-14. ℟ cf. Is 45:8

℟ **Send victory like a dew, you heavens,
and let the clouds rain it down.**

1 I will hear what the Lord God has to say,
a voice that speaks of peace,
peace for his people.
His help is near for those who fear him
and his glory will dwell in our land. ℟

2 Mercy and faithfulness have met;
justice and peace have embraced.
Faithfulness shall spring from the earth
and justice look down from heaven. ℟

Third Week of Advent: Wednesday

3   The Lord will make us prosper
    and our earth shall yield its fruit.
    Justice shall march before him
    and peace shall follow his steps. ℟

Gospel Acclamation Is 55:6
Alleluia, alleluia!
Seek the Lord while he is still to be found,
call to him while he is still near.
Alleluia!

or Is 40:9-10

Alleluia, alleluia!
Shout with a loud voice, joyful messenger to Jerusalem.
Here is the Lord God coming with power.
Alleluia!

GOSPEL

A reading from the holy Gospel according to Luke 7:19-23
Go back and tell John what you have seen and heard.

John, summoning two of his disciples, sent them to the Lord to ask, 'Are you the one who is to come, or must we wait for someone else?' When the men reached Jesus they said, 'John the Baptist has sent us to you, to ask, "Are you the one who is to come or have we to wait for someone else?" ' It was just then that he cured many people of diseases and afflictions and of evil spirits, and gave the gift of sight to many who were blind. Then he gave the messengers their answer, 'Go back and tell John what you have seen and heard: the blind see again, the lame walk, lepers are cleansed, and the deaf hear, the dead are raised to life, the Good News is proclaimed to the poor and happy is the man who does not lose faith in me.'

This is the Gospel of the Lord.

Prayer over the Gifts
Lord,
may the gift we offer in faith and love
be a continual sacrifice in your honour
and truly become our eucharist and our salvation.

Preface of Advent I, P1.

Communion Antiphon: The Lord our God comes in strength and will fill his servants with joy.

Prayer after Communion
God of mercy,
may this eucharist bring us your divine help,
free us from our sins,
and prepare us for the birthday of our Saviour,
who is Lord for ever and ever.

THURSDAY

Special Masses are given for weekdays from 17-24 December. See pp.54ff.

Entrance Antiphon: Lord, you are near, and all your commandments are just; long have I known that you decreed them for ever.

Opening Prayer
Lord,
our sins bring us unhappiness.
Hear our prayer for courage and strength.
May the coming of your Son
bring us the joy of salvation.

FIRST READING

A reading from the prophet Isaiah 54:1-10
Like a forsaken wife, the Lord calls you back.

Shout for joy, you barren women who bore no children!
Break into cries of joy and gladness, you who were never in
   labour!
For the sons of the forsaken one are more in number
than the sons of the wedded wife, says the Lord.

Widen the space of your tent,
stretch out your hangings freely,
lengthen your ropes, make your pegs firm;
for you will burst out to right and to left.
Your race will take possession of the nations,
and people the abandoned cities.

Do not be afraid, you will not be put to shame,
do not be dismayed, you will not be disgraced;
for you will forget the shame of your youth
and no longer remember the curse of your widowhood.
For now your creator will be your husband,
his name, the Lord of hosts;
your redeemer will be the Holy One of Israel,
he is called the God of the whole earth.
Yes, like a forsaken wife, distressed in spirit,
the Lord calls you back.
Does a man cast off the wife of his youth?
says your God.

I did forsake you for a brief moment,
but with great love will I take you back.
In excess of anger, for a moment
I hid my face from you.
But with everlasting love I have taken pity on you,
says the Lord, your redeemer.

I am now as I was in the days of Noah
when I swore that Noah's waters
should never flood the world again.
So now I swear concerning my anger with you
and the threats I made against you;

for the mountains may depart,
the hills be shaken,
but my love for you will never leave you
and my covenant of peace with you will never be shaken,
says the Lord who takes pity on you.

This is the word of the Lord.

Responsional Psalm Ps 29:2. 4-6. 11-13. ℟ v.2

℟ **I will praise you, Lord,
you have rescued me.**

1 I will praise you, Lord, you have rescued me
   and have not let my enemies rejoice over me.
   O Lord, you have raised my soul from the dead,
   restored me to life from those who sink into the grave. ℟

2 Sing psalms to the Lord, you who love him,
   give thanks to his holy name.
   His anger lasts but a moment; his favour through life.
   At night there are tears, but joy comes with dawn. ℟

Third Week of Advent: Thursday

3   The Lord listened and had pity.
    The Lord came to my help.
    For me you have changed my mourning into dancing,
    O Lord my God, I will thank you for ever.   ℟

Gospel Acclamation
    Alleluia, alleluia!
    The day of the Lord is near.
    Look, he comes to save us.
    Alleluia!
or   Lk 3:4.6

    Alleluia, alleluia!
    Prepare a way for the Lord.
    make his paths straight.
    And all mankind shall see the salvation of God.
    Alleluia!

GOSPEL

A reading from the holy Gospel according to Luke   7:24-30
John is the messenger who prepares the way of the Lord.

When John's messengers had gone Jesus began to talk to the people about John, 'What did you go out into the wilderness to see? A reed swaying in the breeze? No? Then what did you go out to see? A man dressed in fine clothes? Oh no, those who go in for fine clothes and live luxuriously are to be found at court! Then what did you go out to see? A prophet? Yes, I tell you, and much more than a prophet: he is the one of whom scripture says: See, I am going to send my messenger before you; he will prepare the way before you. I tell you, of all the children born of women, there is no greater than John: yet the least in the kingdom of God is greater than he is. All the people who heard him, and the tax collectors too, acknowledged God's plan by accepting baptism from John; but by refusing baptism from him the Pharisees and the lawyers had thwarted what God had in mind for them.'

This is the Gospel of the Lord.

Prayer over the Gifts
Father,
from all you give us
we present this bread and wine.

As we serve you now,
accept our offering
and sustain us with your promise of eternal life.

Preface of Advent I, P1.

Communion Antiphon: Let our lives be honest and holy in this present age, as we wait for the happiness to come when our great God reveals himself in glory.

Prayer after Communion
Father,
may our communion
teach us to love heaven.
May its promise and hope
guide our way on earth.

FRIDAY

Speical Masses are given for weekdays from 17-24 December. See pp.54ff.

Entrance Antiphon: The Lord is coming from heaven in splendour to visit his people, and bring them peace and eternal life.

Opening Prayer
All-powerful Father,
guide us with your love
as we await the coming of your Son.
Keep us faithful
that we may be helped through life
and brought to salvation.

FIRST READING

A reading from the prophet Isaiah 56:1-3. 6-8
My house will be called a house of prayer for all the peoples.

Thus says the Lord: Have a care for justice, act with integrity, for soon my salvation will come and my integrity be manifest.

Blessed is the man who does this and the son of man who clings to it: observing the sabbath, not profaning it, and keeping his hand from every evil deed.

Third Week of Advent: Friday

Let no foreigner who has attached himself to the Lord say, 'The Lord will surely exclude me from his people.'

Foreigners who have attached themselves to the Lord to serve him and to love his name and be his servants – all who observe the sabbath, not profaning it, and cling to my covenant – these I will bring to my holy mountain. I will make them joyful in my house of prayer. Their holocausts and their sacrifices will be accepted on my altar, for my house will be called a house of prayer for all the peoples.

It is the Lord God who speaks, who gathers the outcasts of Israel: there are others I will gather besides those already gathered.

This is the word of the Lord.

Responsorial Psalm
Ps 66:2-3. 5. 7-8. R/ v.4

R/ **Let the peoples praise you, O God;
let all the peoples praise you.**

1. O God, be gracious and bless us
   and let your face shed its light upon us.
   So will your ways be known upon earth
   and all nations learn your saving help. R/

2. Let the nations be glad and exult
   for you rule the world with justice.
   With fairness you rule the peoples,
   you guide the nations on earth. R/

3. The earth has yielded its fruit
   for God, our God, has blessed us.
   May God still give us his blessing
   till the ends of the earth revere him. R/

Gospel Acclamation
Ps 84:8

Alleluia, alleluia!
Let us see, O Lord, your mercy
and give us your saving help.
Alleluia!

or

Alleluia, alleluia!
Come to us, Lord, with your peace
that we may rejoice in your presence with sincerity of heart.
Alleluia!

Third Week of Advent: Friday

GOSPEL

A reading from the holy Gospel according to John 5:33-36

John was a lamp alight and shining.

Jesus said to the Jews:

> You sent messengers to John,
> and he gave his testimony to the truth:
> not that I depend on human testimony;
> no, it is for your salvation that I speak of this.
> John was a lamp alight and shining
> and for a time you were content to enjoy the light that he gave.
> But my testimony is greater than John's:
> the works my Father has given me to carry out,
> these same works of mine
> testify that the Father has sent me.

This is the Gospel of the Lord.

Prayer over the Gifts

Lord,
we are nothing without you.
As you sustain us with your mercy,
receive our prayers and offerings.

Preface of Advent I, P1.

Communion Antiphon: We are waiting for our Saviour, the Lord Jesus Christ; he will transfigure our lowly bodies into copies of his own glorious body.

Prayer after Communion

Father,
you give us food from heaven.
Teach us to live by your wisdom
and to love the things of heaven
by our sharing in this mystery.

GOSPEL ACCLAMATIONS
For the weekdays of Advent until 16 December

1   cf. Ps 79:4

Alleluia, alleluia!
God of hosts, bring us back;
let your face shine on us and we shall be saved.
Alleluia!

2   Ps 84:8

Alleluia, alleluia!
Let us see, O Lord, your mercy
and give us your saving help.
Alleluia!

3   Is 33:22

Alleluia, alleluia!
The Lord is our judge, the Lord our lawgiver,
the Lord our king and our saviour.
Alleluia!

4   Is 40:9-10

Alleluia, alleluia!
Shout with a loud voice, joyful messenger to Jerusalem.
Here is the Lord God coming with power.
Alleluia!

5   cf. Is 45:8

Alleluia, alleluia!
Send victory like a dew, you heavens, and let the clouds rain it down.
Let the earth open and bring forth the saviour.
Alleluia!

6   Is 55:6

Alleluia, alleluia!
Seek the Lord while he is still to be found,
call to him while he is still near.
Alleluia!

Gospel Acclamation Weekdays of Advent until 16 December

7   Lk 3:4. 6

Alleluia, alleluia!
Prepare a way for the Lord,
make his paths straight.
And all mankind shall see the salvation of God.
Alleluia!

8

Alleluia, alleluia!
Come Lord! Do not delay.
Forgive the sins of your people.
Alleluia!

9

Alleluia, alleluia!
Behold, our Lord will come with power
and will enlighten the eyes of his servants.
Alleluia!

10

Alleluia, alleluia!
Come to us, Lord, with your peace
that we may rejoice in your presence with sincerity of heart.
Alleluia!

11

Alleluia, alleluia!
See, the king, the Lord of the world, will come.
He will free us from the yoke of our bondage.
Alleluia!

12

Alleluia, alleluia!
The day of the Lord is near;
look, he comes to save us.
Alleluia!

13

Alleluia, alleluia!
The Lord will come, go out to meet him.
Great is his beginning and his reign will have no end.
Alleluia!

Gospel Acclamation Weekdays of Advent until 16 December

14

Alleluia, alleluia!
Look, the Lord will come to save his people.
Blessed those who are ready to meet him.
Alleluia!

WEEKDAYS OF ADVENT
FROM 17 DECEMBER TO 24 DECEMBER

17 DECEMBER

Entrance Antiphon: You heavens, sing for joy, and earth exult! Our Lord is coming; he will take pity on those in distress.

Opening Prayer
Father,
creator and Redeemer of mankind,
you decreed, and your Word became man,
born of the Virgin Mary.
May we come to share the divinity of Christ,
who humbled himself to share our human nature,
for he lives and reigns . . .

FIRST READING

A reading from the book of Genesis   49:2. 8-10
The sceptre shall not pass from Judah.

Jacob called his sons and said,

> 'Gather round, sons of Jacob, and listen;
> listen to Israel your father.
> Judah, your brothers shall praise you:
> you grip your enemies by the neck,
> your father's sons shall do you homage,
> Judah is a lion cub,
> you climb back, my son, from your kill;
> like a lion he crouches and lies down,
> or a lioness: who dare rouse him?
> The sceptre shall not pass from Judah,
> nor the mace from between his feet,
> until he come to whom it belongs,
> to whom the peoples shall render obedience.'

This is the word of the Lord.

Responsorial Psalm   Ps 71:1-4. 7-8. 17. ℟ cf. v.7
℟ **In his days justice shall flourish**
   and peace till the moon fails.

1 O God, give your judgement to the king,
  to a king's son your justice,

Weekdays of Advent: 17 December

that he may judge your people in justice
and your poor in right judgement. ℟

2 May the mountains bring forth peace for the people
and the hills, justice.
May he defend the poor of the people
and save the children of the needy. ℟

3 In his days justice shall flourish
and peace till the moon fails.
He shall rule from sea to sea,
from the Great River to earth's bounds. ℟

4 May his name be blessed for ever
and endure like the sun.
Every tribe shall be blessed in him,
all nations bless his name. ℟

Gospel Acclamation
Alleluia, alleluia!
Wisdom of the Most High,
ordering all things with strength and gentleness,
come and teach us the way of truth.
Alleluia!

GOSPEL

A reading from the holy Gospel according to Matthew 1:1-17
A genealogy of Jesus Christ, son of David.

A genealogy of Jesus Christ, son of David, son of Abraham:

Abraham was the father of Isaac,
Isaac the father of Jacob,
Jacob the father of Judah and his brothers,
Judah was the father of Perez and Zerah, Tamar being their
    mother,
Perez was the father of Hezron,
Hezron the father of Ram,
Ram was the father of Amminadab,
Amminadab the father of Nahshon,
Nahshon the father of Salmon,
Salmon was the father of Boaz, Rahab being his mother,
Boaz was the father of Obed, Ruth being his mother,
Obed was the father of Jesse;
and Jesse was the father of King David.

David was the father of Solomon, whose mother had been
    Uriah's wife,
Solomon was the father of Rehoboam,
Rehoboam the father of Abijah,
Abijah the father of Asa,
Asa was the father of Jehoshaphat,
Jehoshaphat the father of Joram,
Joram the father of Azariah,
Azariah was the father of Jotham,
Jotham the father of Ahaz,
Ahaz the father of Hezekiah
Hezekiah was the father of Manasseh,
Manasseh the father of Amon,
Amon the father of Josiah;
and Josiah was the father of Jechoniah and his brothers.
Then the deportation to Babylon took place.

After the deportation to Babylon:
Jechoniah was the father of Shealtiel,
Shealtiel the father of Zerubbabel,
Zerubbabel was the father of Abiud,
Abiud the father of Eliakim,
Eliakim the father of Azor,
Azor was the father of Zadok,
Zadok the father of Achim,
Achim the father of Eliud,
Eliud was the father of Eleazar,
Eleazar the father of Matthan,
Matthan the father of Jacob;
and Jacob was the father of Joseph the husband of Mary;
of her was born Jesus who is called Christ.

The sum of generations is therefore: fourteen from Abraham to David; fourteen from David to the Babylonian deportation; and fourteen from the Babylonian deportation to Christ.

This is the Gospel of the Lord.

Prayer over the Gifts
Lord,
bless these gifts of your Church
and by this eucharist
renew us with the bread from heaven.

Preface of Advent II, P2.

Communion Antiphon: The Desired of all nations is coming, and the house of the Lord will be filled with his glory.

Prayer after Communion
God our Father,
as you nourish us with the food of life,
give us also your Spirit,
so that we may be radiant with his light
at the coming of Christ your Son,
who is Lord for ever and ever.

18 DECEMBER

Entrance Antiphon: Christ our King is coming, the Lamb whom John proclaimed.

Opening Prayer
All-powerful God,
renew us by the coming feast of your Son
and free us from our slavery to sin.

FIRST READING

A reading from the prophet Jeremiah   23:5-8
I will raise a virtuous Branch for David.

'See, the days are coming – it is the Lord who speaks –
when I will raise a virtuous Branch for David,
who will reign as true king and be wise,
practising honesty and integrity in the land.
In his days Judah will be saved
and Israel dwell in confidence.
And this is the name he will be called:
The Lord-our-integrity.

'So, then, the days are coming – it is the Lord who speaks – when people will no longer say, "As the Lord lives who brought the sons of Israel out of the land of Egypt!" but, "As the Lord lives who led back and brought home the descendants of the House of Israel out of the land of the North and from all the countries to which he had dispersed them, to live on their own soil." '

This is the word of the Lord.

Responsorial Psalm Ps 71:1-2. 12-13. 18-19. ℟ cf. v.7
> ℟ **In his days justice shall flourish
> and peace till the moon fails.**

1. O God, give your judgement to the king,
   to a king's son your justice,
   that he may judge your people in justice
   and your poor in right judgement. ℟

2. For he shall save the poor when they cry
   and the needy who are helpless.
   He will have pity on the weak
   and save the lives of the poor. ℟

3. Blessed be the Lord, God of Israel,
   who alone works wonders,
   ever blessed his glorious name.
   Let his glory fill the earth.
   Amen! Amen! ℟

Gospel Acclamation
Alleluia, alleluia!
Ruler of the House of Israel,
who gave the law to Moses on Sinai,
come and save us with outstretched arm.
Alleluia!

GOSPEL

A reading from the holy Gospel according to Matthew 1:18-24
Jesus is born of Mary who was betrothed to Joseph, son of David.

This is how Jesus Christ came to be born. His mother Mary was betrothed to Joseph, but before they came to live together she was found to be with child through the Holy Spirit. Her husband Joseph, being a man of honour and wanting to spare her publicity, decided to divorce her informally. He had made up his mind to do this when the angel of the Lord appeared to him in a dream and said, 'Joseph son of David, do not be afraid to take Mary home as your wife, because she has conceived what is in her by the Holy Spirit. She will give birth to a son and you must name him Jesus, because he is the one who is to save his people from their sins.' Now all this took place to fulfil the words spoken by the Lord through the prophet:

Weekdays of Advent: 19 December

> The virgin will conceive and give birth to a son
> and they will call him Emmanuel,

a name which means 'God-is-with-us'. When Joseph woke up he did what the angel of the Lord had told him to do: he took his wife to his home.

This is the Gospel of the Lord.

Prayer over the Gifts
Lord,
may this sacrifice
bring us into the eternal life of your Son,
who died to save us from death,
for he is Lord for ever and ever.

Preface of Advent II, P2.

Communion Antiphon: His name will be called Emmanuel, which means God is with us.

Prayer after Communion
Lord,
we receive mercy in your Church.
Prepare us to celebrate with fitting honour
the coming feast of our redemption.

19 DECEMBER

Entrance Antiphon: He who is to come will not delay; and then there will be no fear in our lands, because he is our Saviour.

Opening Prayer
Father,
you show the world the splendour of your glory
in the coming of Christ, born of the Virgin.
Give to us true faith and love
to celebrate the mystery of God made man.

FIRST READING

A reading from the book of Judges 13:2-7. 24-25
The birth of Samson was announced by an angel.

There was a man of Zorah of the tribe of Dan, called Manoah. His wife was barren, she had borne no children. The angel of the Lord appeared to this woman and said to her, 'You are barren and have had no child. But from now on take great care. Take no wine or strong drink, and eat nothing unclean. For you will conceive and bear a son. No razor is to touch his head, for the boy shall be God's nazirite from his mother's womb. It is he who will begin to rescue Israel from the power of the Philistines.' Then the woman went and told her husband, 'A man of God has just come to me; his presence was like the presence of the angel of God, he was so majestic. I did not ask him where he came from, and he did not reveal his name to me. But he said to me, "You will conceive and bear a son. From now on, take no wine or strong drink, and eat nothing unclean. For the boy shall be God's nazirite from his mother's womb to his dying day."'

The woman gave birth to a son and called him Samson. The child grew, and the Lord blessed him; and the spirit of the Lord began to move him.

This is the word of the Lord.

Responsorial Psalm Ps 70:3-6. 16-17. ℟ cf. v.8

℟ **My lips are filled with your praise,
with your glory all the day long.**

1 Be a rock where I can take refuge,
  a mighty stronghold to save me;
  for you are my rock, my stronghold.
  Free me from the hand of the wicked.   ℟

2 It is you, O Lord, who are my hope,
  my trust, O Lord, since my youth.
  On you I have leaned from my birth,
  from my mother's womb you have been my help.   ℟

3 I will declare the Lord's mighty deeds
  proclaiming your justice, yours alone.
  O God, you have taught me from my youth
  and I proclaim your wonders still.   ℟

Gospel Acclamation
Alleluia, alleluia!
Root of Jesse, set up as a sign to the peoples,
come to save us,
and delay no more.
Alleluia!

GOSPEL

A reading from the holy Gospel according to Luke 1:5-25
The birth of John the Baptist was announced by Gabriel.

In the days of King Herod of Judaea there lived a priest called Zechariah who belonged to the Abijah section of the priesthood, and he had a wife, Elizabeth by name, who was a descendant of Aaron. Both were worthy in the sight of God, and scrupulously observed all the commandments and observances of the Lord. But they were childless: Elizabeth was barren and they were both getting on in years.

Now it was the turn of Zechariah's section to serve, and he was exercising his priestly office before God when it fell to him by lot, as the ritual custom was, to enter the Lord's sanctuary and burn incense there. And at the hour of incense the whole congregation was outside, praying.

Then there appeared to him the angel of the Lord, standing on the right of the altar of incense. The sight disturbed Zechariah and he was overcome with fear. But the angel said to him, 'Zechariah, do not be afraid, your prayer has been heard. Your wife Elizabeth is to bear you a son and you must name him John. He will be your joy and delight and many will rejoice at his birth, for he will be great in the sight of the Lord; he must drink no wine, no strong drink. Even from his mother's womb he will be filled with the Holy Spirit, and he will bring back many of the sons of Israel to the Lord their God. With the spirit and power of Elijah, he will go before him to turn the hearts of fathers towards their children and the disobedient back to the wisdom that the virtuous have, preparing for the Lord a people fit for him.' Zechariah said to the angel, 'How can I be sure of this? I am an old man and my wife is getting on in years.' The angel replied, 'I am Gabriel who stand in God's presence, and I have been sent to speak to you and bring you this good news. Listen! Since you have not believed my words, which will come true at their appointed time, you will be silenced and have no power of speech until this has happened.' Meanwhile the people were waiting for Zechariah and were surprised that he stayed in the sanctuary so long. When he came out he could not speak to them, and they realised that he had received a vision in the sanctuary. But he could only make signs to them, and remained dumb.

When his time of service came to an end he returned home. Some time later his wife Elizabeth conceived, and for five months she kept to herself. 'The Lord has done this for me' she said 'now that it has pleased him to take away the humiliation I suffered among men.'

This is the Gospel of the Lord.

Prayer over the Gifts
Lord of mercy,
receive the gifts we bring to your altar.
Let your power take away our weakness
and make our offerings holy.

Preface of Advent II, P2.

Communion Antiphon: The dawn from on high shall break upon us, to guide our feet on the road to peace.

Prayer after Communion
Father,
we give you thanks for the bread of life.
Open our hearts in welcome
to prepare for the coming of our Saviour,
who is Lord for ever and ever.

20 DECEMBER

Entrance Antiphon: A shoot will spring from Jesse's stock, and all mankind will see the saving power of God.

Opening Prayer
God of love and mercy,
help us to follow the example of Mary,
always ready to do your will.
At the message of an angel
she welcomed your eternal Son
and, filled with the light of your Spirit,
she became the temple of your Word,
who lives and reigns . . .

Weekdays of Advent: 20 December

FIRST READING

A reading from the prophet Isaiah   7: 10-14
The maiden is with child.

The Lord spoke to Ahaz and said, 'Ask the Lord your God for a sign for yourself coming either from the depths of Sheol or from the heights above.' 'No,' Ahaz answered 'I will not put the Lord to the test.'

Then Isaiah said:

'Listen now, House of David:
are you not satisfied with trying the patience of men
without trying the patience of my God, too?
The Lord himself, therefore,
will give you a sign.
It is this: the maiden is with child
and will soon give birth to a son
whom she will call Emmanuel,
a name which means "God-is-with-us"'.

This is the word of the Lord.

Responsorial Psalm   Ps 23:1-6. ℟ cf. v.7. 10
 ℟ **Let the Lord enter!**
  He is the king of glory.

1 The Lord's is the earth and its fullness,
  the world and all its peoples.
  It is he who set it on the seas;
  on the waters he made it firm.   ℟

2 Who shall climb the mountain of the Lord?
  Who shall stand in his holy place?
  The man with clean hands and pure heart,
  who desires not worthless things.   ℟

3 He shall receive blessings from the Lord
  and reward from the God who saves him.
  Such are the men who seek him,
  seek the face of the God of Jacob.   ℟

Gospel Acclamation
 Alleluia, alleluia!
 Emmanuel,
 our king and lawgiver,

come and save us,
Lord our God.
Alleluia!

or

Alleluia, alleluia!
Key of David, who open the gates of the eternal kingdom,
come to liberate from prison
the captive who lives in darkness.
Alleluia!

GOSPEL

A reading from the holy Gospel according to Luke — 1:26-38

Listen! You are to conceive and bear a son.

The angel Gabriel was sent by God to a town in Galilee called Nazareth, to a virgin betrothed to a man named Joseph, of the House of David; and the virgin's name was Mary. He went in and said to her, 'Rejoice, so highly favoured! The Lord is with you.' She was deeply disturbed by these words and asked herself what this greeting could mean, but the angel said to her, 'Mary, do not be afraid; you have won God's favour. Listen! You are to conceive and bear a son, and you must name him Jesus. He will be great and will be called Son of the Most High. The Lord God will give him the throne of his ancestor David; he will rule over the House of Jacob for ever and his reign will have no end.' Mary said to the angel, 'But how can this come about, since I am a virgin?' 'The Holy Spirit will come upon you,' the angel answered, 'and the power of the Most High will cover you with its shadow. And so the child will be holy and will be called Son of God. Know this too: your kinswoman Elizabeth has, in her old age, herself conceived a son, and she whom people called barren is now in her sixth month, for nothing is impossible to God.' 'I am the handmaid of the Lord,' said Mary, 'let what you have said be done to me.' And the angel left her.

This is the Gospel of the Lord.

Prayer over the Gifts
Lord,
accept this sacrificial gift.
May the eucharist we share
bring us to the eternal life
we seek in faith and hope.

Preface of Advent II, P2.

Communion Antiphon: The angel said to Mary: you shall conceive and bear a son, and you shall call him Jesus.

Prayer after Communion
Lord,
watch over the people you nourish with this eucharist.
Lead them to rejoice in true peace.

21 DECEMBER

Entrance Antiphon: Soon the Lord God will come, and you will call him Emmanuel, for God is with us.

Opening Prayer
Lord,
hear the prayers of your people.
May we who celebrate the birth of your Son as man
rejoice in the gift of eternal life when he comes in glory,
for he lives and reigns . . .

FIRST READING

A reading from the Song of Songs 2:8-14
See how my beloved comes leaping over the mountains.

I hear my Beloved.
See how he comes
leaping on the mountains,
bounding over the hills.
My Beloved is like a gazelle,
like a young stag.

See where he stands
behind our wall.
He looks in at the window,
he peers through the lattice.

My Beloved lifts up his voice,
he says to me,
'Come then, my love,
my lovely one, come.

For see, winter is past,
the rains are over and gone.
The flowers appear on the earth.
The season of glad songs has come,
the cooing of the turtledove is heard
in our land.
The fig tree is forming its first figs
and the blossoming vines give out their fragrance.
Come then, my love,
my lovely one, come.
My dove, hiding in the clefts of the rock,
in the coverts of the cliff,
show me your face,
let me hear your voice;
for your voice is sweet
and your face is beautiful.'

    This is the word of the Lord.

Alternative First Reading

A reading from the prophet Zephaniah   3:14-18
The Lord, the king of Israel, is in your midst.

Shout for joy, daughter of Zion,
Israel, shout aloud!
Rejoice, exult with all your heart,
daughter of Jerusalem!
The Lord has repealed your sentence;
he has driven your enemies away.
The Lord, the king of Israel, is in your midst;
you have no more evil to fear.
When that day comes, word will come to Jerusalem:
Zion, have no fear,
do not let your hands fall limp.
The Lord your God is in your midst,
a victorious warrior.
He will exult with joy over you,
he will renew you by his love;
he will dance with shouts of joy for you
as on a day of festival.

    This is the word of the Lord.

Weekdays of Advent: 21 December

Responsorial Psalm Ps 32:2-3. 11-12. 20-21. ℟ vv.1. 3
℟ **Ring out your joy to the Lord, O you just;
O sing him a song that is new.**

1 Give thanks to the Lord upon the harp,
  with a ten-stringed lute sing him songs.
  O sing him a song that is new,
  play loudly, with all your skill. ℟

2 His own designs shall stand for ever,
  the plans of his heart from age to age.
  They are happy, whose God is the Lord,
  the people he has chosen as his own. ℟

3 Our soul is waiting for the Lord.
  The Lord is our help and our shield.
  In him do our hearts find joy.
  We trust in his holy name. ℟

Gospel Acclamation
  Alleluia, alleluia!
  Key of David, who open the gates of the eternal kingdom,
  come to liberate from prison
  the captive who lives in darkness.
  Alleluia!

or

  Alleluia, alleluia!
  Emmanuel,
  our king and lawgiver,
  come and save us,
  Lord our God.
  Alleluia!

GOSPEL

A reading from the holy Gospel according to Luke 1:39-45
Why should I be honoured with a visit from the mother of my Lord?

Mary set out and went as quickly as she could to a town in the hill country of Judah. She went into Zechariah's house and greeted Elizabeth. Now as soon as Elizabeth heard Mary's greeting, the child leapt in her womb and Elizabeth was filled with the Holy Spirit. She gave a loud cry and said, 'Of all women you are the most blessed, and blessed is the fruit of your womb. Why should

I be honoured with a visit from the mother of my Lord? For the moment your greeting reached my ears, the child in my womb leapt for joy. Yes, blessed is she who believed that the promise made her by the Lord would be fulfilled.'

This is the Gospel of the Lord.

Prayer over the Gifts
Lord of love,
receive these gifts which you have given to your Church.
Let them become for us
the means of our salvation.

Preface of Advent II, P2.

Communion Antiphon: Blessed are you for your firm believing, that the promises of the Lord would be fulfilled.

Prayer after Communion
Lord,
help us to serve you
that we may be brought to salvation.
May this eucharist be our constant protection.

22 DECEMBER

Entrance Antiphon: Gates, lift up your heads! Stand erect, ancient doors, and let in the King of glory.

Opening Prayer
God our Father,
you sent your Son
to free mankind from the power of death.
May we who celebrate the coming of Christ as man
share more fully in his divine life,
for he lives and reigns . . .

FIRST READING

A reading from the first book of Samuel   1:24-28
Hannah gives thanks for Samuel's birth.

When Hannah had weaned Samuel, she took him up with her together with a three-year old bull, an ephah of flour and a skin of

Weekdays of Advent: 22 December 69

wine, and she brought him to the temple of the Lord at Shiloh; and the child was with them. They slaughtered the bull and the child's mother came to Eli. She said, 'If you please, my lord. As you live, my lord, I am the woman who stood here beside you, praying to the Lord. This is the child I prayed for, and the Lord granted me what I asked him. Now I make him over to the Lord for the whole of his life. He is made over to the Lord.'

There she left him, for the Lord.

This is the word of the Lord.

Responsorial Psalm 1 Sam 2:1. 4-8. ℟ v.1

℟ **My heart exults in the Lord my saviour.**

1. My heart exults in the Lord,
   I find my strength in my God;
   my mouth laughs at my enemies
   as I rejoice in your saving help. ℟

2. The bows of the mighty are broken,
   but the weak are clothed with strength.
   Those with plenty must labour for bread,
   but the hungry need work no more.
   The childless wife has children now
   but the fruitful wife bears no more. ℟

3. It is the Lord who gives life and death,
   he brings men to the grave and back;
   it is the Lord who gives poverty and riches.
   He brings men low and raises them on high. ℟

4. He lifts up the lowly from the dust,
   from the dungheap he raises the poor
   to set him in the company of princes,
   to give him a glorious throne.
   For the pillars of the earth are the Lord's,
   on them he has set the world. ℟

Gospel Acclamation
Alleluia, alleluia!
Root of Jesse,
set up as a sign to the peoples,
come to save us
and delay no more.
Alleluia!

or

> Alleluia, alleluia!
> King of the peoples
> and corner-stone of the Church,
> come and save man
> whom you made from the dust of the earth.
> Alleluia!

GOSPEL

A reading from the holy Gospel according to Luke 1:46-56
The Almighty has done great things for me.

Mary said:

> 'My soul proclaims the greatness of the Lord
> and my spirit exults in God my saviour;
> because he has looked upon his lowly handmaid.
> Yes, from this day forward all generations will call me blessed,
> for the Almighty has done great things for me.
> Holy is his name,
> and his mercy reaches from age to age for those who fear him.
>
> 'He has shown the power of his arm,
> he has routed the proud of heart.
> He has pulled down princes from their thrones and exalted
>   the lowly.
> The hungry he has filled with good things, the rich sent empty
>   away.
> He has come to the help of Israel his servant, mindful of his
>   mercy
> – according to the promise he made to our ancestors –
> of his mercy to Abraham and to his descendants for ever.'

Mary stayed with Elizabeth about three months and then went back home.

This is the Gospel of the Lord.

Prayer over the Gifts
Lord God,
with confidence in your love
we come with gifts to worship at your altar.
By the mystery of this eucharist
purify us and renew your life within us.

Weekdays of Advent: 23 December

Preface of Advent II, P2.

Communion Antiphon: My soul proclaims the greatness of the Lord, for the Almighty has done great things for me.

Prayer after Communion
Lord,
strengthen us by the sacrament we have received.
Help us to go out to meet our Saviour
and to merit eternal life
with lives that witness to our faith.

23 DECEMBER

Entrance Antiphon: A little child is born for us, and he shall be called the mighty God; every race on earth shall be blessed in him.

Opening Prayer
Father,
we contemplate the birth of your Son.
He was born of the Virgin Mary
and came to live among us.
May we receive forgiveness and mercy
through our Lord Jesus Christ, your Son,
who lives and reigns . . .

FIRST READING

A reading from the prophet Malachi 3:1-4. 23-24

I am going to send you Elijah the prophet before the day of the Lord comes.

The Lord God says this: Look, I am going to send my messenger to prepare a way before me. And the Lord you are seeking will suddenly enter his Temple; and the angel of the covenant whom you are longing for, yes, he is coming, says the Lord of hosts. Who will be able to resist the day of his coming? Who will remain standing when he appears? For he is like the refiner's fire and the fullers' alkali. He will take his seat as refiner and purifier; he will purify the sons of Levi and refine them like gold and silver, and then they will make the offering to the Lord as it should be made.

The offering of Judah and Jerusalem will be welcomed by the Lord as in former days, as in the years of old.

Know that I am going to send you Elijah the prophet before my day comes, that great and terrible day. He shall turn the hearts of fathers towards their children and the hearts of the children towards their fathers, lest I come and strike the land with a curse.

This is the word of the Lord.

Responsorial Psalm   Ps 24:4-5. 8-9. 10. 14. ℟ Lk 21:28

℟ **Stand erect, hold your heads high,
   because your liberation is near at hand.**

1. Lord, make me know your ways.
   Lord, teach me your paths.
   Make me walk in your truth, and teach me:
   for you are God my saviour.   ℟

2. The Lord is good and upright.
   He shows the path to those who stray.
   He guides the humble in the right path;
   he teaches his way to the poor.   ℟

3. His ways are faithfulness and love
   for those who keep his covenant and will.
   The Lord's friendship is for those who revere him;
   to them he reveals his covenant.   ℟

Gospel Acclamation
Alleluia, alleluia!
King of the peoples
and corner-stone of the Church,
come and save man
whom you made from the dust of the earth.
Alleluia!

GOSPEL

A reading from the holy Gospel according to Luke   1:57-66
The birth of John the Baptist.

The time came for Elizabeth to have her child, and she gave birth to a son; and when her neighbours and relations heard that the Lord had shown her so great a kindness, they shared her joy.

Now on the eighth day they came to circumcise the child; they

Weekdays of Advent: 23 December

were going to call him Zechariah after his father, but his mother spoke up. 'No,' she said 'he is to be called John.' They said to her, 'But no one in your family has that name', and made signs to his father to find out what he wanted him called. The father asked for a writing-tablet and wrote, 'His name is John'. And they were all astonished. At that instant his power of speech returned and he spoke and praised God. All their neighbours were filled with awe and the whole affair was talked about throughout the hill country of Judaea. All those who heard of it treasured it in their hearts. 'What will this child turn out to be?' they wondered. And indeed the hand of the Lord was with him.

This is the Gospel of the Lord.

Prayer over the Gifts
Lord,
you have given us this memorial
as the perfect form of worship.
Restore us to your peace
and prepare us to celebrate the coming of our Saviour,
for he is Lord for ever and ever.

Preface of Advent II, P2.

Communion Antiphon: I stand at the door and knock, says the Lord. If anyone hears my voice and opens the door, I will come in and sit down to supper with him and he with me.

Prayer after Communion
Lord,
as you nourish us with the bread of life,
give peace to our spirits
and prepare us to welcome your Son with ardent faith.

24 DECEMBER

Mass in the Morning

Entrance Antiphon: The appointed time has come; God has sent his Son into the world.

Opening Prayer
Come Lord Jesus,
do not delay;
give new courage to your people who trust in your love.
By your coming, raise us to the joy of your kingdom,
where you live and reign . . .

FIRST READING

A reading from the second book of Samuel   7:1-5. 8-12. 14. 16
The kingdom of David will always stand secure before the Lord.

Once David had settled into his house and the Lord had given him rest from all the enemies surrounding him, the king said to the prophet Nathan, 'Look, I am living in a house of cedar while the ark of God dwells in a tent.' Nathan said to the king, 'Go and do all that is in your mind, for the Lord is with you.'

But that very night the word of the Lord came to Nathan:
'Go and tell my servant David, "Thus the Lord speaks: Are you the man to build me a house to dwell in? I took you from the pasture, from following the sheep, to be a leader of my people Israel; I have been with you on all your expeditions; I have cut off all your enemies before you. I will give you fame as great as the fame of the greatest on earth. I will provide a place for my people Israel; I will plant them there and they shall dwell in that place and never be disturbed again; nor shall the wicked continue to oppress them as they did, in the days when I appointed judges over my people Israel; I will give them rest from all their enemies. The Lord will make you great; the Lord will make you a House. And when your days are ended and you are laid to rest with your ancestors, I will preserve the offspring of your body after you and make his sovereignty secure. I will be a father to him and he a son to me. Your House and your sovereignty will always stand secure before me and your throne be established for ever".'

This is the word of the Lord.

Responsorial Psalm Ps 88:2-5. 27. 29. ℟ cf. v.2
 ℟ **I will sing for ever of your love, O Lord.**

1 I will sing for ever of your love, O Lord;
   through all ages my mouth will proclaim your truth.
   Of this I am sure, that your love lasts for ever,
   that your truth is firmly established as the heavens. ℟

2 'I have made a covenant with my chosen one;
   I have sworn to David my servant;
   I will establish your dynasty for ever
   and set up your throne through all ages.' ℟

3 He will say to me: 'You are my father,
   my God, the rock who saves me.'
   I will keep my love for him always;
   for him my covenant shall endure. ℟

Gospel Acclamation
  Alleluia, alleluia!
  Morning star, radiance of eternal light,
  sun of justice,
  come and enlighten those who live in darkness
  and in the shadow of death.
  Alleluia!

GOSPEL

A reading from the holy Gospel according to Luke 1:67-79
Our God from on high will bring the rising Sun to visit us.

John's father Zechariah was filled with the Holy Spirit and spoke this prophecy:

  'Blessed be the Lord, the God of Israel,
  for he has visited his people, he has come to their rescue
  and he has raised up for us a power for salvation
  in the House of his servant David,
  even as he proclaimed,
  by the mouth of his holy prophets from ancient times,
  that he would save us from our enemies
  and from the hands of all who hate us.
  Thus he shows mercy to our ancestors,
  thus he remembers his holy covenant,
  the oath he swore

to our father Abraham
that he would grant us, free from fear,
to be delivered from the hands of our enemies,
to serve him in holiness and virtue
in his presence, all our days.
And you, little child,
you shall be called Prophet of the Most High,
for you will go before the Lord
to prepare the way for him.
To give his people knowledge of salvation
through the forgiveness of their sins;
this by the tender mercy of our God
who from on high will bring the rising Sun to visit us,
to give light to those who live
in darkness and the shadow of death,
and to guide our feet
into the way of peace.'

This is the Gospel of the Lord.

Prayer over the Gifts
Father,
accept the gifts we offer.
By our sharing in this eucharist
free us from sin
and help us to look forward in faith
to the glorious coming of your Son,
who is Lord for ever and ever.

Preface of Advent II, P1.

Communion Antiphon: Blessed be the Lord God of Israel, for he has visited and redeemed his people.

Prayer after Communion
Lord,
your gift of the eucharist has renewed our lives.
May we who look forward to the feast of Christ's birth
rejoice for ever in the wonder of his love,
for he is Lord for ever and ever.

GOSPEL ACCLAMATIONS
For the Weekdays of Advent 17-24 December

1

Alleluia, alleluia!
Wisdom of the Most High,
ordering all things with strength and gentleness,
come and teach us the way of truth.
Alleluia!

2

Alleluia, alleluia!
Ruler of the House of Israel,
who gave the law to Moses on Sinai,
come and save us with outstretched arm.
Alleluia!

3

Alleluia, alleluia!
Root of Jesse,
set up as a sign to the peoples,
come to save us
and delay no more.
Alleluia!

4

Alleluia, alleluia!
Key of David, who open the gates of the eternal kingdom,
come to liberate from prison
the captive who lives in darkness.
Alleluia!

5

Alleluia, alleluia!
Morning star, radiance of eternal light,
sun of justice,
come and enlighten those who live in darkness
and in the shadow of death.
Alleluia!

6

Alleluia, alleluia!
King of the peoples
and corner-stone of the Church,
come and save man
whom you made from the dust of the earth.
Alleluia!

7

Alleluia, alleluia!
Emmanuel,
our king and lawgiver,
come and save us,
Lord our God.
Alleluia!

THE SEASON OF CHRISTMAS

O CHRIST

what shall we offer you coming on earth?

ANGELS *offer* PRAISE
HEAVEN *lights up a* STAR
MAGI *bring* GIFTS
SHEPHERDS *their* WONDER
EARTH *a* CAVE
DESERT *a* MANGER

We offer you a

MOTHER

THE NATIVITY OF THE LORD

Vigil Mass　　　　　　　　　　　　　　Solemnity

This Mass is celebrated during the afternoon of 24 December, before or after Evening Prayer I of Christmas.

Entrance Antiphon: Today you will know that the Lord is coming to save us, and in the morning you will see his glory.

Opening Prayer
Let us pray
　　[that Christmas morning will find us at peace]

God our Father,
every year we rejoice
as we look forward to this feast of our salvation.
May we welcome Christ as our Redeemer,
and meet him with confidence when he comes to be our judge,
who lives and reigns . . .

or

Let us pray
　　[and be ready to welcome the Lord]

God of endless ages, Father of all goodness,
we keep vigil for the dawn of salvation
and the birth of your Son.

With gratitude we recall his humanity,
the life he shared with the sons of men.
May the power of his divinity
help us answer his call to forgiveness and life.

FIRST READING

A reading from the prophet Isaiah　　　　　　　　　　　　62:1-5
The Lord takes delight in you.

About Zion I will not be silent,
about Jerusalem I will not grow weary,
until her integrity shines out like the dawn
and her salvation flames like a torch.
The nations then will see your integrity,
all the kings your glory,
and you will be called by a new name,

one which the mouth of the Lord will confer.
You are to be a crown of splendour in the hand of the Lord,
a princely diadem in the hand of your God;
no longer are you to be named 'Forsaken',
nor your land 'Abandoned',
but you shall be called 'My Delight'
and your land 'The Wedded';
for the Lord takes delight in you
and your land will have its wedding.
Like a young man marrying a virgin,
so will the one who built you wed you,
and as the bridegroom rejoices in his bride,
so will your God rejoice in you.

This is the word of the Lord.

Responsional Psalm   Ps 88:4-5. 16-17. 27. 29. ℟ cf. v.2
  ℟   **I will sing for ever of your love, O Lord.**

1 'I have made a covenant with my chosen one;
   I have sworn to David my servant:
   I will establish your dynasty for ever
   and set up your throne through all ages.' ℟

2 Happy the people who acclaim such a king,
   who walk, O Lord, in the light of your face,
   who find their joy every day in your name,
   who make your justice the source of their bliss. ℟

3 'He will say to me: "You are my father,
   my God, the rock who saves me."
   I will keep my love for him always;
   for him my covenant shall endure.' ℟

SECOND READING

A reading from the Acts of the Apostles   13:16-17. 22-25
Paul's witness to Christ, the son of David.

When Paul reached Antioch in Pisidia, he stood up in the synagogue, held up a hand for silence and began to speak:
  'Men of Israel, and fearers of God, listen! The God of our nation Israel chose our ancestors, and made our people great when they were living as foreigners in Egypt; then by divine power he led them out.
  'Then he made David their king, of whom he approved in

The Nativity of the Lord: Vigil Mass

these words, "I have selected David son of Jesse, a man after my own heart, who will carry out my whole purpose". To keep his promise, God has raised up for Israel one of David's descendants, Jesus, as Saviour, whose coming was heralded by John when he proclaimed a baptism of repentance for the whole people of Israel. Before John ended his career he said, "I am not the one you imagine me to be; that one is coming after me and I am not fit to undo his sandal".'

This is the word of the Lord.

Gospel Acclamation
Alleluia, alleluia!
Tomorrow there will be an end to the sin of the world
and the saviour of the world will be our king.
Alleluia!

GOSPEL

A reading from the holy Gospel according to Matthew 1:1-25
The ancestry of Jesus Christ, the son of David.

A genealogy of Jesus Christ, son of David, son of Abraham:
Abraham was the father of Isaac,
Isaac the father of Jacob,
Jacob was the father of Judah and his brothers,
Judah was the father of Perez and Zerah, Tamar being their
  mother,
Perez was the father of Hezron,
Hezron the father of Ram,
Ram was the father of Amminadab,
Amminadab the father of Nahshon,
Nahshon the father of Salmon,
Salmon was the father of Boaz, Rahab being his mother,
Boaz was the father of Obed, Ruth being his mother,
Obed was the father of Jesse;
and Jesse was the father of King David.

David was the father of Solomon, whose mother had been
  Uriah's wife,
Solomon was the father of Rehoboam,
Rehoboam the father of Abijah,
Abijah the father of Asa,
Asa was the father of Jehoshaphat,
Jehoshaphat the father of Joram,

Joram the father of Azariah,
Azariah was the father of Jotham,
Jotham the father of Ahaz,
Ahaz the father of Hezekiah,
Hezekiah was the father of Manasseh,
Manasseh the father of Amon,
Amon the father of Josiah;
and Josiah was the father of Jechoniah and his brothers.
Then the deportation to Babylon took place.

After the deportation to Babylon:
Jechoniah was the father to Shealtiel,
Shealtiel the father of Zerubbabel,
Zerubbabel was the father of Abiud,
Abiud the father of Eliakim,
Eliakim the father of Azor,
Azor was the father of Zadok,
Zadok the father of Achim,
Achim the father of Eliud,
Eliud was the father of Eleazar,
Eleazar the father of Matthan,
Matthan the father of Jacob;
and Jacob was the father of Joseph the husband of Mary; of her was born Jesus who is called Christ.

The sum of generations is therefore: fourteen from Abraham to David; fourteen from David to the Babylonian deportation; and fourteen from the Babylonian deportation to Christ.

*This is how Jesus Christ came to be born. His mother Mary was betrothed to Joseph; but before they came to live together she was found to be with child through the Holy Spirit. Her husband Joseph, being a man of honour and wanting to spare her publicity, decided to divorce her informally. He had made up his mind to do this when the angel of the Lord appeared to him in a dream and said, 'Joseph son of David, do not be afraid to take Mary home as your wife, because she has conceived what is in her by the Holy Spirit. She will give birth to a son and you must name him Jesus, because he is the one who is to save his people from their sins.' Now all this took place to fulfil the words spoken by the Lord through the prophet:

> The Virgin will conceive and give birth to a son
> and they will call him Emmanuel,

a name which means 'God-is-with-us'. When Joseph woke up he did what the angel of the Lord told him to do: he took his wife to

The Nativity of the Lord: Vigil Mass

his home and, though he had not had intercourse with her, she gave birth to a son; and he named him Jesus.

This is the Gospel of the Lord.*

*Shorter form, verses 18-25. Read between *.

In the Profession of Faith, all genuflect at the words, *and was made man*.

Prayer over the Gifts
Lord,
as we keep tonight the vigil of Christmas,
may we celebrate this eucharist
with greater joy than ever
since it marks the beginning of our redemption.

Preface of Christmas I-III, P3-P5.

Communion Antiphon: The glory of the Lord will be revealed, and all mankind will see the saving power of God.

Prayer after Communion
Father,
we ask you to give us a new birth
as we celebrate the beginning
of your Son's life on earth.
Strengthen us in spirit
as we take your food and drink.

Solemn Blessing
Bow your heads and pray for God's blessing.

Lord,
bless and strengthen your people.
May they remain faithful to you
and always rejoice in your mercy.
We ask this in the name of Jesus the Lord. ℟ **Amen.**

May almighty God bless you,
the Father, and the Son, ✠ and the Holy Spirit. ℟ **Amen.**

For the Masses of Christmas Day, and the solemnities of the Christmas Season, see companion volume, *The Sunday Missal*.

For the Masses of 26, 27, 28 December (when these dates do not fall on a Sunday), see below, in the Proper of Saints.

29 DECEMBER

Fifth Day in the Octave of Christmas

Entrance Antiphon: God loved the world so much, he gave his only Son, that all who believe in him might not perish, but might have eternal life.

Opening Prayer
All-powerful and unseen God,
the coming of your light into our world
has made the darkness vanish.
Teach us to proclaim the birth of your Son Jesus Christ,
who lives and reigns . . .

FIRST READING

A reading from the first letter of St John 2:3-11
Anyone who loves his brother is living in the light.

We can be sure that we know Jesus
only by keeping his commandments.
Anyone who says, 'I know him',
and does not keep his commandments,
is a liar,
refusing to admit the truth.
But when anyone does obey what he has said,
God's love comes to perfection in him.
We can be sure
that we are in God
only when the one who claims to be living in him
is living the same kind of life as Christ lived.
My dear people,
this is not a new commandment that I am writing to tell you,
but an old commandment
that you were given from the beginning,
the original commandment which was the message brought to
  you.
Yet in another way, what I am writing to you,
and what is being carried out in your lives as it was in his,

is a new commandment;
because the night is over
and the real light is already shining.
Anyone who claims to be in the light
but hates his brother
is still in the dark.
But anyone who loves his brother is living in the light
and need not be afraid of stumbling;
unlike the man who hates his brother and is in the darkness,
not knowing where he is going,
because it is too dark to see.

This is the word of the Lord.

Responsorial Psalm Ps 95:1-3. 5-6. ℟ v.11

℟ **Let the heavens rejoice and earth be glad.**

1 O sing a new song to the Lord,
sing to the Lord all the earth.
O sing to the Lord, bless his name. ℟

2 Proclaim his help day by day,
tell among the nations his glory
and his wonders among all the peoples. ℟

3 It was the Lord who made the heavens,
his are majesty and state and power
and splendour in his holy place. ℟

Gospel Acclamation Jn 1:14. 12

Alleluia, alleluia!
The Word became flesh, and dwelt among us.
To all who received him he gave power to become children of
  God.
Alleluia!

or Lk 2:32

Alleluia, alleluia!
A light to enlighten the pagans
and the glory of your people Israel.
Alleluia!

Alternative Acclamations p.116.

GOSPEL

A reading from the holy Gospel according to Luke 2:22-35
A light to enlighten the pagans.

When the day came for them to be purified as laid down by the Law of Moses, the parents of Jesus took him up to Jerusalem to present him to the Lord – observing what stands written in the Law of the Lord: Every first-born male must be consecrated to the Lord – and also to offer in sacrifice, in accordance with what is said in the Law of the Lord, a pair of turtledoves or two young pigeons. Now in Jerusalem there was a man called Simeon. He was an upright and devout man; he looked forward to Israel's comforting and the Holy Spirit rested on him. It had been revealed to him by the Holy Spirit that he would not see death until he had set eyes on the Christ of the Lord. Prompted by the Spirit he came to the Temple: and when the parents brought in the child Jesus to do for him what the Law required, he took him into his arms and blessed God; and he said:

> 'Now, Master, you can let your servant go in peace,
> just as you promised;
> because my eyes have seen the salvation
> which you have prepared for all the nations to see,
> a light to enlighten the pagans
> and the glory of your people Israel.'

As the child's father and mother stood there wondering at the things that were being said about him, Simeon blessed them and said to Mary his mother, 'You see this child: he is destined for the fall and for the rising of many in Israel, destined to be a sign that is rejected – and a sword will pierce your own soul too – so that the secret thoughts of many may be laid bare.'

This is the Gospel of the Lord.

Prayer over the Gifts
Lord,
receive our gifts in this wonderful exchange:
from all you have given us
we bring you these gifts,
and in return, you give us yourself.

Preface of Christmas I-III, P3-P5.

Communion Antiphon: Through the tender compassion of our God, the dawn from on high shall break upon us.

Prayer after Communion
Father of love and mercy,
grant that our lives may always be founded
on the power of this holy mystery.

30 DECEMBER

Sixth Day in the Octave of Christmas

When there is no Sunday in the octave of Christmas, the feast of the Holy Family is celebrated today. See companion volume, *The Sunday Missal.*

Entrance Antiphon: When peaceful silence lay over all, and night had run half of her swift course, your all-powerful word, O Lord, leaped down from heaven, from the royal throne.

Opening Prayer
All-powerful God,
may the human birth of your Son
free us from our former slavery to sin
and bring us new life.

FIRST READING

A reading from the first letter of St John 2:12-17
Anyone who does the will of God remains for ever.

I am writing to you, my own children,
whose sins have already been forgiven through his name;
I am writing to you, fathers,
who have come to know the one
who has existed since the beginning;
I am writing to you, young men,
who have already overcome the Evil One;
I have written to you, children,
because you already know the Father;
I have written to you, fathers,
because you have come to know the one
who has existed since the beginning;

I have written to you, young men,
because you are strong and God's word has made its home in you,
and you have overcome the Evil One.
You must not love this passing world
or anything that is in the world.
The love of the Father cannot be
in any man who loves the world,
because nothing the world has to offer
– the sensual body,
the lustful eye,
pride in possessions –
could ever come from the Father
but only from the world;
and the world, with all it craves for,
is coming to an end;
but anyone who does the will of God
remains for ever.

This is the word of the Lord.

Responsorial Psalm
Ps 95:7-10. ℟ v.11

℟ **Let the heavens rejoice and earth be glad.**

1 Give the Lord, you families of peoples,
   give the Lord glory and power,
   give the Lord the glory of his name. ℟

2 Bring an offering and enter his courts,
   worship the Lord in his temple.
   O earth, tremble before him. ℟

3 Proclaim to the nations: 'God is king'.
   The world he made firm in its place;
   he will judge the peoples in fairness. ℟

Gospel Acclamation
Heb 1:1-2

Alleluia, alleluia!
At various times in the past
and in various different ways,
God spoke to our ancestors through the prophets;
but in our own time, the last days,
he has spoken to us through his Son.
Alleluia!

30 December: Sixth Day in the Octave of Christmas

or

Alleluia, alleluia!
A hallowed day has dawned upon us.
Come, you nations, worship the Lord,
for today a great light has shone down upon the earth.
Alleluia!

GOSPEL

A reading from the holy Gospel according to Luke 2:36-40
She spoke of the child to all who looked forward to the deliverance of Jerusalem.

There was a prophetess, Anna the daughter of Phanuel, of the tribe of Asher. She was well on in years. Her days of girlhood over, she had been married for seven years before becoming a widow. She was now eighty-four years old and never left the Temple, serving God night and day with fasting and prayer. She came by just at that moment and began to praise God; and she spoke of the child to all who looked forward to the deliverance of Jerusalem. When they had done everything the Law of the Lord required, they went back to Galilee, to their own town of Nazareth. Meanwhile the child grew to maturity, and he was filled with wisdom; and God's favour was with him.

This is the Gospel of the Lord.

Prayer over the Gifts
Father,
in your mercy accept our gifts.
By sharing in this eucharist
may we come to live more fully the love we profess.

Preface of Christmas I-III, P3-P5.

Communion Antiphon: From his riches we have all received, grace for grace.

Prayer after Communion
God our Father,
in this eucharist you touch our lives.
Keep your love alive in our hearts
that we may become worthy of you.

31 DECEMBER

Seventh Day in the Octave of Christmas

Entrance Antiphon: A child is born for us, a son given to us; dominion is laid on his shoulder, and he shall be called Wonderful-Counsellor.

Opening Prayer
Ever-living God,
in the birth of your Son
our religion has its origin and its perfect fulfilment.
Help us to share in the life of Christ
for he is the salvation of mankind,
who lives and reigns . . .

FIRST READING

A reading from the first letter of St John 2:18-21
You have been anointed by the Holy One and have all received the knowledge.

Children, these are the last days;
you were told that an Antichrist must come,
and now several antichrists have already appeared;
we know from this that these are the last days.
Those rivals of Christ came out of your own number, but they
 had never really belonged;
if they had belonged, they would have stayed with us;
but they left us, to prove that not one of them
ever belonged to us.
But you have been anointed by the Holy One,
and have all received the knowledge.
It is not because you do not know the truth that I am writing to
 you
but rather because you know it already
and know that no lie can come from the truth.

This is the word of the Lord.

Responsorial Psalm Ps 95:1-2. 11-13. ℟ v.11
 ℟ **Let the heavens rejoice and earth be glad.**

1 O sing a new song to the Lord,
 sing to the Lord all the earth.

31 December: Seventh Day in the Octave of Christmas

    O sing to the Lord, bless his name.
    Proclaim his help day by day. ℟

2. Let the heavens rejoice and earth be glad,
   let the sea and all within it thunder praise,
   let the land and all it bears rejoice,
   all the trees of the wood shout for joy
   at the presence of the Lord for he comes,
   he comes to rule the earth. ℟

3. With justice he will rule the world,
   he will judge the peoples with his truth. ℟

Gospel Acclamation

    Alleluia, alleluia!
    A hallowed day has dawned upon us.
    Come, you nations, worship the Lord,
    for today a great light has shone down upon the earth.
    Alleluia!

or   Jn 1:14.12

    Alleluia, alleluia!
    The Word became flesh, and dwelt among us.
    To all who received him he gave power to become children of
        God.
    Alleluia!

GOSPEL

A reading from the holy Gospel according to John   1:1-18
The Word was made flesh.

In the beginning was the Word:
the Word was with God
and the Word was God.
He was with God in the beginning.
Through him all things came to be,
not one thing had its being but through him.
All that came to be had life in him
and that life was the light of men,
a light that shines in the dark,
a light that darkness could not overpower.
A man came, sent by God.
His name was John.
He came as a witness,

as a witness to speak for the light,
so that everyone might believe through him.
He was not the light,
only a witness to speak for the light.

The Word was the true light
that enlightens all men;
and he was coming into the world.
He was in the world
that had its being through him,
and the world did not know him.
He came to his own domain
and his own people did not accept him.
But to all who did accept him
he gave power to become children of God,
to all who believe in the name of him
who was born not out of human stock
or urge of the flesh
or will of man
but of God himself.
The Word was made flesh,
he lived among us,
and we saw his glory,
the glory that is his as the only Son of the Father,
full of grace and truth.

John appears as his witness. He proclaims:
'This is the one of whom I said:
He who comes after me
ranks before me
because he existed before me.'

Indeed, from his fullness we have, all of us, received –
yes, grace in return for grace,
since, though the Law was given through Moses,
grace and truth have come through Jesus Christ.
No one has ever seen God;
it is the only Son, who is nearest to the Father's heart,
who has made him known.

    This is the Gospel of the Lord.

Prayer over the Gifts
Father of peace,
accept our devotion and sincerity,

31 December: Seventh Day in the Octave of Christmas

and by our sharing in this mystery
draw us closer to each other and to you.

Preface of Christmas I-III, P3-P5.

Communion Antiphon: God's love for us was revealed when he sent his only Son into the world, so that we could have life through him.

Prayer after Communion
Lord,
may this sacrament be our strength.
Teach us to value all the good you give us
and help us to strive for eternal life.

> For the Mass of 1 January, Solemnity of Mary, Mother of God, and of the Epiphany, see companion volume, *The Sunday Missal.*

MASS PROPERS FOR WEEKDAYS OF THE CHRISTMAS SEASON
from 2 January to 12 January

MONDAY

Entrance Antiphon: A holy day has dawned upon us. Come, you nations, and adore the Lord. Today a great light has come upon the earth.

Opening Prayer
Before the Epiphany
Lord,
keep us true in the faith,
proclaiming that Christ your Son,
who is one with you in eternal glory,
became man and was born of a virgin mother.
Free us from all evil
and lead us to the joy of eternal life.

After the Epiphany
Lord,
let the light of your glory shine within us,
and lead us through the darkness of this world
to the radiant joy of our eternal home.

READINGS from 2-12 January, see below, pp.102ff.

Prayer over the Gifts
Lord,
receive our gifts in this wonderful exchange:
from all you have given us
we bring you these gifts,
and in return, you give us yourself.

Preface of Christmas I-III, or of the Epiphany, P3-P6.

Communion Antiphon: We have seen his glory, the glory of the Father's only Son, full of grace and truth.

Prayer after Communion
Father of love and mercy,

grant that our lives may always be founded
on the power of this holy mystery.

TUESDAY

Entrance Antiphon: Blessed is he who comes in the name of the Lord; the Lord God shines upon us.

Opening Prayer
Before the Epiphany
God our Father,
when your Son was born of the Virgin Mary
he became like us in all things but sin.
May we who have been reborn in him
be free from our sinful ways.

After the Epiphany
Father,
your Son became like us
when he revealed himself in our nature:
help us to become more like him,
who lives and reigns . . .

READINGS from 2-12 January, see below, pp. 102ff.

Prayer over the Gifts
Father,
in your mercy accept our gifts.
By sharing in this eucharist
may we come to live more fully the love we profess.

Preface of Christmas I-III, or of the Epiphany, P3-P6.

Communion Antiphon: God loved us so much that he sent his own Son in the likeness of sinful flesh.

Prayer after Communion
God our Father,
in this eucharist you touch our lives.
Keep your love alive in our hearts
that we may become worthy of you.

WEDNESDAY

Entrance Antiphon: The people who walked in darkness have seen a great light; on those who lived in the shadow of death, light has shone.

Opening Prayer
Before the Epiphany
All-powerful Father,
you sent your Son Jesus Christ
to bring the new light of salvation to the world.
May he enlighten us with his radiance,
who lives and reigns . . .

After the Epiphany
God, light of all nations,
give us the joy of lasting peace,
and fill us with your radiance
as you filled the hearts of our fathers.

READINGS from 2-12 January, see below pp.102ff.

Prayer over the Gifts
Father of peace,
accept our devotion and sincerity,
and by our sharing in this mystery
draw us closer to each other and to you.

Preface of Christmas I-III, or of the Epiphany, P3-P6.

Communion Antiphon: The eternal life which was with the Father has been revealed to us.

Prayer after Communion
Lord,
may this sacrament be our strength.
Teach us to value all the good you give us
and help us to strive for eternal life.

Weekdays of Christmas Season 2-12 January

THURSDAY

Entrance Antiphon: In the beginning, before all ages, the Word was God; that Word was born a man to save the world.

Opening Prayer
Before the Epiphany
Father,
you make known the salvation of mankind
at the birth of your Son.
Make us strong in faith
and bring us to the glory you promise.

After the Epiphany
God our Father,
through Christ your Son
the hope of eternal life dawned on our world.
Give to us the light of faith
that we may always acknowledge him as our Redeemer
and come to the glory of his kingdom,
where he lives and reigns . . .

READINGS from 2-12 January, see below, pp.102ff.

Prayer over the Gifts
Lord,
receive our gifts in this wonderful exchange:
from all you have given us
we bring you these gifts,
and in return, you give us yourself.

Preface of Christmas I-III, or of the Epiphany, P3-P6.

Communion Antiphon: God loved the world so much, he gave his only Son, that all who believe in him might not perish, but might have eternal life.

Prayer after Communion
Father of love and mercy,
grant that our lives may always be founded
on the power of this holy mystery.

FRIDAY

Entrance Antiphon: The Lord is a light in darkness to the upright; he is gracious, merciful, and just.

Opening Prayer
Before the Epiphany
Lord,
fill our hearts with your light.
May we always acknowledge Christ as our Saviour
and be more faithful to his gospel,
for he lives and reigns . . .

After the Epiphany
All-powerful Father,
you have made known the birth of the Saviour
by the light of a star.
May he continue to guide us with his light,
for he lives and reigns . . .

READINGS from 2-12 January, see below, pp.102ff.

Prayer over the Gifts
Father,
in your mercy accept our gifts.
By sharing in this eucharist
may we come to live more fully the love we profess.

Preface of Christmas I-III, or of the Epiphany, P3-P6.

Communion Antiphon: God's love for us was revealed when he sent his only Son into the world, so that we could have life through him.

Prayer after Communion
God our Father,
in this eucharist you touch our lives.
Keep your love alive in our hearts
that we may become worthy of you.

Weekdays of Christmas Season 2-12 January

SATURDAY

Entrance Antiphon: God sent his own Son, born of a woman, so that we could be adopted as his sons.

Opening Prayer
Before the Epiphany
All-powerful and ever-living God,
you give us a new vision of your glory
in the coming of Christ your Son.
He was born of the Virgin Mary
and came to share our life.
May we come to share his eternal life
in the glory of your kingdom,
where he lives and reigns . . .

After the Epiphany
God our Father,
through your Son you made us a new creation.
He shared our nature and became one of us;
with his help, may we become more like him,
who lives and reigns . . .

READINGS from 2-12 January, see below, pp. 102ff.

Prayer over the Gifts
Father of peace,
accept our devotion and sincerity,
and by our sharing in this mystery
draw us closer to each other and to you.

Preface of Christmas I-III, or of the Epiphany, P3-P6.

Communion Antiphon: From his riches we have all received, grace for grace.

Prayer after Communion
Lord,
may this sacrament be our strength.
Teach us to value all the good you give us
and help us to strive for eternal life.

READINGS FOR WEEKDAYS OF THE CHRISTMAS SEASON

from 2 January – Epiphany

In countries where Epiphany is celebrated on the Sunday between 2 January and 8 January, the readings given below for the days 7-12 January are used after Epiphany, and the following readings for 3-6 January are omitted.

2 JANUARY

FIRST READING

A reading from the first letter of St John   2:22-28

Keep alive in yourselves what you were taught in the beginning.

The man who denies that Jesus is the Christ –
he is the liar,
he is Antichrist;
and he is denying the Father as well as the Son,
because no one who has the Father can deny the Son,
and to acknowledge the Son is to have the Father as well.
Keep alive in yourselves what you were taught in the beginning:
as long as what you were taught in the beginning is alive in you,
you will live in the Son
and in the Father;
and what is promised to you by his own promise
is eternal life.
This is all that I am writing to you about the people
who are trying to lead you astray.
But you have not lost the anointing that he gave you,
and you do not need anyone to teach you;
the anointing he gave teaches you everything;
you are anointed with truth, not with a lie,
and as it has taught you, so you must stay in him.
Live in Christ, then, my children,
so that if he appears, we may have full confidence,
and not turn from him in shame
at his coming.

    This is the word of the Lord.

Readings before Epiphany: 2 January

Responsorial Psalm Ps 97:1-4. ℟ v.3
> ℟ **All the ends of the earth have seen the salvation of our God.**

1. Sing a new song to the Lord
for he has worked wonders.
His right hand and his holy arm
have brought salvation. ℟

2. The Lord has made known his salvation;
has shown his justice to the nations.
He has remembered his truth and love
for the house of Israel. ℟

3. All the ends of the earth have seen
the salvation of our God.
Shout to the Lord all the earth,
ring out your joy. ℟

Gospel Acclamation Jn 1:14. 12
Alleluia, alleluia!
The Word became flesh, and dwelt among us.
To all who received him he gave power to become children of God.
Alleluia!

or Heb 1:1-2

Alleluia, alleluia!
At various times in the past
and in various different ways,
God spoke to our ancestors through the prophets;
but in our own time, the last days,
he has spoken to us through his Son.
Alleluia!

Alternative Acclamations p.116.

GOSPEL

A reading from the holy Gospel according to John 1:19-28
One is coming after me who existed before me.

This is how John appeared as a witness. When the Jews sent priests and Levites from Jerusalem to ask him, 'Who are you?' he not only declared, but he declared quite openly, 'I am not the Christ'. 'Well then,' they asked 'are you Elijah?' 'I am not' he said. 'Are you the Prophet?' He answered, 'No.' So they said to him, 'Who are you? We must take back an answer to those who sent us. What have you to say about yourself?' So John said, 'I am, as Isaiah prophesied:

> a voice that cries in the wilderness:
> Make a straight way for the Lord.'

Now these men had been sent by the Pharisees, and they put this further question to him, 'Why are you baptising if you are not the Christ, and not Elijah, and not the prophet?' John replied, 'I baptise with water; but there stands among you – unkown to you – the one who is coming after me; and I am not fit to undo his sandal-strap.' This happened at Bethany, on the far side of the Jordan, where John was baptising.

This is the Gospel of the Lord.

3 JANUARY

FIRST READING

A reading from the first letter of St John   2:29-3:6
Anyone who lives in God does not sin.

You know that God is righteous –
then you must recognise that everyone whose life is righteous
has been begotten by him.
Think of the love that the Father has lavished on us,
by letting us be called God's children;
and that is what we are.
Because the world refused to acknowledge him,
therefore it does not acknowledge us.
My dear people, we are already the children of God
but what we are to be in the future has not yet been revealed;
all we know is, that when it is revealed
we shall be like him
because we shall see him as he really is.
Surely everyone who entertains this hope
must purify himself, must try to be as pure as Christ.
Anyone who sins at all
breaks the law,
because to sin is to break the law.
Now you know that he appeared in order to abolish sin,

and that in him there is no sin,
and anyone who sins
has never seen him or known him.

This is the word of the Lord.

Responsorial Psalm   Ps 97:1. 3-6. ℟ v.3
℟ **All the ends of the earth have seen
the salvation of our God.**

1 Sing a new song to the Lord
for he has worked wonders.
His right hand and his holy arm
have brought salvation. ℟

2 All the ends of the earth have seen
the salvation of our God.
Shout to the Lord all the earth,
ring out your joy. ℟

3 Sing psalms to the Lord with the harp
with the sound of music.
With trumpets and the sound of the horn
acclaim the King, the Lord. ℟

Gospel Acclamation
Alleluia, alleluia!
A hallowed day has dawned upon us.
Come you nations, worship the Lord,
for today a great light has shone down upon the earth.
Alleluia!

or   Jn 1:14. 12

Alleluia, alleluia!
The Word became flesh, and dwelt among us.
To all who received him he gave power to become children of
    God.
Alleluia!

GOSPEL

A reading from the holy Gospel according to John   1:29-34
Look, there is the lamb of God.

The next day, seeing Jesus coming towards him, John said,
'Look, there is the lamb of God that takes away the sin of the

world. This is the one I spoke of when I said: A man is coming after me who ranks before me because he existed before me. I did not know him myself, and yet it was to reveal him to Israel that I came baptising with water.' John also declared, 'I saw the Spirit coming down on him from heaven like a dove and resting on him. I did not know him myself, but he who sent me to baptise with water had said to me, "The man on whom you see the Spirit come down and rest is the one who is going to baptise with the Holy Spirit". Yes, I have seen and I am the witness that he is the Chosen One of God.'

This is the Gospel of the Lord.

4 JANUARY

FIRST READING

A reading from the first letter of St John 3:7-10
He cannot sin when he has been begotten by God.

My children, do not let anyone lead you astray:
to live a holy life
is to be holy just as God is holy;
to lead a sinful life is to belong to the devil,
since the devil was a sinner from the beginning.
It was to undo all that the devil has done
that the Son of God appeared.
No one who has been begotten by God sins;
because God's seed remains inside him,
he cannot sin when he has been begotten by God.
In this way we distinguish the children of God
from the children of the devil:
anybody not living a holy life
and not loving his brother
is no child of God's.

This is the word of the Lord.

Responsorial Psalm Ps 97:1. 7-9. ℞ v.3
℞ **All the ends of the earth have seen
the salvation of our God.**

1 Sing a new song to the Lord
for he has worked wonders.

His right hand and his holy arm
have brought salvation. ℟

2. Let the sea and all within it, thunder;
the world, and all its peoples.
Let the rivers clap their hands
and the hills ring out their joy
at the presence of the Lord. ℟

3. For the Lord comes,
he comes to rule the earth.
He will rule the world with justice
and the peoples with fairness. ℟

Gospel Acclamation Jn 1:14. 12

Alleluia, alleluia!
The word became flesh, and dwelt among us.
To all who received him he gave power to become children of God.
Alleluia!

or Heb 1:1-2

Alleluia, alleluia!
At various times in the past
and in various different ways,
God spoke to our ancestors through the prophets;
but in our own time, the last days,
he has spoken to us through his Son.
Alleluia!

GOSPEL

A reading from the holy Gospel according to John 1:35-42
We have found the Messiah.

As John stood there with two of his disciples, Jesus passed, and John stared hard at him and said, 'Look, there is the lamb of God.' Hearing this, the two disciples followed Jesus. Jesus turned round, saw them following and said, 'What do you want?' They answered, 'Rabbi,' – which means Teacher – 'where do you live?' 'Come and see' he replied; so they went and saw where he lived, and stayed with him the rest of that day. It was about the tenth hour.

One of these two who became followers of Jesus after hearing what John had said was Andrew, the brother of Simon Peter.

Early next morning, Andrew met his brother and said to him, 'We have found the Messiah' – which means the Christ – and he took Simon to Jesus. Jesus looked hard at him and said, 'You are Simon son of John; you are to be called Cephas' – meaning Rock.

This is the Gospel of the Lord.

5 JANUARY

FIRST READING

A reading from the first letter of St John   3:11-21
We have passed out of death and into life because we love our brothers.

This is the message
as you heard it from the beginning:
that we are to love one another;
not to be like Cain, who belonged to the Evil One
and cut his brother's throat;
cut his brother's throat simply for this reason,
that his own life was evil and his brother lived a good life.
You must not be surprised, brothers, when the world hates you;
we have passed out of death and into life,
and of this we can be sure
because we love our brothers.
If you refuse to love, you must remain dead;
to hate your brother is to be a murderer,
and murderers, as you know, do not have eternal life in them.
This has taught us love –
that he gave up his life for us:
and we, too, ought to give up our lives for our brothers.
If a man who was rich enough in this world's goods
saw that one of his brothers was in need,
but closed his heart to him,
how could the love of God be living in him?
My children,
our love is not to be just words or mere talk,
but something real and active;
only by this can we be certain
that we are children of the truth
and be able to quieten our conscience in his presence,
whatever accusations it may raise against us,
because God is greater than our conscience and he knows
    everything.

Readings before Epiphany: 5 January

My dear people,
if we cannot be condemned by our own conscience,
we need not be afraid in God's presence.

> This is the word of the Lord.

Responsional Psalm Ps 99. ℟ v.1
℟ **Cry out with joy to the Lord, all the earth.**

1. Cry out with joy to the Lord, all the earth.
   Serve the Lord with gladness.
   Come before him, singing for joy. ℟

2. Know that he, the Lord, is God.
   He made us, we belong to him,
   we are his people, the sheep of his flock. ℟

3. Go within his gates, giving thanks.
   Enter his courts with songs of praise.
   Give thanks to him and bless his name. ℟

4. Indeed, how good is the Lord,
   eternal his merciful love.
   He is faithful from age to age. ℟

Gospel Acclamation Heb 1:1-2
Alleluia, alleluia!
At various times in the past
and in various different ways,
God spoke to our ancestors through the prophets;
but in our own time, the last days,
he has spoken to us through his Son.
Alleluia!

or

Alleluia, alleluia!
A hallowed day has dawned upon us.
Come, you nations, worship the Lord,
for today a great light has shone down upon the earth.
Alleluia!

GOSPEL

A reading from the holy Gospel according to John 1:43-51
You are the Son of God, you are the King of Israel.

After Jesus had decided to leave for Galilee, he met Philip and said, 'Follow me.' Philip came from the same town, Bethsaida, as Andrew and Peter. Philip found Nathanael and said to him, 'We have found the one Moses wrote about in the Law, the one about whom the Prophets wrote: he is Jesus son of Joseph, from Nazareth.' 'From Nazareth?' said Nathanael 'Can anything good come from that place?' 'Come and see' replied Philip. When Jesus saw Nathanael coming he said of him, 'There is an Israelite who deserves the name, incapable of deceit.' 'How do you know me?' said Nathanael. 'Before Philip came to call you,' said Jesus 'I saw you under the fig tree.' Nathanael answered, 'Rabbi, you are the Son of God, you are the King of Israel.' Jesus replied, 'You believe that just because I said: I saw you under the fig tree. You will see greater things than that.' And then he added, 'I tell you most solemnly, you will see heaven laid open and, above the Son of Man, the angels of God ascending and descending.'

This is the Gospel of the Lord.

6 JANUARY

For use in countries where Epiphany is celebrated on Sunday 7 or 8 January.

FIRST READING

A reading from the first letter of St John　　　　　　　　5:5-13
There are three witnesses: the Spirit and the water and the blood.

Who can overcome the world?
Only the man who believes that Jesus is the Son of God:
Jesus Christ who came by water and blood,
not with water only,
but with water and blood;
with the Spirit as another witness –
since the Spirit is the truth –
so that there are three witnesses,
the Spirit, the water and the blood,
and all three of them agree.
We accept the testimony of human witnesses,
but God's testimony is much greater,
and this is God's testimony,
given as evidence for his Son.
Everybody who believes in the Son of God
has this testimony inside him;

and anyone who will not believe God
is making God out to be a liar,
because he has not trusted
the testimony God has given about his Son.
This is the testimony:
God has given us eternal life
and this life is in his Son;
anyone who has the Son has life,
anyone who does not have the Son does not have life.
I have written all this to you
so that you who believe in the name of the Son of God
may be sure that you have eternal life.

This is the word of the Lord.

Responsorial Psalm Ps 147:12-15. 19-20. ℟ v.12

℟ **Praise the Lord, Jerusalem.**

or

℟ **Alleluia!**

1 O praise the Lord, Jerusalem!
   Sion, praise your God!
   He has strengthened the bars of your gates,
   he has blessed the children within you. ℟

2 He established peace on your borders,
   he feeds you with finest wheat.
   He sends out his word to the earth
   and swiftly runs his command. ℟

3 He makes his word known to Jacob,
   to Israel his laws and decreees.
   He has not dealt thus with other nations;
   he has not taught them his decrees. ℟

Gospel Acclamation cf. Mk 9:6
Alleluia, alleluia!
The heavens opened and the Father's voice resounded:
'This is my Son, the Beloved. Listen to him.'
Alleluia!

GOSPEL

A reading from the holy Gospel according to Mark 1:6-11
You are my beloved Son, in whom I am well pleased.

In the course of his preaching, John said, 'Someone is following me, someone who is more powerful than I am, and I am not fit to kneel down and undo the strap of his sandals. I have baptised you with water, but he will baptise you with the Holy Spirit.'

It was at this time that Jesus came from Nazareth in Galilee and was baptised in the Jordan by John. No sooner had he come up out of the water than he saw the heavens torn apart and the Spirit, like a dove, descending on him. And a voice came from heaven, 'You are my Son, the Beloved; my favour rests on you.'

This is the Gospel of the Lord.

Alternative Gospel

A reading from the holy Gospel according to Luke 3:23-38
Genealogy of Jesus Christ, son of Adam, Son of God.

When he started to teach, Jesus was about thirty years old, being the son, as it was thought, of Joseph son of Heli, son of Matthat, son of Levi, son of Melchi, son of Jannai, son of Joseph, son of Mattathias, son of Amos, son of Nahum, son of Esli, son of Naggai, son of Maath, son of Mattathias, son of Semein, son of Josech, son of Joda, son of Joanan, son of Rhesa, son of Zerubbabel, son of Shealtiel, son of Neri, son of Melchi, son of Addi, son of Cosam, son of Elmadam, son of Er, son of Joshua, son of Eliezer, son of Jorim, son of Matthat, son of Levi, son of Symeon, son of Judah, son of Joseph, son of Jonam, son of Eliakim, son of Melea, son of Menna, son of Mattatha, son of Nathan, son of David, son of Jesse, son of Obed, son of Boaz, son of Sala, son of Nahshon, son of Amminadab, son of Admin, son of Arni, son of Hezron, son of Perez, son of Judah, son of Jacob, son of Isaac, son of Abraham, son of Terah, son of Nahor, son of Serug, son of Reu, son of Peleg, son of Eber, son of Shelah, son of Cainan, son of Arphaxad, son of Shem, son of Noah, son of Lamech, son of Methuselah, son of Enoch, son of Jared, son of Mahalaleel, son of Cainan, son of Enos, son of Seth, son of Adam, son of God.

This is the Gospel of the Lord.

Shorter form

A reading from the holy Gospel according to Luke

3:23. 31-34. 36. 38

Genealogy of Jesus Christ, son of Adam, Son of God.

When he started to teach, Jesus was about thirty years old, being the son, as it was thought, of Joseph son of Heli, son of Melea, son of Menna, son of Mattatha, son of Nathan, son of David, son of Jesse, son of Obed, son of Boaz, son of Sala, son of Nahshon, son of Amminadab, son of Admin, son of Arni, son of Hezron, son of Perez, son of Judah, son of Jacob, son of Isaac, son of Abraham, son of Terah, son of Nahor, son of Cainan, son of Arphaxad, son of Shem, son of Noah, son of Lamech, son of Enos, son of Seth, son of Adam, son of God.

This is the Gospel of the Lord.

7 JANUARY

For use in countries where Epiphany is celebrated on Sunday 8 January.

FIRST READING

A reading from the first letter of St John 5:14-21

If we ask for anything, he will hear us.

We are quite confident that if we ask the Son of God for anything
and it is in accordance with his will,
he will hear us;
and, knowing that whatever we may ask, he hears us,
we know that we have been granted what we asked of him.
If anybody sees his brother commit a sin
that is not a deadly sin,
he has only to pray, and God will give life to the sinner
– not those who commit a deadly sin;
for there is a sin that is death,
and I will not say that you must pray about that.
Every kind of wrong-doing is sin,
but not all sin is deadly.
We know that anyone who has been begotten by God
does not sin,

because the begotten Son of God protects him,
and the Evil One does not touch him.
We know that we belong to God,
but the whole world lies in the power of the Evil One.
We know, too, that the Son of God has come,
and has given us the power
to know the true God.
We are in the true God,
as we are in his Son, Jesus Christ.
This is the true God,
this is eternal life.
Children, be on your guard against false gods.

> This is the word of the Lord.

Responsional Psalm Ps 149:1-6. 9. ℟ v.4

℟ **The Lord takes delight in his people.**

or

℟ **Alleluia!**

1 Sing a new song to the Lord,
his praise in the assembly of the faithful.
Let Israel rejoice in its Maker,
let Zion's sons exult in their king. ℟

2 Let them praise his name with dancing
and make music with timbrel and harp.
For the Lord takes delight in his people.
He crowns the poor with salvation. ℟

3 Let the faithful rejoice in their glory,
shout for joy and take their rest.
Let the praise of God be on their lips;
this honour is for all his faithful. ℟

Gospel Acclamation Lk 7:16

Alleluia, alleluia!
A great prophet has appeared among us;
God has visited his people.
Alleluia!

GOSPEL

A reading from the holy Gospel according to John 2:1-11

This was the first of the signs given by Jesus, at Cana in Galilee.

There was a wedding at Cana in Galilee. The mother of Jesus was there, and Jesus and his disciples had also been invited. When they ran out of wine, since the wine provided for the wedding was all finished, the mother of Jesus said to him, 'They have no wine.' Jesus said, 'Woman, why turn to me? My hour has not come yet.' His mother said to the servants, 'Do whatever he tells you.' There were six stone water jars standing there, meant for the ablutions that are customary among the Jews: each could hold twenty or thirty gallons. Jesus said to the servants, 'Fill the jars with water,' and they filled them to the brim. 'Draw some out now,' he told them, 'and take it to the steward.' They did this; the steward tasted the water, and it had turned into wine. Having no idea where it came from – only the servants who had drawn the water knew – the steward called the bridegroom and said, 'People generally serve the best wine first, and keep the cheaper sort till the guests have had plenty to drink; but you have kept the best wine till now.'

This was the first of the signs given by Jesus: it was given at Cana in Galilee. He let his glory be seen, and his disciples believed in him.

This is the Gospel of the Lord.

GOSPEL ACCLAMATIONS
for the Weekdays before Epiphany

1   Jn 1:14. 12

Alleluia, alleluia!
The Word became flesh, and dwelt among us.
To all who received him he gave power to become children of God.
Alleluia!

2   Heb 1:1-2

Alleluia, alleluia!
At various times in the past
and in various different ways,
God spoke to our ancestors through the prophets;
but in our own time, the last days,
he has spoken to us through his Son.
Alleluia!

3

Alleluia, alleluia!
A hallowed day has dawned upon us.
Come, you nations, worship the Lord,
for today a great light has shone down upon the earth.
Alleluia!

READINGS FOR
WEEKDAYS OF THE CHRISTMAS SEASON
after Epiphany to the Baptism of the Lord

The readings given for 7-12 January are used only on the weekdays between the Solemnity of the Epiphany and the following Sunday.

The readings for the weekdays of Ordinary Time begin on the Monday following the Sunday on which the Baptism of the Lord is celebrated, i.e. the Sunday following 6 January, and from that day the readings given below for 7-12 January are omitted.

MONDAY AFTER EPIPHANY OR 7 JANUARY

FIRST READING

A reading from the first letter of St John   3:22 – 4:6
Test the spirits, to see if they come from God.

Whatever we ask God,
we shall receive,
because we keep his commandments
and live the kind of life that he wants.
His commandments are these:
that we believe in the name of his Son Jesus Christ
and that we love one another
as he told us to.
Whoever keeps his commandments
lives in God and God lives in him.
We know that he lives in us
by the Spirit that he has given us.

It is not every spirit, my dear people, that you can trust;
test them, to see if they come from God,
there are many false prophets, now, in the world.
You can tell the spirits that come from God by this:
every spirit which acknowledges that Jesus the Christ has come
    in the flesh
is from God;
but any spirit which will not say this of Jesus
is not from God,
but is the spirit of Antichrist,
whose coming you were warned about.

Well, now he is here, in the world.
Children,
you have already overcome these false prophets,
because you are from God and you have in you
one who is greater than anyone in this world;
as for them, they are of the world,
and so they speak the language of the world
and the world listens to them.
But we are children of God,
and those who know God listen to us;
those who are not of God refuse to listen to us.
This is how we can tell
the spirit of truth from the spirit of falsehood.

> This is the word of the Lord.

Responsorial Psalm   Ps 2:7-8. 10-11. ℟ v.8

℟ **I will give you the nations for your heritage.**

1 The Lord said to me: 'You are my Son.
 It is I who have begotten you this day.
 Ask and I shall bequeath you the nations,
 put the ends of the earth in your possession.' ℟

2 Now, O kings, understand,
 take warning, rulers of the earth;
 serve the Lord with awe
 and trembling, pay him your homage. ℟

Gospel Acclamation   Mt 4:16
Alleluia, alleluia!
The people that lived in darkness
has seen a great light;
on those who dwell in the land and shadow of death
a light has dawned.
Alleluia!

or   Mt 4:23

Alleluia, alleluia!
Jesus proclaimed the Good News of the kingdom
and cured all kinds of diseases among the people.
Alleluia!

Alternative Acclamations p.130.

GOSPEL

A reading from the holy Gospel according to Matthew
The kingdom of heaven is close at hand. 4:12-17. 23-25

Hearing that John had been arrested, Jesus went back to Galilee, and leaving Nazareth he went and settled in Capernaum, a lakeside town on the borders of Zebulun and Naphtali. In this way the prophecy of Isaiah was to be fulfilled:

> Land of Zebulun! Land of Naphtali!
> Way of the sea on the far side of Jordan,
> Galilee of the nations!
> The people that lived in darkness
> has seen a great light;
> on those who dwell in the land and shadow of death
> a light has dawned.

From that moment Jesus began his preaching with the message, 'Repent, for the kingdom of heaven is close at hand.'

He went round the whole of Galilee teaching in their synagogues, proclaiming the Good News of the kingdom and curing all kinds of diseases and sickness among the people. His fame spread throughout Syria, and those who were suffering from diseases and painful complaints of one kind or another, the possessed, epileptics, the paralysed, were all brought to him, and he cured them. Large crowds followed him, coming from Galilee, the Decapolis, Jerusalem, Judaea and Transjordania.

This is the Gospel of the Lord.

TUESDAY AFTER EPIPHANY OR 8 JANUARY

FIRST READING

A reading from the first letter of St John 4:7-10
God is love.

My dear people,
let us love one another
since love comes from God
and everyone who loves is begotten by God and knows God.
Anyone who fails to love can never have known God,
because God is love.
God's love for us was revealed

when God sent into the world his only Son
so that we could have life through him;
this is the love I mean:
not our love for God,
but God's love for us when he sent his Son
to be the sacrifice that takes our sins away.

This is the word of the Lord.

Responsorial Psalm   Ps 71:1-4. 7-8. ℟ cf. v.11
    ℟ **All nations shall fall prostrate before you, O Lord.**

1. O God give your judgement to the king,
   to a king's son your justice,
   that he may judge your people in justice
   and your poor in right judgement. ℟

2. May the mountains bring forth peace for the people
   and the hills, justice.
   May he defend the poor of the people
   and save the children of the needy. ℟

3. In his days justice shall flourish
   and peace till the moon fails.
   He shall rule from sea to sea,
   from the Great River to earth's bounds. ℟

Gospel Acclamation   Mt 4:23
Alleluia, alleluia!
Jesus proclaimed the Good News of the kingdom
and cured all kinds of diseases among the people.
Alleluia!

or   Lk 4:18

Alleluia, alleluia!
The Lord has sent me to bring the good news to the poor,
to proclaim liberty to captives.
Alleluia!

GOSPEL

A reading from the holy Gospel according to Mark   6:34-44
By multiplying the loaves Jesus shows that he is a prophet.

As Jesus stepped ashore he saw a large crowd; and he took pity on them because they were like sheep without a shepherd, and he set himself to teach them at some length. By now it was getting very late, and his disciples came up to him and said, 'This is a lonely place and it is getting very late, so send them away, and they can go to the farms and villages round about, to buy themselves something to eat.' He replied, 'Give them something to eat yourselves.' They answered, 'Are we to go and spend two hundred denarii on bread for them to eat?' 'How many loaves have you?' he asked. 'Go and see.' And when they had found out they said, 'Five, and two fish.' Then he ordered them to get all the people together in groups on the green grass, and they sat down on the ground in squares of hundreds and fifties. Then he took the five loaves and the two fish, raised his eyes to heaven and said the blessing; then he broke the loaves and handed them to his disciples to distribute among the people. He also shared out the two fish among them all. They all ate as much as they wanted. They collected twelve basketfuls of scraps of bread and pieces of fish. Those who had eaten the loaves numbered five thousand men.

This is the Gospel of the Lord.

WEDNESDAY AFTER EPIPHANY OR 9 JANUARY

FIRST READING

A reading from the first letter of St John 4:11-18

As long as we love one another God will live in us.

My dear people,
since God has loved us so much,
we too should love one another.
No one has ever seen God;
but as long as we love one another
God will live in us
and his love will be complete in us.
We can know that we are living in him
and he is living in us
because he lets us share his Spirit.
We ourselves saw and we testify
that the Father sent his Son
as saviour of the world.
If anyone acknowledges that Jesus is the Son of God,
God lives in him, and he in God.
We ourselves have known and put our faith in

God's love towards ourselves.
God is love
and anyone who lives in love lives in God,
and God lives in him.
Love will come to its perfection in us
when we can face the day of Judgement without fear;
because even in this world
we have become as he is.
In love there can be no fear,
but fear is driven out by perfect love:
because to fear is to expect punishment,
and anyone who is afraid is still imperfect in love.

This is the word of the Lord.

Responsorial Psalm   Ps 71:1-2. 10-13. ℟ cf. v.11
   ℟ **All nations shall fall prostrate before you, O Lord.**

1 O God, give your judgement to the king,
    to a king's son your justice,
    that he may judge your people in justice
    and your poor in right judgement. ℟

2 The kings of Tarshish and the sea coasts
    shall pay him tribute.
    The kings of Sheba and Seba
    shall bring him gifts.
    Before him all kings shall fall prostrate,
    all nations shall serve him. ℟

3 For he shall save the poor when they cry
    and the needy who are helpless.
    He will have pity on the weak
    and save the lives of the poor. ℟

Gospel Acclamation   Lk 4:18
   Alleluia, alleluia!
   The Lord has sent me to bring the good news to the poor,
   to proclaim liberty to captives.
   Alleluia!

or   cf. 1 Tim 3:16

   Alleluia, alleluia!
   Glory be to you, O Christ,
   proclaimed to the pagans;

glory be to you, O Christ,
believed in by the world.
Alleluia!

GOSPEL

A reading from the holy Gospel according to Mark 6:45-52
They saw him walking on the lake.

After the five thousand had eaten and were filled, Jesus made his disciples get into the boat and go on ahead to Bethsaida, while he himself sent the crowd away. After saying good-bye to them he went off into the hills to pray. When evening came, the boat was far out on the lake, and he was alone on the land. He could see they were worn out with rowing, for the wind was against them; and about the fourth watch of the night he came towards them walking on the lake. He was going to pass them by, but when they saw him walking on the lake they thought it was a ghost and cried out, for they had all seen him and were terrified. But he at once spoke to them, and said, 'Courage! It is I! Do not be afraid.' Then he got into the boat with them, and the wind dropped. They were utterly and completely dumbfounded, because they had not seen what the miracle of the loaves meant; their minds were closed.

This is the Gospel of the Lord.

THURSDAY AFTER EPIPHANY OR 10 JANUARY

FIRST READING

A reading from the first letter of St John 4:19 – 5:4
Anyone who loves God must also love his brother.

We are to love,
because God loved us first.
Anyone who says, 'I love God',
and hates his brother,
is a liar,
since a man who does not love the brother that he can see
cannot love God, whom he has never seen.
So this is the commandment that he has given us,
that anyone who loves God must also love his brother.

Whoever believes that Jesus is the Christ

has been begotten by God:
and whoever loves the Father that begot him
loves the child whom he begets.
We can be sure that we love God's children
if we love God himself and do what he has commanded us;
this is what loving God is –
keeping his commandments;
and his commandments are not difficult,
because anyone who has been begotten by God
has already overcome the world;
this is the victory over the world –
our faith.

    This is the word of the Lord.

Responsorial Psalm   Ps 71:1-2. 14-15. 17. ℟ cf. v.11

   ℟ **All nations shall fall prostrate before you, O Lord.**

1 O God, give your judgement to the king,
   to a king's son your justice,
   that he may judge your people in justice
   and your poor in right judgement. ℟

2 From oppression he will rescue their lives,
   to him their blood is dear.
   They shall pray for him without ceasing
   and bless him all the day. ℟

3 May his name be blessed for ever
   and endure like the sun.
   Every tribe shall be blessed in him,
   All nations bless his name. ℟

Gospel Acclamation   Lk 7:16
   Alleluia, alleluia!
   A great prophet has appeared among us;
   God has visited his people.
   Alleluia!

or   Lk 4:18

   Alleluia, alleluia!
   The Lord has sent me to bring the good news to the poor,
   to proclaim liberty to captives.
   Alleluia!

GOSPEL

A reading from the holy Gospel according to Luke 4:14-22
This text is being fulfilled today.

Jesus, with the power of the Spirit in him, returned to Galilee; and his reputation spread throughout the countryside. He taught in their synagogues and everyone praised him.

He came to Nazara, where he had been brought up, and went into the synagogue on the sabbath day as he usually did. He stood up to read, and they handed him the scroll of the prophet Isaiah. Unrolling the scroll he found the place where it is written:

> The spirit of the Lord has been given to me,
> for he has anointed me.
> He has sent me to bring the good news to the poor,
> to proclaim liberty to captives
> and to the blind new sight,
> to set the downtrodden free,
> to proclaim the Lord's year of favour.

He then rolled up the scroll, gave it back to the assistant and sat down. And all eyes in the synagogue were fixed on him. Then he began to speak to them, 'This text is being fulfilled today even as you listen.' And he won the approval of all, and they were astonished by the gracious words that came from his lips.

This is the Gospel of the Lord.

FRIDAY AFTER EPIPHANY OR 11 JANUARY

FIRST READING

A reading from the first letter of St John 5:5-13
The Spirit, the water and the blood.

Who can overcome the world?
Only the man who believes that Jesus is Son of God:
Jesus Christ who came by water and blood,
not with water only,
but with water and blood;
with the Spirit as another witness –
since the Spirit is the truth –
so that there are three witnesses,
the Spirit, the water and the blood,
and all three of them agree.

We accept the testimony of human witnesses,
but God's testimony is much greater,
and this is God's testimony,
given as evidence for his Son.
Everybody who believes in the Son of God
has this testimony inside him;
and anyone who will not believe God
is making God out to be a liar,
because he has not trusted
the testimony God has given about his Son.
This is the testimony:
God has given us eternal life
and this life is in his Son;
anyone who has the Son has life,
anyone who does not have the Son does not have life.

I have written all this to you
so that you who believe in the name of the Son of God
may be sure that you have eternal life.

 This is the word of the Lord.

Responsorial Psalm   Ps 147:12-15. 19-20. ℟ v.12

 ℟ **O praise the Lord, Jerusalem!**

or

 ℟ **Alleluia!**

1 O praise the Lord, Jerusalem!
  Zion, praise your God!
  He has strengthened the bars of your gates,
  he has blessed the children within you. ℟

2 He established peace on your borders,
  he feeds you with finest wheat.
  He sends out his word to the earth
  and swiftly runs his command. ℟

3 He makes his word known to Jacob,
  to Israel his laws and decrees.
  He has not dealt thus with other nations;
  he has not taught them his decrees. ℟

Gospel Acclamation   cf. 1 Tim 3:16
    Alleluia, alleluia!
    Glory be to you, O Christ, proclaimed to the pagans;
    glory be to you, O Christ, believed in by the world.
    Alleluia!

or   Mt 4:23

    Alleluia, alleluia!
    Jesus proclaimed the Good News of the kingdom
    and cured all kinds of diseases among the people.
    Alleluia!

GOSPEL

A reading from the holy Gospel according to Luke   5:12-16
And the leprosy left him at once.

Jesus was in one of the towns when a man appeared, covered with leprosy. Seeing Jesus he fell on his face and implored him. 'Sir,' he said 'If you want to, you can cure me.' Jesus stretched out his hand, touched him and said, 'Of course I want to! Be cured!' And the leprosy left him at once. He ordered him to tell no one, 'But go and show yourself to the priest and make the offering for your healing as Moses prescribed it, as evidence for them.'

    His reputation continued to grow, and large crowds would gather to hear him and to have their sickness cured, but he would always go off to some place where he could be alone and pray.

    This is the Gospel of the Lord.

SATURDAY AFTER EPIPHANY OR 12 JANUARY

FIRST READING

A reading from the first letter of St John   5:14-21
Whatever we may ask, he hears us.

We are quite confident that if we ask the Son of God for anything,
and it is in accordance with his will,
he will hear us;
and, knowing that whatever we may ask, he hears us,
we know that we have already been granted what we asked of
    him.
If anybody sees his brother commit a sin
that is not a deadly sin,

he has only to pray, and God will give life to the sinner
– not those who commit a deadly sin;
for there is a sin that is death,
and I will not say that you must pray about that.
Every kind of wrong-doing is sin,
but not all sin is deadly.
We know that anyone who has been begotten by God
does not sin,
because the begotten Son of God protects him,
and the Evil One does not touch him.
We know that we belong to God,
but the whole world lies in the power of the Evil One.
We know, too, that the Son of God has come,
and has given us the power
to know the true God.
We are in the true God,
as we are in his Son, Jesus Christ.
This is the true God,
this is eternal life.
Children, be on your guard against false gods.

This is the word of the Lord.

Responsorial Psalm Ps 149:1-6. 9. ℟ v.4

℟ **The Lord takes delight in his people.**

or

℟ **Alleluia!**

1 Sing a new song to the Lord,
his praise in the assembly of the faithful.
Let Israel rejoice in its Maker,
let Zion's sons exult in their king. ℟

2 Let them praise his name with dancing
and make music with timbrel and harp.
For the Lord takes delight in his people.
He crowns the poor with salvation. ℟

3 Let the faithful rejoice in their glory,
shout for joy and take their rest.
Let the praise of God be on their lips;
this honour is for all his faithful. ℟

Readings after Epiphany: Saturday/12 January

Gospel Acclamation   Lk 7:16
    Alleluia, alleluia!
    A great prophet has appeared among us;
    God has visited his people.
    Alleluia!

or   Mt 4:16

    Alleluia, alleluia!
    The people that lived in darkness
    has seen a great light;
    on those who dwell in the land and shadow of death
    a light has dawned.
    Alleluia!

GOSPEL

A reading from the holy Gospel according to John   3:22-30
The bridegroom's friend is glad when he hears the bridegroom's voice.

Jesus went with his disciples into the Judaean countryside and stayed with them there and baptised. At the same time John was baptising at Aenon near Salim, where there was plenty of water, and people were going there to be baptised. This was before John had been put in prison.

  Now some of John's disciples had opened a discussion with a Jew about purification, so they went to John and said, 'Rabbi, the man who was with you on the far side of the Jordan, the man to whom you bore witness, is baptising now; and everyone is going to him.' John replied:

    'A man can lay claim
    only to what is given him from heaven.

'You yourselves can bear me out: I said: I myself am not the Christ; I am the one who has been sent in front of him.

    'The bride is only for the bridegroom;
    and yet the bridegroom's friend,
    who stands there and listens,
    is glad when he hears the bridegroom's voice.
    This same joy I feel, and now it is complete.
    He must grow greater,
    I must grow smaller.'

This is the Gospel of the Lord.

GOSPEL ACCLAMATIONS
for the Weekdays after Epiphany

1   Mt 4:16

Alleluia, alleluia!
The people that lived in darkness
has seen a great light;
on those who dwell in the land and shadow of death
a light has dawned.
Alleluia!

2   cf. Mt 4:23

Alleluia, alleluia!
Jesus proclaimed the Good News of the kingdom
and cured all kinds of diseases among the people.
Alleluia!

3   Lk 4:18

Alleluia, alleluia!
The Lord has sent me to bring the good news to the poor,
to proclaim liberty to captives.
Alleluia!

4   Lk 7:16

Alleluia, alleluia!
A great prophet has appeared among us;
God has visited his people.
Alleluia!

5   cf. 1 Tim 3:16

Alleluia, alleluia!
Glory be to you, O Christ,
proclaimed to the pagans;
glory be to you, O Christ,
believed in by the world.
Alleluia!

THE SEASON OF LENT

Come!
Let us Return to the Lord

For he has torn
that he may heal
he has stricken
that he may bind up

After two days **He will revive us**
on the third day **Raise us up**
that we may **Live** before him

HE · WILL · COME · AS · SURELY · AS · DAY · DAWNS

ASH WEDNESDAY

The ashes used today come from the branches blessed the preceding year for Passion Sunday.

Entrance Antiphon: Lord, you are merciful to all, and hate nothing you have created. You overlook the sins of men to bring them to repentance. You are the Lord our God.

The penitential rite and the Gloria are omitted.

Opening Prayer
Let us pray
    [for the grace to keep Lent faithfully]

Lord,
protect us in our struggle against evil.
As we begin the discipline of Lent,
make this season holy by our self-denial.

or

Let us pray
    [in quiet remembrance of our need for redemption]

Father in heaven,
the light of your truth bestows sight
to the darkness of sinful eyes.
May this season of repentance
bring us the blessing of your forgiveness
and the gift of your light.

When the blessing and distribution of ashes is done apart from Mass these readings may be used for a liturgy of the word before the blessing of ashes.

FIRST READING

A reading from the prophet Joel   2:12-18
Let your hearts be broken, not your garments torn.

'Now, now – it is the Lord who speaks –
come back to me with all your heart,
fasting, weeping, mourning.'
Let your hearts be broken not your garments torn,
turn to the Lord your God again,

for he is all tenderness and compassion,
slow to anger, rich in graciousness,
and ready to relent.
Who knows if he will not turn again, will not relent,
will not leave a blessing as he passes,
oblation and libation
for the Lord your God?
Sound the trumpet in Zion!
Order a fast,
proclaim a solemn assembly,
call the people together,
summon the community,
assemble the elders,
gather the children,
even the infants at the breast.
Let the bridegroom leave his bedroom
and the bride her alcove.
Between vestibule and altar let the priests,
the ministers of the Lord, lament.
Let them say,
'Spare your people, Lord!
Do not make your heritage a thing of shame,
a byword for the nations.
Why should it be said among the nations,
"Where is their God?"'
Then the Lord, jealous on behalf of his land,
took pity on his people.

This is the word of the Lord.

Responsorial Psalm   Ps 50:3-6. 12-14. 17.   v.3
Have mercy on us, O Lord, for we have sinned.

1 Have mercy on me, God, in your kindness.
   In your compassion blot out my offence.
   O wash me more and more from my guilt
   and cleanse me from my sin.

2 My offences truly I know them;
   my sin is always before me.
   Against you, you alone, have I sinned:
   what is evil in your sight I have done.

3 A pure heart create for me, O God,
   put a steadfast spirit within me.

Ash Wednesday

Do not cast me away from your presence,
nor deprive me of your holy spirit. ℟

4   Give me again the joy of your help;
with a spirit of fervour sustain me.
O Lord, open my lips
and my mouth shall declare your praise. ℟

SECOND READING

A reading from the second letter of St Paul
to the Corinthians
5:20 – 6:2

Be reconciled to God...now is the favourable time.

We are ambassadors for Christ; it is as though God were appealing through us, and the appeal that we make in Christ's name is: be reconciled to God. For our sake God made the sinless one into sin, so that in him we might become the goodness of God. As his fellow workers, we beg you once again not to neglect the grace of God that you have received. For he says: At the favourable time, I have listened to you; on the day of salvation I came to your help. Well, now is the favourable time; this is the day of salvation.

This is the word of the Lord.

Gospel Acclamation
Ps 50:12. 14

Praise to you, O Christ, king of eternal glory!
A pure heart create for me, O God,
and give me again the joy of your help.
Praise to you, O Christ, king of eternal glory!

or
cf. Ps 94:8

Praise to you, O Christ, king of eternal glory!
Harden not your hearts today,
but listen to the voice of the Lord.
Praise to you, O Christ, king of eternal glory!

Alternative Acclamations pp.244ff.

GOSPEL

A reading from the holy Gospel according to Matthew 6:1-6. 16-18
Your Father, who sees all that is done in secret, will reward you.

Jesus said to his disciples:
'Be careful not to parade your good deeds before men to

attract their notice; by doing this you will lose all reward from your Father in heaven. So when you give alms, do not have it trumpeted before you; this is what the hypocrites do in the synagogues and in the streets to win men's admiration. I tell you solemnly, they have had their reward. But when you give alms, your left hand must not know what your right is doing; your almsgiving must be secret, and your Father who sees all that is done in secret will reward you.

'And when you pray, do not imitate the hypocrites: they love to say their prayers standing up in the synagogues and at the street corners for people to see them. I tell you solemnly, they have had their reward. But when you pray go to your private room and, when you have shut your door, pray to your Father who is in that secret place, and your Father who sees all that is done in secret will reward you.

'When you fast do not put on a gloomy look as the hypocrites do: they pull long faces to let men know they are fasting. I tell you solemnly, they have had their reward. But when you fast, put oil on your head and wash your face, so that no one will know you are fasting except your Father who sees all that is done in secret; and your Father who sees all that is done in secret will reward you.'

This is the Gospel of the Lord.

Blessing and Giving of Ashes
After the homily the priest joins his hands and says:
Dear friends in Christ,
let us ask our Father
to bless these ashes
which we will use
as the mark of our repentance.

Silent prayer

Lord,
bless the sinner who asks for your forgiveness
and bless ✠ all those who receive these ashes.
May they keep this lenten season
in preparation for the joy of Easter.

or

Lord,
bless these ashes ✠

Ash Wednesday

by which we show that we are dust.
Pardon our sins
and keep us faithful to the discipline of Lent,
for you do not want sinners to die
but to live with the risen Christ,
who reigns with you for ever and ever.

He sprinkles the ashes with holy water in silence.
The priest then places ashes on those who come forward, saying to each:

Turn away from sin and be faithful to the gospel.

or

Remember, man, you are dust
and to dust you will return.

Meanwhile some of the following antiphons or other appropriate songs are sung.

1. Come back to the Lord with all your heart;
   leave the past in ashes,
   and turn to God with tears and fasting,
   for he is slow to anger and ready to forgive.

2. Let the priests and ministers of the Lord
   lament before his altar, and say:
   Spare us, Lord; spare your people!
   Do not let us die for we are crying out to you.

3. Lord, take away our wickedness.

These may be repeated after each verse of Psalm 50, Have mercy on me, God, see above, p.134.

Responsory
Direct our hearts to better things, O Lord;
heal our sin and ignorance.
Lord, do not face us suddenly with death,
but give us time to repent.

℟ **Turn to us with mercy, Lord; we have sinned against you.**
℣ Help us, God our saviour, rescue us for the honour of your name.
℟ **Turn to us with mercy, Lord; we have sinned against you.**

After the giving of ashes the priest washes his hands; the rite concludes with the prayer of the faithful.
The Profession of Faith is omitted.

Prayer over the Gifts
Lord,
help us to resist temptation
by our lenten works of charity and penance.
By this sacrifice
may we be prepared to celebrate
the death and resurrection of Christ our Saviour
and be cleansed from sin and renewed in spirit.

Preface of Lent I-IV, P8-P11.

Communion Antiphon: The man who meditates day and night on the law of the Lord will yield fruit in due season.

Prayer after Communion
Lord,
through this communion
may our lenten penance give you glory
and bring us your protection.

THURSDAY AFTER ASH WEDNESDAY

Entrance Antiphon: When I cry to the Lord, he hears my voice and saves me from the foes who threaten me. Unload your burden onto the Lord, and he will support you.

Opening Prayer
Lord,
may everything we do
begin with your inspiration,
continue with your help,
and reach perfection under your guidance.

FIRST READING

A reading from the book of Deuteronomy 30:15-20
See, I set before you today a blessing and a curse.

Moses said to the people: 'See, today I set before you life and prosperity, death and disaster. If you obey the commandments of the Lord your God that I enjoin on you today, if you love the Lord your God and follow his ways, if you keep his commandments, his laws, his customs, you will live and increase, and the Lord your God will bless you in the land which you are entering to make your own. But if your heart strays, if you refuse to listen, if you let yourself be drawn into worshipping other gods and serving them, I tell you today, you will most certainly perish; you will not live long in the land you are crossing the Jordan to enter and possess. I call heaven and earth to witness against you today: I set before you life or death, blessing or curse. Choose life, then, so that you and your descendants may live in the love of the Lord your God, obeying his voice, clinging to him; for in this your life consists, and on this depends your long stay in the land which the Lord swore to your fathers Abraham, Isaac and Jacob he would give them.'

This is the word of the Lord.

Responsorial Psalm   Ps 1:1-4. 6. ℟ Ps 39:5

℟ **Happy the man who has placed his trust in the Lord.**

1 Happy indeed is the man
who follows not the counsel of the wicked;
nor lingers in the way of sinners
nor sits in the company of scorners,
but whose delight is the law of the Lord,
and who ponders his law day and night. ℟

2 He is like a tree that is planted
beside the flowing waters.
that yields its fruit in due season
and whose leaves shall never fade;
and all that he does shall prosper. ℟

3 Not so are the wicked, not so!
For they like winnowed chaff
shall be driven away by the wind;
for the Lord guards the way of the just
but the way of the wicked leads to doom. ℟

Gospel Acclamation
Ps 50:12. 14

Praise and honour to you, Lord Jesus!
A pure heart create for me, O God,
and give me again the joy of your help.
Praise and honour to you, Lord Jesus!

or
Mt 4:17

Praise and honour to you, Lord Jesus!
Repent, says the Lord,
for the kingdom of heaven is close at hand.
Praise and honour to you, Lord Jesus!

GOSPEL

A reading from the holy Gospel according to Luke 9:22-25
Anyone who loses his life for my sake, that man will save it.

Jesus said to his disciples: 'The Son of Man is destined to suffer grievously, to be rejected by the elders and chief priests and scribes and to be put to death, and to be raised up on the third day.'

Then to all he said, 'If anyone wants to be a follower of mine, let him renounce himself and take up his cross every day and follow me. For anyone who wants to save his life will lose it; but anyone who loses his life for my sake, that man will save it. What gain, then, is it for a man to have won the whole world and to have lost or ruined his very self?'

This is the Gospel of the Lord.

Prayer over the Gifts
Lord,
accept these gifts.
May they bring us your mercy
and give you honour and praise.

Preface of Lent I-V, P8-P11.

Communion Antiphon: Create a clean heart in me, O God; give me a new and steadfast spirit.

Prayer after Communion
Merciful Father,
may the gifts and blessings we receive
bring us pardon and salvation.

FRIDAY AFTER ASH WEDNESDAY

Entrance Antiphon: The Lord heard me and took pity on me. He came to my help.

Opening Prayer

Lord,
with your loving care
guide the penance we have begun.
Help us to persevere with love and sincerity.

FIRST READING

A reading from the prophet Isaiah 58:1-9
Is not this the sort of fast that pleases me?

Thus says the Lord:

> Shout for all you are worth,
> raise your voice like a trumpet.
> Proclaim their faults to my people,
> their sins to the House of Jacob.
>
> They seek me day after day,
> they long to know my ways,
> like a nation that wants to act with integrity
> and not ignore the law of its God.
>
> They ask me for laws that are just,
> they long for God to draw near:
> 'Why should we fast if you never see it,
> why do penance if you never notice?'
>
> Look, you do business on your fastdays,
> you oppress all your workmen;
> look, you quarrel and squabble when you fast
> and strike the poor man with your fist.
>
> Fasting like yours today
> will never make your voice heard on high.
> Is that the sort of fast that pleases me,
> a truly penitential day for men?
>
> Hanging your head like a reed,
> lying down on sackcloth and ashes?
> Is that what you call fasting,
> a day acceptable to the Lord?

Is not this the sort of fast that pleases me
– it is the Lord who speaks –
to break unjust fetters
and undo the thongs of the yoke,

to let the oppressed go free,
and break every yoke,
to share your bread with the hungry,
and shelter the homeless poor,

to clothe the man you see to be naked
and not turn from your own kin?
Then will your light shine like the dawn
and your wound be quickly healed over.

Your integrity will go before you
and the glory of the Lord behind you.
Cry, and the Lord will answer;
call, and he will say, 'I am here.'

This is the word of the Lord.

Responsorial Psalm
Ps 50:3-6. 18-19. ℟ v.19

℟ **A humbled, contrite heart, O God, you will not spurn.**

1 Have mercy on me, God, in your kindness.
   In your compassion blot out my offence.
   O wash me more and more from my guilt
   and cleanse me from my sin.   ℟

2 My offences truly I know them;
   my sin is always before me.
   Against you, you alone, have I sinned;
   what is evil in your sight I have done.   ℟

3 For in sacrifice you take no delight,
   burnt offering from me you would refuse,
   my sacrifice a contrite spirit.
   A humbled, contrite heart you will not spurn.   ℟

Gospel Acclamation
cf. Ps 129:5. 7

Glory and praise to you, O Christ!
My soul is waiting for the Lord,
I count on his word,
because with the Lord there is mercy
and fullness of redemption.
Glory and praise to you, O Christ!

or cf. Amos 5:14

Glory and praise to you, O Christ!
Seek good and not evil so that you may live,
and that the Lord God of hosts may really be with you.
Glory and praise to you, O Christ!

GOSPEL

A reading from the holy Gospel according to Matthew 9:14-15
When the bridegroom is taken from them, then they will fast.

John's disciples came to Jesus and said, 'Why is it that we and the Pharisees fast, but your disciples do not?' Jesus replied, 'Surely the bridegroom's attendants would never think of mourning as long as the bridegroom is still with them? But the time will come for the bridegroom to be taken away from them, and then they will fast.'

This is the Gospel of the Lord.

Prayer over the Gifts
Lord,
through this lenten eucharist
may we grow in your love and service
and become an acceptable offering to you.

Preface of Lent I-IV, P8-P11.

Communion Antiphon: Teach us your ways, O Lord, and lead us in your paths.

Prayer after Communion
Lord,
may our sharing in this mystery
free us from our sins
and make us worthy of your healing.

SATURDAY AFTER ASH WEDNESDAY

Entrance Antiphon: Answer us, Lord, with your loving-kindness, turn to us in your great mercy.

Saturday after Ash Wednesday

Opening Prayer
Father,
look upon our weakness
and reach out to help us with your loving power.

FIRST READING

A reading from the prophet Isaiah 58:9-14
Your light will rise in the darkness.

The Lord says this:

If you do away with the yoke,
the clenched fist, the wicked word,
if you give your bread to the hungry,
and relief to the oppressed,
your light will rise in the darkness,
and your shadows become like noon.
The Lord will always guide you,
giving you relief in desert places.
He will give strength to your bones
and you shall be like a watered garden,
like a spring of water
whose waters never run dry.
You will rebuild the ancient ruins,
build up on the old foundations.
You will be called 'Breach-mender',
'Restorer of ruined houses'.
If you refrain from trampling the sabbath,
and doing business on the holy day,
if you call the sabbath 'Delightful',
and the day sacred to the Lord 'Honourable',
if you honour it by abstaining from travel,
from doing business and from gossip,
then you shall find happiness in the Lord
and I will lead you triumphant over the heights of the land.
I will feed you on the heritage of Jacob your father.
For the mouth of the Lord has spoken.

This is the word of the Lord.

Responsorial Psalm Ps 85:1-6. ℟ v.11
℟ **Show me, Lord, your way
so that I may walk in your truth.**

1 Turn your ear, O Lord, and give answer

for I am poor and needy.
Preserve my life, for I am faithful:
save the servant who trusts in you. ℟

2   You are my God, have mercy on me, Lord,
for I cry to you all the day long.
Give joy to your servant, O Lord,
for to you I lift up my soul. ℟

3   O Lord, you are good and forgiving,
full of love to all who call.
Give heed, O Lord, to my prayer
and attend to the sound of my voice. ℟

Gospel Acclamation cf. Ps 94:8

Glory to you, O Christ, you are the Word of God!
Harden not your hearts today,
but listen to the voice of the Lord.
Glory to you, O Christ, you are the Word of God!

or Ez 33:11

Glory to you, O Christ, you are the Word of God!
I take pleasure, not in the death of a wicked man –
it is the Lord who speaks –
but in the turning back of a wicked man
who changes his ways to win life.
Glory to you, O Christ, you are the Word of God!

GOSPEL

A reading from the holy Gospel according to Luke 5:27-32
I have not come to call the virtuous, but sinners to repentance.

Jesus noticed a tax collector, Levi by name, sitting by the customs house, and said to him, 'Follow me.' And leaving everything he got up and followed him.

In his honour Levi held a great reception in his house, and with them at table was a large gathering of tax collectors and others. The Pharisees and their scribes complained to his disciples and said, 'Why do you eat and drink with tax collectors and sinners?' Jesus said to them in reply, 'It is not those who are well who need the doctor, but the sick. I have not come to call the virtuous, but sinners to repentance.'

This is the Gospel of the Lord.

Prayer over the Gifts
Lord,
receive our sacrifice of praise and reconciliation.
Let it free us from sin
and enable us to give you loving service.

Preface of Lent I-IV, P8-P11.

Communion Antiphon: It is mercy that I want, and not sacrifice, says the Lord; I did not come to call the virtuous, but sinners.

Prayer after Communion
Lord,
we are nourished by the bread of life you give us.
May this mystery we now celebrate
help us to reach eternal life with you.

FIRST WEEK OF LENT

MONDAY

Entrance Antiphon: As the eyes of servants are on the hands of their master, so our eyes are fixed on the Lord our God, pleading for his mercy. Have mercy on us, Lord, have mercy.

Opening Prayer
God our Saviour,
bring us back to you
and fill our minds with your wisdom.
May we be enriched by our observance of Lent.

FIRST READING

A reading from the book of Leviticus   19:1-2. 11-18
You must pass judgement on your neighbour according to justice.

The Lord spoke to Moses; he said: 'Speak to the whole community of the sons of Israel and say to them: "Be holy, for I, the Lord your God, am holy.

"You must not steal nor deal deceitfully or fraudulently with your neighbour. You must not swear falsely by my name, profaning the name of your God. I am the Lord. You must not exploit or rob your neighbour. You must not keep back the labourer's wage until next morning. You must not curse the dumb, nor put an obstacle in the blind man's way, but you must fear your God. I am the Lord.

"You must not be guilty of unjust verdicts. You must neither be partial to the little man nor overawed by the great; you must pass judgement on your neighbour according to justice. You must not slander your own people, and you must not jeopardise your neighbour's life. I am the Lord. You must not bear hatred for your brother in your heart. You must openly tell him, your neighbour, of his offence; this way you will not take a sin upon yourself. You must not exact vengeance, nor must you bear a grudge against the children of your people. You must love your neighbour as yourself. I am the Lord."'

This is the word of the Lord.

Responsorial Psalm Ps 18:8-10. 15. ℟ Jn 6:64

℟ **Your words are spirit, Lord,**
 and they are life.

1 The law of the Lord is perfect,
 it revives the soul.
 The rule of the Lord is to be trusted,
 it gives wisdom to the simple. ℟

2 The precepts of the Lord are right,
 they gladden the heart.
 The command of the Lord is clear,
 it gives light to the eyes. ℟

3 The fear of the Lord is holy,
 abiding for ever.
 The decrees of the Lord are truth
 and all of them just. ℟

4 May the spoken words of my mouth,
 the thoughts of my heart,
 win favour in your sight, O Lord,
 my rescuer, my rock! ℟

Gospel Acclamation Ez 18:31
Praise to you, O Christ, king of eternal glory!
Shake off all your sins – it is the Lord who speaks –
and make yourselves a new heart and a new spirit.
Praise to you, O Christ, king of eternal glory!

or 2 Cor 6:2

Praise to you, O Christ, king of eternal glory!
Now is the favourable time;
this is the day of salvation.
Praise to you, O Christ, king of eternal glory!

GOSPEL

A reading from the holy Gospel according to Matthew 25:31-46
In so far as you did this to one of the least of these brothers of mine you did it to me.

Jesus said to his disciples: 'When the Son of Man comes in his glory, escorted by all the angels, then he will take his seat on his throne of glory. All the nations will be assembled before him and he will separate men one from another as the shepherd separates sheep from goats. He will place the sheep on his right hand and the goats on his left. Then the King will say to those on his right hand, "Come, you whom my Father has blessed, take for your heritage the kingdom prepared for you since the foundation of the world. For I was hungry and you gave me food; I was thirsty and you gave me drink; I was a stranger and you made me welcome; naked and you clothed me, sick and you visited me, in prison and you came to see me." Then the virtuous will say to him in reply, "Lord, when did we see you hungry and feed you; or thirsty and give you drink? When did we see you a stranger and make you welcome; naked and clothe you; sick or in prison and go to see you?" And the King will answer, "I tell you solemnly, in so far as you did this to one of the least of these brothers of mine, you did it to me". Next he will say to those on his left hand, "Go away from me, with your curse upon you, to the eternal fire prepared for the devil and his angels. For I was hungry and you never gave me food; I was thirsty and you never gave me anything to drink; I was a stranger and you never made me welcome, naked and you never clothed me, sick and in prison and you never visited me." Then it will be their turn to ask, "Lord, when did we see you hungry or thirsty, a stranger or naked, sick or in prison, and did not come to your help?" Then he will answer, "I tell you solemnly, in so far as you neglected to do this to one of the least of these, you neglected to do it to me." And they will go away to eternal punishment, and the virtuous to eternal life.'

This is the Gospel of the Lord.

First Week of Lent: Tuesday

Prayer over the Gifts
Lord,
may this offering of our love
be acceptable to you.
Let it transform our lives
and bring us your mercy.

Preface of Lent I-IV, P8-P11.

Communion Antiphon: I tell you, anything you did for the least of my brothers, you did for me, says the Lord. Come, you whom my Father has blessed; inherit the kingdom prepared for you since the foundation of the world.

Prayer after Communion
Lord,
through this sacrament
may we rejoice in your healing power
and experience your saving love in mind and body.

TUESDAY

Entrance Antiphon: In every age, O Lord, you have been our refuge. From all eternity, you are God.

Opening Prayer
Father,
look on us, your children.
Through the discipline of Lent
help us to grow in our desire for you.

FIRST READING

A reading from the prophet Isaiah 55:10-11
My word shall succeed in what it was sent to do.

Thus says the Lord:
As the rain and the snow come down from the heavens and do not return without watering the earth, making it yield and giving growth to provide seed for the sower and bread for the eating, so the word that goes from my mouth does not return to me empty, without carrying out my will and succeeding in what

it was sent to do.

This is the word of the Lord.

Responsorial Psalm   Ps 33:4-7. 16-19. ℟ v.18

℟ **The Lord rescues the just in all their distress.**

1. Glorify the Lord with me.
  Together let us praise his name.
  I sought the Lord and he answered me;
  from all my terrors he set me free. ℟

2. Look towards him and be radiant;
  let your faces not be abashed.
  This poor man called; the Lord heard him
  and rescued him from all his distress. ℟

3. The Lord turns his face against the wicked
  to destroy their remembrance from the earth.
  The Lord turns his eyes to the just
  and his ears to their appeal. ℟

4. They call and the Lord hears
  and rescues them in all their distress.
  The Lord is close to the broken-hearted;
  those whose spirit is crushed he will save. ℟

Gospel Acclamation   Mt 4:4

Praise and honour to you, Lord Jesus!
Man does not live on bread alone,
but on every word that comes from the mouth of God.
Praise and honour to you, Lord Jesus!

GOSPEL

A reading from the holy Gospel according to Matthew   6:7-15
You should pray like this.

Jesus said to his disciples: 'In your prayers do not babble as the pagans do, for they think that by using many words they will make themselves heard. Do not be like them; your Father knows what you need before you ask him. So you should pray like this:

   'Our Father in heaven,
   may your name be held holy,
   your kingdom come,
   your will be done,

on earth as in heaven.
Give us today our daily bread.
And forgive us our debts,
as we have forgiven those who are in debt to us.
And do not put us to the test,
but save us from the evil one.

'Yes, if you forgive others their failings, your heavenly Father will forgive you yours; but if you do not forgive others, your Father will not forgive your failings either.'

This is the Gospel of the Lord.

Prayer over the Gifts
Father of creation,
from all you have given us
we bring you this bread and wine.
May it become for us the food of eternal life.

Preface of Lent I-IV, P8-P11.

Communion Antiphon: My God of justice, you answer my cry; you come to my help when I am in trouble. Take pity on me, Lord, and hear my prayer.

Prayer after Communion
Lord,
may we who receive this sacrament
restrain our earthly desires
and grow in love for the things of heaven.

WEDNESDAY

Entrance Antiphon: Remember your mercies, Lord, your tenderness from ages past. Do not let our enemies triumph over us; O God, deliver Israel from all her distress.

Opening Prayer
Lord,
look upon us and hear our prayer.
By the good works you inspire
help us to discipline our bodies
and to be renewed in spirit.

FIRST READING

A reading from the prophet Jonah 3:1-10
The people of Nineveh renounced their evil behaviour.

The word of the Lord was addressed to Jonah: 'Up!' he said, 'Go to Nineveh, the great city, and preach to them as I told you to.' Jonah set out and went to Nineveh in obedience to the word of the Lord. Now Nineveh was a city great beyond compare: it took three days to cross it. Jonah went on into the city, making a day's journey. He preached in these words, 'Only forty days more and Nineveh is going to be destroyed,' And the people of Nineveh believed in God; they proclaimed a fast and put on sackcloth, from the greatest to the least. The news reached the king of Nineveh, who rose from his throne, took off his robe, put on sackcloth and sat down in ashes. A proclamation was then promulgated throughout Nineveh, by decree of the king and his ministers, as follows: 'Men and beasts, herds and flocks, are to taste nothing; they must not eat, they must not drink water. All are to put on sackcloth and call on God with all their might; and let everyone renounce his evil behaviour and the wicked things he has done. Who knows if God will not change his mind and relent, if he will not renounce his burning wrath, so that we do not perish?' God saw their efforts to renounce their evil behaviour. And God relented: he did not inflict on them the disaster which he had threatened.

This is the word of the Lord.

Responsorial Psalm Ps 50:3-4. 12-13. 18-19. ℟ v.19

℟ **A humbled, contrite heart, O God, you will not spurn.**

1 Have mercy on me, God, in your kindness.
  In your compassion blot out my offence.
  O wash me more and more from my guilt
  and cleanse me from my sin. ℟

2 A pure heart create for me, O God,
  put a steadfast spirit within me.
  Do not cast me away from your presence,
  nor deprive me of your holy spirit. ℟

3 For in sacrifice you take no delight,
  burnt offering from me you would refuse,
  my sacrifice a contrite spirit.
  A humbled, contrite heart you will not spurn. ℟

Gospel Acclamation
Ez 33:11

Glory and praise to you, O Christ!
I take pleasure, not in the death of a wicked man –
it is the Lord who speaks –
but in the turning back of a wicked man
who changes his ways to win life.
Glory and praise to you, O Christ!

or
Joel 2:12-13

Glory and praise to you, O Christ!
Now, now – it is the Lord who speaks –
come back to me with all your heart,
for I am all tenderness and compassion.
Glory and praise to you, O Christ!

GOSPEL

A reading from the holy Gospel according to Luke 11:29-32

The only sign given to this generation is the sign of Jonah.

The crowds got even bigger and Jesus addressed them. 'This is a wicked generation; it is asking for a sign. The only sign it will be given is the sign of Jonah. For just as Jonah became a sign to the Ninevites, so will the Son of Man be to this generation. On Judgement day the Queen of the South will rise up with the men of this generation and condemn them, because she came from the ends of the earth to hear the wisdom of Solomon; and there is something greater than Solomon here. On Judgement day the men of Nineveh will stand up with this generation and condemn it, because when Jonah preached they repented; and there is something greater than Jonah here.'

This is the Gospel of the Lord.

Prayer over the Gifts
Lord,
from all you have given us,
we bring you these gifts in your honour.
Make them the sacrament of our salvation.

Preface of Lent I-IV, P8-P11.

Communion Antiphon: Lord, give joy to all who trust in you; be their defender and make them happy for ever.

Prayer after Communion
Father,
you never fail to give us the food of life.
May this eucharist renew our strength
and bring us to salvation.

THURSDAY

Entrance Antiphon: Let my words reach your ears, Lord; listen to my groaning, and hear the cry of my prayer, O my King, my God.

Opening Prayer
Father,
without you we can do nothing.
By your Spirit help us to know what is right
and to be eager in doing your will.

FIRST READING

A reading from the book of Esther 4:17
I have no helper but you, Lord.

Queen Esther took refuge with the Lord in the mortal peril which had overtaken her. She besought the Lord God of Israel in these words:

'My Lord, our King, the only one,
come to my help, for I am alone
and have no helper but you
and am about to take my life in my hands.

'I have been taught from my earliest years, in the bosom of my
    family, that you, Lord, chose
Israel out of all the nations
and our ancestors out of all the people of old times
to be your heritage for ever;
and that you have treated them as you promised.
Remember, Lord; reveal yourself
in the time of our distress.
'As for me, give me courage,
King of gods and master of all power.
Put persuasive words into my mouth
when I face the lion;

change his feeling into hatred for our enemy,
that the latter and all like him may be brought to their end.

'As for ourselves, save us by your hand,
and come to my help, for I am alone
and have no one but you, Lord.'

This is the word of the Lord.

Responsorial Psalm   Ps 137:1-3. 7-8. ℟ v.3

℟ **On the day I called, you answered me, O Lord.**

1 I thank you, Lord, with all my heart,
   you have heard the words of my mouth.
   Before the angels I will bless you.
   I will adore before your holy temple. ℟

2 I thank you for your faithfulness and love
   which excel all we ever knew of you.
   On the day I called, you answered;
   you increased the strength of my soul. ℟

3 You stretch out your hand and save me,
   your hand will do all things for me.
   Your love, O Lord, is eternal,
   discard not the work of your hands. ℟

Gospel Acclamation   Joel 2:12-13

Glory to you, O Christ, you are the Word of God!
Now, now – it is the Lord who speaks –
come back to me with all your heart,
for I am all tenderness and compassion.
Glory to you, O Christ, you are the Word of God!

or   Ps 50:12.14

Glory to you, O Christ, you are the Word of God!
A pure heart create for me, O God,
and give me again the joy of your help.
Glory to you, O Christ, you are the Word of God!

GOSPEL

A reading from the holy Gospel according to Matthew   7:7-12
The one who asks always receives.

Jesus said to his disciples: 'Ask, and it will be given to you;

search, and you will find; knock, and the door will be opened to you. For the one who asks always receives; the one who searches always finds; the one who knocks will always have the door opened to him. Is there a man among you who would hand his son a stone when he asked for bread? Or would hand him a snake when he asked for a fish? If you, then, who are evil, know how to give your children what is good, how much more will your Father in heaven give good things to those who ask him!

'So always treat others as you would like them to treat you; that is the meaning of the Law and the Prophets.'

This is the Gospel of the Lord.

Prayer over the Gifts
Lord,
be close to your people,
accept our prayers and offerings,
and let us turn to you with all our hearts.

Preface of Lent I-IV, P8-P11.

Communion Antiphon: Everyone who asks will receive; whoever seeks shall find, and to him who knocks it shall be opened.

Prayer after Communion
Lord our God,
renew us by these mysteries.
May they heal us now
and bring us eternal salvation.

FRIDAY

Entrance Antiphon: Lord, deliver me from my distress. See my hardship and my poverty, and pardon all my sins.

Opening Prayer
Lord,
may our observance of Lent
help to renew us and prepare us
to celebrate the death and resurrection of Christ,
who lives and reigns . . .

First Week of Lent: Friday

FIRST READING

A reading from the prophet Ezekiel   18:21-28
Am I likely to take pleasure in the death of a wicked man and not prefer to see him renounce his wickedness and live.

Thus says the Lord:
   If the wicked man renounces all the sins he has committed, respects my laws and is law-abiding and honest, he will certainly live; he will not die. All the sins he committed will be forgotten from then on; he shall live because of the integrity he has practised. What! Am I likely to take pleasure in the death of a wicked man – it is the Lord who speaks – and not prefer to see him renounce his wickedness and live?
   'But if the upright man renounces his integrity, commits sin, copies the wicked man and practises every kind of filth, is he to live? All the integrity he has practised shall be forgotten from then on; but this is because he himself has broken faith and committed sin, and for this he shall die. But you object, "What the Lord does is unjust." Listen, you House of Israel: is what I do unjust? Is it not what you do that is unjust? When the upright man renounces his integrity to commit sin and dies because of this, he dies because of the evil that he himself has committed. When the sinner renounces sin to become law-abiding and honest, he deserves to live. He has chosen to renounce all his previous sins, he shall certainly live; he shall not die.'

   This is the word of the Lord.

Responsorial Psalm   Ps 129. ℟ v.3

  ℟ **If you, O Lord, should mark our guilt,**
     Lord, who would survive?

1 Out of the depths I cry to you, O Lord,
   Lord, hear my voice!
   O let your ears be attentive
   to the voice of my pleading.   ℟

2 If you, O Lord, should mark our guilt,
   Lord, who would survive?
   But with you is found forgiveness:
   for this we revere you.   ℟

3 My soul is waiting for the Lord,
   I count on his word.
   My soul is longing for the Lord

more than watchman for daybreak.
Let the watchman count on daybreak
and Israel on the Lord.

℟ **If you, O Lord, should mark our guilt,
Lord, who would survive?**

4 Because with the Lord there is mercy
and fullness of redemption,
Israel indeed he will redeem
from all its iniquity. ℟

Gospel Acclamation cf. Amos 5:14
Praise to you, O Christ, king of eternal glory!
Seek good and not evil so that you may live,
and that the Lord God of hosts may really be with you.
Praise to you, O Christ, king of eternal glory!

or Ez 18:31

Praise to you, O Christ, king of eternal glory!
Shake off all your sins – it is the Lord who speaks –
and make yourselves a new heart and a new spirit.
Praise to you, O Christ, king of eternal glory!

GOSPEL

A reading from the holy Gospel according to Matthew 5:20-26
Go and be reconciled with your brother first.

Jesus said to his disciples: 'If your virtue goes no deeper than that of the scribes and Pharisees, you will never get into the kingdom of heaven.

'You have learnt how it was said to our ancestors: You must not kill, and if anyone does kill he must answer for it before the court. But I say this to you: anyone who is angry with his brother will answer for it before the court; if a man calls his brother "Fool" he will answer for it before the Sanhedrin, and if a man calls him "Renegade" he will answer for it in hell fire. So then, if you are bringing your offering to the altar and there remember that your brother has something against you, leave your offering there before the altar, go and be reconciled with your brother first, and then come back and present your offering. Come to terms with your opponent in good time while you are still on the way to the court with him, or he may hand you over to the judge and the judge to the officer, and you will be thrown into prison. I

First Week of Lent: Saturday

tell you solemnly, you will not get out till you have paid the last penny.'

This is the Gospel of the Lord.

Prayer over the Gifts
Lord of mercy,
in your love accept these gifts.
May they bring us your saving power.

Preface of Lent I-IV, P8-P11.

Communion Antiphon: By my life, I do not wish the sinner to die, says the Lord, but to turn to me and live.

Prayer after Communion
Lord,
may the sacrament you give us
free us from our sinful ways and bring us new life.
May this eucharist lead us to salvation.

SATURDAY

Entrance Antiphon: The law of the Lord is perfect, reviving the soul; his commandments are the wisdom of the simple.

Opening Prayer
Eternal Father,
turn our hearts to you.
By seeking your kingdom
and loving one another,
may we become a people who worship you
in spirit and truth.

FIRST READING

A reading from the book of Deuteronomy   26:16-19
You will be a people consecrated to the Lord God.

Moses said to the people: 'The Lord your God today commands you to observe these laws and customs; you must keep and observe them with all your heart and with all your soul.

'You have today made this declaration about the Lord; that he will be your God, but only if you follow his ways, keep his statutes, his commandments, his ordinances, and listen to his voice. And the Lord has today made this declaration about you: that you will be his very own people as he promised you, but only if you keep all his commandments; then for praise and renown and honour he will set you high above all the nations he has made, and you will be a people consecrated to the Lord, as he promised.'

This is the word of the Lord.

Responsorial Psalm   Ps 118:1-2. 4-5. 7-8. R/ v.1

℟ **They are happy who follow God's law!**

1. They are happy whose life is blameless,
   who follow God's law!
   They are happy those who do his will,
   seeking him with all their hearts. ℟

2. You have laid down your precepts
   to be obeyed with care.
   May my footsteps be firm
   to obey your statutes. ℟

3. I will thank you with an upright heart
   as I learn your decrees.
   I will obey your statutes;
   do not forsake me. ℟

Gospel Acclamation   cf. Lk 8:15

Praise and honour to you, Lord Jesus!
Blessed are those who, with a noble and generous heart,
take the word of God to themselves
and yield a harvest through their perseverance.
Praise and honour to you, Lord Jesus!

or   2 Cor 6:2

Praise and honour to you, Lord Jesus!
Now is the favourable time;
this is the day of salvation.
Praise and honour to you, Lord Jesus!

First Week of Lent: Saturday

GOSPEL

A reading from the holy Gospel according to Matthew 5:43-48
Be perfect as your heavenly Father is perfect.

Jesus said to his disciples: 'You have learnt how it was said: You must love your neighbour and hate your enemy. But I say this to you: love your enemies and pray for those who persecute you; in this way you will be sons of your Father in heaven, for he causes the sun to rise on bad men as well as good, and his rain to fall on honest and dishonest men alike. For if you love those who love you, what right have you to claim any credit? Even the tax collectors do as much, do they not? And if you save your greetings for your brothers, are you doing anything exceptional? Even the pagans do as much, do they not? You must therefore be perfect just as your heavenly Father is perfect.'

This is the Gospel of the Lord.

Prayer over the Gifts
Lord,
may we be renewed by this eucharist.
May we become more like Christ your Son,
who is Lord for ever and ever.

Preface of Lent I-IV, P8-P11.

Communion Antiphon: Be perfect, as your heavenly Father is perfect, says the Lord.

Prayer after Communion
Lord,
may the word we share
be our guide to peace in your kingdom.
May the food we receive
assure us of your constant love.

SECOND WEEK OF LENT

MONDAY

Entrance Antiphon: Redeem me, Lord, and have mercy on me; my foot is set on the right path, I worship you in the great assembly.

Opening Prayer
God our Father,
teach us to find new life through penance.
Keep us from sin,
and help us live by your commandment of love.

FIRST READING

A reading from the prophet Daniel 9:4-10
We have sinned, we have done wrong.

O Lord, God great and to be feared, you keep the covenant and have kindness for those who love you and keep your commandments: we have sinned, we have done wrong, we have acted wickedly, we have betrayed your commandments and your ordinances and turned away from them. We have not listened to your servants the prophets, who spoke in your name to our kings, our princes, our ancestors, and to all the people of the land. Integrity, Lord, is yours; ours the look of shame we wear today, we, the people of Judah, the citizens of Jerusalem, the whole of Israel, near and far away, in every country to which you have dispersed us because of the treason we have committed against you. To us, Lord, the look of shame belongs, to our kings, our princes, our ancestors, because we have sinned against you. To the Lord our God mercy and pardon belong, because we have betrayed him, and have not listened to the voice of the Lord our God nor followed the laws he has given us through his servants the prophets.

This is the word of the Lord.

Responsorial Psalm
Ps 78:8-9. 11. 13. ℟ Ps 102:10

℟ **Do not treat us according to our sins, O Lord.**

1 Do not hold the guilt of our fathers against us.
  Let your compassion hasten to meet us
  for we are in the depths of distress. ℟

Second Week of Lent: Monday

2 O God our saviour, come to our help,
   come for the sake of the glory of your name.
   O Lord our God, forgive us our sins;
   rescue us for the sake of your name. ℟

3 Let the groans of the prisoners come before you;
   let your strong arm reprieve those condemned to die.
   But we, your people, the flock of your pasture,
   will give you thanks for ever and ever.
   We will tell your praise from age to age. ℟

Gospel Acclamation

   Praise and honour to you, Lord Jesus!
   The seed is the word of God, Christ the sower,
   whoever finds this seed will remain for ever.
   Praise and honour to you, Lord Jesus!

or   cf. Jn 6:63.68

   Praise and honour to you, Lord Jesus!
   Your words are spirit, Lord and they are life;
   you have the message of eternal life.
   Praise and honour to you, Lord Jesus!

GOSPEL

A reading from the holy Gospel according to Luke   6:36-38
Grant pardon, and you will be pardoned.

Jesus said to his disciples: 'Be compassionate as your Father is compassionate. Do not judge, and you will not be judged yourselves; do not condemn, and you will not be condemned yourselves; grant pardon, and you will be pardoned. Give, and there will be gifts for you: a full measure, pressed down, shaken together, and running over, will be poured into your lap; because the amount you measure out is the amount you will be given back.'

   This is the Gospel of the Lord.

Prayer over the Gifts

Father of mercy,
hear our prayer.
May the grace of this mystery
prevent us from becoming absorbed in material things.

Preface of Lent I-IV, P8-P11.

Communion Antiphon: Be merciful as your Father is merciful, says the Lord.

Prayer after Communion

Lord,
may this communion bring us pardon
and lead us to the joy of heaven.

TUESDAY

Entrance Antiphon: Give light to my eyes, Lord, lest I sleep in death, and my enemy say: I have overcome him.

Opening Prayer

Lord,
watch over your Church,
and guide it with your unfailing love.
Protect us from what could harm us
and lead us to what will save us.
Help us always,
for without you we are bound to fail.

FIRST READING

A reading from the prophet Isaiah 1:10. 16-20
Learn to do good, search for justice.

Hear the word of the Lord,
you rulers of Sodom;
listen to the command of our God,
you people of Gomorrah.

'Wash, make yourselves clean.
Take your wrong-doing out of my sight.

'Cease to do evil.
Learn to do good,
search for justice,
help the oppressed,
be just to the orphan,
plead for the widow.

'Come now, let us talk this over,
says the Lord.
Though your sins are like scarlet,

they shall be as white as snow;
though they are red as crimson,
they shall be like wool.

'If you are willing to obey,
you shall eat the good things of the earth.
But if you persist in rebellion,
the sword shall eat you instead.'
The mouth of the Lord has spoken.

This is the word of the Lord.

Responsorial Psalm   Ps 49:8-9. 16-17. 21. 23. ℟ v.23

  ℟ **I will show God's salvation to the upright.**

1 'I find no fault with your sacrifices,
your offerings are always before me.
I do not ask more bullocks from your farms,
nor goats from among your herds. ℟

2 'But how can you recite my commandments
and take my covenant on your lips,
you who despise my law
and throw my words to the winds. ℟

3 'You do this, and should I keep silence?
Do you think that I am like you?
A sacrifice of thanksgiving honours me
and I will show God's salvation to the upright.' ℟

Gospel Acclamation   Mt 4:17
Glory and praise to you, O Christ!
Repent, says the Lord, for the kingdom of heaven is close at hand.
Glory and praise to you, O Christ!

or   Ez 18:31

Glory and praise to you, O Christ!
Shake off all your sins – it is the Lord who speaks –
and make yourselves a new heart and a new spirit.
Glory and praise to you, O Christ!

GOSPEL

A reading from the holy Gospel according to Matthew 23:1-12

They do not practise what they preach.

Addressing the people and his disciples Jesus said, 'The scribes and the Pharisees occupy the chair of Moses. You must therefore do what they tell you and listen to what they say; but do not be guided by what they do, since they do not practise what they preach. They tie up heavy burdens and lay them on men's shoulders, but will they lift a finger to move them? Not they! Everything they do is done to attract attention, like wearing broader phylacteries and longer tassels, like wanting to take the place of honour at banquets and the front seats in the synagogues, being greeted obsequiously in the market squares and having people calling them Rabbi.

'You, however, must not allow yourselves to be called Rabbi, since you have only one Master, and you are all brothers. You must call no one on earth your father, since you have only one Father, and he is in heaven. Nor must you allow yourselves to be called teachers, for you have only one Teacher, the Christ. The greatest among you must be your servant. Anyone who exalts himself will be humbled and anyone who humbles himself will be exalted.'

This is the Gospel of the Lord.

Prayer over the Gifts
Lord,
bring us closer to you by this celebration.
May it cleanse us from our faults
and lead us to the gifts of heaven.

Preface of Lent I-IV, P8-P11.

Communion Antiphon: I will tell all your marvellous works. I will rejoice and be glad in you, and sing to your name, Most High.

Prayer after Communion
Lord,
may the food we receive
bring us your constant assistance
that we may live better lives.

WEDNESDAY

Entrance Antiphon: Do not abandon me, Lord. My God, do not go away from me! Hurry to help me, Lord, my Saviour.

Opening Prayer
Father,
teach us to live good lives,
encourage us with your support
and bring us to eternal life.

FIRST READING

A reading from the prophet Jeremiah 18:18-20
Come on, let us hit at him.

'Come on,' they said 'let us concoct a plot against Jeremiah; the priest will not run short of instruction without him, nor the sage of advice, nor the prophet of the word. Come on, let us hit at him with his own tongue; let us listen carefully to every word he says.'

Listen to me Lord,
hear what my adversaries are saying.
Should evil be returned for good?
For they are digging a pit for me.
Remember how I stood in your presence
to plead on their behalf,
to turn your wrath away from them.

This is the word of the Lord.

Responsorial Psalm Ps 30:5-6. 14-16. R̷ v.17
℟ **Save me in your love, O Lord.**

1. Release me from the snares they have hidden
   for you are my refuge, Lord.
   Into your hands I commend my spirit.
   It is you who will redeem me, Lord. ℟

2. I have heard the slander of the crowd,
   fear is all around me,
   as they plot together against me,
   as they plan to take my life. ℟

3. But as for me, I trust in you, Lord,
   I say: 'You are my God.'

My life is in your hands, deliver me
from the hands of those who hate me.'

℟ **Save me in your love, O Lord.**

Gospel Acclamation cf. Jn 6:63. 68
Glory to you, O Christ, you are the Word of God!
Your words are spirit, Lord, and they are life;
you have the message of eternal life.
Glory to you, O Christ, you are the word of God!

or Jn 8:12

Glory to you, O Christ, you are the Word of God!
I am the light of the world, says the Lord;
anyone who follows me will have the light of life.
Glory to you, O Christ, you are the Word of God!

GOSPEL

A reading from the holy Gospel according to Matthew 20:17-28
They will condemn him to death.

Jesus was going up to Jerusalem, and on the way he took the Twelve to one side and said to them, 'Now we are going up to Jerusalem, and the Son of Man is about to be handed over to the chief priests and scribes. They will condemn him to death and will hand him over to the pagans to be mocked and scourged and crucified; and on the third day he will rise again.'

Then the mother of Zebedee's sons came with her sons to make a request of him, and bowed low; and he said to her, 'What is it you want?' She said to him, 'Promise that these two sons of mine may one sit at your right hand and the other at your left in your kingdom.' 'You do not know what you are asking,' Jesus answered. 'Can you drink the cup that I am going to drink?' They replied, 'We can.' 'Very well,' he said 'you shall drink my cup, but as for seats at my right hand and my left, these are not mine to grant; they belong to those to whom they have been allotted by my Father.'

When the other ten heard this they were indignant with the two brothers. But Jesus called them to him and said, 'You know that among the pagans the rulers lord it over them, and their great men make their authority felt. This is not to happen among you. No; anyone who wants to be great among you must be your servant, and anyone who wants to be first among you must be

Second Week of Lent: Thursday 169

your slave, just as the Son of Man came not to be served but to serve, and to give his life as a ransom for many.'

This is the Gospel of the Lord.

Prayer over the Gifts
Lord,
accept this sacrifice,
and through this holy exchange of gifts
free us from the sins that enslave us.

Preface of Lent I-IV, P8-P11.

Communion Antiphon: The Son of Man did not come to be served, but to serve, and to give his life as a ransom for many.

Prayer after Communion
Lord our God,
may the eucharist you give us
as a pledge of unending life
help us to salvation.

THURSDAY

Entrance Antiphon: Test me, O God, and know my thoughts; see whether I step in the wrong path, and guide me along the everlasting way.

Opening Prayer
God of love,
bring us back to you.
Send your Spirit to make us strong in faith
and active in good works.

FIRST READING

A reading from the prophet Jeremiah 17:5-10
A curse on the man who puts his trust in man, a blessing on the man who puts his trust in the Lord.

The Lord says this:

'A curse on the man who puts his trust in man,
who relies on things of flesh,
whose heart turns from the Lord.

He is like dry scrub in the wastelands:
if good comes, he has no eyes for it,
he settles in the parched places of the wilderness,
a salt land, uninhabited.

'A blessing on the man who puts his trust in the Lord,
with the Lord for his hope.
He is like a tree by the waterside
that thrusts its roots to the stream:
when the heat comes it feels no alarm,
its foliage stays green;
it has no worries in a year of drought,
and never ceases to bear fruit.

'The heart is more devious than any other thing,
perverse too: who can pierce its secrets?
I, the Lord, search the heart,
I probe the loins
to give each man what his conduct
and actions deserve.'

This is the word of the Lord.

Responsorial Psalm
Ps 1:1-4. 6. ℟ Ps. 39:5

℟ **Happy the man who has placed
his trust in the Lord.**

1 Happy indeed is the man
who follows not the counsel of the wicked;
nor lingers in the way of sinners
nor sits in the company of scorners,
but whose delight is the law of the Lord
and who ponders his law day and night. ℟

2 He is like a tree that is planted
beside the flowing waters,
that yields its fruit in due season
and whose leaves shall never fade;
and all that he does shall prosper. ℟

3 Not so are the wicked, not so!
For they like winnowed chaff
shall be driven away by the wind.
For the Lord guards the way of the just
but the way of the wicked leads to doom. ℟

Second Week of Lent: Thursday

Gospel Acclamation   Lk 15:18

Praise to you, O Christ, king of eternal glory!
I will leave this place and go to my father and say:
'Father, I have sinned against heaven and against you.'
Praise to you, O Christ, king of eternal glory!

or   cf. Lk 8:15

Praise to you, O Christ, king of eternal glory!
Blessed are those who, with a noble and generous heart,
take the word of God to themselves
and yield a harvest through their perseverance.
Praise to you, O Christ, king of eternal glory!

GOSPEL

A reading from the holy Gospel according to Luke   16:19-31

Good things came your way, just as bad things came the way of Lazarus. Now he is being comforted here while you are in agony.

Jesus said to the Pharisees: 'There was a rich man who used to dress in purple and fine linen and feast magnificently every day. And at his gate there lay a poor man called Lazarus, covered with sores, who longed to fill himself with the scraps that fell from the rich man's table. Dogs even came and licked his sores. Now the poor man died and was carried away by the angels to the bosom of Abraham. The rich man also died and was buried.

'In his torment in Hades he looked up and saw Abraham a long way off with Lazarus in his bosom. So he cried out, "Father Abraham, pity me and send Lazarus to dip the tip of his finger in water and cool my tongue, for I am in agony in these flames." "My son", Abraham replied "remember that during your life good things came your way, just as bad things came the way of Lazarus. Now he is being comforted here while you are in agony. But that is not all: between us and you a great gulf has been fixed, to stop anyone, if he wanted to, crossing from our side to yours, and to stop any crossing from your side to ours."

'The rich man replied, "Father, I beg you then to send Lazarus to my father's house, since I have five brothers, to give them warning so that they do not come to this place of torment too." "They have Moses and the prophets," said Abraham "let them listen to them." "Ah no, father Abraham," said the rich man "but if someone comes to them from the dead, they will repent." Then Abraham said to him, "If they will not listen either to Moses or to the prophets, they will not be convinced even if someone should rise from the dead."'

This is the Gospel of the Lord.

Prayer over the Gifts
Lord,
may this sacrifice bless our lenten observance.
May it lead us to sincere repentance.

Preface of Lent I-IV, P8-P11.

Communion Antiphon: Happy are those of blameless life, who follow the law of the Lord.

Prayer after Communion
Lord,
may the sacrifice we have offered strengthen our faith
and be seen in our love for one another.

FRIDAY

Entrance Antiphon: To you, Lord, I look for protection, never let me be disgraced. You are my refuge; save me from the trap they have laid for me.

Opening Prayer
Merciful Father,
may our acts of penance bring us your forgiveness,
open our hearts to your love,
and prepare us for the coming feast of the resurrection.

FIRST READING

A reading from the book of Genesis   37:3-4. 12-13. 17-28
Here comes the man of dreams. Come on, let us kill him.

Israel loved Joseph more than all his other sons, for he was the son of his old age, and he had a coat with long sleeves made for him. But his brothers, seeing how his father loved him more than all his other sons, came to hate him so much that they could not say a civil word to him.

His brothers went to pasture their father's flock at Shechem. Then Israel said to Joseph, 'Are not your brothers with the flock

Second Week of Lent: Friday

at Shechem? Come, I am going to send you to them.' So Joseph went after his brothers and found them at Dothan.

They saw him in the distance, and before he reached them they made a plot among themselves to put him to death. 'Here comes the man of dreams' they said to one another. 'Come on, let us kill him and throw him into some well; we can say that a wild beast devoured him. Then we shall see what becomes of his dreams.'

But Reuben heard, and he saved him from their violence. 'We must not take his life' he said. 'Shed no blood,' said Reuben to them 'throw him into this well in the wilderness, but do not lay violent hands on him' – intending to save him from them and to restore him to his father. So, when Joseph reached his brothers, they pulled off his coat, the coat with long sleeves that he was wearing, and catching hold of him they threw him into the well, an empty well with no water in it. They then sat down to eat.

Looking up they saw a group of Ishmaelites who were coming from Gilead, their camels laden with gum, tragacanth, balsam and resin, which they were taking down into Egypt. Then Judah said to his brothers, 'What do we gain by killing our brother and covering up his blood? Come, let us sell him to the Ishmaelites, but let us not do any harm to him. After all, he is our brother, and our own flesh.' His brothers agreed.

Now some Midianite merchants were passing, and they drew Joseph up out of the well. They sold Joseph to the Ishmaelites for twenty silver pieces, and these men took Joseph to Egypt.

This is the word of the Lord.

Responsorial Psalm   Ps 104:16-21. ℟ v.5

  ℟ **Remember the wonders the Lord has done.**

1   God called down a famine on the land;
     he broke the staff that supported them.
     He had sent a man before them,
     Joseph, sold as a slave. ℟

2   His feet were put in chains,
     his neck was bound with iron,
     until what he said came to pass
     and the Lord's word proved him true. ℟

3   Then the king sent and released him;
     the ruler of the peoples set him free,
     making him master of his house
     and ruler of all he possessed. ℟

Gospel Acclamation   Jn 3:16
  Praise and honour to you, Lord Jesus!
  God loved the world so much that he gave his only Son;
  everyone who believes in him has eternal life.
  Praise and honour to you, Lord Jesus!

GOSPEL

A reading from the holy Gospel according to Matthew   21:33-43. 45-46

This is the heir. Come on, let us kill him.

Jesus said to the chief priests and the elders of the people: 'Listen to another parable. There was a man, a landowner, who planted a vineyard; he fenced it round, dug a winepress in it and built a tower; then he leased it to tenants and went abroad. When vintage time drew near he sent his servants to the tenants to collect his produce. But the tenants seized his servants, thrashed one, killed another and stoned a third. Next he sent some more servants, this time a larger number, and they dealt with them in the same way. Finally he sent his son to them. "They will respect my son," he said. But when the tenants saw the son, they said to each other, "This is the heir. Come on, let us kill him and take over his inheritance." So they seized him and threw him out of the vineyard and killed him. Now when the owner of the vineyard comes, what will he do to those tenants?' They answered, 'He will bring those wretches to a wretched end and lease the vineyard to other tenants who will deliver the produce to him when the season arrives.' Jesus said to them, 'Have you never read in the scriptures:

  It was the stone rejected by the builders
  that became the keystone.
  This was the Lord's doing
  and it is wonderful to see?

'I tell you, then, that the kingdom of God will be taken from you and given to a people who will produce its fruit.'

When they heard his parables, the chief priests and the scribes realised he was speaking about them, but though they would have liked to arrest him they were afraid of the crowds, who looked on him as a prophet.

This is the Gospel of the Lord.

Second Week of Lent: Saturday

Prayer over the Gifts
God of mercy,
prepare us to celebrate these mysteries.
Help us to live the love they proclaim.

Preface of Lent I-IV, P8-P11.

Communion Antiphon: God loved us and sent his Son to take away our sins.

Prayer after Communion
Lord,
may this communion so change our lives
that we may seek more faithfully
the salvation it promises.

SATURDAY

Entrance Antiphon: The Lord is loving and merciful, to anger slow, and full of love; the Lord is kind to all, and compassionate to all his creatures.

Opening Prayer
God our Father,
by your gifts to us on earth
we already share in your life.
In all we do,
guide us to the light of your kingdom.

FIRST READING

A reading from the prophet Micah   7:14-15. 18-20
Tread down our faults to the bottom of the sea.

With shepherd's crook, O Lord, lead your people to pasture,
the flock that is your heritage,
living confined in a forest
with meadow land all around.
Let them pasture in Bashan and Gilead
as in the days of old.
As in the days when you came out of Egypt
grant us to see wonders.
What god can compare with you: taking fault away,

pardoning crime,
not cherishing anger for ever
but delighting in showing mercy?
Once more have pity on us,
tread down our faults,
to the bottom of the sea
throw all our sins.
Grant Jacob your faithfulness,
and Abraham your mercy,
as you swore to our fathers
from the days of long ago.

> This is the word of the Lord.

Responsorial Psalm Ps 102:1-4. 9-12. R/ v.8

R/ **The Lord is compassion and love.**

1 My soul, give thanks to the Lord,
   all my being, bless his holy name.
   My soul, give thanks to the Lord
   and never forget all his blessings.   R/

2 It is he who forgives all your guilt,
   who heals every one of your ills,
   who redeems your life from the grave,
   who crowns you with love and compassion.   R/

3 His wrath will come to an end;
   he will not be angry for ever.
   He does not treat us according to our sins
   nor repay us according to our faults.   R/

4 For as the heavens are high above the earth
   so strong is his love for those who fear him.
   As far as the east is from the west
   so far does he remove our sins.   R/

Gospel Acclamation Lk 15:18

Glory and praise to you, O Christ!
I will leave this place and go to my father and say:
'Father, I have sinned against heaven and against you.'
Glory and praise to you, O Christ!

Second Week of Lent: Saturday

GOSPEL

A reading from the holy Gospel according to Luke 15:1-3. 11-32
Your brother here was dead and has come to life.

The tax collectors and the sinners were all seeking the company of Jesus to hear what he had to say, and the Pharisees and the scribes complained. 'This man' they said 'welcomes sinners and eats with them.' So he spoke this parable to them:

'A man had two sons. The younger said to his father, "Father, let me have the share of the estate that would come to me." So the father divided the property between them. A few days later, the younger son got together everything he had and left for a distant country where he squandered his money on a life of debauchery.

'When he had spent it all, that country experienced a severe famine, and now he began to feel the pinch, so he hired himself out to one of the local inhabitants who put him on his farm to feed the pigs. And he would willingly have filled his belly with the husks the pigs were eating but no one offered him anything. Then he came to his senses and said, "How many of my father's paid servants have more food than they want, and here am I dying of hunger! I will leave this place and go to my father and say: Father, I have sinned against heaven and against you; I no longer deserve to be called your son; treat me as one of your paid servants." So he left the place and went back to his father.

'While he was still a long way off, his father saw him and was moved with pity. He ran to the boy, clasped him in his arms and kissed him tenderly. Then his son said, "Father, I have sinned against heaven and against you. I no longer deserve to be called your son." But the father said to his servants. "Quick! Bring out the best robe and put it on him; put a ring on his finger and sandals on his feet. Bring the calf we have been fattening, and kill it; we are going to have a feast, a celebration because this son of mine was dead and has come back to life; he was lost and is found." And they began to celebrate.

'Now the elder son was out in the fields, and on his way back, as he drew near the house, he could hear music and dancing. Calling one of the servants he asked what it was all about. "Your brother has come" replied the servant "and your father has killed the calf we had fattened because he has got him back safe and sound." He was angry then and refused to go in, and his father came out to plead with him; but he answered his father, "Look, all these years I have slaved for you and never once disobeyed your orders, yet you never offered me so much as a kid for me to celebrate with my friends. But, for this son of yours, when he comes back after swallowing up your property – he and his women – you kill the calf we had been fattening."

'The father said, "My son, you are with me always and all I have is yours. But it was only right we should celebrate and rejoice, because your brother here was dead and has come to life; he was lost and is found." '

This is the Gospel of the Lord.

Prayer over the Gifts
Lord,
may the grace of these sacraments
help us to reject all harmful things
and lead us to your spirtual gifts.

Preface of Lent I-IV, P8-P11.

Communion Antiphon: My son, you should rejoice, because your brother was dead and has come back to life; he was lost and is found.

Prayer after Communion
Lord,
give us the spirit of love
and lead us to share in your life.

THIRD WEEK OF LENT
Alternative Readings for Third Week of Lent

The following readings may be used instead of the proper ones any day this week, especially in Years B and C when the Gospel of the Samaritan woman is not read on the Third Sunday of Lent.

FIRST READING

A reading from the book of Exodus 17:1-7
Water will flow from it for the people to drink.

The whole community of the sons of Israel moved from their camp in the desert of Zin at the Lord's command, to travel the further stages; and they pitched camp at Rephidim where there was no water for the people to drink. So they grumbled against

Third Week of Lent: Alternative Readings

Moses. 'Give us water to drink' they said. Moses answered them. 'Why do you grumble against me? Why do you put the Lord to the test?' But tormented by thirst, the people complained against Moses. 'Why did you bring us out of Egypt?' they said. 'Was it so that I should die of thirst, my children too, and my cattle?' Moses appealed to the Lord. 'How am I to deal with this people?' he said. 'A little more and they will stone me!' The Lord said to Moses, 'Take with you some of the elders of Israel and move on to the forefront of the people; take in your hand the staff with which you struck the river, and go. I shall be standing before you there on the rock, at Horeb. You must strike the rock, and water will flow from it for the people to drink.' This is what Moses did, in the sight of the elders of Israel. The place was named Massah and Meribah because of the grumbling of the sons of Israel and because they put the Lord to the test by saying, 'Is the Lord with us, or not?'

This is the word of the Lord.

Responsorial Psalm
Ps 94:1-2. 6-9. ℟ v.8

℟ **O that today you would listen to his voice:
'Harden not your hearts.'**

1 Come, ring out our joy to the Lord;
hail the rock who saves us.
Let us come before him, giving thanks,
with songs let us hail the Lord. ℟

2 Come in; let us bow and bend low;
let us kneel before the God who made us
for he is our God and we
the people who belong to his pasture,
the flock that is led by his hand. ℟

3 O that today you would listen to his voice!
'Harden not your hearts as at Meribah,
as on that day at Massah in the desert
when your fathers put me to the test;
when they tried me, though they saw my work.' ℟

Gospel Acclamation
cf. Ps 94:8

Praise to you, O Christ, king of eternal glory!
Harden not your hearts today,
but listen to the voice of the Lord.
Praise to you, O Christ, king of eternal glory!

or   Jn 4:42. 15

Praise to you, O Christ, king of eternal glory!
Lord, you are really the saviour of the world;
give me the living water, so that I may never get thirsty.
Praise to you, O Christ, king of eternal glory!

GOSPEL

A reading from the holy Gospel according to John   4:5-42
A spring of water, welling up to eternal life.

Jesus came to the Samaritan town called Sychar, near the land that Jacob gave to his son Joseph. Jacob's well is there and Jesus, tired by the journey, sat straight down by the well. It was about the sixth hour. When a Samaritan woman came to draw water, Jesus said to her, 'Give me a drink.' His disciples had gone into the town to buy food. The Samaritan woman said to him, 'What? You are a Jew and you ask me, a Samaritan, for a drink?' – Jews, in fact, do not associate with Samaritans. Jesus replied:

'If you only knew what God is offering
and who it is that is saying to you:
Give me a drink,
you would have been the one to ask,
and he would have given you living water.'

'You have no bucket, sir,' she answered 'and the well is deep: how could you get this living water? Are you a greater man than our father Jacob who gave us this well and drank from it himself with his sons and his cattle?' Jesus replied:

'Whoever drinks this water
will get thirsty again;
but anyone who drinks the water that I shall give
will never be thirsty again:
the water that I shall give
will turn into a spring inside him, welling up to eternal life.'

'Sir,' said the woman 'give me some of that water, so that I may never get thirsty and never have to come here again to draw water.' 'Go and call your husband' said Jesus to her 'and come back here.' The woman answered, 'I have no husband.' He said to her, 'You are right to say, "I have no husband"; for although you have had five, the one you have now is not your husband. You spoke the truth there.' 'I see you are a prophet, sir' said the woman. 'Our fathers worshipped on this mountain, while you

say that Jerusalem is the place where one ought to worship.'
Jesus said:

'Believe me, woman, the hour is coming
when you will worship the Father
neither on this mountain nor in Jerusalem.
You worship what you do not know;
we worship what we do know;
for salvation comes from the Jews.
But the hour will come – in fact is is here already –
when true worshippers will worship the Father in spirit and truth:
that is the kind of worshipper
the Father wants.
God is spirit,
and those who worship
must worship in spirit and truth.'

The woman said to him, 'I know that Messiah – that is, Christ – is coming; and when he comes he will tell us everything.' 'I who am speaking to you,' said Jesus 'I am he.'

At this point his disciples returned, and were surprised to find him speaking to a woman, though none of them asked, 'What do you want from her?' or 'Why are you talking to her.' The woman put down her water jar and hurried back to the town to tell the people. 'Come and see a man who has told me everything I ever did; I wonder if he is the Christ?' This brought people out of the town and they started walking towards him.

Meanwhile, the disciples were urging him, 'Rabbi, do have something to eat'; but he said, 'I have food to eat that you do not know about.' So the disciples asked one another, 'Has someone been bringing him food?' But Jesus said:

'My food
is to do the will of the one who sent me,
and to complete his work.
Have you not got a saying:
Four months and then the harvest?
Well, I tell you:
Look around you, look at the fields;
already they are white, ready for harvest!
Already the reaper is being paid his wages,
already he is bringing in the grain for eternal life,
and thus the sower and reaper rejoice together.

For here the proverb holds good:
one sows, another reaps;
I sent you to reap
a harvest you had not worked for.
Others worked for it;
and you have come into the rewards of their trouble.'

Many Samaritans of that town had believed in him on the strength of the woman's testimony when she said, 'He told me all I have ever done', so, when the Samaritans came up to him, they begged him to stay with them. He stayed for two days, and when he spoke to them many more came to believe; and they said to the woman, 'Now we no longer believe because of what you told us; we have heard him ourselves and we know that he really is the saviour of the world.'

This is the Gospel of the Lord.

MONDAY

Entrance Antiphon: My soul is longing and pining for the courts of the Lord; my heart and my flesh sing for joy to the living God.

Opening Prayer
God of mercy,
free your Church from sin
and protect it from evil.
Guide us, for we cannot be saved without you.

FIRST READING

A reading from the second book of the Kings 5:1-15

There were many lepers in Israel, but none of these was cured, except the Syrian, Naaman.

Naaman, army commander to the king of Aram, was a man who enjoyed his master's respect and favour, since through him the Lord had granted victory to the Aramaeans. But the man was a leper. Now on one of their raids, the Aramaeans had carried off from the land of Israel a little girl who had become a servant of Naaman's wife. She said to her mistress, 'If only my master would approach the prophet of Samaria. He would cure him of his leprosy.' Naaman went and told his master. 'This and this' he reported 'is what the girl from the land of Israel said.' 'Go by all means,' said the king of Aram 'I will send a letter to the king of Israel.' So Naaman left, taking with him ten talents of silver, six thousand shekels of gold and ten festal robes. He presented the letter to the king of Israel. It read: 'With this letter, I am sending my servant Naaman to you for you to cure him of his leprosy.' When the king of Israel read the letter, he tore his garments. 'Am I a god to give death and life,' he said 'that he sends a man to me and asks me to cure him of his leprosy? Listen to this, and take note of it and see how he intends to pick a quarrel with me.'

When Elisha heard that the king of Israel had torn his garments, he sent word to the king, 'Why did you tear your garments? Let him come to me, and he will find there is a prophet in Israel.' So Naaman came with his team and chariot and drew up at the door of Elisha's house. And Elisha sent him a messenger to say, 'Go and bathe seven times in the Jordan, and your flesh will become clean once more.' But Naaman was indignant and went off, saying, 'Here was I thinking he would be sure to come out to me, and stand there, and call on the name of the Lord his God, and wave his hand over the spot and cure the leprous part. Surely Abana and Pharpar, the rivers of Damascus, are better than any water in Israel? Could I not bathe in them and become clean?' And he turned round and went off in a rage. But his servants approached him and said, 'My father, if the prophet had asked you to do something difficult, would you not have done it? All the more reason, then, when he says to you, "Bathe and you will become clean."' So he went down and immersed himself seven times in the Jordan, as Elisha had told him to do. And his flesh became clean once more like the flesh of a little child.

Returning to Elisha with his whole escort, he went in and stood before him. 'Now I know' he said 'that there is no God in all the earth except in Israel.'

This is the word of the Lord.

Responsorial Psalm   Pss 41:2-3; 42:3-4. R╱ Ps 41:3
   R╱ **My soul is thirsting for God, the God of my life;
      when can I enter and see the face of God?**

1 Like the deer that yearns
  for running streams,
  so my soul is yearning
  for you, my God.   R╱

2 My soul is thirsting for God,
   the God of my life;
   when can I enter and see
   the face of God?

   ℟ **My soul is thirsting for God, the God of my life;
   when can I enter and see the face of God?**

3 O send forth your light and your truth;
   let these be my guide.
   Let them bring me to your holy mountain
   to the place where you dwell. ℟

4 And I will come to the altar of God,
   the God of my joy.
   My redeemer, I will thank you on the harp,
   O God, my God. ℟

Gospel Acclamation 2 Cor 6:2
   Praise and honour to you, Lord Jesus!
   Now is the favourable time;
   this is the day of salvation.
   Praise and honour to you, Lord Jesus!

or cf. Ps 129:5.7

   Praise and honour to you, Lord Jesus!
   My soul is waiting for the Lord,
   I count on his word,
   because with the Lord there is mercy
   and fullness of redemption.
   Praise and honour to you, Lord Jesus!

GOSPEL

A reading from the holy Gospel according to Luke 4:24-30

Like Elijah and Elisha, Jesus is not sent to the Jews only.

Jesus came to Nazara and spoke to the people in the synagogue: 'I tell you solemnly, no prophet is ever accepted in his own country.

'There were many widows in Israel, I can assure you, in Elijah's day, when heaven remained shut for three years and six months and a great famine raged throughout the land, but Elijah was not sent to any one of these: he was sent to a widow at Zarephath, a Sidonian town. And in the prophet Elisha's time

Third Week of Lent: Tuesday

there were many lepers in Israel, but none of these was cured, except the Syrian, Naaman.'

When they heard this everyone in the synagogue was enraged. They sprang to their feet and hustled him out of the town; and they took him up to the brow of the hill their town was built on, intending to throw him down the cliff, but he slipped through the crowd and walked away.

This is the Gospel of the Lord.

Prayer over the Gifts
Father,
bless these gifts
that they may become the sacrament of our salvation.

Preface of Lent I-IV, P8-P11.

Communion Antiphon: All you nations, praise the Lord, for steadfast is his kindly mercy to us.

Prayer after Communion
Lord,
forgive the sins of those
who receive your sacrament,
and bring us together in unity and peace.

TUESDAY

Entrance Antiphon: I call upon you, God, for you will answer me; bend your ear and hear my prayer. Guard me as the pupil of your eye; hide me in the shade of your wings.

Opening Prayer
Lord,
you call us to your service
and continue your saving work among us.
May your love never abandon us.

FIRST READING

A reading from the prophet Daniel   3:25. 34-43
May the contrite soul, the humbled spirit be acceptable to you.

Azariah stood in the heart of the fire, and he began to pray:

Oh! Do not abandon us for ever,
for the sake of your name;
do not repudiate your covenant,
do not withdraw your favour from us,
for the sake of Abraham, your friend,
of Isaac your servant,
and of Israel your holy one,
to whom you promised descendants as countless as the stars of heaven
and as the grains of sand on the seashore.
Lord, now we are the least of all the nations,
now we are despised throughout the world, today because of our sins.
We have at this time no leader, no prophet, no prince,
no holocaust, no sacrifice, no oblation, no incense,
no place where we can offer you the first-fruits
and win your favour.
But may the contrite soul, the humbled spirit be as acceptable to you
as holocausts of rams and bullocks,
as thousands of fattened lambs:
such let our sacrifice be to you today,
and may it be your will that we follow you wholeheartedly,
since those who put their trust in you will not be disappointed.
And now we put our whole heart into following you,
into fearing you and seeking your face once more.
Do not disappoint us:
treat us gently, as you yourself are gentle
and very merciful.
Grant us deliverance worthy of your wonderful deeds,
let your name win glory, Lord.

This is the word of the Lord.

Responsorial Psalm   Ps 24:4-9. ℟ v.6

℟ **Remember your mercy, Lord.**

1 Lord, make me know your ways.
  Lord, teach me your paths.
  Make me walk in your truth, and teach me:
  for you are God my saviour.   ℟

2 Remember your mercy, Lord,
   and the love you have shown from of old.
   Do not remember the sins of my youth
   because of your goodness, O Lord.   ℟

3 The Lord is good and upright.
   He shows the path to those who stray.
   He guides the humble in the right path;
   he teaches his way to the poor.   ℟

Gospel Acclamation   cf. Lk 8:15
   Glory and praise to you, O Christ!
   Blessed are those who, with a noble and generous heart,
   take the word of God to themselves
   and yield a harvest through their perseverance.
   Glory and praise to you, O Christ!

or   Joel 2:12-13

   Glory and praise to you, O Christ!
   Now, now – it is the Lord who speaks –
   come back to me with all your heart,
   for I am all tenderness and compassion.
   Glory and praise to you, O Christ!

GOSPEL

A reading from the holy Gospel according to Matthew   18:21-35
Your Father will not forgive you unless you each forgive your brother from your heart.

Peter went up to Jesus and said, 'Lord, how often must I forgive my brother if he wrongs me? As often as seven times?' Jesus answered, 'Not seven, I tell you, but seventy-seven times.

'And so the kingdom of heaven may be compared to a king who decided to settle his accounts with his servants. When the reckoning began, they brought him a man who owed ten thousand talents; but he had no means of paying, so his master gave orders that he should be sold, together with his wife and children and all his possessions, to meet the debt. At this, the servant threw himself down at his master's feet. "Give me time" he said "and I will pay the whole sum." And the servant's master felt so sorry for him that he let him go and cancelled the debt. Now as this servant went out, he happened to meet a fellow servant who owed him one hundred denarii; and he seized him by the throat and began to throttle him. "Pay what you owe me" he said. His fellow servant fell at his feet and implored him, saying, "Give me time and I will pay you." But the other would not agree; on the contrary, he had him thrown into prison till he should pay the debt. His fellow servants were deeply distressed when they saw what had happened, and they went to their master and reported the whole affair to him. Then the master sent for him. "You wicked servant," he said. "I cancelled all that debt of yours when you appealed to me. Were you not bound, then, to have pity on your fellow servant just as I had pity on you?" And in his anger the master handed him over to the torturers till he should pay all his debt. And that is how my heavenly Father will deal with you unless you each forgive your brother from your heart.'

This is the Gospel of the Lord.

Prayer over the Gifts
Lord,
may the saving sacrifice we offer
bring us your forgiveness,
so that freed from sin, we may always please you.

Preface of Lent I-IV, P8-P11.

Communion Antiphon: Lord, who may stay in your dwelling place? Who shall live on your holy mountain? He who walks without blame and does what is right.

Prayer after Communion
Lord,
may our sharing in this holy mystery
bring us your protection, forgiveness and life.

WEDNESDAY

Entrance Antiphon: Lord, direct my steps as you have promised, and let no evil hold me in its power.

Opening Prayer
Lord,

Third Week of Lent: Wednesday

during this lenten season
nourish us with your word of life
and make us one in love and prayer.

FIRST READING

A reading from the book of Deuteronomy 4:1. 5-9
Take notice of the laws and observe them.

Moses said to the people: 'And now, Israel, take notice of the laws and customs that I teach you today, and observe them, that you may have life and may enter and take possession of the land that the Lord the God of your fathers is giving you. See, as the Lord my God has commanded me, I teach you the laws and customs that you are to observe in the land you are to enter and make your own. Keep them, observe them, and they will demonstrate to the peoples your wisdom and understanding. When they come to know of all these laws they will exclaim, "No other people is as wise and prudent as this great nation." And indeed, what great nation is there that has its gods so near as the Lord our God is to us whenever we call to him? And what great nation is there that has laws and customs to match this whole Law that I put before you today?

'But take care what you do and be on your guard. Do not forget the things your eyes have seen, nor let them slip from your heart all the days of your life; rather, tell them to your children and to your children's children.'

This is the word of the Lord.

Responsorial Psalm Ps 147:12-13. 15-16. 19-20. ℟ v.12
 ℟ **O praise the Lord, Jerusalem!**

1 O praise the Lord, Jerusalem!
   Zion, praise your God!
   He has strengthened the bars of your gates,
   he has blessed the children within you. ℟

2 He sends out his word to the earth
   and swiftly runs his command.
   He showers down snow white as wool,
   he scatters hoar-frost like ashes. ℟

3 He makes his word known to Jacob,
   to Israel his laws and decrees.
   He has not dealt thus with other nations;
   he has not taught them his decrees. ℟

Gospel Acclamation Jn 8:12
    Glory to you, O Christ, you are the Word of God!
    I am the light of the world, says the Lord,
    anyone who follows me will have the light of life.
    Glory to you, O Christ, you are the Word of God!

or   cf. Jn 6:63.68

    Glory to you, O Christ, you are the Word of God!
    Your words are spirit, Lord, and they are life;
    you have the message of eternal life.
    Glory to you, O Christ, you are the Word of God!

GOSPEL

A reading from the holy Gospel according to Matthew   5:17-19
The man who keeps these commandments and teaches them will be considered great in the kingdom of heaven.

Jesus said to his disciples: 'Do not imagine that I have come to abolish the Law or the Prophets. I have come not to abolish but to complete them. I tell you solemnly, till heaven and earth disappear, not one dot, not one little stroke, shall disappear from the Law until its purpose is achieved. Therefore, the man who infringes even one of the least of these commandments and teaches others to do the same will be considered the least in the kingdom of heaven; but the man who keeps them and teaches them will be considered great in the kingdom of heaven.'

    This is the Gospel of the Lord.

Prayer over the Gifts
Lord,
receive our prayers and offerings.
In time of danger,
protect all who celebrate this sacrament.

Preface of Lent I-IV, P8-P11.

Communion Antiphon: Lord, you will show me the path of life and fill me with joy in your presence.

Prayer after Communion
Lord,
may this eucharist forgive our sins,

Third Week of Lent: Thursday 191

make us holy,
and prepare us for the eternal life you promise.

THURSDAY

Entrance Antiphon: I am the Saviour of all people, says the Lord. Whatever their troubles, I will answer their cry, and I will always be their Lord.

Opening Prayer
Father,
help us to be ready to celebrate the great paschal mystery.
Make our love grow each day
as we approach the feast of our salvation.

FIRST READING

A reading from the prophet Jeremiah 7:23-28
Here is the nation that will not listen to the voice of the Lord its God.

These were my orders: Listen to my voice, then I will be your God and you shall be my people. Follow right to the end the way that I mark out for you, and you will prosper. But they did not listen, they did not pay attention; they followed the dictates of their own evil hearts, refused to face me, and turned their backs on me from the day your ancestors came out of the land of Egypt until today, day after day I have persistently sent you all my servants the prophets. But they have not listened to me, have not paid attention; they have grown stubborn and behaved worse than their ancestors. You may say all these words to them: they will not listen to you; you may call them: they will not answer. So tell them this, 'Here is the nation that will not listen to the voice of the Lord its God nor take correction. Sincerity is no more, it has vanished from their mouths.'

This is the word of the Lord.

Responsorial Psalm Ps 94:1-2. 6-9. ℟ v.8
 ℟ **O that today you would listen to his voice!**
 'Harden not your hearts.'

1 Come, ring out our joy to the Lord;
 hail the rock who saves us.
 Let us come before him, giving thanks,
 with songs let us hail the Lord. ℟

2 Come in; let us bow and bend low;
let us kneel before the God who made us
for he is our God and we
the people who belong to his pasture,
the flock that is led by his hand.

℟ **O that today you would listen to his voice!
'Harden not your hearts.'**

3 O that today you would listen to his voice!
'Harden not your hearts as at Meribah,
as on that day at Massah in the desert
when your fathers put me to the test;
when they tried me, though they saw my work.' ℟

Gospel Acclamation Ez 18:31
Praise to you, O Christ, king of eternal glory!
Shake off all your sins – it is the Lord who speaks –
and make yourselves a new heart and a new spirit.
Praise to you, O Christ, king of eternal glory!

or Joel 2:12-13

Praise to you, O Christ, king of eternal glory!
Now, now – it is the Lord who speaks –
come back to me with all your heart,
for I am all tenderness and compassion.
Praise to you, O Christ, king of eternal glory!

GOSPEL

A reading from the holy Gospel according to Luke 11:14-23
He who is not with me is against me.

Jesus was casting out a devil and it was dumb; but when the devil had gone out the dumb man spoke, and the people were amazed. But some of them said, 'It is through Beelzebul, the prince of devils, that he casts out devils.' Others asked him, as a test, for a sign from heaven; but, knowing what they were thinking, he said to them, 'Every kingdom divided against itself is heading for ruin, and a household divided against itself collapses. So too with Satan: if he is divided against himself, how can his kingdom stand? – since you assert that it is through Beelzebul that I cast out devils. Now if it is through Beelzebul that I cast out devils, through whom do your own experts cast them out? Let them be

Third Week of Lent: Friday

your judges, then. But if it is through the finger of God that I cast out devils, then know that the kingdom of God has overtaken you. So long as a strong man fully armed guards his own palace, his goods are undisturbed; but when someone stronger than he is attacks and defeats him, the stronger man takes away all the weapons he relied on and shares out his spoil.

'He who is not with me is against me; and he who does not gather with me scatters.'

This is the Gospel of the Lord.

Prayer over the Gifts
Lord,
take away our sinfulness and be pleased with our offerings.
Help us to pursue the true gifts you promise
and not become lost in false joys.

Preface of Lent I-IV, P8-P11.

Communion Antiphon: You have laid down your precepts to be faithfully kept. May my footsteps be firm in keeping your commands.

Prayer after Communion
Lord,
may your sacrament of life
bring us the gift of salvation
and make our lives pleasing to you.

FRIDAY

Entrance Antiphon: Lord, there is no god to compare with you; you are great and do wonderful things, you are the only God.

Opening Prayer
Merciful Father,
fill our hearts with your love
and keep us faithful to the gospel of Christ.
Give us the grace to rise above our human weakness.

FIRST READING

A reading from the prophet Hosea   14:2-10
We will not say any more, 'Our God' to what our own hands have made.

The Lord says this:

> Israel, come back to the Lord your God;
> your iniquity was the cause of your downfall.
> Provide yourself with words
> and come back to the Lord.
> Say to him, 'Take all iniquity away
> so that we may have happiness again
> and offer you our words of praise.
> Assyria cannot save us,
> we will not ride horses any more,
> or say, "Our God!" to what our own hands have made,
> for you are the one in whom orphans find compassion.'
> – I will heal their disloyalty,
> I will love them with all my heart,
> for my anger has turned from them.
> I will fall like dew on Israel.
> He shall bloom like the lily,
> and thrust out roots like the poplar,
> his shoots will spread far;
> he will have the beauty of the olive
> and the fragrance of Lebanon.
> They will come back to live in my shade;
> they will grow corn that flourishes,
> they will cultivate vines
> as renowned as the wine of Helbon.
> What has Ephraim to do with idols any more
> when it is I who hear his prayer and care for him?
> I am like a cypress ever green,
> all your fruitfulness comes from me.
> Let the wise man understand these words.
> Let the intelligent man grasp their meaning.
> For the ways of the Lord are straight,
> and virtuous men walk in them,
> but sinners stumble.
>
> This is the word of the Lord.

Third Week of Lent: Friday

Responsorial Psalm Ps 80:6. 8-11. 14. 17. ℟ vv.9. 11
 ℟ **I am the Lord your God;
    listen to my warning.**

1 A voice I did not know said to me:
   'I freed your shoulder from the burden;
   your hands were freed from the load.
   You called in distress and I saved you. ℟

2 'I answered, concealed in the storm cloud,
   at the waters of Meribah I tested you.
   Listen, my people, to my warning,
   O Israel, if only you would heed! ℟

3 'Let there be no foreign god among you,
   no worship of an alien god.
   I am the Lord your God,
   who brought you from the land of Egypt. ℟

4 'O that my people would heed me,
   that Israel would walk in my ways!
   But Israel I would feed with finest wheat
   and fill them with honey from the rock.' ℟

Gospel Acclamation
Praise and honour to you, Lord Jesus!
The seed is the word of God, Christ the sower;
whoever finds this seed will remain for ever.
Praise and honour to you, Lord Jesus!

or   Mt 4:17

Praise and honour to you, Lord Jesus!
Repent, says the Lord,
for the kingdom of heaven, is close at hand.
Praise and honour to you, Lord Jesus!

GOSPEL

A reading from the holy Gospel according to Mark   12:28-34
The Lord our God is the one Lord, and you must love him.

One of the scribes came up to Jesus and put a question to him, 'Which is the first of all the commandments?' Jesus replied, 'This is the first: Listen, Israel, the Lord our God is the one Lord, and you must love the Lord your God with all your heart, with all your soul, with all your mind, and with all your strength. The second is this: You must love your neighbour as yourself. There is no commandment greater than these.' The scribe said to him, 'Well spoken, Master; what you have said is true: that he is one and there is no other. To love him with all your heart, with all your understanding and strength, and to love your neighbour as yourself, this is far more important than any holocaust or sacrifice.' Jesus, seeing how wisely he had spoken, said, 'You are not far from the kingdom of God.' And after that no one dared to question him any more.

This is the Gospel of the Lord.

Prayer over the Gifts
Lord,
bless the gifts we have prepared.
Make them acceptable to you
and a lasting source of salvation.

Preface of Lent I-IV, P8-P11.

Communion Antiphon: To love God with all your heart, and your neighbour as yourself, is a greater thing than all the temple sacrifices.

Prayer after Communion
Lord,
fill us with the power of your love.
As we share in this eucharist,
may we come to know fully the redemption we have received.

SATURDAY

Entrance Antiphon: Bless the Lord, my soul, and remember all his kindnesses, for he pardons all my faults.

Opening Prayer
Lord,
make this lenten observance
of the suffering, death and resurrection of Christ
bring us to the full joy of Easter

FIRST READING

A reading from the prophet Hosea 5:15 – 6:6
What I want is love, not sacrifice.

The Lord says this:

> They will search for me in their misery:
> 'Come, let us return to the Lord.
> He has torn us to pieces, but he will heal us;
> he has struck us down, but he will bandage our wounds;
> after a day or two he will bring us back to life,
> on the third day he will raise us
> and we shall live in his presence.
> Let us set ourselves to know the Lord;
> that he will come is as certain as the dawn,
> he will come to us as showers come,
> like spring rains watering the earth.'
>
> What am I to do with you, Ephraim?
> What am I to do with you, Judah?
> This love of yours is like a morning cloud,
> like the dew that quickly disappears.
> This is why I have torn them to pieces by the prophets,
> why I slaughtered them with the words from my mouth,
> his judgement will rise like the light,
> since what I want is love, not sacrifice;
> knowledge of God, not holocausts.

This is the word of the Lord.

Responsorial Psalm Ps 50:3-4. 18-21. ℟ cf. Hos 6:6

℟ **What I want is love, not sacrifice.**

1 Have mercy on me, God, in your kindness.
  In your compassion blot out my offence.
  O wash me more and more from my guilt
  and cleanse me from my sin. ℟

2 For in sacrifice you take no delight,
  burnt offering from me you would refuse,
  my sacrifice, a contrite spirit.
  A humbled, contrite heart you will not spurn. ℟

3 In your goodness, show favour to Zion:
  rebuild the walls of Jerusalem.
  Then you will be pleased with lawful sacrifice,
  burnt offerings wholly consumed. ℟

Gospel Acclamation
cf. Ps 94:8

Glory and praise to you, O Christ!
Harden not your hearts today,
but listen to the voice of the Lord.
Glory and praise to you, O Christ!

GOSPEL

A reading from the holy Gospel according to Luke 18:9-14

The tax collector went home again at rights with God; the Pharisee did not.

Jesus spoke the following parable to some people who prided themselves on being virtuous and despised everyone else, 'Two men went up to the Temple to pray, one a Pharisee, the other a tax collector. The Pharisee stood there and said this prayer to himself, "I thank you, God, that I am not grasping, unjust, adulterous like the rest of mankind, and particularly that I am not like this tax collector here. I fast twice a week; I pay tithes on all I get." The tax collector stood some distance away, not daring even to raise his eyes to heaven; but he beat his breast and said, "God, be merciful to me, a sinner." This man, I tell you, went home again at rights with God; the other did not. For everyone who exalts himself will be humbled, but the man who humbles himself will be exalted.'

This is the Gospel of the Lord.

Prayer over the Gifts
Lord,
by your grace you enable us
to come to these mysteries with renewed lives.
May this eucharist give you worthy praise.

Preface of Lent I-IV, P8-P11.

Communion Antiphon: He stood at a distance and beat his breast, saying: O God, be merciful to me, a sinner.

Prayer after Communion
God of mercy,
may the holy gifts we receive
help us to worship you in truth,
and to receive your sacraments with faith.

FOURTH WEEK OF LENT
Alternative Readings for the Fourth Week of Lent

The following readings may be used instead of the proper ones any day this week, especially in Years B and C when the Gospel of the man born blind is not read on the Fourth Sunday of Lent.

FIRST READING

A reading from the prophet Micah 7:7-9
Though I live in darkness, the Lord God is my light.

For my part, I look to the Lord,
my hope is in the God who will save me;
my God will hear me.
Do not gloat over me, my enemy:
though I have fallen, I shall rise;
though I live in darkness,
the Lord is my light.
I must suffer the anger of the Lord,
for I have sinned against him,
until he takes up my cause
and rights my wrongs;
he will bring me out into the light
and I shall rejoice to see the rightness of his ways.

This is the word of the Lord

Responsorial Psalm Ps 26:1. 7-9. 13-14. R̷ v.1

R̷ **The Lord is my light and my help.**

1. The Lord is my light and my help;
   whom shall I fear?
   The Lord is the stronghold of my life;
   before whom shall I shrink? R̷

2. O Lord, hear my voice when I call;
   have mercy and answer.
   Of you my heart has spoken:
   'Seek his face.' R̷

3. It is your face, O Lord, that I seek;
   hide not your face.
   Dismiss not your servant in anger;
   you have been my help. R̷

(continued)

4 I am sure I shall see the Lord's goodness
  in the land of the living.
  Hope in him, hold firm and take heart.
  Hope in the Lord!

  ℟ **The Lord is my light and my help.**

Gospel Acclamation

Jn 8:12

Praise to you, O Christ, king of eternal glory!
I am the light of the world, says the Lord,
anyone who follows me will have the light of life.
Praise to you, O Christ, king of eternal glory!

GOSPEL

A reading from the holy Gospel according to John 9:1-41
He went off and washed himself, and came away with his sight restored.

As Jesus went along, he saw a man who had been blind from birth. His disciples asked him, 'Rabbi, who sinned, this man or his parents, for him to have been born blind?' 'Neither he nor his parents sinned,' Jesus answered 'he was born blind so that the works of God might be displayed in him.

'As long as the day lasts
I must carry out the work of the one who sent me;
the night will soon be here when no one can work.
As long as I am in the world
I am the light of the world.'

Having said this, he spat on the ground, made a paste with the spittle, put this over the eyes of the blind man and said to him, 'Go and wash in the Pool of Siloam' (a name that means 'sent'). So the blind man went off and washed himself, and came away with his sight restored.

His neighbours and people who earlier had seen him begging said, 'Isn't this the man who used to sit and beg?' Some said, 'Yes, it is the same one.' Others said, 'No, he only looks like him.' The man himself said, 'I am the man.' So they said to him, 'Then how do your eyes come to be open?' 'The man called Jesus' he answered 'made a paste, daubed my eyes with it and said to me, "Go and wash at Siloam"; so I went, and when I washed I could see.' They asked, 'Where is he?' 'I don't know' he answered.

They brought the man who had been blind to the Pharisees. It had been a sabbath day when Jesus made the paste and opened the man's eyes, so when the Pharisees asked him how he had come to see, he said, 'He put a paste on my eyes and I washed, and I can see.' Then some of the Pharisees said, 'This man cannot be from God: he does not keep the sabbath.' Others said, 'How could a sinner produce signs like this?' And there was disagreement among them. So they spoke to the blind man again, 'What have you to say about him yourself, now that he has opened your eyes?' 'He is a prophet' replied the man.

However, the Jews would not believe that the man had been blind and had gained his sight, without first sending for his parents and asking them, 'Is this man really your son who you say was born blind?' His parents answered, 'We know he is our son and we know he was born blind, but we don't know how it is that he can see now, or who opened his eyes. He is old enough: let him speak for himself.' His parents spoke like this out of fear of the Jews, who had already agreed to expel from the synagogue anyone who should acknowledge Jesus as the Christ. This was why his parents said, 'He is old enough; ask him.'

So the Jews again sent for the man and said to him, 'Give glory to God! For our part, we know that this man is a sinner.' The man answered, 'I don't know if he is a sinner; I only know that I was blind and now I can see.' They said to him, 'What did he do to you? How did he open your eyes?' He replied, 'I have told you once and you wouldn't listen. Why do you want to hear it all again? Do you want to become his disciples too?' At this they hurled abuse at him: 'You can be his disciple,' they said 'we are disciples of Moses; we know that God spoke to Moses, but as for this man, we don't know where he comes from.' The man replied, 'Now here is an astonishing thing! He has opened my eyes, and you don't know where he comes from! We know that God doesn't listen to sinners, but God does listen to men who are devout and do his will. Ever since the world began it is unheard of for anyone to open the eyes of a man who was born blind; if this man were not from God, he couldn't do a thing.' 'Are you trying to teach us,' they replied 'and you a sinner through and through, since you were born!' And they drove him away.

Jesus heard they had driven him away, and when he found him he said to him 'Do you believe in the Son of Man?' 'Sir,' the man replied 'tell me who he is so that I may believe in him.' Jesus said, 'You are looking at him; he is speaking to you.' The man said, 'Lord I believe', and worshipped him.

Jesus said:

'It is for judgement
that I have come into this world,
so that those without sight may see
and those with sight turn blind.'

Hearing this, some Pharisees who were present said to him, 'We are not blind, surely?' Jesus replied:

'Blind? If you were,
you would not be guilty,
but since you say, "We see",
your guilt remains.'

This is the Gospel of the Lord.

MONDAY

Entrance Antiphon: Lord, I put my trust in you; I shall be glad and rejoice in your mercy, because you have seen my affliction.

Opening Prayer
Father, creator,
you give the world new life by your sacraments.
May we, your Church, grow in your life
and continue to receive your help on earth.

FIRST READING

A reading from the prophet Isaiah   65:17-21
No more will the sound of weeping or the sound of cries be heard.

Thus says the Lord: Now I create new heavens and a new earth, and the past will not be remembered, and will come no more to men's minds. Be glad and rejoice for ever and ever for what I am creating, because I now create Jerusalem 'Joy' and her people 'Gladness'. I shall rejoice over Jerusalem and exult in my people. No more will the sound of weeping or the sound of cries be heard in her; in her, no more will be found the infant living a few days only, or the old man not living to the end of his days. To die at the age of a hundred will be dying young; not to live to be a hundred will be the sign of a curse. They will build houses and inhabit them, plant vineyards and eat their fruit.

This is the word of the Lord.

Responsorial Psalm
Ps 29:2. 4-6. 11-13. ℟ v.2

℟ **I will praise you, Lord,
you have rescued me.**

1 I will praise you, Lord, you have rescued me
and have not let my enemies rejoice over me.
O Lord, you have raised my soul from the dead,
restored me to life from those who sink into the grave. ℟

2 Sing psalms to the Lord, you who love him,
give thanks to his holy name.
His anger lasts but a moment; his favour through life.
At night there are tears, but joy comes with dawn. ℟

3 The Lord listened and had pity.
The Lord came to my help.
For me you have changed my mourning into dancing;
O Lord my God, I will thank you for ever. ℟

Gospel Acclamation
cf. Ps 129:5. 7

Praise and honour to you, Lord Jesus!
My soul is waiting for the Lord,
I count on his word,
because with the Lord there is mercy
and fullness of redemption.
Praise and honour to you, Lord Jesus!

or
cf. Amos 5:14

Praise and honour to you, Lord Jesus!
Seek good and not evil so that you may live,
and that the Lord God of hosts may really be with you.
Praise and honour to you, Lord Jesus!

GOSPEL

A reading from the holy Gospel according to John
4:43-54

Go home, your son will live.

Jesus left Samaria for Galilee. He himself had declared that there is no respect for a prophet in his own country, but on his arrival the Galileans received him well, having seen all that he had done at Jerusalem during the festival which they too had attended.

He went again to Cana in Galilee, where he had changed the water into wine. Now there was a court official there whose son was ill at Capernaum and, hearing that Jesus had arrived in Galilee from Judaea, he went and asked him to come and cure his son as he was at the point of death. Jesus said, 'So you will not believe unless you see signs and portents!' 'Sir,' answered the official 'come down before my child dies.' 'Go home,' said Jesus 'your son will live.' The man believed what Jesus had said and started on his way; and while he was still on the journey back his servants met him with the news that his boy was alive. He asked them when the boy had begun to recover. 'The fever left him yesterday' they said 'at the seventh hour.' The father realised that this was exactly the time when Jesus had said, 'Your son will live'; and he and all his household believed.

This was the second sign given by Jesus, on his return from Judaea to Galilee.

This is the Gospel of the Lord.

Prayer over the Gifts
Lord,
through the gifts we present
may we receive the grace
to cast off the old ways of life
and to redirect our course toward the life of heaven.

Preface of Lent I-IV, P8-P11.

Communion Antiphon: I shall put my spirit within you, says the Lord; you will obey my laws and keep my decrees.

Prayer after Communion
Lord,
may your gifts bring us life and holiness
and lead us to the happiness of eternal life.

TUESDAY

Entrance Antiphon: Come to the waters, all who thirst; though you have no money, come and drink with joy.

Opening Prayer
Father,
may our lenten observance
prepare us to embrace the paschal mystery
and to proclaim your salvation with joyful praise.

FIRST READING

A reading from the prophet Ezekiel 47:1-9. 12

I saw a stream of water coming from the Temple, bringing life to all wherever it flowed.

The angel brought me to the entrance of the Temple, where a stream came out from under the Temple threshold and flowed eastwards, since the Temple faced east. The water flowed from under the right side of the Temple, south of the altar. He took me out by the north gate and led me right round outside as far as the outer east gate where the water flowed out on the right-hand side. The man went to the east holding his measuring line and measured off a thousand cubits; he then made me wade across the stream; the water reached my ankles. He measured off another thousand and made me wade across the stream again; the water reached my knees. He measured off another thousand and made me wade across again; the water reached my waist. He measured off another thousand; it was now a river which I could not cross; the stream had swollen and was now deep water, a river impossible to cross. He then said, 'Do you see, son of man?' He took me further, then brought me back to the bank of the river. When I got back, there were many trees on each bank of the river. He said, 'This water flows east down to the Arabah and to the sea; and flowing into the sea it makes its waters wholesome. Wherever the river flows, all living creatures teeming in it will live. Fish will be very plentiful, for wherever the water goes it brings health, and life teems wherever the river flows. Along the river, on either bank, will grow every kind of fruit tree with leaves that never wither and fruit that never fails; they will bear new fruit every month, because this water comes from the sanctuary. And their fruit will be good to eat and the leaves medicinal.'

This is the word of the Lord.

Responsorial Psalm Ps 45:2-3. 5-6. 8-9. ℟ v.8

℟ **The Lord of hosts is with us:
the God of Jacob is our stronghold.**

1 God is for us a refuge and strength,
 a helper close at hand, in time of distress:
 so we shall not fear though the earth should rock,
 though the mountains fall into the depths of the sea. ℟

2 The waters of a river give joy to God's city,
   the holy place where the Most High dwells.
   God is within, it cannot be shaken;
   God will help it at the dawning of the day.

   ℟ **The Lord of hosts is with us:
       the God of Jacob is our stronghold.**

3 The Lord of hosts is with us:
   the God of Jacob is our stronghold.
   Come, consider the works of the Lord
   the redoubtable deeds he has done on the earth. ℟

Gospel Acclamation   Ps 50:12. 14
Praise and honour to you, Lord Jesus!
A pure heart create for me, O God,
and give me again the joy of your help.
Praise and honour to you, Lord Jesus!

GOSPEL

A reading from the holy Gospel according to John   5:1-3. 5-16
The man was cured at once.

There was a Jewish festival, and Jesus went up to Jerusalem. Now at the Sheep Pool in Jerusalem there is a building, called Bethzatha in Hebrew, consisting of five porticos; and under these were crowds of sick people – blind, lame, paralysed. One man there had an illness which had lasted thirty-eight years, and when Jesus saw him lying there and knew he had been in this condition for a long time, he said, 'Do you want to be well again?' 'Sir,' replied the sick man 'I have no one to put me into the pool when the water is disturbed; and while I am still on the way, someone else gets there before me.' Jesus said 'Get up, pick up your sleeping-mat and walk.' The man was cured at once, and he picked up his mat and walked away.

Now that day happened to be the sabbath, so the Jews said to the man who had been cured, 'It is the sabbath; you are not allowed to carry your sleeping-mat.' He replied, 'But the man who cured me told me, "Pick up your mat and walk." ' They asked, 'Who is the man who said to you, "Pick up your mat and walk"?' The man had no idea who it was since Jesus had disappeared into the crowd that filled the place. After a while Jesus met him in the Temple and said, 'Now you are well again, be sure not to sin any more, or something worse may happen to you.' The man went back and told the Jews that it was Jesus who had cured him. It was because he did things like this on the sabbath that the Jews began to persecute Jesus.

This is the Gospel of the Lord.

Prayer over the Gifts
Lord,
may your gifts of bread and wine
which nourish us here on earth
become the food of our eternal life.

Preface of Lent I-IV, P8-P11.

Communion Antiphon: The Lord is my shepherd; there is nothing I shall want. In green pastures he gives me rest, he leads me beside the waters of peace.

Prayer after Communion
Lord,
may your holy sacraments cleanse and renew us;
may they bring us your help
and lead us to salvation.

WEDNESDAY

Entrance Antiphon: I pray to you, O God, for the time of your favour. Lord, in your great love, answer me.

Opening Prayer
Lord,
you reward virtue
and forgive the repentant sinner.
Grant us your forgiveness
as we come before you confessing our guilt.

FIRST READING

A reading from the prophet Isaiah 49:8-15
I have appointed you as covenant of the people to restore the land.

Thus says the Lord:

At the favourable time I will answer you,

on the day of salvation I will help you.
(I have formed you and have appointed you
as covenant of the people.)
I will restore the land
and assign you the estates that lie waste.
I will say to the prisoners, 'Come out',
to those who are in darkness, 'Show yourselves'.

On every roadway they will graze,
and each bare height shall be their pasture.
They will never hunger or thirst,
scorching wind and sun shall never plague them;
for he who pities them will lead them
and guide them to springs of water.
I will make a highway of all the mountains,
and the high roads shall be banked up.
Some are on their way from afar,
others from the north and the west,
others from the land of Sinim.
Shout for joy, you heavens; exult, you earth!
You mountains, break into happy cries!
For the Lord consoles his people
and takes pity on those who are afflicted.

For Zion was saying, 'The Lord has abandoned me,
the Lord has forgotten me.'
Does a woman forget her baby at the breast,
or fail to cherish the son of her womb?
Yet even if these forget,
I will never forget you.

This the word of the Lord.

Responsorial Psalm   Ps 144:8-9. 13-14. 17-18. R/ v.8
  R/ **The Lord is kind and full of compassion.**

1   The Lord is kind and full of compassion,
    slow to anger, abounding in love.
    How good is the Lord to all,
    compassionate to all his creatures.   R/

2   The Lord is faithful in all his words
    and loving in all his deeds.
    The Lord supports all who fall
    and raises all who are bowed down.   R/

Fourth Week of Lent: Wednesday

3   The Lord is just in all his ways
    and loving in all his deeds.
    He is close to all who call him.
    who call on him from their hearts. ℟

Gospel Acclamation   Jn 3:16

    Glory and praise to you, O Christ!
    God loved the world so much that he gave his only Son;
    everyone who believes in him has eternal life.
    Glory and praise to you, O Christ!

or   Jn 11:25.26

    Glory and praise to you, O Christ!
    I am the resurrection and the life, says the Lord;
    whoever believes in me will never die.
    Glory and praise to you, O Christ!

GOSPEL

A reading from the holy Gospel according to John   5:17-30
As the Father raises the dead and gives them life, so the Son gives life to those he chooses.

Jesus said to the Jews: 'My Father goes on working, and so do I.' But that only made the Jews even more intent on killing him, because, not content with breaking the sabbath, he spoke of God as his own Father, and so made himself God's equal. To this accusation Jesus replied:

    'I tell you most solemnly,
    the Son can do nothing by himself;
    he can do only what he sees the Father doing:
    and whatever the Father does the Son does too.
    For the Father loves the Son
    and shows him everything he does himself,
    and he will show him even greater things than these,
    works that will astonish you.
    Thus, as the Father raises the dead and gives them life,
    so the Son gives life to anyone he chooses;
    for the Father judges no one;
    he has entrusted all judgement to the Son,
    so that all may honour the Son
    as they honour the Father.
    Whoever refuses honour to the Son

refuses honour to the Father who sent him.
I tell you most solemnly,
whoever listens to my words,
and believes in the one who sent me,
has eternal life;
without being brought to judgement
he has passed from death to life.
I tell you most solemnly,
the hour will come – in fact it is here already –
when the dead will hear the voice of the Son of God,
and all who hear it will live.
For the Father, who is the source of life,
has made the Son the source of life;
and, because he is the Son of Man,
has appointed him supreme judge.
Do not be surprised at this,
for the hour is coming
when the dead will leave their graves
at the sound of his voice:
those who did good
will rise again to life;
and those who did evil, to condemnation.
I can do nothing by myself;
I can only judge as I am told to judge,
and my judging is just,
because my aim is to do not my own will,
but the will of him who sent me.'

This is the Gospel of the Lord.

Prayer over the Gifts
Lord God,
may the power of this sacrifice wash away our sins,
renew our lives and bring us to salvation.

Preface of Lent I-IV, P8-P11.

Communion Antiphon: God sent his Son into the world, not to condemn it, but so that the world might be saved through him.

Prayer after Communion
Lord,
may we never misuse your healing gifts,
but always find in them a source of life and salvation.

THURSDAY

Entrance Antiphon: Let hearts rejoice who search for the Lord. Seek the Lord and his strength, seek always the face of the Lord.

Opening Prayer
Merciful Father,
may the penance of our lenten observance
make us your obedient people.
May the love within us be seen in what we do
and lead us to the joy of Easter.

FIRST READING

A reading from the book of Exodus   32:7-14
Do not bring this disaster on your people.

The Lord spoke to Moses, 'Go down now, because your people whom you brought out of Egypt have apostasised. They have been quick to leave the way I marked out for them; they have made themselves a calf of molten metal and have worshipped it and offered it sacrifice. "Here is your God, Israel," they have cried "who brought you up from the land of Egypt!" I can see how headstrong these people are! Leave me now, my wrath shall blaze out against them and devour them; of you, however, I will make a great nation.'

But Moses pleaded with the Lord his God. 'Lord,' he said 'why should your wrath blaze out against this people of yours whom you brought out of the land of Egypt with arm outstretched and mighty hand? Why let the Egyptians say, "Ah, it was in treachery that he brought them out, to do them to death in the mountains and wipe them off the face of the earth"? Leave your burning wrath; relent and do not bring this disaster on your people. Remember Abraham, Isaac and Jacob, your servants to whom by your own self you swore and made this promise: I will make your offspring as many as the stars of heaven, and all this land which I promised I will give to your descendants, and it shall be their heritage for ever.' So the Lord relented and did not bring on his people the disaster he had threatened.

This the word of the Lord.

Responsorial Psalm
Ps 105:19-23. ℟ v.4

℟ **O Lord, remember me
out of the love you have for your people.**

1. They fashioned a calf at Horeb
   and worshipped an image of metal,
   exchanging the God who was their glory
   for the image of a bull that eats grass. ℟

2. They forgot the God who was their saviour,
   who had done such great things in Egypt,
   such portents in the land of Ham,
   such marvels at the Red Sea. ℟

3. For this he said he would destroy them,
   but Moses, the man he had chosen,
   stood in the breach before him,
   to turn back his anger from destruction. ℟

Gospel Acclamation
cf. Jn 6:63. 68

Glory to you, O Christ, you are the Word of God!
Your words are spirit, Lord, and they are life;
you have the message of eternal life.
Glory to you, O Christ, you are the Word of God!

or
Jn 3:16

Glory to you, O Christ, you are the Word of God!
God loved the world so much that he gave his only Son;
everyone who believes in him has eternal life.
Glory to you, O Christ, you are the Word of God!

GOSPEL

A reading from the holy Gospel according to John   5:31-47

You place your hope in Moses, and Moses will be your accuser.

Jesus said to the Jews:

'Were I to testify on my own behalf.
my testimony would not be valid;
but there is another witness who can speak on my behalf,
and I know that his testimony is valid.
You sent messengers to John,
and he gave his testimony to the truth:
not that I depend on human testimony;
no, it is for your salvation that I speak of this.

Fourth Week of Lent: Thursday

John was a lamp alight and shining
and for a time you were content to enjoy the light that he
　gave.
But my testimony is greater than John's:
the works my Father has given me to carry out,
these same works of mine
testify that the Father has sent me.
Besides, the Father who sent me
bears witness to me himself.
You have never heard his voice,
you have never seen his shape,
and his word finds no home in you
because you do not believe
in the one he has sent.

'You study the scriptures,
believing that in them you have eternal life;
now these same scriptures testify to me
and yet you refuse to come to me for life!
As for human approval, this means nothing to me.
Besides, I know you too well:
you have no love of God in you.
I have come in the name of my Father
and you refuse to accept me;
if someone else comes in his own name
you will accept him.

'How can you believe,
since you look to one another for approval
and are not concerned
with the approval that comes from the one God?
Do not imagine that I am going to accuse you before the
　Father:
you place your hopes on Moses,
and Moses will be your accuser.
If you really believed him
you would believe me too,
since it was I that he was writing about;
but if you refuse to believe what he wrote,
how can you believe what I say?'

This is the Gospel of the Lord.

Prayer over the Gifts
All-powerful God,
look upon our weakness.
May the sacrifice we offer
bring us purity and strength.

Preface of Lent I-IV, P8-P11.

Communion Antiphon: I will put my law within them, I will write it on their hearts; then I shall be their God, and they will be my people.

Prayer after Communion
Lord,
may the sacraments we receive
cleanse us of sin and free us from guilt,
for our sins bring us sorrow
but your promise of salvation brings us joy.

FRIDAY

Entrance Antiphon: Save me, O God, by your power, and grant me justice! God, hear my prayer; listen to my plea.

Opening Prayer
Father, our source of life,
you know our weakness.
May we reach out with joy to grasp your hand
and walk more readily in your ways.

FIRST READING

A reading from the book of Wisdom 2:1. 12-22
Let us condemn him to a shameful death.

The godless say to themselves, with their misguided reasoning:

'Let us lie in wait for the virtuous man, since he annoys us
and opposes our way of life,
reproaches us for our breaches of the law
and accuses us of playing false to our upbringing.
He claims to have knowledge of God,
and calls himself a son of the Lord.

Fourth Week of Lent: Friday

Before us he stands, a reproof to our way of thinking,
the very sight of him weighs our spirits down;
his way of life is not like other men's,
the paths he treads are unfamiliar.
In his opinion we are counterfeit;
he holds aloof from our doings as though from filth;
he proclaims the final end of the virtuous as happy
and boasts of having God for his father.
Let us see if what he says is true,
let us observe what kind of end he himself will have.
If the virtuous man is God's son, God will take his part
and rescue him from the clutches of his enemies.
Let us test him with cruelty and with torture,
and thus explore this gentleness of his
and put his endurance to the proof.
Let us condemn him to a shameful death
since he will be looked after – we have his word for it.'

This is the way they reason, but they are misled,
their malice makes them blind.
They do not know the hidden things of God,
they have no hope that holiness will be rewarded,
they can see no reward for blameless souls.

This is the word of the Lord.

Responsorial Psalm Ps 33:16. 18. 19-21. 23. ℟ v. 19

℟ **The Lord is close to the broken-hearted.**

1 The Lord turns his face against the wicked
   to destroy their remembrance from the earth.
   The just call and the Lord hears
   and rescues them in all their distress.   ℟

2 The Lord is close to the broken-hearted;
   those whose spirit is crushed he will save.
   Many are the trials of the just man
   but from them all the Lord will rescue him.   ℟

3 He will keep guard over all his bones,
   not one of his bones shall be broken.
   The Lord ransoms the souls of his servants.
   Those who hide in him shall not be condemned.   ℟

Fourth Week of Lent: Friday

Gospel Acclamation   Joel 2:12-13
   Praise to you, O Christ, king of eternal glory.
   Now, now – it is the Lord who speaks –
   come back to me with all your heart,
   for I am all tenderness and compassion.
   Praise to you, O Christ, king of eternal glory.

or   Mt 4:4

   Praise to you, O Christ, king of eternal glory.
   Man does not live on bread alone,
   but on every word that comes from the mouth of God.
   Praise to you, O Christ, king of eternal glory.

GOSPEL

A reading from the holy Gospel according to John   7:1-2. 10. 25-30
They would have arrested him, but his time had not yet come.

Jesus stayed in Galilee; he could not stay in Judaea, because the Jews were out to kill him.

As the Jewish feast of Tabernacles drew near, after his brothers had left for the festival, Jesus went up as well, but quite privately, without drawing attention to himself.

Meanwhile some of the people of Jerusalem were saying, 'Isn't this the man they want to kill? And here he is, speaking freely, and they have nothing to say to him! Can it be true the authorities have made up their minds that he is the Christ? Yet we all know where he comes from, but when the Christ appears no one will know where he comes from.'

Then, as Jesus taught in the Temple, he cried out:

'Yes, you know me and you know where I came from.
Yet I have not come of myself:
no, there is one who sent me and I really come from him,
and you do not know him,
but I know him
because I have come from him
and it was he who sent me.'

They would have arrested him then, but because his time had not yet come no one laid a hand on him.

This is the Gospel of the Lord.

Prayer over the Gifts
All-powerful God,
may the healing power of this sacrifice
free us from sin
and help us to approach you with pure hearts.

Preface of Lent I-IV, P8-P11.

Communion Antiphon: In Christ, through the shedding of his blood, we have redemption and forgiveness of our sins by the abundance of his grace.

Prayer after Communion
Lord,
in this eucharist we pass from death to life.
Keep us from our old and sinful ways
and help us to continue in the new life.

SATURDAY

Entrance Antiphon: The snares of death overtook me, the ropes of hell tightened around me; in my distress I called upon the Lord, and he heard my voice.

Opening Prayer
Lord,
guide us in your gentle mercy,
for left to ourselves
we cannot do your will.

FIRST READING

A reading from the prophet Jeremiah 11:18-20

I was like a trustful lamb being led to the slaughter-house.

The Lord revealed it to me; I was warned. Lord, that was when you opened my eyes to their scheming. I for my part was like a trustful lamb being led to the slaughter-house, not knowing the schemes they were plotting against me, 'Let us destroy the tree in its strength, let us cut him off from the land of the living, so that his name may be quickly forgotten!'

But you, Lord of hosts, who pronounce a just sentence,

Fourth Week of Lent: Saturday

who probe the loins and heart,
let me see the vengeance you will take on them,
for I have committed my cause to you.

This is the word of the Lord.

Responsorial Psalm   Ps 7:2-3. 9-12. ℟ v.2

℟ **Lord God, I take refuge in you.**

1. Lord God, I take refuge in you.
   From my pursuer save me and rescue me,
   lest he tear me to pieces like a lion
   and drag me off with no one to rescue me. ℟

2. Give judgement for me, Lord; I am just
   and innocent of heart.
   Put an end to the evil of the wicked!
   Make the just stand firm,
   you who test mind and heart,
   O just God! ℟

3. God is the shield that protects me,
   who saves the upright of heart.
   God is a just judge
   slow to anger;
   but he threatens the wicked every day. ℟

Gospel Acclamation   Ez 33:11

Praise and honour to you, Lord Jesus!
I take pleasure, not in the death of a wicked man,
– it is the Lord who speaks –
but in the turning back of a wicked man
who changes his ways to win life.
Praise and honour to you, Lord Jesus!

or   cf. Lk 8:15

Praise and honour to you, Lord Jesus!
Blessed are those who,
with a noble and generous heart,
take the word of God to themselves
and yield a harvest through their perseverance.
Praise and honour to you, Lord Jesus!

GOSPEL

A reading from the holy Gospel according to John 7:40-52
Would the Christ be from Galilee?

Several people who had been listening to Jesus said, 'Surely he must be the prophet', and some said, 'He is the Christ', but others said, 'Would the Christ be from Galilee? Does not scripture say that the Christ must be descended from David and come from the town of Bethlehem?' So the people could not agree about him. Some would have liked to arrest him, but no one actually laid hands on him.

The police went back to the chief priests and Pharisees who said to them, 'Why haven't you brought him?' The police replied, 'There has never been anybody who has spoken like him.' 'So' the Pharisees answered 'you have been led astray as well? Have any of the authorities believed in him? Any of the Pharisees? This rabble knows nothing about the Law – they are damned.' One of them, Nicodemus – the same man who had come to Jesus earlier – said to them, 'But surely the Law does not allow us to pass judgement on a man without giving him a hearing and discovering what he is about?' To this they answered, 'Are you a Galilean too? Go into the matter, and see for yourself: prophets do not come out of Galilee.'

This is the Gospel of the Lord.

Prayer over the Gifts

Father,
accept our gifts
and make our hearts obedient to your will.

Preface of Lent I-IV, P8-P11.

Communion Antiphon: We have been ransomed with the precious blood of Christ, as with the blood of a lamb without blemish or spot.

Prayer after Communion
Lord,
may the power of your holy gifts free us from sin
and help us to please you in our daily lives.

FIFTH WEEK OF LENT
Alternative Readings for the Fifth Week of Lent

The following readings may be used instead of the proper ones any day this week, especially in Years B and C when the Gospel of Lazarus is not read on the Fifth Sunday of Lent.

FIRST READING

A reading from the second book of the Kings 4:18-21. 32-37
As Elisha lowered himself on to him, the child's flesh grew warm.

One day the son of the Shunammitess went out to his father who was with the reapers, and exclaimed to his father, 'Oh, my head! My head!' The father told a servant to carry him to his mother. He lifted him up and took him to his mother, and the boy sat on her knee until midday, when he died. She went upstairs, laid him on the bed of Elisha the man of God, shut the door on him and went out.

Elisha then went to the house, and there on his bed lay the child, dead. He went in and shut the door on the two of them and prayed to the Lord. Then he climbed on to the bed and stretched himself on top of the child, putting his mouth on his mouth, his eyes to his eyes, and his hands on his hands, and as he lowered himself on to him, the child's flesh grew warm. Then he got up and walked to and fro inside the house, and then climbed on to the bed again and lowered himself on to the child seven times in all; then the child sneezed and opened his eyes. He then summoned Gehazi his servant. 'Call our Shunammitess' he said; and he called her. When she came to him, he said, 'Take up your son.' She went in and falling at his feet bowed down to the ground; and taking up her son went out.

This is the word of the Lord.

Responsorial Psalm Ps 16:1. 6-8. 15. ℟ v.15

℟ **I shall be filled, when I awake,**
with the sight of your glory.

1 Lord, hear a cause that is just,
  pay heed to my cry.
  Turn your ear to my prayer:
  no deceit is on my lips. ℟

Fifth Week of Lent: Alternative Readings

2 I am here and I call, you will hear me, O God.
   Turn your ear to me; hear my words.
   Display your great love, you whose right hand saves
   your friends from those who rebel against them. ℟

3 Guard me as the apple of your eye.
   Hide me in the shadow of your wings.
   As for me, in my justice I shall see your face
   and be filled, when I awake, with the sight of your glory. ℟

Gospel Acclamation   Jn 11:25.26

Glory and praise to you, O Christ!
I am the resurrection and the life, says the Lord,
whoever believes in me will never die.
Glory and praise to you, O Christ!

GOSPEL

A reading from the holy Gospel according to John   11:1-45
I am the resurrection and the life.

There was a man named Lazarus who lived in the village of Bethany with the two sisters, Mary and Martha, and he was ill. – It was the same Mary, the sister of the sick man Lazarus, who anointed the Lord with ointment and wiped his feet with her hair. The sisters sent this message to Jesus, 'Lord, the man you love is ill.' On receiving the message, Jesus said, 'This sickness will end not in death but in God's glory, and through it the Son of God will be glorified.'

Jesus loved Martha and her sister and Lazarus, yet when he heard that Lazarus was ill he stayed where he was for two more days before saying to the disciples, 'Let us go to Judaea.' The disciples said, 'Rabbi, it is not long since the Jews wanted to stone you; are you going back again?' Jesus replied:

'Are there not twelve hours in the day?
A man can walk in the daytime without stumbling
because he has the light of the world to see by;
but if he walks at night he stumbles,
because there is no light to guide him.'

He said that and then added, 'Our friend Lazarus is resting, I am going to wake him.' The disciples said to him, 'Lord, if he is able to rest he is sure to get better.' The phrase Jesus used referred to the death of Lazarus; but they thought that by 'rest' he meant 'sleep', so Jesus put it plainly, 'Lazarus is dead; and for your sake I am glad I was not there because now you will believe. But let us go to him.' Then Thomas – known as the Twin – said to the other disciples, 'Let us go too, and die with him.'

On arriving, Jesus found that Lazarus had been in the tomb for four days already. Bethany is only about two miles from Jerusalem, and many Jews had come to Martha and Mary to sympathise with them over their brother. When Martha heard that Jesus had come she went to meet him. Mary remained sitting in the house. Martha said to Jesus, 'If you had been here, my brother would not have died, but I know that, even now, whatever you ask of God, he will grant you.' 'Your brother' said Jesus to her 'will rise again.' Martha said, 'I know he will rise again at the resurrection on the last day.' Jesus said:

> 'I am the resurrection and the life.
> If anyone believes in me, even though he dies he will live,
> and whoever lives and believes in me
> will never die.
> Do you believe this?'

'Yes, Lord,' she said 'I believe that you are the Christ, the Son of God, the one who was to come into this world.'

When she had said this, she went and called her sister Mary, saying in a low voice, 'The Master is here and wants to see you.' Hearing this, Mary got up quickly and went to him. Jesus had not yet come into the village; he was still at the place where Martha had met him. When the Jews who were in the house sympathising with Mary saw her get up so quickly and go out, they followed her, thinking that she was going to the tomb to weep there.

Mary went to Jesus, and as soon as she saw him she threw herself at his feet saying, 'Lord, if you had been here, my brother would not have died.' At the sight of her tears, and those of the Jews who followed her, Jesus said in great distress with a sigh that came straight from the heart, 'Where have you put him?' They said, 'Lord, come and see.' Jesus wept; and the Jews said, 'See how much he loved him!' But there were some who remarked, 'He opened the eyes of the blind man, could he not have prevented this man's death?' Still sighing, Jesus reached the tomb; it was a cave with a stone to close the opening. Jesus said, 'Take the stone away.' Martha said to him, 'Lord, by now he will smell; this is the fourth day.' Jesus replied, 'Have I not told you that if you believe you will see the glory of God?' So they took away the stone. Then Jesus lifted up his eyes and said:

Fifth Week of Lent: Monday

'Father, I thank you for hearing my prayer.
I knew indeed that you always hear me,
but I speak
for the sake of all these who stand round me,
so that they may believe it was you who sent me.'

When he had said this, he cried in a loud voice, 'Lazarus, here! Come out!' The dead man came out, his feet and hands bound with bands of stuff and a cloth round his face. Jesus said to them, 'Unbind him, let him go free.'

Many of the Jews who had come to visit Mary and had seen what he did believed in him.

This is the Gospel of the Lord.

MONDAY

Entrance Antiphon: God, take pity on me! My enemies are crushing me; all day long they wage war on me.

Opening Prayer
Father of love, source of all blessings,
help us to pass from our old life of sin
to the new life of grace.
Prepare us for the glory of your kingdom.

FIRST READING

A reading from the prophet Daniel   13:1-9. 15-17. 19-30. 33-62
Have I to die, innocent as I am?

In Babylon there lived a man named Joakim. He had married Susanna daughter of Hilkiah, a woman of great beauty; and she was God-fearing, because her parents were worthy people and had instructed their daughter in the Law of Moses. Joakim was a very rich man, and had a garden attached to his house; the Jews would often visit him since he was held in greater respect than any other man. Two elderly men had been selected from the people that year to act as judges. Of such the Lord said, 'Wickedness has come to Babylon through the elders and judges posing as guides to the people.' These men were often at Joakim's house, and all who were engaged in litigation used to come to them. At midday, when everyone had gone, Susanna used to take a walk in her husband's garden. The two elders, who used to watch her every day as she came in to take her walk, gradually began to desire her. They threw reason aside, making no effort to turn their eyes to heaven, and forgetting its demands of virtue. So they waited for a favourable moment; and one day Susanna came as usual, accompanied only by two young maidservants. The day was hot and she wanted to bathe in the garden. There was no one about except the two elders, spying on her from their hiding place. She said to the servants, 'Bring me some oil and balsam and shut the garden door while I bathe.'

Hardly were the servants gone than the two elders were there after her. 'Look,' they said 'the garden door is shut, no one can see us. We want to have you, so give in and let us! Refuse, and we will both give evidence that a young man was with you and that was why you sent your maids away.' Susanna sighed. 'I am trapped,' she said 'whatever I do. If I agree, that means my death; if I resist, I cannot get away from you. But I prefer to fall innocent into your power than to sin in the eyes of the Lord.' Then she cried out as loud as she could. The two elders began shouting too, putting the blame on her, and one of them ran to open the garden door. The household, hearing the shouting in the garden, rushed out by the side entrance to see what was happening; once the elders had told their story the servants were thoroughly taken aback, since nothing of this sort had ever been said of Susanna.

Next day a meeting was held at the house of her husband Joakim. The two elders arrived, in their vindictiveness determined to have her put to death. They addressed the company: 'Summon Susanna daughter of Hilkiah and wife of Joakim.' She was sent for, and came accompanied by her parents, her children and all her relations.

All her own people were weeping, and so were all the others who saw her. The two elders stood up, with all the people round them, and laid their hands on the woman's head. Tearfully she turned her eyes to heaven, her heart confident in God. The elders then spoke. 'While we were walking by ourselves in the garden, this woman arrived with two servants. She shut the garden door and then dismissed the servants. A young man who had been hiding went over to her and they lay down together. From the end of the garden where we were, we saw this crime taking place and hurried towards them. Though we saw them together we were unable to catch the man: he was too strong for us; he opened the door and took to his heels. We did, however, catch this woman and ask her who the young man was. She refused to tell us. That is our evidence.'

Fifth Week of Lent: Monday

Since they were elders of the people, and judges, the assembly took their word: *Susanna was condemned to death. She cried out as loud as she could, 'Eternal God, you know all secrets and everything before it happens; you know that they have given false evidence against me. And now have I to die, innocent as I am of everything their malice has invented against me?'

The Lord heard her cry and, as she was being led away to die, he roused the holy spirit residing in a young boy named Daniel who began to shout, 'I am innocent of this woman's death!' At which all the people turned to him and asked, 'What do you mean by these words?' Standing in the middle of the crowd he replied, 'Are you so stupid, sons of Israel, as to condemn a daughter of Israel unheard and without troubling to find out the truth? Go back to the scene of the trial: these men have given false evidence against her.'

All the people hurried back, and the elders said to Daniel, 'Come and sit with us and tell us what you mean, since God has given you the gifts that elders have.' Daniel said 'Keep the men well apart from each other for I want to question them.' When the men had been separated, Daniel had one of them brought to him. 'You have grown old in wickedness,' he said, 'and now the sins of your earlier days have overtaken you, you with your unjust judgements, your condemnation of the innocent, your acquittal of guilty men, when the Lord has said, "You must not put the innocent and the just to death." Now then, since you saw her so clearly, tell me what tree you saw them lying under?' He replied, 'Under a mastic tree.' Daniel said, 'True enough! Your lie recoils on your own head: the angel of God has already received your sentence from him and will slash you in half.' He dismissed the man, ordered the other to be brought and said to him, 'Spawn of Canaan, not of Judah, beauty has seduced you, lust has led your heart astray! This is how you have been behaving with the daughters of Israel and they were too frightened to resist; but here is a daughter of Judah who could not stomach your wickedness! Now then, tell me what tree you surprised them under?' He replied, 'Under a holm oak.' Daniel said, 'True enough! Your lie recoils on your own head: the angel of God is waiting, with a sword to drive home and split you, and destroy the pair of you.'

Then the whole assembly shouted, blessing God, the saviour of those who trust in him. And they turned on the two elders whom Daniel had convicted of false evidence out of their own mouths. As prescribed in the Law of Moses, they sentenced them to the same punishment as they had intended to inflict on their neighbour. They put them to death; the life of an innocent woman was spared that day.

This is the word of the Lord.*

*Shorter form, verses 41-62. Read between *.

Responsorial Psalm   Ps 22. ℟ v.4

℟ **If I should walk in the valley of darkness
no evil would I fear.**

1 The Lord is my shepherd;
there is nothing I shall want.
Fresh and green are the pastures
where he gives me repose.
Near restful waters he leads me,
to revive my drooping spirit. ℟

2 He guides me along the right path;
he is true to his name.
If I should walk in the valley of darkness
no evil would I fear.
You are there with your crook and your staff;
with these you give me comfort. ℟

3 You have prepared a banquet for me
in the sight of my foes.
My head you have anointed with oil;
my cup is overflowing. ℟

4 Surely goodness and kindness shall follow me
all the days of my life.
In the Lord's own house shall I dwell
for ever and ever. ℟

Gospel Acclamation   2 Cor 6:2
Glory to you, O Christ, you are the Word of God!
Now is the favourable time;
this is the day of salvation.
Glory to you, O Christ, you are the Word of God!

or   Ez 33:11

Glory to you, O Christ, you are the Word of God!
I take pleasure, not in the death of a wicked man

> – it is the Lord who speaks –
> but in the turning back of a wicked man
> who changes his ways to win life.
> Glory to you, O Christ, you are the Word of God!

GOSPEL

A reading from the holy Gospel according to John   8:1-11

If there is one of you who has not sinned, let him be the first to throw a stone at her.

Jesus went to the Mount of Olives. At daybreak he appeared in the Temple again; and as all the people came to him, he sat down and began to teach them.

The scribes and Pharisees brought a woman along who had been caught committing adultery; and making her stand there in full view of everybody, they said to Jesus, 'Master, this woman was caught in the very act of committing adultery, and Moses has ordered us in the Law to condemn women like this to death by stoning. What have you to say?' They asked him this as a test, looking for something to use against him. But Jesus bent down and started writing on the ground with his finger. As they persisted with their question, he looked up and said, 'If there is one of you who has not sinned, let him be the first to throw a stone at her.' Then he bent down and wrote on the ground again. When they heard this they went away one by one, beginning with the eldest, until Jesus was left alone with the woman, who remained standing there. He looked up and said, 'Woman, where are they? Has no one condemned you?' 'No one sir,' she replied. 'Neither do I condemn you,' said Jesus 'go away and don't sin any more.'

This is the Gospel of the Lord.

Alternative Gospel

For use in Year C when John 8:1-11 is read on the preceding Sunday.

A reading from the holy Gospel according to John   8:12-20

I am the light of the world.

Jesus said to the people:

> 'I am the light of the world;

anyone who follows me will not be walking in the dark;
he will have the light of life.'

At this the Pharisees said to him, 'You are testifying on your own behalf; your testimony is not valid.' Jesus replied:

'It is true that I am testifying on my own behalf,
but my testimony is still valid,
because I know
where I came from and where I am going;
but you do not know
where I come from or where I am going.
You judge by human standards;
I judge no one,
but if I judge,
my judgement will be sound,
because I am not alone:
the one who sent me is with me;
and in your Law it is written
that the testimony of two witnesses is valid.
I may be testifying on my own behalf,
but the Father who sent me is my witness too.'

They asked him, 'Where is your Father?' Jesus answered:

'You do not know me, nor do you know my Father;
if you did know me, you would know my Father as well.'

He spoke these words in the Treasury, while teaching in the Temple. No one arrested him, because his time had not yet come.

This is the Gospel of the Lord.

Prayer over the Gifts
Lord,
as we come with joy
to celebrate the mystery of the eucharist,
may we offer you hearts
purified by bodily penance.

Preface of the Passion of the Lord I, P17.

Communion Antiphon: (When the gospel of the woman taken in adultery is read): Has no one condemned you? The woman answered: No one, Lord. Neither do I condemn you: go and do not sin again.

or When other gospels are read: I am the light of the world, says the Lord; the man who follows me will have the light of life.

Prayer after Communion
Father,
through the grace of your sacraments
may we follow Christ more faithfully
and come to the joy of your kingdom,
where he is Lord for ever and ever.

TUESDAY

Entrance Antiphon: Put your hope in the Lord. Take courage and be strong.

Opening Prayer
Lord,
help us to do your will
that your Church may grow
and become more faithful in your service.

FIRST READING

A reading from the book of Numbers 21:4-9
If anyone is bitten and looks at the fiery serpent, he shall live.

The Israelites left Mount Hor by the road to the Sea of Suph, to skirt the land of Edom. On the way the people lost patience. They spoke against God and against Moses, 'Why did you bring us out of Egypt to die in this wilderness? For there is neither bread nor water here; we are sick of this unsatisfying food.'

At this God sent fiery serpents among the people; their bite brought death to many in Israel. The people came and said to Moses, 'We have sinned by speaking against the Lord and against you. Intercede for us with the Lord to save us from these serpents.' Moses interceded for the people, and the Lord answered him, 'Make a fiery serpent and put it on a standard. If anyone is bitten and looks at it, he shall live.' So Moses fashioned a bronze serpent which he put on a standard, and if anyone was bitten by a serpent, he looked at the bronze serpent and lived.

This is the word of the Lord.

Responsorial Psalm
Ps 101:2-3. 16-21. ℟ v.2

℟ **O Lord, listen to my prayer
and let my cry for help reach you.**

1 O Lord, listen to my prayer
and let my cry for help reach you.
Do not hide your face from me
in the day of my distress.
Turn your ear towards me
and answer me quickly when I call. ℟

2 The nations shall fear the name of the Lord
and all the earth's kings your glory,
when the Lord shall build up Zion again
and appear in all his glory.
Then he will turn to the prayers of the helpless;
he will not despise their prayers. ℟

3 Let this be written for ages to come
that a people yet unborn may praise the Lord;
for the Lord leaned down from his sanctuary on high.
He looked down from heaven to the earth
that he might hear the groans of the prisoners
and free those condemned to die. ℟

Gospel Acclamation
Jn 8:12

Praise to you, O Christ, king of eternal glory!
I am the light of the world, says the Lord,
anyone who follows me will have the light of life.
Praise to you, O Christ, king of eternal glory!

or

Praise to you, O Christ, king of eternal glory!
The seed is the word of God, Christ the sower;
whoever finds this seed will remain for ever.
Praise to you, O Christ, king of eternal glory!

GOSPEL

A reading from the holy Gospel according to John 8:21-30

When you have lifted up the Son of Man, then you will know that I am He.

Jesus said to the Pharisees:

'I am going away; you will look for me

Fifth Week of Lent: Tuesday

and you will die in your sin.
Where I am going, you cannot come.'

The Jews said to one another, 'Will he kill himself? Is that what he means by saying, "Where I am going, you cannot come"?' Jesus went on:

'You are from below;
I am from above.
You are of this world;
I am not of this world.
I have told you already: You will die in your sins.
Yes, if you do not believe that I am He,
you will die in your sins.'

So they said to him, 'Who are you?' Jesus answered:

'What I have told you from the outset.
About you I have much to say
and much to condemn;
but the one who sent me is truthful,
and what I have learnt from him
I declare to the world.'

They failed to understand that he was talking to them about the Father. So Jesus said:

'When you have lifted up the Son of Man,
then you will know that I am He
and that I do nothing of myself:
what the Father has taught me
is what I preach;
he who sent me is with me,
and has not left me to myself,
for I always do what pleases him.'

As he was saying this, many came to believe in him.

This is the Gospel of the Lord.

Prayer over the Gifts
Merciful Lord,
we offer this gift of reconciliation
so that you will forgive our sins
and guide our wayward hearts.

Preface of the Passion of the Lord I, P17.

Communion Antiphon: When I am lifted up from the earth, I will draw all men to myself, says the Lord.

Prayer after Communion

All-powerful God,
may the holy mysteries we share in this eucharist
make us worthy to attain the gift of heaven.

WEDNESDAY

Entrance Antiphon: Lord, you rescue me from raging enemies, you lift me above my attackers, you deliver me from violent men.

Opening Prayer

Father of mercy,
hear the prayers of your repentant children
who call on you in love.
Enlighten our minds and sanctify our hearts.

FIRST READING

A reading from the prophet Daniel 3:14-20. 24-25. 28
He has sent his angel to rescue his servants.

King Nebuchadnezzar said, 'Shadrach, Meshach and Abednego, is it true that you do not serve my gods, and that you refuse to worship the golden statue I have erected? When you hear the sound of horn, pipe, lyre, trigon, harp, bagpipe, or any other instrument, are you prepared to prostrate yourselves and worship the statue I have made? If you refuse to worship it, you must be thrown straight away into the burning fiery furnace; and where is the god who could save you from my power?' Shadrach, Meshach and Abednego replied to King Nebuchadnezzar, 'Your question hardly requires an answer: if our God, the one we serve, is able to save us from the burning fiery furnace and from your power, O king, he will save us; and even if he does not, then you must know, O king, that we will not serve your god or worship the statue you have erected.' These words infuriated King Nebuchadnezzar; his expression was very different now as he looked at Shadrach, Meshach and Abednego. He gave orders for the furnace to be made seven times hotter than usual, and commanded certain stalwarts from his army to bind Shadrach,

Fifth Week of Lent: Wednesday

Meshach and Abednego and throw them into the burning fiery furnace.

Then King Nebuchadnezzar sprang to his feet in amazement. He said to his advisers, 'Did we not have these three men thrown bound into the fire?' They replied, 'Certainly, O king.' 'But,' he went on 'I can see four men walking about freely in the heart of the fire without coming to any harm. And the fourth looks like a son of the gods.'

Nebuchadnezzar exclaimed, 'Blessed be the God of Shadrach, Meshach and Abednego: he has sent his angel to rescue his servants who, putting their trust in him, defied the order of the king, and preferred to forfeit their bodies rather than serve or worship any god but their own.'

This is the word of the Lord.

Responsional Psalm   Dan 3:52-56. ℟ v.52

1   You are blest, Lord God of our fathers.
    ℟ **To you glory and praise for evermore.**
    Blest your glorious holy name
    ℟ **To you glory and praise for evermore.**

2   You are blest in the temple of your glory.
    ℟ **To you glory and praise for evermore.**
    You are blest on the throne of your kingdom.
    ℟ **To you glory and praise for evermore.**

3   You are blest who gaze into the depths.
    ℟ **To you glory and praise for evermore.**
    You are blest in the firmament of heaven.
    ℟ **To you glory and praise for evermore.**

Gospel Acclamation   Mt 4:4

Praise and honour to you, Lord Jesus!
Man does not live on bread alone,
but on every word that comes from the mouth of God.
Praise and honour to you, Lord Jesus!

or   Lk 8:15

Praise and honour to you, Lord Jesus!
Blessed are those who,
with a noble and generous heart,
take the word of God to themselves
and yield a harvest through their perseverance.
Praise and honour to you, Lord Jesus!

GOSPEL

A reading from the holy Gospel according to John 8:31-42
If the Son of Man makes you free, you will be free indeed.

To the Jews who believed in him Jesus said:

'If you make my word your home
you will indeed be my disciples,
you will learn the truth
and the truth will make you free.'

They answered, 'We are descended from Abraham and we have never been the slaves of anyone; what do you mean, "You will be made free"?' Jesus replied:

'I tell you most solemnly,
everyone who commits sin is a slave.
Now the slave's place in the house is not assured,
but the son's place is assured.
So if the Son makes you free,
you will be free indeed.
I know that you are descended from Abraham;
but in spite of that you want to kill me
because nothing I say has penetrated into you.
What I, for my part, speak of
is what I have seen with my Father;
but you, you put into action
the lessons learnt from your father.'

They repeated, 'Our father is Abraham.' Jesus said to them:

'If you were Abraham's children,
you would do as Abraham did.
As it is, you want to kill me
when I tell you the truth
as I have learnt it from God;
that is not what Abraham did.
What you are doing is what your father does.'

'We were not born of prostitution,' they went on 'we have one father: God.' Jesus answered:

'If God were your father, you would love me,
since I have come here from God; yes, I have come from him;
not that I came because I chose,
no, I was sent, and by him.'

This is the Gospel of the Lord.

Prayer over the Gifts
Lord,
you have given us these gifts to honour your name.
Bless them,
and let them become a source of health and strength.

Preface of the Passion of the Lord I, P17.

Communion Antiphon: God has transferred us into the kingdom of the Son he loves; in him we are redeemed, and find forgiveness of our sins.

Prayer after Communion
Lord,
may the mysteries we receive heal us,
remove sin from our hearts,
and make us grow strong
under your constant protection.

THURSDAY

Entrance Antiphon: Christ is the mediator of a new covenant so that since he has died, those who are called may receive the eternal inheritance promised to them.

Opening Prayer
Lord,
come to us:
free us from the stain of our sins.
Help us to remain faithful to a holy way of life,
and guide us to the inheritance you have promised.

FIRST READING

A reading from the book of Genesis 17:3-9
You shall become the father of a multitude of nations.

Abram bowed to the ground and God said this to him, 'Here now is my covenant with you: you shall become the father of a multitude of nations. You shall no longer be called Abram; your name shall be Abraham, for I will make you father of a multitude of nations. I will make you most fruitful. I will make you into nations, and your issue shall be kings. I will establish my

Covenant between myself and you, and your descendants after you, generation after generation, a Covenant in perpetuity, to be your God and the God of your descendants after you. I will give to you and to your descendants after you the land you are living in, the whole land of Canaan, to own in perpetuity, and I will be your God.'

God said to Abraham, 'You on your part shall maintain my Covenant, yourself and your descendants after you, generation after generation.'

This is the word of the Lord.

Responsorial Psalm   Ps 104:4-9. R/ v.8

R/ **The Lord remembers his covenant for ever.**

1 Consider the Lord and his strength;
constantly seek his face.
Remember the wonders he has done,
his miracles, the judgements he spoke. R/

2 O children of Abraham, his servant,
O sons of the Jacob he chose.
He, the Lord, is our God:
his judgements prevail in all the earth. R/

3 He remembers his covenant for ever,
his promise for a thousand generations,
the covenant he made with Abraham,
the oath he swore to Isaac. R/

Gospel Acclamation   cf. Jn 6:63.68
Glory and praise to you, O Christ!
Your words are spirit, Lord, and they are life;
you have the message of eternal life.
Glory and praise to you, O Christ!

or   cf. Ps 94:8

Glory and praise to you, O Christ!
Harden not your hearts today
but listen to the voice of the Lord.
Glory and praise to you, O Christ!

GOSPEL

A reading from the holy Gospel according to John 8:51-59
Your father Abraham rejoiced to think that he would see my Day.

Jesus said to the Jews:

'I tell you most solemnly,
whoever keeps my word
will never see death.'

The Jews said, 'Now we know for certain that you are possessed. Abraham is dead, and the prophets are dead, and yet you say, "Whoever keeps my word will never know the taste of death." Are you greater than our father Abraham, who is dead? The prophets are dead too. Who are you claiming to be?' Jesus answered:

'If I were to seek my own glory
that would be no glory at all;
my glory is conferred by the Father,
by the one of whom you say, "He is our God"
although you do not know him.
But I know him,
and if I were to say: I do not know him,
I should be a liar, as you are liars yourselves.
But I do know him, and I faithfully keep his word.
Your father Abraham rejoiced
to think that he would see my Day;
he saw it and was glad.'

The Jews then said, 'You are not fifty yet, and you have seen Abraham!' Jesus replied:

'I tell you most solemnly,
before Abraham ever was,
I Am.'

At this they picked up stones to throw at him; but Jesus hid himself and left the Temple.

This is the Gospel of the Lord.

Prayer over the Gifts
Merciful Lord,
accept the sacrifice we offer you
that it may help us grow in holiness
and advance the salvation of the world.

Preface of the Passion of the Lord I, P17.

Communion Antiphon: God did not spare his own Son, but gave him up for us all; with Christ he will surely give us all things.

Prayer after Communion
Lord of mercy,
let the sacrament which renews us
bring us to eternal life.

FRIDAY

Entrance Antiphon: Have mercy on me, Lord, for I am in distress; rescue me from the hands of my enemies. Lord, keep me from shame, for I have called to you.

Opening Prayer
Lord,
grant us your forgiveness,
and set us free from our enslavement to sin.

FIRST READING

A reading from the prophet Jeremiah 20:10-13

The Lord is at my side, a mighty hero.

Jeremiah said:

'I hear so many disparaging me,
" 'Terror from every side!'
Denounce him! Let us denounce him!"
All those who used to be my friends
watched for my downfall,
"Perhaps he will be seduced into error.
Then we will master him
and take our revenge!"
But the Lord is at my side, a mighty hero;
my opponents will stumble, mastered,
confounded by their failure;
everlasting, unforgettable disgrace will be theirs.
But you, Lord of hosts, you who probe with justice,
who scrutinise the loins and heart,
let me see the vengeance you will take on them,

for I have committed my cause to you.
Sing to the Lord,
praise the Lord,
for he has delivered the soul of the needy
from the hands of evil men.'

This is the word of the Lord.

Responsorial Psalm
Ps 17:2-7. ℟ cf v.7

℟ **In my anguish I called to the Lord
and he heard my voice.**

1 I love you, Lord, my strength,
my rock, my fortress, my saviour.
My God is the rock where I take refuge;
my shield, my mighty help, my stronghold.
The Lord is worthy of all praise:
when I call I am saved from my foes. ℟

2 The waves of death rose about me;
the torrents of destruction assailed me;
the snares of the grave entangled me;
the traps of death confronted me. ℟

3 In my anguish I called to the Lord;
I cried to my God for help.
From his temple he heard my voice;
my cry came to his ears. ℟

Gospel Acclamation
Mt 4:17

Glory to you, O Christ, you are the Word of God!
Repent, says the Lord,
for the kingdom of heaven is close at hand.
Glory to you, O Christ, you are the Word of God!

or
cf. Jn 6:63.68

Glory to you, O Christ, you are the Word of God!
Your words are spirit, Lord, and they are life;
you have the message of eternal life.
Glory to you, O Christ, you are the Word of God!

GOSPEL

A reading from the holy Gospel according to John 10:31-42
They wanted to arrest Jesus then, but he eluded them.

The Jews fetched stones to stone him, so Jesus said to them, 'I have done many good works for you to see, works from my Father; for which of these are you stoning me?' The Jews answered him, 'We are not stoning you for doing a good work but for blasphemy: you are only a man and you claim to be God.' Jesus answered:

> 'Is it not written in your Law:
> I said, you are gods?
> So the Law used the word gods
> of those to whom the word of God was addressed,
> and scripture cannot be rejected.
> Yet you say to someone the Father has consecrated and sent
>   into the world,
> "You are blaspheming,"
> because he says, "I am the Son of God."
> If I am not doing my Father's work,
> there is no need to believe me;
> but if I am doing it,
> then even if you refuse to believe in me,
> at least believe in the work I do;
> then you will know for sure
> that the Father is in me and I am in the Father.'

They wanted to arrest him then, but he eluded them.

He went back again to the far side of the Jordan to stay in the district where John had once been baptising. Many people who came to him there said, 'John gave no signs, but all he said about this man was true'; and many of them believed in him.

This is the Gospel of the Lord.

Prayer over the Gifts
God of mercy,
may the gifts we present at your altar
help us to achieve eternal salvation.

Preface of the Passion of the Lord I, P17.

Communion Antiphon: Jesus carried our sins in his own body on the cross so that we could die to sin and live in holiness; by his wounds we have been healed.

Prayer after Communion
Lord,
may we always receive the protection of this sacrifice.
May it keep us safe from all harm.

SATURDAY

Entrance Antiphon: Lord, do not stay away; come quickly to help me! I am a worm and no man: men scorn me, people despise me.

Opening Prayer
God our Father,
you always work to save us,
and now we rejoice in the great love
you give to your chosen people.
Protect all who are about to become your children,
and continue to bless those who are already baptised.

FIRST READING

A reading from the prophet Ezekiel 37:21-28
I will make them into one nation.

The Lord says this: 'I am going to take the sons of Israel from the nations where they have gone. I shall gather them together from everywhere and bring them home to their own soil. I shall make them into one nation in my own land and on the mountains of Israel, and one king is to be king of them all; they will no longer form two nations, nor be two separate kingdoms. They will no longer defile themselves with their idols and their filthy practices and all their sins. I shall rescue them from all the betrayals they have been guilty of; I shall cleanse them; they shall be my people and I will be their God. My servant David will reign over them, one shepherd for all; they will follow my observances, respect my laws and practise them. They will live in the land that I gave my servant Jacob, the land in which your ancestors lived. They will live in it, they, their children, their children's children, for ever. David my servant is to be their prince for ever. I shall make a covenant of peace with them, an eternal covenant with them. I shall resettle them and increase them; I shall settle my sanctuary

Fifth Week of Lent: Saturday

among them for ever. I shall make my home above them; I will be their God, they shall be my people. And the nations will learn that I am the Lord the sanctifier of Israel, when my sanctuary is with them for ever.'

This is the word of the Lord.

Responsorial Psalm   Jer 31:10-13. R̸ v.10
> R̸ **The Lord will guard us
> as a shepherd guards his flock.**

1 O nations, hear the word of the Lord,
   proclaim it to the far-off coasts.
   Say: 'He who scattered Israel will gather him
   and guard him as a shepherd guards his flock.'   R̸

2 For the Lord has ransomed Jacob,
   has saved him from an overpowering hand.
   They will come and shout for joy on Mount Zion,
   they will stream to the blessings of the Lord.   R̸

3 Then the young girls will rejoice and will dance,
   the men, young and old, will be glad.
   I will turn their mourning into joy.
   I will console them, give gladness for grief.   R̸

Gospel Acclamation   Jn 3:16
  Praise to you, O Christ, king of eternal glory!
  God loved the world so much that he gave his only Son;
  everyone who believes in him has eternal life.
  Praise to you, O Christ, king of eternal glory!

or   Ez 18:31
  Praise to you, O Christ, king of eternal glory!
  Shake off all your sins – it is the Lord who speaks –
  and make yourselves a new heart and a new spirit.
  Praise to you, O Christ, king of eternal glory!

GOSPEL

A reading from the holy Gospel according to John   11:45-56
To gather together in unity the scattered children of God

Many of the Jews who had come to visit Mary and had seen what Jesus did believed in him, but some of them went to tell the Pharisees what he had done. Then the chief priests and Pharisees

Fifth Week of Lent: Saturday

called a meeting. 'Here is this man working all these signs' they said 'and what action are we taking? If we let him go on in this way everybody will believe in him, and the Romans will come and destroy the Holy Place and our nation.' One of them, Caiaphas, the high priest that year, said, 'You don't seem to have grasped the situation at all; you fail to see that it is better for one man to die for the people, than for the whole nation to be destroyed.' He did not speak in his own person, it was as high priest that he made this prophecy that Jesus was to die for the nation – and not for the nation only, but to gather together in unity the scattered children of God. From that day they were determined to kill him. So Jesus no longer went about openly among the Jews, but left the district for a town called Ephraim, in the country bordering on the desert, and stayed there with his disciples.

The Jewish Passover drew near, and many of the country people who had gone up to Jerusalem to purify themselves looked out for Jesus, saying to one another as they stood about in the Temple, 'What do you think? Will he come to the festival or not?'

This is the Gospel of the Lord.

Prayer over the Gifts
Ever-living God,
in baptism, the sacrament of our faith,
you restore us to life.
Accept the prayers and gifts of your people:
forgive our sins and fulfill our hopes and desires.

Preface of the Passion of the Lord I, P17.

Communion Antiphon: Christ was sacrificed so that he could gather together the scattered children of God.

Prayer after Communion
Father of mercy and power,
we thank you for nourishing us
with the body and blood of Christ
and for calling us to share in his divine life,
for he is Lord for ever and ever.

GOSPEL ACCLAMATIONS
For the Weekdays of Lent

During Lent, both before and after the Gospel Acclamation, one or other of the following phrases may be used, or another similar phrase:

> Praise to you, O Christ, king of eternal glory!
> Praise and honour to you, Lord Jesus!
> Glory and praise to you, O Christ!
> Glory to you, O Christ, you are the Word of God!

---

1 *Ps 50:12. 14*

A pure heart create for me, O God,
and give me again the joy of your help.

2 *cf. Ps 94:8*

Harden not your hearts today,
but listen to the voice of the Lord.

3 *cf. Ps 129:5.7*

My soul is waiting for the Lord,
I count on his word,
because with the Lord there is mercy
and fullness of redemption.

4 *Ez 18:31*

Shake off all your sins – it is the Lord speaks –
and make yourselves a new heart and a new spirit.

5 *Ez 33:11*

I take pleasure, not in the death of a wicked man
– it is the Lord who speaks –
but in the turning back of a wicked man
who changes his ways to win life.

6 *Joel 2:12-13*

Now, now – it is the Lord who speaks –
came back to me with all your heart,
for I am all tenderness and compassion.

Gospel Acclamation for Weekdays of Lent

7   cf. Amos 5:14

Seek good and not evil so that you may live,
and that the Lord God of hosts may really be with you.

8   Mt 4:4

Man does not live on bread alone,
but on every word that comes from the mouth of God.

9   Mt 4:17

Repent, says the Lord, for the kingdom of heaven is close at hand.

10   cf. Lk 8:15

Blessed are those who, with a noble and generous heart,
take the word of God to themselves
and yield a harvest through their perseverance.

11   Lk 15:18

I will leave this place and go to my father and say:
'Father, I have sinned against heaven and against you.'

12   Jn 3:16

God loved the world so much that he gave his only Son;
everyone who believes in him has eternal life.

13   cf. Jn 6:63. 68

Your words are spirit, Lord, and they are life;
you have the message of eternal life.

14   Jn 8:12

I am the light of the world, says the Lord,
anyone who follows me will have the light of life.

15   Jn 11:25. 26

I am the resurrection and the life, says the Lord,
whoever believes in me will never die.

16   2 Cor 6:2

Now is the favourable time;
this is the day of salvation.

17

The seed is the word of God, Christ the sower;
whoever finds this seed will remain for ever.

HOLY WEEK

MONDAY

Entrance Antiphon: Defend me, Lord, from all my foes: take up your arms and come swiftly to my aid for you have the power to save me.

Opening Prayer
All-powerful God,
by the suffering and death of your Son,
strengthen and protect us in our weakness.

FIRST READING

A reading from the prophet Isaiah 42:1-7
He does not cry out or shout aloud.

Here is my servant whom I uphold,
my chosen one in whom my soul delights.
I have endowed him with my spirit
that he may bring true justice to the nations.

He does not cry out or shout aloud,
or make his voice heard in the streets.
He does not break the crushed reed,
nor quench the wavering flame.

Faithfully he brings true justice;
he will neither waver, nor be crushed
until true justice is established on earth,
for the islands are awaiting his law.

Thus says God, the Lord,
he who created the heavens and spread them out,
who gave shape to the earth and what comes from it,
who gave breath to its people
and life to the creatures that move in it:

> I, the Lord, have called you to serve the cause of right;
> I have taken you by the hand and formed you;
> I have appointed you as covenant of the people and light of
>   the nations,
> to open the eyes of the blind,

to free captives from prison,
and those who live in darkness from the dungeon.

This is the word of the Lord.

Responsorial Psalm   Ps 26:1-3. 13-14. ℟ v.1

℟ **The Lord is my light and my help.**

1 The Lord is my light and my help;
   whom shall I fear?
   The Lord is the stronghold of my life;
   before whom shall I shrink?   ℟

2 When evil-doers draw near
   to devour my flesh,
   it is they, my enemies and foes,
   who stumble and fall.   ℟

3 Though an army encamp against me
   my heart would not fear.
   Though war break out against me
   even then would I trust.   ℟

4 I am sure I shall see the Lord's goodness
   in the land of the living.
   Hope in him, hold firm and take heart.
   Hope in the Lord!   ℟

Gospel Acclamation

Praise and honour to you, Lord Jesus!
Hail to you, our King!
You alone have had compassion on our sins.
Praise and honour to you, Lord Jesus!

GOSPEL

A reading from the holy Gospel according to John   12:1-11
Leave her alone; she had to keep this scent for the day of my burial.

Six days before the Passover, Jesus went to Bethany, where Lazarus was, whom he had raised from the dead. They gave a dinner for him there; Martha waited on them and Lazarus was among those at table. Mary brought in a pound of very costly ointment, pure nard, and with it anointed the feet of Jesus, wiping them with her hair; the house was full of the scent of the ointment. Then Judas Iscariot – one of his disciples, the man who was to betray him – said, 'Why wasn't this ointment sold for three hundred denarii, and the money given to the poor?' He said this, not because he cared about the poor, but because he was a thief; he was in charge of the common fund and used to help himself to the contributions. So Jesus said, 'Leave her alone; she had to keep this scent for the day of my burial. You have the poor with you always, you will not always have me.'

Meanwhile a large number of Jews heard that he was there and came not only on account of Jesus but also to see Lazarus whom he had raised from the dead. Then the chief priests decided to kill Lazarus as well, since it was on his account that many of the Jews were leaving them and believing in Jesus.

This is the Gospel of the Lord.

Prayer over the Gifts

Lord,
look with mercy on our offerings.
May the sacrifice of Christ, your Son,
bring us to eternal life,
for he is Lord for ever and ever.

Preface of the Passion of the Lord II, P18.

Communion Antiphon: When I am in trouble, Lord, do not hide your face from me; hear me when I call, and answer me quickly.

Prayer after Communion

God of mercy,
be close to your people.
Watch over us who receive this sacrament of salvation,
and keep us in your love.

TUESDAY

Entrance Antiphon: **False witnesses have stood up against me, and my enemies threaten violence; Lord, do not surrender me into their power!**

Opening Prayer
Father,
may we receive your forgiveness and mercy
as we celebrate the passion and death of the Lord,
who lives and reigns . . .

FIRST READING

A reading from the prophet Isaiah 49:1-6
I will make you the light of the nations so that my salvation may reach to the ends of the earth.

Islands, listen to me,
pay attention, remotest peoples.
The Lord called me before I was born,
from my mother's womb he pronounced my name.

He made my mouth a sharp sword,
and hid me in the shadow of his hand.
He made me into a sharpened arrow,
and concealed me in his quiver.

He said to me, 'You are my servant Israel,
in whom I shall be glorified';
while I was thinking, 'I have toiled in vain,
I have exhausted myself for nothing';

and all the while my cause was with the Lord,
my reward with my God.
I was honoured in the eyes of the Lord,
my God was my strength.

And now the Lord has spoken,
he who formed me in the womb to be his servant,
to bring Jacob back to him,
to gather Israel to him:

'It is not enough for you to be my servant,
to restore the tribes of Jacob and bring back the survivors of Israel;

Holy Week: Tuesday

I will make you the light of the nations
so that my salvation may reach to the ends of the earth.'

This is the word of the Lord.

Responsorial Psalm   Ps 70:1-6. 15. 17. ℟ v.15

℟ **My lips will tell of your help.**

1. In you, O Lord, I take refuge;
   let me never be put to shame.
   In your justice rescue me, free me:
   pay heed to me and save me. ℟

2. Be a rock where I can take refuge,
   a mighty stronghold to save me;
   for you are my rock, my stronghold.
   Free me from the hand of the wicked. ℟

3. It is you, O Lord, who are my hope,
   my trust, O Lord, since my youth.
   On you I have leaned from my birth,
   from my mother's womb you have been my help. ℟

4. My lips will tell of your justice
   and day by day of your help
   (though I can never tell it all).
   O God, you have taught me from my youth
   and I proclaim your wonders still. ℟

Gospel Acclamation
Glory and praise to you, O Christ!
Hail to you, our King!
Obedient to the Father, you were led to your crucifixion
as a meek lamb is led to the slaughter.
Glory and praise to you, O Christ!

GOSPEL

A reading from the holy Gospel according to John   13:21-33. 36-38
One of you will betray me; before the cock crows, you will have disowned me three times.

While at supper with his disciples, Jesus was troubled in spirit and declared , 'I tell you most solemnly, one of you will betray me.' The disciples looked at one another, wondering which he meant. The disciple Jesus loved was reclining next to Jesus;

Holy Week: Tuesday

Simon Peter signed to him and said, 'Ask who it is he means', so leaning back on Jesus' breast he said, 'Who is it, Lord?' 'It is the one' replied Jesus 'to whom I give the piece of bread that I shall dip in the dish.' He dipped the piece of bread and gave it to Judas son of Simon Iscariot. At that instant, after Judas had taken the bread, Satan entered him. Jesus then said, 'What you are going to do, do quickly.' None of the others at table understood the reason he said this. Since Judas had charge of the common fund, some of them thought Jesus was telling him, 'Buy what we need for the festival', or telling him to give something to the poor. As soon as Judas had taken the piece of bread he went out. Night had fallen.

When he had gone Jesus said:

'Now has the Son of Man been glorified,
and in him God has been glorified.
If God has been glorified in him,
God will in turn glorify him in himself,
and will glorify him very soon.
My little children.
I shall not be with you much longer.
You will look for me,
and, as I told the Jews,
where I am going,
you cannot come.'

Simon Peter said, 'Lord, where are you going?' Jesus replied, 'Where I am going you cannot follow me now; you will follow me later.' Peter said to him, 'Why can't I follow you now? I will lay down my life for you.' 'Lay down your life for me?' answered Jesus. 'I tell you most solemnly, before the cock crows you will have disowned me three times.'

This is the Gospel of the Lord.

Prayer over the Gifts

Lord,
look with mercy on our offerings.
May we who share the holy gifts
receive the life they promise.

Preface of the Passion of the Lord II, P18.

Communion Antiphon: God did not spare his own Son, but gave him up for us all.

Prayer after Communion
God of mercy,
may the sacrament of salvation
which now renews our strength
bring us a share in your life for ever.

WEDNESDAY

Entrance Antiphon: At the name of Jesus every knee must bend, in heaven, on earth, and under the earth; Christ became obedient for us even to death, dying on the cross. Therefore, to the glory of God the Father: Jesus Christ is Lord.

Opening Prayer
Father,
in your plan of salvation
your Son Jesus Christ accepted the cross
and freed us from the power of the enemy.
May we come to share the glory of his resurrection,
for he lives and reigns . . .

FIRST READING

A reading from the prophet Isaiah 50:4-9
I did not cover my face against insult and spittle.

The Lord has given me
a disciple's tongue.
So that I may know how to reply to the wearied
he provides me with speech.
Each morning he wakes me to hear,
to listen like a disciple.
The Lord has opened my ear.
For my part, I made no resistance,
neither did I turn away.
I offered my back to those who struck me,
my cheeks to those who tore at my beard;
I did not cover my face
against insult and spittle.
The Lord comes to my help,
so that I am untouched by the insults.
So, too, I set my face like flint;
I know I shall not be shamed.

My vindicator is here at hand. Does anyone start proceedings
  against me?
Then let us go to court together.
Who thinks he has a case against me?
Let him approach me.
The Lord is coming to my help,
who dare condemn me?

This is the word of the Lord.

Responsorial Psalm   Ps 68:8-10. 21-22. 31. 33-34. ℟ v.14

℟ **In your great love, O Lord,**
  answer my prayer for your favour.

1 It is for you that I suffer taunts,
   that shame covers my face,
   that I have become a stranger to my brothers,
   an alien to my own mother's sons.
   I burn with zeal for your house
   and taunts against you fall on me.   ℟

2 Taunts have broken my heart;
   I have reached the end of my strength.
   I looked in vain for compassion,
   for consolers; not one could I find.
   For food they gave me poison;
   in my thirst they gave me vinegar to drink.   ℟

3 I will praise God's name with a song;
   I will glorify him with thanksgiving.
   The poor when they see it will be glad
   and God-seeking hearts will revive;
   for the Lord listens to the needy
   and does not spurn his servants in their chains.   ℟

Gospel Acclamation

Glory to you, O Christ, you are the Word of God!
Hail to you, our King!
Obedient to the Father, you were led to your crucifixion
as a meek lamb is led to the slaughter.
Glory to you, O Christ, you are the Word of God!

Alternative Acclamation

Glory to you, O Christ, you are the Word of God!
Hail to you, our King!
You alone have had compassion on our sins.
Glory to you, O Christ, you are the Word of God!

GOSPEL

A reading from the holy Gospel according to Matthew 26:14-25

The Son of Man is going to his fate, as the scriptures say he will, but alas for that man by whom he is betrayed.

One of the Twelve, the man called Judas Iscariot, went to the chief priests and said, 'What are you prepared to give me if I hand him over to you?' They paid him thirty silver pieces, and from that moment he looked for an opportunity to betray him.

Now on the first day of Unleavened Bread the disciples came to Jesus to say, 'Where do you want us to make the preparations for you to eat the passover?' 'Go to so-and-so in the city' he replied 'and say to him, "The Master says: My time is near. It is at your house that I am keeping Passover with my disciples." ' The disciples did what Jesus told them and prepared the Passover.

When evening came he was at table with the twelve disciples. And while they were eating he said, 'I tell you solemnly, one of you is about to betray me.' They were greatly distressed and started asking him in turn, 'Not I, Lord, surely?' He answered, 'Someone who has dipped his hand into the dish with me, will betray me. The Son of Man is going to his fate, as the scriptures say he will, but alas for that man by whom the Son of Man is betrayed! Better for that man if he had never been born!' Judas, who was to betray him, asked in his turn, 'Not I, Rabbi surely?' 'They are your own words' answered Jesus.

This is the Gospel of the Lord.

Prayer over the Gifts
Lord,
accept the gifts we present
as we celebrate this mystery
of the suffering and death of your Son.
May we share in the eternal life he won for us,
for he is Lord for ever and ever.

Preface of the Passion of the Lord II, P18.

Communion Antiphon: The Son of Man did not come to be served, but to serve, and to give his life as a ransom for many.

Prayer after Communion
All-powerful God,

the eucharist proclaims the death of your Son.
Increase our faith in its saving power
and strengthen our hope in the life it promises.

HOLY THURSDAY

Chrism Mass

This Mass, which the bishop concelebrates with his presbyterium and at which the oils are blessed, manifests the communion of the priests with their bishop. It is thus desirable that, if possible, all the priests take part in it and receive communion under both kinds. To show the unity of the presbyterium, the priests who concelebrate with the bishop should come from different parts of the diocese.

Entrance Antiphon: Jesus Christ has made us a kingdom of priests to serve his God and Father: glory and kingship be his for ever and ever.

The Gloria is sung or said.

Opening Prayer
Father,
by the power of the Holy Spirit
you anointed your only Son Messiah and Lord of creation;
you have given us a share in his consecration
to priestly service in your Church.
Help us to be faithful witnesses in the world
to the salvation Christ won for all mankind.

FIRST READING

A reading from the prophet Isaiah   61:1-3. 6. 8-9

The Lord has anointed me and has sent me to bring Good News to the poor, to give them the oil of gladness.

The spirit of the Lord has been given to me,
for the Lord has anointed me.
He has sent me to bring good news to the poor,
to bind up hearts that are broken;

to proclaim liberty to captives,

freedom to those in prison;
to proclaim a year of favour from the Lord,
a day of vengeance for our God;

to comfort all those who mourn and to give them
for ashes a garland;
for mourning robe the oil of gladness,
for despondency, praise.

But you, you will be named 'priests of the Lord',
they will call you 'ministers of our God'.
I reward them faithfully
and make an everlasting covenant with them.

Their race will be famous throughout the nations,
their descendants throughout the peoples.
All who see them will admit
that they are a race whom the Lord has blessed.

>   This is the word of the Lord.

Responsorial Psalm   Ps 88:21-22. 25. 27. ℟ v.2

> ℟ **I will sing for ever of your love, O Lord.**

1 I have found David my servant
and with my holy oil anointed him.
My hand shall always be with him
and my arm shall make him strong.   ℟

2 My truth and my love shall be with him;
by my name his might shall be exalted.
He will say to me: 'You are my father,
my God, the rock who saves me.'   ℟

SECOND READING

A reading from the book of the Apocalypse   1:5-8
He made us a line of kings, priests to serve his God and Father.

Grace and peace to you from Jesus Christ, the faithful witness, the First-born from the dead, the Ruler of the kings of the earth. He loves us and has washed away our sins with his blood, and made us a line of kings, priests to serve his God and Father; to him, then, be glory and power for ever and ever. Amen. It is he who is coming on the clouds; everyone will see him, even those who pierced him, and all the races of the earth will mourn over

Holy Thursday: Chrism Mass

him. This is the truth. Amen. 'I am the Alpha and the Omega' says the Lord God, who is, who was, and who is to come, the Almighty.

This is the word of the Lord.

Gospel Acclamation   Is 61:1 (Lk 4:18)
Praise to you, O Christ, king of eternal glory!
The spirit of the Lord has been given to me;
he has sent me to bring the good news to the poor.
Praise to you, O Christ, king of eternal glory.

GOSPEL

A reading from the holy Gospel according to Luke   4:16-21
The spirit of the Lord has been given to me, for he has anointed me.

Jesus came to Nazara, where he had been brought up, and went into the synagogue on the sabbath day as he usually did. He stood up to read, and they handed him the scroll of the prophet Isaiah. Unrolling the scroll he found the place where it is written:

> The spirit of the Lord has been given to me,
> for he has anointed me.
> He has sent me to bring the good news to the poor,
> to proclaim liberty to captives
> and to the blind new sight,
> to set the downtrodden free,
> to proclaim the Lord's year of favour.

He then rolled up the scroll, gave it back to the assistant and sat down. And all eyes in the synagogue were fixed on him. Then he began to speak to them, 'This text is being fulfilled today even as you listen.'

This is the Gospel of the Lord.

Renewal of Commitment to Priestly Service
After the homily, the bishop speaks to the priests, inviting them to renew publicly their priestly promises. He uses these, or similar, words:
My brothers,
today we celebrate the memory of the first eucharist,
at which our Lord Jesus Christ
shared with his apostles and with us
his call to the priestly service of his Church.

Now, in the presence of your bishop and God's holy people,
are you ready to renew your own dedication to Christ
as priests of his new covenant?
Priests I am.

At your ordination
you accepted the responsibilities of the priesthood
out of love for the Lord Jesus and his Church.
Are you resolved to unite yourselves more closely to Christ
and to try to become more like him
by joyfully sacrificing your own pleasure and ambition
to bring his peace and love to your brothers and sisters?
Priests I am.

Are you resolved
to be faithful ministers of the mysteries of God,
to celebrate the eucharist and the other liturgical services
with sincere devotion?
Are you resolved to imitate Jesus Christ,
the head and shepherd of the Church,
by teaching the Christian faith
without thinking of your own profit,
solely for the well-being of the people
you were sent to serve?
Priests I am.

Then the bishop addresses the people:
My brothers and sisters,
pray for your priests.
Ask the Lord to bless them with the fullness of his love,
to help them be faithful ministers of Christ the High Priest,
so that they will be able to lead you to him,
the fountain of your salvation.
People **Lord Jesus Christ, hear us and answer our prayer.**

Pray also for me
that despite my own unworthiness
I may faithfully fulfil the office of apostle
which Jesus Christ has entrusted to me.
Pray that I may become more like
our High Priest and Good Shepherd,
the teacher and servant of all,
and so be a genuine sign
of Christ's loving presence among you.
People **Lord Jesus Christ, hear us and answer our prayer.**

Holy Thursday: Chrism Mass

May the Lord in his love
keep you close to him always,
and may he bring all of us,
his priests and people,
to eternal life.
All **Amen.**

The Profession of Faith and General Intercessions are omitted.

Prayer over the Gifts
Lord God,
may the power of this sacrifice
cleanse the old weakness of our human nature.
Give us a newness of life
and bring us to salvation.

Preface of the Priesthood (Chrism Mass), P20.

Communion Antiphon: For ever I will sing the goodness of the Lord; I will proclaim your faithfulness to all generations.

Prayer after Communion
Lord God almighty,
you have given us fresh strength
in these sacramental gifts.
Renew in us the image of Christ's goodness

Solemn Blessing
Father,
look with love upon your people,
the love which our Lord Jesus Christ showed us
when he delivered himself to evil men
and suffered the agony of the cross.
Grant this through Christ our Lord.

May almighty God bless you,
the Father, and the Son, ✠ and the Holy Spirit.   ℟   **Amen.**

THE EASTER TRIDUUM: Celebrations for the Easter Triduum: Holy Thursday, Good Friday, Easter Vigil, will be found in companion volume, *The Sunday Missal*.

THE SEASON OF EASTER

THE SEASON OF EASTER

he is RISEN Alleluia

OCTAVE OF EASTER

EASTER MONDAY

Entrance Antiphon: The Lord brought you to a land flowing with milk and honey, so that his law would always be given honour among you, alleluia.

or

The Lord has risen from the dead, as he foretold. Let there be happiness and rejoicing for he is our King for ever, alleluia.

The Gloria is said or sung.

Opening Prayer
Father,
you give your Church constant growth
by adding new members to your family.
Help us put into action in our lives
the baptism we have received with faith.

FIRST READING

A reading from the Acts of the Apostles   2:14. 22-33
God raised this man Jesus to life, and all of us are witnesses to that.

On the day of Pentecost, Peter stood up with the Eleven and addressed the crowd in a loud voice: 'Men of Israel, listen to what I am going to say: Jesus the Nazarene was a man commended to you by God by the miracles and portents and signs that God worked through him when he was among you, as you all know. This man, who was put into your power by the deliberate intention and foreknowledge of God, you took and had crucified by men outside the Law. You killed him, but God raised him to life, freeing him from the pangs of Hades; for it was impossible for him to be held in its power since, as David says of him:

> I saw the Lord before me always,
> for with him at my right hand nothing can shake me.
> So my heart was glad
> and my tongue cried out with joy;
> my body, too, will rest in the hope
> that you will not abandon my soul to Hades
> nor allow your holy one to experience corruption.
> You have made known the way of life to me,

you will fill me with gladness through your presence.

'Brothers, no one can deny that the patriarch David himself is dead and buried: his tomb is still with us. But since he was a prophet, and knew that God had sworn him an oath to make one of his descendants succeed him on the throne, what he foresaw and spoke about was the resurrection of the Christ: he is the one who was not abandoned to Hades, and whose body did not experience corruption. God raised this man Jesus to life, and all of us are witnesses to that.

'Now raised to the heights by God's right hand, he has received from the Father the Holy Spirit, who was promised, and what you see and hear is the outpouring of that Spirit.'

This is the word of the Lord.

Responsorial Psalm   Ps 15:1-2. 5. 7-11. ℟ v.1

  ℟ **Preserve me, Lord, I take refuge in you.**

or

  ℟ **Alleluia, alleluia, alleluia!**

1. Preserve me, God, I take refuge in you.
   I say to the Lord: 'You are my God.
   O Lord, it is you who are my portion and cup;
   it is you yourself who are my prize.' ℟

2. I will bless the Lord who gives me counsel,
   who even at night directs my heart.
   I keep the Lord ever in my sight:
   since he is at my right hand, I shall stand firm. ℟

3. And so my heart rejoices, my soul is glad;
   even my body shall rest in safety.
   For you will not leave my soul among the dead,
   nor let your beloved know decay. ℟

4. You will show me the path of life,
   the fullness of joy in your presence,
   at your right hand happiness for ever. ℟

Sequence
The sequence is optional on the weekdays of the Octave of Easter.

    Christians, to the Paschal Victim offer sacrifice and praise.
    The sheep are ransomed by the Lamb;
    and Christ, the undefiled,

hath sinners to his Father reconciled.
Death with life contended: combat strangely ended!
Life's own Champion, slain, yet lives to reign.
Tell us, Mary: say what thou didst see upon the way.
The tomb the Living did enclose;
I saw Christ's glory as he rose!
The angels there attesting;
shroud with grave-clothes resting.
Christ, my hope, has risen: he goes before you into Galilee.
That Christ is truly risen from the dead we know.
Victorious king, thy mercy show!

Gospel Acclamation Ps 117:24
Alleluia, alleluia!
This day was made by the Lord;
we rejoice and are glad.
Alleluia!

GOSPEL

A reading from the Gospel according to Matthew 28:8-15
Tell my brothers that they must leave for Galilee; they will see me there.

Filled with awe and great joy the women came quickly away from the tomb and ran to tell the disciples.

And there, coming to meet them, was Jesus. 'Greetings' he said. And the women came up to him and, falling down before him, clasped his feet. Then Jesus said to them, 'Do not be afraid; go and tell my brothers that they must leave for Galilee; they will see me there.'

While they were on their way, some of the guard went off into the city to tell the chief priests all that had happened. These held a meeting with the elders and, after some discussion, handed a considerable sum of money to the soldiers with these instructions, 'This is what you must say, "His disciples came during the night and stole him away while we were asleep." And should the governor come to hear of this, we undertake to put things right with him ourselves and to see that you do not get into trouble.' The soldiers took the money and carried out their instructions, and to this day that is the story among the Jews.

This is the Gospel of the Lord.

The Profession of Faith is not made.

Prayer over the Gifts
Father,
you have given us new light by baptism
and the profession of your name.
Accept the gifts of your children
and bring us to eternal joy in your presence.

Preface of Easter I, P21.

Communion Antiphon: Christ now raised from the dead will never die again; death no longer has power over him, alleluia.

Prayer after Communion
Lord,
may the life we receive in these Easter sacraments
continue to grow in our hearts.
As you lead us along the way of eternal salvation,
make us worthy of your many gifts.

EASTER TUESDAY

Entrance Antiphon: If men desire wisdom, she will give them the water of knowledge to drink. They will never waver from the truth; they will stand firm for ever, alleluia.

The Gloria is said or sung.

Opening Prayer
Father,
by this Easter mystery you touch our lives
with the healing power of your love.
You have given us the freedom of the sons of God.
May we who now celebrate your gift
find joy in it for ever in heaven.

FIRST READING

A reading from the Acts of the Apostles 2:36-41

You must repent and every one of you must be baptised in the name of Jesus.

On the day of Pentecost, Peter spoke to the Jews: 'The whole House of Israel can be certain that God has made this Jesus whom you crucified both Lord and Christ.'

Hearing this, they were cut to the heart and said to Peter and the apostles, 'What must we do, brothers?' 'You must repent,' Peter answered 'and every one of you must be baptised in the name of Jesus Christ for the forgiveness of your sins, and you will receive the gift of the Holy Spirit. The promise that was made is for you and your children, and for all those who are far away, for all those whom the Lord our God will call to himself.' He spoke to them for a long time using many arguments, and he urged them, 'Save yourselves from this perverse generation.' They were convinced by his arguments, and they accepted what he said and were baptised. That very day about three thousand were added to their number.

This is the word of the Lord.

Responsorial Psalm   Ps 32:4-5. 18-20. 22. ℟ v.5

℟ **The Lord fills the earth with his love.**

or

℟ **Alleluia, alleluia, alleluia!**

1 The word of the Lord is faithful
 and all his works to be trusted.
 The Lord loves justice and right
 and fills the earth with his love.   ℟

2 The Lord looks on those who revere him,
 on those who hope in his love,
 to rescue their souls from death,
 to keep them alive in famine.   ℟

3 Our soul is waiting for the Lord.
 The Lord is our help and our shield.
 May your love be upon us, O Lord,
 as we place all our hope in you.   ℟

The sequence may be used. See above p.264.

Gospel Acclamation   Ps 117:24

Alleluia, alleluia!
This day was made by the Lord;
we rejoice and are glad.
Alleluia!

Easter Tuesday

GOSPEL

A reading from the holy Gospel according to John 20:11-18
I have seen the Lord and he has spoken to me.

Mary stayed outside near the tomb, weeping. Then, still weeping, she stooped to look inside, and saw two angels in white sitting where the body of Jesus had been, one at the head, the other at the feet. They said, 'Woman, why are you weeping?' 'They have taken my Lord away,' she replied, 'and I don't know where they have put him.' As she said this she turned round and saw Jesus standing there, though she did not recognise him. Jesus said, 'Woman, why are you weeping? Who are you looking for?' Supposing him to be the gardener, she said, 'Sir, if you have taken him away, tell me where you have put him, and I will go and remove him.' Jesus said, 'Mary!' She knew him then and said to him in Hebrew, 'Rabbuni!' – which means Master. Jesus said to her 'Do not cling to me, because I have not yet ascended to the Father. But go and find the brothers, and tell them: I am ascending to my Father and your Father, to my God and your God.' So Mary of Magdala went and told the disciples that she had seen the Lord and that he had said these things to her.

This is the Gospel of the Lord.

The Profession of Faith is not made.

Prayer over the Gifts
Lord,
accept these gifts from your family.
May we hold fast to the life you have given us
and come to the eternal gifts you promise.

Preface of Easter I, P21.

Communion Antiphon: If you have been raised with Christ, seek the things that are above, where Christ is seated at the right hand of God, alleluia.

Prayer after Communion
All-powerful Father,
hear our prayers.
Prepare for eternal joy
the people you have renewed in baptism.

EASTER WEDNESDAY

Entrance Antiphon: Come, you whom my Father has blessed; inherit the kingdom prepared for you since the foundation of the world, alleluia.

The Gloria is said or sung.

Opening Prayer
God our Father,
on this solemn feast you give us the joy of recalling
the rising of Christ to new life.
May the joy of our annual celebration
bring us to the joy of eternal life.

FIRST READING

A reading from the Acts of the Apostles 3:1-10
I will give you what I have: in the name of Jesus stand up and walk!

Once, when Peter and John were going up to the Temple for the prayers at the ninth hour, it happened that there was a man being carried past. He was a cripple from birth; and they used to put him down every day near the Temple entrance called the Beautiful Gate so that he could beg from the people going in. When this man saw Peter and John on their way into the Temple he begged from them. Both Peter and John looked straight at him and said, 'Look at us.' He turned to them expectantly, hoping to get something from them, but Peter said, 'I have neither silver nor gold, but I will give you what I have: in the name of Jesus Christ the Nazarene, walk!' Peter then took him by the hand and helped him to stand up. Instantly his feet and ankles became firm, he jumped up, stood, and began to walk, and he went with them into the Temple, walking and jumping and praising God. Everyone could see him walking and praising God, and they recognised him as the man who used to sit begging at the Beautiful Gate of the Temple. They were all astonished and unable to explain what had happened to him.

This is the word of the Lord.

Responsorial Psalm
Ps 104:1-4. 6-9. ℟ v.3

℟ **Let the hearts that seek the Lord rejoice.**

or

℟ **Alleluia, alleluia, alleluia!**

1. Give thanks to the Lord, tell his name,
   make known his deeds among the peoples.
   O sing to him, sing his praise;
   tell all his wonderful works! ℟

2. Be proud of his holy name,
   let the hearts that seek the Lord rejoice.
   Consider the Lord and his strength;
   constantly seek his face. ℟

3. O children of Abraham, his servant,
   O sons of the Jacob he chose.
   He, the Lord, is our God:
   his judgements prevail in all the earth. ℟

4. He remembers his covenant for ever,
   his promise for a thousand generations,
   the covenant he made with Abraham,
   the oath he swore to Isaac. ℟

The sequence may be used. See above p.264.

Gospel Acclamation
Ps 117:24

Alleluia, alleluia!
This day was made by the Lord;
we rejoice and are glad.
Alleluia!

GOSPEL

A reading from the holy Gospel according to Luke 24:13-35
They recognised Jesus at the breaking of bread.

Two of the disciples of Jesus were on their way to a village called Emmaus, seven miles from Jerusalem, and they were talking together about all that had happened. Now as they talked this over, Jesus himself came up and walked by their side; but something prevented them from recognising him. He said to them, 'What matters are you discussing as you walk along?' They stopped short, their faces downcast.

Easter Wednesday

Then one of them, called Cleopas, answered him, 'You must be the only person staying in Jerusalem who does not know the things that have been happening there these last few days.' 'What things?' he asked. 'All about Jesus of Nazareth' they answered 'who proved he was a great prophet by the things he said and did in the sight of God and of the whole people; and how our chief priests and our leaders handed him over to be sentenced to death, and had him crucified. Our own hope had been that he would be the one to set Israel free. And this is not all: two whole days have gone by since it all happened; and some women from our group have astounded us; they went to the tomb in the early morning, and when they did not find the body, they came back to tell us they had seen a vision of angels who declared he was alive. Some of our friends went to the tomb and found everything exactly as the women had reported, but of him they saw nothing.'

Then he said to them, 'You foolish men! So slow to believe the full message of the prophets! Was it not ordained that the Christ should suffer and so enter into his glory?' Then, starting with Moses and going through all the prophets, he explained to them the passages throughout the scriptures that were about himself.

When they drew near to the village to which they were going, he made as if to go on; but they pressed him to stay with them. 'It is nearly evening' they said 'and the day is almost over.' So he went in to stay with them. Now while he was with them at table, he took the bread and said the blessing; then he broke it and handed it to them. And their eyes were opened and they recognised him; but he had vanished from their sight. Then they said to each other, 'Did not our hearts burn within us as he talked to us on the road and explained the scriptures to us?'

They set out that instant and returned to Jerusalem. There they found the Eleven assembled together with their companions, who said to them, 'Yes, it is true. The Lord has risen and has appeared to Simon.' Then they told their story of what had happened on the road and how they had recognised him at the breaking of bread.

This is the Gospel of the Lord.

The Profession of Faith is not made.

Prayer over the Gifts
Lord,

accept this sacrifice of our redemption
and accomplish in us salvation of mind and body.

Preface of Easter I, P21.

Communion Antiphon: The disciples recognised the Lord Jesus in the breaking of bread, alleluia.

Prayer after Communion
Lord,
may this sharing in the sacrament of your Son
free us from our old life of sin
and make us your new creation.

EASTER THURSDAY

Entrance Antiphon: Your people praised your great victory, O Lord. Wisdom opened the mouth that was dumb, and made the tongues of babies speak, alleluia.

The Gloria is said or sung.

Opening Prayer
Father,
you gather the nations to praise your name.
May all who are reborn in baptism
be one in faith and love.

FIRST READING

A reading from the Acts of the Apostles 3:11-26
You killed the prince of life. God, however, raised him from the dead.

Everyone came running towards Peter and John in great excitement, to the Portico of Solomon, as it is called, where the man was still clinging to them. When Peter saw the people he addressed them, 'Why are you so surprised at this? Why are you staring at us as though we had made this man walk by our own power or holiness? You are Israelites, and it is the God of Abraham, Isaac and Jacob, the God of our ancestors, who has glorified his servant Jesus, the same Jesus you handed over and then disowned in the presence of Pilate, after Pilate had decided to release him. It was you who accused the Holy One, the Just

Easter Thursday

One, you who demanded the reprieve of a murderer while you killed the prince of life. God, however, raised him from the dead, and to that fact we are the witnesses; and it is the name of Jesus which, through our faith in it, has brought back the strength of this man whom you see here and who is well known to you. It is faith in that name that has restored this man to health, as you can all see.

'Now I know, brothers, that neither you nor your leaders had any idea what you were really doing; this was the way God carried out what he had foretold, when he said through all his prophets that Christ would suffer. Now you must repent and turn to God, so that your sins may be wiped out, and so that the Lord may send the time of comfort. Then he will send you the Christ he has predestined, that is Jesus, whom heaven must keep till the universal restoration comes which God proclaimed, speaking through his holy prophets. Moses, for example, said: The Lord God will raise up a prophet like myself for you, from among your own brothers; you must listen to whatever he tells you. The man who does not listen to that prophet is to be cut off from the people. In fact, all the prophets that have ever spoken, from Samuel onwards, have predicted these days.

'You are the heirs of the prophets, the heirs of the covenant God made with our ancestors when he told Abraham: in your offspring all the families of the earth will be blessed. It was for you in the first place that God raised up his servant and sent him to bless you by turning every one of you from your wicked ways.'

This is the word of the Lord.

Responsorial Psalm   Ps 8:2. 5-9. ℟ v.2

   ℟ **How great is your name, O Lord our God, through all the earth!**

or

   ℟ **Alleluia, alleluia, alleluia!**

1. How great is your name, O Lord our God,
   through all the earth!
   What is man that you should keep him in mind,
   mortal man that you care for him? ℟

2. Yet you have made him little less than a god;
   with glory and honour you crowned him,
   gave him power over the works of your hand,
   put all things under his feet. ℟

(continued)

3. All of them, sheep and cattle,
yes, even the savage beasts,
birds of the air, and fish
that make their way through the waters.

℟ **How great is your name, O Lord our God, through all the earth!**

The sequence may be used. See above p.264.

Gospel Acclamation   Ps 117:24
Alleluia, alleluia!
This day was made by the Lord;
we rejoice and are glad.
Alleluia!

GOSPEL

A reading from the holy Gospel according to Luke   24:35-48
It is written that the Christ would suffer and on the third day rise from the dead.

The disciples told their story of what had happened on the road and how they had recognised Jesus at the breaking of bread.

They were still talking about all this when Jesus himself stood among them and said to them, 'Peace be with you!' In a state of alarm and fright, they thought they were seeing a ghost. But he said, 'Why are you so agitated, and why are these doubts rising in your hearts? Look at my hands and feet; yes, it is I indeed. Touch me and see for yourselves; a ghost has no flesh and bones as you can see I have.' And as he said this he showed them his hands and feet. Their joy was so great that they still could not believe it, and they stood there dumbfounded; so he said to them, 'Have you anything here to eat?' And they offered him a piece of grilled fish, which he took and ate before their eyes.

Then he told them, 'This is what I meant when I said, while I was still with you, that everything written about me, in the Law of Moses, in the Prophets and in the Psalms, has to be fulfilled.' He then opened their minds to understand the scriptures, and he said to them, 'So you see how it is written that the Christ would suffer and on the third day rise from the dead, and that, in his name, repentance for the forgiveness of sins would be preached to all the nations, beginning from Jerusalem. You are witnesses to this.'

This is the Gospel of the Lord.

Easter Friday 275

The Profession of Faith is not made.

Prayer over the Gifts
Lord,
accept our gifts
and grant your continuing protection
to all who have received new life in baptism.

Preface of Easter I, P21.

Communion Antiphon: You are a people God claims as his own, to praise him who called you out of darkness into his marvellous light, alleluia.

Prayer after Communion
Lord,
may this celebration of our redemption
help us in this life
and lead us to eternal happiness.

EASTER FRIDAY

Entrance Antiphon: The Lord led his people out of slavery. He drowned their enemies in the sea, alleluia.

The Gloria is said or sung.

Opening Prayer
Eternal Father,
you gave us the Easter mystery
as our covenant of reconciliation.
May the new birth we celebrate
show its effects in the way we live.

FIRST READING

A reading from the Acts of the Apostles 4:1-12
This is the only name by which we can be saved.

While Peter and John were talking to the people the priests came up to him, accompanied by the captain of the Temple and the Sadducees. They were extremely annoyed at their teaching the people the doctrine of the resurrection from the dead by proclaiming the resurrection of Jesus. They arrested them, but as it was already late, they held them till the next day. But many of those who had listened to their message became believers, the total number of whom had now risen to something like five thousand.

The next day the rulers, elders and scribes had a meeting in Jerusalem with Annas the high priest, Caiaphas, Jonathan, Alexander and all the members of the high-priestly families. They made the prisoners stand in the middle and began to interrogate them, 'By what power, and by whose name have you men done this?' Then Peter, filled with the Holy Spirit, addressed them. 'Rulers of the people, and elders! If you are questioning us today about an act of kindness to a cripple, and asking us how he was healed, then I am glad to tell you all, and would indeed be glad to tell the whole people of Israel, that it was by the name of Jesus Christ the Nazarene, the one you crucified, whom God raised from the dead, by this name and by no other that this man is able to stand up perfectly healthy, here in your presence today. This is the stone rejected by you the builders, but which has proved to be the keystone. For of all the names in the world given to men, this is the only one by which we can be saved.'

This is the word of the Lord.

Responsorial Psalm   Ps 117:1-2. 4. 22-27. R̷ v.22

  R̷ **The stone which the builders rejected
has become the corner stone.**

or

  R̷ **Alleluia, alleluia, alleluia!**

1 Give thanks to the Lord for he is good,
for his love has no end.
Let the sons of Israel say:
'His love has no end.'
Let those who fear the Lord say:
'His love has no end.'   R̷

2 The stone which the builders rejected
has become the corner stone.
This is the work of the Lord,
a marvel in our eyes.
This day was made by the Lord;
we rejoice and are glad.   R̷

3 O Lord, grant us salvation;
O Lord, grant success.
Blessed in the name of the Lord
is he who comes.
We bless you from the house of the Lord;
the Lord God is our light. ℟

The sequence may be used. See above p.264.

Gospel Acclamation Ps 117:24
Alleluia, alleluia!
This day was made by the Lord;
we rejoice and are glad.
Alleluia!

GOSPEL

A reading from the holy Gospel according to John 21:1-14

Jesus stepped forward, took the bread and gave it to them, and the same with the fish.

Jesus showed himself again to the disciples. It was by the Sea of Tiberias, and it happened like this: Simon Peter, Thomas called the Twin, Nathanael from Cana in Galilee, the sons of Zebedee and two more of his disciples were together. Simon Peter said, 'I'm going fishing.' They replied, 'We'll come with you.' They went out and got into the boat but caught nothing that night.

It was light by now and there stood Jesus on the shore, though the disciples did not realise that it was Jesus. Jesus called out, 'Have you caught anything, friends?' And when they answered, 'No', he said, 'Throw the net out to starboard and you'll find something.' So they dropped the net, and there were so many fish that they could not haul it in. The disciple Jesus loved said to Peter, 'It is the Lord'. At these words 'It is the Lord,' Simon Peter, who had practically nothing on, wrapped his cloak round him and jumped into the water. The other disciples came on in the boat, towing the net and the fish; they were only about a hundred yards from land.

As soon as they came ashore they saw that there was some bread there, and a charcoal fire with fish cooking on it. Jesus said, 'Bring some of the fish you have just caught.' Simon Peter went aboard and dragged the net to the shore, full of big fish, one hundred and fifty-three of them; and in spite of there being so many the net was not broken. Jesus said to them, 'Come and have breakfast.' None of the disciples was bold enough to ask, 'Who are you?'; they knew quite well it was the Lord. Jesus then stepped forward, took the bread and gave it to them, and the same with the fish. This was the third time that Jesus showed himself to the disciples after rising from the dead.

This is the Gospel of the Lord.

The Profession of Faith is not made.

Prayer over the Gifts
Lord,
bring to perfection the spirit of life
we receive from these Easter gifts.
Free us from seeking after the passing things in life
and help us set our hearts on the kingdom of heaven.

Preface of Easter I, P21.

Communion Antiphon: Jesus said to his disciples: Come and eat. And he took the bread, and gave it to them, alleluia.

Prayer after Communion
Lord,
watch over those you have saved in Christ.
May we who are redeemed by his suffering and death
always rejoice in his resurrection,
for he is Lord for ever and ever.

SATURDAY

Entrance Antiphon: The Lord led his people to freedom and they shouted with joy and gladness, alleluia.

The Gloria is said or sung.

Opening Prayer
Father of love,
by the outpouring of your grace
you increase the number of those who believe in you.
Watch over your chosen family.
Give undying life to all
who have been born again in baptism.

FIRST READING

A reading from the Acts of the Apostles 4:13-21
We cannot promise to stop proclaiming what we have seen and heard.

The rulers, elders and scribes were astonished at the assurance shown by Peter and John, considering they were uneducated laymen; and they recognised them as associates of Jesus; but when they saw the man who had been cured standing by their side, they could find no answer. So they ordered them to stand outside while the Sanhedrin had a private discussion. 'What are we going to do with these men?' they asked. 'It is obvious to everybody in Jerusalem that a miracle has been worked through them in public, and we cannot deny it. But to stop the whole thing spreading any further among the people, let us caution them never to speak to anyone in this name again.'

So they called them in and gave them a warning on no account to make statements or to teach in the name of Jesus. But Peter and John retorted, 'You must judge whether in God's eyes it is right to listen to you and not to God. We cannot promise to stop proclaiming what we have seen and heard.' The court repeated the warnings and then released them; they could not think of any way to punish them, since all the people were giving glory to God for what had happened.

This is the word of the Lord.

Responsorial Psalm Ps 117:1. 14-21. ℟ v.21

℟ **I will thank you, Lord,
for you have given answer.**

or

℟ **Alleluia, alleluia, alleluia!**

1 Give thanks to the Lord for he is good,
   for his love has no end.
   The Lord is my strength and my song;
   he was my saviour.
   There are shouts of joy and victory
   in the tents of the just. ℟

2 The Lord's right hand has triumphed;
   his right hand raised me up.
   I shall not die, I shall live
   and recount his deeds.

(continued)

I was punished, I was punished by the Lord,
but not doomed to die.

℟ **I will thank you, Lord,
for you have given answer.**

or

℟ **Alleluia, alleluia, alleluia!**

3 Open to me the gates of holiness:
I will enter and give thanks.
This is the Lord's own gate
where the just may enter.
I will thank you for you have given answer
and you are my saviour.   ℟

The sequence may be used. See above, p.264.

Gospel Acclamation   Ps 117:24
Alleluia, alleluia!
This day was made by the Lord;
we rejoice and are glad.
Alleluia!

GOSPEL

A reading from the holy Gospel according to Mark   16:9-15
Go out to the whole world; proclaim the Good News.

Having risen in the morning on the first day of the week, Jesus appeared first to Mary of Magdala from whom he had cast out seven devils. She then went to those who had been his companions, and who were mourning and in tears, and told them. But they did not believe her when they heard her say that he was alive and that she had seen him.

After this, he showed himself under another form to two of them as they were on their way into the country. These went back and told the others, who did not believe them either.

Lastly, he showed himself to the Eleven themselves while they were at table. He reproached them for their incredulity and obstinacy, because they had refused to believe those who had seen him after he had risen. And he said to them, 'Go out to the whole world; proclaim the Good News to all creation.'

This is the Gospel of the Lord.

Second Week of Easter: Monday

The Profession of Faith is not made.

Prayer over the Gifts
Lord,
give us joy by these Easter mysteries.
Let the continuous offering of this sacrifice
by which we are renewed
bring us to eternal happiness.

Preface of Easter I, P21.

Communion Antiphon: All you who have been baptised have been clothed in Christ, alleluia.

Prayer after Communion
Lord,
look on your people with kindness
and by these Easter mysteries
bring us to the glory of the resurrection.

SECOND WEEK OF EASTER

MONDAY

Entrance Antiphon: Christ now raised from the dead will never die again; death no longer has power over him, alleluia.

Opening Prayer
Almighty and ever-living God,
your Spirit made us your children,
confident to call you Father.
Increase your Spirit of love within us
and bring us to our promised inheritance.

FIRST READING

A reading from the Acts of the Apostles 4:23-31
As they prayed, they were all filled with the Holy Spirit and began to proclaim the word of God boldly.

As soon as Peter and John were released they went to the community and told them everything the chief priests and elders had said to them. When they heard it they lifted up their voice to

God all together. 'Master,' they prayed 'it is you who made heaven and earth and sea, and everything in them; you it is who said through the Holy Spirit and speaking through our ancestor David, your servant:

> Why this arrogance among the nations,
> these futile plots among the peoples?
> Kings on earth setting out to war,
> princes making an alliance,
> against the Lord and against his Anointed.

'This is what has come true: in this very city Herod and Pontius Pilate made an alliance with the pagan nations and the peoples of Israel, against your holy servant Jesus whom you anointed, but only to bring about the very thing that you in your strength and your wisdom had predetermined should happen. And now, Lord, take note of their threats and help your servants to proclaim your message with all boldness, by stretching out your hand to heal and to work miracles and marvels through the name of your holy servant Jesus.' As they prayed, the house where they were assembled rocked; they were all filled with the Holy Spirit and began to proclaim the word of God boldly.

This is the word of the Lord.

Responsorial Psalm

Ps 2:1-9. ℟ cf. v.13

℟ **Blessed are they who put their trust in God.**

or

℟ **Alleluia!**

1 Why this tumult among nations,
among peoples this useless murmuring?
They arise, the kings of the earth,
princes plot against the Lord and his Anointed.
'Come, let us break their fetters,
come, let us cast off their yoke.' ℟

2 He who sits in the heavens laughs;
the Lord is laughing them to scorn.
Then he will speak in his anger,
his rage will strike them with terror.
'It is I who have set up my king
on Zion, my holy mountain.' ℟

Second Week of Easter: Monday

3 I will announce the decree of the Lord:
The Lord said to me: 'You are my Son.
It is I who have begotten you this day.
Ask and I shall bequeath you the nations,
put the ends of the earth in your possession.
With a rod of iron you will break them,
shatter them like a potter's jar.' ℟

Gospel Acclamation

Col 3:1

Alleluia, alleluia!
Since you have been brought back to true life with Christ,
you must look for the things that are in heaven where Christ is,
sitting at God's right hand.
Alleluia!

Alternative Acclamations pp.386ff.

GOSPEL

A reading from the holy Gospel according to John 3:1-8
Unless a man is born from above, he cannot see the kingdom of God.

There was one of the Pharisees called Nicodemus, a leading Jew, who came to Jesus by night and said, 'Rabbi, we know that you are a teacher who comes from God; for no one could perform the signs that you do unless God were with him.' Jesus answered:

'I tell you most solemnly,
unless a man is born from above,
he cannot see the kingdom of God.'

Nicodemus said, 'How can a grown man be born? Can he go back into his mother's womb and be born again?' Jesus replied:

'I tell you most solemnly,
unless a man is born through water and the Spirit,
he cannot enter the kingdom of God:
what is born of the flesh is flesh;
what is born of the Spirit is spirit.
Do not be surprised when I say:
You must be born from above.
The wind blows wherever it pleases;
you hear its sound,

but you cannot tell where it comes from or where it is going. That is how it is with all who are born of the Spirit.'

This is the Gospel of the Lord.

Prayer over the Gifts

Lord,
receive these gifts from your Church.
May the great joy you give us
come to perfection in heaven.

Preface of Easter II-V, P22-P25.

Communion Antiphon: Jesus came and stood among his disciples and said to them: Peace be with you, alleluia.

Prayer after Communion

Lord,
look on your people with kindness
and by these Easter mysteries
bring us to the glory of the resurrection.

TUESDAY

Entrance Antiphon: Let us shout out our joy and happiness, and give glory to God, the Lord of all, because he is our King, alleluia.

Opening Prayer

All-powerful God,
help us to proclaim the power of the Lord's resurrection.
May we who accept this sign of the love of Christ
come to share the eternal life he reveals,
for he lives and reigns . . .

FIRST READING

A reading from the Acts of the Apostles 4:32-37
United, heart and soul.

The whole group of believers was united, heart and soul; no one claimed for his own use anything that he had, as everything they owned was held in common.

The apostles continued to testify to the resurrection of the Lord Jesus with great power, and they were all given great respect.

None of their members was ever in want, as all those who owned land or houses would sell them, and bring the money from them, to present it to the apostles; it was then distributed to any members who might be in need.

There was a Levite of Cypriot origin called Joseph whom the apostles surnamed Barnabas (which means 'son of encouragement'). He owned a piece of land and he sold it and brought the money, and presented it to the apostles.

This is the word of the Lord.

Responsorial Psalm   Ps 91:1-2. 5. ℟ v.1

℟ **The Lord is king, with majesty enrobed.**

or

℟ **Alleluia!**

1. The Lord is king, with majesty enrobed;
the Lord has robed himself with might,
he has girded himself with power. ℟

2. The world you made firm, not to be moved;
your throne has stood firm from of old.
From all eternity, O Lord, you are. ℟

3. Truly your decrees are to be trusted.
Holiness is fitting to your house,
O Lord, until the end of time. ℟

Gospel Acclamation   cf. Apoc 1:5

Alleluia, alleluia!
You, O Christ, are the faithful witness,
the First-born from the dead;
you have loved us and have washed away our sins with your blood.
Alleluia!

or   Jn 3:15

Alleluia, alleluia!
The Son of Man must be lifted up
so that everyone who believes in him
may have eternal life.
Alleluia!

GOSPEL

A reading from the holy Gospel according to John 3:7-15

No one has gone up to heaven except the one who came down from heaven, the Son of Man.

Jesus said to Nicodemus:

'Do not be surprised when I say:
You must be born from above.
The wind blows wherever it pleases;
you hear its sound,
but you cannot tell where it comes from or where it is going.
That is how it is with all who are born of the Spirit.'

'How can that be possible?' asked Nicodemus. 'You, a teacher in Israel, and you do not know these things!' replied Jesus.

'I tell you most solemnly,
we speak only about what we know
and witness only to what we have seen
and yet you people reject our evidence.
If you do not believe me
when I speak about things in this world,
how are you going to believe me
when I speak to you about heavenly things?
No one has gone up to heaven
except the one who came down from heaven,
the Son of Man who is in heaven;
and the Son of Man must be lifted up
as Moses lifted up the serpent in the desert,
so that everyone who believes may have eternal life in him.'

This is the Gospel of the Lord.

Prayer over the Gifts
Lord,
give us joy by these Easter mysteries.
Let the continuous offering of this sacrifice
by which we are renewed
bring us to eternal happiness.

Preface of Easter II-V, P22-P25.

Communion Antiphon: Christ had to suffer and to rise from the dead, and so enter into his glory, alleluia.

Prayer after Communion
Lord,
may this celebration of our redemption
help us in this life
and lead us to eternal happiness.

WEDNESDAY

Entrance Antiphon: I will be a witness to you in the world, O Lord. I will spread the knowledge of your name among my brothers, alleluia.

Opening Prayer
God of mercy,
you have filled us with the hope of resurrection
by restoring man to his original dignity.
May we who relive this mystery each year
come to share it in perpetual love.

FIRST READING

A reading from the Acts of the Apostles   5:17-26
The men you imprisoned are in the Temple, preaching to the people.

The high priest intervened with all his supporters from the party of the Sadducees. Prompted by jealousy, they arrested the apostles and had them put in the common gaol.

But at night the angel of the Lord opened the prison gates and said as he led them out, 'Go and stand in the Temple, and tell the people all about this new Life.' They did as they were told; they went into the Temple at dawn and began to preach.

When the high priest arrived, he and his supporters convened the Sanhedrin – this was the full Senate of Israel – and sent to the gaol for them to be brought. But when the officials arrived at the prison they found they were not inside, so they went back and reported, 'We found the gaol securely locked and the warders on duty at the gates, but when we unlocked the door we found no one inside.' When the captain of the Temple and the chief priests heard this news they wondered what this could mean. Then a man arrived with fresh news. 'At this very moment,' he said 'the men you imprisoned are in the Temple. They are standing there preaching to the people.' The captain went with his men and fetched them. They were afraid to use force in case the people stoned them.

This is the word of the Lord.

Responsorial Psalm   Ps 33:2-9. R̷ v.7
> R̷ **This poor man called
> and the Lord heard him.**

or

> R̷ **Alleluia!**

1 I will bless the Lord at all times,
 his praise always on my lips;
 in the Lord my soul shall make its boast.
 The humble shall hear and be glad.   R̷

2 Glorify the Lord with me.
 Together let us praise his name.
 I sought the Lord and he answered me;
 from all my terrors he set me free.   R̷

3 Look towards him and be radiant;
 let your faces not be abashed.
 This poor man called; the Lord heard him
 and rescued him from all his distress.   R̷

4 The angel of the Lord is encamped
 around those who revere him, to rescue them.
 Taste and see that the Lord is good.
 He is happy who seeks refuge in him.   R̷

Gospel Acclamation
 Alleluia, alleluia!
 Christ has risen and shone upon us
 whom he redeemed with his blood.
 Alleluia!

or   Jn 3:16

 Alleluia, alleluia!
 God loved the world so much that he gave his only Son;
 everyone who believes in him has eternal life.
 Alleluia!

Second Week of Easter: Wednesday

GOSPEL

A reading from the holy Gospel according to John 3:16-21
God sent his Son into the world so that through him the world might be saved.

Jesus said to Nicodemus:

'God loved the world so much
that he gave his only Son,
so that everyone who believes in him may not be lost
but may have eternal life.
For God sent his Son into the world
not to condemn the world,
but so that through him the world might be saved.
No one who believes in him will be condemned;
but whoever refuses to believe is condemned already,
because he has refused to believe
in the name of God's only Son.
On these grounds is sentence pronounced:
that though the light has come into the world
men have shown they prefer
darkness to the light
because their deeds were evil.
And indeed, everybody who does wrong
hates the light and avoids it,
for fear his actions should be exposed;
but the man who lives by the truth
comes out into the light,
so that it may be plainly seen that what he does is done in God.'

This is the Gospel of the Lord.

Prayer over the Gifts

Lord God
by this holy exchange of gifts
you share with us your divine life.
Grant that everything we do
may be directed by the knowledge of your truth.

Preface of Easter II-V, P22-P25.

Communion Antiphon: The Lord says, I have chosen you from the world to go and bear fruit that will last, alleluia.

Prayer after Communion

Merciful Father,
may these mysteries give us new purpose
and bring us to a new life in you.

THURSDAY

Entrance Antiphon: When you walked at the head of your people, O God, and lived with them on their journey, the earth shook at your presence, and the skies poured forth their rain, alleluia.

Opening Prayer

God of mercy,
may the Easter mystery we celebrate
be effective throughout our lives.

FIRST READING

A reading from the Acts of the Apostles 5:27-33
We are witnesses to all this, we and the Holy Spirit.

When the officials had brought the apostles in to face the Sanhedrin, the high priest demanded an explanation. 'We gave you a formal warning' he said 'not to preach in this name, and what have you done? You have filled Jerusalem with your teaching, and seem determined to fix the guilt of this man's death on us.' In reply Peter and the apostles said, 'Obedience to God comes before obedience to men; it was the God of our ancestors who raised up Jesus, but it was you who had him executed by hanging on a tree. By his own right hand God has now raised him up to be leader and saviour, to give repentance and forgiveness of sins through him to Israel. We are witnesses to all this, we and the Holy Spirit whom God has given to those who obey him.'

This so infuriated them that they wanted to put them to death.

This is the word of the Lord.

Responsorial Psalm Ps 33:2. 9. 17-20. R̷ v.7

   R̷ **This poor man called
      and the Lord heard him.**

or

   R̷ **Alleluia!**

Second Week of Easter: Thursday

1 I will bless the Lord at all times,
 his praise always on my lips.
 Taste and see that the Lord is good.
 He is happy who seeks refuge in him. ℟

2 The Lord turns his eyes to the just
 and his ears to their appeal.
 They call and the Lord hears
 and rescues them in all their distress. ℟

3 The Lord is close to the broken-hearted;
 those whose spirit is crushed he will save.
 Many are the trials of the just man
 but from them all the Lord will rescue him. ℟

Gospel Acclamation

Alleluia, alleluia!
Christ has risen: he who created all things,
and has granted his mercy to men.
Alleluia!

or   Jn 20:29

Alleluia, alleluia!
You believe, Thomas, because you can see me,
Happy are those who have not seen and yet believe.
Alleluia!

GOSPEL

A reading from the holy Gospel according to John   3:31-36
The Father loves the Son and has entrusted everything to him.

John the Baptist said to his disciples:

'He who comes from above
is above all others;
he who is born of the earth
is earthly himself and speaks in an earthly way.
He who comes from heaven
bears witness to the things he has seen and heard,
even if his testimony is not accepted;
though all who do accept his testimony
are attesting the truthfulness of God,
since he whom God has sent
speaks God's own words:

God gives him the Spirit without reserve.
The Father loves the Son
and has entrusted everything to him.
Anyone who believes in the Son has eternal life,
but anyone who refuses to believe in the Son will never see life:
the anger of God stays on him.'

This is the Gospel of the Lord.

Prayer over the Gifts
Lord,
accept our prayers and offerings.
Make us worthy of your sacraments of love
by granting us your forgiveness.

Preface of Easter II-V, P22-P25.

Communion Antiphon: I, the Lord, am with you always, until the end of the world, alleluia.

Prayer after Communion
Almighty and ever-living Lord,
you restored us to life
by raising Christ from death.
Strengthen us by this Easter sacrament;
may we feel its saving power in our daily life.

FRIDAY

Entrance Antiphon: By your blood, O Lord, you have redeemed us from every tribe and tongue, from every nation and people: you have made us into the kingdom of God, alleluia.

Opening Prayer
Father,
in your plan of salvation
your Son Jesus Christ accepted the cross
and freed us from the power of the enemy.
May we come to share the glory of his resurrection,
for he lives and reigns . . .

FIRST READING

A reading from the Acts of the Apostles 5:34-42

They left, glad to have had the honour of suffering humiliation for the sake of the name of Jesus.

One member of the Sanhedrin, a Pharisee called Gamaliel, who was a doctor of the Law and respected by the whole people, stood up and asked to have the apostles taken outside for a time. Then he addressed the Sanhedrin, 'Men of Israel, be careful how you deal with these people. There was Theudas who became notorious not so long ago. He claimed to be someone important, and he even collected about four hundred followers; but when he was killed, all his followers scattered and that was the end of them. And then there was Judas the Galilean, at the time of the census, who attracted crowds of supporters; but he got killed too, and all his followers dispersed. What I suggest, therefore, is that you leave these men alone and let them go. If this enterprise, this movement of theirs, is of human origin it will break up of its own accord; but if it does in fact come from God you will not only be unable to destroy them, but you might find yourselves fighting against God.'

His advice was accepted; and they had the apostles called in, gave orders for them to be flogged, warned them not to speak in the name of Jesus and released them. And so they left the presence of the Sanhedrin glad to have had the honour of suffering humiliation for the sake of the name.

They preached every day both in the Temple and in private houses, and their proclamation of the Good News of Christ Jesus was never interrupted.

This is the word of the Lord.

Responsorial Psalm Ps 26:1. 4. 13-14. ℟ cf. v.4

   ℟ **There is one thing I ask of the Lord,**
      to live in the house of the Lord.

or

   ℟ **Alleluia!**

1   The Lord is my light and my help;
    whom shall I fear?
    The Lord is the stronghold of my life;
    before whom shall I shrink? ℟

2. There is one thing I ask of the Lord,
for this I long,
to live in the house of the Lord,
all the days of my life,
to savour the sweetness of the Lord,
to behold his temple.

℟ **There is one thing I ask of the Lord,
to live in the house of the Lord.**

or

℟ **Alleluia!**

3. I am sure I shall see the Lord's goodness
in the land of the living.
Hope in him, hold firm and take heart.
Hope in the Lord!   ℟

Gospel Acclamation

Alleluia, alleluia!
We know that Christ is truly risen from the dead;
have mercy on us, triumphant King.
Alleluia!

or

Mt 4:4

Alleluia, alleluia!
Man does not live on bread alone, but on every word
that comes from the mouth of God.
Alleluia!

GOSPEL

A reading from the holy Gospel according to John   6:1-15

To all who were sitting there he gave out as much as they wanted.

Jesus went off to the other side of the Sea of Galilee – or of Tiberias – and a large crowd followed him, impressed by the signs he gave by curing the sick. Jesus climbed the hillside, and sat down there with his disciples. It was shortly before the Jewish feast of Passover.

Looking up, Jesus saw the crowds approaching and said to Philip, 'Where can we buy some bread for these people to eat?' He only said this to test Philip; he himself knew exactly what he was going to do. Philip answered, 'Two hundred denarii would only buy enough to give them a small piece each.' One of his disciples, Andrew, Simon Peter's brother, said, 'There is a small boy here with five barley loaves and two fish; but what is that between so many?' Jesus said to them, 'Make the people sit down.' There was plenty of grass there, and as many as five thousand men sat down. Then Jesus took the loaves, gave thanks, and gave them out to all who were sitting ready; he then did the same with the fish, giving out as much as they wanted. When they had eaten enough he said to the disciples, 'Pick up the pieces left over, so that nothing gets wasted.' So they picked them up, and filled twelve hampers with scraps left over from the meal of five barley loaves. The people, seeing this sign that he had given, said, 'This really is the prophet who is come into the world.' Jesus, who could see they were about to come and take him by force and make him king, escaped back to the hills by himself.

This is the Gospel of the Lord.

Prayer over the Gifts
Lord,
accept these gifts from your family.
May we hold fast to the life you have given us
and come to the eternal gifts you promise.

Preface of Easter II-V, P22-P25.

Communion Antiphon: Christ our Lord was put to death for our sins; and he rose again to make us worthy of life, alleluia.

Prayer after Communion
Lord,
watch over those you have saved in Christ.
May we who are redeemed by his suffering and death
always rejoice in his resurrection,
for he is Lord for ever and ever.

SATURDAY

Entrance Antiphon: You are a people God claims as his own, to praise him who called you out of darkness into his marvellous light, alleluia.

Opening Prayer
God our Father,

look upon us with love.
You redeem us and make us your children in Christ.
Give us true freedom
and bring us to the inheritance you promised.

FIRST READING

A reading from the Acts of the Apostles 6:1-7
They elected seven men full of the Holy Spirit.

About this time, when the number of disciples was increasing, the Hellenists made a complaint against the Hebrews: in the daily distribution their own widows were being overlooked. So the Twelve called a full meeting of the disciples and addressed them, 'It would not be right for us to neglect the word of God so as to give out food; you, brothers, must select from among yourselves seven men of good reputation, filled with the Spirit and with wisdom; we will hand over this duty to them, and continue to devote ourselves to prayer and to the service of the word.' The whole assembly approved of this proposal and elected Stephen, a man full of faith and of the Holy Spirit, together with Philip, Prochorus, Nicanor, Timon, Parmenas, and Nicolaus of Antioch, a convert to Judaism. They presented these to the apostles, who prayed and laid their hands on them.

The word of the Lord continued to spread: the number of disciples in Jerusalem was greatly increased, and a large group of priests made their submission to the faith.

This is the word of the Lord.

Responsorial Psalm Ps 32:1-2. 4-5. 18-19. ℟ v.22

℟ **May your love be upon us, O Lord,
as we place all our hope in you.**

or

℟ **Alleluia!**

1 Ring out your joy to the Lord, O you just;
 for praise is fitting for loyal hearts.
 Give thanks to the Lord upon the harp,
 with a ten-stringed lute sing him songs. ℟

2 For the word of the Lord is faithful
 and all his works to be trusted.
 The Lord loves justice and right
 and fills the earth with his love. ℟

3 The Lord looks on those who revere him,
   on those who hope in his love,
   to rescue their souls from death,
   to keep them alive in famine. ℟

Gospel Acclamation   Rom 6:9
   Alleluia, alleluia!
   Christ, having been raised from the dead, will never die again.
   Death has no power over him any more.
   Alleluia!

or

   Alleluia, alleluia!
   Christ has risen: he who created all things,
   and has granted his mercy to men.
   Alleluia!

GOSPEL

A reading from the holy Gospel according to John   6:16-21
They saw Jesus walking on the lake.

In the evening the disciples went down to the shore of the lake and got into a boat to make for Capernaum on the other side of the lake. It was getting dark by now and Jesus had still not rejoined them. The wind was strong, and the sea was getting rough. They had rowed three or four miles when they saw Jesus walking on the lake and coming towards the boat. This frightened them, but he said, 'It is I. Do not be afraid.' They were for taking him into the boat, but in no time it reached the shore at the place they were making for.

   This is the Gospel of the Lord.

Prayer over the Gifts
Merciful Lord,
make holy these gifts
and let our spiritual sacrifice
make us an everlasting gift to you.

Preface of Easter II-V, P22-P25.

Communion Antiphon: Father, I want the men you have given me to be with me where I am, so that they may see the glory you have given me, alleluia.

Prayer after Communion
Lord,
may this eucharist,
which we have celebrated in memory of your Son,
help us to grow in love.

THIRD WEEK OF EASTER

MONDAY

Entrance Antiphon: The Good Shepherd is risen! He who laid down his life for his sheep, who died for his flock, he is risen, alleluia.

Opening Prayer
God our Father,
your light of truth
guides us to the way of Christ.
May all who follow him
reject what is contrary to the gospel.

FIRST READING

A reading from the Acts of the Apostles 6:8-15
They could not get the better of Stephen because of his wisdom, and because it was the Spirit that prompted what he said.

Stephen was filled with grace and power and began to work miracles and great signs among the people. But then certain people came forward to debate with Stephen, some from Cyrene and Alexandria who were members of the synagogue called the Synagogue of Freedmen, and others from Cilicia and Asia. They found they could not get the better of him because of his wisdom, and because it was the Spirit that prompted what he said. So they procured some men to say, 'We heard him using blasphemous language against Moses and against God.' Having in this way turned the people against him as well as the elders and scribes, they took Stephen by surprise, and arrested him and brought him before the Sanhedrin. There they put up false witnesses to say, 'This man is always making speeches against this Holy Place and the Law. We have heard him say that Jesus the Nazarene is going to destroy this Place and alter the traditions that Moses handed down to us.' The members of the Sanhedrin all looked intently at Stephen, and his face appeared to them like the face of an angel.

This is the word of the Lord.

Third Week of Easter: Monday

Responsorial Psalm Ps 118:23-24. 26-27. 29-30. ℟ v.1
  ℟ **They are happy whose life is blameless.**

or

  ℟ **Alleluia!**

1. Though princes sit plotting against me
   I ponder on your statutes.
   Your will is my delight;
   your statutes are my counsellors. ℟

2. I declared my ways and you answered:
   teach me your statutes.
   Make me grasp the way of your precepts
   and I will muse on your wonders. ℟

3. Keep me from the way of error
   and teach me your law.
   I have chosen the way of truth
   with your decrees before me. ℟

Gospel Acclamation Jn 20:29
  Alleluia, alleluia!
  You believe, Thomas, because you can see me.
  Happy are those who have not seen and yet believe.
  Alleluia!

or Mt 4:4

  Alleluia, alleluia!
  Man does not live on bread alone, but on every word
  that comes from the mouth of God.
  Alleluia!

GOSPEL

A reading from the holy Gospel according to John 6:22-29

Do not work for food that cannot last, but work for food that endures to eternal life.

After Jesus had fed the five thousand, his disciples saw him walking on the water. Next day, the crowd that had stayed on the other side saw that only one boat had been there, and that Jesus had not got into the boat with his disciples, but that the disciples had set off by themselves. Other boats, however, had put in from Tiberias, near the place where the bread had been eaten. When the people saw that neither Jesus nor his disciples were there, they got into those boats and crossed to Capernaum to look for Jesus. When they found him on the other side, they said to him, 'Rabbi, when did you come here?' Jesus answered:

> 'I tell you most solemnly,
> you are not looking for me
> because you have seen the signs
> but because you had all the bread you wanted to eat.
> Do not work for food that cannot last,
> but work for food that endures to eternal life,
> the kind of food the Son of Man is offering you,
> for on him the Father, God himself, has set his seal.'

Then they said to him, 'What must we do if we are to do the works that God wants?' Jesus gave them this answer, 'This is working for God: you must believe in the one he has sent.'

This is the Gospel of the Lord.

Prayer over the Gifts
Lord,
accept our prayers and offerings.
Make us worthy of your sacraments of love
by granting us your forgiveness.

Preface of Easter II-V, P22-P25.

Communion Antiphon: The Lord says, peace I leave with you, my own peace I give you; not as the world gives, do I give, alleluia.

Prayer after Communion
Almighty and ever-living Lord,
you restored us to life
by raising Christ from death.
Strengthen us by this Easter sacrament;
may we feel its saving power in our daily life.

TUESDAY

Entrance Antiphon: All you who fear God, both the great and the small, give praise to him! For his salvation and strength have come, the power of Christ, alleluia.

Opening Prayer
Father,
you open the kingdom of heaven
to those born again by water and the Spirit.
Increase your gift of love in us.
May all who have been freed from sins in baptism
receive all that you have promised.

FIRST READING

A reading from the Acts of the Apostles 7:51 – 8:1

Lord Jesus, receive my spirit.

Stephen said to the people, the elders and the scribes: 'You stubborn people, with your pagan hearts and pagan ears. You are always resisting the Holy Spirit, just as your ancestors used to do. Can you name a single prophet your ancestors never persecuted? In the past they killed those who foretold the coming of the Just One, and now you have become his betrayers, his murderers. You who had the Law brought to you by angels are the very ones who have not kept it.'

They were infuriated when they heard this, and ground their teeth at him.

But Stephen, filled with the Holy Spirit, gazed into heaven and saw the glory of God, and Jesus standing at God's right hand. 'I can see heaven thrown open' he said 'and the Son of Man standing at the right hand of God.' At this all the members of the council shouted out and stopped their ears with their hands; then they all rushed at him, sent him out of the city and stoned him. The witnesses put down their clothes at the feet of a young man called Saul. As they were stoning him, Stephen said in invocation, 'Lord Jesus, receive my spirit.' Then he knelt down and said aloud, 'Lord, do not hold this sin against them'; and with these words he fell asleep. Saul entirely approved of the killing.

This is the word of the Lord.

Third Week of Easter: Tuesday

Responsorial Psalm Ps 30:3-4. 6-8. 17. 21. ℟ v.6

℟ **Into your hands, O Lord,
I commend my spirit.**

or

℟ **Alleluia!**

1 Be a rock of refuge for me,
a mighty stronghold to save me,
for you are my rock, my stronghold.
For your name's sake, lead me and guide me. ℟

2 Into your hands I commend my spirit.
It is you who will redeem me, Lord.
As for me, I trust in the Lord:
let me be glad and rejoice in your love. ℟

3 Let your face shine on your servant.
Save me in your love.
You hide those who trust you in the shelter of your presence
from the plotting of men. ℟

Gospel Acclamation Jn 10:14

Alleluia, alleluia!
I am the good shepherd, says the Lord,
I know my sheep and my own know me.
Alleluia!

or Jn 6:35

Alleluia, alleluia!
I am the bread of life, says the Lord.
He who comes to me will never be hungry;
he who believes in me will never thirst.
Alleluia!

GOSPEL

A reading from the holy Gospel according to John 6:30-35

It was not Moses who gave you bread from heaven, it is my Father who gives you the bread from heaven, the true bread.

The people said to Jesus: 'What sign will you give to show us that we should believe in you? What work will you do? Our fathers had manna to eat in the desert; as scripture says: He gave them bread from heaven to eat.'
  Jesus answered:

Third Week of Easter: Wednesday

> 'I tell you most solemnly,
> it was not Moses who gave you bread from heaven,
> it is my Father who gives you the bread from heaven,
> the true bread;
> for the bread of God
> is that which comes down from heaven
> and gives life to the world.'

'Sir,' they said, 'give us that bread always.' Jesus answered:

> 'I am the bread of life.
> He who comes to me will never be hungry;
> he who believes in me will never thirst.'

This is the Gospel of the Lord.

Prayer over the Gifts
Lord,
receive these gifts from your Church.
May the great joy you give us
come to perfection in heaven.

Preface of Easter II-V, P22-P25.

Communion Antiphon: Because we have died with Christ, we believe that we shall also come to life with him, alleluia.

Prayer after Communion
Lord,
look on your people with kindness
and by these Easter mysteries
bring us to the glory of the resurrection.

WEDNESDAY

Entrance Antiphon: Fill me with your praise and I will sing your glory; songs of joy will be on my lips, alleluia.

Opening Prayer
Merciful Lord,
hear the prayers of your people.
May we who have received your gift of faith
share for ever in the new life of Christ.

FIRST READING

A reading from the Acts of the Apostles 8:1-8

They went from place to place preaching the Good News.

That day a bitter persecution started against the church in Jerusalem, and everyone except the apostles fled to the country districts of Judaea and Samaria.

There were some devout people, however, who buried Stephen and made great mourning for him.

Saul then worked for the total destruction of the Church; he went from house to house arresting both men and women and sending them to prison.

Those who had escaped went from place to place preaching the Good News. One of them was Philip who went to a Samaritan town and proclaimed the Christ to them. The people united in welcoming the message Philip preached, either because they had heard of the miracles he worked or because they saw them for themselves. There were, for example, unclean spirits that came shrieking out of many who were possessed, and several paralytics and cripples were cured. There was great rejoicing in that town as a result.

This is the word of the Lord.

Responsorial Psalm Ps 65:1-7. ℟ v.1

℟ **Cry out with joy to God all the earth.**

or

℟ **Alleluia!**

1 Cry out with joy to God all the earth,
 O sing to the glory of his name.
 O render him glorious praise.
 Say to God: 'How tremendous your deeds!' ℟

2 'Before you all the earth shall bow;
 shall sing to you, sing to your name.'
 Come and see the works of God,
 tremendous his deeds among men. ℟

3 He turned the sea into dry land,
 they passed through the river dry-shod.
 Let our joy then be in him;
 he rules for ever by his might. ℟

Third Week of Easter: Wednesday

Gospel Acclamation   Jn 10:27

    Alleluia, alleluia!
    The sheep that belong to me listen to my voice,
    says the Lord;
    I know them and they follow me.
    Alleluia!

or   cf. Jn 6:40

    Alleluia, alleluia!
    It is my Father's will, says the Lord,
    that whoever believes in the Son shall have eternal life,
    and that I shall raise him up on the last day.
    Alleluia!

GOSPEL

A reading from the holy Gospel according to John   6:35-40

It is my Father's will that whoever sees the Son shall have eternal life.

Jesus said to the crowd:

    'I am the bread of life.
    He who comes to me will never be hungry;
    he who believes in me will never thirst.
    But, as I have told you,
    you can see me and still you do not believe.
    All that the Father gives me will come to me,
    and whoever comes to me
    I shall not turn him away;
    because I have come from heaven,
    not to do my own will,
    but to do the will of the one who sent me.
    Now the will of him who sent me
    is that I should lose nothing
    of all that he has given to me,
    and that I should raise it up on the last day.
    Yes, it is my Father's will
    that whoever sees the Son and believes in him
    shall have eternal life,
    and that I shall raise him up on the last day.'

This is the Gospel of the Lord.

Prayer over the Gifts
Lord,

restore us by these Easter mysteries.
May the continuing work of our Redeemer
bring us eternal joy.

Preface of Easter II-V, P22-P25.

Communion Antiphon: Christ has risen and shines upon us, whom he has redeemed by his blood, alleluia.

Prayer after Communion
Lord,
may this celebration of our redemption
help us in this life
and lead us to eternal happiness.

THURSDAY

Entrance Antiphon: Let us sing to the Lord, he has covered himself in glory! The Lord is my strength, and I praise him: he is the Saviour of my life, alleluia.

Opening Prayer
Father,
in this holy season
we come to know the full depth of your love.
You have freed us from the darkness of error and sin.
Help us to cling to your truths with fidelity.

FIRST READING

A reading from the Acts of the Apostles 8:26-40
If you believe with all your heart, you may be baptised.

The angel of the Lord spoke to Philip saying, 'Be ready to set out at noon along the road that goes from Jerusalem down to Gaza, the desert road.' So he set off on his journey. Now it happened that an Ethiopian had been on pilgrimage to Jerusalem; he was a eunuch and an officer at the court of the kandake, or queen, of Ethiopia, and was in fact her chief treasurer. He was now on his way home; and as he sat in his chariot he was reading the prophet Isaiah. The Spirit said to Philip, 'Go up and meet that chariot.' When Philip ran up, he heard him reading Isaiah the prophet and asked, 'Do you understand what you are reading?'

'How can I' he replied 'unless I have someone to guide me?' So he invited Philip to get in and sit by his side. Now the passage of scripture he was reading was this:

> Like a sheep that is led to the slaughter-house,
> like a lamb that is dumb in front of its shearers,
> like these he never opens his mouth.
> He has been humiliated and has no one to defend him.
> Who will ever talk about his descendants,
> since his life on earth has been cut short!

The eunuch turned to Philip and said, 'Tell me, is the prophet referring to himself or someone else?' Starting, therefore, with this text of scripture Philip proceeded to explain the Good News of Jesus to him.

Further along the road they came to some water, and the eunuch said, 'Look, there is some water here; is there anything to stop me being baptised?' He ordered the chariot to stop, then Philip and the eunuch both went down to the water and Philip baptised him. But after they had come up out of the water again Philip was taken away by the Spirit of the Lord, and the eunuch never saw him again but went on his way rejoicing. Philip found that he had reached Azotus and continued his journey proclaiming the Good News in every town as far as Caesarea.

This is the word of the Lord.

Responsorial Psalm   Ps 65:8-9. 16-17. 20. R̸ v.1

℟ **Cry out with joy to God all the earth.**

or

℟ **Alleluia!**

1. O peoples, bless our God,
   let the voice of his praise resound,
   of the God who gave life to our souls
   and kept our feet from stumbling. ℟

2. Come and hear, all who fear God.
   I will tell what he did for my soul:
   to him I cried aloud,
   with high praise ready on my tongue. ℟

3. Blessed be God
   who did not reject my prayer
   nor withhold his love from me. ℟

Gospel Acclamation

Alleluia, alleluia!
The Lord, who hung for us upon the tree,
has risen from the tomb.
Alleluia!

or　　　　　　　　　　　　　　　　　　　　　　　　　　　　　Jn 6:51

Alleluia, alleluia!
I am the living bread which has come down from heaven,
says the Lord.
Anyone who eats this bread will live for ever.
Alleluia!

GOSPEL

A reading from the holy Gospel according to John　　　　　6:44-51
I am the living bread which has come down from heaven.

Jesus said to the crowd:

'No one can come to me
unless he is drawn by the Father who sent me,
and I will raise him up at the last day.
It is written in the prophets:
They will all be taught by God,
and to hear the teaching of the Father,
and learn from it,
is to come to me.
Not that anybody has seen the Father,
except the one who comes from God:
he has seen the Father.
I tell you most solemnly,
everybody who believes has eternal life.
I am the bread of life.
Your fathers ate the manna in the desert
and they are dead;
but this is the bread that comes down from heaven,
so that a man may eat it and not die.
I am the living bread which has come down from heaven.
Anyone who eats this bread will live for ever;
and the bread that I shall give
is my flesh, for the life of the world.'

This is the Gospel of the Lord.

Third Week of Easter: Friday

Prayer over the Gifts
Lord God,
by this holy exchange of gifts
you share with us your divine life.
Grant that everything we do
may be directed by the knowledge of your truth.

Preface of Easter II-V, P22-P25.

Communion Antiphon: Christ died for all, so that living men should not live for themselves, but for Christ who died and was raised to life for them, alleluia.

Prayer after Communion
Merciful Father,
may these mysteries give us new purpose
and bring us to a new life in you.

FRIDAY

Entrance Antiphon: The Lamb who was slain is worthy to receive strength and divinity, wisdom and power and honour, alleluia.

Opening Prayer
Father,
by the love of your Spirit,
may we who have experienced
the grace of the Lord's resurrection
rise to the newness of life in joy.

FIRST READING

A reading from the Acts of the Apostles 9:1-20
This man is my chosen instrument to bring my name before pagans.

Saul was still breathing threats to slaughter the Lord's disciples. He had gone to the high priest and asked for letters addressed to the synagogues in Damascus, that would authorise him to arrest and take to Jerusalem any followers of the Way, men or women, that he could find.

Suddenly, while he was travelling to Damascus and just before he reached the city, there came a light from heaven all round him. He fell to the ground, and then he heard a voice saying, 'Saul, Saul, why are you persecuting me?' 'Who are you, Lord?' he asked, and the voice answered, 'I am Jesus, and you are persecuting me. Get up now and go into the city, and you will be told what you have to do.' The men travelling with Saul stood there speechless, for though they heard the voice they could see no one. Saul got up from the ground, but even with his eyes wide open he could see nothing at all, and they had to lead him into Damascus by the hand. For three days he was without his sight, and took neither food nor drink.

A disciple called Ananias who lived in Damascus had a vision in which he heard the Lord say to him, 'Ananias!' When he replied, 'Here I am, Lord,' the Lord said, 'You must go to Straight Street and ask at the house of Judas for someone called Saul, who comes from Tarsus. At this moment he is praying, having had a vision of a man called Ananias coming in and laying hands on him to give him back his sight.'

When he heard that, Ananias said, 'Lord, several people have told me about this man and all the harm he has been doing to your saints in Jerusalem. He has only come here because he holds a warrant from the chief priests to arrest everybody who invokes your name.' The Lord replied, 'You must go all the same, because this man is my chosen instrument to bring my name before pagans and pagan kings and before the people of Israel; I myself will show him how much he himself must suffer for my name.' Then Ananias went. He entered the house, and at once laid his hands on Saul and said, 'Brother Saul, I have been sent by the Lord Jesus who appeared to you on your way here so that you may recover your sight and be filled with the Holy Spirit.' Immediately it was as though scales fell away from Saul's eyes and he could see again. So he was baptised there and then, and after taking some food he regained his strength.

After he had spent only a few days with the disciples in Damascus, he began preaching in the synagogues, 'Jesus is the Son of God.'

This is the word of the Lord.

Responsional Psalm   Ps 116. ℟ Mk 16:15

    ℟   **Go out to the whole world;**
         proclaim the Good News.

or

    ℟   **Alleluia!**

Third Week of Easter: Friday 311

1. O praise the Lord, all you nations,
   acclaim him all you peoples! ℟

2. Strong is his love for us;
   he is faithful for ever. ℟

Gospel Acclamation cf. Lk 24:46. 26
Alleluia, alleluia!
It was ordained that the Christ should suffer
and rise from the dead,
and so enter into his glory.
Alleluia!

or Jn 6:56

Alleluia, alleluia!
He who eats my flesh and drinks my blood
lives in me and I live in him, says the Lord.
Alleluia!

GOSPEL

A reading from the holy Gospel according to John 6:52-59
My flesh is real food and my blood is real drink.

The Jews started arguing with one another: 'How can this man give us his flesh to eat?' they said. Jesus replied:

'I tell you most solemnly,
if you do not eat the flesh of the Son of Man
and drink his blood,
you will not have life in you.
Anyone who does eat my flesh and drink my blood
has eternal life,
and I shall raise him up on the last day.
For my flesh is real food
and my blood is real drink.
He who eats my flesh and drinks my blood
lives in me
and I live in him.
As I, who am sent by the living Father,
myself draw life from the Father,
so whoever eats me will draw life from me.
This is the bread come down from heaven;
not like the bread our ancestors ate:
they are dead,

but anyone who eats this bread will live for ever.'

He taught this doctrine at Capernaum, in the synagogue.

This is the Gospel of the Lord.

Prayer over the Gifts
Merciful Lord,
make holy these gifts
and let our spiritual sacrifice
make us an everlasting gift to you.

Preface of Easter II-V, P22-P25.

Communion Antiphon: The man who died on the cross has risen from the dead, and has won back our lives from death, alleluia.

Prayer after Communion
Lord,
may this eucharist,
which we have celebrated in memory of your Son,
help us to grow in love.

SATURDAY

Entrance Antiphon: In baptism we have died with Christ, and we have risen to new life in him, because we believed in the power of God who raised him from the dead, alleluia.

Opening Prayer
God our Father,
by the waters of baptism
you give new life to the faithful.
May we not succumb to the influence of evil
but remain true to your gift of life.

FIRST READING

A reading from the Acts of the Apostles 9:31-42
The churches built themselves up and were filled with the consolation of the Holy Spirit.

The churches throughout Judaea, Galilee and Samaria were now left in peace, building themselves up, living in the fear of the

Lord, and filled with the consolation of the Holy Spirit.

Peter visited one place after another and eventually came to the saints living down in Lydda. There he found a man called Aeneas, a paralytic who had been bedridden for eight years. Peter said to him, 'Aeneas, Jesus Christ cures you: get up and fold up your sleeping mat.' Aeneas got up immediately; everybody who lived in Lydda and Sharon saw him, and they were all converted to the Lord.

At Jaffa there was a woman disciple called Tabitha, or Dorcas in Greek, who never tired of doing good or giving in charity. But the time came when she got ill and died, and they washed her and laid her out in a room upstairs. Lydda is not far from Jaffa, so when the disciples heard that Peter was there, they sent two men with an urgent message for him, 'Come and visit us as soon as possible.'

Peter went back with them straightaway, and on his arrival they took him up to the upstairs room, where all the widows stood round him in tears, showing him tunics and other clothes Dorcas had made when she was with them. Peter sent them all out of the room and knelt down and prayed. Then he turned to the dead woman and said 'Tabitha, stand up.' She opened her eyes, looked at Peter and sat up. Peter helped her to her feet, then he called in the saints and widows and showed them she was alive. The whole of Jaffa heard about it and many believed in the Lord.

This is the word of the Lord.

Responsorial Psalm   Ps 115:12-17. ℟ v.12

  ℟ **How can I repay the Lord
for his goodness to me?**

or

  ℟ **Alleluia!**

1 How can I repay the Lord
for his goodness to me?
The cup of salvation I will raise;
I will call on the Lord's name. ℟

2 My vows to the Lord I will fulfil
before all his people.
O precious in the eyes of the Lord
is the death of his faithful. ℟

(continued)

3 Your servant, Lord, your servant am I;
   you have loosened my bonds.
   A thanksgiving sacrifice I make:
   I will call on the Lord's name.

   ℟ **How can I repay the Lord
       for his goodness to me?**

or

   ℟ **Alleluia!**

Gospel Acclamation
Alleluia, alleluia!
We know that Christ is truly risen from the dead;
have mercy on us, triumphant King.
Alleluia!

or cf. Jn 6:63. 68

Alleluia, alleluia!
Your words are spirit, Lord, and they are life:
you have the message of eternal life.
Alleluia!

GOSPEL

A reading from the holy Gospel according to John 6:60-69
Who shall we go to? You have the message of eternal life.

After hearing his doctrine, many of the followers of Jesus said, 'This is intolerable language. How could anyone accept it?' Jesus was aware that his followers were complaining about it and said, 'Does this upset you? What if you should see the Son of Man ascend to where he was before?

'It is the spirit that gives life,
the flesh has nothing to offer.
The words I have spoken to you are spirit
and they are life.

'But there are some of you who do not believe.' For Jesus knew from the outset those who did not believe, and who it was that would betray him. He went on, 'This is why I told you that no one could come to me unless the Father allows him.' After this, many of his disciples left him and stopped going with him.

Then Jesus said to the Twelve, 'What about you, do you want to go away too?' Simon Peter answered, 'Lord, who shall we go to? You have the message of eternal life, and we believe; we know that you are the Holy One of God.'

This is the Gospel of the Lord.

Prayer over the Gifts
Lord,
accept these gifts from your family.
May we hold fast to the life you have given us
and come to the eternal gifts you promise.

Preface of Easter II-V, P22-P25.

Communion Antiphon: Father, I pray for them: may they be one in us, so that the world may believe it was you who sent me, alleluia.

Prayer after Communion
Lord,
watch over those you have saved in Christ.
May we who are redeemed by his suffering and death
always rejoice in his resurrection,
for he is Lord for ever and ever.

FOURTH WEEK OF EASTER

MONDAY

Entrance Antiphon: Christ now raised from the dead will never die again; death no longer has power over him, alleluia.

Opening Prayer
Father,
through the obedience of Jesus,
your servant and your Son,
you raised a fallen world.
Free us from sin
and bring us the joy that lasts for ever.

FIRST READING

A reading from the Acts of the Apostles 11:1-18

God can grant even the pagans the repentance that leads to life.

The apostles and the brothers in Judaea heard that the pagans too had accepted the word of God, and when Peter came up to Jerusalem the Jews criticised him and said, 'So you have been visiting the uncircumcised and eating with them, have you?' Peter in reply gave them the details point by point: 'One day, when I was in the town of Jaffa,' he began 'I fell into a trance as I was praying and had a vision of something like a big sheet being let down from heaven by its four corners. This sheet reached the ground quite close to me. I watched it intently and saw all sorts of animals and wild beasts – everything possible that could walk, crawl or fly. Then I heard a voice that said to me, "Now Peter; kill and eat!" But I answered: Certainly not, Lord; nothing profane or unclean has ever crossed my lips. And a second time the voice spoke from heaven. "What God has made clean, you have no right to call profane." This was repeated three times, before the whole of it was drawn up to heaven again.

'Just at that moment, three men stopped outside the house where we were staying; they had been sent from Caesarea to fetch me, and the Spirit told me to have no hesitation about going back with them. The six brothers here came with me as well, and we entered the man's house. He told us he had seen an angel standing in his house who said, "Send to Jaffa and fetch Simon known as Peter; he has a message for you that will save you and your entire household."

'I had scarcely begun to speak when the Holy Spirit came down on them in the same way as it came on us at the beginning, and I remembered that the Lord had said, "John baptised with water, but you will be baptised with the Holy Spirit." I realised then that God was giving them the identical thing he gave to us when we believed in the Lord Jesus Christ; and who was I to stand in God's way?'

This account satisfied them, and they gave glory to God. 'God' they said, 'can evidently grant even the pagans the repentance that leads to life.'

This is the word of the Lord.

Responsorial Psalm Pss 41:2-3; 42:3-4. ℟ cf. Ps 41:3
  ℟ **My soul is thirsting for God,
  the God of my life.**

or

  ℟ **Alleluia!**

1 Like the deer that yearns
  for running streams,
  so my soul is yearning
  for you, my God.   ℟

2 My soul is thirsting for God,
  the God of my life;
  when can I enter and see
  the face of God?   ℟

3 O send forth your light and your truth;
  let these be my guide.
  Let them bring me to your holy mountain
  to the place where you dwell.   ℟

4 And I will come to the altar of God,
  the God of my joy.
  My redeemer, I will thank you on the harp,
  O God, my God.   ℟

Gospel Acclamation Jn 10:14
  Alleluia, alelluia!
  I am the good shepherd, says the Lord,
  I know my sheep and my own know me.
  Alleluia!

GOSPEL

A reading from the holy Gospel according to John 10:1-10
I am the gate of the sheepfold.

Jesus said: 'I tell you most solemnly, anyone who does not enter the sheepfold through the gate, but gets in some other way, is a thief and a brigand. The one who enters through the gate is the shepherd of the flock; the gatekeeper lets him in, the sheep hear his voice, one by one he calls his own sheep and leads them out. When he has brought out his flock, he goes ahead of them, and the sheep follow because they know his voice. They never follow a stranger but run away from him: they do not recognise the voice of strangers.'

Jesus told them this parable but they failed to understand what he meant by telling it to them.

So Jesus spoke to them again:

'I tell you most solemnly,
I am the gate of the sheepfold.
All others who have come
are thieves and brigands;
but the sheep took no notice of them.
I am the gate.
Anyone who enters through me will be safe:
he will go freely in and out
and be sure of finding pasture.
The thief comes
only to steal and kill and destroy.
I have come
so that they may have life
and have it to the full.'

This is the Gospel of the Lord.

Alternative Gospel

For use in Year A, when John 10:1-10 was read on the preceding Sunday.

A reading from the holy Gospel according to John   10:11-18
The good shepherd is one who lays down his life for his sheep.

Jesus said:

'I am the good shepherd:
the good shepherd is one who lays down his life for his sheep.
The hired man, since he is not the shepherd
and the sheep do not belong to him,
abandons the sheep and runs away
as soon as he sees a wolf coming,
and then the wolf attacks and scatters the sheep;
this is because he is only a hired man
and has no concern for the sheep.
I am the good shepherd;
I know my own

and my own know me,
just as the Father knows me
and I know the Father;
and I lay down my life for my sheep.
And there are other sheep I have
that are not of this fold,
and these I have to lead as well.
They too will listen to my voice,
and there will be only one flock,
and one shepherd.
The Father loves me,
because I lay down my life
in order to take it up again.
No one takes it from me;
I lay it down of my own free will,
and as it is in my power to lay it down,
so it is in my power to take it up again;
and this is the command I have been given by my Father.'

This is the Gospel of the Lord.

Prayer over the Gifts
Lord,
receive these gifts from your Church.
May the great joy you give us
come to perfection in heaven.

Preface of Easter II-V, P22-P25.

Communion Antiphon: Jesus came and stood among his disciples and said to them: Peace be with you, alleluia.

Prayer after Communion
Lord,
look on your people with kindness
and by these Easter mysteries
bring us to the glory of the resurrection.

TUESDAY

Entrance Antiphon: Let us shout out our joy and happiness, and give glory to God, the Lord of all, because he is our King, alleluia.

Fourth Week of Easter: Tuesday

Opening Prayer
Almighty God,
as we celebrate the resurrection,
may we share with each other
the joy the risen Christ has won for us.

FIRST READING

A reading from the Acts of the Apostles 11:19-26
They started preaching to the Greeks, proclaiming the Lord Jesus.

Those who had escaped during the persecution that happened because of Stephen travelled as far as Phoenicia and Cyprus and Antioch, but they usually proclaimed the message only to Jews. Some of them, however, who came from Cyprus and Cyrene, went to Antioch where they started preaching to the Greeks, proclaiming the Good News of the Lord Jesus to them as well. The Lord helped them, and a great number believed and were converted to the Lord.

The church in Jerusalem heard about this and they sent Barnabas to Antioch. There he could see for himself that God had given grace, and this pleased him, and he urged them all to remain faithful to the Lord with heartfelt devotion; for he was a good man, filled with the Holy Spirit and with faith. And a large number of people were won over to the Lord.

Barnabas then left for Tarsus to look for Saul, and when he found him he brought him to Antioch. As things turned out they were to live together in that church a whole year, instructing a large number of people. It was at Antioch that the disciples were first called 'Christians'.

This is the word of the Lord.

Responsorial Psalm Ps 86:1-7. ℟ Ps 116:1

℟ **O praise the Lord, all you nations!**

or

℟ **Alleluia!**

1 On the holy mountain is his city
 cherished by the Lord.
 The Lord prefers the gates of Zion
 to all Jacob's dwellings.
 Of you are told glorious things,
 O city of God! ℟

Fourth Week of Easter: Tuesday

2 'Babylon and Egypt I will count
among those who know me;
Philistia, Tyre, Ethiopia,
these will be her children
and Zion shall be called "Mother"
for all shall be her children.' ℟

3 It is he, the Lord Most High,
who gives each his place.
In his register of peoples he writes:
'These are her children'
and while they dance they will sing:
'In you all find their home.' ℟

Gospel Acclamation   Jn 10:27
Alleluia, alleluia!
The sheep that belong to me listen to my voice,
says the Lord;
I know them and they follow me.
Alleluia!

GOSPEL

A reading from the holy Gospel according to John   10:22-30
The Father and I are one.

It was the time when the feast of Dedication was being celebrated in Jerusalem. It was winter, and Jesus was in the Temple walking up and down in the Portico of Solomon. The Jews gathered round him and said, 'How much longer are you going to keep us in suspense? If you are the Christ, tell us plainly.' Jesus replied:

'I have told you, but you do not believe.
The works I do in my Father's name are my witness;
but you do not believe,
because you are no sheep of mine.
The sheep that belong to me listen to my voice;
I know them and they follow me.
I give them eternal life;
they will never be lost
and no one will ever steal them from me.
The Father who gave them to me is greater than anyone,
and no one can steal from the Father.
The Father and I are one.'

This is the Gospel of the Lord.

Prayer over the Gifts
Lord,
give us joy by these Easter mysteries;
let the continuous offering of this sacrifice
by which we are renewed
bring us to eternal happiness.

Preface of Easter II-V, P22-P25.

Communion Antiphon: Christ had to suffer and to rise from the dead, and so enter into his glory, alleluia.

Prayer after Communion
Lord,
may this celebration of our redemption
help us in this life
and lead us to eternal happiness.

WEDNESDAY

Entrance Antiphon: I will be a witness to you in the world, O Lord. I will spread the knowledge of your name among my brothers, alleluia.

Opening Prayer
God our Father,
life of the faithful,
glory of the humble,
happiness of the just,
hear our prayer.
Fill our emptiness
with the blessing of this eucharist,
the foretaste of eternal joy.

FIRST READING

A reading from the Acts of the Apostles 12:24 – 13:5
Set Barnabas and Saul apart.

The word of God continued to spread and to gain followers. Barnabas and Saul completed their task and came back from Jerusalem, bringing John Mark with them.

In the church at Antioch the following were prophets and

teachers: Barnabas, Simeon called Niger, and Lucius of Cyrene, Manaen, who had been brought up with Herod the tetrarch, and Saul. One day while they were offering worship to the Lord and keeping a fast, the Holy Spirit said, 'I want Barnabas and Saul set apart for the work to which I have called them.' So it was that after fasting and prayer they laid their hands on them and sent them off.

So these two, sent on their mission by the Holy Spirit, went down to Seleucia and from there sailed to Cyprus. They landed at Salamis and proclaimed the word of God in the synagogues of the Jews. John acted as their assistant.

This is the word of the Lord.

Responsorial Psalm Ps 66:2-3. 5-6. 8. ℟ v.4

℟ **Let the peoples praise you, O God;**
let all the peoples praise you,

or

℟ **Alleluia!**

1 O God, be gracious and bless us
and let your face shed its light upon us.
So will your ways be known upon earth
and all nations learn your saving help. ℟

2 Let the nations be glad and exult
for you rule the world with justice.
With fairness you rule the peoples,
you guide the nations on earth. ℟

3 Let the peoples praise you, O God;
let all the peoples praise you.
May God still give us his blessing
till the ends of the earth revere him. ℟

Gospel Acclamation Jn 20:29
Alleluia, alleluia!
You believe, Thomas, because you can see me.
Happy are those who have not seen and yet believe.
Alleluia!

or Jn 8:12

Alleluia, alleluia!
I am the light of the world, says the Lord,

Fourth Week of Easter: Wednesday

anyone who follows me will have the light of life.
Alleluia!

GOSPEL

A reading from the holy Gospel according to John 12:44-50
I, the light, have come into the world.

Jesus declared publicly:

> 'Whoever believes in me
> believes not in me
> but in the one who sent me,
> and whoever sees me,
> sees the one who sent me.
> I, the light, have come into the world,
> so that whoever believes in me
> need not stay in the dark any more.
> If anyone hears my words and does not keep them faithfully,
> it is not I who shall condemn him,
> since I have come not to condemn the world,
> but to save the world:
> he who rejects me and refuses my words
> has his judge already:
> the word itself that I have spoken
> will be his judge on the last day.
> For what I have spoken does not come from myself;
> no, what I was to say, what I had to speak,
> was commanded by the Father who sent me,
> and I know that his commands mean eternal life.
> And therefore what the Father has told me
> is what I speak.'

This is the Gospel of the Lord.

Prayer over the Gifts
Lord God,
by this holy exchange of gifts
you share with us your divine life.
Grant that everything we do
may be directed by the knowledge of your truth.

Preface of Easter II-V, P22-P25.

Communion Antiphon: The Lord says, I have chosen you from the world to go and bear fruit that will last, alleluia.

Prayer after Communion
Merciful Father,
may these mysteries give us new purpose
and bring us to a new life in you.

THURSDAY

Entrance Antiphon: When you walked at the head of your people, O God, and lived with them on their journey, the earth shook at your presence and the skies poured forth their rain, alleluia.

Opening Prayer
Father,
in restoring human nature
you have given us a greater dignity
than we had in the beginning.
Keep us in your love
and continue to sustain those
who have received new life in baptism.

FIRST READING

A reading from the Acts of the Apostles 13:13-25
God has raised up one of David's descendants, Jesus, as Saviour.

Paul and his friends went by sea from Paphos to Perga in Pamphylia where John left them to go back to Jerusalem. The others carried on from Perga till they reached Antioch in Pisidia. Here they went to synagogue on the sabbath and took their seats. After the lessons from the Law and the Prophets had been read, the presidents of the synagogue sent them a message: 'Brothers, if you would like to address some words of encouragement to the congregation, please do so.' Paul stood up, held up a hand for silence and began to speak:

'Men of Israel, and fearers of God, listen! The God of our nation Israel chose our ancestors, and made our people great when they were living as foreigners in Egypt; then by divine power he led them out, and for about forty years took care of them in the wilderness. When he had destroyed seven nations in Canaan, he put them in possession of their land for about four hundred and fifty years. After this he gave them judges, down from the prophet Samuel. Then they demanded a king, and God gave them Saul son of Kish, a man of the tribe of Benjamin. After forty years, he deposed him and made David their king, of whom he approved in these words: "I have selected David son of Jesse, a man after my own heart, who will carry out my whole purpose." To keep his promise, God has raised up for Israel one of David's descendants, Jesus, as Saviour, whose coming was heralded by John when he proclaimed a baptism of repentance for the whole people of Israel. Before John ended his career he said, "I am not the one you imagine me to be; that one is coming after me and I am not fit to undo his sandal."'

This is the word of the Lord.

Responsorial Psalm   Ps 88:2-3. 21-22. 25. 27. ℟ cf. v.2
    ℟ **I will sing for ever of your love, O Lord.**

or

      ℟ **Alleluia!**

1   I will sing for ever of your love, O Lord;
    through all ages my mouth will proclaim your truth.
    Of this I am sure, that your love lasts for ever,
    that your truth is firmly established as the heavens.   ℟

2   I have found David my servant
    and with my holy oil anointed him.
    My hand shall always be with him
    and my arm shall make him strong.   ℟

3   My truth and my love shall be with him;
    by my name his might shall be exalted.
    He will say to me: 'You are my father,
    my God, the rock who saves me.'   ℟

Gospel Acclamation   cf. Apoc 1:5
    Alleluia, alleluia!
    You, O Christ, are the faithful witness, the First-born from the dead;
    you have loved us and have washed away our sins with your blood.
    Alleluia!

Fourth Week of Easter: Thursday

GOSPEL

A reading from the holy Gospel according to John 13:16-20
Whoever welcomes the one I send welcomes me.

After he had washed the feet of his disciples, Jesus said to them:

'I tell you most solemnly,
no servant is greater than his master,
no messenger is greater than the man who sent him.

'Now that you know this, happiness will be yours if you behave accordingly. I am not speaking about all of you: I know the ones I have chosen; but what scripture says must be fulfilled: Someone who shares my table rebels against me.

'I tell you this now, before it happens,
so that when it does happen
you may believe that I am He.
I tell you most solemnly,
whoever welcomes the one I send welcomes me,
and whoever welcomes me welcomes the one who sent me.'

This is the Gospel of the Lord.

Prayer over the Gifts
Lord,
accept our prayers and offerings.
Make us worthy of your sacraments of love
by granting us your forgiveness.

Preface of Easter II-V, P22-P25.

Communion Antiphon: I, the Lord, am with you always, until the end of the world, alleluia.

Prayer after Communion
Almighty and ever-living Lord,
you restored us to life
by raising Christ from death.
Strengthen us by this Easter sacrament;
may we feel its saving power in our daily life.

FRIDAY

Entrance Antiphon: By your blood, O Lord, you have redeemed us from every tribe and tongue, from every nation and people: you have made us into the kingdom of God, alleluia.

Opening Prayer
Father of our freedom and salvation,
hear the prayers of those redeemed by your Son's suffering.
Through you may we have life;
with you may we have eternal joy.

FIRST READING

A reading from the Acts of the Apostles 13:26-33
God has fulfilled his promise by raising Jesus from the dead.

Paul stood up in the synagogue at Antioch in Pisidia, held up a hand for silence and began to speak: 'My brothers, sons of Abraham's race, and all you who fear God, this message of salvation is meant for you. What the people of Jerusalem and their rulers did, though they did not realise it, was in fact to fulfil the prophecies read on every sabbath. Though they found nothing to justify his death, they condemned him and asked Pilate to have him executed. When they had carried out everything that scripture foretells about him they took him down from the tree and buried him in a tomb. But God raised him from the dead, and for many days he appeared to those who had accompanied him from Galilee to Jerusalem: and it is these same companions of his who are now his witnesses before our people.

'We have come here to tell you the Good News. It was to our ancestors that God made the promise but it is to us, their children, that he has fulfilled it, by raising Jesus from the dead. As scripture says in the first psalm: You are my son: today I have become your father.'

This is the word of the Lord.

Responsorial Psalm
Ps 2:6-11. ℟ v.7

℟ **You are my Son.**
It is I who have begotten you this day.

or

℟ **Alleluia!**

Fourth Week of Easter: Friday

1. 'It is I who have set up my king
   on Zion, my holy mountain.'
   I will announce the decree of the Lord:
   The Lord said to me: 'You are my Son.
   It is I who have begotten you this day.' ℟

2. 'Ask and I shall bequeath you the nations,
   Put the ends of the earth in your possession.
   With a rod of iron you will break them,
   shatter them like a potter's jar.' ℟

3. Now, O kings, understand,
   take warning rulers of the earth;
   serve the Lord with awe
   and trembling, pay him your homage. ℟

Gospel Acclamation   Col 3:1
Alleluia, alleluia!
Since you have been brought back to true life with Christ,
you must look for the things that are in heaven where Christ is,
sitting at God's right hand.
Alleluia!

or   Jn 14:6

Alleluia, alleluia!
I am the Way, the Truth and the Life, says the Lord;
no one can come to the Father except through me.
Alleluia!

GOSPEL

A reading from the holy Gospel according to John   14:1-6
I am the Way, the Truth and the Life.

Jesus said to his disciples:

'Do not let your hearts be troubled.
Trust in God still, and trust in me.
There are many rooms in my Father's house;
if there were not, I should have told you.
I am going now to prepare a place for you,
and after I have gone and prepared you a place,
I shall return to take you with me;
so that where I am

you may be too.
You know the way to the place where I am going.'

Thomas said, 'Lord, we do not know where you are going, so how can we know the way?' Jesus said:

'I am the Way, the Truth and the Life.
No one can come to the Father except through me.'

This is the Gospel of the Lord.

Prayer over the Gifts
Lord,
accept these gifts from your family.
May we hold fast to the life you have given us
and come to the eternal gifts you promise.

Preface of Easter II-V, P22-P25.

Communion Antiphon: Christ our Lord was put to death for our sins; and he rose again to make us worthy of life, alleluia.

Prayer after Communion
Lord,
watch over those you have saved in Christ.
May we who are redeemed by his suffering and death
always rejoice in his resurrection,
for he is Lord for ever and ever.

SATURDAY

Entrance Antiphon: You are a people God claims as his own, to praise him who called you out of darkness into his marvellous light, alleluia.

Opening Prayer
Father,
may we whom you renew in baptism
bear witness to our faith by the way we live.
By the suffering, death, and resurrection of your Son
may we come to eternal joy.

Fourth Week of Easter: Saturday

FIRST READING

A reading from the Acts of the Apostles 13:44-52
We must turn to the pagans.

The next sabbath almost the whole town of Antioch assembled to hear the word of God. When they saw the crowds, the Jews, prompted by jealousy, used blasphemies and contradicted everything Paul said. Then Paul and Barnabas spoke out boldly 'We had to proclaim the word of God to you first, but since you have rejected it, since you do not think yourselves worthy of eternal life, we must turn to the pagans. For this is what the Lord commanded us to do when he said:

> I have made you a light for the nations,
> so that my salvation may reach the ends of the earth.'

It made the pagans very happy to hear this and they thanked the Lord for his message; all who were destined for eternal life became believers. Thus the word of the Lord spread through the whole countryside.

But the Jews worked upon some of the devout women of the upper classes and the leading men of the city and persuaded them to turn against Paul and Barnabas and expel them from their territory. So they shook the dust from their feet in defiance and went off to Iconium; but the disciples were filled with joy and the Holy Spirit.

This is the word of the Lord.

Responsorial Psalm Ps 97:1-4. R̸ v.3

R̸ **All the ends of the earth have seen the salvation of our God.**

or

R̸ **Alleluia!**

1 Sing a new song to the Lord
  for he has worked wonders.
  His right hand and his holy arm
  have brought salvation. R̸

2 The Lord has made known his salvation;
  has shown his justice to the nations.
  He has remembered his truth and love
  for the house of Israel. R̸

(continued)

Fourth Week of Easter: Saturday

3 All the ends of the earth have seen
the salvation of our God.
Shout to the Lord all the earth,
ring out your joy.

℟ **All the ends of the earth have seen the salvation of our God.**

or

℟ **Alleluia!**

Gospel Acclamation
Rom 6:9

Alleluia, alleluia!
Christ, having been raised from the dead will never die again.
Death has no power over him any more.
Alleluia!

or
Jn 8:31. 32.

Alleluia, alleluia!
If you make my word your home you will indeed be my disciples,
and you will learn the truth, says the Lord.
Alleluia!

GOSPEL

A reading from the holy Gospel according to John 14:7-14
To have seen me is to have seen the Father.

Jesus said to his disciples:

'If you know me, you know my Father too.
From this moment you know him and have seen him.'

Philip said, 'Lord, let us see the Father and then we shall be satisfied.' 'Have I been with you all this time, Philip,' said Jesus to him, 'and you still do not know me?'

'To have seen me is to have seen the Father,
so how can you say, "Let us see the Father"?
Do you not believe
that I am in the Father and the Father is in me?
The words I say to you I do not speak as from myself:
it is the Father, living in me, who is doing this work.
You must believe me when I say
that I am in the Father and the Father is in me;

believe it on the evidence of this work, if for no other reason.

'I tell you most solemnly,
whoever believes in me
will perform the same works as I do myself,
he will perform even greater works,
because I am going to the Father.
Whatever you ask for in my name I will do,
so that the Father may be glorified in the Son.
If you ask for anything in my name,
I will do it.'

This is the Gospel of the Lord.

Prayer over the Gifts
Merciful Lord,
make holy these gifts
and let our spiritual sacrifice
make us an everlasting gift to you.

Preface of Easter II-V, P22-P25.

Communion Antiphon: Father, I want the men you have given me to be with me where I am, so that they may see the glory you have given me, alleluia.

Prayer after Communion
Lord,
may this eucharist,
which we have celebrated in memory of your Son,
help us to grow in love.

FIFTH WEEK OF EASTER

MONDAY

Entrance Antiphon: The Good Shepherd is risen! He who laid down his life for his sheep, who died for his flock, he is risen, alleluia.

Opening Prayer
Father,
help us to seek the values

that will bring us eternal joy in this changing world.
In our desire for what you promise
make us one in mind and heart.

FIRST READING

A reading from the Acts of the Apostles 14:5-18
We have come with good news to make you turn from these empty idols to the living God.

With the connivance of the authorities a move was made by pagans as well as Jews to make attacks on Paul and Barnabas and to stone them. When the apostles came to hear of this, they went off for safety to Lycaonia where, in the towns of Lystra and Derbe and in the surrounding country, they preached the Good News.

A man sat there who had never walked in his life, because his feet were crippled from birth; and as he listened to Paul preaching, he managed to catch his eye. Seeing that the man had the faith to be cured, Paul said in a loud voice, 'Get to your feet – stand up,' and the cripple jumped up and began to walk.

When the crowd saw what Paul had done they shouted in the language of Lycaonia, 'These people are gods who have come down to us disguised as men.' They addressed Barnabas as Zeus, and since Paul was the principal speaker they called him Hermes. The priests of Zeus-outside-the-Gate, proposing that all the people should offer sacrifice with them, brought garlanded oxen to the gates. When the apostles Barnabas and Paul heard what was happening they tore their clothes, and rushed into the crowd, shouting, 'Friends, what do you think you are doing? We are only human beings like you. We have come with good news to make you turn from these empty idols to the living God who made heaven and earth and the sea and all that these hold. In the past he allowed each nation to go its own way; but even then he did not leave you without evidence of himself in the good things he does for you: he sends you rain from heaven, he makes your crops grow when they should, he gives you food and makes you happy.' Even this speech, however, was scarcely enough to stop the crowd offering them sacrifice.

This is the word of the Lord.

Fifth Week of Easter: Monday

Responsorial Psalm   Ps 113B:1-4. 15-16. ℞ v.1

℞   **Not to us, Lord,
but to your name give the glory.**

or

℞   **Alleluia!**

1. Not to us, Lord, not to us,
but to your name give the glory
for the sake of your love and your truth,
lest the heathen say: 'Where is their God?' ℞

2. Our God he is in the heavens;
he does whatever he wills.
Their idols are silver and gold,
the work of human hands. ℞

3. May you be blessed by the Lord,
the maker of heaven and earth.
The heavens belong to the Lord
but the earth he has given to men. ℞

Gospel Acclamation
Alleluia, alleluia!
Christ has risen and shone upon us
whom he redeemed with his blood.
Alleluia!

or   Jn 14:26

Alleluia, alleluia!
The Holy Spirit will teach you everything
and remind you of all I have said to you.
Alleluia!

GOSPEL

A reading from the holy Gospel according to John   14:21-26
The Advocate, whom the Father will send in my name, will teach you everything.

Jesus said to his disciples:

'Anybody who receives my commandments and keeps them
will be one who loves me;
and anybody who loves me will be loved by my Father,
and I shall love him and show myself to him.'

Judas – this was not Judas Iscariot – said to him, 'Lord, what is all this about? Do you intend to show yourself to us and not to the world?' Jesus replied:

'If anyone loves me he will keep my word,
and my Father will love him,
and we shall come to him
and make our home with him.
Those who do not love me do not keep my words.
And my word is not my own:
it is the word of the one who sent me.
I have said these things to you
while still with you;
but the Advocate, the Holy Spirit,
whom the Father will send in my name,
will teach you everything
and remind you of all I have said to you.'

This is the Gospel of the Lord.

Prayer over the Gifts
Lord,
accept our prayers and offerings.
Make us worthy of your sacraments of love
by granting us your forgiveness.

Preface of Easter II-V, P22-P25.

Communion Antiphon: The Lord says, peace I leave with you, my own peace I give you; not as the world gives, do I give, alleluia.

Prayer after Communion
Almighty and ever-living Lord,
you restored us to life
by raising Christ from death.
Strengthen us by this Easter sacrament;
may we feel its saving power in our daily life.

TUESDAY

Entrance Antiphon: All you who fear God, both the great and the small, give praise to him! For his salvation and strength have come, the power of Christ, alleluia.

Opening Prayer
Father,
you restored your people to eternal life
by raising Christ your Son from death.
Make our faith strong and our hope sure.
May we never doubt that you will fulfil
the promises you have made.

FIRST READING

A reading from the Acts of the Apostles 14:19-28
They gave an account to the church of all that God had done with them.

Some Jews arrived from Antioch and Iconium, and turned the people against the apostles. They stoned Paul and dragged him outside the town, thinking he was dead. The disciples came crowding round him but, as they did so, he stood up and went back to the town. The next day he and Barnabas went off to Derbe.

Having preached the Good News in that town and made a considerable number of disciples, they went back through Lystra and Iconium to Antioch. They put fresh heart into the disciples, encouraging them to persevere in the faith. 'We all have to experience many hardships' they said 'before we enter the kingdom of God.' In each of these churches they appointed elders, and with prayer and fasting they commended them to the Lord in whom they had come to believe.

They passed through Pisidia and reached Pamphylia. Then after proclaiming the word at Perga they went down to Attalia and from there sailed for Antioch, where they had originally been commended to the grace of God for the work they had now completed.

On their arrival they assembled the church and gave an account of all that God had done with them, and how he had opened the door of faith to the pagans. They stayed there with the disciples for some time.

This is the word of the Lord.

Responsorial Psalm

Ps 144:10-13. 21. ℟ cf. v.12

℟ **Your friends, O Lord, shall make known
the glorious splendour of your reign.**

or

℟ **Alleluia!**

1. All your creatures shall thank you, O Lord,
   and your friends shall repeat their blessing.
   They shall speak of the glory of your reign
   and declare your might, O God,
   to make known to men your mighty deeds
   and the glorious splendour of your reign. ℟

2. Yours is an everlasting kingdom;
   your rule lasts from age to age. ℟

3. Let me speak the praise of the Lord,
   let all mankind bless his holy name
   for ever, for ages unending. ℟

Gospel Acclamation

cf. Lk 24:46. 26

Alleluia, alleluia!
It was ordained that the Christ should suffer
and rise from the dead,
and so enter into his glory.
Alleluia!

GOSPEL

A reading from the holy Gospel according to John 14:27-31
My own peace I give you.

Jesus said to his disciples:

'Peace I bequeath to you,
my own peace I give you,
a peace the world cannot give, this is my gift to you.
Do not let your hearts be troubled or afraid.
You heard me say:
I am going away, and shall return.
If you loved me you would have been glad to know that I am
    going to the Father,
for the Father is greater than I.
I have told you this now before it happens,
so that when it does happen you may believe.

I shall not talk with you any longer,
because the prince of this world is on his way.
He has no power over me,
but the world must be brought to know that I love the Father
and that I am doing exactly what the Father told me.'

This is the Gospel of the Lord.

Prayer over the Gifts
Lord,
receive these gifts from your Church.
May the great joy you give us
come to perfection in heaven.

Preface of Easter II-V, P22-P25.

Communion Antiphon: Because we have died with Christ, we believe that we shall also come to life with him, alleluia.

Prayer after Communion
Lord,
look on your people with kindness
and by these Easter mysteries
bring us to the glory of the resurrection.

WEDNESDAY

Entrance Antiphon: Fill me with your praise and I will sing your glory; songs of joy will be on my lips, alleluia.

Opening Prayer
Father of all holiness,
guide our hearts to you.
Keep in the light of your truth
all those you have freed from the darkness of unbelief.

FIRST READING

A reading from the Acts of the Apostles 15:1-6
It was arranged that they should go up to Jerusalem and discuss the problem with the apostles and elders.

Some men came down from Judaea and taught the brothers, 'Unless you have yourselves circumcised in the tradition of

Moses you cannot be saved.' This led to disagreement, and after Paul and Barnabas had had a long argument with these men it was arranged that Paul and Barnabas and others of the church should go up to Jerusalem and discuss the problem with the apostles and elders.

All the members of the church saw them off, and as they passed through Phoenicia and Samaria they told how the pagans had been converted, and this news was received with the greatest satisfaction by the brothers. When they arrived in Jerusalem they were welcomed by the church and by the apostles and elders, and gave an account of all that God had done with them.

But certain members of the Pharisees' party who had become believers objected, insisting that the pagans should be circumcised and instructed to keep the Law of Moses. The apostles and elders met to look into the matter.

This is the word of the Lord.

Responsorial Psalm
Ps 121:1-5. ℟ cf. v.1

℟ **I rejoiced when I heard them say: 'Let us go to God's house.'**

or

℟ **Alleluia!**

1. I rejoiced when I heard them say:
'Let us go to God's house.'
And now our feet are standing
within your gates, O Jerusalem. ℟

2. Jerusalem is built as a city
strongly compact.
It is there that the tribes go up,
the tribes of the Lord. ℟

3. For Israel's law it is,
there to praise the Lord's name.
There were set the thrones of judgement
of the house of David. ℟

Gospel Acclamation
Jn 10:14
Alleluia, alleluia!
I am the good shepherd, says the Lord,
I know my sheep and my own know me.
Alleluia!

Fifth Week of Easter: Wednesday

or Jn 15:4-5

Alleluia, alleluia!
Make your home in me, as I make mine in you, says the Lord;
whoever remains in me bears fruit in plenty.
Alleluia!

GOSPEL

A reading from the holy Gospel according to John 15:1-8
Whoever remains in me, with me in him, bears fruit in plenty.

Jesus said to his disciples:

'I am the true vine,
and my Father is the vinedresser.
Every branch in me that bears no fruit
he cuts away,
and every branch that does bear fruit he prunes
to make it bear even more.
You are pruned already,
by means of the word that I have spoken to you.
Make your home in me, as I make mine in you.
As a branch cannot bear fruit all by itself,
but must remain part of the vine,
neither can you unless you remain in me.
I am the vine,
you are the branches.
Whoever remains in me, with me in him,
bears fruit in plenty;
for cut off from me you can do nothing.
Anyone who does not remain in me
is like a branch that has been thrown away
– he withers;
these branches are collected and thrown on the fire,
and they are burnt.
If you remain in me
and my words remain in you,
you may ask what you will
and you shall get it.
It is to the glory of my Father that you should bear much fruit,
and then you will be my disciples.'

This is the Gospel of the Lord.

Prayer over the Gifts
Lord,
restore us by these Easter mysteries.
May the continuing work of our Redeemer
bring us eternal joy.

Preface of Easter II-V, P22-P25.

Communion Antiphon: Christ has risen and shines upon us, whom he has redeemed by his blood, alleluia.

Prayer after Communion
Lord,
may this celebration of our redemption
help us in this life
and lead us to eternal happiness.

THURSDAY

Entrance Antiphon: Let us sing to the Lord, he has covered himself in glory! The Lord is my strength, and I praise him: he is the Saviour of my life, alleluia.

Opening Prayer
Father,
in your love you have brought us
from evil to good and from misery to happiness.
Through your blessings
give the courage of perseverance
to those you have called and justified by faith.

FIRST READING

A reading from the Acts of the Apostles 15:7-21
I rule that we do not make things difficult for pagans who turn to God.

After the discussion had gone on a long time, Peter stood up and addressed the apostles and elders.

'My brothers,' he said 'you know perfectly well that in the early days God made his choice among you: the pagans were to learn the Good News from me and so become believers. In fact God, who can read everyone's heart, showed his approval of them by giving the Holy Spirit to them just as he had to us. God made no distinction between them and us, since he purified their hearts by faith. It would only provoke God's anger now, surely, if you imposed on the disciples the very burden that neither we nor our ancestors were strong enough to support? Remember, we believe that we are saved in the same way as they are: through the grace of the Lord Jesus.'

This silenced the entire assembly, and they listened to Barnabas and Paul describing all the signs and wonders God had worked through them among the pagans.

When they had finished it was James who spoke. 'My brothers,' he said 'listen to me. Simeon has described how God first arranged to enlist a people for his name out of the pagans. This is entirely in harmony with the words of the prophets, since the scriptures say:

> After that I shall return
> and rebuild the fallen House of David;
> I shall rebuild it from its ruins
> and restore it.
> Then the rest of mankind,
> all the pagans who are consecrated to my name,
> will look for the Lord,
> says the Lord who made this known so long ago.

'I rule, then, that instead of making things more difficult for pagans who turn to God, we send them a letter telling them merely to abstain from anything polluted by idols, from fornication, from the meat of strangled animals and from blood. For Moses has always had his preachers in every town, and is read aloud in the synagogues every sabbath.'

This is the word of the Lord.

Responsorial Psalm   Ps 95:1-3. 10. ℟ cf. v.3
℟ **Proclaim the wonders of the Lord
among all the peoples.**

or

℟ **Alleluia!**

1 O sing a new song to the Lord,
   sing to the Lord all the earth.
   O sing to the Lord, bless his name.   ℟

2. Proclaim his help day by day,
   tell among the nations his glory
   and his wonders among all the peoples.

   ℟ **Proclaim the wonders of the Lord
   among all the peoples.**

or

   ℟ **Alleluia!**

3. Proclaim to the nations: 'God is king.'
   The world he made firm in its place;
   he will judge the peoples in fairness. ℟

Gospel Acclamation

Alleluia, alleluia!
Christ has risen: he who created all things,
and has granted his mercy to men.
Alleluia!

or
Jn 10:27

Alleluia, alleluia!
The sheep that belong to me listen to my voice,
says the Lord;
I know them and they follow me.
Alleluia!

GOSPEL

A reading from the holy Gospel according to John   15:9-11
Remain in my love, and let your joy be complete.

Jesus said to his disciples:

'As the Father has loved me,
so I have loved you.
Remain in my love.
If you keep my commandments
you will remain in my love,
just as I have kept my Father's commandments
and remain in his love.
I have told you this
so that my own joy may be in you
and your joy be complete.'

This is the Gospel of the Lord.

Fifth Week of Easter: Friday

Prayer over the Gifts
Lord God,
by this holy exchange of gifts
you share with us your divine life.
Grant that everything we do
may be directed by the knowledge of your truth.

Preface of Easter II-V, P22-P25.

Communion Antiphon: Christ died for all, so that living men should not live for themselves, but for Christ who died and was raised to life for them, alleluia.

Prayer after Communion
Merciful Father,
may these mysteries give us new purpose
and bring us to a new life in you.

FRIDAY

Entrance Antiphon: The Lamb who was slain is worthy to receive strength and divinity, wisdom and power and honour, alleluia.

Opening Prayer
Lord,
by this Easter mystery
prepare us for eternal life.
May our celebration of Christ's death and resurrection
guide us to salvation.

FIRST READING

A reading from the Acts of the Apostles 15:22-31

It has been decided by the Holy Spirit and by ourselves not to saddle you with any burden beyond essentials.

The apostles and elders decided to choose delegates to send to Antioch with Paul and Barnabas; the whole church concurred with this. They chose Judas known as Barsabbas and Silas, both leading men in the brotherhood, and gave them this letter to take with them:

  'The apostles and elders, your brothers, send greetings to the brothers of pagan birth in Antioch, Syria and Cilicia. We hear that some of our members have disturbed you with their demands and have unsettled your minds. They acted without any authority from us, and so we have decided unanimously to elect delegates and to send them to you with Barnabas and Paul, men we highly respect who have dedicated their lives to the name of our Lord Jesus Christ. Accordingly we are sending you Judas and Silas, who will confirm by word of mouth what we have written in this letter. It has been decided by the Holy Spirit and by ourselves not to saddle you with any burden beyond these essentials: you are to abstain from food sacrificed to idols, from blood, from the meat of strangled animals and from fornication. Avoid these, and you will do what is right. Farewell.'

The party left and went down to Antioch, where they summoned the whole community and delivered the letter. The community read it and were delighted with the encouragement it gave them.

This is the word of the Lord.

Responsorial Psalm Ps 56:8-12. ℟ v.10

℟ **I will thank you, Lord, among the peoples.**

or

℟ **Alleluia!**

1 My heart is ready, O God,
my heart is ready.
I will sing, I will sing your praise.
Awake my soul,
awake lyre and harp,
I will awake the dawn. ℟

2 I will thank you Lord among the peoples,
praise you among the nations;
for your love reaches to the heavens
and your truth to the skies.
O God, arise above the heavens;
may your glory shine on earth! ℟

Gospel Acclamation Jn 10:27

Alleluia, alleluia!
The sheep that belong to me listen to my voice,
says the Lord;
I know them and they follow me.
Alleluia!

Fifth Week of Easter: Friday

or Jn 15:15

Alleluia, alleluia!
I call you friends, says the Lord,
because I have made known to you everything I have learnt
  from my Father.
Alleluia!

GOSPEL

A reading from the holy Gospel according to John 15:12-17
What I command you is to love one another.

Jesus said to his disciples:

'This is my commandment:
love one another,
as I have loved you.
A man can have no greater love
than to lay down his life for his friends.
You are my friends,
if you do what I command you.
I shall not call you servants any more,
because a servant does not know
his master's business;
I call you friends,
because I have made known to you
everything I have learnt from my Father.
You did not choose me,
no, I chose you;
and I commissioned you
to go out and to bear fruit,
fruit that will last;
and then the Father will give you
anything you ask him in my name.
What I command you
is to love one another.'

This is the Gospel of the Lord.

Prayer over the Gifts
Merciful Lord,
make holy these gifts
and let our spiritual sacrifice
make us an everlasting gift to you.

Preface of Easter II-V, P22-P25.

Communion Antiphon: The man who died on the cross has risen from the dead, and has won back our lives from death, alleluia.

Prayer after Communion
Lord,
may this eucharist,
which we have celebrated in memory of your Son,
help us to grow in love.

SATURDAY

Entrance Antiphon: In baptism we have died with Christ, and we have risen to new life in him, because we believed in the power of God who raised him from the dead, alleluia.

Opening Prayer
Loving Father,
through our rebirth in baptism
you give us your life and promise immortality.
By your unceasing care,
guide our steps towards the life of glory.

FIRST READING

A reading from the Acts of the Apostles   16:1-10
Come across to Macedonia and help us.

From Cilicia Paul went to Derbe, and then on to Lystra. Here there was a disciple called Timothy, whose mother was a Jewess who had become a believer; but his father was a Greek. The brothers at Lystra and Iconium spoke well of Timothy, and Paul, who wanted to have him as a travelling companion, had him circumcised. This was on account of the Jews in the locality where everyone knew his father was a Greek.

As they visited one town after another, they passed on the decisions reached by the apostles and elders in Jerusalem, with instructions to respect them.

So the churches grew strong in the faith, as well as growing daily in numbers.

They travelled through Phrygia and the Galatian country, having been told by the Holy Spirit not to preach the word in

Fifth Week of Easter: Saturday

Asia. When they reached the frontier of Mysia they thought to cross it into Bithynia, but as the Spirit of Jesus would not allow them, they went through Mysia and came down to Troas.

One night Paul had a vision: a Macedonian appeared and appealed to him in these words, 'Come across to Macedonia and help us.' Once he had seen this vision we lost no time in arranging a passage to Macedonia, convinced that God had called us to bring them the Good News.

This is the word of the Lord.

Responsorial Psalm   Ps 99:1-3. 5. ℟ v.1

    ℟ **Cry out with joy to the Lord, all the earth.**

or

    ℟ **Alleluia!**

1. Cry out with joy to the Lord, all the earth.
   Serve the Lord with gladness.
   Come before him, singing for joy. ℟

2. Know that he, the Lord, is God.
   He made us, we belong to him,
   we are his people, the sheep of his flock. ℟

3. Indeed, how good is the Lord,
   eternal his merciful love.
   He is faithful from age to age. ℟

Gospel Acclamation

    Alleluia, alleluia!
    The Lord, who hung for us upon the tree,
    has risen from the tomb.
    Alleluia!

or   Col 3:1

    Alleluia, alleluia!
    Since you have been brought back to true life with Christ,
    you must look for the things that are in heaven where Christ is,
    sitting at God's right hand.
    Alleluia!

GOSPEL

A reading from the holy Gospel according to John 15:18-21

You do not belong to the world because my choice withdrew you from the world.

Jesus said to his disciples:

'If the world hates you,
remember that it hated me before you.
If you belonged to the world,
the world would love you as its own;
but because you do not belong to the world,
because my choice withdrew you from the world,
therefore the world hates you.
Remember the words I said to you:
A servant is not greater than his master.
If they persecuted me,
they will persecute you too;
if they kept my word,
they will keep yours as well.
But it will be on my account that they will do all this,
because they do not know the one who sent me.'

This is the Gospel of the Lord.

Prayer over the Gifts

Lord,
accept these gifts from your family.
May we hold fast to the life you have given us
and come to the eternal gifts you promise.

Preface of Easter II-V, P22-P25.

Communion Antiphon: Father, I pray for them: may they be one in us, so that the world may believe it was you who sent me, alleluia.

Prayer after Communion

Lord,
watch over those you have saved in Christ.
May we who are redeemed by his suffering and death
always rejoice in his resurrection,
for he is Lord for ever and ever.

SIXTH WEEK OF EASTER

MONDAY

Entrance Antiphon: Christ now raised from the dead will never die again; death no longer has power over him, alleluia.

Opening Prayer
God of mercy,
may our celebration of your Son's resurrection
help us to experience its effect in our lives.

FIRST READING

A reading from the Acts of the Apostles 16:11-15
The Lord opened her heart to accept what Paul was saying.

Sailing from Troas we made a straight run for Samothrace; the next day for Neapolis, and from there for Philippi, a Roman colony and the principal city of that particular district of Macedonia. After a few days in this city we went along the river outside the gates as it was the sabbath and this was a customary place for prayer. We sat down and preached to the women who had come to the meeting. One of these women was called Lydia, a devout woman from the town of Thyatira who was in the purple-dye trade. She listened to us, and the Lord opened her heart to accept what Paul was saying. After she and her household had been baptised she sent us an invitation: 'If you really think me a true believer in the Lord,' she said 'come and stay with us'; and she would take no refusal.

This is the word of the Lord.

Responsorial Psalm
Ps 149:1-6. 9. ℟ v.4

℟ **The Lord takes delight in his people.**

or

℟ **Alleluia!**

1 Sing a new song to the Lord,
his praise in the assembly of the faithful.
Let Israel rejoice in its Maker,
let Zion's sons exult in their king. ℟

2 Let them praise his name with dancing
and make music with timbrel and harp.

For the Lord takes delight in his people.
He crowns the poor with salvation.

℟ **The Lord takes delight in his people.**

or

℟ **Alleluia!**

3 Let the faithful rejoice in their glory,
shout for joy and take their rest.
Let the praise of God be on their lips:
this honour is for all his faithful.   ℟

Gospel Acclamation Lk 24:46. 26
Alleluia, alleluia!
It was ordained that the Christ should suffer
and rise from the dead,
and so enter into his glory.
Alleluia!

or Jn 15: 26-27

Alleluia, alleluia!
The Spirit of truth will be my witness;
and you too will be witnesses, says the Lord.
Alleluia!

GOSPEL

A reading from the holy Gospel according to John   15:26 – 16:4
The Spirit of truth will be my witness.

Jesus said to his disciples:

'When the Advocate comes,
whom I shall send to you from the Father,
the Spirit of truth who issues from the Father,
he will be my witness.
And you too will be witnesses,
because you have been with me from the outset.

'I have told you all this
so that your faith may not be shaken.
They will expel you from the synagogues,
and indeed the hour is coming
when anyone who kills you will think he is doing a holy duty
    for God.
They will do these things

because they have never known either the Father or myself.
But I have told you all this,
so that when the time for it comes
you may remember that I told you.'

This is the Gospel of the Lord.

Prayer over the Gifts
Lord,
receive these gifts from your Church.
May the great joy you give us
come to perfection in heaven.

Preface of Easter II-V, P22-P25.

Communion Antiphon: Jesus came and stood among his disciples and said to them: Peace be with you, alleluia.

Prayer after Communion
Lord,
look on your people with kindness
and by these Easter mysteries
bring us to the glory of the resurrection.

TUESDAY

Entrance Antiphon: Let us shout out our joy and happiness, and give glory to God, the Lord of all, because he is our King, alleluia.

Opening Prayer
God our Father,
may we look forward with hope to our resurrection,
for you have made us your sons and daughters,
and restored the joy of our youth.

FIRST READING

A reading from the Acts of the Apostles 16:22-34
Become a believer in the Lord Jesus, and you will be saved, and your household too.

The crowd of Philippians joined in and showed its hostility to Paul and Silas, so the magistrates had them stripped and ordered them to be flogged. They were given many lashes and then thrown into prison, and the gaoler was told to keep a close watch on them. So, following his instructions, he threw them into the inner prison and fastened their feet in the stocks.

Late that night Paul and Silas were praying and singing God's praises, while the other prisoners listened. Suddenly there was an earthquake that shook the prison to its foundations. All the doors flew open and the chains fell from all the prisoners. When the gaoler woke and saw the doors wide open he drew his sword and was about to commit suicide, presuming that the prisoners had escaped. But Paul shouted at the top of his voice, 'Don't do yourself any harm; we are all here.'

The gaoler called for lights, then rushed in, threw himself trembling at the feet of Paul and Silas, and escorted them out, saying, 'Sirs, what must I do to be saved?' They told him, 'Become a believer in the Lord Jesus, and you will be saved, and your household too.' Then they preached the word of the Lord to him and to all his family. Late as it was, he took them to wash their wounds, and was baptised then and there with all his household. Afterwards he took them home and gave them a meal, and the whole family celebrated their conversion to belief in God.

This is the word of the Lord.

Responsorial Psalm   Ps 137:1-3. 7-8. ℟ v.7
    ℟   **You stretch out your hand and save me, O Lord.**

or

    ℟   **Alleluia!**

1 I thank you, Lord, with all my heart,
you have heard the words of my mouth.
Before the angels I will bless you.
I will adore before your holy temple.   ℟

2 I thank you for your faithfulness and love
which excel all we ever knew of you.
On the day I called, you answered;
you increased the strength of my soul.   ℟

3 You stretch out your hand and save me,
your hand will do all things for me.
Your love, O Lord, is eternal,
discard not the work of your hands.   ℟

Gospel Acclamation
Alleluia, alleluia!
Christ has risen and shone upon us
whom he redeemed with his blood.
Alleluia!

or Jn 16:7. 13

Alleluia, alleluia!
I will send you the Spirit of truth, says the Lord;
he will lead you to the complete truth.
Alleluia!

GOSPEL

A reading from the holy Gospel according to John 16:5-11
Unless I go, the Advocate will not come to you.

Jesus said to his disciples:

'Now I am going to the one who sent me.
Not one of you has asked, "Where are you going?"
Yet you are sad at heart because I have told you this.
Still, I must tell you the truth:
it is for your own good that I am going
because unless I go,
the Advocate will not come to you;
but if I do go,
I will send him to you.
And when he comes,
he will show the world how wrong it was,
about sin,
and about who was in the right,
and about judgement:
about sin:
proved by their refusal to believe in me;
about who was in the right:
proved by my going to the Father
and your seeing me no more;
about judgement:
proved by the prince of this world being already condemned.'

This is the Gospel of the Lord.

Prayer over the Gifts
Lord,

give us joy by these Easter mysteries;
let the continuous offering of this sacrifice
by which we are renewed
bring us to eternal happiness.

Preface of Easter II-V, P22-P25.

Communion Antiphon: Christ had to suffer and to rise from the dead, and so enter into his glory, alleluia.

Prayer after Communion
Lord,
may this celebration of our redemption
help us in this life
and lead us to eternal happiness.

WEDNESDAY

Entrance Antiphon: I will be a witness to you in the world, O Lord. I will spread the knowledge of your name among my brothers, alleluia.

Opening Prayer
Lord,
as we celebrate your Son's resurrection,
so may we rejoice with all the saints
when he returns in glory,
who lives and reigns . . .

FIRST READING

A reading from the Acts of the Apostles   17:15. 22 – 18:1
The God whom I proclaim is in fact the one whom you already worship without knowing it.

Paul's escort took him as far as Athens, and went back with instructions for Silas and Timothy to rejoin Paul as soon as they could.

Paul stood before the whole Council of the Areopagus and made this speech:

'Men of Athens, I have seen for myself how extremely scrupulous you are in all religious matters, because I noticed, as I

Sixth Week of Easter: Wednesday

strolled round admiring your sacred monuments, that you had an altar inscribed: To An Unknown God. Well, the God whom I proclaim is in fact the one whom you already worship without knowing it.

'Since the God who made the world and everything in it is himself Lord of heaven and earth, he does not make his home in shrines made by human hands. Nor is he dependent on anything that human hands can do for him, since he can never be in need of anything; on the contrary, it is he who gives everything – including life and breath – to everyone. From one single stock he not only created the whole human race so that they could occupy the entire earth, but he decreed how long each nation should flourish and what the boundaries of its territory should be. And he did this so that all nations might seek the deity and, by feeling their way towards him, succeed in finding him. Yet in fact he is not far from any of us, since it is in him that we live, and move, and exist, as indeed some of your own writers have said:

"We are all his children."

'Since we are the children of God, we have no excuse for thinking that the deity looks like anything in gold, silver or stone that has been carved and designed by a man.

'God overlooked that sort of thing when men were ignorant, but now he is telling everyone everywhere that they must repent, because he has fixed a day when the whole world will be judged, and judged in righteousness, and he has appointed a man to be the judge. And God has publicly proved this by raising this man from the dead.'

At this mention of rising from the dead, some of them burst out laughing; others said, 'We would like to hear you talk about this again.' After that Paul left them, but there were some who attached themselves to him and became believers, among them Dionysius the Areopagite and a woman called Damaris, and others besides. After this Paul left Athens and went to Corinth.

This is the word of the Lord.

Responsorial Psalm
Ps 148:1-2. 11-14

℟ **Your glory fills all heaven and earth.**

or

℟ **Alleluia!**

1 Praise the Lord from the heavens,
   praise him in the heights.
   Praise him, all his angels,
   praise him, all his host. ℟

2 All earth's kings and peoples,
   earth's princes and rulers;
   young men and maidens,
   old men together with children. ℟

3 Let them praise the name of the Lord
   for he alone is exalted.
   The splendour of his name
   reaches beyond heaven and earth. ℟

4 He exalts the strength of his peoples.
   He is the praise of all his saints,
   of the sons of Israel,
   of the people to whom he comes close. ℟

Gospel Acclamation
Col 3:1

Alleluia, alleluia!
Since you have been brought back to true life with Christ,
you must look for the things that are in heaven where Christ is,
sitting at God's right hand.
Alleluia!

or
Jn 14:16

Alleluia, alleluia!
I shall ask the Father
and he will give you another Advocate
to be with you for ever.
Alleluia!

GOSPEL

A reading from the holy Gospel according to John 16:12-15
The Spirit of truth will lead you to the complete truth.

Jesus said to his disciples:

'I still have many things to say to you
but they would be too much for you now.
But when the Spirit of truth comes
he will lead you to the complete truth,
since he will not be speaking as from himself
but will say only what he has learnt;
and he will tell you of the things to come.
He will glorify me,
since all he tells you
will be taken from what is mine.
Everything the Father has is mine;
that is why I said:
All he tells you
will be taken from what is mine.'

This is the Gospel of the Lord.

Prayer over the Gifts
Lord God,
by this holy exchange of gifts
you share with us your divine life.
Grant that everything we do
may be directed by the knowledge of your truth.

Preface of Easter II-V, P22-P25.

Communion Antiphon: The Lord says, I have chosen you from the world, to go and bear fruit that will last, alleluia.

Prayer after Communion
Merciful Father,
may these mysteries give us new purpose
and bring us to a new life in you.

THURSDAY

This Mass is celebrated in countries where the celebration of the Ascension is transferred to the Seventh Sunday of Easter.

Entrance Antiphon: When you walked at the head of your people, O God, and lived with them on their journey, the earth shook at your presence, and the skies poured forth their rain, alleluia.

Opening Prayer
Father,
may we always give you thanks
for raising Christ our Lord to glory,
because we are his people
and share the salvation he won,
for he lives and reigns . . .

FIRST READING

A reading from the Acts of the Apostles 18:1-8
Paul lodged with them and worked, and he used to hold debates in the synagogues.

Paul left Athens and went to Corinth, where he met a Jew called Aquila whose family came from Pontus. He and his wife Priscilla had recently left Italy because an edict of Claudius had expelled all the Jews from Rome. Paul went to visit them, and when he found they were tentmakers, of the same trade as himself, he lodged with them, and they worked together. Every sabbath he used to hold debates in the synagogues, trying to convert Jews as well as Greeks.

After Silas and Timothy had arrived from Macedonia, Paul devoted all his time to preaching, declaring to the Jews that Jesus was the Christ. When they turned against him and started to insult him, he took his cloak and shook it out in front of them, saying, 'Your blood be on your own heads; from now on I can go to the pagans with a clear conscience.' Then he left the synagogue and moved to the house next door that belonged to a worshipper of God called Justus. Crispus, president of the synagogue, and his whole household, all became believers in the Lord. A great many Corinthians who had heard him became believers and were baptised.

This is the word of the Lord.

Responsorial Psalm
Ps 97:1-4. ℟ cf.v.2

℟ **The Lord has shown his salvation to the nations.**

or

℟ **Alleluia!**

1. Sing a new song to the Lord
for he has worked wonders.
His right hand and his holy arm
have brought salvation. ℟

2. The Lord has made known his salvation;
has shown his justice to the nations.
He has remembered his truth and love
for the house of Israel. ℟

3. All the ends of the earth have seen
the salvation of our God.
Shout to the Lord all the earth,
ring out your joy. ℟

Gospel Acclamation
Rom 6:9

Alleluia, alleluia!
Christ, having been raised from the dead, will never die again.
Death has no power over him any more.
Alleluia!

or

cf. Jn 14:18

Alleluia, alleluia!
I will not leave you orphans, says the Lord;
I go, but I will come back to you,
and your hearts will be full of joy.
Alleluia!

GOSPEL

A reading from the holy Gospel according to John 16:16-20
You will be sorrowful, but your sorrow will turn to joy.

Jesus said to his disciples:

'In a short time you will no longer see me,
and then a short time later you will see me again.'

Then some of his disciples said to one another, 'What does he mean, "In a short time you will no longer see me, and then a short time later you will see me again" and, "I am going to the

Father?" What is this "short time"? We don't know what he means.' Jesus knew that they wanted to question him, so he said, 'You are asking one another what I meant by saying: In a short time you will no longer see me, and then a short time later you will see me again.

> 'I tell you most solemnly,
> you will be weeping and wailing
> while the world will rejoice;
> you will be sorrowful,
> but your sorrow will turn to joy.'

This is the Gospel of the Lord.

Prayer over the Gifts
Lord,
accept our prayers and offerings.
Make us worthy of your sacraments of love
by granting us your forgiveness.

Preface of Easter II-V, P22-P25.

Communion Antiphon: I, the Lord, am with you always, until the end of the world, alleluia.

Prayer after Communion
Almighty and ever-living Lord,
you restored us to life
by raising Christ from death.
Strengthen us by this Easter sacrament;
may we feel its saving power in our daily life.

For the Mass of the Ascension, see companion volume, *The Sunday Missal.*

FRIDAY

Entrance Antiphon: By your blood, O Lord, you have redeemed us from every tribe and tongue, from every nation and people: you have made us into the kingdom of God, alleluia.

Opening Prayer
When the Ascension is celebrated on the Thursday.

Father,
you have given us eternal life
through Christ your Son who rose from the dead
and now sits at your right hand.
When he comes again in glory,
may he clothe with immortality
all who have been born again in baptism.

When the Ascension is celebrated on the 7th Sunday of Easter.

Lord,
hear our prayer
that your gospel may reach all men
and that we who receive salvation through your Word
may be your children in deed as well as in name.

FIRST READING

A reading from the Acts of the Apostles 18:9-18
I have many people on my side in this city.

At Corinth one night the Lord spoke to Paul in a vision, 'Do not be afraid to speak out, nor allow yourself to be silenced: I am with you. I have so many people on my side in this city that no one will even attempt to hurt you.' So Paul stayed at Corinth preaching the word of God among them for eighteen months.

But while Gallio was proconsul of Achaia, the Jews made a concerted attack on Paul and brought him before the tribunal. 'We accuse this man' they said 'of persuading people to worship God in a way that breaks the Law.' Before Paul could open his mouth, Gallio said to the Jews, 'Listen, you Jews. If this were a misdemeanour or a crime, I would not hesitate to attend to you; but if it is only quibbles about words and names, and about your own Law, then you must deal with it yourselves – I have no intention of making legal decisions about things like that.' Then he sent them out of the court, and at once they all turned on Sosthenes, the synagogue president, and beat him in front of the court house. Gallio refused to take any notice at all.

After staying on for some time, Paul took leave of the brothers and sailed for Syria, accompanied by Priscilla and Aquila. At Cenchreae he had his hair cut off, because of a vow he had made.

This is the word of the Lord.

Responsorial Psalm   Ps 46:2-7. ℟ v.8

  ℟ **God is king of all the earth.**

or

  ℟ **Alleluia!**

1. All peoples, clap your hands,
   cry to God with shouts of joy!
   For the Lord, the Most High, we must fear,
   great king over all the earth. ℟

2. He subdues peoples under us
   and nations under our feet.
   Our inheritance, our glory, is from him,
   given to Jacob out of love. ℟

3. God goes up with shouts of joy;
   the Lord goes up with trumpet blast.
   Sing praise for God, sing praise,
   sing praise to our king, sing praise. ℟

Gospel Acclamation
To be used where the Ascension of the Lord is celebrated on the Thursday:

                                                                      Jn 14:26

Alleluia, alleluia!
The Holy Spirit will teach you everything
and remind you of all I have said to you.
Alleluia!

or   cf. Lk 24:46. 26

Alleluia, alleluia!
It was ordained that the Christ should suffer
and rise from the dead,
and so enter into his glory.
Alleluia!

Sixth Week of Easter: Friday

To be used where the Ascension of the Lord is celebrated on the Seventh Sunday of Easter:
> Alleluia, alleluia!
> Christ has risen; he who created all things,
> and has granted his mercy to men.
> Alleluia!

GOSPEL

A reading from the holy Gospel according to John   16:20-23
No one shall take your joy from you.

Jesus said to his disciples:

> 'I tell you most solemnly,
> you will be weeping and wailing
> while the world will rejoice;
> you will be sorrowful
> but your sorrow will turn to joy.
> A woman in childbirth suffers,
> because her time has come;
> but when she has given birth to the child she forgets the suffering
> in her joy that a man has been born into the world.
> So it is with you: you are sad now,
> but I shall see you again, and your hearts will be full of joy,
> and that joy no one shall take from you.
> When that day comes,
> you will not ask me any questions.'

This is the Gospel of the Lord.

Prayer over the Gifts
Lord,
accept these gifts from your family.
May we hold fast to the life you have given us
and come to the eternal gifts you promise.

Preface of Easter II-V, P22-P25, or of Ascension I or II, P26 or P27.

Communion Antiphon: Christ our Lord was put to death for our sins; and he rose again to make us worthy of life, alleluia.

Prayer after Communion
Lord,
watch over those you have saved in Christ.
May we who are redeemed by his suffering and death
always rejoice in his resurrection,
for he is Lord for ever and ever.

SATURDAY

Entrance Antiphon: You are a people God claims as his own, to praise him who called you out of darkness into his marvellous light, alleluia.

Opening Prayer
When the Ascension is celebrated on the Thursday.
Father,
at your Son's ascension into heaven
you promised to send the Holy Spirit on your apostles.
You filled them with heavenly wisdom:
fill us also with the gift of your Spirit.

When the Ascension is celebrated on the 7th Sunday of Easter.
Lord,
teach us to know you better
by doing good to others.
Help us to grow in your love
and come to understand the eternal mystery
of Christ's death and resurrection.

FIRST READING

A reading from the Acts of the Apostles 18:23-28
Apollos demonstrated from the scriptures that Jesus was the Christ.

Paul came down to Antioch where he spent a short time before continuing his journey through the Galatian country and then through Phrygia, encouraging all the followers.

An Alexandrian Jew named Apollos now arrived in Ephesus. He was an eloquent man, with a sound knowledge of the scriptures, and yet, though he had been given instruction in the Way of the Lord and preached with great earnestness and was accurate in all the details he taught about Jesus, he had only experienced the baptism of John. When Priscilla and Aquila heard him speak boldly in the synagogue, they took an interest in him and gave him further instruction about the Way.

When Apollos thought of crossing over to Achaia, the brothers encouraged him and wrote asking the disciples to welcome him. When he arrived there he was able by God's grace to help the believers considerably by the energetic way he refuted the Jews in public and demonstrated from the scriptures that Jesus was the Christ.

This is the word of the Lord.

Responsorial Psalm   Ps 46:2-3. 8-10. ℟ v.8

℟ **God is king of all the earth.**

or

℟ **Alleluia!**

1 All peoples, clap your hands,
 cry to God with shouts of joy!
 For the Lord, the Most High, we must fear,
 great king over all the earth. ℟

2 God is king of all the earth.
 Sing praise with all your skill.
 God is king over the nations:
 God reigns on his holy throne. ℟

3 The princes of the peoples are assembled
 with the people of Abraham's God.
 The rulers of the earth belong to God,
 to God who reigns over all. ℟

Gospel Acclamation

To be used where the Ascension of the Lord is celebrated on the Thursday:

                                                                     Jn 14:16

Alleluia, alleluia!
I shall ask the Father,
and he will give you another Advocate
to be with you for ever.
Alleluia!

or Jn 16:28

> Alleluia, alleluia!
> I came from the Father
> and have come into the world,
> and now I leave the world
> to go to the Father.
> Alleluia!

To be used where the Ascension of the Lord is celebrated on the Seventh Sunday of Easter:

> Alleluia, alleluia!
> The Lord, who hung for us upon the tree,
> has risen from the tomb.
> Alleluia!

GOSPEL

A reading from the holy Gospel according to John 16:23-28
The Father loves you for loving me and believing.

Jesus said to his disciples:

> 'I tell you most solemnly,
> anything you ask for from the Father
> he will grant in my name.
> Until now you have not asked for anything in my name.
> Ask and you will receive,
> and so your joy will be complete.
> I have been telling you all this in metaphors;
> the hour is coming
> when I shall no longer speak to you in metaphors,
> but tell you about the Father in plain words.
> When that day comes
> you will ask in my name;
> and I do not say that I shall pray to the Father for you,
> because the Father himself loves you
> for loving me
> and believing that I came from God.
> I came from the Father and have come into the world
> and now I leave the world to go to the Father.'

This is the Gospel of the Lord.

Prayer over the Gifts
Merciful Lord,
make holy these gifts,
and let our spiritual sacrifice
make us an everlasting gift to you.

Preface of Easter II-V, P22-P25, or of Ascension I or II, P26-P27.

Communion Antiphon: Father, I want the men you have given me to be with me where I am, so that they may see the glory you have given me, alleluia.

Prayer after Communion
Lord,
may this eucharist,
which we have celebrated in memory of your Son,
help us to grow in love.

SEVENTH WEEK OF EASTER

MONDAY

Entrance Antiphon: You will receive power when the Holy Spirit comes upon you. You will be my witnesses to all the world, alleluia.

Opening Prayer
Lord,
send the power of your Holy Spirit upon us
that we may remain faithful
and do your will in our daily lives.

FIRST READING

A reading from the Acts of the Apostles 19:1-8
Did you receive the Holy Spirit when you became believers?

While Apollos was in Corinth, Paul made his way overland as far as Ephesus, where he found a number of disciples. When he asked, 'Did you receive the Holy Spirit when you became believers?' they answered, 'No, we were never even told there was such a thing as a Holy Spirit.' 'Then how were you baptised?'

he asked. 'With John's baptism' they replied. 'John's baptism' said Paul 'was a baptism of repentance; but he insisted that the people should believe in the one who was to come after him – in other words Jesus.' When they heard this, they were baptised in the name of the Lord Jesus, and the moment Paul had laid hands on them the Holy Spirit came down on them, and they began to speak with tongues and to prophesy. There were about twelve of these men.

He began by going to the synagogue, where he spoke out boldly and argued persuasively about the kingdom of God. He did this for three months.

This is the word of the Lord.

Responsorial Psalm
Ps 67:2-7. ℟ v.33

℟ **Kingdoms of the earth, sing to God.**

or

℟ **Alleluia!**

1 Let God arise, let his foes be scattered.
   Let those who hate him flee before him.
   As smoke is blown away so will they be blown away;
   like wax that melts before the fire,
   so the wicked shall perish at the presence of God. ℟

2 But the just shall rejoice at the presence of God,
   they shall exult and dance for joy.
   O sing to the Lord, make music to his name;
   rejoice in the Lord, exult at his presence. ℟

3 Father of the orphan, defender of the widow,
   such is God in his holy place.
   God gives the lonely a home to live in;
   he leads the prisoners forth into freedom. ℟

Gospel Acclamation
Jn 16:28

Alleluia, alleluia!
I came from the Father and have come into the world,
and now I leave the world to go to the Father.
Alleluia!

or

Col 3:1

Alleluia, alleluia!
Since you have been brought back to true life with Christ,

Seventh Week of Easter: Monday

you must look for the things that are in heaven where Christ
   is,
sitting at God's right hand.
Alleluia!

GOSPEL

A reading from the holy Gospel according to John 16:29-33
Be brave: I have conquered the world.

His disciples said to Jesus, 'Now you are speaking plainly and not using metaphors! Now we see that you know everything, and do not have to wait for questions to be put into words; because of this we believe that you came from God.' Jesus answered them:

'Do you believe at last?
Listen; the time will come – in fact it has come already –
when you will be scattered, each going his own way
and leaving me alone.
And yet I am not alone,
because the Father is with me.
I have told you all this
so that you may find peace in me.
In the world you will have trouble,
but be brave:
I have conquered the world.'

This is the Gospel of the Lord.

Prayer over the Gifts
Lord,
may these gifts cleanse us from sin
and make our hearts live with your gift of grace.

Preface of Ascension I or II, P26 or P27.

Communion Antiphon: The Lord said: I will not leave you orphans. I will come back to you, and your hearts will rejoice, alleluia.

Prayer after Communion
Merciful Father,
may these mysteries give us new purpose
and bring us to a new life in you.

TUESDAY

Entrance Antiphon: I am the beginning and the end of all things. I have met death, but I am alive, and I shall live for eternity, alleluia.

Opening Prayer

God of power and mercy,
send your Holy Spirit
to live in our hearts
and make us temples of his glory.

FIRST READING

A reading from the Acts of the Apostles 20:17-27

I am finishing my race and carrying out the mission the Lord Jesus gave me.

From Miletus Paul sent for the elders of the church of Ephesus. When they arrived he addressed these words to them:

'You know what my way of life has been ever since the first day I set foot among you in Asia, how I have served the Lord in all humility, with all the sorrows and trials that came to me through the plots of the Jews. I have not hesitated to do anything that would be helpful to you; I have preached to you, and instructed you both in public and in your homes, urging both Jews and Greeks to turn to God and to believe in our Lord Jesus.

'And now you see me a prisoner already in spirit; I am on my way to Jerusalem, but have no idea what will happen to me there, except that the Holy Spirit, in town after town, has made it clear enough that imprisonment and persecution await me. But life to me is not a thing to waste words on, provided that when I finish my race I have carried out the mission the Lord Jesus gave me – and that was to bear witness to the Good News of God's grace.

'I now feel sure that none of you among whom I have gone about proclaiming the kingdom will ever see my face again. And so here and now I swear that my conscience is clear as far as all of you are concerned, for I have without faltering put before you the whole of God's purpose.'

This is the word of the Lord.

Responsorial Psalm
Ps 67:10-11. 20-21. ℟ v.33

℟ **Kingdoms of the earth, sing to God.**

or

℟ **Alleluia!**

1. You poured down, O God, a generous rain:
   when your people were starved you gave them new life.
   It was there that your people found a home,
   prepared in your goodness, O God, for the poor. ℟

2. May the Lord be blessed day after day.
   He bears our burdens, God our saviour.
   This God of ours is a God who saves.
   The Lord our God holds the keys of death. ℟

Gospel Acclamation
Jn 14:18

Alleluia, alleluia!
I will not leave you orphans, says the Lord;
I go, but I will come back to you,
and your hearts will be full of joy.
Alleluia!

or
Jn 14:16

Alleluia, alleluia!
I shall ask the Father,
and he will gave you another Advocate
to be with you for ever.
Alleluia!

GOSPEL

A reading from the holy Gospel according to John 17:1-11
Father, glorify your Son.

Jesus raised his eyes to heaven and said:

'Father, the hour has come:
glorify your Son
so that your Son may glorify you;
and, through the power over all mankind that you have given him,
let him give eternal life to all those you have entrusted to him.
And eternal life is this:
to know you,

the only true God,
and Jesus Christ whom you have sent.
I have glorified you on earth
and finished the work
that you gave me to do.

'Now, Father, it is time for you to glorify me
with the glory I had with you
before ever the world was.
I have made your name known
to the men you took from the world to give me.
They were yours and you gave them to me,
and they have kept your word.
Now at last they know
that all you have given me comes indeed from you;
for I have given them
the teaching you gave to me,
and they have truly accepted this, that I came from you,
and have believed that it was you who sent me.
I pray for them;
I am not praying for the world
but for those you have given me,
because they belong to you:
all I have is yours
and all you have is mine
and in them I am glorified.
I am not in the world any longer,
but they are in the world,
and I am coming to you.'

This is the Gospel of the Lord.

Prayer over the Gifts
Father,
accept the prayers and offerings of your people
and bring us to the glory of heaven,
where Jesus is Lord for ever and ever.

Preface of Ascension I or II, P26 or P27.

Communion Antiphon: The Lord says: The Holy Spirit whom the Father will send in my name will teach you all things, and remind you of all I have said to you, alleluia.

Prayer after Communion
Lord,
may this eucharist,
which we have celebrated in memory of your Son,
help us to grow in love.

WEDNESDAY

Entrance Antiphon: All nations, clap your hands. Shout with a voice of joy to God, alleluia.

Opening Prayer
God of mercy,
unite your Church in the Holy Spirit
that we may serve you with all our hearts
and work together with unselfish love.

FIRST READING

A reading from the Acts of the Apostles 20:28-38
I commend you to God, who has power to build you up and to give you your inheritance.

Paul addressed these words to the elders of the church of Ephesus: 'Be on your guard for yourselves and for all the flock of which the Holy Spirit has made you the overseers, to feed the Church of God which he bought with his own blood. I know quite well that when I have gone fierce wolves will invade you and will have no mercy on the flock. Even from your own ranks there will be men coming forward with a travesty of the truth on their lips to induce the disciples to follow them. So be on your guard, remembering how night and day for three years I never failed to keep you right, shedding tears over each one of you. And now I commend you to God, and to the word of his grace that has power to build you up and to give you your inheritance among all the sanctified.

'I have never asked anyone for money or clothes; you know for yourselves that the work I did earned enough to meet my needs and those of my companions. I did this to show you that is how we must exert ourselves to support the weak, remembering the words of the Lord Jesus, who himself said, "There is more happiness in giving than in receiving." '

When he had finished speaking he knelt down with them all and prayed. By now they were all in tears; they put their arms round Paul's neck and kissed him; what saddened them most was his saying they would never see his face again. Then they escorted him to the ship.

This is the word of the Lord.

Responsorial Psalm   Ps 67:29-30. 33-36. ℟ v.33

   ℟ **Kingdoms of the earth, sing to God.**

or

   ℟ **Alleluia!**

1   Show forth, O God, show forth your might,
your might, O God, which you have shown for us.
For the sake of your temple high in Jerusalem
may kings come to you bringing their tribute.   ℟

2   Kingdoms of the earth, sing to God, praise the Lord
who rides on the heavens, the ancient heavens.
He thunders his voice, his mighty voice.
Come, acknowledge the power of God.   ℟

3   His glory is over Israel; his might is in the skies.
God is to be feared in his holy place.
He is the Lord, Israel's God.
He gives strength and power to his people.
Blessed be God!   ℟

Gospel Acclamation   Mt 28:10. 20

Alleluia, alleluia!
Go, make disciples of all the nations:
I am with you always; yes, to the end of time.
Alleluia!

or   Jn 17:17

Alleluia, alleluia!
Your word is truth, O Lord,
consecrate us in the truth.
Alleluia!

Seventh Week of Easter: Wednesday

GOSPEL

A reading from the holy Gospel according to John 17:11-19
May they be one like us.

Jesus raised his eyes to heaven and said:

'Holy Father,
keep those you have given me true to your name,
so that they may be one like us.
While I was with them,
I kept those you had given me true to your name.
I have watched over them and not one is lost
except the one who chose to be lost,
and this was to fulfil the scriptures.
But now I am coming to you
and while still in the world I say these things
to share my joy with them to the full.
I passed your word on to them,
and the world hated them
because they belong to the world
no more than I belong to the world.
I am not asking you to remove them from the world,
but to protect them from the evil one.
They do not belong to the world
any more than I belong to the world.
Consecrate them in the truth;
your word is truth.
As you sent me into the world,
I have sent them into the world,
and for their sake I consecrate myself
so that they too may be consecrated in truth.

This is the Gospel of the Lord.

Prayer over the Gifts
Lord,
accept this offering we make at your command.
May these sacred mysteries by which we worship you
bring your salvation to perfection within us.

Preface of Ascension I or II, P26 or P27.

Communion Antiphon: The Lord says: When the Holy Spirit comes to you, the Spirit whom I shall send, the Spirit of truth who proceeds from the Father, he will bear witness to me, and you also will be my witnesses, alleluia.

Prayer after Communion
Lord,
may our participation in the eucharist
increase your life in us,
cleanse us from sin,
and make us increasingly worthy of this holy sacrament.

THURSDAY

Entrance Antiphon: Let us come to God's presence with confidence, because we will find mercy, and strength when we need it, alleluia.

Opening Prayer
Father,
let your Spirit come upon us with power
to fill us with his gifts.
May he make our hearts pleasing to you,
and ready to do your will.

FIRST READING

A reading from the Acts of the Apostles 22:30; 23:6-11
Now you must bear witness in Rome.

Since the tribune wanted to know what precise charge the Jews were bringing against Paul, he freed him and gave orders for a meeting of the chief priests and the entire Sanhedrin; then he brought Paul down and stood him in front of them.

Now Paul was well aware that one section was made up of Sadducees and the other of Pharisees, so he called out in the Sanhedrin, 'Brothers, I am a Pharisee and the son of Pharisees. It is for our hope in the resurrection of the dead that I am on trial.' As soon as he said this a dispute broke out between the Pharisees and Sadducees, and the assembly was split between the two parties. For the Sadducees say there is neither resurrection, nor angel, nor spirit, while the Pharisees accept all three. The shouting grew louder, and some of the scribes from the Pharisees' party stood up and protested strongly, 'We find nothing wrong with this man. Suppose a spirit has spoken to him, or an angel?' Feeling was running high, and the tribune, afraid that they would tear Paul to pieces, ordered his troops to go down and haul him out and bring him into the fortress.

Next night, the Lord appeared to him and said, 'Courage! You have borne witness for me in Jerusalem, now you must do the same in Rome.'

This is the word of the Lord.

Responsorial Psalm   Ps 15:1-2. 5. 7-11. ℟ v.1

℟ **Preserve me, Lord, I take refuge in you.**

or

℟ **Alleluia!**

1 Preserve me, God, I take refuge in you.
I say to the Lord: 'You are my God.'
O Lord, it is you who are my portion and cup;
it is you yourself who are my prize.   ℟

2 I will bless the Lord who gives me counsel,
who even at night directs my heart.
I keep the Lord ever in my sight:
since he is at my right hand, I shall stand firm.   ℟

3 And so my heart rejoices, my soul is glad;
even my body shall rest in safety.
For you will not leave my soul among the dead,
nor let your beloved know decay.   ℟

4 You will show me the path of life,
the fullness of joy in your presence.
at your right hand happiness for ever.   ℟

Gospel Acclamation   cf Jn 16:7. 13
Alleluia, alleluia!
I will send you the Spirit of truth, says the Lord;
he will lead you to the complete truth.
Alleluia!

or   Jn 17:21

Alleluia, alleluia!
With me in them and you in me,
may they be so completely one
that the world will realise that it was you who sent me,
says the Lord.
Alleluia!

Seventh Week of Easter: Thursday

GOSPEL

A reading from the holy Gospel according to John 17:20-26
May they be completely one.

Jesus raised his eyes to heaven and said:

'Holy Father,
I pray not only for these,
but for those also
who through their words will believe in me.
May they all be one.
Father, may they be one in us,
as you are in me and I am in you,
so that the world may believe it was you who sent me.
I have given them the glory you gave to me,
that they may be one as we are one.
With me in them and you in me,
may they be so completely one
that the world will realise that it was you who sent me
and that I have loved them as much as you loved me.

'Father,
I want those you have given me
to be with me where I am,
so that they may always see the glory
you have given me
because you loved me
before the foundation of the world.
Father, Righteous One,
the world has not known you,
but I have known you,
and these have known
that you have sent me.
I have made your name known to them
and will continue to make it known,
so that the love with which you loved me may be in them,
and so that I may be in them.'

This is the Gospel of the Lord.

Prayer over the Gifts
Merciful Lord,
make holy these gifts,
and let our spiritual sacrifice
make us an everlasting gift to you.

Preface of Ascension I or II, P26 or P27.

Communion Antiphon: This is the word of Jesus: It is best for me to leave you; because if I do not go, the Spirit will not come to you, alleluia.

Prayer after Communion
Lord,
renew us by the mysteries we have shared.
Help us to know you
and prepare us for the gifts of the Spirit.

FRIDAY

Entrance Antiphon: Christ loved us and has washed away our sins with his blood, and has made us a kingdom of priests to serve his God and Father, alleluia.

Opening Prayer
Father,
in glorifying Christ and sending us your Spirit,
you open the way to eternal life.
May our sharing in this gift increase our love
and make our faith grow stronger.

FIRST READING

A reading from the Acts of the Apostles 25:13-21
A dead man called Jesus whom Paul alleged to be alive.

King Agrippa and Bernice arrived in Caesarea and paid their respects to Festus. Their visit lasted several days, and Festus put Paul's case before the king. 'There is a man here' he said 'whom Felix left behind in custody, and while I was in Jerusalem the chief priests and elders of the Jews laid information against him, demanding his condemnation. But I told them that Romans are not in the habit of surrendering any man, until the accused confronts his accusers and is given an opportunity to defend himself against the charge. So they came here with me, and I wasted no time but took my seat on the tribunal the very next day and had the man brought in. When confronted with him, his accusers did not charge him with any of the crimes I had expected; but they had some argument or other with him about their own religion and about a dead man called Jesus whom Paul alleged to be alive. Not feeling qualified to deal with questions of this sort, I asked him if he would be willing to go to Jerusalem, to be tried there on this issue. But Paul put in an appeal for his case to be reserved for the judgement of the august emperor, so I ordered him to be remanded until I could send him to Caesar.'

This is the word of the Lord.

Responsorial Psalm   Ps 102:1-2. 11-12. 19-20. ℟ v.19

   ℟ **The Lord has set his sway in heaven.**

or

   ℟ **Alleluia!**

1 My soul, give thanks to the Lord,
    all my being, bless his holy name.
    My soul, give thanks to the Lord
    and never forget all his blessings. ℟

2 For as the heavens are high above the earth
    so strong is his love for those who fear him.
    As far as the east is from the west
    so far does he remove our sins. ℟

3 The Lord has set his sway in heaven
    and his kingdom is ruling over all.
    Give thanks to the Lord, all his angels,
    mighty in power, fulfilling his word. ℟

Gospel Acclamation   Jn 14:26
Alleluia, alleluia!
The Holy Spirit will teach you everything
and remind you of all I have said to you.
Alleluia!

GOSPEL

A reading from the holy Gospel according to John   21:15-19
Feed my lambs, feed my sheep.

Jesus showed himself to his disciples, and after they had eaten he said to Simon Peter, 'Simon son of John, do you love me more than these others do?' He answered, 'Yes Lord, you know I love you.' Jesus said to him, 'Feed my lambs.' A second time he said to him, 'Simon son of John, do you love me?' He replied, 'Yes, Lord, you know I love you.' Jesus said to him, 'Look after my sheep.' Then he said to him a third time, 'Simon son of John, do you love me?' Peter was upset that he asked him the third time, 'Do you love me?' and said, 'Lord, you know everything; you know I love you.' Jesus said to him, 'Feed my sheep.

> 'I tell you most solemnly,
> when you were young
> you put on your own belt
> and walked where you liked;
> but when you grow old
> you will stretch out your hands,
> and somebody else will put a belt round you
> and take you where you would rather not go.'

In these words he indicated the kind of death by which Peter would give glory to God. After this he said, 'Follow me.'

This is the Gospel of the Lord.

Prayer over the Gifts
Father of love and mercy,
we place our offering before you.
Send your Holy Spirit to cleanse our lives
so that our gifts may be acceptable.

Preface of Ascension I or II, P26 or P27.

Communion Antiphon: When the Spirit of truth comes, says the Lord, he will lead you to the whole truth, alleluia.

Prayer after Communion
God our Father,
the eucharist is our bread of life
and the sacrament of our forgiveness.
May our sharing in this mystery
bring us to eternal life,
where Jesus is Lord for ever and ever.

SATURDAY

Morning Mass

Entrance Antiphon: The disciples were constantly at prayer together, with Mary the mother of Jesus, the other women, and the brothers of Jesus, alleluia.

Opening Prayer
Almighty Father,
let the love we have celebrated in this Easter season
be put into practice in our daily lives.

FIRST READING

A reading from the Acts of the Apostles 28:16-20. 30-31
Paul stayed in Rome, proclaiming the kingdom of God.

On our arrival in Rome Paul was allowed to stay in lodgings of his own with the soldier who guarded him.

After three days he called together the leading Jews. When they had assembled, he said to them, 'Brothers, although I have done nothing against our people or the customs of our ancestors, I was arrested in Jerusalem and handed over to the Romans. They examined me and would have set me free, since they found me guilty of nothing involving the death penalty; but the Jews lodged an objection, and I was forced to appeal to Caesar, not that I had any accusation to make against my own nation. That is why I have asked to see you and talk to you, for it is on account of the hope of Israel that I wear this chain.'

Paul spent the whole of the two years in his own rented lodging. He welcomed all who came to visit him, proclaiming the kingdom of God and teaching the truth about the Lord Jesus Christ with complete freedom and without hindrance from anyone.

This is the word of the Lord.

Responsorial Psalm Ps 10:4-5. 7. R̷ cf. v. 7
  R̷ **The upright shall see your face, O Lord.**

or

  R̷ **Alleluia!**

1 The Lord is in his holy temple,
  the Lord, whose throne is in heaven.

> His eyes look down on the world;
> his gaze tests mortal men.   ℟

2 The Lord tests the just and the wicked:
   the lover of violence he hates.   ℟

3 The Lord is just and loves justice:
   the upright shall see his face.   ℟

Gospel Acclamation Col 3:1
   Alleluia, alleluia!
   Since you have been brought back to true life with Christ,
   you must look for the things that are in heaven where Christ is,
   sitting at God's right hand.
   Alleluia!

or   Jn 16:7. 13

   Alleluia, alleluia!
   I will send you the Spirit of truth, says the Lord;
   he will lead you to the complete truth.
   Alleluia!

GOSPEL

A reading from the holy Gospel according to John   21:20-25
This disciple is the one who has written these things down, and we know that his testimony is true.

Peter turned and saw the disciple Jesus loved following them – the one who had leaned on his breast at the supper and had said to him, 'Lord, who is it that will betray you?' Seeing him, Peter said to Jesus, 'What about him, Lord?' Jesus answered, 'If I want him to stay behind till I come, what does it matter to you? You are to follow me.' The rumour then went out among the brothers that this disciple would not die. Yet Jesus had not said to Peter, 'He will not die,' but, 'If I want him to stay behind till I come.'

   This disciple is the one who vouches for these things and has written them down, and we know that his testimony is true.

   There were many other things that Jesus did; if all were written down, the world itself, I suppose, would not hold all the books that would have to written.

   This is the Gospel of the Lord.

Prayer over the Gifts
Lord,
may the coming of the Holy Spirit
prepare us to receive these holy sacraments,
for he is our forgiveness.

Preface of Ascension I or II, P26 or P27.

Communion Antiphon: The Lord says: The Holy Spirit will give glory to me, because he takes my words from me and will hand them on to you, alleluia.

Prayer after Communion
Father of mercy,
hear our prayers
that we may leave our former selves behind
and serve you with holy and renewed hearts.

GOSPEL ACCLAMATIONS
for the Weekdays before the Ascension

1   Mt 4:4

    Alleluia, alleluia!
    Man does not live on bread alone, but on every word
    that comes from the mouth of God.
    Alleluia!

2   cf. Lk 24:46. 26

    Alleluia, alleluia!
    It was ordained that the Christ should suffer
    and rise from the dead,
    and so enter into his glory.
    Alleluia!

3   Jn 3:15

    Alleluia, alleluia!
    The Son of Man must be lifted up
    so that everyone who believes in him
    may have eternal life.
    Alleluia!

4   Jn 3:16

Alleluia, alleluia!
God loved the world so much that he gave his only Son;
everyone who believes in him has eternal life.
Alleluia!

5   Jn 6:35

Alleluia, alleluia!
I am the bread of life, says the Lord.
He who comes to me will never be hungry;
he who believes in me will never thirst.
Alleluia!

6   cf. Jn 6:40

Alleluia, alleluia!
It is my Father's will, says the Lord,
that whoever believes in the Son shall have eternal life,
and that I shall raise him up on the last day.
Alleluia!

7   Jn 6:51

Alleluia, alleluia!
I am the living bread which has come down from heaven,
says the Lord.
Anyone who eats this bread will live for ever.
Alleluia!

8   Jn 6:56

Alleluia, alleluia!
He who eats my flesh and drinks my blood
lives in me and I live in him, says the Lord.
Alleluia!

9   cf. Jn 6:63. 68

Alleluia, alleluia!
Your words are spirit, Lord, and they are life:
you have the message of eternal life.
Alleluia!

10   Jn 8:12

Alleluia, alleluia!
I am the light of the world, says the Lord,
anyone who follows me will have the light of life.
Alleluia!

11   Jn 8:31.32

Alleluia, alleluia!
If you make my word your home you will indeed be my
    disciples,
and you will learn the truth, says the Lord.
Alleluia!

12   Jn 10:14

Alleluia, alleluia!
I am the good shepherd, says the Lord,
I know my sheep and my own know me.
Alleluia!

13   Jn 10:27

Alleluia, alleluia!
The sheep that belong to me listen to my voice, says the Lord;
I know them and they follow me.
Alleluia!

14   Jn 14:6

Alleluia, alleluia!
I am the Way, the Truth and the Life, says the Lord;
no one can come to the Father except through me.
Alleluia!

15   Jn 15:4-5

Alleluia, alleluia!
Make your home in me, as I make mine in you, says the Lord;
whoever remains in me bears fruit in plenty.
Alleluia!

16   Jn 15:15

Alleluia, alleluia!
I call you friends, says the Lord,
because I have made known to you everything I have learnt from my Father.
Alleluia!

17   Jn 20:29

Alleluia, alleluia!
Jesus said: 'You believe because you can see me.
Happy are those who have not seen and yet believe.'
Alleluia!

or

Alleluia, alleluia!
Jesus said: 'You believe, Thomas, because you can see me.
Happy are those who have not seen and yet believe.'
Alleluia!

18   Rom 6:9

Alleluia, alleluia!
Christ, having been raised from the dead, will never die again.
Death has no power over him any more.
Alleluia!

19   Col 3:1

Alleluia, alleluia!
Since you have been brought back to true life with Christ,
you must look for the things that are in heaven where Christ is,
sitting at God's right hand.
Alleluia!

20   cf. Apoc 1:5

Alleluia, alleluia!
You, O Christ, are the faithful witness, the First-born from the dead;
you have loved us and have washed away our sins with your blood.
Alleluia!

21

Alleluia, alleluia!
We know that Christ is truly risen from the dead;
have mercy on us, triumphant King.
Alleluia!

22

Alleluia, alleluia!
The Lord, who hung for us upon the tree,
has risen from the tomb.
Alleluia!

23

Alleluia, alleluia!
Christ has risen and shone upon us
whom he redeemed with his blood.
Alleluia!

24

Alleluia, alleluia!
Christ has risen: he who created all things,
and has granted his mercy to men.
Alleluia!

GOSPEL ACCLAMATIONS
For the Weekdays after the Ascension

1   Mt 28:19. 20

Alleluia, alleluia!
Go, make disciples of all the nations:
I am with you always: yes, to the end of time.
Alleluia!

2   Jn 14:16

Alleluia, alleluia!
I shall ask the Father,
 and he will give you another Advocate to be with you for
  ever.
Alleluia!

Gospel Acclamations Weekdays after Ascension

3   cf. Jn 14:18

Alleluia, alleluia!
I will not leave you orphans, says the Lord;
I go, but I will come back to you, and your hearts will be full of joy.
Alleluia!

4   Jn 14:26

Alleluia, alleluia!
The Holy Spirit will teach you everything
and remind you of all I have said to you.
Alleluia!

5   Jn 15:26.27

Alleluia, alleluia!
The Spirit of truth will be my witness,
and you too will be witnesses, says the Lord.
Alleluia!

6   cf. Jn 16:7. 13

Alleluia, alleluia!
I will send you the Spirit of truth, says the Lord;
he will lead you to the complete truth.
Alleluia!

7   Jn 16:28

Alleluia, alleluia!
I came from the Father and have come into the world,
and now I leave the world to go to the Father.
Alleluia!

8   Jn 17:17

Alleluia, alleluia!
Your word is truth, O Lord,
consecrate us in the truth.
Alleluia!

9   Jn 17:21

Alleluia, alleluia!
May they all be one.
Father, may they be one in us, as you are in me and I am in you,
so that the world may believe it was you who sent me, says the Lord.
Alleluia!

10   Col 3:1

Alleluia, alleluia!
Since you have been brought back to true life with Christ,
you must look for the things that are in heaven where Christ is,
sitting at God's right hand.
Alleluia!

PENTECOST

Vigil Mass

On Saturday evening before or after Evening Prayer I of Pentecost.

Entrance Antiphon: The love of God has been poured into our hearts by his Spirit living in us, alleluia.

Opening Prayer
Let us pray
    [that the Holy Spirit
    may bring peace and unity to all mankind]

Almighty and ever-living God,
you fulfilled the Easter promise
by sending us your Holy Spirit.
May that Spirit unite the races and nations on earth
to proclaim your glory.

or

God our Father,
you have given us new birth.
Strengthen us with your Holy Spirit
and fill us with your light.

or

Let us pray
    [that the flame of the Spirit will descend upon us]

Father in heaven,
fifty days have celebrated the fullness
of the mystery of your revealed love.
See your people gathered in prayer,
open to receive the Spirit's flame.
May it come to rest in our hearts
and disperse the divisions of word and tongue.
With one voice and one song
may we praise your name in joy and thanksgiving.

The Gloria is said.

Pentecost: Vigil Mass

FIRST READING

Any of these readings from the Old Testament may be chosen.

1

A reading from the book of Genesis 11:1-9

It was named Babel because there the language of the whole earth was confused.

Throughout the earth men spoke the same language, with the same vocabulary. Now as they moved eastwards they found a plain in the land of Shinar where they settled. They said to one another, 'Come, let us make bricks and bake them in the fire.' – For stone they used bricks, and for mortar they used bitumen. – 'Come,' they said 'let us build ourselves a town and a tower with its top reaching heaven. Let us make a name for ourselves, so that we may not be scattered about the whole earth.'

Now the Lord came down to see the town and the tower that the sons of man had built. 'So they are all a single people with a single language!' said the Lord. 'This is but the start of their undertakings! There will be nothing too hard for them to do. Come, let us go down and confuse their language on the spot so that they can no longer understand one another.' The Lord scattered them thence over the whole face of the earth, and they stopped building the town. It was named Babel therefore, because there the Lord confused the language of the whole earth. It was from there that the Lord scattered them over the whole face of the earth.

This is the word of the Lord.

2

A reading from the book of Exodus 19:3-8, 16-20

Th Lord came down on the mountain of Sinai before all the people.

Moses went up to God, and the Lord called to him from the mountain, saying, 'Say this to the House of Jacob, declare this to the sons of Israel, "You yourselves have seen what I did with the Egyptians, how I carried you on eagle's wings and brought you to myself. From this you know that now, if you obey my voice and hold fast to my covenant, you of all the nations shall be my very own, for all the earth is mine. I will count you a kingdom of priests, a consecrated nation." Those are the words you are to speak to the sons of Israel.' So Moses went and summoned the elders of the people, putting before them all that the Lord had bidden him. Then all the people answered as one, 'All that the Lord has said, we will do.'

Now at daybreak on the third day there were peals of thunder on the mountain and lightning flashes, a dense cloud, and a loud trumpet blast, and inside the camp all the people trembled. Then Moses led the people out of the camp to meet God; and they stood at the bottom of the mountain. The mountain of Sinai was entirely wrapped in smoke, because the Lord had descended on it in the form of fire. Like smoke from a furnace the smoke went up, and the whole mountain shook violently. Louder and louder grew the sound of the trumpet. Moses spoke, and God answered him with peals of thunder. The Lord came down on the mountain of Sinai, on the mountain top, and the Lord called Moses to the top of the mountain.

This is the word of the Lord.

3

A reading from the prophet Ezekiel 37:1-14
Dry bones, I am going to make the breath enter you, and you will live.

The hand of the Lord was laid on me, and he carried me away by the spirit of the Lord and set me down in the middle of a valley, a valley full of bones. He made me walk up and down among them. There were vast quantities of these bones on the ground the whole length of the valley; and they were quite dried up. He said to me, 'Son of man, can these bones live?' I said, 'You know, Lord.' He said, 'Prophesy over these bones. Say, "Dry bones, hear the word of the Lord. The Lord says this to these bones: I am now going to make the breath enter you, and you will live. I shall put sinews on you, I shall make flesh grow on you, I shall cover you with skin and give you breath, and you will live; and you will learn that I am the Lord." ' I prophesied as I had been ordered. While I was prophesying, there was a noise, a sound of clattering; and the bones joined together. I looked, and saw that they were covered with sinews; flesh was growing on them and skin was covering them, but there was no breath in them. He said to me, 'Prophesy to the breath; prophesy, son of man. Say to the breath, "The Lord says this: Come from the four winds, breath; breathe on these dead; let them live!" ' I prophesied as he had ordered me, and the breath entered them; they came to life again and stood up on their feet, a great, an immense army.

Then he said, 'Son of man, these bones are the whole House

of Israel. They keep saying, "Our bones are dried up, our hope has gone; we are as good as dead." So prophesy. Say to them, "The Lord says this: I am now going to open your graves; I mean to raise you from your graves, my people, and lead you back to the soil of Israel. And you will know that I am the Lord, when I open your graves and raise you from your graves, my people. And I shall put my spirit in you, and you will live, and I shall resettle you on your own soil; and you will know that I, the Lord, have said and done this – it is the Lord who speaks."'

This is the word of the Lord.

4

A reading from the prophet Joel 3:1-5

I will pour out my spirit on all people.

Thus says the Lord:

'I will pour out my spirit on all mankind.
Your sons and daughters shall prophesy,
your old men shall dream dreams,
and your young men see visions.
Even on the slaves, men and women,
will I pour out my spirit in those days.
I will display portents in heaven and on earth.
blood and fire and columns of smoke.'

The sun will be turned into darkness,
and the moon into blood,
before the day of the Lord dawns,
that great and terrible day.
All who call on the name of the Lord will be saved,
for on Mount Zion there will be some who have escaped,
as the Lord has said,
and in Jerusalem some survivors whom the Lord will call.

This is the word of the Lord.

Responsorial Psalm Ps 103:1-2. 24. 27-30. 35. R̸ cf. v.30

 R̸ **Send forth your Spirit, O Lord,
  and renew the face of the earth.**

or

 R̸ **Alleluia!**

Pentecost: Vigil Mass

1. Bless the Lord, my soul!
   Lord God, how great you are,
   clothed in majesty and glory,
   wrapped in light as in a robe! ℟

2. How many are your works, O Lord!
   In wisdom you have made them all.
   The earth is full of your riches.
   Bless the Lord, my soul. ℟

3. All of these look to you
   to give them their food in due season.
   You give it, they gather it up:
   you open your hand, they have their fill. ℟

4. You take back your spirit, they die,
   returning to the dust from which they came.
   You send forth your spirit, they are created;
   and you renew the face of the earth. ℟

SECOND READING

A reading from the letter of St Paul to the Romans   8:22-27

The Spirit himself expresses our plea in a way that could never be put into words.

From the beginning till now the entire creation, as we know, has been groaning in one great act of giving birth; and not only creation, but all of us who possess the first-fruits of the Spirit, we too groan inwardly as we wait for our bodies to be set free. For we must be content to hope that we shall be saved – our salvation is not in sight, we should not have to be hoping for it if it were – but, as I say, we must hope to be saved since we are not saved yet – it is something we must wait for with patience.

The Spirit too comes to help us in our weakness. For when we cannot choose words in order to pray properly, the Spirit himself expresses our plea in a way that could never be put into words, and God who knows everything in our hearts knows perfectly well what he means, and that the pleas of the saints expressed by the Spirit are according to the mind of God.

This is the word of the Lord.

Gospel Acclamation
Alleluia, alleluia!
Come, Holy Spirit, fill the hearts of your faithful

and kindle in them the fire of your love.
Alleluia!

GOSPEL

A reading from the holy Gospel according to John 7:37-39
From his breast shall flow fountains of living water.

On the last day and greatest day of the festival, Jesus stood there and cried out:

'If any man is thirsty, let him come to me!
Let the man come and drink who believes in me!'

As scripture says: From his breast shall flow fountains of living water.

He was speaking of the Spirit which those who believed in him were to receive; for there was no Spirit as yet because Jesus had not yet been glorified.

This is the Gospel of the Lord.

Prayer over the Gifts
Lord,
send your Spirit on these gifts
and through them help the Church you love
to show your salvation to all the world.

Preface of Pentecost, P28.

Communion Antiphon: On the last day of the festival, Jesus stood and cried aloud: If anyone is thirsty, let him come to me and drink, alleluia.

Prayer after Communion
Lord,
through this eucharist,
send the Holy Spirit of Pentecost into our hearts
to keep us always in your love.

For Pentecost Sunday, see
companion volume, *The Sunday Missal*.

WEEKDAY MASSES IN ORDINARY TIME

There may be thirty-three or thirty-four Weeks in Ordinary Time. The cycle begins with the Monday after the Baptism of the Lord (the Sunday which follows 6 January), and continues until Ash Wednesday. It recommences on the Monday after Pentecost Sunday, and ends on the Saturday before the First Sunday of Advent.

To ascertain the number of Weeks in Ordinary Time before Lent, and the Week with which the cycle recommences after Pentecost, see the Table of Principal Celebrations, p.ix.

Choice of texts

'On weekdays of ordinary time, the prayers may be taken from the preceding Sunday, from another Sunday of ordinary time, or from the prayers for various occasions given in the missal. It is always permissible to use only the opening prayer from these Masses.

'This makes available a wider selection of texts and affords an opportunity to restate the themes of prayer for the liturgical assembly. It also permits adaptation of the prayer to the needs of the people, the Church, and the world' (*General Instruction* n 323).

'In the weekday lectionary, readings are provided for each day of the year. Unless a solemnity or feast occurs, these readings are to be used regularly on the days to which they are assigned' (*General Instruction* n 319).

In the pages which follow, the proper prayers and chants of the 34 Masses for ordinary time are given. These are followed by the readings for weekdays in ordinary time Year I, and then by Year II. Year I is read in odd-numbered years, and Year II in even-numbered years.

The Gloria and the Profession of Faith are not said on weekdays.

Weekday Prefaces I-VI, P37-P42, are used.

Two antiphons are given for communion, the first from the Psalms, the second for the most part from the Gospel. Either one may be selected, but preference should be given to the antiphon which may happen to come from the Gospel of the Mass.

MASSES FOR WEEKDAYS
in Ordinary Time

I

Entrance Antiphon: I saw a man sitting on a high throne, being worshipped by a great number of angels who were singing together: This is he whose kingdom will last for ever.

Opening Prayer

Let us pray
  [that we will know and do what God wills]

Father of love,
hear our prayers.
Help us to know your will
and to do it with courage and faith.

Prayer over the Gifts

Lord,
accept our offering.
Make us grow in holiness
and grant what we ask you in faith.

Weekday Prefaces I-VI, P37-P42.

Communion Antiphon: Lord, you are the source of life, and in the light of your glory we find happiness.

or

I came that men may have life, and have it to the full, says the Lord.

Prayer after Communion

All-powerful God,
you renew us with your sacraments.
Help us to thank you by lives of faithful service.

Masses for Weekdays in Ordinary Time

II

Entrance Antiphon: May all the earth give you worship and praise, and break into song to your name, O God, Most High.

Opening Prayer
Let us pray
   [to our Father for the gift of peace]

Father of heaven and earth,
hear our prayers,
and show us the way to peace in the world.

or

Let us pray
   [for the gift of peace]

Almighty and ever-present Father,
your watchful care reaches from end to end
and orders all things in such power
that even the tensions and the tragedies of sin
cannot frustrate your loving plans.

Help us to embrace your will,
give us the strength to follow your call,
so that your truth may live in our hearts
and reflect peace to those who believe in your love.

Prayer over the Gifts
Father,
may we celebrate the eucharist
with reverence and love,
for when we proclaim the death of the Lord
you continue the work of his redemption,
who is Lord for ever and ever.

Communion Antiphon: The Lord has prepared a feast for me: given wine in plenty for me to drink.

or

We know and believe in God's love for us.

Prayer after Communion
Lord,
you have nourished us with bread from heaven.
Fill us with your Spirit,
and make us one in peace and love.

III

Entrance Antiphon: Sing a new song to the Lord! Sing to the Lord, all the earth. Truth and beauty surround him, he lives in holiness and glory.

Opening Prayer
Let us pray
   [for unity and peace]

All-powerful and ever-living God,
direct your love that is within us,
that our efforts in the name of your Son
may bring mankind to unity and peace.

or

Let us pray
   [pleading that our vision
   may overcome our weakness]

Almighty Father,
the love you offer
always exceeds the furthest expression of our human longing,
for you are greater than the human heart.

Direct each thought, each effort of our life,
so that the limits of our faults and weaknesses
may not obscure the vision of your glory
or keep us from the peace you have promised.

Prayer over the Gifts
Lord,
receive our gifts.
Let our offerings make us holy
and bring us salvation.

Communion Antiphon: Look up at the Lord with gladness and smile; your face will never be ashamed.

or

I am the light of the world, says the Lord; the man who follows me will have the light of life.

Prayer after Communion
God, all-powerful Father,
may the new life you give us increase our love
and keep us in the joy of your kingdom.

IV

Entrance Antiphon: Save us, Lord our God, and gather us together from the nations, that we may proclaim your holy name and glory in your praise.

Opening Prayer
Let us pray
   [for a greater love of God
   and of our fellow men]

Lord our God,
help us to love you with all our hearts
and to love all men as you love them.

or

Let us pray
   [joining in the praise of the living God
   for we are his people]

Father in heaven,
from the days of Abraham and Moses
until this gathering of your Church in prayer,
you have formed a people in the image of your Son.

Bless this people with the gift of your kingdom.
May we serve you with our every desire
and show love for one another
even as you have loved us.

Prayer over the Gifts
Lord,
be pleased with the gifts we bring to your altar,
and make them the sacrament of our salvation.

Communion Antiphon: Let your face shine on your servant, and save me by your love. Lord, keep me from shame, for I have called to you.

or

Happy are the poor in spirit; the kingdom of heaven is theirs! Happy are the lowly; they shall inherit the land.

Prayer after Communion
Lord,
you invigorate us with this help to our salvation.
By this eucharist give the true faith continued growth
throughout the world.

V

Entrance Antiphon: Come, let us worship the Lord. Let us bow down in the presence of our maker, for he is the Lord our God.

Opening Prayer
Let us pray
    [that God will watch over us and protect us]

Father,
watch over your family
and keep us safe in your care,
for all our hope is in you.

or
Let us pray
    [with reverence in the presence of the living God]

In faith and love we ask you, Father,
to watch over your family gathered here.
In your mercy and loving kindness
no thought of ours is left unguarded,
no tear unheeded, no joy unnoticed.

Through the prayer of Jesus
may the blessings promised to the poor in spirit
lead us to the treasures of your heavenly kingdom.

Prayer over the Gifts
Lord our God,
may the bread and wine
you give us for our nourishment on earth
become the sacrament of our eternal life.

Communion Antiphon: Give praise to the Lord for his kindness, for his wonderful deeds towards men. He has filled the hungry with good things, he has satisfied the thirsty.

or
Happy are the sorrowing; they shall be consoled. Happy those who hunger and thirst for what is right; they shall be satisfied.

Prayer after Communion
God our Father,
you give us a share in the one bread and the one cup
and make us one in Christ.
Help us to bring your salvation and joy
to all the world.

Masses for Weekdays in Ordinary Time

VI

Entrance Antiphon: Lord, be my rock of safety, the stronghold that saves me. For the honour of your name, lead me and guide me.

Opening Prayer

Let us pray
   [that everything we do
   will be guided by God's law of love]

God our Father,
you have promised to remain for ever
with those who do what is just and right.
Help us to live in your presence.

or

Let us pray
   [for the wisdom that is greater than human words]

Father in heaven,
the loving plan of your wisdom took flesh in Jesus Christ,
and changed mankind's history
by his command of perfect love.

May our fulfilment of his command reflect your wisdom
and bring your salvation to the ends of the earth.

Prayer over the Gifts

Lord,
we make this offering in obedience to your word.
May it cleanse and renew us,
and lead us to our eternal reward.

Communion Antiphon: They ate and were filled; the Lord gave them what they wanted: they were not deprived of their desire.

or

God loved the world so much, he gave his only Son, that all who believe in him might not perish, but might have eternal life.

Prayer after Communion

Lord,
you give us food from heaven.
May we always hunger
for the bread of life.

VII

Entrance Antiphon: Lord, your mercy is my hope, my heart rejoices in your saving power. I will sing to the Lord for his goodness to me.

Opening Prayer
Let us pray
   [that God will make us more like Christ, his Son]
Father,
keep before us the wisdom and love
you have revealed in your Son.
Help us to be like him
in word and deed,
for he lives and reigns . . .
or
Let us pray
   [to the God of power and might,
   for his mercy is our hope]
Almighty God,
Father of our Lord Jesus Christ,
faith in your word is the way to wisdom,
and to ponder your divine plan is to grow in the truth.
Open our eyes to your deeds,
our ears to the sound of your call,
so that our every act may increase our sharing
in the life you have offered us.

Prayer over the Gifts
Lord,
as we make this offering,
may our worship in Spirit and truth
bring us salvation.

Communion Antiphon: I will tell all your marvellous works. I will rejoice and be glad in you, and sing to your name, Most High.
or
Lord, I believe that you are the Christ, the Son of God, who was to come into this world.

Prayer after Communion
Almighty God,
help us to live the example of love
we celebrate in this eucharist,
that we may come to its fulfilment in your presence.

VIII

Entrance Antiphon: The Lord has been my strength; he has led me into freedom. He saved me because he loves me.

Opening Prayer

Let us pray
   [that God will bring peace to the world
   and freedom to his Church]

Lord,
guide the course of world events
and give your Church the joy and peace
of serving you in freedom.

or

Let us pray
   [that the peace of Christ
   may find welcome in the world]

Father in heaven,
form in us the likeness of your Son
and deepen his life within us.
Send us as witnesses of gospel joy
into a world of fragile peace and broken promises.
Touch the hearts of all men with your love
that they in turn may love one another.

Prayer over the Gifts

God our Creator,
may this bread and wine we offer
as a sign of our love and worship
lead us to salvation.

Communion Antiphon: I will sing to the Lord for his goodness to me, I will sing the name of the Lord, Most High.

or

I, the Lord, am with you always, until the end of the world.

Prayer after Communion

God of salvation,
may this sacrament which strengthens us here on earth
bring us to eternal life.

IX

Entrance Antiphon: O look at me and be merciful, for I am wretched and alone. See my hardship and my poverty, and pardon all my sins.

Opening Prayer

Let us pray
 [for God's care and protection]
Father,
your love never fails.
Hear our call.
Keep us from danger
and provide for all our needs.

or

Let us pray
 [for the confidence born of faith]
God our Father,
teach us to cherish the gifts that surround us.
Increase our faith in you
and bring our trust to its promised fulfilment
in the joy of your kingdom.

Prayer over the Gifts

Lord,
as we gather to offer our gifts
confident in your love,
make us holy by sharing your life with us
and by this eucharist forgive our sins.

Communion Antiphon: I call upon you, God, for you will answer me; bend your ear and hear my prayer.

or

I tell you solemnly, whatever you ask for in prayer, believe that you have received it, and it will be yours, says the Lord.

Prayer after Communion

Lord,
as you give us the body and blood of your Son,
guide us with your Spirit
that we may honour you
not only with our lips,
but also with the lives we lead,
and so enter your kingdom.

X

Entrance Antiphon: The Lord is my light and my salvation. Who shall frighten me? The Lord is the defender of my life. Who shall make me tremble?

Opening Prayer
Let us pray
    [for the guidance of the Holy Spirit]

God of wisdom and love,
source of all good,
send your Spirit to teach us your truth
and guide our actions
in your way of peace.

or

Let us pray
    [to our Father
    who calls us to freedom in Jesus his Son]

Father in heaven,
words cannot measure the boundaries of love
for those born to new life in Christ Jesus.
Raise us beyond the limits this world imposes,
so that we may be free to love as Christ teaches
and find our joy in your glory.

Prayer over the Gifts
Lord,
look with love on our service.
Accept the gifts we bring
and help us grow in Christian love.

Communion Antiphon: I can rely on the Lord; I can always turn to him for shelter. It was he who gave me my freedom. My God, you are always there to help me!

or

God is love, and he who lives in love, lives in God, and God in him.

Prayer after Communion
Lord,
may your healing love
turn us from sin
and keep us on the way that leads to you.

XI

Entrance Antiphon: Lord, hear my voice when I call to you. You are my help; do not cast me off, do not desert me, my Saviour God.

Opening Prayer
Let us pray
   [for the grace to follow Christ more closely]

Almighty God,
our hope and our strength,
without you we falter.
Help us to follow Christ
and to live according to your will.

or
Let us pray
   [to the Father,
   whose love gives us strength to follow his Son]

God our Father,
we rejoice in the faith that draws us together,
aware that selfishness can drive us apart.
Let your encouragement be our constant strength.
Keep us one in the love that has sealed our lives,
help us to live as one family
the gospel we profess.

Prayer over the Gifts
Lord God,
in this bread and wine
you give us food for body and spirit.
May the eucharist renew our strength
and bring us health of mind and body.

Communion Antiphon: One thing I seek: to dwell in the house of the Lord all the days of my life.

or
Father, keep in your name those you have given me, that they may be one as we are one, says the Lord.

Prayer after Communion
Lord,
may this eucharist
accomplish in your Church
the unity and peace it signifies.

Masses for Weekdays in Ordinary Time

XII

Entrance Antiphon: God is the strength of his people. In him, we his chosen live in safety. Save us, Lord, who share in your life, and give us your blessing; be our shepherd for ever.

Opening Prayer
Let us pray
    [that we may grow in the love of God]

Father,
guide and protector of your people,
grant us an unfailing respect for your name,
and keep us always in your love.
or
Let us pray
    [to God whose fatherly love keeps us safe]

God of the universe,
we worship you as Lord.
God, ever close to us,
we rejoice to call you Father.
From this world's uncertainty we look to your covenant.
Keep us one in your peace, secure in your love.

Prayer over the Gifts
Lord,
receive our offering,
and may this sacrifice of praise
purify us in mind and heart
and make us always eager to serve you.

Communion Antiphon: The eyes of all look to you, O Lord, and you give them food in due season.
or
I am the Good Shepherd; I give my life for my sheep, says the Lord.

Prayer after Communion
Lord,
you give us the body and blood of your Son
to renew your life within us.
In your mercy, assure our redemption
and bring us to the eternal life
we celebrate in this eucharist.

XIII

Entrance Antiphon: All nations, clap your hands. Shout with a voice of joy to God.

Opening Prayer

Let us pray
   [that Christ may be our light]

Father,
you call your children
to walk in the light of Christ.
Free us from darkness
and keep us in the radiance of your truth.
   or
Let us pray
   [for the strength to reject the darkness of sin]

Father in heaven,
the light of Jesus
has scattered the darkness of hatred and sin.
Called to that light
we ask for your guidance.
Form our lives in your truth, our hearts in your love.

Prayer over the Gifts

Lord God,
through your sacraments
you give us the power of your grace.
May this eucharist
help us to serve you faithfully.

Communion Antiphon: O, bless the Lord, my soul, and all that is within me bless his holy name.
   or
Father, I pray for them: may they be one in us, so that the world may believe it was you who sent me.

Prayer after Communion

Lord,
may this sacrifice and communion
give us a share in your life
and help us bring your love to the world.

XIV

Entrance Antiphon: Within your temple, we ponder your loving kindness, O God. As your name, so also your praise reaches to the ends of the earth; your right hand is filled with justice.

Opening Prayer
Let us pray
    [for forgiveness through the grace of Jesus Christ]
Father,
through the obedience of Jesus,
your servant and your Son,
you raised a fallen world.
Free us from sin
and bring us the joy that lasts for ever.

or

Let us pray
    [for greater willingness
    to serve God and our fellow man]
Father,
in the rising of your Son
death gives birth to new life.
The sufferings he endured restored hope to a fallen world.
Let sin never ensnare us
with empty promises of passing joy.
Make us one with you always,
so that our joy may be holy,
and our love may give life.

Prayer over the Gifts
Lord,
let this offering to the glory of your name
purify us and bring us closer to eternal life.

Communion Antiphon: Taste and see the goodness of the Lord; blessed is he who hopes in God.

or

Come to me, all you that labour and are burdened, and I will give you rest, says the Lord.

Prayer after Communion
Lord,
may we never fail to praise you
for the fullness of life and salvation
you give us in this eucharist.

XV

Entrance Antiphon: In my justice I shall see your face, O Lord; when your glory appears, my joy will be full.

Opening Prayer
Let us pray
 [that the gospel may be our rule of life]

God our Father,
your light of truth
guides us to the way of Christ.
May all who follow him
reject what is contrary to the gospel.
or
Let us pray
 [to be faithful to the light we have received,
 to the name we bear]

Father,
let the light of your truth
guide us to your kingdom
through a world filled with lights contrary to your own.
Christian is the name and the gospel we glory in.
May your love make us what you have called us to be.

Prayer over the Gifts
Lord,
accept the gifts of your Church.
May this eucharist
help us grow in holiness and faith.

Communion Antiphon: The sparrow even finds a home, the swallow finds a nest wherein to place her young, near to your altars, Lord of hosts, my King, my God! How happy they who dwell in your house! For ever they are praising you.
or
Whoever eats my flesh and drinks my blood will live in me and I in him, says the Lord.

Prayer after Communion
Lord,
by our sharing in the mystery of this eucharist,
let your saving love grow within us.

Masses for Weekdays in Ordinary Time

XVI

Entrance Antiphon: God himself is my help. The Lord upholds my life. I will offer you a willing sacrifice; I will praise your name, O Lord, for its goodness.

Opening Prayer
Let us pray
   [to be kept faithful in the service of God]
Lord,
be merciful to your people.
Fill us with your gifts
and make us always eager to serve you
in faith, hope, and love.
or
Let us pray
   [that God will continue to bless us
   with his compassion and love]
Father,
let the gift of your life
continue to grow in us,
drawing us from death to faith, hope, and love.
Keep us alive in Christ Jesus.
Keep us watchful in prayer
and true to his teaching
till your glory is revealed in us.

Prayer over the Gifts
Lord,
bring us closer to salvation
through these gifts which we bring in your honour.
Accept the perfect sacrifice you have given us,
bless it as you blessed the gifts of Abel.

Communion Antiphon: The Lord keeps in our minds the wonderful things he has done. He is compassion and love; he always provides for his faithful.
or
I stand at the door and knock, says the Lord. If anyone hears my voice and opens the door, I will come in and sit down to supper with him, and he with me.

Prayer after Communion
Merciful Father,
may these mysteries
give us new purpose
and bring us to a new life in you.

XVII

Entrance Antiphon: God is in his holy dwelling; he will give a home to the lonely, he gives power and strength to his people.

Opening Prayer
Let us pray
   [that we will make good use of the gifts that God has given us]
God our Father and protector,
without you nothing is holy,
nothing has value.
Guide us to everlasting life
by helping us to use wisely
the blessings you have given to the world.

or

Let us pray
   [for the faith to recognise God's presence in our world]
God our Father,
open our eyes to see your hand at work
in the splendour of creation,
in the beauty of human life.
Touched by your hand our world is holy.
Help us to cherish the gifts that surround us,
to share your blessings with our brothers and sisters,
and to experience the joy of life in your presence.

Prayer over the Gifts
Lord,
receive these offerings
chosen from your many gifts.
May these mysteries make us holy
and lead us to eternal joy.

Communion Antiphon: O bless the Lord, my soul, and remember all his kindness.

or

Happy are those who show mercy; mercy shall be theirs. Happy are the pure of heart, for they shall see God.

Prayer after Communion
Lord,
we receive the sacrament
which celebrates the memory
of the death and resurrection of Christ your Son.
May this gift bring us closer to our eternal salvation.

XVIII

Entrance Antiphon: God, come to my help, Lord, quickly give me assistance. You are the one who helps me and sets me free: Lord, do not be long in coming.

Opening Prayer

Let us pray
  [for the gift of God's forgiveness and love]

Father of everlasting goodness,
our origin and guide,
be close to us
and hear the prayers of all who praise you.
Forgive our sins and restore us to life.
Keep us safe in your love.
or
Let us pray
  [to the Father whose kindness never fails]

God our Father,
gifts without measure flow from your goodness
to bring us your peace.
Our life is your gift.
Guide our life's journey,
for only your love makes us whole.
Keep us strong in your love.

Prayer over the Gifts

Merciful Lord,
make holy these gifts,
and let our spiritual sacrifice
make us an everlasting gift to you.

Communion Antiphon: You gave us bread from heaven, Lord: a sweet-tasting bread that was very good to eat.
or
The Lord says: I am the bread of life. A man who comes to me will not go away hungry, and no one who believes in me will thirst.

Prayer after Communion

Lord,
you give us the strength of new life
by the gift of the eucharist.
Protect us with your love
and prepare us for eternal redemption.

XIX

Entrance Antiphon: Lord, be true to your covenant, forget not the life of your poor ones for ever. Rise up, O God, and defend your cause; do not ignore the shouts of your enemies.

Opening Prayer

Let us pray
   [in the Spirit
   that we may grow in the love of God]
Almighty and ever-living God,
your Spirit made us your children,
confident to call you Father.
Increase your Spirit within us
and bring us to our promised inheritance.

or

Let us pray
   [that through us
   others may find the way of life in Christ]
Father,
we come, reborn in the Spirit,
to celebrate our sonship in the Lord Jesus Christ.
Touch our hearts,
help them grow towards the life you have promised.
Touch our lives,
make them signs of your love for all men.

Prayer over the Gifts

God of power,
giver of the gifts we bring,
accept the offering of your Church
and make it the sacrament of our salvation.

Communion Antiphon: Praise the Lord, Jerusalem; he feeds you with the finest wheat.

or

The bread I shall give is my flesh for the life of the world, says the Lord.

Prayer after Communion

Lord,
may the eucharist you give us
bring us to salvation
and keep us faithful to the light of your truth.

XX

Entrance Antiphon: God, our protector, keep us in mind; always give strength to your people. For if we can be with you even one day, it is better than a thousand without you.

Opening Prayer

Let us pray
   [that the love of God
   may raise us beyond what we see
   to the unseen glory of his kingdom]

God our Father,
may we love you in all things and above all things
and reach the joy you have prepared for us
beyond all our imagining.

or

Let us pray
   [with humility and persistence]

Almighty God, ever-loving Father,
your care extends beyond the boundaries of race and nation
to the hearts of all who live.

May the walls, which prejudice raises between us,
crumble beneath the shadow of your outstretched arm.

Prayer over the Gifts

Lord,
accept our sacrifice
as a holy exchange of gifts.
By offering what you have given us
may we receive the gift to yourself.

Communion Antiphon: With the Lord there is mercy, and fullness of redemption.

or

I am the living bread from heaven, says the Lord; if anyone eats this bread he will live for ever.

Prayer after Communion

God of mercy,
by this sacrament you make us one with Christ.
By becoming more like him on earth,
may we come to share his glory in heaven,
where he lives and reigns for ever and ever.

XXI

Entrance Antiphon: Listen, Lord, and answer me. Save your servant who trusts in you. I call to you all day long, have mercy on me, O Lord.

Opening Prayer

Let us pray
  [that God will make us one in mind and heart]
Father,
help us to seek the values
that will bring us enduring joy in this changing world.
In our desire for what you promise
make us one in mind and heart.
or
Let us pray
  [with minds fixed on eternal truth]
Lord our God,
all truth is from you,
and you alone bring oneness of heart.
Give your people the joy
of hearing your word in every sound
and of longing for your presence more than for life itself.
May all the attractions of a changing world
serve only to bring us
the peace of your kingdom which this world does not give.

Prayer over the Gifts

Merciful God,
the perfect sacrifice of Jesus Christ
make us your people.
In your love,
grant peace and unity to your Church.

Communion Antiphon: Lord, the earth is filled with your gift from heaven; man grows bread from earth, and wine to cheer his heart.
or
The Lord says: The man who eats my flesh and drinks my blood will live for ever; I shall raise him to life on the last day.

Prayer after Communion

Lord,
may this eucharist increase within us
the healing power of your love.
May it guide and direct our efforts
to please you in all things.

Masses for Weekdays in Ordinary Time

XXII

Entrance Antiphon: I call to you all day long, have mercy on me, O Lord. You are good and forgiving, full of love for all who call to you.

Opening Prayer
Let us pray
    [that God will increase our faith
    and bring to perfection the gifts he has given us]
Almighty God,
every good thing comes from you.
Fill our hearts with love for you,
increase our faith,
and by your constant care
protect the good you have given us.

or

Let us pray
    [to God who forgives all who call upon him]
Lord God of power and might,
nothing is good which is against your will,
and all is of value which comes from your hand.
Place in our hearts a desire to please you
and fill our minds with insight into love,
so that every thought may grow in wisdom
and all our efforts may be filled with your peace.

Prayer over the Gifts
Lord,
may this holy offering
bring us your blessing
and accomplish within us
its promise of salvation.

Communion Antiphon: O Lord, how great is the depth of the kindness which you have shown to those who love you.

or

Happy are the peacemakers; they shall be called sons of God. Happy are they who suffer persecution for justice' sake; the kingdom of heaven is theirs.

Prayer after Communion
Lord,
you renew us at your table with the bread of life.
May this food strengthen us in love
and help us to serve you in each other.

XXIII

Entrance Antiphon: Lord, you are just, and the judgements you make are right. Show mercy when you judge me, your servant.

Opening Prayer
Let us pray
   [that we may realise the freedom God has given us
   in making us his sons and daughters]
God our Father,
you redeem us
and make us your children in Christ.
Look upon us,
give us true freedom
and bring us to the inheritance you promised.
  or
Let us pray
   [to our just and merciful God]
Lord our God,
in you justice and mercy meet.
With unparalleled love you have saved us from death
and drawn us into the circle of your life.
Open our eyes to the wonders this life sets before us,
that we may serve you free from fear
and address you as God our Father.

Prayer over the Gifts
God of peace and love,
may our offering bring you true worship
and make us one with you.

Communion Antiphon: Like a deer that longs for running streams, my soul longs for you, my God. My soul is thirsting for the living God.
  or
I am the light of the world, says the Lord; the man who follows me will have the light of life.

Prayer after Communion
Lord,
your word and your sacrament
give us food and life.
May this gift of your Son
lead us to share his life for ever.

Masses for Weekdays in Ordinary Time

XXIV

Entrance Antiphon: Give peace, Lord, to those who wait for you, and your prophets will proclaim you as you deserve. Hear the prayers of your servant and of your people Israel.

Opening Prayer
Let us pray
   [that God will keep us faithful in his service]

Almighty God,
our creator and guide,
may we serve you with all our heart
and know your forgiveness in our lives.
or
Let us pray
   [for the peace which is born of faith and hope]

Father in heaven, Creator of all,
look down upon your people in their moments of need,
for you alone are the source of our peace.
Bring us to the dignity which distinguishes the poor in spirit
and show us how great is the call to serve,
that we may share in the peace of Christ
who offered his life in the service of all.

Prayer over the Gifts
Lord,
hear the prayers of your people
and receive our gifts.
May the worship of each one here
bring salvation to all.

Communion Antiphon: O God, how much we value your mercy! All mankind can gather under your protection.
or
The cup that we bless is a communion with the blood of Christ; and the bread that we break is a communion with the body of the Lord.

Prayer after Communion
Lord,
may the eucharist you have given us
influence our thoughts and actions.
May your Spirit guide and direct us in your way.

XXV

Entrance Antiphon: I am the Saviour of all people, says the Lord. Whatever their troubles, I will answer their cry, and I will always be their Lord.

Opening Prayer
Let us pray
 [that we will grow in the love of God and of one another]
Father,
guide us, as you guide creation
according to your law of love.
May we love one another
and come to perfection
in the eternal life prepared for us.

or

Let us pray
 [to the Lord who is a God of love to all peoples]
Father in heaven,
the perfection of justice is found in your love
and all mankind is in need of your law.
Help us to find this love in each other
that justice may be attained
through obedience to your law.

Prayer over the Gifts
Lord,
may these gifts which we now offer
to show our belief and our love
be pleasing to you.
May they become for us
the eucharist of Jesus Christ your Son,
who is Lord for ever and ever.

Communion Antiphon: You have laid down your precepts to be faithfully kept. May my footsteps be firm in keeping your commands.

or

I am the Good Shepherd, says the Lord; I know my sheep, and mine know me.

Prayer after Communion
Lord,
help us with your kindness.
Make us strong through the eucharist.
May we put into action
the saving mystery we celebrate.

XXVI

Entrance Antiphon: O Lord, you had just cause to judge men as you did: because we sinned against you and disobeyed your will. But now show us your greatness of heart, and treat us with your unbounded kindness.

Opening Prayer

Let us pray
   [for God's forgiveness
   and for the happiness it brings]
Father,
you show your almighty power
in your mercy and forgiveness.
Continue to fill us with your gifts of love.
Help us to hurry towards the eternal life your promise
and come to share in the joys of your kingdom.
or
Let us pray
   [for the peace of the kingdom
   which we have been promised]
Father of our Lord Jesus Christ,
in your unbounded mercy
you have revealed the beauty of your power
through your constant forgiveness of our sins.
May the power of this love be in our hearts
to bring your pardon and your kingdom to all we meet.

Prayer over the Gifts

God of mercy,
accept our offering
and make it a source of blessing for us.

Communion Antiphon: O Lord, remember the words you spoke to me, your servant, which made me live in hope and consoled me when I was downcast.
or
This is how we know what love is: Christ gave up his life for us; and we too must give up our lives for our brothers.

Prayer after Communion

Lord,
may this eucharist
in which we proclaim the death of Christ
bring us salvation
and make us one with him in glory,
for he is Lord for ever and ever.

XXVII

Entrance Antiphon: O Lord, you have given everything its place in the world, and no one can make it otherwise. For it is your creation, the heavens and the earth and the stars: you are the Lord of all.

Opening Prayer
Let us pray
   [that God will forgive our failings and bring us peace]
Father,
your love for us
surpasses all our hopes and desires.
Forgive our failings,
keep us in your peace
and lead us in the way of salvation.
or
Let us pray
   [before the face of God, in trusting faith]
Almighty and eternal God,
Father of the world to come,
your goodness is beyond what our spirit can touch
and your strength is more than the mind can bear.
Lead us to seek beyond our reach
and give us the courage to stand before your truth.

Prayer over the Gifts
Father,
receive these gifts
which our Lord Jesus Christ
has asked us to offer in his memory.
May our obedient service
bring us to the fullness of your redemption.

Communion Antiphon: The Lord is good to those who hope in him, to those who are searching for his love.
or
Because there is one bread, we, though many, are one body, for we all share in the one loaf and in the one cup.

Prayer after Communion
Almighty God,
let the eucharist we share fill us with your life.
May the love of Christ
which we celebrate here
touch our lives and lead us to you.

XXVIII

Entrance Antiphon: If you, O Lord, laid bare our guilt, who could endure it? But you are forgiving, God of Israel.

Opening Prayer
Let us pray
   [that God will help us to love one another]

Lord,
our help and guide,
make your love the foundation of our lives.
May our love for you express itself
in our eagerness to do good for others.

or
Let us pray
   [in quiet for the grace of sincerity]

Father in heaven,
the hand of your loving kindness
powerfully yet gently guides all the moments of our day.

Go before us in our pilgrimage of life,
anticipate our needs and prevent our failing.
Send your Spirit to unite us in faith,
that sharing in your service,
we may rejoice in your presence.

Prayer over the Gifts
Lord,
accept the prayers and gifts
we offer in faith and love.
May this eucharist bring us to your glory.

Communion Antiphon: The rich suffer want and go hungry, but nothing shall be lacking to those who fear the Lord.

or
When the Lord is revealed we shall be like him, for we shall see him as he is.

Prayer after Communion
Almighty Father,
may the body and blood of your Son
give us a share in his life,
for he is Lord for ever and ever.

XXIX

Entrance Antiphon: I call upon you, God, for you will answer me; bend your ear and hear my prayer. Guard me as the pupil of your eye; hide me in the shade of your wings.

Opening Prayer
Let us pray
   [for the gift of simplicity and joy
   in our service of God and man]

Almighty and ever-living God,
our source of power and inspiration,
give us strength and joy
in serving you as followers of Christ,
who lives and reigns . . .

or

Let us pray
   [to the Lord who bends close to hear our prayer]

Lord our God, Father of all,
you guard us under the shadow of your wings
and search into the depths of our hearts.

Remove the blindness that cannot know you
and relieve the fear that would hide us from your sight.

Prayer over the Gifts
Lord God,
may the gifts we offer
bring us your love and forgiveness
and give us freedom to serve you with our lives.

Communion Antiphon: See how the eyes of the Lord are on those who fear him, on those who hope in his love, that he may rescue them from death and feed them in time of famine.

or

The Son of Man came to give his life as a ransom for many.

Prayer after Communion
Lord,
may this eucharist help us to remain faithful.
May it teach us the way to eternal life.

XXX

Entrance Antiphon: Let hearts rejoice who search for the Lord. Seek the Lord and his strength, seek always the face of the Lord.

Opening Prayer

Let us pray
    [for the strength to do God's will]

Almighty and ever-living God,
strengthen our faith, hope, and love.
May we do with loving hearts
what you ask of us
and come to share the life you promise.

or

Let us pray
    [in humble hope for salvation]

Praised be you, God and Father of our Lord Jesus Christ.
There is no power for good
which does not come from your covenant,
and no promise to hope in
that your love has not offered.
Strengthen our faith to accept your covenant
and give us the love to carry out your command.

Prayer over the Gifts

Lord God of power and might,
receive the gifts we offer
and let our service give you glory.

Communion Antiphon: We will rejoice at the victory of God and make our boast in his great name.

or

Christ loved us and gave himself up for us as a fragrant offering to God.

Prayer after Communion

Lord,
bring to perfection within us
the communion we share in this sacrament.
May our celebration have an effect in our lives.

XXXI

Entrance Antiphon: Do not abandon me, Lord. My God, do not go away from me! Hurry to help me, Lord, my Saviour.

Opening Prayer
Let us pray
  [that our lives will reflect our faith]

God of power and mercy,
only with your help
can we offer you fitting service and praise.
May we live the faith we profess
and trust your promise of eternal life.
or
Let us pray
  [in the presence of God, the source of every good]

Father in heaven, God of power and Lord of mercy,
from whose fullness we have received,
direct our steps in our everyday efforts.
May the changing moods of the human heart
and the limits which our failings impose on hope
never blind us to you, source of every good.

Faith gives us the promise of peace
and makes known the demands of love.
Remove the selfishness that blurs the vision of faith.

Prayer over the Gifts
God of mercy,
may we offer a pure sacrifice
for the forgiveness of our sins.

Communion Antiphon: Lord, you will show me the path of life and fill me with joy in your presence.
or
As the living Father sent me, and I live because of the Father, so he who eats my flesh and drinks my blood will live because of me.

Prayer after Communion
Lord,
you give us new hope in this eucharist.
May the power of your love
continue its saving work among us
and bring us to the joy you promise.

Masses for Weekdays in Ordinary Time

XXXII

Entrance Antiphon: Let my prayer come before you, Lord; listen, and answer me.

Opening Prayer

Let us pray
 [for health of mind and body]
God of power and mercy,
protect us from all harm.
Give us freedom of spirit
and health in mind and body
to do your work on earth.

or

Let us pray
 [that our prayer rise like incense
 in the presence of the Lord]
Almighty Father,
strong is your justice and great is your mercy.
Protect us in the burdens and challenges of life.
Shield our minds from the distortion of pride
and enfold our desire with the beauty of truth.
Help us to become more aware of your loving design
so that we may more willingly give our lives in service to all.

Prayer over the Gifts

God of mercy,
in this eucharist we proclaim the death of the Lord.
Accept the gifts we present
and help us follow him with love,
for he is Lord for ever and ever.

Communion Antiphon: The Lord is my shepherd; there is nothing I shall want. In green pastures he gives me rest, he leads me beside the waters of peace.

or

The disciples recognised the Lord Jesus in the breaking of bread.

Prayer after Communion

Lord,
we thank you for the nourishment you give us
through your holy gift.
Pour out your Spirit upon us
and in the strength of this food from heaven
keep us single-minded in your service.

XXXIII

Entrance Antiphon: The Lord says: my plans for you are peace and not disaster; when you call to me, I will listen to you, and I will bring you back to the place from which I exiled you.

Opening Prayer

Let us pray
 [that God will help us to be faithful]

Father of all that is good,
keep us faithful in serving you,
for to serve you is our lasting joy.
 or
Let us pray
 [with hearts that long for peace]

Father in heaven,
ever-living source of all that is good,
from the beginning of time you promised man salvation
through the future coming of your Son, our Lord Jesus Christ.

Help us to drink of his truth
and expand our hearts with the joy of his promises,
so that we may serve you in faith and in love
and know for ever the joy of your presence.

Prayer over the Gifts

Lord God,
may the gifts we offer
increase our love for you
and bring us to eternal life.

Communion Antiphon: It is good for me to be with the Lord and to put my hope in him.
 or
I tell you solemnly, whatever you ask for in prayer, believe that you have received it, and it will be yours, says the Lord.

Prayer after Communion

Father,
may we grow in love
by the eucharist we have celebrated
in memory of the Lord Jesus,
who is Lord for ever and ever.

XXXIV

Entrance Antiphon: The Lord speaks of peace to his holy people, to those who turn to him with all their heart.

Opening Prayer
Let us pray
  [that the Spirit of God will renew our lives]

Lord,
increase our eagerness to do your will
and help us to know the saving power of your love.

Prayer over the Gifts
God of love,
may the sacrifice we offer
in obedience to your command
renew our resolution to be faithful to your word.

Communion Antiphon: All you nations, praise the Lord, for steadfast is his kindly mercy to us.

or

I, the Lord, am with you always, until the end of the world.

Prayer after Communion
Almighty God,
in this eucharist
you give us the joy of sharing your life.
Keep us in your presence.
Let us never be separated from you.

READINGS FOR WEEKDAYS IN ORDINARY TIME
Year I

ENTER THE KINGDOM AS A CHILD
IT IS NOT HERE OR THERE BUT INSIDE
YOU

FIRST WEEK IN ORDINARY TIME
Year I

MONDAY

FIRST READING

A reading from the letter to the Hebrews 1:1-6
God has spoken to us through his Son.

At various times in the past and in various different ways, God spoke to our ancestors through the prophets; but in our own time, the last days, he has spoken to us through his Son, the Son that he has appointed to inherit everything and through whom he made everything there is. He is the radiant light of God's glory and the perfect copy of his nature, sustaining the universe by his powerful command; and now that he has destroyed the defilement of sin, he has gone to take his place in heaven at the right hand of divine Majesty. So he is now as far above the angels as the title he has inherited is higher than their own name.

God has never said to any angel: You are my Son, today I have become your father; or: I will be a father to him and he a son to me. Again, when he brings the First-born into the world, he says: Let all the angels of God worship him.

This is the word of the Lord.

Responsorial Psalm Ps 96:1-2. 6-7. 9. ℟ cf. v.7

℟ **All you angels, worship the Lord.**

1 The Lord is king, let earth rejoice,
  the many coastlands be glad.
  Cloud and darkness are his raiment;
  his throne, justice and right. ℟

2 The skies proclaim his justice;
  all peoples see his glory.
  All you spirits, worship him. ℟

3 For you indeed are the Lord
  most high above all the earth
  exalted far above all spirits. ℟

Gospel Acclamation cf. Acts 16:14
> Alleluia, alleluia!
> Open our heart, O Lord,
> to accept the words of your Son.
> Alleluia!

or Mk 1:15

> Alleluia, alleluia!
> The kingdom of God is close at hand,
> repent and believe the Good News
> Alleluia!

Alternative Acclamations pp.1277ff.

GOSPEL

A reading from the holy Gospel according to Mark 1:14-20
Repent and believe the Good News.

After John had been arrested, Jesus went into Galilee. There he proclaimed the Good News from God. 'The time has come' he said 'and the kingdom of God is close at hand. Repent, and believe the Good News.'

As he was walking along by the Sea of Galilee he saw Simon and his brother Andrew casting a net in the lake – for they were fishermen. And Jesus said to them, 'Follow me and I will make you into fishers of men.' And at once they left their nets and followed him.

Going on a little further, he saw James son of Zebedee and his brother John; they too were in their boat, mending their nets. He called them at once and, leaving their father Zebedee in the boat with the men he employed, they went after him.

This is the Gospel of the Lord.

In years when the feast of the Baptism of the Lord occurs on Monday of the first week in Ordinary Time, the readings given for Monday may be added to those given for Tuesday, so that the beginning of each book is read.

TUESDAY

FIRST READING

A reading from the letter to the Hebrews 2:5-12
It was appropriate that God should make perfect through suffering the leader who would take them to their salvation.

God did not appoint angels to be rulers of the world to come, and that world is what we are talking about. Somewhere there is a passage that shows us this. It runs: What is man that you should spare a thought for him, the son of man that you should care for him? For a short while you made him lower than the angels; you crowned him with glory and splendour. You have put him in command of everything. Well then, if he has put him in command of everything, he has left nothing which is not under his command. At present, it is true, we are not able to see that everything has been put under his command, but we do see in Jesus one who was for a short while made lower than the angels and is now crowned with glory and splendour because he submitted to death; by God's grace he had to experience death for all mankind.

As it was his purpose to bring a great many of his sons into glory, it was appropriate that God, for whom everything exists and through whom everything exists, should make perfect, through suffering, the leader who would take them to their salvation. For the one who sanctifies, and the ones who are sanctified, are of the same stock; that is why he openly calls them brothers in the text: I shall announce your name to my brothers, praise you in full assembly.

This is the word of the Lord.

Responsorial Psalm Ps 8:2. 5-9. ℟ v.7

℟ **You gave your Son power
over the works of your hand.**

1 How great is your name, O Lord our God,
through all the earth!
What is man that you should keep him in mind,
mortal man that you care for him? ℟

2 Yet you have made him little less than a god;
with glory and honour you crowned him,
gave him power over the works of your hand,
put all things under his feet. ℟

(continued)

3 All of them, sheep and cattle,
yes, even the savage beasts,
birds of the air, and fish
that make their way through the waters.

℟ **You gave your Son power
over the works of your hand.**

Gospel Acclamation   James 1:21
Alleluia, alleluia!
Accept and submit to the word
which has been planted in you
and can save your souls.
Alleluia!

or   cf. 1 Thess 2:13

Alleluia, alleluia!
Accept God's message for what it really is:
God's message, and not some human thinking.
Alleluia!

GOSPEL

A reading from the holy Gospel according to Mark   1:21-28
He taught them with authority.

Jesus and his disciples went as far as Capernaum, and as soon as the sabbath came he went to the synagogue and began to teach. And his teaching made a deep impression on them because, unlike the scribes, he taught them with authority.

In their synagogue just then there was a man possessed by an unclean spirit, and it shouted, 'What do you want with us, Jesus of Nazareth? Have you come to destroy us? I know who you are: the Holy One of God.' But Jesus said sharply, 'Be quiet! Come out of him!' And the unclean spirit threw the man into convulsions and with a loud cry went out of him. The people were so astonished that they started asking each other what it all meant. 'Here is a teaching that is new' they said 'and with authority behind it: he gives orders even to unclean spirits and they obey him.' And his reputation rapidly spread everywhere, through all the surrounding Galilean countryside.

This is the Gospel of the Lord.

WEDNESDAY

FIRST READING

A reading from the letter to the Hebrews 2:14-18

It was essential that he should in this way become completely like his brothers so that he could be compassionate.

Since all the children share the same blood and flesh, Jesus too shared equally in it, so that by his death he could take away all the power of the devil, who had power over death, and set free all those who had been held in slavery all their lives by the fear of death. For it was not the angels that he took to himself; he took to himself descent from Abraham. It was essential that he should in this way become completely like his brothers so that he could be a compassionate and trustworthy high priest of God's religion, able to atone for human sins. That is, because he has himself been through temptation he is able to help others who are tempted.

This is the word of the Lord.

Responsorial Psalm Ps 104:1-4. 6-9. ℟ v.8

℟ **The Lord remembers his covenant for ever.**

or

℟ **Alleluia!**

1 Give thanks to the Lord, tell his name,
 make known his deeds among the peoples.
 O sing to him, sing his praise;
 tell all his wonderful works! ℟

2 Be proud of his holy name,
 let the hearts that seek the Lord rejoice.
 Consider the Lord and his strength;
 constantly seek his face. ℟

3 O children of Abraham, his servant,
 O sons of the Jacob he chose.
 He, the Lord, is our God:
 his judgements prevail in all the earth. ℟

4 He remembers his covenant for ever,
 his promise for a thousand generations,
 the covenant he made with Abraham,
 the oath he swore to Isaac. ℟

Gospel Acclamation   cf. Col 3:16. 17

Alleluia, alleluia!
Let the message of Christ, in all its richness,
find a home with you;
through him give thanks to God the Father.
Alleluia!

or   Jn 10:27

Alleluia, alleluia!
The sheep that belong to me listen to my voice,
says the Lord,
I know them and they follow me.
Alleluia!

GOSPEL

A reading from the holy Gospel according to Mark   1:29-39
He cured many who were suffering from diseases of one kind or another.

On leaving the synagogue, Jesus went with James and John straight to the house of Simon and Andrew. Now Simon's mother-in-law had gone to bed with fever, and they told him about her straightaway. He went to her, took her by the hand and helped her up. And the fever left her and she began to wait on them.

That evening, after sunset, they brought to him all who were sick and those who were possessed by devils. The whole town came crowding round the door, and he cured many who were suffering from diseases of one kind or another; he also cast out many devils, but he would not allow them to speak, because they knew who he was.

In the morning, long before dawn, he got up and left the house, and went off to a lonely place and prayed there. Simon and his companions set out in search of him, and when they found him they said, 'Everybody is looking for you.' He answered, 'Let us go elsewhere, to the neighbouring country towns, so that I can preach there too, because that is why I came.' And he went all through Galilee, preaching in their synagogues and casting out devils.

This is the Gospel of the Lord.

THURSDAY

FIRST READING

A reading from the letter to the Hebrews 3:7-14
As long as this 'today' lasts, keep encouraging one another.

The Holy Spirit says: If only you would listen to him today; do not harden your hearts, as happened in the Rebellion, on the Day of Temptation in the wilderness, when your ancestors challenged me and tested me, though they had seen what I could do for forty years. That was why I was angry with that generation and said: How unreliable these people who refuse to grasp my ways! And so, in anger, I swore that not one would reach the place of rest I had for them. Take care, brothers, that there is not in any one of your community a wicked mind, so unbelieving as to turn away from the living God. Every day, as long as this 'today' lasts, keep encouraging one another so that none of you is hardened by the lure of sin, because we shall remain co-heirs with Christ only if we keep a grasp on our first confidence right to the end.

This is the word of the Lord.

Responsorial Psalm Ps 94:6-11. R̷ v.8

R̷ **O that today you would listen to his voice!**
 'Harden not your hearts.'

1 Come in; let us bow and bend low;
 let us kneel before the God who made us
 for he is our God and we
 the people who belong to his pasture,
 the flock that is led by his hand. R̷

2 O that today you would listen to his voice!
 'Harden not your hearts as at Meribah,
 as on that day at Massah in the desert
 when your fathers put me to the test;
 when they tried me, though they saw my work. R̷

3 For forty years I was wearied of these people
 and I said: ''Their hearts are astray,
 these people do not know my ways.''
 Then I took an oath in my anger:
 ''Never shall they enter my rest.'' ' R̷

Gospel Acclamation Ps 118:88

Alleluia, alleluia!
Because of your love give me life,
and I will do your will.
Alleluia!

or cf. Mt 4:23

Alleluia, alleluia!
Jesus proclaimed the Good News of the kingdom,
and cured all kinds of sickness among the people.
Alleluia!

GOSPEL

A reading from the holy Gospel according to Mark 1:40-45
The leprosy left him and he was cured.

A leper came to Jesus and pleaded on his knees: 'If you want to' he said 'you can cure me.' Feeling sorry for him, Jesus stretched out his hand and touched him. 'Of course I want to!' he said. 'Be cured!' And the leprosy left him at once and he was cured. Jesus immediately sent him away and sternly ordered him, 'Mind you say nothing to anyone, but go and show yourself to the priest, and make the offering for your healing prescribed by Moses as evidence of your recovery.' The man went away, but then started talking about it freely and telling the story everywhere, so that Jesus could no longer go openly into any town, but had to stay outside in places where nobody lived. Even so, people from all around would come to him.

This is the Gospel of the Lord.

FRIDAY

FIRST READING

A reading from the letter to the Hebrews 4:1-5. 11
We must therefore do everything we can to reach this place of rest.

Be careful: the promise of reaching the place of rest God had for the Israelites still holds good, and none of you must think that he has come too late for it. We received the Good News exactly as they did; but hearing the message did them no good because they did not share the faith of those who listened. We, however, who have faith, shall reach a place of rest, as in the text: And so, in anger, I swore that not one would reach the place of rest I had for them. God's work was undoubtedly all finished at the beginning of the world; as one text says, referring to the seventh day: After all his work God rested on the seventh day. The text we are considering says: they shall not reach the place of rest I had for them.

We must therefore do everything we can to reach this place of rest, or some of you might copy this example of disobedience and be lost.

This is the word of the Lord.

Responsorial Psalm   Ps 77:3-4. 6-8. ℟ cf. v.7

℟ **Never forget the deeds of the Lord.**

1. The things we have heard and understood,
   the things our fathers have told us
   we will not hide from their children
   but will tell them to the next generation:
   the glories of the Lord and his might
   and the marvellous deeds he has done. ℟

2. They too should arise and tell their sons
   that they too should set their hope in God
   and never forget God's deeds
   but keep every one of his commands. ℟

3. So that they might not be like their fathers,
   a defiant and rebellious race,
   a race whose heart was fickle,
   whose spirit was unfaithful to God. ℟

Gospel Acclamation   cf. Eph 1:17. 18

Alleluia, alleluia!
May the Father of our Lord Jesus Christ
enlighten the eyes of our mind,
so that we can see what hope his call holds for us.
Alleluia!

or   Lk 7:16

Alleluia, alleluia!
A great prophet has appeared among us;
God has visited his people.
Alleluia!

GOSPEL

A reading from the holy Gospel according to Mark   2:1-12
The Son of Man has authority on earth to forgive sins.

When Jesus returned to Capernaum, word went round that he was back; and so many people collected there that there was no room left, even in front of the door. He was preaching the word to them when some people came bringing him a paralytic carried by four men, but as the crowd made it impossible to get the man to him, they stripped the roof over the place where Jesus was; and when they had made an opening, they lowered the stretcher on which the paralytic lay. Seeing their faith, Jesus said to the paralytic, 'My child, your sins are forgiven.' Now some scribes were sitting there, and they thought to themselves, 'How can this man talk like that? He is blaspheming. Who can forgive sins but God?' Jesus, inwardly aware that this was what they were thinking, said to them, 'Why do you have these thoughts in your hearts? Which of these is easier: to say to the paralytic, "Your sins are forgiven" or to say, "Get up, pick up your stretcher and walk"? But to prove to you that the Son of Man has authority on earth to forgive sins,' – he said to the paralytic – 'I order you: get up, pick up your stretcher, and go off home.' And the man got up, picked up his stretcher at once and walked out in front of everyone, so that they were all astounded and praised God saying, 'We have never seen anything like this.'

This is the Gospel of the Lord.

SATURDAY

FIRST READING

A reading from the letter to the Hebrews   4:12-16
Let us be confident in approaching the throne of grace.

The word of God is something alive and active: it cuts like any double-edged sword but more finely: it can slip through the place where the soul is divided from the spirit, or joints from the marrow; it can judge the secret emotions and thoughts. No created thing can hide from him; everything is uncovered and open to the eyes of the one to whom we must give account of ourselves.

Since in Jesus, the Son of God, we have the supreme high

priest who has gone through to the highest heaven, we must never let go of the faith that we have professed. For it is not as if we had a high priest who was incapable of feeling our weaknesses with us; but we have one who has been tempted in every way that we are, though he is without sin. Let us be confident, then, in approaching the throne of grace, that we shall have mercy from him and find grace when we are in need of help.

This is the word of the Lord.

Responsorial Psalm
Ps 18:8-10. 15. ℟ cf. Jn 6:63

℟ **Your words are spirit, Lord,
and they are life.**

1 The law of the Lord is perfect,
it revives the soul.
The rule of the Lord is to be trusted,
it gives wisdom to the simple. ℟

2 The precepts of the Lord are right,
they gladden the heart.
The command of the Lord is clear,
it gives light to the eyes. ℟

3 The fear of the Lord is holy,
abiding for ever.
The decrees of the Lord are truth
and all of them just. ℟

4 May the spoken words of my mouth,
the thoughts of my heart,
win favour in your sight, O Lord,
my rescuer, my rock! ℟

Gospel Acclamation
Ps 118:29. 35

Alleluia, alleluia!
Bend my heart to your will, O Lord,
and teach me your law.
Alleluia!

or
Lk 4:18

Alleluia, alleluia!
The Lord has sent me to bring the good news to the poor,
to proclaim liberty to captives.
Alleluia!

GOSPEL

A reading from the holy Gospel according to Mark 2:13-17
I did not come to call the virtuous, but sinners.

Jesus went out to the shore of the lake; and all the people came to him, and he taught them. As he was walking on he saw Levi the son of Alphaeus, sitting by the customs house, and he said to him, 'Follow me.' And he got up and followed him.

When Jesus was at dinner in his house, a number of tax collectors and sinners were also sitting at the table with Jesus and his disciples; for there were many of them among his followers. When the scribes of the Pharisee party saw him eating with sinners and tax collectors, they said to his disciples, 'Why does he eat with tax collectors and sinners?' When Jesus heard this he said to them, 'It is not the healthy who need the doctor, but the sick. I did not come to call the virtuous, but sinners.'

This is the Gospel of the Lord.

SECOND WEEK IN ORDINARY TIME
Year I

MONDAY

FIRST READING

A reading from the letter to the Hebrews 5:1-10
Although he was Son, he learnt to obey through suffering.

Every high priest has been taken out of mankind and is appointed to act for men in their relations with God, to offer gifts and sacrifices for sins; and so he can sympathise with those who are ignorant or uncertain because he too lives in the limitations of weakness. That is why he has to make sin offerings for himself as well as for the people. No one takes this honour on himself, but each one is called by God, as Aaron was. Nor did Christ give himself the glory of becoming high priest, but he had it from the one who said to him: You are my son, today I have become your father, and in another text: You are a priest of the order of

Melchizedek, and for ever. During his life on earth, he offered up prayer and entreaty, aloud and in silent tears, to the one who had the power to save him out of death, and he submitted so humbly that his prayer was heard. Although he was Son, he learnt to obey through suffering; but having been made perfect, he became for all who obey him the source of eternal salvation and was acclaimed by God with the title of high priest of the order of Melchizedek.

This is the word of the Lord.

Responsional Psalm

Ps 109:1-4. ℟ v.4

℟ **You are a priest for ever,
a priest like Melchizedek of old.**

1 The Lord's revelation to my Master:
'Sit on my right:
I will put your foes beneath your feet.' ℟

2 The Lord will send from Zion
your sceptre of power:
rule in the midst of all your foes. ℟

3 A prince from the day of your birth
on the holy mountains;
from the womb before the daybreak I begot you. ℟

4 The Lord has sworn an oath he will not change.
'You are a priest for ever,
a priest like Melchizedek of old.' ℟

Gospel Acclamation

cf. 1 Thess 2:13

Alleluia, alleluia!
Accept God's message for what it really is:
God's message, and not some human thinking.
Alleluia!

or

Heb 4:12

Alleluia, alleluia!
The word of God is something alive and active;
it can judge secret emotions and thoughts.
Alleluia!

GOSPEL

A reading from the holy Gospel according to Mark   2:18-22

The bridegroom is with them.

One day when John's disciples and the Pharisees were fasting, some people came and said to Jesus, 'Why is it that John's disciples and the disciples of the Pharisees fast, but your disciples do not?' Jesus replied, 'Surely the bridegroom's attendants would never think of fasting while the bridegroom is still with them? As long as they have the bridegroom with them, they could not think of fasting. But the time will come for the bridegroom to be taken away from them, and then, on that day, they will fast. No one sews a piece of unshrunken cloth on an old cloak; if he does, the patch pulls away from it, the new from the old, and the tear gets worse. And nobody puts new wine into old wineskins; if he does, the wine will burst the skins, and the wine is lost and the skins too. No! New wine, fresh skins!'

This is the Gospel of the Lord.

TUESDAY

FIRST READING

A reading from the letter to the Hebrews   6:10-20

In the hope that is held out to us we have an anchor for our soul, as sure as it is firm.

God would not be so unjust as to forget all you have done, the love that you have for his name or the services you have done, and are still doing, for the saints. Our one desire is that every one of you should go on showing the same earnestness to the end, to the perfect fulfilment of our hopes, never growing careless, but imitating those who have the faith and the perseverance to inherit the promises.

When God made the promise to Abraham, he swore by his own self, since it was impossible for him to swear by anyone greater: I will shower blessings on you and give you many descendants. Because of that, Abraham persevered and saw the promise fulfilled. Men, of course, swear an oath by something greater than themselves, and between men, confirmation by an oath puts an end to all dispute. In the same way, when God wanted to make the heirs to the promise thoroughly realise that

Second Week in Ordinary Time, Year I: Tuesday

his purpose was unalterable, he conveyed this by an oath; so that there would be two unalterable things in which it was impossible for God to be lying, and so that we, now we have found safety, should have a strong encouragement to take a firm grip on the hope that is held out to us. Here we have an anchor for our soul, as sure as it is firm, and reaching right through beyond the veil where Jesus has entered before us and on our behalf, to become a high priest of the order of Melchizedek, and for ever.

This is the word of the Lord.

Responsorial Psalm   Ps 100:1-2. 4-5. 9. 10. ℟ v.5

℟ **The Lord keeps his covenant ever in mind.**

or

℟ **Alleluia!**

1 I will thank the Lord with all my heart
 in the meeting of the just and their assembly.
 Great are the works of the Lord;
 to be pondered by all who love them. ℟

2 He makes us remember his wonders.
 The Lord is compassion and love.
 He gives food to those who fear him;
 keeps his covenant ever in mind. ℟

3 He sent deliverance to his people
 and established his covenant for ever.
 Holy his name, to be feared.
 His praise shall last for ever! ℟

Gospel Acclamation   Ps 118:18
Alleluia, alleluia!
Open my eyes, O Lord, that I may consider
the wonders of your law.
Alleluia!

or   cf. Eph 1:17. 18

Alleluia, alleluia!
May the Father of our Lord Jesus Christ
enlighten the eyes of our mind,
so that we can see what hope his call holds for us
Alleluia!

GOSPEL

A reading from the holy Gospel according to Mark   2:23-28

The sabbath was made for man, not man for the sabbath.

One sabbath day Jesus happened to be taking a walk through the cornfields, and his disciples began to pick ears of corn as they went along. And the Pharisees said to him, 'Look, why are they doing something on the sabbath day that is forbidden?' And he replied, 'Did you never read what David did in his time of need when he and his followers were hungry – how he went into the house of God when Abiathar was high priest, and ate the loaves of offering which only the priests are allowed to eat, and how he also gave some to the men with him?'

And he said to them, 'The sabbath was made for man, not man for the sabbath; so the Son of Man is master even of the sabbath.'

This is the Gospel of the Lord.

WEDNESDAY

FIRST READING

A reading from the letter to the Hebrews   7:1-3. 15-17

You are a priest of the order of Melchizedek, and for ever.

You remember that Melchizedek, king of Salem, a priest of God most High, went to meet Abraham who was on his way back after defeating the kings, and blessed him; and also that it was to him that Abraham gave a tenth of all that he had. By the interpretation of his name, he is, first, 'king of righteousness' and also king of Salem, that is, 'king of peace'; he has no father, mother or ancestry, and his life has no beginning or ending; he is like the Son of God. He remains a priest for ever.

This becomes even more clearly evident when there appears a second Melchizedek, who is a priest not by virtue of a law about physical descent, but by the power of an indestructible life. For it was about him that the prophecy was made: You are a priest of the order of Melchizedek, and for ever.

This is the word of the Lord.

Second Week in Ordinary Time, Year I: Wednesday

Responsorial Psalm   Ps 109:1-4. ℟ v.4

  ℟ **You are a priest for ever,**
     a priest like Melchizedek of old.

1. The Lord's revelation to my Master:
   'Sit on my right:
   I will put your foes beneath your feet.'   ℟

2. The Lord will send from Zion
   your sceptre of power;
   rule in the midst of all your foes.   ℟

3. A prince from the day of your birth
   on the holy mountains;
   from the womb before the daybreak I begot you.   ℟

4. The Lord has sworn an oath he will not change.
   'You are a priest for ever,
   a priest like Melchizedek of old.'   ℟

Gospel Acclamation   Heb 4:12
   Alleluia, alleluia!
   The word of God is something alive and active;
   it can judge secret emotions and thoughts.
   Alleluia!

or   cf. Mt 4:23

   Alleluia, alleluia!
   Jesus proclaimed the Good News of the kingdom,
   and cured all kinds of sickness among the people.
   Alleluia!

GOSPEL

A reading from the holy Gospel according to Mark   3:1-6
Is it against the law on the sabbath day to save life?

Jesus went into a synagogue, and there was a man there who had a withered hand. And they were watching him to see if he would cure him on the sabbath day, hoping for something to use against him. He said to the man with the withered hand, 'Stand up out in the middle!' Then he said to them, 'Is it against the law on the sabbath day to do good, or to do evil; to save life, or to kill?' But they said nothing. Then, grieved to find them so obstinate, he looked angrily round at them, and said to the man, 'Stretch out your hand.' He stretched it out and his hand was better. The

Pharisees went out and at once began to plot with the Herodians against him, discussing how to destroy him.

This is the Gospel of the Lord.

THURSDAY

FIRST READING

A reading from the letter to the Hebrews 7:25–8:6
He offered sacrifices by offering himself once and for all.

The power of Jesus to save is utterly certain, since he is living for ever to intercede for all who come to God through him.

To suit us, the ideal high priest would have to be holy, innocent and uncontaminated, beyond the influence of sinners, and raised up above the heavens; one who would not need to offer sacrifices every day, as the other high priests do for their own sins and then for those of the people, because he has done this once and for all by offering himself. The Law appoints high priests who are men subject to weakness; but the promise on oath, which came after the Law, appointed the Son who is made perfect for ever.

The great point of all that we have said is that we have a high priest of exactly this kind. He has his place at the right of the throne of divine Majesty in the heavens, and he is the minister of the sanctuary and of the true Tent of Meeting which the Lord, and not any man, set up. It is the duty of every high priest to offer gifts and sacrifices, and so this one too must have something to offer. In fact, if he were on earth, he would not be a priest at all, since there are others who make the offerings laid down by the Law and these only maintain the service of a model or a reflection of the heavenly realities. For Moses, when he had the Tent to build, was warned by God who said: See that you make everything according to the pattern shown you on the mountain.

We have seen that he has been given a ministry of a far higher order, and to the same degree it is a better covenant of which he is the mediator, founded on better promises.

This is the word of the Lord.

Second Week in Ordinary Time, Year I: Thursday

Responsorial Psalm   Ps 39:7-10. 17. ℟ cf. vv.8. 9

℟   **Here I am, Lord!**
     I come to do your will.

1. You do not ask for sacrifice and offerings,
   but an open ear.
   You do not ask for holocaust and victim.
   Instead, here am I. ℟

2. In the scroll of the book it stands written
   that I should do your will.
   My God, I will delight in your law
   in the depth of my heart. ℟

3. Your justice I have proclaimed
   in the great assembly.
   My lips I have not sealed;
   you know it, O Lord. ℟

4. O let there be rejoicing and gladness
   for all who seek you.
   Let them ever say: 'The Lord is great',
   who love your saving help. ℟

Gospel Acclamation   cf. Jn 6:63. 68

Alleluia, alleluia!
Your words are spirit, Lord,
and they are life:
you have the message of eternal life.
Alleluia!

or   cf. 2 Tim 1:10

Alleluia, alleluia!
Our Saviour Christ Jesus abolished death,
and he has proclaimed life through the Good News.
Alleluia!

GOSPEL

A reading from the holy Gospel according to Mark   3:7-12

The unclean spirits would shout, 'You are the son of God!' But he warned them strongly not to make him known.

Jesus withdrew with his disciples to the lakeside, and great crowds from Galilee followed him. From Judaea, Jerusalem, Idumaea, Transjordania and the region of Tyre and Sidon, great numbers who had heard of all he was doing came to him. And he asked his disciples to have a boat ready for him because of the crowd, to keep him from being crushed. For he had cured so many that all who were afflicted in any way were crowding forward to touch him. And the unclean spirits, whenever they saw him, would fall down before him and shout, 'You are the Son of God!' But he warned them strongly not to make him known.

This is the Gospel of the Lord.

FRIDAY

FIRST READING

A reading from the letter to the Hebrews 8:6-13
It is a better covenant of which he is the mediator.

We have seen that Jesus has been given a ministry of a far higher order, and to the same degree it is a better covenant of which he is the mediator, founded on better promises. If that first covenant had been without a fault, there would have been no need for a second one to replace it. And in fact God does find fault with them; he says:

> See, the days are coming – it is the Lord who speaks –
> when I will establish a new covenant
> with the House of Israel and the House of Judah,
> but not a covenant like the one I made with their ancestors
> on the day I took them by the hand
> to bring them out of the land of Egypt.
> They abandoned that covenant of mine,
> and so I on my side deserted them. It is the Lord who speaks.
> No, this is the covenant I will make
> with the House of Israel
> when those days arrive – it is the Lord who speaks.
> I will put my laws into their minds
> and write them on their hearts.
> Then I will be their God
> and they shall be my people.
> There will be no further need for neighbour to try to teach neighbour,
> or brother to say to brother,
> 'Learn to know the Lord.'
> No, they will all know me,
> the least no less than the greatest,

since I will forgive their iniquities
and never call their sins to mind.

By speaking of a new covenant, he implies that the first one is already old. Now anything old only gets more antiquated until in the end it disappears.

This is the word of the Lord.

Responsorial Psalm
Ps 84:8. 10-14. ℟ v.11

℟ **Mercy and faithfulness have met.**

1 Let us see, O Lord, your mercy
 and give us your saving help.
 His help is near for those who fear him
 and his glory will dwell in our land. ℟

2 Mercy and faithfulness have met;
 justice and peace have embraced.
 Faithfulness shall spring from the earth
 and justice look down from heaven. ℟

3 The Lord will make us prosper
 and our earth shall yield its fruit.
 Justice shall march before him
 and peace shall follow his steps. ℟

Gospel Acclamation
cf. 2 Thess 2:14

Alleluia, alleluia!
Through the Good News God called us
to share the glory of our Lord Jesus Christ.
Alleluia!

or
2 Cor 5:19

Alleluia, alleluia!
God in Christ was reconciling the world to himself,
and he has entrusted to us the news that they are reconciled.
Alleluia!

GOSPEL

A reading from the holy Gospel according to Mark
3:13-19
He summoned those he wanted to be his companions.

Jesus went up into the hills and summoned those he wanted. So they came to him and he appointed twelve; they were to be his companions and to be sent out to preach, with power to cast out devils. And so he appointed the Twelve: Simon to whom he gave the name Peter, James the son of Zebedee and John the brother of James, to whom he gave the name Boanerges or 'Sons of Thunder'; then Andrew, Philip, Bartholomew, Matthew, Thomas, James the son of Alphaeus, Thaddaeus, Simon the Zealot and Judas Iscariot, the man who was to betray him.

This is the Gospel of the Lord.

SATURDAY

FIRST READING

A reading from the letter to the Hebrews 9:2-3. 11-14
He has entered the sanctuary once and for all through his own blood.

There was a tent which comprised two compartments: the first, in which the lamp-stand, the table and the presentation loaves were kept, was called the Holy Place; then beyond the second veil, an innermost part which was called the Holy of Holies.

But now Christ has come, as the high priest of all the blessings which were to come. He has passed through the greater, the more perfect tent, which is better than the one made by men's hands because it is not of this created order; and he has entered the sanctuary once and for all, taking with him not the blood of goats and bull calves, but his own blood, having won an eternal redemption for us. The blood of goats and bulls and the ashes of a heifer are sprinkled on those who have incurred defilement and they restore the holiness of their outward lives; how much more effectively the blood of Christ, who offered himself as the perfect sacrifice to God through the eternal Spirit, can purify our inner self from dead actions so that we do our service to the living God.

This is the word of the Lord.

Responsorial Psalm Ps 46:2-3. 6-9. ℟ v.6

℟ **God goes up with shouts of joy;**
the Lord goes up with trumpet blast.

1 All peoples, clap your hands,
cry to God with shouts of joy!
For the Lord, the Most High, we must fear,
great king over all the earth. ℟

2 God goes up with shouts of joy;
the Lord goes up with trumpet blast.

Sing praise for God, sing praise,
sing praise to our king, sing praise. ℟

3 God is king of all the earth.
Sing praise with all your skill.
God is king over the nations;
God reigns on his holy throne. ℟

Gospel Acclamation   2 Cor 5:19
Alleluia, alleluia!
God in Christ was reconciling the world to himself,
and he has entrusted to us the news that they are reconciled.
Alleluia!

or   cf. Acts 16:14

Alleluia, alleluia!
Open our heart, O Lord,
to accept the words of your Son.
Alleluia!

GOSPEL

A reading from the holy Gospel according to Mark   3:20-21
His relatives said he was out of his mind.

Jesus went home, and such a crowd collected that they could not even have a meal. When his relatives heard of this, they set out to take charge of him, convinced he was out of his mind.

This is the Gospel of the Lord.

THIRD WEEK IN ORDINARY TIME
Year I
MONDAY

FIRST READING

A reading from the letter of the Hebrews   9:15. 24-28
He sacrificed himself once and for all to do away with sin; when he appears a second time it will be to those who are waiting for him.

Christ brings a new covenant, as the mediator, only so that the people who were called to an eternal inheritance may actually receive what was promised: his death took place to cancel the sins that infringed the earlier covenant. It is not as though Christ had entered a man-made sanctuary which was only modelled on the real one; but it was heaven itself, so that he could appear in the actual presence of God on our behalf. And he does not have to offer himself again and again, like the high priest going into the sanctuary year after year with the blood that is not his own, or else he would have had to suffer over and over again since the world began. Instead of that, he has made his appearance once and for all, now at the end of the last age, to do away with sin by sacrificing himself. Since men only die once, and after that comes judgement, so Christ, too, offers himself only once to take the faults of many on himself, and when he appears a second time, it will not be to deal with sin but to reward with salvation those who are waiting for him.

This is the word of the Lord.

Responsorial Psalm

Ps 97:1-6. ℟ v.1

℟ **Sing a new song to the Lord
for he has worked wonders.**

1   Sing a new song to the Lord
    for he has worked wonders.
    His right hand and his holy arm
    have brought salvation.   ℟

2   The Lord has made known his salvation;
    has shown his justice to the nations.
    He has remembered his truth and love
    for the house of Israel.   ℟

3   All the ends of the earth have seen
    the salvation of our God.
    Shout to the Lord all the earth,
    ring out your joy.   ℟

4   Sing psalms to the Lord with the harp
    with the sound of music.
    With trumpets and the sound of the horn
    acclaim the King, the Lord.   ℟

Gospel Acclamation

Ps 24:4. 5

Alleluia, alleluia!
Teach me your paths, my God,

make me walk in your truth.
Alleluia!

or   cf. 2 Tim 1:10

Alleluia, alleluia!
Our Saviour Christ Jesus abolished death,
and he has proclaimed life through the Good News.
Alleluia!

GOSPEL

A reading from the holy Gospel according to Mark   3:22-30
It is the end of Satan.

The scribes who had come down from Jerusalem were saying: 'Beelzebul is in him' and, 'It is through the prince of devils that he casts devils out.' So Jesus called them to him and spoke to them in parables, 'How can Satan cast out Satan? If a kingdom is divided against itself, that kingdom cannot last. And if a household is divided against itself, that household can never stand. Now if Satanhas rebelled against himself and is divided, he cannot stand either – it is the end of him. But no one can make his way into a strong man's house and burgle his property unless he has tied up the strong man first. Only then can he burgle his house.

'I tell you solemnly, all men's sins will be forgiven, and all their blasphemies: but let anyone blaspheme against the Holy Spirit and he will never have forgiveness: he is guilty of an eternal sin.' This was because they were saying, 'An unclean spirit is in him.'

This is the Gospel of the Lord.

TUESDAY

FIRST READING

A reading from the letter to the Hebrews   10:1-10
God, here I am! I am coming to obey your will.

Since the Law has no more than a reflection of these realities, and no finished picture of them, it is quite incapable of bringing the worshippers to perfection, with the same sacrifices repeatedly offered year after year. Otherwise, the offering of them would have stopped, because the worshippers, when they had been purified once, would have no awareness of sins. Instead of that, the sins are recalled year after year in the sacrifices. Bulls' blood and goats' blood are useless for taking away sins, and this is what he said, on coming into the world:

> You who wanted no sacrifice or oblation,
> prepared a body for me.
> You took no pleasure in holocausts or sacrifices for sin;
> then I said,
> just as I was commanded in the scroll of the book,
> 'God, here I am! I am coming to obey your will.'

Notice that he says first: You did not want what the Law lays down as the things to be offered, that is: the sacrifices, the oblations, the holocausts and the sacrifices for sin, and you took no pleasure in them; and then he says: Here I am! I am coming to obey your will. He is abolishing the first sort to replace it with the second. And this will was for us to be made holy by the offering of his body made once and for all by Jesus Christ.

This is the word of the Lord.

Responsorial Psalm   Ps 39:2. 4. 7-8. 10.11. ℟ cf. vv.8. 9

℟ **Here I am, Lord!**
I come to do your will.

1. I waited, I waited for the Lord
   and he stooped down to me;
   he heard my cry.
   He put a new song into my mouth,
   praise of our God. ℟

2. You do not ask for sacrifice and offerings,
   but an open ear.
   You do not ask for holocaust and victim.
   Instead, here am I. ℟

3. Your justice I have proclaimed
   in the great assembly.
   My lips I have not sealed;
   you know it, O Lord. ℟

4. I have not hidden your justice in my heart
   but declared your faithful help.
   I have not hidden your love and your truth
   from the great assembly. ℟

Gospel Acclamation Ps 118:135

Alleluia, alleluia!
Let your face shine on your servant,
and teach me your decrees.
Alleluia!

or cf. Mt 11:25

Alleluia, alleluia!
Blessed are you, Father,
Lord of heaven and earth,
for revealing the mysteries of the kingdom
to mere children.
Alleluia!

GOSPEL

A reading from the holy Gospel according to Mark 3:31-35
Anyone who does the will of God, that person is my brother and sister and mother.

The mother and brothers of Jesus arrived and, standing outside, sent in a message asking for him. A crowd was sitting round him at the time the message was passed to him, 'Your mother and brothers and sisters are outside asking for you.' He replied, 'Who are my mother and my brothers?' And looking round at those sitting in a circle about him, he said, 'Here are my mother and my brothers. Anyone who does the will of God, that person is my brother and sister and mother.'

This is the Gospel of the Lord.

WEDNESDAY

FIRST READING

A reading from the letter to the Hebrews 10:11-18
He achieved the eternal perfection of all whom he is sanctifying.

All the priests stand at their duties every day, offering over and over again the same sacrifices which are quite incapable of taking sins away. Jesus, on the other hand, has offered one single sacrifice for sins, and then taken his place for ever, at the right hand of God, where he is now waiting until his enemies are made into a footstool for him. By virtue of that one single offering, he has achieved the eternal perfection of all whom he is sanctifying.

The Holy Spirit assures us of this; for he says, first:

> This is the covenant I will make with them
> when those days arrive;

and the Lord then goes on to say:

> I will put my laws into their hearts
> and write them on their minds.
> I will never call their sins to mind,
> or their offences.

When all sins have been forgiven, there can be no more sin offerings.

This is the word of the Lord.

Responsorial Psalm   Ps 109:1-4. ℟ v.4

℟ **You are a priest for ever,
a priest like Melchizedek of old.**

1. The Lord's revelation to my Master:
'Sit on my right:
I will put your foes beneath your feet.'   ℟

2. The Lord will send from Zion
your sceptre of power:
rule in the midst of all your foes.   ℟

3. A prince from the day of your birth
on the holy mountains;
from the womb before the daybreak I begot you.   ℟

4. The Lord has sworn an oath he will not change.
'You are a priest for ever,
a priest like Melchizedek of old.'   ℟

Gospel Acclamation   1 Sam 3:9; Jn 6:68

Alleluia, alleluia!
Speak, Lord, your servant is listening:
you have the message of eternal life.
Alleluia!

or

Alleluia, alleluia!
The seed is the word of God, Christ the sower;
whoever finds this seed will remain for ever.
Alleluia!

GOSPEL

A reading from the holy Gospel according to Mark 4:1-20

Imagine a sower going out to sow.

Jesus began to teach by the lakeside, but such a huge crowd gathered round him that he got into a boat on the lake and sat there. The people were all along the shore, at the water's edge. He taught them many things in parables, and in the course of his teaching he said to them, 'Listen! Imagine a sower going out to sow. Now it happened that, as he sowed, some of the seed fell on the edge of the path, and the birds came and ate it up. Some seed fell on rocky ground where it found little soil and sprang up straightaway, because there was no depth of earth; and when the sun came up it was scorched and, not having any roots, it withered away. Some seed fell into thorns, and the thorns grew up and choked it, and it produced no crop. And some seed fell into rich soil and, growing tall and strong, produced crop; and yielded thirty, sixty, even a hundredfold.' And he said, 'Listen, anyone who has ears to hear!'

When he was alone, the Twelve, together with the others who formed his company, asked what the parables meant. He told them, 'The secret of the kingdom of God is given to you, but to those who are outside everything comes in parables, so that they may see and see again, but not perceive; may hear and hear again, but not understand; otherwise they might be converted and be forgiven.'

He said to them, 'Do you not understand this parable? Then how will you understand any of the parables? What the sower is sowing is the word. Those on the edge of the path where the word is sown are people who have no sooner heard it than Satan comes and carries away the word that was sown in them. Similarly, those who receive the seed on patches of rock are people who, when first they hear the word, welcome it at once with joy. But they have no root in them, they do not last; should some trial come, or some persecution on account of the word, they fall away at once. Then there are others who receive the seed in thorns. These have heard the word, but the worries of this world, the lure of riches and all the other passions come in to choke the word, and so it produces nothing. And there are those who have received the seed in rich soil: they hear the word and accept it and yield a harvest, thirty and sixty and a hundredfold.'

This is the Gospel of the Lord.

THURSDAY

FIRST READING

A reading from the letter to the Hebrews 10:19-25
Let us keep firm in the hope we profess and be concerned for each other, to stir a response in love.

Through the blood of Jesus we have the right to enter the sanctuary, by a new way which he has opened for us, a living opening through the curtain, that is to say, his body. And we have the supreme high priest over all the house of God. So as we go in, let us be sincere in heart and filled with faith, our minds sprinkled and free from any trace of bad conscience and our bodies washed with pure water. Let us keep firm in the hope we profess, because the one who made the promise is faithful. Let us be concerned for each other, to stir a response in love and good works. Do not stay away from the meetings of the community, as some do, but encourage each other to go; the more so as you see the Day drawing near.

This is the word of the Lord.

Responsorial Psalm
Ps 23:1-6. ℟ cf. v.6

℟ **Such are the men who seek your face, O Lord.**

1 The Lord's is the earth and its fullness,
   the world and all its peoples.
   It is he who set it on the seas;
   on the waters he made it firm.   ℟

2 Who shall climb the mountain of the Lord?
   Who shall stand in his holy place?
   The man with clean hands and pure heart,
   who desires not worthless things.   ℟

3 He shall receive blessings from the Lord
   and reward from the God who saves him.
   Such are the men who seek him,
   seek the face of the God of Jacob.   ℟

Gospel Acclamation
Phil 2:15-16
Alleluia, alleluia!
You will shine in the world like bright stars
because you are offering it the word of life.
Alleluia!

or   Ps 118:105

Alleluia, alleluia!
Your word is a lamp for my steps
and a light for my path.
Alleluia!

GOSPEL

A reading from the holy Gospel according to Mark   4:21-25
A lamp is to be put on a lamp-stand. The amount you measure out is the amount you will be given.

Jesus said to the crowd: 'Would you bring in a lamp to put it under a tub or under the bed? Surely you will put it on the lampstand? For there is nothing hidden but it must be disclosed, nothing kept secret except to be brought to light. If anyone has ears to hear, let him listen to this.'

He also said to them, 'Take notice of what you are hearing. The amount you measure out is the amount you will be given – and more besides; for the man who has will be given more; from the man who has not, even what he has will be taken away.'

This is the Gospel of the Lord.

FRIDAY

FIRST READING

A reading from the letter to the Hebrews   10:32-39
Remember all the sufferings you had to meet. Be as confident now.

Remember all the sufferings that you had to meet after you received the light, in earlier days: sometimes by being yourselves publicly exposed to insults and violence, and sometimes as associates of others who were treated in the same way. For you not only shared in the sufferings of those who were in prison, but you happily accepted being stripped of your belongings, knowing that you owned something that was better and lasting. Be as confident now, then, since the reward is so great. You will need endurance to do God's will and gain what he has promised.

Only a little while now, a very little while,
and the one that is coming will have come; he will not delay.
The righteous man will live by faith,

but if he draws back, my soul will take no pleasure in him.

You and I are not the sort of people who draw back, and are lost by it; we are the sort who keep faithful until our souls are saved.

This is the word of the Lord.

Responsorial Psalm   Ps 36:3-6. 23-24. 39-40. ℟ v.39

   ℟ **The salvation of the just comes from the Lord.**

1. If you trust in the Lord and do good,
   then you will live in the land and be secure.
   If you find your delight in the Lord,
   he will grant your heart's desire. ℟

2. Commit your life to the Lord,
   trust in him and he will act,
   so that your justice breaks forth like the light,
   your cause like the noon-day sun. ℟

3. The Lord guides the steps of a man
   and makes safe the path of one he loves.
   Though he stumble he shall never fall
   for the Lord holds him by the hand. ℟

4. The salvation of the just comes from the Lord,
   their stronghold in time of distress.
   The Lord helps them and delivers them
   and saves them: for their refuge is in him. ℟

Gospel Acclamation   Ps 118:27

   Alleluia, alleluia!
   Make me grasp the way of your precepts,
   and I will muse on your wonders.
   Alleluia!

or   cf. Mt 11:25

   Alleluia, alleluia!
   Blessed are you, Father,
   Lord of heaven and earth,
   for revealing the mysteries of the kingdom
   to mere children.
   Alleluia!

GOSPEL

A reading from the holy Gospel according to Mark   4:26-34
A man throws seed on the land. While he sleeps the seed is growing; how, he does not know.

Jesus said to the crowd: 'This is what the kingdom of God is like. A man throws seed on the land. Night and day, while he sleeps, when he is awake, the seed is sprouting and growing; how, he does not know. Of its own accord the land produces first the shoot, then the ear, then the full grain in the ear. And when the crop is ready, he loses no time: he starts to reap because the harvest has come.'

He also said, 'What can we say the kingdom of God is like? What parable can we find for it? It is like a mustard seed which at the time of its sowing in the soil is the smallest of all the seeds on earth; yet once it is sown it grows into the biggest shrub of them all and puts out big branches so that the birds of the air can shelter in its shade.'

Using many parables like these, he spoke the word to them, so far as they were capable of understanding it. He would not speak to them except in parables, but he explained everything to his disciples when they were alone.

This is the Gospel of the Lord.

SATURDAY

FIRST READING

A reading from the letter to the Hebrews   11:1-2. 8-19
He looked forward to a city founded, designed and built by God.

Only faith can guarantee the blessings that we hope for, or prove the existence of the realities that at present remain unseen. It was for faith that our ancestors were commended.

It was by faith that Abraham obeyed the call to set out for a country that was the inheritance given to him and his descendants, and that he set out without knowing where he was going. By faith he arrived, as a foreigner, in the Promised Land, and lived there as if in a strange country, with Isaac and Jacob, who were heirs with him of the same promise. They lived there in tents while he looked forward to a city founded, designed and built by God.

It was equally by faith that Sarah, in spite of being past the age, was made able to conceive, because she believed that he who had made the promise would be faithful to it. Because of this, there came from one man, and one who was already as good as dead himself, more descendants than could be counted, as many as the stars of heaven or the grains of sand on the seashore.

All these died in faith, before receiving any of the things that had been promised, but they saw them in the far distance and welcomed them, recognising that they were only strangers and nomads on earth. People who use such terms about themselves make it quite plain that they are in search of their real homeland. They can hardly have meant the country they came from, since they had the opportunity to go back to it; but in fact they were longing for a better homeland, their heavenly homeland. That is why God is not ashamed to be called their God, since he has founded the city for them.

It was by faith that Abraham, when put to the test, offered up Isaac. He offered to sacrifice his only son even though the promises had been made to him and he had been told: It is through Isaac that your name will be carried on. He was confident that God had the power even to raise the dead; and so, figuratively speaking, he was given back Isaac from the dead.

This is the word of the Lord.

Responsorial Psalm Lk 1:69-75. ℟ cf. v.68

℟ **Blessed be the Lord, the God of Israel!**
He has visited his people and redeemed them.

1 He has raised up for us a mighty saviour
in the house of David his servant,
as he promised by the lips of holy men,
those who were his prophets from of old.   ℟

2 A saviour who would free us from our foes,
from the hands of all who hate us.
So his love for our fathers is fulfilled
and his holy covenant remembered.   ℟

3 He swore to Abraham our father
to grant us, that free from fear,
and saved from the hands of our foes,
we might serve him in holiness and justice
all the days of our life in his presence.   ℟

Gospel Acclamation cf. Ps. 26:11
> Alleluia, alleluia!
> Instruct me, Lord, in your way;
> on an even path lead me.
> Alleluia!

or Jn 3:16

> Alleluia, alleluia!
> God loved the world so much that he gave his only Son;
> everyone who believes in him has eternal life.
> Alleluia!

GOSPEL

A reading from the holy Gospel according to Mark 4:35-41
Who can this be? Even the wind and the sea obey him.

With the coming of evening, Jesus said to his disciples, 'Let us cross over to the other side.' And leaving the crowd behind they took him, just as he was, in the boat; and there were other boats with him. Then it began to blow a gale and the waves were breaking into the boat so that it was almost swamped. But he was in the stern, his head on the cushion, asleep. They woke him and said to him, 'Master, do you not care? We are going down!' And he woke up and rebuked the wind and said to the sea, 'Quiet now! Be calm!' And the wind dropped, and all was calm again. Then he said to them, 'Why are you so frightened? How is it that you have no faith?' They were filled with awe and said to one another, 'Who can this be? Even the wind and the sea obey him.'

This is the Gospel of the Lord.

FOURTH WEEK IN ORDINARY TIME
Year I
MONDAY

FIRST READING

A reading from the letter to the Hebrews 11:32-40
Through faith they conquered kingdoms. God will make provision for us to have something better.

Gideon, Barak, Samson, Jephthah, David, Samuel and the

prophets – these were men who through faith conquered kingdoms, did what is right and earned the promises. They could keep a lion's mouth shut, put out blazing fires and emerge unscathed from battle. They were weak people who were given strength, to be brave in war and drive back foreign invaders. Some came back to their wives from the dead, by resurrection; and others submitted to torture, refusing release so that they would rise again to a better life. Some had to bear being pilloried and flogged, or even chained up in prison. They were stoned, or sawn in half, or beheaded; they were homeless, and dressed in the skins of sheep and goats; they were penniless and were given nothing but ill-treatment. They were too good for the world and they went out to live in deserts and mountains and in caves and ravines. These are all heroes of faith, but they did not receive what was promised, since God had made provision for us to have something better, and they were not to reach perfection except with us.

This is the word of the Lord.

Responsorial Psalm   Ps 30:20-24. R v.25

℟ **Let your heart take courage,**
   all who hope in the Lord.

1 How great is the goodness, Lord,
that you keep for those who fear you,
that you show to those who trust you
in the sight of men. ℟

2 You hide them in the shelter of your presence
from the plotting of men:
you keep them safe within your tent
from disputing tongues. ℟

3 Blessed be the Lord who has shown me
the wonders of his love
in a fortified city. ℟

4 'I am far removed from your sight'
I said in my alarm.
Yet you heard the voice of my plea
when I cried for help. ℟

5 Love the Lord, all you saints.
He guards the faithful
but the Lord will repay to the full
those who act with pride. ℟

Gospel Acclamation cf. Jn 17:17

Alleluia, alleluia!
Your word is truth, O Lord,
consecrate us in the truth.
Alleluia!

or Lk 7:16

Alleluia, alleluia!
A great prophet has appeared among us;
God has visited his people.
Alleluia!

GOSPEL

A reading from the holy Gospel according to Mark 5:1-20
Come out of that man, unclean spirit.

Jesus and his disciples reached the country of the Gerasenes on the other side of the lake, and no sooner had he left the boat than a man with an unclean spirit came out from the tombs towards him. The man lived in the tombs and no one could secure him any more, even with a chain, because he had often been secured with fetters and chains but had snapped the chains and broken the fetters, and no one had the strength to control him. All night and all day, among the tombs and in the mountains, he would howl and gash himself with stones. Catching sight of Jesus from a distance, he ran up and fell at his feet and shouted at the top of his voice, 'What do you want with me, Jesus, son of the Most High God? Swear by God you will not torture me!' – For Jesus had been saying to him, 'Come out of the man, unclean spirit.' 'What is your name?' Jesus asked. 'My name is legion,' he answered 'for there are many of us.' And he begged him earnestly not to send them out of the district. Now there was there on the mountainside a great herd of pigs feeding and the unclean spirits begged him, 'Send us to the pigs, let us go into them.' So he gave them leave. With that, the unclean spirits came out and went into the pigs, and the herd of about two thousand pigs charged down the cliff into the lake, and there they were drowned. The swineherds ran off and told their story in the town and in the country round about; and the people came to see what had really happened. They came to Jesus and saw the demoniac sitting there, clothed and in his full senses – the very man who had had the legion in him before – and they were afraid. And those who had witnessed it reported what had happened to the demoniac and what had become of the pigs. Then they began to implore Jesus to leave the neighbourhood. As he was getting into the boat, the man who had been possessed begged to be allowed to stay with him. Jesus would not let him but said to him, 'Go home to your people and tell them all that the Lord in his mercy has done for you.' So the man went off and proceeded to spread throughout the Decapolis all that Jesus had done for him. And everyone was amazed.

This is the Gospel of the Lord.

TUESDAY

FIRST READING

A reading from the letter to the Hebrews 12:1-4
We should keep running steadily in the race we have started.

With so many witnesses in a great cloud on every side of us, we too, then, should throw off everything that hinders us, especially the sin that clings so easily, and keep running steadily in the race we have started. Let us not lose sight of Jesus, who leads us in our faith and brings it to perfection: for the sake of the joy which was still in the future, he endured the cross, disregarding the shamefulness of it, and from now on has taken his place at the right of God's throne. Think of the way he stood such opposition from sinners and then you will not give up for want of courage. In the fight against sin, you have not yet had to keep fighting to the point of death.

This is the word of the Lord.

Responsorial Psalm Ps 21:26-28. 30-32. R̸ cf. v.27
  R̸ **They shall praise you, Lord,**
      those who seek you.

1 My vows I will pay before those who fear him.
   The poor shall eat and shall have their fill.
   They shall praise the Lord, those who seek him.
   May their hearts live for ever and ever! R̸

2 All the earth shall remember and return to the Lord,
   all families of the nations worship before him.
   They shall worship him, all the mighty of the earth;
   before him shall bow all who go down to the dust. R̸

3 And my soul shall live for him, my children serve him.
They shall tell of the Lord to generations yet to come,
declare his faithfulness to peoples yet unborn:
'These things the Lord has done.' ℟

Gospel Acclamation   Jn 14:6
Alleluia, alleluia!
I am the Way, the Truth and the Life, says the Lord;
no one can come to the Father except through me.
Alleluia!

or   Mt 8:17
Alleluia, alleluia!
He took our sicknesses away,
and carried our diseases for us.
Alleluia!

GOSPEL

A reading from the holy Gospel according to Mark   5:21-43
Little girl, I tell you get up.

When Jesus had crossed in the boat to the other side a large crowd gathered round him and he stayed by the lakeside. Then one of the synagogue officials came up, Jairus by name, and seeing him, fell at his feet and pleaded with him earnestly, saying, 'My little daughter is desperately sick. Do come and lay your hands on her to make her better and save her life.' Jesus went with him and a large crowd followed him; they were pressing all round him.

Now there was a woman who had suffered from a haemorrhage for twelve years; after long and painful treatment under various doctors, she had spent all she had without being any the better for it, in fact, she was getting worse. She had heard about Jesus, and she came up behind him through the crowd and touched his cloak. 'If I can touch even his clothes,' she had told herself 'I shall be well again.' And the source of the bleeding dried up instantly, and she felt in herself that she was cured of her complaint. Immediately aware that power had gone out from him, Jesus turned round in the crowd and said; 'Who touched my clothes?' His disciples said to him, 'You see how the crowd is pressing round you and yet you say, "Who touched me?" ' But he continued to look all round to see who had done it. Then the woman came forward, frightened and trembling because she knew what had happened to her, and she fell at his feet and told him the whole truth. 'My daughter,' he said 'your faith has restored you to health; go in peace and be free from your complaint.'

While he was still speaking some people arrived from the house of the synagogue official to say, 'Your daughter is dead: why put the Master to any further trouble?' But Jesus had overheard this remark of theirs and he said to the official, 'Do not be afraid; only have faith.' And he allowed no one to go with him except Peter and James and John the brother of James. So they came to the official's house and Jesus noticed all the commotion, with people weeping and wailing unrestrainedly. He went in and said to them, 'Why all this commotion and crying? The child is not dead, but asleep.' But they laughed at him. So he turned them all out and, taking with him the child's father and mother and his own companions, he went into the place where the child lay. And taking the child by the hand he said to her, 'Talitha, kum!' which means, 'Little girl, I tell you to get up.' The little girl got up at once and began to walk about, for she was twelve years old. At this they were overcome with astonishment, and he ordered them strictly not to let anyone know about it, and told them to give her something to eat.

This is the Gospel of the Lord.

WEDNESDAY

FIRST READING

A reading from the letter to the Hebrews   12:4-7. 11-15

The Lord trains the ones that he loves.

In the fight against sin, you have not yet had to keep fighting to the point of death.

Have you forgotten that encouraging text in which you are addressed as sons? My son, when the Lord corrects you, do not treat it lightly; but do not get discouraged when he reprimands you. For the Lord trains the ones that he loves and he punishes all those that he acknowledges as his son. Suffering is part of your training; God is treating you as his sons. Has there ever been any son whose father did not train him?

Of course, any punishment is most painful at the time, and far from pleasant; but later, in those on whom it has been used, it

Fourth Week in Ordinary Time, Year I: Wednesday

bears fruit in peace and goodness. So hold up your limp arms and steady your trembling knees and smooth out the path you tread; then the injured limb will not be wrenched, it will grow strong again.

Always be wanting peace with all people, and the holiness without which no one can ever see the Lord. Be careful that no one is deprived of the grace of God and that no root of bitterness should begin to grow and make trouble; this can poison a whole community.

This is the word of the Lord.

Responsorial Psalm   Ps 102:1-2. 13-14. 17-18. ℟ cf. v.17

℟ **The love of the Lord is everlasting upon those who hold him in fear.**

1 My soul, give thanks to the Lord,
all my being, bless his holy name.
My soul, give thanks to the Lord
and never forget all his blessings. ℟

2 As a father has compassion on his sons,
the Lord has pity on those who fear him;
for he knows of what we are made,
he remembers that we are dust. ℟

3 But the love of the Lord is everlasting
upon those who hold him in fear;
his justice reaches out to children's children
when they keep his covenant in truth. ℟

Gospel Acclamation   Mt 4:4
Alleluia, alleluia!
Man does not live on bread alone,
but on every word that comes from the mouth of God.
Alleluia!

or   Jn 10:27

Alleluia, alleluia!
The sheep that belong to me listen to my voice,
says the Lord,
I know them and they follow me.
Alleluia!

GOSPEL

A reading from the holy Gospel according to Mark   6:1-6
A prophet is only despised in his own country.

Jesus went to his home town and his disciples accompanied him. With the coming of the sabbath he began teaching in the synagogue and most of them were astonished when they heard him. They said, 'Where did the man get all this? What is this wisdom that has been granted him, and these miracles that are worked through him? This is the carpenter, surely, the son of Mary, the brother of James and Joset and Jude and Simon? His sisters, too, are they not here with us?' And they would not accept him. And Jesus said to them, 'A prophet is only despised in his own country, among his own relations and in his own house'; and he could work no miracle there, though he cured a few sick people by laying his hands on them.

    This is the Gospel of the Lord.

THURSDAY

FIRST READING

A reading from the letter to the Hebrews   12:18-19. 21-24
What you have come to is Mount Zion and the city of the living God.

What you have come to is nothing known to the senses: not a blazing fire, or a gloom turning to total darkness, or a storm; or trumpeting thunder or the great voice speaking which made everyone that heard it beg that no more should be said to them. The whole scene was so terrible that Moses said: I am afraid, and was trembling with fright. But what you have come to is Mount Zion and the city of the living God, the heavenly Jerusalem where the millions of angels have gathered for the festival, with the whole Church in which everyone is a 'first-born son' and a citizen of heaven. You have come to God himself, the supreme Judge, and been placed with spirits of the saints who have been made perfect; and to Jesus, the mediator who brings a new covenant and a blood for purification which pleads more insistently than Abel's.

    This is the word of the Lord.

Fourth Week in Ordinary Time, Year I: Thursday

Responsorial Psalm   Ps 47:2-4. 9-11. ℟ cf. v.10

℟ **O God, we ponder your love within your temple.**

1 The Lord is great and worthy to be praised
in the city of our god.
His holy mountain rises in beauty,
the joy of all the earth. ℟

2 Mount Zion, true pole of the earth,
the Great King's city!
God, in the midst of its citadels,
has shown himself its stronghold. ℟

3 As we have heard, so we have seen
in the city of our God,
in the city of the Lord of hosts
which God upholds for ever. ℟

4 O God, we ponder your love
within your temple.
Your praise, O God, like your name
reaches to the ends of the earth.
With justice your right hand is filled. ℟

Gospel Acclamation   Jn 15:15

Alleluia, alleluia!
I call you friends, says the Lord,
because I have made known to you
everything I have learnt from my Father.
Alleluia!

or   Mk 1:15

Alleluia, alleluia!
The kingdom of God is close at hand,
repent and believe the Good News.
Alleluia!

GOSPEL

A reading from the holy Gospel according to Mark   6:7-13
He began to send them out.

Jesus made a tour round the villages, teaching. Then he summoned the Twelve and began to send them out in pairs giving them authority over the unclean spirits. And he instructed them to take nothing for the journey except a staff – no bread, no haversack, no coppers for their purses. They were to wear sandals but, he added, 'Do not take a spare tunic.' And he said to them, 'If you enter a house anywhere, stay there until you leave the district. And if any place does not welcome you and people refuse to listen to you, as you walk away shake off the dust from under your feet as a sign to them.' So they set off to preach repentance; and they cast out many devils, and anointed many sick people with oil and cured them.

This is the Gospel of the Lord.

FRIDAY

FIRST READING

A reading from the letter to the Hebrews   13:1-8

Jesus Christ is the same today as he was yesterday and as he will be for ever.

Continue to love each other like brothers, and remember always to welcome strangers, for by doing this, some people have entertained angels without knowing it. Keep in mind those who are in prison, as though you were in prison with them; and those who are being badly treated, since you too are in the one body. Marriage is to be honoured by all, and marriages are to be kept undefiled, because fornicators and adulterers will come under God's judgement. Put greed out of your lives and be content with whatever you have; God himself has said: I will not fail you or desert you, and so we can say with confidence: With the Lord to help me, I fear nothing: what can man do to me?

Remember your leaders, who preached the word of God to you, and as you reflect on the outcome of their lives, imitate their faith. Jesus Christ is the same today as he was yesterday and as he will be for ever.

This is the word of the Lord.

Responsorial Psalm   Ps 26:1. 3. 5. 8-9. ℟ v.1
 ℟ **The Lord is my light and my help.**

1   The Lord is my light and my help;
    whom shall I fear?
    The Lord is the stronghold of my life;
    before whom shall I shrink? ℟

Fourth Week in Ordinary Time, Year I: Friday

2 Though an army encamp against me
   my heart would not fear.
   Though war break out against me
   even then would I trust.   ℞

3 For there he keeps me safe in his tent
   in the day of evil.
   He hides me in the shelter of his tent,
   on a rock he sets me safe.   ℞

4 It is your face, O Lord, that I seek;
   hide not your face.
   Dismiss not your servant in anger;
   you have been my help.   ℞

Gospel Acclamation   cf. Lk 8:15
Alleluia, alleluia!
Blessed are those who,
with a noble and generous heart,
take the word of God to themselves
and yield a harvest through their perseverance.
Alleluia!

GOSPEL

A reading from the holy Gospel according to Mark   6:14-29
It is John whose head I have cut off. He has risen from the dead.

King Herod had heard about Jesus, since by now his name was well-known. Some were saying, 'John the Baptist has risen from the dead, and that is why miraculous powers are at work in him.' Others said, 'He is Elijah'; others again, 'He is a prophet, like the prophets we used to have.' But when Herod heard this he said, 'It is John whose head I cut off; he has risen from the dead.'

Now it was this same Herod who had sent to have John arrested, and had him chained up in prison because of Herodias, his brother Philip's wife whom he had married. For John had told Herod, 'It is against the law for you to have your brother's wife.' As for Herodias, she was furious with him and wanted to kill him; but she was not able to, because Herod was afraid of John, knowing him to be a good and holy man, and gave him his protection. When he had heard him speak he was greatly perplexed, and yet he liked to listen to him.

An opportunity came on Herod's birthday when he gave a

banquet for the nobles of his court, for his army officers and for the leading figures in Galilee. When the daughter of this same Herodias came in and danced, she delighted Herod and his guests; so the king said to the girl, 'Ask me anything you like and I will give it you.' And he swore her an oath, 'I will give you anything you ask, even half my kingdom.' She went out and said to her mother, 'What shall I ask for?' She replied, 'The head of John the Baptist.' The girl hurried straight back to the king and made her request, 'I want you to give me John the Baptist's head, here and now, on a dish.' The king was deeply distressed but, thinking of the oaths he had sworn and of his guests, he was reluctant to break his word to her. So the king at once sent one of the bodyguard with orders to bring John's head. The man went off and beheaded him in prison; then he brought the head on a dish and gave it to the girl, and the girl gave it to her mother. When John's disciples heard about this, they came and took his body and laid it in a tomb.

This is the Gospel of the Lord.

SATURDAY

FIRST READING

A reading from the letter to the Hebrews   13:15-17. 20-21

May the God of peace, who brought back from the dead the great Shepherd, make you ready to do his will in any kind of good action.

Through Jesus, let us offer God an unending sacrifice of praise, a verbal sacrifice that is offered every time we acknowledge his name. Keep doing good works and sharing your resources, for these are sacrifices that please God.

Obey your leaders and do as they tell you, because they must give an account of the way they look after your souls; make this a joy for them to do, and not a grief – you yourselves would be the losers.

I pray that the God of peace, who brought our Lord Jesus back from the dead to become the great Shepherd of the sheep by the blood that sealed an eternal covenant, may make you ready to do his will in any kind of good action; and turn us all into whatever is acceptable to himself through Jesus Christ, to whom be glory for ever and ever, Amen.

This is the word of the Lord.

Fourth Week in Ordinary Time, Year I: Saturday

Responsional Psalm Ps 22. ℟ v.1

℟ **The Lord is my shepherd;
there is nothing I shall want.**

1 The Lord is my shepherd;
   there is nothing I shall want.
   Fresh and green are the pastures
   where he gives me repose.
   Near restful waters he leads me,
   to revive my drooping spirit. ℟

2 He guides me along the right path;
   he is true to his name.
   If I should walk in the valley of darkness
   no evil would I fear.
   You are there with your crook and your staff;
   with these you give me comfort. ℟

3 You have prepared a banquet for me
   in the sight of my foes.
   My head you have anointed with oil;
   my cup is overflowing. ℟

4 Surely goodness and kindness shall follow me
   all the days of my life.
   In the Lord's own house shall I dwell
   for ever and ever. ℟

Gospel Acclamation Jn 10:27

Alleluia, alleluia!
The sheep that belong to me listen to my voice,
says the Lord,
I know them and they follow me.
Alleluia!

GOSPEL

A reading from the holy Gospel according to Mark 6:30-34
They were like sheep without a shepherd.

The apostles rejoined Jesus and told him all they had done and taught. Then he said to them, 'You must come away to some lonely place all by yourselves and rest for a while'; for there were so many coming and going that the apostles had no time even to eat. So they went off in a boat to a lonely place where they could be by themselves. But people saw them going, and many could guess where; and from every town they all hurried to the place on foot and reached it before them. So as he stepped ashore he saw a large crowd; and he took pity on them because they were like sheep without a shepherd, and he set himself to teach them at some length.

This is the Gospel of the Lord.

FIFTH WEEK IN ORDINARY TIME
Year I

MONDAY

FIRST READING

A reading from the book of Genesis 1:1-19
God said, and so it was.

In the beginning God created the heavens and the earth. Now the earth was a formless void, there was darkness over the deep, and God's spirit hovered over the water.

God said, 'Let there be light,' and there was light. God saw that light was good, and God divided light from darkness. God called light 'day,' and darkness he called 'night'. Evening came and morning came: the first day.

God said, 'Let there be a vault in the waters to divide the waters in two.' And so it was. God made the vault, and it divided the waters above the vault from the waters under the vault. God called the vault 'heaven'. Evening came and morning came: the second day.

God said, 'Let the waters under heaven come together into a single mass, and let dry land appear.' And so it was. God called the dry land 'earth' and the mass of waters 'seas', and God saw that it was good.

God said, 'Let the earth produce vegetation: seed-bearing plants, and trees bearing fruit with their seed inside, on the earth.' And so it was. The earth produced vegetation: plants bearing seed in their several kinds, and trees bearing fruit with their seed inside in their several kinds. God saw that it was good. Evening came and morning came: the third day.

God said, 'Let there be lights in the vault of heaven to divide day from night, and let them indicate festivals, days and years. Let them be lights in the vault of heaven to shine on the earth.'

Fifth Week in Ordinary Time, Year I: Monday

And so it was God made the two great lights: the greater light to govern the day, the smaller light to govern the night, and the stars. God set them in the vault of heaven to shine on the earth, to govern the day and the night and to divide light from darkness. God saw that it was good. Evening came and morning came: the fourth day.

This is the word of the Lord.

Responsorial Psalm Ps 103:1-2. 5-6. 10. 12. 24. 35. ℟ v.31

℟ **May the Lord rejoice in his works!**

1 Bless the Lord, my soul!
   Lord God, how great you are,
   clothed in majesty and glory,
   wrapped in light as in a robe! ℟

2 You founded the earth on its base,
   to stand firm from age to age.
   You wrapped it with the ocean like a cloak:
   the waters stood higher than the mountains. ℟

3 You make springs gush forth in the valleys:
   they flow in between the hills.
   On their banks dwell the birds of heaven;
   from the branches they sing their song. ℟

4 How many are your works, O Lord!
   In wisdom you have made them all.
   The earth is full of your riches.
   Bless the Lord, my soul! ℟

Gospel Acclamation Jn 8:12
Alleluia, alleluia!
I am the light of the world, says the Lord
anyone who follows me
will have the light of life.
Alleluia!

or cf. Mt 4:23

Alleluia, alleluia!
Jesus proclaimed the Good News of the kingdom,
and cured all kinds of sickness among the people.
Alleluia!

GOSPEL

A reading from the holy Gospel according to Mark 6:53-56
All those who touched him were cured.

Having made the crossing, Jesus and his disciples came to land at Genessaret and tied up. No sooner had they stepped out of the boat than people recognised him, and started hurrying all through the countryside and brought the sick on stretchers to wherever they heard he was. And wherever he went, to village, or town, or farm, they laid down the sick in the open spaces, begging him to let them touch even the fringe of his cloak. And all those who touched him were cured.

This is the Gospel of the Lord.

TUESDAY

FIRST READING

A reading from the book of Genesis 1:20–2:4
Let us make man in our own image, in the likeness of ourselves.

God said, 'Let the waters teem with living creatures, and let birds fly above the earth within the vault of heaven.' And so it was. God created great sea-serpents and every kind of living creature with which the waters teem, and every kind of winged creature.

God saw that it was good. God blessed them, saying, 'Be fruitful, multiply, and fill the waters of the seas; and let the birds multiply upon the earth.' Evening came and morning came: the fifth day.

God said, 'Let the earth produce every kind of living creature: cattle, reptiles, and every kind of wild beast.' And so it was. God made every kind of wild beast, every kind of cattle, and every kind of land reptile. God saw that it was good.

God said, 'Let us make man in our own image, in the likeness of ourselves, and let them be masters of the fish of the sea, the birds of heaven, the cattle, all the wild beasts and all the reptiles that crawl upon the earth.'

God created man in the image of himself,
in the image of God he created him,
male and female he created them.

God blessed them, saying to them, 'Be fruitful, multiply, fill the earth and conquer it. Be masters of the fish of the sea, the birds of heaven and all living animals on the earth.' God said, 'See, I give you all the seed-bearing plants that are upon the whole earth, and all the trees with seed-bearing fruit; this shall be your food. To all wild beasts, all birds of heaven and all living reptiles on the earth I give all the foliage of plants for food.' And so it was. God saw all he had made, and indeed it was very good. Evening came and morning came: the sixth day.

Thus heaven and earth were completed with all their array. On the seventh day God completed the work he had been doing. He rested on the seventh day after all the work he had been doing. God blessed the seventh day and made it holy, because on that day he had rested after all his work of creating.

Such were the origins of heaven and earth when they were created.

This is the word of the Lord.

Responsorial Psalm   Ps 8:4-9. ℟ v.2

℟ **How great is your name,
O Lord our God,
through all the earth!**

1 When I see the heavens, the work of your hands,
the moon and the stars which you arranged,
what is man that you should keep him in mind,
mortal man that you care for him? ℟

2 Yet you have made him little less than a god;
with glory and honour you crowned him,
gave him power over the works of your hand,
put all things under his feet. ℟

3 All of them, sheep and cattle,
yes, even the savage beasts,
birds of the air, and fish
that make their way through the waters. ℟

Gospel Acclamation   Ps 118:34

Alleluia, alleluia!
Train me, Lord, to observe your law,
to keep it with my heart.
Alleluia!

or   Ps 118:36. 29

> Alleluia, alleluia!
> Bend my heart to your will, O Lord,
> and teach me your law.
> Alleluia!

GOSPEL

A reading from the holy Gospel according to Mark 7:1-13
You put aside the commandment of God to cling to human traditions.

The Pharisees and some of the scribes who had come from Jerusalem gathered round Jesus, and they noticed that some of his disciples were eating with unclean hands, that is, without washing them. For the Pharisees, and the Jews in general, follow the tradition of the elders and never eat without washing their arms as far as the elbow; and on returning from the market place they never eat without first sprinkling themselves. There are also many other observances which have been handed down to them concerning the washing of cups and pots and bronze dishes. So these Pharisees and scribes asked him, 'Why do your disciples not respect the tradition of the elders but eat their food with unclean hands?' He answered, 'It was of you hypocrites that Isaiah so rightly prophesied in this passage of scripture:

> This people honours me only with lip-service,
> while their hearts are far from me.
> The worship they offer me is worthless,
> the doctrines they teach are only human regulations.

You put aside the commandment of God to cling to human traditions.' And he said to them. 'How ingeniously you get round the commandment of God in order to preserve your own tradition! For Moses said: Do your duty to your father and your mother, and, Anyone who curses father or mother must be put to death. But you say, "If a man says to his father or mother: Anything I have that I might have used to help you is Corban (that is, dedicated to God), then he is forbidden from that moment to do anything for his father or mother." In this way you make God's word null and void for the sake of your tradition which you have handed down. And you do many other things like this.'

This is the Gospel of the Lord.

WEDNESDAY

FIRST READING

A reading from the book of Genesis 2:4-9. 15-17

The Lord God took the man and settled him in the garden of Eden.

At the time when the Lord God made earth and heaven there was as yet no wild bush on the earth nor had any wild plant yet sprung up, for the Lord God had not sent rain on the earth, nor was there any man to till the soil. However, a flood was rising from the earth and watering all the surface of the soil. The Lord God fashioned man of dust from the soil. Then he breathed into his nostrils a breath of life, and thus man became a living being.

The Lord God planted a garden in Eden which is in the east, and there he put the man he had fashioned. The Lord God caused to spring up from the soil every kind of tree, enticing to look at and good to eat, with the tree of life and the tree of the knowledge of good and evil in the middle of the garden. The Lord God took the man and settled him in the garden of Eden to cultivate and take care of it. Then the Lord God gave the man this admonition, 'You may eat indeed of all the trees in the garden. Nevertheless of the tree of the knowledge of good and evil you are not to eat, for on the day you eat of it you shall most surely die.'

This is the word of the Lord.

Responsorial Psalm Ps 103:1-2. 27-30. R̷ v.1

℟ **Bless the Lord, my soul!**

1 Bless the Lord my soul!
  Lord God, how great you are,
  clothed in majesty and glory,
  wrapped in light as in a robe. ℟

2 All of these look to you
  to give them their food in due season.
  You give it, they gather it up:
  you open your hand, they have their fill. ℟

3 You take back your spirit, they die,
  returning from the dust from which they came.
  You send forth your spirit, they are created;
  and you renew the face of the earth. ℟

Gospel Acclamation cf. 2 Tim 1:10
> Alleluia, alleluia!
> Our Saviour Christ Jesus abolished death,
> and he has proclaimed life through the Good News.
> Alleluia!

or cf. Jn 17:17
> Alleluia, alleluia!
> Your word is truth, O Lord,
> consecrate us in the truth.
> Alleluia!

GOSPEL

A reading from the holy Gospel according to Mark 7:14-23

It is what comes out of a man that makes him unclean.

Jesus called the people to him and said, 'Listen to me, all of you, and understand. Nothing that goes into a man from outside can make him unclean; it is the things that come out of a man that make him unclean. If anyone has ears to hear, let him listen to this.'

When he had gone back into the house, away from the crowd, his disciples questioned him about the parable. He said to them, 'Do you not understand either? Can you not see that whatever goes into a man from outside cannot make him unclean, because it does not go into his heart but through his stomach and passes out in the sewer?' (Thus he pronounced all foods clean.) And he went on, 'It is what comes out of a man that makes him unclean. For it is from within, from men's hearts, that evil intentions emerge: fornication, theft, murder, adultery, avarice, malice, deceit, indecency, envy, slander, pride, folly. All these evil things come from within and make a man unclean.'

This is the Gospel of the Lord.

THURSDAY

FIRST READING

A reading from the book of Genesis 2:18-25

He brought her to the man. They became one body.

The Lord God said, 'It is not good that the man should be alone. I will make him a helpmate.' So from the soil the Lord God fashioned all the wild beasts and all the birds of heaven. These he brought to the man to see what he would call them; each one was to bear the name the man would give it. The man gave names to all the cattle, all the birds of heaven, and all the wild beasts. But no helpmate suitable for man was found for him. So the Lord God made the man fall into a deep sleep. And while he slept, he took one of his ribs and enclosed it in flesh. The Lord God built the rib he had taken from the man into a woman, and brought her to the man. The man exclaimed:

'This at last is bone from my bones,
and flesh from my flesh!
This is to be called woman,
for this was taken from man.'

This is why a man leaves his father and mother and joins himself to his wife, and they become one body.

Now both of them were naked, the man and his wife, but they felt no shame in front of each other.

This is the word of the Lord.

Responsorial Psalm
Ps 127:1-5. ℟ cf. v.1

℟ **O blessed are those who fear the Lord.**

1 O blessed are those who fear the Lord
and walk in his ways!
By the labour of your hands you shall eat.
You will be happy and prosper. ℟

2 Your wife like a fruitful vine
in the heart of your house;
your children like shoots of the olive
around your table. ℟

3 Indeed thus shall be blessed
the man who fears the Lord.
May the Lord bless you from Zion
all the days of your life! ℟

Gospel Acclamation
Ps 144:13
Alleluia, alleluia!
The Lord is faithful in all his words
and loving in all his deeds.
Alleluia!

or James 1:21

Alleluia, alleluia!
Accept and submit to the word
which has been planted in you
and can save your souls.
Alleluia!

GOSPEL

A reading from the holy Gospel according to Mark 7:24-30

The house-dogs under the table can eat the children's scraps.

Jesus left Gennesaret and set out for the territory of Tyre. There he went into a house and did not want anyone to know he was there, but he could not pass unrecognised. A woman whose little daughter had an unclean spirit heard about him straightaway and came and fell at his feet. Now the woman was a pagan, by birth a Syrophoenician, and she begged him to cast the devil out of her daughter. And he said to her, 'The children should be fed first, because it is not fair to take the children's food and throw it to the house-dogs.' But she spoke up: 'Ah yes, sir,' she replied, 'but the house-dogs under the table can eat the children's scraps.' And he said to her, 'For saying this, you may go home happy: the devil has gone out of your daughter.' So she went off to her home and found the child lying on the bed and the devil gone.

This is the Gospel of the Lord.

FRIDAY

FIRST READING

A reading from the book of Genesis 3:1-8

You will be like gods, knowing good and evil.

The serpent was the most subtle of all the wild beasts that the Lord God had made. It asked the woman, 'Did God really say you were not to eat from any of the trees in the garden?' The woman answered the serpent, 'We may eat the fruit of the trees in the garden. But of the fruit of the tree in the middle of the garden God said, "You must not eat it, nor touch it, under pain of death." ' Then the serpent said to the woman, 'No! You will not die! God knows in fact that on the day you eat it your eyes will be opened and you will be like gods, knowing good and evil.' The

Fifth Week in Ordinary Time, Year I: Friday

woman saw that the tree was good to eat and pleasing to the eye, and that it was desirable for the knowledge that it could give. So she took some of its fruit and ate it. She gave some also to her husband who was with her, and he ate it. Then the eyes of both of them were opened and they realised that they were naked. So they sewed fig-leaves together to make themselves loin-cloths.

The man and his wife heard the sound of the Lord God walking in the garden in the cool of the day, and they hid from the Lord God among the trees of the garden.

This is the word of the Lord.

Responsorial Psalm   Ps 31:1-2. 5-7. R/ v.1

℟ **Happy the man whose offence is forgiven.**

1. Happy the man whose offence is forgiven,
   whose sin is remitted.
   O happy the man to whom the Lord
   imputes no guilt,
   in whose spirit is no guile.   ℟

2. But now I have acknowledged my sins;
   my guilt I did not hide.
   I said: 'I will confess
   my offence to the Lord.'
   And you, Lord, have forgiven
   the guilt of my sin.   ℟

3. So let every good man pray to you
   in the time of need.
   The floods of water may reach high
   but him they shall not reach.   ℟

4. You are my hiding place, O Lord;
   you save me from distress.
   You surround me with cries of deliverance.   ℟

Gospel Acclamation   cf. Jn 6:63. 68
Alleluia, alleluia!
Your words are spirit, Lord,
and they are life:
you have the message of eternal life.
Alleluia!

or   cf. Acts 16:14

Alleluia, alleluia!
Open our heart, O Lord,
to accept the words of your Son.
Alleluia!

GOSPEL

A reading from the holy Gospel according to Mark   7:31-37
He makes the deaf hear and the dumb speak.

Returning from the district of Tyre, Jesus went by way of Sidon towards the Sea of Galilee, right through the Decapolis region. And they brought him a deaf man who had an impediment in his speech; and they asked him to lay his hand on him. He took him aside in private, away from the crowd, put his fingers into the man's ears and touched his tongue with spittle. Then looking up to heaven he sighed; and he said to him, 'Ephphatha,' that is, 'Be opened.' And his ears were opened, and the ligament of his tongue was loosened and he spoke clearly. And Jesus ordered them to tell no one about it, but the more he insisted, the more widely they published it. Their admiration was unbounded. 'He has done all things well,' they said 'he makes the deaf hear and the dumb speak.'

This is the Gospel of the Lord.

SATURDAY

FIRST READING

A reading from the book of Genesis   3:9-24
The Lord God expelled him from the garden of Eden, to till the soil.

The Lord God called to the man. 'Where are you?' he asked. 'I heard the sound of you in the garden,' he replied 'I was afraid because I was naked, so I hid.' 'Who told you that you were naked?' he asked. 'Have you been eating of the tree I forbade you to eat?' The man replied, 'It was the woman you put with me; she gave me the fruit, and I ate it.' Then the Lord God asked the woman, 'What is this you have done?' The woman replied, 'The serpent tempted me and I ate.'

Then the Lord God said to the serpent, 'Because you have done this,

'Be accursed beyond all cattle,
all wild beasts.
You shall crawl on your belly and eat dust
every day of your life.
I will make you enemies of each other:
you and the woman,
your offspring and her offspring.
It will crush your head
and you will strike its heel.'

To the woman he said:

'I will multiply your pains in childbearing,
you shall give birth to your children in pain.
Your yearning shall be for your husband,
yet he will lord it over you.'

To the man he said, 'Because you listened to the voice of your wife and ate from the tree of which I had forbidden you to eat,

'Accursed be the soil because of you.
With suffering shall you get your food from it
every day of your life.
It shall yield you brambles and thistles,
and you shall eat wild plants.
With sweat on your brow
shall you eat your bread,
until you return to the soil,
as you were taken from it.
For dust you are
and to dust you shall return.'

The man named his wife 'Eve' because she was the mother of all those who live. The Lord God made clothes out of skins for the man and his wife, and they put them on. Then the Lord God said, 'See, the man has become like one of us, with his knowlege of good and evil. He must not be allowed to stretch his hand out next and pick from the tree of life also, and eat some and live for ever.' So the Lord God expelled him from the garden of Eden, to till the soil from which he had been taken. He banished the man, and in front of the garden of Eden he posted cherubs, and the flame of a flashing sword, to guard the way to the tree of life.

This is the word of the Lord.

Responsorial Psalm   Ps 89:2-6. 12-13. R̸ v.1

    R̸ **O Lord, you have been our refuge
from one generation to the next.**

1 Before the mountains were born
or the earth or the world brought forth,
you are God, without beginning or end.   R̸

2 You turn men back into dust
and say: 'Go back, sons of men.'
To your eyes a thousand years
are like yesterday, come and gone,
no more than a watch in the night.   R̸

3 You sweep men away like a dream,
like grass which springs up in the morning.
In the morning it springs up and flowers:
by evening it withers and fades.   R̸

4 Make us know the shortness of our life
that we may gain wisdom of heart.
Lord, relent! Is your anger for ever?
Show pity on your servants.   R̸

Gospel Acclamation   Mt 4:4
Alleluia, alleluia!
Man does not live on bread alone,
but on every word that comes from the mouth of God.
Alleluia!

GOSPEL

A reading from the holy Gospel according to Mark   8:1-10
They ate as much as they wanted.

A great crowd had gathered, and they had nothing to eat. So Jesus called his disciples to him and said to them, 'I feel sorry for all these people; they have been with me for three days now and have nothing to eat. If I send them off home hungry they will collapse on the way; some have come a great distance.' His disciples replied, 'Where could anyone get bread to feed these people in a deserted place like this?' He asked them, 'How many loaves have you?' 'Seven' they said. Then he instructed the crowd to sit down on the ground, and he took the seven loaves, and after giving thanks he broke them and handed them to his disciples to distribute; and they distributed them among the crowd. They had a few small fish as well, and over these he said a blessing and ordered them to be distributed also. They ate as much as they wanted, and they collected seven basketfuls of the scraps left over. Now there had been about four thousand people. He sent them away and immediately, getting into the boat with his disciples, went to the region of Dalmanutha.

This is the Gospel of the Lord.

SIXTH WEEK IN ORDINARY TIME
Year I

MONDAY

FIRST READING

A reading from the book of Genesis 4:1-15. 25

Cain set on his brother Abel and killed him.

The man had intercourse with his wife Eve, and she conceived and gave birth to Cain. 'I have acquired a man with the help of the Lord' she said. She gave birth to a second child, Abel, the brother of Cain. Now Abel became a shepherd and kept flocks, while Cain tilled the soil. Time passed and Cain brought some of the produce of the soil as an offering for the Lord, while Abel for his part brought the first-born of his flock and some of their fat as well. The Lord looked with favour on Abel and his offering. But he did not look with favour on Cain and his offering, and Cain was very angry and downcast. The Lord asked Cain, 'Why are you angry and downcast? If you are well disposed, ought you not to lift up your head? But if you are ill disposed, is not sin at the door like a crouching beast hungering for you, which you must master?' Cain said to his brother Abel, 'Let us go out'; and while they were in the open country, Cain set on his brother Abel and killed him.

The Lord asked Cain, 'Where is your brother Abel?' 'I do not know' he replied. 'Am I my brother's guardian?' 'What have you done?' the Lord asked. 'Listen to the sound of your brother's blood, crying out to me from the ground. Now be accursed and driven from the ground that has opened its mouth to receive your brother's blood at your hands. When you till the ground it shall no longer yield you any of its produce. You shall be a fugitive and a wanderer over the earth.' Then Cain said to the Lord, 'My punishment is greater than I can bear. See! Today you drive me from this ground. I must hide from you, and be a fugitive and a wanderer over the earth. Why, whoever comes across me will kill me!' 'Very well, then,' the Lord replied 'if anyone kills Cain, sevenfold vengeance shall be taken from him.' So the Lord put a mark on Cain, to prevent whoever might come across him from striking him down.

Adam had intercourse with his wife, and she gave birth to a son whom she named Seth, 'because God has granted me other offspring' she said 'in place of Abel, since Cain has killed him.'

This is the word of the Lord.

Responsorial Psalm Ps 49:1. 8. 16-17. 20-21. R̸ v.14
  R̸ **Pay your sacrifice of thanksgiving to God.**

1 The God of gods, the Lord,
  has spoken and summoned the earth,
  from the rising of the sun to its setting.
  'I find no fault with your sacrifices,
  your offerings are always before me.' R̸

2 'But how can you recite my commandments
  and take my covenant on your lips,
  you who despise my law
  and throw my words to the winds. R̸

3 'You who sit and malign your brother
  and slander your own mother's son.
  You do this, and should I keep silence?
  Do you think that I am like you?' R̸

Gospel Acclamation cf. Ps 94:8
  Alleluia, alleluia!
  Harden not your hearts today,
  but listen to the voice of the Lord.
  Alleluia!

or Jn 14:6

  Alleluia, alleluia!
  I am the Way, the Truth and the Life, says the Lord;
  no one can come to the Father except through me.
  Alleluia!

Sixth Week in Ordinary Time, Year I: Tuesday

GOSPEL

A reading from the holy Gospel according to Mark 8:11-13
Why does this generation demand a sign?

The Pharisees came up and started a discussion with Jesus; they demanded of him a sign from heaven, to test him. And with a sigh that came straight from the heart he said, 'Why does this generation demand a sign? I tell you solemnly, no sign shall be given to this generation.' And leaving them again and re-embarking he went away to the opposite shore.

This is the Gospel of the Lord.

TUESDAY

FIRST READING

A reading from the book of Genesis 6:5-8; 7:1-5. 10
I will rid the earth's face of man, my own creation.

The Lord saw that the wickedness of man was great on the earth, and that the thoughts in his heart fashioned nothing but wickedness all day long. The Lord regretted having made man on the earth, and his heart grieved. 'I will rid the earth's face of man, my own creation,' the Lord said 'and of animals also, reptiles too, and the birds of heaven; for I regret having made them.' But Noah had found favour with the Lord.

The Lord said to Noah, 'Go aboard the ark, you and all your household, for you alone among this generation do I see as a good man in my judgement. Of all the clean animals you must take seven of each kind, both male and female; of the unclean animals you must take two, a male and its female (and of the birds of heaven also, seven of each kind, both male and female), to propagate their kind over the whole earth. For in seven days' time I mean to make it rain on the earth for forty days and nights, and I will rid the earth of every living thing that I made.' Noah did all that the Lord ordered.

Seven days later the waters of the flood appeared on the earth.

This is the word of the Lord.

Responsorial Psalm Ps 28:1-4. 9-10. R/ v.11

  R/ **The Lord will bless his people with peace.**

1 O give the Lord you sons of God,
   give the Lord glory and power;
   give the Lord the glory of his name.
   Adore the Lord in his holy court. R/

2 The Lord's voice resounding on the waters,
   the Lord on the immensity of waters;
   the voice of the Lord, full of power,
   the voice of the Lord, full of splendour. R/

3 The God of glory thunders.
   In his temple they all cry: 'Glory!'
   The Lord sat enthroned over the flood;
   the Lord sits as king for ever. R/

Gospel Acclamation cf. Acts 16:14
   Alleluia, alleluia!
   Open our heart, O Lord,
   to accept the words of your Son.
   Alleluia!

or Jn 14:23

   Alleluia, alleluia!
   If anyone loves me he will keep my word,
   and my Father will love him,
   and we shall come to him.
   Alleluia!

GOSPEL

A reading from the holy Gospel according to Mark 8:14-21
Be on your guard against the yeast of the Pharisees and the yeast of Herod.

The disciples had forgotten to take any food and they had only one loaf with them in the boat. Then Jesus gave them this warning, 'Keep your eyes open; be on your guard against the yeast of the Pharisees and the yeast of Herod.' And they said to one another, 'It is because we have no bread.' And Jesus knew it, and he said to them, 'Why are you talking about having no bread? Do you not yet understand? Have you no perception? Are your minds closed? Have you eyes that do not see, ears that do not hear? Or do you not remember? When I broke the five loaves among the five thousand, how many baskets full of scraps did you collect?' They answered, 'Twelve.' 'And when I broke the seven loaves for the four thousand, how many baskets full of scraps did you collect?' And they answered, 'Seven.' Then he said to them, 'Are you still without perception?'

This is the Gospel of the Lord.

WEDNESDAY

FIRST READING

A reading from the book of Genesis   8:6-13. 20-22

He looked out; the surface of the ground was dry.

At the end of forty days Noah opened the porthole he had made in the ark and he sent out the raven. This went off, and flew back and forth until the waters dried up from the earth. Then he sent out the dove, to see whether the waters were receding from the surface of the earth. The dove, finding nowhere to perch, returned to him in the ark, for there was water over the whole surface of the earth; putting out his hand he took hold of it and brought it back into the ark with him. After waiting seven more days, again he sent out the dove from the ark. In the evening, the dove came back to him and there it was with a new olive-branch in its beak. So Noah realised that the waters were receding from the earth. After waiting seven more days he sent out the dove, and now it returned to him no more.

It was in the six hundred and first year of Noah's life, in the first month and on the first of the month, that the water dried up from the earth. Noah lifted back the hatch of the ark and looked out. The surface of the ground was dry!

Noah built an altar for the Lord, and choosing from all the clean animals and all the clean birds he offered burnt offerings on the altar. The Lord smelt the appeasing fragrance and said to himself, 'Never again will I curse the earth because of man, because his heart contrives evil from his infancy. Never again will I strike down every living thing as I have done.

'As long as earth lasts,
sowing and reaping,
cold and heat,
summer and winter,
day and night
shall cease no more.'

This is the word of the Lord.

Responsorial Psalm   Ps 115:12-15. 18-19. ℟ v.17

   ℟ **A thanksgiving sacrifice I make to you, O Lord.**

or

   ℟ **Alleluia!**

1. How can I repay the Lord
for his goodness to me?
The cup of salvation I will raise;
I will call on the Lord's name.   ℟

2. My vows to the Lord I will fulfil
before all his people.
O precious in the eyes of the Lord
is the death of his faithful.   ℟

3. My vows to the Lord I will fulfil
before all his people,
in the courts of the house of the Lord,
in your midst, O Jerusalem.   ℟

Gospel Acclamation   Ps 118:29. 35
Alleluia, alleluia!
Your word is a lamp for my steps
and a light for my path.
Alleluia!

or   cf. Eph 1:17. 18

Alleluia, alleluia!
May the Father of our Lord Jesus Christ
enlighten the eyes of our mind,
so that we can see what hope his call holds for us.
Alleluia!

GOSPEL

A reading from the holy Gospel according to Mark   8:22-26

He was cured and he could see everything plainly and distinctly.

Jesus and his disciples came to Bethsaida, and some people brought to him a blind man whom they begged him to touch. He took the blind man by the hand and led him outside the village. Then putting spittle on his eyes and laying his hands on him, he asked, 'Can you see anything?' The man, who was beginning to see, replied, 'I can see people; they look like trees to me, but they are walking about.' Then he laid his hands on the man's eyes again and he saw clearly; he was cured, and he could see everything plainly and distinctly. And Jesus sent him home, saying, 'Do not even go into the village.'

This is the Gospel of the Lord.

THURSDAY

FIRST READING

A reading from the book of Genesis 9:1-13

I set my bow in the clouds and it shall be a sign of the covenant between me and the earth.

God blessed Noah and his sons, saying to them, 'Be fruitful, multiply and fill the earth. Be the terror and the dread of all the wild beasts and all the birds of heaven, of everything that crawls on the ground and all the fish of the sea; they are handed over to you. Every living and crawling thing shall provide food for you, no less than the foliage of plants. I give you everything, with this exception: you must not eat flesh with life, that is to say blood, in it. I will demand an account of your life-blood. I will demand an account from every beast and from man. I will demand an account of every man's life from his fellow men.

'He who sheds man's blood,
shall have his blood shed by man,
for in the image of God
man was made.

'As for you, be fruitful, multiply, teem over the earth and be lord of it.'

God spoke to Noah and his sons, 'See, I establish my Covenant with you, and with your descendants after you; also with every living creature to be found with you, birds, cattle and every wild beast with you: everthing that came out of the ark, everything that lives on the earth. I establish my Covenant with you: no thing of flesh shall be swept away again by the waters of the flood. There shall be no flood to destroy the earth again.'

God said, 'Here is the sign of the Covenant I make between myself and you and every living creature with you for all generations: I set my bow in the clouds and it shall be a sign of the Covenant between me and the earth.'

This is the word of the Lord.

Responsorial Psalm   Ps 101:16-21. 29. 22-23. ℟ v.20

    ℟ **The Lord looked down from heaven to the earth.**

1   The nations shall fear the name of the Lord
and all the earth's kings your glory,
when the Lord shall build up Zion again
and appear in all his glory.
Then he will turn to the prayers of the helpless;
he will not despise their prayers.   ℟

2   Let this be written for ages to come
that a people yet unborn may praise the Lord;
for the Lord leaned down from his sanctuary on high.
He looked down from heaven to the earth
that he might hear the groans of the prisoners
and free those condemned to die.   ℟

3   The sons of your servants shall dwell untroubled
and their race shall endure before you
that the name of the Lord may be proclaimed in Zion
and his praise in the heart of Jerusalem,
when peoples and kingdoms are gathered together
to pay their homage to the Lord.   ℟

Gospel Acclamation   James 1:18
    Alleluia, alleluia!
By his own choice the Father made us his children
by the message of the truth,
so that we should be a sort of first-fruits
of all that he created.
Alleluia!

or   cf. Jn 6:63. 68

    Alleluia, alleluia!
Your words are spirit, Lord,
and they are life:
you have the message of eternal life.
Alleluia!

GOSPEL

A reading from the holy Gospel according to Mark   8:27-33
You are the Christ. The Son of Man is destined to suffer greviously.

Jesus and his disciples left for the villages round Caesarea Philippi. On the way he put this question to his disciples, 'Who do people say I am?' And they told him, 'John the Baptist,' they said, 'others Elijah; others again, one of the prophets.' 'But you,' he asked, 'who do you say I am?' Peter spoke up and said to him, 'You are the Christ.' And he gave them strict orders not to tell anyone about him.

And he began to teach them that the Son of Man was destined to suffer grievously, to be rejected by the elders and the chief priests and the scribes, and to be put to death, and after three days to rise again; and he said all this quite openly. Then, taking him aside, Peter started to remonstrate with him. But, turning and seeing his disciples, he rebuked Peter and said to him, 'Get behind me, Satan! Because the way you think is not God's way but man's.'

This is the Gospel of the Lord.

FRIDAY

FIRST READING

A reading from the book of Genesis 11:1-9
Let us go down and confuse their language.

Throughout the earth men spoke the same language, with the same vocabulary. Now as they moved eastwards they found a plain in the land of Shinar where they settled. They said to one another, 'Come, let us make bricks and bake them in the fire.' – For stone they used bricks, and for mortar they used bitumen. – 'Come,' they said, 'let us build ourselves a town and a tower with its top reaching heaven. Let us make a name for ourselves, so that we may not be scattered about the whole earth.'

Now the Lord came down to see the town and the tower that the sons of man had built. 'So they are all a single people with a single language!' said the Lord. 'This is but the start of their undertakings! There will be nothing too hard for them to do. Come, let us go down and confuse their language on the spot so that they can no longer understand one another.' The Lord scattered them hence over the whole face of the earth, and they stopped building the town. It was named Babel therefore, because there the Lord confused the language of the whole earth. It was from there that the Lord scattered them over the whole face of the earth.

This is the word of the Lord.

Responsorial Psalm Ps 32:10-15. R v.12

℟ **Happy the people the Lord has chosen as his own.**

1 He frustrates the designs of the nations,
   he defeats the plans of the peoples.
   His own designs shall stand for ever,
   the plans of his heart from age to age. ℟

2 They are happy, whose God is the Lord,
   the people he has chosen as his own.
   From the heavens the Lord looks forth,
   he sees all the children of men. ℟

3 From the place where he dwells he gazes
   on all the dwellers on the earth,
   he who shapes the hearts of them all
   and considers all their deeds. ℟

Gospel Acclamation 1 Jn 2:5
Alleluia, alleluia!
When anyone obeys what Christ has said,
God's love comes to perfection in him.
Alleluia!

or Jn 15:15

Alleluia, alleluia!
I call you friends, says the Lord,
because I have made known to you
everything I have learnt from my Father.
Alleluia!

GOSPEL

A reading from the holy Gospel according to Mark 8:34 – 9:1
Anyone who loses his life for my sake, and for the sake of the gospel, will save it.

Jesus called the people and his disciples to him and said, 'If anyone wants to be a follower of mine, let him renounce himself and take up his cross and follow me. For anyone who wants to save his life will lose it; but anyone who loses his life for my sake, and for the sake of the gospel, will save it. What gain, then, is it for a man to win the whole world and ruin his life? And indeed what can man offer in exchange for his life? For if anyone in this adulterous and sinful generation is ashamed of me and of my words, the Son of Man will also be ashamed of him when he comes in the glory of his Father with the holy angels.'

And he said to them, 'I tell you solemnly, there are some standing here who will not taste death before they see the kingdom of God come with power.'

This is the Gospel of the Lord.

SATURDAY

FIRST READING

A reading from the letter to the Hebrews 11:1-7

It is by faith that we understand that the world was created by one word from God.

Only faith can guarantee the blessings that we hope for, or prove the existence of the realities that at present remain unseen. It was for faith that our ancestors were commended.

It is by faith that we understand that the world was created by one word from God, so that no apparent cause can account for the things we can see.

It was because of his faith that Abel offered God a better sacrifice than Cain, and for that he was declared to be righteous when God made acknowledgement of his offerings. Though he is dead, he still speaks by faith.

It was because of his faith that Enoch was taken up and did not have to experience death: he was not to be found because God had taken him. This was because before his assumption it is attested that he had pleased God. Now it is impossible to please God without faith, since anyone who comes to him must believe that he exists and rewards those who try to find him.

It was through his faith that Noah, when he had been warned by God of something that had never been seen before, felt a holy fear and built an ark to save his family. By his faith the world was convicted, and he was able to claim the righteousness which is the reward of faith.

This is the word of the Lord.

Responsorial Psalm Ps 144:2-5. 10-11. ℟ cf. v.1

℟ **I will bless your name for ever, O Lord.**

1 I will bless you day after day
and praise your name for ever.
The Lord is great, highly to be praised,
his greatness cannot be measured. ℟

2   Age to age shall proclaim your works,
    shall declare your mighty deeds,
    shall speak of your splendour and glory,
    tell the tale of your wonderful works.

    ℟ **I will bless your name for ever, O Lord.**

3   All your creatures shall thank you, O Lord,
    and your friends shall repeat their blessing.
    They shall speak of the glory of your reign
    and declare your might, O God. ℟

Gospel Acclamation   Ps 147:12. 15
    Alleluia, alleluia!
    O praise the Lord, Jerusalem!
    He sends out his word to the earth.
    Alleluia.

or   cf. Mk 9:6

    Alleluia, alleluia!
    The heavens opened and the Father's voice resounded:
    'This is my Son, the Beloved. Listen to him.'
    Alleluia!

GOSPEL

A reading from the holy Gospel according to Mark   9:2-13
In their presence he was transfigured.

Jesus took with him Peter and James and John and led them up a high mountain where they could be alone by themselves. There in their presence he was transfigured: his clothes became dazzlingly white, whiter than any earthly bleacher could make them. Elijah appeared to them with Moses; and they were talking with Jesus. Then Peter spoke to Jesus: 'Rabbi,' he said, 'it is wonderful for us to be here; so let us make three tents, one for you, one for Moses and one for Elijah.' He did not know what to say; they were so frightened. And a cloud came, covering them in shadow; and there came a voice from the cloud, 'This is my Son, the Beloved. Listen to him.' Then suddenly, when they looked round, they saw no one with them any more but only Jesus.

As they came down from the mountain he warned them to tell no one what they had seen, until after the Son of Man had risen from the dead. They observed the warning faithfully, though among themselves they discussed what 'rising from the dead' could mean. And they put this question to him, 'Why do the scribes say that Elijah has to come first?' 'True,' he said, 'Elijah is to come first and to see that everything is as it should be; yet how is it that the scriptures say about the Son of Man that he is to suffer grievously and be treated with contempt? However, I tell you that Elijah has come and they have treated him as they pleased, just as the scriptures say about him.'

This is the Gospel of the Lord.

SEVENTH WEEK IN ORDINARY TIME
Year I

MONDAY

FIRST READING

A reading from the book of Ecclesiasticus   1:1-10

Before all other things, wisdom was created.

All wisdom is from the Lord,
and it is his own for ever.
The sand of the sea and the raindrops,
and the days of eternity, who can assess them?
The height of the sky and the breadth of the earth,
and the depth of the abyss, who can probe them?
Before all other things wisdom was created,
shrewd understanding is everlasting.
For whom has the root of wisdom ever been uncovered?
Her resourceful ways, who knows them?
One only is wise, terrible indeed,
seated on his throne, the Lord.
He himself has created her, looked on her and assessed her,
and poured her out on all his works
to be with all mankind as his gift,
and he conveyed her to those who love him.

This is the word of the Lord.

Responsorial Psalm   Ps 92:1-2. 5. ℟ v.1

℟ **The Lord is king, with majesty enrobed.**

1 The Lord is king, with majesty enrobed;
   the Lord has robed himself with might,
   he has girded himself with power.   ℟

2 The world you made firm, not to be moved;
your throne has stood firm from of old.
From all eternity, O Lord, you are.

℟ **The Lord is king, with majesty enrobed.**

3 Truly your decrees are to be trusted.
Holiness is fitting to your house,
O Lord, until the end of time. ℟

Gospel Acclamation 1 Peter 1:25

Alleluia, alleluia!
The word of the Lord remains for ever:
What is this word?
It is the Good News that has been brought to you.
Alleluia!

or cf. 2 Tim 1:10

Alleluia, alleluia!
Our Saviour Christ Jesus abolished death,
and he has proclaimed life through the Good News.
Alleluia!

GOSPEL

A reading from the holy Gospel according to Mark 9:14-29
I do have faith. Help the little faith I have.

When Jesus, with Peter, James and John came down from the mountain and rejoined the disciples they saw a large crowd round them and some scribes arguing with them. The moment they saw him the whole crowd were struck with amazement and ran to greet him. 'What are you arguing about with them?' he asked. A man answered him from the crowd, 'Master, I have brought my son to you; there is a spirit of dumbness in him, and when it takes hold of him it throws him to the ground, and he foams at the mouth and grinds his teeth and goes rigid. And I asked your disciples to cast it out and they were unable to.' 'You faithless generation,' he said to them in reply. 'How much longer must I be with you? How much longer must I put up with you? Bring him to me.' They brought the boy to him, and as soon as the spirit saw Jesus it threw the boy into convulsions, and he fell to the ground and lay writhing there, foaming at the mouth. Jesus asked the father, 'How long has this been happening to him?' 'From childhood,' he replied, 'and it has often thrown him into the fire and into the water, in order to destroy him. But if you can do anything, have pity on us and help us.' 'If you can?' retorted Jesus. 'Everything is possible for anyone who has faith.' Immediately the father of the boy cried out, 'I do have faith. Help the little faith I have!' And when Jesus saw how many people were pressing round him, he rebuked the unclean spirit. 'Deaf and dumb spirit,' he said, 'I command you: come out of him and never enter him again.' Then throwing the boy into violent convulsions it came out shouting, and the boy lay there so like a corpse that most of them said, 'He is dead.' But Jesus took him by the hand and helped him up, and he was able to stand. When he had gone indoors his disciples asked him privately, 'Why were we unable to cast it out?' 'This is the kind,' he answered 'that can only be driven out by prayer.'

This is the Gospel of the Lord.

TUESDAY

FIRST READING

A reading from the book of Ecclesiasticus 2:1-11

Prepare yourself for an ordeal.

My son, if you aspire to serve the Lord,
prepare yourself for an ordeal.
Be sincere of heart, be steadfast,
and do not be alarmed when disaster comes.
Cling to him and do not leave him,
so that you may be honoured at the end of your days.
Whatever happens to you, accept it,
and in the uncertainties of your humble state, be patient,
since gold is tested in the fire,
and chosen men in the furnace of humiliation.
Trust him and he will uphold you,
follow a straight path and hope in him.
You who fear the Lord, wait for his mercy;
do not turn aside in case you fall.
You who fear the Lord, trust him,
you who will not be baulked of your reward.
You who fear the Lord hope for good things,
for everlasting happiness and mercy.
Look at the generations of old and see:
who ever trusted in the Lord and was put to shame?

Or who ever feared him steadfastly and was left forsaken?
Or who ever called out to him, and was ignored?
For the Lord is compassionate and merciful,
he forgives sins, and saves in days of distress.

This is the word of the Lord.

Responsorial Psalm Ps 36:3-4. 18-19. 27-28. 39-40. R̷ v.5

R̷ **Commit your life to the Lord,
trust him and he will act.**

1 If you trust in the Lord and do good,
then you will live in the land and be secure.
If you find your delight in the Lord,
he will grant your heart's desire. R̷

2 He protects the lives of the upright,
their heritage will last for ever.
They shall not be put to shame in evil days,
in time of famine their food shall not fail. R̷

3 Then turn away from evil and do good
and you shall have a home for ever;
for the Lord loves justice
and will never forsake his friends. R̷

4 The salvation of the just comes from the Lord,
their stronghold in time of distress.
The Lord helps them and delivers them
and saves them: for their refuge is in him. R̷

Gospel Acclamation Jn 14:23
Alleluia, alleluia!
If anyone loves me he will keep my word,
and my Father will love him,
and we shall come to him.
Alleluia!

or   Gal 6:14

Alleluia, alleluia!
The only thing I can boast about
is the cross of our Lord Jesus Christ,
through whom the world is crucified to me,
and I to the world.
Alleluia!

Seventh Week in Ordinary Time, Year I: Wednesday

GOSPEL

A reading from the holy Gospel according to Mark   9:30-37
The Son of Man will be delivered into the hands of men. If anyone wants to be first, he must make himself the last of all.

Jesus and his disciples made their way through Galilee; and he did not want anyone to know, because he was instructing his disciples; he was telling them, 'The Son of Man will be delivered into the hands of men; they will put him to death; and three days after he has been put to death he will rise again.' But they did not understand what he said and were afraid to ask him.

They came to Capernaum, and when he was in the house he asked them, 'What were you arguing about on the road?' They said nothing because they had been arguing which of them was the greatest. So he sat down, called the Twelve to him and said, 'If anyone wants to be first, he must make himself last of all and servant of all.' He then took a little child, set him in front of them, put his arms round him, and said to them, 'Anyone who welcomes one of these little children in my name, welcomes me; and anyone who welcomes me welcomes not me but the one who sent me.'

This is the Gospel of the Lord.

WEDNESDAY

FIRST READING

A reading from the book of Ecclesiasticus   4:11-19
The Lord loves those who love wisdom.

Wisdom brings up her own sons,
and cares for those who seek her.
Whoever loves her loves life,
those who wait on her early will be filled with happiness.
Whoever holds her close will inherit honour,
and wherever he walks the Lord will bless him.
Those who serve her minister to the Holy One,
and the Lord loves those who love her.
Whoever obeys her judges aright,
and whoever pays attention to her dwells secure.
If he trusts himself to her he will inherit her,
and his descendants will remain in possession of her;
for though she takes him at first through winding ways,

bringing fear and faintness on him,
plaguing him with her discipline until she can trust him,
and testing him with her ordeals,
in the end she will lead him back to the straight road,
and reveal her secrets to him.
If he wanders away she will abandon him,
and hand him over to his fate.

This is the word of the Lord.

Responsorial Psalm   Ps 118:165. 168. 171-2. 174-5. ℟ v.165

℟ **The lovers of your law
have great peace, O Lord.**

1 The lovers of your law have great peace;
 they never stumble.
 I obey your precepts and your will;
 all that I do is before you. ℟

2 Let my lips proclaim your praise
 because you teach me your statutes.
 Let my tongue sing your promise
 for your commands are just. ℟

3 Give life to my soul that I may praise you.
 Let your decrees give me help.
 Lord, I long for your saving help
 and your law is my delight. ℟

Gospel Acclamation   Jn 14:16
Alleluia, alleluia!
I am the Way, the Truth and the Life, says the Lord;
no one can come to the Father except through me.
Alleluia!

GOSPEL

A reading from the holy Gospel according to Mark   9:38-40
Anyone who is not against us is for us.

John said to Jesus, 'Master, we saw a man who is not one of us casting out devils in your name; and because he was not one of us we tried to stop him.' But Jesus said, 'You must not stop him: no one who works a miracle in my name is likely to speak evil of me. Anyone who is not against us is for us.'

This is the Gospel of the Lord.

Seventh Week in Ordinary Time, Year I: Thursday 515

THURSDAY

FIRST READING

A reading from the book of Ecclesiasticus 5:1-8
Do not delay your return to the Lord.

Do not give your heart to your money,
or say, 'With this I am self-sufficient.'
Do not be led by your appetites and energy
to follow the passions of your heart.
And do not say, 'Who has authority over me?'
for the Lord will certainly be avenged on you.
Do not say, 'I sinned, and what happened to me?'
for the Lord's forbearance is long.
Do not be so sure of forgiveness
that you add sin to sin.
And do not say, 'His compassion is great,
he will forgive me my many sins';
for with him are both mercy and wrath,
and his rage bears heavy on sinners.
Do not delay your return to the Lord,
do not put it off day after day;
for suddenly the Lord's wrath will blaze out,
and at the time of vengeance you will be utterly destroyed.
Do not set your heart on ill-gotten gains,
they will be of no use to you on the day of disaster.

This is the word of the Lord.

Responsorial Psalm Ps 1:1-4. 6. ℟ Ps 39:5
 ℟ **Happy the man who has placed
  his trust in the Lord.**

1 Happy indeed is the man
 who follows not the counsel of the wicked;
 nor lingers in the way of sinners
 nor sits in the company of scorners,
 but whose delight is the law of the Lord
 and who ponders his law day and night. ℟

2 He is like a tree that is planted
 beside the flowing waters,
 that yields its fruit in due season
 and whose leaves shall never fade;
 and all that he does shall prosper. ℟ (continued)

3   Not so are the wicked, not so!
    For they like winnowed chaff
    shall be driven away by the wind.
    For the Lord guards the way of the just
    but the way of the wicked leads to doom.

    ℟ **Happy the man who has placed
    his trust in the Lord.**

Gospel Acclamation   cf. Lk 8:15

Alleluia, alleluia!
Blessed are those who,
with a noble and generous heart,
take the word of God to themselves
and yield a harvest through their perseverance.
Alleluia!

or   cf. 1 Thess 2:13

Alleluia, alleluia!
Accept God's message for what is really is:
God's message, and not some human thinking.
Alleluia!

GOSPEL

A reading from the holy Gospel according to Mark   9:41-50
It is better to enter into life crippled, than to have two hands and go to hell.

Jesus said to his disciples: 'If anyone gives you a cup of water to drink just because you belong to Christ, then I tell you solemnly, he will most certainly not lose his reward.

'But anyone who is an obstacle to bring down one of these little ones who have faith, would be better thrown into the sea with a great millstone round his neck. And if your hand should cause you to sin, cut it off; it is better for you to enter into life crippled, than to have two hands and go to hell, into the fire that cannot be put out. And if your foot should cause you to sin, cut it off; it is better for you to enter into life lame, than to have two feet and be thrown into hell. And if your eye should cause you to sin, tear it out; it is better for you to enter into the kingdom of God with one eye, than to have two eyes and be thrown into hell where their worm does not die nor their fire go out. For everyone will be salted with fire. Salt is a good thing, but if salt has become insipid, how can you season it again? Have salt in yourselves and be at peace with one another.'

This is the Gospel of the Lord.

FRIDAY

FIRST READING

A reading from the book of Ecclesiasticus 6:5-17
A faithful friend is something beyond price.

A kindly turn of speech multiplies a man's friends,
and a courteous way of speaking invites many a friendly reply.
Let your acquaintances be many,
but your advisers one in a thousand.
If you want to make a friend, take him on trial,
and be in no hurry to trust him;
for one kind of friend is only so when it suits him
but will not stand by you in your day of trouble.
Another kind of friend will fall out with you
and to your dismay make your quarrel public,
and a third kind of friend will share your table,
but not stand by you in your day of trouble:
when you are doing well he will be your second self,
ordering your servants about;
but if ever you are brought low he will turn against you
and will hide himself from you.
Keep well clear of your enemies,
and be wary of your friends.
A faithful friend is a sure shelter,
whoever finds one has found a rare treasure.
A faithful friend is something beyond price,
there is no measuring his worth.
A faithful friend is the elixir of life,
and those who fear the Lord will find one.
Whoever fears the Lord makes true friends,
for as a man is, so is his friend.

This is the word of the Lord.

Responsorial Psalm   Ps 118:12. 16. 18. 27. 34-35. ℟ v.35
   ℟   **Guide me, Lord, in the path of your commands.**

1. Blessed are you, O Lord;
teach me your statutes.
I take delight in your statutes;
I will not forget your word. ℟

2. Open my eyes that I may consider
the wonders of your law.
Make me grasp the way of your precepts
and I will muse on your wonders. ℟

3. Train me to observe your law,
to keep it with my heart.
Guide me in the path of your commands;
for there is my delight. ℟

Gospel Acclamation   Ps 110:7. 8
Alleluia, alleluia!
Your precepts, O Lord, are all of them sure;
they stand firm for ever and ever.
Alleluia!

or   cf. Jn 17:17

Alleluia, alleluia!
Your word is truth, O Lord,
consecrate us in the truth.
Alleluia!

GOSPEL

A reading from the holy Gospel according to Mark   10:1-12
What God has united, man must not divide.

Jesus came to the district of Judaea and the far side of the Jordan. And again crowds gathered round him, and again he taught them, as his custom was. Some Pharisees approached him and asked, 'Is it against the law for a man to divorce his wife?' They were testing him. He answered them, 'What did Moses command you?' 'Moses allowed us' they said 'to draw up a writ of dismissal and so to divorce.' Then Jesus said to them, 'It was because you were so unteachable that he wrote this commandment for you. But from the beginning of creation God made them male and female. This is why a man must leave father and mother, and the two become one body. They are no longer two, therefore, but one body. So then, what God has united, man must not divide.' Back in the house the disciples questioned him again about this, and he said to them, 'The man who divorces his wife and marries another is guilty of adultery against her. And if a woman divorces her husband and marries another she is guilty of adultery too.'

This is the Gospel of the Lord.

SATURDAY

FIRST READING

A reading from the book of Ecclesiasticus 17:1-15
The Lord God made man in his own image.

The Lord fashioned man from the earth,
to consign him back to it.
He gave them so many days' determined time,
he gave them authority over everything on earth.
He clothed them with strength like his own,
and made them in his own image.
He filled all living things with dread of man,
making him master over beasts and birds.
He shaped for them a mouth and tongue, eyes and ears,
and gave them a heart to think with.
He filled them with knowledge and understanding,
and revealed to them good and evil.
He put his own light in their hearts
to show them the magnificence of his works.
They will praise his holy name,
as they tell of his magnificent works.
He set knowledge before them,
he endowed them with the law of life.
He established an eternal covenant with them,
and revealed his judgements to them.
Their eyes saw his glorious majesty,
and their ears heard the glory of his voice.
He said to them, 'Beware of all wrong-doing';
he gave each a commandment concerning his neighbour.
Their ways are always under his eye,
they cannot be hidden from his sight.

This is the word of the Lord.

Readings for Weekdays in Ordinary Time

Responsorial Psalm Ps 102:13-18. ℟ cf. v.17

℟ **The love of the Lord is everlasting**
upon those who hold him in fear.

1 As a father has compassion on his sons,
the Lord has pity on those who fear him;
for he knows of what we are made,
he remembers that we are dust. ℟

2 As for man, his days are like grass;
he flowers like the flower of the field
the wind blows and he is gone
and his place never sees him again. ℟

3 But the love of the Lord is everlasting
upon those who hold him in fear;
his justice reaches out to children's children
when they keep his covenant in truth. ℟

Gospel Acclamation cf. Mt 11:25
Alleluia, alleluia!
Blessed are you, Father,
Lord of heaven and earth,
for revealing the mysteries of the kingdom
to mere children.
Alleluia!

GOSPEL

A reading from the holy Gospel according to Mark 10:13-16
Anyone who does not welcome the kingdom of God like a little child will never enter it.

People were bringing little children to Jesus, for him to touch them. The disciples turned them away, but when Jesus saw this he was indignant and said to them, 'Let the little children come to me; do not stop them; for it is to such as these that the kingdom of God belongs. I tell you solemnly, anyone who does not welcome the kingdom of God like a little child will never enter it.' Then he put his arms round them, laid his hands on them and gave them his blessing.

This is the Gospel of the Lord.

EIGHTH WEEK IN ORDINARY TIME
Year I

MONDAY

FIRST READING

A reading from the book of Ecclesiasticus 17:24-29
Return to the Lord and leave sin behind.

To those who repent God permits return,
and he encourages those who were losing hope.
Return to the Lord and leave sin behind,
plead before his face and lessen your offence.
Come back to the Most High and turn away from iniquity,
and hold in abhorrence all that is foul.
Who will praise the Most High in Sheol,
if the living do not do so by giving glory to him?
To the dead, as to those who do not exist, praise is unknown,
only those with life and health can praise the Lord.
How great is the mercy of the Lord,
his pardon on all those who turn towards him!

This is the word of the Lord.

Responsorial Psalm Ps 31:1-2. 5-7. ℟ v.11

℟ **Rejoice, rejoice in the Lord,
exult, you just!**

1 Happy the man whose offence is forgiven,
 whose sin is remitted.
 O happy the man to whom the Lord
 imputes no guilt,
 in whose spirit is no guile. ℟

2 But now I have acknowledged my sins;
 my guilt I did not hide.
 I said: 'I will confess
 my offence to the Lord.'
 And you, Lord, have forgiven
 the guilt of my sin. ℟

3 So let every good man pray to you
 in the time of need.
 The floods of water may reach high

(continued)

but him they shall not reach.

℟ **Rejoice, rejoice in the Lord,
exult, you just!**

4 You are my hiding place, O Lord;
you save me from distress.
You surround me with cries of deliverance. ℟

Gospel Acclamation cf. 1 Thess 2:13
Alleluia, alleluia!
Accept God's message for what it really is:
God's message, and not some human thinking.
Alleluia!

or 2 Cor 8:9

Alleluia, alleluia!
Jesus Christ was rich,
but he became poor for your sake,
to make you rich out of his poverty.
Alleluia!

GOSPEL

A reading from the holy Gospel according to Mark 10:17-27
Sell everything you own and follow me.

Jesus was setting out on a journey when a man ran up, knelt before him and put this question to him, 'Good master, what must I do to inherit eternal life?' Jesus said to him, 'Why do you call me good? No one is good but God alone. You know the commandments: You must not kill; You must not commit adultery; You must not steal; You must not bring false witness; You must not defraud; Honour your father and mother.' And he said to him, 'Master, I have kept all these from my earliest days.' Jesus looked steadily at him and loved him, and he said, 'There is one thing you lack. Go and sell everything you own and give the money to the poor, and you will have treasure in heaven; then come, follow me.' But his face fell at these words and he went away sad, for he was a man of great wealth.

Jesus looked round and said to his disciples, 'How hard it is for those who have riches to enter the kingdom of God!' The disciples were astounded by these words, but Jesus insisted, 'My children,' he said to them 'how hard it is to enter the kingdom of

God! It is easier for a camel to pass through the eye of a needle than for a rich man to enter the kingdom of God.' They were more astonished than ever. 'In that case' they said to one another 'who can be saved?' Jesus gazed at them. 'For men' he said 'it is impossible, but not for God: because everything is possible for God.'

This is the Gospel of the Lord.

TUESDAY

FIRST READING

A reading from the book of Ecclesiasticus 35:1-12

A man offers communion sacrifices by following the commandments.

A man multiplies offerings by keeping the Law;
he offers communion sacrifices by following the commandments.
By showing gratitude he makes an offering of fine flour,
by giving alms he offers a sacrifice of praise.
Withdraw from wickedness and the Lord will be pleased,
withdraw from injustice and you make atonement.
Do not appear empty-handed in the Lord's presence;
for all these things are due under the commandment.
A virtuous man's offering graces the altar,
and its savour rises before the Most High.
A virtuous man's sacrifice is acceptable,
its memorial will not be forgotten.
Honour the Lord with generosity,
do not stint the first fruits you bring.
Add a smiling face to all your gifts,
and be cheerful as you dedicate your tithes.
Give to the Most High as he has given to you,
generously as your means can afford;
for the Lord is a good rewarder,
he will reward you seven times over.
Offer him no bribe, he will not accept it,
do not put your faith in an unvirtuous sacrifice;
since the Lord is a judge
who is no respecter of personages.

This is the word of the Lord.

Responsorial Psalm   Ps 49:5-8. 14. 23. R̸ v.23

   R̸ **I will show God's salvation to the upright.**

1 'Summon before me my people
   who made covenant with me by sacrifice.'
   The heavens proclaim his justice,
   for he, God, is the judge.   R̸

2 'Listen, my people, I will speak;
   Israel, I will testify against you,
   for I am God your God.
   I find no fault with your sacrifices,
   your offerings are always before me.   R̸

3 'Pay your sacrifice of thanksgiving to God
   and render him your votive offerings.
   A sacrifice of thanksgiving honours me
   and I will show God's salvation to the upright.'   R̸

Gospel Acclamation   Phil 2:15-16
   Alleluia, alleluia!
   You will shine in the world like bright stars
   because you are offering it the word of life.
   Alleluia!

or   cf. Mt 11:25
   Alleluia, alleluia!
   Blessed are you, Father,
   Lord of heaven and earth,
   for revealing the mysteries of the kingdom
   to mere children.
   Alleluia!

GOSPEL

A reading from the holy Gospel according to Mark   10:28-31

You will be repaid a hundred times over, not without persecutions, now in this present time and, in the world to come, eternal life.

'What about us?' Peter asked Jesus. 'We have left everything and followed you.' Jesus said, 'I tell you solemnly, there is no one who has left house, brothers, sisters, father, children or land for my sake and for the sake of the gospel who will not be repaid a hundred times over, houses, brothers, sisters, mothers, children and land – not without persecutions – now in this present time and, in the world to come, eternal life.

   'Many who are first will be last, and the last first.'

This is the Gospel of the Lord.

WEDNESDAY

FIRST READING

A reading from the book of Ecclesiasticus   36:1. 4-5. 10-17
Let the nations know that there is no God but you, Lord.

Have mercy on us, Master, Lord of all, and look on us,
cast the fear of yourself over every nation.
Let them acknowledge you, just as we have acknowledged
that there is no God but you, Lord.
Send new portents, do fresh wonders,
win glory for your hand and your right arm.
Gather together all the tribes of Jacob,
restore them their inheritance as in the beginning.
Have mercy, Lord, on the people who have invoked your name,
on Israel whom you have treated as a first-born.
Show compassion on your holy city,
on Jerusalem the place of your rest.
Fill Zion with songs of your praise,
and your sanctuary with your glory.
Bear witness to those you created in the beginning,
and bring about what has been prophesied in your name.
Give those who wait for you their reward,
and let your prophets be proved worthy of belief.
Grant, Lord, the prayer of your servants,
in accordance with Aaron's blessing on your people,
so that all the earth's inhabitants may acknowledge
that you are the Lord, the everlasting God.

    This is the word of the Lord.

Responsorial Psalm   Ps 78:8-9. 11. 13. ℟ Ecclus 36:1
  ℟ **Have mercy on us, Lord,**
    and look on us.

1 Do not hold the guilt of our fathers against us.
   Let your compassion hasten to meet us
   for we are in the depths of distress. ℟

2 O God our saviour, come to our help,
   come for the sake of the glory of your name.
   O Lord our God, forgive us our sins
   rescue us for the sake of your name. ℟   (continued)

3 Let the groans of the prisoners come before you;
let your strong arm reprieve those condemned to die.
But we, your people, the flock of your pasture,
will give you thanks for ever and ever.
We will tell your praise from age to age.

℟ **Have mercy on us, Lord,
and look on us.**

Gospel Acclamation 1 Jn 2:5
Alleluia, alleluia!
When anyone obeys what Christ has said,
God's love comes to perfection in him.
Alleluia!

or Mk 10:45

Alleluia, alleluia!
The Son of Man came to serve,
and to give his life as a ransom for many.
Alleluia!

GOSPEL

A reading from the holy Gospel according to Mark 10:32-45

Now we are going up to Jerusalem and the Son of Man is about to be handed over.

The disciples were on the road, going up to Jerusalem; Jesus was walking on ahead of them; they were in a daze, and those who followed were apprehensive. Once more taking the Twelve aside he began to tell them what was going to happen to him: 'Now we are going up to Jerusalem, and the Son of Man is about to be handed over to the chief priests and the scribes. They will condemn him to death and will hand him over to the pagans, who will mock him and spit at him and scourge him and put him to death; and after three days he will rise again.'

James and John, the sons of Zebedee, approached him. 'Master,' they said to him 'we want you to do us a favour.' He said to them, 'What is it you want me to do for you?' They said to him, 'Allow us to sit one at your right hand and the other at your left in your glory.' 'You do not know what you are asking' Jesus said to them. 'Can you drink the cup that I must drink, or be baptised with the baptism with which I must be baptised?' They replied, 'We can.' Jesus said to them, 'The cup that I must drink you shall drink, and with the baptism with which I must be baptised you shall be baptised, but as for seats at my right hand or my left, these are not mine to grant; they belong to those to whom they have been allotted.'

When the other ten heard this they began to feel indignant with James and John, so Jesus called them to him and said to them, 'You know that among the pagans their so-called rulers lord it over them, and their great men make their authority felt. This is not to happen among you. No; anyone who wants to become great among you must be your servant, and anyone who wants to be first among you must be slave to all. For the Son of Man himself did not come to be served but to serve, and to give his life as a ransom for many.'

This is the Gospel of the Lord.

THURSDAY

FIRST READING

A reading from the book of Ecclesiasticus 42:15-25

The work of the Lord is full of his glory.

I will remind you of the works of the Lord,
and tell of what I have seen.
By the words of the Lord his works come into being
and all creation obeys his will.
As the sun in shining looks on all things,
so the work of the Lord is full of his glory.
The Lord has not granted to the holy ones
to tell of all his marvels
which the Almighty Lord has solidly constructed
for the universe to stand firm in his glory.
He has fathomed the deep and the heart,
and seen into their devious ways;
for the Most High knows all the knowledge there is,
and has observed the signs of the times.
He declares what is past and what will be,
and uncovers the traces of hidden things.
Not a thought escapes him,
not a single word is hidden from him.
He has imposed an order on the magnificent works of his wisdom,
he is from everlasting to everlasting,

nothing can be added to him, nothing taken away.
He needs no one's advice.
How desirable are all his works,
how dazzling to the eye!
They all live and last for ever,
whatever the circumstances all obey him.
All things go in pairs, by opposites,
and he has made nothing defective;
the one consolidates the excellence of the other,
who could ever be sated with gazing at his glory?

This is the word of the Lord.

Responsorial Psalm Ps 32:2-9. ℟ v.6

℟ **By the word of the Lord the heavens were made.**

1 Give thanks to the Lord upon the harp,
   with a ten-stringed lute sing him songs.
   O sing him a song that is new,
   play loudly, with all your skill.   ℟

2 For the word of the Lord is faithful
   and all his works to be trusted.
   The Lord loves justice and right
   and fills the earth with his love.   ℟

3 By his word the heavens were made,
   by the breath of his mouth all the stars.
   He collects the waves of the ocean;
   he stores up the depths of the sea.   ℟

4 Let all the earth fear the Lord,
   all who live in the world revere him.
   He spoke; and it came to be.
   He commanded; it sprang into being.   ℟

Gospel Acclamation Ps 129:5

Alleluia, alleluia!
My soul is waiting for the Lord,
I count on his word,
Alleluia!

or Jn 8:12

Alleluia, alleluia!
I am the light of the world, says the Lord,
anyone who follows me

Eighth Week in Ordinary Time, Year I: Friday 529

will have the light of life.
Alleluia!

GOSPEL

A reading from the holy Gospel according to Mark 10:46-52
Master, let me see again.

As Jesus was leaving Jericho with his disciples and a large crowd, Bartimaeus (that is, the son of Timaeus), a blind beggar, was sitting at the side of the road. When he heard that it was Jesus of Nazareth, he began to shout and to say, 'Son of David, Jesus, have pity on me.' And many of them scolded him and told him to keep quiet, but he only shouted all the louder, 'Son of David, have pity on me.' Jesus stopped and said, 'Call him here.' So they called the blind man. 'Courage,' they said 'get up; he is calling you.' So throwing off his cloak, he jumped up and went to Jesus. Then Jesus spoke, 'What do you want me to do for you?' 'Rabbuni,' the blind man said to him 'Master, let me see again.' Jesus said to him, 'Go; your faith has saved you.' And immediately his sight returned and he followed him along the road.

This is the Gospel of the Lord.

FRIDAY

FIRST READING

A reading from the book of Ecclesiasticus 44:1. 9-13
Our ancestors were generous men, and their name lives on for all generations.

Let us praise illustrious men,
our ancestors in their successive generations.
While others have left no memory,
and disappeared as though they had not existed,
they are now as though they had never been,
and so too, their children after them.

But here is a list of generous men
whose good works have not been forgotten.
In their descendants there remains
a rich inheritance born of them.
Their descendants stand by the covenants
and, thanks to them, so do their children's children.

Their offspring will last for ever,
their glory will not fade.

This is the word of the Lord.

Responsorial Psalm Ps 149:1-6. 9. ℟ v.4

℟ **The Lord takes delight in his people.**

or

℟ **Alleluia!**

1 Sing a new song to the Lord,
his praise in the assembly of the faithful.
Let Israel rejoice in its Maker,
let Zion's sons exult in their king. ℟

2 Let them praise his name with dancing
and make music with timbrel and harp.
For the Lord takes delight in his people.
He crowns the poor with salvation. ℟

3 Let the faithful rejoice in their glory,
shout for joy and take their rest.
Let the praise of God be on their lips;
this honour is for all his faithful. ℟

Gospel Acclamation Ps 118:29. 35

Alleluia, alleluia!
Bend my heart to your will, O Lord,
and teach me your law.
Alleluia!

or cf. Jn 15:16

Alleluia, alleluia!
I chose you from the world
to go out and to bear fruit,
fruit that will last.
Alleluia!

GOSPEL

A reading from the holy Gospel according to Mark 11:11-26
My house will be called a house of prayer for all people. Have faith in God.

After he had been acclaimed by the crowds, Jesus entered

Jerusalem and went into the Temple. He looked all round him, but as it was now late, he went out to Bethany with the Twelve.

Next day as they were leaving Bethany, he felt hungry. Seeing a fig tree in leaf some distance away, he went to see if he could find any fruit on it, but when he came up to it he found nothing but leaves; for it was not the season for figs. And he addressed the fig tree. 'May no one ever eat fruit from you again' he said. And his disciples heard him say this.

So they reached Jerusalem and he went into the Temple and began driving out those who were selling and buying there; he upset the tables of the money changers and the chairs of those who were selling pigeons. Nor would he allow anyone to carry anything through the Temple. And he taught them and said, 'Does not scripture say: My house will be called a house of prayer for all the peoples? But you have turned it into a robber's den.' This came to the ears of the chief priests and the scribes, and they tried to find some way of doing away with him; they were afraid of him because the people were carried away by his teaching. And when evening came he went out of the city.

Next morning, as they passed by, they saw the fig tree withered to the roots. Peter remembered. 'Look, Rabbi,' he said to Jesus 'the fig tree you cursed has withered away.' Jesus answered, 'Have faith in God. I tell you solemnly, if anyone says to this mountain, "Get up and throw yourself into the sea," with no hesitation in his heart but believing that what he says will happen, it will be done for him. I tell you therefore: everything you ask and pray for, believe that you have it already, and it will be yours. And when you stand in prayer, forgive whatever you have against anybody, so that your Father in heaven may forgive your failings too. But if you do not forgive, your Father in heaven will not forgive your failings either.'

This is the Gospel of the Lord.

SATURDAY

FIRST READING

A reading from the book of Ecclesiasticus 51:12-20
Glory be to him who has given me wisdom.

I will thank you and praise you,
and bless the name of the Lord.
When I was still a youth, before I went travelling,

in my prayers I asked outright for wisdom.
Outside the sanctuary I would pray for her,
and to the last I will continue to seek her.
From her blossoming to the ripening of her grape
my heart has taken its delight in her.
My foot has pursued a straight path,
I have been following her steps ever since my youth.
By bowing my ear a little I have received her,
and have found much instruction.
Thanks to her I have advanced;
the glory be to him who has given me wisdom!
For I am determined to put her into practice,
I have earnestly pursued what is good, I will not be put to shame.
My soul has fought to possess her,
I have been scrupulous in keeping the law;
I have stretched out my hands to heaven
and bewailed my ignorance of her;
I have directed my soul towards her,
and in purity have found her.

    This is the word of the Lord.

Responsorial Psalm   Ps 18:8-11. ℟ v.9
   ℟ **The precepts of the Lord gladden the heart.**

1. The law of the Lord is perfect,
   it revives the soul.
   The rule of the Lord is to be trusted,
   it gives wisdom to the simple. ℟

2. The precepts of the Lord are right,
   they gladden the heart.
   The command of the Lord is clear,
   it gives light to the eyes. ℟

3. The fear of the Lord is holy,
   abiding for ever.
   The decrees of the Lord are truth
   and all of them just. ℟

4. They are more to be desired than gold,
   than the purest of gold,
   and sweeter are they than honey,
   than honey from the comb. ℟

Gospel Acclamation
1 Peter 1:25

> Alleluia, alleluia!
> The word of the Lord remains for ever:
> What is this word?
> It is the Good News that has been brought to you.
> Alleluia!

or
cf. Col 3:16. 17

> Alleluia, alleluia!
> Let the message of Christ, in all its richness,
> find a home with you;
> through him give thanks to God the Father.
> Alleluia!

GOSPEL

A reading from the holy Gospel according to Mark 11:27-33
What authority have you for acting like this?

Jesus and his disciples came to Jerusalem, and as Jesus was walking in the Temple, the chief priests and the scribes and the elders came to him, and they said to him, 'What authority have you for acting like this? Or who gave you authority to do these things?' Jesus said to them, 'I will ask you a question, only one; answer me and I will tell you my authority for acting like this. John's baptism: did it come from heaven, or from man? Answer me that.' And they argued it out this way among themselves: 'If we say from heaven, he will say, "Then why did you refuse to believe him?" But dare we say from man?' – they had the people to fear, for everyone held that John was a real prophet. So their reply to Jesus was, 'We do not know.' And Jesus said to them, 'Nor will I tell you my authority for acting like this.'

This is the Gospel of the Lord.

NINTH WEEK IN ORDINARY TIME
Year I

MONDAY

FIRST READING

A reading from the book of Tobit   1:3; 2:1-8
Tobit feared God more than he feared the king.

I, Tobit, have walked in paths of truth and in good works all the days of my life. I have given much in alms to my brothers and fellow countrymen, exiled like me to Nineveh in the country of Assyria.

At our feast of Pentecost (the feast of Weeks) there was a good dinner. I took my place for the meal; the table was brought to me and various dishes were brought. Then I said to my son Tobias, 'Go, my child, and seek out some poor, loyal-hearted man among our brothers exiled in Nineveh, and bring him to share my meal. I will wait until you come back, my child.' So Tobias went out to look for some poor man among our brothers, but he came back again and said, 'Father!' I answered, 'What is it, my child?' He went on, 'Father, one of our nation has just been murdered; he has been strangled and then thrown down in the market place; he is there still.' I sprang up at once, left my meal untouched, took the man from the market place and laid him in one of my rooms, waiting until sunset to bury him. I came in again and washed myself and ate my bread in sorrow, remembering the words of the prophet Amos concerning Bethel:

> Your feasts will be turned to mourning,
> and all your songs to lamentation.

And I wept. When the sun was down, I went and dug a grave and buried him. My neighbours laughed and said, 'See! He is not afraid any more.' (You must remember that a price had been set on my head earlier for this very thing.) 'The time before this he had to flee, yet here he is, beginning to bury the dead again.'

This the word of the Lord.

Responsorial Psalm
Ps 111:1-6. ℟ v.1

℟ **Happy the man who fears the Lord.**

or

℟ **Alleluia!**

1 Happy the man who fears the Lord,
   who takes delight in his commands.
   His sons will be powerful on earth;
   the children of the upright are blessed ℟

2 Riches and wealth are in his house;
   his justice stands firm for ever.
   He is a light in the darkness for the upright:
   he is generous, merciful and just. ℟

3 The good man takes pity and lends,
   he conducts his affairs with honour.
   The just man will never waver:
   he will be remembered for ever. ℟

Gospel Acclamation
cf. Col 3:16. 17

Alleluia, alleluia!
Let the message of Christ, in all its richness,
find a home with you;
through him give thanks to God the Father.
Alleluia!

or

cf. Apoc 1:5

Alleluia, alleluia!
Jesus Christ, the faithful witness,
the First-born from the dead,
loves us and has washed away our sins with his blood.
Alleluia!

GOSPEL

A reading from the holy Gospel according to Mark   12:1-12
They seized the beloved son, killed him, and threw him out of the vineyard.

Jesus began to speak to the chief priests, the scribes and the elders in parables, 'A man planted a vineyard; he fenced it round, dug out a trough for the winepress and built a tower; then he leased it to tenants and went abroad. When the time came, he sent a servant to the tenants to collect from them his share of the produce from the vineyard. But they seized the man, thrashed him and sent him away empty-handed. Next he sent another servant to them; him they beat about the head and treated shamefully. And he sent another and him they killed; then a number of others, and they thrashed some and killed the rest. He had still someone left: his beloved son. He sent him to them last of all. 'They will respect my son' he said. But those tenants said to each other, 'This is the heir. Come on, let us kill him, and the inheritance will be ours.' So they seized him and killed him and threw him out of the vineyard. Now what will the owner of the vineyard do? He will come and make an end to the tenants and give the vineyard to others. Have you not read this text of scripture:

> It was the stone rejected by the builders
> that became the keystone.
> This was the Lord's doing
> and it is wonderful to see'?

And they would have liked to arrest him, because they realised that the parable was aimed at them, but they were afraid of the crowds. So they left him alone and went away.

This is the Gospel of the Lord.

TUESDAY

FIRST READING

A reading from the book of Tobit 2:9-14

Tobit did not complain against God at being struck blind.

I, Tobit, took a bath; then I went into the courtyard and lay down by the courtyard wall. Since it was hot I left my face uncovered. I did not know that there were sparrows in the wall above my head; their hot droppings fell into my eyes. White spots then formed which I was obliged to have treated by the doctors. But the more ointments they tried me with, the more the spots blinded me, and in the end I became blind altogether. I remained without sight four years; all my brothers were distressed; and Ahikar provided for my upkeep for two years, till he left for Elymais.

My wife Anna then undertook woman's work; she would spin wool and take cloth to weave; she used to deliver whatever had been ordered from her and then receive payment. Now on March the seventh she finished a piece of work and delivered it to her customers. They paid her all that was due, and into the bargain presented her with a kid for a meal. When the kid came into my house, it began to bleat. I called to my wife and said, 'Where does this creature come from? Suppose it has been stolen! Quick, let the owners have it back; we have no right to eat stolen goods.' She said, 'No, it was a present given me over and above my wages.' I did not believe her, and told her to give it back to the owners (I blushed at this in her presence). Then she answered, 'What about your own alms? What about your own good works? Everyone knows what return you have had for them.'

This is the word of the Lord.

Responsorial Psalm   Ps 111:1-2. 7-9. R̷ cf. v.7

℟ **With a firm heart he trusts in the Lord.**

or

℟ **Alleluia!**

1. Happy the man who fears the Lord,
   who takes delight in his commands.
   His sons will be powerful on earth;
   the children of the upright are blessed. ℟

2. He has no fear of evil news:
   with a firm heart he trusts in the Lord.
   With a steadfast heart he will not fear;
   he will see the downfall of his foes. ℟

3. Open-handed, he gives to the poor;
   his justice stands firm for ever.
   His head will be raised in glory. ℟

Gospel Acclamation   Heb 4:12

Alleluia, alleluia!
The word of God is something alive and active;
it can judge secret emotions and thoughts.
Alleluia!

or   cf. Eph 1:17. 18

Alleluia, alleluia!
May the Father of our Lord Jesus Christ

enlighten the eyes of our mind,
so that we can see what hope his call holds for us.
Alleluia!

GOSPEL

A reading from the holy Gospel according to Mark 12:13-17
Give back to Caesar what belongs to Caesar - and to God what belongs to God.

The chief priests and the scribes and the elders sent to Jesus some Pharisees and some Herodians to catch him out in what he said. These came and said to him, 'Master, we know you are an honest man, that you are not afraid of anyone, because a man's rank means nothing to you, and that you teach the way of God in all honesty. Is it permissible to pay taxes to Caesar or not? Should we pay, yes or no?' Seeing through their hypocrisy he said to them, 'Why do you set this trap for me? Hand me a denarius and let me see it.' They handed him one and he said, 'Whose head is this? Whose name?' 'Caesar's' they told him. Jesus said to them, 'Give back to Caesar what belongs to Caesar – and to God what belongs to God.' This reply took them completely by surprise.

This is the Gospel of the Lord.

WEDNESDAY

FIRST READING

A reading from the book of Tobit 3:1-11. 16-17
The prayer of each of them found favour before the glory of God.

Sad at heart, I, Tobit, sighed and wept, and began this prayer of lamentation:

'You are just, O Lord,
and just are all your works.
All your ways are grace and truth,
and you are the Judge of the world.

'Therefore, Lord,
remember me, look on me.
Do not punish me for my sins
or for my heedless faults
or for those of my fathers.

'For we have sinned against you

and broken your commandments;
and you have given us over to be plundered,
to captivity and death,
to be the talk, the laughing-stock and scorn
of all the nations among whom you have dispersed us.

'Whereas all your decrees are true
when you deal with me as my faults deserve,
and those of my fathers,
since we have neither kept your commandments
nor walked in truth before you;
so now, do with me as you will;
be pleased to take my life from me;
I desire to be delivered from earth
and to become earth again.
For death is better for me than life.
I have been reviled without a cause
and I am distressed beyond measure.

'Lord, I wait for the sentence you will give
to deliver me from this affliction.
Let me go away to my everlasting home;
do not turn your face from me, O Lord.
For it is better to die than still to live
in the face of trouble that knows no pity;
I am weary of hearing myself traduced.'

It chanced on the same day that Sarah the daughter of Raguel, who lived in Media at Ecbatana, also heard insults from one of her father's maids. You must know that she had been given in marriage seven times, and that Asmodeus, that worst of demons, had killed her bridegrooms one after another before ever they had slept with her as man with wife. The servant-girl said, 'Yes, you kill your bridegrooms yourself. That makes seven already to whom you have been given, and you have not once been in luck yet. Just because your bridegrooms have died, that is no reason for punishing us. Go and join them, and may we be spared the sight of any child of yours!' That day she grieved, she sobbed, and went up to her father's room intending to hang herself. But then she thought, 'Suppose they blamed my father! They will say, "You had an only daughter whom you loved, and now she has hanged herself for grief." I cannot cause my father a sorrow which would bring down his old age to the dwelling of the dead. I should do better not to hang myself, but to beg the Lord to let gave them a warmhearted welcome.

They washed and bathed and sat down to table. Then Tobias said to Raphael, 'Brother Azarias, will you ask Raguel to give me my sister Sarah?' Raguel overheard the words, and said to the young man, 'Eat and drink, and make the most of your evening; no one else has the right to take my daughter Sarah – no one but you, my brother. In any case I, for my own part, am not at liberty to give her to anyone else, since you are her next of kin. However, my boy, I must be frank with you: I have tried to find a husband for her seven times among our kinsmen, and all of them have died the first evening, on going to her room. But for the present, my boy, eat and drink; the Lord will grant you his grace and peace.' Tobias spoke out, 'I will not hear of eating and drinking till you have come to a decision about me.' Raguel answered, 'Very well. Since, as prescribed by the Book of Moses, she is given to you, heaven itself decrees she shall be yours. I therefore entrust your sister to you. From now you are her brother and she is your sister. She is given to you from today for ever. The Lord of heaven favour you tonight, my child, and grant you his grace and peace.' Raguel called for his daughter Sarah, took her by the hand and gave her to Tobias with these words, 'I entrust her to you; the law and the ruling recorded in the Book of Moses assign her to you as your wife. Take her; take her home to your father's house with a good conscience. The God of heaven grant you a good journey in peace.' Then he turned to her mother and asked her to fetch him writing paper. He drew up the marriage contract, how he gave his daughter as bride to Tobias according to the ordinance in the Law of Moses.

After this they began to eat and drink. The parents meanwhile had gone out and shut the door behind them. Tobias said to Sarah, 'Get up, my sister! You and I must pray and petition our Lord to win his grace and his protection.' She stood up, and they began praying for protection, and this was how he began:

'You are blessed, O God of our fathers;
blessed, too, is your name
for ever and ever.
Let the heavens bless you
and all things you have made
for evermore.
It was you who created Adam,
you who created Eve his wife
to be his help and support;

and from these two the human race was born.
It was you who said,
"It is not good that the man should be alone;
let us make him a helpmate like himself."
And so I do not take my sister
for any lustful motive;
I do it in singleness of heart.
Be kind enough to have pity on her and on me
and bring us to old age together.'

And together they said 'Amen, Amen', and lay down for the night.

This is the word of the Lord.

Responsorial Psalm   Ps 127:1-5. ℟ cf. v.1

℟ **O blessed are those who fear the Lord.**

1 O blessed are those who fear the Lord
   and walk in his ways!
   By the labour of your hands you shall eat.
   You will be happy and prosper.   ℟

2 Your wife like a fruitful vine
   in the heart of your house;
   your children like shoots of the olive,
   around your table.   ℟

3 Indeed thus shall be blessed
   the man who fears the Lord.
   May the Lord bless you from Zion
   all the days of your life!   ℟

Gospel Acclamation   cf. Jn 6:63. 68

Alleluia, alleluia!
Your words are spirit, Lord,
and they are life:
you have the message of eternal life.
Alleluia!

or   cf. 2 Tim 1:10

Alleluia, alleluia!
Our Saviour Christ Jesus abolished death,
and he has proclaimed life through the Good News.
Alleluia!

GOSPEL

A reading from the holy Gospel according to Mark 12:28-34
This is the first commandment. The second is like it.

One of the scribes came up to Jesus and put a question to him, 'Which is the first of all the commandments?' Jesus replied, 'This is the first: Listen, Israel, the Lord our God is the one Lord, and you must love the Lord your God with all your heart, with all your soul, with all your mind and with all your strength. The second is this: you must love your neighbour as yourself. There is no commandment greater than these.' The scribe said to him, 'Well spoken, Master; what you have said is true: that he is one and there is no other. To love him with all your heart, with all your understanding and strength, and to love your neighbour as yourself, this is far more important than any holocaust or sacrifice.' Jesus, seeing how wisely he had spoken, said, 'You are not far from the kingdom of God.' And after that no one dared to question him any more.

This is the Gospel of the Lord.

FRIDAY

FIRST READING

A reading from the book of Tobit 11:5-17
He had scourged me and has had pity on me, and now I see my son.

Anna was sitting, watching the road by which her son would come. She was sure at once it must be he and said to the father, 'Here comes your son, with his companion.'

Raphael said to Tobias before he reached his father, 'I give you my word that your father's eyes will open. You must put the fish's gall to his eyes; the medicine will smart and will draw a filmy white skin off his eyes. And your father will be able to see and look on the light.'

The mother ran forward and threw her arms round her son's neck. 'Now I can die,' she said 'I have seen you again.' And she wept. Tobit rose to his feet and stumbled across the courtyard through the door. Tobias came on towards him (he had the fish's gall in his hand). He blew into his eyes and said, steadying him, 'Take courage, father!' With this he applied the medicine, left it there a while, then with both hands peeled away a filmy skin from the corners of his eyes. Then his father fell on his neck and

Ninth Week in Ordinary Time, Year I: Friday

wept. He exclaimed, 'I can see, my son, the light of my eyes!' And he said:

> 'Blessed be God!
> Blessed be his great name!
> Blessed be all his holy angels!
> Blessed be his great name
> for evermore!
> For he had scourged me
> and now has had pity on me
> and I see my son Tobias.'

Tobias went into the house, and with a loud voice joyfully blessed God. Then he told his father everything: how his journey had been successful and he had brought the silver back; how he had married Sarah, the daughter of Raguel; how she was following him now, close behind, and could not be far from the gates of Nineveh.

Tobit set off to the gates of Nineveh to meet his daughter-in-law, giving joyful praise to God as he went. When the people of Nineveh saw him walking without a guide and stepping forward as briskly as of old, they were astonished. Tobit described to them how God had taken pity on him and had opened his eyes. Then Tobit met Sarah, the bride of his son Tobias, and blessed her in these words, 'Welcome, daughter! Blessed be your God for sending you to us, my daughter. Blessings on your father, blessings on my son Tobias, blessings on yourself, my daughter. Welcome now to your own house in joyfulness and in blessedness. Come in, my daughter.' He held a feast that day for all the Jews of Nineveh.

This is the word of the Lord.

Responsorial Psalm   Ps 145:2. 7-10. ℟ v.2

  ℟ **My soul, give praise to the Lord.**

or

  ℟ **Alleluia!**

1 My soul, give praise to the Lord;
 I will praise the Lord all my days,
 make music to my God while I live. ℟

2 It is the Lord who keeps faith for ever,
 who is just to those who are oppressed.
 It is he who gives bread to the hungry,

(continued)

the Lord, who sets prisoners free.

℟ **My soul, give praise to the Lord.**

or

℟ **Alleluia!**

3 It is the Lord who gives sight to the blind,
 who raises up those who are bowed down,
 the Lord, who protects the stranger
 and upholds the widow and orphan. ℟

4 It is the Lord who loves the just
 but thwarts the path of the wicked.
 The Lord will reign for ever,
 Zion's God, from age to age. ℟

Gospel Acclamation cf. Ps 18:9
 Alleluia, alleluia!
 Your words gladden the heart, O Lord,
 they give light to the eyes.
 Alleluia!

or Jn 14:23

 Alleluia, alleluia!
 If anyone loves me he will keep my word,
 and my Father will love him,
 and we shall come to him.
 Alleluia!

GOSPEL

A reading from the holy Gospel according to Mark 12:35-37
How can they maintain that the Christ is the son of David?

While teaching in the Temple, Jesus said, 'How can the scribes maintain that the Christ is the son of David? David himself, moved by the Holy Spirit, said:

 The Lord said to my Lord:
 Sit at my right hand
 and I will put your enemies
 under your feet.

David himself calls him Lord, in what way then can he be his son?' And the great majority of the people heard this with delight.

This is the Gospel of the Lord.

SATURDAY

FIRST READING

A reading from the book of Tobit   12:1. 5-15. 20
I am about to return to him who sent me. Give thanks to God.

When the feasting was over, Tobit called his son Tobias and said, 'My son, you ought to think about paying the amount due to your fellow traveller; give him more than the figure agreed on.' So Tobias called his companion and said, 'Take half of what you brought back, in payment for all you have done, and go in peace.'

Then Raphael took them both aside and said, 'Bless God, utter his praise before all the living for all the favours he has given you. Bless and extol his name. Proclaim before all men the deeds of God as they deserve, and never tire of giving him thanks. It is right to keep the secret of a king, yet right to reveal and publish the works of God. Thank him worthily. Do what is good, and no evil can befall you.

'Prayer with fasting and alms with right conduct are better than riches with iniquity. Better to practise almsgiving than to hoard up gold. Almsgiving saves from death and purges every kind of sin. Those who give alms have their fill of days; those who commit sin and do evil, bring harm on themselves.

'I am going to tell you the whole truth, hiding nothing from you. I have already told you that it is right to keep the secret of a king, yet right too to reveal in worthy fashion the works of God. So you must know that when you and Sarah were at prayer, it was I who offered your supplications before the glory of the Lord and who read them; so too when you were burying the dead. When you did not hesitate to get up and leave the table to go and bury a dead man, I was sent to test your faith, and at the same time God sent me to heal you and your daughter-in-law Sarah. I am Raphael, one of the seven angels who stand ever ready to enter the presence of the glory of the Lord.

'Now bless the Lord on earth and give thanks to God. I am about to return to him above who sent me.'

This is the word of the Lord.

Responsorial Psalm   Tob 13:2. 6-8. ℟ v.1

   ℟ **Blessed be God who lives for ever.**

1. By turns he punishes and pardons;
   he sends men down to the depths of the underworld
   and draws them up from supreme Destruction;
   no one can escape his hand. ℟

2. If you return to him
   with all your heart and all your soul,
   behaving honestly towards him,
   then he will return to you
   and hide his face from you no longer. ℟

3. Consider how well he has treated you;
   loudly give him thanks.
   Bless the Lord of justice
   and extol the King of the ages. ℟

4. I for my part sing his praise
   in the country of my exile;
   I make his power and greatness known
   to a nation that has sinned. ℟

5. Sinners, return to him;
   let your conduct be upright before him;
   perhaps he will be gracious to you
   and take pity on you. ℟

Gospel Acclamation   cf. Lk 8:15

Alleluia, alleluia!
Blessed are those who,
with a noble and generous heart,
take the word of God to themselves
and yield a harvest through their perseverance.
Alleluia!

or   Mt 5:3

Alleluia, alleluia!
How happy are the poor in spirit;
theirs is the kingdom of heaven.
Alleluia!

GOSPEL

A reading from the holy Gospel according to Mark 12:38-44
This poor widow had put more in than all of them.

In his teaching Jesus said, 'Beware of the scribes who like to walk about in long robes, to be greeted obsequiously in the market squares, to take the front seats in the synagogues and the places of honour at banquets; these are the men who swallow the property of widows, while making a show of lengthy prayers. The more severe will be the sentence they receive.'

He sat down opposite the treasury and watched the people putting money into the treasury, and many of the rich put in a great deal. A poor widow came and put in two small coins, the equivalent of a penny. Then he called his disciples and said to them, 'I tell you solemnly, this poor widow has put more in than all who have contributed to the treasury; for they have all put in money they had over, but she from the little she had has put in everything she possessed, all she had to live on.'

This is the Gospel of the Lord.

TENTH WEEK IN ORDINARY TIME
Year I

MONDAY

FIRST READING

A reading from the second letter of St Paul 1:1-7
to the Corinthians
God comforts us, so that we can offer others consolation in their sorrows.

From Paul, appointed by God to be an apostle of Christ Jesus, and from Timothy, one of the brothers, to the church of God at Corinth and to all the saints in the whole of Achaia. Grace and peace to you from God our Father and the Lord Jesus Christ.

Blessed be the God and Father of our Lord Jesus Christ, a gentle Father and the God of all consolation, who comforts us in all our sorrows, so that we can offer others, in their sorrows, the consolation that we have received from God ourselves. Indeed, as the sufferings of Christ overflow to us, so, through Christ, does our consolation overflow. When we are made to suffer, it is for your consolation and salvation. When, instead, we are comforted, this should be a consolation to you, supporting you in patiently bearing the same sufferings as we bear. And our hope for you is confident, since we know that, sharing our sufferings, you will also share our consolations.

This is the word of the Lord.

Responsorial Psalm   Ps 33:2-9. ℟ v.9

℟ **Taste and see that the Lord is good.**

1. I will bless the Lord at all times,
 his praise always on my lips;
 in the Lord my soul shall make its boast.
 The humble shall hear and be glad. ℟

2. Glorify the Lord with me.
 Together let us praise his name.
 I sought the Lord and he answered me;
 from all my terrors he set me free. ℟

3. Look towards him and be radiant;
 let your faces not be abashed.
 This poor man called; the Lord heard him
 and rescued him from all his distress. ℟

4. The angel of the Lord is encamped
 around those who revere him, to rescue them.
 Taste and see that the Lord is good.
 He is happy who seeks refuge in him. ℟

Gospel Acclamation   cf. 2 Thess 2:14

Alleluia, alleluia!
Through the Good News God called us
to share the glory of our Lord Jesus Christ.
Alleluia!

or   Mt 5:12

Alleluia, alleluia!
Rejoice and be glad:
your reward will be great in heaven.
Alleluia!

GOSPEL

A reading from the holy Gospel according to Matthew   5:1-12

How happy are the poor in spirit.

Seeing the crowds, Jesus went up the hill. There he sat down and was joined by his disciples. Then he began to speak. This is what he taught them:

> 'How happy are the poor in spirit;
> theirs is the kingdom of heaven.
> Happy the gentle:
> they shall have the earth for their heritage.
> Happy those who mourn:
> they shall be comforted.
> Happy those who hunger and thirst for what is right:
> they shall be satisfied.
> Happy the merciful:
> they shall have mercy shown them.
> Happy the pure in heart:
> they shall see God.
> Happy the peacemakers:
> they shall be called sons of God.
> Happy those who are persecuted in the cause of right:
> theirs is the kingdom of heaven.

'Happy are you when people abuse you and persecute you and speak all kinds of calumny against you on my account. Rejoice and be glad, for your reward will be great in heaven; this is how they persecuted the prophets before you.'

This is the Gospel of the Lord.

TUESDAY

FIRST READING

A reading from the second letter of St Paul to the Corinthians   1:18-22

Jesus was never Yes and No: with him it was always Yes.

I swear by God's truth, there is no Yes and No about what we say to you. The Son of God, the Christ Jesus that we proclaimed among you – I mean Silvanus and Timothy and I – was never Yes and No: with him it was always Yes, and however many the promises God made, the Yes to them all is in him. That is why it is 'through him' that we answer Amen to the praise of God. Remember it is God himself who assures us all, and you, of our standing in Christ, and has anointed us, marking us with his seal and giving us the pledge, the Spirit, that we carry in our hearts.

This is the word of the Lord.

Responsorial Psalm   Ps 118:129-133. 135. R/ v.135

    R/ **Let your face shine on your servant.**

1. Your will is wonderful indeed;
    therefore I obey it.
    The unfolding of your word gives light
    and teaches the simple. R/

2. I open my mouth and I sigh
    as I yearn for your commands.
    Turn and show me your mercy;
    show justice to your friends. R/

3. Let my steps be guided by your promise;
    let no evil rule me.
    Let your face shine on your servant
    and teach me your decrees. R/

Gospel Acclamation   Phil 2:15-16

    Alleluia, alleluia!
    You will shine in the world like bright stars
    because you are offering it the word of life.
    Alleluia!

or   Mt 5:16

    Alleluia, alleluia!
    Your light must shine in the sight of men,
    so that, seeing your good works,
    they may give the praise to your Father in heaven.
    Alleluia!

GOSPEL

A reading from the holy Gospel according to Matthew   5:13-16
You are the light of the world.

Jesus said to his disciples: 'You are the salt of the earth. But if salt becomes tasteless, what can make it salty again? It is good for nothing, and can only be thrown out to be trampled underfoot by men.

'You are the light of the world. A city built on a hill-top cannot be hidden. No one lights a lamp to put it under a tub; they put it on the lamp-stand where it shines for everyone in the house. In the same way your light must shine in the sight of men, so that, seeing your good works, they may give the praise to your Father in heaven.'

This is the Gospel of the Lord.

WEDNESDAY

FIRST READING

A reading from the second letter of St Paul to the Corinthians   3:4-11

God is the one who has given us the qualifications to be the administrators of the new covenant, which is not a covenant of written letters but of the Spirit.

Before God, we are confident of this through Christ: not that we are qualified in ourselves to claim anything as our own work: all our qualifications come from God. He is the one who has given us the qualifications to be the administrators of this new covenant, which is not a covenant of written letters but of the Spirit: the written letters bring death, but the Spirit gives life. Now if the administering of death, in the written letters engraved on stones, was accompanied by such a brightness that the Israelites could not bear looking at the face of Moses, though it was a brightness that faded, then how much greater will be the brightness that surrounds the administering of the Spirit! For if there was any splendour in administering condemnation, there must be very much greater splendour in administering justification. In fact, compared with this greater splendour, the thing that used to have such splendour now seems to have none; and if what was so temporary had any splendour, there must be much more in what is going to last for ever.

This is the word of the Lord.

Responsorial Psalm
Ps 98:5-9. ℟ v.9

℟ **You are holy, O Lord our God.**

1. Exalt the Lord our God;
   bow down before Zion, his footstool.
   He the Lord is holy. ℟

2. Among his priests were Aaron and Moses,
   among those who invoked his name was Samuel.
   They invoked the Lord and he answered. ℟

3. To them he spoke in the pillar of cloud.
   They did his will; they kept the law,
   which he, the Lord, had given. ℟

4. O Lord our God, you answered them.
   For them you were a God who forgives;
   yet you punished all their offences. ℟

5. Exalt the Lord our God;
   bow down before his holy mountain
   for the Lord our God is holy. ℟

Gospel Acclamation
Ps 118:27

Alleluia, alleluia!
Make me grasp the way of your precepts,
and I will muse on your wonders.
Alleluia!

or
Ps 24:4. 5

Alleluia, alleluia!
Teach me your paths, my God,
make me walk in your truth.
Alleluia!

GOSPEL

A reading from the holy Gospel according to Matthew 5:17-19

I have come not to abolish the Law or the Prophets but to complete them.

Jesus said to his disciples: 'Do not imagine that I have come to abolish the Law or the Prophets. I have come not to abolish but to complete them. I tell you solemnly, till heaven and earth disappear, not one dot, not one little stroke, shall disappear from the Law until its purpose is achieved. Therefore, the man who infringes even one of the least of these commandments and teaches others to do the same will be considered the least in the kingdom of heaven; but the man who keeps them and teaches them will be considered great in the kingdom of heaven.'

This is the Gospel of the Lord.

THURSDAY

FIRST READING

A reading from the second letter of St Paul to the Corinthians   3:15–4:1, 3-6

God has shone in our minds to radiate the light of the knowledge of God's glory.

Even today, whenever Moses is read, the veil is over the minds of the Israelites. It will not be removed until they turn to the Lord. Now this Lord is the Spirit, and where the Spirit of the Lord is, there is freedom. And we, with our unveiled faces reflecting like mirrors the brightness of the Lord, all grow brighter and brighter as we are turned into the image that we reflect; this is the work of the Lord who is Spirit.

Since we have by an act of mercy been entrusted with this work of administration, there is no weakening on our part. If our gospel does not penetrate the veil, then the veil is on those who are not on the way to salvation; the unbelievers whose minds the god of this world has blinded, to stop them seeing the light shed by the Good News of the glory of Christ, who is the image of God. For it is not ourselves that we are preaching, but Christ Jesus as the Lord, and ourselves as your servants for Jesus' sake. It is the same God that said, 'Let there be light shining out of darkness,' who has shone in our minds to radiate the light of the knowledge of God's glory, the glory on the face of Christ.

This is the word of the Lord.

Responsorial Psalm   Ps 84:9-14. ℟ cf. v.10

  ℟ **The glory of the Lord will dwell in our land.**

1 I will hear what the Lord God has to say,
   a voice that speaks of peace.
   His help is near for those who fear him
   and his glory will dwell in our land. ℟

2 Mercy and faithfulness have met,

justice and peace have embraced.
Faithfulness shall spring from the earth
and justice look down from heaven.

℟ **The glory of the Lord will dwell in our land.**

3 The Lord will make us prosper
and our earth shall yield its fruit.
Justice shall march before him
and peace shall follow his steps. ℟

Gospel Acclamation　　　　　　　　　　　　　　　cf. 1 Thess 2:13
Alleluia, alleluia!
Accept God's message for what it really is:
God's message, and not some human thinking.
Alleluia!

or　　　　　　　　　　　　　　　　　　　　　　　　　Jn 13:34

Alleluia, alleluia!
I give you a new commandment:
love one another just as I have loved you,
says the Lord.
Alleluia!

GOSPEL

A reading from the holy Gospel according to Matthew　　5:20-26
Anyone who is angry with his brother will answer for it before the court.

Jesus said to his disciples: 'If your virtue goes no deeper than that of the scribes and Pharisees, you will never get into the kingdom of heaven.

'You have learnt how it was said to our ancestors: You must not kill; and if anyone does kill he must answer for it before the court. But I say this to you: anyone who is angry with his brother will answer for it before the court; if a man calls his brother "Fool" he will answer for it before the Sanhedrin; and if a man calls him "Renegade" he will answer for it in hell fire. So then, if you are bringing your offering to the altar and there remember that your brother has something against you, leave your offering there before the altar, go and be reconciled with your brother first, and then come back and present your offering. Come to terms with your opponent in good time while you are still on the way to the court with him, or he may hand you over to the judge and the judge to the officer, and you will be thrown into prison. I tell you solemnly, you will not get out till you have paid the last penny.'

This is the Gospel of the Lord.

FRIDAY

FIRST READING

A reading from the second letter of St Paul to the Corinthians 4:7-15

He who raised Jesus to life will raise us with Jesus in our turn, and put us by his side and you with us.

We are only the earthenware jars that hold this treasure, to make it clear that such an overwhelming power comes from God and not from us. We are in difficulties on all sides, but never cornered; we see no answer to our problems, but never despair; we have been persecuted, but never deserted; knocked down, but never killed; always, wherever we may be, we carry with us in our body the death of Jesus, so that the life of Jesus, too, may always be seen in our body. Indeed, while we are still alive, we are consigned to our death every day, for the sake of Jesus, so that in our mortal flesh the life of Jesus, too, may be openly shown. So death is at work in us, but life in you.

But as we have the same spirit of faith that is mentioned in scripture – I believed, and therefore I spoke – we too believe and therefore we too speak, knowing that he who raised the Lord Jesus to life will raise us with Jesus in our turn, and put us by his side and you with us. You see, all this is for your benefit, so that the more grace is multiplied among people, the more thanksgiving there will be to the glory of God.

This is the word of the Lord.

Responsorial Psalm Ps 115:10-11. 15-18. ℟ v.17

℟ **A thanksgiving sacrifice I make to you, O Lord.**

or

℟ **Alleluia!**

1 I trusted, even when I said:
   'I am sorely afflicted,'
   and when I said in my alarm:
   'No man can be trusted.' ℟

(continued)

2 O precious in the eyes of the Lord
   is the death of his faithful.
   Your servant, Lord, your servant am I;
   you have loosened my bonds.

   ℟ **A thanksgiving sacrifice I make to you, O Lord.**

or

   ℟ **Alleluia!**

3 A thanksgiving sacrifice I make:
   I will call on the Lord's name.
   My vows to the Lord I will fulfil
   before all his people.   ℟

Gospel Acclamation   Jn 10:27
Alleluia, alleluia!
The sheep that belong to me listen to my voice,
says the Lord,
I know them and they follow me.
Alleluia!

or   Phil 2:15. 16

Alleluia, alleluia!
You will shine in the world like bright stars
because you are offering it the word of life.
Alleluia!

GOSPEL

A reading from the holy Gospel according to Matthew   5:27-32
If a man looks at a woman lustfully, he has already committed adultery.

Jesus said to his disciples: 'You have learnt how it was said: You must not commit adultery. But I say this to you: if a man looks at a woman lustfully, he has already committed adultery with her in his heart. If your right eye should cause you to sin, tear it out and throw it away; for it will do you less harm to lose one part of you than to have your whole body thrown into hell. And if your right hand should cause you to sin, cut it off and throw it away; for it will do you less harm to lose one part of you than to have your whole body go to hell.

   'It has also been said: Anyone who divorces his wife must give her a writ of dismissal. But I say this to you: everyone who

Tenth Week in Ordinary Time, Year I: Saturday

divorces his wife, except for the case of fornication, makes her an adulteress; and anyone who marries a divorced woman commits adultery.'

This is the Gospel of the Lord.

SATURDAY

FIRST READING

A reading from the second letter of St Paul to the Corinthians 5:14-21

For our sake God made the sinless one into sin.

The love of Christ overwhelms us when we reflect that if one man has died for all, then all men should be dead; and the reason he died for all was so that living men should live no longer for themselves but for him who died and was raised to life for them.

From now onwards, therefore, we do not judge anyone by the standards of the flesh. Even if we did once know Christ in the flesh, that is not how we know him now. And for anyone who is in Christ, there is a new creation; the old creation has gone, and now the new one is here. It is all God's work. It was God who reconciled us to himself through Christ and gave us the work of handing on this reconciliation. In other words, God in Christ was reconciling the world to himself, not holding men's faults against them, and he has entrusted to us the news that they are reconciled. So we are ambassadors for Christ; it is as though God were appealing through us, and the appeal that we make in Christ's name is: be reconciled to God. For our sake God made the sinless one into sin, so that in him we might become the goodness of God.

This is the word of the Lord.

Responsorial Psalm Ps 102:1-4. 8-9. 11-12. ℟ v.8

℟ **The Lord is compassion and love.**

1 My soul, give thanks to the Lord,
   all my being, bless his holy name.
   My soul, give thanks to the Lord
   and never forget all his blessings. ℟

2 It is he who forgives all your guilt,
   who heals every one of your ills,

who redeems your life from the grave,
who crowns you with love and compassion.

℞ **The Lord is compassion and love.**

3 The Lord is compassion and love,
slow to anger and rich in mercy.
His wrath will come to an end;
he will not be angry for ever. ℞

4 For as the heavens are high above the earth
so strong is his love for those who fear him.
As far as the east is from the west
so far does he remove our sins. ℞

Gospel Acclamation   Ps 118:18

Alleluia, alleluia!
Open my eyes, O Lord, that I may consider
the wonders of your law.
Alleluia!

or   Ps 118:36. 29

Alleluia, alleluia!
Bend my heart to your will, O Lord,
and teach me your law.
Alleluia!

GOSPEL

A reading from the holy Gospel according to Matthew   5:33-37
I say to you do not swear at all.

Jesus said to his disciples: 'You have learnt how it was said to our ancestors: You must not break your oath, but must fulfil your oaths to the Lord. But I say this to you: do not swear at all, either by heaven, since that is God's throne; or by the earth, since that is his footstool; or by Jerusalem, since that is the city of the great king. Do not swear by your own head either, since you cannot turn a single hair white or black. All you need say is "Yes" if you mean yes, "No" if you mean no; anything more than this comes from the evil one.'

This is the Gospel of the Lord.

ELEVENTH WEEK IN ORDINARY TIME
Year I

MONDAY

FIRST READING

A reading from the second letter of St Paul to the Corinthians 6:1-10

Let us prove we are servants of God.

As God's fellow workers we beg you once again not to neglect the grace of God that you have received. For he says: At the favourable time, I have listened to you; on the day of salvation I came to your help. Well, now is the favourable time; this is the day of salvation.

We do nothing that people might object to, so as not to bring discredit on our function as God's servants. Instead, we prove we are servants of God by great fortitude in times of suffering: in times of hardship and distress; when we are flogged, or sent to prison, or mobbed; labouring, sleepless, starving. We prove we are God's servants by our purity, knowledge, patience and kindness; by a spirit of holiness, by a love free from affectation; by the word of truth and by the power of God; by being armed with the weapons of righteousness in the right hand and in the left, prepared for honour or disgrace, for blame or praise; taken for impostors while we are genuine; obscure yet famous; said to be dying and here are we alive; rumoured to be executed before we are sentenced; thought most miserable and yet we are always rejoicing; taken for paupers though we make others rich, for people having nothing though we have everything.

This is the word of the Lord.

Responsorial Psalm Ps 97:1-4. ℟ v.2

℟ **The Lord has made known his salvation.**

1 Sing a new song to the Lord
  for he has worked wonders.
  His right hand and his holy arm
  have brought salvation. ℟

2 The Lord has made known his salvation;
  has shown his justice to the nations.

(continued)

He has remembered his truth and love
for the house of Israel.

℟ **The Lord has made known his salvation.**

3 All the ends of the earth have seen
the salvation of our God.
Shout to the Lord all the earth,
ring out your joy. ℟

Gospel Acclamation   Jn 14:23

Alleluia, alleluia!
If anyone loves me he will keep my word,
and my Father will love him,
and we shall come to him.
Alleluia!

or   Ps 118:105

Alleluia, alleluia!
Your word is a lamp for my steps
and a light for my path.
Alleluia!

GOSPEL

A reading from the holy Gospel according to Matthew   5:38-42

I say this to you: offer the wicked man no resistance.

Jesus said to his disciples: 'You have learnt how it was said: Eye for eye and tooth for tooth. But I say this to you: offer the wicked man no resistance. On the contrary, if anyone hits you on the right cheek, offer him the other as well; if a man takes you to law and would have your tunic, let him have your cloak as well. And if anyone orders you to go one mile, go two miles with him. Give to anyone who asks, and if anyone wants to borrow, do not turn away.'

This is the Gospel of the Lord.

TUESDAY

FIRST READING

A reading from the second letter of St Paul 8:1-9
to the Corinthians
Christ became poor for your sake.

Here, brothers, is the news of the grace of God which was given in the churches in Macedonia; and of how, throughout great trials by suffering, their constant cheerfulness and their intense poverty have overflowed in a wealth of generosity. I can swear that they gave not only as much as they could afford, but far more, and quite spontaneously, begging and begging us for the favour of sharing in this service to the saints and, what was quite unexpected, they offered their own selves first to God and, under God, to us.

Because of this, we have asked Titus, since he has already made a beginning, to bring this work of mercy to the same point of success among you. You always have the most of everything – of faith, of eloquence, of understanding, of keenness for any cause, and the biggest share of our affection – so we expect you to put the most into this work of mercy too. It is not an order that I am giving you ; I am just testing the genuineness of your love against the keenness of others. Remember how generous the Lord Jesus was: he was rich, but he became poor for your sake, to make you rich out of his poverty.

This is the word of the Lord.

Responsorial Psalm   Ps 145:2.5-9. ℟ v.2
    ℟ **My soul, give praise to the Lord.**

or

    ℟   **Alleluia!**

1   I will praise the Lord all my days,
     make music to my God while I live.   ℟

2   He is happy who is helped by Jacob's God,
     whose hope is in the Lord his God,
     who alone made heaven and earth,
     the seas and all they contain.   ℟

3   It is he who keeps faith for ever,
     who is just to those who are oppressed.

(continued)

It is he who gives bread to the hungry,
the Lord, who sets prisoners free.

℟ **My soul, give praise to the Lord.**

or

℟ **Alleluia!**

4 It is the Lord who gives sight to the blind,
who raises up those who are bowed down,
the Lord, who protects the stranger
and upholds the widow and orphan.   ℟

Gospel Acclamation   2 Cor 5:19
Alleluia, alleluia!
God in Christ was reconciling the world to himself,
and he has entrusted to us the news that they are reconciled.
Alleluia!

or   Jn 13:34

Alleluia, alleluia!
I give you a new commandment:
love one another just as I have loved you,
says the Lord.
Alleluia!

GOSPEL

A reading from the holy Gospel according to Matthew   5:43-48
Love your enemies.

Jesus said to his disciples: 'You have learnt how it was said: You must love your neighbour and hate your enemy. But I say to you: love your enemies and pray for those who persecute you; in this way you will be sons of your Father in heaven, for he causes his sun to rise on bad men as well as good, and his rain to fall on honest and dishonest men alike. For if you love those who love you, what right have you to claim any credit? Even the tax collectors do as much, do they not? And if you save your greetings for your brothers, are you doing anything exceptional? Even the pagans do as much, do they not? You must therefore be perfect just as your heavenly Father is perfect.'

This is the Gospel of the Lord.

WEDNESDAY

FIRST READING

A reading from the second letter of St Paul to the Corinthians 9:6-11

God loves a cheerful giver.

Do not forget: thin sowing means thin reaping; the more you sow, the more you reap. Each one should give what he has decided in his own mind, not grudgingly or because he is made to, for God loves a cheerful giver. And there is no limit to the blessings which God can send you – he will make sure that you will always have all you need for yourselves in every possible circumstance, and still have something to spare for all sorts of good works. As scripture says: He was free in almsgiving, and gave to the poor: his good deeds will never be forgotten.

The one who provides seed for the sower and bread for food will provide you with all the seed you want and make the harvest of your good deeds a larger one, and, made richer in every way, you will be able to do all the generous things which, through us, are the cause of thanksgiving to God.

This is the word of the Lord.

Responsorial Psalm   Ps 111:1-4. 9. ℟ v.1

  ℟ **Happy the man who fears the Lord.**

or

  ℟ **Alleluia!**

1. Happy the man who fears the Lord,
   who takes delight in his commands.
   His sons will be powerful on earth;
   the children of the upright are blessed. ℟

2. Riches and wealth are in his house;
   his justice stands firm for ever.
   He is a light in the darkness for the upright:
   he is generous, merciful and just. ℟

3. Open-handed, he gives to the poor;
   his justice stands firm for ever.
   His head will be raised in glory. ℟

Gospel Acclamation   Col 3:16. 17

Alleluia, alleluia!
Let the message of Christ, in all its richness,
find a home with you;
through him give thanks to God the Father.
Alleluia!

or   Jn 14:23

Alleluia, alleluia!
If anyone loves me he will keep my word,
and my Father will love him,
and we shall come to him.
Alleluia!

GOSPEL

A reading from the holy Gospel according to Matthew   6:1-6. 16-18

Your Father who sees all that is done in secret will reward you.

Jesus said to his disciples: 'Be careful not to parade your good deeds before men to attract their notice; by doing this you will lose all reward from your Father in heaven. So when you give alms, do not have it trumpeted before you ; that is what the hypocrites do in the synagogues and in the streets to win men's admiration. I tell you solemnly, they have had their reward. But when you give alms, your left hand must not know what your right is doing; your almsgiving must be secret, and your Father who sees all that is done in secret will reward you.

'And when you pray, do not imitate the hypocrites: they love to say their prayers standing up in the synagogues and at the street corners for people to see them. I tell you solemnly, they have had their reward. But when you pray, go to your private room and, when you have shut your door, pray to your Father who is in that secret place, and your Father who sees all that is done in secret will reward you.

'When you fast do not put on a gloomy look as the hypocrites do: they pull long faces to let men know they are fasting. I tell you solemnly, they have had their reward. But when you fast, put oil on your head and wash your face, so that no one will know you are fasting except your Father who sees all that is done in secret; and your Father who sees all that is done in secret will reward you.'

This is the Gospel of the Lord.

THURSDAY

FIRST READING

A reading from the second letter of St Paul to the Corinthians
11:1-11
I preached the gospel of God to you and took no fee for it.

I only wish you were able to tolerate a little foolishness from me. But of course: you are tolerant towards me. You see, the jealousy that I feel for you is God's own jealousy: I arranged for you to marry Christ so that I might give you away as a chaste virgin to this one husband. But the serpent, with his cunning, seduced Eve, and I am afraid that in the same way your ideas may get corrupted and turned away from simple devotion to Christ. Because any newcomer has only to proclaim a new Jesus, different from the one that we preached, or you have only to receive a new spirit, different from the one you have already received, or a new gospel, different from the one you have already accepted – and you welcome it with open arms. As far as I can tell, these arch-apostles have nothing more than I have. I may not be a polished speechmaker, but as for knowledge, that is a different matter; surely we have made this plain, speaking on every subject in front of all of you.

Or was I wrong, lowering myself so as to lift you high, by preaching the gospel of God to you and taking no fee for it? I was robbing other churches, living on them so that I could serve you. When I was with you and ran out of money, I was no burden to anyone; the brothers who came from Macedonia provided me with everything I wanted. I was very careful, and I always shall be, not to be a burden to you in any way, and by Christ's truth in me, this cause of boasting will never be taken from me in the regions of Achaia. Would I do that if I did not love you? God knows I do.

This is the word of the Lord.

Responsorial Psalm   Ps 110:1-4. 7-8. ℟ v.7

   ℟ **Your works, O Lord, are justice and truth.**

or

    ℟ **Alleluia!**

1. I will thank the Lord with all my heart
   in the meeting of the just and their assembly.
   Great are the works of the Lord;
   to be pondered by all who love them. ℟

2. Majestic and glorious his work,
   his justice stands firm for ever.
   He makes us remember his wonders.
   The Lord is compassion and love. ℟

3. His works are justice and truth:
   his precepts are all of them sure,
   standing firm for ever and ever:
   they are made in uprightness and truth. ℟

Gospel Acclamation   1 Sam 3:9; Jn 6:68
Alleluia, alleluia!
Speak, Lord, your servant is listening:
you have the message of eternal life.
Alleluia!

or   Rom 8:15

Alleluia, alleluia!
The spirit you received is the spirit of sons,
and it makes us cry out, 'Abba, Father!'
Alleluia!

GOSPEL

A reading from the holy Gospel according to Matthew   6:7-15
You should pray like this.

Jesus said to his disciples: 'In your prayers do not babble as the pagans do, for they think that by using many words they will make themselves heard. Do not be like them; your Father knows what you need before you ask him. So you should pray like this·

   Our Father in heaven,
   may your name be held holy,
   your kingdom come,

your will be done,
on earth as in heaven.
Give us today our daily bread.
And forgive us our debts,
as we have forgiven those who are in debt to us.
And do not put us to the test,
but save us from the evil one.

'Yes, if you forgive others their failings, your heavenly Father will forgive you yours; but if you do not forgive others, your Father will not forgive your failings either.'

This is the Gospel of the Lord.

FRIDAY

FIRST READING

A reading from the second letter of St Paul to the Corinthians   11:18. 21-30

To leave out much more, there is my preoccupation: my anxiety for all the churches.

So many others have been boasting of their worldly achievements, that I will boast myself. But if anyone wants some brazen speaking – I am still talking as a fool – then I can be as brazen as any of them, and about the same things. Hebrews, are they? So am I. Israelites? So am I. Descendants of Abraham? So am I. The servants of Christ? I must be mad to say this, but so am I, and more than they: more, because I have worked harder, I have been sent to prison more often, and whipped so many times more, often almost to death. Five times I had the thirty-nine lashes from the Jews; three times I have been beaten with sticks; once I was stoned; three times I have been shipwrecked and once adrift in the open sea for a night and a day. Constantly travelling, I have been in danger from rivers and in danger from brigands, in danger from my own people and in danger from pagans; in danger in the towns, in danger in the open country, danger at sea and danger from so-called brothers. I have worked and laboured, often without sleep; I have been hungry and thirsty and often starving; I have been in the cold without clothes. And, to leave out much more, there is my daily preoccupation: my anxiety for all the churches. When any man has had scruples, I have had scruples with him; when any man is made to fall, I am tortured.

If I am to boast, then let me boast of my own feebleness.

This is the word of the Lord.

Responsorial Psalm   Ps 33:2-7. ℟ cf. v.18

℟ **The Lord rescues the just**
in all their distress.

1. I will bless the Lord at all times,
his praise always on my lips;
in the Lord my soul shall make its boast.
The humble shall hear and be glad. ℟

2. Glorify the Lord with me.
Together let us praise his name.
I sought the Lord and he answered me;
from all my terrors he set me free. ℟

3. Look towards him and be radiant;
let your faces not be abashed.
This poor man called; the Lord heard him
and rescued him from all his distress. ℟

Gospel Acclamation   Jn 8:12

Alleluia, alleluia!
I am the light of the world, says the Lord,
anyone who follows me
will have the light of life.
Alleluia!

or   Mt 5:3

Alleluia, alleluia!
How happy are the poor in spirit;
theirs is the kingdom of heaven.
Alleluia!

GOSPEL

A reading from the holy Gospel according to Matthew   6:19-23
Where your treasure is, there will your heart be also.

Jesus said to his disciples: 'Do not store up treasures for yourselves on earth, where moths and woodworms destroy them and thieves can break in and steal. But store up treasures for yourselves in heaven, where neither moth or woodworms destroy them and thieves cannot break in and steal. For where your treasure is, there will your heart be also.

'The lamp of the body is the eye. It follows that if your eye is sound, your whole body will be filled with light. But if your eye is diseased, your whole body will be all darkness. If then, the light inside you is darkness, what darkness that will be!'

This is the Gospel of the Lord.

SATURDAY

FIRST READING

A reading from the second letter of St Paul 12:1-10
to the Corinthians
I shall be very happy to make my weaknesses my special boast.

Must I go on boasting, though there is nothing to be gained by it? But I will move on to the visions and revelations I have had from the Lord. I know a man in Christ who, fourteen years ago, was caught up – whether still in the body or out of the body, I do not know; God knows – right into the third heaven. I do know, however, that this same person – whether in the body or out of the body, I do not know; God knows – was caught up into paradise and heard things which must not and cannot be put into human language. I will boast about a man like that, but not about anything of my own except my weaknesses. If I should decide to boast, I should not be made to look foolish, because I should only be speaking the truth; but I am not going to, in case anyone should begin to think I am better than he can actually see and hear me to be.

In view of the extraordinary nature of these revelations, to stop me from getting too proud I was given a thorn in the flesh, an angel of Satan to beat me and stop me from getting too proud! About this thing, I have pleaded with the Lord three times for it to leave me, but he has said, 'My grace is enough for you: my power is at its best in weakness.' So I shall be very happy to make my weaknesses my special boast so that the power of Christ may stay over me, and that is why I am quite content with my weaknesses, and with insults, hardships, persecutions, and the agonies I go through for Christ's sake. For it is when I am weak that I am strong.

This is the word of the Lord.

Responsorial Psalm
Ps 33:8-13. ℟ v.9

℟ **Taste and see that the Lord is good.**

1. The angel of the Lord is encamped
around those who revere him, to rescue them.
Taste and see that the Lord is good.
He is happy who seeks refuge in him. ℟

2. Revere the Lord, you his saints.
They lack nothing, those who revere him.
Strong lions suffer want and go hungry
but those who seek the Lord lack no blessing. ℟

3. Come, children, and hear me
that I may teach you the fear of the Lord.
Who is he who longs for life
and many days, to enjoy his prosperity? ℟

Gospel Acclamation
Mt 4:4

Alleluia, alleluia!
Man does not live on bread alone,
but on every word that comes from the mouth of God.
Alleluia!

or
2 Cor 8:9

Alleluia, alleluia!
Jesus Christ was rich,
but he became poor for your sake,
to make you rich out of his poverty.
Alleluia!

GOSPEL

A reading from the holy Gospel according to Matthew 6:24-34
Do not worry about tomorrow.

Jesus said to his disciples: 'No one can be the slave of two masters: he will either hate the first and love the second, or treat the first with respect and the second with scorn. You cannot be the slave both of God and money.

'That is why I am telling you not to worry about your life and what you are to eat, nor about your body and how you are to clothe it. Surely life means more than food, and the body more than clothing! Look at the birds in the sky. They do not sow or reap or gather into barns; yet your heavenly Father feeds them. Are you not worth much more than they are? Can any of you, for all his worrying, add one single cubit to his span of life? And why worry about clothing? Think of the flowers growing in the fields; they never have to work or spin; yet I assure you that not even Solomon in all his regalia was robed like one of these. Now if that is how God clothes the grass in the field which is there today and thrown into the furnace tomorrow, will he not much more look after you, you men of little faith? So do not worry; do not say, "What are we to eat? What are we to drink? How are we to be clothed?" It is the pagans who set their hearts on all these things. Your heavenly Father knows you need them all. Set your hearts on his kingdom first, and on his righteousness, and all these other things will be given you as well. So do not worry about tomorrow: tomorrow will take care of itself. Each day has enough trouble of its own.'

This is the Gospel of the Lord.

TWELFTH WEEK IN ORDINARY TIME
Year I

MONDAY

FIRST READING

A reading from the book of Genesis 12:1-9
Abram went as the Lord told him.

The Lord said to Abram, 'Leave your country, your family and your father's house, for the land I will show you. I will make you a great nation; I will bless you and make your name so famous that it will be used as a blessing.

'I will bless those who bless you:
I will curse those who slight you.
All the tribes of the earth
shall bless themselves by you.'

So Abram went as the Lord told him, and Lot went with him. Abram was seventy-five years old when he left Haran. Abram took his wife Sarai, his nephew Lot, all the possessions they had amassed and the people they had acquired in Haran. They set off for the land of Canaan, and arrived there.

Abram passed through the land as far as Shechem's holy place, the Oak of Moreh. At that time the Canaanites were in the land. The Lord appeared to Abram and said, 'It is to your descendants that I will give this land.' So Abram built there an altar for the Lord who had appeared to him. From there he moved on to the mountainous district east of Bethel, where he pitched his tent, with Bethel to the west and Ai to the east. There he built an altar to the Lord and invoked the name of the Lord. Then Abram made his way stage by stage to the Negeb.

This is the word of the Lord.

Responsional Psalm   Ps 32:12-13. 18-20. 22. ℟ v.12

   ℟ **Happy the people the Lord has chosen as his own.**

1. They are happy, whose God is the Lord,
   the people he has chosen as his own.
   From the heavens the Lord looks forth,
   he sees all the children of men. ℟

2. The Lord looks on those who revere him,
   on those who hope in his love,
   to rescue their souls from death,
   to keep them alive in famine. ℟

3. Our soul is waiting for the Lord.
   The Lord is our help and our shield.
   May your love be upon us, O Lord,
   as we place all our hope in you. ℟

Gospel Acclamation   cf. Jn 17:17

Alleluia, alleluia!
Your word is truth, O Lord,
consecrate us in the truth.
Alleluia!

or   Heb 4:12

Alleluia, alleluia!
The word of God is something alive and active;
it can judge secret emotions and thoughts.
Alleluia!

GOSPEL

A reading from the holy Gospel according to Matthew   7:1-5
Take the plank out of your own eye first.

Jesus said to his disciples: 'Do not judge, and you will not be judged; because the judgements you give are the judgements you will get, and the amount you measure out is the amount you will be given. Why do you observe the splinter in your brother's eye and never notice the plank in your own? How dare you say to your brother, "Let me take the splinter out of your eye", when all the time there is a plank in your own? Hypocrite! Take the plank out of your own eye first, and then you will see clearly enough to take the splinter out of your brother's eye.'

This is the Gospel of the Lord.

TUESDAY

FIRST READING

A reading from the book of Genesis 13:2. 5-18
Let there be no dispute between me and you, for we are brothers.

Abram was a very rich man, with livestock, silver and gold. Lot, who was travelling with Abram, had flocks and cattle of his own, and tents too. The land was not sufficient to accommodate them both at once, for they had too many possessions to be able to live together. Dispute broke out between the herdsmen of Abram's livestock and those of Lot's. (The Canaanites and the Perizzites were then living in the land.) Accordingly Abram said to Lot, 'Let there be no dispute between me and you, nor between my herdsmen and yours, for we are brothers. Is not the whole land open before you? Part company with me: if you take the left, I will go right; if you take the right, I will go left.'

Looking round, Lot saw all the Jordan plain, irrigated everywhere – this was before the Lord destroyed Sodom and Gomorrah – like the garden of the Lord or the land of Egypt, as far as Zoar. So Lot chose all the Jordan plain for himself and moved off eastwards. Thus they parted company: Abram settled in the land of Canaan; Lot settled among the towns of the plain, pitching his tents on the outskirts of Sodom. Now the people of Sodom were vicious men, great sinners against the Lord.

The Lord said to Abram after Lot had parted company with him, 'Look all round from where you are towards the north and the south, towards the east and the west. All the land within sight I will give to you and your descendants for ever. I will make your descendants like the dust on the ground: when men succeed in counting the specks of dust on the ground, then they will be able to count your descendants! Come, travel through the length and breadth of the land, for I mean to give it to you.'

So Abram went with his tents to settle at the Oak of Mamre, at Hebron, and there he built an altar to the Lord.

This is the word of the Lord.

Responsorial Psalm Ps 14:2-5. ℟ v.1

℟ **The just will live in the presence of the Lord.**

1. Lord, who shall dwell on your holy mountain?
   He who walks without fault;
   he who acts with justice
   and speaks the truth from his heart;
   he who does not slander with his tongue. ℟

2. He who does no wrong to his brother,
   who casts no slur on his neighbour,
   who holds the godless in disdain,
   but honours those who fear the Lord. ℟

3. He who keeps his pledge, come what may;
   who takes no interest on a loan
   and accepts no bribes against the innocent.
   Such a man will stand firm for ever. ℟

Gospel Acclamation cf. Mt 11:25

Alleluia, alleluia!
Blessed are you, Father,
Lord of heaven and earth,
for revealing the mysteries of the kingdom
to mere children.
Alleluia!

or Jn 8:12

Alleluia, alleluia!
I am the light of the world, says the Lord,
anyone who follows me
will have the light of life.
Alleluia!

GOSPEL

A reading from the holy Gospel according to Matthew 7:26. 12-14

Always treat others as you would like them to treat you.

Jesus said to his disciples: 'Do not give dogs what is holy; and do not throw your pearls in front of pigs, or they may trample them and then turn on you and tear you to pieces.

'So always treat others as you would like them to treat you; that is the meaning of the Law and the Prophets.

'Enter by the narrow gate, since the road that leads to perdition is wide and spacious, and many take it; but it is a narrow gate and a hard road that leads to life, and only a few find it.'

This is the Gospel of the Lord.

WEDNESDAY

FIRST READING

A reading from the book of Genesis 15:1-12. 17-18

Abraham put his faith in God, and his faith was considered as justifying him. The Lord made a Covenant with Abraham.

It happened that the word of the Lord was spoken to Abram in a vision, 'Have no fear, Abram, I am your shield; your reward will be very great.'

'My Lord,' Abram replied 'what do you intend to give me? I go childless ... ' Then Abram said, 'See, you have given me no descendants; some man of my household will be my heir.' And then this word of the Lord was spoken to him, 'He shall not be your heir; your heir shall be of your own flesh and blood.' Then taking him outside he said, 'Look up to heaven and count the stars if you can. Such will be your descendants' he told him. Abram put his faith in the Lord, who counted this as making him justified.

'I am the Lord' he said to him 'who brought you out of Ur of the Chaldaeans to make you heir to this land.' 'My Lord,' Abram replied 'how am I to know that I shall inherit it?' He said to him, 'Get me a three-year-old heifer, a three-year-old goat, a three-year-old ram, a turtledove and a young pigeon.' He brought him all these, cut them in half and put half on one side and half facing it on the other; but the birds he did not cut in half. Birds of prey came down on the carcases but Abram drove them off.

Now as the sun was setting Abram fell into a deep sleep, and terror seized him. When the sun had set and darkness had fallen, there appeared a smoking furnace and a firebrand that went between the halves. That day the Lord made a Covenant with Abram in these terms:

> 'To your descendants I give this land,
> from the wadi of Egypt to the Great River,
> the river Euphrates.'

This is the word of the Lord.

Responsorial Psalm   Ps 104:1-4. 6-9. R̸ v.8

    R̸ **The Lord remembers his covenant for ever.**

or

    R̸ **Alleluia!**

1. Give thanks to the Lord, tell his name,
   make known his deeds among the peoples.
   O sing to him, sing his praise;
   tell all his wonderful works!   R̸

2. Be proud of his holy name,
   let the hearts that seek the Lord rejoice.
   Consider the Lord and his strength;
   constantly seek his face.   R̸

3. O children of Abraham, his servant,
   O sons of the Jacob he chose.
   He, the Lord, is our God:
   his judgements prevail in all the earth.   R̸

4. He remembers his covenant for ever,
   his promise for a thousand generations,
   the covenant he made with Abraham,
   the oath he swore to Isaac.   R̸

Gospel Acclamation   Ps 118:88
    Alleluia, alleluia!
    Because of your love give me life,
    and I will do your will.
    Alleluia!

or   Jn 15:4. 5

    Alleluia, alleluia!
    Make your home in me, as I make mine in you,
    says the Lord;

whoever remains in me bears fruit in plenty.
Alleluia!

GOSPEL

A reading from the holy Gospel according to Matthew 7:15-20
You will be able to tell them by their fruits.

Jesus said to his disciples: 'Beware of false prophets who come to you disguised as sheep but underneath are ravenous wolves. You will be able to tell them by their fruits. Can people pick grapes from thorns, or figs from thistles? In the same way, a sound tree produces good fruit but a rotten tree bad fruit. A sound tree cannot bear bad fruit, nor a rotten tree bear good fruit. Any tree that does not produce good fruit is cut down and thrown on the fire. I repeat, you will be able to tell them by their fruits.'

This is the Gospel of the Lord.

THURSDAY

FIRST READING

A reading from the book of Genesis 16:1-12. 15-16
Hagar bore Abram a son, and Abram gave him the name Ishmael.

Abram's wife Sarai had borne him no child, but she had an Egyptian maidservant named Hagar. So Sarai said to Abram, 'Listen, now! Since the Lord has kept me from having children, go to my slave-girl. Perhaps I shall get children through her.' Abram agreed to what Sarai had said.

Thus after Abram had lived in the land of Canaan for ten years Sarai took Hagar her Egyptian slave-girl and gave her to Abram as his wife. He went to Hagar and she conceived. And once she knew she had conceived, her mistress counted for nothing in her eyes. Then Sarai said to Abram, 'May this insult to me come home to you! It was I who put my slave-girl into your arms but now she knows that she has conceived, I count for nothing in her eyes. Let the Lord judge between me and you.' 'Very well,' Abram said to Sarai, 'your slave-girl is at your disposal. Treat her as you think fit.' Sarai accordingly treated her so badly that she ran away from her.

The angel of the Lord met Hagar near a spring in the wilderness, the spring that is on the road to Shur. He said, 'Hagar, slave-girl of Sarai, where have you come from, and where are you going?' 'I am running away from my mistress Sarai' she replied. The angel of the Lord said to her, 'Go back to your mistress and submit to her.' The angel of the Lord said to her, 'I will make your descendants too numerous to be counted.' Then the angel of the Lord said to her:

'Now you have conceived, and you will bear a son,
and you shall name him Ishmael,
for the Lord has heard your cries of distress.
A wild-ass of a man he will be,
against every man, and every man against him,
setting himself to defy all his brothers.'

Hagar bore Abram a son, and Abram gave to the son that Hagar bore the name Ishmael. Abram was eighty-six years old when Hagar bore him Ishmael.

This is the word of the Lord.*

*Shorter form, verses 6-12. 15-16. Read between *.

Responsorial Psalm   Ps 105:1-5. ℟ v.1

  ℟ **O give thanks to the Lord for he is good.**

or

  ℟ **Alleluia!**

1 O give thanks to the Lord for he is good;
for his great love is without end.
Who can tell the Lord's mighty deeds?
Who can recount all his praise? ℟

2 They are happy who do what is right,
who at all times do what is just.
O Lord, remember me
out of the love you have for your people. ℟

3 Come to me, Lord, with your help
that I may see the joy of your chosen ones
and may rejoice in the gladness of your nation
and share the glory of your people. ℟

Gospel Acclamation   Heb 4:12
Alleluia, alleluia!
The word of God is something alive and active;
it can judge secret emotions and thoughts.
Alleluia!

Twelfth Week in Ordinary Time, Year I: Friday 581

or Jn 14:23

Alleluia, alleluia!
If anyone loves me he will keep my word,
and my Father will love him,
and we shall come to him.
Alleluia!

GOSPEL

A reading from the holy Gospel according to Matthew 7:21-29
The house built on rock and the house built on sand.

Jesus said to his disciples: 'It is not those who say to me, "Lord, Lord," who will enter the kingdom of heaven, but the person who does the will of my Father in heaven. When the day comes many will say to me, "Lord, Lord, did we not prophesy in your name, cast out demons in your name, work miracles in your name?" Then I shall tell them to their faces: I have never known you; away from me, you evil men!

'Therefore, everyone who listens to these words of mine and acts on them will be like a sensible man who built his house on rock. Rain came down, floods rose, gales blew and hurled themselves against the house, and it did not fall: it was founded on rock. But everyone who listens to these words of mine and does not act on them will be like a stupid man who built his house on sand. Rain came down, floods rose, gales blew and struck that house, and it fell; and what a fall it had!'

Jesus had now finished what he wanted to say, and his teaching made a deep impression on the people because he taught them with authority, and not like their own scribes.

This is the Gospel of the Lord.

FRIDAY

FIRST READING

A reading from the book of Genesis 17:1. 9-10. 15-22
All your males must be circumcised, and this shall be the sign of the Covenant. Sarah shall bear you a son.

When Abram was ninety-nine years old the Lord appeared to him and said, 'I am El Shaddai. Bear yourself blameless in my presence.

'You shall maintain my Covenant, yourself and your descendants after you, generation after generation. Now this is my Covenant which you are to maintain between myself and you, and your descendants after you: all your males must be circumcised.

'As for Sarai your wife, you shall not call her Sarai, but Sarah. I will bless her and moreover give you a son by her. I will bless her and nations shall come out of her; kings of peoples shall descend from her.' Abraham bowed to the ground, and he laughed, thinking to himself, 'Is a child to be born to a man one hundred years old, and will Sarah have a child at the age of ninety?' Abraham said to God, 'Oh, let Ishmael live in your presence!' But God replied, 'No, but your wife Sarah shall bear you a son whom you are to name Isaac. With him I will establish my Covenant, a Covenant in perpetuity, to be his God and the God of his descendants after him. For Ishmael too I grant you your request: I bless him and I will make him fruitful and greatly increased in numbers. He shall be the father of twelve princes, and I will make him into a great nation. But my Covenant I will establish with Isaac, whom Sarah will bear you at this time next year.' When he had finished speaking to Abraham God went up from him.

This is the word of the Lord.

Responsorial Psalm Ps 127:1-5. ℟ v.4

℟ **Indeed thus shall be blessed
the man who fears the Lord.**

1 O blessed are those who fear the Lord
and walk in his ways!
By the labour of your hands you shall eat.
You will be happy and prosper. ℟

2 Your wife like a fruitful vine
in the heart of your house;
your children like shoots of the olive,
around your table. ℟

3 Indeed thus shall be blessed
the man who fears the Lord.
May the Lord bless you from Zion
all the days of your life! ℟

Gospel Acclamation   Ps 144:13

    Alleluia, alleluia!
    The Lord is faithful in all his words
    and loving in all his deeds.
    Alleluia!

or   Mt 8:17

    Alleluia, alleluia!
    He took our sicknesses away,
    and carried our diseases for us.
    Alleluia!

GOSPEL

A reading from the holy Gospel according to Matthew   8:1-4
If you want to, you can cure me.

After Jesus had come down from the mountain large crowds followed him. A leper now came up and bowed low in front of him. 'Sir,' he said, 'if you want to, you can cure me.' Jesus stretched out his hand, touched him and said, 'Of course I want to! Be cured!' And his leprosy was cured at once. Then Jesus said to him, 'Mind you do not tell anyone, but go and show yourself to the priest and make the offering prescribed by Moses, as evidence for them.'

    This is the Gospel of the Lord.

SATURDAY

FIRST READING

A reading from the book of Genesis   18:1-15
Is anything too wonderful for the Lord? I shall visit you again and Sarah will have a son.

The Lord appeared to Abraham at the Oak of Mamre while he was sitting by the entrance of the tent during the hottest part of the day. He looked up, and there he saw three men standing near him. As soon as he saw them he ran from the entrance of the tent to meet them, and bowed to the ground. 'My lord,' he said 'I beg you, if I find favour with you, kindly do not pass your servant by. A little water shall be brought; you shall wash your feet and lie down under the tree. Let me fetch a little bread and you shall refresh yourselves before going further. That is why you have come in your servant's direction.' They replied, 'Do as you say.'

Abraham hastened to the tent to find Sarah. 'Hurry,' he said 'knead three bushels of flour and make loaves.' Then running to the cattle Abraham took a fine and tender calf and gave it to the servant, who hurried to prepare it. Then taking cream, milk and the calf he had prepared, he laid all before them, and they ate while he remained standing near them under the tree.

'Where is your wife Sarah?' they asked him. 'She is in the tent' he replied. Then his guest said, 'I shall visit you again next year without fail, and your wife will then have a son.' Sarah was listening at the entrance of the tent behind him. Now Abraham and Sarah were old, well on in years, and Sarah had ceased to have her monthly periods. So Sarah laughed to herself, thinking, 'Now that I am past the age of child-bearing, and my husband is an old man, is pleasure to come my way again!' But the Lord asked Abraham, 'Why did Sarah laugh and say, "Am I really going to have a child now that I am old?" Is anything too wonderful for the Lord? At the same time next year I shall visit you again and Sarah will have a son.' 'I did not laugh' Sarah said, lying because she was afraid. But he replied, 'Oh yes, you did laugh.'

This is the word of the Lord.

Responsorial Psalm   Lk 1:46-50. 53-55. ℟ cf. v.54

   ℟ **The Lord remembered his mercy.**

1. My soul glorifies the Lord,
   my spirit rejoices in God my saviour.   ℟

2. He looks on his servant in her nothingness;
   henceforth all ages will call me blessed.
   The Almighty works marvels for me.
   Holy his name!   ℟

3. His mercy is from age to age,
   on those who fear him.
   He fills the starving with good things,
   sends the rich away empty.   ℟

4. He protects Israel, his servant,
   remembering his mercy,
   the mercy promised to our fathers,
   to Abraham and his sons for ever.   ℟

Gospel Acclamation
cf. 2 Tim 1:10

Alleluia, alleluia!
Our Saviour Christ Jesus abolished death,
and he has proclaimed life through the Good News.
Alleluia!

or
Mt 8:17

Alleluia, alleluia!
He took our sicknesses away,
and carried our diseases for us.
Alleluia!

GOSPEL

A reading from the holy Gospel according to Matthew 8:5-17

Many will come from east and west to take their places with Abraham and Isaac and Jacob.

When Jesus went into Capernaum a centurion came up and pleaded with him. 'Sir,' he said 'my servant is lying at home paralysed, and in great pain.' 'I will come myself and cure him' said Jesus. The centurion replied, 'Sir, I am not worthy to have you under my roof; just give the word and my servant will be cured. For I am under authority myself, and have soldiers under me; and I say to one man: Go, and he goes; to another: Come here, and he comes; to my servant: Do this, and he does it.' When Jesus heard this he was astonished and said to those following him, 'I tell you solemnly, nowhere in Israel have I found faith like this. And I tell you that many will come from east and west to take their places with Abraham and Isaac and Jacob at the feast in the kingdom of heaven; but the subjects of the kingdom will be turned out into the dark, where there will be weeping and grinding of teeth.' And to the centurion Jesus said, 'Go back, then; you have believed, so let this be done for you.' And the servant was cured at that moment.

And going into Peter's house Jesus found Peter's mother-in-law in bed with fever. He touched her hand and the fever left her, and she got up and began to wait on him.

That evening they brought him many who were possessed by devils. He cast out the spirits with a word and cured all who were sick. This was to fulfil the prophecy of Isaiah:

He took our sicknesses away and carried our diseases for us.

This is the Gospel of the Lord.

LOOK AT THE BIRDS
GOD FEEDS
LOOK AT THE FLOWERS
GOD CLOTHES
BE CONCERNED FOR THE KINGDOM
HE WILL PROVIDE FOR YOU

THIRTEENTH WEEK IN ORDINARY TIME
Year I

MONDAY

FIRST READING

A reading from the book of Genesis 18:16-33
Are you going to destroy the just man with the sinner?

From Mamre the men set out and arrived within sight of Sodom, with Abraham accompanying them to show them the way. Now the Lord had wondered, 'Shall I conceal from Abraham what I am going to do, seeing that Abraham will become a great nation with all the nations of the earth blessing themselves by him? For I have singled him out to command his sons and his household after him to maintain the way of the Lord by just and upright living. In this way the Lord will carry out for Abraham what he has promised him.' Then the Lord said, 'How great an outcry there is against Sodom and Gomorrah! How grievous is their sin! I propose to go down and see whether or not they have done all that is alleged in the outcry against them that has come up to me. I am determined to know.'

The men left there and went to Sodom while Abraham remained standing before the Lord. Approaching him he said, 'Are you really going to destroy the just man with the sinner? Perhaps there are fifty just men in the town. Will you really overwhelm them, will you not spare the place for the fifty just men in it? Do not think of doing such a thing: to kill the just man with the sinner, treating just and sinner alike! Do not think of it! Will the judge of the whole earth not administer justice?' The Lord replied, 'If at Sodom I find fifty just men in the town, I will spare the whole place because of them.'

Abraham replied, 'I am bold indeed to speak like this to my Lord, I who am dust and ashes. But perhaps the fifty just men lack five: will you destroy the whole city for five?' 'No,' he replied, 'I will not destroy it if I find forty-five just men there.' Again Abraham said to him, 'Perhaps there will only be forty there.' 'I will not do it,' he replied 'for the sake of the forty.'

Abraham said, 'I trust my Lord will not be angry, but give me leave to speak: perhaps there will only be thirty there.' 'I will not do it' he replied 'if I find thirty there.' He said, 'I am bold indeed to speak like this, but perhaps there will only be twenty there.' 'I will not destroy it' he replied 'for the sake of the twenty.' He said, 'I trust my Lord will not be angry if I speak once more: perhaps there will only be ten.' 'I will not destroy it' he replied 'for the sake of the ten.'

When he had finished talking to Abraham the Lord went away, and Abraham returned home.

This is the word of the Lord.

Responsorial Psalm Ps 102:1-4. 8-11. ℟ v.8

℟ **The Lord is compassion and love.**

1 My soul, give thanks to the Lord,
   all my being, bless his holy name.
   My soul, give thanks to the Lord
   and never forget all his blessings. ℟

2 It is he who forgives all your guilt,
   who heals every one of your ills,
   who redeems your life from the grave,
   who crowns you with love and compassion. ℟

3 The Lord is compassion and love,
   slow to anger and rich in mercy.
   His wrath will come to an end;
   he will not be angry for ever. ℟

4 He does not treat us according to our sins
   nor repay us according to our faults.
   For as the heavens are high above the earth
   so strong is his love for those who fear him. ℟

Gospel Acclamation Jn 8:12

Alleluia, alleluia!
I am the light of the world, says the Lord,
anyone who follows me
will have the light of life.
Alleluia!

or cf. Ps 94:8

Alleluia, alleluia!
Harden not your hearts today,
but listen to the voice of the Lord.
Alleluia!

Thirteenth Week in Ordinary Time, Year I: Tuesday

GOSPEL

A reading from the holy Gospel according to Matthew 8:18-22
Follow me.

When Jesus saw the great crowds all about him he gave orders to leave for the other side. One of the scribes then came up and said to him, 'Master, I will follow you wherever you go.' Jesus replied, 'Foxes have holes and the birds of the air have nests, but the Son of Man has nowhere to lay his head.'

Another man, one of his disciples, said to him, 'Sir, let me go and bury my father first.' But Jesus replied, 'Follow me, and leave the dead to bury their dead.'

This is the Gospel of the Lord.

TUESDAY

FIRST READING

A reading from the book of Genesis 19:15-29
The Lord rained brimstone and fire on Sodom and Gomorrah.

The angels urged Lot, 'Come, take your wife and these two daughters of yours, or you will be overwhelmed in the punishment of the town.' And as he hesitated, the men took him by the hand, and his wife and his two daughters, because of the pity the Lord felt for him. They led him out and left him outside the town.

As they were leading him out he said, 'Run for your life. Neither look behind you nor stop anywhere on the plain. Make for the hills if you would not be overwhelmed.' 'No, I beg you, my lord,' Lot said to them 'your servant has won your favour and you have shown great kindness to me in saving my life. But I could not reach the hills before this calamity overtook me, and death with it. The town over there is near enough to flee to, and is a little one. Let me make for that – is it not little? – and my life will be saved.' He answered, 'I grant you this favour too, and will not destroy the town you speak of. Hurry, escape to it, for I can do nothing until you reach it.' That is why the town is named Zoar.

As the sun rose over the land and Lot entered Zoar, the Lord rained on Sodom and Gomorrah brimstone and fire from the Lord. He overthrew these towns and the whole plain, with all the inhabitants of the towns, and everything that grew there. But the wife of Lot looked back, and was turned into a pillar of salt.

Rising early in the morning Abraham went to the place where he had stood before the Lord, and looking towards Sodom and Gomorrah, and across all the plain, he saw the smoke rising from the land, like smoke from a furnace.

Thus it was that when God destroyed the towns of the plain, he kept Abraham in mind and rescued Lot out of disaster when he overwhelmed the towns where Lot lived.

This is the word of the Lord.

Responsorial Psalm Ps 25:2-3. 9-12. ℟ v.3

℟ **Your love, O Lord, is before my eyes.**

1 Examine me, Lord, and try me;
  O test my heart and my mind,
  for your love is before my eyes
  and I walk according to your truth. ℟

2 Do not sweep me away with sinners,
  nor my life with bloodthirsty men
  in whose hands are evil plots,
  whose right hands are filled with gold. ℟

3 As for me, I walk the path of perfection.
  Redeem me and show me your mercy.
  My foot stands on level ground:
  I will bless the Lord in the assembly. ℟

Gospel Acclamation Ps 147:12. 15

Alleluia, alleluia!
O praise the Lord, Jerusalem!
He sends out his word to the earth.
Alleluia!

or Ps 129:5

Alleluia, alleluia!
My soul is waiting for the Lord,
I count on his word.
Alleluia!

GOSPEL

A reading from the holy Gospel according to Matthew 8:23-27
He stood up and rebuked the winds and the seas; and all was calm again.

Jesus got into the boat followed by his disciples. Without warning a storm broke over the lake, so violent that the waves were breaking right over the boat. But he was asleep. So they went to him and woke him saying, 'Save us, Lord, we are going down!' And he said to them, 'Why are you so frightened, you men of little faith?' And with that he stood up and rebuked the winds and the seas; and all was calm again. The men were astounded and said, 'Whatever kind of man is this? Even the winds and the sea obey him.'

This is the Gospel of the Lord.

WEDNESDAY

FIRST READING

A reading from the book of Genesis 21:5. 8-20

The slave-girl's son is not to share the inheritance with my son Isaac.

Abraham was a hundred years old when his son Isaac was born to him. The child grew and was weaned, and Abraham gave a great banquet on the day Isaac was weaned. Now Sarah watched the son that Hagar the Egyptian had borne to Abraham, playing with her son Isaac. 'Drive away that slave-girl and her son,' she said to Abraham; 'this slave-girl's son is not to share the inheritance with my son Isaac.' This greatly distressed Abraham because of his son, but God said to him, 'Do not distress yourself on account of the boy and your slave-girl. Grant Sarah all she asks of you, for it is through Isaac that your name will be carried on. But the slave-girl's son I will also make into a nation, for he is your child too.' Rising early next morning Abraham took some bread and a skin of water and, giving them to Hagar, he put the child on her shoulder and sent her away.

She wandered off into the wilderness of Beersheba. When the skin of water was finished she abandoned the child under a bush. Then she went and sat down at a distance, about a bowshot away, saying to herself, 'I cannot see the child die.' So she sat at a distance; and the child wailed and wept.

But God heard the boy wailing, and the angel of God called to Hagar from heaven. 'What is wrong, Hagar?' he asked, 'Do not be afraid, for God has heard the boy's cry where he lies. Come, pick up the boy and hold him safe, for I will make him into a great nation.' Then God opened Hagar's eyes and she saw a well, so she went and filled the skin with water and gave the boy a drink.

God was with the boy. He grew up and made his home in the wilderness, and he became a bowman.

This is the word of the Lord.

Responsorial Psalm Ps 33:7-8. 10-13. ℟ v.7

℟ **This poor man called; the Lord heard him.**

1 This poor man called; the Lord heard him
and rescued him from all his distress.
The angel of the Lord is encamped
around those who revere him, to rescue them. ℟

2 Revere the Lord, you his saints.
They lack nothing, those who revere him.
Strong lions suffer want and go hungry
but those who seek the Lord lack no blessing. ℟

3 Come, children, and hear me
that I may teach you the fear of the Lord.
Who is he who longs for life
and many days, to enjoy his prosperity? ℟

Gospel Acclamation Jn 14:6

Alleluia, alleluia!
I am the Way, the Truth and the Life, says the Lord;
no one can come to the Father except through me.
Alleluia!

or James 1:18

Alleluia, alleluia!
By his own choice the Father made us his children
by the message of the truth,
so that we should be a sort of first-fruits
of all that he created.
Alleluia!

GOSPEL

A reading from the holy Gospel according to Matthew 8:28-34

Have you come here to torture the devils before the time?

When Jesus reached the country of the Gadarenes on the other side of the lake, two demoniacs came towards him out of the tombs – creatures so fierce that no one could pass that way. They stood there shouting, 'What do you want with us, Son of God? Have you come here to torture us before the time?' Now some distance away there was a large herd of pigs feeding, and the devils pleaded with Jesus, 'If you cast us out, send us into the herd of pigs.' And he said to them, 'Go then,' and they came out and made for the pigs; and at that the whole herd charged down the cliff into the lake and perished in the water. The swineherds ran off and made for the town, where they told the whole story, including what had happened to the demoniacs. At this the whole town set out to meet Jesus; and as soon as they saw him they implored him to leave the neighbourhood.

This is the Gospel of the Lord.

THURSDAY

FIRST READING

A reading from the book of Genesis 22:1-19

The sacrifice of our father Abraham.

It happened that God put Abraham to the test. 'Abraham, Abraham,' he called. 'Here I am' he replied. 'Take your son,' God said 'your only child Isaac, whom you love, and go to the land of Moriah. There you shall offer him as a burnt offering on a mountain I will point out to you.'

Rising early next morning Abraham saddled his ass and took with him two of his servants and his son Isaac. He chopped wood for the burnt offering and started on his journey to the place God had pointed out to him. On the third day Abraham looked up and saw the place in the distance. Then Abraham said to his servants, 'Stay here with the donkey. The boy and I will go over there; we will worship and come back to you.'

Abraham took the wood for the burnt offering, loaded it on Isaac, and carried in his own hands the fire and the knife. Then the two of them set out together. Isaac spoke to his father Abraham. 'Father' he said. 'Yes, my son' he replied. 'Look,' he said 'here are the fire and the wood, but where is the lamb for the burnt offering?' Abraham answered, 'My son, God himself will provide the lamb for the burnt offering.' Then the two of them went on together.

When they arrived at the place God had pointed out to him, Abraham built an altar there, and arranged the wood. Then he bound his son Isaac and put him on the altar on top of the wood.

Abraham stretched out his hands and seized the knife to kill his son.

But the angel of the Lord called to him from heaven. 'Abraham, Abraham' he said. 'I am here' he replied. 'Do not raise your hand against the boy' the angel said. 'Do not harm him, for now I know you fear God. You have not refused me your son, your only son.' Then looking up, Abraham saw a ram caught by its horns in a bush. Abraham took the ram and offered it as a burnt-offering in place of his son. Abraham called this place 'The Lord provides', and hence the saying today: On the mountain the Lord provides.

The angel of the Lord called Abraham a second time from heaven. 'I swear by my own self – it is the Lord who speaks – because you have done this, because you have not refused me your son, your only son, I will shower blessings on you, I will make your descendants as many as the stars of heaven and the grains of sand on the seashore. Your descendants shall gain possession of the gates of their enemies. All the nations of the earth shall bless themselves by your descendants, as a reward for your obedience.'

Abraham went back to his servants, and together they set out for Beersheba, and he settled in Beersheba.

This is the word of the Lord.

Responsorial Psalm
Ps 114:1-6. 8-9. ℟ v.9

℟ **I will walk in the presence of the Lord in the land of the living.**

or

℟ **Alleluia!**

1 I love the Lord for he has heard
the cry of my appeal;
for he turned his ear to me
in the day when I called him. ℟

2 They surrounded me, the snares of death,
with the anguish of the tomb;
they caught me, sorrow and distress.
I called on the Lord's name.
O Lord my God, deliver me! ℟

3 How gracious is the Lord, and just;
our God has compassion.

Thirteenth Week in Ordinary Time, Year I: Thursday

The Lord protects the simple hearts;
I was helpless so he saved me. ℟

4 He has kept my soul from death,
(my eyes from tears)
and my feet from stumbling.
I will walk in the presence of the Lord
in the land of the living. ℟

Gospel Acclamation cf. Mt 11:25

Alleluia, alleluia!
Blessed are you, Father,
Lord of heaven and earth,
for revealing the mysteries of the kingdom
to mere children.
Alleluia!

or 2 Cor 5:19

Alleluia, alleluia!
God in Christ was reconciling the world to himself,
and he has entrusted to us the news that they are reconciled.
Alleluia!

GOSPEL

A reading from the holy Gospel according to Matthew 9:1-8
They praised God for giving such power to men.

Jesus got in the boat, crossed the water and came to his own town. Then some people appeared, bringing him a paralytic stretched out on a bed. Seeing their faith, Jesus said to the paralytic, 'Courage, my child, your sins are forgiven.' And at this some scribes said to themselves, 'This man is blaspheming.' Knowing what was in their minds Jesus said, 'Why do you have such wicked thoughts in your hearts? Now, which of these is easier: to say, "Your sins are forgiven", or to say, "Get up and walk"? But to prove to you that the Son of Man has authority on earth to forgive sins,' – he said to the paralytic – 'get up, and pick up your bed and go off home.' And the man got up and went home. A feeling of awe came over the crowd when they saw this, and they praised God for giving such power to men.

This is the Gospel of the Lord.

FRIDAY

FIRST READING

A reading from the book of Genesis 23:1-4. 19; 24:1-8. 62-67

Isaac loved Rebekah and so was consoled for the loss of his mother.

The length of Sarah's life was a hundred and twenty-seven years. She died at Kiriath-arba, or Hebron, in the land of Canaan, and Abraham went to mourn and grieve for her.

Then leaving his dead, Abraham spoke to the sons of Heth: 'I am a stranger and a settler among you' he said. 'Let me own a burial-plot among you, so that I may take my dead wife and bury her.'

After this Abraham buried his wife Sarah in the cave of the field of Machpelah opposite Mamre, in the country of Canaan.

By now Abraham was an old man well on in years, and the Lord had blessed him in every way. Abraham said to the eldest servant of his household, the steward of all his property, 'Place your hand under my thigh, I would have you swear by the Lord God of heaven and God of earth, that you will not choose a wife for my son from the daughters of the Canaanites among whom I live. Instead, go to my own land and my own kinsfolk to choose a wife for my son Isaac.' The servant asked him, 'What if the woman does not want to come with me to this country? Must I take your son back to the country from which you came?' Abraham answered, 'On no account take my son back there. The Lord, God of heaven and God of earth, took me from my father's home, and from the land of my father's home, and from the land of my kinsfolk, and he swore to me that he would give this country to my descendants. He will now send his angel ahead of you, so that you may choose a wife for my son there. And if the woman does not want to come with you, you will be free from this oath of mine. Only do not take my son back there.'

Isaac, who lived in the Negeb, had meanwhile come into the wilderness of the well of Lahai Roi. Now Isaac went walking in the fields as evening fell, and looking up saw camels approaching. And Rebekah looked up and saw Isaac. She jumped down from her camel, and asked the servant, 'Who is that man walking through the fields to meet us?' The servant replied, 'That is my master'; then she took her veil and hid her face. The servant told Isaac the whole story, and Isaac led Rebekah into his tent and made her his wife; and he loved her.

Thirteenth Week in Ordinary Time, Year I: Friday

And so Isaac was consoled for the loss of his mother.

This is the word of the Lord.

Responsorial Psalm   Ps 105:1-5. ℟ v.1

   ℟ **O give thanks to the Lord for he is good.**

or

      ℟ **Alleuia!**

1. O give thanks to the Lord for he is good;
for his great love is without end.
Who can tell the Lord's mighty deeds?
Who can recount all his praise? ℟

2. They are happy who do what is right,
who at all times do what is just.
O Lord, remember me
out of the love you have for your people. ℟

3. Come to me, Lord, with your help
that I may see the joy of your chosen ones
and may rejoice in the gladness of your nation
and share the glory of your people. ℟

Gospel Acclamation   Ps 24:4, 5
Alleluia, alleluia!
Teach me your paths, my God,
make me walk in your truth.
Alleluia!

or   Mt 11:28

Alleluia, alleluia!
Come to me, all you who labour and are overburdened,
and I will give you rest, says the Lord.
Alleluia!

GOSPEL

A reading from the holy Gospel according to Matthew   9:9-13

It is not the healthy who need the doctor; what I want is mercy, not sacrifice.

As Jesus was walking he saw a man named Matthew sitting by the customs house, and he said to him, 'Follow me.' And he got up and followed him.

While he was at dinner in the house it happened that a number of tax collectors and sinners came to sit at the table with Jesus and his disciples. When the Pharisees saw this, they said to his disciples, 'Why does your master eat with tax collectors and sinners?' When he heard this he replied, 'It is not the healthy who need the doctor, but the sick. Go and learn the meaning of the words: What I want is mercy, not sacrifice. And indeed I did not come to call the virtuous, but sinners.'

This is the Gospel of the Lord.

SATURDAY

FIRST READING

A reading from the book of Genesis   27:1-5. 15-29
Jacob supplanted his brother and took his brother's blessing.

Isaac had grown old, and his eyes were so weak that he could no longer see. He summoned his elder son Esau. 'My son!' he said to him, and the latter answered, 'I am here.' Then he said, 'See, I am old and do not know when I may die. Now take your weapons, your quiver and bow; go out into the country and hunt me some game. Make me the kind of savoury I like and bring it to me, so that I may eat, and give you my blessing before I die.'

Rebekah happened to be listening while Isaac was talking to his son Esau. So when Esau went into the country to hunt game for his father, Rebekah took her elder son Esau's best clothes, which she had in the house, and dressed her younger son Jacob in them, covering his arms and the smooth part of his neck with the skins of the kids. Then she handed the savoury and the bread she had made to her son Jacob.

He presented himself before his father and said, 'Father.' 'I am here' was the reply, 'who are you, my son?' Jacob said to his father, 'I am Esau your firstborn; I have done as you told me. Please get up and take your place and eat the game I have brought and then give me your blessing.' Isaac said to his son, 'How quickly you found it, my son!' 'It was the Lord your God' he answered 'who put it in my path.' Isaac said to Jacob, 'Come here, then, and let me touch you, my son, to know if you are my son Esau or not.' Jacob came close to his father Isaac, who touched him and said, 'The voice is Jacob's voice but the arms are the arms of Esau!' He did not recognise him, for his arms were hairy like his brother Esau's, and so he blessed him. He said, 'Are you really my son Esau?' And he replied, 'I am.' Isaac said, 'Bring it here that I may eat the game my son has brought, and so may give you my blessing.' He brought it to him and he ate; he offered him wine, and he drank. His father Isaac said to him, 'Come closer, and kiss me, my son.' He went closer and kissed his father, who smelled the smell of his clothes.

He blessed him saying:

'Yes, the smell of my son
is like the smell of a fertile field blessed by the Lord.
May God give you
dew from heaven,
and the richness of the earth,
abundance of grain and wine!
May nations serve you
and peoples bow down before you!
Be master of your brothers;
may the sons of your mother bow down before you!
Cursed be he who curses you;
blessed be he who blesses you!'

This is the word of the Lord.

Responsorial Psalm Ps 134:1-6. ℟ v.3

℟ **Praise the Lord for the Lord is good.**

or

℟ **Alleluia!**

1 Praise the name of the Lord,
praise him, servants of the Lord,
who stand in the house of the Lord
in the courts of the house of our God. ℟

2 Praise the Lord for the Lord is good.
Sing a psalm to his name for he is loving.
For the Lord has chosen Jacob for himself
and Israel for his own possession. ℟

3 For I know the Lord is great,
that our Lord is high above all gods.
The Lord does whatever he wills,
in heaven, on earth, in the seas. ℟

Gospel Acclamation   Ps 118:135

    Alleluia, alleluia!
    Let your face shine on your servant,
    and teach me your decrees.
    Alleluia!

or   Jn 10:27

    Alleluia, alleluia!
    The sheep that belong to me listen to my voice,
    says the Lord,
    I know them and they follow me.
    Alleluia!

GOSPEL

A reading from the holy Gospel according to Matthew   9:14-17

Surely the bridegroom's attendants would never think of mourning as long as the bridegroom is still with them?

John's disciples came to Jesus and said, 'Why is it that we and the Pharisees fast, but your disciples do not?' Jesus replied, 'Surely the bridegroom's attendants would never think of mourning as long as the bridegroom is still with them? But the time will come for the bridegroom to be taken away from them, and then they will fast. No one puts a piece of unshrunken cloth on to an old cloak, because the patch pulls away from the cloak and the tear gets worse. Nor do people put new wine into old wineskins; if they do, the skins burst, the wine runs out, and the skins are lost. No; they put new wine into fresh skins and both are preserved.'

    This is the Gospel of the Lord.

FOURTEENTH WEEK IN ORDINARY TIME

Year I

MONDAY

FIRST READING

A reading from the book of Genesis   28:10-22

He saw a ladder standing there, and there were angels of God going up it and coming down, and God was speaking.

Jacob left Beersheba and set out for Haran. When he had reached a certain place he passed the night there, since the sun had set.

Fourteenth Week in Ordinary Time, Year I: Monday

Taking one of the stones to be found at that place, he made it his pillow and lay down where he was. He had a dream: a ladder was there, standing on the ground with its top reaching to heaven; and there were angels of God going up it and coming down. And the Lord was there, standing over him, saying, 'I am the Lord, the God of Abraham your father, and the God of Isaac. I will give to you and your descendants the land on which you are lying. Your descendants shall be like the specks of dust on the ground; you shall spread to the west and the east, to the north and the south, and all the tribes of the earth shall bless themselves by you and your descendants. Be sure that I am with you; I will keep you safe wherever you go, and bring you back to this land, for I will not desert you before I have done all that I have promised you.' Then Jacob awoke from his sleep and said, 'Truly, the Lord is in this place and I never knew it!' He was afraid and said, 'How awe-inspiring this place is! This is nothing less than a house of God; this is the gate of heaven!' Rising early in the morning, Jacob took the stone he had used for his pillow, and set it up as a monument, pouring oil over the top of it. He named the place Bethel, but before that the town was called Luz.

Jacob made this vow, 'If God goes with me and keeps me safe on this journey I am making, if he gives me bread to eat and clothes to wear, and if I return home safely to my father, then the Lord shall be my God. This stone I have set up as a monument shall be a house of God.'

This is the word of the Lord.

Responsorial Psalm   Ps 90:1-4. 14-15. ℟ cf. v.2

℟ **My God, in you I trust.**

1 He who dwells in the shelter of the Most High
 and abides in the shade of the Almighty
 says to the Lord: 'My refuge,
 my stronghold, my God in whom I trust!' ℟

2 It is he who will free you from the snare
 of the fowler who seeks to destroy you;
 he will conceal you with his pinions
 and under his wings you will find refuge. ℟

3 His love he set on me, so I will rescue him;
 protect him for he knows my name.
 When he calls I shall answer: 'I am with you.'
 I will save him in distress. ℟

Gospel Acclamation cf. Jn 6:63. 68

Alleluia, alleluia!
Your words are spirit, Lord,
and they are life:
you have the message of eternal life.
Alleluia!

or cf. 2 Tim 1:10

Alleluia, alleluia!
Our Saviour Christ Jesus abolished death,
and he has proclaimed life through the Good News.
Alleluia!

GOSPEL

A reading from the holy Gospel according to Matthew 9:18-26
My daughter has just died, but come and her life will be saved.

While Jesus was speaking, up came one of the officials, who bowed low in front of him and said, 'My daughter has just died, but come and lay your hand on her and her life will be saved.' Jesus rose and, with his disciples, followed him.

Then from behind him came a woman, who had suffered from a haemorrhage for twelve years, and she touched the fringe of his cloak, for she said to herself, 'If I can only touch his cloak I shall be well again.' Jesus turned round and saw her; and he said to her, 'Courage, my daughter, your faith has restored you to health.' And from that moment the woman was well again.

When Jesus reached the official's house and saw the flute-players, with the crowd making a commotion he said, 'Get out of here; the little girl is not dead, she is asleep.' And they laughed at him. But when the people had been turned out he went inside and took the little girl by the hand; and she stood up. And the news spread all round the countryside.

This is the Gospel of the Lord.

TUESDAY

FIRST READING

A reading from the book of Genesis 32:23-33
Your name shall be Israel, because you have been strong against God.

Jacob rose, and taking his two wives and his two slave-girls and his eleven children he crossed the ford of the Jabbok. He took them and sent them across the stream and sent all his possessions over too. And Jacob was left alone.

And there was one that wrestled with him until daybreak who, seeing that he could not master him, struck him in the socket of his hip, and Jacob's hip was dislocated as he wrestled with him. He said, 'Let me go, for day is breaking.' But Jacob answered, 'I will not let you go unless you bless me.' He then asked, 'What is your name?' 'Jacob,' he replied. He said, 'Your name shall no longer be Jacob, but Israel; because you have been strong against God, you shall prevail against men.' Jacob then made this request, 'I beg you, tell me your name,' but he replied, 'Why do you ask my name?' And he blessed him there.

Jacob named the place Peniel, 'Because I have seen God face to face,' he said 'and I have survived.' The sun rose as he left Peniel, limping because of his hip. That is the reason why to this day the Israelites do not eat the sciatic nerve which is in the socket of the hip, because he had struck Jacob in the socket of the hip on the sciatic nerve.

This is the word of the Lord.

Responsorial Psalm   Ps 16:1-3. 6-8. 15. ℟ v.15

℟ **Lord, in my justice I shall see your face.**

1 Lord, hear a cause that is just,
  pay heed to my cry.
  Turn your ear to my prayer:
  no deceit is on my lips.   ℟

2 From you may my judgement come forth.
  Your eyes discern the truth.
  You search my heart, you visit me by night.
  You test me and you find in me no wrong.   ℟

3 I am here and I call, you will hear me, O God.
  Turn your ear to me; hear my words.
  Display your great love, you whose right hand saves
  your friends from those who rebel against them.   ℟

4 Guard me as the apple of your eye.
  Hide me in the shadow of your wings.
  In my justice I shall see your face
  and be filled, when I awake, with the sight of your glory.   ℟

Gospel Acclamation cf. Eph 1:17. 18
Alleluia, alleluia!
May the Father of our Lord Jesus Christ
enlighten the eyes of our mind,
so that we can see what hope his call holds for us.
Alleluia!

or Jn 10:14

Alleluia, alleluia!
I am the good shepherd, says the Lord;
I know my own sheep, and my own know me.
Alleluia!

GOSPEL

A reading from the holy Gospel according to Matthew 9:32-38
The harvest is rich but the labourers are few.

A man was brought to Jesus, a dumb demoniac. And when the devil was cast out, the dumb man spoke and the people were amazed. 'Nothing like this has ever been seen in Israel' they said. But the Pharisees said, 'It is through the prince of devils that he casts out devils.'

Jesus made a tour through all the towns and villages, teaching in their synagogues, proclaiming the Good News of the kingdom and curing all kinds of diseases and sickness.

And when he saw the crowds he felt sorry for them because they were harassed and dejected, like sheep without a shepherd. Then he said to his disciples, 'The harvest is rich but the labourers are few, so ask the Lord of the harvest to send labourers to his harvest.'

This is the Gospel of the Lord.

WEDNESDAY

FIRST READING

A reading from the book of Genesis 41:55-57; 42:5-7. 17-24
Truly we are being called to account for our brother.

When the country of Egypt began to feel the famine, the people cried out to Pharaoh for bread. But Pharaoh told all the Egyptians, 'Go to Joseph and do what he tells you.' – There was famine all over the world. – Then Joseph opened all the granaries

Fourteenth Week in Ordinary Time, Year I: Wednesday

and sold grain to the Egyptians. The famine grew worse in the land of Egypt. People came to Egypt from all over the world to buy grain from Joseph, for the famine had grown severe throughout the world.

Israel's sons with others making the same journey went to buy grain, for there was famine in the land of Canaan. It was Joseph, as the man in authority over the country, who sold the grain to all comers. So Joseph's brothers went and bowed down before him, their faces touching the ground. When Joseph saw his brothers he recognised them. Then he kept them all in custody for three days.

On the third day Joseph said to them, 'Do this and you shall keep your lives, for I am a man who fears God. If you are honest men let one of your brothers be kept in the place of your detention; as for you, go and take grain to relieve the famine of your families. You shall bring me your youngest brother; this way your words will be proved true, and you will not have to die!' This they did. They said to one another, 'Truly we are being called to account for our brother. We saw his misery of soul when he begged our mercy, but we did not listen to him and now this misery has come home to us.' Reuben answered them, 'Did I not tell you not to wrong the boy? But you did not listen, and now we are brought to account for his blood.' They did not know that Joseph understood, because there was an interpreter between them. He left them and wept.

This is the word of the Lord.

Responsorial Psalm   Ps 32:2-3. 10-11. 18-19. ℟ v.22

  ℟ **May your love be upon us, O Lord,**
     as we place all our hope in you.

1. Give thanks to the Lord upon the harp,
with a ten-stringed lute sing him songs.
O sing him a song that is new,
play loudly, with all your skill.   ℟

2. He frustrates the designs of the nations,
he defeats the plans of the peoples.
His own designs shall stand for ever,
the plans of his heart from age to age.   ℟

3. The Lord looks on those who revere him,
on those who hope in his love,
to rescue their souls from death,
to keep them alive in famine.   ℟

Gospel Acclamation James 1:18
Alleluia, alleluia!
By his own choice the Father made us his children
by the message of the truth,
so that we should be a sort of first-fruits
of all that he created.
Alleluia!

or Mk 1:15

Alleluia, alleluia!
The kingdom of God is close at hand,
repent and believe the Good News.
Alleluia!

GOSPEL

A reading from the holy Gospel according to Matthew 10:1-7

Go to the lost sheep of the house of Israel.

Jesus summoned his twelve disciples, and gave them authority over unclean spirits with power to cast them out and to cure all kinds of diseases and sickness.

These are the names of the twelve apostles: first, Simon who is called Peter, and his brother Andrew; James the son of Zebedee, and his brother John; Philip and Bartholomew; Thomas, and Matthew the tax collector; James the son of Alphaeus, and Thaddaeus; Simon the Zealot and Judas Iscariot, the one who was to betray him. These twelve Jesus sent out, instructing them as follows:

'Do not turn your steps to pagan territory, and do not enter any Samaritan town; go rather to the lost sheep of the House of Israel. And as you go, proclaim that the kingdom of heaven is close at hand.'

This is the Gospel of the Lord.

THURSDAY

FIRST READING

A reading from the book of Genesis 44:18-21. 23-29; 45:1-5

God sent me into Egypt to preserve your lives.

Judah went up to Joseph and said, 'May it please my lord, let your servant have a word privately with my lord. Do not be angry with your servant, for you are like Pharaoh himself. My lord questioned his servants, "Have you father or brother?" And we said to my lord, "We have an old father, and a younger brother born of his old age. His brother is dead, so he is the only one left of his mother, and his father loves him." Then you said to your servants, "Bring him down to me that my eyes may look on him. If your youngest brother does not come down with you, you will not be admitted to my presence again." When we went back to your servant my father, we repeated to him what my lord had said. So when our father said, "Go back and buy us a little food," we said, "We cannot go down. If our youngest brother is with us, we will go down, for we cannot be admitted to the man's presence unless our youngest brother is with us." So your servant our father said to us, "You know that my wife bore me two children. When one left me, I said that he must have been torn to pieces. And I have not seen him to this day. If you take this one from me too and any harm comes to him, you will send me down to Sheol with my white head bowed in misery."'

Then Joseph could not control his feelings in front of all his retainers, and he exclaimed, 'Let everyone leave me.' No one therefore was present with him while Joseph made himself known to his brothers, but he wept so loudly that all the Egyptians heard, and the news reached Pharaoh's palace.

Joseph said to his brothers, 'I am Joseph. Is my father really still alive?' His brothers could not answer him, they were so dismayed at the sight of him. Then Joseph said to his brothers, 'Come closer to me.' When they had come closer to him he said, 'I am your brother Joseph whom you sold into Egypt. But now, do not grieve, do not reproach yourselves for having sold me here, since God sent me before you to preserve your lives.'

This is the word of the Lord.

Responsorial Psalm   Ps 104:16-21. ℟ v.5

    ℟ **Remember the wonders the Lord has done.**

or

    ℟ **Alleluia!**

1 The Lord called down a famine on the land;
    he broke the staff that supported them.
    He had sent a man before them,
    Joseph, sold as a slave. ℟

2 His feet were put in chains,
   his neck was bound with iron,
   until what he said came to pass
   and the Lord's word proved him true.

   ℟ **Remember the wonders the Lord has done.**

   or

   ℟ **Alleluia!**

3 Then the king sent and released him;
   the ruler of the peoples set him free,
   making him master of his house
   and ruler of all he possessed. ℟

Gospel Acclamation cf. Ps 94:8
   Alleluia, alleluia!
   Harden not your hearts today,
   but listen to the voice of the Lord.
   Alleluia!

or Mk 1:15

   Alleluia, alleluia!
   The kingdom of God is close at hand,
   repent and believe the Good News.
   Alleluia!

GOSPEL

A reading from the holy Gospel according to Matthew 10:7-15

You received without charge, give without charge.

Jesus instructed the Twelve as follows: 'As you go, proclaim that the kingdom of heaven is close at hand. Cure the sick, raise the dead, cleanse the lepers, cast out devils. You received without charge, give without charge. Provide yourselves with no gold or silver, not even with a few coppers for your purses, with no haversack for the journey or spare tunic or footwear or a staff, for the workman deserves his keep.

'Whatever town or village you go into, ask for someone trustworthy and stay with him until you leave. As you enter his house, salute it, and if the house deserves it, let your peace descend upon it; if it does not, let your peace come back to you. And if anyone does not welcome you or listen to what you have to say, as you walk out of the house or town shake the dust from your feet. I tell you solemnly, on the day of Judgement it will not go as hard with the land of Sodom and Gomorrah as with that town.'

This is the Gospel of the Lord.

FRIDAY

FIRST READING

A reading from the book of Genesis 46:1-7. 28-30
I can die, now that I have seen you.

Israel left Canaan with his possessions, and reached Beersheba. There he offered sacrifices to the God of his father Isaac. God spoke to Israel in a vision at night, 'Jacob, Jacob,' he said. 'I am here,' he replied. 'I am God, the God of your father,' he continued. 'Do not be afraid of going down to Egypt, for I will make you a great nation there. I myself will go down to Egypt with you. I myself will bring you back again, and Joseph's hand shall close your eyes.' Then Jacob left Beersheba. Israel's sons conveyed their father Jacob, their little children and their wives in the waggons Pharaoh had sent to fetch him.

Taking their livestock and all that they had acquired in the land of Canaan, they went to Egypt, Jacob and all his family with him: his sons and his grandsons, his daughters and his granddaughters, in a word, all his children he took with him to Egypt.

Israel sent Judah ahead to Joseph, so that the latter might present himself to him in Goshen. When they arrived in the land of Goshen, Joseph had his chariot made ready and went up to meet his father Israel in Goshen. As soon as he appeared he threw his arms round his neck and for a long time wept on his shoulder. Israel said to Joseph, 'Now I can die, now that I have seen you again, and seen you still alive.'

This is the word of the Lord.

Responsorial Psalm Ps 36:3-4. 18-19. 27-28. 39-40. ℟ v.39
  ℟ **The salvation of the just comes from the Lord.**

1 If you trust in the Lord and do good,
  then you will live in the land and be secure.
  If you find your delight in the Lord,
  he will grant your heart's desire. ℟

2 He protects the lives of the upright,
  their heritage will last for ever.

They shall not be put to shame in evil days,
in time of famine their food shall not fail.

℟ **The salvation of the just comes from the Lord.**

3 Then turn away from evil and do good
and you shall have a home for ever;
for the Lord loves justice
and will never forsake his friends. ℟

4 The salvation of the just comes from the Lord,
their stronghold in time of distress.
The Lord helps them and delivers them
and saves them: for their refuge is in him. ℟

Gospel Acclamation 1 Peter 1:25
Alleluia, alleluia!
The word of the Lord remains for ever:
What is this word?
It is the Good News that has been brought to you.
Alleluia!

or Jn 16:13; 14:26

Alleluia, alleluia!
When the Spirit of truth comes
he will lead you to the complete truth,
and he will remind you of all I have said to you.
Alleluia!

GOSPEL

A reading from the holy Gospel according to Matthew 10:16-23
It is not you who will be speaking; the Spirit of the Father will be speaking in you.

Jesus instructed the Twelve as follows: 'Remember, I am sending you out like sheep among wolves; so be cunning as serpents and yet as harmless as doves.

'Beware of men: they will hand you over to sanhedrins and scourge you in their synagogues. You will be dragged before governors and kings for my sake, to bear witness before them and the pagans. But when they hand you over, do not worry about how to speak or what to say; what you are to say will be given to you when the time comes; because it is not you who will be speaking; the Spirit of your Father will be speaking in you.

'Brother will betray brother to death, and the father his child;

children will rise against their parents and have them put to death. You will be hated by all men on account of my name; but the man who stands firm to the end will be saved. If they persecute you in one town, take refuge in the next; and if they persecute you in that, take refuge in another. I tell you solemnly, you will not have gone the round of the towns of Israel before the Son of Man comes.'

This is the Gospel of the Lord.

SATURDAY

FIRST READING

A reading from the book of Genesis 49:29-33; 50:15-26

God will be sure to remember you kindly and take you back from this country.

Jacob gave his sons these instructions, 'I am about to be gathered to my people. Bury me near my fathers, in the cave that is in the field of Ephron the Hittite, in the cave in the field at Machpelah, opposite Mamre, in the land of Canaan, which Abraham bought from Ephron the Hittite as a burial-plot. There Abraham was buried and his wife Sarah. There Isaac was buried and his wife Rebekah. There I buried Leah. I mean the field and the cave in it that were bought from the sons of Heth.'

When Jacob had finished giving his instructions to his sons, he drew his feet up into the bed, and breathing his last was gathered to his people.

Seeing that their father was dead, Joseph's brothers said, 'What if Joseph intends to treat us as enemies and repay us in full for all the wrong we did him?' So they sent this message to Joseph: 'Before your father died he gave us this order: "You must say to Joseph: Oh forgive your brothers their crime and their sin and all the wrong they did you." Now therefore, we beg you, forgive the crime of the servants of your father's God.' Joseph wept at the message they sent to him.

His brothers came themselves and fell down before him. 'We present ourselves before you' they said 'as your slaves.' But Joseph answered them, 'Do not be afraid; is it for me to put myself in God's place? The evil you planned to do me has by God's design been turned to good, that he might bring about, as indeed he has, the deliverance of a numerous people. So you need not be afraid; I myself will provide for you and your dependants.' In this way he reassured them with words that touched their hearts.

So Joseph stayed in Egypt with his father's family; and Joseph lived a hundred and ten years. Joseph saw the third generation of Ephraim's children, as also the children of Machir, Manasseh's son, who were born on Joseph's lap. At length Joseph said to his brothers, 'I am about to die; but God will be sure to remember you kindly and take you back from this country to the land that he promised on oath to Abraham, Isaac and Jacob.' And Joseph made Israel's sons swear an oath, 'When God remembers you with kindness be sure to take my bones from here.'

Joseph died at the age of a hundred and ten; they embalmed him and laid him in his coffin in Egypt.

This is the word of the Lord.

Responsorial Psalm   Ps 104:1-4. 6-7. ℟ cf. Ps 68:33

℟ **Seek the Lord, you who are poor,
and your hearts will revive.**

1 Give thanks to the Lord, tell his name,
make known his deeds among the peoples.
O sing to him, sing his praise;
tell all his wonderful works! ℟

2 Be proud of his holy name,
let the hearts that seek the Lord rejoice.
Consider the Lord and his strength;
constantly seek his face. ℟

3 O children of Abraham, his servant,
O sons of the Jacob he chose.
He, the Lord, is our God:
his judgements prevail in all the earth. ℟

Gospel Acclamation   1 Jn 2:5
Alleluia, alleluia!
When anyone obeys what Christ has said,
God's love comes to perfection in him.
Alleluia!

or   1 Peter 4:14

Alleluia, alleluia!
It is a blessing for you,
when they insult you

for bearing the name of Christ,
for the Spirit of God rests on you.
Alleluia!

GOSPEL

A reading from the holy Gospel according to Matthew 10:24-38
Do not be afraid of those who can kill the body.

Jesus instructed the Twelve as follows: 'The disciple is not superior to his teacher, nor the slave to his master. It is enough for the disciple that he should grow to be like his teacher, and the slave like his master. If they have called the master of the house Beelzebul, what will they not say of his household?

'Do not be afraid of them therefore. For everything that is now covered will be uncovered, and everything now hidden will be made clear. What I say to you in the dark, tell in the daylight; what you hear in whispers, proclaim from the housetops.

'Do not be afraid of those who kill the body but cannot kill the soul; fear him rather who can destroy both body and soul in hell. Can you not buy two sparrows for a penny? And yet not one falls to the ground without your Father knowing. Why, every hair on your head has been counted. So there is no need to be afraid; you are worth more than hundreds of sparrows.

'So if anyone declares himself for me in the presence of men, I will declare myself for him in the presence of my Father in heaven. But the one who disowns me in the presence of men, I will disown in the presence of my Father in heaven.'

This is the Gospel of the Lord.

FIFTEENTH WEEK IN ORDINARY TIME
Year I

MONDAY

FIRST READING

A reading from the book of Exodus 1:8-14. 22
We must take steps against Israel increasing any further.

There came to power in Egypt a new king who knew nothing of Joseph. 'Look,' he said to his subjects 'these people, the sons of Israel, have become so numerous and strong that they are a threat to us. We must be prudent and take steps against their increasing any further, or if war should break out, they might add to the number of our enemies. They might take arms against us and so escape out of the country.' Accordingly they put slave-drivers over the Israelites to wear them down under heavy loads. In this way they built the store-cities of Pithom and Rameses for Pharaoh. But the more they were crushed, the more they increased and spread, and men came to dread the sons of Israel. The Egyptians forced the sons of Israel into slavery, and made their lives unbearable with hard labour, work with clay and with brick, all kinds of work in the fields; they forced on them every kind of labour.

Pharaoh then gave his subjects this command: 'Throw all the boys born to the Hebrews into the river, but let all the girls live.'

This is the word of the Lord.

Responsorial Psalm
Ps 123. R̸ v.8

R̸ **Our help is in the name of the Lord.**

1 'If the Lord had not been on our side,'
 this is Israel's song.
 'If the Lord had not been on our side
 when men rose against us,
 then would they have swallowed us alive
 when their anger was kindled. R̸

2 Then would the waters have engulfed us,
 the torrent gone over us;
 over our head would have swept
 the raging waters.'
 Blessed be the Lord who did not give us
 a prey to their teeth! R̸

3 Our life, like a bird, has escaped
 from the snare of the fowler.
 Indeed the snare has been broken
 and we have escaped.
 Our help is in the name of the Lord,
 who made heaven and earth. R̸

Gospel Acclamation
cf. Acts 16:14

Alleluia, alleluia!
Open our heart, O Lord,
to accept the words of your Son.
Alleluia!

Fifteenth Week in Ordinary Time, Year I: Tuesday

or Mt 5:10

Alleluia, alleluia!
Happy those who are persecuted
in the cause of right,
for theirs is the kingdom of heaven.
Alleluia!

GOSPEL

A reading from the holy Gospel according to Matthew 10:34–11:1

It is not peace I have come to bring, but a sword.

Jesus instructed the Twelve as follows: 'Do not suppose that I have come to bring peace to the earth: it is not peace I have come to bring, but a sword. For I have come to set a man against his father, a daughter against her mother, a daughter-in-law against her mother-in-law. A man's enemies will be those of his own household.

'Anyone who prefers father or mother to me is not worthy of me. Anyone who prefers son or daughter to me is not worthy of me. Anyone who does not take his cross and follow in my footsteps is not worthy of me. Anyone who finds his life will lose it; anyone who loses his life for my sake will find it.

'Anyone who welcomes you welcomes me; and those who welcome me welcome the one who sent me.

'Anyone who welcomes a prophet because he is a prophet will have a prophet's reward; and anyone who welcomes a holy man because he is a holy man will have a holy man's reward.

'If anyone gives so much as a cup of cold water to one of these little ones because he is a disciple, then I tell you solemnly, he will most certainly not lose his reward.'

When Jesus had finished instructing his twelve disciples he moved on from there to teach and preach in their towns.

This is the Gospel of the Lord.

TUESDAY
FIRST READING

A reading from the book of Exodus   2:1-15

Pharaoh's daughter named him Moses because, she said, 'I drew him out of the water.' Later, when he was a man, he set out to visit his countrymen.

There was a man of the tribe of Levi who had taken a woman of Levi as his wife. She conceived and gave birth to a son and, seeing what a fine child he was, she kept him hidden for three months. When she could hide him no longer, she got a papyrus basket for him; coating it with bitumen and pitch, she put the child inside and laid it among the reeds at the river's edge. His sister stood some distance away to see what would happen to him.

Now Pharaoh's daughter went down to bathe in the river, and the girls attending her were walking along by the riverside. Among the reeds she noticed the basket, and she sent her maid to fetch it. She opened it and looked, and saw a baby boy, crying; and she was sorry for him. 'This is a child of one of the Hebrews' she said. Then the child's sister said to Pharaoh's daughter, 'Shall I go and find you a nurse among the Hebrew women to suckle the child for you?' 'Yes, go' Pharaoh's daughter said to her; and the girl went off to find the baby's own mother. To her the daughter of Pharaoh said, 'Take this child away and suckle it for me. I will see you are paid.' So the woman took the child and suckled it. When the child grew up, she brought him to Pharaoh's daughter who treated him like a son; she named him Moses because, she said, 'I drew him out of the water.'

Moses, a man by now, set out at this time to visit his countrymen, and he saw what a hard life they were having; and he saw an Egyptian strike a Hebrew, one of his countrymen. Looking round he could see no one in sight, so he killed the Egyptian and hid him in the sand. On the following day he came back, and there were two Hebrews, fighting. He said to the man who was in the wrong, 'What do you mean by hitting your fellow countryman?' 'And who appointed you' the man retorted 'to be prince over us, and judge? Do you intend to kill me as you killed the Egyptian?' Moses was frightened. 'Clearly that business has come to light' he thought. When Pharaoh heard of the matter he would have killed Moses, but Moses fled from Pharaoh and made for the land of Midian.

This is the word of the Lord.

Fifteenth Week in Ordinary Time, Year I: Tuesday 617

Responsorial Psalm   Ps 68:3. 14. 30-31. 33-34. R̷ cf. v.33

  R̷ **Seek the Lord, you who are poor,
and your hearts will revive.**

1 I have sunk into the mud of the deep
and there is no foothold.
I have entered the waters of the deep
and the waves overwhelm me.   R̷

2 This is my prayer to you,
my prayer for your favour.
In your great love, answer me, O God,
with your help that never fails.   R̷

3 As for me in my poverty and pain
let your help, O God, lift me up.
I will praise God's name with a song;
I will glorify him with thanksgiving.   R̷

4 The poor when they see it will be glad
and God-seeking hearts will revive;
for the Lord listens to the needy
and does not spurn his servants in their chains.   R̷

Gospel Acclamation   Ps 118:34

Alleluia, alleluia!
Train me, Lord, to observe your law,
to keep it with my heart.
Alleluia!

or   cf. Ps 94:8

Alleluia, alleluia!
Harden not your hearts today,
but listen to the voice of the Lord.
Alleluia!

GOSPEL

A reading from the holy Gospel according to Matthew   11:20-24

It will not go as hard on Judgement day with Tyre and Sidon and with the land of Sodom as with you.

Jesus began to reproach the towns in which most of his miracles had been worked, because they refused to repent.

   'Alas for you, Chorazin! Alas for you, Bethsaida! For if the miracles done in you had been done in Tyre and Sidon, they would have repented long ago in sackcloth and ashes. And still, I tell you that it will not go as hard on Judgement day with Tyre and Sidon as with you. And as for you, Capernaum, did you want to be exalted as high as heaven? You shall be thrown down to hell. For if the miracles done in you had been done in Sodom, it would have been standing yet. And still, I tell you that it will not go as hard with the land of Sodom on Judgement day as with you.'

This is the Gospel of the Lord.

WEDNESDAY

FIRST READING

A reading from the book of Exodus 3:1-6. 9-12

The Lord appeared to Moses in the shape of a flame of fire, coming from the middle of a bush.

Moses was looking after the flock of Jethro, his father-in-law, priest of Midian. He led his flock to the far side of the wilderness and came to Horeb, the mountain of God. There the angel of the Lord appeared to him in the shape of a flame of fire, coming from the middle of a bush. Moses looked; there was the bush blazing but it was not being burnt up. 'I must go and look at this strange sight,' Moses said 'and see why the bush is not burnt.' Now the Lord saw him go forward to look, and God called to him from the middle of the bush. 'Moses, Moses!' he said. 'Here I am' he answered. 'Come no nearer' he said. 'Take off your shoes, for the place on which you stand is holy ground. I am the God of your father,' he said 'the God of Abraham, the God of Isaac and the God of Jacob.' At this Moses covered his face, afraid to look at God.

And the Lord said, 'And now the cry of the sons of Israel has come to me, and I have witnessed the way in which the Egyptians oppress them, so come, I send you to Pharaoh to bring the sons of Israel, my people, out of Egypt.'

Moses said to God, 'Who am I to go to Pharaoh and bring the sons of Israel out of Egypt?' 'I shall be with you,' was the answer 'and this is the sign by which you shall know that it is I who have sent you ... After you have led the people out of Egypt, you are to offer worship to God on this mountain.'

This is the word of the Lord.

Responsorial Psalm
Ps 102:1-4. 6-7. ℟ v.8

℟ **The Lord is compassion and love.**

1. My soul, give thanks to the Lord,
   all my being, bless his holy name.
   My soul, give thanks to the Lord
   and never forget all his blessings. ℟

2. It is he who forgives all your guilt,
   who heals every one of your ills,
   who redeems your life from the grave,
   who crowns you with love and compassion. ℟

3. The Lord does deeds of justice,
   gives judgement for all who are oppressed.
   He made known his ways to Moses
   and his deeds to Israel's sons. ℟

Gospel Acclamation
cf. Mt 11:25

Alleluia, alleluia!
Blessed are you, Father, Lord of heaven and earth,
for revealing the mysteries of the kingdom to mere children.
Alleluia!

GOSPEL

A reading from the holy Gospel according to Matthew 11:25-27

You have hidden these things from the learned and revealed them to mere children.

Jesus exclaimed, 'I bless you, Father, Lord of heaven and of earth, for hiding these things from the learned and the clever and revealing them to mere children. Yes, Father, for that is what it pleased you to do. Everything has been entrusted to me by my Father; and no one knows the Son except the Father, just as no one knows the Father except the Son and those to whom the Son chooses to reveal him.'

This is the Gospel of the Lord.

THURSDAY

FIRST READING

A reading from the book of Exodus 3:13-20
I Am who I Am. I Am has sent me to you.

Moses, hearing the voice of God coming from the middle of the bush, said to him 'I am to go, then, to the sons of Israel and say to them, "The God of your fathers has sent me to you." But if they ask me what his name is, what am I to tell them?' And God said to Moses, 'I Am who I Am. This' he added 'is what you must say to the sons of Israel: "I Am has sent me to you." ' And God also said to Moses, 'You are to say to the sons of Israel: "The Lord, the God of your fathers, the God of Abraham, the God of Isaac, and the God of Jacob, has sent me to you." This is my name for all time; by this name I shall be invoked for all generations to come.

'Go and gather the elders of Israel together and tell them, "The Lord, the God of your fathers, has appeared to me, – the God of Abraham, of Isaac, and of Jacob; and he has said to me: I have visited you and seen all that the Egyptians are doing to you. And so I have resolved to bring you up out of Egypt where you are oppressed, into the land of the Canaanites, the Hittites, the Amorites, the Perizzites. the Hivites and the Jebusites, to a land where milk and honey flow." They will listen to your words, and with the elders of Israel you are to go to the king of Egypt and say to him, "The Lord, the God of the Hebrews, has come to meet us. Give us leave, then, to make a three days' journey into the wilderness to offer sacrifice to the Lord our God." For myself, knowing that the king of Egypt will not let you go unless he is forced by a mighty hand, I shall show my power and strike Egypt with all the wonders I am going to work there. After this he will let you go.'

This is the word of the Lord.

Responsorial Psalm Ps 104:1. 5. 8-9. 24-27. ℟ v.8

℟ **The Lord remembers his covenant for ever.**

or

℟ **Alleluia!**

1 Give thanks to the Lord, tell his name,
 make known his deeds among the peoples.
 Remember the wonders he has done,
 his miracles, the judgements he spoke. ℟

Fifteenth Week in Ordinary Time, Year I: Thursday

2 He remembers his covenant for ever,
 his promise for a thousand generations,
 the covenant he made with Abraham,
 the oath he swore to Isaac.   ℟

3 He gave his people increase;
 he made them stronger than their foes,
 whose hearts he turned to hate his people
 and to deal deceitfully with his servants.   ℟

4 Then he sent Moses his servant
 and Aaron the man he had chosen.
 Through them he showed his marvels
 and his wonders in the country of Ham.   ℟

Gospel Acclamation   Ps 129:5

Alleluia, alleluia!
My soul is waiting for the Lord, I count on his word.
Alleluia!

or   Mt 11:28

Alleluia, alleluia!
Come to me, all you who labour and are overburdened,
and I will give you rest, says the Lord.
Alleluia!

GOSPEL

A reading from the holy Gospel according to Matthew   11:28-30
I am gentle and humble in heart.

Jesus exclaimed: 'Come to me, all you who labour and are overburdened, and I will give you rest. Shoulder my yoke and learn from me, for I am gentle and humble in heart, and you will find rest for your souls. Yes, my yoke is easy and my burden light.'

This is the Gospel of the Lord.

FRIDAY

FIRST READING

A reading from the book of Exodus 11:10–12:14
You shall slaughter a lamb between the two evenings; and when I see the blood I will pass over you.

Moses and Aaron worked many wonders in the presence of Pharaoh. But the Lord made Pharaoh's heart stubborn, and he did not let the sons of Israel leave his country.

The Lord said to Moses and Aaron in the land of Egypt, 'This month is to be the first of all the others for you, the first month of your year. Speak to the whole community of Israel and say, 'On the tenth day of this month each man must take an animal from the flock, one for each family: one animal for each household. If the household is too small to eat the animal, a man must join with his neighbour, the nearest to his house, as the number of persons requires. You must take into account what each can eat in deciding the number for the animal. It must be an animal without blemish, a male one year old; you may take it from either sheep or goats. You must keep it till the fourteenth day of the month when the whole assembly of the community of Israel shall slaughter it between the two evenings. Some of the blood must then be taken and put on the two doorposts and the lintel of the houses where it is eaten. That night, the flesh is to be eaten, roasted over the fire; it must be eaten with unleavened bread and bitter herbs. Do not eat any of it raw or boiled, but roasted over the fire, head, feet and entrails. You must not leave any over till the morning: whatever is left till morning you are to burn. You shall eat it like this: with a girdle round your waist, sandals on your feet, a staff in your hand. You shall eat it hastily: it is a passover in honour of the Lord. That night, I will go through the land of Egypt and strike down all the first-born in the land of Egypt, man and beast alike, and I shall deal out punishment to all the gods of Egypt. I am the Lord! The blood shall serve to mark the houses that you live in. When I see the blood I will pass over you and you shall escape the destroying plague when I strike the land of Egypt. This day is to be a day of remembrance for you, and you must celebrate it as a feast in the Lord's honour. For all generations you are to declare it a day of festival, for ever.'

This is the word of the Lord.

Fifteenth Week in Ordinary Time, Year I: Friday

Responsorial Psalm   Ps 115:12-13. 15-18. ℟ v.13

> ℟ **The cup of salvation I will raise;**
> **I will call on the Lord's name.**

or

> ℟ **Alleluia!**

1. How can I repay the Lord
   for his goodness to me?
   The cup of salvation I will raise;
   I will call on the Lord's name.   ℟

2. O precious in the eyes of the Lord
   is the death of his faithful.
   Your servant, Lord, your servant am I;
   you have loosened my bonds.   ℟

3. A thanksgiving sacrifice I make:
   I will call on the Lord's name.
   My vows to the Lord I will fulfil
   before all his people.   ℟

Gospel Acclamation   cf. Ps 26:1
Alleluia, alleluia!
Instruct me, Lord, in your way;
on an even path lead me.
Alleluia!

or   Jn 10:27

Alleluia, alleluia!
The sheep that belong to me listen to my voice,
says the Lord,
I know them and they follow me.
Alleluia!

GOSPEL

A reading from the holy Gospel according to Matthew   12:1-8
The Son of Man is master of the sabbath.

Jesus took a walk one sabbath day through the cornfields. His disciples were hungry and began to pick ears of corn and eat them. The Pharisees noticed it and said to him, 'Look, your disciples are doing something that is forbidden on the sabbath.' But he said to them, 'Have you not read what David did when he and his followers were hungry - how he went into the house of

God and how they ate the loaves of offering which neither he nor his followers were allowed to eat, but which were for the priests alone? Or again, have you not read in the Law that on the sabbath day the Temple priests break the sabbath without being blamed for it? Now here, I tell you, is something greater than the Temple. And if you had understood the meaning of the words: What I want is mercy, not sacrifice, you would not have condemned the blameless. For the Son of Man is master of the sabbath.'

This is the Gospel of the Lord.

SATURDAY

FIRST READING

A reading from the book of Exodus 12:37-42
It was night when the Lord brought Israel out of the land of Egypt.

The sons of Israel left Rameses for Succoth, about six hundred thousand on the march – all men – not counting their families. People of various sorts joined them in great numbers; there were flocks, too, and herds in immense droves. They baked cakes with the dough which they had brought from Egypt, unleavened because the dough was not leavened; they had been driven out of Egypt, with no time for dallying, and had not provided themselves with food for the journey. The time that the sons of Israel had spent in Egypt was four hundred and thirty years. And on the very day the four hundred and thirty years ended, all the array of the Lord left the land of Egypt. The night, when the Lord kept vigil to bring them out of the land of Egypt, must be kept as a vigil in honour of the Lord for all their generations.

This is the word of the Lord.

Responsorial Psalm Ps 135:1. 10-15. 23-24

1 O give thanks to the Lord for he is good.
   ℟ **Great is his love, love without end.**
   He remembered us in our distress.
   ℟ **Great is his love, love without end.**
   And he snatched us away from our foes.
   ℟ **Great is his love, love without end.**

2 The first-born of the Egyptians he smote.
   ℟ **Great is his love, love without end.**

He brought Israel out from their midst.
℟ **Great is his love, love without end.**
Arm outstretched, with power in his hand.
℟ **Great is his love, love without end.**

3 He divided the Red Sea in two.
℟ **Great is his love, love without end.**
He made Israel pass through the midst.
℟ **Great is his love, love without end.**
He flung Pharaoh and his force in the sea.
℟ **Great is his love, love without end.**

or ℟ **Alleluia!**

Gospel Acclamation   Ps 118:27

Alleluia, alleluia!
Make me grasp the way of your precepts,
and I will muse on your wonders.
Alleluia!

or   2 Cor 5:19

Alleluia, alleluia!
God in Christ was reconciling the world to himself,
and he has entrusted to us the news that they are reconciled.
Alleluia!

GOSPEL

A reading from the holy Gospel according to Matthew   12:14-21
Jesus warned them not to make him known; this was to fulfil the prophecy.

The Pharisees went out and began to plot against Jesus, discussing how to destroy him.

Jesus knew this and withdrew from the district. Many followed him and he cured them all, but warned them not to make him known. This was to fulfil the prophecy of Isaiah:

Here is my servant whom I have chosen,
my beloved, the favourite of my soul.
I will endow him with my spirit,
and he will proclaim the true faith to the nations.
He will not brawl or shout,
nor will anyone hear his voice in the streets.
He will not break the crushed reed,

nor put out the smouldering wick
till he has led the truth to victory:
in his name the nations will put their hope.

This is the Gospel of the Lord.

SIXTEENTH WEEK IN ORDINARY TIME
Year I

MONDAY

FIRST READING

A reading from the book of Exodus 14:5-18
When I have won glory for myself at the expense of Pharaoh, the Egyptians will learn that I am the Lord.

When Pharaoh, king of Egypt, was told that the Israelites had made their escape, he and his courtiers changed their minds about the people. 'What have we done,' they said 'allowing Israel to leave our service?' So Pharaoh had his chariot harnessed and gathered his troops about him, taking six hundred of the best chariots and all the other chariots in Egypt, each manned by a picked team. The Lord made Pharaoh, king of Egypt, stubborn, and he gave chase to the sons of Israel as they made their triumphant escape. So the Egyptians gave chase and came up with them where they lay encamped beside the sea – all the horses, the chariots of Pharaoh, his horsemen, his army – near Pi-hahiroth, facing Baal-zephon. And as Pharaoh approached, the sons of Israel looked round – and there were the Egyptians in pursuit of them! The sons of Israel were terrified and cried out to the Lord. To Moses they said, 'Were there no graves in Egypt that you must lead us out to die in the wilderness? What good have you done us, bringing us out of Egypt? We spoke of this in Egypt, did we not? Leave us alone, we said, we would rather work for the Egyptians! Better to work for the Egyptians than die in the wilderness!' Moses answered the people, 'Have no fear! Stand firm, and you will see what the Lord will do to save you today: the Egyptians you see today, you will never see again. The Lord will do the fighting for you: you have only to keep still.'

The Lord said to Moses, 'Why do you cry to me so? Tell the sons of Israel to march on. For yourself, raise your staff and stretch out your hand over the sea and part it for the sons of Israel to walk through the sea on dry ground. I for my part will make the heart of the Egyptians so stubborn that they will follow them. So shall I win myself glory at the expense of Pharaoh, of all his army, his chariots, his horsemen. And when I have won glory for myself, at the expense of Pharaoh and his chariots and his army, the Egyptians will learn that I am the Lord.'

This is the word of the Lord.

Responsional Psalm   Ex 15:1-6. ℟ v.1

℟ **I will sing to the Lord, glorious his triumph!**

1. I will sing to the Lord, glorious his triumph!
   Horse and rider he has thrown into the sea!
   The Lord is my strength, my song, my salvation.
   This is my God and I extol him,
   my father's God and I give him praise.   ℟

2. The Lord is a warrior! The Lord is his name.
   The chariots of Pharaoh he hurled into the sea,
   the flower of his army is drowned in the sea.   ℟

3. The deeps hide them; they sank like a stone.
   Your right hand, Lord, glorious in its power,
   your right hand, Lord, has shattered the enemy.   ℟

Gospel Acclamation   cf. 2 Tim 1:10

Alleluia, alleluia!
Our Saviour Christ Jesus abolished death,
and he has proclaimed life through the Good News.
Alleluia!

or   cf. Ps 94:8

Alleluia, alleluia!
Harden not your heart today,
but listen to the voice of the Lord.
Alleluia!

GOSPEL

A reading from the holy Gospel according to Matthew   12:38-42
The Queen of the South will rise up with this generation and condemn it.

Some of the scribes and Pharisees spoke up. 'Master,' they said 'we should like to see a sign from you.' Jesus replied, 'It is an evil and unfaithful generation that asks for a sign! The only sign it will be given is the sign of the prophet Jonah. For as Jonah was in the belly of the sea-monster for three days and three nights, so will the Son of Man be in the heart of the earth for three days and three nights. On Judgement day the men of Nineveh will stand up with this generation and condemn it, because when Jonah preached they repented; and there is something greater than Jonah here. On Judgement day the Queen of the South will rise up with this generation and condemn it, because she came from the ends of the earth to hear the wisdom of Solomon; and there is something greater than Solomon here.'

This is the Gospel of the Lord.

TUESDAY

FIRST READING

A reading from the book of Exodus   14:21–15:1

The sons of Israel went on dry ground right into the sea.

Moses stretched out his hand over the sea. The Lord drove back the sea with a strong easterly wind all night, and he made dry land of the sea. The waters parted and the sons of Israel went on dry ground right into the sea, walls of water to right and to left of them. The Egyptians gave chase: after them they went, right into the sea, all Pharaoh's horses, his chariots, and his horsemen. In the morning watch, the Lord looked down on the army of the Egyptians from the pillar of fire and of cloud, and threw the army into confusion. He so clogged their chariot wheels that they could scarcely make headway. 'Let us flee from the Israelites,' the Egyptians cried 'the Lord is fighting for them against the Egyptians!' 'Stretch out your hand over the sea,' the Lord said to Moses 'that the waters may flow back on the Egyptians and their chariots and their horsemen.' Moses stretched out his hand over the sea and, as day broke, the sea returned to its bed. The fleeing Egyptians marched right into it, and the Lord overthrew the Egyptians in the very middle of the sea. The returning waters overwhelmed the chariots and the horsemen of Pharaoh's whole army, which had followed the Israelites into the sea; not a single one of them was left. But the sons of Israel had marched through the sea on dry ground, walls of water to right and to left of them. That day, the Lord rescued Israel from the Egyptians, and Israel

Sixteenth Week in Ordinary Time, Year I: Tuesday

saw the Egyptians lying dead on the shore. Israel witnessed the great act that the Lord had performed against the Egyptians, and the people venerated the Lord; they put their faith in the Lord and in Moses, his servant.

It was then that Moses and the sons of Israel sang this song in honour of the Lord:*

*The Responsorial Psalm may follow immediately, as at the Easter Vigil.

Responsorial Psalm　　　　　　　　　　　Ex 15:8-10. 12. 17. ℟ v.1

℟ **I will sing to the Lord, glorious his triumph!**

1. At the breath of your anger the waters piled high;
   the moving waters stood up like a dam.
   The deeps turned solid in the midst of the sea.
   The enemy said: 'I will pursue and overtake them,
   I will divide the plunder, I shall have my will.
   I will draw my sword, my hand shall destroy them.　℟

2. You blew with your breath, the sea closed over them.
   They went down like lead into the mighty waters.
   You stretched forth your hand, the earth engulfed them.　℟

3. You will lead your people and plant them on your mountain,
   the place, O Lord, where you have made your home,
   the sanctuary, Lord, which your hands have made.　℟

Gospel Acclamation　　　　　　　　　　　　　　　　　　1 Jn 2:5

Alleluia, alleluia!
When anyone obeys what Christ has said,
God's love comes to perfection in him.
Alleluia!

or　　　　　　　　　　　　　　　　　　　　　　　　　　Jn 14:23

Alleluia, alleluia!
If anyone loves me he will keep my word,
and my Father will love him,
and we shall come to him.
Alleluia!

GOSPEL

A reading from the holy Gospel according to Matthew 12:46-50

Stretching out his hand towards his disciples he said, 'Here are my mother and my brothers.'

Jesus was speaking to the crowds when his mother and his brothers appeared; they were standing outside and were anxious to have a word with him. But to the man who told him this Jesus replied, 'Who is my mother? Who are my brothers?' And stretching out his hand towards his disciples he said, 'Here are my mother and my brothers. Anyone who does the will of my Father in heaven, he is my brother and sister and mother.'

This is the Gospel of the Lord.

WEDNESDAY

FIRST READING

A reading from the book of Exodus 16:1-5. 9-15

I will rain down bread for you from the heavens.

From Elim they set out, and the whole community of the sons of Israel reached the wilderness of Sin – between Elim and Sinai – on the fifteenth day of the second month after they had left Egypt. And the whole community of the sons of Israel began to complain against Moses and Aaron in the wilderness and said to them, 'Why did we not die at the Lord's hand in the land of Egypt, when we were able to sit down to pans of meat and could eat bread to our heart's content! As it is, you have brought us to this wilderness to starve this whole company to death!'

Then the Lord said to Moses, 'Now I will rain down bread for you from the heavens. Each day the people are to go out and gather the day's portion; I propose to test them in this way to see whether they will follow my law or not. On the sixth day, when they prepare what they have brought in, this will be twice as much as the daily gathering.'

Moses said to Aaron, 'To the whole community of the sons of Israel say this, "Present yourselves before the Lord, for he has heard your complaints."' As Aaron was speaking to the whole community of the sons of Israel, they turned towards the wilderness, and there was the glory of the Lord appearing in the form of a cloud. Then the Lord spoke to Moses and said, 'I have heard the complaints of the sons of Israel. Say this to them, "Between the two evenings you shall eat meat, and in the morning you shall have bread to your heart's content. Then you will learn that I, the Lord, am your God." ' And so it came about: quails flew up in the evening, and they covered the camp; in the morning there was a coating of dew all round the camp. When the coating of dew lifted, there on the surface of the desert was a thing delicate, powdery, as fine as hoarfrost on the ground. When they saw this, the sons of Israel said to one another, 'What is that?' not knowing what it was. 'That' said Moses to them 'is the bread the Lord gives you to eat.'

This is the word of the Lord.

Responsorial Psalm Ps 77:18-19. 23-28. R̷ v.24
 R̷ **The Lord gave them bread from heaven.**

1 In their heart they put God to the test
 by demanding the food they craved.
 They even spoke against God.
 They said: 'Is it possible for God
 to prepare a table in the desert?' R̷

2 Yet he commanded the clouds above
 and opened the gates of heaven.
 He rained down manna for their food,
 and gave them bread from heaven. R̷

3 Mere men ate the bread of angels.
 He sent them abundance of food;
 he made the east wind blow from heaven
 and roused the south wind by his might. R̷

4 He rained food on them like dust,
 winged fowl like the sands of the sea.
 He let it fall in the midst of their camp
 and all around their tents. R̷

Gospel Acclamation Ps 118:29. 35
 Alleluia, alleluia!
 Bend my heart to your will, O Lord,
 and teach me your law.
 Alleluia!

or

Alleluia, alleluia!
The seed is the word of God, Christ the sower;
whoever finds this seed will remain for ever.
Alleluia!

GOSPEL

A reading from the holy Gospel according to Matthew 13:1-9
It produced crop a hundredfold.

Jesus left the house and sat by the lakeside, but such crowds gathered round him that he got into a boat and sat there. The people all stood on the beach, and he told them many things in parables.

He said, 'Imagine a sower going out to sow. As he sowed, some seeds fell on the edge of the path, and the birds came and ate them up. Others fell on patches of rock where they found little soil and sprang up straight away, because there was no depth of earth; but as soon as the sun came up they were scorched and, not having any roots, they withered away. Others fell among thorns, and the thorns grew up and choked them. Others fell on rich soil and produced their crop, some a hundredfold, some sixty, some thirty. Listen, anyone who has ears!'

This is the Gospel of the Lord.

THURSDAY

FIRST READING

A reading from the book of Exodus 19:1-2. 9-11. 16-20
The Lord will descend on the mountain of Sinai in the sight of all the people.

Three months after they came out of the land of Egypt, on that day the sons of Israel came to the wilderness of Sinai. From Rephidim they set out again; and when they reached the wilderness of Sinai, there in the wilderness they pitched their camp; there facing the mountain Israel pitched camp.

The Lord said to Moses, 'I am coming to you in a dense cloud so that the people may hear when I speak to you and may trust you always.' And Moses took the people's reply back to the Lord.

The Lord said Moses, 'Go to the people and tell them to

Sixteenth Week in Ordinary Time, Year I: Thursday 633

prepare themselves today and tomorrow. Let them wash their clothing and hold themselves in readiness for the third day, because on the third day the Lord will descend on the mountain of Sinai in the sight of all the people.'

Now at daybreak on the third day there were peals of thunder on the mountain and lightning flashes, a dense cloud, and a loud trumpet blast, and inside the camp all the people trembled. Then Moses led the people out of the camp to meet God; and they stood at the bottom of the mountain. The mountain of Sinai was entirely wrapped in smoke, because the Lord had descended on it in the form of fire. Like smoke from a furnace the smoke went up, and the whole mountain shook violently. Louder and louder grew the sound of the trumpet. Moses spoke, and God answered him with peals of thunder. The Lord came down on the mountain of Sinai, on the mountain top, and the Lord called Moses to the top of the mountain.

This is the word of the Lord.

Responsorial Psalm   Dan 3:52-56. ℟ v.52

1 You are blest, Lord God of our fathers.
   ℟ **To you glory and praise for evermore.**
   Blest your glorious holy name.
   ℟ **To you glory and praise for evermore.**

2 You are blest in the temple of your glory.
   ℟ **To you glory and praise for evermore.**
   You are blest on the throne of your kingdom.
   ℟ **To you glory and praise for evermore.**

3 You are blest who gaze into the depths.
   ℟ **To you glory and praise for evermore.**
   You are blest in the firmament of heaven.
   ℟ **To you glory and praise for evermore.**

Gospel Acclamation   cf. Ps 94:8
   Alleluia, alleluia!
   Harden not your hearts today,
   but listen to the voice of the Lord.
   Alleluia!

or   cf. Mt 11:25

   Alleluia, alleluia!
   Blessed are you, Father,

Lord of heaven and earth,
for revealing the mysteries of the kingdom
to mere children.
Alleluia!

GOSPEL

A reading from the holy Gospel according to Matthew 13:10-17

The mysteries of the kingdom of heaven are revealed to you, but they are not revealed to them.

The disciples went up to Jesus and asked, 'Why do you talk to the crowds in parables?' 'Because' he replied, 'the mysteries of the kingdom of heaven are revealed to you, but they are not revealed to them. For anyone who has will be given more, and he will have more than enough; but from anyone who has not, even what he has will be taken away. The reason I talk to them in parables is that they look without seeing and listen without hearing or understanding. So in their case the prophecy of Isaiah is being fulfilled:

You will listen and listen again, but not understand,
see and see again, but not perceive.
For the heart of this nation has grown coarse,
their ears are dull of hearing, and they have shut their eyes
for fear they should see with their eyes,
hear with their ears,
understand with their heart,
and be converted
and be healed by me.

But happy are your eyes because they see, your ears because they hear! I tell you solemnly, many prophets and holy men longed to see what you see, and never saw it; to hear what you hear, and never heard it.'

This is the Gospel of the Lord.

FRIDAY

FIRST READING

A reading from the book of Exodus 20:1-17
The law was given through Moses.

The Lord spoke all these words. He said, 'I am the Lord your God

Sixteenth Week in Ordinary Time, Year I: Friday

who brought you out of the land of Egypt, out of the house of slavery.

'You shall have no gods except me.

'You shall not make yourself a carved image or any likeness of anything in heaven or earth beneath or in the waters under the earth; you shall not bow down to them or serve them. For I, the Lord your God, am a jealous God and I punish the father's fault in the sons, the grandsons, and the great-grandsons of those who hate me; but I show kindness to thousands of those who love me and keep my commandments.

'You shall not utter the name of the Lord your God to misuse it, for the Lord will not leave unpunished the man who utters his name to misuse it.

'Remember the sabbath day and keep it holy. For six days you shall labour and do all your work, but the seventh day is a sabbath for the Lord your God. You shall do no work that day, neither you nor your son nor your daughter nor your servants, men or women, nor your animals nor the stranger who lives with you. For in six days the Lord made the heavens and the earth and the sea and all that these hold, but on the seventh day he rested; that is why the Lord has blessed the sabbath day and made it sacred.

'Honour your father and your mother so that you may have a long life in the land that the Lord your God has given you.

'You shall not kill.

'You shall not commit adultery.

'You shall not steal.

'You shall not bear false witness against your neighbour.

'You shall not covet your neighbour's house. You shall not covet your neighbour's wife, or his servant, man or woman, or his ox, or his donkey, or anything that is his.'

This is the word of the Lord.

Responsorial Psalm Ps 18:8-11. ℟ Jn 6:68

℟ **Lord, you have the message of eternal life.**

1 The law of the Lord is perfect,
 it revives the soul.
 The rule of the Lord is to be trusted,
 it gives wisdom to the simple. ℟

2 The precepts of the Lord are right,
 they gladden the heart.

(continued)

The command of the Lord is clear,
it gives light to the eyes.

℟ **Lord, you have the message of eternal life.**

3 The fear of the Lord is holy,
abiding for ever.
The decrees of the Lord are truth
and all of them just. ℟

4 They are more to be desired than gold,
than the purest of gold
and sweeter are they than honey,
than honey from the comb. ℟

Gospel Acclamation James 1:21
Alleluia, alleluia!
Accept and submit to the word
which has been planted in you
and can save your souls.
Alleluia!

or cf. Lk 8:15

Alleluia, alleluia!
Blessed are those who,
with a noble and generous heart,
take the word of God to themselves
and yield a harvest through their perseverance.
Alleluia!

GOSPEL

A reading from the holy Gospel according to Matthew 13:18-23

The man who hears the word and understands it, he is the one who yields a harvest.

Jesus said to his disciples: 'You are to hear the parable of the sower. When anyone hears the word of the kingdom without understanding, the evil one comes and carries off what was sown in his heart; this is the man who received the seed on the edge of the path. The one who received it on patches of rock is the man who hears the word and welcomes it at once with joy. But he has no root in him, he does not last; let some trial come, or some persecution on account of the word, and he falls away at once. The one who received the seed in thorns is the man who hears the word, but the worries of this world and the lure of riches choke the word and so he produces nothing. And the one who received the seed in rich soil is the man who hears the word and understands it; he is the one who yields a harvest and produces now a hundredfold, now sixty, now thirty.'

This is the Gospel of the Lord.

SATURDAY

FIRST READING

A reading from the book of Exodus   24:3-8
This is the blood of the Covenant that the Lord has made with you.

Moses went and told the people all the commands of the Lord and all the ordinances. In answer, all the people said with one voice, 'We will observe all the commands that the Lord has decreed.' Moses put all the commands of the Lord into writing, and early next morning he built an altar at the foot of the mountain, with twelve standing-stones for the twelve tribes of Israel. Then he directed certain young Israelites to offer holocausts and to immolate bullocks to the Lord as communion sacrifices. Half of the blood Moses took up and put into basins, the other half he cast on the altar. And taking the Book of the Covenant he read it to the listening people, and they said, 'We will observe all that the Lord has decreed; we will obey.' Then Moses took the blood and cast it towards the people. 'This' he said 'is the blood of the Covenant that the Lord has made with you, containing all these rules.'

This is the word of the Lord.

Responsorial Psalm   Ps 49:1-2. 5-6. 14-15. ℟ v.14
    ℟ **Pay your sacrifice of thanksgiving to God.**

1   The God of gods, the Lord,
     has spoken and summoned the earth,
     from the rising of the sun to its setting.
     Out of Zion's perfect beauty he shines.   ℟

2   'Summon before me my people
     who made covenant with me by sacrifice.'
     The heavens proclaim his justice,
     for he, God, is the judge.   ℟

(continued)

3 Pay your sacrifice of thanksgiving to God
and render him your votive offerings.
'Call on me in the day of distress.
I will free you and you shall honour me.'

℟ **Pay your sacrifice of thanksgiving to God.**

Gospel Acclamation   Heb 4:12

Alleluia, alleluia!
The word of God is something alive and active;
it can judge secret emotions and thoughts.
Alleluia!

or   James 1:21

Alleluia, alleluia!
Accept and submit to the word
which has been planted in you
and can save your souls.
Alleluia!

GOSPEL

A reading from the holy Gospel according to Matthew   13:24-30
Let them both grow till the harvest.

Jesus put a parable before the crowds, 'The kingdom of heaven may be compared to a man who sowed good seed in his field. While everybody was asleep his enemy came, sowed darnel all among the wheat, and made off. When the new wheat sprouted and ripened, the darnel appeared as well. The owner's servants went to him and said, "Sir, was it not good seed that you sowed in your field? If so, where does the darnel come from?" "Some enemy has done this" he answered. And the servants said, "Do you want us to go and weed it out?" But he said, "No, because when you weed out the darnel you might pull up the wheat with it. Let them both grow till the harvest; and at harvest time I shall say to the reapers: First collect the darnel and tie it in bundles to be burnt, then gather the wheat into my barn."'

This is the Gospel of the Lord.

SEVENTEENTH WEEK IN ORDINARY TIME
Year I

MONDAY

FIRST READING

A reading from the book of Exodus 32:15-24. 30-34
This people has committed a grave sin, making themselves a god of gold.

Moses made his way back down the mountain with the two tablets of the Testimony in his hands, tablets inscribed on both sides, inscribed on the front and on the back. These tablets were the work of God, and the writing on them was God's writing engraved on the tablets.

Joshua heard the noise of the people shouting. 'There is the sound of battle in the camp,' he told Moses. Moses answered him:

'No song of victory is this sound,
no wailing for defeat this sound;
it is the sound of chanting that I hear.'

As he approached the camp and saw the calf and the groups dancing, Moses' anger blazed. He threw down the tablets he was holding and broke them at the foot of the mountain. He seized the calf they had made and burned it, grinding it into powder which he scattered on the water; and he made the sons of Israel drink it. To Aaron Moses said, 'What has this people done to you, for you to bring such a great sin on them?' 'Let not my lord's anger blaze like this' Aaron answered. 'You know yourself how prone this people is to evil. They said to me, "Make us a god to go at our head; this Moses, the man who brought us up from Egypt, we do not know what has become of him." So I said to them, "Who has gold?" and they took it off and brought it to me. I threw it into the fire and out came this calf.'

On the following day Moses said to the people, 'You have committed a grave sin. But now I shall go up to the Lord: perhaps I can make atonement for your sin.' And Moses returned to the Lord. 'I am grieved,' he cried 'this people has committed a grave sin making themselves a god of gold. And yet, if it pleased you to forgive this sin of theirs . . . ! But if not, then blot me out from the book that you have written.' The Lord answered Moses, 'It is the man who has sinned against me that I shall blot out from my book. Go now, lead the people to the place of which I told you.

My angel shall go before you but, on the day of my visitation, I shall punish them for their sin.'

This is the word of the Lord.

Responsorial Psalm   Ps 105:19-23. R v.1

    R **O give thanks to the Lord for he is good.**

or

    R **Alleluia!**

1. They fashioned a calf at Horeb
and worshipped an image of metal,
exchanging the God who was their glory
for the image of a bull that eats grass. R

2. They forgot the God who was their saviour,
who had done such great things in Egypt,
such portents in the land of Ham,
such marvels at the Red Sea. R

3. For this he said he would destroy them,
but Moses, the man he had chosen,
stood in the breach before him,
to turn back his anger from destruction. R

Gospel Acclamation   cf. 2 Thess 2:14
Alleluia, alleluia!
Through the Good News God called us
to share the glory of our Lord Jesus Christ.
Alleluia!

or   James 1:18

Alleluia, alleluia!
By his own choice the Father made us his children
by the message of the truth,
so that we should be a sort of first-fruits
of all that he created.
Alleluia!

GOSPEL

A reading from the holy Gospel according to Matthew   13:31-35

A mustard seed becomes a tree so that the birds of the air shelter in its branches.

Jesus put a parable before the crowds, 'The kingdom of heaven is like a mustard seed which a man took and sowed in his field. It is the smallest of all the seeds, but when it has grown it is the biggest shrub of all and becomes a tree so that the birds of the air come and shelter in its branches.'

He told them another parable, 'The kingdom of heaven is like the yeast a woman took and mixed in with three measures of flour till it was leavened all through.'

In all this Jesus spoke to the crowds in parables; indeed, he would never speak to them except in parables. This was to fulfill the prophecy:

I will speak to you in parables
and expound things hidden since the foundation of the world.

This is the Gospel of the Lord.

TUESDAY

FIRST READING

A reading from the book of Exodus 33:7-11; 34:5-9. 28

The Lord would speak to Moses face to face.

Moses used to take the Tent and pitch it outside the camp, at some distance from the camp. He called it the Tent of Meeting. Anyone who had to consult the Lord would go out to the Tent of Meeting, outside the camp. Whenever Moses went out to the Tent, all the people would rise. Every man would stand at the door of his tent and watch Moses until he reached the Tent; the pillar of cloud would come down and station itself at the entrance to the Tent, and the Lord would speak with Moses. When they saw the pillar of cloud stationed at the entrance to the Tent, all the people would rise and bow low, each at the door of his tent. The Lord would speak with Moses face to face, as a man speaks with his friend. Then Moses would turn back to the camp, but the young man who was his servant, Joshua son of Nun, would not leave the Tent.

Moses stood with the Lord on the mountain. He called on the name of the Lord. The Lord passed before him and proclaimed, 'The Lord, the Lord, a God of tenderness and compassion, slow to anger, rich in kindness and faithfulness; for thousands he maintains his kindness, forgives faults, transgression, sin; yet he lets nothing go unchecked, punishing the father's fault in the sons and in the grandsons to the third and fourth generation.'

And Moses bowed down to the ground at once and worshipped. 'If I have indeed won your favour, Lord,' he said 'let my Lord come with us, I beg. True, they are a headstrong people, but forgive us our faults and our sins, and adopt us as your heritage.'

He stayed there with the Lord for forty days and forty nights, eating and drinking nothing. He inscribed on the tablets the words of the Covenant – the Ten Words.

This is the word of the Lord.

Responsional Psalm Ps 102:6-13. ℟ v.8

℟ **The Lord is compassion and love.**

1 The Lord does deeds of justice,
   gives judgement for all who are oppressed.
   He made known his ways to Moses
   and his deeds to Israel's sons. ℟

2 The Lord is compassion and love,
   slow to anger and rich in mercy.
   His wrath will come to an end:
   he will not be angry for ever. ℟

3 He does not treat us according to our sins
   nor repay us according to our faults.
   For as the heavens are high above the earth
   so strong is his love for those who fear him. ℟

4 As far as the east is from the west
   so far does he remove our sins.
   As a father has compassion on his sons,
   the Lord has pity on those who fear him. ℟

Gospel Acclamation 1 Peter 1:25

Alleluia, alleluia!
The word of the Lord remains for ever:
What is this word?
It is the Good News that has been brought to you.
Alleluia!

or

Alleluia, alleluia!
The seed is the word of God, Christ the sower;
whoever finds this seed will remain for ever.
Alleluia!

Seventeenth Week in Ordinary Time, Year I: Wednesday

GOSPEL

A reading from the holy Gospel according to Matthew 13:36-43

Just as the darnel is gathered up and burnt in the fire, so it will be at the end of time.

Leaving the crowds, Jesus went to the house; and his disciples came to him and said, 'Explain the parable about the darnel in the field to us.' He said in reply, 'The sower of the good seed is the Son of Man. The field is the world; the good seed is the subjects of the kingdom; the darnel, the subjects of the evil one; the enemy who sowed them, the devil; the harvest is the end of the world; the reapers are the angels. Well then, just as the darnel is gathered up and burnt in the fire, so it will be at the end of time. The Son of Man will send his angels and they will gather out of his kingdom all things that provoke offences and all who do evil, and throw them into the blazing furnace, where there will be weeping and grinding of teeth. Then the virtuous will shine like the sun in the kingdom of their Father. Listen, anyone who has ears!'

This is the Gospel of the Lord.

WEDNESDAY

FIRST READING

A reading from the book of Exodus 34:29-35

When they saw Moses, they would not venture near him.

When Moses came down from the mountain of Sinai – as he came down from the mountain, Moses had the two tablets of the Testimony in his hands – he did not know that the skin on his face was radiant after speaking with the Lord. And when Aaron and all the sons of Israel saw Moses, the skin on his face shone so much that they would not venture near him. But Moses called to them, and Aaron with all the leaders of the community came back to him; and he spoke to them. Then all the sons of Israel came closer, and he passed on to them all the orders that the Lord had given him on the mountain of Sinai. And when Moses had finished speaking to them, he put a veil over his face. Whenever he went into the Lord's presence to speak with him, Moses would remove the veil until he came out again. And when he came out, he would tell the sons of Israel what he had been ordered to pass on to them, and the sons of Israel would see the face of Moses radiant. Then Moses would put the veil back over his face until he returned to speak with the Lord.

This is the word of the Lord.

Responsorial Psalm   Ps 98:5-7. 9. ℟ cf. v.9

℟ **You are holy, O Lord our God.**

1. Exalt the Lord our God;
   bow down before Zion, his footstool.
   He the Lord is holy. ℟

2. Among his priests were Aaron and Moses,
   among those who invoked his name were Samuel.
   They invoked the Lord and he answered. ℟

3. To them he spoke in the pillar of cloud.
   They did his will; they kept the law,
   which he, the Lord, had given. ℟

4. Exalt the Lord our God;
   bow down before his holy mountain
   for the Lord our God is holy. ℟

Gospel Acclamation   Ps 118:105

Alleluia, alleluia!
Your word is a lamp for my steps
and a light for my path.
Alleluia!

or   Jn 15:15

Alleluia, alleluia!
I call you friends, says the Lord,
because I have made known to you
everything I have learnt from my Father.
Alleluia!

GOSPEL

A reading from the holy Gospel according to Matthew   13:44-46

He sells everything he owns and buys the field.

Jesus said to the crowds: 'The kingdom of heaven is like treasure hidden in a field which someone has found; he hides it again, goes off happy, sells everything he owns and buys the field.

'Again, the kingdom of heaven is like a merchant looking for fine pearls; when he finds one of great value he goes and sells everything he owns and buys it.'

This is the Gospel of the Lord.

THURSDAY

FIRST READING

A reading from the book of Exodus 40:16-21. 34-38
The cloud covered the Tent of Meeting and the glory of the Lord God filled the tabernacle.

Moses did exactly as the Lord had directed him. The tabernacle was set up on the first day of the first month in the second year. Moses erected the tabernacle. He fixed the sockets for it, put up its frames, put its cross-bars in position, set up its posts. He spread the tent over the tabernacle and on top of this the covering for the tent, as the Lord had directed Moses. He took the Testimony and placed it inside the ark. He set the shafts to the ark and placed the throne of mercy on it. He brought the ark into the tabernacle and put the screening veil in place; thus he screened the ark of the Lord, as the Lord had directed Moses.

The cloud covered the Tent of Meeting and the glory of the Lord filled the tabernacle. Moses could not enter the Tent of Meeting because of the cloud that rested on it and because of the glory of the Lord that filled the tabernacle.

At every stage of their journey, whenever the cloud rose from the tabernacle the sons of Israel would resume their march. If the cloud did not rise, they waited and would not march until it did. For the cloud of the Lord rested on the tabernacle by day, and a fire shone within the cloud by night, for all the House of Israel to see. And so it was for every stage of their journey.

This is the word of the Lord.

Responsorial Psalm Ps 83:3-6. 8. 11. ℟ v.2
℟ **How lovely is your dwelling place, Lord, God of hosts.**

1 My soul is longing and yearning,
 is yearning for the courts of the Lord.
 My heart and my soul ring out their joy
 to God, the living God. ℟

2 The sparrow herself finds a home
   and the swallow a nest for her brood;
   she lays her young by your altars,
   Lord of hosts, my king and my God.

   ℟ **How lovely is your dwelling place,
       Lord, God of hosts.**

3 They are happy, who dwell in your house,
   for ever singing your praise.
   They are happy, whose strength is in you,
   they walk with ever growing strength. ℟

4 One day within your courts
   is better than a thousand elsewhere.
   The threshold of the house of God
   I prefer to the dwellings of the wicked. ℟

Gospel Acclamation   Jn 15:15
   Alleluia, alleluia!
   I call you friends, says the Lord,
   because I have made known to you
   everything I have learnt from my Father.
   Alleluia!

or   cf. Acts 16:14

   Alleluia, alleluia!
   Open our heart, O Lord,
   to accept the words of your Son.
   Alleluia!

GOSPEL

A reading from the holy Gospel according to Matthew   13:47-53
They collect the good ones in a basket and throw away those that are no use.

Jesus said to the crowds: 'The kingdom of heaven is like a dragnet cast into the sea that brings in a haul of all kinds. When it is full, the fishermen haul it ashore; then, sitting down, they collect the good ones in a basket and throw away those that are no use. This is how it will be at the end of time; the angels will appear and separate the wicked from the just to throw them into the blazing furnace where there will be weeping and grinding of teeth.

'Have you understood all this?' They said, 'Yes.' And he said to them, 'Well then, every scribe who becomes a disciple of the kingdom of heaven is like a householder who brings out from his storeroom things both new and old.'

When Jesus had finished these parables he left the district.

This is the Gospel of the Lord.

FRIDAY

FIRST READING

A reading from the book of Leviticus   23:1. 4-11. 15-16. 27. 34-37
You are to call these the most solemn festivals of the Lord.

The Lord spoke to Moses; he said:

'These are the Lord's solemn festivals, the sacred assemblies to which you are to summon the sons of Israel on the appointed day.

'The fourteenth day of the first month, between the two evenings, is the Passover of the Lord; and the fifteenth day of the same month is the feast of Unleavened Bread for the Lord. For seven days you shall eat bread without leaven. On the first day you are to hold a sacred assembly; you must do no heavy work. For seven days you shall offer a burnt offering to the Lord. The seventh day is to be a day of sacred assembly; you must do no work.'

The Lord spoke to Moses; he said:

'Speak to the sons of Israel and say to them:

'When you enter the land that I give you, and gather in the harvest there, you must bring the first sheaf of your harvest to the priest, and he is to present it to the Lord with the gesture of offering, so that you may be acceptable. The priest shall make this offering on the day after the sabbath.

'From the day after the sabbath, the day on which you bring the sheaf of offering, you are to count seven full weeks. You are to count fifty days, to the day after the seventh sabbath, and then you are to offer the Lord a new oblation.

'But the tenth day of this seventh month shall be the Day of Atonement. You are to hold a sacred assembly. You must fast, and you must offer a burnt offering to the Lord.

'The fifteenth day of this seventh month shall be the feast of Tabernacles for the Lord, lasting seven days. The first day is a day of sacred assembly; you must do no heavy work. For seven days you must offer a burnt offering to the Lord. On the eighth day you are to hold a sacred assembly, you must offer a burnt offering to the Lord. It is a day of solemn meeting; you must do no heavy work.

'These are the solemn festivals of the Lord to which you are to summon the children of Israel, sacred assemblies for the purpose of offering burnt offerings, holocausts, oblations, sacrifices and libations to the Lord, according to the ritual of each day.'

This is the word of the Lord.

Responsorial Psalm   Ps 80:3-6. 10-11. ℟ v.2

℟ **Ring out your joy to God our strength.**

1. Raise a song and sound the timbrel,
   the sweet-sounding harp and the lute,
   blow the trumpet at the new moon,
   when the moon is full, on our feast.   ℟

2. For this is Israel's law,
   a command of the God of Jacob.
   He imposed it as a rule on Joseph,
   when he went out against the land of Egypt.   ℟

2. Let there be no foreign god among you,
   no worship of an alien god.
   I am the Lord your God,
   who brought you from the land of Egypt.   ℟

Gospel Acclamation   cf. 1 Thess 2:13
    Alleluia, alleluia!
    Accept God's message for what it really is:
    God's message, and not some human thinking.
    Alleluia!

or   1 Peter 1:25
    Alleluia, alleluia!
    The word of the Lord remains for ever:
    What is this word?
    It is the Good News that has been brought to you.
    Alleluia!

GOSPEL

A reading from the holy Gospel according to Matthew   13:54-58
This is the carpenter's son, surely? Where did the man get his wisdom and these miraculous powers?

Coming to his home town, Jesus taught the people in their

synagogue in such a way that they were astonished and said, 'Where did the man get this wisdom and these miraculous powers? This is the carpenter's son, surely? Is not his mother the woman called Mary, and his brothers James and Joseph and Simon and Jude? His sisters, too, are they not all here with us? So where did the man get it all?' And they would not accept him. But Jesus said to them, 'A prophet is only despised in his own country and in his own house,' and he did not work many miracles there because of their lack of faith.

This is the Gospel of the Lord.

SATURDAY

FIRST READING

A reading from the book of Leviticus   25:1. 8-17
In the year of jubilee each of you is to return to his ancestral home.

The Lord spoke to Moses on Mount Sinai; he said: 'You are to count seven weeks of years – seven times seven years, that is to say a period of seven weeks of years, forty-nine years. And on the tenth day of the seventh month you shall sound the trumpet; on the Day of Atonement you shall sound the trumpet throughout the land. You will declare this fiftieth year sacred and proclaim the liberation of all the inhabitants of the land. This is to be a jubilee for you; each of you will return to his ancestral home, each to his own clan. This fiftieth year is to be a jubilee year for you: you will not sow, you will not harvest the ungathered corn, you will not gather from the untrimmed vine. The jubilee is to be a holy thing to you, you will eat what comes from the fields.

'In this year of jubilee each of you is to return to his ancestral home. If you buy or sell with your neighbour, let no one wrong his brother. If you buy from your neighbour, this must take into account the number of years since the jubilee: according to the number of productive years he will fix the price. The greater the number of years, the higher shall be the price demanded; the less the number of years, the greater the reduction; for what he is selling you is a certain number of harvests. Let none of you wrong his neighbour, but fear your God; I am the Lord your God.'

This is the word of the Lord.

Responsorial Psalm   Ps 66:2-3. 5. 7-8. ℟ v.4

  ℟ **Let the peoples praise you, O God;**
     let all the peoples praise you.

1. O God, be gracious and bless us
and let your face shed its light upon us.
So will your ways be known upon earth
and all nations learn your saving help. ℟

2. Let the nations be glad and exult
for you rule the world with justice.
With fairness you rule the peoples,
you guide the nations on earth. ℟

3. The earth has yielded its fruit
for God, our God, has blessed us.
May God still give us his blessing
till the ends of the earth revere him. ℟

Gospel Acclamation   cf. Lk 8:15

Alleluia, alleluia!
Blessed are those who,
with a noble and generous heart,
take the word of God to themselves
and yield a harvest through their perseverance.
Alleluia!

or   Mt 5:10

Alleluia, alleluia!
Happy those who are persecuted
in the cause of right,
for theirs is the kingdom of heaven.
Alleluia!

GOSPEL

A reading from the holy Gospel according to Matthew   14:1-12
Herod sent and had John beheaded. John's disciples went off to tell Jesus.

Herod the tetrarch heard about the reputation of Jesus, and said to his court, 'This is John the Baptist himelf; he has risen from the dead, and that is why miraculous powers are at work in him.'
    Now it was Herod who had arrested John, chained him up and put him in prison because of Herodias, his brother Philip's

Eighteenth Week in Ordinary Time, Year I: Monday

wife. For John had told him, 'It is against the Law for you to have her.' He had wanted to kill him but was afraid of the people, who regarded John as a prophet. Then, during the celebrations for Herod's birthday, the daughter of Herodias danced before the company, and so delighted Herod that he promised on oath to give her anything she asked. Prompted by her mother she said, 'Give me John the Baptist's head, here, on a dish.' The king was distressed but, thinking of the oaths he had sworn and of his guests, he ordered it to be given her, and sent and had John beheaded in the prison. The head was brought in on a dish and given to the girl who took it to her mother. John's disciples came and took the body and buried it; then they went off to tell Jesus.

This is the Gospel of the Lord.

EIGHTEENTH WEEK IN ORDINARY TIME
Year I

MONDAY

FIRST READING

A reading from the book of Numbers   11:4-15
I am not able to carry this nation by myself alone.

The sons of Israel began to wail, 'Who will give us meat to eat?' they said. 'Think of the fish we used to eat free in Egypt, the cucumbers, melons, leeks, onions and garlic! Here we are wasting away, stripped of everything; there is nothing but manna for us to look at!'

The manna was like coriander seed, and had the appearance of bdellium. The people went round gathering it, and ground it in a mill or crushed it with a pestle; it was then cooked in a pot and made into pancakes. It tasted like cake made with oil. When the dew fell on the camp at night-time, the manna fell with it.

Moses heard the people wailing, every family at the door of its tent. The anger of the Lord flared out, and Moses greatly worried over this. And he spoke to the Lord:

'Why do you treat your servant so badly? Why have I not found favour with you, so that you load on me the weight of all this nation? Was it I who conceived all this people, was it I who gave them birth, that you should say to me, "Carry them in your bosom, like a nurse with a baby at the breast, to the land that I swore to give their fathers?" Where am I to find meat to give to all this people, when they come worrying me so tearfully and say, "Give us meat to eat"? I am not able to carry this nation by myself alone; the weight is too much for me. If this is how you want to deal with me, I would rather you killed me! If only I had found favour in your eyes, and not lived to see such misery as this!'

This is the word of the Lord.

Responsorial Psalm   Ps 80:12-17. ℟ v.2

℟ **Ring out your joy to God our strength.**

1 My people did not heed my voice
  and Israel would not obey,
  so I left them in their stubbornness of heart
  to follow their own designs. ℟

2 O that my people would heed me,
  that Israel would walk in my ways!
  At once I would subdue their foes,
  turn my hand against their enemies. ℟

3 The Lord's enemies would cringe at their feet
  and their subjection would last for ever.
  But Israel I would feed with finest wheat
  and fill them with honey from the rock. ℟

Gospel Acclamation   Jn 14:6

Alleluia, alleluia!
I am the Way, the Truth and the Life, says the Lord;
no one can come to the Father except through me.
Alleluia!

or   Mt 4:4

Alleluia, alleluia!
Man does not live on bread alone,
but on every word that comes from the mouth of God.
Alleluia!

Eighteenth Week in Ordinary Time, Year I: Monday

GOSPEL

A reading from the holy Gospel according to Matthew 14:13-21

Jesus raised his eyes to heaven and said the blessing. He handed the loaves to his disciples who gave them to the crowds.

When Jesus received the news of John the Baptist's death he withdrew by boat to a lonely place where they could be by themselves. But the people heard of this and, leaving the towns, went after him on foot. So as he stepped ashore he saw a large crowd; and he took pity on them and healed their sick.

When evening came, the disciples went to him and said, 'This is a lonely place, and the time has slipped by; so send the people away, and they can go to the villages to buy themselves some food.' Jesus replied, 'There is no need for them to go: give them something to eat yourselves.' But they answered, 'All we have with us is five loaves and two fish.' 'Bring them here to me,' he said. He gave orders that the people were to sit down on the grass; then he took the five loaves and the two fish, raised his eyes to heaven and said the blessing. And breaking the loaves he handed them to his disciples who gave them to the crowds. They all ate as much as they wanted, and they collected the scraps remaining, twelve baskets full. Those who ate numbered about five thousand men, to say nothing of women and children.

This is the Gospel of the Lord.

Alternative Gospel

This is to be used in Year A, when the Gospel given above is read on the preceding Sunday.

A reading from the holy Gospel according to Matthew 14:22-36

Tell me to come to you across the water.

When Jesus heard of the death of John the Baptist, he made the disciples get into the boat, and go on ahead to the other side while he would send the crowds away. After sending the crowds away he went up into the hills by himself to pray. When evening came, he was there alone, while the boat, by now far out on the lake, was battling with a heavy sea, for there was a head-wind. In the fourth watch of the night he went towards them, walking on the lake, and when the disciples saw him on the lake they were terrified. 'It is a ghost' they said, and cried out in fear. But at once Jesus called out to them, saying, 'Courage! It is I! Do not be afraid.' It was Peter who answered. 'Lord', he said 'if it is you, tell me to come to you across the water.' 'Come' said Jesus. Then Peter got out of the boat and started walking towards Jesus across the water, but as soon as he felt the force of the wind, he took fright and began to sink. 'Lord! Save me!' he cried. Jesus put out his hand at once and held him. 'Man of little faith,' he said 'why did you doubt?' And as they got into the boat the wind dropped. The men in the boat bowed down before him and said, 'Truly, you are the Son of God.'

Having made the crossing, they came to land at Gennesaret. When the local people recognised him they spread the news through the whole neighbourhood and took all that were sick to him, begging him just to let them touch the fringe of his cloak. And all those who touched it were completely cured.

This is the Gospel of the Lord.

TUESDAY

FIRST READING

A reading from the book of Numbers   12:1-13

There has never been such a prophet as Moses; how have you dared to speak against him?

Miriam, and Aaron too, spoke against Moses in connexion with the Cushite woman he had taken. (For he had married a Cushite woman.) They said, 'Has the Lord spoken to Moses only? Has he not spoken to us too?' The Lord heard this. Now Moses was the most humble of men, the humblest man on earth.

Suddenly, the Lord said to Moses and Aaron and Miriam, 'Come, all three of you, to the Tent of Meeting.' They went, all three of them, and the Lord came down in a pillar of cloud and stood at the entrance of the Tent. He called Aaron and Miriam and they both came forward. The Lord said, 'Listen now to my words:

If any man among you is a prophet
I make myself known to him in a vision,
I speak to him in a dream.
Not so with my servant Moses:
he is at home in my house;
I speak with him face to face,

Eighteenth Week in Ordinary Time, Year I: Tuesday 655

plainly and not in riddles,
and he sees the form of the Lord.

How then have you dared to speak against my servant Moses?'

The anger of the Lord blazed out against them. He departed, and as soon as the cloud withdrew from the Tent, there was Miriam a leper, white as snow! Aaron turned to look at her; she had become a leper.

Aaron said to Moses:

'Help me, my lord! Do not punish us for a sin committed in folly of which we are guilty. I entreat you, do not let her be like a monster, coming from its mother's womb with flesh half corrupted.'

Moses cried to the Lord, 'O God,' he said 'please heal her, I beg you!'

This is the word of the Lord.

Responsorial Psalm   Ps 50:3-7. 12-13. ℟ cf. v.3

℟ **Have mercy on us, Lord, for we have sinned.**

1 Have mercy on me, God, in your kindness.
 In your compassion blot out my offence.
 O wash me more and more from my guilt
 and cleanse me from my sin.   ℟

2 My offences truly I know them;
 my sin is always before me.
 Against you, you alone, have I sinned;
 what is evil in your sight I have done.   ℟

3 That you may be justified when you give sentence
 and be without reproach when you judge,
 O see, in guilt I was born,
 a sinner was I conceived.   ℟

4 A pure heart create for me, O God,
 put a steadfast spirit within me.
 Do not cast me away from your presence,
 nor deprive me of your holy spirit.   ℟

Gospel Acclamation   Jn 8:12
Alleluia, alleluia!
I am the light of the world, says the Lord,
anyone who follows me
will have the light of life.
Alleluia!

or Jn 1:49

Alleluia, alleluia!
Rabbi, you are the Son of God,
you are the King of Israel.
Alleluia!

GOSPEL

A reading from the holy Gospel according to Matthew 14:22-36
Tell me to come to you across the water.

Jesus made the disciples get into the boat and go on ahead to the other side while he would send the crowds away. After sending the crowds away he went up into the hills by himself to pray. When evening came, he was there alone, while the boat, by now far out on the lake, was battling with a heavy sea, for there was a head-wind. In the fourth watch of the night he went towards them, walking on the lake, and when the disciples saw him walking on the lake they were terrified. 'It is a ghost' they said, and cried out in fear. But at once Jesus called out to them, saying, 'Courage! It is I! Do not be afraid.' It was Peter who answered. 'Lord,' he said 'if it is you, tell me to come to you across the water.' 'Come' said Jesus. Then Peter got out of the boat and started walking towards Jesus across the water, but as soon as he felt the force of the wind he took fright and began to sink. 'Lord! Save me!' he cried. Jesus put out his hand at once and held him. 'Man of little faith,' he said 'why did you doubt?' And as they got into the boat the wind dropped. The men in the boat bowed down before him and said, 'Truly, you are the Son of God.'

Having made the crossing, they came to land at Gennesaret. When the local people recognised him they spread the news through the whole neighbourhood and took all that were sick to him, begging him just to let them touch the fringe of his cloak. And all those who touched it were completely cured.

This is the Gospel of the Lord.

Alternative Gospel

This is to be used in Year A, when the Gospel given above is read on the preceding Monday.

A reading from the holy Gospel according to Matthew
15:1-2. 10-14
Any plant my Father has not planted will be pulled up by the roots.

Pharisees and scribes from Jerusalem came to Jesus and said, 'Why do your disciples break away from the tradition of the elders? They do not wash their hands when they eat food.'

He called the people to him and said, 'Listen, and understand. What goes into the mouth does not make a man unclean; it is what comes out of the mouth that makes him unclean.'

Then the disciples came to him and said, 'Do you know that the Pharisees were shocked when they heard what you said?' He replied, 'Any plant my heavenly Father has not planted will be pulled up by the roots. Leave them alone. They are blind men leading blind men; and if one blind man leads another, both will fall into a pit.'

This is the Gospel of the Lord.

WEDNESDAY

FIRST READING

A reading from the book of Numbers   13:1-2. 25–14:1. 26-29. 34-35
They refused a land of delight.

The Lord spoke to Moses in the wilderness of Paran and said, 'Send out men, one from each tribe, to make a reconnaissance of this land of Canaan which I am giving to the sons of Israel. Send the leader of each tribe.' At the end of forty days, they came back from their reconnaissance of the land. They sought out Moses, Aaron and the whole community of Israel, in the wilderness of Paran, at Kadesh. They made their report to them, and to the whole community, and showed them the produce of the country.

They told them this story, 'We went into the land to which you sent us. It does indeed flow with milk and honey; this is its produce. At the same time, its inhabitants are a powerful people; the towns are fortified and very big; yes, and we saw the descendants of Anak there. The Amalekite holds the Negeb area, the Hittite, Amorite and Jebusite the highlands, and the Canaanite the sea coast and the banks of the Jordan.'

Caleb harangued the people gathered about Moses: 'We must march in,' he said 'and conquer this land: we are well able to do it.' But the men who had gone up with him answered, 'We are not able to march against this people; they are stronger than we are.' And they began to disparage the country they had reconnoitred to the sons of Israel, 'The country we went to reconnoitre is a country that devours its inhabitants. Every man we saw there was of enormous size. Yes, and we saw giants there (the sons of Anak, descendants of the Giants). We felt like grasshoppers, and so we seemed to them.'

At this, the whole community raised their voices and cried aloud, and the people wailed all that night. The Lord spoke to Moses and Aaron. He said:

'How long does this perverse community complain against me? I have heard the complaints which the sons of Israel make against me. Say to them, "As I live – it is the Lord who speaks – I will deal with you according to the very words you have used in my hearing. In this wilderness your dead bodies will fall, all you men of the census, all you who were numbered from the age of twenty years and over, you who have complained against me. For forty days you reconnoitred the land. Each day shall count for a year: for forty years you shall bear the burden of your sins, and you shall learn what it means to reject me." I, the Lord, have spoken: this is how I will deal with this perverse community that has conspired against me. Here in this wilderness, to the last man, they shall die.'

This is the word of the Lord.

Responsorial Psalm   Ps 105:6-7. 13-14. 21-23. ℟ v.4

  ℟ **O Lord, remember me
out of the love you have for your people.**

or

  ℟ **Alleluia!**

1 Our sin is the sin of our fathers;
we have done wrong, our deeds have been evil.
Our fathers when they were in Egypt
paid no heed to your wonderful deeds. ℟

Eighteenth Week in Ordinary Time, Year I: Wednesday 659

2 But they soon forgot his deeds
 and would not wait upon his will.
 They yielded to their cravings in the desert
 and put God to the test in the wilderness. ℟

3 They forgot the God who was their saviour,
 who had done such great things in Egypt,
 such portents in the land of Ham,
 such marvels at the Red Sea. ℟

4 For this he said he would destroy them,
 but Moses, the man he had chosen,
 stood in the breach before him,
 to turn back his anger from destruction. ℟

Gospel Acclamation James 1:18
 Alleluia, alleluia!
 By his own choice the Father made us his children
 by the message of the truth,
 so that we should be a sort of first-fruits
 of all that he created.
 Alleluia!

or Lk 7:16

 Alleluia, alleluia!
 A great prophet has appeared among us;
 God has visited his people.
 Alleluia!

GOSPEL

A reading from the holy Gospel according to Matthew 15:21-28
Woman, you have great faith.

Jesus left Gennesaret and withdrew to the region of Tyre and Sidon. Then out came a Canaanite woman from that district and started shouting, 'Sir, Son of David, take pity on me. My daughter is tormented by a devil.' But he answered her not a word. And his disciples went and pleaded with him. 'Give her what she wants,' they said 'because she is shouting after us.' He said in reply, 'I was sent only to the lost sheep of the House of Israel.' But the woman had come up and was kneeling at his feet. 'Lord,' she said 'help me.' He replied, 'It is not fair to take the children's food and throw it to the house-dogs.' She retorted, 'Ah yes, sir, but even house-dogs can eat the scraps that fall from their master's table.' Then Jesus answered her, 'Woman, you have great faith. Let your wish be granted.' And from that moment her daughter was well again.

This is the Gospel of the Lord.

THURSDAY

FIRST READING

A reading from the book of Numbers 20:1-13
Make water flow for the community out of the rock.

The sons of Israel, the whole community, arrived in the first month at the desert of Zin. The people settled at Kadesh. It was there that Miriam died and was buried.

There was no water for the community, and they were all united against Moses and Aaron. The people challenged Moses: 'We would rather have died,' they said 'as our brothers died before the Lord! Why did you bring the assembly of the Lord into this wilderness, only to let us die here, ourselves and our cattle? Why did you lead us out of Egypt, only to bring us to this wretched place? It is a place unfit for sowing, it has no figs, no vines, no pomegranates, and there is not even water to drink!'

Leaving the assembly, Moses and Aaron went to the door of the Tent of Meeting. They threw themselves face downward on the ground, and the glory of the Lord appeared to them. The Lord spoke to Moses and said, 'Take the branch and call the community together, you and your brother Aaron. Then, in full view of them, order this rock to give water. You will make water flow for them out of the rock, and provide drink for the community and their cattle.'

Moses took up the branch from before the Lord, as he had directed him. Then Moses and Aaron called the assembly together in front of the rock and addressed them, 'Listen now, you rebels. Shall we make water gush from this rock for you?' And Moses raised his hand and struck the rock twice with the branch; water gushed in abundance, and the community drank and their cattle too.

Then the Lord said to Moses and Aaron, 'Because you did not believe that I could proclaim my holiness in the eyes of the sons of Israel, you shall not lead this assembly into the land I am

giving them.'
These are the waters of Meribah, where the sons of Israel challenged the Lord and he proclaimed his holiness.

This is the word of the Lord.

Responsorial Psalm   Ps 94:1-2. 6-9. ℟ v.8
℟ **O that today you would listen to his voice!
Harden not your hearts.**

1 Come, ring out our joy to the Lord:
hail the rock who saves us.
Let us come before him, giving thanks,
with songs let us hail the Lord. ℟

2 Come in; let us bow and bend low;
let us kneel before the God who made us
for he is our God and we
the people who belong to his pasture,
the flock that is led by his hand. ℟

3 O that today you would listen to his voice!
'Harden not your hearts as at Meribah,
as on that day at Massah in the desert
when your fathers put me to the test;
when they tried me, though they saw my work.' ℟

Gospel Acclamation   Ps 144:13
Alleluia, alleluia!
The Lord is faithful in all his words
and loving in all his deeds.
Alleluia!

or   Mt 16:18

Alleluia, alleluia!
You are Peter and on this rock I will build my Church.
And the gates of the underworld can never hold out against it.
Alleluia!

GOSPEL

A reading from the holy Gospel according to Matthew   16:13-23
You are Peter, and I will give you the keys of the kingdom of heaven.

When Jesus came to the region of Casesarea Philippi he put this question to his disciples, 'Who do people say the Son of Man is?'

And they said, 'Some say he is John the Baptist, some Elijah, and others Jeremiah or one of the prophets.' 'But you,' he said, 'who do you say I am?' Then Simon Peter spoke up, 'You are the Christ,' he said 'the Son of the living God.' Jesus replied, 'Simon son of Jonah, you are a happy man! Because it was not flesh and blood that revealed this to you but my Father in heaven. So I now say to you: You are Peter and on this rock I will build my Church. And the gates of the underworld can never hold out against it. I will give you the keys of the kingdom of heaven; whatever you bind on earth shall be considered bound in heaven; whatever you loose on earth shall be considered loosed in heaven.' Then he gave the disciples strict orders not to tell anyone that he was the Christ.

From that time Jesus began to make it clear to his disciples that he was destined to go to Jerusalem and suffer grievously at the hands of the elders and chief priests and scribes, to be put to death and to be raised up on the third day. Then, taking him aside, Peter started to remonstrate with him. 'Heaven preserve you, Lord,' he said 'this must not happen to you.' But he turned and said to Peter, 'Get behind me, Satan! You are an obstacle in my path, because the way you think is not God's way but man's.'

This is the Gospel of the Lord.

FRIDAY

FIRST READING

A reading from the book of Deuteronomy 4:32-40
God loved your fathers and chose their descendants after them.

Moses said to the people: 'Put this question to the ages that are past, that went before you, from the time God created man on earth: Was there ever a word so majestic, from one end of heaven to the other? Was anything ever heard? Did ever a people hear the voice of the living God speaking from the heart of the fire, as you heard it, and remain alive? Has any god ventured to take to himself one nation from the midst of another by ordeals, signs, wonders, war with mighty hand and outstretched arm, by fearsome terrors – all this that the Lord your God did for you before your eyes in Egypt?

'This he showed you so that you might know that the Lord is God indeed and that there is no other. He let you hear his voice out of heaven for your instruction; on earth he let you see his

Eighteenth Week in Ordinary Time, Year I: Friday

great fire, and from the heart of the fire you heard his word. Because he loved your fathers and chose their descendants after them, he brought you out from Egypt, openly showing his presence and his great power, driving out in front of you nations greater and more powerful than yourself, and brought you into their land to give it you for your heritage, as it is still today.

'Understand this today, therefore, and take it to heart: the Lord is God indeed, in heaven above as on earth beneath, he and no other. Keep his laws and commandments as I give them to you today, so that you and your children may prosper and live long in the land that the Lord your God gives you for ever.'

This is the word of the Lord.

Responsional Psalm   Ps 76:12-16. 21. ℟ v.12

℟ **I remember the deeds of the Lord.**

1 I remember the deeds of the Lord,
   I remember your wonders of old,
   I muse on all your works
   and ponder your mighty deeds.   ℟

2 Your ways, O God, are holy.
   What god is great as our God?
   You are the God who works wonders
   You showed your power among the peoples.   ℟

3 Your strong arm redeemed your people,
   the sons of Jacob and Joseph.
   You guided your people like a flock
   by the hand of Moses and Aaron.   ℟

Gospel Acclamation   1 Sam 3:9; Jn 6:68

Alleluia, alleluia!
Speak, Lord, your servant is listening:
you have the message of eternal life.
Alleluia!

or   Mt 5:10

Alleluia, alleluia!
Happy those who are persecuted
in the cause of right,
for theirs is the kingdom of heaven.
Alleluia!

GOSPEL

A reading from the holy Gospel according to Matthew   16:24-28
What has a man to offer in exchange for his life?

Jesus said to his disciples, 'If anyone wants to be a follower of mine, let him renounce himself and take up his cross and follow me. For anyone who wants to save his life will lose it; but anyone who loses his life for my sake will find it. What, then, will a man gain if he wins the whole world and ruins his life? Or what has a man to offer in exchange for his life?

'For the Son of Man is going to come in the glory of his Father with his angels, and, when he does, he will reward each one according to his behaviour. I tell you solemnly, there are some of these standing here who will not taste death before they see the Son of Man coming with his kingdom.'

This is the Gospel of the Lord.

SATURDAY

FIRST READING

A reading from the book of Deuteronomy   6:4-13
You shall love the Lord your God with all your heart.

Moses said to the people: 'Listen, Israel: the Lord our God is the one Lord. You shall love the Lord your God with all your heart, with all your soul, with all your strength. Let these words I urge on you today be written on you heart. You shall repeat them to your children and say them over to them whether at rest in your house or walking abroad, at your lying down or at your rising; you shall fasten them on your hands as a sign and on your forehead as a circlet; you shall write them on the doorposts of your house and on your gates.

'When the Lord has brought you into the land which he swore to your fathers Abraham, Isaac and Jacob that he would give you, with great and prosperous cities not of your building, houses full of good things not furnished by you, wells you did not dig, vineyards and olives you did not plant, when you have eaten these and had your fill, then take care you do not forget the Lord who brought you out of the land of Egypt, out of the house of slavery. You must fear the Lord your God, you must serve him, by his name you must swear.'

This is the word of the Lord.

Eighteenth Week in Ordinary Time, Year I: Saturday

Responsorial Psalm Ps 17:2-4. 47. 51. ℟ v.2

℟ **I love you, Lord, my strength.**

1 I love you, Lord, my strength,
my rock, my fortress, my saviour. ℟

2 My God is the rock where I take refuge;
my shield, my mighty help, my stronghold.
The Lord is worthy of all praise:
when I call I am saved from my foes. ℟

3 Long life to the Lord, my rock!
Praised be the God who saves me.
He has given great victories to his king
and shown his love for his anointed. ℟

Gospel Acclamation cf. Eph 1:17, 18

Alleluia, alleluia!
May the Father of our Lord Jesus Christ
enlighten the eyes of our mind,
so that we can see what hope his call holds for us.
Alleluia!

or cf. 2 Tim 1:10

Alleluia, alleluia!
Our Saviour Christ Jesus abolished death,
and he has proclaimed life through the Good News.
Alleluia!

GOSPEL

A reading from the holy Gospel according to Matthew 17:14-20
If you had faith, nothing would be impossible for you.

A man came up to Jesus and went down on his knees before him. 'Lord,' he said 'take pity on my son: he is a lunatic and in a wretched state; he is always falling into the fire or into the water. I took him to your disciples and they were unable to cure him.' 'Faithless and perverse generation!' Jesus said in reply 'How much longer must I be with you? How much longer must I put up with you? Bring him here to me.' And when Jesus rebuked it the devil came out of the boy who was cured from that moment.

Then the disciples came privately to Jesus. 'Why were we unable to cast it out?' they asked. He answered, 'Because you have little faith. I tell you solemnly, if your faith were the size of a mustard seed you could say to this mountain, "Move from here to there", and it would move; nothing would be impossible for you.'

This is the Gospel of the Lord.

NINETEENTH WEEK IN ORDINARY TIME
Year I

MONDAY

FIRST READING

A reading from the book of Deuteronomy 10:12-22
Circumcise your heart. Love the stranger, for you were strangers.

Moses said to the people: 'What does the Lord your God ask of you? Only this: to fear the Lord our God, to follow all his ways, to love him, to serve the Lord your God with all your heart and all your soul, to keep the commandments and laws of the Lord that for your good I lay down for you today.

'To the Lord your God belong indeed heaven and the heaven of heavens, and the earth and all it contains; yet it was on your fathers that the Lord set his heart for love of them, and after them of all the nations chose their descendants, you yourselves up to the present day. Circumcise your heart then and be obstinate no longer; for the Lord your God is God of gods and Lord of lords, the great God, triumphant and terrible, never partial, never to be bribed. It is he who sees justice done for the orphan and the widow, who loves the stranger and gives him food and clothing. Love the stranger then, for you were strangers in the land of Egypt. It is the Lord your God you must fear and serve; you must cling to him; in his name take your oaths. He it is you must praise, he is your God: for you he has done these great and terrible things you have seen with your own eyes; and though your fathers numbered only seventy when they went down to Egypt, the Lord your God has made you as many as the stars of heaven.'

This is the word of the Lord.

Responsorial Psalm   Ps 147:12-15. 19-20. ℟ v.12

   ℟ **O praise the Lord, Jerusalem!**

or

   ℟ **Alleluia!**

1. O praise the Lord, Jerusalem!
   Zion, praise your God!
   He has strengthened the bars of your gates,
   he has blessed the children within you. ℟

2. He established peace on your borders,
   he feeds you with finest wheat.
   He sends out his word to the earth
   and swiftly runs his command. ℟

3. He makes his word known to Jacob,
   to Israel his laws and decrees.
   He has not dealt thus with other nations;
   he has not taught them his decrees. ℟

Gospel Acclamation   Ps 147:12. 15
Alleluia, alleluia!
O praise the Lord, Jerusalem!
He sends out his word to the earth.
Alleluia!

or   cf. 2 Thess 2:14

Alleluia, alleluia!
Through the Good News God called us
to share the glory of our Lord Jesus Christ.
Alleluia!

GOSPEL

A reading from the holy Gospel according to Matthew   17:22-27

They will put the Son of Man to death, and he will be raised to life again. The sons are exempt from tribute.

One day when they were together in Galilee, Jesus said to his disciples 'The Son of Man is going to be handed over into the power of men; they will put him to death, and on the third day he will be raised to life again.' And a great sadness came over them.

When they reached Capernaum, the collectors of the half-shekel came to Peter and said, 'Does your master not pay the half-shekel?' 'Oh yes' he replied, and went into the house. But before he could speak, Jesus said, 'Simon, what is your opinion? From whom do the kings of the earth take toll or tribute? From their sons or from foreigners?' And when he replied, 'From foreigners,' Jesus said, 'Well then, the sons are exempt. However, so as not to offend these people, go to the lake and cast a hook; take the first fish that bites, open its mouth and there you will find a shekel; take it and give it to them for me and for you.'

This is the Gospel of the Lord.

TUESDAY

FIRST READING

A reading from the book of Deuteronomy 31:1-8

Be strong, Joshua, stand firm; you are going with this people into the land.

Moses proceeded to address these words to the whole of Israel, 'I am one hundred and twenty years old now, and can no longer come and go as I will. The Lord has said to me, "You shall not cross this Jordan." It is the Lord your God who will cross it at your head to destroy these nations facing you and dispossess them; and Joshua too shall cross at your head, as the Lord has said. The Lord will treat them as he treated Sihon and Og the Amorite kings and their land, destroying them. The Lord will hand them over to you, and you will deal with them in exact accordance with the commandments I have enjoined on you. Be strong, stand firm, have no fear of them, no terror, for the Lord your God is going with you; he will not fail you or desert you.'

Then Moses summoned Joshua and in the presence of all Israel said to him, 'Be strong, stand firm; you are going with this people into the land the Lord swore to their fathers he would give them; you are to give it into their possession. The Lord himself will lead you; he will be with you; he will not fail you or desert you. Have no fear, do not be disheartened by anything.'

This is the word of the Lord.

Responsorial Psalm Deut 32:3-4. 7-9. ℟ v.9

℟ **The Lord's portion was his people.**

1 I proclaim the name of the Lord.
  Oh, tell the greatness of our God!

> He is the Rock, his work is perfect,
> for all his ways are Equity. ℟

2. Think back on the days of old,
   think over the years, down the ages.
   Ask of your father, let him teach you;
   of your elders, let them enlighten you. ℟

3. When the Most High gave the nations their inheritance,
   when he divided the sons of men,
   he fixed their bounds according to the number of the sons of God;
   but the Lord's portion was his people,
   Jacob his share of inheritance. ℟

4. The Lord alone is his guide,
   with him is no alien god. ℟

Gospel Acclamation cf. Mt 11:25

> Alleluia, alleluia!
> Blessed are you, Father,
> Lord of heaven and earth,
> for revealing the mysteries of the kingdom
> to mere children.
> Alleluia!

or Mt 11:29

> Alleluia, alleluia!
> Shoulder my yoke and learn from me, says the Lord,
> for I am gentle and humble in heart.
> Alleluia!

GOSPEL

A reading from the holy Gospel according to Matthew 18:1-5. 10. 12-14

See that you never despise any of these little ones.

The disciples came to Jesus and said, 'Who is the greatest in the kingdom of heaven?' So he called a little child to him and set the child in front of them. Then he said, 'I tell you solemnly, unless you change and become like little children you will never enter the kingdom of heaven. And so, the one who makes himself as little as this little child is the greatest in the kingdom of heaven.

  'Anyone who welcomes a little child like this in my name

welcomes me.

'See that you never despise any of these little ones, for I tell you that their angels in heaven are continually in the presence of my Father in heaven.

'Tell me. Suppose a man has a hundred sheep and one of them strays; will he not leave the ninety-nine on the hillside and go in search of the stray? I tell you solemnly, if he finds it, it gives him more joy than do the ninety-nine that did not stray at all. Similarly, it is never the will of your Father in heaven that one of these little ones should be lost.'

This is the Gospel of the Lord.

WEDNESDAY

FIRST READING

A reading from the book of Deuteronomy 34:1-12

Moses died as the Lord decreed, and there has never been such a prophet as him.

Leaving the plains of Moab, Moses went up Mount Nebo, the peak of Pisgah opposite Jericho, and the Lord showed him the whole land; Gilead as far as Dan, all Naphtali, the land of Ephraim and Manasseh, all the land of Judah as far as the Western Sea, the Negeb, and the stretch of the Valley of Jericho, city of palm trees, as far as Zoar. The Lord said to him, 'This is the land I swore to give to Abraham, Isaac and Jacob, saying: I will give it to your descendants. I have let you see it with your own eyes, but you shall not cross into it.' There in the land of Moab, Moses the servant of the Lord died as the Lord decreed; he buried him in the valley, in the land of Moab, opposite Beth-peor; but to this day no one has ever found his grave. Moses was a hundred and twenty years old when he died, his eye undimmed, his vigour unimpaired. The sons of Israel wept for Moses in the plains of Moab for thirty days. The days of weeping for the mourning rites of Moses came to an end. Joshua son of Nun was filled with the spirit of wisdom, for Moses had laid his hands on him. It was he that the sons of Israel obeyed, carrying out the order that the Lord had given to Moses.

Since then, never has there been such a prophet in Israel as Moses, the man the Lord knew face to face. What signs and wonders the Lord caused him to perform in the land of Egypt against Pharaoh and all his servants and his whole land! How

Nineteenth Week in Ordinary Time, Year I: Wednesday

mighty the hand and great the fear that Moses wielded in the sight of all Israel!

This is the word of the Lord.

Responsorial Psalm   Ps 65:1-3. 5. 16-17. ℟ cf. vv.20. 9

℟ **Blessed be God who gave life to my soul.**

1. Cry out with joy to God all the earth,
   O sing to the glory of his name.
   O render him glorious praise.
   Say to God: 'How tremendous your deeds!' ℟

2. Come and see the works of God,
   tremendous his deeds among men.
   Come and hear, all who fear God.
   I will tell what he did for my soul:
   to him I cried aloud,
   with high praise ready on my tongue. ℟

Gospel Acclamation   Ps 110:7. 8

Alleluia, alleluia!
Your precepts, O Lord, are all of them sure;
they stand firm for ever and ever.
Alleluia!

or   2 Cor 5:19

Alleluia, alleluia!
God in Christ was reconciling the word to himself,
and he has entrusted to us the news that they are reconciled.
Alleluia!

GOSPEL

A reading from the holy Gospel according to Matthew   18:15-20

If he listens to you, you have won back your brother.

Jesus said to his disciples: 'If your brother does something wrong, go and have it out with him alone, between your two selves. If he listens to you, you have won back your brother. If he does not listen, take one or two others along with you: the evidence of two or three witnesses is required to sustain any charge. But if he refuses to listen to these, report it to the community; and if he refuses to listen to the community, treat him like a pagan or a tax collector.

'I tell you solemnly, whatever you bind on earth shall be considered bound in heaven; whatever you loose on earth shall be considered loosed in heaven.

'I tell you solemnly once again, if two of you on earth agree to ask anything at all, it will be granted to you by my Father in heaven. For where two or three meet in my name, I shall be there with them.'

This is the Gospel of the Lord.

THURSDAY

FIRST READING

A reading from the book of Joshua 3:7-11. 13-17
The ark of the Lord is about to cross the Jordan at your head.

The Lord said to Joshua, 'This very day I will begin to make you a great man in the eyes of all Israel, to let them be sure that I am going to be with you even as I was with Moses. As for you, give this order to the priests carrying the ark of the covenant: "When you have reached the brink of the waters of the Jordan, you are to stand still in the Jordan itself." ' Then Joshua said to the Israelites, 'Come closer and hear the words of the Lord your God.' Joshua said, 'By this you shall know that a living God is with you and without a doubt will expel the Canaanite. Look, the ark of the Lord, the Lord of the whole earth, is about to cross the Jordan at your head. As soon as the priests with the ark of the Lord, the Lord of the whole earth, have set their feet in the waters of the Jordan, the upper waters of the Jordan flowing down will be stopped in their course and stand still in one mass.'

Accordingly, when the people struck camp to cross the Jordan, the priests carried the ark of the covenant in front of the people. As soon as the bearers of the ark reached the Jordan and the feet of the priests who carried it touched the waters (the Jordan overflows the whole length of its banks throughout the harvest season) the upper waters stood still and made one heap over a wide space – from Adam to the fortress of Zarethan – while those flowing down to the Sea of the Arabah, that is, the Salt Sea, stopped running altogether. The people crossed opposite Jericho. The priests who carried the ark of the covenant of the Lord stood still on dry ground in mid-Jordan, and all Israel continued to cross dry-shod till the whole nation had finished its crossing of the river.

This is the word of the Lord.

Responsorial Psalm
Ps 113A:1-6

℞ **Alleluia!**

1 When Israel came forth from Egypt,
   Jacob's sons from an alien people,
   Judah became the Lord's temple,
   Israel became his kingdom. ℞

2 The sea fled at the sight:
   the Jordan turned back on its course,
   the mountains leapt like rams
   and the hills like yearling sheep? ℞

3 Why was it, sea, that you fled,
   that you turned back, Jordan, on your course?
   Mountains, that you leapt like rams,
   hills, like yearling sheep? ℞

Gospel Acclamation
Ps 118:88

Alleluia, alleluia!
Because of your love give me life,
and I will do your will.
Alleluia!

or
Ps 118:135

Alleluia, alleluia!
Let your face shine on your servant,
and teach me your decrees.
Alleluia!

GOSPEL

A reading from the holy Gospel according to Matthew 18:21–19:1
Do not forgive seven times, I tell you, but seventy-seven times.

Peter went up to Jesus and said, 'Lord, how often must I forgive my brother if he wrongs me? As often as seven times?' Jesus answered, 'Not seven, I tell you, but seventy-seven times.

'And so the kingdom of heaven may be compared to a king who decided to settle his accounts with his servants. When the reckoning began, they brought him a man who owed ten thousand talents; but he had no means of paying, so his master gave orders that he should be sold, together with his wife and children and all his possessions, to meet the debt. At this, the servant threw himself down at his master's feet. "Give me time" he said "and I will pay the whole sum." And the servant's master felt so sorry for him that he let him go and cancelled the debt. Now as this servant went out, he happened to meet a fellow servant who owed him one hundred denarii; and he seized him by the throat and began to throttle him. "Pay what you owe me" he said. His fellow servant fell at his feet and implored him, saying, "Give me time and I will pay you." But the other would not agree; on the contrary, he had him thrown into prison till he should pay the debt. His fellow servants were deeply distressed when they saw what had happened, and they went to their master and reported the whole affair to him. Then the master sent for him. "You wicked servant," he said, "I cancelled all that debt of yours when you appealed to me. Were you not bound, then, to have pity on your fellow servant just as I had pity on you?" And in his anger the master handed him over to the torturers till he should pay all his debt. And that is how my heavenly Father will deal with you unless you each forgive your brother from your heart.'

Jesus had now finished what he wanted to say, and he left Galilee and came into the part of the Judaea which is on the far side of the Jordan.

This is the Gospel of the Lord.

FRIDAY

FIRST READING

A reading from the book of Joshua 24:1-13

I brought your father from beyond the River – I brought you out of Egypt – I brought you into the land.

Joshua gathered all the tribes of Israel together at Shechem; then he called the elders, leaders, judges and scribes of Israel, and they presented themselves before God. Then Joshua said to all the people:

'The Lord the God of Israel says this, "In ancient days your ancestors lived beyond the River – such was Terah the father of

Nineteenth Week in Ordinary Time, Year I: Friday 675

Abraham and of Nahor – and they served other gods. Then I brought your father Abraham from beyond the River and led him through all the land of Canaan. I increased his descendants and gave him Isaac. To Isaac I gave Jacob and Esau. To Esau I gave the mountain country of Seir as his possession. Jacob and his sons went down into Egypt. Then I sent Moses and Aaron and plagued Egypt with the wonders that I worked there. So I brought you out of it. I brought your ancestors out of Egypt, and you came to the Sea; the Egyptians pursued your ancestors with chariots and horsemen as far as the Sea of Reeds. There they called to the Lord, and he spread a thick fog between you and the Egyptians, and made the sea go back on them and cover them. You saw with your own eyes the things I did in Egypt. Then for a long time you lived in the wilderness, until I brought you into the land of the Amorites who lived beyond the Jordan; they made war on you and I gave them into your hands; you took possession of their country because I destroyed them before you. Next, Balak son of Zippor the king of Moab arose to make war on Israel, and sent for Balaam son of Beor to come and curse you. But I would not listen to Balaam; instead, he had to bless you, and I saved you from his hand.

"When you crossed the Jordan and came to Jericho, those who held Jericho fought against you, as did the Amorites and Perizzites, the Canaanites, Hittites, Girgashites, Hivites and Jebusites, but I put them all into your power. I sent out hornets in front of you, which drove the two Amorite kings before you; this was not the work of your sword or your bow. I gave you a land where you never toiled, you live in towns you never built; you eat now from vineyards and olive groves you never planted." '

This is the word of the Lord.

Responsorial Psalm   Ps 135:1-3, 16-18, 21-22, 24

1 O give thanks to the Lord for he is good.
 ℟ **Great is his love, love without end.**
 Give thanks to the God of gods.
 ℟ **Great is his love, love without end.**
 Give thanks to the Lord of lords.
 ℟ **Great is his love, love without end.**

2 Through the desert his people he led.
 ℟ **Great is his love, love without end.**
 Nations in their greatness he struck.
 ℟ **Great is his love, love without end.**

Kings in their splendour he slew.
℟ **Great is his love, love without end.**

3 He let Israel inherit their land.
℟ **Great is his love, love without end.**
On his servant their land he bestowed.
℟ **Great is his love, love without end.**
And he snatched us away from our foes.
℟ **Great is his love, love without end.**

or ℟ **Alleluia!**

Gospel Acclamation   Ps 110:7. 8
Alleluia, alleluia!
Your precepts, O Lord, are all of them sure;
they stand firm for ever and ever.
Alleluia!

or   cf. 1 Thess 2:13

Alleluia, alleluia!
Accept God's message for what is really is:
God's message, and not some human thinking.
Alleluia!

GOSPEL

A reading from the holy Gospel according to Matthew   19:3-12

You were so unteachable that Moses allowed you to divorce your wives; it was not like this from the beginning.

Some Pharisees approached Jesus, and to test him they said, 'Is it against the Law for a man to divorce his wife on any pretext whatever?' He answered, 'Have you not read that the creator from the beginning made them male and female and that he said: This is why a man must leave father and mother, and cling to his wife, and the two become one body? They are no longer two, therefore, but one body. So then, what God has united, man must not divide.'

They said to him, 'Then why did Moses command that a writ of dismissal should be given in cases of divorce?' 'It was because you were so unteachable' he said 'that Moses allowed you to divorce your wives, but it was not like this from the beginning. Now I say this to you: the man who divorces his wife – I am not speaking of fornication – and marries another, is guilty of adultery.'

The disciples said to him, 'If that is how things are between husband and wife, it is not advisable to marry.' But he replied, 'It is not everyone who can accept what I have said, but only those to whom it is granted. There are eunuchs born that way from their mother's womb, there are eunuchs made so by men and there are eunuchs who have made themselves that way for the sake of the kingdom of heaven. Let anyone accept this who can.'

This is the Gospel of the Lord.

SATURDAY

FIRST READING

A reading from the book of Joshua 24:14-29

Choose today whom you wish to serve.

Joshua said to all the people: 'Fear the Lord and serve him perfectly and sincerely; put away the gods that your ancestors served beyond the River and in Egypt, and serve the Lord. But if you will not serve the Lord, choose today whom you wish to serve, whether the gods that your ancestors served beyond the River, or the gods of the Amorites in whose land you are now living. As for me in my House, we will serve the Lord.'

The people answered, 'We have no intention of deserting the Lord and serving other gods! Was it not the Lord our God who brought us and our ancestors out of the land of Egypt, the house of slavery, who worked those great wonders before our eyes and preserved us all along the way we travelled and among all the peoples through whom we journeyed? What is more, the Lord drove all those people out before us, as well as the Amorites who used to live in this country. We too will serve the Lord, for he is our God.'

Then Joshua said to the people, 'You cannot serve the Lord, because he is a holy God, he is a jealous God who will not forgive your transgressions or your sins. If you desert the Lord to follow alien gods he in turn will afflict and destroy you after the goodness he has shown you.' The people answered Joshua, 'No; it is the Lord we wish to serve.' Then Joshua said to the people, 'You are witnesses against yourselves that you have chosen the Lord, to serve him.' They answered, 'We are witnesses.' 'Then cast away the alien gods among you and give your hearts to the Lord the God of Israel!' The people answered Joshua, 'It is the

Lord our God we choose to serve; it is his voice that we will obey.'

That day, Joshua made a covenant for the people; he laid down a statute and ordinance for them at Shechem. Joshua wrote these words in the Book of the Law of God. Then he took a great stone and set it up there, under the oak in the sanctuary of the Lord, and Joshua said to all the people, 'See! This stone shall be a witness against us because it has heard all the words that the Lord has spoken to us: it shall be a witness against you in case you deny your God.' Then Joshua sent the people away, and each returned to his own inheritance.

After these things Joshua son of Nun, the servant of the Lord, died; he was a hundred and ten years old.

This is the word of the Lord.

Responsorial Psalm Ps 15:1-2. 5. 7-8. 11. ℟ cf. v.5

℟ **You are my inheritance, O Lord.**

1 Preserve me, God, I take refuge in you.
   I say to the Lord: 'You are my God.'
   O Lord, it is you who are my portion and cup;
   it is you yourself who are my prize.   ℟

2 I will bless the Lord who gives me counsel,
   who even at night directs my heart.
   I keep the Lord ever in my sight:
   since he is at my right hand, I shall stand firm.   ℟

3 You will show me the path of life,
   the fullness of joy in your presence,
   at your right hand happiness for ever.   ℟

Gospel Acclamation cf. Col 3:16. 17

Alleluia, allelua!
Let the message of Christ, in all its richness,
find a home with you;
through him give thanks to God the Father.
Alleluia!

or cf. Mt 11:25

Alleluia, alleluia!
Blessed are you, Father,
Lord of heaven and earth,
for revealing the mysteries of the kingdom
to mere children.
Alleluia!

GOSPEL

A reading from the holy Gospel according to Matthew 19:13-15

Do not stop the little children coming to me: for it is to such as these that the kingdom of heaven belongs.

People brought little children to Jesus, for him to lay his hands on them and say a prayer. The disciples turned them away, but Jesus said, 'Let the little children alone, and do not stop them coming to me; for it is to such as these that the kingdom of heaven belongs.' Then he laid his hands on them and went on his way.

This is the Gospel of the Lord.

TWENTIETH WEEK IN ORDINARY TIME
Year I

MONDAY

FIRST READING

A reading from the book of Judges 2:11-19

The Lord appointed judges but they would not listen to them.

The sons of Israel did what displeases the Lord and served the Baals. They deserted the Lord, the God of their ancestors, who had brought them out of the land of Egypt, and followed other gods from the gods of the peoples round them. They bowed down to these; they provoked the Lord; they deserted the Lord to serve Baal and Astarte. Then the Lord's anger flamed out against Israel. He handed them over to pillagers who plundered them; he delivered them to the enemies surrounding them, and they were not able to resist them. In every warlike venture, the hand of the Lord was there to foil them, as the Lord had warned, as the Lord had sworn to them. Thus he reduced them to dire distress.

Then the Lord appointed judges for them, and rescued the men of Israel from the hands of their plunderers. But they would not listen to their judges. They prostituted themselves to other gods, and bowed down before these. Very quickly they left the path their ancestors had trodden in obedience to the orders of the Lord; they did not follow their example. When the Lord appointed judges for them, the Lord was with the judge and rescued them from the hands of their enemies as long as the judge lived, for the Lord felt pity for them as they groaned under the iron grip of their oppressors. But once the judge was dead, they relapsed and behaved even worse than their ancestors. They followed other gods; they served them and bowed before them, and would not give up the practices and stubborn ways of their ancestors at all.

This is the word of the Lord.

Responsorial Psalm   Ps 105: 34-37. 39-40. 43-44. ℟ v.4

  ℟ **O Lord, remember me**
     out of the love you have for your people.

1. They failed to destroy the peoples
 as the Lord had given command,
 but instead they mingled with the nations
 and learned to act like them. ℟

2. They worshipped the idols of the nations
 and these became a snare to entrap them.
 They even offered their own sons
 and their daughters in sacrifice to demons. ℟

3. So they defiled themselves by their deeds
 and broke their marriage bond with the Lord
 till his anger blazed against his people:
 he was filled with horror at his chosen ones. ℟

4. Time after time he rescued them,
 but in their malice they dared to defy him.
 In spite of this he paid heed to their distress,
 so often as he heard their cry. ℟

Gospel Acclamation   Ps 118:34

  Alleluia, alleluia!
  Train me, Lord, to observe your law,
  to keep it with my heart.
  Alleluia!

or   Mt 5:3

  Alleluia, alleluia!
  How happy are the poor in spirit;
  theirs is the kingdom of heaven.
  Alleluia!

GOSPEL

A reading from the holy Gospel according to Matthew 19:16–22

If you wish to be perfect, sell what you own and you will have treasure in heaven.

There was a man who came to Jesus and asked, 'Master, what good deed must I do to possess eternal life?' Jesus said to him, 'Why do you ask me about what is good? There is one alone who is good. But if you wish to enter into life, keep the commandments.' He said, 'Which?' 'These,' Jesus replied, 'You must not kill. You must not commit adultery. You must not steal. You must not bring false witness. Honour your father and mother, and: You must love your neighbour as yourself.' The young man said to him 'I have kept all these. What more do I need to do?' Jesus said, 'If you wish to be perfect, go and sell what you own and give the money to the poor, and you will have treasure in heaven; then come, follow me.' But when the young man heard these words he went away sad, for he was a man of great wealth.

This is the Gospel of the Lord.

TUESDAY

A reading from the book of Judges 6:11–24

Gideon, you will rescue Israel: do I not send you myself?

The angel of the Lord came and sat under the terebinth at Ophrah which belonged to Joash of Abiezer. Gideon his son was threshing wheat inside the winepress to keep it hidden from Midian, when the angel of the Lord appeared to him and said, 'The Lord is with you, valiant warrier!' Gideon answered him, 'Forgive me, my lord, but if the Lord is with us, then why is it that all this is happening to us now? And where are all the wonders our ancestors tell us of when they say, "Did not the Lord bring us out of Egypt?" But now the Lord has deserted us; he has abandoned us to Midian.'

At this the Lord turned to him and said, 'Go in the strength now upholding you, and you will rescue Israel from the power of Midian. Do I not sent you myself?' Gideon answered him, 'Forgive me, my lord, but how can I deliver Israel? My clan, you must know, is the weakest in Manasseh and I am the least important in my family,' The Lord answered him, 'I will be with you and you shall crush Midian as though it were a single man.' Gideon said to him, 'If I have found favour in your sight, give me a sign that it is you who speak to me. I beg you, do not go away until I come back, I will bring you my offering and set it down before you.' And he answered, 'I will stay until you return.'

Gideon went away and prepared a young goat and made unleavened cakes with an ephah of flour. He put the meat into a basket and the broth into a pot, then brought it all to him under the terebinth. As he came near, the angel of the Lord said to him, 'Take the meat and unleavened cakes, put them on this rock and pour the broth over them.' Gideon did so. Then the angel of the Lord reached out the tip of the staff in his hand and touched the meat and unleavened cakes. Fire sprang from the rock and consumed the meat and unleavened cakes, and the angel of the Lord vanished before his eyes. Then Gideon knew this was the angel of the Lord, and he said, 'Alas, my Lord! I have seen the angel of the Lord face to face!' The Lord answered him, 'Peace be with you; have no fear; you will not die.' Gideon built an altar there to the Lord and called it The-Lord-is-Peace.

This is the word of the Lord.

Responsorial Psalm   Ps 84:9. 11-14. ℟ v.9

℟ **The Lord speaks peace to his people.**

1 I will hear what the Lord God has to say,
   a voice that speaks of peace,
   peace for his people and his friends
   and those who turn to him in their hearts.   ℟

2 Mercy and faithfulness have met;
   justice and peace have embraced.
   Faithfulness shall spring from the earth
   and justice look down from heaven.   ℟

3 The Lord will make us prosper
   and our earth shall yield its fruit.
   Justice shall march before him
   and peace shall follow his steps.   ℟

Gospel Acclamation   Ps 24:4. 5

Alleluia, alleluia!
Teach me your paths, my God,

make me walk in your truth.
Alleluia!

or 2 Cor 8:9

Alleluia, alleluia!
Jesus Christ was rich,
but he became poor for your sake,
to make you rich out of his poverty.
Alleluia!

GOSPEL

A reading from the holy Gospel according to Matthew 19:23-30

It is easier for a camel to pass through the eye of a needle than for a rich man to enter the kingdom of heaven.

Jesus said to his disciples, 'I tell you solemnly, it will be hard for a rich man to enter the kingdom of heaven. Yes, I tell you again, it is easier for a camel to pass through the eye of a needle than for a rich man to enter the kingdom of heaven.' When the disciples heard this they were astonished. 'Who can be saved, then?' they said. Jesus gazed at them. 'For men' he told them 'this is impossible; for God everything is possible.'

Then Peter spoke. 'What about us?' he said to him. 'We have left everything and followed you. What are we to have, then?' Jesus said to him, 'I tell you solemnly, when all is made new and the Son of Man sits on his throne of glory, you will yourselves sit on twelve thrones to judge the twelve tribes of Israel. And everyone who has left houses, brothers, sisters, father, mother, children or land for the sake of my name will be repaid a hundred times over, and also inherit eternal life.

'Many who are first will be last, and the last, first.'

This is the Gospel of the Lord.

WEDNESDAY

FIRST READING

A reading from the book of Judges 9:6-15

You said, 'A king must rule over us' - although the Lord your God himself is your king.

All the leading men of Shechem and all Bethmillo gathered, and proclaimed Abimelech king by the terebinth of the pillar at Shechem.

News of this was brought to Jotham. He came and stood on the top of Mount Gerizim and shouted aloud for them to hear:

'Hear me, leaders of Shechem,
that God may also hear you!

'One day the trees went out
to anoint a king to rule over them.
They said to the olive tree, "Be our king!"

'The olive tree answered them,
"Must I forego my oil
which gives honour to gods and men,
to stand swaying above the trees?"

'Then the trees said to the fig tree,
"Come now, you be our king!"

'The fig tree answered them,
"Must I forego my sweetness,
forego my excellent fruit,
to stand swaying above the trees?"

'Then the trees said to the vine,
"Come now, you be our king!"

'The vine answered them,
"Must I forego my wine
which cheers the heart of gods and men,
to stand swaying above the trees?"

'Then all the trees said to the thorn bush,
"Come now, you be our king!"

'And the thorn bush answered the trees,
"If in all good faith you anoint me king to reign over you,
then come and shelter in my shade.
If not, fire will come from the thorn bush
and devour the cedars of Lebanon." '

This is the word of the Lord.

Responsorial Psalm Ps 20:2-7. ℞ v.2

℞ **O Lord, your strength gives joy to the king.**

1 O Lord, your strength gives joy to the king;

how your saving help makes him glad!
You have granted him his heart's desire;
you have not refused the prayer of his lips. ℟

2 You came to meet him with the blessings of success,
you have set on his head a crown of pure gold.
He asked you for life and this you have given,
days that will last from age to age. ℟

3 Your saving help has given him glory.
You have laid upon him majesty and splendour,
you have granted your blessings to him for ever.
You have made him rejoice with the joy of your presence. ℟

Gospel Acclamation Ps 118:135

Alleluia! alleluia!
Let your face shine on your servant,
and teach me your decrees.
Alleluia!

or Heb 4:12

Alleluia, alleluia!
The word of God is something alive and active;
it can judge secret emotions and thoughts.
Alleluia!

GOSPEL

A reading from the holy Gospel according to Matthew 20:1-16
Why be envious because I am generous.

Jesus said to his disciples: 'The kingdom of heaven is like a landowner going out at daybreak to hire workers for his vineyard. He made an agreement with the workers for one denarius a day, and sent them to his vineyard. Going out at about the third hour he saw others standing idle in the market place and said to them, "You go to my vineyard too and I will give you a fair wage." So they went. At about the sixth hour and again at about the ninth hour, he went out and did the same. Then at about the eleventh hour he went out and found more men standing round, and he said to them, "Why have you been standing here idle all day?" "Because no one has hired us" they answered. He said to them, "You go into my vineyard too." In the evening, the owner of the vineyard said to his bailiff, "Call the workers and pay them their wages, starting with the last arrivals and ending with the first." So those who were hired at about the eleventh hour came forward and received one denarius each. When the first came, they expected to get more, but they too received one denarius each. They took it, but grumbled at the landowner. "The men who came last" they said "have done only one hour, and you have treated them the same as us, though we have done a heavy day's work in all the heat." He answered one of them and said, "My friend, I am not being unjust to you; did we not agree on one denarius? Take your earnings and go. I choose to pay the last-comer as much as I pay you. Have I no right to do what I like with my own? Why be envious because I am generous?" Thus the last will be first, and the first, last.'

This is the Gospel of the Lord.

THURSDAY

FIRST READING

A reading from the book of Judges 11:29-39

I will offer up the first person to meet me from the door of my house as a holocaust to the Lord.

The spirit of the Lord came on Jephthah, who crossed Gilead and Manasseh, passed through to Mizpah in Gilead and from Mizpah in Gilead made his way to the rear of the Ammonites. And Jephthah made a vow to the Lord, 'If you deliver the Ammonites into my hands, then the first person to meet me from the door of my house when I return in triumph from fighting the Ammonites shall belong to the Lord, and I will offer him up as a holocaust.' Jephthah marched against the Ammonites to attack them, and the Lord delivered them into his power. He harassed them from Aroer almost to Minnith (twenty towns) and to Abel-keramim. It was a very severe defeat, and the Ammonites were humbled before the Israelites.

As Jephthah returned to his house at Mizpah, his daughter came out from it to meet him; she was dancing to the sound of timbrels. This was his only child; apart from her he had neither son nor daughter. When he saw her, he tore his clothes and exclaimed, 'Oh my daughter, what sorrow you are bringing me! Must it be you, the cause of my ill-fortune! I have given a promise to the Lord, and I cannot unsay what I have said.' She answered him, 'My father, you have given a promise to the Lord; treat me as the vow you took binds you to, since the Lord has given you vengeance on your enemies the Ammonites.' Then she said to her father, 'Grant me one request. Let me be free for two months. I shall go and wander in the mountains, and with my companions bewail my virginity.' He answered, 'Go,' and let her depart for two months. So she went away with her companions and bewailed her virginity in the mountains. When the two months were over, she returned to her father, and he treated her as the vow he had uttered bound him.

This is the word of the Lord.

Responsorial Psalm   Ps 39:5. 7-10. R̷ vv.8-9

    R̷ **Here I am, Lord!**
       I come to do your will.

1. Happy the man who has placed
his trust in the Lord
and has not gone over to the rebels
who follow false gods. R̷

2. You do not ask for sacrifice and offerings,
but an open ear.
You do not ask for holocaust and victim.
Instead, here am I. R̷

3. In the scroll of the book it stands written
that I should do your will.
My God, I delight in your law
in the depth of my heart. R̷

4. Your justice I have proclaimed
in the great assembly.
My lips I have not sealed;
you know it, O Lord. R̷

Gospel Acclamation   Ps 118:27
    Alleluia, alleluia!
    Make me grasp the way of your precepts,
    and I will muse on your wonders.
    Alleluia!

or   cf. Ps 94:8

    Alleluia, alleluia!
    Harden not your hearts today,
    but listen to the voice of the Lord.
    Alleluia!

GOSPEL

A reading from the holy Gospel according to Matthew   22:1-14

Invite everyone you can find to the wedding.

Jesus began to speak to the chief priests and the elders of the people in parables, 'The kingdom of heaven may be compared to a king who gave a feast for his son's wedding. He sent his servants to call those who had been invited, but they would not come. Next he sent some more servants. "Tell those who have been invited" he said "that I have my banquet all prepared, my oxen and fattened cattle have been slaughtered, everything is ready. Come to the wedding." But they were not interested: one went off to his farm, another to his business, and the rest seized his servants, maltreated them and killed them. The king was furious. He despatched his troops, destroyed those murderers and burnt their town. Then he said to his servants, "The wedding is ready; but as those who were invited proved to be unworthy, go to the crossroads in the town and invite everyone you can find to the wedding." So these servants went out on to the roads and collected together everyone they could find, bad and good alike; and the wedding hall was filled with guests. When the king came in to look at the guests he noticed one man who was not wearing a wedding garment, and said to him, "How did you get in here, my friend, without a wedding garment?" And the man was silent. Then the king said to the attendants, "Bind him hand and foot and throw him out into the dark, where there will be weeping and grinding of teeth." For many are called, but few are chosen.'

This is the Gospel of the Lord.

FRIDAY

FIRST READING

A reading from the book of Ruth   1:1. 3-6. 14-16. 22

Naomi came back with Ruth the Moabitess and came to Bethlehem.

In the days of the Judges famine came to the land and a certain man from Bethlehem of Judah went – he, his wife and his two sons – to live in the country of Moab. Elimelech, Naomi's husband, died, and she and her two sons were left. These married Moabite women: one was named Orpah and the other

Ruth. They lived there about ten years. Then both Mahlon and Chilion also died and the woman was bereft of her two sons and her husband. So she and her daughters-in-law prepared to return from the country of Moab, for she had heard that the Lord had visited his people and given them food. Then Orpah kissed her mother-in-law and went back to her people. But Ruth clung to her.

Naomi said to her, 'Look, your sister-in-law has gone back to her people and to her god. You must return too; follow your sister-in-law.'

But Ruth said, 'Do not press me to leave you and to turn back from your company, for

'wherever you go, I will go,
wherever you live, I will live.
Your people shall be my people,
and your God, my God.'

This was how Naomi, she who returned from the country of Moab, came back with Ruth the Moabitess her daughter-in-law. And they came to Bethlehem at the beginning of the barley harvest.

This is the word of the Lord.

Responsorial Psalm   Ps 145:5-10. ℟ v.2

    ℟ **My soul, give praise to the Lord.**

or

    ℟ **Alleluia!**

1. He is happy who is helped by Jacob's God,
   whose hope is in the Lord his God,
   who alone made heaven and earth,
   the seas and all they contain.   ℟

2. It is he who keeps faith for ever,
   who is just to those who are oppressed.
   It is he who gives bread to the hungry,
   the Lord, who sets prisoners free.   ℟

3. It is the Lord who gives sight to the blind,
   who raises up those who are bowed down,
   the Lord, who protects the stranger
   and upholds the widow and orphan.   ℟

(continued)

4   It is the Lord who loves the just
    but thwarts the path of the wicked.
    The Lord will reign for ever,
    Zion's God, from age to age.

    ℟ **My soul, give praise to the Lord.**

or

    ℟ **Alleluia!**

Gospel Acclamation   Ps 118:18
Alleluia, alleluia!
Open my eyes, O Lord, that I may consider
the wonders of your law.
Alleluia!

or   Ps 24:4. 5

Alleluia, alleluia!
Teach me your paths, my God,
make me walk in your truth.
Alleluia!

GOSPEL

A reading from the holy Gospel according to Matthew   22:34-40
You must love the Lord your God, and your neighbour as yourself.

When the Pharisees heard that Jesus had silenced the Sadducees they got together and, to disconcert him, one of them put a question, 'Master, which is the greatest commandment of the Law?' Jesus said, 'You must love the Lord your God with all your heart, with all your soul, and with all your mind. This is the greatest and the first commandment. The second resembles it: You must love your neighbour as yourself. On these two commandments hang the whole Law, and the Prophets also.'

This is the Gospel of the Lord.

SATURDAY

FIRST READING

A reading from the book of Ruth 2:1-3. 8-11; 4:13-17

The Lord has not left the dead man without next of kin to perpetuate his name This was the father of David's father, Jesse.

Naomi had a kinsman on her husband's side, well-to-do and of Elimelech's clan. His name was Boaz.

Ruth the Moabitess said to Naomi, 'Let me go into the fields and glean among the ears of corn in the footsteps of some man who will look on me with favour.' And she said to her, 'Go, my daughter.' So she set out and went to glean in the fields after the reapers. And it chanced that she came to that part of the fields which belonged to Boaz of Elimelech's clan.

Boaz said to Ruth, 'Listen, my daughter, and understand this. You are not to glean in any other field, do not leave here but stay with my servants. Keep your eyes on whatever part of the field they are reaping and follow behind. I have ordered my servants not to molest you. And if you are thirsty, go to the pitchers and drink what the servants have drawn.' Then she fell on her face, bowing to the ground. And she said to him, 'How have I so earned your favour that you take notice of me, even though I am a foreigner?' And Boaz answered her, 'I have been told all you have done for your mother-in-law since your husband's death, and how you left your own father and mother and the land where you were born to come among a people whom you knew nothing about before you came here.'

So Boaz took Ruth and she became his wife. And when they came together, the Lord made her conceive and she bore a son. And the woman said to Naomi, 'Blessed be the Lord who has not left the dead man without next of kin this day to perpetuate his name in Israel. The child will be a comfort to you and the prop of your old age, for your daughter-in-law who loves you and is more to you than seven sons has given him birth.' And Naomi took the child to her own bosom and she became his nurse.

And the women of the neighbourhood gave him a name. 'A son has been born for Naomi' they said; and they named him Obed. This was the father of David's father, Jesse.

This is the word of the Lord.

Responsorial Psalm Ps 127:1-5. ℟ v.4

℟ **Indeed thus shall be blessed
the man who fears the Lord.**

1 O blessed are those who fear the Lord
   and walk in his ways!
   By the labour of your hands you shall eat.
   You will be happy and prosper. ℟

2 Your wife like a fruitful vine
   in the heart of your house;
   your children like shoots of the olive,
   around your table. ℟

3 Indeed thus shall be blessed
   the man who fears the Lord.
   May the Lord bless you from Zion
   all the days of your life! ℟

Gospel Acclamation Ps 118:29. 35

Alleluia, alleluia!
Bend my heart to your will, O Lord,
and teach me your law.
Alleluia!

or Mt 23:9. 10

Alleluia, alleluia!
You have only one Father,
and he is in heaven;
you have only one Teacher,
the Christ.
Alleluia!

GOSPEL

A reading from the holy Gospel according to Matthew 23:1-12
They do not practise what they preach.

Addressing the people and his disciples Jesus said, 'The scribes and the Pharisees occupy the chair of Moses. You must therefore do what they tell you and listen to what they say; but do not be guided by what they do: since they do not practise what they preach. They tie up heavy burdens and lay them on men's shoulders, but will they lift a finger to move them? Not they! Everything they do is done to attract attention, like wearing broader phylacteries and longer tassels, like wanting to take the place of honour at banquets and the front seats in the synagogues, being greeted obsequiously in the market squares and having people call them Rabbi.

'You, however, must not allow yourselves to be called Rabbi, since you have only one Master, and you are all brothers. You must call no one on earth your father, since you have only one Father, and he is in heaven. Nor must you allow yourselves to be called teachers, for you have only one Teacher, the Christ. The greatest among you must be your servant. Anyone who exalts himself will be humbled, and anyone who humbles himself will be exalted.'

This is the Gospel of the Lord.

TWENTY-FIRST WEEK IN ORDINARY TIME
Year I

MONDAY

FIRST READING

A reading from the first letter of St Paul to the Thessalonians 1:1-5. 8-10

You broke with idolatry when you were converted to God and you are waiting for his Son, whom he raised from the dead.

From Paul, Silvanus and Timothy, to the Church in Thessalonika which is in God our Father and the Lord Jesus Christ; wishing you grace and peace from God the Father and the Lord Jesus Christ.

We always mention you in our prayers and thank God for you all, and constantly remember before God our Father how you have shown your faith in action, worked for love and persevered through hope, in our Lord Jesus Christ.

We know, brothers, that God loves you and that you have been chosen, because when we brought the Good News to you, it came to you not only as words, but as power and as the Holy Spirit and as utter conviction. And you observed the sort of life we lived when we were with you, which was for your instruction. We do not need to tell other people about it: other people tell us how we started the work among you, how you broke with idolatry when you were converted to God and became servants of the real, living God; and how you are now waiting for Jesus, his

Son, whom he raised from the dead, to come from heaven to save us from the retribution which is coming.

This is the word of the Lord.

Responsorial Psalm   Ps 149:1-6. 9. R̷ v.4
℟ **The Lord takes delight in his people.**

or

℟ **Alleluia!**

1. Sing a new song to the Lord,
   his praise in the assembly of the faithful.
   Let Israel rejoice in its Maker,
   let Zion's sons exult in their king. ℟

2. Let them praise his name with dancing
   and make music with timbrel and harp.
   For the Lord takes delight in his people.
   He crowns the poor with salvation. ℟

3. Let the faithful rejoice in their glory,
   shout for joy and take their rest.
   Let the praise of God be on their lips:
   this honour is for all his faithful. ℟

Gospel Acclamation   cf. Jn 17:17
Alleluia, alleluia!
Your word is truth, O Lord,
consecrate us in the truth.
Alleluia!

or   Jn 10:27

Alleluia, alleluia!
The sheep that belong to me listen to my voice,
says the Lord,
I know them and they follow me.
Alleluia!

GOSPEL

A reading from the holy Gospel according to Matthew   23:13-22
Alas for you, blind guides!

Jesus said: 'Alas for you, scribes and Pharisees, you hypocrites! You who shut up the kingdom of heaven in men's faces, neither going in yourselves nor allowing others to go in who want to.

'Alas for you, scribes and Pharisees, you hypocrites! You who travel over sea and land to make a single proselyte, and when you have him you make him twice as fit for hell as you are.

'Alas for you, blind guides! You who say, "If a man swears by the Temple, it has no force; but if a man swears by the gold of the Temple, he is bound." Fools and blind! For which is of greater worth, the gold or the Temple that makes the gold sacred? Or else, "If a man swears by the altar he has no force; but if a man swears by the offering that is on the altar, he is bound." You blind men! For which is of greater worth, the offering or the altar that makes the offering sacred? Therefore, when a man swears by the altar he is swearing by that and by everything on it. And when a man swears by the Temple he is swearing by that and by the One who dwells in it. And when a man swears by heaven he is swearing by the throne of God and by the One who is seated there.'

This is the Gospel of the Lord.

TUESDAY

FIRST READING

A reading from the first letter of St Paul 2:1-8
to the Thessalonians

We were eager to hand over to you not only the Good News but our whole lives as well.

You know yourselves, my brothers, that our visit to you has not proved ineffectual.

We had, as you know, been given rough treatment and been grossly insulted at Philippi, and it was our God who gave us the courage to proclaim his Good News to you in the face of great opposition. We have not taken to preaching because we are deluded, or immoral, or trying to deceive anyone; it was God who decided that we were fit to be entrusted with the Good News, and when we are speaking, we are not trying to please men but God, who can read our inmost thoughts. You know very well, and we can swear it before God, that never at any time have our speeches been simply flattery, or a cover for trying to get money; nor have we ever looked for any special honour from men, either from you or anybody else, when we could have imposed ourselves on you with full weight, as apostles of Christ.

Instead, we were unassuming. Like a mother feeding and looking after her own children, we felt so devoted and protective towards you, and had come to love you so much, that we were eager to hand over to you not only the Good News but our whole lives as well.

This is the word of the Lord.

Responsorial Psalm
Ps 138:1-3. 4-6. ℟ v.1

℟ **O Lord, you search me and you know me.**

1 O Lord, you search me and you know me,
 you know my resting and my rising,
 you discern my purpose from afar. ℟

2 You mark when I walk or lie down,
 all my ways lie open to you.
 Before ever a word is on my tongue
 you know it, O Lord, through and through. ℟

3 Behind and before you besiege me,
 your hand ever laid upon me.
 Too wonderful for me, this knowledge,
 too high, beyond my reach. ℟

Gospel Acclamation
cf. Acts 16:14

Alleluia, alleluia!
Open our heart, O Lord,
to accept the words of your Son.
Alleluia!

or
Heb 4:12

Alleluia, alleluia!
The word of God is something alive and active;
it can judge secret emotions and thoughts.
Alleluia!

GOSPEL

A reading from the holy Gospel according to Matthew 23:23-26

You should have practised these matters of the Law, without neglecting the others.

Jesus said, 'Alas for you, scribes and Pharisees, you hypocrites! You who pay your tithe of mint and dill and cummin and have neglected the weightier matters of the Law – justice, mercy, good faith! These you should have practised, without neglecting the others. You blind guides! Straining out gnats and swallowing camels!

'Alas for you, scribes and Pharisees, you hypocrites! You who clean the outside of cup and dish and leave the inside full of extortion and intemperance. Blind Pharisee! Clean the inside of cup and dish first so that the outside may become clean as well.'

This is the Gospel of the Lord.

WEDNESDAY

FIRST READING

A reading from the first letter of St Paul 2:9-13
to the Thessalonians
Slaving night and day, we were proclaiming the Good News to you.

Let me remind you, brothers, how hard we used to work, slaving night and day so as not to be a burden on any one of you while we were proclaiming God's Good News to you. You are witnesses, and so is God, that our treatment of you, since you became believers, has been impeccably right and fair. You can remember how we treated every one of you as a father treats his children, teaching you what was right, encouraging you and appealing to you to live a life worthy of God, who is calling you to share the glory of his kingdom.

Another reason why we constantly thank God for you is that as soon as you heard the message that we brought you as God's message, you accepted it for what it really is, God's message and not some human thinking; and it is still a living power among you who believe it.

This is the word of the Lord.

Responsorial Psalm Ps 138:7-12. ℟ v.1

℟ **O Lord, you search me and you know me.**

1 O where can I go from your spirit,
 or where can I flee from your face?
 If I climb the heavens, you are there.
 If I lie in the grave, you are there. ℟

2 If I take the wings of the dawn
 and dwell at the sea's furthest end,

    even there your hand would lead me,
    your right hand would hold me fast.

    ℟ **O Lord, you search me and you know me.**

3   If I say: 'Let the darkness hide me
    and the light around me be night,'
    even darkness is not dark for you
    and the night is as clear as the day.   ℟

Gospel Acclamation   Mt 4:4
    Alleluia, alleluia!
    Man does not live on bread alone,
    but on every word that comes from the mouth of God.
    Alleluia!

or   1 Jn 2:5

    Alleluia, alleluia!
    When anyone obeys what Christ has said,
    God's love comes to perfection in him,
    Alleluia!

GOSPEL

A reading from the holy Gospel according to Matthew   23:27-32
You are the sons of those who murdered the prophets.

Jesus said, 'Alas for you, scribes and Pharisees, you hypocrites! You who are like whitewashed tombs that look handsome on the outside, but inside are full of dead men's bones and every kind of corruption. In the same way you appear to people from the outside like good honest men, but inside you are full of hypocrisy and lawlessness.

 'Alas for you, scribes and Pharisees, you hypocrites! You who build the sepulchres of the prophets and decorate the tombs of holy men, saying, "We would never have joined in shedding the blood of the prophets, had we lived in our fathers' day." So! Your own evidence tells against you! You are the sons of those who murdered the prophets! Very well then, finish off the work that your fathers began.'

   This is the Gospel of the Lord.

THURSDAY

FIRST READING

A reading from the first letter of St Paul to the Thessalonians   3:7-13

May the Lord be generous in increasing your love and make you love one another and the whole human race.

Brothers, your faith has been a great comfort to us in the middle of our own troubles and sorrows; now we can breathe again, as you are still holding firm in the Lord. How can we thank God enough for you, for all the joy we feel before our God on your account? We are earnestly praying night and day to be able to see you face to face again and make up any shortcomings in your faith.

May God our Father himself, and our Lord Jesus Christ, make it easy for us to come to you. May the Lord be generous in increasing your love and make you love one another and the whole human race as much as we love you. And may he so confirm your hearts in holiness that you may be blameless in the sight of our God and Father when our Lord Jesus Christ comes with all his saints.

This is the word of the Lord.

Responsorial Psalm   Ps 89:3-4. 12-14. 17. ℟ v.14

℟ **Fill us with your love that we may rejoice.**

1. You turn men back into dust
   and say: 'Go back, sons of men.'
   To your eyes a thousand years
   are like yesterday, come and gone,
   no more than a watch in the night.   ℟

2. Make us know the shortness of our life
   that we may gain wisdom of heart.
   Lord, relent! Is your anger for ever?
   Show pity to your servants.   ℟

3. In the morning, fill us with your love;
   we shall exult and rejoice all our days.
   Let the favour of the Lord be upon us:
   give success to the work of our hands.   ℟

Gospel Acclamation Jn 15:15
> Alleluia, alleluia!
> I call you friends, says the Lord,
> because I have made known to you
> everything I have learnt from my Father.
> Alleluia!

or Mt 24:42. 44

> Alleluia, alleluia!
> Stay awake and stand ready,
> because you do not know the hour
> when the Son of Man is coming.
> Alleluia!

GOSPEL

A reading from the holy Gospel according to Matthew 24:42-51
Stand ready.

Jesus said to his disciples: 'Stay awake, because you do not know the day when your master is coming. You may be quite sure of this, that if the householder had known at what time of the night the burglar would come, he would have stayed awake and would not have allowed anyone to break the wall of his house. Therefore, you too must stand ready because the Son of Man is coming at an hour you do not expect.

'What sort of servant, then, is faithful and wise enough for the master to place him over his household to give them their food at the proper time? Happy that servant if his master's arrival finds him at this employment. I tell you solemnly, he will place him over everything he owns. But as for the dishonest servant who says to himself, "My master is taking his time," and sets about beating his fellow servants and eating and drinking with drunkards, his master will come on a day he does not expect and at an hour he does not know. The master will cut him off and send him to the same fate as the hypocrites, where there will be weeping and grinding of teeth.'

This is the Gospel of the Lord.

FRIDAY

FIRST READING

A reading from the first letter of St Paul to the Thessalonians   4:1-8

What God wants is for you all to be holy.

Brothers, we urge you and appeal to you in the Lord Jesus to make more and more progress in the kind of life that you are meant to live: the life that God wants, as you learnt from us, and as you are already living it. You have not forgotten the instructions we gave you on the authority of the Lord Jesus.

What God wants is for you all to be holy. He wants you to keep away from fornication, and each one of you to know how to use the body that belongs to him in a way that is holy and honourable, not giving way to selfish lust like the pagans who do not know God. He wants nobody at all ever to sin by taking advantage of a brother in these matters; the Lord always punishes sins of that sort, as we told you before and assured you. We have been called by God to be holy, not to be immoral; in other words, anyone who objects is not objecting to a human authority, but to God, who gives you his Holy Spirit.

This is the word of the Lord.

Responsorial Psalm   Ps 96:1-2. 5-6. 10-12. ℟ v.12

    ℟   **Rejoice, you just, in the Lord.**

1. The Lord is king, let earth rejoice,
   the many coastlands be glad.
   Cloud and darkness are his raiment;
   his throne, justice and right. ℟

2. The mountains melt like wax
   before the Lord of all the earth.
   The skies proclaim his justice;
   all peoples see his glory. ℟

3. The Lord loves those who hate evil:
   he guards the souls of his saints;
   he sets them free from the wicked. ℟

4. Light shines forth for the just
   and joy for the upright of heart.
   Rejoice, you just, in the Lord;
   give glory to his holy name. ℟

Gospel Acclamation   Ps 129:5
Alleluia, alleluia!
My soul is waiting for the Lord,
I count on his word.
Alleluia!

or   Lk 21:36

Alleluia, alleluia!
Stay awake, praying at all times
for the strength to stand with confidence
before the Son of Man.
Alleluia!

GOSPEL

A reading from the holy Gospel according to Matthew   25:1-13
The bridegroom is here, go out and meet him.

Jesus said to his disciples: 'The kingdom of heaven will be like this: Ten bridesmaids took their lamps and went to meet the bridegroom. Five of them were foolish and five were sensible: the foolish ones did take their lamps, but they brought no oil, whereas the sensible ones took flasks of oil as well as their lamps. The bridegroom was late, and they all grew drowsy and fell asleep. But at midnight there was a cry, "The bridegroom is here! Go out and meet him." At this, all those bridesmaids woke up and trimmed their lamps, and the foolish ones said to the sensible ones, "Give us some of your oil: our lamps are going out." But they replied, "There may not be enough for us and for you; you had better go to those who sell it and buy some for yourselves." They had gone off to buy it when the bridegroom arrived. Those who were ready went in with him to the wedding hall and the door was closed. The other bridesmaids arrived later. "Lord, Lord," they said, "open the door for us." But he replied, "I tell you solemnly, I do not know you." So stay awake, because you do not know either the day or the hour.'

This is the Gospel of the Lord.

SATURDAY

FIRST READING

A reading from the first letter of St Paul to the Thessalonians 4:9-11

You have learnt from God yourselves to love one another.

As for loving our brothers, there is no need for anyone to write to you about that, since you have learnt from God yourselves to love one another, and in fact this is what you are doing with all the brothers throughout the whole of Macedonia. However, we do urge you, brothers, to go on making even greater progress and to make a point of living quietly, attending to your own business and earning your living, just as we told you to.

This is the word of the Lord.

Responsorial Psalm
Ps 97:1. 7-9. ℟ v.9

℟ **The Lord comes to rule the people with fairness.**

1. Sing a new song to the Lord
   for he has worked wonders.
   His right hand and his holy arm
   have brought salvation. ℟

2. Let the sea and all within it, thunder;
   the world, and all its peoples.
   Let the rivers clap their hands
   and the hills ring out their joy
   at the presence of the Lord. ℟

3. For the Lord comes,
   he comes to rule the earth.
   He will rule the world with justice
   and the peoples with fairness. ℟

Gospel Acclamation
Phil 2:15-16

Alleluia, alleluia!
You will shine in the world like bright stars
because you are offering it the word of life.
Alleluia!

or
Jn 13:34

Alleluia, alleluia!
I give you a new commandment:

love one another just as I have loved you,
says the Lord.
Alleluia!

GOSPEL

A reading from the holy Gospel according to Matthew 25:14-30
You have shown you can be faithful in small things, come and join in your master's happiness.

Jesus told his disciples this parable: 'A man on his way abroad summoned his servants and entrusted his property to them. To one he gave five talents, to another two, to a third one; each in proportion to his ability. Then he set out. The man who had received the five talents promptly went and traded with them and made five more. The man who had received two made two more in the same way. But the man who had received one went off and dug a hole in the ground and hid his master's money. Now a long time after, the master of those servants came back and went through his accounts with them. The man who had received the five talents came forward bringing five more. "Sir," he said, "you entrusted me with five talents; here are five more that I have made." His master said to him, "Well done, good and faithful servant; you have shown you can be faithful in small things, I will trust you with greater; come and join in your master's happiness." Next the man with the two talents came forward. "Sir," he said, "you entrusted me with two talents; here are two more that I have made." His master said to him, "Well done, good and faithful servant; you have shown you can be faithful in small things, I will trust you with greater; come and join in your master's happiness." Last came forward the man who had the one talent. "Sir," said he, "I heard you were a hard man, reaping where you have not sown and gathering where you have not scattered; so I was afraid, and I went off and hid your talent in the ground. Here it is; it was yours, you have it back." But his master answered him, "You wicked and lazy servant! So you knew that I reap where I have not sown and gather where I have not scattered? Well then, you should have deposited my money with the bankers, and on my return I would have recovered my capital with interest. So now, take the talent from him and give it to the man who has the five talents. For to everyone who has will be given more, and he will have more than enough; but from the man who has not, even what he has will be

Twenty-second Week in Ordinary Time, Year I: Monday 705

taken away. As for this good-for-nothing servant, throw him out into the dark, where there will be weeping and grinding of teeth."'

This is the Gospel of the Lord.

TWENTY-SECOND WEEK IN ORDINARY TIME
Year I

MONDAY

FIRST READING

A reading from the first letter of St Paul 4:13-18
to the Thessalonians
God will bring those who have died in Jesus with him.

We want you to be quite certain, brothers, about those who have died, to make sure that you do not grieve about them, like the other people who have no hope. We believe that Jesus died and rose again, and that it will be the same for those who have died in Jesus: God will bring them with him. We can tell you this from the Lord's own teaching, that any of us who are left alive until the Lord's coming will not have any advantage over those who have died. At the trumpet of God, the voice of the archangel will call out the command and the Lord himself will come down from heaven; those who have died in Christ will be the first to rise, and then those of us who are still alive will be taken up in the clouds, together with them, to meet the Lord in the air. So we shall stay with the Lord for ever. With such thoughts as these you should comfort one another.

This is the word of the Lord.

Responsorial Psalm Ps 95:1. 3-5. 11-13. ℟ v.13
  ℟ **The Lord comes to rule the earth.**

1 O sing a new song to the Lord,
 sing to the Lord all the earth.
 Tell among the nations his glory
 and his wonders among all the peoples.   ℟

2 The Lord is great and worthy of praise,
 to be feared above all gods;

the gods of the heathens are naught.
It was the Lord who made the heavens.

℟ **The Lord comes to rule the earth.**

3 Let the heavens rejoice and earth be glad,
let the sea and all within it thunder praise,
let the land and all it bears rejoice,
all the trees of the wood shout for joy
at the presence of the Lord for he comes,
he comes to rule the earth.   ℟

4 With justice he will rule the world,
he will judge the peoples with his truth.   ℟

Gospel Acclamation   Jn 8:12

Alleluia, alleluia!
I am the light of the world, says the Lord,
anyone who follows me
will have the light of life.
Alleluia!

or   Lk 4:18

Alleluia, alleluia!
The Lord has sent me to bring the good news to the poor,
to proclaim liberty to captives.
Alleluia!

GOSPEL

A reading from the holy Gospel according to Luke   4:16-30

He has sent me to bring the good news to the poor. No prophet is accepted in his own country.

Jesus came to Nazara, where he had been brought up, and went into the synagogue on the sabbath day as he usually did. He stood up to read, and they handed him the scroll of the prophet Isaiah. Unrolling the scroll he found the place where it is written:

The spirit of the Lord has been given to me,
for he has anointed me.
He has sent me to bring the good news to the poor,
to proclaim liberty to captives
and to the blind new sight,
to set the downtrodden free,
to proclaim the Lord's year of favour.

He then rolled up the scroll, gave it back to the assistant and sat down. And all eyes in the synagogue were fixed on him. Then he began to speak to them, 'This text is being fulfilled today even as you listen.' And he won the approval of all, and they were astonished by the gracious words that came from his lips.

They said, 'This is Joseph's son, surely?' But he replied, 'No doubt you will quote me the saying, "Physician, heal yourself" and tell me, "We have heard all that happened in Capernaum, do the same here in your own countryside." ' And he went on, 'I tell you solemnly, no prophet is ever accepted in his own country.

'There were many widows in Israel, I can assure you, in Elijah's day, when heaven remained shut for three years and six months and a great famine raged throughout the land, but Elijah was not sent to any one of these: he was sent to a widow at Zarephath, a Sidonian town. And in the prophet Elisha's time there were many lepers in Israel, but none of these was cured, except the Syrian, Naaman.'

When they heard this everyone in the synagogue was enraged. They sprang to their feet and hustled him out of the town; and they took him up to the brow of the hill their town was built on, intending to throw him down the cliff, but he slipped through the crowd and walked away.

This is the Gospel of the Lord.

TUESDAY

FIRST READING

A reading from the first letter of St Paul 5:1-6. 9-11
to the Thessalonians
Christ died for us so that we should live united to him.

You will not be expecting us to write anything to you, brothers, about 'times and seasons', since you know very well that the Day of the Lord is going to come like a thief in the night. It is when people are saying, 'How quiet and peaceful it is' that the worst suddenly happens, as suddenly as labour pains come on a pregnant woman; and there will be no way for anybody to evade it.

But it is not as if you live in the dark, my brothers, for that Day to overtake you like a thief. No, you are all sons of light and sons of the day: we do not belong to the night or to darkness, so we should not go on sleeping, as everyone else does, but stay wide awake and sober. God never meant us to experience the Retribution, but to win salvation through our Lord Jesus Christ, who died for us so that, alive or dead, we should still live united to him. So give encouragement to each other, and keep strengthening one another, as you do already.

This is the word of the Lord.

Responsorial Psalm
Ps 26:1. 4. 13-14. ℟ v.13

℟ **I am sure I shall see the Lord's goodness in the land of the living.**

1. The Lord is my light and my help;
   whom shall I fear?
   The Lord is the stronghold of my life;
   before whom shall I shrink? ℟

2. There is one thing I ask of the Lord,
   for this I long,
   to live in the house of the Lord,
   all the days of my life,
   to savour the sweetness of the Lord,
   to behold his temple. ℟

3. I am sure I shall see the Lord's goodness
   in the land of the living.
   Hope in him, hold firm and take heart.
   Hope in the Lord! ℟

Gospel Acclamation
Heb 4:12

Alleluia, alleluia!
The word of God is something alive and active;
it can judge secret emotions and thoughts.
Alleluia!

or
Lk 7:16

Alleluia, alleluia!
A great prophet has appeared among us;
God has visited his people.
Alleluia!

Twenty-second Week in Ordinary Time, Year I: Wednesday

GOSPEL

A reading from the holy Gospel according to Luke   4:31-37
I know who you are, the Holy One of God.

Jesus went down to Capernaum, a town in Galilee, and taught them on the sabbath. And his teaching made a deep impression on them because he spoke with authority.

In the synagogue there was a man who was possessed by the spirit of an unclean devil, and it shouted at the top of its voice, 'Ha! What do you want with us, Jesus of Nazareth? Have you come to destroy us? I know who you are: the Holy One of God.' But Jesus said sharply, 'Be quiet! Come out of him!' And the devil, throwing the man down in front of everyone, went out of him without hurting him at all. Astonishment seized them and they were all saying to one another, 'What teaching! He gives orders to unclean spirits with authority and power and they come out.' And reports of him went all through the surrounding countryside.

This is the Gospel of the Lord.

WEDNESDAY

FIRST READING

A reading from the letter of St Paul to the Colossians   1:1-8
The message of the truth has reached you and is spreading all over the world.

From Paul, appointed by God to be an apostle of Christ Jesus, and from our brother Timothy to the saints in Colossae, our faithful brothers in Christ: Grace and peace to you from God our Father.

We have never failed to remember you in our prayers and to give thanks for you to God, the Father of our Lord Jesus Christ, ever since we heard about your faith in Christ and the love that you show towards all the saints because of the hope which is stored up for you in heaven. It is only recently that you heard of this, when it was announced in the message of the truth. The Good News which has reached you is spreading all over the world and producing the same results as it has among you ever since the day when you heard about God's grace and understood what this really is. Epaphras, who taught you, is one of our closest fellow workers and a faithful deputy for us as Christ's servant, and it was he who told us all about your love in the Spirit.

This is the word of the Lord.

Responsorial Psalm   Ps 51:10-11. ℟ v.10
  ℟ **I trust in the goodness of God
     for ever and ever.**

1 I am like a growing olive tree
   in the house of God.
   I trust in the goodness of God
   for ever and ever.   ℟

2 I will thank you for evermore;
   for this is your doing.
   I will proclaim that your name is good,
   in the presence of your friends.   ℟

Gospel Acclamation   1 Peter 1:25
  Alleluia, alleluia!
  The word of the Lord remains for ever:
  What is this word?
  It is the Good News that has been brought to you.
  Alleluia!

or   Lk 4:18

  Alleluia, alleluia!
  The Lord has sent me to bring the good news to the poor,
  to proclaim liberty to captives.
  Alleluia!

GOSPEL

A reading from the holy Gospel according to Luke   4:38-44
I must proclaim the Good News to the other towns too, because that is what I was sent to do.

Leaving the synagogue Jesus went to Simon's house. Now Simon's mother-in-law was suffering from a high fever and they asked him to do something for her. Leaning over her he rebuked the fever and it left her. And she immediately got up and began to wait on them.

At sunset all those who had friends suffering from diseases of one kind or another brought them to him, and laying his hands on each he cured them. Devils too came out of many people, howling, 'You are the Son of God.' But he rebuked them and would not allow them to speak because they knew that he was the Christ.

When daylight came he left the house and made his way to a lonely place. The crowds went to look for him, and when they had caught up with him they wanted to prevent him leaving them, but he answered, 'I must proclaim the Good News of the kingdom of God to the other towns too, because that is what I was sent to do.' And he continued his preaching in the synagogues of Judaea.

This is the Gospel of the Lord.

THURSDAY

FIRST READING

A reading from the letter of St Paul to the Colossians 1:9-14

God has taken us out of the power of darkness and created a place for us in the kingdom of the Son that he loves.

Ever since the day we heard about you, we have never failed to pray for you, and what we ask God is that through perfect wisdom and spiritual understanding you should reach the fullest knowledge of his will. So you will be able to lead the kind of life which the Lord expects of you, a life acceptable to him in all its aspects; showing the results in all the good actions you do and increasing your knowledge of God. You will have in you the strength, based on his own glorious power, never to give in, but to bear anything joyfully, thanking the Father who has made it possible for you to join the saints and with them to inherit the light.

Because that is what he has done: he has taken us out of the power of darkness and created a place for us in the kingdom of the Son that he loves, and in him, we gain our freedom, the forgiveness of our sins.

This is the word of the Lord.

Responsorial Psalm
Ps 97:2-6. ℟ v.2

℟ **The Lord has made known his salvation.**

1. The Lord has made known his salvation;
   has shown his justice to the nations.
   He has remembered his truth and love
   for the house of Israel. ℟

2. All the ends of the earth have seen
   the salvation of our God.
   Shout to the Lord all the earth,
   ring out your joy. ℟

3. Sing psalms to the Lord with the harp
   with the sound of music.
   With trumpets and the sound of the horn
   acclaim the King, the Lord. ℟

Gospel Acclamation
cf. 2 Thess 2:14

Alleluia, alleluia!
Through the Good News God called us
to share the glory of our Lord Jesus Christ.
Alleluia!

or
Mt 4:19

Alleluia, alleluia!
Follow me, says the Lord,
and I will make you fishers of men.
Alleluia!

GOSPEL

A reading from the holy Gospel according to Luke   5:1-11
They left everything and followed him.

Jesus was standing one day by the Lake of Gennesaret, with the crowd pressing round him listening to the word of God, when he caught sight of two boats close to the bank. The fishermen had gone out of them and were washing their nets. He got into one of the boats – it was Simon's – and asked him to put out a little from the shore. Then he sat down and taught the crowds from the boat.

When he had finished speaking he said to Simon, 'Put out into deep water and pay out your nets for a catch.' 'Master,' Simon replied 'we worked hard all night long and caught nothing, but if you say so, I will pay out the nets.' And when they had done this they netted such a huge number of fish that their nets began to tear, so they signalled to their companions in the other boat to come and help them; when these came, they filled the two boats to sinking point.

When Simon Peter saw this he fell at the knees of Jesus saying, 'Leave me, Lord; I am a sinful man.' For he and all his companions were completely overcome by the catch they had made; so also were James and John, sons of Zebedee, who were Simon's partners. But Jesus said to Simon, 'Do not be afraid; from now on it is men you will catch.' Then, bringing their boats back to land, they left everything and followed him.

This is the Gospel of the Lord.

FRIDAY

FIRST READING

A reading from the letter of St Paul to the Colossians 1:15-20
All things were created through him and for him.

Christ Jesus is the image of the unseen God
and the first-born of all creation,
for in him were created
all things in heaven and on earth:
everything visible and everything invisible,
Thrones, Dominations, Sovereignties, Powers –
all things were created through him and for him.
Before anything was created, he existed,
and he holds all things in unity.
Now the Church is his body,
he is its head.
As he is the Beginning,
he was first to be born from the dead,
so that he should be first in every way;
because God wanted all perfection
to be found in him
and all things to be reconciled through him and for him,
everything in heaven and everything on earth,
when he made peace
by his death on the cross.

This is the word of the Lord.

Responsorial Psalm   Ps 99:2-5. ℟ v.2

   ℟ **Come before the Lord, singing for joy.**

1. Cry out with joy to the Lord, all the earth.
Serve the Lord with gladness.
Come before him, singing for joy. ℟

2. Know that he, the Lord, is God.
He made us, we belong to him,
we are his people, the sheep of his flock. ℟

3. Go within his gates, giving thanks.
Enter his courts with songs of praise.
Give thanks to him and bless his name. ℟

4. Indeed, how good is the Lord,
eternal his merciful love.
He is faithful from age to age. ℟

Gospel Acclamation   Ps 18:9

Alleluia, alleluia!
Your words gladden the heart, O Lord,
they give light to the eyes.
Alleluia!

or   Jn 8:12

Alleluia, alleluia!
I am the light of the world, says the Lord,
anyone who follows me
will have the light of life.
Alleluia!

GOSPEL

A reading from the holy Gospel according to Luke   5:33-39
When the bridegroom is taken from them, then they will fast.

The Pharisees and the scribes said to Jesus, 'John's disciples are always fasting and saying prayers, and the disciples of the Pharisees too, but yours go on eating and drinking.' Jesus replied, 'Surely you cannot make the bridegroom's attendants fast while the bridegroom is still with them? But the time will come, the time for the bridegroom to be taken away from them; that will be the time when they will fast.'

He also told them this parable. 'No one tears a piece from a new cloak to put it on an old cloak; if he does, not only will he have torn the new one, but the piece taken from the new will not match the old.

'And nobody puts new wine into old skins; if he does, the new wine will burst the skins and then run out, and the skins will be lost. No; new wine must be put into fresh skins. And nobody who has been drinking old wine wants new. "The old is good" he says.'

This is the Gospel of the Lord.

SATURDAY

FIRST READING

A reading from the letter of St Paul to the Colossians   1:21-23
God has reconciled you so that you may appear holy and pure.

Not long ago, you were foreigners and enemies, in the way that you used to think and the evil things that you did; but now God has reconciled you, by Christ's death in his mortal body. Now you are able to appear before him holy, pure and blameless – as long as you persevere and stand firm on the solid base of the faith, never letting yourselves drift away from the hope promised by the Good News, which you have heard, which has been preached to the whole human race, and of which I, Paul, have become the servant.

This is the word of the Lord.

Responsorial Psalm   Ps 53:3-4. 6. 8. ℟ v.6
    ℟ **I have God for my help.**

1 O God, save me by your name;
   by your power, uphold my cause.
   O God, hear my prayer;
   listen to the words of my mouth.   ℟

2 But I have God for my help.
   The Lord upholds my life.
   I will sacrifice to you with willing heart
   and praise your name for it is good.   ℟

Gospel Acclamation   cf. Ps 26:11
    Alleluia, alleluia!
    Instruct me, Lord, in your way;
    on an even path lead me.
    Alleluia!

or   Jn 14:6

> Alleluia, alleluia!
> I am the Way, the Truth and the Life, says the Lord;
> no one can come to the Father except through me.
> Alleluia!

GOSPEL

A reading from the holy Gospel according to Luke   6:1-5
Why are you doing something that is forbidden on the sabbath day?

One sabbath Jesus happened to be taking a walk through the cornfields, and his disciples were picking ears of corn, rubbing them in their hands and eating them. Some of the Pharisees said, 'Why are you doing something that is forbidden on the sabbath day?' Jesus answered them, 'So you have not read what David did when he and his followers were hungry – how he went into the House of God, took the loaves of offering and ate them and gave them to his followers, loaves which only the priests are allowed to eat?' And he said to them, 'The Son of Man is master of the sabbath.'

This is the Gospel of the Lord.

TWENTY-THIRD WEEK IN ORDINARY TIME
Year I

MONDAY

FIRST READING

A reading from the letter of St Paul to the Colossians   1:24 – 2:3
I became the servant of the Church to deliver a mystery hidden for centuries.

It makes me happy to suffer for you, as I am suffering now, and in my own body to do what I can to make up all that has still to be undergone by Christ for the sake of his body, the Church. I became the servant of the Church when God made me responsible for delivering God's message to you, the message which was a mystery hidden for generations and centuries and has now been revealed to his saints. It was God's purpose to reveal it to them and to show all the rich glory of this mystery to pagans. The

Twenty-third Week in Ordinary Time, Year I: Monday 717

mystery is Christ among you, your hope of glory: this is the Christ we proclaim, this is the wisdom in which we thoroughly train everyone and instruct everyone, to make them all perfect in Christ. It is for this I struggle wearily on, helped only by his power driving me irresistibly.

Yes, I want you to know that I do have to struggle hard for you, and for those in Laodicea, and for so many others who have never seen me face to face. It is all to bind you together in love and to stir your minds, so that your understanding may come to full development, until you really know God's secret in which all the jewels of wisdom and knowledge are hidden.

This is the word of the Lord.

Responsorial Psalm   Ps 61:6-7.9. R̷ v.8
 R̷ **In God is my safety and glory.**

1 In God alone be at rest, my soul;
 for my hope comes from him.
 He alone is my rock, my stronghold,
 my fortress; I stand firm.   R̷

2 Take refuge in God all you people.
 Trust him at all times.
 Pour out your hearts before him
 for God is our refuge.   R̷

Gospel Acclamation   Ps 118:105
 Alleluia, alleluia!
 Your word is a lamp for my steps
 and a light for my path.
 Alleluia!
or   Jn 10:27
 Alleluia, alleluia!
 The sheep that belong to me listen to my voice,
 says the Lord,
 I know them and they follow me.
 Alleluia!

GOSPEL

A reading from the holy Gospel according to Luke   6:6-11
They were watching Jesus to see if he would cure a man on the sabbath.

On the sabbath Jesus went into the synagogue and began to teach, and a man was there whose right hand was withered. The scribes and the Pharisees were watching him to see if he would cure a man on the sabbath, hoping to find something to use against him. But he knew their thoughts; and he said to the man with the withered hand, 'Stand up! Come out into the middle.' And he came out and stood there. Then Jesus said to them, 'I put it to you: is it against the law on the sabbath to do good, or to do evil; to save life, or to destroy it?' Then he looked around at them all and said to the man, 'Stretch out your hand.' He did so, and his hand was better. But they were furious, and began to discuss the best way of dealing with Jesus.

This is the Gospel of the Lord.

TUESDAY

FIRST READING

A reading from the letter of St Paul to the Colossians 2:6-15
The Lord has brought you to life with him, he has forgiven you all your sins.

You must live your whole life according to the Christ you have received – Jesus the Lord; you must be rooted in him and built on him and held firm by the faith you have been taught, and full of thanksgiving.

Make sure that no one traps you and deprives you of your freedom by some secondhand, empty, rational philosophy based on the principles of this world instead of on Christ.

In his body lives the fullness of divinity, and in him you too find your own fulfilment, in the one who is the head of every Sovereignty and Power.

In him you have been circumcised, with circumcision not performed by human hand, but by the complete stripping of your body of flesh. This is circumcision according to Christ. You have been buried with him, when you were baptised; and by baptism, too, you have been raised up with him through your belief in the power of God who raised him from the dead. You were dead, because you were sinners and had not been circumcised: he has brought you to life with him, he has forgiven us all our sins.

He has overridden the Law, and cancelled every record of the debt that we had to pay; he has done away with it by nailing it to the cross; and so he got rid of the Sovereignties and the Powers,

Twenty-third Week in Ordinary Time, Year I: Tuesday

and paraded them in public, behind him in his triumphal procession.

This is the word of the Lord.

Responsorial Psalm   Ps 144:1-2. 8-11. ℟ v.9

℟ **How good is the Lord to all.**

1. I will give you glory, O God my King,
   I will bless your name for ever.
   I will bless you day after day
   and praise your name for ever. ℟

2. The Lord is kind and full of compassion,
   slow to anger, abounding in love.
   How good is the Lord to all,
   compassionate to all his creatures. ℟

3. All your creatures shall thank you, O Lord,
   and your friends shall repeat their blessing.
   They shall speak of the glory of your reign
   and declare your might, O God. ℟

Gospel Acclamation   Phil 2:15-16
Alleluia, alleluia!
You will shine in the world like bright stars
because you are offering it the word of life.
Alleluia!

or   cf. Jn 15:16

Alleluia, alleluia!
I chose you from the world
to go out and to bear fruit,
fruit that will last.
Alleluia!

GOSPEL

A reading from the holy Gospel according to Luke   6:12-19
Jesus spent the whole night in prayer and he picked twelve whom he called 'apostles'.

Jesus went out into the hills to pray; and he spent the whole night in prayer to God. When day came he summoned his disciples and picked out twelve of them; he called them 'apostles': Simon whom he called Peter, and his brother Andrew; James, John, Philip, Bartholomew, Matthew, Thomas, James son of Alphaeus,

Simon called the Zealot, Judas son of James, and Judas Iscariot who became a traitor.

He then came down with them and stopped at a piece of level ground where there was a large gathering of his disciples with a great crowd of people from all parts of Judaea and from Jerusalem and from the coastal region of Tyre and Sidon who had come to hear him and to be cured of their diseases. People tormented by unclean spirits were also cured, and everyone in the crowd was trying to touch him because power came out of him that cured them all.

This is the Gospel of the Lord.

WEDNESDAY

FIRST READING

A reading from the letter of St Paul to the Colossians   3:1-11

You have died with Christ. That is why you must kill everything in you that belongs only to earthly life.

Since you have been brought back to true life with Christ, you must look for the things that are in heaven, where Christ is, sitting at God's right hand. Let your thoughts be on heavenly things, not on the things that are on the earth, because you have died, and now the life you have is hidden with Christ in God. But when Christ is revealed – and he is your life – you too will be revealed in all your glory with him.

That is why you must kill everything in you that belongs only to earthly life: fornication, impurity, guilty passion, evil desires and especially greed, which is the same thing as worshipping a false god; all this is the sort of behaviour that makes God angry. And it is the way in which you used to live when you were surrounded by people doing the same thing, but now you, of all people, must give all these things up: getting angry, being bad-tempered, spitefulness, abusive language and dirty talk; and never tell each other lies. You have stripped off your old behaviour with your old self, and you have put on a new self which will progress towards true knowledge the more it is renewed in the image of its creator; and in that image there is no room for distinction between Greek and Jew, between the circumcised or the uncircumcised, or between barbarian and Scythian, slave and free man. There is only Christ: he is every-

Twenty-second Week in Ordinary Time, Year I: Wednesday 721

thing and he is in everything.

This is the word of the Lord.

Responsorial Psalm   Ps 144:2-3. 10-13. ℟ v.9

℟ **How good is the Lord to all.**

1. I will bless you day after day
   and praise your name for ever.
   The Lord is great, highly to be praised,
   his greatness cannot be measured. ℟

2. All your creatures shall thank you, O Lord,
   and your friends shall repeat their blessing.
   They shall speak of the glory of your reign
   and declare your might, O God. ℟

3. To make known to men your mighty deeds
   and the glorious splendour of your reign.
   Yours is an everlasting kingdom;
   your rule lasts from age to age. ℟

Gospel Acclamation   1 Jn 2:5

Alleluia, alleluia!
When anyone obeys what Christ has said,
God's love comes to perfection in him.
Alleluia!

or   Lk 6:23

Alleluia, alleluia!
Rejoice and be glad:
your reward will be great in heaven.
Alleluia!

GOSPEL

A reading from the holy Gospel according to Luke   6:20-26
How happy are you who are poor. But alas for you who are rich.

Fixing his eyes on his disciples Jesus said:

'How happy are you who are poor: yours is the kingdom of God.
Happy you who are hungry now: you shall be satisfied.
Happy you who weep now: you shall laugh.

'Happy are you when people hate you, drive you out, abuse you, denounce your name as criminal, on account of the Son of Man. Rejoice when that day comes and dance for joy, for then your reward will be great in heaven. This was the way their ancestors treated the prophets.

'But alas for you who are rich: you are having your consolation now.
Alas for you who have your fill now: you shall go hungry.
Alas for you who laugh now: you shall mourn and weep.

'Alas for you when the world speaks well of you! This was the way their ancestors treated the false prophets.'

This is the Gospel of the Lord.

THURSDAY

FIRST READING

A reading from the letter of St Paul to the Colossians 3:12-17
Put on love.

You are God's chosen race, his saints; he loves you, and you should be clothed in sincere compassion, in kindness and humility, gentleness and patience. Bear with one another; forgive each other as soon as a quarrel begins. The Lord has forgiven you; now you must do the same. Over all these clothes, to keep them together and complete them, put on love. And may the peace of Christ reign in your hearts, because it is for this that you were called together as parts of one body. Always be thankful.

Let the message of Christ, in all its richness, find a home with you. Teach each other, and advise each other, in all wisdom. With gratitude in your hearts sing psalms and hymns and inspired songs to God; and never say or do anything except in the name of the Lord Jesus, giving thanks to God the Father through him.

This is the word of the Lord.

Responsorial Psalm

Ps 150:1-6. ℟ v.6

℟ **Let everything that breathes
give praise to the Lord.**

or

℟ **Alleluia!**

1. Praise God in his holy place,
   praise him in his mighty heavens.
   Praise him for his powerful deeds,
   praise his surpassing greatness. ℟

2. O praise him with sound of trumpet,
   praise him with lute and harp.
   Praise him with timbrel and dance,
   praise him with strings and pipes. ℟

3. O praise him with resounding cymbals,
   praise him with clashing of cymbals.
   Let everything that lives and that breathes
   give praise to the Lord. ℟

Gospel Acclamation

James 1:21

Alleluia, alleluia!
Accept and submit to the word
which has been planted in you
and can save your souls.
Alleluia!

or

1 Jn 4:12

Alleluia, alleluia!
As long as we love one another
God will live in us,
and his love will be complete in us.
Alleluia!

GOSPEL

A reading from the holy Gospel according to Luke 6:27-38

Be compassionate as your Father is compassionate.

Jesus said to his disciples: 'I say this to you who are listening: Love your enemies, do good to those who hate you, bless those who curse you, pray for those who treat you badly. To the man who slaps you on one cheek, present the other cheek too; to the man who takes your cloak from you, do not refuse your tunic. Give to everyone who asks you, and do not ask for your property back from the man who robs you. Treat others as you would like them to treat you. If you love those who love you, what thanks can you expect? Even sinners love those who love them. And if you do good to those who do good to you, what thanks can you expect? For even sinners do that much. And if you lend to those from whom you hope to receive, what thanks can you expect? Even sinners lend to get back the same amount. Instead, love your enemies and do good, and lend without any hope of return. You will have a great reward, and you will be sons of the Most High, for he himself is kind to the ungrateful and the wicked.

'Be compassionate as your Father is compassionate. Do not judge, and you will not be judged yourselves; do not condemn, and you will not be condemned yourselves; grant pardon, and you will be pardoned. Give, and there will be gifts for you: a full measure, pressed down, shaken together, and running over, will be poured into your lap; because the amount you measure out is the amount you will be given back.'

This is the Gospel of the Lord.

FRIDAY

FIRST READING

A reading from the first letter of St Paul to Timothy 1:1-2. 12-14
I used to be a blasphemer, but the mercy of God was shown me.

From Paul, apostle of Christ Jesus appointed by the command of God our saviour and of Christ Jesus our hope, to Timothy, true child of mine in the faith; wishing you grace, mercy and peace from God the Father and from Christ Jesus our Lord.

I thank Christ Jesus our Lord, who has given me strength, and who judged me faithful enough to call me into his service even though I used to be a blasphemer and did all I could to injure and discredit the faith. Mercy, however, was shown me, because until I became a believer I had been acting in ignorance; and the grace of our Lord filled me with faith and with the love that is in Christ Jesus.

This is the word of the Lord.

Twenty-third Week in Ordinary Time, Year I: Friday

Responsorial Psalm   Ps 15:1-2. 5. 7-8. 11. ℟ cf. v.5
   ℟ **You are my inheritance, O Lord.**

1. Preserve me, God, I take refuge in you.
   I say to the Lord: 'You are my God.
   My happiness lies in you alone.'
   O Lord, it is you who are my portion and cup;
   it is you yourself who are my prize.   ℟

2. I will bless the Lord who gives me counsel,
   who even at night directs my heart.
   I keep the Lord ever in my sight:
   since he is at my right hand, I shall stand firm.   ℟

3. You will show me the path of life,
   the fullness of joy in your presence,
   at your right hand happiness for ever.   ℟

Gospel Acclamation   Ps 147:12. 15
   Alleluia, alleluia!
   O praise the Lord, Jerusalem!
   He sends out his word to the earth.
   Alleluia!

or   cf. Jn 17:17
   Alleluia, alleluia!
   Your word is truth, O Lord,
   consecrate us in the truth.
   Alleluia!

GOSPEL

A reading from the holy Gospel according to Luke   6:39-42
Can one blind man guide another?

Jesus told a parable to the disciples, 'Can one blind man guide another? Surely both will fall into a pit? The disciple is not superior to his teacher; the fully trained disciple will always be like his teacher. Why do you observe the splinter in your brother's eye and never notice the plank in your own? How can you say to your brother, "Brother, let me take out the splinter that is in your eye", when you cannot see the plank in your own? Hypocrite! Take the plank out of your own eye first, and then you will see clearly enough to take out the splinter that is in your brother's eye.'

   This is the Gospel of the Lord.

SATURDAY

FIRST READING

A reading from the first letter of St Paul to Timothy 1:15-17

Christ Jesus came into the world to save sinners.

Here is a saying that you can rely on and nobody should doubt: that Christ Jesus came into the world to save sinners. I myself am the greatest of them; and if mercy has been shown to me, it is because Jesus Christ meant to make me the greatest evidence of his inexhaustible patience for all the other people who would later have to trust in him to come to eternal life. To the eternal King, the undying, invisible and only God, be honour and glory for ever and ever. Amen.

This is the word of the Lord.

Responsorial Psalm   Ps 112:1-7. R̷ v.2

R̷ **May the name of the Lord be blessed for evermore!**

or

R̷ **Alleluia!**

1 Praise, O servants of the Lord,
 praise the name of the Lord!
 May the name of the Lord be blessed
 both now and for evermore! R̷

2 From the rising of the sun to its setting
 praised be the name of the Lord!
 High above all nations is the Lord,
 above the heavens his glory. R̷

3 Who is like the Lord, our God,
 who has risen on high to his throne
 yet stoops from the heights to look down,
 to look down upon heaven and earth?
 From the dust he lifts up the lowly,
 from the dungheap he raises the poor. R̷

Gospel Acclamation   Jn 14:6
 Alleluia, alleluia!
 I am the Way, the Truth and the Life, says the Lord;
 no one can come to the Father except through me.
 Alleluia!

or Jn 14:23

Alleluia, alleluia!
If anyone loves me he will keep my word,
and my Father will love him,
and we shall come to him.
Alleluia!

GOSPEL

A reading from the holy Gospel according to Luke 6:43-49
Why do you call me, 'Lord, Lord' and not do what I say?

Jesus said to his disciples: 'There is no sound tree that produces rotten fruit, nor again a rotten tree that produces sound fruit. For every tree can be told by its own fruit: people do not pick figs from thorns, nor gather grapes from brambles. A good man draws what is good from the store of goodness in his heart; a bad man draws what is bad from the store of badness. For a man's words flow out of what fills his heart.

'Why do you call me, "Lord, Lord" and not do what I say?'

'Everyone who comes to me and listens to my words and acts on them – I will show you what he is like. He is like the man who when he built his house dug, and dug deep, and laid the foundations on rock; when the river was in flood it bore down on that house but could not shake it, it was so well built. But the one who listens and does nothing is like the man who built his house on soil, with no foundations: as soon as the river bore down on it, it collapsed; and what a ruin that house became!'

This is the Gospel of the Lord.

TWENTY-FOURTH WEEK IN ORDINARY TIME
Year I

MONDAY

FIRST READING

A reading from the first letter of St Paul to Timothy 2:1-8
There should be prayers offered for everyone to God, who wants everyone to be saved.

My advice is that, first of all, there should be prayers offered for everyone – petitions, intercessions and thanksgiving – and especially for kings and others in authority, so that we may be able to live religious and reverent lives in peace and quiet. To do this is right, and will please God our saviour: he wants everyone to be saved and reach full knowledge of the truth. For there is only one God, and there is only one mediator between God and mankind, himself a man, Christ Jesus, who sacrificed himself as a ransom for them all. He is the evidence of this, sent at the appointed time, and I have been named a herald and apostle of it and – I am telling the truth and no lie – a teacher of the faith and the truth to the pagans.

In every place, then, I want the men to lift their hands up reverently in prayer, with no anger or argument.

This is the word of the Lord.

Responsorial Psalm   Ps 27:2. 7-9. R̷ v.6

R̷ **Blessed be the Lord,
for he has heard my cry.**

1   Hear the voice of my pleading
    as I call for help,
    as I lift up my hands in prayer
    to your holy place. R̷

2   The Lord is my strength and my shield;
    in him my heart trusts.
    I was helped, my heart rejoices
    and I praise him with my song. R̷

3   The Lord is the strength of his people,
    the stronghold where his anointed find salvation.
    Save your people; bless Israel your heritage.
    Be their shepherd and carry them for ever. R̷

Gospel Acclamation   Ps 118:27

Alleluia, alleluia!
Make me grasp the way of your precepts,
and I will muse on your wonders.
Alleluia!

or   Jn 3:16

Alleluia, alleluia!
God loved the world so much that he gave his only Son;
everyone who believes in him has eternal life.
Alleluia!

GOSPEL

A reading from the holy Gospel according to Luke   7:1-10
Not even in Israel have I found faith like this.

When Jesus had come to the end of all he wanted the people to hear, he went into Capernaum. A centurion there had a servant, a favourite of his, who was sick and near death. Having heard about Jesus he sent some Jewish elders to him to ask him to come and heal his servant. When they came to Jesus they pleaded earnestly with him. 'He deserves this of you' they said 'because he is friendly towards our people; in fact, he is the one who built the synagogue.' So Jesus went with them, and was not very far from the house when the centurion sent word to him by some friends: 'Sir,' he said 'do not put yourself to trouble; because I am not worthy to have you under my roof; and for this same reason I did not presume to come to you myself; but give the word and let my servant be cured. For I am under authority myself, and have soldiers under me; and I say to one man: Go, and he goes; to another: Come here, and he comes; to my servant: Do this, and he does it.' When Jesus heard these words he was astonished at him and, turning round, said to the crowd following him, 'I tell you, not even in Israel have I found faith like this.' And when the messengers got back to the house they found the servant in perfect health.

This is the Gospel of the Lord.

TUESDAY

FIRST READING

A reading from the first letter of St Paul to Timothy   3:1-13
The president must have an impeccable character. In the same way, deacons must be conscientious believers in the mystery of the faith.

Here is a saying that you can rely on: To want to be a presiding elder is to want to do a noble work. That is why the president must have an impeccable character. He must not have been married more than once, and he must be temperate, discreet and courteous, hospitable and a good teacher; not a heavy drinker, not hot-tempered, but kind and peaceable. He must not be a lover of money. He must be a man who manages his own family well and brings his children up to obey him and be well-behaved:

how can any man who does not understand how to manage his own family have responsibility for the church of God? He should not be a new convert, in case pride might turn his head and then he might be condemned as the devil was condemned. It is also necessary that people outside the Church should speak well of him, so that he never gets a bad reputation and falls into the devil's trap.

In the same way, deacons must be respectable men whose word can be trusted, moderate in the amount of wine they drink and with no squalid greed for money. They must be conscientious believers in the mystery of the faith. They are to be examined first, and only admitted to serve as deacons if there is nothing against them. In the same way, the women must be respectable, not gossips but sober and quite reliable. Deacons must not have been married more than once, and must be men who manage their children and families well. Those of them who carry out their duties well as deacons will earn a high standing for themselves and be rewarded with great assurance in their work for the faith in Christ Jesus.

This is the word of the Lord.

Responsorial Psalm Ps 100:1-3. 5. 6. ℟ v.2
℟ **I will walk with blameless heart.**

1 My song is of mercy and justice;
   I sing to you, O Lord.
   I will walk in the way of perfection.
   O when, Lord, will you come?   ℟

2 I will walk with blameless heart
   within my house;
   I will not set before my eyes
   whatever is base.   ℟

3 The man who slanders his neighbour in secret
   I will bring to silence.
   The man of proud looks and haughty heart
   I will never endure.   ℟

4 I look to the faithful in the land
   that they may dwell with me.
   He who walks in the way of perfection
   shall be my friend.   ℟

Gospel Acclamation cf. 2 Tim 1:10
> Alleluia, alleluia!
> Our Saviour Christ Jesus abolished death,
> and he has proclaimed life through the Good News.
> Alleluia!

or Lk 7:16

> Alleluia, alleluia!
> A great prophet has appeared among us;
> God has visited his people.
> Alleluia!

GOSPEL

A reading from the holy Gospel according to Luke 7:11-17
Young man, I tell you to get up.

Jesus went to a town called Nain, accompanied by his disciples and a great number of people. When he was near the gate of the town it happened that a dead man was being carried out for burial, the only son of his mother, and she was a widow. And a considerable number of the townspeople were with her. When the Lord saw her he felt sorry for her. 'Do not cry' he said. Then he went up and put his hand on the bier and the bearers stood still, and he said, 'Young man, I tell you to get up.' And the dead man sat up and began to talk, and Jesus gave him to his mother. Everyone was filled with awe and praised God saying, 'A great prophet has appeared among us; God has visited his people.' And this opinion of him spread throughout Judaea and all over the countryside.

This is the Gospel of the Lord.

WEDNESDAY

FIRST READING

A reading from the first letter of St Paul to Timothy 3:14-16
The mystery of our religion is very deep.

At the moment of writing to you, I am hoping that I may be with you soon; but in case I should be delayed, I wanted you to know how people ought to behave in God's family - that is, in the Church of the living God, which upholds the truth and keeps it safe. Without any doubt, the mystery of our religion is very deep indeed:

> He was made visible in the flesh,
> attested by the Spirit,
> seen by angels,
> proclaimed to the pagans,
> believed in by the world,
> taken up in glory.

This is the word of the Lord.

Responsorial Psalm   Ps 110:1-6. R̥ v.2

R̥ **Great are the works of the Lord.**

or

R̥ **Alleluia!**

1. I will thank the Lord with all my heart
   in the meeting of the just and their assembly.
   Great are the works of the Lord;
   to be pondered by all who love them. R̥

2. Majestic and glorious his work,
   his justice stands firm for ever.
   He makes us remember his wonders.
   The Lord is compassion and love. R̥

3. He gives food to those who fear him;
   keeps his covenant ever in mind.
   He has shown his might to his people
   by giving them the lands of the nations. R̥

Gospel Acclamation   cf. 1 Thess 2:13

Alleluia, alleluia!
Accept God's message for what it really is:
God's message, and not some human thinking.
Alleluia!

or   cf. Jn 6:63. 68

Alleluia, alleluia!
Your words are spirit, Lord,
and they are life:
you have the message of eternal life.
Alleluia!

GOSPEL

A reading from the holy Gospel according to Luke 7:31-35

We played the pipes for you, and you wouldn't dance; we sang dirges, and you wouldn't cry.

Jesus said to the people: 'What description can I find for the men of this generation? What are they like? They are like children shouting to one another while they sit in the market place:

> "We played the pipes for you,
> and you wouldn't dance;
> we sang dirges,
> and you wouldn't cry."

'For John the Baptist comes, not eating bread, not drinking wine, and you say, "He is possessed." The Son of Man comes, eating and drinking, and you say, "Look, a glutton and a drunkard, a friend of tax collectors and sinners." Yet Wisdom has been proved right by all her children.'

This is the Gospel of the Lord.

THURSDAY

FIRST READING

A reading from the first letter of St Paul to Timothy 4:12-16

Always take great care about what you do and what you teach; in this way you will save both yourself and those who listen to you.

Do not let people disregard you because you are young, but be an example to all the believers in the way you speak and behave, and in your love, your faith and your purity. Make use of the time until I arrive by reading to the people, preaching and teaching. You have in you a spiritual gift which was given to you when the prophets spoke and the body of elders laid their hands on you; do not let it lie unused. Think hard about all this, and put it into practice, and everyone will be able to see how you are advancing. Take great care about what you do and what you teach; always do this, and in this way you will save both yourself and those who listen to you.

This is the word of the Lord.

Responsorial Psalm   Ps 110:7-10. ℟ v.2

   ℟ **Great are the works of the Lord.**

or

   ℟ **Alleluia!**

1. His works are justice and truth:
   his precepts are all of them sure,
   standing firm for ever and ever:
   they are made in uprightness and truth. ℟

2. He has sent deliverance to his people
   and established his covenant for ever.
   Holy his name, to be feared. ℟

3. To fear the Lord is the beginning of wisdom;
   all who do so prove themselves wise.
   His praise shall last for ever! ℟

Gospel Acclamation   2 Cor 5:19
Alleluia, alleluia!
God in Christ was reconciling the world to himself,
and he has entrusted to us the news that they are reconciled.
Alleluia!

or   Mt 11:28

Alleluia, alleluia!
Come to me, all you who labour and are overburdened,
and I will give you rest, says the Lord.
Alleluia!

GOSPEL

A reading from the holy Gospel according to Luke   7:36-50
Her many sins must have been forgiven her, or she would not have shown such great love.

One of the Pharisees invited Jesus to a meal. When he arrived at the Pharisee's house and took his place at table, a woman came in, who had a bad name in the town. She had heard he was dining with the Pharisee and had brought with her an alabaster jar of ointment. She waited behind him at his feet, weeping, and her tears fell on his feet, and she wiped them away with her hair; then she covered his feet with kisses and anointed them with the ointment.

When the Pharisee who had invited him saw this, he said to himself, 'If this man were a prophet, he would know who this woman is that is touching him and what a bad name she has.' Then Jesus took him up and said, 'Simon, I have something to say to you.' 'Speak, Master' was the reply. 'There was once a creditor who had two men in his debt; one owed him five hundred denarii, the other fifty. They were unable to pay, so he pardoned them both. Which of them will love him more?' 'The one who was pardoned more, I suppose' answered Simon. Jesus said, 'You are right.'

Then he turned to the woman. 'Simon,' he said 'you see this woman? I came into your house, and you poured no water over my feet, but she has poured out her tears over my feet and wiped them away with her hair. You gave me no kiss, but she has been covering my feet with kisses ever since I came in. You did not anoint my head with oil, but she has anointed my feet with ointment. For this reason I tell you that her sins, her many sins, must have been forgiven her, or she would not have shown such great love. It is the man who is forgiven little who shows little love.' Then he said to her, 'Your sins are forgiven.' Those who were with him at table began to say to themselves, 'Who is this man, that he even forgives sins?' But he said to the woman, 'Your faith has saved you; go in peace.'

This is the Gospel of the Lord.

FRIDAY

FIRST READING

A reading from the first letter of St Paul to Timothy 6:2-12
As a man dedicated to God you must aim to be saintly.

This is what you are to teach the brothers to believe and persuade them to do. Anyone who teaches anything different, and does not keep to the sound teaching which is that of our Lord Jesus Christ, the doctrine which is in accordance with true religion, is simply ignorant and must be full of self-conceit – with a craze for questioning everything and arguing about words. All that can come of this is jealousy, contention, abuse and wicked mistrust of one another; and unending disputes by people who are neither rational nor informed and imagine that religion is a way of making a profit. Religion, of course, does bring large profits, but only to those who are content with what they have. We brought nothing into the world, and we can take nothing out of it; but as long as we have food and clothing, let us be content with that. People who long to be rich are a prey to temptation; they get trapped into all sorts of foolish and dangerous ambitions which eventually plunge them into ruin and destruction. 'The love of money is the root of all evils' and there are some who, pursuing it, have wandered away from the faith, and so given their souls any number of fatal wounds.

But, as a man dedicated to God, you must avoid all that. You must aim to be saintly and religious, filled with faith and love, patient and gentle. Fight the good fight of the faith and win for yourself the eternal life to which you were called when you made your profession and spoke up for the truth in front of many witnesses.

This is the word of the Lord.

Responsorial Psalm Ps 48:6-10. 17-20. ℟ Mt 5:3

℟ **How happy are the poor in spirit;**
theirs is the kingdom of heaven.

1 Why should I fear in evil days
the malice of the foes who surround me,
men who trust in their wealth,
and boast of the vastness of their riches? ℟

2 For no man can buy his own ransom,
or pay a price to God for his life.
The ransom of his soul is beyond him.
He cannot buy life without end,
nor avoid coming to the grave. ℟

3 Then do not fear when a man grows rich,
when the glory of his house increases.
He takes nothing with him when he dies,
his glory does not follow him below. ℟

4 Though he flattered himself while he lived:
'Men will praise me for doing well for myself,'
yet he will go to join his fathers,
who will never see the light any more. ℟

Gospel Acclamation cf. Ps 94:8

Alleluia, alleluia!
Harden not your hearts today,

but listen to the voice of the Lord.
Alleluia!

or   cf. Mt 11:25

Alleluia, alleluia!
Blessed are you, Father,
Lord of heaven and earth,
for revealing the mysteries of the kingdom
to mere children.
Alleluia!

GOSPEL

A reading from the holy Gospel according to Luke   8:1-3
With Jesus went several women who provided for him out of their own resources.

Jesus made his way through towns and villages preaching, and proclaiming the Good News of the kingdom of God. With him went the Twelve, as well as certain women who had been cured of evil spirits and ailments: Mary surnamed the Magdalene, from whom seven demons had gone out, Joanna the wife of Herod's steward Chuza, Susanna, and several others who provided for them out of their own resources.

This is the Gospel of the Lord.

SATURDAY

FIRST READING

A reading from the first letter of St Paul to Timothy   6:13-16
Do all that you have been told, with no faults or failures, until the Appearing of the Lord.

Before God the source of all life and before Jesus Christ, who spoke up as a witness for the truth in front of Pontius Pilate, I put to you the duty of doing all that you have been told, with no faults or failures, until the Appearing of our Lord Jesus Christ,

who at the due time will be revealed
by God, the blessed and only Ruler of all,
the King of kings and the Lord of lords,
who alone is immortal,
whose home is in inaccessible light,

whom no man has seen and no man is able to see:
to him be honour and everlasting power. Amen.

This is the word of the Lord.

Responsional Psalm Ps 99. ℟ v.2

℟ **Come before the Lord, singing for joy.**

1. Cry out with joy to the Lord, all the earth.
   Serve the Lord with gladness.
   Come before him, singing for joy. ℟

2. Know that he, the Lord, is God.
   He made us, we belong to him,
   we are his people, the sheep of his flock. ℟

3. Go within his gates, giving thanks.
   Enter his courts with songs of praise.
   Give thanks to him and bless his name. ℟

4. Indeed, how good is the Lord,
   eternal his merciful love.
   He is faithful from age to age. ℟

Gospel Acclamation Ps 118:18

Alleluia, alleluia!
Open my eyes, O Lord, that I may consider
the wonders of your law.
Alleluia!

or cf. Lk 8:15

Alleluia, alleluia!
Blessed are those who,
with a noble and generous heart,
take the word of God to themselves
and yield a harvest through their perseverance.
Alleluia!

GOSPEL

A reading from the holy Gospel according to Luke 8:4-15

The part in the rich soil is people who take the word to themselves and yield a harvest through their perseverance.

With a large crowd gathering and people from every town finding their way to him, Jesus used this parable:
  'A sower went out to sow his seed. As he sowed, some fell on

the edge of the path and was trampled on; and the birds of the air ate it up. Some seed fell on rock, and when it came up it withered away, having no moisture. Some seed fell amongst thorns and the thorns grew with it and choked it. And some seed fell into rich soil and grew and produced its crop a hundredfold.' Saying this he cried, 'Listen, anyone who has ears to hear!'

His disciples asked him what this parable might mean, and he said, 'The mysteries of the kingdom of God are revealed to you; for the rest there are only parables, so that

they may see but not perceive,
listen but not understand.

'This, then, is what the parable means: the seed is the word of God. Those on the edge of the path are people who have heard it, and then the devil comes and carries away the word from their hearts in case they should believe and be saved. Those on the rock are people who, when they first hear it, welcome the word with joy. But these have no root; they believe for a while, and in time of trial they give up. As for the part that fell into thorns, this is people who have heard, but as they go on their way they are choked by the worries and riches and pleasures of life and do not reach maturity. As for the part in the rich soil, this is people with a noble and generous heart who have heard the word and take it to themselves and yield a harvest through their perseverance.'

This is the Gospel of the Lord.

TWENTY-FIFTH WEEK IN ORDINARY TIME
Year I

MONDAY

FIRST READING

A reading from the book of Ezra   1:1-6
Whoever is of the Lord's people, let him go up to Jerusalem to build the Temple of the Lord.

In the first year of Cyrus king of Persia, to fulfil the word of the Lord that was spoken through Jeremiah, the Lord roused the spirit of Cyrus king of Persia to issue a proclamation and to have it publicly displayed throughout his kingdom: 'Thus speaks Cyrus king of Persia, "The Lord, the God of heaven, has given me all the kingdoms of the earth; he has ordered me to build him a Temple in Jerusalem, in Judah. Whoever there is among you of all his people, may his God be with him! Let him go up to Jerusalem in Judah to build the Temple of the Lord, the God of Israel – he is the God who is in Jerusalem. And let each survivor, wherever he lives, be helped by the people of that place with silver and gold, with goods and cattle, as well as voluntary offerings for the Temple of God which is in Jerusalem."'

Then the heads of families of Judah and of Benjamin, the priests and the Levites, in fact all whose spirit had been roused by God, prepared to go and rebuild the Temple of the Lord in Jerusalem; and all their neighbours gave them every assistance with silver, gold, goods, cattle, quantities of costly gifts and with voluntary offerings of every kind.

This is the word of the Lord.

Responsorial Psalm

Ps 125. ℟ v.3

℟ **What marvels the Lord worked for us.**

1 When the Lord delivered Zion from bondage,
 it seemed like a dream.
 Then was our mouth filled with laughter,
 on our lips there were songs. ℟

2 The heathens themselves said: 'What marvels
 the Lord worked for them!'
 What marvels the Lord worked for us!
 Indeed we were glad. ℟

3 Deliver us, O Lord, from our bondage
 as streams in dry land.
 Those who are sowing in tears
 will sing when they reap. ℟

4 They go out, they go out, full of tears,
 carrying seed for the sowing:
 they come back, they come back, full of song,
 carrying their sheaves. ℟

Gospel Acclamation

James 1:18

Alleluia, alleluia!
By his own choice the Father made us his children
by the message of the truth,

so that we should be a sort of first-fruits
of all that he created.
Alleluia!

or																					Mt 5:16

Alleluia, alleluia!
Your light must shine in the sight of men,
so that, seeing your good works,
they may give the praise to your Father in heaven.
Alleluia!

GOSPEL

A reading from the holy Gospel according to Luke		8:16-18
A lamp is put on a lamp-stand so that people may see the light when they come in.

Jesus said to his disciples: 'No one lights a lamp to cover it with a bowl or to put it under a bed. No, he puts it on a lamp-stand so that people may see the light when they come in. For nothing is hidden but it will be made clear, nothing secret but it will be known and brought to light. So take care how you hear; for anyone who has will be given more; from anyone who has not, even what he thinks he has will be taken away.'

This is the Gospel of the Lord.

TUESDAY

FIRST READING

A reading from the book of Ezra		6:7-8. 12. 14-20
The Jews finished the temple and celebrated the Passover.

King Darius wrote to the satrap of Transeuphrates and his colleagues: 'Leave the high commissioner of Judah and the elders of the Jews to work on this Temple of God; they are to rebuild this Temple of God on its ancient site. This, I decree, is how you must assist the elders of the Jews in the reconstruction of this Temple of God: the expenses of these people are to be paid, promptly and without fail, from the royal revenue – that is, from the tribute of Transeuphrates. I, Darius, have issued this decree. Let it be obeyed to the letter!'

The elders of the Jews, for their part, prospered with their building, inspired by Haggai the prophet and Zechariah son of

Iddo. They finished the building in accordance with the order of the God of Israel and the order of Cyrus and of Darius. This temple was finished on the twenty-third day of the month of Adar; it was the sixth year of the reign of King Darius. The Israelites – the priests, the Levites and the remainder of the exiles – joyfully dedicated this Temple of God; for the dedication of this Temple of God they offered one hundred bulls, two hundred rams, four hundred lambs and, as a sacrifice for sin for the whole of Israel, twelve he-goats, corresponding to the number of the tribes of Israel. Then they installed the priests according to their orders in the service of the Temple of God in Jerusalem, as is written in the Book of Moses.

The exiles celebrated the Passover on the fourteenth day of the first month. The Levites, as one man, had purified themselves; all were pure, so they sacrificed the passover for all the exiles, for their brothers the priests and for themselves.

This is the word of the Lord.

Responsorial Psalm Ps 121:1-5. ℟ v.1

℟ **I rejoiced when I heard them say:**
    'Let us go to God's house.'

1   I rejoiced when I heard them say:
    'Let us go to God's house.'
    And now our feet are standing
    within your gates, O Jerusalem. ℟

2   Jerusalem is built as a city
    strongly compact.
    It is there that the tribes go up,
    the tribes of the Lord. ℟

3   For Israel's law it is,
    there to praise the Lord's name.
    There were set the thrones of judgement
    of the house of David. ℟

Gospel Acclamation Ps 129:5
    Alleluia, alleluia!
    My soul is waiting for the Lord,
    I count on his word.
    Alleluia!

or   Lk 11:28

Alleluia, alleluia!
Happy are those who hear the word of God
and keep it!
Alleluia!

GOSPEL

A reading from the holy Gospel according to Luke   8:19-21
My mother and my brothers are those who hear the word of God and put it into practice.

The mother and the brothers of Jesus came looking for him, but they could not get to him because of the crowd. He was told, 'Your mother and brothers are standing outside and want to see you.' But he said in answer, 'My mother and my brothers are those who hear the word of God and put it into practice.'

This is the Gospel of the Lord.

WEDNESDAY

FIRST READING

A reading from the book of Ezra   9:5-9
God has not forgotten us in our slavery.

At the evening sacrifice I, Ezra, came out of my stupor and falling on my knees, with my garment and cloak torn, I stretched out my hands to the Lord my God, and said:

'My God, I am ashamed, I blush to lift my face to you, my God. For our crimes have increased, until they are higher than our heads, and our sin has piled up to heaven. From the days of our ancestors until now our guilt has been great; on account of our crimes we, our kings and our priests, were given into the power of the kings of other countries, given to the sword, to captivity, to pillage and to shame, as is the case today. But now, suddenly, the Lord our God by his favour has left us a remnant and granted us a refuge in his holy place; this is how our God has cheered our eyes and given us a little respite in our slavery. For we are slaves: but God has not forgotten us in our slavery; he has shown us kindness in the eyes of the kings of Persia, obtaining permission for us to rebuild the Temple of our God and restore its ruins, and he has found us safety and shelter in Judah and in Jerusalem.'

This is the word of the Lord.

Responsorial Psalm   Tob 13:2. 4. 6-8. ℟ v.1

℟ **Blessed be God who lives for ever.**

1. God punishes, he also has mercy,
   he leads men to the depths of the grave,
   he restores them from the great destruction.
   No man can escape his hand. ℟

2. It is he who scattered us among the nations.
   Among them must we show forth his greatness
   and exalt him in the presence of all living;
   for he is our Lord and our God,
   our Father and our God for ever. ℟

3. Now think what he has done for you,
   give thanks to him with all your voice.
   Give praise to the Lord for his justice
   and exalt the king of all ages. ℟

4. In this land of exile I will thank him,
   and show forth his greatness and might
   to the race of sinful men. ℟

5. Sinners, come back to him,
   do what is right before him.
   Who knows but he will receive you with pity? ℟

Gospel Acclamation   Col 3:16. 17

Alleluia, alleluia!
Let the message of Christ, in all its richness,
find a home with you;
through him give thanks to God the Father.
Alleluia!

or   Mk 1:15

Alleluia, alleluia!
The kingdom of God is close at hand,
repent and believe the Good News.
Alleluia!

Twenty-fifth Week in Ordinary Time, Year I: Thursday

GOSPEL

A reading from the holy Gospel according to Luke 9:1-6
Jesus sent them out to proclaim the kingdom of God and to heal.

Jesus called the Twelve together and gave them power and authority over all devils and to cure diseases, and he sent them out to proclaim the kingdom of God and to heal. He said to them, 'Take nothing for the journey: neither staff, nor haversack, nor bread, nor money; and let none of you take a spare tunic. Whatever house you enter, stay there; and when you leave, let it be from there. As for those who do not welcome you, when you leave their town shake the dust from your feet as a sign to them.' So they set out and went from village to village proclaiming the Good News and healing everywhere.

This is the Gospel of the Lord.

THURSDAY

FIRST READING

A reading from the prophet Haggai 1:1-8
Rebuild the House: I shall then take pleasure in it.

In the second year of King Darius, on the first day of the sixth month, the word of the Lord was addressed through the prophet Haggai to Zerubbabel son of Shealtiel, high commissioner of Judah, and to Joshua son of Jehozadak, the high priest, as follows, 'The Lord of hosts says this, "This people says: The time has not yet come to rebuild the Temple of the Lord. (And the word of the Lord was addressed through the prophet Haggai, as follows:) Is this a time for you to live in your panelled houses, when this House lies in ruins? So now, the Lord of hosts says this: Reflect carefully how things have gone for you. You have sown much and harvested little; you eat but never have enough, drink but never have your fill, put on clothes but do not feel warm. The wage earner gets his wages only to put them in a purse riddled with holes. Reflect carefully how things have gone for you. So go to the hill country, fetch wood, and rebuild the House: I shall then take pleasure in it, and be glorified there, says the Lord."'

This is the word of the Lord.

Responsorial Psalm   Ps 149:1-6. 9. ℟ v.4

℟ **The Lord takes delight in his people.**

or

℟ **Alleluia!**

1 Sing a new song to the Lord,
his praise in the assembly of the faithful.
Let Israel rejoice in its Maker,
let Zion's sons exult in their king. ℟

2 Let them praise his name with dancing
and make music with timbrel and harp.
For the Lord takes delight in his people.
He crowns the poor with salvation. ℟

3 Let the faithful rejoice in their glory,
shout for joy and take their rest.
Let the praise of God be on their lips,
this honour is for all his faithful. ℟

Gospel Acclamation   Ps 118:18

Alleluia, alleluia!
Open my eyes, O Lord, that I may consider
the wonders of your law.
Alleluia!

or   Jn 14:6

Alleluia, alleluia!
I am the Way, the Truth and the Life, says the Lord;
no one can come to the Father except through me.
Alleluia!

GOSPEL

A reading from the holy Gospel according to Luke   9:7-9
I beheaded John, so who is this I hear such reports about?

Herod the tetrarch had heard about all that was being done by Jesus; and he was puzzled, because some people were saying that John had risen from the dead, others that Elijah had reappeared, still others that one of the ancient prophets had come back to life. But Herod said, 'John? I beheaded him. So who is this I hear such reports about?' And he was anxious to see Jesus.

This is the Gospel of the Lord.

FRIDAY

FIRST READING

A reading from the prophet Haggai 1:15 – 2:9

A little while now, and I will fill this Temple with glory.

In the second year of King Darius, on the twenty-first day of the seventh month, the word of the Lord was addressed through the prophet Haggai, as follows, 'You are to speak to Zerubbabel son of Shealtiel, the high commissioner of Judah, to Joshua son of Jehozadak, the high priest, and to all the remnant of the people. Say this, "Who is there left among you that saw this Temple in its former glory? And how does it look to you now? Does it seem nothing to you? But take courage now, Zerubbabel – it is the Lord who speaks. Courage, High Priest Joshua son of Jehozadak! Courage, all you people of the country! – it is the Lord who speaks. To work! I am with you – it is the Lord of hosts who speaks – and my spirit remains among you. Do not be afraid! For the Lord of hosts says this: A little while now, and I am going to shake the heavens and the earth, the sea and the dry land. I will shake all the nations and the treasures of all the nations shall flow in, and I will fill this Temple with glory, says the Lord of hosts. Mine is the silver, mine the gold! – it is the Lord of hosts who speaks. The new glory of this Temple is going to surpass the old, says the Lord of hosts, and in this place I will give peace – it is the Lord of hosts who speaks."'

This is the word of the Lord.

Responsorial Psalm Ps 42:1-4. R/ cf. v.5

R/ **Hope in God; I will praise him still,**
my saviour and my God.

1 Defend me, O God, and plead my cause
against a godless nation.
From deceitful and cunning men
rescue me, O God. R/

2 Since you, O God, are my stronghold,
why have you rejected me?
Why do I go mourning
oppressed by the foe? R/

3 O send forth your light and your truth;
let these be my guide.

(continued)

Let them bring me to your holy mountain
to the place where you dwell.

℟ **Hope in God, I will praise him still,
my saviour and my God.**

4 And I will come to the altar of God,
the God of my joy.
My redeemer, I will thank you on the harp,
O God, my God. ℟

Gospel Acclamation cf. Eph 1:17. 18
Alleluia, alleluia!
May the Father of our Lord Jesus Christ
enlighten the eyes of our mind,
so that we can see what hope his call holds for us.
Alleluia!

or Mk 10:45

Alleluia, alleluia!
The Son of Man came to serve,
and to give his life as a ransom for many.
Alleluia!

GOSPEL

A reading from the holy Gospel according to Luke 9:18-22
You are the Christ of God. The Son of Man is destined to suffer grievously.

One day when Jesus was praying alone in the presence of his disciples he put this question to them, 'Who do the crowds say I am?' And they answered, 'John the Baptist; others Elijah; and others say one of the ancient prophets come back to life.' 'But you,' he said 'who do you say I am?' It was Peter who spoke up. 'The Christ of God' he said. But he gave them strict orders not to tell anyone anything about this.

'The Son of Man' he said 'is destined to suffer grievously, to be rejected by the elders and chief priests and scribes and to be put to death, and to be raised up on the third day.'

This is the Gospel of the Lord.

SATURDAY

FIRST READING

A reading from the prophet Zechariah 2:5-9. 14-15
I am coming to dwell in the middle of you.

Raising my eyes, I saw a vision. It was this: there was a man with a measuring line in his hand. I asked him, 'Where are you going?' He said, 'To measure Jerusalem, to find out her breadth and her length.' And then, while the angel who was talking to me stood still, another angel came forward to meet him. He said to him, 'Run, and tell that young man this, "Jerusalem is to remain unwalled, because of the great number of men and cattle there will be in her. But I – it is the Lord who speaks – I will be a wall of fire for her all round her, and I will be her glory in the midst of her."'

Sing, rejoice,
daughter of Zion;
for I am coming
to dwell in the middle of you
– it is the Lord who speaks.
Many nations will join the Lord,
on that day;
they will become his people.

This is the word of the Lord.

Responsorial Psalm Jer 31:10-13. ℟ v.10

℟ **The Lord will guard us,
as a shepherd guards his flock.**

1 O nations, hear the word of the Lord,
   proclaim it to the far-off coasts.
   Say: 'He who scattered Israel will gather him,
   and guard him as a shepherd guards his flock.' ℟

2 For the Lord has ransomed Jacob,
   has saved him from an overpowering hand.
   They will come and shout for joy on Mount Zion,
   they will stream to the blessings of the Lord. ℟

3 Then the young girls will rejoice and will dance,
   the men, young and old, will be glad.
   I will turn their mourning into joy,
   I will console them, give gladness for grief. ℟

Gospel Acclamation   cf. Acts 16:14

> Alleluia, alleluia!
> Open our heart, O Lord,
> to accept the words of your Son.
> Alleluia!

or   cf. 2 Tim 1:10

> Alleluia, alleluia!
> Our Saviour Christ Jesus abolished death,
> and he has proclaimed life through the Good News.
> Alleluia!

GOSPEL

A reading from the holy Gospel according to Luke   9:43-45

The Son of Man is going to be handed over. They were afraid to ask him about what he had said.

At a time when everyone was full of admiration for all he did, Jesus said to his disciples, 'For your part, you must have these words constantly in your mind: The Son of Man is going to be handed over into the power of men.' But they did not understand him when he said this; it was hidden from them so that they should not see the meaning of it, and they were afraid to ask him about what he had just said.

This is the Gospel of the Lord.

TWENTY-SIXTH WEEK IN ORDINARY TIME
Year I

MONDAY

FIRST READING

A reading from the prophet Zechariah   8:1-8

I am going to save my people from the countries of the East and the West.

The word of the Lord of hosts was addressed to me as follows:

> 'The Lord of hosts says this.
> I am burning with jealousy for Zion,
> with great anger for her sake.
>
> 'The Lord of hosts says this.

I am coming back to Zion
and shall dwell in the middle of Jerusalem.
Jerusalem will be called Faithful City
and the mountain of the Lord of hosts, the Holy Mountain.

'The Lord of hosts says this.
Old men and old women will again sit down
in the squares of Jerusalem;
every one of them staff in hand
because of their great age.
And the squares of the city will be full
of boys and girls
playing in the squares.

'The Lord of hosts says this.
If this seems a miracle
to the remnant of this people (in those days),
will it seem one to me?
It is the Lord of hosts who speaks.
The Lord of hosts says this.
Now I am going to save my people
from the countries of the East
and from the countries of the West.
I will bring them back
to live inside Jerusalem.
They shall be my people
and I will be their God
in faithfulness and integrity.'

This is the word of the Lord.

Responsorial Psalm Ps 101:16-21. 29. 22-23. ℟ v.17

℟ **The Lord shall build up Zion again
and appear in all his glory.**

1 The nations shall fear the name of the Lord
and all the earth's kings your glory,
when the Lord shall build up Zion again
and appear in all his glory.
Then he will turn to the prayers of the helpless;
he will not despise their prayers. ℟

2 Let this be written for ages to come
that a people yet unborn may praise the Lord;
for the Lord leaned down from his sanctuary on high.

(continued)

He looked down from heaven to the earth
that he might hear the groans of the prisoners
and free those condemned to die.

℟ **The Lord shall build up Zion again
and appear in all his glory.**

3 The sons of your servants shall dwell untroubled
and their race shall endure before you
that the name of the Lord may be proclaimed in Zion
and his praise in the heart of Jerusalem,
when peoples and kingdoms are gathered together
to pay their homage to the Lord. ℟

Gospel Acclamation Jn 14:23
Alleluia, alleluia!
If anyone loves me he will keep my word,
and my Father will love him,
and we shall come to him.
Alleluia!

or Mk 10:45

Alleluia, alleluia!
The Son of Man came to serve,
and to give his life as a ransom for many.
Alleluia!

GOSPEL

A reading from the holy Gospel according to Luke 9:46-50
The least among you all, that is the one who is great.

An argument started between the disciples about which of them was the greatest. Jesus knew what thoughts were going through their minds, and he took a little child and set him by his side and then said to them, 'Anyone who welcomes this little child in my name welcomes me; and anyone who welcomes me welcomes the one who sent me. For the least among you all, that is the one who is great.'

John spoke up. 'Master,' he said 'we saw a man casting out devils in your name, and because he is not with us we tried to stop him.' But Jesus said to him, 'You must not stop him: anyone who is not against you is for you.'

This is the Gospel of the Lord.

TUESDAY

FIRST READING

A reading from the prophet Zechariah 8:20-23
Many peoples will come to seek the Lord in Jerusalem.

The Lord of hosts says this. 'There will be other peoples yet, and citizens of great cities. And the inhabitants of one city will go to the next and say, "Come, let us go and entreat the favour of the Lord, and seek the Lord of hosts; I am going myself." And many peoples and great nations will come to seek the Lord of hosts in Jerusalem and to entreat the favour of the Lord.'

The Lord of hosts says this. 'In those days, ten men of nations of every language will take a Jew by the sleeve and say, "We want to go with you, since we have learnt that God is with you." '

This is the word of the Lord.

Responsorial Psalm   Ps 86. ℟ Zech 8:23

℟ **God is with us.**

1 On the holy mountain is his city
 cherished by the Lord.
 The Lord prefers the gates of Zion
 to all Jacob's dwellings.
 Of you are told glorious things,
 O city of God! ℟

2 Babylon and Egypt I will count
 among those who know me;
 Philistia, Tyre, Ethiopia,
 these will be her children
 and Zion shall be called 'Mother'
 for all shall be her children. ℟

3 It is he, the Lord Most High,
 who gives each his place.
 In his register of peoples he writes:
 'These are her children'
 and while they dance they will sing;
 'In you all find their home.' ℟

Gospel Acclamation   Ps 118:29. 35

Alleluia, alleluia!
Bend my heart to your will, O Lord,

and teach me your law.
Alleluia!

or   Mk 10:45

Alleluia, alleluia!
The Son of Man came to serve,
and to give his life as a ransom for many.
Alleluia!

GOSPEL

A reading from the holy Gospel according to Luke   9:51-56
Jesus resolutely took the road for Jerusalem.

As the time drew near for him to be taken up to heaven, Jesus resolutely took the road for Jerusalem and sent messengers ahead of him. These set out, and they went into a Samaritan village to make preparations for him, but the people would not receive him because he was making for Jerusalem. Seeing this, the disciples James and John said, 'Lord, do you want us to call down fire from heaven to burn them up?' But he turned and rebuked them, and they went off to another village.

This is the Gospel of the Lord.

WEDNESDAY

FIRST READING

A reading from the book of Nehemiah   2:1-8
If it pleases the king, give me leave to go to the city of my ancestors and rebuild it.

In the month of Nisan, in the twentieth year of King Artaxerxes, the wine being my concern, I took up the wine and offered it to the king. Now I had never been downcast before. So the king said, 'Why is your face so sad? You are not sick, surely? This must be a sadness of your heart.' A great fear came over me and I said to the king, 'May the king live for ever! How could my face be other than sad when the city where the tombs of my ancestors are lies in ruins, and its gates have been burnt down?' 'What' the king asked 'is your request?' I called on the God of heaven and made this reply to the king, 'If it pleases the king, and if you are satisfied with your servant, give me leave to go to Judah, to the city of my ancestors' tombs, and rebuild it.' The king, with the queen sitting there beside him, said, 'How long will your journey take, and when will you return?' So I named a date that seemed acceptable to the king and he gave me leave to go. I spoke to the king once more, 'If it pleases the king, could letters be given me for the governors of Transeuphrates to allow me to pass through to Judah? And also a letter for Asaph, keeper of the king's park, to supply me with timber for the gates of the citadel of the Temple, for the city walls and for the house I am to occupy?' This the king granted me, for the kindly favour of my God was with me.

This is the word of the Lord.

Responsorial Psalm   Ps 136:1-6. ℟ v.6

℟ **O let my tongue cleave to my mouth
if I remember you not!**

1 By the rivers of Babylon
   there we sat and wept,
   remembering Zion;
   on the poplars that grew there
   we hung up our harps. ℟

2 For it was there that they asked us,
   our captors, for songs,
   our oppressors, for joy.
   'Sing to us,' they said,
   'one of Zion's songs.' ℟

3 O how could we sing
   the song of the Lord
   on alien soil?
   If I forget you, Jerusalem,
   let my right hand wither! ℟

4 O let my tongue
   cleave to my mouth
   if I remember you not,
   if I prize not Jerusalem
   above all my joys! ℟

Gospel Acclamation   Ps 118:105
Alleluia, alleluia!
Your word is a lamp for my steps
and a light for my path.
Alleluia!

or Phil 3:8-9

Alleluia, alleluia!
I have accepted the loss of everything
and I look on everything as so much rubbish
if only I can have Christ
and be given a place in him.
Alleluia!

GOSPEL

A reading from the holy Gospel according to Luke 9:57-62
I will follow you wherever you go.

As Jesus and his disciples travelled along they met a man on the road who said to him, 'I will follow you wherever you go.' Jesus answered, 'Foxes have holes and the birds of the air have nests, but the Son of Man has nowhere to lay his head.'

Another to whom he said, 'Follow me', replied, 'Let me go and bury my father first.' But he answered, 'Leave the dead to bury the dead; your duty is to go and spread the news of the kingdom of God.'

Another said, 'I will follow you, sir, but first let me go and say good-bye to my people at home.' Jesus said to him, 'Once the hand is laid on the plough, no one who looks back is fit for the kingdom of God.'

This is the Gospel of the Lord.

THURSDAY

FIRST READING

A reading from the book of Nehemiah 8:1-12
Ezra opened the Book of the Law, blessed the Lord, and all the people responded, 'Amen! Amen!'

When the seventh month came, all the people gathered as one man on the square before the Water Gate. They asked Ezra the scribe to bring the Book of the Law of Moses which the Lord had prescribed for Israel. Accordingly Ezra the priest brought the Law before the assembly, consisting of men, women, and children old enough to understand. This was the first day of the seventh month. On the square before the Water Gate, in the presence of the men and women, and children old enough to understand, he read from the book from early morning till noon; all the people listened attentively to the Book of the Law.

Ezra the scribe stood on a wooden dais erected for the purpose. In full view of all the people – since he stood higher than all the people – Ezra opened the book; and when he opened it all the people stood up. Then Ezra blessed the Lord, the great God, and all the people raised their hands and answered, 'Amen! Amen!'; then they bowed down and, face to the ground, prostrated themselves before the Lord.

The Levites explained the Law to the people while the people remained standing. And Ezra read from the Law of God, translating and giving the sense, so that the people understood what was read.

Then Nehemiah – His Excellency – and Ezra, priest and scribe (and the Levites who were instructing the people) said to all the people, 'This day is sacred to the Lord your God. Do not be mournful, do not weep.' For the people were all in tears as they listened to the words of the Law.

He then said, 'Go, eat the fat, drink the sweet wine, and send a portion to the man who has nothing prepared ready. For this day is sacred to our Lord. Do not be sad: the joy of the Lord is your stronghold.' And the Levites calmed all the people, saying, 'Be at ease; this is a sacred day. Do not be sad.' And all the people went off to eat and drink and give shares away and begin to enjoy themselves since they had understood the meaning of what had been proclaimed to them.

This is the word of the Lord.

Responsorial Psalm Ps 18:8-11. ℟ v.9

℟ **The precepts of the Lord gladden the heart.**

1   The law of the Lord is perfect,
    it revives the soul.
    The rule of the Lord is to be trusted,
    it gives wisdom to the simple. ℟

2   The precepts of the Lord are right,
    they gladden the heart.
    The command of the Lord is clear,
    it gives light to the eyes. ℟

3   The fear of the Lord is holy,
    abiding for ever.
    The decrees of the Lord are truth
    and all of them just. ℟

(continued)

4   They are more to be desired than gold,
    than the purest of gold
    and sweeter are they than honey,
    than honey from the comb.

℟ **The precepts of the Lord gladden the heart.**

Gospel Acclamation   Mt 4:4
Alleluia, alleluia!
Man does not live on bread alone,
but on every word that comes from the mouth of God.
Alleluia!

or   Mk 1:15

Alleluia, alleluia!
The kingdom of God is close at hand,
repent and believe the Good News.
Alleluia!

GOSPEL

A reading from the holy Gospel according to Luke   10:1-12
Your peace will rest on him.

The Lord appointed seventy-two others and sent them out ahead of him, in pairs, to all the towns and places he himself was to visit. He said to them, 'The harvest is rich but the labourers are few, so ask the Lord of the harvest to send labourers to his harvest. Start off now, but remember, I am sending you out like lambs among wolves. Carry no purse, no haversack, no sandals. Salute no one on the road. Whatever house you go into, let your first words be, "Peace to this house!" And if a man of peace lives there, your peace will go and rest on him; if not, it will come back to you. Stay in the same house, taking what food and drink they have to offer, for the labourer deserves his wages; do not move from house to house. Whenever you go into a town where they make you welcome, eat what is set before you. Cure those in it who are sick, and say, "The kingdom of God is very near to you." But whenever you enter a town and they do not make you welcome, go into its street and say, "We wipe off the very dust of your town that clings to our feet, and leave it with you. Yet be sure of this: the kingdom of God is very near." I tell you, on that day it will not go as hard with Sodom as with that town.

This is the Gospel of the Lord.

FRIDAY

FIRST READING

A reading from the book of Baruch   1:15-22
We have sinned in the sight of the Lord and have disobeyed him.

Integrity belongs to the Lord our God; to us the look of shame we wear today, to us, the people of Judah and the citizens of Jerusalem, to our kings and princes, our priests, our prophets, as to our ancestors, because we have sinned in the sight of the Lord, have disobeyed him, and have not listened to the voice of the Lord our God telling us to follow the commandments which the Lord had ordained for us. From the day when the Lord brought our ancestors out of the land of Egypt until today we have been disobedient to the Lord our God, we have been disloyal, refusing to listen to his voice. And so the disasters, and the curse which the Lord pronounced through his servant Moses the day he brought our fathers out of Egypt to give us a land where milk and honey flow, have seized on us, disasters we experience today. Despite all the words of those prophets whom he sent us, we have not listened to the voice of the Lord our God, but, each following the dictates of his evil heart, we have taken to serving alien gods, and doing what is displeasing to the Lord our God.

This is the word of the Lord.

Responsorial Psalm   Ps 78:1-5. 8-9. ℟ v.9

℟   **Rescue us, O Lord,
for the glory of your name.**

1 O God, the nations have invaded your land,
   they have profaned your holy temple.
   They have made Jerusalem a heap of ruins.
   They have handed over the bodies of your servants as food
   to feed the birds of heaven
   and the flesh of your faithful to the beasts of the earth.   ℟

2 They have poured out blood like water in Jerusalem,
   leaving no one to bury the dead.
   We have become the taunt of our neighbours,
   the mockery and scorn of those who surround us.
   How long, O Lord? Will you be angry for ever,
   how long will your anger burn like fire?   ℟   (continued)

3 Do not hold the guilt of our fathers against us.
   Let your compassion hasten to meet us
   for we are in the depths of distress.

   ℟ **Rescue us, O Lord,
        for the glory of your name.**

4 O God our saviour, come to our help,
   come for the sake of the glory of your name.
   O Lord our God, forgive us our sins;
   rescue us for the sake of your name.   ℟

Gospel Acclamation   Ps 144:13
   Alleluia, alleluia!
   The Lord is faithful in all his words
   and loving in all his deeds.
   Alleluia!

or   cf. Ps 94:8

   Alleluia, alleluia!
   Harden not your hearts today,
   but listen to the voice of the Lord.
   Alleluia!

GOSPEL

A reading from the holy Gospel according to Luke   10:13-16
Anyone who rejects me rejects the one who sent me.

Jesus said to his disciples: 'Alas for you, Chorazin! Alas for you, Bethsaida! For if the miracles done in you had been done in Tyre and Sidon, they would have repented long ago, sitting in sackcloth and ashes. And still, it will not go as hard with Tyre and Sidon at the Judgement as with you. And as for you, Capernaum, did you want to be exalted high as heaven? You shall be thrown down to hell.

   'Anyone who listens to you listens to me; anyone who rejects you rejects me, and those who reject me reject the one who sent me.'

   This is the Gospel of the Lord.

SATURDAY

FIRST READING

A reading from the book of Baruch 4:5-12. 27-29
He who brought disaster on you will give you eternal joy.

Take courage, my people,
constant reminder of Israel.
You were sold to the nations,
but not for extermination.
You provoked God;
and so were delivered to your enemies,
since you had angered your creator
by offering sacrifices to demons, not to God.
You had forgotten the eternal God who reared you.
You had also grieved Jerusalem who nursed you,
for when she saw the anger fall on you
from God, she said:

Listen, you neighbours of Zion:
God has sent me great sorrow.
I have seen my sons and daughters taken into captivity,
to which they have been sentenced by the Eternal.
I had reared them joyfully;
in tears, in sorrow, I watched them go away.
Do not, any of you, exult over me,
a widow, deserted by so many;
I suffer loneliness because of the sins of my own children,
who turned away from the Law of God.

Take courage, my children, call on God:
he who brought disaster on you will remember you.
As by your will you first strayed away from God,
so now turn back and search for him ten times as hard;
for as he brought down those disasters on you,
so will he rescue you and give you eternal joy.

This is the word of the Lord.

Responsorial Psalm Ps 68:33-37. ℟ v.34

℟ **The Lord listens to the needy.**

1 The poor when they see it will be glad
and God-seeking hearts will revive;
for the Lord listens to the needy

and does not spurn his servants in their chains.
Let the heavens and the earth give him praise,
the sea and all its living creatures.

℟ **The Lord listens to the needy.**

2 For God will bring help to Zion
and rebuild the cities of Judah
and men shall dwell there in possession.
The sons of his servants shall inherit it;
those who love his name shall dwell there. ℟

Gospel Acclamation cf. Mt 11:25
Alleluia, alleluia!
Blessed are you, Father, Lord of heaven and earth,
for revealing the mysteries of the kingdom to mere children.
Alleluia!

GOSPEL

A reading from the holy Gospel according to Luke 10:17-24
Rejoice that your names are written in heaven.

The seventy-two came back rejoicing. 'Lord,' they said 'even the devils submit to us when we use your name.' Jesus said to them, 'I watched Satan fall like lightning from heaven. Yes. I have given you power to tread underfoot serpents and scorpions and the whole strength of the enemy; nothing shall ever hurt you. Yet do not rejoice that the spirits submit to you; rejoice rather that your names are written in heaven.'

It was then that, filled with joy by the Holy Spirit, he said, 'I bless you, Father, Lord of heaven and of earth, for hiding these things from the learned and the clever and revealing them to mere children. Yes, Father, for that is what it pleased you to do. Everything has been entrusted to me by my Father; and no one knows who the Son is except the Father, and who the Father is except the Son and those to whom the Son chooses to reveal him.'

Then turning to his disciples he spoke to them in private, 'Happy the eyes that see what you see, for I tell you that many prophets and kings wanted to see what you see, and never saw it; to hear what you hear, and never heard it.'

This is the Gospel of the Lord.

TWENTY-SEVENTH WEEK IN ORDINARY TIME
Year I
MONDAY

FIRST READING

A reading from the prophet Jonah 1:1 – 2:1.11

Jonah ran away from the Lord.

The word of the Lord was addressed to Jonah son of Amittai:
'Up!' he said 'Go to Nineveh, the great city, and inform them that their wickedness has become known to me.' Jonah decided to run away from the Lord, and to go to Tarshish. He went down to Joppa and found a ship bound for Tarshish; he paid his fare and went aboard, to go with them to Tarshish, to get away from the Lord. But the Lord unleashed a violent wind on the sea, and there was such a great storm at sea that the ship threatened to break up. The sailors took fright, and each of them called on his own god, and to lighten the ship they threw the cargo overboard. Jonah, however, had gone below and lain down in the hold and fallen fast asleep. The boatswain came upon him and said 'What do you mean by sleeping? Get up! Call on your God! Perhaps he will spare us a thought, and not leave us to die.' Then they said to each other, 'Come on, let us draw lots to find out who is responsible for bringing this evil on us.' So they cast lots, and the lot fell to Jonah. Then they said to him, 'Tell us, what is your business? Where do you come from? What is your country? What is your nationality?' He replied, 'I am a Hebrew, and I worship the Lord, the God of heaven, who made the sea and the land.' The sailors were seized with terror at this and said, 'What have you done?' They knew that he was trying to escape from the Lord, because he had told them so. They then said, 'What are we to do with you, to make the sea grow calm for us?' For the sea was growing rougher and rougher. He replied, 'Take me and throw me into the sea, and then it will grow calm for you. For I can see it is my fault this violent storm has happened to you.' The sailors rowed hard in an effort to reach the shore, but in vain, since the sea grew still rougher for them. They then called on the Lord and said, 'O Lord, do not let us perish for taking this man's life; do not hold us guilty of innocent blood; for you, Lord, have acted as you thought right.' And taking hold of Jonah they threw him into the sea; and the sea grew calm again. At this the men were seized with dread of the Lord; they offered a sacrifice to the

Lord and made vows. The Lord had arranged that a great fish should be there to swallow Jonah; and Jonah remained in the belly of the fish for three days and three nights. The Lord spoke to the fish, which then vomited Jonah on to the shore.

This is the word of the Lord.

Responsorial Psalm   Jonah 2:3-5. 8. ℟ v.7

℟ **You lifted my life from the pit, O Lord.**

1. Out of my distress I cried to the Lord
and he answered me;
from the belly of Sheol I cried,
and you have heard my voice. ℟

2. You cast me into the abyss, into the heart of the sea,
and the flood surrounded me.
All your waves, your billows,
washed over me. ℟

3. And I said: I am cast out
from your sight.
How shall I ever look again
on your Holy Temple? ℟

4. While my soul was fainting within me,
I remembered the Lord,
and my prayer came before you
into your holy Temple. ℟

Gospel Acclamation   cf. Jn 6:63. 68

Alleluia, alleluia!
Your words are spirit, Lord,
and they are life:
you have the message of eternal life.
Alleluia!

or   Jn 13:34

Alleluia, alleluia!
I give you a new commandment:
love one another just as I have loved you,
says the Lord.
Alleluia!

GOSPEL

A reading from the holy Gospel according to Luke 10:25-37
Who is my neighbour?

There was a lawyer who, to disconcert Jesus, stood up and said to him, 'Master, what must I do to inherit eternal life?' He said to him, 'What is written in the Law? What do you read there?' He replied, 'You must love the Lord your God with all your heart, with all your soul, with all your strength, and with all your mind, and your neighbour as yourself.' 'You have answered right,' said Jesus 'do this and life is yours.'

But the man was anxious to justify himself and said to Jesus, 'And who is my neighbour?' Jesus replied, 'A man was once on his way down from Jerusalem to Jericho and fell into the hands of brigands; they took all he had, beat him and then made off, leaving him half dead. Now a priest happened to be travelling down the same road, but when he saw the man, he passed by on the other side. In the same way a Levite who came to the place saw him, and passed by on the other side. But a Samaritan traveller who came upon him was moved with compassion when he saw him. He went up and bandaged his wounds, pouring oil and wine on them. He then lifted him on to his own mount, carried him to the inn and looked after him. Next day, he took out two denarii and handed them to the innkeeper. "Look after him," he said "and on my way back I will make good any extra expense you have." Which of these three, do you think, proved himself a neighbour to the man who fell into the brigands' hands?' 'The one who took pity on him' he replied. Jesus said to him, 'Go, and do the same yourself.'

This is the Gospel of the Lord.

TUESDAY

FIRST READING

A reading from the prophet Jonah 3:1-10
The people of Nineveh renounced their evil behaviour, and God relented.

The word of the Lord was addressed to Jonah: 'Up!' he said. 'Go to Nineveh, the great city, and preach to them as I told you to.' Jonah set out and went to Nineveh in obedience to the word of the Lord. Now Nineveh was a city great beyond compare: it took three days to cross it. Jonah went on into the city, making a day's journey. He preached in these words, 'Only forty days more and Nineveh is going to be destroyed.' And the people of Nineveh believed in God; they proclaimed a fast and put on sackcloth from the greatest to the least. The news reached the king of Nineveh, who rose from his throne, took off his robe, put on sackcloth and sat down in ashes. A proclamation was then promulgated throughout Nineveh, by decree of the king and his ministers, as follows: 'Men and beasts, herds and flocks, are to taste nothing; they must not eat, they must not drink water. All are to put on sackcloth and call on God with all their might; and let everyone renounce his evil behaviour and the wicked things he has done. Who knows if God will not change his mind and relent, if he will not renounce his burning wrath, so that we do not perish?' God saw their efforts to renounce their evil behaviour. And God relented: he did not inflict on them the disaster which he had threatened.

This is the word of the Lord.

Responsorial Psalm   Ps 129:1-4. 7-8. R/ v.3

R/ **If you, O Lord, should mark our guilt,
Lord, who would survive?**

1   Out of the depths I cry to you, O Lord,
     Lord, hear my voice!
     O let your ears be attentive
     to the voice of my pleading.   R/

2   If you, O Lord, should mark our guilt,
     Lord, who would survive?
     But with you is found forgiveness:
     for this we revere you.   R/

3   Because with the Lord there is mercy
     and fullness of redemption,
     Israel indeed he will redeem
     from all its iniquity.   R/

Gospel Acclamation   Jn 15:15
     Alleluia, alleluia!
     I call you friends, says the Lord,
     because I have made known to you
     everything I have learnt from my Father,
     Alleluia!

Twenty-seventh Week in Ordinary Time, Year I: Wednesday 767

or   Lk 11:28

Alleluia, alleluia!
Happy are those who hear the word of God
and keep it!
Alleluia!

GOSPEL

A reading from the holy Gospel according to Luke   10:38-42
Martha welcomed Jesus into her house.
It is Mary who has chosen the better part.

Jesus came to a village, and a woman named Martha welcomed him into her house. She had a sister called Mary, who sat down at the Lord's feet and listened to him speaking. Now Martha who was distracted with all the serving said, 'Lord, do you not care that my sister is leaving me to do the serving all by myself? Please tell her to help me.' But the Lord answered: 'Martha, Martha,' he said 'you worry and fret about so many things, and yet few are needed, indeed only one. It is Mary who has chosen the better part; it is not to be taken from her.'

This is the Gospel of the Lord.

WEDNESDAY

FIRST READING

A reading from the prophet Jonah   4:1-11
You are only upset about a castor-oil plant.
Am I not to feel sorry for Nineveh, the great city!

Jonah was very indignant; he fell into a rage. He prayed to the Lord and said, 'Ah! Lord, is not this just as I said would happen when I was still at home? That was why I went and fled to Tarshish: I knew that you were a God of tenderness and compassion, slow to anger, rich in graciousness, relenting from evil. So now Lord, please take away my life, for I might as well be dead as go on living.' The Lord replied, 'Are you right to be angry?' Jonah then went out of the city and sat down to the east of the city. There he made himself a shelter and sat under it in the shade, to see what would happen to the city. Then the Lord God arranged that a castor-oil plant should grow up over Jonah to give shade for his head and soothe his ill-humour; Jonah was delighted with the castor-oil plant. But at dawn the next day, God arranged that a worm should attack the castor-oil plant – and it withered. Next, when the sun rose, God arranged that there should be a scorching east wind; the sun beat down so hard on Jonah's head that he was overcome and begged for death, saying, 'I might as well be dead as go on living.' God said to Jonah, 'Are you right to be angry about the castor-oil plant?' He replied, 'I have every right to be angry, to the point of death.' The Lord replied, 'You are only upset about a castor-oil plant which cost you no labour, which you did not make grow, which sprouted in a night and has perished in a night. And am I not to feel sorry for Nineveh, the great city, in which there are more than a hundred and twenty thousand people who cannot tell their right hand from their left, to say nothing of all the animals?'

This is the word of the Lord.

Responsorial Psalm   Ps 85:3-6. 9-10. ℟ v.15

   ℟ **You, O Lord, have mercy and compassion.**

1 You are my God, have mercy on me, Lord,
    for I cry to you all the day long.
    Give joy to your servant, O Lord,
    for to you I lift up my soul. ℟

2 O Lord, you are good and forgiving,
    full of love to all who call.
    Give heed, O Lord, to my prayer
    and attend to the sound of my voice. ℟

3 All the nations shall come to adore you
    and glorify your name, O Lord:
    for you are great and do marvellous deeds,
    you who alone are God. ℟

Gospel Acclamation   Ps 118:34
   Alleluia, alleluia!
   Train me, Lord, to observe your law,
   to keep it with my heart.
   Alleluia!
or   Rom 8:15
   Alleluia, alleluia!
   The spirit you received is the spirit of sons,
   and it makes us cry out, 'Abba, Father!'
   Alleluia!

Twenty-seventh Week in Ordinary Time, Year I: Thursday

GOSPEL

A reading from the holy Gospel according to Luke 11:1-4
Lord, teach us to pray.

Once Jesus was in a certain place praying, and when he had finished, one of his disciples said, 'Lord, teach us to pray, just as John taught his disciples.' He said to them, 'Say this when you pray:

"Father, may your name be held holy,
your kingdom come;
give us each day our daily bread,
and forgive us our sins,
for we ourselves forgive each one who is in debt to us.
And do not put us to the test." '

This is the Gospel of the Lord.

THURSDAY

FIRST READING

A reading from the prophet Malachi 3:13-20
The day is coming now, burning like a furnace.

You say harsh things about me, says the Lord. You ask, 'What have we said against you?' You say, 'It is useless to serve God; what is the good of keeping his commands or of walking mournfully before the Lord of hosts? Now we have reached the point when we call the arrogant blessed; yes, they prosper, these evildoers; they try God's patience and yet go free.' This is what those who fear the Lord used to say to one another. But the Lord took note and heard them: a book of remembrance was written in his presence recording those who fear him and take refuge in his name. On the day which I am preparing, says the Lord of hosts, they are going to be my own special possession. I will make allowances for them as a man makes allowances for the son who obeys him. Then once again you will see the difference between an upright man and a wicked one, between the one who serves God and the one who does not serve him. For the day is coming now, burning like a furnace; and all the arrogant and the evil-doers will be like stubble. The day that is coming is going to burn them up, says the Lord of hosts, leaving them neither root nor stalk. But for you who fear my name, the sun of righteousness will shine out with healing in its rays.

This is the word of the Lord.

Responsorial Psalm   Ps 1. ℟ Ps 39:5
   ℟ **Happy the man who has placed his trust in the Lord.**

1. Happy indeed is the man
who follows not the counsel of the wicked;
nor lingers in the way of sinners
nor sits in the company of scorners,
but whose delight is the law of the Lord
and who ponders his law day and night.   ℟

2. He is like a tree that is planted
beside the flowing waters,
that yields its fruit in due season
and whose leaves shall never fade;
and all that he does shall prosper.   ℟

3. Not so are the wicked, not so!
For they like winnowed chaff
shall be driven away by the wind.
For the Lord guards the way of the just
but the way of the wicked leads to doom.   ℟

Gospel Acclamation   Jn 14:6
   Alleluia, alleluia!
I am the Way, the Truth and the Life, says the Lord;
no one can come to the Father except through me.
Alleluia!

or   cf. Acts 16:14

   Alleluia, alleluia!
Open our heart, O Lord,
to accept the words of your Son.
Alleluia!

GOSPEL

A reading from the holy Gospel according to Luke   11:5-13
Ask, and it will be given to you.

Jesus said to his disciples: 'Suppose one of you has a friend and goes to him in the middle of the night to say, "My friend, lend me three loaves, because a friend of mine on his travels has just arrived at my house and I have nothing to offer him;" and the man answers from inside the house, "Do not bother me. The door is bolted now, and my children and I are in bed; I cannot get up to give it you." I tell you, if the man does not get up and give it him for friendship's sake, persistence will be enough to make him get up and give his friend all he wants.

'So I say to you: Ask, and it will be given to you; search, and you will find; knock, and the door will be opened to you. For the one who asks always receives; the one who searches always finds; the one who knocks will always have the door opened to him. What father among you would hand his son a stone when he asked for bread? Or hand him a snake instead of a fish? Or hand him a scorpion if he asked for an egg? If you then, who are evil, know how to give your children what is good, how much more will the heavenly Father give the Holy Spirit to those who ask him!'

This is the Gospel of the Lord.

FRIDAY

FIRST READING

A reading from the prophet Joel 1:13-15; 2:1-2
The day of the Lord, the day of darkness and gloom.

Priests, put on sackcloth and lament.
Ministers of the altar, wail.
Come, pass the night in sackcloth,
you ministers of my God.
For the house of our God has been deprived
of oblation and libation.
Order a fast,
proclaim a solemn assembly;
elders, call together
all the inhabitants of the country
to the house of the Lord your God.
Cry out to the Lord,
'Oh, what a day!
For the day of the Lord is near,
it comes as a devastation from Shaddai.'

Sound the trumpet in Zion,

give the alarm on my holy mountain!
Let all the inhabitants of the country tremble,
for the day of the Lord is coming,
yes, it is near.

Day of darkness and gloom,
day of cloud and blackness.
Like the dawn there spreads across the mountains
a vast and mighty host,
such as has never been before,
such as will never be again
to the remotest ages.

    This is the word of the Lord.

Responsorial Psalm   Ps 9:2-3. 6. 16. 8-9. ℟ v.9

  ℟ **The Lord will judge the world with justice.**

1 I will praise you, Lord, with all my heart;
   I will recount all your wonders.
   I will rejoice in you and be glad,
   and sing psalms to your name O Most High.   ℟

2 You have checked the nations, destroyed the wicked;
   you have wiped out their name for ever and ever.
   The nations have fallen in the pit which they made,
   their feet caught in the snare they laid.   ℟

3 But the Lord sits enthroned for ever.
   He has set up his throne for judgement;
   he will judge the world with justice,
   he will judge the peoples with his truth.   ℟

Gospel Acclamation   Jn 10:27

  Alleluia, alleluia!
  The sheep that belong to me listen to my voice,
  says the Lord,
  I know them and they follow me.
  Alleluia!

or   Jn 12:31-32

  Alleluia, alleluia!
  Now the prince of this world is to be overthrown,
  says the Lord;
  and when I am lifted up from the earth
  I shall draw all men to myself.
  Alleluia!

GOSPEL

A reading from the holy Gospel according to Luke 11:15-26

If it is through the finger of God that I cast out devils, then know that the kingdom of God has overtaken you.

When Jesus had cast out a devil, some of the people said, 'It is through Beelzebul, the prince of devils, that he casts out devils.' Others asked Jesus, as a test, for a sign from heaven; but, knowing what they were thinking, he said to them, 'Every kingdom divided against itself is heading for ruin, and a household divided against itself collapses. So too with Satan: if he is divided against himself, how can his kingdom stand? – since you assert that it is through Beelzebul that I cast out devils. Now if it is through Beelzebul that I cast out devils, through whom do your own experts cast them out? Let them be your judges, then. But if it is through the finger of God that I cast out devils, then know that the kingdom of God has overtaken you. So long as a strong man fully armed guards his own palace, his goods are undisturbed; but when someone stronger than he is attacks and defeats him, the stronger man takes away all the weapons he relied on and shares out his spoil.

'He who is not with me is against me; and he who does not gather with me scatters.

'When an unclean spirit goes out of a man it wanders through waterless country looking for a place to rest, and not finding one it says, "I will go back to the home I came from." But on arrival, finding it swept and tidied, it then goes off and brings seven other spirits more wicked than itself, and they go in and set up house there, so that the man ends up by being worse than he was before.'

This is the Gospel of the Lord.

SATURDAY

FIRST READING

A reading from the prophet Joel 4:12-21

Put the sickle in; the harvest is ripe.

The Lord says this:

'Let the nations rouse themselves, let them march
to the Valley of Jehoshaphat,

for I am going to sit in judgement there
on all the nations round.
Put the sickle in:
the harvest is ripe;
come and tread:
the winepress is full,
the vats are overflowing,
so great is their wickedness!'

Host on host
in the Valley of Decision!
For the day of the Lord is near
in the Valley of Decision!
Sun and moon grow dark,
the stars lose their brilliance.
The Lord roars from Zion,
makes his voice heard from Jerusalem;
heaven and earth tremble.
But the Lord will be a shelter for his people,
a stronghold for the sons of Israel

'You will learn then that I am the Lord your God,
dwelling in Zion, my holy mountain.
Jerusalem will be a holy place,
no alien will ever pass through it again.'

When that day comes,
the mountains will run with new wine
and the hills flow with milk,
and all the river beds of Judah
will run with water.
A fountain will spring from the house of the Lord
to water the wadi of Acacias.
Egypt will become a desolation,
Edom a desert waste
on account of the violence done to the sons of Judah
whose innocent blood they shed in their country.
But Judah will be inhabited for ever,
Jerusalem from age to age.
'I will avenge their blood and let none go unpunished,'
and the Lord shall make his home in Zion.

This is the word of the Lord.

Twenty-seventh Week in Ordinary Time, Year I: Saturday

Responsorial Psalm   Ps 96:1-2. 5-6. 11-12. ℟ v.12

   ℟ **Rejoice, you just, in the Lord.**

1. The Lord is king, let earth rejoice,
   the many coastlands be glad.
   Cloud and darkness are his raiment;
   his throne, justice and right. ℟

2. The mountains melt like wax
   before the Lord of all the earth.
   The skies proclaim his justice;
   all peoples see his glory. ℟

3. Light shines forth for the just
   and joy for the upright of heart,
   Rejoice, you just, in the Lord;
   give glory to his holy name. ℟

Gospel Acclamation   Jn 14:23

Alleluia, alleluia!
If anyone loves me he will keep my word,
and my Father will love him,
and we shall come to him.
Alleluia!

or   Lk 11:28

Alleluia, alleluia!
Happy are those who hear the word of God
and keep it!
Alleluia!

GOSPEL

A reading from the holy Gospel according to Luke   11:27-28

Happy the womb that bore you! Still happier those who hear the word of God.

As Jesus was speaking, a woman in the crowd raised her voice and said, 'Happy the womb that bore you and the breasts you sucked!' But he replied, 'Still happier those who hear the word of God and keep it!'

This is the Gospel of the Lord.

TWENTY-EIGHTH WEEK IN ORDINARY TIME
Year I

MONDAY

FIRST READING

A reading from the letter of St Paul to the Romans 1:1-7
Through Christ we received grace and our apostolic mission to preach the obedience of faith to all pagan nations.

From Paul, a servant of Christ Jesus who has been called to be an apostle, and specially chosen to preach the Good News that God promised long ago through his prophets in the scriptures.

This news is about the Son of God who, according to the human nature he took, was a descendant of David: it is about Jesus Christ our Lord who, in the order of the spirit, the spirit of holiness that was in him, was proclaimed Son of God in all his power through his resurrection from the dead. Through him we received grace and our apostolic mission to preach the obedience of faith to all pagan nations in honour of his name. You are one of these nations, and by his call belong to Jesus Christ. To you all, then, who are God's beloved in Rome, called to be saints, may God our Father and the Lord Jesus Christ send grace and peace.

This is the word of the Lord.

Responsorial Psalm Ps 97: 1-4. ℟ v.2

℟ **The Lord has made known his salvation.**

1 Sing a new song to the Lord
  for he has worked wonders.
  His right hand and his holy arm
  have brought salvation. ℟

2 The Lord has made known his salvation;
  has shown his justice to the nations.
  He has remembered his truth and love
  for the house of Israel. ℟

3 All the ends of the earth have seen
  the salvation of our God.
  Shout to the Lord all the earth,
  ring out your joy. ℟

Twenty-eighth Week in Ordinary Time, Year I: Tuesday

Gospel Acclamation — Ps 118:88

> Alleluia, alleluia!
> Because of your love give me life,
> and I will do your will.
> Alleluia!

or — cf. Ps 94:8

> Alleluia, alleluia!
> Harden not your hearts today,
> but listen to the voice of the Lord.
> Alleluia!

GOSPEL

A reading from the holy Gospel according to Luke — 11:29-32

The only sign which will be given to this wicked generation is the sign of Jonah.

The crowds got even bigger and Jesus addressed them, 'This is a wicked generation; it is asking for a sign. The only sign it will be given is the sign of Jonah. For just as Jonah became a sign to the Ninevites, so will the Son of Man be to this generation. On Judgement day the Queen of the South will rise up with the men of this generation and condemn them, because she came from the ends of the earth to hear the wisdom of Solomon; and there is something greater than Solomon here. On Judgement day the men of Nineveh will stand up with this generation and condemn it, because when Jonah preached they repented; and there is something greater than Jonah here.'

This is the Gospel of the Lord.

TUESDAY

FIRST READING

A reading from the letter of St Paul to the Romans — 1:16-25

Men knew God and yet refused to honour him as God.

I am not ashamed of the Good News: it is the power of God saving all who have faith – Jews first, but Greeks as well – since this is what reveals the justice of God to us: it shows how faith leads to faith, or as scripture says: The upright man finds life through faith.

The anger of God is being revealed from heaven against all the impiety and depravity of men who keep truth imprisoned in their wickedness. For what can be known about God is perfectly plain to them since God himself has made it plain. Ever since God created the world his everlasting power and deity – however invisible – have been there for the mind to see in the things he has made. That is why such people are without excuse: they knew God and yet refused to honour him as God or to thank him; instead, they made nonsense out of logic and their empty minds were darkened. The more they called themselves philosophers, the more stupid they grew, until they exchanged the glory of the immortal God for a worthless imitation, for the image of mortal man, of birds, of quadrupeds and reptiles. That is why God left them to their filthy enjoyments and the practices with which they dishonour their own bodies, since they have given up divine truth for a lie and have worshipped and served creatures instead of the creator, who is blessed for ever. Amen!

This is the word of the Lord.

Responsorial Psalm   Ps 18:2-5. R̸ v.2
R̸ **The heavens proclaim the glory of God.**

1 The heavens proclaim the glory of God
   and the firmament shows forth the work of his hands.
   Day unto day takes up the story
   and night unto night makes known the message.   R̸

2 No speech, no word, no voice is heard
   yet their span goes forth through all the earth,
   their words to the utmost bounds of the world.   R̸

Gospel Acclamation   Ps 118:135
Alleluia, alleluia!
Let your face shine on your servant,
and teach me your decrees.
Alleluia!

or   Heb 4:12

Alleluia, alleluia!
The word of God is something alive and active;
it can judge secret emotions and thoughts.
Alleluia!

GOSPEL

A reading from the holy Gospel according to Luke 11:37-41

Give alms and then indeed everything will be clean for you.

Jesus had just finished speaking when a Pharisee invited him to dine at his house. He went in and sat down at the table. The Pharisee saw this and was surprised that he had not first washed before the meal. But the Lord said to him, 'Oh, you Pharisees! You clean the outside of cup and plate, while inside yourselves you are filled with extortion and wickedness. Fools! Did not he who made the outside make the inside too? Instead, give alms from what you have and then indeed everything will be clean for you.'

This is the Gospel of the Lord.

WEDNESDAY

FIRST READING

A reading from the letter of St Paul to the Romans 2:1-11

God will repay each one as his works deserve – Jews first, but Greeks as well.

No matter who you are, if you pass judgement you have no excuse. In judging others you condemn yourself, since you behave no differently from those you judge. We know that God condemns that sort of behaviour impartially: and when you judge those who behave like this while you are doing exactly the same, do you think you will escape God's judgement? Or are you abusing his abundant goodness, patience and toleration, not realising that this goodness of God is meant to lead you to repentance? Your stubborn refusal to repent is only adding to the anger God will have towards you on that day of anger when his just judgements will be made known. He will repay each one as his works deserve. For those who sought renown and honour and immortality by always doing good there will be eternal life; for the unsubmissive who refused to take truth for their guide and took depravity instead, there will be anger and fury. Pain and suffering will come to every human being who employs himself in evil – Jews first, but Greeks as well; renown, honour and peace will come to everyone who does good – Jews first, but Greeks as well. God has no favourites.

This is the word of the Lord.

Responsional Psalm   Ps 61:2-3. 6-7. 9. ℟ v.13

  ℟ **Lord, you repay each man according to his deeds.**

1. In God alone is my soul at rest;
   my help comes from him.
   He alone is my rock, my stronghold,
   my fortress: I stand firm. ℟

2. In God alone be at rest, my soul;
   for my hope comes from him.
   He alone is my rock, my stronghold,
   my fortress: I stand firm. ℟

3. Take refuge in God all you people.
   Trust him at all times,
   Pour out your hearts before him
   for God is our refuge. ℟

Gospel Acclamation   cf. Ps 26:11

Alleluia, alleluia!
Instruct me, Lord, in your way;
on an even path lead me.
Alleluia!

or   Jn 10:27

Alleluia, alleluia!
The sheep that belong to me listen to my voice,
says the Lord,
I know them and they follow me.
Alleluia!

GOSPEL

A reading from the holy Gospel according to Luke   11:42-46
Alas for you Pharisees! And alas for you lawyers also!

The Lord said to the Pharisees: 'Alas for you Pharisees! You who pay your tithe of mint and rue and all sorts of garden herbs and overlook justice and the love of God! These you should have practised, without leaving the others undone. Alas for you Pharisees who like taking the seats of honour in the synagogues and being greeted obsequiously in the market squares! Alas for you, because you are like the unmarked tombs that men walk on without knowing it!'

A lawyer then spoke up. 'Master,' he said 'when you speak like this you insult us too.' 'Alas for you lawyers also,' he replied, 'because you load on men burdens that are unendurable, burdens that you yourselves do not move a finger to lift.'

This is the Gospel of the Lord.

THURSDAY

FIRST READING

A reading from the letter of St Paul to the Romans　　3:21-30
A man is justified by faith and not by doing something the Law tells him to do.

God's justice that was made known through the Law and the Prophets has now been revealed outside the Law, since it is the same justice of God that comes through faith to everyone, Jew and pagan alike, who believes in Jesus Christ. Both Jew and pagan sinned and forfeited God's glory, and both are justified through the free gift of his grace by being redeemed in Christ Jesus who was appointed by God to sacrifice his life so as to win reconciliation through faith. In this way God makes his justice known; first, for the past, when sins went unpunished because he held his hand, then, for the present age, by showing positively that he is just, and that he justifies everyone who believes in Jesus.

So what becomes of our boasts? There is no room for them. What sort of law excludes them? The sort of law that tells us what to do? On the contrary, it is the law of faith, since, as we see it, a man is justified by faith and not by doing something the Law tells him to do. Is God the God of Jews alone and not of the pagans too? Of the pagans too, most certainly, since there is only one God.

This is the word of the Lord.

Responsorial Psalm　　Ps 129:1-6. ℟ v.7

℟　**With the Lord there is mercy,
　　and fullness of redemption.**

1　Out of the depths I cry to you, O Lord,
　　Lord, hear my voice!
　　O let your ears be attentive
　　to the voice of my pleading.　℟

2 If you, O Lord, should mark our guilt,
   Lord, who would survive?
   But with you is found forgiveness:
   for this we revere you.

   ℟ **With the Lord there is mercy,
   and fullness of redemption.**

3 My soul is waiting for the Lord,
   I count on his word.
   My soul is longing for the Lord
   more than watchman for daybreak. ℟

Gospel Acclamation   Ps 110:7. 8
Alleluia, alleluia!
Your precepts, O Lord, are all of them sure;
they stand firm for ever and ever.
Alleluia!

or   Jn 14:6

Alleluia, alleluia!
I am the Way, the Truth and the Life, says the Lord;
no one can come to the Father except through me.
Alleluia!

GOSPEL

A reading from the holy Gospel according to Luke   11:47-54
This generation will have to answer for every prophet's blood, from the blood of Abel to the blood of Zechariah.

Jesus said: 'Alas for you who build the tombs of the prophets, the men your ancestors killed! In this way you both witness what your ancestors did and approve it; they did the killing, you do the building.

'And that is why the Wisdom of God said, "I will send them prophets and apostles; some they will slaughter and persecute, so that this generation will have to answer for every prophet's blood that has been shed since the foundation of the world, from the blood of Abel to the blood of Zechariah, who was murdered between the altar and the sanctuary." Yes, I tell you, this generation will have to answer for it all.

'Alas for you lawyers who have taken away the key of knowledge! You have not gone in yourselves, and have prevented others going in who wanted to.'

Twenty-eighth Week in Ordinary Time, Year I: Friday

When he left the house, the scribes and the Pharisees began a furious attack on him and tried to force answers from him on innumerable questions, setting traps to catch him out in something he might say.

This is the Gospel of the Lord.

FRIDAY

FIRST READING

A reading from the letter of St Paul to the Romans   4:1-8
Abraham put his faith in God, and this faith was considered as justifying him.

What shall we say about Abraham, the ancestor from whom we are all descended? If Abraham was justified as a reward for doing something, he would really have had something to boast about, though not in God's sight because scripture says: Abraham put his faith in God, and this faith was considered as justifying him. If a man has work to show, his wages are not considered as a favour but as his due; but when a man has nothing to show except faith in the one who justifies sinners, then his faith is considered as justifying him. And David says the same: a man is happy if God considers him righteous, irrespective of good deeds:

Happy those whose crimes are forgiven,
whose sins are blotted out;
happy the man whom the Lord considers sinless.

This is the word of the Lord.

Responsorial Psalm   Ps 31:1-2. 5. 11. ℟ cf. v.7
  ℟ **You are my refuge, O Lord;**
    you fill me with the joy of salvation.

1 Happy the man whose offence is forgiven,
   whose sin is remitted.
   O happy the man to whom the Lord
   imputes no guilt,
   in whose spirit is no guile. ℟

2 But now I have acknowledged my sins;
   my guilt I did not hide.
   I said: 'I will confess

my offence to the Lord.'
And you, Lord, have forgiven
the guilt of my sin.

℟ **You are my refuge, O Lord;
you fill me with the joy of salvation.**

3 Rejoice, rejoice in the Lord,
exult, you just!
O come, ring out your joy,
all you upright of heart. ℟

Gospel Acclamation cf. Ps 18:9

Alleluia, alleluia!
Your words gladden the heart, O Lord,
they give light to the eyes.
Alleluia!

or Ps 32:22

Alleluia, alleluia!
May your love to be upon us, O Lord,
as we place all our hope in you.
Alleluia!

GOSPEL

A reading from the holy Gospel according to Luke 12:1-7
Every hair on your head has been counted.

The people had gathered in their thousands so that they were treading on one another. And Jesus began to speak, first of all to his disciples. 'Be on your guard against the yeast of the Pharisees – that is, their hypocrisy. Everything that is now covered will be uncovered, and everything now hidden will be made clear. For this reason, whatever you have said in the dark will be heard in the daylight, and what you have whispered in hidden places will be proclaimed on the housetops.

'To you my friends I say: Do not be afraid of those who kill the body and after that can do no more. I will tell you whom to fear: *fear him who, after he has killed, has the power to cast into hell.* Yes, I tell you, fear him. Can you not buy five sparrows for two pennies? And yet not one is forgotten in God's sight. Why, every hair on your head has been counted. There is no need to be afraid: you are worth more than hundreds of sparrows.'

This is the Gospel of the Lord.

SATURDAY

FIRST READING
A reading from the letter of St Paul to the Romans 4:13. 16-18

Though it seemed Abraham's hope could not be fulfilled, he hoped and he believed.

The promise of inheriting the world was not made to Abraham and his descendants on account of any law but on account of the righteousness which consists in faith. That is why what fulfils the promise depends on faith, so that it may be a free gift and be available to all of Abraham's descendants, not only those who belong to the Law but also those who belong to the faith of Abraham who is the father of all of us. As scripture says: I have made you the ancestor of many nations – Abraham is our father in the eyes of God, in whom he put his faith, and who brings the dead to life and calls into being what does not exist.

Though it seemed Abraham's hope could not be fulfilled, he hoped and he believed, and through doing so he did become the father of many nations exactly as he had been promised: Your descendants will be as many as the stars.

This is the word of the Lord.

Responsorial Psalm Ps 104:6-9. 42-43. R̥ v.8

℟ **The Lord remembers his covenant for ever.**

or

℟ **Alleluia!**

1 O children of Abraham, his servant,
   O sons of the Jacob he chose.
   He, the Lord, is our God:
   his judgements prevail in all the earth. ℟

2 He remembers his covenant for ever,
   his promise for a thousand generations,
   the covenant he made with Abraham,
   the oath he swore to Isaac. ℟

3 For he remembered his holy word,
   which he gave to Abraham his servant.
   So he brought out his people with joy,
   his chosen ones with shouts of rejoicing. ℟

Gospel Acclamation 1 Sam 3:9; Jn 6:68
> Alleluia, alleluia!
> Speak, Lord, your servant is listening:
> you have the message of eternal life.
> Alleluia!

or Jn 15:26. 27
> Alleluia, alleluia!
> The Spirit of truth will be my witness,
> and you too will be witnesses,
> says the Lord.
> Alleluia!

GOSPEL

A reading from the holy Gospel according to Luke 12:9-12
When the time comes, the Holy Spirit will teach you what you must say.

Jesus said to his disciples, 'I tell you, if anyone openly declares himself for me in the presence of men, the Son of Man will declare himself for him in the presence of God's angels. But the man who disowns me in the presence of men will be disowned in the presence of God's angels.

'Everyone who says a word against the Son of Man will be forgiven, but he who blasphemes against the Holy Spirit will not be forgiven.

'When they take you before synagogues and magistrates and authorities, do not worry about how to defend yourselves or what to say, because when the time comes, the Holy Spirit will teach you what you must say.'

This is the Gospel of the Lord.

TWENTY-NINTH WEEK IN ORDINARY TIME
Year I
MONDAY

FIRST READING

A reading from the letter of St Paul to the Romans 4:20-25
Scripture says that our faith too will be 'considered' if we believe in him.

Since God had made him a promise, Abraham refused either to

Twenty-ninth Week in Ordinary Time, Year I: Monday

deny it or even to doubt it, but drew strength from faith and gave glory to God, convinced that God had power to do what he had promised. This is the faith that was 'considered as justifying him'. Scripture however does not refer only to him but to us as well when it says that his faith was thus 'considered'; our faith too will be 'considered' if we believe in him who raised Jesus our Lord from the dead, Jesus who was put to death for our sins and raised to life to justify us.

This is the word of the Lord.

Responsorial Psalm Lk 1:69-75. ℟ cf. v.68

℟ **Blessed be the Lord, the God of Israel!
He has visited his people.**

1 He has raised up for us a mighty saviour
 in the house of David his servant,
 as he promised by the lips of holy men,
 those who were his prophets from of old. ℟

2 A saviour who would free us from our foes,
 from the hands of all who hate us.
 So his love for our fathers is fulfilled
 and his holy covenant remembered. ℟

3 He swore to Abraham our father
 to grant us, that free from fear,
 and saved from the hands of our foes,
 we might serve him in holiness and justice
 all the days of our life in his presence. ℟

Gospel Acclamation Ps 24:4. 5

Alleluia, alleluia!
Teach me your paths, my God,
make me walk in your truth.
Alleluia!

or Mt 5:3

Alleluia, alleluia!
How happy are the poor in spirit;
theirs is the kingdom of heaven.
Alleluia!

GOSPEL

A reading from the holy Gospel according to Luke 12:13-21
This hoard of yours, whose will it be?

A man in the crowd said to Jesus, 'Master, tell my brother to give me a share of our inheritance.' 'My friend,' he replied 'who appointed me your judge, or the arbitrator of your claims?' Then he said to them, 'Watch, and be on your guard against avarice of any kind, for a man's life is not made secure by what he owns, even when he has more than he needs.'

Then he told them a parable: 'There was once a rich man who, having had a good harvest from his land, thought to himself "What am I to do? I have not enough room to store my crops." Then he said, "This is what I will do: I will pull down my barns and build bigger ones, and store all my grain and my goods in them, and I will say to my soul: My soul, you have plenty of good things laid by for many years to come; take things easy, eat, drink, have a good time." But God said to him, "Fool! This very night the demand will be made for your soul; and this hoard of yours, whose will it be then?" So it is when a man stores up treasure for himself in place of making himself rich in the sight of God.'

This is the Gospel of the Lord.

TUESDAY

FIRST READING

A reading from the letter of St Paul to the Romans 5:12. 15. 17-21
If death reigned over everyone as the consequence of one man's fall, it is even more certain that everyone will reign in life.

Sin entered the world through one man, and through sin death, and thus death has spread through the whole human race because everyone has sinned.

If it is certain that through one man's fall so many died, it is even more certain that divine grace, coming through the one man, Jesus Christ, came to so many as an abundant free gift. If it is certain that death reigned over everyone as the consequence of one man's fall, it is even more certain that one man, Jesus Christ, will cause everyone to reign in life who receives the free gift that he does not deserve, of being made righteous. Again, as one

Twenty-ninth Week in Ordinary Time, Year I: Tuesday

man's fall brought condemnation on everyone, so the good act of one man brings everyone life and makes them justified. As by one man's disobedience many were made sinners, so by one man's obedience many will be made righteous. But however great the number of sins committed, grace was even greater; and so, just as sin reigned wherever there was death, so grace will reign to bring eternal life, thanks to the righteousness that comes through Jesus Christ our Lord.

This is the word of the Lord.

Responsorial Psalm   Ps 39:7-10. 17. ℟ cf. vv.8. 9

℟ **Here I am, Lord!**
   I come to do your will.

1 You do not ask for sacrifice and offerings,
   but an open ear.
   You do not ask for holocaust and victim.
   Instead, here am I.   ℟

2 In the scroll of the book it stands written
   that I should do your will.
   My God, I delight in your law
   in the depth of my heart.   ℟

3 Your justice I have proclaimed
   in the great assembly.
   My lips I have not sealed;
   you know it, O Lord.   ℟

4 O let there be rejoicing and gladness
   for all who seek you.
   Let them ever say: 'The Lord is great',
   who love your saving help.   ℟

Gospel Acclamation   cf. Lk 8:15
Alleluia, alleluia!
Blessed are those who,
with a noble and generous heart,
take the word of God to themselves
and yield a harvest through their perseverance.
Alleluia!

or   Lk 21:36

Alleluia, alleluia!
Stay awake, praying at all times
for the strength to stand with confidence

before the Son of Man
Alleluia!

GOSPEL

A reading from the holy Gospel according to Luke 12:35-38
Happy those servants whom the master finds awake when he comes.

Jesus said to his disciples: 'See that you are dressed for action and have your lamps lit. Be like men waiting for their master to return from the wedding feast, ready to open the door as soon as he comes and knocks. Happy those servants whom the master finds awake when he comes. I tell you solemnly, he will put on an apron, sit them down at table and wait on them. It may be in the second watch he comes, or in the third, but happy those servants if he finds them ready.'

This is the Gospel of the Lord.

WEDNESDAY

FIRST READING

A reading from the letter of St Paul to the Romans 6:12-18
Offer yourselves to God, and consider yourselves dead men brought back to life.

You must not let sin reign in your mortal bodies or command your obedience to bodily passions, you must not let any part of your body turn into an unholy weapon fighting on the side of sin; you should, instead, offer yourselves to God, and consider yourselves dead men brought back to life; you should make every part of your body into a weapon fighting on the side of God; and then sin will no longer dominate your life, since you are living by grace and not by law.

Does the fact that we are living by grace and not by law mean that we are free to sin? Of course not. You know that if you agree to serve and obey a master you become his slaves. You cannot be slaves of sin that leads to death and at the same time slaves of obedience that leads to righteousness. You were once slaves of sin, but thank God you submitted without reservation to the creed you were taught. You may have been freed from the slavery of sin, but only to become 'slaves' of righteousness.

This is the word of the Lord.

Responsorial Psalm
Ps 123. ℟ v.8

℟ **Our help is in the name of the Lord.**

1 'If the Lord had not been on our side,'
   this is Israel's song.
   'If the Lord had not been on our side
   when men rose against us,
   then would they have swallowed us alive
   when their anger was kindled. ℟

2 'Then would the waters have engulfed us,
   the torrent gone over us;
   over our head would have swept
   the raging waters.'
   Blessed be the Lord who did not give us
   a prey to their teeth! ℟

3 Our life, like a bird, has escaped
   from the snare of the fowler.
   Indeed the snare has been broken
   and we have escaped.
   Our help is in the name of the Lord,
   who made heaven and earth. ℟

Gospel Acclamation
Jn 10:27

Alleluia, alleluia!
The sheep that belong to me listen to my voice,
says the Lord,
I know them and they follow me.
Alleluia!

or
Mt 24:42. 44

Alleluia, alleluia!
Stay awake and stand ready,
because you do not know the hour
when the Son of Man is coming.
Alleluia!

GOSPEL

A reading from the holy Gospel according to Luke 12:39-48
When a man has had a great deal given him, a great deal will be demanded of him.

Jesus said to his disciples: 'You may be quite sure of this, that if the householder had known at what hour the burglar would come, he would not have let anyone break through the wall of his house. You too must stand ready, because the Son of Man is coming at an hour you do not expect.'

Peter said, 'Lord, do you mean this parable for us, or for everyone?' The Lord replied, 'What sort of steward, then, is faithful and wise enough for the master to place him over his household to give them their allowance of food at the proper time? Happy that servant if his master's arrival finds him at this employment. I tell you truly, he will place him over everything he owns. But as for the servant who says to himself, "My master is taking his time coming", and sets about beating the menservants and the maids, and eating and drinking and getting drunk, his master will come on a day he does not expect and at an hour he does not know. The master will cut him off and send him to the same fate as the unfaithful.

'The servant who knows what his master wants, but has not even started to carry out those wishes, will receive very many strokes of the lash. The one who did not know, but deserves to be beaten for what he has done, will receive fewer strokes. When a man has had a great deal given him, a great deal will be demanded of him; when a man has had a great deal given him on trust, even more will be expected of him.'

This is the Gospel of the Lord.

THURSDAY

FIRST READING

A reading from the letter of St Paul to the Romans 6:19-23

Now you have been set free from sin, you have been made slaves of God.

If I may use human terms to help your natural weakness: as once you put your bodies at the service of vice and immorality, so now you must put them at the service of righteousness for your sanctification.

When you were slaves of sin, you felt no obligation to righteousness, and what did you get from this? Nothing but experiences that now make you blush, since that sort of behaviour ends in death. Now, however, you have been set free from sin, you have been made slaves of God, and you get a reward leading to your sanctification and ending in eternal life. For the wage paid by sin is death; the present given by God is eternal life in Christ Jesus our Lord.

This is the word of the Lord.

Twenty-ninth Week in Ordinary Time, Year 1: Thursday

Responsorial Psalm   Ps 1:1-4. 6. ℟ Ps 39:5

℟ **Happy the man who has placed his trust in the Lord.**

1. Happy indeed is the man
who follows not the counsel of the wicked;
nor lingers in the way of sinners
nor sits in the company of scorners,
but whose delight is the law of the Lord
and who ponders his law day and night. ℟

2. He is like a tree that is planted
beside the flowing waters,
that yields its fruit in due season
and whose leaves shall never fade;
and all that he does shall prosper. ℟

3. Not so are the wicked, not so!
For they like winnowed chaff
shall be driven away by the wind.
For the Lord guards the way of the just
but the way of the wicked leads to doom. ℟

Gospel Acclamation   Jn 8:12

Alleluia, alleluia!
I am the light of the world, says the Lord,
anyone who follows me
will have the light of life.
Alleluia!

or   Phil 3:8-9

Alleluia, alleluia!
I have accepted the loss of everything
and I look on everything as so much rubbish
if only I can have Christ
and be given a place in him.
Alleluia!

GOSPEL

A reading from the holy Gospel according to Luke   12:49-53

I am here not to bring peace but division.

Jesus said to his disciples: 'I have come to bring fire to the earth, and how I wish it were blazing already! There is a baptism I must still receive, and how great is my distress till it is over!

'Do you suppose that I am here to bring peace on earth? No, I tell you, but rather division. For from now on a household of five will be divided: three against two and two against three; the father divided against the son, son against father, mother against daughter, daughter against mother, mother-in-law against daughter-in-law, daughter-in-law against mother-in-law.'

This is the Gospel of the Lord.

FRIDAY

FIRST READING

A reading from the letter of St Paul to the Romans 7:18-25
Who will rescue me from this body doomed to death?

I know of nothing good living in me – living, that is, in my unspiritual self – for though the will to do what is good is in me, the performance is not, with the result that instead of doing the good things I want to do, I carry out the sinful things I do not want. When I act against my will, then, it is not my true self doing it, but sin which lives in me.

In fact, this seems to be the rule, that every single time I want to do good it is something evil that comes to hand. In my inmost self I dearly love God's Law, but I can see that my body follows a different law that battles against the law which my reason dictates. This is what makes me a prisoner of that law of sin which lives inside my body.

What a wretched man I am! Who will rescue me from this body doomed to death? Thanks be to God through Jesus Christ our Lord!

This is the word of the Lord.

Responsorial Psalm   Ps 118:66. 68. 76-77. 93-94. ℟ v.68
  ℟ **Lord, teach me your statutes.**

1 Teach me discernment and knowledge
  for I trust in your commands.
  You are good and your deeds are good;
  teach me your statutes. ℟

2 Let your love be ready to console me
  by your promise to your servant.
  Let your love come to me and I shall live
  for your law is my delight. ℟

3 I will never forget your precepts
   for with them you give me life.
   Save me, for I am yours
   since I seek your precepts. ℟

Gospel Acclamation cf. Ps 94:8
  Alleluia, alleluia!
  Harden not your hearts today,
  but listen to the voice of the Lord.
  Alleluia!

or cf. Mt 11:25

  Alleluia, alleluia!
  Blessed are you, Father,
  Lord of heaven and earth,
  for revealing the mysteries of the kingdom
  to mere children.
  Alleluia!

GOSPEL

A reading from the holy Gospel according to Luke 12:54-59

You know how to interpret the face of the earth and the sky. How is it you do not know how to interpret these times?

Jesus said to the crowds, 'When you see a cloud looming up in the west you say at once that rain is coming, and so it does. And when the wind is from the south you say it will be hot, and it is. Hypocrites! You know how to interpret the face of the earth and the sky. How is it you do not know how to interpret these times?

'Why not judge for yourselves what is right? For example: when you go to court with your opponent, try to settle with him on the way, or he may drag you before the judge and the judge hand you over to the bailiff and the bailiff have you thrown into prison. I tell you, you will not get out till you have paid the very last penny.'

This is the Gospel of the Lord.

SATURDAY

FIRST READING

A reading from the letter of St Paul to the Romans 8:1-11
The Spirit of him who raised Jesus from the dead is living in you.

The reason why those who are in Christ Jesus are not condemned, is that the law of the spirit of life in Christ Jesus has set you free from the law of sin and death. God has done what the Law, because of our unspiritual nature, was unable to do. God dealt with sin by sending his own Son in a body as physical as any sinful body, and in that body God condemned sin. He did this in order that the Law's just demands might be satisfied in us, who behave not as our unspiritual nature but as the spirit dictates.

The unspiritual are interested only in what is unspiritual, but the spiritual are interested in spiritual things. It is death to limit oneself to what is unspiritual; life and peace can only come with concern for the spiritual. That is because to limit oneself to what is unspiritual is to be at enmity with God: such a limitation never could and never does submit to God's law. People who are interested only in unspiritual things can never be pleasing to God. Your interests, however, are not in the unspiritual, but in the spiritual, since the Spirit of God has made his home in you. In fact, unless you possessed the Spirit of Christ you would not belong to him. Though your body may be dead it is because of sin, but if Christ is in you then your spirit is life itself because you have been justified; and if the Spirit of him who raised Jesus from the dead is living in you, then he who raised Jesus from the dead will give life to your own mortal bodies through his Spirit living in you.

This is the word of the Lord.

Responsorial Psalm
Ps 23:1-6. ℟ v.6

℟ **Such are the men who seek your face, O Lord.**

1 The Lord's is the earth and its fullness,
  the world and all its peoples.
  It is he who set it on the seas;
  on the waters he made it firm. ℟

2 Who shall climb the mountain of the Lord?
  Who shall stand in his holy place?
  The man with clean hands and pure heart,
  who desires not worthless things. ℟

Twenty-ninth Week in Ordinary Time, Year I: Saturday

3 He shall receive blessings from the Lord
   and reward from the God who saves him.
   Such are the men who seek him,
   seek the face of the God of Jacob.   ℟

Gospel Acclamation   Ps 144:13
   Alleluia, alleluia!
   The Lord is faithful in all his words
   and loving in all his deeds.
   Alleluia!

or   Ez 33:11

   Alleluia, alleluia!
   I take pleasure, not in the death of a wicked man,
   says the Lord,
   but in the turning back of a wicked man
   who changes his ways to win life.
   Alleluia!

GOSPEL

A reading from the holy Gospel according to Luke   13:1-9
Unless you repent, you will all perish as they did.

Some people arrived and told Jesus about the Galileans whose blood Pilate had mingled with that of their sacrifices. At this he said to them, 'Do you suppose these Galileans who suffered like that were greater sinners than any other Galileans? They were not, I tell you. No; but unless you repent you will all perish as they did. Or those eighteen on whom the tower at Siloam fell and killed them? Do you suppose that they were more guilty than all the other people living in Jerusalem? They were not, I tell you. No; but unless you repent you will all perish as they did.'

He told this parable: 'A man had a fig tree planted in his vineyard, and he came looking for fruit on it but found none. He said to the man who looked after the vineyard, "Look here, for three years now I have been coming to look for fruit on this fig tree and finding none. Cut it down: why should it be taking up the ground?" "Sir," the man replied "leave it one more year and give me time to dig round it and manure it: it may bear fruit next year; if not, then you can cut it down." '

This is the Gospel of the Lord.

THIRTIETH WEEK IN ORDINARY TIME
Year I

MONDAY

FIRST READING

A reading from the letter of St Paul to the Romans 8:12-17
The spirit you received is the spirit of sons, and it makes us cry out, 'Abba, Father!'

My brothers, there is no necessity for us to obey our unspiritual selves or to live unspiritual lives. If you do live in that way, you are doomed to die; but if by the Spirit you put an end to the misdeeds of the body you will live.

Everyone moved by the Spirit is a son of God. The spirit you received is not the spirit of slaves bringing fear into your lives again; it is the spirit of sons, and it makes us cry out, 'Abba, Father!' The Spirit himself and our spirit bear united witness that we are children of God. And if we are children we are heirs as well: heirs of God and coheirs with Christ, sharing his sufferings so as to share his glory.

This is the word of the Lord.

Responsorial Psalm Ps 67:2. 4. 6-7. 20-21. ℟ v.21

℟ **This God of ours is a God who saves.**

1 Let God arise, let his foes be scattered.
  Let those who hate him flee before him.
  But the just shall rejoice at the presence of God,
  they shall exult and dance for joy. ℟

2 Father of the orphan, defender of the widow,
  such is God in his holy place.
  God gives the lonely a home to live in;
  he leads the prisoners forth into freedom. ℟

3 May the Lord be blessed day after day.
  He bears our burdens, God our saviour.
  This God of ours is a God who saves.
  The Lord our God holds the keys of death. ℟

Gospel Acclamation
cf. Jn 17:17

Alleluia, alleluia!
Your word is truth, O Lord,
consecrate us in the truth.
Alleluia!

GOSPEL

A reading from the holy Gospel according to Luke 13:10-17

This woman, a daughter of Abraham – was it not right to untie her bonds on the sabbath day?

One sabbath day Jesus was teaching in one of the synagogues, and a woman was there who for eighteen years had been possessed by a spirit that left her enfeebled: she was bent double and quite unable to stand upright. When Jesus saw her he called her over and said, 'Woman, you are rid of your infirmity' and he laid his hands on her. And at once she straightened up, and she glorified God.

But the synagogue official was indignant because Jesus had healed on the sabbath, and he addressed the people present. 'There are six days' he said 'when work is to be done. Come and be healed on one of those days and not on the sabbath.' But the Lord answered him. 'Hypocrites!' he said 'Is there one of you who does not untie his ox or his donkey from the manger on the sabbath and take it out for watering? And this woman, a daughter of Abraham whom Satan has held bound these eighteen years – was it not right to untie her bonds on the sabbath day?' When he said this, all his adversaries were covered with confusion, and all the people were overjoyed at all the wonders he worked.

This is the Gospel of the Lord.

TUESDAY

FIRST READING

A reading from the letter of St Paul to the Romans 8:18-25

The whole creation is eagerly waiting for God to reveal his sons.

I think that what we suffer in this life can never be compared to the glory, as yet unrevealed, which is waiting for us. The whole creation is eagerly waiting for God to reveal his sons. It was not for any fault on the part of creation that it was made unable to attain its purpose, it was made so by God; but creation still retains the hope of being freed, like us, from its slavery to decadence, to enjoy the same freedom and glory as the children of God. From the beginning till now the entire creation, as we know, has been groaning in one great act of giving birth; and not only creation, but all of us who possess the first-fruits of the Spirit, we too groan inwardly as we wait for our bodies to be set free. For we must be content to hope that we shall be saved – our salvation is not in sight, we should not have to be hoping for it if it were – but, as I say, we must hope to be saved since we are not saved yet – it is something we must wait for with patience.

This is the word of the Lord.

Responsorial Psalm   Ps 125. ℟ v.3

℟ **What marvels the Lord worked for us!**

1 When the Lord delivered Zion from bondage,
   it seemed like a dream.
   Then was our mouth filled with laughter,
   on our lips there were songs.   ℟

2 The heathens themselves said: 'What marvels
   the Lord worked for them!'
   What marvels the Lord worked for us!
   Indeed we were glad.   ℟

3 Deliver us, O Lord, from our bondage
   as streams in dry land.
   Those who are sowing in tears.
   will sing when they reap.   ℟

4 They go out, they go out, full of tears,
   carrying seed for the sowing:
   they come back, they come back, full of song,
   carrying their sheaves.   ℟

Gospel Acclamation   Jn 15:15

Alleluia, alleluia!
I call you friends, says the Lord,
because I have made known to you
everything I have learnt from my Father.
Alleluia!

or cf. Mt 11:25
Alleluia, alleluia!
Blessed are you, Father,
Lord of heaven and earth,
for revealing the mysteries of the kingdom
to mere children.
Alleluia!

GOSPEL

A reading from the holy Gospel according to Luke 13:18-21

The seed grew and became a tree.

Jesus said, 'What is the kingdom of God like? What shall I compare it with? It is like a mustard seed which a man took and threw into his garden: it grew and became a tree, and the birds of the air sheltered in its branches.'

Another thing he said, 'What shall I compare the kingdom of God with? It is like the yeast a woman took and mixed in with three measures of flour till it was leavened all through.'

This is the Gospel of the Lord.

WEDNESDAY

FIRST READING

A reading from the letter of St Paul to the Romans 8:26-30

By turning everything to their good God co-operates with all those who love him.

The Spirit comes to help us in our weakness. For when we cannot choose words in order to pray properly, the Spirit himself expresses our plea in a way that could never be put into words, and God who knows everything in our hearts knows perfectly well what he means, and that the pleas of the saints expressed by the Spirit are according to the mind of God.

We know that by turning everything to their good God co-operates with all those who love him, with all those that he has called according to his purpose. They are the ones he chose specially long ago and intended to become true images of his Son, so that his Son might be the eldest of many brothers. He called those he intended for this; those he called he justified, and with those he justified he shared his glory.

This is the word of the Lord.

Responsorial Psalm   Ps 12:4-6. ℟ v.6

   ℟ **Lord, I trust in your mercy.**

1. Look at me, answer me, Lord my God!
   Give light to my eyes lest I fall asleep in death,
   lest my enemy say: 'I have overcome him';
   lest my foes rejoice to see my fall. ℟

2. As for me, I trust in your merciful love.
   Let my heart rejoice in your saving help:
   Let me sing to the Lord for his goodness to me,
   singing psalms to the name of the Lord, the Most High. ℟

Gospel Acclamation   Jn 14:6
Alleluia, alleluia!
I am the Way, the Truth and the Life, says the Lord;
no one can come to the Father except through me.
Alleluia!

or   cf. 2 Thess 2:14

Alleluia, alleluia!
Through the Good News God called us
to share the glory of our Lord Jesus Christ.
Alleluia!

GOSPEL

A reading from the holy Gospel according to Luke   13:22-30
Men from east and west will come to take their places in the kingdom of God.

Through towns and villages Jesus went teaching, making his way to Jerusalem. Someone said to him, 'Sir, will there be only a few saved?' He said to them, 'Try your best to enter by the narrow door, because, I tell you, many will try to enter and will not succeed.

'Once the master of the house has got up and locked the door, you may find yourself knocking on the door, saying, "Lord, open to us" but he will answer, "I do not know where you come from." Then you will find yourself saying, "We once ate and drank in your company; you taught in our streets" but he will reply, "I do not know where you come from. Away from me, all you wicked men!"

'Then there will be weeping and grinding of teeth, when you see Abraham and Isaac and Jacob and all the prophets in the kingdom of God, and yourselves turned outside. And men from east and west, from north and south, will come to take their places at the feast in the kingdom of God.

'Yes, there are those now last who will be first, and those now first who will be last.'

This is the Gospel of the Lord.

THURSDAY

FIRST READING

A reading from the letter of St Paul to the Romans 8:31-39

No created thing can ever come between us and the love of God made visible in Christ.

With God on our side who can be against us? Since God did not spare his own Son, but gave him up to benefit us all, we may be certain, after such a gift, that he will not refuse anything he can give. Could anyone accuse those that God has chosen? When God acquits, could anyone condemn? Could Christ Jesus? No! He not only died for us – he rose from the dead, and there at God's right hand he stands and pleads for us.

Nothing therefore can come between us and the love of Christ, even if we are troubled or worried, or being persecuted, or lacking food or clothes, or being threatened or even attacked. As scripture promised: For your sake we are being massacred daily, and reckoned as sheep for the slaughter. These are the trials through which we triumph, by the power of him who loved us.

For I am certain of this: neither death nor life, no angel, no prince, nothing that exists, nothing still to come, not any power, or height or depth, nor any created thing, can ever come between us and the love of God made visible in Christ Jesus our Lord.

This is the word of the Lord.

Responsorial Psalm   Ps 108:21-22. 26-27. 30-31. ℟ v.26
   ℟ **Save me, O Lord, because of your love.**

1 For your name's sake act in my defence;
   in the goodness of your love be my rescuer.
   For I am poor and needy
   and my heart is pierced within me.   ℟

2 Help me, Lord my God;
  save me because of your love.
  Let them know that this is your work,
  that this is your doing, O Lord.

  ℟ **Save me, O Lord, because of your love.**

3 Loud thanks to the Lord are on my lips.
  I will praise him in the midst of the throng,
  for he stands at the poor man's side
  to save him from those who condemn him.   ℟

Gospel Acclamation   Ps 147:12. 15
  Alleluia, alleluia!
  O praise the Lord, Jerusalem!
  He sends out his word to the earth.
  Alleluia!

or   cf. Lk 19:38; 2:14
  Alleluia, alleluia!
  Blessings on the King who comes,
  in the name of the Lord!
  Peace in heaven
  and glory in the highest heavens!
  Alleluia!

GOSPEL

A reading from the holy Gospel according to Luke   13:31-35
It would not be right for a prophet to die outside Jerusalem.

Some Pharisees came up to Jesus. 'Go away' they said. 'Leave this place, because Herod means to kill you.' He replied, 'You may go and give that fox this message: Learn that today and tomorrow I cast out devils and on the third day attain my end. But for today and tomorrow and the next day I must go on, since it would not be right for a prophet to die outside Jerusalem.

'Jerusalem, Jerusalem, you that kill the prophets and stone those who are sent to you! How often have I longed to gather your children, as a hen gathers her brood under her wings, and you refused! So be it! Your house will be left to you. Yes, I promise you, you shall not see me till the time comes when you say:

Blessings on him who comes in the name of the Lord!'

This is the Gospel of the Lord.

FRIDAY

FIRST READING

A reading from the letter of St Paul to the Romans   9:1-5
I would willingly be condemned if it could help my brothers.

What I want to say now is no pretence; I say it in union with Christ – it is the truth – my conscience in union with the Holy Spirit assures me of it too. What I want to say is this: my sorrow is so great, my mental anguish so endless, I would willingly be condemned and be cut off from Christ if it could help my brothers of Israel, my own flesh and blood. They were adopted as sons, they were given the glory and the covenants; the Law and the ritual were drawn up for them, and the promises were made to them. They are descended from the patriarchs and from their flesh and blood came Christ who is above all, God for ever blessed! Amen.

This is the word of the Lord.

Responsorial Psalm   Ps 147:12-15. 19-20. ℟ v.12

℟ **O praise the Lord, Jerusalem!**

1. O praise the Lord, Jerusalem!
   Zion, praise your God!
   He has strengthened the bars of your gates,
   he has blessed the children within you. ℟

2. He established peace on your borders,
   he feeds you with finest wheat.
   He sends out his word to the earth
   and swiftly runs his command. ℟

3. He makes his word known to Jacob,
   to Israel his laws and decrees.
   He has not dealt thus with other nations;
   he has not taught them his decrees. ℟

Gospel Acclamation   cf. 1 Thess 2:13

Alleluia, alleluia!
Accept God's message for what it really is:
God's message, and not some human thinking.
Alleluia!

or Jn 10:27

Alleluia, alleluia!
The sheep that belong to me listen to my voice,
says the Lord,
I know them and they follow me.
Alleluia!

GOSPEL

A reading from the holy Gospel according to Luke 14:1-6

Which of you here, if his son falls into a well, or his ox, will not pull him out on a sabbath day?

Now on a sabbath day Jesus had gone for a meal to the house of one of the leading Pharisees; and they watched him closely. There in front of him was a man with dropsy, and Jesus addressed the lawyers and Pharisees. 'Is it against the law' he asked 'to cure a man on the sabbath, or not?' But they remained silent, so he took the man and cured him and sent him away. Then he said to them, 'Which of you here, if his son falls into a well, or his ox, will not pull him out on a sabbath day without hesitation?' And to this they could find no answer.

This is the Gospel of the Lord.

SATURDAY

FIRST READING

A reading from the letter of St Paul to the Romans
 11:1-2, 11-12, 25-29

Since the rejection of the Jews meant the reconciliation of the world, their admission will mean nothing less than a resurrection from the dead.

Let me put a question: is it possible that God has rejected his people? Of course not. I, an Israelite, descended from Abraham through the tribe of Benjamin, could never agree that God had rejected his people, the people he chose specially long ago.

Let me put another question then: have the Jews fallen for ever, or have they just stumbled? Obviously they have not fallen for ever: their fall, though, has saved the pagans in a way the Jews may now well emulate. Think of the extent to which the world, the pagan world, has benefited from their fall and defection – then think how much more it will benefit from the conversion of them all.

There is a hidden reason for all this, brothers, of which I do not want you to be ignorant, in case you think you know more than you do. One section of Israel has become blind, but this will last only until the whole pagan world has entered, and then after this the rest of Israel will be saved as well. As scripture says: The liberator will come from Zion, he will banish godlessness from Jacob. And this is the covenant I will make with them when I take their sins away.

The Jews are enemies of God only with regard to the Good News, and enemies only for your sake; but as the chosen people, they are still loved by God, loved for the sake of their ancestors. God never takes back his gifts or revokes his choice.

This is the word of the Lord.

Responsorial Psalm Ps 93:12-15. 17-18. ℞ v.14

℞ **The Lord will not abandon his people.**

1 Happy the man whom you teach, O Lord,
  whom you train by means of your law:
  to him you give peace in evil days. ℞

2 The Lord will not abandon his people
  nor forsake those who are his own:
  for judgement shall again be just
  and all true hearts shall uphold it. ℞

3 If the Lord were not to help me,
  I would soon go down into the silence.
  When I think: 'I have lost my foothold;'
  your mercy, Lord, holds me up. ℞

Gospel Acclamation cf. Col 3:16. 17

Alleluia, alleluia!
Let the message of Christ, in all its richness,
find a home with you;
through him give thanks to God the Father.
Alleluia!

or

Alleluia, alleluia!
Shoulder my yoke and learn from me, says the Lord,
for I am gentle and humble in heart.
Alleluia!

GOSPEL

A reading from the holy Gospel according to Luke   14:1, 7-11

Everyone who exalts himself will be humbled, and the man who humbles himself will be exalted.

Now on a sabbath day Jesus had gone for a meal to the house of one of the leading Pharisees; and they watched him closely.

He then told the guests a parable, because he had noticed how they picked the places of honour. He said this, 'When someone invites you to a wedding feast, do not take your seat in the place of honour. A more distinguished person than you may have been invited, and the person who invited you both may come and say, "Give up your place to this man." And then, to your embarrassment, you would have to go and take the lowest place. No; when you are a guest, make your way to the lowest place and sit there, so that, when your host comes, he may say, "My friend, move up higher." In that way, everyone with you at the table will see you honoured. For everyone who exalts himself will be humbled, and the man who humbles himself will be exalted.'

This is the Gospel of the Lord.

THIRTY-FIRST WEEK IN ORDINARY TIME
Year I
MONDAY

FIRST READING

A reading from the letter of St Paul to the Romans   11:29-36

God has imprisoned all men in their own disobedience only to show mercy to all mankind.

God never takes back his gifts or revokes his choice.

Just as you changed from being disobedient to God, and now enjoy mercy because of their disobedience, so those who are disobedient now – and only because of the mercy shown to you – will also enjoy mercy eventually. God has imprisoned all men in their own disobedience only to show mercy to all mankind.

How rich are the depths of God – how deep his wisdom and knowledge – and how impossible to penetrate his motives or understand his methods! Who could ever know the mind of the

Lord? Who could ever be his counsellor? Who could ever give him anything or lend him anything? All that exists comes from him; all is by him and for him. To him be glory for ever! Amen.

This is the word of the Lord.

Responsorial Psalm Ps 68:30-31. 33-34. 36-37. ℟ v.14

℟ **In your great love, answer me, O God.**

1. As for me in my poverty and pain
let your help, O God, lift me up.
I will praise God's name with a song;
I will glorify him with thanksgiving. ℟

2. The poor when they see it will be glad
and God-seeking hearts will revive;
for the Lord listens to the needy
and does not spurn his servants in their chains. ℟

3. For God will bring help to Zion
and rebuild the cities of Judah
and men shall dwell there in possession.
The sons of his servants shall inherit it;
those who love his name shall dwell there. ℟

Gospel Acclamation Ps 118:18

Alleluia, alleluia!
Open my eyes, O Lord, that I may consider
the wonders of your law.
Alleluia!

or Jn 8:31-32

Alleluia, alleluia!
If you make my word your home
you will indeed be my disciples,
and you will learn the truth, says the Lord.
Alleluia!

GOSPEL

A reading from the holy Gospel according to Luke 14:12-14
Do not invite your friends; invite the poor and the crippled.

Jesus said to his host, one of the leading Pharisees, 'When you give a lunch or a dinner, do not ask your friends, brothers, relations or rich neighbours, for fear they repay your courtesy by inviting you in return. No; when you have a party, invite the poor, the crippled, the lame, the blind; that they cannot pay you back means that you are fortunate, because repayment will be made to you when the virtuous rise again.'

This is the Gospel of the Lord.

TUESDAY

FIRST READING

A reading from the letter of St Paul to the Romans 12:5-16
We belong to each other as parts.

All of us, in union with Christ, form one body, and as parts of it we belong to each other. Our gifts differ according to the grace given us. If your gift is prophecy, then use it as your faith suggests; if administration, then use it for administration; if teaching, then use it for teaching. Let the preachers deliver sermons, the almsgivers give freely, the officials be diligent, and those who do works of mercy do them cheerfully.

Do not let your love be a pretence, but sincerely prefer good to evil. Love each other as much as brothers should, and have a profound respect for each other. Work for the Lord with untiring effort and with great earnestness of spirit. If you have hope, this will make you cheerful. Do not give up if trials come; and keep on praying. If any of the saints are in need you must share with them; and you should make hospitality your special care.

Bless those who persecute you: never curse them, bless them. Rejoice with those who rejoice and be sad with those in sorrow. Treat everyone with equal kindness; never be condescending but make real friends with the poor.

This is the word of the Lord.

Responsorial Psalm Ps 130

℟ **Keep my soul in peace before you, O Lord.**

1 O Lord, my heart is not proud
nor haughty my eyes.
I have not gone after things too great
nor marvels beyond me. ℟

2 Truly I have set my soul
in silence and peace.
A weaned child on its mother's breast,

even so is my soul. ℟

3 O Israel, hope in the Lord
both now and for ever. ℟

Gospel Acclamation cf. Eph 1:17. 18
Alleluia, alleluia!
May the Father of our Lord Jesus Christ
enlighten the eyes of our mind,
so that we can see what hope his call holds for us.
Alleluia!

or Mt 11:28
Alleluia, alleluia!
Come to me, all you who labour and are overburdened,
and I will give you rest, says the Lord.
Alleluia!

GOSPEL

A reading from the holy Gospel according to Luke 14:15-24

Go to the open roads and the hedgerows and force people to come in to make sure my house is full.

One of those gathered round the table said to Jesus, 'Happy the man who will be at the feast in the kingdom of God!' But he said to him, 'There was a man who gave a great banquet, and he invited a large number of people. When the time for the banquet came, he sent his servant to say to those who had been invited, "Come along: everything is ready now." But all alike started to make excuses. The first said, "I have bought a piece of land and must go and see it. Please accept my apologies." Another said, "I have bought five yoke of oxen and am on my way to try them out. Please accept my apologies." Yet another said, "I have just got married and so am unable to come."

'The servant returned and reported this to his master. Then the householder, in a rage, said to his servant, "Go out quickly into the streets and alleys of the town and bring in here the poor, the crippled, the blind and the lame." "Sir," said the servant "your orders have been carried out and there is still room." Then the master said to his servant, "Go to the open roads and the hedgerows and force people to come in to make sure my house is full; because, I tell you, not one of those who were invited shall have a taste of my banquet." '

This is the Gospel of the Lord.

WEDNESDAY

FIRST READING

A reading from the letter of St Paul to the Romans 13:8-10
Love is the answer to every one of the commandments.

Avoid getting into debt, except the debt of mutual love. If you love your fellow men you have carried out your obligations. All the commandments: You shall not commit adultery, you shall not kill, you shall not steal, you shall not covet, and so on, are summed up in this single command: You must love your neighbour as yourself. Love is the one thing that cannot hurt your neighbour; that is why it is the answer to every one of the commandments.

This is the word of the Lord.

Responsorial Psalm
Ps 111:1-2. 4-5. 9. ℞ v.5

℞ **Happy the man who takes pity and lends.**

or

℞ **Alleluia!**

1. Happy the man who fears the Lord,
   who takes delight in his commands.
   His sons will be powerful on earth;
   the children of the upright are blessed. ℞

2. He is a light in the darkness for the upright:
   he is generous, merciful and just.
   The good man takes pity and lends,
   he conducts his affairs with honour. ℞

3. Open-handed, he gives to the poor;
   his justice stands firm for ever.
   His head will be raised in glory. ℞

Gospel Acclamation
Ps 118:88
Alleluia, alleluia!
Because of your love give me life,
and I will do your will.
Alleluia!

or 1 Peter 4:14

Alleluia, alleluia!
It is a blessing for you,
when they insult you
for bearing the name of Christ,
for the Spirit of God rests on you.
Alleluia!

GOSPEL

A reading from the holy Gospel according to Luke 14:25-33

None of you can be my disciples unless he gives up all his possessions.

Great crowds accompanied Jesus on his way and he turned and spoke to them. 'If any man comes to me without hating his father, mother, wife, children, brothers, sisters, yes and his own life too, he cannot be my disciple. Anyone who does not carry his cross and come after me cannot be my disciple.

'And indeed, which of you here, intending to build a tower, would not first sit down and work out the cost to see if he had enough to complete it? Otherwise, if he laid the foundation and then found himself unable to finish the work, the onlookers would all start making fun of him and saying, "Here is a man who started to build and was unable to finish." Or again, what king marching to war against another king would not first sit down and consider whether with ten thousand men he could stand up to the other who advanced against him with twenty thousand? If not, then while the other king was still a long way off, he would send envoys to sue for peace. So in the same way, none of you can be my disciples unless he gives up all his possessions.'

This is the Gospel of the Lord.

THURSDAY

FIRST READING

A reading from the letter of St Paul to the Romans 14:7-12

Alive or dead we belong to the Lord.

The life and death of each of us has its influence on others; if we live, we live for the Lord; and if we die, we die for the Lord, so that alive or dead we belong to the Lord. This explains why Christ both died and came to life, it was so that he might be Lord both of the dead and of the living. This is also why you should never pass judgement on a brother or treat him with contempt, as some of you have done. We shall all have to stand before the judgement seat of God; as scripture says: By my life – it is the Lord who speaks – every knee shall bend before me, and every tongue shall praise God. It is to God, therefore, that each of us must give an account of himself.

This is the word of the Lord.

Responsorial Psalm Ps 26:1. 4. 13-14. R/ v.13

R/ **I am sure I shall see the Lord's goodness in the land of the living.**

1 The Lord is my light and my help;
whom shall I fear?
The Lord is the stronghold of my life;
before whom shall I shrink? R/

2 There is one thing I ask of the Lord,
for this I long,
to live in the house of the Lord,
all the days of my life,
to savour the sweetness of the Lord,
to behold his temple. R/

3 I am sure I shall see the Lord's goodness
in the land of the living.
Hope in him, hold firm and take heart.
Hope in the Lord! R/

Gospel Acclamation Ps 129:5

Alleluia, alleluia!
My soul is waiting for the Lord,
I count on his word.
Alleluia!

or Mt 11:28

Alleluia, alleluia!
Come to me, all you who labour and are overburdened,
and I will give you rest, says the Lord.
Alleluia!

Thirty-first Week in Ordinary Time, Year I: Friday

GOSPEL

A reading from the holy Gospel according to Luke   15:1-10
There will be rejoicing in heaven over one repentant sinner.

The tax collectors and the sinners were all seeking the company of Jesus to hear what he had to say, and the Pharisees and the scribes complained. 'This man' they said 'welcomes sinners and eats with them.' So he spoke this parable to them:

'What man among you with a hundred sheep, losing one, would not leave the ninety-nine in the wilderness and go after the missing one till he found it? And when he found it, would he not joyfully take it on his shoulders and then, when he got home, call together his friends and neighbours? "Rejoice with me," he would say "I have found my sheep that was lost." In the same way, I tell you, there will be more rejoicing in heaven over one repentant sinner than over ninety-nine virtuous men who have no need of repentance.

'Or again, what woman with ten drachmas would not, if she lost one, light a lamp and sweep out the house and search thoroughly till she found it? And then, when she had found it, call together her friends and neighbours. "Rejoice with me," she would say "I have found the drachma I lost." In the same way, I tell you, there is rejoicing among the angels of God over one repentant sinner.'

This is the Gospel of the Lord.

FRIDAY

FIRST READING

A reading from the letter of St Paul to the Romans   15:14-21
I am a priest of Jesus Christ among the pagans so as to make them acceptable as an offering.

My brothers, I am quite certain that you are full of good intentions, perfectly well instructed and able to advise each other. The reason why I have written to you, and put some things rather strongly, is to refresh your memories, since God has given me this special position. He has appointed me as a priest of Jesus Christ, and I am to carry out my priestly duty by bringing the Good News from God to the pagans, and so make them acceptable as an offering, made holy by the Holy Spirit.

I think I have some reason to be proud of what I, in union with Christ Jesus, have been able to do for God. What I am presuming to speak of, of course, is only what Christ himself has done to win the allegiance of the pagans, using what I have said and done by the power of signs and wonders, by the power of the Holy Spirit. Thus, all the way along, from Jerusalem to Illyricum, I have preached Christ's Good News to the utmost of my capacity. I have always, however, made it an unbroken rule never to preach where Christ's name has already been heard. The reason for that was that I had no wish to build on other men's foundations; on the contrary, my chief concern has been to fulfil the text: Those who have never been told about him will see him, and those who have never heard about him will understand.

This is the word of the Lord.

Responsorial Psalm

Ps 97:1-4. ℟ cf. v.2

℟ **The Lord has shown his salvation to the nations.**

1. Sing a new song to the Lord
  for he has worked wonders.
  His right hand and his holy arm
  have brought salvation. ℟

2. The Lord has made known his salvation;
  has shown his justice to the nations.
  He has remembered his truth and love
  for the house of Israel. ℟

3. All the ends of the earth have seen
  the salvation of our God.
  Shout to the Lord all the earth,
  ring out your joy. ℟

Gospel Acclamation

2 Cor 5:19

Alleluia, alleluia!
God in Christ was reconciling the world to himself,
and he has entrusted to us the news that they are reconciled.
Alleluia!

or

1 Jn 2:5

Alleluia, alleluia!
When anyone obeys what Christ has said,
God's love comes to perfection in him.
Alleluia!

Thirty-first Week in Ordinary Time, Year I: Saturday

GOSPEL

A reading from the holy Gospel according to Luke 16:1-8

The children of this world are more astute in dealing with their own kind than are the children of light.

Jesus said to his disciples, 'There was a rich man and he had a steward who was denounced to him for being wasteful with his property. He called for the man and said, "What is this I hear about you? Draw me up an account of your stewardship because you are not to be my steward any longer." Then the steward said to himself, "Now that my master is taking the stewardship from me, what am I to do? Dig? I am not strong enough. Go begging? I should be too ashamed. Ah, I know what I will do to make sure that when I am dismissed from office there will be some to welcome me into their homes."

'Then he called his master's debtors one by one. To the first he said, "How much do you owe my master?" "One hundred measures of oil" was the reply. The steward said, "Here, take your bond; sit down straight away and write fifty." To another he said, "And you, sir, how much do you owe?" "One hundred measures of wheat" was the reply. The steward said, "Here, take your bond and write eighty."

'The master praised the dishonest steward for his astuteness. For the children of this world are more astute in dealing with their own kind than are the children of light.'

This is the Gospel of the Lord.

SATURDAY

FIRST READING

A reading from the letter of St Paul to the Romans 16:3-9. 16. 22-27

Greet each other with a holy kiss.

My greetings to Prisca and Aquila, my fellow workers in Christ Jesus, who risked death to save my life: I am not the only one to owe them a debt of gratitude, all the churches among the pagans do as well. My greetings also to the church that meets at their house.

Greetings to my friend Epaenetus, the first of Asia's gifts to Christ; greetings to Mary who worked so hard for you; to those outstanding apostles Andronicus and Junias, my compatriots and fellow prisoners who became Christians before me; to Ampliatus, my friend in the Lord; to Urban, my fellow worker in Christ; to my friend Stachys. Greet each other with a holy kiss. All the churches of Christ send greetings.

I, Tertius, who wrote out this letter, greet you in the Lord. Greetings from Gaius, who is entertaining me and from the whole church that meets in his house. Erastus, the city treasurer, sends his greetings; so does our brother Quartus.

Glory to him who is able to give you the strength to live according to the Good News I preach, and in which I proclaim Jesus Christ, the revelation of a mystery kept secret for endless ages, but now so clear that it must be broadcast to pagans everywhere to bring them to the obedience of faith. This is only what scripture has predicted, and it is all part of the way the eternal God wants things to be. He alone is wisdom; give glory therefore to him through Jesus Christ for ever and ever. Amen.

This is the word of the Lord.

Responsorial Psalm   Ps 144:2-5. 10-11. R/ v.1

℟ **I will bless your name for ever, O Lord.**

1 I will bless you day after day
   and praise your name for ever.
   The Lord is great, highly to be praised,
   his greatness cannot be measured. ℟

2 Age to age shall proclaim your works,
   shall declare your mighty deeds,
   shall speak of your splendour and glory,
   tell the tale of your wonderful works. ℟

3 All your creatures shall thank you, O Lord,
   and your friends shall repeat their blessing.
   They shall speak of the glory of your reign
   and declare your might, O God. ℟

Gospel Acclamation   cf. Acts 16:14

Alleluia, alleluia!
Open our heart, O Lord,
to accept the words of your Son.
Alleluia!

or   2 Cor 8:9

Alleluia, alleluia!
Jesus Christ was rich,

but he became poor for your sake,
to make you rich out of his poverty.
Alleluia!

GOSPEL

A reading from the holy Gospel according to Luke 16:9-15
If you cannot be trusted with money, that tainted thing, who will trust you with genuine riches?

Jesus said to his disciples, 'I tell you this: use money, tainted as it is, to win you friends, and thus make sure that when it fails you, they will welcome you into the tents of eternity. The man who can be trusted in little things can be trusted in great; the man who is dishonest in little things will be dishonest in great. If then you cannot be trusted with money, that tainted thing, who will trust you with genuine riches? And if you cannot be trusted with what is not yours, who will give you what is your very own?

'No servant can be the slave of two masters: he will either hate the first and love the second, or treat the first with respect and the second with scorn. You cannot be the slave both of God and of money.'

The Pharisees, who loved money, heard all this and laughed at him. He said to them, 'You are the very ones who pass yourselves off as virtuous in people's sight, but God knows your hearts. For what is thought highly of by men is loathsome in the sight of God.'

This is the Gospel of the Lord.

THIRTY-SECOND WEEK IN ORDINARY TIME
Year I

MONDAY

FIRST READING

A reading from the book of Wisdom 1:1-7
Wisdom is a spirit, a friend to man. The Spirit of the Lord fills the whole world.

Love virtue, you who are judges on earth,
let honesty prompt your thinking about the Lord,

seek him in simplicity of heart;
since he is to be found by those who do not put him to the test,
he shows himself to those who do not distrust him.
But selfish intentions divorce from God;
and Omnipotence, put to the test, confounds the foolish.
No, Wisdom will never make its way into a crafty soul
nor stay in a body that is in debt to sin;
the holy spirit of instruction shuns deceit,
it stands aloof from reckless purposes,
is taken aback when iniquity appears.

Wisdom is a spirit, a friend to man,
though she will not pardon the words of a blasphemer,
since God sees into the innermost parts of him,
truly observes his heart,
and listens to his tongue.
The Spirit of the Lord, indeed, fills the whole world,
and that which holds all things together knows every word that is said.

This is the word of the Lord.

Responsorial Psalm   Ps 138:1-10. ℟ v.24

℟ **Lead me, O Lord, in the path of life eternal.**

1 O Lord, you search me and you know me,
   you know my resting and my rising,
   you discern my purpose from afar.
   You mark when I walk or lie down,
   all my ways lie open to you. ℟

2 Before ever a word is on my tongue
   you know it, O Lord, through and through.
   Behind and before you besiege me,
   your hand ever laid upon me.
   Too wonderful for me, this knowledge,
   too high, beyond my reach. ℟

3 O where can I go from your spirit,
   or where can I flee from your face?
   If I climb the heavens, you are there.
   If I lie in the grave, you are there. ℟

4 If I take the wings of the dawn
   and dwell at the sea's furthest end,

even there your hand would lead me,
your right hand would hold me fast. ℟

Gospel Acclamation   Phil 2:15-16
Alleluia, alleluia!
You will shine in the world like bright stars
because you are offering it the word of life.
Alleluia!

GOSPEL

A reading from the holy Gospel according to Luke   17:1-6

If your brother comes back to you seven times a day and says, 'I am sorry,' you must forgive him.

Jesus said to his disciples, 'Obstacles are sure to come, but alas for the one who provides them! It would be better for him to be thrown into the sea with a millstone put round his neck than that he should lead astray a single one of these little ones. Watch yourselves!

'If your brother does something wrong, reprove him and, if he is sorry, forgive him. And if he wrongs you seven times a day and seven times comes back to you and says, "I am sorry," you must forgive him.'

The apostles said to the Lord, 'Increase our faith.' The Lord replied, 'Were your faith the size of a mustard seed you could say to this mulberry tree, "Be uprooted and planted in the sea," and it would obey you.'

This is the Gospel of the Lord.

TUESDAY

FIRST READING

A reading from the book of Wisdom   2:23 – 3:9

In the eyes of the unwise, they did appear to die, but they are in peace.

God made man imperishable,
he made him in the image of his own nature;
it was the devil's envy that brought death into the world,
as those who are his partners will discover.

But the souls of the virtuous are in the hands of God,

no torment shall ever touch them.
In the eyes of the unwise, they did appear to die,
their going looked like a disaster;
their leaving us, like annihilation;
but they are in peace.
If they experienced punishment as men see it,
their hope was rich with immortality;
slight was their affliction, great will their blessing be.
God has put them to the test
and proved them worthy to be with him;
he has tested them like gold in a furnace,
and accepted them as a holocaust.
When the time comes for his visitation they will shine out;
as sparks run through the stubble, so will they.
They shall judge nations, rule over peoples,
and the Lord will be their king for ever.
They who trust in him will understand the truth,
those who are faithful will live with him in love;
for grace and mercy await those he has chosen.

This is the word of the Lord.

Responsorial Psalm   Ps 33:2-3. 16-19. R̸ v.2

R̸ **I will bless the Lord at all times.**

1 I will bless the Lord at all times,
   his praise always on my lips;
   in the Lord my soul shall make its boast.
   The humble shall hear and be glad.   R̸

2 The Lord turns his face against the wicked
   to destroy their remembrance from the earth.
   The Lord turns his eyes to the just
   and his ears to their appeal.   R̸

3 They call and the Lord hears
   and rescues them in all their distress.
   The Lord is close to the broken-hearted;
   those whose spirit is crushed he will save.   R̸

Gospel Acclamation   Mt 4:4
Alleluia, alleluia!
Man does not live on bread alone,
but on every word that comes from the mouth of God.
Alleluia!

or   Jn 14:23

Alleluia, alleluia!
If anyone loves me he will keep my word,
and my Father will love him,
and we shall come to him.
Alleluia!

GOSPEL

A reading from the holy Gospel according to Luke   17:7-10
We are merely servants: we have done no more than our duty.

Jesus said to his disciples: 'Which of you, with a servant ploughing or minding sheep, would say to him when he returned from the fields, "Come and have your meal immediately?" Would he not be more likely to say, "Get my supper laid; make yourself tidy and wait on me while I eat and drink. You can eat and drink yourself afterwards"? Must he be grateful to the servant for doing what he was told? So with you: when you have done all you have been told to do, say, "We are merely servants: we have done no more than our duty." '

This is the Gospel of the Lord.

WEDNESDAY

FIRST READING

A reading from the book of Wisdom   6:1-11
Listen, kings, that you may learn what wisdom is.

Listen, kings, and understand;
rulers of remotest lands, take warning;
hear this, you who have thousands under your rule,
who boast of your hordes of subjects.
For power is a gift to you from the Lord,
sovereignty is from the Most High;
he himself will probe your acts and scrutinise your intentions.

If, as administrators of his kingdom, you have not governed
   justly
nor observed the law,
nor behaved as God would have you behave,
he will fall on you swiftly and terribly.

Ruthless judgement is reserved for the high and mighty;
the lowly will be compassionately pardoned,
the mighty will be mightily punished.
For the Lord of All does not cower before a personage,
he does not stand in awe of greatness,
since he himself has made small and great
and provides for all alike;
but strict scrutiny awaits those in power.

Yes, despots, my words are for you,
that you may learn what wisdom is and not transgress;
for they who observe holy things holily will be adjudged holy,
and, accepting instruction from them, will find their defence in them.
Look forward, therefore, to my words;
yearn for them, and they will instruct you.

    This is the word of the Lord.

Responsorial Psalm
Ps 81:3-4. 6-7. ℟ v.8

  ℟ **Arise, O God, judge the earth.**

1. Do justice for the weak and the orphan,
defend the afflicted and the needy.
Rescue the weak and the poor;
set them free from the hand of the wicked. ℟

2. I have said to you: 'You are gods
and all of you, sons of the Most High.'
And yet, you shall die like men,
you shall fall like any of the princes. ℟

Gospel Acclamation
cf. 2 Thess 2:14

Alleluia, alleluia!
Through the Good News God called us
to share the glory of our Lord Jesus Christ.
Alleluia!

or

1 Thess 5:18

Alleluia, alleluia!
For all things give thanks,
because this is what God expects you to do in Christ Jesus.
Alleluia!

GOSPEL

A reading from the holy Gospel according to Luke 17:11-19

No one has come back to give praise to God, except this foreigner.

On the way to Jerusalem Jesus travelled along the border between Samaria and Galilee. As he entered one of the villages, ten lepers came to meet him. They stood some way off and called to him, 'Jesus! Master! Take pity on us.' When he saw them he said, 'Go and show yourselves to the priests.' Now as they were going away they were cleansed. Finding himself cured, one of them turned back praising God at the top of his voice and threw himself at the feet of Jesus and thanked him. The man was a Samaritan. This made Jesus say, 'Were not all ten made clean? The other nine, where are they? It seems that no one has come back to give praise to God, except this foreigner.' And he said to the man, 'Stand up and go on your way. Your faith has saved you.'

This is the Gospel of the Lord.

THURSDAY

FIRST READING

A reading from the book of Wisdom 7:22 – 8:1

Wisdom is a reflection of the eternal light, untarnished mirror of God's power.

Within Wisdom is a spirit intelligent, holy,
unique, manifold, subtle,
active, incisive, unsullied,
lucid, invulnerable, benevolent, sharp,
irresistible, beneficent, loving to man,
steadfast, dependable, unperturbed,
almighty, all-surveying,
penetrating all intelligent, pure
and most subtle spirits;
for Wisdom is quicker to move than any motion;
she is so pure, she pervades and permeates all things.

She is a breath of the power of God,
pure emanation of the glory of the Almighty;
hence nothing impure can find a way into her.
She is a reflection of the eternal light,

untarnished mirror of God's active power,
image of his goodness.

Although alone, she can do all;
herself unchanging, she makes all things new.
In each generation she passes into holy souls,
she makes them friends of God and prophets;
for God loves only the man who lives with Wisdom.
She is indeed more splendid than the sun,
she outshines all the constellations;
compared with light, she takes first place,
for light must yield to night,
but over Wisdom evil can never triumph.
She deploys her strength from one end of the earth to the other,
ordering all things for good.

This is the word of the Lord.

Responsorial Psalm   Ps 118:89-91. 130. 135. 175. ℟ v.89

℟ **Your word, O Lord, stands for ever.**

1 Your word, O Lord, for ever
  stands firm in the heavens:
  your truth lasts from age to age,
  like the earth you created.   ℟

2 By your decree it endures to this day;
  for all things serve you.
  The unfolding of your word gives light
  and teaches the simple.   ℟

3 Let your face shine on your servant
  and teach me your decrees.
  Give life to my soul that I may praise you.
  Let your decrees give me help.   ℟

Gospel Acclamation   1 Peter 1:25
Alleluia, alleluia!
The word of the Lord remains for ever:
What is this word?
It is the Good News that has been brought to you.
Alleluia!

or　　　　　　　　　　　　　　　　　　　　　　　　　　　　Jn 15:5

Alleluia, alleluia!
I am the vine,
you are the branches.
Whoever remains in me, with me in him,
bears fruit in plenty, says the Lord.
Alleluia!

GOSPEL

A reading from the holy Gospel according to Luke　　　17:20-25
The kingdom of God is among you.

Asked by the Pharisees when the kingdom of God was to come, Jesus gave them this answer, 'The coming of the kingdom of God does not admit of observation and there will be no one to say, "Look here! Look there!" For, you must know, the kingdom of God is among you.'

He said to the disciples, 'A time will come when you will long to see one of the days of the Son of Man and will not see it. They will say to you, "Look there!" or, "Look here!" Make no move; do not set off in pursuit; for as the lightning flashing from one part of heaven lights up the other, so will be the Son of Man when his day comes. But first he must suffer grievously and be rejected by this generation.'

This is the Gospel of the Lord.

FRIDAY

FIRST READING

A reading from the book of Wisdom　　　　　　　　　　　13:1-9
If they are capable of investigating the world, how have they been so slow to find its Master?

Naturally stupid are all men who have not known God
and who, from the good things that are seen, have not been able
　　to discover Him-who-is,
or, by studying the works, have failed to recognise the Artificer.
Fire however, or wind, or the swift air,
the sphere of the stars, impetuous water, heaven's lamps,
are what they have held to be the gods who govern the world.

If, charmed by their beauty, they have taken things for gods,
let them know how much the Lord of these excels them,
since the very Author of beauty has created them.
And if they have been impressed by their power and energy,
let them deduce from these how much mightier is he that has
    formed them,
since through the grandeur and beauty of the creatures
we may, by analogy, contemplate their Author.

Small blame, however, attaches to these men,
for perhaps they only go astray
in their search for God and their eagerness to find him;
living among his works, they strive to comprehend them
and fall victim to appearances, seeing so much beauty.

Even so, they are not to be excused:
if they are capable of acquiring enough knowledge
to be able to investigate the world,
how have they been so slow to find its Master?

> This is the word of the Lord.

Responsorial Psalm
Ps 18:2-5. R̷ v.2

R̷ **The heavens proclaim the glory of God.**

1. The heavens proclaim the glory of God
   and the firmament shows forth the work of his hands.
   Day unto day takes up the story
   and night unto night makes known the message. R̷

2. No speech, no word, no voice is heard
   yet their span extends through all the earth,
   their words to the utmost bounds of the world. R̷

Gospel Acclamation
Heb 4:12

> Alleluia, alleluia!
> The word of God is something alive and active;
> it can judge secret emotions and thoughts.
> Alleluia!

or
Lk 21:28

> Alleluia, alleluia!
> Stand erect, hold your heads high,
> because your liberation is near at hand.
> Alleluia!

Thirty-second Week in Ordinary Time, Year I: Saturday 829

GOSPEL

A reading from the holy Gospel according to Luke 17:26-37
When the day comes for the Son of Man to be revealed.

Jesus said to the disciples: 'As it was in Noah's day, so will it also be in the days of the Son of Man. People were eating and drinking, marrying wives and husbands, right up to the day Noah went into the ark, and the Flood came and destroyed them all. It will be the same as it was in Lot's day: people were eating and drinking, buying and selling, planting and building, but the day Lot left Sodom, God rained fire and brimstone from heaven and it destroyed them all. It will be the same when the day comes for the Son of Man to be revealed.

'When that day comes, anyone on the housetop, with his possessions in the house, must not come down to collect them, nor must anyone in the fields turn back either. Remember Lot's wife. Anyone who tries to preserve his life will lose it; and anyone who loses it will keep it safe. I tell you, on that night two will be in one bed: one will be taken, the other left; two women will be grinding corn together: one will be taken, the other left.' The disciples interrupted. 'Where Lord?' they asked. He said, 'Where the body is, there too will the vultures gather.'

This is the Gospel of the Lord.

SATURDAY

FIRST READING

A reading from the book of Wisdom 18:14-16; 19:6-9
The Red Sea became an unimpeded way, and they skipped like lambs.

When peaceful silence lay over all,
and night had run the half of her swift course,
down from the heavens, from the royal throne, leapt your
    all-powerful Word;
into the heart of a doomed land the stern warrior leapt.
Carrying your unambiguous command like a sharp sword,
he stood, and filled the universe with death;
he touched the sky, yet trod the earth.
For, to keep your children from all harm,
the whole creation, obedient to your commands,
was once more, and newly, fashioned in its nature.

Overshadowing the camp there was the cloud,
where water had been, dry land was seen to rise,
the Red Sea became an unimpeded way,
the tempestuous flood a green plain;
sheltered by your hand, the whole nation passd across,
gazing at these amazing miracles.
They were like horses at pasture,
they skipped like lambs,
singing your praises, Lord, their deliverer.

    This is the word of the Lord.

Responsorial Psalm   Ps 104: 2-3. 36-37. 42-43. R̸ v.5

  R̸ **Remember the wonders the Lord has done.**

or

    R̸   **Alleluia!**

1. O sing to the Lord, sing his praise;
   tell all his wonderful works!
   Be proud of his holy name,
   let the hearts that seek the Lord rejoice.   R̸

2. He struck all the first-born in their land,
   the finest flower of their sons.
   He led out Israel with silver and gold.
   In his tribes were none who fell behind.   R̸

3. For he remembered his holy word,
   which he gave to Abraham his servant.
   So he brought out his people with joy,
   his chosen ones with shouts of rejoicing.   R̸

Gospel Acclamation   James 1:21

Alleluia, alleluia!
Accept and submit to the word
which has been planted in you
and can save your souls.
Alleluia!

or   cf. 2 Thess 2:14

Alleluia, alleluia!
Through the Good News God called us
to share the glory of our Lord Jesus Christ.
Alleluia!

GOSPEL

A reading from the holy Gospel according to Luke   18:1-8
God will see justice done to his chosen who cry to him.

Jesus told his disciples a parable about the need to pray continually and never lose heart. 'There was a judge in a certain town' he said 'who had neither fear of God nor respect for men. In the same town there was a widow who kept on coming to him and saying, "I want justice from you against my enemy!" For a long time he refused, but at last he said to himself, "Maybe I have neither fear of God nor respect for man, but since she keeps pestering me I must give the widow her just rights, or she will persist in coming and worry me to death."'

And the Lord said, 'You notice what the unjust judge has to say? Now will not God see justice done to his chosen who cry to him day and night even when he delays to help them? I promise you, he will see justice done to them, and done speedily. But when the Son of Man comes, will he find any faith on earth?'

This is the Gospel of the Lord.

THIRTY-THIRD WEEK IN ORDINARY TIME
Year I

MONDAY

FIRST READING

A reading from the first book   1:10-15. 41-43. 54-57. 62-64
of Maccabees
It was a dreadful wrath that visited Israel.

There grew a sinful offshoot, Antiochus Epiphanes, son of King Antiochus; once a hostage in Rome, he became king in the one hundred and thirty-seventh year of the kingdom of the Greeks. It was then that there emerged from Israel a set of renegades who led many people astray. 'Come,' they said 'let us reach an understanding with the pagans surrounding us. For since we separated ourselves from them many misfortunes have overtaken us.' This proposal proved acceptable, and a number of the people eagerly approached the king, who authorised them to practise the pagan observances. So they built a gymnasium in Jerusalem, such as the pagans have, disguised their circumcision, and abandoned the holy covenant, submitting to the heathen rule as willing slaves of impiety.

Then the king issued a proclamation to his whole kingdom that all were to become a single people, each renouncing his particular customs. All the pagans conformed to the king's decree, and many Israelites chose to accept his religion, sacrificing to idols and profaning the sabbath. On the fifteenth day of Chislev in the year one hundred and forty-five the king erected the abomination of desolation above the altar; and altars were built in the surrounding towns of Judah and incense offered at the doors of houses and in the streets. Any books of the Law that came to light were torn up and burned. Whenever anyone was discovered possessing a copy of the covenant or practising the Law, the king's decree sentenced him to death.

Yet there were many in Israel who stood firm and found the courage to refuse unclean food. They chose death rather than contamination by such fare or profanation of the holy covenant, and they were executed. It was a dreadful wrath that visited Israel.

This is the word of the Lord.

Responsorial Psalm   Ps 118:53. 61. 134. 150. 155. 158. ℟ cf. v.88

℟ **Give me life, O Lord,**
and I will do your will.

1   I am seized with indignation at the wicked
    who forsake your law.
    Though the nets of the wicked ensnared me
    I remembered your law.   ℟

2   Redeem me from man's oppression
    and I will keep your precepts.
    Those who harm me unjustly draw near:
    they are far from your law.   ℟

3   Salvation is far from the wicked
    who are heedless of your statutes.
    I look at the faithless with disgust;
    they ignore your promise.   ℟

Gospel Acclamation   Jn 8:12
Alleluia, alleluia!
I am the light of the world, says the Lord,

anyone who follows me
will have the light of life.
Alleluia!

GOSPEL

A reading from the holy Gospel according to Luke 18:35-43
What do you want me to do for you? – Let me see again.

As Jesus drew near to Jericho there was a blind man sitting at the side of the road begging. When he heard the crowd going past he asked what it was all about, and they told him that Jesus the Nazarene was passing by. So he called out, 'Jesus, Son of David, have pity on me.' The people in front scolded him and told him to keep quiet, but he shouted all the louder, 'Son of David, have pity on me.' Jesus stopped and ordered them to bring the man to him, and when he came up, asked him, 'What do you want me to do for you?' 'Sir,' he replied 'let me see again.' Jesus said to him,' 'Receive your sight. Your faith has saved you.' And instantly his sight returned and he followed him praising God, and all the people who saw it gave praise to God for what had happened.

This is the Gospel of the Lord.

TUESDAY

FIRST READING

A reading from the second book of Maccabees 6:18-31
I shall have left an example of how to make a good death for the holy laws.

Eleazar, one of the foremost teachers of the Law, a man already advanced in years and of most noble appearance, was being forced to open his mouth wide to swallow pig's flesh. But he, resolving to die with honour rather than to live disgraced, went to the block of his own accord, spitting the stuff out, the plain duty of anyone with the courage to reject what it is not lawful to taste, even from a natural tenderness for his own life. Those in charge of the impious banquet, because of their long-standing friendship with him, took him aside and privately urged him to have meat brought of a kind he could properly use, prepared by himself, and only pretend to eat the portions of sacrificial meat as prescribed by the king; this action would enable him to escape death, by availing himself of an act of kindness prompted by their long friendship. But having taken a noble decision worthy of his years and the dignity of his great age and the well earned distinction of his grey hairs, worthy too of his impeccable conduct from boyhood, and above all of the holy legislation established by God himself, he publicly stated his convictions, telling them to send him at once to Hades. 'Such pretence' he said 'does not square with our time of life; many young people would suppose that Eleazar at the age of ninety had conformed to the foreigners' way of life, and because I had played this part for the sake of a paltry brief spell of life might themselves be led astray on my account; I should only bring defilement and disgrace on my old age. Even though for the moment I avoid execution by man, I can never, living or dead, elude the grasp of the Almighty. Therefore if I am man enough to quit this life here and now I shall prove myself worthy of my old age, and I shall have left the young a noble example of how to make a good death, eagerly and generously, for the venerable and holy laws.'

With these words he went straight to the block. His escorts, so recently well disposed towards him, turned against him after this declaration, which they regarded as sheer madness. Just before he died under the blows, he groaned aloud and said, 'The Lord whose knowledge is holy sees clearly that, though I might have escaped death, whatever agonies of body I now endure under this bludgeoning, in my soul I am glad to suffer, because of the awe which he inspires in me.'

This was how he died, leaving his death as an example of nobility and a record of virtue not only for the young but for the great majority of the nation.

This is the word of the Lord.

Responsorial Psalm   Ps 3:2-7. ℟ v.6
℟ **The Lord upholds me.**

1 How many are my foes, O Lord!
   How many are rising up against me!
   How many are saying about me:
   'There is no help for him in God.' ℟

2 But you, Lord, are a shield about me,
   my glory, who lift up my head.
   I cry aloud to the Lord.
   He answers from his holy mountain. ℟

3 I lie down to rest and I sleep.
   I wake, for the Lord upholds me.

Thirty-third Week in Ordinary Time, Year I: Tuesday

I will not fear even thousands of people
who are ranged on every side against me.   ℟

Gospel Acclamation   Ps 129:5
Alleluia, alleluia!
My soul is waiting for the Lord,
I count on his word.
Alleluia!

or   1 Jn 4:10

Alleluia, alleluia!
God so loved us when he sent his Son
to be the sacrifice that takes our sins away.
Alleluia!

GOSPEL

A reading from the holy Gospel according to Luke   19:1-10
The Son of Man has come to seek out and save what was lost.

Jesus entered Jericho and was going through the town when a man whose name was Zacchaeus made his appearance; he was one of the senior tax collectors and a wealthy man. He was anxious to see what kind of man Jesus was, but he was too short and could not see him for the crowd; so he ran ahead and climbed a sycamore tree to catch a glimpse of Jesus who was to pass that way. When Jesus reached the spot he looked up and spoke to him: 'Zacchaeus, come down. Hurry, because I must stay at your house today.' And he hurried down and welcomed him joyfully. They all complained when they saw what was happening. 'He has gone to stay at a sinner's house' they said. But Zacchaeus stood his ground and said to the Lord, 'Look, sir, I am going to give half my property to the poor, and if I have cheated anybody I will pay him back four times the amount.' And Jesus said to him, 'Today salvation has come to this house, because this man too is a son of Abraham; for the Son of Man has come to seek out and save what was lost.'

This is the Gospel of the Lord.

WEDNESDAY

FIRST READING

A reading from the second book of Maccabees 7:1. 20-31
The creator of the world will give you back both breath and life.

There were seven brothers who were arrested with their mother. The king tried to force then to taste pig's flesh, which the Law forbids, by torturing them with whips and scourges.

The mother was especially admirable and worthy of honourable remembrance, for she watched the death of seven sons in the course of a single day, and endured it resolutely because of her hopes in the Lord. Indeed she encouraged each of them in the language of their ancestors; filled with noble conviction, she reinforced her womanly argument with manly courage, saying to them, 'I do not know how you appeared in my womb; it was not I who endowed you with breath and life, I had not the shaping of your every part. 'It is the creator of the world, ordaining the process of man's birth and presiding over the origin of all things, who in his mercy will most surely give you back both breath and life, seeing that you now despise your own existence for the sake of his laws.'

Antiochus thought he was being ridiculed, suspecting insult in the tone of her voice; and as the youngest was still alive he appealed to him not with mere words but with promises on oath to make him both rich and happy if he would abandon the traditions of his ancestors; he would make him his Friend and entrust him with public office. The young man took no notice at all, and so the king then appealed to the mother, urging her to advise the youth to save his life. After a great deal of urging on his part she agreed to try persuasion on her son. Bending over him, she fooled the cruel tyrant with these words, uttered in the language of their ancestors, 'My son, have pity on me; I carried you nine months in my womb and suckled you three years, fed you and reared you to the age you are now and cherished you. I implore you, my child, observe heaven and earth, consider all that is in them, and acknowledge that God made them out of what did not exist, and that mankind comes into being in the same way. Do not fear this executioner, but prove yourself worthy of your brothers, and make death welcome, so that in the day of mercy I may receive you back in your brothers' company.'

She had scarcely ended when the young man said, 'What are you all waiting for? I will not comply with the king's ordinance; I

Thirty-third Week in Ordinary Time, Year I: Wednesday 837

obey the ordinance of the Law given to our ancestors through Moses. As for you, sir, who have contrived every kind of evil against the Hebrews, you will certainly not escape the hands of God.'

This is the word of the Lord.

Responsorial Psalm Ps 16:1. 5-6. 8. 15. ℟ v.15

℟ **I shall be filled, when I awake, with the sight of your glory, O Lord.**

1. Lord, hear a cause that is just,
pay heed to my cry.
Turn your ear to my prayer:
no deceit is on my lips. ℟

2. I kept my feet firmly in your paths;
there was no faltering in my steps.
I am here and I call, you will hear me, O God.
Turn your ear to me; hear my words. ℟

3. Guard me as the apple of your eye.
Hide me in the shadow of your wings.
As for me, in my justice I shall see your face
and be filled, when I awake, with the sight of your glory. ℟

Gospel Acclamation 1 Jn 2:5

Alleluia, alleluia!
When anyone obeys what Christ has said,
God's love comes to perfection in him.
Alleluia!

or cf. Jn 15:16

Alleluia, alleluia!
I chose you from the world
to go out and to bear fruit,
fruit that will last.
Alleluia!

GOSPEL

A reading from the holy Gospel according to Luke 19:11-28
Why did you not put my money in the bank?

While the people were listening, Jesus went on to tell a parable, because he was near Jerusalem and they imagined that the kingdom of God was going to show itself then and there. Accordingly he said, 'A man of noble birth went to a distant country to be appointed king and afterwards return. He summoned ten of his servants and gave them ten pounds. "Do business with these" he told them "until I get back." But his compatriots detested him and sent a delegation to follow him with this message, "We do not want this man to be our king."

'Now on his return, having received his appointment as king, he sent for those servants to whom he had given the money, to find out what profit each had made. The first came in and said, "Sir, your one pound has brought in ten." "Well done, my good servant!" he replied. "Since you have proved yourself faithful in a very small thing, you shall have the government of ten cities." Then came the second and said, "Sir, your one pound has made five." To this one also he said, "And you shall be in charge of five cities." Next came the other and said, "Sir, here is your pound. I put it away safely in a piece of linen because I was afraid of you; for you are an exacting man: you pick up what you have not put down and reap what you have not sown." "You wicked servant!" he said "Out of your own mouth I condemn you. So you knew I was an exacting man, picking up what I have not put down and reaping what I have not sown? Then why did you not put my money in the bank? On my return I could have drawn it out with interest." And he said to those standing by, "Take the pound from him and give it to the man who has ten pounds." And they said to him, "But, sir, he has ten pounds . . ." "I tell you, to everyone who has will be given more; but from the man who has not, even what he has will be taken away.

' "But as for my enemies who did not want me for their king, bring them here and execute them in my presence." '

When he had said this he went on ahead, going up to Jerusalem.

This is the Gospel of the Lord.

THURSDAY

FIRST READING

A reading from the first book of Maccabees 2:15-29
We will follow the covenant of our ancestors.

The commissioners of King Antiochus who were enforcing the

apostasy came to the town of Modein to make the Israelites sacrifice. Many Israelites gathered round them, but Mattathias and his sons drew apart. The king's commissioners then addressed Mattathias as follows, 'You are a respected leader, a great man in this town; you have sons and brothers to support you. Be the first to step forward and conform to the king's decree, as all the nations have done, and the leaders of Judah and the survivors in Jerusalem; you and your sons shall be reckoned among the Friends of the King, you and your sons shall be honoured with gold and silver and many presents.' Raising his voice, Mattathias retorted, 'Even if every nation living in the king's dominions obeys him, each forsaking its ancestral religion to conform to his decrees, I, my sons and my brothers will still follow the covenant of our ancestors. Heaven preserve us from forsaking the Law and its observances. As for the king's orders, we will not follow them; we will not swerve from our own religion either to right or to left.' As he finished speaking, a Jew came forward in the sight of all to offer sacrifice on the altar in Modein as the royal edict required. When Mattathias saw this, he was fired with zeal; stirred to the depth of his being, he gave vent to his legitimate anger, threw himself on the man and slaughtered him on the altar. At the same time he killed the king's commissioner who was there to enforce the sacrifice, and tore down the altar. In his zeal for the Law he acted as Phinehas did against Zimri son of Salu. Then Mattathias went through the town, shouting at the top of his voice, 'Let everyone who has a fervour for the Law and takes his stand on the covenant come out and follow me.' Then he fled with his sons into the hills, leaving all their possessions behind in the town.

At this many who were concerned for virtue and justice went down to the desert and stayed there.

This is the word of the Lord.

Responsorial Psalm   Ps 49:1-2. 5-6. 14-15. R/ v.23

℟ **I will show God's salvation to the upright.**

1 The God of gods, the Lord,
 has spoken and summoned the earth,
 from the rising of the sun to its setting.
 Out of Zion's perfect beauty he shines. ℟

2 'Summon before me my people
 who made covenant with me by sacrifice.'
 The heavens proclaim his justice,
 for he, God, is the judge. ℟

(continued)

3 'Pay your sacrifice of thanksgiving to God
and render him your votive offerings.
Call on me in the day of distress.
I will free you and you shall honour me.'

℟ **I will show God's salvation to the upright.**

Gospel Acclamation   Ps 118:135

Alleluia, alleluia!
Let your face shine on your servant,
and teach me your decrees.
Alleluia!

or   cf. Ps 94:8

Alleluia, alleluia!
Harden not your hearts today,
but listen to the voice of the Lord.
Alleluia!

GOSPEL

A reading from the holy Gospel according to Luke   19:41-44
If you had only understood the message of peace!

As Jesus drew near Jerusalem and came in sight of the city he shed tears over it and said, 'If you in your turn had only understood on this day the message of peace! But, alas, it is hidden from your eyes! Yes, a time is coming when your enemies will raise fortifications all round you, when they will encircle you and hem you in on every side; they will dash you and the children inside your walls to the ground; they will leave not one stone standing on another within you – and all because you did not recognise your opportunity when God offered it!'

This is the Gospel of the Lord.

FRIDAY

FIRST READING

A reading from the first book of Maccabees   4:36-37. 52-59
They celebrated the dedication of the altar, joyfully offering holocausts.

Judas and his brothers said, 'Now that our enemies have been defeated, let us go up to purify the sanctuary and dedicate it.' So they marshalled the whole army, and went up to Mount Zion.

Thirty-third Week in Ordinary Time, Year I: Friday

On the twenty-fifth of the ninth month, Chislev, in the year one hundred and forty-eight, they rose at dawn and offered a lawful sacrifice on the new altar of holocausts which they had made. The altar was dedicated, to the sound of zithers, harps and cymbals, at the same time of year and on the same day on which the pagans had originally profaned it. The whole people fell prostrate in adoration, praising to the skies him who had made them so successful. For eight days they celebrated the dedication of the altar, joyfully offering holocausts, communion sacrifices and thanksgivings. They ornamented the front of the Temple with crowns and bosses of gold, repaired the gates and the storerooms and fitted them with doors. There was no end to the rejoicing among the people, and the reproach of the pagans was lifted from them. Judas, with his brothers and the whole assembly of Israel, made it a law that the days of the dedication of the altar should be celebrated yearly at the proper season, for eight days beginning on the twenty-fifth of the month Chislev, with rejoicing and gladness.

This is the word of the Lord.

Responsorial Psalm
1 Chron 29:10-12. ℟ v.13

℟ **We praise your glorious name, O Lord.**

1 Blessed are you, O Lord,
 the God of Israel our father,
 for ever, for ages unending. ℟

2 Yours, Lord, are greatness and power,
 and splendour, triumph and glory.
 All is yours, in heaven and on earth. ℟

3 Yours, O Lord, is the kingdom,
 you are supreme over all.
 Both honour and riches come from you. ℟

4 You are the ruler of all,
 from your hand come strength and power,
 from your hand come greatness and might. ℟

Gospel Acclamation
cf. 2 Tim 1:10

Alleluia, alleluia!
Our Saviour Christ Jesus abolished death,
and he has proclaimed life through the Good News.
Alleluia!

or Jn 10:27

Alleluia, alleluia!
The sheep that belong to me listen to my voice,
says the Lord,
I know them and they follow me.
Alleluia!

GOSPEL

A reading from the holy Gospel according to Luke 19:45-48
You have turned the house of God into a robbers' den.

Jesus went into the Temple and began driving out those who were selling. 'According to scripture,' he said 'my house will be a house of prayer. But you have turned it into a robbers' den.'

He taught in the Temple every day. The chief priests and the scribes, with the support of the leading citizens, tried to do away with him, but they did not see how they could carry this out because the people as a whole hung on his words.

This is the Gospel of the Lord.

SATURDAY

FIRST READING

A reading from the first book of Maccabees 6:1-13
I am dying of melancholy because of the wrong I did in Jerusalem.

King Antiochus was making his way across the upper provinces; he had heard that in Persia there was a city called Elymais, renowned for its riches, its silver and gold, and its very wealthy temple containing golden armour, breastplates and weapons, left there by Alexander son of Philip, the king of Macedon, the first to reign over the Greeks. He therefore went and attempted to take the city and pillage it, but without success, since the citizens learnt of his intention, and offered him a stiff resistance, whereupon he turned about and retreated, disconsolate, in the direction of Babylon. But while he was still in Persia news reached him that the armies that had invaded the land of Judah had been defeated, and that Lysias in particular had advanced in massive strength, only to be forced to turn and flee before the Jews; these had been strengthened by the acquisition of arms, supplies and abundant spoils from the armies they had cut to pieces; they had

Thirty-third Week in Ordinary Time, Year I: Saturday

overthrown the abomination he had erected over the altar in Jerusalem, and had encircled the sanctuary with high walls as in the past, and had fortified Bethzur, one of his cities. When the king heard this news he was amazed and profoundly shaken; he threw himself on his bed and fell into a lethargy from acute disappointment, because things had not turned out for him as he had planned. And there he remained for many days, subject to deep and recurrent fits of melancholy, until he understood that he was dying. Then summoning all his Friends, he said to them, 'Sleep evades my eyes, and my heart is cowed by anxiety. I have been asking myself how I could have come to such a pitch of distress, so great a flood as that which now engulfs me – I who was so generous and well-loved in my heyday. But now I remember the wrong I did in Jerusalem when I seized all the vessels of silver and gold there, and ordered the extermination of the inhabitants of Judah for no reason at all. This, I am convinced, is why these misfortunes have overtaken me, and why I am dying of melancholy in a foreign land.'

This is the word of the Lord.

Responsorial Psalm
Ps 9:2-4. 6. 16. 19. ℟ cf. v.16

℟ **I will rejoice in your saving help, O Lord.**

1 I will praise you, Lord, with all my heart;
   I will recount all your wonders.
   I will rejoice in you and be glad,
   and sing psalms to your name, O Most High.   ℟

2 See how my enemies turn back,
   how they stumble and perish before you.
   You have checked the nations, destroyed the wicked;
   you have wiped out their name for ever and ever.   ℟

3 The nations' feet have been caught
   in the snare they laid;
   for the needy shall not always be forgotten
   nor the hopes of the poor be in vain.   ℟

Gospel Acclamation
cf. Lk 8:15

Alleluia, alleluia!
Blessed are those who,
with a noble and generous heart,
take the word of God to themselves
and yield a harvest through their perseverance.
Alleluia!

or   cf. 2 Tim 1:10

> Alleluia, alleluia!
> Our Saviour Christ Jesus abolished death,
> and he has proclaimed life through the Good News.
> Alleluia!

GOSPEL

A reading from the holy Gospel according to Luke   20:27-40
He is God not of the dead, but of the living.

Some Sadducees – those who say that there is no resurrection – approached Jesus and they put this question to him, 'Master, we have it from Moses in writing, that if a man's married brother dies childless, the man must marry the widow to raise up children for his brother. Well then, there were seven brothers. The first, having married a wife, died childless. The second and then the third married the widow. And the same with all seven, they died leaving no children. Finally the woman herself died. Now, at the resurrection, to which of them will she be wife since she had been married to all seven?'

Jesus replied, 'The children of this world take wives and husbands, but those who are judged worthy of a place in the other world and in the resurrection from the dead do not marry because they can no longer die, for they are the same as the angels, and being children of the resurrection they are sons of God. And Moses himself implies that the dead rise again, in the passage about the bush where he calls the Lord the God of Abraham, the God of Isaac and the God of Jacob. Now he is God, not of the dead, but of the living; for to him all men are in fact alive.'

Some scribes then spoke up. 'Well put, Master' they said – because they would not dare to ask him any more questions.

This is the Gospel of the Lord.

LAST WEEK IN ORDINARY TIME
Year I

MONDAY

FIRST READING

A reading from the prophet Daniel   1:1-6. 8-20
The king found none to equal Daniel, Hananiah, Mishael and Azariah.

In the third year of the reign of Jehoiakim king of Judah, Nebuchadnezzar king of Babylon marched on Jerusalem and besieged it. The Lord delivered Jehoiakim king of Judah into his hands, with some of the furnishings of the Temple of God. He took them away to the land of Shinar, and stored the sacred vessels in the treasury of his own gods.

The king ordered Ashpenaz, his chief eunuch, to select from the Israelites a certain number of boys of either royal or noble descent; they had to be without any physical defect, of good appearance, trained in every kind of wisdom, well-informed, quick at learning, suitable for service in the palace of the king. Ashpenaz himself was to teach them the language and literature of the Chaldaeans. The king assigned them a daily allowance of food and wine from his own royal table. They were to receive an education lasting for three years, after which they were expected to be fit for the king's society. Among them were Daniel, Hananiah, Mishael and Azariah, who were Judaeans. Daniel, who was most anxious not to defile himself with the food and wine from the royal table, begged the chief eunuch to spare him this defilement; and by the grace of God Daniel met goodwill and sympathy on the part of the chief eunuch. But he warned Daniel, 'I am afraid of my lord the king: he has assigned you food and drink, and if he sees you looking thinner in the face than the other boys of your age, my head will be in danger with the king because of you.' At this Daniel turned to the guard whom the chief eunuch had assigned to Daniel, Hananiah, Mishael and Azariah. He said, 'Please allow your servants a ten days' trial, during which we are given only vegetables to eat and water to drink. You can then compare our looks with those of the boys who eat the king's food; go by what you see, and treat your servants accordingly.' The man agreed to do what they asked and put them on ten days' trial. When the ten days were over they looked and were in better health than any of the boys who had eaten their allowance from the royal table; so the guard withdrew their allowance of food and the wine they were to drink, and gave them vegetables. And God favoured these four boys with knowledge and intelligence in everything connected with literature, and in wisdom; while Daniel had the gift of interpreting every kind of vision and dream. When the period stipulated by the king for the boys' training was over, the chief eunuch presented them to Nebuchadnezzar. The king conversed with them, and among all the boys found none to equal Daniel, Hananiah, Mishael and Azariah. So they became members of the king's court, and on whatever point of wisdom or information he might question them, he found them ten times better than all the magicians and enchanters in his entire kingdom.

This is the word of the Lord.

Responsorial Psalm
Dan 3: 52-56. R̷ v.52

1 You are blest, Lord God of our fathers.
   R̷ **To you glory and praise for evermore.**
   Blest your glorious holy name.
   R̷ **To your glory and praise for evermore.**

2 You are blest in the temple of your glory.
   R̷ **To you glory and praise for evermore.**
   You are blest on the throne of your kingdom.
   R̷ **To you glory and praise for evermore.**

3 You are blest who gaze into the depths.
   R̷ **To you glory and praise for evermore.**
   You are blest in the firmament of heaven.
   R̷ **To you glory and praise for evermore.**

Gospel Acclamation
Apoc 2:10

Alleluia, alleluia!
Even if you have to die, says the Lord,
keep faithful, and I will give you
the crown of life.
Alleluia!

or
Mt 24:42. 44

Alleluia, alleluia!
Stay awake and stand ready,
because you do not know the hour
when the Son of Man is coming.
Alleluia!

GOSPEL

A reading from the holy Gospel according to Luke 21:1-4

He noticed a poverty-stricken widow putting in two small coins.

As Jesus looked up he saw rich people putting their offerings into the treasury; then he happened to notice a poverty-stricken widow putting in two small coins, and he said, 'I tell you truly, this poor widow has put in more than any of them; for these have all contributed money they had over, but she from the little she had has put in all she had to live on.'

This is the Gospel of the Lord.

TUESDAY

FIRST READING

A reading from the prophet Daniel 2:31-45

God will set up a kingdom which shall never be destroyed; it will absorb all kingdoms.

Daniel said to Nebuchadnezzar, 'You have had a vision, O king; this is what you saw: a statue, a great statue of extreme brightness, stood before you, terrible to see. The head of this statue was of fine gold, its chest and arms were of silver, its belly and thighs of bronze, its legs of iron, its feet part iron, part earthenware. While you were gazing, a stone broke away, untouched by any hand, and struck the statue, struck its feet of iron and earthenware and shattered them. And then, iron and earthenware, bronze, silver, gold all broke into small pieces as fine as chaff on the threshing-floor in summer. The wind blew them away, leaving not a trace behind. And the stone that had struck the statue grew into a great mountain, filling the whole earth. This was the dream; now we will explain to the king what it means. You, O king, king of kings, to whom the God of heaven has given sovereignty, power, strength and glory – the sons of men, the beasts of the field, the birds of heaven, wherever they live, he has entrusted to your rule, making you king of them all – you are the golden head. And after you another kingdom will rise, not so great as you, and then a third, of bronze, which will rule the whole world. There will be a fourth kingdom, hard as iron, as iron that shatters and crushes all. Like iron that breaks everything to pieces, it will crush and break all the earlier kingdoms. The feet you saw, part earthenware, part iron, are a kingdom which will be split in two, but which will retain something of the strength of iron, just as you saw the iron and the clay of the earthenware mixed together. The feet were part iron, part earthenware; the kingdom will be partly strong and partly weak. And just as you saw the iron and the clay of the earthenware mixed together, so the two will be mixed together in the seed of man; but they will not hold together any more than iron will blend with earthenware. In the time of these kings the God of heaven will set up a kingdom which shall never be destroyed, and this kingdom will not pass into the hands of another race: it will shatter and absorb all the previous kingdoms, and itself last for ever – just as you saw the stone untouched by hand break from the mountain and shatter iron, bronze, earthenware, silver and gold. The great God has shown the king what is to take place. The dream is true, the interpretation exact.'

This is the word of the Lord.

Responsorial Psalm   Dan 3:57-61. ℟ v.59

1. All things the Lord has made, bless the Lord.
    ℟ **Give glory and eternal praise to him!**

2. Angels of the Lord! all bless the Lord.
    ℟ **Give glory and eternal praise to him!**

3. Heavens! bless the Lord.
    ℟ **Give glory and eternal praise to him!**

4. Waters above the heavens! bless the Lord.
    ℟ **Give glory and eternal praise to him!**

5. Powers of the Lord! all bless the Lord.
    ℟ **Give glory and eternal praise to him.**

Gospel Acclamation   Lk 21:28
Alleluia, alleluia!
Stand erect, hold your heads high,
because your liberation is near at hand.
Alleluia!

or   Apoc 2:10

Alleluia, alleluia!
Even if you have to die, says the Lord,
keep faithful, and I will give you
the crown of life.
Alleluia!

GOSPEL

A reading from the holy Gospel according to Luke 21:5-11

Not a single stone will be left on another.

When some were talking about the Temple, remarking how it was adorned with fine stonework and votive offerings, Jesus said, 'All these things you are staring at now – the time will come when not a single stone will be left on another: everything will be destroyed.' And they put to him this question: 'Master,' they said 'when will this happen, then, and what sign will there be that this is about to take place?'

'Take care not to be deceived,' he said 'because many will come using my name and saying, "I am he" and, "The time is near at hand." Refuse to join them. And when you hear of wars and revolutions, do not be frightened, for this is something that must happen but the end is not so soon.' Then he said to them, 'Nation will fight against nation, and kingdom against kingdom. There will be great earthquakes, and plagues and famines here and there; there will be fearful sights and great signs from heaven.'

This is the Gospel of the Lord.

WEDNESDAY

FIRST READING

A reading from the prophet Daniel 5:1-6. 13-14. 16-17. 23-28

The fingers of a human hand appeared and began to write.

King Belshazzar gave a great banquet for his noblemen; a thousand of them attended, and he drank wine in company with this thousand. As he sipped his wine, Belshazzar gave orders for the gold and silver vessels to be brought which his father Nebuchadnezzar had looted from the sanctuary in Jerusalem, so that the king, his noblemen, his wives and his singing women could drink out of them. The gold and silver vessels looted from the sanctuary of the Temple of God in Jerusalem were brought in, and the king, his noblemen, his wives and his singing women drank out of them. They drank their wine and praised their gods of gold and silver, of bronze and iron, of wood and stone. Suddenly the fingers of a human hand appeared, and began to write on the plaster of the palace wall, directly behind the lamp-stand; and the king could see the hand as it wrote. The king turned pale with alarm; his thigh-joints went slack and his knees began to knock. Daniel was brought into the king's presence; the king said to Daniel, 'Are you the Daniel who was one of the Judean exiles brought by my father the king from Judah? I am told that the spirit of God Most Holy lives in you, and that you are known for your perception, intelligence and marvellous wisdom. As I am told that you are able to give interpretations and to unravel difficult problems, if you can read the writing and tell me what it means, you shall be dressed in purple, and have a chain of gold put round your neck, and be third in rank in the kingdom.'

Then Daniel spoke up in the presence of the king. 'Keep your gifts for yourself,' he said 'and give your rewards to others. I will read the writing to the king without them, and tell him what it means. You have defied the Lord of heaven, you have had the vessels from his Temple brought to you, and you, your noblemen, your wives and your singing women have drunk your wine out of them. You have praised gods of gold and silver, of bronze and iron, of wood and stone, which cannot either see, hear or understand; but you have given no glory to the God who holds your breath and all your fortunes in his hands. That is why he has sent the hand which, by itself, has written these words. The writing reads: Mene, Mene, Tekel and Parsin: The meaning of the words is this: Mene: God has measured your sovereignty and put an end to it; Tekel: you have been weighed in the balance and found wanting; Parsin: your kingdom has been divided and given to the Medes and the Persians.'

This is the word of the Lord.

Responsorial Psalm   Dan 3:62-67. R̷ v.59

1 Sun and moon! bless the Lord.
    R̷   **Give glory and eternal praise to him!**
    Stars of heaven! bless the Lord.
    R̷   **Give glory and eternal praise to him!**

2 Showers and dews! all bless the Lord.
    R̷   **Give glory and eternal praise to him!**
    Winds! all bless the Lord.
    R̷   **Give glory and eternal praise to him!**

3 Fire and heat! bless the Lord.
    R̷   **Give glory and eternal praise to him!**

Cold and heat! bless the Lord.
℟ **Give glory and eternal praise to him!**

Gospel Acclamation
Lk 21:36
Alleluia, alleluia!
Stay awake, praying at all times
for the strength to stand with confidence
before the Son of Man.
Alleluia!

or
Apoc 2:10
Alleluia, alleluia!
Even if you have to die, says the Lord,
keep faithful, and I will give you
the crown of life.
Alleluia!

GOSPEL

A reading from the holy Gospel according to Luke 21:12-19
You will be hated by all men on account of my name, but not a hair of your head will be lost.

Jesus said to his disciples: 'Men will seize you and persecute you; they will hand you over to the synagogues and to imprisonment, and bring you before kings and governors because of my name – and that will be your opportunity to bear witness. Keep this carefully in mind: you are not to prepare your defence, because I myself shall give you an eloquence and a wisdom that none of your opponents will be able to resist or contradict. You will be betrayed even by parents and brothers, relations and friends; and some of you will be put to death. You will be hated by all men on account of my name, but not a hair of your head will be lost. Your endurance will win you your lives.'

This is the Gospel of the Lord.

THURSDAY

FIRST READING

A reading from the prophet Daniel 6:12-28
God sent his angel who sealed the lions' jaws.

The presidents and satraps came along in a body and found Daniel praying and pleading with God. They then came to the king and said, 'Have you not just signed an edict forbidding any man for the next thirty days to pray to anyone, god or man, other than to yourself, O king, on pain of being thrown into the lions' den?' 'The decision stands,' the king replied 'as befits the law of the Medes and the Persians, which cannot be revoked.' Then they said to the king, 'O king, this man Daniel, one of the exiles from Judah, disregards both you and the edict which you have signed: he is at his prayers three times each day.' When the king heard these words he was deeply distressed, and determined to save Daniel; he racked his brains until sunset to find some way out. But the men came back in a body to the king and said, 'O king, remember that in conformity with the law of the Medes and the Persians, no edict or decree can be altered when once issued by the king.'

The king then ordered Daniel to be fetched and thrown into the lion pit. The king said to Daniel, 'Your God himself, whom you have served so faithfully, will have to save you.' A stone was then brought and laid over the mouth of the pit; and the king sealed it with his own signet and with that of his noblemen, so that there could be no going back on the original decision about Daniel. The king returned to his palace, spent the night in fasting and refused to receive any of his concubines. Sleep eluded him, and at the first sign of dawn he was up, and hurried off to the lion pit. As he approached the pit he shouted in anguished tones, 'Daniel, servant of the living God! Has your God, whom you serve so faithfully, been able to save you from the lions?' Daniel replied, 'O king, live for ever! My God sent his angel who sealed the lions' jaws, they did me no harm, since in his sight I am blameless, and I have never done you any wrong either, O king.' The king was overjoyed, and ordered Daniel to be released from the pit. Daniel was released from the pit, and found to be quite unhurt, because he had trusted in his God. The king sent for the men who had accused Daniel and had them thrown into the lion pit, they, their wives and their children: and they had not reached the floor of the pit before the lions had seized them and crushed their bones to pieces.

King Darius then wrote to men of all nations, peoples and languages throughout the world. 'May peace be always with you! I decree: in every kingdom of my empire let all tremble with fear before the God of Daniel:

'He is the living God, he endures for ever,
his sovereignty will never be destroyed

and his kingship never end.
He saves, sets free, and works signs and wonders
in the heavens and on earth;
he has saved Daniel from the power of the lions.'

This is the word of the Lord.

Responsorial Psalm   Dan 3:68-74. ℟ v.59

1. Dews and sleets! bless the Lord.
   ℟ **Give glory and eternal praise to him!**

2. Frost and cold! bless the Lord.
   ℟ **Give glory and eternal praise to him!**

3. Ice and snow! bless the Lord.
   ℟ **Give glory and eternal praise to him!**

4. Nights and days! bless the Lord.
   ℟ **Give glory and eternal praise to him!**

5. Light and darkness! bless the Lord.
   ℟ **Give glory and eternal praise to him!**

6. Lightning and clouds! bless the Lord.
   ℟ **Give glory and eternal praise to him!**

7. Let the earth bless the Lord.
   ℟ **Give glory and eternal praise to him!**

Gospel Acclamation   Mt 24:42. 44
    Alleluia, alleluia!
    Stay awake and stand ready,
    because you do not know the hour when the Son of Man is
        coming.
    Alleluia!

or   Lk 21:28
    Alleluia, alleluia!
    Stand erect, hold your heads high,
    because your liberation is near at hand.
    Alleluia!

GOSPEL

A reading from the holy Gospel according to Luke   21:20-28

Jerusalem will be trampled down by the pagans until the age of the pagans is completely over.

Jesus said to his disciples: 'When you see Jerusalem surrounded by armies, you must realise that she will soon be laid desolate. Then those in Judaea must escape to the mountains, those inside the city must leave it, and those in country districts must not take refuge in it. For this is the time of vengeance when all that scripture says must be fulfilled. Alas for those with child, or with babies at the breast, when those days come!

'For great misery will descend on the land and wrath on this people. They will fall by the edge of the sword and be led captive to every pagan country; and Jerusalem will be trampled down by the pagans until the age of the pagans is completely over.

'There will be signs in the sun and moon and stars; on earth nations in agony, bewildered by the clamour of the ocean and its waves; men dying of fear as they await what menaces the world, for the powers of heaven will be shaken. And then they will see the Son of Man coming in a cloud with power and great glory. When these things begin to take place, stand erect, hold your heads high, because your liberation is near at hand.'

This is the Gospel of the Lord.

FRIDAY

FIRST READING

A reading from the prophet Daniel 7:2-14

I saw, coming on the clouds of heaven, one like a son of man.

I, Daniel, have been seeing visions in the night. I saw that the four winds of heaven were stirring up the great sea; four great beasts emerged from the sea, each different from the other. The first was like a lion with eagle's wings; and as I looked its wings were torn off, and it was lifted from the ground and set standing on its feet like a man; and it was given a human heart. The second beast I saw was different, like a bear, raised up on one of its sides, with three ribs in its mouth, between its teeth. 'Up!' came the command 'Eat quantities of flesh!' After this I looked, and saw another beast, like a leopard, and with four bird's wings on its flanks; it had four heads, and power was given to it. Next I saw another vision in the visions of the night: I saw a fourth beast, fearful, terrifying, very strong; it had great iron teeth, and it ate, crushed and trampled underfoot what remained. It was different from the previous beasts and had ten horns.

While I was looking at these horns, I saw another horn sprouting among them, a little one; three of the original horns were pulled out by the roots to make way for it; and in this horn I saw eyes like human eyes, and a mouth that was full of boasts. As I watched:

> Thrones were set in place
> and one of great age took his seat.
> His robe was white as snow,
> the hair of his head as pure as wool.
> His throne was a blaze of flames,
> its wheels were a burning fire.
> A stream of fire poured out,
> issuing from his presence.
> A thousand thousand waited on him,
> ten thousand times ten thousand stood before him.
> A court was held
> and the books were opened.

The great things the horn was saying were still ringing in my ears, and as I watched, the beast was killed, and its body destroyed and committed to the flames. The other beasts were deprived of their power, but received a lease of life for a season and a time.

> I gazed into the visions of the night.
> And I saw, coming on the clouds of heaven,
> one like a son of man.
> He came to the one of great age
> and was led into his presence.
> On him was conferred sovereignty,
> glory and kingship,
> and men of all peoples, nations and languages became his
>   servants.
> His sovereignty is an eternal sovereignty
> which shall never pass away,
> nor will his empire ever be destroyed.

This is the word of the Lord.

Responsorial Psalm   Dan 3:75-81. ℟ v.59

1 Mountains and hills! bless the Lord.
    ℟ **Give glory and eternal praise to him!**

2 Everything that grows on the earth! bless the Lord.
    ℟ **Give glory and eternal praise to him!**   (continued)

3 Springs of water! bless the Lord.
   ℟ **Give glory and eternal praise to him!**

4 Seas and rivers! bless the Lord.
   ℟ **Give glory and eternal praise to him!**

5 Sea beasts and everything that lives in water! bless the Lord.
   ℟ **Give glory and eternal praise to him!**

6 Birds of heaven! bless the Lord.
   ℟ **Give glory and eternal praise to him!**

7 Animals, wild and tame! bless the Lord.
   ℟ **Give glory and eternal praise to him!**

Gospel Acclamation   Lk 21:28

Alleluia, alleluia!
Stand erect, hold your heads high,
because your liberation is near at hand.
Alleluia!

GOSPEL

A reading from the holy Gospel according to Luke   21:29-33
When you see these things happening, know that the kingdom of God is near.

Jesus told his disciples a parable. 'Think of the fig tree and indeed every tree. As soon as you see them bud, you know that summer is now near. So with you when you see these things happening: know that the kingdom of God is near. I tell you solemnly, before this generation has passed away all will have taken place. Heaven and earth will pass away, but my words will never pass away.'

This is the Gospel of the Lord.

SATURDAY

FIRST READING

A reading from the prophet Daniel   7:15-27
Sovereignty and kingship will be given to the people of the saints of the Most High.

I, Daniel, was deeply disturbed and the visions that passed through my head alarmed me. So I approached one of those who were standing by and asked him to tell me the truth about all this. And in reply he revealed to me what these things meant. 'These four great beasts are four kings who will rise from the earth. Those who are granted sovereignty are the saints of the Most High, and the kingdom will be theirs for ever, for ever and ever.' Then I asked to know the truth about the fourth beast, different from all the rest, very terrifying, with iron teeth, and bronze claws, eating, crushing and trampling underfoot what remained; and the truth about the ten horns on its head – and why the other horn sprouted and the three original horns fell, and why this horn had eyes and a mouth that was full of boasts, and why it made a greater show than the other horns. This was the horn I had watched making war on the saints and proving the stronger, until the coming of the one of great age who gave judgement in favour of the saints of the Most High, when the time came for the saints to take over the kingdom. This is what he said:

> The fourth beast
> is to be a fourth kingdom on earth,
> different from all other kingdoms.
> It will devour the whole earth,
> trample it underfoot and crush it.
> As for the ten horns: from this kingdom
> will rise ten kings, and another after them;
> this one will be different from the previous ones
> and will bring down three kings;
> he is going to speak words against the Most High,
> and harass the saints of the Most High.
> He will consider changing seasons and the Law,
> and the saints will be put into his power
> for a time, two times, and half a time.
> But a court will be held and his power will be stripped from him,
> consumed, and utterly destroyed.
> And sovereignty and kingship,
> and the splendours of all the kingdoms under heaven
> will be given to the people of the saints of the Most High.
> His sovereignty is an eternal sovereignty
> and every empire will serve and obey him.

This is the word of the Lord.

Responsorial Psalm   Dan 3:82-87. R̷ v.59

1. Sons of men! bless the Lord.
   R̷ **Give glory and eternal praise to him!**
   Israel! bless the Lord.
   R̷ **Give glory and eternal praise to him!**

2. Priests! bless the Lord.
   R̷ **Give glory and eternal praise to him!**
   Servants of the Lord! bless the Lord.
   R̷ **Give glory and eternal praise to him!**

3. Spirits and souls of the virtuous! bless the Lord.
   R̷ **Give glory and eternal praise to him!**
   Devout and humble-hearted men! bless the Lord.
   R̷ **Give glory and eternal praise to him!**

Gospel Acclamation   Mt 24:42. 44

Alleluia, alleluia!
Stay awake and stand ready,
because you do not know the hour when the Son of Man is coming.
Alleluia!

or   Lk 21:36

Alleluia, alleluia!
Stay awake, praying at all times
for the strength to stand with confidence
before the Son of Man.
Alleluia!

GOSPEL

A reading from the holy Gospel according to Luke   21:34-36

Stay awake, praying for the strength to survive all that is going to happen.

Jesus said to his disciples: 'Watch yourselves, or your hearts will be coarsened with debauchery and drunkenness and the cares of life, and that day will be sprung on you suddenly, like a trap. For it will come down on every living man on the face of the earth. Stay awake, praying at all times for the strength to survive all that is going to happen, and to stand with confidence before the Son of Man.'

This is the Gospel of the Lord.

READINGS FOR WEEKDAYS IN ORDINARY TIME
Year II

LET THERE BE LIGHT

HE WHO FOLLOWS ME SHALL NOT WALK IN DARKNESS

WALK AS CHILDREN OF LIGHT

FIRST WEEK IN ORDINARY TIME
Year II

MONDAY

FIRST READING

A reading from the first book of Samuel   1:1-8
Hannah's rival would taunt her because the Lord had made her barren.

There was a man of Ramathaim, a Zuphite from the highlands of Ephraim whose name was Elkanah son of Jeroham, son of Elihu, son of Tohu, son of Zuph, an Ephraimite. He had two wives, one called Hannah, the other Peninnah; Peninnah had children but Hannah had none. Every year this man used to go up from his town to worship and to sacrifice to the Lord of hosts in Shiloh. The two sons of Eli, Hophni and Phinehas, were there as priests of the Lord.

One day Elkanah offered sacrifice. He used to give portions to Peninnah and to all her sons and daughters; to Hannah, however, he would give only one portion, although he loved her more, since the Lord had made her barren. Her rival would taunt her to annoy her, because the Lord had made her barren. And this went on year after year: every time they went up to the temple of the Lord she used to taunt her. And so Hannah wept and would not eat. Then Elkanah her husband said to her, 'Hannah, why are you crying and why are you not eating? Why so sad? Am I not more to you than ten sons?'

This is the word of the Lord.

Responsorial Psalm   Ps 115:12-19. ℟ v.17

  ℟ **A thanksgiving sacrifice I make to you, O Lord.**

or

  ℟ **Alleluia!**

1 How can I repay the Lord
   for his goodness to me?
   The cup of salvation I will raise;
   I will call on the Lord's name. ℟

2 My vows to the Lord I will fulfil
   before all his people.

O precious in the eyes of the Lord
is the death of his faithful.

℟ **A thanksgiving sacrifice I make to you O Lord.**

or

℟ **Alleluia!**

3 Your servant, Lord, your servant am I;
you have loosened my bonds.
A thanksgiving sacrifice I make;
I will call on the Lord's name. ℟

4 My vows to the Lord I will fulfil
before all his people,
in the courts of the house of the Lord,
in your midst, O Jerusalem. ℟

Gospel Acclamation   cf. Acts 16:14

Alleluia, alleluia!
Open our heart, O Lord,
to accept the words of your Son.
Alleluia!

or   Mk 1:15

Alleluia, alleluia!
The kingdom of God is close at hand,
repent and believe the Good News.
Alleluia!

Alternative Acclamations pp. 1277ff.

GOSPEL

A reading from the holy Gospel according to Mark   1:14-20
Repent and believe the Good News.

After John had been arrested, Jesus went into Galilee. There he proclaimed the Good News from God. 'The time has come' he said 'and the kingdom of God is close to hand. Repent, and believe the Good News.'

As he was walking along by the Sea of Galilee he saw Simon and his brother Andrew casting a net in the lake – for they were fishermen. And Jesus said to them, 'Follow me and I will make you into fishers of men.' And at once they left their nets and followed him.

First Week in Ordinary Time, Year II: Tuesday

Going on a little further, he saw James son of Zebedee and his brother John: they too were in their boat, mending their nets. He called them at once and, leaving their father Zebedee in the boat with the men he employed, they went after him.

This is the Gospel of the Lord.

In years when the feast of the Baptism of the Lord is celebrated on Monday of the first week in Ordinary Time, the readings given for the Monday may be added to those given for Tuesday, so that the beginning of each book may be read.

TUESDAY

FIRST READING

A reading from the first book of Samuel 1:9-20
The Lord was mindful of Hannah and she gave birth to Samuel.

After they had eaten in the hall, Hannah rose and took her stand before the Lord, while Eli the priest was sitting on his seat by the doorpost of the temple of the Lord. In the bitterness of her soul she prayed to the Lord with many tears and made a vow, saying, 'Lord of hosts! If you will take notice of the distress of your servant, and bear me in mind and not forget your servant and give her a man-child, I will give him to the Lord for the whole of his life and no razor shall ever touch his head.'

While she prayed before the Lord which she did for some time, Eli was watching her mouth, for she was speaking under her breath; her lips were moving but her voice could not be heard. He therefore supposed that she was drunk and said to her, 'How long are you going to be in this drunken state? Rid yourself of your wine'. 'No, my lord,' Hannah replied 'I am a woman in great trouble; I have taken neither wine nor strong drink – I was pouring out my soul before the Lord. Do not take your maidservant for a worthless woman; all this time I have been speaking from the depth of my grief and my resentment.' Then Eli answered her: 'Go in peace,' he said 'and may the God of Israel grant what you have asked of him.' And she said, 'May your maidservant find favour in your sight'; and with that the woman went away; she returned to the hall and ate and was dejected no longer.

They rose early in the morning and worshipped before the

Lord and then set out and returned to their home in Ramah. Elkanah had intercourse with Hannah his wife and the Lord was mindful of her. She conceived and gave birth to a son, and called him Samuel 'since' she said 'I asked the Lord for him.'

This is the word of the Lord.

Responsorial Psalm   1 Sam 2:1. 4-8. ℟ cf. v.1

    ℟ **My heart exults in the Lord.**

1. My heart exults in the Lord.
I find my strength in my God;
my mouth laughs at my enemies
as I rejoice in your saving help.   ℟

2. The bows of the mighty are broken,
but the weak are clothed with strength.
Those with plenty must labour for bread,
but the hungry need work no more.
The childless wife has children now
but the fruitful wife bears no more.   ℟

3. It is the Lord who gives life and death,
he brings men to the grave and back;
it is the Lord who gives poverty and riches.
He brings men low and raises them on high.   ℟

4. He lifts up the lowly from the dust,
from the dungheap he raises the poor
to set him in the company of princes,
to give him a glorious throne.   ℟

Gospel Acclamation   James 1:21

    Alleluia, alleluia!
    Accept and submit to the word
    which has been planted in you
    and can save your souls.
    Alleluia!

or   cf. 1 Thess 2:13

    Alleluia, alleluia!
    Accept God's message for what is really is:
    God's message, and not some human thinking.
    Alleluia!

GOSPEL

A reading from the holy Gospel according to Mark 1:21-28

He taught them with authority.

Jesus and his disciples went as far as Capernaum, and as soon as the sabbath came he went to the synagogue and began to teach. And his teaching made a deep impression on them because, unlike the scribes, he taught them with authority.

In their synagogue just then there was a man possessed by an unclean spirit, and it shouted, 'What do you want with us, Jesus of Nazareth? Have you come to destroy us? I know who you are: the Holy One of God.' But Jesus said sharply, 'Be quiet! Come out of him!' And the unclean spirit threw the man into convulsions and with a loud cry went out of him. The people were so astonished that they started asking each other what it all meant. 'Here is a teaching that is new' they said 'and with authority behind it: he gives orders even to unclean spirits and they obey him.' And his reputation rapidly spread everywhere, through all the surrounding Galilean countryside.

This is the Gospel of the Lord.

WEDNESDAY

FIRST READING

A reading from the first book of Samuel 3:1-10. 19-20

Speak, Lord, your servant is listening.

The boy Samuel was ministering to the Lord in the presence of Eli; it was rare for the Lord to speak in those days; visions were uncommon. One day, it happened that Eli was lying down in his room. His eyes were beginning to grow dim; he could no longer see. The lamp of God had not yet gone out, and Samuel was lying in the sanctuary of the Lord where the ark of God was, when the Lord called, 'Samuel! Samuel!' He answered, 'Here I am.' Then he ran to Eli and said, 'Here I am, since you called me.' Eli said, 'I did not call. Go back and lie down.' So he went and lay down. Once again the Lord called, 'Samuel! Samuel!' Samuel got up and went to Eli and said, 'Here I am, since you called me.' He replied, 'I did not call you, my son; go back and lie down.' Samuel had as yet no knowledge of the Lord and the word of the Lord had not yet been revealed to him. Once again the Lord called, the third time. He got up and went to Eli and said, 'Here I am, since you called me.' Eli then understood that it was the Lord who was calling the boy, and he said to Samuel, 'Go and lie down, and if someone calls say, "Speak, Lord, your servant is listening." ' So Samuel went and lay down in his place.

The Lord then came and stood by, calling as he had done before, 'Samuel! Samuel!' Samuel answered, 'Speak, Lord, your servant is listening.'

Samuel grew up and the Lord was with him and let no word of his fall to the ground. All Israel from Dan to Beersheba came to know that Samuel was accredited as a prophet of the Lord.

This is the word of the Lord.

Responsorial Psalm   Ps 39:2. 5. 7-10. ℟ vv.8. 9

℟ **Here I am Lord!,**
    I come to do your will.

1 I waited, I waited for the Lord
and he stooped down to me;
he heard my cry.
Happy the man who has placed
his trust in the Lord
and has not gone over to the rebels
who follow false gods. ℟

2 You do not ask for sacrifice and offerings,
but an open ear.
You do not ask for holocaust and victim.
Instead, here am I. ℟

3 In the scroll of the book it stands written
that I should do your will.
My God, I delight in your law
in the depth of my heart. ℟

4 Your justice I have proclaimed
in the great assembly.
My lips I have not sealed;
you know it, O Lord. ℟

Gospel Acclamation   cf. Col 3:16. 17
Alleluia, alleluia!
Let the message of Christ, in all its richness,
find a home with you;
through him give thanks to God the Father.
Alleluia!

or Jn 10:27

Alleluia, alleluia!
The sheep that belong to me listen to my voice,
says the Lord,
I know them and they follow me.
Alleluia!

GOSPEL

A reading from the holy Gospel according to Mark 1:29-39
He cured many who were suffering from diseases of one kind or another.

On leaving the synagogue, Jesus went with James and John straight to the house of Simon and Andrew. Now Simon's mother-in-law had gone to bed with fever, and they told him about her straightaway. He went to her, took her by the hand and helped her up. And the fever left her and she began to wait on them.

That evening, after sunset, they brought to him all who were sick and those who were possessed by devils. The whole town came crowding round the door, and he cured many who were suffering from diseases of one kind or another; he also cast out many devils, but he would not allow them to speak, because they knew who he was.

In the morning, long before dawn, he got up and left the house, and went off to a lonely place and prayed there. Simon and his companions set out in search of him, and when they found him they said, 'Everybody is looking for you.' He answered, 'Let us go elsewhere, to the neighbouring country towns, so that I can preach there too, because that is why I came.' And he went all through Galilee, preaching in their synagogues and casting out devils.

This is the Gospel of the Lord.

THURSDAY

FIRST READING

A reading from the first book of Samuel 4:1-11
Israel was defeated and the ark of God was captured.

It happened that the Philistines mustered to fight Israel and Israel went out to meet them in battle, encamping near Ebenezer while the Philistines were encamped at Aphek. The Philistines drew up their battle line against Israel, the battle was hotly engaged, and Israel was defeated by the Philistines and about four thousand of their army were killed on the field. The troops returned to the camp and the elders of Israel said, 'Why has the Lord allowed us to be defeated today by the Philistines? Let us fetch the ark of our God from Shiloh so that it may come among us and rescue us from the power of our enemies.' So the troops sent to Shiloh and brought away the ark of the Lord of hosts, he who is seated on the cherubs; the two sons of Eli, Hophni and Phinehas, came with the ark. When the ark of the Lord arrived in the camp, all Israel gave a great shout so that the earth resounded. When the Philistines heard the noise of the shouting, they said, 'What can this great shouting in the Hebrew camp mean?' And they realised that the ark of the Lord had come into the camp. At this the Philistines were afraid; and they said, 'God has come to the camp.' 'Alas!' they cried 'This has never happened before. Alas! Who will save us from the power of this mighty God? It was he who struck down Egypt with every kind of plague! But take courage and be men, Philistines, or you will become slaves to the Hebrews as they have been slaves to you. Be men and fight.' So the Philistines joined battle and Israel was defeated, each man fleeing to his tent. The slaughter was great indeed, and there fell of the Israelites thirty thousand foot soldiers. The ark of God was captured too, and the two sons of Eli died, Hophni and Phinehas.

This is the word of the Lord.

Responsorial Psalm Ps 43:10-11. 14-15. 24-25. ℟ v.27

℟ **Redeem us, O Lord,**
because of your love.

1 Yet now you have rejected us, disgraced us:
you no longer go forth with our armies.
You make us retreat from the foe
and our enemies plunder us at will. ℟

2 You make us the taunt of our neighbours,
the mockery and scorn of all who are near.
Among the nations, you make us a byword,
among the peoples a thing of derision. ℟

3 Awake, O Lord, why do you sleep?
Arise, do not reject us for ever!
Why do you hide your face
and forget our oppression and misery. ℟

First Week in Ordinary Time, Year II: Friday 869

Gospel Acclamation Ps 118:88

Alleluia, alleluia!
Because of your love give me life,
and I will do your will.
Alleluia!

or cf. Mt 4:23

Alleluia, alleluia!
Jesus proclaimed the Good News of the kingdom,
and cured all kinds of sickness among the people.
Alleluia!

GOSPEL

A reading from the holy Gospel according to Mark 1:40-45
The leprosy left him and he was cured.

A leper came to Jesus and pleaded on his knees: 'If you want to' he said 'you can cure me.' Feeling sorry for him, Jesus stretched out his hand and touched him. 'Of course I want to!' he said. 'Be cured!' And the leprosy left him at once and he was cured. Jesus immediately sent him away and sternly ordered him, 'Mind you say nothing to anyone, but go and show yourself to the priest, and make the offering for your healing prescribed by Moses as evidence of your recovery.' The man went away, but then started talking about it freely and telling the story everywhere, so that Jesus could no longer go openly into any town, but had to stay outside in places where nobody lived. Even so, people from all around would come to him.

This is the Gospel of the Lord.

FRIDAY

FIRST READING

A reading from the first book of Samuel 8:4-7. 10-22
You will cry out on account of the king you have chosen for yourselves, but God will not answer you.

All the elders of Israel gathered together and came to Samuel at Ramah. 'Look,' they said to him 'you are old, and your sons do not follow your ways. So give us a king to rule over us, like the other nations.' It displeased Samuel that they should say, 'Let us have a king to rule us,' so he prayed to the Lord. But the Lord said to Samuel, 'Obey the voice of the people in all that they say to you, for it is not you they have rejected; they have rejected me from ruling over them.'

All that the Lord had said Samuel repeated to the people who were asking him for a king. He said, 'These will be the rights of the king who is to reign over you. He will take your sons and assign them to his chariotry and cavalry, and they will run in front of his chariot. He will use them as leaders of a thousand and leaders of fifty; he will make them plough his ploughland and harvest his harvest and make his weapons of war and the gear for his chariots. He will also take your daughters as perfumers, cooks and bakers. He will take the best of your fields, of your vineyards and olive groves and give them to his officials. He will tithe your crops and vineyards to provide for his eunuchs and his officials. He will take the best of your manservants and maidservants, of your cattle and your donkeys, and make them work for him. He will tithe your flocks, and you yourselves will become his slaves. When that day comes, you will cry out on account of the king you have chosen for yourselves, but on that day God will not answer you.'

The people refused to listen to the words of Samuel. They said, 'No! We want a king, so that we in our turn can be like the other nations; our king shall rule us and be our leader and fight our battles.' Samuel listened to all that the people had to say and repeated it in the ears of the Lord. The Lord then said to Samuel, 'Obey their voice and give them a king.'

This is the word of the Lord.

Responsorial Psalm Ps 88:16-19. ℟ cf. v.2

℟ **I will sing for ever of your love, O Lord.**

1 Happy the people who acclaim such a king,
   who walk, O Lord, in the light of your face,
   who find their joy every day in your name,
   who make your justice the source of their bliss. ℟

2 For it is you, O Lord, who are the glory of their strength;
   it is by your favour that our might is exalted:
   for our ruler is in the keeping of the Lord;
   our king in the keeping of the Holy One of Israel. ℟

Gospel Acclamation
cf. Eph 1:17. 18

Alleluia, alleluia!
May the Father of our Lord Jesus Christ
enlighten the eyes of our mind,
so that we can see what hope his call holds for us.
Alleluia!

or
Lk 7:16

Alleluia, alleluia!
A great prophet has appeared among us;
God has visited his people.
Alleluia!

GOSPEL

A reading from the holy Gospel according to Mark 2:1-12

The Son of Man has authority on earth to forgive sins.

When Jesus returned to Capernaum, word went round that he was back; and so many people collected there that there was no room left, even in front of the door. He was preaching the word to them when some people came bringing him a paralytic carried by four men, but as the crowd made it impossible to get the man to him, they stripped the roof over the place where Jesus was; and when they had made an opening, they lowered the stretcher on which the paralytic lay. Seeing their faith, Jesus said to the paralytic, 'My child, your sins are forgiven.' Now some scribes were sitting there, and they thought to themselves, 'How can this man talk like that? He is blaspheming. Who can forgive sins but God?' Jesus, inwardly aware that this was what they were thinking, said to them, 'Why do you have these thoughts in your hearts? Which of these is easier: to say to the paralytic, "Your sins are forgiven" or to say, "Get up, pick up your stretcher and walk"? But to prove to you that the Son of Man has authority on earth to forgive sins,' – he said to the paralytic – 'I order you: get up, pick up your stretcher, and go off home.' And the man got up, picked up his stretcher at once and walked out in front of everyone, so that they were all astounded and praised God saying, 'We have never seen anything like this.'

This is the Gospel of the Lord.

SATURDAY

FIRST READING

A reading from the first book of Samuel 9:1-4. 17-19; 10:1

The Lord told Samuel, 'That is the man of whom I told you; Saul shall rule my people.'

Among the men of Benjamin there was a man named Kish son of Abiel, son of Zeror, son of Becorath, son of Aphiah; a Benjaminite and a man of rank. He had a son named Saul, a handsome man in the prime of life. Of all the Israelites there was no one more handsome than he; he stood head and shoulders taller than the rest of the people. Now some of the she-donkeys of Saul's father Kish had strayed, so Kish said to Saul, 'My son, take one of the servants with you and be off; go and look for the she-donkeys.' They passed through the highlands of Ephraim and passed through the land of Shalishah, but did not find them; they passed through the land of Shaalim, they were not there; they passed through the land of Benjamin, but did not find them.

When Samuel saw Saul, the Lord told him, 'That is the man of whom I told you; he shall rule my people.' Saul accosted Samuel in the gateway and said, 'Tell me, please, where the seer's house is?' Samuel replied to Saul, 'I am the seer. Go up ahead of me to the high place. You are to eat with me today. In the morning I shall take leave of you and tell you all that is in your heart.'

Samuel took a phial of oil and poured it on Saul's head; then he kissed him, saying, 'Has not the Lord anointed you prince over his people Israel? You are the man who must rule the Lord's people, and who must save them from the power of the enemies surrounding them.'

This is the word of the Lord.

Responsorial Psalm   Ps 20:2-7. ℟ v.2

℟ **O Lord, your strength gives joy to the king.**

1 O Lord, your strength gives joy to the king;
   how your saving help makes him glad!
   You have granted him his heart's desire;
   you have not refused the prayer of his lips. ℟

2 You came to meet him with the blessings of success,
   you have set on his head a crown of pure gold.
   He asked you for life and this you have given,
   days that will last from age to age. ℟

First Week in Ordinary Time, Year II: Saturday

3 Your saving help has given him glory.
   You have laid upon him majesty and splendour,
   you have granted your blessings to him for ever.
   You have made him rejoice with the joy of your presence. ℟

Gospel Acclamation Ps 118:29. 35
   Alleluia, alleluia!
   Bend my heart to your will, O Lord,
   and teach me your law.
   Alleluia!

or Lk 4:18

   Alleluia, alleluia!
   The Lord has sent me to bring the good news to the poor,
   to proclaim liberty to captives.
   Alleluia!

GOSPEL

A reading from the holy Gospel according to Mark 2:13-17
I did not come to call the virtuous, but sinners.

Jesus went out to the shore of the lake; and all the people came to him, and he taught them. As he was walking on he saw Levi the son of Alphaeus, sitting by the customs house, and he said to him, 'Follow me.' And he got up and followed him.

When Jesus was at dinner in his house, a number of tax collectors and sinners were also sitting at the table with Jesus and his disciples; for there were many of them among his followers. When the scribes of the Pharisee party saw him eating with sinners and tax collectors, they said to his disciples, 'Why does he eat with tax collectors and sinners?' When Jesus heard this he said to them, 'It is not the healthy who need the doctor, but the sick. I did not come to call the virtuous, but sinners.'

This is the Gospel of the Lord.

SECOND WEEK IN ORDINARY TIME
Year II

MONDAY

FIRST READING

A reading from the first book of Samuel 15:16-23
Obedience is better than sacrifice. The Lord has rejected you as king.

Samuel said to Saul, 'Stop! Let me tell you what the Lord said to me last night.' Saul said, 'Tell me.' Samuel continued, 'Small as you may be in your own eyes, are you not head of the tribes of Israel? The Lord has anointed you king over Israel. The Lord sent you on a mission and said to you, "Go, put these sinners, the Amalekites, under the ban and make war on them until they are exterminated." Why then did you not obey the voice of the Lord? Why did you fall on the booty and do what is displeasing to the Lord?' Saul replied to Samuel, 'But I did obey the voice of the Lord. I went on the mission which the Lord gave me; I brought back Agag king of the Amalekites; I put the Amalekites under the ban. From the booty the people took the best sheep and oxen of what was under the ban to sacrifice them to the Lord your God in Gilgal.' But Samuel replied:

'Is the pleasure of the Lord in holocausts and sacrifices
or in obedience to the voice of the Lord?
Yes, obedience is better than sacrifice,
submissiveness better than the fat of rams.
Rebellion is a sin of sorcery,
presumption a crime of teraphim.

'Since you have rejected the word of the Lord, he has rejected you as king.'

This is the word of the Lord.

Responsorial Psalm Ps 49:8-9. 16-17. 21. 23. ℟ v.23
℟ **I will show God's salvation to the upright.**

1 'I find no fault with your sacrifices,
your offerings are always before me.
I do not ask more bullocks from your farms,
nor goats from among your herds. ℟

2 'But how can you recite my commandments
and take my covenant on your lips,

you who despise my law
and throw my words to the winds. ℟

3 'You do this, and should I keep silence?
Do you think that I am like you?
a sacrifice of thanksgiving honours me
and I will show God's salvation to the upright.' ℟

Gospel Acclamation cf. 1 Thess 2:13
Alleluia, alleluia!
Accept God's message for what it really is:
God's message, and not some human thinking.
Alleluia!

or Heb 4:12

Alleluia, alleluia!
The word of God is something alive and active;
it can judge secret emotions and thoughts.
Alleluia!

GOSPEL

A reading from the holy Gospel according to Mark 2:18-22
The bridegroom is with them.

One day when John's disciples and the Pharisees were fasting, some people came and said to Jesus, 'Why is it that John's disciples and the disciples of the Pharisees fast, but your disciples do not?' Jesus replied, 'Surely the bridegroom's attendants would never think of fasting while the bridegroom is still with them? As long as they have the bridegroom with them, they could not think of fasting. But the time will come for the bridegroom to be taken away from them, and then, on that day, they will fast. No one sews a piece of unshrunken cloth on an old cloak; if he does, the patch pulls away from it, the new from the old, and the tear gets worse. And nobody puts new wine into old wineskins; if he does, the wine will burst the skins, and the wine is lost and the skins too. No! New wine, fresh skins!'

This is the Gospel of the Lord.

TUESDAY

FIRST READING

A reading from the first book of Samuel 16:1-13
Samuel anointed David where he stood with his brothers; and the Spirit of the Lord seized on David.

The Lord said to Samuel, 'How long will you go on mourning over Saul when I have rejected him as king of Israel? Fill your horn with oil and go. I am sending you to Jesse of Bethlehem, for I have chosen myself a king among his sons.' Samuel replied, 'How can I go? When Saul hears of it he will kill me.' Then the Lord said, 'Take a heifer with you and say, "I have come to sacrifice to the Lord." Invite Jesse to the sacrifice, and then I myself will tell you what you must do; you must anoint to me the one I point out to you.'

Samuel did what the Lord ordered and went to Bethlehem. The elders of the town came trembling to meet him and asked, 'Seer, have you come with good intentions towards us?' 'Yes,' he replied 'I have come to sacrifice to the Lord. Purify yourselves and come with me to the sacrifice.' He purified Jesse and his sons and invited them to the sacrifice.

When they arrived, he caught sight of Eliab and thought, 'Surely the Lord's anointed one stands there before him,' but the Lord said to Samuel, 'Take no notice of his appearance or his height for I have rejected him; God does not see as man sees; man looks at appearances but the Lord looks at the heart.' Jesse then called Abinadab and presented him to Samuel, who said, 'The Lord has not chosen this one either.' Jesse then presented Shammah, but Samuel said, 'The Lord has not chosen this one either.' Jesse presented his seven sons to Samuel, but Samuel said to Jesse, 'The Lord has not chosen these.' He then asked Jesse, 'Are these all the sons you have?' He answered, 'There is still one left, the youngest; he is out looking after the sheep.' Then Samuel said to Jesse, 'Send for him; we will not sit down to eat until he comes.' Jesse had him sent for, a boy of fresh complexion, with fine eyes and pleasant bearing. The Lord said, *'Come, anoint him, for this is the one.'* At this, Samuel took the horn of oil and anointed him where he stood with his brothers; and the spirit of the Lord seized on David and stayed with him from that day on. As for Samuel, he rose and went to Ramah.

This is the word of the Lord.

Second Week in Ordinary Time, Year II: Tuesday

Responsorial Psalm   Ps 88:20-22. 27-28. ℟ v.21

    ℟ **I have found David, my servant.**

1. Of old you spoke in a vision.
To your friends the prophets you said:
'I have set the crown on a warrior,
I have exalted one chosen from the people.'   ℟

2. 'I have found David my servant
and with my holy oil anointed him.
My hand shall always be with him
and my arm shall make him strong.'   ℟

3. 'He will say to me: "You are my father,
my God, the rock who saves me."
And I will make him my first-born,
the highest of the kings of the earth.'   ℟

Gospel Acclamation   Ps 118:18

Alleluia, alleluia!
Open my eyes, O Lord, that I may consider
the wonders of your law.
Alleluia!

or   cf. Eph 1:17. 18

Alleluia, alleluia!
May the Father of our Lord Jesus Christ
enlighten the eyes of our mind,
so that we can see what hope his call holds for us
Alleluia!

GOSPEL

A reading from the holy Gospel according to Mark   2:23-28

The sabbath was made for man, not man for the sabbath.

One sabbath day Jesus happened to be taking a walk through the cornfields, and his disciples began to pick ears of corn as they went along. And the Pharisees said to him, 'Look, why are they doing something on the sabbath day that is forbidden?' And he replied, 'Did you never read what David did in his time of need when he and his followers were hungry – how he went into the house of God when Abiathar was high priest, and ate the loaves of offering which only the priests are allowed to eat, and how he also gave some to the men with him?'

And he said to them, 'The sabbath was made for man, not

man for the sabbath; so the Son of Man is master even of the sabbath.'

This is the Gospel of the Lord.

WEDNESDAY

FIRST READING

A reading from the first book of Samuel   17:32-33. 37. 40-51
David triumphed over the Philistine with a sling and a stone.

David said to Saul, 'Let no one lose heart on his account; your servant will go and fight this Philistine.' But Saul answered David, 'You cannot go and fight the Philistine; you are only a boy and he has been a warrior from his youth.' 'The Lord who rescued me from the claws of lion and bear,' David said, 'will rescue me from the power of this Philistine.' Then Saul said to David, 'Go, and the Lord be with you!'

He took his staff in his hand, picked five smooth stones from the river bed, put them in his shepherd's bag, in his pouch, and with his sling in his hand he went to meet the Philistine. The Philistine, his shield-bearer in front of him, came nearer and nearer to David; and the Philistine looked at David, and what he saw filled him with scorn, because David was only a youth, a boy of fresh complexion and pleasant bearing. The Philistine said to him, 'Am I a dog for you to come against me with sticks?' And the Philistine cursed David by his gods. The Philistine said to David, 'Come over here and I will give your flesh to the birds of the air and the beasts of the field.' But David answered the Philistine, 'You come against me with sword and spear and javelin, but I come against you in the name of the Lord of hosts, the God of the armies of Israel that you have dared to insult. Today the Lord will deliver you into my hand and I shall kill you; I will cut off your head, and this very day I will give your dead body and the bodies of the Philistine army to the birds of the air and the wild beasts of the earth, so that all the earth may know that there is a God in Israel, and that all this assembly may know that it is not by sword or by spear that the Lord gives the victory, for he is lord of the battle and he will deliver you into our power.'

No sooner had the Philistine started forward to confront David than David left the line of battle and ran to meet the Philistine. Putting his hand in his bag, he took out a stone and slung it and struck the Philistine on the forehead; the stone penetrated his forehead and he fell on his face to the ground. Thus David triumphed over the Philistine with a sling and a stone and struck the Philistine down and killed him. David had no sword in his hand. Then David ran and, standing over the Philistine, seized his sword and drew it from the scabbard, and with this he killed him, cutting off his head. The Philistines saw that their champion was dead and took to flight.

This is the word of the Lord.

Responsorial Psalm   Ps 143:1-2. 9-10. ℟ v.1
   ℟ **Blessed be the Lord, my rock.**

1. Blessed be the Lord, my rock
who trains my arms for battle,
who prepares my hands for war. ℟

2. He is my love, my fortress;
he is my stronghold, my saviour,
my shield, my place of refuge.
He brings peoples under my rule. ℟

3. To you, O God, will I sing a new song;
I will play on the ten-stringed lute
to you who give kings their victory,
who set David your servant free. ℟

Gospel Acclamation   Heb 4:12
Alleluia, alleluia!
The word of God is something alive and active;
it can judge secret emotions and thoughts.
Alleluia!

or   cf. Mt 4:23

Alleluia, alleluia!
Jesus proclaimed the Good News of the kingdom,
and cured all kinds of sickness among the people.
Alleluia!

GOSPEL

A reading from the holy Gospel according to Mark   3:1-6
Is it against the law on the sabbath day to save life?

Jesus went into a synagogue, and there was a man there who had a withered hand. And they were watching him to see if he would cure him on the sabbath day, hoping for something to use against him. He said to the man with the withered hand, 'Stand up out in the middle!' Then he said to them, 'Is it against the law on the sabbath day to do good or to do evil; to save life, or to kill?' But they said nothing. Then, grieved to find them so obstinate, he looked angrily round at them, and said to the man, 'Stretch out your hand.' He stretched it out and his hand was better. The Pharisees went out and at once began to plot with the Herodians against him, discussing how to destroy him.

This is the Gospel of the Lord.

THURSDAY

FIRST READING

A reading from the first book of Samuel   18:6-9; 19:1-7
My father Saul is looking for a way to kill you.

On their way back, as David was returning after killing the Philistine, the women came out to meet King Saul from all the towns of Israel, singing and dancing to the sound of tambourine and lyre and cries of joy; and as they danced the women sang:

'Saul has killed his thousands,
and David his tens of thousands.'

Saul was very angry; the incident was not to his liking. 'They have given David the tens of thousands,' he said, 'but me only the thousands; he has all but the kingship now.' And Saul turned a jealous eye on David from that day forward.

Saul told Jonathan his son and all his servants of his intention to kill David. Now Jonathan, Saul's son, held David in great affection; and so Jonathan warned David; 'My father Saul is looking for a way to kill you,' he said, 'so be on your guard tomorrow morning; hide away in some secret place. Then I will go and keep my father company in the fields where you are hiding, and will talk to my father about you; I will find out what the situation is and let you know.'

So Jonathan spoke well of David to Saul his father; he said, 'Let not the king sin against his servant David, for he has not sinned against you, and what he has done has been greatly to your advantage. He took his life in his hands when he killed the Philistine, and the Lord brought about a great victory for all

Israel. You saw it yourself and rejoiced; why then sin against innocent blood in killing David without cause?' Saul was impressed by Jonathan's words and took an oath, 'As the Lord lives, I will not kill him.' Jonathan called David and told him all these things. Then Jonathan brought him to Saul, and David attended on him as before.

This is the word of the Lord.

Responsorial Psalm   Ps 55:2-3. 9-14. ℟ v.5

℟ **In God I trust;**
   I shall not fear.

1 Have mercy on me, God, men crush me;
   they fight me all day long and oppress me.
   My foes crush me all the day long,
   for many fight proudly against me.   ℟

2 You have kept an account of my wanderings;
   you have kept a record of my tears;
   (are they not written in your book?)
   Then my foes will be put to flight
   on the day I call to you.   ℟

3 This I know, that God is on my side.
   In God, whose word I praise,
   in the Lord, whose word I praise,
   in God I trust; I shall not fear;
   what can mortal man do to me?   ℟

4 I am bound by the vows I have made you.
   O God, I will offer you praise
   for you rescued my soul from death,
   you kept my feet from stumbling
   that I may walk in the presence of God
   in the light of the living.   ℟

Gospel Acclamation   cf. Jn 6:63. 68

Alleluia, alleluia!
Your words are spirit, Lord,
and they are life:
you have the message of eternal life.
Alleluia!

or   cf. 2 Tim 1:10

Alleluia, alleluia!
Our Saviour Christ Jesus abolished death,
and he has proclaimed life through the Good News.
Alleluia!

GOSPEL

A reading from the holy Gospel according to Mark   3:7-12
The unclean spirits would shout, 'You are the Son of God!' But he warned them strongly not to make him known.

Jesus withdrew with his disciples to the lakeside, and great crowds from Galilee followed him. From Judaea, Jerusalem, Idumaea, Transjordania and the region of Tyre and Sidon, great numbers who had heard of all he was doing came to him. And he asked his disciples to have a boat ready for him because of the crowd, to keep him from being crushed. For he had cured so many that all who were afflicted in any way were crowding forward to touch him. And the unclean spirits, whenever they saw him, would fall down before him and shout, 'You are the Son of God!' But he warned them strongly not to make him known.

This is the Gospel of the Lord.

FRIDAY

FIRST READING

A reading from the first book of Samuel   24:3-21
I will not raise my hand against him, for he is the anointed of the Lord.

Saul took three thousand men chosen from the whole of Israel and went in search of David and his men east of the Rocks of the Wild Goats. He came to the sheep-folds along the route where there was a cave, and went in to cover his feet. Now David and his men were sitting in the recesses of the cave; David's men said to him, 'Today is the day of which the Lord said to you, "I will deliver your enemy into your power, do what you like with him." ' David stood up and, unobserved, cut off the border of Saul's cloak. Afterwards David reproached himself for having cut off the border of Saul's cloak. He said to his men, 'The Lord preserve me from doing such a thing to my lord and raising my hand against him, for he is the anointed of the Lord.' David gave his men strict instructions, forbidding them to attack Saul.

Saul then left the cave and went on his way. After this, David too left the cave and called after Saul, 'My lord king!' Saul looked behind him and David bowed to the ground and did homage. Then David said to Saul, 'Why do you listen to the men who say to you, "David means to harm you"? Why, your own eyes have seen today how the Lord put you in my power in the cave and how I refused to kill you, but spared you. "I will not raise my hand against my lord," I said, "for he is the anointed of the Lord." O my father, see, look at the border of your cloak in my hand. Since I cut off the border of your cloak, yet did not kill you, you must acknowledge frankly that there is neither malice nor treason in my mind. I have not offended against you, yet you hunt me down to take my life. May the Lord be judge between me and you, and may the Lord avenge me on you; but my hand shall not be laid on you. (As the old proverb says: Wickedness goes out from the wicked, and my hand will not be laid on you.) On whose trail has the king of Israel set out? On whose trail are you in hot pursuit? On the trail of a dead dog! On the trail of a single flea! May the Lord be the judge and decide between me and you ; may he take up my cause and defend it and give judgement for me, freeing me from your power.'

When David had finished saying these words to Saul, Saul said, 'Is that your voice, my son David?' And Saul wept aloud. 'You are a more upright man than I,' he said to David, 'for you have repaid me with good while I have repaid you with evil. Today you have crowned your goodness towards me since the Lord had put me in your power yet you did not kill me. When a man comes on his enemy, does he let him go unmolested? May the Lord reward you for the goodness you have shown me today. Now I know you will indeed reign and that the sovereignty in Israel will be secure in your hands.'

This is the word of the Lord.

Responsorial Psalm   Ps 56:2-4. 6. 11. ℟ v.2

℟ **Have mercy on me, God, have mercy.**

1 Have mercy on me, God, have mercy
for in you my soul has taken refuge.
In the shadow of your wings I take refuge
till the storms of destruction pass by. ℟

2   I call to God the Most High,
    to God who has always been my help.
    May he send from heaven and save me
    and shame those who assail me.
    May God send his truth and his love.

    ℟ **Have mercy on me, God, have mercy.**

3   O God, arise above the heavens;
    may your glory shine on earth,
    for your love reaches to the heavens
    and your truth to the skies.   ℟

Gospel Acclamation   cf. 2 Thess 2:14
    Alleluia, alleluia!
    Through the Good News God called us
    to share the glory of our Lord Jesus Christ.
    Alleluia!

or   2 Cor 5:19

    Alleluia, alleluia!
    God in Christ was reconciling the world to himself,
    and he has entrusted to us the news that they are reconciled.
    Alleluia!

GOSPEL

A reading from the holy Gospel according to Mark   3:13-19
He summoned those he wanted to be his companions.

Jesus went up into the hills and summoned those he wanted. So they came to him and he appointed twelve; they were to be his companions and to be sent out to preach, with power to cast out devils. And so he appointed the Twelve: Simon to whom he gave the name Peter, James the son of Zebedee and John the brother of James, to whom he gave the name Boanerges or 'Sons of Thunder'; then Andrew, Philip, Bartholomew, Matthew, Thomas, James the son of Alphaeus, Thaddaeus, Simon the Zealot and Judas Iscariot, the man who was to betray him.

   This is the Gospel of the Lord.

SATURDAY

FIRST READING

A reading from the second book of Samuel   1:1-4. 11-12. 17. 19. 23-27

How did the heroes fall in the thick of the battle.

David returned from his rout of the Amalekites and spent two days in Ziklag. On the third day a man came from the camp where Saul had been, his garments torn and earth on his head. When he came to David, he fell to the ground and did homage. 'Where do you come from?' David asked him. 'I have escaped from the Israelite camp,' he said. David said to him, 'What happened? Tell me.' He replied, 'The people have fled from the battlefield and many of them have fallen. Saul and his son Jonathan are dead too.'

Then David took hold of his garments and tore them, and all the men did the same. They mourned and wept and fasted until the evening for Saul and his son Jonathan, for the people of the Lord and for the House of Israel, because they had fallen by the sword.

Then David made this lament over Saul and his son Jonathan:

Alas, the glory of Israel has been slain on your heights!
How did the heroes fall?
Saul and Jonathan, loved and lovely,
neither in life, nor in death, were divided.
Swifter than eagles were they,
stronger were they than lions.
O daughters of Israel, weep for Saul
who clothed you in scarlet and fine linen,
who set brooches of gold
on your garments.
How did the heroes fall
in the thick of the battle?
O Jonathan, in your death I am stricken,
I am desolate for you, Jonathan my brother.
Very dear to me you were,
your love to me more wonderful
than the love of a woman.
How did the heroes fall
and the battle armour fail?

This is the word of the Lord.

Responsorial Psalm Ps 79:2-3. 5-7. ℟ v.4

℟ **Let your face shine on us, O Lord,
and we shall be saved.**

1 O shepherd of Israel, hear us,
you who lead Joseph's flock,
shine forth from your cherubim throne
upon Ephraim, Benjamin, Manasseh.
O Lord, rouse up your might,
O Lord, come to our help. ℟

2 Lord God of hosts, how long
will you frown on your people's plea?
You have fed them with tears for their bread,
an abundance of tears for their drink.
You have made us the taunt of our neighbours,
our enemies laugh us to scorn. ℟

Gospel Acclamation 2 Cor 15:19

Alleluia, alleluia!
God in Christ was reconciling the world to himself,
and he has entrusted to us the news that they are reconciled.
Alleluia!

or cf. Acts 16:14

Alleluia, alleluia!
Open our heart, O Lord,
to accept the words of your Son.
Alleluia!

GOSPEL

A reading from the holy Gospel according to Mark 3:20-21
His relatives said he was out of his mind.

Jesus went home, and such a crowd collected that they could not even have a meal. When his relatives heard of this, they set out to take charge of him, convinced he was out of his mind.

This is the Gospel of the Lord.

THIRD WEEK IN ORDINARY TIME
Year II

MONDAY

FIRST READING

A reading from the second book of Samuel 5:1-7. 10
You shall be shepherd of my people Israel.

All the tribes of Israel came to David at Hebron. 'Look' they said 'we are your own flesh and blood. In days past when Saul was our king, it was you who led Israel in all their exploits; and the Lord said to you, "You are the man who shall be shepherd of my people Israel, you shall be the leader of Israel." ' So all the elders of Israel came to the king at Hebron, and King David made a pact with them at Hebron in the presence of the Lord, and they anointed David king of Israel.

David was thirty years old when he became king, and he reigned for forty years. He reigned in Hebron over Judah for seven years and six months; then he reigned in Jerusalem over all Israel and Judah for thirty-three years.

David and his men marched on Jerusalem against the Jebusites living there. These said to David, 'You will not get in here. The blind and the lame will hold you off.' (That is to say: David will never get in here.) But David captured the fortress of Zion, that is, the Citadel of David.

He grew greater and greater, and the Lord, the God of hosts, was with him.

This is the word of the Lord.

Responsorial Psalm Ps 88:20-22. 25-26. ℟ v.25

℟ **My truth and my love shall be with him.**

1. Of old you spoke in a vision.
   To your friends the prophets you said:
   'I have set the crown on a warrior,
   I have exalted one chosen from the people. ℟

2. 'I have found David my servant
   and with my holy oil anointed him.
   My hand shall always be with him
   and my arm shall make him strong. ℟

(continued)

3. 'My truth and my love shall be with him;
by my name his might shall be exalted.
I will stretch out his hand to the Sea
and his right hand as far as the River.'

℟ **My truth and my love shall be with him.**

Gospel Acclamation   Ps 24:4. 5
Alleluia, alleluia!
Teach me your paths, my God,
make me walk in your truth.
Alleluia!

or   cf. 2 Tim 1:10

Alleluia, alleluia!
Our Saviour Christ Jesus abolished death,
and he has proclaimed life through the Good News.
Alleluia!

GOSPEL

A reading from the holy Gospel according to Mark   3:22-30
It is the end of Satan.

The scribes who had come down from Jerusalem were saying: 'Beelzebul is in him' and, 'It is through the prince of devils that he casts devils out.' So Jesus called them to him and spoke to them in parables, 'How can Satan cast out Satan? If a kingdom is divided against itself, that kingdom cannot last. And if a household is divided against itself, that household can never stand. Now if Satan has rebelled against himself and is divided, he cannot stand either – it is the end of him. But no one can make his way into a strong man's house and burgle his property unless he has tied up the strong man first. Only then can he burgle his house.

'I tell you solemnly, all men's sins will be forgiven, and all their blasphemies; but let anyone blaspheme against the Holy Spirit and he will never have forgiveness: he is guilty of an eternal sin.' This was because they were saying, 'An unclean spirit is in him.'

This is the Gospel of the Lord.

TUESDAY

FIRST READING

A reading from the second book of Samuel 6:12-15. 17-19
David and all the house of Israel brought up the ark of the Lord with acclaim.

David went and brought the ark of God up from Obed-edom's house to the Citadel of David with great rejoicing. When the bearers of the ark of the Lord had gone six paces, he sacrificed an ox and a fat sheep. And David danced whirling round before the Lord with all his might, wearing a linen loincloth round him. Thus David and all the House of Israel brought up the ark of the Lord with acclaim and the sound of the horn. They brought the ark of the Lord and put it in position inside the tent that David had pitched for it; and David offered holocausts before the Lord, and communion sacrifices. And when David had finished offering holocausts and communion sacrifices, he blessed the people in the name of the Lord of hosts. He then distributed among all the people, among the whole multitude of Israelites, men and women, a roll of bread to each, a portion of dates, and a raisin cake. Then they all went away, each to his own house.

This is the word of the Lord.

Responsorial Psalm Ps 23:7-10. ℟ v.8
℟ **Who is the king of glory?**
He, the Lord, he is the king of glory.

1. O gates, lift high your heads;
grow higher, ancient doors.
Let him enter, the king of glory! ℟

2. Who is the king of glory?
The Lord, the mighty, the valiant,
the Lord, the valiant in war. ℟

3. O gates, lift high your heads;
grow higher, ancient doors.
Let him enter, the king of glory! ℟

4. Who is he, the king of glory?
He, the Lord of armies,
he is the king of glory. ℟

Gospel Acclamation   Ps 118:135
> Alleluia, alleluia!
> Let your face shine on your servant,
> and teach me your decrees.
> Alleluia!

or   cf. Mt 11:25

> Alleluia, alleluia!
> Blessed are you, Father,
> Lord of heaven and earth,
> for revealing the mysteries of the kingdom
> to mere children.
> Alleluia!

GOSPEL

A reading from the holy Gospel according to Mark   3:31-35

Anyone who does the will of God, that person is my brother and sister and mother.

The mother and brothers of Jesus arrived and, standing outside, sent in a message asking for him. A crowd was sitting round him at the time the message was passed to him, 'Your mother and brothers and sisters are outside asking for you.' He replied, 'Who are my mother and my brothers?' And looking round at those sitting in a circle about him, he said, 'Here are my mother and my brothers. Anyone who does the will of God, that person is my brother and sister and mother.'

This is the Gospel of the Lord.

WEDNESDAY

FIRST READING

A reading from the second book of Samuel   7:4-17

Your House and your sovereignty will always stand secure before me.

The word of the Lord came to Nathan:

'Go and tell my servant David, "Thus the Lord speaks: Are you the man to build me a house to dwell in? I have never stayed in a house from the day I brought the Israelites out of Egypt until today, but have always led a wanderer's life in a tent. In all my journeying with the whole people of Israel, did I say to any one of the judges of Israel, whom I had appointed as shepherds of Israel my people: Why have you not built me a house of cedar?" This is what you must say to my servant David, "The Lord of hosts says this: I took you from the pasture, from following the sheep, to be leader of my people Israel; I have been with you on all your expeditions; I have cut off all your enemies before you. I will give you fame as great as the fame of the greatest on earth. I will provide a place for my people Israel; I will plant them there and they shall dwell in that place and never be disturbed again; nor shall the wicked continue to oppress them as they did, in the days when I appointed judges over my people Israel; I will give them rest from all their enemies. The Lord will make you great; the Lord will make you a House. And when your days are ended and you are laid to rest with your ancestors, I will preserve the offspring of your body after you and make his sovereignty secure. (It is he who shall build a house for my name, and I will make his royal throne secure for ever.) I will be a father to him and he a son to me; if he does evil, I will punish him with the rod such as men use, with strokes such as mankind gives. Yet I will not withdraw my favour from him, as I withdrew it from your predecessor. Your House and your sovereignty will always stand secure before me and your throne be established for ever."'

Nathan related all these words to David and this whole revelation.

This is the word of the Lord.

Responsorial Psalm Ps 88:4-5. 27-30. R̸ v.29
 R̸ **I will keep my love for him always.**

1 I have made a covenant with my chosen one;
   I have sworn to David my servant:
   I will establish your dynasty for ever
   and set up your throne through all ages. R̸

2 He will say to me: 'You are my father,
   my God, the rock who saves me.'
   And I will make him my first-born,
   the highest of the kings of the earth. R̸

3 I will keep my love for him always;
   for him my covenant shall endure.
   I will establish his dynasty for ever,
   make his throne as lasting as the heavens. R̸

Gospel Acclamation 1 Sam 3:9; Jn 6:68
> Alleluia, alleluia!
> Speak, Lord, your servant is listening:
> you have the message of eternal life.
> Alleluia!

or

> Alleluia, alleluia!
> The seed is the word of God, Christ the sower;
> whoever finds the seed will remain for ever.
> Alleluia!

GOSPEL

A reading from the holy Gospel according to Mark 4:1-20
Imagine a sower going out to sow.

Jesus began to teach by the lakeside, but such a huge crowd gathered round him that he got into a boat on the lake and sat there. The people were all along the shore, at the water's edge. He taught them many things in parables, and in the course of his teaching he said to them, 'Listen! Imagine a sower going out to sow. Now it happened that, as he sowed, some of the seed fell on the edge of the path, and the birds came and ate it up. Some seed fell on rocky ground where it found little soil and sprang up straightaway, because there was no depth of earth; and when the sun came up it was scorched and, not having any roots, it withered away. Some seed fell into thorns, and the thorns grew up and choked it, and it produced no crop. And some seed fell into rich soil and, growing tall and strong, produced crop; and yielded thirty, sixty, even a hundredfold.' And he said, 'Listen, anyone who has ears to hear.'

When he was alone, the Twelve, together with the others who formed his company, asked what the parables meant. He told them, 'The secret of the kingdom of God is given to you, but to those who are outside everything comes in parables, so that they may see and see again, but not perceive; may hear and hear again, but not understand; otherwise they might be converted and be forgiven.'

He said to them, 'Do you not understand this parable? Then how will you understand any of the parables? What the sower is sowing is the word. Those on the edge of the path where the word is sown are people who have no sooner heard it than Satan comes and carries away the word that was sown in them.

Similarly, those who receive the seed on patches of rock are people who, when first they hear the word, welcome it at once with joy. But they have no root in them, they do not last; should some trial come, or some persecution on account of the word, they fall away at once. Then there are others who receive the seed in thorns. These have heard the word, but the worries of this world, the lure of riches and all the other passions come in to choke the word, and so it produces nothing. And there are those who have received the seed in rich soil: they hear the word and accept it and yield a harvest, thirty and sixty and a hundredfold.'

This is the Gospel of the Lord.

THURSDAY

FIRST READING

A reading from the second book of Samuel 7:18-19. 24-29
Who am I, Lord, and what is my House?

After Nathan had spoken to David, the King went in and, seated before the Lord, said:

'Who am I, Lord, and what is my House, that you have led me as far as this? Yet in your sight, Lord, this is still not far enough, and you make your promises extend to the House of your servant for a far-distant future. You have constituted your people Israel to be your own people for ever; and you, Lord, have become their God. Now, Lord, always keep the promise you have made your servant and his House, and do as you have said. Your name will be exalted for ever and men will say, "The Lord of hosts is God over Israel." The House of your servant David will be made secure in your presence, since you yourself, Lord of hosts, God of Israel, have made this revelation to your servant, "I will build you a House;" hence your servant has ventured to offer this prayer to you. Yes, Lord, you are God indeed, your words are true and you have made this fair promise to your servant. Be pleased, then, to bless the House of your servant, that it may continue for ever in your presence; for you, Lord, have spoken; and with your blessing the House of your servant will be for ever blessed.'

This is the word of the Lord.

Responsorial Psalm
Ps 131:1-5. 11-14. ℟ Lk 1:32

℟ **The Lord God will give him
the throne of his father David.**

1 O Lord, remember David
and all the hardships he endured,
the oath he swore to the Lord,
his vow to the Strong One of Jacob. ℟

2 'I will not enter the house where I live
nor go to the bed where I rest.
I will give no sleep to my eyes
to my eyelids will give no slumber
till I find a place for the Lord,
a dwelling for the Strong One of Jacob.' ℟

3 The Lord swore an oath to David;
he will not go back on his word:
'A son, the fruit of your body,
will I set upon your throne. ℟

4 'If they keep my covenant in truth
and my laws that I have taught them,
their sons also shall rule
on your throne from age to age.' ℟

5 For the Lord has chosen Zion;
he has desired it for his dwelling:
'This is my resting-place for ever,
here have I chosen to live.' ℟

Gospel Acclamation
Phil 2:15-16

Alleluia, alleluia!
You will shine in the world like bright stars
because you are offering it the word of life.
Alleluia!

or
Ps 118:105

Alleluia, alleluia!
Your word is a lamp for my steps
and a light for my path.
Alleluia!

Third Week in Ordinary Time, Year II: Friday

GOSPEL

A reading from the holy Gospel according to Mark   4:21-25
A lamp is to be put on a lamp-stand. The amount you measure out is the amount you will be given.

Jesus said to the crowd: 'Would you bring in a lamp to put it under a tub or under the bed? Surely you will put it on the lamp-stand? For there is nothing hidden but it must be disclosed, nothing kept secret except to be brought to light. If anyone has ears to hear, let him listen to this.'

He also said to them, 'Take notice of what you are hearing. The amount you measure out is the amount you will be given – and more besides; for the man who has will be given more; from the man who has not, even what he has will be taken away.'

This is the Gospel of the Lord.

FRIDAY

FIRST READING

A reading from the second book of Samuel   11:1-10. 13-17
You have shown contempt for me and taken the wife of Uriah to be your wife.

At the turn of the year, the time when kings go campaigning, David sent Joab and with him his own guards and the whole of Israel. They massacred the Ammonites and laid siege to Rabbah. David however remained in Jerusalem.

It happened towards evening when David had risen from his couch and was strolling on the palace roof, that he saw from the roof a woman bathing; the woman was very beautiful. David made inquiries about this woman and was told, 'Why, that is Bathsheba, Eliam's daughter, the wife of Uriah the Hittite.' Then David sent messengers and had her brought. She came to him, and he slept with her. She then went home again. The woman conceived and sent word to David, 'I am with child.'

Then David sent Joab a message, 'Send me Uriah the Hittite,' whereupon Joab sent Uriah to David. When Uriah came into his presence, David asked after Joab and the army and how the war was going. David then said to Uriah, 'Go down to your house and enjoy yourself.' Uriah left the palace, and was followed by a present from the king's table. Uriah however slept by the palace door with his master's bodyguard and did not go down to his house.

This was reported to David; 'Uriah' they said 'did not go down to his house.' The next day David invited him to eat and drink in his presence and made him drunk. In the evening Uriah went out and lay on his couch with his master's bodyguard, but he did not go down to his house.

Next morning David wrote a letter to Joab and sent it by Uriah. In the letter he wrote, 'Station Uriah in the thick of the fight and then fall back behind him so that he may be struck down and die.' Joab, then besieging the town, posted Uriah in a place where he knew there were fierce fighters. The men of the town sallied out and engaged Joab; the army suffered casualties, including some of David's bodyguard; and Uriah the Hittite was killed too.

This is the word of the Lord.

Responsorial Psalm Ps 50:3-7. 10-11. ℟ cf. v.3

℟ **Have mercy on us, Lord, for we have sinned.**

1 Have mercy on me, God, in your kindness.
   In your compassion blot out my offence.
   O wash me more and more from my guilt
   and cleanse me from my sin. ℟

2 My offences truly I know them;
   my sin is always before me.
   Against you, you alone, have I sinned;
   what is evil in your sight I have done. ℟

3 That you may be justified when you give sentence
   and be without reproach when you judge,
   O see, in guilt I was born,
   a sinner was I conceived. ℟

4 Make me hear rejoicing and gladness,
   that the bones you have crushed may thrill.
   From my sins turn away your face
   and blot out all my guilt. ℟

Gospel Acclamation Ps 118:27
   Alleluia, alleluia!
   Make me grasp the way of your precepts,
   and I will muse on your wonders.
   Alleluia!

Third Week in Ordinary Time, Year II: Saturday

or   cf. Mt 11:25

> Alleluia, alleluia!
> Blessed are you, Father,
> Lord of heaven and earth,
> for revealing the mysteries of the kingdom
> to mere children.
> Alleluia!

GOSPEL

A reading from the holy Gospel according to Mark   4:26-34

A man throws seed on the land. While he sleeps the seed is growing; how, he does not know.

Jesus said to the crowd: 'This is what the kingdom of God is like. A man throws seed on the land. Night and day, while he sleeps, when he is awake, the seed is sprouting and growing; how, he does not know. Of its own accord the land produces first the shoot, then the ear, then the full grain in the ear. And when the crop is ready, he loses no time: he starts to reap because the harvest has come.'

He also said, 'What can we say the kingdom of God is like? What parable can we find for it? It is like a mustard seed which at the time of its sowing in the soil is the smallest of all the seeds on earth; yet once it is sown it grows into the biggest shrub of them all and puts out big branches so that the birds of the air can shelter in its shade.'

Using many parables like these, he spoke the word to them, so far as they were capable of understanding it. He would not speak to them except in parables, but he explained everything to his disciples when they were alone.

This is the Gospel of the Lord.

SATURDAY

FIRST READING

A reading from the second book of Samuel   12:1-7. 10-17

I have sinned against the Lord.

The Lord sent Nathan the prophet to David. He came to him and said:

> 'In the same town were two men,

one rich, the other poor.
The rich man had flocks and herds
in great abundance;
the poor man had nothing but a ewe lamb,
one only, a small one he had bought.
This he fed, and it grew up with him and his children,
eating his bread, drinking from his cup,
sleeping on his breast; it was like a daughter to him.
When there came a traveller to stay the rich man
refused to take one of his own flock or herd
to provide for the wayfarer who had come to him.
Instead he took the poor man's lamb
and prepared it for his guest.'

David's anger flared up against the man. 'As the Lord lives,' he said to Nathan 'the man who did this deserves to die! He must make fourfold restitution for the lamb, for doing such a thing and showing no compassion.'

Then Nathan said to David, 'You are the man. So now the sword will never be far from your House, since you have shown contempt for me and taken the wife of Uriah the Hittite to be your wife.

'Thus the Lord speaks, "I will stir up evil for you out of your own House. Before your very eyes I will take your wives and give them to your neighbour, and he shall lie with your wives in the sight of this sun. You worked in secret, I will work this in the face of all Israel and in the face of the sun." '

David said to Nathan, 'I have sinned against the Lord.' Then Nathan said to David, 'The Lord, for his part, forgives your sin; you are not to die. Yet because you have outraged the Lord by doing this, the child that is born to you is to die.' Then Nathan went home.

The Lord struck the child that Uriah's wife had borne to David and it fell gravely ill. David pleaded with the Lord for the child; he kept a strict fast and went home and spent the night on the bare ground, covered with sacking. The officials of his household came and stood round him to get him to rise from the ground, but he refused, nor would he take food with them.

This is the word of the Lord.

Responsorial Psalm
Ps 50:12-17. ℟ v.12

℟ **A pure heart create for me, O God.**

1 A pure heart create for me, O God,
  put a steadfast spirit within me.
  Do not cast me away from your presence,
  nor deprive me of your holy spirit. ℟

2 Give me again the joy of your help;
  with a spirit of fervour sustain me,
  that I may teach transgressors your ways
  and sinners may return to you. ℟

3 O rescue me, God, my helper,
  and my tongue shall ring out your goodness.
  O Lord, open my lips
  and my mouth shall declare your praise. ℟

Gospel Acclamation
Ps 26:11

Alleluia, alleluia!
Instruct me, Lord, in your way;
on an even path lead me.
Alleluia!

or
Jn 3:16

Alleluia, alleluia!
God loved the world so much that he gave his only Son;
everyone who believes in him has eternal life.
Alleluia!

GOSPEL

A reading from the holy Gospel according to Mark 4:35-41
Who can this be? Even the wind and the sea obey him.

With the coming of evening, Jesus said to his disciples, 'Let us cross over to the other side.' And leaving the crowd behind they took him, just as he was, in the boat; and there were other boats with him. Then it began to blow a gale and the waves were breaking into the boat so that it was almost swamped. But he was in the stern, his head on the cushion, asleep. They woke him and said to him, 'Master, do you not care? We are going down!' And he woke up and rebuked the wind and said to the sea, 'Quiet now! Be calm!' And the wind dropped, and all was calm again. Then he said to them, 'Why are you so frightened? How is it that you have no faith?' They were filled with awe and said to one another, 'Who can this be? Even the wind and the sea obey him.'

This is the Gospel of the Lord.

FOURTH WEEK IN ORDINARY TIME
Year II

MONDAY

FIRST READING

A reading from the second book of Samuel 15:13-14. 30; 16:5-13
Let us fly, or we shall never escape Absalom.

A messenger came to tell David, 'The hearts of the men of Israel are now with Absalom.' So David said to all his officers who were with him in Jerusalem, 'Let us be off, let us fly, or we shall never escape from Absalom. Leave as quickly as you can in case he mounts a surprise attack and worsts us and puts the city to the sword.'

David then made his way up the Mount of Olives, weeping as he went, his head covered and his feet bare. And all the people with him had their heads covered and made their way up, weeping as they went.

As David was reaching Bahurim, out came a man of the same clan as Saul's family. His name was Shimei son of Gera, and as he came he uttered curse after curse and threw stones at David and at all King David's officers, though the whole army and all the champions flanked the king right and left. The words of his curse were these, 'Be off, be off, man of blood, scoundrel! The Lord has brought on you all the blood of the House of Saul whose sovereignty you have usurped; and the Lord has transferred that same sovereignty to Absalom your son. Now your doom has overtaken you, man of blood that you are.' Abishai son of Zeruiah said to the king, 'Is this dead dog to curse my lord the king? Let me go over and cut his head off.' But the king replied, 'What business is it of mine and yours, son of Zeruiah? Let him curse. If the Lord said to him, "Curse David," what right has anyone to say, "Why have you done this?" ' David said to Abishai and all his officers, 'Why, my own son, sprung from my body, is now seeking my life; so now how much the more this Benjaminite? Let him curse on if the Lord has told him to. Perhaps the Lord will look on my misery and repay me with good for his curse today.' So David and his men went on their way.

This is the word of the Lord.

Responsorial Psalm   Ps 3:2-8. ℟ v.8

℟ **Arise, Lord; save me, my God.**

1. How many are my foes, O Lord!
   How many are rising up against me!
   How many are saying about me:
   'There is no help for him in God.' ℟

2. But you, Lord, are a shield about me,
   my glory, who lift up my head.
   I cry aloud to the Lord.
   He answers from his holy mountain. ℟

3. I lie down to rest and I sleep.
   I wake, for the Lord upholds me.
   I will not fear even thousands of people
   who are ranged on every side against me.
   Arise, Lord; save me, my God. ℟

Gospel Acclamation   cf. Jn 17:17

Alleluia, alleluia!
Your word is truth, O Lord,
consecrate us in the truth.
Alleluia!

or   Lk 7:16

Alleluia, alleluia!
A great prophet has appeared among us;
God has visited his people.
Alleluia!

GOSPEL

A reading from the holy Gospel according to Mark   5:1-20
Come out of that man, unclean spirit.

Jesus and his disciples reached the country of the Gerasenes on the other side of the lake, and no sooner had he left the boat than a man with an unclean spirit came out from the tombs towards him. The man lived in the tombs and no one could secure him any more, even with a chain, because he had often been secured with fetters and chains but had snapped the chains and broken the fetters, and no one had the strength to control him. All night and all day, among the tombs and in the mountains, he would howl and gash himself with stones. Catching sight of Jesus from a distance, he ran up and fell at his feet and shouted at the top of his voice, 'What do you want with me, Jesus, son of the Most High God? Swear by God you will not torture me!' – For Jesus had been saying to him, 'Come out of the man, unclean spirit.' 'What is your name?' Jesus asked. 'My name is legion,' he answered 'for there are many of us.' And he begged him earnestly not to send them out of the district. Now there was there on the mountainside a great herd of pigs feeding, and the unclean spirits begged him, 'Send us to the pigs, let us go into them.' So he gave them leave. With that, the unclean spirits came out and went into the pigs, and the herd of about two thousand pigs charged down the cliff into the lake, and there they were drowned. The swineherds ran off and told their story in the town and in the country round about; and the people came to see what had really happened. They came to Jesus and saw the demoniac sitting there, clothed and in his full senses – the very man who had had the legion in him before – and they were afraid. And those who had witnessed it reported what had happened to the demoniac and what had become of the pigs. Then they began to implore Jesus to leave the neighbourhood. As he was getting into the boat, the man who had been possessed begged to be allowed to stay with him. Jesus would not let him but said to him, 'Go home to your people and tell them all that the Lord in his mercy has done for you.' So the man went off and proceeded to spread throughout the Decapolis all that Jesus had done for him. And everyone was amazed.

This is the Gospel of the Lord.

TUESDAY

FIRST READING

A reading from the second book of Samuel
                                        18:9-10. 14. 24-25. 30 – 19:3
My son Absalom! Would I had died in your place.

Absalom happened to run into some of David's followers. Absalom was riding a mule and the mule passed under the thick branches of a great oak. Absalom's head caught fast in the oak and he was left hanging between heaven and earth, while the mule he was riding went on. Someone saw this and told Joab. 'I have just seen Absalom,' he said 'hanging from an oak.' And Joab took three lances in his hand and thrust them into Absalom's heart while he was still alive there in the oak tree.

David was sitting between the two gates. The look-out had gone up to the roof of the gate, on the ramparts; he looked up and saw a man running all by himself. The watch called out to the king and told him. The king said, 'Move aside and stand there.' He moved aside and stood waiting.

Then the Cushite arrived. 'Good news for my lord the king!' cried the Cushite. 'The Lord has vindicated your cause today by ridding you of all who rebelled against you.' 'Is all well with young Absalom?' the king asked the Cushite. 'May the enemies of my lord the king,' the Cushite answered, 'and all who rebelled against you to your hurt, share the lot of that young man.'

The king shuddered. He went up to the room over the gate and burst into tears, and weeping said, 'My son Absalom! My son! My son Absalom! Would I had died in your place! Absalom, my son, my son!' Word was brought to Joab, 'The king is now weeping and mourning for Absalom.' And the day's victory was turned to mourning for all the troops, because they learned that the king was grieving for his son. And the troops returned stealthily that day to the town, as troops creep back ashamed when routed in battle.

This is the word of the Lord.

Responsorial Psalm   Ps 85:1-6. ℟ v.1

℟ **Turn your ear, O Lord, and give answer.**

1. Turn your ear, O Lord, and give answer
for I am poor and needy.
Preserve my life, for I am faithful:
save the servant who trusts in you.   ℟

2. You are my God, have mercy on me, Lord,
for I cry to you all the day long.
Give joy to your servant, O Lord,
for to you I lift up my soul.   ℟

3. O Lord, you are good and forgiving,
full of love to all who call.
Give heed, O Lord, to my prayer
and attend to the sound of my voice.   ℟

Gospel Acclamation Jn 14:6
Alleluia, alleluia!
I am the Way, the Truth and the Life, says the Lord;
no one can come to the Father except through me.
Alleluia!

or Mt 8:17

Alleluia, alleluia!
He took our sicknesses away,
and carried our diseases for us.
Alleluia!

GOSPEL

A reading from the holy Gospel according to Mark 5:21-43
Little girl, I tell you get up.

When Jesus had crossed in the boat to the other side, a large crowd gathered round him and he stayed by the lakeside. Then one of the synagogue officials came up, Jairus by name, and seeing him, fell at his feet and pleaded with him earnestly, saying, 'My little daughter is desperately sick. Do come and lay your hands on her to make her better and save her life.' Jesus went with him and a large crowd followed him; they were pressing all round him.

Now there was a woman who had suffered from a haemorrhage for twelve years; after long and painful treatment under various doctors, she had spent all she had without being any the better for it, in fact, she was getting worse. She had heard about Jesus, and she came up behind him through the crowd and touched his cloak. 'If I can touch even his clothes,' she had told herself 'I shall be well again.' And the source of the bleeding dried up instantly, and she felt in herself that she was cured of her complaint. Immediately aware that power had gone out from him, Jesus turned round in the crowd and said, 'Who touched my clothes?' His disciples said to him, 'You see how the crowd is pressing round you and yet you say, "Who touched me?" ' But he continued to look all round to see who had done it. Then the woman came forward, frightened and trembling because she knew what had happened to her, and she fell at his feet and told him the whole truth. 'My daughter,' he said 'your faith has restored you to health; go in peace and be free from your complaint.'

While he was still speaking some people arrived from the

house of the synagogue official to say, 'Your daughter is dead: why put the Master to any further trouble?' But Jesus had overheard this remark of theirs and he said to the official, 'Do not be afraid; only have faith.' And he allowed no one to go with him except Peter and James and John the brother of James. So they came to the official's house and Jesus noticed all the commotion, with people weeping and wailing unrestrainedly. He went in and said to them, 'Why all this commotion and crying? The child is not dead, but asleep.' But they laughed at him. So he turned them all out and, taking with him the child's father and mother and his own companions, he went into the place where the child lay. And taking the child by the hand he said to her, 'Talitha, kum!' which means, 'Little girl, I tell you to get up.' The little girl got up at once and began to walk about, for she was twelve years old. At this they were overcome with astonishment, and he ordered them strictly not to let anyone know about it, and told them to give her something to eat.

This is the Gospel of the Lord.

WEDNESDAY

FIRST READING

A reading from the second book of Samuel 24:2. 9-17

It was I who sinned, taking a census of the people. But these, this flock, what have they done?

King David said to Joab and to the senior army officers who were with him, 'Now go throughout the tribes of Israel from Dan to Beersheba and take a census of the people; I wish to know the size of the population.'

Joab gave the king the figures for the census of the people; Israel numbered eight hundred thousand armed men capable of drawing sword, and Judah five hundred thousand men.

But afterwards David's heart misgave him for having taken a census of the people. 'I have committed a grave sin,' David said to the Lord. 'But now, Lord, I beg you to forgive your servant for this fault. I have been very foolish.' But when David got up the next morning, the following message had come from the Lord to the prophet Gad, David's seer, 'Go and say to David, "The Lord says this: I offer you three things; choose one of them for me to do to you."'

So Gad went to David and told him. 'Are three years of famine to come on you in your country,' he said, 'or will you flee for three months before your pursuing enemy, or would you rather have three days' pestilence in your country? Now think, and decide how I am to answer him who sends me.' David said to Gad, 'This is a hard choice. But let us rather fall into the power of the Lord, since his mercy is great, and not into the power of men.' So David chose pestilence.

It was the time of the wheat harvest. The Lord sent a pestilence on Israel from the morning till the time appointed and plague ravaged the people, and from Dan to Beersheba seventy thousand men of them died. The angel stretched out his hand towards Jerusalem to destroy it, but the Lord thought better of this evil, and he said to the angel who was destroying the people, 'Enough! now withdraw your hand.' The angel of the Lord was beside the threshing-floor of Araunah the Jebusite. When David saw the angel who was ravaging the people, he spoke to the Lord. 'It was I who sinned;' he said, 'I who did this wicked thing. But these, this flock, what have they done? Let your hand lie heavy on me then, and on my family.'

This is the word of the Lord.

Responsorial Psalm Ps 31:1-2. 5-7. ℟ cf. v.5

℟ **Forgive, Lord, the guilt of my sin.**

1 Happy the man whose offence is forgiven,
   whose sin is remitted.
   O happy the man to whom the Lord
   imputes no guilt,
   in whose spirit is no guile. ℟

2 But now I have acknowledged my sins,
   my guilt I did not hide.
   I said: 'I will confess
   my offence to the Lord.'
   And you, Lord, have forgiven
   the guilt of my sin. ℟

3 So let every good man pray to you
   in the time of need.
   The floods of water may reach high
   but him they shall not reach. ℟

4 You are my hiding place, O Lord;
   you save me from distress.
   You surround me with cries of deliverance. ℟

Gospel Acclamation   Mt 4:4

    Alleluia, alleluia!
    Man does not live on bread alone,
    but on every word that comes from the mouth of God.
    Alleluia!

or   Jn 10:27

    Alleluia, alleluia!
    The sheep that belong to me listen to my voice,
    says the Lord,
    I know them and they follow me.
    Alleluia!

GOSPEL

A reading from the holy Gospel according to Mark   6:1-6

A prophet is only despised in his own country.

Jesus went to his home town and his disciples accompanied him. With the coming of the sabbath he began teaching in the synagogue and most of them were astonished when they heard him. They said, 'Where did the man get all this? What is this wisdom that has been granted him, and these miracles that are worked through him? This is the carpenter, surely, the son of Mary, the brother of James and Joset and Jude and Simon? His sisters, too, are they not here with us?' And they would not accept him. And Jesus said to them, 'A prophet is only despised in his own country, among his own relations and in his own house'; and he could work no miracle there, though he cured a few sick people by laying his hands on them. He was amazed at their lack of faith.

    This is the Gospel of the Lord.

THURSDAY

FIRST READING

A reading from the first book of the Kings   2:1-4. 10-12

I am going the way of all the earth; be strong, Solomon, and show yourself a man.

As David's life drew to its close he laid this charge on his son Solomon, 'I am going the way of all the earth. Be strong and show yourself a man. Observe the injunctions of the Lord your God, following his ways and keeping his laws, his commandments, his customs and his decrees, as it stands written in the Law of Moses, that so you may be successful in all you do and undertake, so that the Lord may fulfil the promise he made me, "If your sons are careful how they behave, and walk loyally before me with all their heart and soul, you shall never lack for a man on the throne of Israel." '

So David slept with his ancestors and was buried in the Citadel of David. David's reign over Israel lasted forty years: he reigned in Hebron for seven years, and in Jerusalem for thirty-three.

Solomon was seated upon the throne of David, and his sovereignty was securely established.

This is the word of the Lord.

Responsorial Psalm   1 Chron 29:10-12. ℟ v.12

   ℟ **You, Lord, are the ruler of all.**

1. Blessed are you, O Lord,
   the God of Israel, our father,
   for ever, for ages unending.   ℟

2. Yours, Lord, are greatness and power,
   and splendour, triumph and glory.
   All is yours, in heaven and on earth.   ℟

3. Yours, O Lord, is the kingdom,
   you are supreme over all.
   Both honour and riches come from you.   ℟

4. You are the ruler of all,
   from your hand come strength and power,
   from your hand come greatness and might.   ℟

Gospel Acclamation   Jn 15:15

   Alleluia, alleluia!
   I call you friends, says the Lord,
   because I have made known to you
   everything I have learnt from my Father.
   Alleluia!

or   Mk 1:15

   Alleluia, alleluia!
   The kingdom of God is close at hand,

repent and believe the Good News.
Alleluia!

GOSPEL

A reading from the holy Gospel according to Mark 6:7-13
He began to send them out.

Jesus made a tour round the villages, teaching. Then he summoned the Twelve and began to send them out in pairs giving them authority over the unclean spirits. And he instructed them to take nothing for the journey except a staff – no bread, no haversack, no coppers for their purses. They were to wear sandals but, he added, 'Do not take a spare tunic.' And he said to them, 'If you enter a house anywhere, stay there until you leave the district. And if any place does not welcome you and people refuse to listen to you, as you walk away shake off the dust from under your feet as a sign to them.' So they set off to preach repentance; and they cast out many devils, and anointed many sick people with oil and cured them.

This is the Gospel of the Lord.

FRIDAY

FIRST READING

A reading from the book of Ecclesiasticus 47:2-11
David put all his heart into his songs out of love for his Maker.

As the fat is set apart from the communion sacrifice,
so David was chosen out of all the sons of Israel.
He played with lions as though with kids,
and with bears as though with lambs of the flock.
While still a boy, did he not slay the giant,
and relieve the people of their shame,
by putting out a hand to sling a stone
which brought down the arrogance of Goliath?
For he called on the Lord Most High,
who gave strength to his right arm
to put a mighty warrior to death,
and lift up the horn of his people.
Hence they gave him credit for ten thousand,
and praised him while they blessed the Lord,
by offering him a crown of glory;

for he massacred enemies on every side,
he annihilated his foes the Philistines,
and crushed their horn to this very day.
In all his activities he gave thanks
to the Holy One, the Most High, in words of glory;
he put all his heart into his songs
out of love for his Maker.
He placed harps before the altar
to make the singing sweeter with their music;
he gave the feasts their splendour,
the festivals their solemn pomp,
causing the Lord's holy name to be praised
and the sanctuary to resound from dawn.
The Lord took away his sins,
and exalted his horn for ever;
he gave him a royal covenant,
and a glorious throne in Israel.

This is the word of the Lord.

Responsorial Psalm
Ps 17:31. 47. 50-51. ℟ cf. v.47

℟ **Praised be the God who saves me.**

1 The ways of God are perfect;
the word of the Lord, purest gold.
He indeed is the shield
of all who make him their refuge. ℟

2 Long life to the Lord, my rock!
Praised be the God who saves me.
I will praise you, Lord, among the nations:
I will sing a psalm to your name. ℟

3 He has given great victories to his king
and shown his love for his anointed,
for David and his sons for ever. ℟

Gospel Acclamation
cf. Lk 8:15

Alleluia, alleluia!
Blessed are those who,
with a noble and generous heart,
take the word of God to themselves
and yield a harvest through their perseverance.
Alleluia!

Fourth Week in Ordinary Time, Year II: Friday

GOSPEL

A reading from the holy Gospel according to Mark 6:14-29

It is John whose head I cut off. He has risen from the dead.

King Herod had heard about Jesus, since by now his name was well-known. Some were saying, 'John the Baptist has risen from the dead, and that is why miraculous powers are at work in him.' Others said, 'He is Elijah'; others again, 'He is a prophet, like the prophets we used to have.' But when Herod heard this he said, 'It is John whose head I cut off; he has risen from the dead.'

Now it was this same Herod who had sent to have John arrested, and had him chained up in prison because of Herodias, his brother Philip's wife whom he had married. For John had told Herod, 'It is against the law for you to have your brother's wife.' As for Herodias, she was furious with him and wanted to kill him; but she was not able to, because Herod was afraid of John, knowing him to be a good and holy man, and gave him his protection. When he had heard him speak he was greatly perplexed, and yet he liked to listen to him.

An opportunity came on Herod's birthday when he gave a banquet for the nobles of his court, for his army officers and for the leading figures in Galilee. When the daughter of this same Herodias came in and danced, she delighted Herod and his guests; so the king said to the girl, 'Ask me anything you like and I will give it you.' And he swore her an oath, 'I will give you anything you ask, even half my kingdom.' She went out and said to her mother, 'What shall I ask for?' She replied, 'The head of John the Baptist.' The girl hurried straight back to the king and made her request. 'I want you to give me John the Baptist's head, here and now, on a dish.' The king was deeply distressed but, thinking of the oaths he had sworn and of his guests, he was reluctant to break his word to her. So the king at once sent one of the bodyguard with orders to bring John's head. The man went off and beheaded him in prison; then he brought the head on a dish and gave it to the girl, and the girl gave it to her mother. When John's disciples heard about this, they came and took his body and laid it in a tomb.

This is the Gospel of the Lord.

SATURDAY

FIRST READING

A reading from the first book of the Kings 3:4-13
Give your servant a heart to understand how to discern between good and evil.

King Solomon went to Gibeon to sacrifice there, since that was the greatest of the high places – he offered a thousand holocausts on that altar. At Gibeon the Lord appeared in a dream to Solomon during the night. God said, 'Ask what you would like me to give you.' Solomon replied, 'You showed great kindness to your servant David, my father, when he lived his life before you in faithfulness and justice and integrity of heart; you have continued this great kindness to him by allowing a son of his to sit on his throne today. Now, Lord my God, you have made your servant king in succession to David my father. But I am a very young man, unskilled in leadership. Your servant finds himself in the midst of this people of yours that you have chosen, a people so many its number cannot be counted or reckoned. Give your servant a heart to understand how to discern between good and evil, for who could govern this people of yours that is so great?' It pleased the Lord that Solomon should have asked for this. 'Since you have asked for this' the Lord said 'and not asked for long life for yourself or riches or the lives of your enemies, but have asked for a discerning judgement for yourself, here and now I do what you ask. I give you a heart wise and shrewd as none before you has had and none will have after you. What you have not asked I shall give you too: such riches and glory as no other king ever had.'

This is the word of the Lord.

Responsorial Psalm
Ps 118:9-14. ℟ 12

℟ **Lord, teach me your statutes.**

1 How shall the young remain sinless?
   By obeying your word.
   I have sought you with all my heart:
   let me not stray from your commands. ℟

2 I treasure your promise in my heart
   lest I sin against you.
   Blessed are you, O Lord:
   teach me your statutes. ℟

3. With my tongue I have recounted
   the decrees of your lips.
   I rejoiced to do your will
   as though all riches were mine. ℟

Gospel Acclamation   Jn 10:27
Alleluia, alleluia!
The sheep that belong to me listen to my voice,
says the Lord,
I know them and they follow me.
Alleluia!

GOSPEL

A reading from the holy Gospel according to Mark   6:30-34

They were like sheep without a shepherd.

The apostles rejoined Jesus and told him all they had done and taught. Then he said to them, 'You must come away to some lonely place all by yourselves and rest for a while'; for there were so many coming and going that the apostles had no time even to eat. So they went off in a boat to a lonely place where they could be by themselves. But people saw them going, and many could guess where; and from every town they all hurried to the place on foot and reached it before them. So as he stepped ashore he saw a large crowd; and he took pity on them because they were like sheep without a shepherd, and he set himself to teach them at some length.

This is the Gospel of the Lord.

FIFTH WEEK IN ORDINARY TIME
Year II
MONDAY

FIRST READING

A reading from the first book of the Kings   8:1-7. 9-13

They brought the ark of the covenant into the Holy of Holies, and the cloud filled the Temple of the Lord.

Solomon called the elders of Israel together in Jerusalem to bring the ark of the covenant of the Lord up from the Citadel of David, which is Zion. All the men of Israel assembled round King

Solomon in the month of Ethanim, at the time of the feast (that is, the seventh month), and the priests took up the ark and the Tent of Meeting with all the sacred vessels that were in it. In the presence of the ark, King Solomon and all Israel sacrificed sheep and oxen, countless, innumerable. The priests brought the ark of the covenant of the Lord to its place, in the Debir of the Temple, that is, in the Holy of Holies, under the cherubs' wings. For there where the ark was placed the cherubs spread out their wings and sheltered the ark and its shafts. There was nothing in the ark except the two stone tablets Moses had placed in it at Horeb, the tablets of the covenant which the Lord had made with the Israelites when they came out of the land of Egypt; they are still there today.

Now when the priests came out of the sanctuary, the cloud filled the Temple of the Lord, and because of the cloud the priests could no longer perform their duties: the glory of the Lord filled the Lord's Temple.

Then Solomon said:

'The Lord has chosen to dwell in the thick cloud.
Yes, I have built you a dwelling,
a place for you to live in for ever.'

This is the word of the Lord.

Responsorial Psalm

Ps 131:6-10. ℟ v.8

℟ **Go up, Lord, to the place of your rest!**

1. At Ephrata we heard of the ark;
   we found it in the plains of Yearim.
   'Let us go to the place of his dwelling;
   let us go to kneel at his footstool.' ℟

2. Go up, Lord, to the place of your rest,
   you and the ark of your strength.
   Your priests shall be clothed with holiness;
   your faithful shall ring out their joy.
   For the sake of David your servant
   do not reject your anointed. ℟

Gospel Acclamation

Jn 8:12

Alleluia, alleluia!
I am the light of the world, says the Lord,
anyone who follows me
will have the light of life.
Alleluia!

or cf. Mt 4:23

Alleluia, alleluia!
Jesus proclaimed the Good News of the kingdom,
and cured all kinds of sickness among the people.
Alleluia!

GOSPEL

A reading from the holy Gospel according to Mark 6:53-56
All those who touched him were cured.

Having made the crossing, Jesus and his disciples came to land at Genessaret and tied up. No sooner had they stepped out of the boat than people recognised him, and started hurrying all through the countryside and brought the sick on stretchers to wherever they heard he was. And wherever he went, to village, or town, or farm, they laid down the sick in the open spaces, begging him to let them touch even the fringe of his cloak. And all those who touched him were cured.

This is the Gospel of the Lord.

TUESDAY

FIRST READING

A reading from the first book of the Kings 8:22-23. 27-30
You have said, 'My name shall be there.' Hear the entreaty of your people Israel.

In the presence of the whole assembly of Israel, Solomon stood before the altar of the Lord and, stretching out his hands towards heaven, said, 'Lord God of Israel, not in heaven above nor on earth beneath is there such a God as you, true to your covenant and your kindness towards your servants when they walk wholeheartedly in your way. Yet will God really live with men on the earth? Why, the heavens and their own heavens cannot contain you. How much less this house that I have built! Listen to the prayer and entreaty of your servant, Lord my God; listen to the cry and to the prayer your servant makes to you today. Day and night let your eyes watch over this house, over this place of which you have said, "My name shall be there." Listen to the prayer that your servant will offer in this place.

'Hear the entreaty of your servant and of Israel your people as they pray in this place. From heaven where your dwelling is, hear; and as you hear, forgive.'

This is the word of the Lord.

Responsorial Psalm   Ps 83:3-5. 10-11. R̷ v.2

    R̷ **How lovely is your dwelling place, Lord, God of hosts.**

1 My soul is longing and yearning,
is yearning for the courts of the Lord.
My heart and my soul ring out their joy
to God, the living God.   R̷

2 The sparrow herself finds a home
and the swallow a nest for her brood;
she lays her young by your altars,
Lord of hosts, my king and my God.   R̷

3 They are happy, who dwell in your house,
for ever singing your praise.
Turn your eyes, O God, our shield,
look on the face of your anointed.   R̷

4 One day within your courts
is better than a thousand elsewhere.
The threshold of the house of God
I prefer to the dwellings of the wicked.   R̷

Gospel Acclamation   Ps 118:34

Alleluia, alleluia!
Train me, Lord, to observe your law,
to keep it with my heart.
Alleluia!

or   Ps 118:36. 29

Alleluia, alleluia!
Bend my heart to your will, O Lord,
and teach me your law.
Alleluia!

Fifth Week in Ordinary Time, Year II: Tuesday

GOSPEL

A reading from the holy Gospel according to Mark 7:1-13
You put aside the commandment of God to cling to human traditions.

The Pharisees and some of the scribes who had come from Jerusalem gathered round Jesus, and they noticed that some of his disciples were eating with unclean hands, that is without washing them. For the Pharisees, and the Jews in general, follow the tradition of the elders and never eat without washing their arms as far as the elbow; and on returning from the market place they never eat without first sprinkling themselves. There are also many other observances which have been handed down to them concerning the washing of cups and pots and bronze dishes. So these Pharisees and scribes asked him, 'Why do your disciples not respect the tradition of the elders but eat their food with unclean hands?' He answered, 'It was of you hypocrites that Isaiah so rightly prophesised in this passage of scripture:

This people honours me only with lip-service,
while their hearts are far from me.
The worship they offer me is worthless,
the doctrines they teach are only human regulations.

You put aside the commandment of God to cling to human traditions.' And he said to them, 'How ingeniously you get round the commandment of God in order to preserve your own tradition! For Moses said: Do your duty to your father and your mother, and, Anyone who curses father or mother must be put to death. But you say, "If a man says to his father or mother: Anything I have that I might have used to help you is Corban (that is, dedicated to God), then he is forbidden from that moment to do anything for his father or mother." In this way you make God's word null and void for the sake of your tradition which you have handed down. And you do many other things like this.'

This is the Gospel of the Lord.

WEDNESDAY

FIRST READING

A reading from the first book of the Kings 10:1-10

The queen of Sheba saw all the wisdom of Solomon.

The fame of Solomon having reached the queen of Sheba, she came to test him with difficult questions. She brought immense riches to Jerusalem with her, camels laden with spices, great quantities of gold, and precious stones. On coming to Solomon, she opened her mind freely to him; and Solomon had an answer for all her questions, not one of them was too obscure for the king to expound. When the queen of Sheba saw all the wisdom of Solomon, the palace he had built, the food at his table, the accommodation for his officials, the organisation of his staff and the way they were dressed, his cup-bearers, and the holocausts he offered in the Temple of the Lord, it left her breathless, and she said to the king, 'What I heard in my own country about you and your wisdom was true, then! Until I came and saw it with my own eyes I could not believe what they told me, but clearly they told me less than half: for wisdom and prosperity you surpass the report I heard. How happy your wives are! How happy are these servants of yours who wait on you always and hear your wisdom! Blessed be the Lord your God who has granted you his favour, setting you on the throne of Israel! Because of the Lord's everlasting love for Israel, he has made you king to deal out law and justice.' And she presented the king with a hundred and twenty talents of gold and great quantities of spices and precious stones; no such wealth of spices ever came again as those given to King Solomon by the queen of Sheba.

This is the word of the Lord.

Responsorial Psalm Ps 36:5-6. 30-31. 39-40. ℟ v.30

℟ **The just man's mouth utters wisdom.**

1 Commit your life to the Lord,
trust in him and he will act,
so that your justice breaks forth like the light,
your cause like the noon-day sun. ℟

2 The just man's mouth utters wisdom
and his lips speak what is right;
the law of his God is in his heart,
his steps shall be saved from stumbling. ℟

Fifth Week in Ordinary Time, Year II: Wednesday

3   The salvation of the just comes from the Lord,
    their stronghold in time of distress.
    The Lord helps them and delivers them
    and saves them: for their refuge is in him.   ℟

Gospel Acclamation   cf. 2 Tim 1:10
    Alleluia, alleluia!
    Our Saviour Christ Jesus abolished death,
    and he has proclaimed life through the Good News.
    Alleluia!

or   cf. Jn 17:17

    Alleluia, alleluia!
    Your word is truth, O Lord,
    consecrate us in the truth.
    Alleluia!

GOSPEL

A reading from the holy Gospel according to Mark   7:14-23
It is what comes out of a man that makes him unclean.

Jesus called the people to him and said, 'Listen to me, all of you, and understand. Nothing that goes into a man from outside can make him unclean; it is the things that come out of a man that make him unclean. If anyone has ears to hear, let him listen to this.'

When he had gone back into the house, away from the crowd, his disciples questioned him about the parable. He said to them, 'Do you not understand either? Can you not see that whatever goes into a man from outside cannot make him unclean, because it does not go into his heart but through his stomach and passes out into the sewer?' (Thus he pronounced all foods clean.) And he went on, 'It is what comes out of a man that makes him unclean. For it is from within, from men's hearts, that evil intentions emerge; fornication, theft, murder, adultery, avarice, malice, deceit, indecency, envy, slander, pride, folly. All these evil things come from within and make a man unclean.'

This is the Gospel of the Lord.

THURSDAY

FIRST READING

A reading from the first book of the Kings   11:4-13
Since you do not keep my covenant I will tear the kingdom away from you. For the sake of my servant David, I will leave your son one tribe.

When Solomon grew old his wives swayed his heart to other gods; and his heart was not wholly with the Lord his God as his father David's had been. Solomon became a follower of Astarte, the goddess of the Sidonians, and of Milcom, the Ammonite abomination. He did what was displeasing to the Lord, and was not a wholehearted follower of the Lord, as his father David had been. Then it was that Solomon built a high place for Chemosh the god of Moab on the mountain to the east of Jerusalem, and to Milcom the god of the Ammonites. He did the same for all his foreign wives, who offered incense and sacrifice to their gods.

The Lord was angry with Solomon because his heart had turned from the Lord the God of Israel who had twice appeared to him and who had then forbidden him to follow other gods; but he did not carry out the Lord's order. The Lord therefore said to Solomon, 'Since you behave like this and do not keep my covenant or the laws I laid down for you, I will most surely tear the kingdom away from you and give it to one of your servants. For your father David's sake, however, I will not do this during your lifetime, but will tear it out of your son's hands. Even so, I will not tear the whole kingdom from him. For the sake of my servant David, and for the sake of Jerusalem which I have chosen, I will leave your son one tribe.'

This is the word of the Lord.

Responsorial Psalm   Ps 105:3-4. 35-37. 40. ℟ v.4

  ℟ **O Lord, remember me**
     out of the love you have for your people.

1. They are happy who do what is right,
who at all times do what is just.
O Lord, remember me
out of the love you have for your people.   ℟

2. But instead they mingled with the nations
and learned to act like them.
They worshipped the idols of the nations
and these became a snare to entrap them.   ℟

3   They even offered their own sons
    and their daughters in sacrifice to demons,
    till his anger blazed against his people:
    he was filled with horror at his chosen ones. ℟

Gospel Acclamation Ps 144:13

Alleluia, alleluia!
The Lord is faithful in all his words
and loving in all his deeds.
Alleluia!

or James 1:21

Alleluia, alleluia!
Accept and submit to the word
which has been planted in you
and can save your souls.
Alleluia!

GOSPEL

A reading from the holy Gospel according to Mark 7:24-30

The house-dogs under the table can eat the children's scraps.

Jesus left Gennesaret and set out for the territory of Tyre. There he went into a house and did not want anyone to know he was there, but he could not pass unrecognised. A woman whose little daughter had an unclean spirit heard about him straightaway and came and fell at his feet. Now the woman was a pagan, by birth a Syrophoenician, and she begged him to cast the devil out of her daughter. And he said to her, 'The children should be fed first, because it is not fair to take the children's food and throw it to the house-dogs.' But she spoke up: 'Ah yes, sir,' she replied 'but the house-dogs under the table can eat the children's scraps.' And he said to her, 'For saying this, you may go home happy: the devil has gone out of your daughter.' So she went off to her home and found the child lying on the bed and the devil gone.

This is the Gospel of the Lord.

FRIDAY

FIRST READING

A reading from the first book of the Kings   11:29-32; 12:19
Israel has been separated from the House of David.

One day when Jeroboam had gone out of Jerusalem, the prophet Ahijah of Shiloh accosted him on the road. Ahijah was wearing a new cloak; the two of them were in the open country by themselves. Ahijah took the new cloak he was wearing and tore it into twelve strips, saying to Jeroboam, 'Take ten strips for yourself, for thus the Lord God speaks, the God of Israel, "I am going to tear the kingdom from Solomon's hand and give ten tribes to you. He shall keep one tribe for the sake of my servant David and for the sake of Jerusalem, the city I have chosen out of all the tribes of Israel." ' And Israel has been separated from the House of David until the present day.

This is the word of the Lord.

Responsorial Psalm   Ps 80:10-15. R/ vv.11. 9

℟ **I am the Lord your God;**
   listen to my warning.

1. Let there be no foreign god among you,
no worship of an alien god.
I am the Lord your God,
who brought you from the land of Egypt. ℟

2. But my people did not heed my voice
and Israel would not obey,
so I left them in their stubbornness of heart
to follow their own designs. ℟

3. O that my people would heed me,
that Israel would walk in my ways!
At once I would subdue their foes,
turn my hand against their enemies. ℟

Gospel Acclamation   cf. Jn 6:63. 68
Alleluia, alleluia!
Your words are spirit, Lord,
and they are life:
you have the message of eternal life.
Alleluia!

Fifth Week in Ordinary Time, Year II: Saturday

or   cf. Acts 16:14

Alleluia, alleluia!
Open our heart, O Lord,
to accept the words of your Son.
Alleluia!

GOSPEL

A reading from the holy Gospel according to Mark   7:31-37
He makes the deaf hear and the dumb speak.

Returning from the district of Tyre, Jesus went by way of Sidon towards the Sea of Galilee, right through the Decapolis region. And they brought him a deaf man who had an impediment in his speech; and they asked him to lay his hand on him. He took him aside in private, away from the crowd, put his fingers into the man's ears and touched his tongue with spittle. Then looking up to heaven he sighed; and he said to him, 'Ephphatha,' that is, 'Be opened.' And his ears were opened, and the ligament of his tongue was loosened and he spoke clearly. And Jesus ordered them to tell no one about it, but the more he insisted, the more widely they published it. Their admiration was unbounded. 'He has done all things well,' they said 'he makes the deaf hear and the dumb speak.'

This is the Gospel of the Lord.

SATURDAY

FIRST READING

A reading from the first book of the Kings   12:26-32; 13:33-34
Jeroboam made two golden calves.

Jeroboam thought to himself, 'As things are, the kingdom will revert to the House of David. If this people continues to go up to the Temple of the Lord in Jerusalem to offer sacrifices, the people's heart will turn back again to their lord, Rehoboam king of Judah, and they will put me to death.' So the king thought this over and then made two golden calves; he said to the people, 'You have been going up to Jerusalem long enough. Here are your gods, Israel; these brought you up out of the land of Egypt!' He set up one in Bethel and the people went in procession all the way to Dan in front of the other. He set up the temple of the high places and appointed priests from ordinary families, who were not of the sons of Levi. Jeroboam also instituted a feast in the eighth month, on the fifteenth of the month, like the feast that was kept in Judah, and he went up to the altar. That was how he behaved in Bethel, sacrificing to the calves he had made; and at Bethel he put the priests of the high places he had established.

Jeroboam did not give up his wicked ways after this incident, but went on appointing priests for the high places from the common people. He consecrated as priests of the high places any who wished to be. Such conduct made the House of Jeroboam a sinful House, and caused its ruin and extinction from the face of the earth.

This the word of the Lord.

Responsorial Psalm   Ps 105:6-7. 19-22. R̷ v.4

R̷ **O Lord, remember me
out of the love you have for your people.**

1 Our sin is the sin of our fathers;
we have done wrong, our deeds have been evil.
Our fathers when they were in Egypt
paid no heed to your wonderful deeds. R̷

2 They fashioned a calf at Horeb
and worshipped an image of metal,
exchanging the God who was their glory
for the image of a bull that eats grass. R̷

3 They forgot the God who was their saviour,
who had done such great things in Egypt,
such portents in the land of Ham,
such marvels at the Red Sea. R̷

Gospel Acclamation   Mt 4:4

Alleluia, alleluia!
Man does not live on bread alone,
but on every word that comes from the mouth of God.
Alleluia!

Fifth Week in Ordinary Time, Year II: Saturday

GOSPEL

A reading from the holy Gospel according to Mark 8:1-10

They ate as much as they wanted.

A great crowd had gathered, and they had nothing to eat. So Jesus called his disciples to him and said to them, 'I feel sorry for all these people; they have been with me for three days now and have nothing to eat. If I send them off home hungry they will collapse on the way; some have come a great distance.' His disciples replied, 'Where could anyone get bread to feed these people in a deserted place like this?' He asked them, 'How many loaves have you?' 'Seven,' they said. Then he instructed the crowd to sit down on the ground, and he took the seven loaves, and after giving thanks he broke them and handed them to his disciples to distribute; and they distributed them among the crowd. They had a few small fish as well, and over these he said a blessing and ordered them to be distributed also. They ate as much as they wanted, and they collected seven basketfuls of the scraps left over. Now there had been about four thousand people. He sent them away and immediately, getting into the boat with his disciples, went to the region of Dalmanutha.

This is the Gospel of the Lord.

SIXTH WEEK IN ORDINARY TIME
Year II

MONDAY

FIRST READING

A reading from the letter of St James 1:1-11

Your faith is only put to the test to make you patient so that you will become fully-developed, complete.

From James, servant of God and of the Lord Jesus Christ. Greetings to the twelve tribes of the Dispersion.

My brothers, you will always have your trials but, when they come, try to treat them as a happy privilege; you understand that your faith is only put to the test to make you patient, but patience too is to have its practical results so that you will become fully-developed, complete, with nothing missing.

If there is any one of you who needs wisdom, he must ask God, who gives to all freely and ungrudgingly; it will be given to him. But he must ask with faith, and no trace of doubt, because a person who has doubts is like the waves thrown up in the sea when the wind drives. That sort of person, in two minds, wavering between going different ways, must not expect that the Lord will give him anything.

It is right for the poor brother to be proud of his high rank, and the rich one to be thankful that he has been humbled, because riches last no longer than the flowers in the grass; the scorching sun comes up, and the grass withers, the flower falls; what looked so beautiful now disappears. It is the same with the rich man: his business goes on; he himself perishes.

This is the word of the Lord.

Responsorial Psalm Ps 118:67-68. 71-72. 75-76. ℟ v.77

℟ **Let your love come to me and I shall live.**

1 Before I was afflicted I went astray
  but now I keep your word.
  You are good and your deeds are good;
  teach me your statutes.   ℟

2 It was good for me to be afflicted,
  to learn your statutes.
  The law from your mouth means more to me
  than silver and gold.   ℟

3. Lord, I know that your decrees are right,
   that you afflicted me justly.
   Let your love be ready to console me
   by your promise to your servant. ℟

Gospel Acclamation   cf. Ps 94:8

Alleluia, alleluia!
Harden not your hearts today,
but listen to the voice of the Lord.
Alleluia!

or   Jn 14:6

Alleluia, alleluia!
I am the Way, the Truth and the Life, says the Lord;
no one can come to the Father except through me.
Alleluia!

GOSPEL

A reading from the holy Gospel according to Mark   8:11-13
Why does this generation demand a sign?

The Pharisees came up and started a discussion with Jesus; they demanded of him a sign from heaven, to test him. And with a sigh that came straight from the heart he said, 'Why does this generation demand a sign? I tell you solemnly, no sign shall be given to this generation.' And leaving them again and re-embarking he went away to the opposite shore.

This is the Gospel of the Lord.

TUESDAY

FIRST READING

A reading from the letter of St James   1:12-18
God does not tempt anybody.

Happy the man who stands firm when trials come. He has proved himself, and will win the prize of life, the crown that the Lord has promised to those who love him.

Never, when you have been tempted, say, 'God sent the temptation'; God cannot be tempted to do anything wrong, and he does not tempt anybody. Everyone who is tempted is attracted and seduced by his own wrong desire. Then the desire conceives and gives birth to sin, and when sin is fully grown, it too has a child, and the child is death.

Make no mistake about this, my dear brothers; it is all that is good, everything that is perfect, which is given us from above; it comes down from the Father of all light; with him there is no such thing as alteration, no shadow of a change. By his own choice he made us his children by the message of the truth so that we should be a sort of first-fruits of all that he had created.

This is the word of the Lord.

Responsorial Psalm   Ps 93:12-15. 18-19. ℟ v.12

℟ **Happy the man whom you teach, O Lord.**

1. Happy the man whom you teach, O Lord,
   whom you train by means of your law:
   to him you give peace in evil days. ℟

2. The Lord will not abandon his people
   nor forsake those who are his own;
   for judgement shall again be just
   and all true hearts shall uphold it. ℟

3. When I think: 'I have lost my foothold',
   your mercy, Lord, holds me up.
   When cares increase in my heart
   your consolation calms my soul. ℟

Gospel Acclamation   cf. Acts 16:14

Alleluia, alleluia!
Open our heart, O Lord,
to accept the words of your Son.
Alleluia!

or   Jn 14:23

Alleluia, alleluia!
If anyone loves me he will keep my word,
and my Father will love him.
Alleluia!

GOSPEL

A reading from the holy Gospel according to Mark   8:14-21
Be on your guard against the yeast of the Pharisees and the yeast of Herod.

The disciples had forgotten to take any food and they had only one loaf with them in the boat. Then Jesus gave them this warning, 'Keep your eyes open; be on your guard against the yeast of the Pharisees and the yeast of Herod.' And they said to one another, 'It is because we have no bread.' And Jesus knew it, and he said to them, 'Why are you talking about having no bread? Do you not yet understand? Have you no perception? Are your minds closed? Have you eyes that do not see, ears that do not hear? Or do you not remember? When I broke the five loaves among the five thousand, how many baskets full of scraps did you collect?' They answered, 'Twelve.' 'And when I broke the seven loaves for the four thousand, how many baskets full of scraps did you collect?' And they answered, 'Seven'. Then he said to them, 'Are you still without perception?'

This is the Gospel of the Lord.

WEDNESDAY

FIRST READING

A reading from the letter of St James   1:19-27
You must do what the word tells you, and not just listen to it.

Remember this, my dear brothers: be quick to listen but slow to speak and slow to rouse your temper; God's righteousness is never served by man's anger; so do away with all the impurities and bad habits that are still left in you – accept and submit to the word which has been planted in you and can save your souls. But you must do what the word tells you, and not just listen to it and deceive yourselves. To listen to the word and not obey is like looking at your own features in a mirror and then, after a quick look, going off and immediately forgetting what you looked like. But the man who looks steadily at the perfect law of freedom and makes that his habit – not listening and then forgetting, but actively putting it into practice – will be happy in all that he does.

Nobody must imagine that he is religious while he still goes on deceiving himself and not keeping control over his tongue; anyone who does this has the wrong idea of religion. Pure, unspoilt religion, in the eyes of God our Father is this: coming to the help of orphans and widows when they need it, and keeping oneself uncontaminated by the world.

This is the word of the Lord.

Responsorial Psalm Ps 14:2-5. ℟ v.1

℟ **The just will live in the presence of the Lord.**

1 Lord, who shall dwell on your holy mountain?
  He who walks without fault;
  he who acts with justice
  and speaks the truth from his heart;
  he who does not slander with his tongue. ℟

2 He who does no wrong to his brother,
  who casts no slur on his neighbour,
  who holds the godless in disdain.
  but honours those who fear the Lord. ℟

3 He who keep his pledge, come what may;
  who takes no interest on a loan
  and accepts no bribes against the innocent.
  Such a man will stand firm for ever. ℟

Gospel Acclamation Ps 118:105

Alleluia, alleluia!
Your word is a lamp for my steps
and a light for my path.
Alleluia!

or cf. Eph 1:17. 18

Alleluia, alleluia!
May the Father of our Lord Jesus Christ
enlighten the eyes of our mind,
so that we can see what hope his call holds for us.
Alleluia!

GOSPEL

A reading from the holy Gospel according to Mark   8:22-26
He was cured and he could see everything plainly and distinctly.

Jesus and his disciples came to Bethsaida, and some people brought to him a blind man whom they begged him to touch. He took the blind man by the hand and led him outside the village. Then putting spittle on his eyes and laying his hands on him, he asked, 'Can you see anything?' The man, who was beginning to see, replied, 'I can see people; they look like trees to me, but they are walking about.' Then he laid his hands on the man's eyes again and he saw clearly; he was cured, and he could see everything plainly and distinctly. And Jesus sent him home, saying, 'Do not even go into the village.'

This is the Gospel of the Lord.

THURSDAY

FIRST READING

A reading from the letter of St James   2:1-9
Did not God choose those who are poor? But you have no respect for anybody who is poor.

My brothers, do not try to combine faith in Jesus Christ, our glorified Lord, with the making of distinctions between classes of people. Now suppose a man comes into your synagogue, beautifully dressed and with a gold ring on, and at the same time a poor man comes in, in shabby clothes, and you take notice of the well-dressed man, and say, 'Come this way to the best seats'; then you tell the poor man, 'Stand over there' or 'You can sit on the floor by my foot-rest.' Can't you see that you have used two different standards in your mind, and turned yourselves into judges, and corrupt judges at that?

Listen, my dear brothers: it was those who are poor according to the world that God chose, to be rich in faith and to be the heirs to the kingdom which he promised to those who love him. In spite of this, you have no respect for anybody who is poor. Isn't it always the rich who are against you? Isn't it always their doing when you are dragged before the court? Aren't they the ones who insult the honourable name to which you have been dedicated? Well, the right thing to do is to keep the supreme law of scripture:

you must love your neighbour as yourself; but as soon as you make distinctions between classes of people, you are committing sin, and under condemnation for breaking the Law.

This is the word of the Lord.

Responsorial Psalm   Ps 33:2-7. R/ v.7

   R/ **This poor man called;**
      the Lord heard him.

1. I will bless the Lord at all times,
   his praise always on my lips;
   in the Lord my soul shall make its boast.
   The humble shall hear and be glad.   R/

2. Glorify the Lord with me.
   Together let us praise his name.
   I sought the Lord and he answered me;
   from all my terrors he set me free.   R/

3. Look towards him and be radiant;
   let your faces not be abashed.
   This poor man called; the Lord heard him
   and rescued him from all his distress.   R/

Gospel Acclamation   James 1:18
   Alleluia, alleluia!
   By his own choice the Father made us his children
   by the message of the truth,
   so that we should be a sort of first-fruits
   of all that he created.
   Alleluia!

or   cf. Jn 6:63. 68
   Alleluia, alleluia!
   Your words are spirit, Lord,
   and they are life:
   you have the message of eternal life.
   Alleluia!

GOSPEL

A reading from the holy Gospel according to Mark   8:27-33
You are the Christ. The Son of Man is destined to suffer grievously.

Jesus and his disciples left for the villages round Caesarea

Philippi. On the way he put this question to his disciples, 'Who do people say I am?' And they told him, 'John the Baptist,' they said 'others Elijah; others again, one of the prophets.' 'But you,' he asked 'who do you say I am?' Peter spoke up and said to him, 'You are the Christ.' And he gave them strict orders not to tell anyone about him.

And he began to teach them that the Son of Man was destined to suffer grievously, to be rejected by the elders and the chief priests and the scribes, and to be put to death, and after three days to rise again; and he said all this quite openly. Then, taking him aside, Peter started to remonstrate with him. But, turning and seeing his disciples, he rebuked Peter and said to him, 'Get behind me, Satan! Because the way you think is not God's way but man's.'

This is the Gospel of the Lord.

FRIDAY

FIRST READING

A reading from the letter of St James   2:14-24. 26

A body dies when it is separated from the spirit, and in the same way faith is dead if it is separated from good deeds.

Take the case, my brothers, of someone who has never done a single good act but claims that he has faith. Will that faith save him? If one of the brothers or one of the sisters is in need of clothes and has not enough food to live on, and one of you says to them, 'I wish you well; keep yourself warm and eat plenty,' without giving them these bare necessities of life, then what good is that? Faith is like that: if good works do not go with it, it is quite dead.

This is the way to talk to people of that kind: 'You say you have faith and I have good deeds; I will prove to you that I have faith by showing you my good deeds – now you prove to me that you have faith without any good deeds to show. You believe in the one God – that is creditable enough, but the demons have the same belief, and they tremble with fear. Do realise, you senseless man, that faith without good deeds is useless. You surely know that Abraham our father was justified by his deed, because he offered his son Isaac on the altar? There you see it: faith and deeds were working together; his faith became perfect by what he did. This is what scripture really means when it says: Abraham put his faith in God, and this was counted as making him justified; and that is why he was called 'the friend of God.'

You see now that it is by doing something good, and not only by believing, that a man is justified. A body dies when it is separated from the spirit, and in the same way faith is dead if it is separated from good deeds.

This is the word of the Lord.

Responsorial Psalm Ps 111:1-6. ℟ cf. v.1

℟ **Happy the man who takes delight in the commands of the Lord.**

1 Happy the man who fears the Lord,
  who takes delight in his commands.
  His sons will be powerful on earth;
  the children of the upright are blessed. ℟

2 Riches and wealth are in his house;
  his justice stands firm for ever.
  He is a light in the darkness for the upright:
  he is generous, merciful and just. ℟

3 The good man takes pity and lends,
  he conducts his affairs with honour.
  The just man will never waver:
  he will be remembered for ever. ℟

Gospel Acclamation 1 Jn 2:5

Alleluia, alleluia!
When anyone obeys what Christ has said,
God's love comes to perfection in him.
Alleluia!

or Jn 15:15

Alleluia, alleluia!
I call you friends, says the Lord,
because I have made known to you
everything I have learnt from my Father.
Alleluia!

GOSPEL

A reading from the holy Gospel according to Mark   8:34 – 9:1

Anyone who loses his life for my sake, and for the sake of the gospel, will save it.

Jesus called the people and his disciples to him and said, 'If anyone wants to be a follower of mine, let him renounce himself and take up his cross and follow me. For anyone who wants to save his life will lose it: but anyone who loses his life for my sake, and for the sake of the gospel, will save it. What gain, then, is it for a man to win the whole world and ruin his life? And indeed what can man offer in exchange for his life? For if anyone in this adulterous and sinful generation is ashamed of me and of my words, the Son of Man will also be ashamed of him when he comes in the glory of his Father with the holy angels.'

And he said to them, 'I tell you solemnly, there are some standing here who will not taste death before they see the kingdom of God come with power.'

This is the Gospel of the Lord.

SATURDAY

FIRST READING

A reading from the letter of St James   3:1-10

Nobody can tame the tongue.

Only a few of you, my brothers, should be teachers, bearing in mind that those of us who teach can expect a stricter judgement.

After all, every one of us does something wrong, over and over again; the only man who could reach perfection would be someone who never said anything wrong – he would be able to control every part of himself. Once we put a bit into the horse's mouth, to make it do what we want, we have the whole animal under our control. Or think of ships: no matter how big they are, even if a gale is driving them, the man at the helm can steer them anywhere he likes by controlling a tiny rudder. So is the tongue only a tiny part of the body, but it can proudly claim that it does great things. Think how small a flame can set fire to a huge forest; the tongue is a flame like that. Among all the parts of the body, the tongue is a whole wicked world in itself: it infects the whole body; catching fire from hell, it sets fire to the whole wheel of creation. Wild animals and birds, reptiles and fish can all be tamed by man, and often are; but nobody can tame the tongue – it is a pest that will not keep still, full of deadly poison. We use it to bless the Lord and Father, but we also use it to curse men who are made in God's image: the blessing and the curse come out of the same mouth. My brothers, this must be wrong.

This is the word of the Lord.

Responsorial Psalm Ps 11:2-5. 7-8. ℟ v.8

℟ **It is you, O Lord,
who will take us in your care.**

1 Help, O Lord, for good men have vanished:
 truth has gone from the sons of men.
 Falsehood they speak one to another,
 with lying lips, with a false heart. ℟

2 May the Lord destroy all lying lips,
 the tongue speaking high-sounding words,
 those who say: 'Our tongue is our strength;
 our lips are our own, who is our master?' ℟

3 The words of the Lord are words without alloy,
 silver from the furnace, seven times refined.
 It is you, O Lord, who will take us in your care
 and protect us for ever from this generation. ℟

Gospel Acclamation Ps 147:12. 15

Alleluia, alleluia!
O praise the Lord, Jerusalem!
He sends out his word to the earth.
Alleluia!

or cf. Mk 9:6

Alleluia, alleluia!
The heavens opened and the Father's voice resounded:
'This is my Son, the Beloved. Listen to him.'
Alleluia!

GOSPEL

A reading from the holy Gospel according to Mark 9:2-13

In their presence he was transfigured.

Jesus took with him Peter and James and John and led them up a high mountain where they could be alone by themselves. There in their presence he was transfigured: his clothes became dazzlingly white, whiter than any earthly bleacher could make them. Elijah appeared to them with Moses; and they were talking with Jesus. Then Peter spoke to Jesus: 'Rabbi,' he said 'it is wonderful for us to be here; so let us make three tents, one for you, one for Moses and one for Elijah.' He did not know what to say; they were so frightened. And a cloud came, covering them in shadow; and there came a voice from the cloud, 'This is my Son, the Beloved. Listen to him.' Then suddenly, when they looked round, they saw no one with them any more but only Jesus.

As they came down from the mountain he warned them to tell no one what they had seen, until after the Son of Man had risen from the dead. They observed the warning faithfully, though among themselves they discussed what 'rising from the dead' could mean. And they put this question to him, 'Why do the scribes say that Elijah has to come first?' 'True,' he said 'Elijah is to come first and to see that everything is as it should be; yet how is it that the scriptures say about the Son of Man that he is to suffer grievously and be treated with contempt? However, I tell you that Elijah has come and they have treated him as they pleased, just as the scriptures say about him.'

This is the Gospel of the Lord.

SEVENTH WEEK IN ORDINARY TIME
Year II

MONDAY

FIRST READING

A reading from the letter of St James 3:13-18

If at heart you have a self-seeking ambition, never make any claims for yourself.

If there are any wise or learned men among you, let them show it by their good lives, with humility and wisdom in their actions. But if at heart you have the bitterness of jealousy, or a self-seeking ambition, never make any claims for yourself or cover up the truth with lies – principles of this kind are not the wisdom that comes down from above: they are only earthly, animal and devilish. Wherever you find jealousy and ambition, you find disharmony, and wicked things of every kind being done; whereas the wisdom that comes down from above is essentially something pure; it also makes for peace, and is kindly and considerate; it is full of compassion and shows itself by doing good; nor is there any trace of partiality or hypocrisy in it. Peacemakers, when they work for peace, sow the seeds which will bear fruit in holiness.

This is the word of the Lord.

Responsorial Psalm Ps 18:8-10. 15. ℟ v.9

℟ **The precepts of the Lord gladden the heart.**

1. The law of the Lord is perfect,
it revives the soul.
The rule of the Lord is to be trusted,
it gives wisdom to the simple. ℟

2. The precepts of the Lord are right,
they gladden the heart.
The command of the Lord is clear,
it gives light to the eyes. ℟

3. The fear of the Lord is holy,
abiding for ever,
The decrees of the Lord are truth
and all of them just. ℟

4. May the spoken words of my mouth,
the thoughts of my heart,
win favour in your sight. O Lord,
my rescuer, my rock. ℟

Gospel Acclamation 1 Peter 1:25

Alleluia, alleluia!
The word of the Lord remains for ever:
What is this word?
It is the Good News that has been brought to you.
Alleluia!

or cf. 2 Tim 1:10

Alleluia, alleluia!
Our Saviour Christ Jesus abolished death,
and he has proclaimed life through the Good News.
Alleluia!

GOSPEL

A reading from the holy Gospel according to Mark · 9:14-29

I do have faith. Help the little faith I have.

When Jesus, with Peter, James and John came down from the mountain and rejoined the disciples they saw a large crowd round them and some scribes arguing with them. The moment they saw him the whole crowd were struck with amazement and ran to greet him. 'What are you arguing about with them?' he asked. A man answered him from the crowd, 'Master, I have brought my son to you; there is a spirit of dumbness in him, and when it takes hold of him it throws him to the ground, and he foams at the mouth and grinds his teeth and goes rigid. And I asked your disciples to cast it out and they were unable to.' 'You faithless generation' he said to them in reply. 'How much longer must I be with you? How much longer must I put up with you? Bring him to me.' They brought the boy to him, and as soon as the spirit saw Jesus it threw the boy into convulsions, and he fell to the ground and lay writhing there, foaming at the mouth. Jesus asked the father, 'How long has this been happening to him?' 'From childhood,' he replied 'and it has often thrown him into the fire and into the water, in order to destroy him. But if you can do anything, have pity on us and help us.' 'If you can?' retorted Jesus. 'Everything is possible for anyone who has faith.' Immediately the father of the boy cried out, 'I do have faith. Help the little faith I have!' And when Jesus saw how many people were pressing round him, he rebuked the unclean spirit. 'Deaf and dumb spirit,' he said 'I command you: come out of him and never enter him again.' Then throwing the boy into violent convulsions it came out shouting, and the boy lay there so like a corpse that most of them said, 'He is dead.' But Jesus took him by the hand and helped him up, and he was able to stand. When he had gone indoors his disciples asked him privately, 'Why were we unable to cast it out?' 'This is the kind' he answered 'that can only be driven out by prayer.'

This is the Gospel of the Lord.

TUESDAY

FIRST READING

A reading from the letter of St James 4:1-10

When you do pray and don't get it, it is because you have not prayed properly.

Where do these wars and battles between yourselves first start? Isn't it precisely in the desires fighting inside your own selves? You want something and you haven't got it; so you are prepared to kill. You have an ambition that you cannot satisfy; so you fight to get your way by force. Why you don't have what you want is because you don't pray for it; when you do pray and don't get it, it is because you have not prayed properly, you have prayed for something to indulge your own desires.

You are as unfaithful as adulterous wives; don't you realise that making the world your friend is making God your enemy? Anyone who chooses the world for his friend turns himself into God's enemy. Surely you don't think scripture is wrong when it says: the spirit which he sent to live in us wants us for himself alone? But he has been even more generous to us, as scripture says: God opposes the proud but he gives generously to the humble. Give in to God, then; resist the devil, and he will run away from you. The nearer you go to God, the nearer he will come to you. Clean your hands, you sinners, and clear your minds, you waverers. Look at your wretched condition, and weep for it in misery; be miserable instead of laughing, gloomy instead of happy. Humble yourselves before the Lord and he will lift you up.

This is the word of the Lord.

Responsorial Psalm Ps 54:7-11. 23. ℟ v.23

℟ **Entrust your cares to the Lord
and he will support you.**

1 O that I had wings like a dove
   to fly away and be at rest.
   So I would escape far away
   and take refuge in the desert. ℟

2 I would hasten to find a shelter
   from the raging wind,
   from the destructive storm, O Lord,
   and from their plotting tongues. ℟

3 For I can see nothing but violence
 and strife in the city.
 Night and day they patrol
 high on the city walls. ℟

4 Entrust your cares to the Lord
 and he will support you.
 He will never allow
 the just man to stumble. ℟

Gospel Acclamation   Jn 14:23
   Alleluia, alleluia!
   If anyone loves me he will keep my word,
   and my Father will love him,
   and we shall come to him.
   Alleluia!

or   Gal 6:14

   Alleluia, alleluia!
   The only thing I can boast about
   is the cross of our Lord Jesus Christ,
   through whom the world is crucified to me,
   and I to the world.
   Alleluia!

GOSPEL

A reading from the holy Gospel according to Mark   9:30-37
The Son of Man will be delivered into the hands of men. If anyone wants to be first, he must make himself the last of all.

Jesus and his disciples made their way through Galilee; and he did not want anyone to know, because he was instructing his disciples; he was telling them, 'The Son of Man will be delivered into the hands of men; they will put him to death; and three days after he has been put to death he will rise again.' But they did not understand what he said and were afraid to ask him.

They came to Capernaum, and when he was in the house he asked them, 'What were you arguing about on the road?' They said nothing because they had been arguing which of them was the greatest. So he sat down, called the Twelve to him and said, 'If anyone wants to be first, he must make himself last of all and servant of all.' He then took a little child, set him in front of them, put his arms round him, and said to them, 'Anyone who welcomes one of these little children in my name, welcomes me;

WEDNESDAY

FIRST READING

A reading from the letter of St James 4:13-17

You never know what will happen tomorrow. The most you should ever say is: 'If it is the Lord's will.'

Here is the answer for those of you who talk like this: 'Today or tomorrow, we are off to this or that town; we are going to spend a year there, trading, and make some money.' You never know what will happen tomorrow: you are no more than a mist that is here for a little while and then disappears. The most you should ever say is: 'If it is the Lord's will, we shall still be alive to do this or that.' But how proud and sure of yourselves you are now! Pride of this kind is always wicked. Everyone who knows what is the right thing to do and doesn't do it commits a sin.

This is the word of the Lord.

Responsorial Psalm Ps 48:2-3. 6-11. ℟ Mt 5:3

℟ **How happy are the poor in spirit;
theirs is the kingdom of heaven.**

1 Hear this, all you peoples,
 give heed, all who dwell in the world,
 men both low and high,
 rich and poor alike! ℟

2 Why should I fear in evil days
 the malice of the foes who surround me,
 men who trust in their wealth,
 and boast of the vastness of their riches? ℟

3 For no man can buy his own ransom,
 or pay a price to God for his life.
 The ransom of his soul is beyond him.
 He cannot buy life without end,
 nor avoid coming to the grave. ℟

4 He knows that wise men and fools must both perish
 and leave their wealth to others. ℟

Seventh Week in Ordinary Time, Year II: Thursday

Gospel Acclamation Jn 14:6
Alleluia, alleluia!
I am the Way, the Truth and the Life, says the Lord;
no one can come to the Father except through me.
Alleluia!

GOSPEL

A reading from the holy Gospel according to Mark 9:38-40
Anyone who is not against us is for us.

John said to Jesus, 'Master, we saw a man who is not one of us casting out devils in your name; and because he was not one of us we tried to stop him.' But Jesus said, 'You must not stop him: no one who works a miracle in my name is likely to speak evil of me Anyone who is not against us is for us.'

This is the Gospel of the Lord.

THURSDAY

FIRST READING

A reading from the letter of St James 5:1-6
The cries of the reapers you cheated have reached the ears of the Lord.

The answer for the rich: start crying, weep for the miseries that are coming to you. Your wealth is all rotting, your clothes are all eaten up by moths. All your gold and your silver are corroding away, and the same corrosion will be your own sentence, and eat into your body. It was a burning fire that you stored up as your treasure for the last days. Labourers mowed your fields, and you cheated them – listen to the wages that you kept back, calling out; realise that the cries of the reapers have reached the ears of the Lord of hosts. On earth you have had a life of comfort and luxury; in the time of slaughter you went on eating to your heart's content. It was you who condemned the innocent and killed them; they offered you no resistance.

This is the word of the Lord.

Responsorial Psalm   Ps 48:14-20. ℟ Mt 5:3

> ℟ **How happy are the poor in spirit;**
> **theirs is the kingdom of heaven.**

1. This is the lot of the self-confident,
   who have others at their beck and call.
   Like sheep they are driven to the grave,
   where death shall be their shepherd
   and the just shall become their rulers. ℟

2. With the morning their outward show vanishes
   and the grave becomes their home.
   But God will ransom me from death
   and take my soul to himself. ℟

3. Then do not fear when a man grows rich,
   when the glory of his house increases.
   He takes nothing with him when he dies,
   his glory does not follow him below. ℟

4. Though he flattered himself while he lived:
   'Men will praise me for doing well for myself,'
   yet he will go to join his fathers,
   who will never see the light any more. ℟

Gospel Acclamation   cf. Lk 8:15

Alleluia, alleluia!
Blessed are those who,
with a noble and generous heart,
take the word of God to themselves
and yield a harvest through their perseverance.
Alleluia!

or   cf. 1 Thess 2:13

Alleluia, alleluia!
Accept God's message for what it really is:
God's message, and not some human thinking.
Alleluia!

GOSPEL

A reading from the holy Gospel according to Mark   9:41-50

It is better for you to enter into life crippled, than to have two hands and go to hell.

Jesus said to his disciples: 'If anyone gives you a cup of water to drink just because you belong to Christ, then I tell you solemnly, he will most certainly not lose his reward.

'But anyone who is an obstacle to bring down one of these little ones who have faith, would be better thrown into the sea with a great millstone round his neck. And if your hand should cause you to sin, cut it off; it is better for you to enter into life crippled, than to have two hands and go to hell, into the fire that cannot be put out. And if your foot should cause you to sin, cut it off; it is better for you to enter into life lame, than to have two feet and be thrown into hell. And if your eye should cause you to sin, tear it out; it is better for you to enter into the kingdom of God with one eye, than to have two eyes and be thrown into hell where their worm does not die nor their fire go out. For everyone will be salted with fire. Salt is a good thing, but if salt has become insipid, how can you season it again? Have salt in yourselves and be at peace with one another.'

This is the Gospel of the Lord.

FRIDAY

FIRST READING

A reading from the letter of St James 5:9-12

The Judge is already to be seen waiting at the gates.

Do not make complaints against one another, brothers, so as not to be brought to judgement yourselves; the Judge is already to be seen waiting at the gates. For your example, brothers, in submitting with patience, take the prophets who spoke in the name of the Lord; remember it is those who had endurance that we say are the blessed ones. You have heard of the patience of Job, and understood the Lord's purpose, realising that the Lord is kind and compassionate.

Above all, my brothers, do not swear by heaven or by the earth, or use any oaths at all. If you mean 'yes', you must say 'yes'; if you mean 'no', say 'no'. Otherwise you make yourselves liable to judgement.

This is the word of the Lord.

Responsorial Psalm   Ps 102:1-4. 8-9. 11-12. ℟ v.8

℟   **The Lord is compassion and love.**

1. My soul, give thanks to the Lord,
   all my being, bless his holy name.
   My soul, give thanks to the Lord
   and never forget all his blessings. ℟

2. It is he who forgives all your guilt,
   who heals every one of your ills,
   who redeems your life from the grave,
   who crowns you with love and compassion. ℟

3. The Lord is compassion and love,
   slow to anger and rich in mercy.
   His wrath will come to an end;
   he will not be angry for ever. ℟

4. For as the heavens are high above the earth
   so strong is his love for those who fear him.
   As far as the east is from the west
   so far does he remove our sins. ℟

Gospel Acclamation   Ps 110:7. 8

Alleluia, alleluia!
Your precepts, O Lord, are all of them sure;
they stand firm for ever and ever.
Alleluia!

or   cf. Jn 17:17

Alleluia, alleluia!
Your word is truth, O Lord,
consecrate us in the truth.
Alleluia!

GOSPEL

A reading from the holy Gospel according to Mark   10:1-12
What God has united, man must not divide.

Jesus came to the district of Judaea and the far side of the Jordan. And again crowds gathered round him, and again he taught them, as his custom was. Some Pharisees approached him and asked, 'Is it against the law for a man to divorce his wife?' They were testing him. He answered them, 'What did Moses command you?' 'Moses allowed us' they said 'to draw up a writ of dismissal and so to divorce.' Then Jesus said to them, 'It was because you were so unteachable that he wrote this commandment for you. But from the beginning of creation God made them male and female. This is why a man must leave father and mother, and the two become one body. They are no longer two, therefore, but one body. So then, what God has united, man must not divide.' Back in the house the disciples questioned him again about this, and he said to them, 'The man who divorces his wife and marries another is guilty of adultery against her. And if a woman divorces her husband and marries another she is guilty of adultery too.'

This is the Gospel of the Lord.

SATURDAY

FIRST READING

A reading from the letter of St James 5:13-20
The heartfelt prayer of a good man works very powerfully.

If any one of you is in trouble, he should pray; if anyone is feeling happy, he should sing a psalm. If one of you is ill, he should send for the elders of the church, and they must anoint him with oil in the name of the Lord and pray over him. The prayer of faith will save the sick man and the Lord will raise him up again; and if he has committed any sins, he will be forgiven. So confess your sins to one another, and pray for one another, and this will cure you; the heartfelt prayer of a good man works very powerfully. Elijah was a human being like ourselves – he prayed hard for it not to rain, and no rain fell for three-and-a-half years; then he prayed again and the sky gave rain and the earth gave crops.

My brothers, if one of you strays away from the truth, and another brings him back to it, he may be sure that anyone who can bring back a sinner from the wrong way that he has taken will be saving a soul from death and covering up a great number of sins.

This is the word of the Lord.

Responsorial Psalm Ps 140:1-3. 8. ℟ v.2
℟ **Let my prayer come before you like incense, O Lord.**

1 I have called to you, Lord; hasten to help me!
 Hear my voice when I cry to you.
 Let my prayer come before you like incense,
 the raising of my hands like an evening oblation. ℟

2 Lord, set a guard over my mouth;
 keep watch at the door of my lips!
 To you, Lord God, my eyes are turned;
 in you I take refuge; spare my soul! ℟

Gospel Acclamation cf. Mt 11:25
 Alleluia, alleluia!
 Blessed are you, Father,
 Lord of heaven and earth,
 for revealing the mysteries of the kingdom
 to mere children.
 Alleluia!

GOSPEL

A reading from the holy Gospel according to Mark 10:13-16
Anyone who does not welcome the kingdom of God like a little child will never enter it.

People were bringing little children to Jesus, for him to touch them. The disciples turned them away, but when Jesus saw this he was indignant and said to them, 'Let the little children come to me; do not stop them; for it is to such as these that the kingdom of God belongs. I tell you solemnly, anyone who does not welcome the kingdom of God like a little child will never enter it.' Then he put his arms round them, laid his hands on them and gave them his blessing.

This is the Gospel of the Lord.

EIGHTH WEEK IN ORDINARY TIME
Year II

MONDAY

FIRST READING

A reading from the first letter of St Peter 1:3-9

You did not see Christ, yet you love him; and you are already filled with joy that cannot be described, because you believe.

Blessed be God the Father of our Lord Jesus Christ, who in his great mercy has given us a new birth as his sons, by raising Jesus Christ from the dead, so that we have a sure hope and the promise of an inheritance that can never be spoilt or soiled and never fade away, because it is being kept for you in the heavens. Through your faith, God's power will guard you until the salvation which has been prepared is revealed at the end of time. This is a cause of great joy for you, even though you may for a short time have to bear being plagued by all sorts of trials; so that, when Jesus Christ is revealed, your faith will have been tested and proved like gold – only it is more precious than gold, which is corruptible even though it bears testing by fire – and then you will have praise and glory and honour. You did not see him, yet you love him; and still without seeing him, you are already filled with a joy so glorious that it cannot be described, because you believe; and you are sure of the end to which your faith looks forward, that is, the salvation of your souls.

This is the word of the Lord.

Responsorial Psalm Ps 110:1-2. 5-6. 9-10. ℟ v.5

℟ **The Lord keeps his covenant ever in mind.**

or

℟ **Alleluia!**

1. I will thank the Lord with all my heart
in the meeting of the just and their assembly.
Great are the works of the Lord;
to be pondered by all who love them. ℟

2. He gives food to those who fear him;
keeps his covenant ever in mind.
He has shown his might to his people
by giving them the lands of the nations.

(continued)

3   He has sent deliverance to his people
    and established his covenant for ever.
    Holy his name, to be feared.

    ℞ **The Lord keeps his covenant in mind.**

or

    ℞ **Alleluia!**

4   To fear the Lord is the beginning of wisdom;
    all who do so prove themselves wise.
    His praise shall last for ever!   ℞

Gospel Acclamation   cf. 1 Thess 2:13
    Alleluia, alleluia!
    Accept God's message for what it really is:
    God's message, and not some human thinking.
    Alleluia!

or   2 Cor 8:9

    Alleluia, alleluia!
    Jesus Christ was rich,
    but he became poor for your sake,
    to make you rich out of his poverty.
    Alleluia!

GOSPEL

A reading from the holy Gospel according to Mark   10:17-27
Sell everything you own and follow me.

Jesus was setting out on a journey when a man ran up, knelt before him and put this question to him, 'Good master, what must I do to inherit eternal life?' Jesus said to him, 'Why do you call me good? No one is good but God alone. You know the commandments: You must not kill; You must not commit adultery; You must not steal; You must not bring false witness; You must not defraud; Honour your father and mother.' And he said to him, 'Master, I have kept all these from my earliest days.' Jesus looked steadily at him and loved him, and he said, 'There is one thing you lack. Go and sell everything you own and give the money to the poor, and you will have treasure in heaven; then come, follow me.' But his face fell at these words and he went away sad, for he was a man of great wealth.

Jesus looked round and said to his disciples, 'How hard it is for those who have riches to enter the kingdom of God!' The disciples were astounded by these words, but Jesus insisted, 'My children,' he said to them 'how hard it is to enter the kingdom of God! It is easier for a camel to pass through the eye of a needle than for a rich man to enter the kingdom of God.' They were more astonished than ever. 'In that case' they said to one another 'who can be saved?' Jesus gazed at them. 'For men' he said 'it is impossible, but not for God: because everything is possible for God.'

This is the Gospel of the Lord.

TUESDAY

FIRST READING

A reading from the first letter of St Peter   1:10-16

Their prophecies were about the grace which was to come to you. Free your minds then of encumbrances.

It was this salvation that the prophets were looking and searching so hard for; their prophecies were about the grace which was to come to you. The Spirit of Christ which was in them foretold the sufferings of Christ and the glories that would come after them, and they tried to find out at what time and in what circumstances all this was to be expected. It was revealed to them that the news they brought of all the things which have now been announced to you, by those who preached to you the Good News through the Holy Spirit sent from heaven, was for you and not for themselves. Even the angels long to catch a glimpse of these things.

Free your minds, then, of encumbrances; control them, and put your trust in nothing but the grace that will be given you when Jesus Christ is revealed. Do not behave in the way that you liked to before you learnt the truth; make a habit of obedience: be holy in all you do, since it is the Holy One who has called you, and scripture says: Be holy, for I am holy.

This is the word of the Lord.

Responsorial Psalm
Ps 97:1-4. ℟ v.2

℟ **The Lord has made known his salvation.**

1 Sing a new song to the Lord
  for he has worked wonders.
  His right hand and his holy arm
  have brought salvation. ℟

2 The Lord has made known his salvation;
  has shown his justice to the nations.
  He has remembered his truth and love
  for the house of Israel. ℟

3 All the ends of the earth have seen
  the salvation of our God.
  Shout to the Lord all the earth,
  ring out your joy. ℟

Gospel Acclamation
Phil 2:15-16

Alleluia, alleluia!
You will shine in the world like bright stars
because you are offering it the word of life.
Alleluia!

or
cf. Mt 11:25

Alleluia, alleluia!
Blessed are you, Father,
Lord of heaven and earth,
for revealing the mysteries of the kingdom
to mere children.
Alleluia!

GOSPEL

A reading from the holy Gospel according to Mark 10:28-31

You will be repaid a hundred times over, not without persecutions, now in this present time and, in the world to come, eternal life.

'What about us?' Peter asked Jesus. 'We have left everything and followed you.' Jesus said, 'I tell you solemnly, there is no one who has left house, brothers, sisters, father, children or land for my sake and for the sake of the gospel who will not be repaid a hundred times over, houses, brothers, sisters, mothers, children and land – not without persecution – now in this present time and, in the world to come, eternal life.

'Many who are first will be last, and the last first.'

This is the Gospel of the Lord.

WEDNESDAY

FIRST READING

A reading from the first letter of St Peter 1:18-25

You were ransomed in the precious blood of a lamb without spot or stain, namely Christ.

Remember, the ransom that was paid to free you from the useless way of life your ancestors handed down was not paid in anything corruptible, neither in silver nor gold, but in the precious blood of a lamb without spot or stain, namely Christ; who, though known since before the world was made, has been revealed only in our time, the end of the ages, for your sake. Through him you now have faith in God, who raised him from the dead and gave him glory for that very reason – so that you would have faith and hope in God.

You have been obedient to the truth and purified your souls until you can love like brothers, in sincerity; let your love for each other be real and from the heart – your new birth was not from any mortal seed but from the everlasting word of the living and eternal God. All flesh is grass and its glory like the wild flower's. The grass withers, the flower falls, but the word of the Lord remains for ever. What is this word? It is the Good News that has been brought to you.

This is the word of the Lord.

Responsorial Psalm Ps 147:12-15. 19-20. ℟ v.12

    ℟ **O praise the Lord, Jerusalem!**

or

    ℟ **Alleluia!**

1. O praise the Lord, Jerusalem!
   Zion, praise your God!
   He has strengthened the bars of your gates,
   he has blessed the children within you. ℟

2. He established peace on your borders,
   he feeds you with finest wheat.
   He sends out his word to the earth
   and swiftly runs his command. ℟

(continued)

3   He makes his word known to Jacob,
    to Israel his laws and decrees.
    He has not dealt thus with other nations,
    he has not taught them his decrees.

   ℟ **O praise the Lord, Jerusalem!**

or

   ℟ **Alleluia!**

Gospel Acclamation   1 Jn 2:5
   Alleluia, alleluia!
   When anyone obeys what Christ has said,
   God's love comes to perfection in him.
   Alleluia!

or   Mk 10:45

   Alleluia, alleluia!
   The Son of Man came to serve,
   and to give his life as a ransom for many.
   Alleluia!

GOSPEL

A reading from the holy Gospel according to Mark   10:32-45
Now we are going up to Jerusalem and the Son of Man is about to be handed over.

The disciples were on the road, going up to Jerusalem; Jesus was walking on ahead of them; they were in a daze, and those who followed were apprehensive. Once more taking the Twelve aside he began to tell them what was going to happen to him: 'Now we are going up to Jerusalem, and the Son of Man is about to be handed over to the chief priests and the scribes. They will condemn him to death and will hand him over to the pagans, who will mock him and spit at him and scourge him and put him to death; and after three days he will rise again.'

  James and John, the sons of Zebedee, approached him. 'Master,' they said to him 'we want you to do us a favour.' He said to them, 'What is it you want me to do for you?' They said to him, 'Allow us to sit one at your right hand and the other at your left in your glory.' 'You do not know what you are asking' Jesus said to them. 'Can you drink the cup that I must drink, or be baptised with the baptism with which I must be baptised?' They replied, 'We can.' Jesus said to them. 'The cup that I must drink you shall drink, and with the baptism with which I must be baptised you shall be baptised, but as for seats at my right hand or my left, these are not mine to grant; they belong to those to whom they have been allotted.'

When the other ten heard this they began to feel indignant with James and John, so Jesus called them to him and said to them, 'You know that among the pagans their so-called rulers lord it over them, and their great men make their authority felt. This is not to happen among you. No; anyone who wants to become great among you must be your servant, and anyone who wants to be first among you must be slave to all. For the Son of Man himself did not come to be served but to serve, and to give his life as a ransom for many.'

This is the Gospel of the Lord.

THURSDAY

FIRST READING

A reading from the first letter of St Peter 2:2-5. 9-12

You are a royal priesthood, a people set apart to sing the praises of him who called you.

You are new born, and, like babies, you should be hungry for nothing but milk – the spiritual honesty which will help you to grow up to salvation – now that you have tasted the goodness of the Lord.

He is the living stone, rejected by men but chosen by God and precious to him; set yourselves close to him so that you too, the holy priesthood that offers the spiritual sacrifices which Jesus Christ has made acceptable to God, may be living stones making a spiritual house.

But you are a chosen race, a royal priesthood, a consecrated nation, a people set apart to sing the praises of God who called you out of the darkness into his wonderful light. Once you were not a people at all and now you are the People of God; once you were outside the mercy and now you have been given mercy.

I urge you, my dear people, while you are visitors and pilgrims to keep yourselves free from the selfish passions that attack the soul. Always behave honourably among pagans so that they can see your good works for themselves and, when the day of reckoning comes, give thanks to God for the things which now make them denounce you as criminals.

This is the word of the Lord.

Responsorial Psalm   Ps 99:2-5. ℟ v.2

℟ **Come before the Lord,
singing for joy.**

1. Cry out with joy to the Lord, all the earth.
Serve the Lord with gladness.
Come before him, singing for joy. ℟

2. Know that he, the Lord, is God.
He made us, we belong to him,
we are his people, the sheep of his flock. ℟

3. Go within his gates, giving thanks.
Enter his courts with songs of praise.
Give thanks to him and bless his name. ℟

4. Indeed, how good is the Lord,
eternal his merciful love.
He is faithful from age to age. ℟

Gospel Acclamation   Ps 129:5

Alleluia, alleluia!
My soul is waiting for the Lord,
I count on his word.
Alleluia!

or   Jn 8:12

Alleuia, alleluia!
I am the light of the world, says the Lord,
anyone who follows me
will have the light of life.
Alleluia!

GOSPEL

A reading from the holy Gospel according to Mark   10:46-52
Master, let me see again.

As Jesus was leaving Jericho with his disciples and a large crowd, Bartimaeus (that is, the son of Timaeus), a blind beggar, was sitting at the side of the road. When he heard that it was Jesus of Nazareth, he began to shout and to say, 'Son of David, Jesus, have pity on me.' And many of them scolded him and told him to keep quiet, but he only shouted all the louder, 'Son of David, have pity on me.' Jesus stopped and said, 'Call him here'. So they called the blind man. 'Courage,' they said 'get up; he is calling you.' So throwing off his cloak, he jumped up and went to Jesus. Then Jesus spoke, 'What do you want me to do for you?' 'Rabbuni,' the blind man said to him 'Master, let me see again.' Jesus said to him, 'Go; your faith has saved you.' And immediately his sight returned and he followed him along the road.

This is the Gospel of the Lord.

FRIDAY

FIRST READING

A reading from the first letter of St Peter 4:7-13

Like good stewards responsible for all these different graces of God, put yourselves at the service of others.

Everything will soon come to an end, so, to pray better, keep a calm and sober mind. Above all, never let your love for each other grow insincere, since love covers over many a sin. Welcome each other into your houses without grumbling. Each one of you has received a special grace, so, like good stewards responsible for all these different graces of God, put yourselves at the service of others. If you are a speaker, speak in words which seem to come from God; if you are a helper, help as though every action was done at God's orders; so that in everything God may receive the glory, through Jesus Christ, since to him alone belong all glory and power for ever and ever. Amen.

My dear people, you must not think it unaccountable that you should be tested by fire. There is nothing extraordinary in what has happened to you. If you can have some share in the sufferings of Christ, be glad, because you will enjoy a much greater gladness when his glory is revealed.

This is the word of the Lord.

Responsorial Psalm Ps 95:10-13. ℟ v.13

℟ **The Lord comes to rule the earth.**

1 Proclaim to the nations: 'God is king.'
  The world he made firm in its place;
  he will judge the peoples in fairness. ℟

2 Let the heavens rejoice and earth be glad.
  Let the sea and all within it thunder praise,
  let the land and all it bears rejoice,

all the trees of the wood shout for joy
at the presence of the Lord for he comes,
he comes to rule the earth.

℟ **The Lord comes to rule the earth.**

3 With justice he will rule the world,
he will judge the peoples with his truth. ℟

Gospel Acclamation
Ps 118:29. 35

Alleluia, alleluia!
Bend my heart to your will, O Lord,
and teach me your law.
Alleluia!

or
cf. Jn 15:16

Alleluia, alleluia!
I chose you from the world
to go out and to bear fruit,
fruit that will last.
Alleluia!

GOSPEL

A reading from the holy Gospel according to Mark 11:11-26
My house will be called a house of prayer for all the people. Have faith in God.

After he had been acclaimed by the crowds, Jesus entered Jerusalem and went into the Temple. He looked all round him, but as it was now late, he went out to Bethany with the Twelve.

Next day as they were leaving Bethany, he felt hungry. Seeing a fig tree in leaf some distance away, he went to see if he could find any fruit on it, but when he came up to it he found nothing but leaves; for it was not the season for figs. And he addressed the fig tree. 'May no one ever eat fruit from you again' he said. And his disciples heard him say this.

So they reached Jerusalem and he went into the Temple and began driving out those who were selling and buying there; he upset the tables of the money changers and the chairs of those who were selling pigeons. Nor would he allow anyone to carry anything through the Temple. And he taught them and said, 'Does not scripture say: My house will be called a house of prayer for all the peoples? But you have turned it into a robber's den.'

This came to the ears of the chief priests and the scribes, and they tried to find some way of doing away with him; they were afraid of him because the people were carried away by his teaching. And when evening came he went out of the city.

Next morning, as they passed by, they saw the fig tree withered to the roots. Peter remembered. 'Look, Rabbi,' he said to Jesus 'the fig tree you cursed has withered away.' Jesus answered, 'Have faith in God. I tell you solemnly, if anyone says to this mountain, "Get up and throw yourself into the sea," with no hesitation in his heart but believing that what he says will happen, it will be done for him. I tell you therefore: everything you ask and pray for, believe that you have it already, and it will be yours. And when you stand in prayer, forgive whatever you have against anybody, so that your Father in heaven may forgive your failings too. But if you do not forgive, your Father in heaven will not forgive your failings either.'

This is the Gospel of the Lord.

SATURDAY

FIRST READING

A reading from the letter of St Jude   17. 20-25
God can keep you from falling and bring you safe to his glorious presence, innocent and happy.

Remember, my dear friends, what the apostles of our Lord Jesus Christ told you to expect. You must use your holy faith as your foundation and build on that, praying in the Holy Spirit; keep yourselves within the love of God and wait for the mercy of our Lord Jesus Christ to give you eternal life. When there are some who have doubts, reassure them; when there are some to be saved from the fire, pull them out; but there are others to whom you must be kind with great caution, keeping your distance even from outside clothing which is contaminated by vice.

Glory be to him who can keep you from falling and bring you safe to his glorious presence, innocent and happy. To God, the only God, who saves us through Jesus Christ our Lord, be the glory, majesty, authority and power, which he had before time began, now and for ever. Amen.

This is the word of the Lord.

Responsorial Psalm
Ps 62:2-6. ℟ v.2

℟ **For you my soul is thirsting,
O Lord, my God.**

1 O God, you are my God, for you I long;
for you my soul is thirsting.
My body pines for you.
like a dry weary land without water. ℟

2 So I gaze on you in the sanctuary
to see your strength and your glory.
For your love is better than life,
my lips will speak your praise. ℟

3 So I will bless you all my life,
in your name I will lift up my hands.
My soul shall be filled as with a banquet,
my mouth shall praise you with joy. ℟

Gospel Acclamation
1 Peter 1:25

Alleluia, alleluia!
The word of the Lord remains for ever:
What is this word?
It is the Good News that has been brought to you.
Alleluia!

or
cf. Col 3:16. 17

Alleluia, alleluia!
Let the message of Christ, in all its richness,
find a home with you;
through him give thanks to God the Father.
Alleluia!

GOSPEL

A reading from the holy Gospel according to Mark 11:27-33
What authority have you for acting like this?

Jesus and his disciples came to Jerusalem, and as Jesus was walking in the Temple, the chief priests and the scribes and the elders came to him, and they said to him, 'What authority have you for acting like this? Or who gave you authority to do these things?' Jesus said to them, 'I will ask you a question, only one; answer me and I will tell you my authority for acting like this. John's baptism: did it come from heaven, or from man? Answer me that.' And they argued it out this way among themselves: 'If we say from heaven, he will say, "Then why did you refuse to believe him?" But dare we say from man?' – they had the people to fear, for everyone held that John was a real prophet. So their reply to Jesus was, 'We do not know.' And Jesus said to them, 'Nor will I tell you my authority for acting like this.'

This is the Gospel of the Lord.

NINTH WEEK IN ORDINARY TIME
Year II

MONDAY

FIRST READING

A reading from the second letter of St Peter 1:2-7

He has given us the guarantee of something very great: to be able to share the divine nature.

May you have more and more grace and peace as you come to know our Lord more and more.

By his divine power, he has given us all the things that we need for life and for true devotion, bringing us to know God himself, who has called us by his own glory and goodness. In making these gifts, he has given us the guarantee of something very great and wonderful to come: through them you will be able to share the divine nature and to escape corruption in a world that is sunk in vice. But to attain this, you will have to do your utmost yourselves, adding goodness to the faith that you have, understanding to your goodness, self-control to your understanding, patience to your self-control, true devotion to your patience, kindness towards your fellow men to your devotion, and, to this kindness, love.

This is the word of the Lord.

Responsorial Psalm Ps 90:1-2. 14-16. ℟ v. cf. 2

℟ **My God, in you I trust.**

1 He who dwells in the shelter of the Most High
   and abides in the shade of the Almighty
   says to the Lord: 'My refuge,
   my stronghold, my God in whom I trust!' ℟

2 His love he set on me, so I will rescue him;
protect him for he knows my name.
When he calls I shall answer: 'I am with you.'

℞ **My God, in you I trust.**

3 I will save him in distress and give him glory.
With length of life I will content him;
I shall let him see my saving power. ℞

Gospel Acclamation cf. Col 3:16. 17
Alleluia, alleluia!
Let the message of Christ, in all its richness,
find a home with you;
through him give thanks to God the Father.
Alleluia!

or cf. Apoc 1:5

Alleluia, alleluia!
Jesus Christ, the faithful witness,
the First-born from the dead,
loves us and has washed away our sins with his blood.
Alleluia!

GOSPEL

A reading from the holy Gospel according to Mark 12:1-12
They seized the beloved son and killed him and threw him out of the vineyard.

Jesus began to speak to the chief priests, the scribes and the elders in parables, 'A man planted a vineyard; he fenced it round, dug out a trough for the winepress and built a tower; then he leased it to tenants and went abroad. When the time came, he sent a servant to the tenants to collect from them his share of the produce from the vineyard. But they seized the man, thrashed him and sent him away empty-handed. Next he sent another servant to them; him they beat about the head and treated shamefully. And he sent another and him they killed; then a number of others, and they thrashed some and killed the rest. He had still someone left: his beloved son. He sent him to them last of all. 'They will respect my son' he said. But those tenants said to each other, 'This is the heir. Come on, let us kill him, and the inheritance will be ours.' So they seized him and killed him and threw him out of the vineyard. Now what will the owner of the vineyard do? He will come and make an end of the tenants and give the vineyard to others. Have you not read this text of scripture:

> It was the stone rejected by the builders
> that became the keystone.
> This was the Lord's doing
> and it is wonderful to see?'

And they would have liked to arrest him, because they realised that the parable was aimed at them, but they were afraid of the crowds. So they left him alone and went away.

This is the Gospel of the Lord.

TUESDAY

FIRST READING

A reading from the second letter of St Peter 3:11-15. 17-18
We are waiting for the new heavens and the new earth.

You should be living holy and saintly lives while you wait and long for the Day of God to come, when the sky will dissolve in flames and the elements melt in the heat. What we are waiting for is what he promised: the new heavens and new earth, the place where righteousness will be at home. So then, my friends, while you are waiting, do your best to live lives without spot or stain so that he will find you at peace. Think of our Lord's patience as your opportunity to be saved. You have been warned about this, my friends; be careful not to get carried away by the errors of unprincipled people, from the firm ground that you are standing on. Instead, go on growing in the grace and in the knowledge of our Lord and saviour Jesus Christ. To him be glory, in time and in eternity. Amen.

This is the word of the Lord.

Responsorial Psalm Ps 89:2-4. 10. 14. 16. ℟ v.1

℟ **O Lord, you have been our refuge
from one generation to the next.**

1 Before the mountains were born
   or the earth or the world brought forth,
   you are God, without beginning or end. ℟

2 You turn men back into dust
   and say: 'Go back, sons of men.'

(continued)

To your eyes a thousand years
are like yesterday, come and gone,
no more than a watch in the night.

℟ **O Lord, you have been our refuge
from one generation to the next.**

3 Our span is seventy years
or eighty for those who are strong.
And most of these are emptiness and pain.
They pass swiftly and we are gone. ℟

4 In the morning, fill us with your love;
we shall exult and rejoice all our days.
Show forth your work to your servants;
let your glory shine on their children. ℟

Gospel Acclamation Heb 4:12

Alleluia, alleluia!
The word of God is something alive and active;
it can judge secret emotions and thoughts.
Alleluia!

or cf. Eph 1:17. 18

Alleluia, alleluia!
May the Father of our Lord Jesus Christ
enlighten the eyes of our mind,
so that we can see what hope his call holds for us.
Alleluia!

GOSPEL

A reading from the holy Gospel according to Mark 12:13-17

Give back to Caesar what belongs to Caesar — and to God what belongs to God.

The chief priests and the scribes and the elders sent to Jesus some Pharisees and some Herodians to catch him out in what he said. These came and said to him, 'Master, we know you are an honest man, that you are not afraid of anyone, because a man's rank means nothing to you, and that you teach the way of God in all honesty. Is it permissible to pay taxes to Caesar or not? Should we pay, yes or no?' Seeing through their hypocrisy he said to them, 'Why do you set this trap for me? Hand me a denarius and let me see it.' They handed him one and he said, 'Whose head is this? Whose name?' 'Caesar's' they told him. Jesus said to them,

'Give back to Caesar what belongs to Caesar – and to God what belongs to God.' This reply took them completely by surprise.

This is the Gospel of the Lord.

WEDNESDAY

FIRST READING

A reading from the second letter of St Paul to Timothy   1:1-3. 6-12

Fan into a flame the gift that God gave you when I laid my hands on you.

From Paul, appointed by God to be an apostle of Christ Jesus in his design to promise life in Christ Jesus; to Timothy, dear child of mine, wishing you grace, mercy and peace from God the Father and from Christ Jesus our Lord.

Night and day I thank God, keeping my conscience clear and remembering my duty to him as my ancestors did, and always I remember you in my prayers.

This is why I am reminding you now to fan into a flame the gift that God gave you when I laid my hands on you. God's gift was not a spirit of timidity, but the Spirit of power, and love, and self-control. So you are never to be ashamed of witnessing to the Lord, or ashamed of me for being his prisoner; but with me bear the hardships for the sake of the Good News, relying on the power of God who has saved us and called us to be holy – not because of anything we ourselves have done but for his own purpose and by his own grace. This grace had already been granted to us, in Christ Jesus, before the beginning of time, but it has only been revealed by the Appearing of our saviour Christ Jesus. He abolished death, and he has proclaimed life and immortality through the Good News; and I have been named its herald, its apostle and its teacher.

It is only on account of this that I am experiencing fresh hardships here now; but I have not lost confidence, because I know who it is that I have put my trust in, and I have no doubt at all that he is able to take care of all that I have entrusted to him until that Day.

This is the word of the Lord.

Responsorial Psalm   Ps 122:1-2. ℟ v.1

℟ **To you, O Lord, I lift up my eyes.**

1 To you have I lifted up my eyes,
you who dwell in the heavens:
my eyes, like the eyes of slaves
on the hand of their lord. ℟

2 Like the eyes of a servant
on the hand of her mistress,
so our eyes are on the Lord our God
till he show us his mercy. ℟

Gospel Acclamation   cf. Jn 17:17

Alleluia, alleluia!
Your word is truth, O Lord,
consecrate us in the truth.
Alleluia!

or   Jn 11:25. 26

Alleluia, alleluia!
I am the resurrection and the life,
says the Lord,
whoever believes in me will never die.
Alleluia!

GOSPEL

A reading from the holy Gospel according to Mark   12:18-27

He is God, not of the dead, but of the living.

Some Sadducees – who deny that there is a resurrection – came to Jesus and they put this question to him, 'Master, we have it from Moses in writing, if a man's brother dies leaving a wife but no child, the man must marry the widow to raise up children for his brother. Now there were seven brothers. The first married a wife and then died leaving no children. The second married the widow, and he too died leaving no children; with the third it was the same, and none of the seven left any children. Last of all the woman herself died. Now at the resurrection, when they rise again, whose wife will she be, since she had been married to all seven?'

Jesus said to them, 'Is not the reason why you go wrong, that you understand neither the scriptures nor the power of God? For when they rise from the dead, men and women to not marry; no, they are like the angels in heaven. Now about the dead rising again, have you never read in the Book of Moses, in the passage about the Bush, how God spoke to him and said: I am the God of Abraham, the God of Isaac and the God of Jacob? He is God, not of the dead, but of the living. You are very much mistaken.'

This is the Gospel of the Lord.

THURSDAY

FIRST READING

A reading from the second letter of St Paul to Timothy 2:8-15

They cannot chain up God's news. If we have died with him, then we shall live with him.

Remember the Good News that I carry, 'Jesus Christ risen from the dead, sprung from the race of David'; it is on account of this that I have my own hardships to bear, even to being chained like a criminal – but they cannot chain up God's news. So I bear it all for the sake of those who are chosen, so that in the end they may have the salvation that is in Christ Jesus and the eternal glory that comes with it.

Here is a saying that you can rely on:

If we have died with him, then we shall live with him.
If we hold firm, then we shall reign with him.
If we disown him, then he will disown us.
We may be unfaithful, but he is always faithful,
for he cannot disown his own self.

Remind them of this; and tell them in the name of God that there is to be no wrangling about words: all that this ever achieves is the destruction of those who are listening. Do all you can to present yourself in front of God as a man who has come through his trials, and a man who has no cause to be ashamed of his life's work and has kept a straight course with the message of the truth.

This is the word of the Lord.

Responsional Psalm   Ps 24:4-5. 8-10. 14. ℟ v.4

  ℟ **Lord, make me know your ways.**

1. Lord, make me know your ways.
   Lord, teach me your paths.
   Make me walk in your truth, and teach me:
   for you are God my saviour. ℟

2. The Lord is good and upright.
   He shows the path to those who stray,
   he guides the humble in the right path;
   he teaches his way to the poor. ℟

3. His ways are faithfulness and love
   for those who keep his covenant and will.
   The Lord's friendship is for those who revere him;
   to them he reveals his covenant. ℟

Gospel Acclamation   cf. Jn 6:63. 68

Alleluia, alleluia!
Your words are spirit, Lord,
and they are life:
you have the message of eternal life.
Alleluia!

or   cf. 2 Tim 1:10

Alleluia, alleluia!
Our Saviour Christ Jesus abolished death,
and he has proclaimed life through the Good News.
Alleluia!

GOSPEL

A reading from the holy Gospel according to Mark   12:28-34
This is the first commandment. The second is like it.

One of the scribes came up to Jesus and put a question to him, 'Which is the first of all the commandments?' Jesus replied, 'This is the first: Listen, Israel, the Lord our God is the one Lord, and you must love the Lord your God with all your heart, with all your soul, with all your mind and with all your strength. The second is this: You must love your neighbour as yourself. There is no commandment greater than these.' The scribe said to him, 'Well spoken, Master; what you have said is true: that he is one and there is no other. To love him with all your heart, with all your understanding and strength, and to love your neighbour as

Ninth Week in Ordinary Time, Year II: Friday

yourself, this is far more important than any holocaust or sacrifice.' Jesus, seeing how wisely he had spoken, said, 'You are not far from the kingdom of God.' And after that no one dared to question him any more.

This is the Gospel of the Lord.

FRIDAY

FIRST READING

A reading from the second letter of St Paul to Timothy   3:10-17
Anybody who tries to live in devotion to Christ is certain to be attacked.

You know what I have taught, how I have lived, what I have aimed at; you know my faith, my patience and my love; my constancy and the persecutions and hardships that came to me in places like Antioch, Iconium and Lystra – all the persecutions I have endured; and the Lord has rescued me from every one of them. You are well aware, then, that anybody who tries to live in devotion to Christ is certain to be attacked; while these wicked impostors will go from bad to worse, deceiving others and deceived themselves.

You must keep to what you have been taught and know to be true; remember who your teachers were, and how, ever since you were a child, you have known the holy scriptures – from these you can learn the wisdom that leads to salvation through faith in Christ Jesus. All scripture is inspired by God and can profitably be used for teaching, for refuting error, for guiding people's lives and teaching them to be holy. This is how the man who is dedicated to God becomes fully equipped and ready for any good work.

This is the word of the Lord.

Responsorial Psalm   Ps 118:157. 160-161. 165-166. 168. ℟ v.165

  ℟ **The lovers of your law have great peace.**

1 Though my foes and oppressors are countless
  I have not swerved from your will.
  Your word is founded on truth:
  your decrees are eternal.   ℟

2 Though princes oppress me without cause
  I stand in awe of your word.

The lovers of your law have great peace;
they never stumble.

℟ **The lovers of your law have great peace.**

3 I await your saving help, O Lord,
I fulfil your commands.
I obey your precepts and your will;
all that I do is before you. ℟

Gospel Acclamation Ps 18:9
Alleluia, alleluia!
Your words gladden the heart, O Lord,
they give light to the eyes.
Alleluia!

or Jn 14:23

Alleluia, alleluia!
If anyone loves me he will keep my word,
and my Father will love him,
and we shall come to him.
Alleluia!

GOSPEL

A reading from the holy Gospel according to Mark 12:35-37
How can they maintain that the Christ is the son of David?

While teaching in the Temple, Jesus said, 'How can the scribes maintain that the Christ is the son of David? David himself, moved by the Holy Spirit, said:

The Lord said to my Lord:
Sit at my right hand
and I will put your enemies
under your feet.

David himself calls him Lord, in what way then can he be his son?' And the great majority of the people heard this with delight.

This is the Gospel of the Lord.

SATURDAY

FIRST READING

A reading from the second letter of St Paul to Timothy 4:1-8

Make the preaching of the Good News your life's work. As for me, my life is already being poured away and the Lord will give me the crown of righteousness.

Before God and before Christ Jesus who is to be judge of the living and the dead, I put this duty to you, in the name of his Appearing and of his kingdom: proclaim the message and, welcome or unwelcome, insist on it. Refute falsehood, correct error, call to obedience – but do all with patience and with the intention of teaching. The time is sure to come when, far from being content with sound teaching, people will be avid for the latest novelty and collect themselves a whole series of teachers according to their own tastes; and then, instead of listening to the truth, they will turn to myths. Be careful always to choose the right course; be brave under trials; make the preaching of the Good News your life's work, in thoroughgoing service.

As for me, my life is already being poured away as a libation, and the time has come for me to be gone. I have fought the good fight to the end; I have run the race to the finish; I have kept the faith; all there is to come now is the crown of righteousness reserved for me, which the Lord, the righteous judge, will give me on that Day; and not only to me but to all those who have longed for his Appearing.

This is the word of the Lord.

Responsorial Psalm   Ps 70:8-9. 14-17. 22. ℟ cf. v.15

  ℟ **My lips will tell of your justice, O Lord.**

1. My lips are filled with your praise,
   with your glory all the day long.
   Do not reject me now that I am old;
   when my strength fails do not forsake me.   ℟

2. But as for me, I will always hope
   and praise you more and more.
   My lips will tell of your justice
   and day by day of your help
   (though I can never tell it all).   ℟   (continued)

3. I will declare the Lord's mighty deeds
proclaiming your justice, yours alone.
O God, you have taught me from my youth
and I proclaim your wonders still.

℟ **My lips will tell of your justice, O Lord.**

4. So I will give thanks on the lyre
for your faithful love, my God.
To you will I sing with the harp
to you, the Holy One of Israel. ℟

Gospel Acclamation cf. Lk 8:15
Alleluia, alleluia!
Blessed are those who,
with a noble and generous heart,
take the word of God to themselves
and yield a harvest through their perseverance.
Alleluia!

or Mt 5:3

Alleluia, alleluia!
How happy are the poor in spirit;
theirs is the kingdom of heaven.
Alleluia!

GOSPEL

A reading from the holy Gospel according to Mark 12:38-44
This poor widow has put more in than all of them.

In his teaching Jesus said, 'Beware of the scribes who like to walk about in long robes, to be greeted obsequiously in the market squares, to take the front seats in the synagogues and the places of honour at banquets; these are the men who swallow the property of widows, while making a show of lengthy prayers. The more severe will be the sentence they receive.'

He sat down opposite the treasury and watched the people putting money into the treasury, and many of the rich put in a great deal. A poor widow came and put in two small coins, the equivalent of a penny. Then he called his disciples and said to them, 'I tell you solemnly, this poor widow has put more in than all who have contributed to the treasury; for they have all put in money they had over, but she from the little she had has put in everything she possessed, all she had to live on.'

This is the Gospel of the Lord.

TENTH WEEK IN ORDINARY TIME
Year II

MONDAY

FIRST READING

A reading from the first book of the Kings 17:1-6
Elijah served the Lord God of Israel.

Elijah the Tishbite, of Tishbe in Gilead said to Ahab, 'As the Lord lives, the God of Israel whom I serve, there shall be neither dew nor rain these years except at my order.'

The word of the Lord came to him, 'Go away from here, go eastwards, and hide yourself in the wadi Cherith which lies east of Jordan. You can drink from the stream, and I have ordered the ravens to bring you food there.' He did as the Lord had said; he went and stayed in the wadi Cherith which lies east of Jordan. The ravens brought him bread in the morning and meat in the evening, and he quenched his thirst at the stream.

This is the word of the Lord.

Responsorial Psalm Ps 120:1-8. ℟ cf. v.2

℟ **Our help is in the name of the Lord,
who made heaven and earth.**

1 I lift up my eyes to the mountains:
from where shall come my help?
My help shall come from the Lord
who made heaven and earth. ℟

2 May he never allow you to stumble!
Let him sleep not, your guard.
No, he sleeps not nor slumbers,
Israel's guard. ℟

3 The Lord is your guard and your shade;
at your right side he stands.
By day the sun shall not smite you
nor the moon in the night. ℟

4 The Lord will guard you from evil,
he will guard your soul.
The Lord will guard your going and coming
both now and for ever. ℟

Gospel Acclamation   cf. 2 Thess 2:14

> Alleluia, alleluia!
> Through the Good News God called us
> to share the glory of our Lord Jesus Christ.
> Alleluia!

or   Mt 5:12

> Alleluia, alleluia!
> Rejoice and be glad:
> your reward will be great in heaven.
> Alleluia!

GOSPEL

A reading from the holy Gospel according to Matthew   5:1-12

How happy are the poor in spirit.

Seeing the crowds, Jesus went up the hill. There he sat down and was joined by his disciples. Then he began to speak. This is what he taught them:

> 'How happy are the poor in spirit;
> theirs is the kingdom of heaven.
> Happy the gentle:
> they shall have the earth for their heritage.
> Happy those who mourn:
> they shall be comforted.
> Happy those who hunger and thirst for what is right:
> they shall be satisfied.
> Happy the merciful:
> they shall have mercy shown them.
> Happy the pure in heart:
> they shall see God.
> Happy the peacemakers:
> they shall be called sons of God.
> Happy those who are persecuted in the cause of right:
> theirs is the kingdom of heaven.

'Happy are you when people abuse you and persecute you and speak all kinds of calumny against you on my account. Rejoice and be glad, for your reward will be great in heaven; this is how they persecuted the prophets before you.'

This is the Gospel of the Lord.

TUESDAY

FIRST READING

A reading from the first book of the Kings 17:7-16

The jar of meal was not spent, just as the Lord had foretold through Elijah.

The stream in the place where Elijah lay hidden dried up, for the country had no rain. And then the word of the Lord came to Elijah, 'Up and go to Zarephath, a Sidonian town, and stay there. I have ordered a widow there to give you food.' So he went off to Sidon. And when he reached the city gate, there was a widow gathering sticks; addressing her he said, 'Please bring a little water in a vessel for me to drink.' She was setting off to bring it when he called after her. 'Please' he said 'bring me a scrap of bread in your hand.' 'As the Lord your God lives,' she replied 'I have no baked bread, but only a handful of meal in a jar and a little oil in a jug; I am just gathering a stick or two to go and prepare this for myself and my son to eat, and then we shall die.' But Elijah said to her, 'Do not be afraid, go and do as you have said; but first make a little scone of it for me and bring it to me, and then make some for yourself and for your son. For thus the Lord speaks, the God of Israel:

> "Jar of meal shall not be spent,
> jug of oil shall not be emptied,
> before the day when the Lord sends
> rain on the face of the earth"'

The woman went and did as Elijah told her and they ate the food, she, himself and her son. The jar of meal was not spent nor the jug of oil emptied, just as the Lord had foretold through Elijah.

This is the word of the Lord.

Responsional Psalm Ps 4:2-5. 7-8. ℟ v.7

℟ **Lift up the light of your face on us, O Lord.**

1 When I call, answer me, O God of justice;
  from anguish you released me, have mercy and hear me!
  O men, how long will your hearts be closed,
  will you love what is futile and seek what is false? ℟

2 It is the Lord who grants favours to those whom he loves;

the Lord hears me whenever I call him.
Fear him; do not sin: ponder on your bed and be still.

℟ **Lift up the light of your face on us, O Lord.**

3 'What can bring us happiness?' many say.
Lift up the light of your face on us, O Lord.
You have put into my heart a greater joy
than they have from abundance of corn and new wine. ℟

Gospel Acclamation   Phil 2:15-16

Alleluia, alleluia!
You will shine in the world like bright stars
because you are offering it the word of life.
Alleluia!

or   Mt 5:16

Alleluia, alleluia!
Your light must shine in the sight of men,
so that, seeing your good works,
they may give the praise to your Father in heaven.
Alleluia!

GOSPEL

A reading from the holy Gospel according to Matthew   5:13-16
You are the light of the world.

Jesus said to his disciples: 'You are the salt of the earth. But if salt becomes tasteless, what can make it salty again? It is good for nothing, and can only be thrown out to be trampled underfoot by men.
  'You are the light of the world. A city built on a hilltop cannot be hidden. No one lights a lamp to put it under a tub; they put it on the lamp-stand where it shines for everyone in the house. In the same way your light must shine in the sight of men, so that, seeing your good works, they may give the praise to your Father in heaven.'

This is the Gospel of the Lord.

WEDNESDAY

FIRST READING

A reading from the first book of the Kings   18:20-39

May this people know that you, Lord, are God and are winning back their hearts.

King Ahab called all Israel together and assembled the prophets of Baal on Mount Carmel. Elijah stepped out in front of all the people. 'How long' he said 'do you mean to hobble first on one leg then on the other? If the Lord is God, follow him; if Baal, follow him.' But the people never said a word. Elijah then said to them, 'I, I alone, am left as a prophet of the Lord, while the prophets of Baal are four hundred and fifty. Let two bulls be given us; let them choose one for themselves, dismember it and lay it on the wood, but not set fire to it. I in my turn will prepare the other bull, but not set fire to it. You must call on the name of your god, and I shall call on the name of mine; the god who answers with fire, is God indeed.' The people all answered, 'Agreed!' Elijah then said to the prophets of Baal, 'Choose one bull and begin, for there are more of you. Call on the name of your god but light no fire.' They took the bull and prepared it, and from morning to midday they called on the name of Baal. 'O Baal, answer us!' they cried, but there was no voice, no answer, as they performed their hobbling dance round the altar they had made. Midday came, and Elijah mocked them. 'Call louder,' he said 'for he is a god: he is preoccupied or he is busy, or he has gone on a journey; perhaps he is asleep and will wake up.' So they shouted louder and gashed themselves, as their custom was, with swords and spears until the blood flowed down them. Midday passed, and they ranted on until the time the offering is presented; but there was no voice, no answer, no attention given to them.

Then Elijah said to all the people, 'Come closer to me,' and all the people came closer to him. He repaired the altar of the Lord which had been broken down. Elijah took twelve stones, corresponding to the number of the tribes of the sons of Jacob, to whom the word of the Lord had come, 'Israel shall be your name,' and built an altar in the name of the Lord. Round the altar he dug a trench of a size to hold two measures of seed. He then arranged the wood, dismembered the bull, and laid it on the wood. Then he said, 'Fill four jars with water and pour it on the holocaust and on the wood'; this they did. He said, 'Do it a second time';they did it a second time. He said, 'Do it a third time'; they did it a third time. The water flowed round the altar and the trench itself was full of water. At the time when the offering is presented, Elijah the prophet stepped forward, 'Lord, God of Abraham, Isaac and Israel,' he said 'let them know today that you are God in Israel, and that I am your servant, that I have done all these things at your command. Answer me, Lord, answer me, so that this people may know that you, Lord, are God and are winning back their hearts.'

Then the fire of the Lord fell and consumed the holocaust and wood and licked up the water in the trench. When all the people saw this they fell on their faces. 'The Lord is God,' they cried 'the Lord is God.'

This is the word of the Lord.

Responsorial Psalm   Ps 15:1-2. 4-5. 8. 11. ℟ v.1

  ℟ **Save me, Lord, I take refuge in you.**

1. Preserve me, God, I take refuge in you.
   I say to the Lord: 'You are my God.'   ℟

2. Those who choose other gods increase their sorrows.
   Never will I offer their offerings of blood.
   Never will I take their name upon my lips.   ℟

3. O Lord, it is you who are my portion and cup;
   it is you yourself who are my prize.
   I keep the Lord ever in my sight:
   since he is at my right hand, I shall stand firm.   ℟

4. You will show me the path of life,
   the fullness of joy in your presence,
   at your right hand happiness for ever.   ℟

Gospel Acclamation   Ps 118:27
Alleluia, alleluia!
Make me grasp the way of your precepts,
and I will muse on your wonders.
Alleluia!

or   Ps 24:4. 5
Alleluia, alleluia!
Teach me your paths, my God,
make me walk in your truth.
Alleluia!

GOSPEL

A reading from the holy Gospel according to Matthew   5:17-19
I have come not to abolish the Law or the Prophets but to complete them.

Jesus said to his disciples: 'Do not imagine that I have come to abolish the Law or the Prophets. I have come not to abolish but to complete them. I tell you solemnly, till heaven and earth disappear, not one dot, not one little stroke, shall disappear from the Law until its purpose is achieved. Therefore, the man who infringes even one of the least of these commandments and teaches others to do the same will be considered the least in the kingdom of heaven; but the man who keeps them and teaches them will be considered great in the kingdom of heaven.'

This is the Gospel of the Lord.

THURSDAY

FIRST READING

A reading from the first book of the Kings   18:41-46
Elijah prayed and the sky gave rain.

Elijah said to Ahab, 'Go back, eat and drink; for I hear the sound of rain.' While Ahab went back to eat and drink, Elijah climbed to the top of Carmel and bowed down to the earth, putting his face be- tween his knees. 'Now go up,' he told his servant 'and look out to the sea.' He went up and looked. 'There is nothing at all' he said. 'Go back seven times' Elijah said. The seventh time, the servant said, 'Now there is a cloud, small as a man's hand, rising from the sea.' Elijah said, 'Go and say to Ahab, "Harness the chariot and go down before the rain stops you." ' And with that the sky grew dark with cloud and storm, and rain fell in torrents. Ahab mounted his chariot and made for Jezreel. The hand of the Lord was on Elijah, and tucking up his cloak he ran in front of Ahab as far as the outskirts of Jezreel.

This is the word of the Lord.

Responsorial Psalm   Ps 64:10-13. ℟ v.2

    ℟ **To you our praise is due in Zion, O God.**

1   You care for the earth, give it water,
    you fill it with riches.
    Your river in heaven brims over
    to provide its grain.   ℟

2 And thus you provide for the earth;
   you drench its furrows,
   you level it, soften it with showers,
   you bless its growth.

   ℟ **To you our praise is due i Zion, O God.**

3 You crown the year with your goodness.
   Abundance flows in your steps,
   in the pastures of the wilderness it flows.
   The hills are girded with joy.   ℟

Gospel Acclamation   cf. 1 Thess 2:13
   Alleluia, alleluia!
   Accept God's message for what it really is:
   God's message, and not some human thinking.
   Alleluia!

or   Jn 13:34

   Alleluia, alleluia!
   I give you a new commandment:
   love one another just as I have loved you,
   says the Lord.
   Alleluia!

GOSPEL

A reading from the holy Gospel according to Matthew   5:20-26

Anyone who is angry with his brother will answer for it before the court.

Jesus said to his disciples: 'If your virtue goes no deeper than that of the scribes and Pharisees, you will never get into the kingdom of heaven.

'You have learnt how it was said to our ancestors: You must not kill; and if anyone does kill he must answer for it before the court. But I say this to you: anyone who is angry with his brother will answer for it before the court; if a man calls his brother, "Fool" he will answer for it before the Sanhedrin; and if a man calls him "Renegade" he will answer for it in hell fire. So then, if you are bringing your offering to the altar and there remember that your brother has something against you, leave your offering there before the altar, go and be reconciled with your brother first, and then come back and present your offering. Come to terms with your opponent in good time while you are still on the way to the court with him, or he may hand you over to the judge and the judge to the officer, and you will be thrown into prison. I tell you solemnly, you will not get out till you have paid the last penny.'

This is the Gospel of the Lord.

FRIDAY

FIRST READING

A reading from the first book of the Kings   19:9. 11-16
Stand on the mountain before the Lord God.

When Elijah reached Horeb, the mountain of God, he went into the cave and spent the night in it. Then he was told, 'Go out and stand on the mountan before the Lord.' Then the Lord himself went by. There came a mighty wind, so strong it tore the mountains and shattered the rocks before the Lord. But the Lord was not in the wind. After the wind came an earthquake. But the Lord was not in the eathquake. After the earthquake came a fire. But the Lord was not in the fire. And after the fire there came the sound of a gentle breeze. And when Elijah heard this, he covered his face with his cloak and went out and stood at the entrance of the cave. Then a voice came to him, which said, 'What are you doing here, Elijah?' He replied, 'I am filled with jealous zeal for the Lord of hosts, because the sons of Israel have deserted you, broken down your altars and put your prophets to the sword. I am the only one left and they want to kill me.'

'Go,' the Lord said 'go back by the same way to the wilderness of Damascus. You are to go and anoint Hazael as king of Aram. You are to anoint Jehu son of Nimshi as king of Israel, and to anoint Elisha son of Shaphat, of Abel Meholah, as prophet to succeed you.'

This is the word of the Lord.

Responsorial Psalm   Ps 26:7-9. 13-14. ℟ v.8
  ℟ **It is your face, O Lord, that I seek.**

1 O Lord, hear my voice when I call;
   have mercy and answer.
   Of you my heart has spoken:
   'Seek his face.' ℟

2 It is your face, O Lord, that I seek;
   hide not your face.
   Dismiss not your servant in anger;
   you have been my help.

   ℟ **It is your face, O Lord, that I seek.**

3 I am sure I shall see the Lord's goodness
   in the land of the living.
   Hope in him, hold firm and take heart.
   Hope in the Lord!   ℟

Gospel Acclamation   Jn 10:27
Alleluia, alleluia!
The sheep that belong to me listen to my voice,
says the Lord,
I know them and they follow me.
Alleluia!

or   Phil 2:15. 16

Alleluia, alleluia!
You will shine in the world like bright stars
because you are offering it in the word of life.
Alleluia!

GOSPEL

A reading from the holy Gospel according to Matthew   5:27-32
If a man looks at a woman lustfully, he has already committed adultery.

Jesus said to his disciples: 'You have learnt how it was said: You must not commit adultery. But I say this to you: if a man looks at a woman lustfully, he has already committed adultery with her in his heart. If your right eye should cause you to sin, tear it out and throw it away; for it will do you less harm to lose one part of you than to have your whole body thrown into hell. And if your right hand should cause you to sin, cut it off and throw it away; for it will do you less harm to lose one part of you than to have your whole body go to hell.

It has also been said: Anyone who divorces his wife must give her a writ of dismissal. But I say this to you: everyone who divorces his wife, except for the case of fornication, makes her an adulteress; and anyone who marries a divorced woman commits adultery.'

This is the Gospel of the Lord.

SATURDAY

FIRST READING

A reading from the first book of the Kings 19:19-21
Elisha rose and followed Elijah.

Leaving Mount Horeb, Elijah came on Elisha son of Shaphat as he was ploughing behind twelve yoke of oxen, he himself being with the twelfth. Elijah passed near to him and threw his cloak over him. Elisha left his oxen and ran after Elijah. 'Let me kiss my father and mother, then I will follow you' he said. Elijah answered, 'Go, go back; for have I done anything to you?' Elisha turned away, took the pair of oxen and slaughtered them. He used the plough for cooking the oxen, then gave to his men, who ate. He then rose, and followed Elijah and became his servant.

This is the word of the Lord.

Responsorial Psalm Ps 15:1-2. 5. 7-10. ℟ cf. v.5

℟ **You are my inheritance, O Lord.**

1. Preserve me, God, I take refuge in you.
   I say to the Lord: 'You are my God.'
   O Lord, it is you who are my portion and cup;
   it is you yourself who are my prize. ℟

2. I will bless the Lord who gives me counsel,
   who even at night directs my heart.
   I keep the Lord ever in my sight:
   since he is at my right hand, I shall stand firm. ℟

3. And so my heart rejoices, my soul is glad;
   even my body shall rest in safety.
   For you will not leave my soul among the dead,
   nor let your beloved know decay. ℟

Gospel Acclamation Ps 118:18
Alleluia, alleluia!
Open my eyes, O Lord, that I may consider
the wonders of your law.
Alleluia!

or Ps 118:36. 29

Alleluia, alleluia!
Bend my heart to your will, O Lord,

and teach me your law.
Alleluia!

GOSPEL

A reading from the holy Gospel according to Matthew   5:33-37
I say to you: do not swear at all.

Jesus said to his disciples: 'You have learnt how it was said to our ancestors: You must not break your oath, but must fulfil your oaths to the Lord. But I say this to you: do not swear at all, either by heaven, since that is God's throne; or by the earth, since that is his footstool; or by Jerusalem, since that is the city of the great king. Do not swear by your own head either, since you cannot turn a single hair white or black. All you need say is "Yes" if you mean yes, "No" if you mean no; anything more than this comes from the evil one.'

This is the Gospel of the Lord.

ELEVENTH WEEK IN ORDINARY TIME
Year II

MONDAY

FIRST READING

A reading from the first book of the Kings   21:1-16
Naboth has been stoned to death.

Naboth of Jezreel had a vineyard close by the palace of Ahab king of Samaria, and Ahab said to Naboth, 'Give me your vineyard to be my vegetable garden, since it adjoins my house; I will give you a better vineyard for it or, if you prefer, I will give you its worth in money.' But Naboth answered Ahab, 'The Lord forbid that I should give you the inheritance of my ancestors!'

Ahab went home gloomy and out of temper at the words of Naboth of Jezreel, 'I will not give you the inheritance of my fathers.' He lay down on his bed and turned his face away and refused to eat. His wife Jezebel came to him. 'Why are you so dispirited' she said 'that you will not eat?' He said, 'I have been speaking to Naboth of Jezreel; I said: Give me your vineyard either for money or, if you prefer, for another vineyard in exchange. But he said, "I will not give you my vineyard." ' Then his wife Jezebel said, 'You make a fine king of Israel, and no mistake! Get up and eat; cheer up, and you will feel better; I will get you the vineyard of Naboth of Jezreel myself.'

So she wrote letters in Ahab's name and sealed them with his seal, sending them to the elders and nobles who lived where Naboth lived. In the letters she wrote, 'Proclaim a fast, and put Naboth in the forefront of the people. Confront him with a couple of scoundrels who will accuse him like this, "You have cursed God and the king". Then take him outside and stone him to death.'

The men of Naboth's town, the elders and nobles who lived in his town, did what Jezebel ordered, what was written in the letters she had sent them. They proclaimed a fast and put Naboth in the forefront of the people. Then the two scoundrels came and stood in front of him and made their accusation, 'Naboth has cursed God and the king.' They led him outside the town and stoned him to death. They then sent word to Jezebel, 'Naboth has been stoned to death.' When Jezebel heard that Naboth had been stoned to death, she said to Ahab, 'Get up! Take possession of the vineyard which Naboth of Jezreel would not give you for money, for Naboth is no longer alive, he is dead.' When Ahab heard that Naboth was dead, he got up to go down to the vineyard of Naboth of Jezreel and take possession of it.

This is the word of the Lord.

Responsorial Psalm   Ps 5:2-3. 5-7. ℟ v.2

℟ **Give heed to my groaning, O Lord.**

1. To my words give ear, O Lord,
   give heed to my groaning.
   Attend to the sound of my cries,
   my King and my God.   ℟

2. You are no God who loves evil;
   no sinner is your guest.
   The boastful shall not stand their ground
   before your face.   ℟

3. You hate all who do evil:
   you destroy all who lie.
   The deceitful and bloodthirsty man
   the Lord detests.   ℟

Gospel Acclamation Jn 14:23

Alleluia, alleluia!
If anyone loves me he will keep my word,
and my Father will love him,
and we shall come to him.
Alleluia!

or Ps 118:105

Alleluia, alleluia!
Your word is a lamp for my steps
and a light for my path.
Alleluia!

GOSPEL

A reading from the holy Gospel according to Matthew 5:38-42
I say this to you: offer the wicked man no resistance.

Jesus said to his disciples: 'You have learnt how it was said: Eye for eye and tooth for tooth. But I say this to you: offer the wicked man no resistance. On the contrary, if anyone hits you on the right cheek, offer him the other as well; if a man takes you to law and would have your tunic, let him have your cloak as well. And if anyone orders you to go one mile, go two miles with him. Give to anyone who asks, and if anyone wants to borrow, do not turn away.'

This is the Gospel of the Lord.

TUESDAY

FIRST READING

A reading from the first book of the Kings 21:17-29
You led Israel into sin.

After the death of Naboth, the word of the Lord came to Elijah the Tishbite. 'Up! Go down to meet Ahab king of Israel, in Samaria. You will find him in Naboth's vineyard; he has gone down to take possession of it. You are to say this to him. "The Lord says this: You have committed murder; now you usurp as well. For this – and the Lord says this – in the place where the dogs licked the blood of Naboth, the dogs will lick your blood too." ' Ahab said to Elijah, 'So you have found me out, O my enemy!' Elijah answered, 'I have found you out. For your double dealing, and since you have done what is displeasing to the Lord, I will now bring disaster down on you; I will sweep away your descendants, and wipe out every male belonging to the family of Ahab, fettered or free in Israel. I will treat your House as I treated the House of Jeroboam son of Nebat and of Baasha son of Ahijah, for provoking my anger and leading Israel into sin. (Against Jezebel too the Lord spoke these words: The dogs will eat Jezebel in the Field of Jezreel.) Those of Ahab's family who die in the city, the dogs will eat; and those who die in the open country, the birds of the air will eat.'

And indeed there never was anyone like Ahab for double dealing and for doing what is displeasing to the Lord, urged on by Jezebel his wife. He behaved in the most abominable way, adhering to idols, just as the Amorites used to do whom the Lord had dispossessed for the sons of Israel.

When Ahab heard these words, he tore his garments and put sackcloth next his skin and fasted; he slept in the sackcloth; he walked with slow steps. Then the word of the Lord came to Elijah the Tishbite, 'Have you seen how Ahab has humbled himself before me? Since he has humbled himself before me, I will not bring the disaster in his days; I will bring the disaster down on his House in the days of his son.'

This is the word of the Lord.

Responsorial Psalm   Ps 50:3-6. 11. 16. ℟ cf. v.3
   ℟ **Have mercy on us, Lord, for we have sinned.**

1 Have mercy on me, God, in your kindness.
   In your compassion blot out my offence.
   O wash me more and more from my guilt
   and cleanse me from sin. ℟

2 My offences truly I know them;
   my sin is always before me.
   Against you, you alone, have I sinned;
   what is evil in your sight I have done. ℟

3 From my sins turn away your face
   and blot out all my guilt.
   O rescue me, God, my helper,
   and my tongue shall ring out your goodness. ℟

Gospel Acclamation 2 Cor 5:19

Alleluia, alleluia!
God in Christ was reconciling the world to himself,
and he has entrusted to us the news that they are reconciled.
Alleluia!

or Jn 13:34

Alleluia, alleluia!
I give you a new commandment:
love one another just as I have loved you,
says the Lord.
Alleluia!

GOSPEL

A reading from the holy Gospel according to Matthew 5:43-48

Love your enemies.

Jesus said to his disciples: 'You have learnt how it was said: You must love your neighbour and hate your enemy. But I say this to you: love your enemies and pray for those who persecute you; in this way you will be sons of your Father in heaven, for he causes his sun to rise on bad men as well as good, and his rain to fall on honest and dishonest men alike. For if you love those who love you, what right have you to claim any credit? Even the tax collectors do as much, do they not? And if you save your greetings for your brothers, are you doing anything exceptional? Even the pagans do as much, do they not? You must therefore be perfect just as your heavenly Father is perfect.'

This is the Gospel of the Lord.

WEDNESDAY

FIRST READING

A reading from the second book of the Kings 2:1. 6-14

A chariot of fire appeared and Elijah went up to heaven.

This is what happened when the Lord took Elijah up to heaven in the whirlwind: Elijah and Elisha set out from Gilgal. Elijah said, 'Elisha, please stay here, the Lord is only sending me to the Jordan.' But he replied, 'As the Lord lives and as you yourself live, I will not leave you!' And they went on together.

Eleventh Week in Ordinary Time, Year II: Wednesday 989

Fifty of the brotherhood of prophets followed them, halting some distance away as the two of them stood beside the Jordan. Elijah took his cloak, rolled it up and struck the water; and the water divided to left and right, and the two of them crossed over dry-shod. When they had crossed, Elijah said to Elisha, 'Make your request. What can I do for you before I am taken from you?' Elisha answered, 'Let me inherit a double share of your spirit.' 'Your request is a difficult one' Elijah said. 'If you see me while I am being taken from you, it shall be as you ask; if not, it will not be so.' Now as they walked on, talking as they went, a chariot of fire appeared and horses of fire, coming between the two of them; and Elijah went up to heaven in the whirlwind. Elisha saw it, and shouted, 'My father! My father! Chariot of Israel and its chargers!' Then he lost sight of him, and taking hold of his clothes he tore them in half. He picked up the cloak of Elijah which had fallen, and went back and stood on the bank of the Jordan.

He took the cloak of Elijah and struck the water. 'Where is the Lord, the God of Elijah?' he cried. He struck the water, and it divided to right and left, and Elisha crossed over.

This is the word of the Lord.

Responsorial Psalm
Ps 30:20. 21. 24. ℟ v.25

℟ **Let your heart take courage,
all who hope in the Lord.**

1 How great is the goodness, Lord,
that you keep for those who fear you,
that you show to those who trust you
in the sight of men. ℟

2 You hide them in the shelter of your presence
from the plotting of men:
you keep them safe within your tent
from disputing tongues. ℟

3 Love the Lord, all you saints.
He guards his faithful
but the Lord will repay to the full
those who act with pride. ℟

Gospel Acclamation
cf. Col 3:16. 17

Alleluia, alleluia!
Let the message of Christ, in all its richness,
find a home with you;

through him give thanks to God the Father.
Alleluia!

or   Jn 14:23

Alleluia, alleluia!
If anyone loves me he will keep my word,
and my Father will love him,
and we shall come to him.
Alleluia!

GOSPEL

A reading from the holy Gospel according to Matthew   6:1-6. 16-18

Your Father who sees all that is done in secret will reward you.

Jesus said to his disciples: 'Be careful not to parade your good deeds before men to attract their notice; by doing this you will lose all reward from your Father in heaven. So when you give alms, do not have it trumpeted before you ; this is what the hypocrites do in the synagogues and in the streets to win men's admiration. I tell you solemnly, they have had their reward. But when you give alms, your left hand must not know what your right is doing; your almsgiving must be secret, and your Father who sees all that is done in secret will reward you.

'And when you pray, do not imitate the hypocrites: they love to say their prayers standing up in the synagogues and at the street corners for people to see them. I tell you solemnly, they have had their reward. But when you pray, go to your private room and, when you have shut your door, pray to your Father who is in that secret place, and your Father who sees all that is done in secret will reward you.

'When you fast do not put on a gloomy look as the hypocrites do: they pull long faces to let men know they are fasting. I tell you solemnly, they have had their reward. But when you fast, put oil on your head and wash your face, so that no one will know you are fasting except your Father who sees all that is done in secret; and your Father who sees all that is done in secret will reward you.'

This is the Gospel of the Lord.

THURSDAY

FIRST READING

A reading from the book of Ecclesiasticus 48:1-14

Elijah was shrouded in the whirlwind, and Elisha was filled with his spirit.

The prophet Elijah arose like a fire,
his word flaring like a torch.
It was he who brought famine on them,
and who decimated them in his zeal.
By the word of the Lord, he shut up the heavens,
he also, three times, brought down fire.
How glorious you were in your miracles, Elijah!
Has anyone reason to boast as you have? –
rousing a corpse from death,
from Sheol by the word of the Most High;
dragging kings down to destruction,
and high dignitaries from their beds;
hearing reproof on Sinai,
and decrees of punishment on Horeb;
anointing kings as avengers,
and prophets to succeed you;
taken up in the whirlwind of fire,
in a chariot with fiery horses;
designated in the prophecies of doom
to allay God's wrath before the fury breaks,
to turn the hearts of fathers towards their children,
and to restore the tribes of Jacob.
Happy shall they be who see you,
and those who have fallen asleep in love;
for we too will have life.

Elijah was shrouded in the whirlwind,
and Elisha was filled with his spirit;
throughout his life no ruler could shake him,
and no one could subdue him.
No task was too hard for him,
and even in death his body prophesied.
In his lifetime he performed wonders,
and in death his works were marvellous.

This is the word of the Lord.

Responsorial Psalm   Ps 96:1-7. ℟ v.12

  ℟ **Rejoice, you just, in the Lord.**

1. The Lord is king, let earth rejoice,
   the many coastlands be glad.
   Cloud and darkness are his raiment;
   his throne, justice and right. ℟

2. A fire prepares his path;
   it burns up his foes on every side.
   His lightnings light up the world,
   the earth trembles at the sight. ℟

3. The mountains melt like wax
   before the Lord of all the earth.
   The skies proclaim his justice;
   all peoples see his glory. ℟

4. Let those who serve idols be ashamed,
   those who boast of their worthless gods.
   All you spirits, worship him. ℟

Gospel Acclamation   1 Sam 3:9; Jn 6:68

Alleluia, alleluia!
Speak, Lord, your servant is listening:
you have the message of eternal life.
Alleluia!

or   Rom 8:15

Alleluia, alleluia!
The spirit you received is the spirit of sons,
and it makes us cry out, 'Abba, Father!'
Alleluia!

GOSPEL

A reading from the holy Gospel according to Matthew   6:7-15
You should pray like this.

Jesus said to his disciples: 'In your prayers do not babble as the pagans do, for they think that by using many words they will make themselves heard. Do not be like them; your Father knows what you need before you ask him. So you should pray like this:

    Our Father in heaven,
    may your name be held holy,
    your kingdom come,

your will be done,
on earth as in heaven.
Give us today our daily bread.
And forgive us our debts,
as we have forgiven those who are in debt to us.
And do not put us to the test,
but save us from the evil one.

'Yes, if you forgive others their failings, your heavenly Father will forgive you yours; but if you do not forgive others, your Father will not forgive your failings either.'

This is the Gospel of the Lord.

FRIDAY

FIRST READING

A reading from the second book of the Kings   11:1-4. 9-18. 20

They anointed Jehoash and shouted, 'Long live the king!'

When Althaliah the mother of Ahaziah learned that her son was dead, she promptly did away with all those of royal stock. But Jehosheba, daughter of King Jehoram and sister of Ahaziah, secretly took away Jehoash, her brother's son, from among the sons of the king who were being murdered, and put him with his nurse in the sleeping quarters; in this way she hid him from Athaliah, and he was not put to death. He stayed with her for six years, hidden in the Temple of the Lord, while Athaliah governed the country.

In the seventh year, Jehoiada sent for the commanders of hundreds of the Carians and of the guards, and had them brought to him in the Temple of the Lord. He made a pact with them, and, putting them under oath, showed them the king's son.

The commanders of hundreds did everything as Jehoiada the priest had ordered. They brought their men, those coming off duty on the sabbath together with those mounting guard on the sabbath, and came to Jehoiada the priest. The priests equipped the commanders of hundreds with King David's spears and shields which were in the Temple of the Lord. The guards formed up, each man with his weapon in his hand, from the south corner to the north corner of the Temple, surrounding the altar and the Temple. Then Jehoiada brought out the king's son, put the crown and armlets on him, and he anointed him king. They clapped their hands and shouted, 'Long live the king!'

Athaliah, on hearing the shouts of the people, made for the Temple of the Lord where the people were. When she saw the king standing there beside the pillar, as the custom was, with the captains and trumpeters at the king's side, and all the country people rejoicing and sounding trumpets, Athaliah tore her garments and shouted, 'Treason, treason!' Then Jehoiada the priest gave the order to the army officers: 'Take her ouside the precincts and put to death anyone who follows her.' 'For,' the priest had reasoned, 'she must not be put to death in the Temple of the Lord.' They seized her, and when she had reached the palace through the Entry of the Horses, she was put to death there.

Jehoiada made a covenant between the Lord and king and people, by which the latter undertook to be the people of the Lord; and also between king and people. All the country people then went to the temple of Baal and demolished it; they smashed his altars and his images and killed Mattan, priest of Baal, in front of the altars.

The priest posted entries to guard the Temple of the Lord. All the country people were delighted, and the city made no move. And they put Athaliah to death in the royal palace.

This is the word of the Lord.

Responsorial Psalm Ps 131:11-14. 17-18. ℟ v.13

℟ **The Lord has chosen Zion;**
he has desired it for his dwelling.

1 The Lord swore an oath to David;
he will not go back on his word:
'A son, the fruit of your body,
will I set upon your throne.   ℟

2 'If they keep my covenant in truth
and my laws that I have taught them,
their sons also shall rule
on your throne from age to age.'   ℟

3 For the Lord has chosen Zion;
he has desired it for his dwelling:
'This is my resting-place for ever,
here have I chosen to live.'   ℟

4 There the stock of David will flower:
'I will prepare a lamp for my anointed.
I will cover his enemies with shame
but on him my crown shall shine.' ℟

Gospel Acclamation Jn 8:12
   Alleluia, alleluia!
   I am the light of the world, says the Lord,
   anyone who follows me
   will have the light of life.
   Alleluia!

or Mt 5:3

   Alleluia, alleluia!
   How happy are the poor in spirit;
   theirs is the kingdom of heaven.
   Alleluia!

GOSPEL

A reading from the holy Gospel according to Matthew 6:19-23
Where your treasure is, there will your heart be also.

Jesus said to his disciples: 'Do not store up treasures for yourselves on earth, where moths and woodworms destroy them and thieves can break in and steal. But store up treasures for yourselves in heaven, where neither moth or woodworms destroy them and thieves cannot break in and steal. For where your treasure is, there will your heart be also.

'The lamp of the body is the eye. It follows that if your eye is sound, your whole body will be filled with light. But if your eye is diseased, your whole body will be all darkness. If then, the light inside you is darkness, what darkness that will be!'

This is the Gospel of the Lord.

SATURDAY

FIRST READING

A reading from the second book of Chronicles 24:17-25
You murdered Zechariah between the sanctuary and the altar.

After the death of Jehoiada, the officials of Judah came to pay court to the king, and the king now turned to them for advice.

The Judaeans abandoned the Temple of the Lord, the God of their ancestors, for the worship of sacred poles and idols. Because of their guilt, God's anger fell on Judah and Jerusalem. He sent them prophets to bring them back to the Lord, but when these gave their message, they would not listen. The spirit of God took possession of Zechariah son of Jehoiada the priest. He stood up before the people and said, 'God says this, "Why do you transgress the commandments of the Lord to no good purpose? You have deserted the Lord, now he deserts you." ' They then plotted against him and by order of the king stoned him in the court of the Temple of the Lord. King Joash, forgetful of the kindness that Jehoiada, the father of Zechariah, had shown him, killed Jehoiada's son who cried out as he died, 'The Lord sees and he will avenge!'

When a year had gone by, the Aramaean army made war on Joash. They reached Judah and Jerusalem, and executed all the officials among the people, sending back to the king at Damascus all that they had plundered from them. Though the Aramaean army had by no means come in force, the Lord delivered into its power an army of great size for having deserted him, the God of their ancestors.

The Aramaeans treated Joash as he had deserved, and when they retired they left him a very sick man; and his officers, plotting against him to avenge the death of the son of Jehoiada the priest, murdered him in his bed. So he died, and they buried him in the Citadel of David, though not in the tombs of the kings.

This is the word of the Lord.

Responsorial Psalm Ps 88:4-5. 29-34. ℟ v.29
  ℟ **I will keep my love for him always.**

1 'I have made a covenant with my chosen one;
  I have sworn to David my servant:
  I will establish your dynasty for ever
  and set up your throne through all ages. ℟

2 'I will keep my love for him always;
  for him my covenant shall endure.
  I will establish his dynasty for ever,
  make his throne as lasting as the heavens. ℟

3 'If his sons forsake my law
  and refuse to walk as I decree
  and if ever they violate my statutes,

Eleventh Week in Ordinary Time, Year II: Saturday

    refusing to keep my commands;
    then I will punish their offences with the rod,
    then I will scourge them on account of their guilt. ℞

4 'But I will never take back my love:
    my truth will never fail.' ℞

Gospel Acclamation   Mt 4:4
    Alleluia, alleluia!
    Man does not live on bread alone,
    but on every word that comes from the mouth of God.
    Alleluia!
or   2 Cor 8:9
    Alleluia, alleluia!
    Jesus Christ was rich,
    but he became poor for your sake,
    to make you rich out of his poverty.
    Alleluia!

GOSPEL

A reading from the holy Gospel according to Matthew   6:24-34
Do not worry about tomorrow.

Jesus said to his disciples: 'No one can be the slave of two masters: he will either hate the first and love the second, or treat the first with respect and the second with scorn. You cannot be the slave both of God and money.
    'That is why I am telling you not to worry about your life and what you are to eat, nor about your body and how you are to clothe it. Surely life means more than food, and the body more than clothing! Look at the birds in the sky. They do not sow or reap or gather into barns; yet your heavenly Father feeds them. Are you not worth much more than they are? Can any of you, for all his worrying, add one single cubit to his span of life? And why worry about clothing? Think of the flowers growing in the fields: they never have to work or spin; yet I assure you that not even Solomon in all his regalia was robed like one of these. Now if that is how God clothes the grass in the field which is there today and thrown into the furnace tomorrow, will he not much more look after you, you men of little faith? So do not worry; do not say, "What are we to eat? What are we to drink? How are we to be clothed?" It is the pagans who set their hearts on all these things. Your heavenly Father knows you need them all. Set your hearts on his kingdom first, and on his righteousness, and all these

other things will be given you as well. So do not worry about tomorrow: tomorrow will take care of itself. Each day has enough trouble of its own.'

This is the Gospel of the Lord.

TWELFTH WEEK IN ORDINARY TIME
Year II

MONDAY

FIRST READING

A reading from the second book of the Kings   17:5-8. 13-15. 18
The Lord thrust Israel away from him and there was none left but the tribe of Judah.

The king of Assyria invaded the whole country and, coming to Samaria, laid seige to it for three years. In the ninth year of Hoshea, the king of Assyria captured Samaria and deported the Israelites to Assyria. He settled them in Halah on the Habor, a river of Gozan, and in the cities of the Medes.

This happened because the Israelites had sinned against the Lord their God who had brought them out of the land of Egypt, out of the grip of Pharaoh, king of Egypt. They worshipped other gods, they followed the practices of the nations that the Lord had dispossessed for them.

And yet through all the prophets and all the seers the Lord had given Israel and Judah this warning, 'Turn from your wicked ways and keep my commandments and my law in accordance with the entire Law I laid down for your fathers and delivered to them through my servants the prophets.' But they would not listen, they were more stubborn than their ancestors had been who had no faith in the Lord their God. They despised his laws and the covenant he had made with their ancestors, and the warnings he had given them. For this, the Lord was enraged with Israel and thrust them away from him. There was none left but the tribe of Judah only.

This is the word of the Lord.

Twelfth Week in Ordinary Time, Year II: Monday

Responsorial Psalm   Ps 59:3-5. 12-13. ℟ v.7

℟ **Hear us, O Lord, and help us.**

1. O God you have rejected us and broken us.
   You have been angry; come back to us. ℟

2. You have made the earth quake, torn it open.
   Repair what is shattered for it sways.
   You have inflicted hardships on your people
   and made us drink a wine that dazed us. ℟

3. Will you utterly reject us, O God,
   and no longer march with our armies?
   Give us help against the foe:
   for the help of man is vain. ℟

Gospel Acclamation   cf. Jn 17:17

Alleluia, alleluia!
Your word is truth, O Lord,
consecrate us in the truth.
Alleluia!

or   Heb 4:12

Alleluia, alleluia!
The word of God is something alive and active;
it can judge secret emotions and thoughts.
Alleluia!

GOSPEL

A reading from the holy Gospel according to Matthew   7:1-5

Take the plank out of your own eye first.

Jesus said to his disciples: 'Do not judge, and you will not be judged; because the judgements you give are the judgements you will get, and the amount you measure out is the amount you will be given. Why do you observe the splinter in your brother's eye and never notice the plank in your own? How dare you say to your brother, "Let me take the splinter out of your eye", when all the time there is a plank in your own? Hypocrite! Take the plank out of your own eye first, and then you will see clearly enough to take the splinter out of your brother's eye.'

This is the Gospel of the Lord.

TUESDAY

FIRST READING

A reading from the second book of the Kings   19:9-11. 14-21. 31-36

I will protect this city and save it for my own sake and for the sake of David.

Sennacherib, King of the Assyrians, sent messengers to Hezekiah saying, 'Tell this to Hezekiah king of Judah, "Do not let your God on whom you are relying deceive you, when he says: Jerusalem shall not fall into the power of the king of Assyria. You have learnt by now what the kings of Assyria have done to every country, putting them all under the ban. Are you likely to be spared?" '

Hezekiah took the letter from the hands of the messenger and read it; he then went up to the Temple of the Lord and spread it out before the Lord. Hezekiah said this prayer in the presence of the Lord, 'Lord of hosts, God of Israel, enthroned on the cherubs, you alone are God of all the kingdoms of the earth, you have made heaven and earth.

'Give ear, Lord, and listen.
Open your eyes, Lord, and see.
Hear the words of Sennacherib
who has sent to insult the living God.

'It is true, Lord, that the kings of Assyria have exterminated all the nations, they have thrown their gods on the fire, for these were not gods but the work of men's hands, wood and stone, and hence they have destroyed them. But now, Lord our God, save us from his hand, I pray you, and let all the kingdoms of the earth know that you alone are God, Lord.'

Then Isaiah son of Amoz sent to Hezekiah. 'The Lord, the God of Israel' he said 'says this, "I have heard the prayer you have addressed to me about Sennacherib king of Assyria." Here is the oracle that the Lord has pronounced against him:

' "She despises you, she scorns you,
the virgin daughter of Zion:
she tosses her head behind you,
the daughter of Jerusalem.
A remnant shall go out from Jerusalem,
and survivors from Mount Zion.
The jealous love of the Lord of Hosts shall accomplish this."

Twelfth Week in Ordinary Time, Year II: Tuesday

'This, then, is what the Lord says about the king of Assyria:

' "He will not enter this city,
he will let fly no arrow against it,
confront it with no shield,
throw up no earthwork against it.
By the road that he came on he will return;
he shall not enter this city. It is the Lord who speaks.
I will protect this city and save it
for my own sake and for the sake of my servant David." '

That same night the angel of the Lord went out and struck down a hundred and eighty-five thousand men in the Assyrian camp. Sennacherib struck camp and left; he returned home and stayed in Nineveh.

This is the word of the Lord.

Responsorial Psalm   Ps 47:2-4. 10-11. ℟ cf. v.9
   ℟ **God upholds his city for ever.**

1 The Lord is great and worthy to be praised
in the city of our God.
His holy mountain rises in beauty,
the joy of all the earth.   ℟

2 Mount Zion, true pole of the earth,
the Great King's city!
God, in the midst of its citadels,
has shown himself its stronghold.   ℟

3 O God, we ponder your love
within your temple.
Your praise, O God, like your name
reaches to the ends of the earth.   ℟

Gospel Acclamation   cf. Mt 11:25
Alleluia, alleluia!
Blessed are you, Father,
Lord of heaven and earth,
for revealing the mysteries of the kingdom
to mere children.
Alleluia!

or   Jn 8:12
Alleluia, alleluia!
I am the light of the world, says the Lord,

anyone who follows me
will have the light of life.
Alleluia!

GOSPEL

A reading from the holy Gospel according to Matthew   7:6. 12-14
Always treat others as you would like them to treat you.

Jesus said to his disciples: 'Do not give dogs what is holy; and do not throw your pearls in front of pigs, or they may trample them and then turn on you and tear you to pieces.

'So always treat others as you would like them to treat you; that is the meaning of the Law and the Prophets.

'Enter by the narrow gate, since the road that leads to perdition is wide and spacious, and many take it; but it is a narrow gate and a hard road that leads to life, and only a few find it.'

This is the Gospel of the Lord.

WEDNESDAY

FIRST READING

A reading from the second book of the Kings   22:8-13; 23:1-3
In the people's hearing the king read out everything that was said in the book of the covenant found in the Temple of the Lord, and in the presence of the Lord he made a covenant.

The high priest Hilkiah said to Shaphan the secretary, 'I have found the Book of the Law in the Temple of the Lord.' And Hilkiah gave the book to Shaphan, who read it. Shaphan the secretary went to King Josiah and reported to him as follows. 'Your servants' he said 'have melted down the silver which was in the Temple and have handed it over to the masters of works attached to the Temple of the Lord.' Then Shaphan the secretary informed the king, 'Hilkiah the priest has given me a book'; and Shaphan read it aloud in the king's presence.

On hearing the contents of the Book of the Law, the king tore his garments, and gave the following order to Hilkiah the priest, Ahikam son of Shaphan, Achbor son of Micaiah, Shaphan the secretary and Asaiah the king's minister: 'Go and consult the Lord, on behalf of me and the people, about the contents of this book that has been found. Great indeed must be the anger of the

Lord blazing out against us because our ancestors did not obey what this book says by practising everything written in it.'

The king then had all the elders of Judah and of Jerusalem summoned to him, and the king went up to the Temple of the Lord with all the men of Judah and all the inhabitants of Jerusalem, priests, prophets and all the people, of high or low degree. In their hearing he read out everything that was said in the book of the covenant found in the Temple of the Lord. The king stood beside the pillar, and in the presence of the Lord he made a covenant to follow the Lord and keep his commandments and decrees and laws with all his heart and soul, in order to enforce the terms of the covenant as written in that book. All the people gave their allegiance to the covenant.

This is the word of the Lord.

Responsorial Psalm   Ps 118:33-37. 40. ℟ v.33

℟ **Lord, teach me your statutes.**

1 Teach me the demands of your statutes
and I will keep them to the end.
Train me to observe your law,
to keep it with my heart. ℟

2 Guide me in the path of your commands;
for there is my delight.
Bend my heart to your will
and not to love of gain. ℟

3 Keep my eyes from what is false:
by your word, give me life.
See, I long for your precepts:
then in your justice, give me life. ℟

Gospel Acclamation   Ps 118:88
Alleluia, alleluia!
Because of your love give me life,
and I will do your will.
Alleluia!

or   Jn 15:4. 5

Alleluia, alleluia!
Make your home in me, as I make mine in you,
says the Lord;
whoever remains in me bears fruit in plenty.
Alleluia!

GOSPEL

A reading from the holy Gospel according to Matthew 7:15-20
You will be able to tell them by their fruits.

Jesus said to his disciples: 'Beware of false prophets who come to you disguised as sheep but underneath are ravenous wolves. You will be able to tell them by their fruits. Can people pick grapes from thorns, or figs from thistles? In the same way, a sound tree produces good fruit but a rotten tree bad fruit. A sound tree cannot bear bad fruit, nor a rotten tree bear good fruit. Any tree that does not produce good fruit is cut down and thrown on the fire. I repeat, you will be able to tell them by their fruits.'

This is the Gospel of the Lord.

THURSDAY

FIRST READING

A reading from the second book of the Kings 24:8-17
The king of Babylon deported Jehoiachin and all the nobility of the country to Babylon.

Jehoiachin was eighteen years old when he came to the throne, and he reigned for three months in Jerusalem. His mother's name was Nehushta, daughter of Elnathan, from Jerusalem. He did what is displeasing to the Lord, just as his father had done.

At that time the troops of Nebuchadnezzar king of Babylon marched on Jerusalem, and the city was besieged. Nebuchadnezzar king of Babylon himself came to attack the city while his troops were besieging it. Then Jehoiachin king of Judah surrendered to the king of Babylon, he, his mother, his officers, his nobles and his eunuchs, and the king of Babylon took them prisoner. This was in the eighth year of King Nebuchadnezzar.

The latter carried off all the treasures of the Temple of the Lord and the treasures of the royal palace, and broke up all the golden furnishings that Solomon king of Israel had made for the sanctuary of the Lord, as the Lord had foretold. He carried off all Jerusalem into exile, all the nobles and all the notables, ten thousand of these were exiled, with all the blacksmiths and metalworkers; only the poorest people in the country were left behind. He deported Jehoiachin to Babylon, as also the king's mother, his eunuchs and the nobility of the country; he made them all leave Jerusalem for exile in Babylon. All the men of distinction, seven thousand of them, the blacksmiths and metal-workers, one thousand of them, all of them men capable of bearing arms, were led into exile in Babylon by the king of Babylon.

The king of Babylon made Mattaniah, Jehoiachin's uncle, king in succession to him, and changed his name to Zedekiah.

This is the word of the Lord.

Responsorial Psalm   Ps 78:1-5. 8-9. ℟ v.9

℟ **Rescue us, O Lord,**
for the glory of your name.

1. O God, the nations have invaded your land,
they have profaned your holy temple.
they have made Jerusalem a heap of ruins.
They have handed over the bodies of your servants
as food to feed the birds of heaven
and the flesh of your faithful to the beasts of the earth. ℟

2. They have poured out blood like water in Jerusalem,
leaving no one to bury the dead.
We have become the taunt of our neighbours,
the mockery and scorn of those who surround us.
How long, O Lord? Will you be angry for ever,
how long will your anger burn like fire? ℟

3. Do not hold the guilt of our fathers against us.
Let your compassion hasten to meet us
for we are in the depths of distress. ℟

4. O God our saviour, come to our help,
come for the sake of the glory of your name.
O Lord our God, forgive us our sins;
rescue us for the sake of your name. ℟

Gospel Acclamation   Heb 4:12

Alleluia, alleluia!
The word of God is something alive and active;
it can judge secret emotions and thoughts.
Alleluia!

or   Jn 14:23

Alleluia, alleluia,
If anyone loves me he will keep my word,
and my Father will love him,
and we shall come to him.
Alleluia!

GOSPEL

A reading from the holy Gospel according to Matthew 7:21-29
The house built on rock and the house built on sand.

Jesus said to his disciples: 'It is not those who say to me, "Lord, Lord," who will enter the kingdom of heaven, but the person who does the will of my Father in heaven. When the day comes many will say to me, "Lord, Lord, did we not prophesy in your name, cast out demons in your name, work many miracles in your name?" Then I shall tell them to their faces: I have never known you; away from me, you evil men!

'Therefore, everyone who listens to these words of mine and acts on them will be like a sensible man who built his house on rock. Rain came down, floods rose, gales blew and hurled themselves against that house, and it did not fall: it was founded on rock. But everyone who listens to these words of mine and does not act on them will be like a stupid man who built his house on sand. Rain came down, floods rose, gales blew and struck that house, and it fell; and what a fall it had!'

Jesus had now finished what he wanted to say, and his teaching made a deep impression on the people because he taught them with authority, and not like their own scribes.

This is the Gospel of the Lord.

FRIDAY

FIRST READING

A reading from the second book of the Kings 25:1-12
Judah was deported from its land.

In the ninth year of Zedekiah's reign, in the tenth month, on the tenth day of the month, Nebuchadnezzar king of Bablyon came with his whole army to attack Jerusalem; he pitched camp in front of the city and threw up earthworks round it. The city lay under siege till the eleventh year of King Zedekiah. In the fourth month, on the ninth day of the month, when famine was raging in the city and there was no food for the populace, a breach was made in the city wall. At once, the king made his escape under cover of dark, with all the fighting men, by way of the gate between the two walls, which is near the king's garden – the Chaldaeans had surrounded the city – and made his way towards the Arabah. The

Chaldaean troops pursued the king and caught up with him in the plains of Jericho, where all his troops deserted. The Chaldaeans captured the king and took him to the king of Babylon at Riblah, who passed sentence on him. He had the sons of Zedekiah slaughtered before his eyes, then put out Zedekiah's eyes and, loading him with chains, carried him off to Babylon.

In the fifth month, on the seventh day of the month – it was in the nineteenth year of Nebuchadnezzar king of Babylon – Nebuzaradan, commander of the guard, an officer of the king of Babylon, entered Jerusalem. He burned down the Temple of the Lord, the royal palace and all the houses in Jerusalem. The Chaldaean troops who accompanied the commander of the guard demolished the walls surrounding Jerusalem. Nebuzaradan, commander of the guard, deported the remainder of the population left behind in the city, the deserters who had gone over to the king of Babylon, and the rest of the common people. The commander of the guard left some of the humbler country people as vineyard workers and ploughmen.

This is the word of the Lord.

Responsional Psalm Ps 136:1-6. ℟ v.6

℟ **O let my tongue
cleave to my mouth
if I remember you not.**

1 By the rivers of Babylon
there we sat and wept,
remembering Zion;
on the poplars that grew there
we hung up our harps. ℟

2 For it was there that they asked us,
our captors, for songs,
our oppressors, for joy.
'Sing to us,' they said,
'one of Zion's songs.' ℟

3 O how could we sing
the song of the Lord
on alien soil?
If I forget you, Jerusalem,
let my right hand wither! ℟

4 O let my tongue
cleave to my mouth

(continued)

if I remember you not,
if I prize not Jerusalem
above all my joys!

℟ **O let my tongue
cleave to my mouth
if I remember you not.**

Gospel Acclamation
Ps 144:13

Alleluia, alleluia!
The Lord is faithful in all his words
and loving in all his deeds.
Alleluia!

or
Mt 8:17

Alleluia, alleluia!
He took our sicknesses away,
and carried our diseases for us.
Alleluia!

GOSPEL

A reading from the holy Gospel according to Matthew 8:1-4
If you want to, you can cure me.

After Jesus had come down from the mountain large crowds followed him. A leper now came up and bowed low in front of him, 'Sir,' he said 'if you want to, you can cure me.' Jesus stretched out his hand, touched him and said, 'Of course I want to! Be cured!' And his leprosy was cured at once. Then Jesus said to him, 'Mind you do not tell anyone, but go and show yourself to the priest and make the offering prescribed by Moses, as evidence for them.'

This is the Gospel of the Lord.

SATURDAY

FIRST READING

A reading from the book of Lamentations 2:2. 10-14. 18-19
Cry aloud to the Lord, daughter of Zion.

The Lord has pitilessly destroyed
all the homes of Jacob;
in his displeasure he has shattered

the strongholds of the daughter of Judah;
he has thrown to the ground, he has left accursed
the kingdom and its rulers.

Mutely they sit on the ground,
the elders of the daughter of Zion;
they have put dust on their heads,
and wrapped themselves in sackcloth.
The virgins of Jerusalem hang their heads
down to the ground.

My eyes wasted away with weeping,
my entrails shuddered,
my liver spilled on the ground
at the ruin of the daughters of my people,
as children, mere infants, fainted
in the squares of the Citadel.

They kept saying to their mothers,
'Where is the bread?'
as they fainted like wounded men
in the squares of the City,
as they poured out their souls
on their mother's breasts.

How can I describe you, to what compare you,
daughter of Jerusalem?
Who can rescue and comfort you,
virgin daughter of Zion?
For huge as the sea is your affliction;
who can possibly cure you?

The visions your prophets had on your behalf
were delusive, tinsel things,
they never pointed out your sin,
to ward off your exile.
The visions they proffered you were false,
fallacious, misleading.

Cry aloud, then, to the Lord,
groan, daughter of Zion;
let your tears flow like a torrent,
day and night;
give yourself no relief,
grant your eyes no rest.

Up, cry out in the night-time,
in the early hours of darkness;
pour your heart out like water
before the Lord.
Stretch out your hands to him
for the lives of your children
who faint with hunger at the entrance to every street.

    This is the word of the Lord.

Responsorial Psalm   Ps 73:1-7. 20-21. ℟ v.19

  ℟ **Do not forget your poor servants for ever.**

1. Why, O God, have you cast us off for ever?
Why blaze with anger against the sheep of your pasture?
Remember your people whom you chose long ago,
the tribe you redeemed to be your own possession,
the mountain of Zion where you made your dwelling. ℟

2. Turn your steps to these places that are utterly ruined!
The enemy has laid waste the whole of the sanctuary.
Your foes have made uproar in your house of prayer:
they have set up their emblems, their foreign emblems,
high above the entrance to the sanctuary. ℟

3. Their axes have battered the wood of its doors.
They have struck together with hatchet and pickaxe.
O God, they have set your sanctuary on fire:
they have razed and profaned the place where you dwell. ℟

4. Remember your covenant; every cave in the land
is a place where violence makes its home.
Do not let the oppressed return disappointed:
let the poor and the needy bless your name. ℟

Gospel Acclamation   cf. 2 Tim 1:10
Alleluia, alleluia!
Our Saviour Christ Jesus abolished death,
and he has proclaimed life through the Good News.
Alleluia!

or   Mt 8:17

Alleluia, alleluia!
He took our sicknesses away,
and carried our diseases for us.
Alleluia!

Twelfth Week in Ordinary Time, Year II: Saturday

GOSPEL

A reading from the holy Gospel according to Matthew 8:5-17

Many will come from east and west to take their places with Abraham and Isaac and Jacob.

When Jesus went into Capernaum, a centurion came up and pleaded with him. 'Sir,' he said, 'my servant is lying at home paralysed, and in great pain.' 'I will come myself and cure him,' said Jesus. The centurion replied, 'Sir, I am not worthy to have you under my roof; just give the word and my servant will be cured. For I am under authority myself, and have soldiers under me; and I say to one man: Go, and he goes; to another: Come here, and he comes; to my servant: Do this, and he does it.' When Jesus heard this he was astonished and said to those following him, 'I tell you solemnly, nowhere in Israel have I found faith like this. And I tell you that many will come from east and west to take their places with Abraham and Isaac and Jacob at the feast in the kingdom of heaven; but the subjects of the kingdom will be turned out into the dark, where there will be weeping and grinding of teeth.' And to the centurion Jesus said, 'Go back, then; you have believed, so let this be done for you.' And the servant was cured at that moment.

And going into Peter's house Jesus found Peter's mother-in-law in bed with fever. He touched her hand and the fever left her, and she got up and began to wait on him.

That evening they brought him many who were possessed by devils. He cast out the spirits with a word and cured all who were sick. This was to fulfill the prophecy of Isaiah:

He took our sicknesses away and carried our diseases for us.

This is the Gospel of the Lord.

THIRTEENTH WEEK IN ORDINARY TIME
Year II

MONDAY

FIRST READING

A reading from the prophet Amos   2:6-10. 13-16
They trample on the heads of ordinary people.

The Lord says this:

> For the three crimes, the four crimes, of Israel
> I have made my decree and will not relent:
> because they have sold the virtuous man for silver
> and the poor man for a pair of sandals,
> because they trample on the heads of ordinary people
> and push the poor out of their path,
> because father and son have both resorted to the same girl,
> profaning my holy name,
> because they stretch themselves out by the side of every altar
> on clothes acquired as pledges,
> and drink the wine of the people they have fined
> in the house of their god . . .
> Yet it was I who overthrew the Amorites when they attacked,
> men tall as cedars and strong as oaks,
> I who destroyed them,
> both fruit above ground
> and root below.
> It was I who brought you out of the land of Egypt
> and for forty years led you through the wilderness
> to take possession of the Amorite's country.
> See then how I am going to crush you into the ground
> as the threshing-sledge crushes when clogged by straw;
> flight will not save even the swift,
> the strong man will find his strength useless,
> the mighty man will be powerless to save himself.
> The bowman will not stand his ground,
> the fast runner will not escape,
> the horseman will not save himself,
> the bravest warriors will run away naked that day.
> It is the Lord who speaks.

This is the word of the Lord.

Responsorial Psalm

Ps 49:16-23. ℟ v.22

℟ **Mark this, you who never think of God.**

1. 'How can you recite my commandments
   and take my covenant on your lips,
   you who despise my law
   and throw my words to the winds? ℟

2. 'You who see a thief and go with him;
   who throw in your lot with adulterers,
   who unbridle your mouth for evil
   and whose tongue is plotting crime. ℟

3. 'You who sit and malign your brother
   and slander your own mother's son.
   You do this, and should I keep silence?
   Do you think I am like you? ℟

4. 'Mark this, you who never think of God,
   lest I seize you and you cannot escape;
   a sacrifice of thanksgiving honours me
   and I will show God's salvation to the upright.' ℟

Gospel Acclamation

Jn 8:12

Alleluia, alleluia!
I am the light of the world, says the Lord,
anyone who follows me
will have the light of life.
Alleluia!

or

cf. Ps 94:8

Alleluia, alleluia!
Harden not your hearts today,
but listen to the voice of the Lord,
Alleluia!

GOSPEL

A reading from the holy Gospel according to Matthew 8:18-22

Follow me.

When Jesus saw the great crowds all about him he gave orders to leave for the other side. One of the scribes then came up and said to him, 'Master, I will follow you wherever you go.' Jesus replied, 'Foxes have holes and the birds of the air have nests, but the Son of Man has nowhere to lay his head.'

Another man, one of his disciples, said to him, 'Sir, let me go and bury my father first.' But Jesus replied, 'Follow me, and leave the dead to bury their dead.'

This is the Gospel of the Lord.

TUESDAY

FIRST READING

A reading from the prophet Amos   3:1-8; 4:11-12
The Lord speaks: who can refuse to prophesy?

Listen, sons of Israel, to this oracle the Lord speaks against you, against the whole family I brought out of the land of Egypt:

> You alone, of all the families of earth, have I acknowledged, therefore it is for all your sins that I mean to punish you.
> Do two men take the road together
> if they have not planned to do so?
> Does the lion roar in the jungle
> if no prey has been found?
> Does the young lion growl in his lair
> if he has captured nothing?
> Does the bird fall to the ground
> if no trap has been set?
> Does the snare spring up from the ground
> if nothing has been caught?
> Does the trumpet sound in the city
> without the populace becoming alarmed?
> Does misfortune come to a city
> if the Lord has not sent it?
> No more does the Lord do anything
> without revealing his plans to his servants the prophets.
> The lion roars: who can help feeling afraid?
> The Lord speaks: who can refuse to prophesy?
>
> I overthrew you as God overthrew Sodom and Gomorrah,
> and you were like a brand snatched from the blaze;
> and yet you never came back to me.
> It is the Lord who speaks.
> This therefore, Israel, is what I plan to do to you,
> and because I am going to do this to you,
> Israel, prepare to meet your God!

This is the word of the Lord.

Responsorial Psalm

Ps 5:5-8. ℟ v.9

℟ **Lead me, Lord, in your justice.**

1. You are no God who loves evil;
   no sinner is your guest.
   The boastful shall not stand their ground
   before your face. ℟

2. You hate all who do evil:
   you destroy all who lie.
   The deceitful and bloodthirsty man
   the Lord detests. ℟

3. But I through the greatness of your love
   have access to your house.
   I bow down before your holy temple,
   filled with awe. ℟

Gospel Acclamation

Ps 147:12. 15

Alleluia, alleluia!
O praise the Lord, Jerusalem!
He sends out his word to the earth.
Alleluia!

or

Ps 129:5

Alleuia, alleluia!
My soul is waiting for the Lord,
I count on his word.
Alleluia!

GOSPEL

A reading from the holy Gospel according to Matthew 8:23-27

He stood up and rebuked the winds and the sea; and all was calm again.

Jesus got into the boat followed by his disciples. Without warning a storm broke over the lake, so violent that the waves were breaking right over the boat. But he was asleep. So they went to him and woke him saying, 'Save us, Lord, we are going down!' And he said to them, 'Why are you so frightened, you men of little faith?' And with that he stood up and rebuked the winds and the sea; and all was calm again. The men were astounded and said, 'Whatever kind of man is this? Even the winds and the sea obey him.'

This is the Gospel of the Lord.

WEDNESDAY

FIRST READING

A reading from the prophet Amos   5:14-15. 21-24

Let me have no more of the din of your chanting, but let integrity flow like an unfailing stream.

Seek good and not evil
so that you may live,
and that the Lord, God of hosts, may really be with you
as you claim he is.
Hate evil, love good,
maintain justice at the city gate,
and it may be that the Lord, God of hosts, will take pity
on the remnant of Joseph.

The Lord says this:
I hate and despise your feasts,
I take no pleasure in your solemn festivals.
When you offer me holocausts,
I reject your oblations,
and refuse to look at your sacrifices of fattened cattle.
Let me have no more of the din of your chanting,
no more of your strumming on harps.
But let justice flow like water,
and integrity like an unfailing stream.

    This is the word of the Lord.

Responsorial Psalm   Ps 49:7-13. 16-17. ℟ v.23

    ℟ **I will show God's salvation to the upright.**

1   'Listen, my people, I will speak;
     Israel, I will testify against you,
     for I am God your God.   ℟

2   'I find no fault with your sacrifices,
     your offerings are always before me.
     I do not ask more bullocks from your farms,
     nor goats from among your herds.   ℟

3   'I own all the beasts of the forest,
     beasts in their thousands on my hills.
     I know all the birds in the sky,
     all that moves in the field belongs to me.   ℟

4 'Were I hungry, I would not tell you,
  for I own the world and all it holds.
  Do you think I eat the flesh of bulls,
  or drink the blood of goats? ℟

5 'How can you recite my commandments
  and take my covenant on your lips,
  you who despise my law
  and throw my words to the winds?' ℟

Gospel Acclamation   Jn 14:6
Alleluia, alleluia!
I am the Way, the Truth and the Life, says the Lord;
no one can come to the Father except through me.
Alleluia!

or   James 1:18
Alleluia, alleluia!
By his own choice the Father made us his children
by the message of the truth,
so that we should be sort of first-fruits
of all that he created.
Alleluia!

GOSPEL

A reading from the holy Gospel according to Matthew   8:28-34
Have you come here to torture the devils before the time?

When Jesus reached the country of the Gadarenes on the other side of the Lake, two demoniacs came towards him out of the tombs – creatures so fierce that no one could pass that way. They stood there shouting, 'What do you want with us, Son of God? Have you come here to torture us before the time?' Now some distance away there was a large herd of pigs feeding, and the devils pleaded with Jesus, 'If you cast us out, send us into the herd of pigs.' And he said to them, 'Go then,' and they came out and made for the pigs; and at that the whole herd charged down the cliff into the lake and perished in the water. The swineherds ran off and made for the town, where they told the whole story, including what had happened to the demoniacs. At this the whole town set out to meet Jesus; and as soon as they saw him they implored him to leave the neighbourhood.

This is the Gospel of the Lord.

THURSDAY

FIRST READING

A reading from the prophet Amos 7:10-17
Go prophesy to my people.

Amaziah the priest of Bethel sent word to Jeroboam king of Israel as follows. 'Amos is plotting against you in the heart of the House of Israel; the country can no longer tolerate what he keeps saying. For this is what he says, "Jeroboam is going to die by the sword, and Israel go into exile far from its country." ' To Amos, Amaziah said, 'Go away, seer; get back to the land of Judah; earn your bread there, do your prophesying there. We want no more prophesying in Bethel; this is the royal sanctuary, the national temple.' 'I was no prophet, neither did I belong to any of the brotherhoods of prophets,' Amos replied to Amaziah. 'I was a shepherd, and looked after sycamores: but it was the Lord who took me from herding the flock, and the Lord who said, "Go, prophesy to my people Israel." So listen to the word of the Lord. You say:

"Do not prophesy against Israel,
utter no oracles against the House of Isaac."

Very well, this is what the Lord says,
"Your wife will be forced to go on the streets,
your sons and daughters will fall by the sword,
your land will be parcelled out by measuring line.
and you yourself die on unclean soil
and Israel will go into exile far distant from its own land." '

This is the word of the Lord.

Responsorial Psalm Ps 18:8-11. ℟ v.10

℟ **The decrees of the Lord are truth
and all of them just.**

1 The law of the Lord is perfect,
it revives the soul.
The rule of the Lord is to be trusted,
it gives wisdom to the simple. ℟

2 The precepts of the Lord are right,
they gladden the heart.
The command of the Lord is clear,

Thirteenth Week in Ordinary Time, Year II: Thursday 1019

it gives light to the eyes. ℟

3 The fear of the Lord is holy,
abiding for ever.
The decrees of the Lord are truth
and all of them just. ℟

4 They are more to be desired than gold,
than the purest of gold
and sweeter are they than honey,
than honey from the comb. ℟

Gospel Acclamation cf. Mt 11:25
Alleluia, alleluia!
Blessed are you, Father,
Lord of heaven and earth,
for revealing the mysteries of the kingdom
to mere children.
Alleluia!

or 2 Cor 5:19

Alleluia, alleluia!
God in Christ was reconciling the world to himself,
and he has entrusted to us the news that they are reconciled.
Alleluia!

GOSPEL

A reading from the holy Gospel according to Matthew 9:1-8
They praised God for giving power to men.

Jesus got back in the boat, crossed the water and came to his own town. Then some people appeared, bringing him a paralytic stretched out on a bed. Seeing their faith, Jesus said to the paralytic, 'Courage, my child, your sins are forgiven.' And at this some scribes said to themselves, 'This man is blaspheming.' Knowing what was in their minds Jesus said, 'Why do you have such wicked thoughts in your hearts? Now, which of these is easier: to say, "Your sins are forgiven", or to say, "Get up and walk"? But to prove to you that the Son of Man has authority on earth to forgive sins,' – he said to the paralytic – 'get up, and pick up your bed and go off home.' And the man got up and went home. A feeling of awe came over the crowd when they saw this, and they praised God for giving such power to men.

This is the Gospel of the Lord.

FRIDAY

FIRST READING

A reading from the prophet Amos   8:4-6. 9-12

I will bring famine on the country, a famine not of bread, but of hearing the word of the Lord.

Listen to this, you who trample on the needy
and try to suppress the poor people of the country,
you who say, 'When will New Moon be over
so that we can sell our corn,
and sabbath, so that we can market our wheat?
Then by lowering the bushel, raising the shekel,
by swindling and tampering with the scales,
we can buy up the poor for money,
and the needy for a pair of sandals,
and get a price even for the sweepings of the wheat.'

'That day – it is the Lord who speaks –
I will make the sun go down at noon,
and darken the earth in broad daylight.
I am going to turn your feasts into funerals,
all your singing into lamentation;
I will have your loins all in sackcloth,
your heads all shaved.
I will make it a mourning like the mourning for an only son,
as long as it lasts it will be like a day of bitterness.
See what days are coming – it is the Lord who speaks –
days when I will bring famine on the country,
a famine not of bread, a drought not of water,
but of hearing the word of the Lord.
They will stagger from sea to sea,
wander from north to east,
seeking the word of the Lord
and failing to find it.'

    This is the word of the Lord.

Responsorial Psalm   Ps 118:2. 10. 20. 30. 40. 131. ℟ Mt 4:4
  ℟   **Man does not live on bread alone
      but on every word that comes from the mouth of God.**

1   They are happy those who do his will,
    seeking him with all their hearts.

Thirteenth Week in Ordinary Time, Year II: Friday

I have sought you with all my heart:
let me not stray from your commands. ℟

2 My soul is ever consumed
in longing for your decrees.
I have chosen the way of truth
with your decrees before me. ℟

3 See, I long for your precepts:
then in your justice, give me life.
I open my mouth and I sigh
as I yearn for your commands. ℟

Gospel Acclamation   Ps 24:4. 5
Alleluia, alleluia!
Teach me your paths, my God,
make me walk in your truth.
Alleluia!

or   Mt 11:28

Alleluia, alleluia!
Come to me, all you who labour and are overburdened,
and I will give you rest, says the Lord.
Alleluia!

GOSPEL

A reading from the holy Gospel according to Matthew   9:9-13
It is not the healthy who need the doctor. What I want is mercy, not sacrifice.

As Jesus was walking he saw a man named Matthew sitting by the customs house, and he said to him, 'Follow me.' And he got up and followed him.

While he was at dinner in the house it happened that a number of tax collectors and sinners came to sit at the table with Jesus and his disciples. When the Pharisees saw this, they said to his disciples, 'Why does your master eat with tax collectors and sinners?' When he heard this he replied, 'It is not the healthy who need the doctor, but the sick. Go and learn the meaning of the word: What I want is mercy, not sacrifice. And indeed I did not come to call the virtuous, but sinners.'

This is the Gospel of the Lord.

SATURDAY

FIRST READING

A reading from the prophet Amos   9:11-15

I mean to restore the fortunes of my captive people, and I will plant them in their own country.

It is the Lord who speaks:

> 'That day I will re-erect the tottering hut of David,
> make good the gaps in it, restore its ruins
> and rebuild it as it was in the days of old,
> so that they can conquer the remnant of Edom
> and all the nations that belonged to me.'

It is the Lord who speaks, and he will carry this out.

> 'The days are coming now – it is the Lord who speaks –
> when harvest will follow directly after ploughing,
> the treading of grapes soon after sowing,
> when the mountains will run with new wine
> and the hills all flow with it.
> I mean to restore the fortunes of my people Israel;
> they will rebuild the ruined cities and live in them,
> plant vineyards and drink their wine,
> dig gardens and eat their produce.
> I will plant them in their own country,
> never to be rooted up again
> out of the land I have given them,
> says the Lord, your God.'

This is the word of the Lord.

Responsorial Psalm   Ps 84:9. 11-14. ℟ v.9

  ℟   **The Lord speaks peace to his people.**

1. I will hear what the Lord God has to say,
   a voice that speaks of peace,
   peace for his people and his friends
   and those who turn to him in their hearts.   ℟

2. Mercy and faithfulness have met;
   justice and peace have embraced.
   Faithfulness shall spring from the earth
   and justice look down from heaven.   ℟

Thirteenth Week in Ordinary Time, Year II: Saturday

3 The Lord will make us prosper
   and our earth shall yield its fruit.
   Justice shall march before him
   and peace shall follow his steps. ℟

Gospel Acclamation   Ps 118:135
   Alleluia, alleluia!
   Let your face shine on your servant,
   and teach me your decrees.
   Alleluia!

or   Jn 10:27

   Alleluia, alleluia!
   The sheep that belong to me listen to my voice,
   says the Lord,
   I know them and they follow me.
   Alleluia!

GOSPEL

A reading from the holy Gospel according to Matthew   9:14-17
Surely the bridegroom's attendants would never think of mourning as long as the bridegroom is still with them?

John's disciples came to Jesus and said, 'Why is it that we and the Pharisees fast, but your disciples do not?' Jesus replied, 'Surely the bridegroom's attendants would never think of mourning as long as the bridegroom is still with them? But the time will come for the bridegroom to be taken away from them, and then they will fast. No one puts a piece of unshrunken cloth on to an old cloak, because the patch pulls away from the cloak and the tear gets worse. Nor do people put new wine into old wineskins; if they do, the skins burst, the wine runs out, and the skins are lost. No; they put new wine into fresh skins and both are preserved.'

This is the Gospel of the Lord.

FOURTEENTH WEEK IN ORDINARY TIME
Year II

MONDAY

FIRST READING

A reading from the prophet Hosea 2:16-18. 21-22
I will betroth you to myself for ever.

It is the Lord who speaks:

> I am going to lure her
> and lead her out into the wilderness
> and speak to her heart.
> There she will respond to me as she did when she was young,
> as she did when she came out of the land of Egypt.
> When that day comes – it is the Lord who speaks –
> she will call me, 'My husband',
> no longer will she call me, 'My Baal.'
> I will betroth you to myself for ever,
> betroth you with integrity and justice,
> with tenderness and love;
> I will betroth you to myself with faithfulness,
> and you will come to know the Lord.

This is the word of the Lord.

Responsorial Psalm Ps 144:2-9. ℟ v.8

℟ **The Lord is kind and full of compassion.**

1. I will bless you day after day
   and praise your name for ever.
   The Lord is great, highly to be praised,
   his greatness cannot be measured. ℟

2. Age to age shall proclaim your works,
   shall declare your mighty deeds,
   shall speak of your splendour and glory,
   tell the tale of your wonderful works. ℟

3. They will speak of your terrible deeds,
   recount your greatness and might.
   They will recall your abundant goodness;
   age to age shall ring out your justice. ℟

4. The Lord is kind and full of compassion,
   slow to anger, abounding in love.

Fourteenth Week in Ordinary Time, Year II: Monday

How good is the Lord to all,
compassionate to all his creatures. ℟

Gospel Acclamation *cf. Jn 6:63-68*
Alleluia, alleluia!
Your words are spirit, Lord,
and they are life:
you have the message of eternal life.
Alleluia!

or *cf. 2 Tim 1:10*

Alleluia, alleluia!
Our Saviour Christ Jesus abolished death,
and he has proclaimed life through the Good News.
Alleluia!

GOSPEL

A reading from the holy Gospel according to Matthew 9:18-26
My daughter has just died, but come and her life will be saved.

While Jesus was speaking, up came one of the officials, who bowed low in front of him and said, 'My daughter has just died, but come and lay your hand on her and her life will be saved.' Jesus rose and, with his disciples, followed him.

Then from behind him came a woman, who had suffered from a haemorrhage for twelve years, and she touched the fringe of his cloak, for she said to herself, 'If I can only touch his cloak I shall be well again.' Jesus turned round and saw her; and he said to her, 'Courage, my daughter, your faith has restored you to health.' And from that moment the woman was well again.

When Jesus reached the official's house, and saw the flute-players, with the crowd making a commotion he said, 'Get out of here; the little girl is not dead, she is asleep.' And they laughed at him. But when the people had been turned out he went inside and took the little girl by the hand; and she stood up. And the news spread all round the countryside.

This is the Gospel of the Lord.

TUESDAY

FIRST READING

A reading from the prophet Hosea 8:4-7. 11-13
They sow the wind, they will reap the whirlwind.

Thus says the Lord:

> They have set up kings, but not with my consent,
> and appointed princes, but without my knowledge.
> Out of their own silver and gold they have made idols,
> which are doomed to destruction.
> I spurn your calf, Samaria,
> my anger blazes against it.
> (How long will it be before they purge themselves of this,
> the sons of Israel?)
> A workman made the thing,
> this cannot be God!
> Yes, the calf of Samaria shall go up in flames.
>
> They sow the wind, they will reap the whirlwind;
> their wheat will yield no ear,
> the ear will yield no flour,
> or, if it does, foreigners will swallow it.
> Ephraim has built altar after altar,
> they have only served him as occasion for sin.
> Were I to write out the thousand precepts of my Law for him,
> they would be paid no more attention than those of a stranger.
> They love sacrificing; right, let them sacrifice!
> They love meat; right, let them eat it!
> The Lord takes no pleasure in these.
> He is now going to remember their iniquity
> and punish their sins;
> they will have to go back to Egypt.

This is the word of the Lord.

Responsorial Psalm Ps 113B:3-10. ℟ v.9
℟ **Sons of Israel, trust in the Lord.**

or

℟ **Alleluia!**

1 Our God, he is in the heavens;
he does whatever he wills.

Fourteenth Week in Ordinary Time, Year II: Tuesday

The idols of the heathen are silver and gold,
the work of human hands. ℟

2 They have mouths but they cannot speak;
they have eyes but they cannot see;
they have ears but they cannot hear;
they have nostrils but they cannot smell. ℟

3 With their hands they cannot feel;
with their feet they cannot walk.
Their makers will become like them:
so will all who trust in them. ℟

4 Sons of Israel, trust in the Lord;
he is their help and their shield.
Sons of Aaron, trust in the Lord;
he is their help and their shield. ℟

Gospel Acclamation cf. Eph 1:17. 18

Alleluia, alleluia!
May the Father of our Lord Jesus Christ
enlighten the eyes of our mind,
so that we can see what hope his call holds for us.
Alleluia!

or Jn 10:14

Alleluia, alleluia!
I am the good shepherd, says the Lord;
I know my own sheep, and my own know me.
Alleluia!

GOSPEL

A reading from the holy Gospel according to Matthew 9:32-38
The harvest is rich but the labourers are few.

A man was brought to Jesus, a dumb demoniac. And when the devil was cast out, the dumb man spoke and the people were amazed. 'Nothing like this has ever been seen in Israel' they said. But the Pharisees said, 'It is through the prince of devils that he casts out devils.'

Jesus made a tour through all the towns and villages, teaching in their synagogues, proclaiming the Good News of the kingdom and curing all kinds of diseases and sickness.

And when he saw the crowds he felt sorry for them because they were harassed and dejected, like sheep without a shepherd.

Then he said to his disciples, 'The harvest is rich but the labourers are few, so ask the Lord of the harvest to send labourers to his harvest.'

This is the Gospel of the Lord.

WEDNESDAY

FIRST READING

A reading from the prophet Hosea 10:1-3. 7-8. 12

It is time to go seeking the Lord.

Israel was a luxuriant vine
yielding plenty of fruit.
The more his fruit increased,
the more altars he built;
the richer his land became,
the richer he made the sacred stones.
Their heart is a divided heart;
very well, they must pay for it;
the Lord is going to break their altars down
and destroy their sacred stones.
Then they will say,
'We have no king
because we have not feared the Lord.'
But what can a king do for us?

Samaria has had her day.
Her king is like a straw drifting on the water.
The idolatrous high places shall be destroyed –
that sin of Israel;
thorn and thistle will grow on their altars.
Then they will say to the mountains, 'Cover us!'
and to the hills, 'Fall on us!'

Sow integrity for yourselves,
reap a harvest of kindness,
break up your fallow ground:
it is time to go seeking the Lord
until he comes to rain salvation on you.

This is the word of the Lord.

Fourteenth Week in Ordinary Time, Year II: Wednesday 1029

Responsorial Psalm Ps 104:2-7. ℟ v.4

℟ **Constantly seek the face of the Lord.**

or

℟ **Alleluia!**

1 O sing to him, sing his praise;
  tell all his wonderful works!
  Be proud of his holy name,
  let the hearts that seek the Lord rejoice. ℟

2 Consider the Lord and his strength;
  constantly seek his face.
  Remember the wonders he has done,
  his miracles, the judgements he spoke. ℟

3 O children of Abraham, his servant,
  O sons of the Jacob he chose.
  He, the Lord, is our God:
  his judgements prevail in all the earth. ℟

Gospel Acclamation James 1:18
  Alleluia, alleluia!
  By his own choice the Father made us his children
  by the message of the truth,
  so that we should be a sort of first-fruits
  of all that he created.
  Alleluia!

or Mk 1:15

  Alleluia, alleluia!
  The kingdom of God is close at hand,
  repent and believe the Good News.
  Alleluia!

GOSPEL

A reading from the holy Gospel according to Matthew 10:1-7
Go to the lost sheep of the House of Israel.

Jesus summoned his twelve disciples, and gave them authority over unclean spirits with power to cast them out and to cure all kinds of diseases and sickness.

  These are the names of the twelve apostles: first, Simon who is called Peter, and his brother Andrew; James the son of Zebedee, and his brother John; Philip and Bartholomew; Thomas, and Matthew the tax collector; James the son of Alphaeus, and Thaddaeus; Simon the Zealot and Judas Iscariot, the one who was to betray him. These twelve Jesus sent out, instructing them as follows:

'Do not turn your steps to pagan territory, and do not enter any Samaritan town; go rather to the lost sheep of the House of Israel. And as you go, proclaim that the kingdom of heaven is close at hand.'

This is the Gospel of the Lord.

THURSDAY

FIRST READING

A reading from the prophet Hosea 11:1-4. 8-9
My heart recoils from it.

Thus says the Lord:

When Israel was a child I loved him,
and I called my son out of Egypt,
But the more I called to them, the further they went from me;
they have offered sacrifice to the Baals
and set their offerings smoking before the idols.
I myself taught Ephraim to walk,
I took them in my arms;
yet they have not understood that I was the one looking after them.
I led them with reins of kindness,
with leading-strings of love.

I was like someone who lifts an infant close against his cheek;
stooping down to him I gave him his food.
My heart recoils from it,
my whole being trembles at the thought.
I will not give rein to my fierce anger,
I will not destroy Ephraim again,
for I am God, not man:
I am the Holy One in your midst
and have no wish to destroy.

This is the word of the Lord.

Fourteenth Week in Ordinary Time, Year II: Thursday

Responsorial Psalm   Ps 79:2-3. 15-16. ℟ v.4

   ℟ **Let your face shine on us, O Lord,**
       and we shall be saved.

1   O shepherd of Israel, hear us,
     shine forth from your cherubim throne.
     O Lord, rouse up your might,
     O Lord, come to our help.   ℟

2   God of hosts, turn again, we implore,
     look down from heaven and see.
     Visit this vine and protect it,
     the vine your right hand has planted.   ℟

Gospel Acclamation   cf. Ps 94:8

    Alleluia, alleluia!
    Harden not your hearts today,
    but listen to the voice of the Lord.
    Alleluia!

or   Mk 1:15

    Alleluia, alleluia!
    The kingdom of God is close at hand,
    repent and believe the Good News.
    Alleluia!

GOSPEL

A reading from the holy Gospel according to Matthew   10:7-15
You received without charge, give without charge.

Jesus instructed the Twelve as follows: 'As you go, proclaim that the kingdom of heaven is close at hand. Cure the sick, raise the dead, cleanse the lepers, cast out devils. You received without charge, give without charge. Provide yourselves with no gold or silver, not even with a few coppers for your purses, with no haversack for the journey or spare tunic or footwear or a staff, for the workman deserves his keep.

   'Whatever town or village you go into, ask for someone trustworthy and stay with him until you leave. As you enter his house, salute it, and if the house deserves it, let your peace descend upon it; if it does not, let your peace come back to you. And if anyone does not welcome you or listen to what you have to say, as you walk out of the house or town shake the dust from your feet. I tell you solemnly, on the day of Judgement it will not go as hard with the land of Sodom and Gomorrah as with that town.'

This is the Gospel of the Lord.

FRIDAY

FIRST READING

A reading from the prophet Hosea 14:2-10
We will not say any more, 'Our God!' to what our own hands have made.

The Lord says this:

> Israel, come back to the Lord your God;
> your iniquity was the cause of your downfall.
> Provide yourself with words
> and come back to the Lord.
> Say to him, 'Take all iniquity away
> so that we may have happiness again
> and offer you our words of praise.
> Assyria cannot save us,
> we will not ride horses any more,
> or say, "Our God!" to what our own hands have made,
> for you are the one in whom orphans find compassion.'
> – I will heal their disloyalty,
> I will love them with all my heart,
> for my anger has turned from them.
> I will fall like dew on Israel.
> He shall bloom like the lily,
> and thrust out roots like the poplar,
> his shoots will spread far;
> he will have the beauty of the olive
> and the fragrance of Lebanon.
> They will come back to live in my shade;
> they will grow corn that flourishes,
> they will cultivate vines
> as renowned as the wine of Helbon.
> What has Ephraim to do with idols any more
> when it is I who hear his prayer and care for him?
> I am like a cypress ever green,
> all your fruitfulness comes from me.

Let the wise man understand these words.

Fourteenth Week in Ordinary Time, Year II: Friday   1033

Let the intelligent man grasp their meaning.
For the ways of the Lord are straight,
and virtuous men walk in them,
but sinners stumble.

This is the word of the Lord.

Responsorial Psalm   Ps 50:3-4. 8-9. 12-14. 17. ℟ v.17
   ℟ **My mouth shall declare your praise.**

1. Have mercy on me, God, in your kindness.
   In your compassion blot out my offence.
   O wash me more and more from my guilt
   and cleanse me from my sin.   ℟

2. Indeed you love truth in the heart;
   then in the secret of my heart teach me wisdom.
   O purify me, then I shall be clean;
   O wash me, I shall be whiter than snow.   ℟

3. A pure heart create for me, O God,
   put a steadfast spirit within me.
   Do not cast me away from your presence,
   nor deprive me of your holy spirit.   ℟

4. Give me again the joy of your help;
   with a spirit of fervour sustain me.
   O Lord, open my lips
   and my mouth shall declare your praise.   ℟

Gospel Acclamation   1 Peter 1:25
   Alleluia, alleluia!
   The word of the Lord remains for ever:
   What is this word?
   It is the Good News that has been brought to you.
   Alleluia!

or   Jn 16:13; 14:26
   Alleluia, alleluia!
   When the Spirit of truth comes
   he will lead you to the complete truth,
   and he will remind you of all I have said to you.
   Alleluia!

GOSPEL

A reading from the holy Gospel according to Matthew   10:16-23

It is not you who will be speaking; the Spirit of your Father will be speaking in you.

Jesus instructed the Twelve as follows: 'Remember, I am sending you out like sheep among wolves; so be cunning as serpents and yet as harmless as doves.

'Beware of men: they will hand you over to sanhedrins and scourge you in their synagogues. You will be dragged before governors and kings for my sake, to bear witness before them and the pagans. But when they hand you over, do not worry about how to speak or what to say; what you are to say will be given to you when the time comes; because it is not you who will be speaking; the Spirit of your Father will be speaking in you.

'Brother will betray brother to death, and the father his child; children will rise against their parents and have them put to death. You will be hated by all men on account of my name; but the man who stands firm to the end will be saved. If they persecute you in one town, take refuge in the next; and if they persecute you in that, take refuge in another. I tell you solemnly, you will not have gone the round of the towns of Israel before the Son of Man comes.'

This is the Gospel of the Lord.

SATURDAY

FIRST READING

A reading from the prophet Isaiah   6:1-8

I am a man of unclean lips, and my eyes have looked at the King, the Lord of hosts.

In the year of King Uzziah's death I saw the Lord seated on a high throne; his train filled the sanctuary; above him stood seraphs, each one with six wings: two to cover its face, two to cover its feet and two for flying.

    And they cried out to one another in this way,
'Holy, holy, holy is the Lord of hosts.
His glory fills the whole earth.'

The foundations of the threshold shook with the voice of the one who cried out, and the Temple was filled with smoke. I said:

Fourteenth Week in Ordinary Time, Year II: Saturday 1035

'What a wretched state I am in! I am lost,
for I am a man of unclean lips
and I live among a people of unclean lips,
and my eyes have looked at the King, the Lord of hosts.'

Then one of the seraphs flew to me, holding in his hand a live coal which he had taken from the altar with a pair of tongs. With this he touched my mouth and said:

'See now, this has touched your lips,
your sin is taken away,
your iniquity is purged.'

Then I heard the voice of the Lord saying:

'Whom shall I send? Who will be our messenger?'

I answered, 'Here I am, send me.'

This is the word of the Lord.

Responsional Psalm
Ps 92:1-2. 5. R̷ v.1

R̷ **The Lord is king, with majesty enrobed.**

1. The Lord is king, with majesty enrobed;
the Lord has robed himself with might,
he has girded himself with power. R̷

2. The world you made firm, not to be moved;
your throne has stood firm from of old.
From all eternity, O Lord, you are. R̷

3. Truly your decrees are to be trusted.
Holiness is fitting to your house,
O Lord, until the end of time. R̷

Gospel Acclamation
1 Jn 2:5

Alleluia, alleluia!
When anyone obeys what Christ has said,
God's love comes to perfection in him.
Alleluia!

or
1 Peter 4:14

Alleluia, alleluia!
It is a blessing for you,
when they insult you
for bearing the name of Christ,
for the Spirit of God rests on you.
Alleluia!

GOSPEL

A reading from the holy Gospel according to Matthew   10:24-33
Do not be afraid of those who kill the body.

Jesus instructed the Twelve as follows: 'The disciple is not superior to his teacher, nor the slave to his master. It is enough for the disciple that he should grow to be like his teacher, and the slave like his master. If they have called the master of the house Beelzebul, what will they not say of his household?

'Do not be afraid of them therefore. For everything that is now covered will be uncovered, and everything now hidden will be made clear. What I say to you in the dark, tell in the daylight; what you hear in whispers, proclaim from the housetops.

'Do not be afraid of those who kill the body but cannot kill the soul; fear him rather who can destroy both body and soul in hell. Can you not buy two sparrows for a penny? And yet not one falls to the ground without your Father knowing. Why, every hair on your head has been counted. So there is no need to be afraid; you are worth more than hundreds of sparrows.

'So if anyone declares himself for me in the presence of men, I will declare myself for him in the presence of my Father in heaven. But the one who disowns me in the presence of men, I will disown in the presence of my Father in heaven.'

This is the Gospel of the Lord.

FIFTEENTH WEEK IN ORDINARY TIME
Year II

MONDAY

FIRST READING

A reading from the prophet Isaiah   1:10-17
Make yourselves clean. Take your wrong-doing out of my sight.

Hear the word of the Lord,
you rulers of Sodom:
listen to the command of our God,
you people of Gomorrah.

   'What are your endless sacrifices to me?
says the Lord.

I am sick of holocausts of rams
and the fat of calves.
The blood of bulls and of goats revolts me.
When you come to present yourselves before me,
who asked you to trample over my courts?
Bring me your worthless offerings no more,
the smoke of them fills me with disgust.
New Moons, sabbaths, assemblies –
I cannot endure festival and solemnity.
Your New Moons and your pilgrimages
I hate with all my soul.
They lie heavy on me,
I am tired of bearing them.

'When you stretch out your hands
I turn my eyes away.
You may multiply your prayers,
I shall not listen.
Your hands are covered with blood,
wash, make yourselves clean.

'Take your wrong-doing out of my sight.
Cease to do evil.
Learn to do good,
search for justice,
help the oppressed,
be just to the orphan,
plead for the widow.'

This is the word of the Lord.

Responsorial Psalm   Ps 49:8-9. 16-17. 21. 23. ℟ v.23

℟ **I will show God's salvation to the upright.**

1 'I find no fault with your sacrifices,
your offerings are always before me.
I do not ask more bullocks from your farms,
nor goats from among your herds.' ℟

2 'How can you recite my commandments
and take my covenant on your lips,
you who despise my law
and throw my words to the winds?' ℟

3 'You do this, and should I keep silence?
Do you think that I am like you? (continued)

A sacrifice of thanksgiving honours me
and I will show God's salvation to the upright.'

℞ **I will show God's salvation to the upright.**

Gospel Acclamation cf. Acts 16:14
Alleluia, alleluia!
Open our heart, O Lord,
to accept the words of your Son.
Alleluia!

or Mt 5:10

Alleluia, alleluia!
Happy those who are persecuted
in the cause of right,
for theirs is the kingdom of heaven.
Alleluia!

GOSPEL

A reading from the holy Gospel according to Matthew 10:34 – 11:1
It is not peace I have come to bring, but a sword.

Jesus instructed the Twelve as follows: 'Do not suppose that I have come to bring peace to the earth: it is not peace I have come to bring, but a sword. For I have come to set a man against his father, a daughter against her mother, a daughter-in-law against her mother-in-law. A man's enemies will be those of his own household.

'Anyone who prefers father or mother to me is not worthy of me. Anyone who prefers son or daughter to me is not worthy of me. Anyone who does not take his cross and follow in my footsteps is not worthy of me. Anyone who finds his life will lose it; anyone who loses his life for my sake will find it.

'Anyone who welcomes you welcomes me; and those who welcome me welcome the one who sent me.

'Anyone who welcomes a prophet because he is a prophet will have a prophet's reward; and anyone who welcomes a holy man because he is a holy man will have a holy man's reward.

'If anyone gives so much as a cup of cold water to one of these little ones because he is a disciple, then I tell you solemnly, he will most certainly not lose his reward.'

When Jesus had finished instructing his twelve disciples he moved on from there to teach and preach in their towns.

This is the Gospel of the Lord.

TUESDAY

FIRST READING

A reading from the prophet Isaiah 7:1-9

If you do not stand by me, you will not stand at all.

In the reign of Ahaz son of Jotham, son of Uzziah, king of Judah, Razon the king of Aram went up against Jerusalem with Pekah son of Remaliah, king of Israel, to lay siege to it; but he was unable to capture it.

The news was brought to the House of David. 'Aram,' they said, 'has reached Ephraim.' Then the heart of the king and the hearts of the people shuddered as the trees of the forest shudder in front of the wind. The Lord said to Isaiah, 'Go with your son Shear-jashub, and meet Ahaz at the end of the conduit of the upper pool on the Fuller's Field road, and say to him:

> "Pay attention, keep calm, have no fear,
> do not let your heart sink
> because of these two smouldering stumps of firebrands,
> or because Aram, Ephraim and the son of Remaliah
> have plotted to ruin you, and have said:
> Let us invade Judah and terrorise it
> and seize it for ourselves,
> and set up a king there,
> the son of Tabeel.
> The Lord says this:
> It shall not come true; it shall not be.
> The capital of Aram is Damascus,
> the head of Damascus, Razon;
> the capital of Ephraim, Samaria,
> the head of Samaria, the son of Remaliah.
> Six or five years more
> and shattered Ephraim shall no longer be a people.
> But if you do not stand by me,
> you will not stand at all."'

This is the word of the Lord.

Responsorial Psalm   Ps 47:2-8. R℣ v.9
   R℣ **God upholds his city for ever.**

1. The Lord is great and worthy to be praised
in the city of our God.
His holy mountain rises in beauty,
the joy of all the earth. R℣

2. Mount Zion, true pole of the earth,
the Great King's city!
God, in the midst of its citadels,
has shown himself its stronghold. R℣

3. For the kings assembled together,
together they advanced.
They saw; at once they were astounded;
dismayed, they fled in fear. R℣

4. A trembling seized them there,
like the pangs of birth,
or as the east wind destroys
the ships of Tarshish. R℣

Gospel Acclamation   Ps 118:34
Alleluia, alleluia!
Train me, Lord, to observe your law,
to keep it with my heart.
Alleluia!

or   cf. Ps 94:8
Alleluia, alleluia!
Harden not your hearts today,
but listen to the voice of the Lord.
Alleluia!

GOSPEL

A reading from the holy Gospel according to Matthew   11:20-24
It will not go as hard on Judgement day with Tyre and Sidon and with the land of Sodom as with you.

Jesus began to reproach the towns in which most of his miracles had been worked, because they refused to repent.

  'Alas for you, Chorazin! Alas for you, Bethsaida! For if the miracles done in you had been done in Tyre and Sidon, they would have repented long ago in sackcloth and ashes. And still, I tell you that it will not go as hard on Judgement day with Tyre and Sidon as with you. And as for you, Capernaum, did you want to be exalted as high as heaven? You shall be thrown down to hell. For if the miracles done in you had been done in Sodom, it would have been standing yet. And still, I tell you it will not go as hard with the land of Sodom on Judgement day as with you.'

This is the Gospel of the Lord.

WEDNESDAY

FIRST READING

A reading from the prophet Isaiah 10:5-7. 13-16
Does the axe claim more credit than the man who wields it?

The Lord of hosts says this:

'Woe to Assyria, the rod of my anger,
the club brandished by me in my fury!
I sent him against a godless nation;
I gave him commission against a people that provokes me,
to pillage and to plunder freely
and to stamp down like the mud in the streets.
But he did not intend this,
his heart did not plan it so.
No, in his heart was to destroy,
to go on cutting nations to pieces without limit.'

For he has said:

'By the strength of my own arm I have done this
and by my own intelligence, for understanding is mine;
I have pushed back the frontiers of peoples
and plundered their treasures.
I have brought their inhabitants down to the dust.
As if they were a bird's nest, my hand has seized
the riches of the peoples.
As people pick up deserted eggs
I have picked up the whole earth,
with not a wing fluttering,
not a beak opening, not a chirp.'

Does the axe claim more credit than the man who wields it,
or the saw more strength than the man who handles it?
It would be like the cudgel controlling the man who raises it,

or the club moving what is not made of wood!
And so the Lord of hosts is going to send
a wasting sickness on his stout warriors;
beneath his plenty, a burning will burn
like a consuming fire.

    This is the word of the Lord.

Responsorial Psalm Ps 93:5-10. 14-15. ℟ v.14
℟ **The Lord will not abandon his people.**

1. They crush your people, Lord,
   they afflict the ones you have chosen.
   They kill the widow and the stranger
   and murder the fatherless child. ℟

2. And they say: 'The Lord does not see;
   the God of Jacob pays no heed.'
   Mark this, most senseless of people;
   fools, when will you understand? ℟

3. Can he who made the ear not hear?
   Can he who formed the eye not see?
   Will he who trains nations not punish?
   Will he who teaches men not have knowledge? ℟

4. The Lord will not abandon his people
   nor forsake those who are his own:
   for judgement shall again be just
   and all true hearts shall uphold it. ℟

Gospel Acclamation cf. Mt 11:25
Alleluia, alleluia!
Blessed are you, Father, Lord of heaven and earth,
for revealing the mysteries of the kingdom to mere children.
Alleluia!

GOSPEL

A reading from the holy Gospel according to Matthew   11:25-27
You have hidden these things from the learned and revealed them to mere children.

Jesus exclaimed, 'I bless you, Father, Lord of heaven and of earth, for hiding these things from the learned and the clever and revealing them to mere children. Yes, Father, for that is what it pleased you to do. Everything has been entrusted to me by my Father; and no one knows the Son except the Father, just as no one knows the Father except the Son and those to whom the Son chooses to reveal him.'

This is the Gospel of the Lord.

THURSDAY

FIRST READING

A reading from the prophet Isaiah   26:7-9. 12. 16-19
Awake, exult, all you who lie in the dust.

The path of the upright man is straight,
you smooth the way of the upright.
Following the path of your judgements,
we hoped in you, Lord,
your name, your memory are all my soul desires.

At night my soul longs for you
and my spirit in me seeks for you;
when your judgements appear on earth
the inhabitants of the world learn the meaning of integrity.

Lord, you are giving us peace,
since you treat us
as our deeds deserve.

Distressed, we search for you, Lord;
the misery of oppression was your punishment for us.
As a woman with child near her time
writhes and cries out in her pangs,

so are we, O Lord, in your presence:
we have conceived, we writhe
as if we were giving birth;
we have not given the spirit of salvation to the earth,
no more inhabitants of the world are born.

Your dead will come to life,
their corpses will rise;
awake, exult,
all you who lie in the dust,
for your dew is a radiant dew
and the land of ghosts will give birth.

This is the word of the Lord.

Responsorial Psalm   Ps 101:13-21. R̷ v.20

   R̷ **The Lord looked down from heaven to the earth.**

1. You, O Lord, will endure for ever
and your name from age to age.
You will arise and have mercy on Zion:
for this is the time to have mercy,
for your servants love her very stones,
are moved with pity even for her dust. R̷

2. The nations shall fear the name of the Lord
and all the earth's kings your glory,
when the Lord shall build up Zion again
and appear in all his glory.
Then he will turn to the prayers of the helpless;
he will not despise their prayers. R̷

3. Let this be written for ages to come
that a people yet unborn may praise the Lord;
for the Lord leaned down from his sanctuary on high.
He looked down from heaven to the earth
that he might hear the groans of the prisoners
and free those condemned to die. R̷

Gospel Acclamation   Ps 129:5

   Alleluia, alleluia!
My soul is waiting for the Lord, I count on his word.
Alleluia!

or   Mt 11:28

   Alleluia, alleluia!
Come to me, all you who labour and are overburdened,
and I will give you rest, says the Lord.
Alleluia!

GOSPEL

A reading from the holy Gospel according to Matthew   11:28-30

I am gentle and humble in heart.

Jesus exclaimed: 'Come to me, all you who labour and are overburdened, and I will give you rest. Shoulder my yoke and learn from me, for I am gentle and humble in heart, and you will find rest for your souls. Yes, my yoke is easy and my burden light.'

   This is the Gospel of the Lord.

FRIDAY

FIRST READING

A reading from the prophet Isaiah 38:1-6. 21-22. 7-8

I have heard your prayer and seen your tears.

Hezekiah fell ill and was at the point of death. The prophet Isaiah son of Amoz came and said to him, 'The Lord says this, "Put your affairs in order, for you are going to die, you will not live." ' Hezekiah turned his face to the wall and addressed this prayer to the Lord, 'Ah, Lord, remember, I beg you, how I have behaved faithfully and with sincerity of heart in your presence and done what is right in your eyes.' And Hezekiah shed many tears.

Then the word of the Lord came to Isaiah, 'Go and say to Hezekiah, "The Lord, the God of David your ancestor, says this: I have heard your prayer and seen your tears. I will cure you: in three days' time you shall go up to the Temple of the Lord. I will add fifteen years to your life. I will save you from the hands of the king of Assyria, I will protect this city." '

'Bring a fig poultice,' Isaiah said. 'Apply it to the ulcer and he will recover.' Hezekiah said, 'What is the sign to tell me that I shall be going up to the Temple of the Lord?' 'Here' Isaiah replied 'is the sign from the Lord that he will do what he has said. Look, I shall make the shadow cast by the declining sun go back ten steps on the steps of Ahaz.' And the sun went back the ten steps by which it had declined.

This is the word of the Lord.

Responsorial Psalm
Is 38:10-12. 16. ℟ cf. v.27

℟ **You have held back my life, O Lord, from the pit of doom.**

1. I said, 'So I must go away,
my life half spent,
assigned to the world below
for the rest of my years.' ℟

2. I said, 'No more shall I see the Lord
in the land of the living,
no more shall I look upon men
within this world. ℟

3. 'My home is pulled up and removed
like a shepherd's tent.

(continued)

Like a weaver you have rolled up my life,
you cut it from the loom.

℟ **You have held back my life, O Lord, from the pit of doom.**

4 'For you, Lord, my heart will live,
you gave me back my spirit;
you cured me, kept me alive,
changed my sickness into health.' ℟

Gospel Acclamation   Ps 26:11
Alleluia, alleluia!
Instruct me, Lord, in your way;
on an even path lead me.
Alleluia!

or   Jn 10:27

Alleluia, alleluia!
The sheep that belong to me listen to my voice,
says the Lord,
I know them and they follow me.
Alleluia!

GOSPEL

A reading from the holy Gospel according to Matthew   12:1-8
The Son of Man is master of the sabbath.

Jesus took a walk one sabbath day through the cornfields. His disciples were hungry and began to pick ears of corn and eat them. The Pharisees noticed it and said to him, 'Look, your disciples are doing something that is forbidden on the sabbath.' But he said to them, 'Have you not read what David did when he and his followers were hungry – how he went into the house of God and how they ate the loaves of offering which neither he nor his followers were allowed to eat, but which were for the priests alone? Or again, have you not read in the Law that on the sabbath day the Temple priests break the sabbath without being blamed for it? Now here, I tell you, is something greater than the Temple. And if you had understood the meaning of the words: What I want is mercy, not sacrifice, you would not have condemned the blameless. For the Son of Man is master of the sabbath.'

This is the Gospel of the Lord.

SATURDAY

FIRST READING

A reading from the prophet Micah 2:1-5

They seized the fields and took over the houses.

Woe to those who plot evil,
who lie in bed planning mischief!
No sooner is it dawn than they do it
– their hands have the strength for it.
Seizing the fields that they covet,
they take over houses as well,
owner and house they confiscate together,
taking both man and inheritance.
So the Lord says this:
Now it is I who plot
such mischief against this breed
as your necks will not escape;
nor will you be able to walk proudly,
so evil will the time be.
On that day they will make a satire on you,
sing a dirge and say,
'We are stripped of everything;
my people's portion is measured out and shared,
no one will give it back to them,
our fields are awarded to our despoiler.'
Therefore you will have no one
to measure out a share
in the community of the Lord.

This is the word of the Lord.

Responsorial Psalm Ps 9B:1-4. 7-8. 14. ℟. v.12

℟ **Lord, do not forget the poor.**

1 Lord, why do you stand afar off
 and hide yourself in times of distress?
 The poor man is devoured by the pride of the wicked:
 he is caught in the schemes that others have made. ℟

2 For the wicked man boasts of his heart's desires;
 the covetous blasphemes and spurns the Lord.
 In his pride the wicked says: 'He will not punish.
 There is no God.' Such are his thoughts. ℟ (continued)

3 His mouth is full of cursing, guile, oppression,
  mischief and deceit under his tongue.
  He lies in wait among the reeds;
  the innocent he murders in secret.

  ℟ **Lord, do not forget the poor.**

4 But you have seen the trouble and sorrow,
  you note it, you take it in hand.
  The helpless trusts himself to you;
  for you are the helper of the orphan. ℟

Gospel Acclamation Ps 118:27
Alleluia, alleluia!
Make me grasp the way of your precepts,
and I will muse on your wonders.
Alleluia!

or 2 Cor 5:19

Alleluia, alleluia!
God in Christ was reconciling the world by himself,
and he has entrusted to us the news that they are reconciled.
Alleluia!

GOSPEL

A reading from the holy Gospel according to Matthew 12:14-21
Jesus warned them not to make him known; this was to fulfil the prophecy.

The Pharisees went out and began to plot against Jesus, discussing how to destroy him.

Jesus knew this and withdrew from the district. Many followed him and he cured them all, but warned them not to make him known. This was to fulfil the prophecy of Isaiah:

> Here is my servant whom I have chosen,
> my beloved, the favourite of my soul.
> I will endow him with my spirit,
> and he will proclaim the true faith to the nations.
> He will not brawl or shout,
> nor will anyone hear his voice in the streets.
> He will not break the crushed reed,
> nor put out the smouldering wick
> till he has led the truth to victory:
> in his name the nations will put their hope.

This is the Gospel of the Lord.

SIXTEENTH WEEK IN ORDINARY TIME
Year II

MONDAY

FIRST READING

A reading from the prophet Micah 6:1-4. 6-8
It has been explained to you, man, what the Lord asks of you.

Listen to what the Lord is saying:

> Stand up and let the case begin in the hearing of the mountains
> and let the hills hear what you say.
> Listen, you mountains, to the Lord's accusation,
> give ear, you foundations of the earth,
> for the Lord is accusing his people,
> pleading against Israel:
> My people, what have I done to you,
> how have I been a burden to you? Answer me.
> I brought you out of the land of Egypt,
> I rescued you from the house of slavery;
> I sent Moses to lead you,
> with Aaron and Miriam.

– 'With what gift shall I come into the Lord's presence
and bow down before God on high?
Shall I come with holocausts,
with calves one year old?
Will he be pleased with rams by the thousand,
with libations of oil in torrents?
Must I give my first-born for what I have done wrong,
the fruit of my body for my own sin?'

– What is good has been explained to you, man;
this is what the Lord asks of you:
only this, to act justly,
to love tenderly
and to walk humbly with your God.

This is the word of the Lord.

Responsorial Psalm   Ps 49:5-6. 8-9. 16-17. 21. 23. ℟ v.23

  ℟   **I will show God's salvation to the upright.**

1. 'Summon before me my people
who made covenant with me by sacrifice.'
The heavens proclaim his justice,
you forgave the guilt of your people
and covered all their sins.
You averted all your rage,
you calmed the heat of your anger. ℟

2. Revive us now, God, our helper!
Put an end to your grievance against us.
Will you be angry with us for ever,
will your anger never cease? ℟

3. Will you not restore again our life
that your people may rejoice in you?
Let us see, O Lord, your mercy
and give us your saving help. ℟

Gospel Acclamation   cf. 2 Tim 1:10

Alleluia, alleluia!
Our Saviour Christ Jesus abolished death,
and he has proclaimed life through the Good News.
Alleluia!

or   cf. Ps 94:8

Alleluia, alleluia!
Harden not your hearts today,
but listen to the voice of the Lord.
Alleluia!

GOSPEL

A reading from the holy Gospel according to Matthew   12:38-42
The Queen of the South will rise up with this generation and condemn it.

Some of the scribes and Pharisees spoke up. 'Master,' they said 'we should like to see a sign from you.' Jesus replied, 'It is an evil and unfaithful generation that asks for a sign! The only sign it will be given is the sign of the prophet Jonah. For as Jonah was in the belly of the sea-monster for three days and three nights, so will the Son of Man be in the heart of the earth for three days and three nights. On Judgement day the men of Nineveh will stand up with this generation and condemn it, because when Jonah preached they repented; and there is something greater than Jonah here. On Judgement day the Queen of the South will rise up with this generation and condemn it, because she came from the ends of the earth to hear the wisdom of Solomon; and there is something greater than Solomon here.'

This is the Gospel of the Lord.

TUESDAY

FIRST READING

A reading from the prophet Micah 7:14-15. 18-20
To the bottom of the sea throw all our sins.

With shepherd's crook, O Lord, lead your people to pasture
the flock that is your heritage,
living confined in a forest
with meadow land all around.
Let them pasture in Bashan and Gilead
as in the days of old.
As in the days when you came out of Egypt
grant us to see wonders.
What god can compare with you: taking fault away,
pardoning crime,
not cherishing anger for ever
but delighting in showing mercy?
Once more have pity on us,
tread down our faults,
to the bottom of the sea
throw all our sins.
Grant Jacob your faithfulness,
and Abraham your mercy,
as you swore to our fathers
from the days of long ago.

This is the word of the Lord.

Responsorial Psalm
Ps 84:2-8. ℟ v.8
℟ **Let us see, O Lord, your mercy.**

1 O Lord, you once favoured your land
and revived the fortunes of Jacob,
you forgave the guilt of your people
and covered all their sins.

(continued)

You averted all your rage,
you calmed the heat of your anger.

℟ **Let us see, O Lord, your mercy.**

2 Revive us now, God, our helper!
Put an end to your grievance against us.
Will you be angry with us for ever,
will your anger never cease? ℟

3 Will you not restore again our life
that your people may rejoice in you?
Let us see, O Lord, your mercy
and give us your saving help. ℟

Gospel Acclamation 1 Jn 2:5

Alleluia, alleluia!
When anyone obeys what Christ has said,
God's love comes to perfection in him.
Alleluia!

or Jn 14:23

Alleluia, alleluia!
If anyone loves me he will keep my word,
and my Father will love him,
and we shall come to him.
Alleluia!

GOSPEL

A reading from the holy Gospel according to Matthew 12:46-50

Stretching out his hand towards his disciples he said, 'Here are my mother and my brothers.'

Jesus was speaking to the crowds when his mother and his brothers appeared; they were standing outside and were anxious to have a word with him. But to the man who told him this Jesus replied, 'Who is my mother? Who are my brothers?' And stretching out his hand towards his disciples he said, 'Here are my mother and my brothers. Anyone who does the will of my Father in heaven, he is my brother and sister and mother.'

This is the Gospel of the Lord.

WEDNESDAY

FIRST READING

A reading from the prophet Jeremiah 1:1. 4-10
I have appointed you as prophet to the nations.

The words of Jeremiah son of Hilkiah, of a priestly family living at Anathoth in the territory of Benjamin.

The word of the Lord was addressed to me, saying,

'Before I formed you in the womb I knew you;
before you came to birth I consecrated you;
I have appointed you as prophet to the nations.'

I said, 'Ah, Lord; look, I do not know how to speak: I am a child!' But the Lord replied,

'Do not say, "I am a child."
Go now to those to whom I send you
and say whatever I command you.
Do not be afraid of them,
for I am with you to protect you –
it is the Lord who speaks!'

Then the Lord put out his hand and touched my mouth and said to me:

'There! I am putting my words into your mouth.
Look, today I am setting you
over nations and over kingdoms,
to tear up and to knock down,
to destroy and to overthrow,
to build and to plant.'

This is the word of the Lord.

Responsional Psalm Ps 70:1-6. 15. 17. ℟ cf. v.15

℟ **My lips will tell of your justice, O Lord.**

1 In you, O Lord, I take refuge;
let me never be put to shame.
In your justice rescue me, free me:
pay heed to me and save me. ℟

2 Be a rock where I can take refuge,
a mighty stronghold to save me;
for you are my rock, my stronghold.
Free me from the hand of the wicked. ℟

(continued)

3 It is you, O Lord, who are my hope,
   my trust, O Lord, since my youth.
   On you I have leaned from my birth,
   from my mother's womb you have been my help.

   ℟ **My lips will tell of your justice, O Lord.**

4 My lips will tell of your justice
   and day by day of your help.
   O God, you have taught me from my youth
   and I proclaim your wonders still. ℟

Gospel Acclamation   Ps 118:29. 35
   Alleluia alleluia!
   Bend my heart to your will, O Lord,
   and teach me your law.
   Alleluia!

or

   Alleluia, alleluia!
   The seed is the word of God, Christ the sower;
   whoever finds this seed will remain for ever.
   Alleluia!

GOSPEL

A reading from the holy Gospel according to Matthew   13:1-9
It produced crop a hundredfold.

Jesus left the house and sat by the lakeside, but such crowds gathered round him that he got into a boat and sat there. The people all stood on the beach, and he told them many things in parables.

He said, 'Imagine a sower going out to sow. As he sowed, some seeds fell on the edge of the path, and the birds came and ate them up. Others fell on patches of rock where they found little soil and sprang up straight away, because there was no depth of earth; but as soon as the sun came up they were scorched and, not having any roots, they withered away. Others fell among thorns, and the thorns grew up and choked them. Others fell on rich soil and produced their crop, some a hundredfold, some sixty, some thirty. Listen, anyone who has ears!'

This is the Gospel of the Lord.

THURSDAY

FIRST READING

A reading from the prophet Jeremiah   2:1-3. 7-8. 12-13

My people have abandoned me, the fountain of living water, only to dig cisterns for themselves, leaky cisterns that hold no water.

The word of the Lord was addressed to me saying, 'Go and shout this in the hearing of Jerusalem:

> ' "The Lord says this:
> I remember the affection of your youth,
> the love of your bridal days:
> you followed me through the wilderness,
> through a land unsown.
> Israel was sacred to the Lord,
> the first-fruits of his harvest;
> anyone who ate of this had to pay for it,
> misfortune came to them –
> it is the Lord who speaks."

> 'I brought you to a fertile country
> to enjoy its produce and good things;
> but no sooner had you entered than you defiled my land,
> and made my heritage detestable.
> The priests have never asked, "Where is the Lord?"
> Those who administer the Law have no knowledge of me.
> The shepherds have rebelled against me;
> the prophets have prophesied in the name of Baal,
> following things with no power in them.

> 'You heavens, stand aghast at this,
> stand stupefied, stand utterly appalled
> – it is the Lord who speaks –
> since my people have committed a double crime:
> they have abandoned me,
> the fountain of living water,
> only to dig cisterns for themselves,
> leaky cisterns
> that hold no water.'

This is the word of the Lord

Responsorial Psalm   Ps 35:6-11. R̥ v.10

   R̥ **In you, Lord, is the source of life.**

1. Your love, Lord, reaches to heaven;
   your truth to the skies.
   Your justice is like God's mountain,
   your judgements like the deep. R̥

2. O Lord, how precious is your love.
   My God, the sons of men
   find refuge in the shelter of your wings.
   They feast on the riches of your house;
   they drink from the stream of your delight. R̥

3. In you is the source of life
   and in your light we see light.
   Keep on loving those who know you,
   doing justice for upright hearts. R̥

Gospel Acclamation   cf. Ps 94:8

   Alleluia, alleluia!
   Harden not your hearts today,
   but listen to the voice of the Lord.
   Alleluia!

or   cf. Mt 11:25

   Alleluia, alleluia!
   Blessed are you, Father,
   Lord of heaven and earth,
   for revealing the mysteries of the kingdom
   to mere children.
   Alleluia!

GOSPEL

A reading from the holy Gospel according to Matthew   13:10-17

The mysteries of the kingdom of heaven are revealed to you, but they are not revealed to them.

The disciples went up to Jesus and asked, 'Why do you talk to the crowds in parables?' 'Because' he replied, 'the mysteries of the kingdom of heaven are revealed to you, but they are not revealed to them. For anyone who has will be given more, and he will have more than enough; but from anyone who has not, even what he has will be taken away. The reason I talk to them in parables is that they look without seeing and listen without hearing or understanding. So in their case this prophecy of Isaiah is being fulfilled:

> You will listen and listen again, but not understand,
> see and see again, but not perceive.
> For the heart of this nation has grown coarse,
> their ears are dull of hearing and they have shut their eyes
> for fear they should see with their eyes,
> hear with their ears,
> understand with their heart,
> and be converted
> and be healed by me.

But happy are your eyes because they see, your ears because they hear! I tell you solemnly, many prophets and holy men longed to see what you see, and never saw it; to hear what you hear, and never heard it.'

This is the Gospel of the Lord.

FRIDAY

FIRST READING

A reading from the prophet Jeremiah   3:14-17
I will give you shepherds after my own heart; all the nations will gather in Jerusalem.

'Come back, disloyal children – it is the Lord who speaks – for I alone am your Master. I will take one from a town, two from a clan, and bring you to Zion. I will give you shepherds after my own heart, and these shall feed you on knowledge and discretion. And when you have increased and become many in the land, then – it is the Lord who speaks – no one will ever say again: Where is the ark of the covenant of the Lord? There will be no thought of it, no memory of it, no regret for it, no making of another. When that time comes, Jerusalem shall be called: The Throne of the Lord; all the nations will gather there in the name of the Lord and will no longer follow the dictates of their own stubborn hearts.'

This is the word of the Lord.

Responsorial Psalm   Jer 31:10-13. ℟ cf. v.10

  ℟ **The Lord will guard us
as a shepherd guards his flock.**

1 O nations, hear the word of the Lord,
proclaim it to the far-off coasts.
Say: 'He who scattered Israel will gather him
and guard him as a shepherd guards his flock.'   ℟

2 For the Lord has ransomed Jacob,
has saved him from an overpowering hand.
They will come and shout for joy on Mount Zion,
they will stream to the blessings of the Lord.   ℟

3 Then the young girls will rejoice and dance,
the men, young and old, will be glad.
I will turn their mourning into joy,
I will console them, give gladness for grief.   ℟

Gospel Acclamation   James 1:21
Alleluia, alleluia!
Accept and submit to the word
which has been planted in you
and can save your souls.
Alleluia!

or   cf. Lk 8:15

Alleluia, alleluia!
Blessed are those who,
with a noble and generous heart,
take the word of God to themselves
and yield a harvest through their perseverance.
Alleluia!

GOSPEL

A reading from the holy Gospel according to Matthew   13:18-23
The man who hears the word and understands it, he is the one who yields a harvest.

Jesus said to his disciples: 'You are to hear the parable of the sower. When anyone hears the word of the kingdom without understanding, the evil one comes and carries off what was sown in his heart: this is the man who received the seed on the edge of the path. The one who received it on patches of rock is the man who hears the word and welcomes it at once with joy. But he has no root in him, he does not last; let some trial come, or some persecution on account of the word, and he falls away at once. The one who received the seed in thorns is the man who hears the word, but the worries of this world and the lure of riches choke the word and so he produces nothing. And the one who received the seed in rich soil is the man who hears the word and understands it; he is the one who yields a harvest and produces now a hundredfold, now sixty, now thirty.'

This is the Gospel of the Lord.

SATURDAY

FIRST READING

A reading from the prophet Jeremiah 7:1-11
Do you take this temple that bears my name for a robber's den?

The word that was addressed to Jeremiah by the Lord, 'Go and stand at the gate of the Temple of the Lord and there proclaim this message. Say, "Listen to the word of the Lord, all you men of Judah who come in by these gates to worship the Lord. The Lord of hosts, the God of Israel, says this: Amend your behaviour and your actions and I will stay with you here in this place. Put no trust in delusive words like these: This is the sanctuary of the Lord, the sanctuary of the Lord, the sanctuary of the Lord! But if you do amend your behaviour and your actions, if you treat each other fairly, if you do not exploit the stranger, the orphan and the widow (if you do not shed innocent blood in this place), and if you do not follow alien gods, to your own ruin, then here in this place I will stay with you, in the land that long ago I gave to your father for ever. Yet here you are, trusting in delusive words, to no purpose! Steal, would you, murder, commit adultery, perjure yourselves, burn incense to Baal, follow alien gods that you do not know? – and then come presenting yourselves in this Temple that bears my name, saying: Now we are safe – safe to go on committing all these abominations! Do you take this Temple that bears my name for a robbers' den? I, at any rate, am not blind – it is the Lord who speaks."'

This is the word of the Lord.

Responsorial Psalm   Ps 83:3-6. 8. 11. R̷ v.2

   R̷ **How lovely is your dwelling place, Lord, God of hosts.**

1. My soul is longing and yearning,
is yearning for the courts of the Lord.
My heart and my soul ring out their joy
to God, the living God.   R̷

2. The sparrow herself finds a home
and the swallow a nest for her brood;
she lays her young by your altars,
Lord of hosts, my king and my God.   R̷

3. They are happy, who dwell in your house,
for ever singing your praise.
They are happy, whose strength is in you;
they walk with ever growing strength.   R̷

4. One day within your courts
is better than a thousand elsewhere.
The threshold of the house of God
I prefer to the dwellings of the wicked.   R̷

Gospel Acclamation   Heb 4:12
   Alleluia, alleluia!
   The word of God is something alive and active;
   it can judge secret emotions and thoughts.
   Alleluia!

or   James 1:21

   Alleluia, alleluia!
   Accept and submit to the word
   which has been planted in you
   and can save your souls.
   Alleluia!

GOSPEL

A reading from the holy Gospel according to Matthew   13:24-30
Let them both grow till the harvest.

Jesus put a parable before the crowds, 'The kingdom of heaven may be compared to a man who sowed good seed in his field. While everybody was asleep his enemy came, sowed darnel all among the wheat, and made off. When the new wheat sprouted and ripened, the darnel appeared as well. The owner's servants went to him and said, "Sir, was it not good seed that you sowed in your field? If so, where does the darnel come from?" "Some enemy has done this," he answered. And the servants said, "Do you want us to go and weed it out?" But he said, "No, because when you weed out the darnel you might pull up the wheat with it. Let them both grow till the harvest; and at harvest time I shall say to the reapers: First collect the darnel and tie it in bundles to be burnt, then gather the wheat into my barn." '

This is the Gospel of the Lord.

SEVENTEENTH WEEK IN ORDINARY TIME
Year II

MONDAY

FIRST READING

A reading from the prophet Jeremiah 13:1-11

The people will become like this loincloth, good for nothing.

The Lord said this to me, 'Go and buy a linen loincloth and put it round your waist. But do not dip it in water.' And so, as the Lord has ordered, I bought a loincloth and put it round my waist. A second time the word of the Lord was spoken to me, 'Take the loincloth that you have bought and are wearing round your waist; up! Go to the Euphrates and hide it in a hole in the rock.' So I went and hid it near the Euphrates as the Lord had ordered me. Many days afterwards the Lord said to me, 'Get up and go to the Euphrates and fetch the loincloth I ordered you to hide there.' So I went to the Euphrates, and I searched, and I took the loincloth from the place where I had hidden it. The loincloth was spoilt, good for nothing. Then the word of the Lord was addressed to me, 'Thus says the Lord: In the same way I will spoil the arrogance of Judah and Jerusalem. This evil people who refuse to listen to my words, who follow the dictates of their own hard hearts, who have followed alien gods, and served them and worship- ped them, let them become like this loincloth, good for nothing. For just as a loincloth clings to a man's waist, so I had intended the whole House of Judah to cling to me – it is the Lord who speaks – to be my people, my glory, my honour and my boast. But they have not listened.'

This is the word of the Lord.

Responsorial Psalm   Deut 32:18-21. ℟ cf. v.18

   ℟ **You forget the God who fathered you.**

1. You forget the Rock who begot you,
   unmindful now of the God who fathered you.
   The Lord had seen this, and in his anger
   cast off his sons and his daughters. ℟

2. 'I shall hide my face from them,' he says
   'and see what becomes of them.
   For they are a deceitful brood,
   children with no loyalty in them. ℟

3. 'They have roused me to jealousy with what is no god,
   they have angered me with their beings of nothing;
   I, then, will rouse them to jealousy with what is no people.
   I will anger them with an empty-headed nation.' ℟

Gospel Acclamation   cf. 2 Thess 2:14

   Alleluia, alleluia!
   Through the Good News God called us
   to share the glory of our Lord Jesus Christ.
   Alleluia!

or   James 1:18

   Alleluia, alleluia!
   By his own choice the Father made us his children
   by the message of the truth,
   so that we should be a sort of first-fruits
   of all that he created.
   Alleluia!

GOSPEL

A reading from the holy Gospel according to Matthew   13:31-35

A mustard seed becomes a tree so that the birds of the air shelter in its branches.

Jesus put a parable before the crowds, 'The kingdom of heaven is like a mustard seed which a man took and sowed in his field. It is the smallest of all the seeds, but when it has grown it is the biggest shrub of all and becomes a tree so that the birds of the air come and shelter in its branches.'

   He told them another parable, 'The kingdom of heaven is like the yeast a woman took and mixed in with three measures of flour till it was leavened all through.'

In all this Jesus spoke to the crowds in parables; indeed, he would never speak to them except in parables. This was to fulfil the prophecy:

> I will speak to you in parables
> and expound things hidden since the foundation of the world.

This is the Gospel of the Lord.

TUESDAY

FIRST READING

A reading from the prophet Jeremiah 14:17-22
Remember, Lord, do not break your covenant with us.

The Lord said to me:

Say this word to the people:
'Tears flood my eyes
night and day, unceasingly,
since a crushing blow falls on the daughter of my people,
a most grievous injury.
If I go into the countryside,
there lie men killed by the sword;
if I go into the city,
I see people sick with hunger;
even prophets and priests
plough the land: they are at their wit's end.'

'Have you rejected Judah altogether?
Does your very soul revolt at Zion?
Why have you struck us down without hope of cure?
We were hoping for peace – no good came of it!
For the moment of cure – nothing but terror!
Lord, we do confess our wickedness
and our father's guilt:
we have indeed sinned against you.
For your name's sake do not reject us,
do not dishonour the throne of your glory.
Remember us; do not break your covenant with us.
Can any of the pagan Nothings make it rain?
Can the heavens produce showers?
No, it is you, Lord.
O our God, you are our hope,

since it is you who do all this.'

This is the word of the Lord.

Responsorial Psalm   Ps 78:8-9. 11. 13. ℟ v.9

℟ **Rescue us, O Lord,**
   for the glory of your name.

1. Do not hold the guilt of our fathers against us.
   Let your compassion hasten to meet us.
   for we are in the depths of distress. ℟

2. O God our saviour, come to our help,
   come for the sake of the glory of your name.
   O Lord our God, forgive us our sins;
   rescue us for the sake of your name. ℟

3. Let the groans of the prisoners come before you;
   let your strong arm reprieve those condemned to die.
   But we, your people, the flock of your pasture,
   will give you thanks for ever and ever.
   We will tell your praise from age to age. ℟

Gospel Acclamation   1 Peter 1:25

Alleluia, alleluia!
The word of the Lord remains for ever:
What is this word?
It is the Good News that has been brought to you.
Alleluia!

or

Alleluia, alleluia!
The seed is the word of God, Christ the sower;
whoever finds this seed will remain for ever.
Alleluia!

GOSPEL

A reading from the holy Gospel according to Matthew   13:36-43

Just as the darnel is gathered up and burnt in the fire, so it will be at the end of the time.

Leaving the crowds, Jesus went to the house, and his disciples came to him and said, 'Explain the parable about the darnel in the field to us.' He said in reply, 'The sower of the good seed is the Son of Man. The field is the world; the good seed is the subjects of the kingdom; the darnel, the subjects of the evil one; the enemy who sowed them, the devil; the harvest is the end of the world; the reapers are the angels. Well then, just as the darnel is gathered up and burnt in the fire, so it will be at the end of time. The Son of Man will send his angels and they will gather out of his kingdom all things that provoke offences and all who do evil, and throw them into the blazing furnace, where there will be weeping and grinding of teeth. Then the virtuous will shine like the sun in the kingdom of their Father. Listen, anyone who has ears!'

This is the Gospel of the Lord.

WEDNESDAY

FIRST READING

A reading from the prophet Jeremiah 15:10. 16-21

Why is my suffering continual? If you come back, I will take you back into my service.

Woe is me, my mother, for you have borne me
to be a man of strife and of dissension for all the land.
I neither lend nor borrow,
yet all of them curse me
and avenge me on my persecutors.
Your anger is very slow: do not let me be snatched away.
Realise that I suffer insult for your sake.
When your words came, I devoured them:
your word was my delight
and the joy of my heart;
for I was called by your name,
Lord, God of hosts.
I never took pleasure in sitting in scoffers' company;
with your hand on me I held myself aloof,
since you had filled me with indignation.
Why is my suffering continual,
my wound incurable, refusing to be healed?
Do you mean to be for me a deceptive stream
with inconstant waters?

To which the Lord replied,

'If you come back,
I will take you back into my service;

and if you utter noble, not despicable, thoughts,
you shall be as my own mouth.
They will come back to you,
but you must not go back to them.
I will make you
a bronze wall fortified against this people.
They will fight against you
but they will not overcome you,
because I am with you
to save you and to deliver you
– it is the Lord who speaks.
I mean to deliver you from the hands of the wicked
and redeem you from the clutches of the violent.'

This is the word of the Lord.

Responsorial Psalm   Ps 58:2-5. 10-11. 17-18. ℞ v.17

℞ **O God, you have been a refuge in the day of my distress.**

1. Rescue me, God, from my foes;
   protect me from those who attack me.
   O rescue me from those who do evil
   and save me from blood-thirsty men. ℞

2. See, they lie in wait for my life;
   powerful men band together against me.
   For no offence, no sin of mine, Lord,
   for no guilt of mine they rush to take their stand. ℞

3. O my Strength, it is you to whom I turn,
   for you, O God, are my stronghold,
   the God who shows me love. ℞

4. As for me, I will sing of your strength
   and each morning acclaim your love
   for you have been my stronghold,
   a refuge in the day of my distress. ℞

5. O my Strength, it is you to whom I turn,
   for you, O God, are my stronghold,
   the God who shows me love. ℞

Gospel Acclamation   Ps 118:105
Alleluia, alleluia!
Your word is a lamp for my steps
and a light for my path.
Alleluia!

Seventeenth Week in Ordinary Time, Year II: Thursday

or   Jn 15:15

Alleluia, alleluia!
I call you friends, says the Lord,
because I have made known to you
everything I have learnt from my Father.
Alleluia!

GOSPEL

A reading from the holy Gospel according to Matthew   13:44-46
He sells everything he owns and buys the field.

Jesus said to the crowds: 'The kingdom of heaven is like treasure hidden in a field which someone has found; he hides it again, goes off happy, sells everything he owns and buys the field.

'Again, the kingdom of heaven is like a merchant looking for fine pearls; when he finds one of great value he goes and sells everything he owns and buys it.'

This is the Gospel of the Lord.

THURSDAY

FIRST READING

A reading from the prophet Jeremiah   18:1-6
As the clay is in the potter's hand, so are you in mine.

The word that was addressed to Jeremiah by the Lord, 'Get up and make your way down to the potter's house; there I shall let you hear what I have to say.' So I went down to the potter's house; and there he was, working at the wheel. And whenever the vessel he was making came out wrong, as happens with the clay handled by potters, he would start afresh and work it into another vessel, as potters do. Then this word of the Lord was addressed to me, 'House of Israel, can not I do to you what this potter does? – it is the Lord who speaks. Yes, as the clay is in the potter's hand, so you are in mine, House of Israel.'

This is the word of the Lord.

Responsorial Psalm   Ps 145:2-6. ℟ v.5

   ℟ **He is happy who is helped by Jacob's God.**

or

   ℟ **Alleluia!**

1. My soul, give praise to the Lord;
I will praise the Lord all my days,
make music to my God while I live. ℟

2. Put no trust in princes,
in mortal men in whom there is no help.
Take their breath, they return to clay
and their plans that day come to nothing. ℟

3. He is happy who is helped by Jacob's God,
whose hope is in the Lord his God,
who alone made heaven and earth,
the seas and all they contain. ℟

Gospel Acclamation   Jn 15:15
Alleluia, alleluia!
I call you friends, says the Lord,
because I have made known to you
everything I have learnt from my Father.
Alleluia!

or   cf. Acts 16:14

Alleluia, alleluia!
Open our heart, O Lord,
to accept the words of your Son.
Alleluia!

GOSPEL

A reading from the holy Gospel according to Matthew   13:47-53
They collect the good ones in a basket and throw away those that are no use.

Jesus said to the crowds: 'The kingdom of heaven is like a dragnet cast into the sea that brings in a haul of all kinds. When it is full, the fishermen haul it ashore; then, sitting down, they collect the good ones in a basket and throw away those that are no use. This is how it will be at the end of time; the angels will appear and separate the wicked from the just to throw them into the blazing furnace where there will be weeping and grinding of teeth.

'Have you understood all this?' They said, 'Yes.' And he said to them, 'Well then, every scribe who becomes a disciple of the kingdom of heaven is like a householder who brings out from his storeroom things both new and old.'

When Jesus had finished these parables he left the district.

This is the Gospel of the Lord.

FRIDAY

FIRST READING

A reading from the prophet Jeremiah 26:1-9

The people were all crowding round in the Temple of the Lord.

At the beginning of the reign of Jehoiakim son of Josiah, king of Judah, this word was addressed to Jeremiah by the Lord. 'The Lord says this: Stand in the court of the Temple of the Lord. To all the people of the towns of Judah who come to worship in the Temple of the Lord you must speak all the words I have commanded you to tell them; do not omit one syllable. Perhaps they will listen and each turn from his evil way: if so, I shall relent and not bring the disaster on them which I intended for their misdeeds. Say to them, "The Lord says this: If you will not listen to me by following my Law which I put before you, by paying attention to the words of my servants the prophets whom I send so persistently to you, without you ever listening to them, I will treat this Temple as I treated Shiloh, and make this city a curse for all the nations of the earth."'

The priests and prophets and all the people heard Jeremiah say these words in the Temple of the Lord. When Jeremiah had finished saying everything that the Lord had ordered him to say to all the people, the priests and prophets seized hold of him and said, 'You shall die! Why have you made this prophecy in the name of the Lord, "This Temple will be like Shiloh, and this city will be desolate, and uninhabited"?' And the people were all crowding round Jeremiah in the Temple of the Lord.

This is the word of the Lord.

Responsorial Psalm Ps 68:5. 8-10. 14. ℟ v.14

℟ **In your great love, answer me, O God.**

1 More numerous than the hairs on my head
  are those who hate me without cause.

Those who attack me with lies
are too much for my strength.
How can I restore
what I have never stolen?

℟ **In your great love, answer me, O God.**

2 It is for you that I suffer taunts,
that shame covers my face,
that I have become a stranger to my brothers,
an alien to my own mother's sons.
I burn with zeal for your house
and taunts against you fall on me. ℟

3 This is my prayer to you,
my prayer for your favour.
In your great love, answer me, O God,
with your help that never fails. ℟

Gospel Acclamation cf. 1 Thess 2:13
Alleluia, alleluia!
Accept God's message for what it really is:
God's message, and not some human thinking.
Alleluia!

or 1 Peter 1:25
Alleluia, alleluia!
The word of the Lord remains for ever:
What is this word?
It is the Good News that has been brought to you.
Alleluia!

GOSPEL

A reading from the holy Gospel according to Matthew 13:54-58

This is the carpenter's son, surely? Where did the man get this wisdom and these miraculous powers?

Coming to his home town, Jesus taught the people in their synagogue in such a way that they were astonished and said, 'Where did the man get this wisdom and these miraculous powers? This is the carpenter's son, surely? Is not his mother the woman called Mary, and his brothers James and Joseph and Simon and Jude? His sisters, too, are they not all here with us? So where did the man get it all?' And they would not accept him. But Jesus said to them, 'A prophet is only despised in his own country and in his own house,' and he did not work many miracles there because of their lack of faith.

This is the Gospel of the Lord.

SATURDAY

FIRST READING

A reading from the prophet Jeremiah 26:11-16. 24
The Lord has truly sent me to you to say all these words.

The priests and prophets addressed the officials and all the people: 'This man deserves to die, since he has prophesied against this city, as you have heard with your own ears.' Jeremiah, however, replied to the people as follows, 'The Lord himself sent me to say all the things you have heard against this Temple and this city. So now amend your behaviour and actions, listen to the voice of the Lord your God: if you do, he will relent and not bring down on you the disaster he has pronounced against you. For myself, I am as you see in your hands. Do whatever you please or think right with me. But be sure of this, that if you put me to death, you will be bringing innocent blood on yourselves, on this city and on its citizens, since the Lord has truly sent me to you to say all these words in your hearing.'

The officials and all the people then said to the priests and prophets, 'This man does not deserve to die: he has spoken to us in the name of the Lord our God.' And Jeremiah had a protector in Ahikam son of Shaphan, so he was not handed over to the people to be put to death.

This is the word of the Lord.

Responsorial Psalm Ps 68:15-16. 30-31. 33-34. ℟ cf. v.14

℟ **In your great love, answer me, O God.**

1 Rescue me from sinking in the mud;
  save me from my foes.
  Save me from the waters of the deep
  lest the waves overwhelm me.
  Do not let the deep engulf me
  nor death close its mouth on me. ℟

2 As for me in my poverty and pain
  let your help, O God, lift me up.

(continued)

I will praise God's name with a song;
I will glorify him with thanksgiving.

℟ **In your great love, answer me, O God.**

3 The poor when they see it will be glad
and God-seeking hearts will revive;
for the Lord listens to the needy
and does not spurn his servants in their chains. ℟

Gospel Acclamation Lk 8:15
Alleluia, alleluia!
Blessed are those who,
with a noble and generous heart,
take the word of God to themselves
and yield a harvest through their perseverance.
Alleluia!

or Mt 5:10

Alleluia, alleluia!
Happy those who are persecuted
in the cause of right.
for theirs is the kingdom of heaven.
Alleluia!

GOSPEL

A reading from the holy Gospel according to Matthew 14:1-12
Herod sent and had John beheaded. John's disciples went off to tell Jesus.

Herod the tetrarch heard about the reputation of Jesus, and said to his court, 'This is John the Baptist himself; he has risen from the dead, and that is why miraculous powers are at work in him.'

Now it was Herod who had arrested John, chained him up and put him in prison because of Herodias, his brother Philip's wife. For John had told him, 'It is against the Law for you to have her.' He had wanted to kill him but was afraid of the people, who regarded John as a prophet. Then, during the celebrations for Herod's birthday, the daughter of Herodias danced before the company, and so delighted Herod that he promised on oath to give her anything she asked. Prompted by her mother she said, 'Give me John the Baptist's head, here, on a dish.' The king was distressed but, thinking of the oaths he had sworn and of his guests, he ordered it to be given her, and sent and had John beheaded in the prison. The head was brought in on a dish and given to the girl who took it to her mother. John's disciples came and took the body and buried it; then they went off to tell Jesus.

This is the Gospel of the Lord.

EIGHTEENTH WEEK IN ORDINARY TIME
Year II

MONDAY

FIRST READING

A reading from the prophet Jeremiah   28:1-17

Hananiah, the Lord has not sent you; and thanks to you this people are now relying on what is false.

At the beginning of the reign of Zedekiah king of Judah in the fifth month of the fourth year, the prophet Hananiah son of Azzur, a Gibeonite, spoke as follows to Jeremiah in the Temple of the Lord in the presence of the priests and of all the people. 'The Lord, the God of Israel, says this, "I have broken the yoke of the king of Babylon. In two years' time I will bring back all the vessels of the Temple of the Lord which Nebuchadnezzar king of Babylon carried off from this place and took to Babylon. And I will also bring back Jeconiah son of Jehoiakim, king of Judah, and all the exiles of Judah who have gone to Babylon – it is the Lord who speaks. Yes, I am going to break the yoke of the king of Babylon." '

The prophet Jeremiah then replied to the prophet Hananiah in front of the priests and all the people there in the Temple of the Lord. 'I hope so' the prophet Jeremiah said. 'May the Lord do so. May he fulfil the words that you have prophesied and bring the vessels of the Temple of the Lord and all the exiles back to this place from Babylon. Listen carefully, however, to this word I am now going to say for you and all the people to hear: From remote times, the prophets who preceded you and me prophesied war, famine and plague for many countries and for great kingdoms; but the prophet who prophesies peace can only be recognised as one truly sent by the Lord when his word comes true.'

The prophet Hananiah then took the yoke off the neck of the prophet Jeremiah and broke it. In front of all the people Hananiah then said, 'The Lord says this, "This is how, two years hence, I will break the yoke of Nebuchadnezzar king of Babylon and take it off the necks of all the nations." ' At this, the prophet Jeremiah went away.

After the prophet Hananiah had broken the yoke which he had taken off the neck of the prophet Jeremiah the word of the Lord was addressed to Jeremiah, 'Go to Hananiah and tell him this, "The Lord says this: You can break wooden yokes? Right, I will make them iron yokes instead! For the Lord of hosts, the God of Israel, says this: An iron yoke is what I now lay on the necks of all these nations to subject them to Nebuchadnezzar king of Babylon. (They will be subject to him; I have even given him the wild animals.)"'

The prophet Jeremiah said to the prophet Hananiah, 'Listen carefully Hananiah: the Lord has not sent you; and thanks to you this people are now relying on what is false. Hence – the Lord says this, "I am going to throw you off the face of the earth: you are going to die this year (since you have preached apostasy from the Lord)."'

The prophet Hananiah died the same year, in the seventh month.

This is the word of the Lord.

Responsorial Psalm   Ps 118:29. 43. 79-80. 95. 102. R/ v.68

R/ **Lord, teach me your statutes.**

1 Keep me from the way of error
   and teach me your law.
   Do not take the word of truth from my mouth
   for I trust in your decrees.   R/

2 Let your faithful turn to me,
   those who know your will.
   Let my heart be blameless in your statutes
   lest I be ashamed.   R/

3 Though the wicked lie in wait to destroy me
   yet I ponder on your will.
   I have not turned away from your decrees;
   you yourself have taught me.   R/

Gospel Acclamation   Jn 14:6
Alleluia, alleluia!
I am the Way, the Truth and the Life, says the Lord;
no one can come to the Father except through me.
Alleluia!

Eighteenth Week in Ordinary Time, Year II: Monday

or   Mt 4:4

Alleluia, alleluia!
Man does not live on bread alone,
but on every word that comes from the mouth of God.
Alleluia!

GOSPEL

A reading from the holy Gospel according to Matthew   14:13-21

Jesus raised his eyes to heaven and said the blessing. He handed the loaves to his disciples who gave them to the crowds.

When Jesus received the news of John the Baptist's death he withdrew by boat to a lonely place where they could be by themselves. But the people heard of this and, leaving the towns, went after him on foot. So as he stepped ashore he saw a large crowd; and he took pity on them and healed their sick.

When evening came, the disciples went to him and said, 'This is a lonely place, and the time has slipped by; so send the people away, and they can go to the villages to buy themselves some food.' Jesus replied, 'There is no need for them to go: give them something to eat yourselves.' But they answered, 'All we have with us is five loaves and two fish.' 'Bring them here to me,' he said. He gave orders that the people were to sit down on the grass; then he took the five loaves and the two fish, raised his eyes to heaven and said the blessing. And breaking the loaves he handed them to his disciples who gave them to the crowds. They all ate as much as they wanted, and they collected the scraps remaining, twelve baskets full. Those who ate numbered about five thousand men, to say nothing of women and children.

This is the Gospel of the Lord.

Alternative Gospel

This is to be used in Year A, when the Gospel given above is read on the preceding Sunday.

A reading from the holy Gospel according to Matthew   14:22-36

Tell me to come to you across the water.

When Jesus heard of the death of John the Baptist, he made the disciples get into the boat and go on ahead to the other side while he would send the crowds away. After sending the crowds away he went up into the hills by himself to pray. When evening came, he was there alone, while the boat, by now far out on the lake, was battling with a heavy sea, for there was a head-wind. In the fourth watch of the night he went towards them, walking on the lake, and when the disciples saw him on the lake they were terrified. 'It is a ghost' they said, and cried out in fear. But at once Jesus called out to them, saying, 'Courage! It is I! do not be afraid.' It was Peter who answered. 'Lord,' he said 'if it is you, tell me to come to you across the water.' 'Come' said Jesus. Then Peter got out of the boat and started walking towards Jesus across the water, but as soon as he felt the force of the wind, he took fright and began to sink. 'Lord! Save me!' he cried. Jesus put out his hand at once and held him. 'Man of little faith,' he said 'why did you doubt?' And as they got into the boat the wind dropped. The men in the boat bowed down before him and said, 'Truly, you are the Son of God.'

Having made the crossing, they came to land at Gennesaret. When the local people recognised him they spread the news through the whole neighbourhood and took all that were sick to him, begging him just to let them touch the fringe of his cloak. And all those who touched it were completely cured.

This is the Gospel of the Lord.

TUESDAY

FIRST READING

A reading from the prophet Jeremiah 30:1-2. 12-15. 18-22

So many are your sins, that I have done this to you. I will restore the tents of Jacob.

The word addressed to Jeremiah by the Lord: The Lord, the God of Israel says this: Write all the words I have spoken to you in a book.

Yes, the Lord says this:
Your wound is incurable,
your injury past healing.
There is no one to care for your sore,
no medicine to make you well again.
All your lovers have forgotten you,
they look for you no more.

Eighteenth Week in Ordinary Time, Year II: Tuesday

Yes, I have struck you as an enemy strikes,
with harsh punishment
(so great is your guilt, so many your sins).
Why bother to complain about your wound?
Your pain is incurable.
So great is your guilt, so many your sins,
that I have done all this to you.

The Lord says this:
Now I will restore the tents of Jacob,
and take pity on his dwellings:
the city shall be rebuilt on its ruins,
the citadel restored on its site.
From them will come thanksgiving
and shouts of joy.
I will make them increase, and not diminish them,
make them honoured, and not disdained.
Their sons shall be as once they were,
their community fixed firm in my presence,
and I will punish all their oppressors.
Their prince will be one of their own,
their ruler come from their own people.
I will let him come freely into my presence and he can come
 close to me;
who else, indeed, would risk his life
by coming close to me? – it is the Lord who speaks.
And you shall be my people and I will be your God.

This is the word of the Lord.

Responsorial Psalm   Ps 101:16-21. 29. 22-3. ℟ v.17

℟ **The Lord shall build up Zion again
and appear in all his glory.**

1 The nations shall fear the name of the Lord
 and all the earth's kings your glory,
 when the Lord shall build up Zion again
 and appear in all his glory.
 Then he will turn to the prayers of the helpless;
 he will not despise their prayers. ℟

2 Let this be written for ages to come
 that a people yet unborn may praise the Lord;
 for the Lord leaned down from his sanctuary on high.
 He looked down from heaven to the earth

that he might hear the groans of the prisoners
and free those condemned to die.

℟ **The Lord shall build up Zion again
and appear in all his glory.**

3 The sons of your servants shall dwell untroubled
and their race shall endure before you
that the name of the Lord may be proclaimed to Zion
and his praise in the heart of Jerusalem,
when peoples and kingdoms are gathered together
to pay their homage to the Lord.   ℟

Gospel Acclamation   Jn 8:12
Alleluia, alleluia!
I am the light of the world, says the Lord,
anyone who follows me
will have the light of life.
Alleluia!

or   Jn 1:49

Alleluia, alleluia!
Rabbi, you are the Son of God,
you are the King of Israel.
Alleluia!

GOSPEL

A reading from the holy Gospel according to Matthew   14:22-36
Tell me to come to you across the water.

When the crowds had eaten their fill Jesus made the disciples get into the boat and go on ahead to the other side while he would send the crowds away. After sending the crowds away he went up into the hills by himself to pray. When evening came, he was there alone, while the boat, by now far out on the lake, was battling with a heavy sea, for there was a headwind. In the fourth watch of the night he went towards them, walking on the lake, and when the disciples saw him walking on the lake they were terrified. 'It is a ghost' they said, and cried out in fear. But at once Jesus called out to them, saying, 'Courage! It is I! Do not be afraid.' It was Peter who answered. 'Lord,' he said 'if it is you, tell me to come to you across the water.' 'Come' said Jesus. Then Peter got out of the boat and started walking towards Jesus across the water, but as soon as he felt the force of the wind, he took fright and began to sink. 'Lord! Save me!' he cried. Jesus put out his hand at once and held him. 'Man of little faith,' he said 'why did you doubt?' And as they got into the boat the wind dropped. The men in the boat bowed down before him and said, 'Truly, you are the Son of God.'

Having made the crossing, they came to land at Gennesaret. When the local people recognised him they spread the news through the whole neighbourhood and took all that were sick to him, begging him just to let them touch the fringe of his cloak. And all those who touched it were completely cured.

This is the Gospel of the Lord.

Alternative Gospel

This is to be used in Year A, when the Gospel given above is read on the preceding Monday.

A reading from the holy Gospel according to Matthew 15:1-2. 10-14

Any plant my Father has not planted will be pulled up by the roots.

Pharisees and scribes from Jerusalem came to Jesus and said, 'Why do your disciples break away from the tradition of the elders? They do not wash their hands when they eat food.'

He called the people to him and said, 'Listen, and understand. What goes into the mouth does not make a man unclean; it is what comes out of the mouth that makes him unclean.'

Then the disciples came to him and said, 'Do you know that the Pharisees were shocked when they heard what you said?' He replied, 'Any plant my heavenly Father has not planted will be pulled up by the roots. Leave them alone. They are blind men leading blind men; and if one blind man leads another, both will fall into a pit.'

This is the Gospel of the Lord.

WEDNESDAY

FIRST READING

A reading from the prophet Jeremiah 31:1-7
I have loved you with an everlasting love.

I will be the God of all the clans of Israel – it is the Lord who speaks – they shall be my people.

> The Lord says this:
> They have found pardon in the wilderness,
> those who have survived the sword.
> Israel is marching to his rest.
> The Lord has appeared to him from afar:
> I have loved you with an everlasting love,
> so I am constant in my affection for you.
> I build you once more; you shall be rebuilt,
> virgin of Israel.
> Adorned once more, and with your tambourines,
> you will go out dancing gaily.
> You will plant vineyards once more
> on the mountains of Samaria
> (the planters have done their planting: they will gather the fruit).
> Yes, a day will come when the watchmen shout
> on the mountains of Ephraim,
> 'Up! Let us go up to Zion,
> to the Lord our God!'
>
> For the Lord says this:
> Shout with joy for Jacob!
> Hail the chief of nations!
> Proclaim! Praise! Shout:
> 'The Lord has saved his people,
> the remnant of Israel!'

This is the word of the Lord.

Responsorial Psalm
Jer 31:10-13. ℟ cf. v.10

℟ **The Lord will guard us
as a shepherd guards his flock.**

1 O nations, hear the word of the Lord,
   proclaim it to the far-off coasts.
   Say: 'He who scattered Israel will gather him

Eighteenth Week in Ordinary Time, Year II: Wednesday

and guard him as a shepherd guards his flock.'   ℟

2 For the Lord has ransomed Jacob,
   has saved him from an overpowering hand.
   They will come and shout for joy on Mount Zion,
   they will stream to the blessings of the Lord.   ℟

3 Then the young girls will rejoice and dance,
   the men, young and old, will be glad.
   I will turn their mourning into joy,
   I will console them, give gladness for grief.   ℟

Gospel Acclamation   James 1:18

Alleluia, alleluia!
By his own choice the Father made us his children
by the message of the truth,
so that we should be a sort of first-fruits
of all that he created.
Alleluia!

or   Lk 7:16

Alleluia, alleluia!
A great prophet has appeared among us;
God has visited his people.
Alleluia!

GOSPEL

A reading from the holy Gospel according to Matthew   15:21-28
Woman, you have great faith.

Jesus left Gennesaret and withdrew to the region of Tyre and Sidon. Then out came a Canaanite woman from that district and started shouting, 'Sir, Son of David, take pity on me. My daughter is tormented by a devil.' But he answered her not a word. And his disciples went and pleaded with him. 'Give her what she wants,' they said 'because she is shouting after us.' He said in reply, 'I was sent only to the lost sheep of the House of Israel.' But the woman had come up and was kneeling at his feet. 'Lord,' she said 'help me.' He replied. 'It is not fair to take the children's food and throw it to the house-dogs.' She retorted, 'Ah yes, sir; but even house-dogs can eat the scraps that fall from their master's table.' Then Jesus answered her, 'Woman, you have great faith. Let your wish be granted.' And from that moment her daughter was well again.

This is the Gospel of the Lord.

THURSDAY

FIRST READING

A reading from the prophet Jeremiah 31:31-34

I will make a new covenant and will never call their sin to mind.

See, the days are coming – it is the Lord who speaks – when I will make a new covenant with the House of Israel and the House of Judah, but not a covenant like the one I made with their ancestors on the day I took them by the hand to bring them out of the land of Egypt. They broke that covenant of mine, so I had to show them who was master. It is the Lord who speaks. No, this is the covenant I will make with the House of Israel when those days arrive – it is the Lord who speaks. Deep within them I will plant my law, writing it on their hearts. Then I will be their God and they shall be my people. There will be no further need for neighbour to try to teach neighbour, or brother to say to brother, 'Learn to know the Lord!' No, they will all know me, the least no less than the greatest – it is the Lord who speaks – since I will forgive their iniquity and never call their sin to mind.

This is the word of the Lord.

Responsorial Psalm

Ps 50:12-15. 18-19. R/ v.12

R/ **A pure heart create for me, O God.**

1 A pure heart create for me, O God,
 put a steadfast spirit within me.
 Do not cast me away from your presence,
 nor deprive me of your holy spirit. R/

2 Give me again the joy of your help;
 with a spirit of fervour sustain me,
 that I may teach transgressors your ways
 and sinners may return to you. R/

3 For in sacrifice you take no delight,
 burnt offering from me you would refuse,
 my sacrifice, a contrite spirit.
 A humbled, contrite heart you will not spurn. R/

Gospel Acclamation

Ps 144:13

Alleluia, alleluia!
The Lord is faithful in all his words
and loving in all his deeds.
Alleluia!

or   Mt 16:18

Alleluia, alleluia!
You are Peter and on this rock I will build my Church.
And the gates of the underworld can never hold out against it.
Alleluia!

GOSPEL

A reading from the holy Gospel according to Matthew   16:13-23
You are Peter, and I will give you the keys of the kingdom of heaven.

When Jesus came to the region of Caesarea Philippi he put this question to his disciples, 'Who do people say the Son of Man is?' And they said, 'Some say he is John the Baptist, some Elijah, and others Jeremiah or one of the prophets.' 'But you,' he said 'who do you say I am?' Then Simon Peter spoke up, 'You are the Christ,' he said 'the Son of the living God.' Jesus replied, 'Simon son of Jonah, you are a happy man! Because it was not flesh and blood that revealed this to you but my Father in heaven. So I now say to you: You are Peter and on this rock I will build my Church. And the gates of the underworld can never hold out against it. I will give you the keys of the kingdom of heaven; whatever you bind on earth shall be considered bound in heaven; whatever you loose on earth shall be considered loosed in heaven.' Then he gave the disciples strict orders not to tell anyone that he was the Christ.

From that time Jesus began to make it clear to his disciples that he was destined to go to Jerusalem and suffer grievously at the hands of the elders and chief priests and scribes, to be put to death and to be raised up on the third day. Then, taking him aside, Peter started to remonstrate with him. 'Heaven preserve you, Lord,' he said 'this must not happen to you.' But he turned and said to Peter, 'Get behind me, Satan! You are an obstacle in my path, because the way you think is not God's way but man's.'

This is the Gospel of the Lord.

FRIDAY

FIRST READING

A reading from the prophet Nahum   2:1. 3; 3:1-3. 6-7
Woe to the city soaked in blood.

See, over the mountains the messenger hurries!

'Peace!' he proclaims.
Judah, celebrate your feasts,
carry out your vows,
for Belial will never pass through you again;
he is utterly annihilated.
Yes, the Lord is restoring the vineyard of Jacob
and the vineyard of Israel.
For the plunderers had plundered them,
they had broken off their branches.
Woe to the city soaked in blood,
full of lies,
stuffed with booty,
whose plunderings know no end!
The crack of the whip!
The rumble of wheels!
Galloping horse,
jolting chariot,
charging cavalry,
flash of swords,
gleam of spears . . .
a mass of wounded,
hosts of dead,
countless corpses;
they stumble over the dead.
I am going to pelt you with filth,
shame you, make you a public show.
And all who look on you
will turn their backs on you and say,
'Nineveh is a ruin.'
Could anyone pity her?
Where can I find anyone to comfort her?

   This is the word of the Lord.

Responsional Psalm   Deut 32:35-36. 39. 41. ℟ v.39
   ℟   **It is the Lord who deals death and life.**

1 It is close, the day of their ruin;
   their doom comes at speed.
   For the Lord will see his people righted,
   he will take pity on his servants.   ℟

2 See now that I, I am He,
   and beside me there is no other god.

It is I who deal death and life:
when I have struck it is I who heal. ℟

3 When I have whetted my flashing sword
I will take up the cause of Right,
I will give my foes as good again,
I will repay those who hate me. ℟

Gospel Acclamation   1 Sam 3:9; Jn 6:68
Alleluia, alleluia!
Speak, Lord, your servant is listening:
you have the message of eternal life.
Alleluia!

or   Mt 5:10

Alleluia, alleluia!
Happy those who are persecuted
in the cause of right,
for theirs is the kingdom of heaven.
Alleluia!

GOSPEL

A reading from the holy Gospel according to Matthew   16:24-28
What has a man to offer in exchange for his life?

Jesus said to his disciples, 'If anyone wants to be a follower of mine, let him renounce himself and take up his cross and follow me. For anyone who wants to save his life will lose it; but anyone who loses his life for my sake will find it. What, then, will a man gain if he wins the whole world and ruins his life? Or what has a man to offer in exchange for his life?

'For the Son of Man is going to come in the glory of his Father with his angels, and, when he does, he will reward each one according to his behaviour. I tell you solemnly, there are some of these standing here who will not taste death before they see the Son of Man coming with his kingdom.'

This is the Gospel of the Lord.

SATURDAY

FIRST READING

A reading from the prophet Habakkuk 1:12 – 2:4

The upright man will live by his faithfulness.

Are not you, from ancient times Lord,
my God, my Holy One, who never dies?
Lord, you have made this people an instrument of justice,
set it firm as a rock in order to punish.

Your eyes are too pure to rest on wickedness,
you cannot look on at tyranny.
Why do you look on while men are treacherous,
and stay silent while the evil man swallows a better man than he?
You treat mankind like fishes in the sea,
like creeping, masterless things.

A people, these, who catch all on their hook,
who draw them with their net,
in their dragnet gather them,
and so, triumphantly, rejoice.

At this, they offer a sacrifice to their net,
and burn incense to their dragnet,
for providing them with luxury
and lavish food.
Are they then to empty their net unceasingly,
slaughtering nations without pity?

I will stand on my watchtower,
and take up my post on my battlements,
watching to see what he will say to me,
what answer he will make to my complaints.

Then the Lord answered and said,
  'Write the vision down,
  inscribe it on tablets
  to be easily read,
  since this vision is for its own time only:
  eager for its own fulfilment, it does not deceive;
  if it comes slowly, wait,
  for come it will, without fail.

  'See, how he flags, he whose soul is not at rights,
  but the upright man will live by his faithfulness.'

This is the word of the Lord.

Eighteenth Week in Ordinary Time, Year II: Saturday

Responsorial Psalm   Ps 9:8-13. ℟ v.11

℟ **You will never forsake those who seek you, O Lord.**

1 The Lord sits enthroned for ever.
   He has set up his throne for judgement;
   he will judge the world with justice,
   he will judge the peoples with his truth. ℟

2 For the oppressed let the Lord be a stronghold,
   a stronghold in times of distress.
   Those who know your name will trust you:
   you will never forsake those who seek you. ℟

3 Sing psalms to the Lord who dwells in Zion.
   Proclaim his mighty works among the peoples;
   for the Avenger of blood has remembered them,
   and has not forgotten the cry of the poor. ℟

Gospel Acclamation   cf. Eph 1:17. 18
Alleluia, alleluia!
May the Father of our Lord Jesus Christ
enlighten the eyes of our mind,
so that we can see what hope his call holds for us.
Alleluia!

or   cf. 2 Tim 1:10

Alleluia, alleluia!
Our Saviour Christ Jesus abolished death,
and he has proclaimed life through the Good News.
Alleluia!

GOSPEL

A reading from the holy Gospel according to Matthew   17:14-20

If you had faith, nothing would be impossible for you.

A man came up to Jesus and went down on his knees before him. 'Lord,' he said 'take pity on my son: he is a lunatic and in a wretched state; he is always falling into the fire or into the water. I took him to your disciples and they were unable to cure him.' 'Faithless and perverse generation!' Jesus said in reply 'How much longer must I be with you? How much longer must I put up with you? Bring him here to me.' And when Jesus rebuked it the devil came out of the boy who was cured from that moment.

    Then the disciples came privately to Jesus. 'Why were we

unable to cast it out?' they asked. He answered, 'Because you have little faith. I tell you solemnly, if your faith were the size of a mustard seed you could say to this mountain, "Move from here to there", and it would move; nothing would be impossible for you.'

This is the Gospel of the Lord.

NINETEENTH WEEK IN ORDINARY TIME
Year II

MONDAY

FIRST READING

A reading from the prophet Ezekiel   1:2-5. 24-28
It was something that looked like the glory of the Lord.

On the fifth of the month – it was the fifth year of exile for King Jehoiachin – the word of the Lord was addressed to the priest Ezekiel son of Buzi, in the land of the Chaldaeans, on the bank of the river Chebar.

There the hand of the Lord came on me. I looked; a stormy wind blew from the north, a great cloud with light around it, a fire from which flashes of lightning darted, and in the centre a sheen like bronze at the heart of the fire. In the centre I saw what seemed four animals. They looked like this. They were of human form. I heard the noise of their wings as they moved; it sounded like rushing water, like the voice of Shaddai, a noise like a storm, like the noise of a camp; when they halted, they folded their wings, and there was a noise.

Above the vault over their heads was something that looked like a sapphire; it was shaped like a throne and high up on this throne was a being that looked like a man. I saw him shine like bronze, and close to and all around him from what seemed his loins upwards was what looked like fire; and from what seemed his loins downwards I saw what looked like fire, and a light all round like a bow in the clouds on rainy days; that is how the surrounding light appeared. It was something that looked like the glory of the Lord. I looked, and prostrated myself.

This is the word of the Lord.

Nineteenth Week in Ordinary Time, Year II: Monday 1089

Responsorial Psalm Ps 148:1-2. 11-14
℟ **Your glory fills all heaven and earth.**

or

℟ **Alleluia!**

1 Praise the Lord from the heavens,
 praise him, in the heights.
 Praise him, all his angels,
 praise him, all his host. ℟

2 All earth's kings and peoples, praise him,
 earth's princes and rulers;
 young men and maidens,
 old men together with children. ℟

3 Let them praise the name of the Lord
 for he alone is exalted.
 The splendour of his name
 reaches beyond heaven and earth. ℟

4 He exalts the strength of his people.
 He is the praise of all his saints,
 of the sons of Israel,
 of the people to whom he comes close. ℟

Gospel Acclamation Ps 147:12.15
 Alleluia, alleluia!
 O praise the Lord, Jerusalem!
 He sends out his word to the earth.
 Alleluia!

or cf. 2 Thess 2:14

 Alleluia, alleluia!
 Through the Good News God called us
 to share the glory of our Lord Jesus Christ.
 Alleluia!

GOSPEL

A reading from the holy Gospel according to Matthew 17:22-27
They will put the Son of Man to death, and he will be raised to life again. The sons are exempt from tribute.

One day when they were together in Galilee, Jesus said to his disciples 'The Son of Man is going to be handed over into the power of men; they will put him to death, and on the third day he will be raised to life again.' And a great sadness came over them.

When they reached Capernaum, the collectors of the half-shekel came to Peter and said, 'Does your master not pay the half-shekel?' 'Oh yes' he replied, and went into the house. But before he could speak, Jesus said, 'Simon, what is your opinion? From whom do the kings of the earth take toll or tribute? From their sons or from foreigners?' And when he replied, 'From foreigners,' Jesus said, 'Well then, the sons are exempt. However, so as not offend these people, go to the lake and cast a hook; take the first fish that bites, open its mouth and there you will find a shekel; take it and give it to them for me and for you.'

This is the Gospel of the Lord.

TUESDAY

FIRST READING

A reading from the prophet Ezekiel 2:8 – 3:4

He gave me the scroll to eat, and it tasted as sweet as honey.

I, Ezekiel, heard a voice speaking. It said, 'You, son of man, listen to the words I say; do not be a rebel like that rebellious set. Open your mouth and eat what I am about to give you.' I looked. A hand was there, stretching out to me and holding a scroll. He unrolled it in front of me; it was written on back and front; on it was written 'lamentations, wailings, moanings'. He said, 'Son of man, eat what is given to you; eat this scroll, then go and speak to the House of Israel.' I opened my mouth; he gave me the scroll to eat and said, 'Son of man, feed and be satisfied by the scroll I am giving you.' I ate it, and it tasted sweet as honey.

Then he said, 'Son of man, go to the House of Israel and tell them what I have said.'

This is the word of the Lord.

Responsorial Psalm Ps 118:14. 24. 72. 103. 111. 131. ℟ v.103

℟ **Your promise is sweet to my taste, O Lord.**

1 I rejoice to do your will
  as though all riches were mine.
  Your will is my delight;
  your statutes are my counsellors. ℟

Nineteenth Week in Ordinary Time, Year II: Tuesday 1091

2 The law from your mouth means more to me
 than silver and gold.
 Your promise is sweeter to my taste
 than honey in the mouth. ℟

3 Your will is my heritage for ever,
 the joy of my heart.
 I open my mouth and I sigh
 as I yearn for your commands. ℟

Gospel Acclamation cf. Mt 11:25
 Alleluia, alleluia!
 Blessed are you, Father,
 Lord of heaven and earth,
 for revealing the mysteries of the kingdom
 to mere children.
 Alleluia!

or Mt 11:29

 Alleuia, alleluia!
 Shoulder my yoke and learn from me, says the Lord,
 for I am gentle and humble in heart.
 Alleluia!

GOSPEL

A reading from the holy Gospel according 18:1-5. 10. 12-14
to Matthew
See that you never despise any of these little ones.

The disciples came to Jesus and said, 'Who is the greatest in the kingdom of heaven?' So he called a little child to him and set the child in front of them. Then he said, 'I tell you solemnly, unless you change and become like little children you will never enter the kingdom of heaven. And so, the one who makes himself as little as this little child is the greatest in the kingdom of heaven.

'Anyone who welcomes a little child like this in my name welcomes me.

'See that you never despise any of these little ones, for I tell you that their angels in heaven are continually in the presence of my Father in heaven.

'Tell me. Suppose a man has a hundred sheep and one of them strays; will he not leave the ninety-nine on the hillside and go in search of the stray? I tell you solemnly, if he finds it, it gives him more joy than do the ninety-nine that did not stray at all.

Similarly, it is never the will of your Father in heaven that one of these little ones should be lost.'

This is the Gospel of the Lord.

WEDNESDAY

FIRST READING

A reading from the prophet Ezekiel 9:1-7; 10:18-22

Mark a cross on the foreheads of all who deplore the filth practised in Jerusalem.

As I, Ezekiel, listened God shouted, 'Come here, you scourges of the city, and bring your weapons of destruction.' Immediately six men advanced from the upper north gate, each holding a deadly weapon. In the middle of them was a man in white, with a scribe's ink horn in his belt. They came in and halted in front of the bronze altar. The glory of the God of Israel rose off the cherubs where it had been and went up to the threshold of the Temple. He called the man in white with a scribe's ink horn in his belt and said, 'Go all through the city, all through Jerusalem, and mark a cross on the foreheads of all who deplore and disapprove of all the filth practised in it.' I heard him say to the others, 'Follow him through the city, and strike. Show neither pity nor mercy; old men, young men, virgins, children, women, kill and exterminate them all. But do not touch anyone with a cross on his forehead. Begin at my sanctuary.' So they began with the old men in front of the Temple. He said to them, 'Defile the Temple; fill the courts with corpses, and go.' They went out and hacked their way through the city.

The glory of the Lord came out from the Temple threshold and paused over the cherubs. The cherubs spread their wings and rose from the ground to leave, and as I watched the wheels rose with them. They paused at the entrance to the east gate of the Temple of the Lord, and the glory of the God of Israel hovered over them. This was the creature that I had seen supporting the God of Israel beside the river Chebar, and I was now certain that these were cherubs. Each had four faces and four wings and what seemed to be human hands under their wings. Their faces were just as I had seen them beside the river Chebar. Each moved straight forward.

This is the word of the Lord.

Responsorial Psalm
Ps 112:1-6. ℟ v.4

℟ **Above the heavens is the glory of the Lord.**

or

℟ **Alleluia!**

1 Praise, O servants of the Lord,
 praise the name of the Lord!
 May the name of the Lord be blessed
 both now and for evermore! ℟

2 From the rising of the sun to its setting
 praised be the name of the Lord!
 High above all nations is the Lord,
 above the heavens his glory. ℟

3 Who is like the Lord, our God,
 who has risen on high to his throne
 yet stoops from the heights to look down,
 to look down upon heaven and earth? ℟

Gospel Acclamation
Ps 110:7. 8

Alleluia, alleluia!
Your precepts, O Lord, are all of them sure;
they stand firm for ever and ever,
Alleluia!

or
2 Cor 5:19

Alleluia, alleluia!
God in Christ was reconciling the world to himself,
and he has entrusted to us the news that they are reconciled.
Alleluia!

GOSPEL

A reading from the holy Gospel according to Matthew 18:15-20
If he listens to you, you have won back your brother.

Jesus said to his disciples: If your brother does something wrong, go and have it out with him alone, between your two selves. If he listens to you, you have won back your brother. If he does not listen, take one or two others along with you: the evidence of two or three witnesses is required to sustain any charge. But if he refuses to listen to these, report it to the community; and if he refuses to listen to the community, treat him like a pagan or a tax collector.

'I tell you solemnly, whatever you bind on earth shall be considered bound in heaven; whatever you loose on earth shall be considered loosed in heaven.

'I tell you solemnly once again, if two of you on earth agree to ask anything at all, it will be granted to you by my Father in heaven. For where two or three meet in my name, I shall be there with them.'

This is the Gospel of the Lord.

THURSDAY

FIRST READING

A reading from the prophet Ezekiel 12:1-12
Emigrate by daylight when they can see you.

The word of the Lord was addressed to me as follows, 'Son of man, you are living with that set of rebels who have eyes and never see, ears and never hear, for they are a set of rebels. You, son of man, pack an exile's bundle and emigrate by daylight when they can see you, emigrate from where you are to somewhere else while they watch. Perhaps they will admit then that they are a set of rebels. You will pack your baggage like an exile's bundle, by daylight, for them to see, and leave like an exile in the evening, making sure that they are looking. As they watch, make a hole in the wall and go out through it. As they watch, you will shoulder your pack and go out into the dark; you will cover your face so that you cannot see the country, since I have made you a symbol for the House of Israel.'

I did as I had been told. I packed my baggage like an exile's bundle, by daylight; and in the evening I made a hole through the wall with my hand. I went out into the dark and shouldered my pack as they watched.

The next morning the word of the Lord was addressed to me as follows, 'Son of man, did not the House of Israel, did not that set of rebels, ask you what you were doing? Say, "The Lord says this: This oracle is directed against Jerusalem and the whole House of Israel wherever they are living." Say, "I am a symbol of you; the thing I have done will be done to them; they will go into exile, into banishment." Their ruler will shoulder his pack in the dark and go out through the wall; a hole will be made to let him out; he will cover his face rather than see the country.'

This is the word of the Lord.

Nineteenth Week in Ordinary Time, Year II: Thursday 1095

Responsorial Psalm Ps 77:56-59. 61-62. ℟ cf. v.7

℟ **Never forget the deeds of the Lord..**

1 They put God to the proof and defied him;
  they refused to obey the Most High.
  They strayed, as faithless as their fathers,
  like a bow on which the archer cannot count. ℟

2 With their mountain shrines they angered him;
  made him jealous with the idols they served.
  God saw and was filled with fury:
  he utterly rejected Israel. ℟

3 He gave his ark into captivity,
  his glorious ark into the hand of the foe.
  He gave up his people to the sword,
  in his anger against his chosen ones. ℟

Gospel Acclamation Ps 118:88

Alleluia, alleluia!
Because of your love give me life,
and I will do your will.
Alleluia!

or Ps 118:135

Allluia, alleluia!
Let your face shine on your servant,
and teach me your decrees.
Alleluia!

GOSPEL

A reading from the holy Gospel according to Matthew 18:21 – 19:1
Do not forgive seven times, I tell you, but seventy-seven times.

Peter went up to Jesus and said, 'Lord, how often must I forgive my brother if he wrongs me? As often as seven times?' Jesus answered, 'Not seven, I tell you, but seventy-seven times.

  'And so the kingdom of heaven may be compared to a king who decided to settle his accounts with his servants. When the reckoning began, they brought him a man who owed ten thousand talents; but he had no means of paying, so his master gave orders that he should be sold, together with his wife and children and all his possessions, to meet the debt. At this, the servant threw himself down at his master's feet. "Give me time" he said "and I will pay the whole sum." And the servant's master felt so sorry for him that he let him go and cancelled the debt. Now as this servant went out, he happened to meet a fellow servant who owed him one hundred denarii; and he seized him by the throat and began to throttle him. "Pay what you owe me" he said. His fellow servant fell at his feet and implored him, saying, "Give me time and I will pay you." But the other would not agree; on the contrary, he had him thrown into prison till he should pay the debt. His fellow servants were deeply distressed when they saw what had happened, and they went to their master and reported the whole affair to him. Then the master sent for him. "You wicked servant," he said. "I cancelled all that debt of yours when you appealed to me. Were you not bound, then, to have pity on your fellow servant just as I had pity on you?" And in his anger the master handed him over to the torturers till he should pay all his debt. And that is how my heavenly Father will deal with you unless you each forgive your brother from your heart.'

Jesus had now finished what he wanted to say, and he left Galilee and came into the part of Judaea which is on the far side of the Jordan.

This is the Gospel of the Lord.

FRIDAY

FIRST READING

A reading from the prophet Ezekiel 16:1-15. 60. 63

You were perfect in beauty because I had clothed you with my own splendour; and you have made yourself a prostitute.

The word of the Lord was addressed to me as follows, 'Son of man, confront Jerusalem with her filthy crimes. Say, "The Lord says this: By origin and birth you belong to the land of Canaan. Your father was an Amorite and your mother a Hittite. At birth, the very day you were born, there was no one to cut your navel-string, or wash you in cleansing water, or rub you with salt, or wrap you in napkins. No one leaned kindly over you to do anything like that for you. You were exposed in the open fields; you were as unloved as that on the day you were born.

"I saw you struggling in your blood as I was passing, and I said to you as you lay in your blood: Live, and grow like the grass of the fields. You developed, you grew, you reached marriageable age. Your breasts and your hair both grew, but you were quite naked. Then I saw you as I was passing. Your time had come, the time for love. I spread part of my cloak over you and covered your nakedness; I bound myself by oath, I made a covenant with you – it is the Lord who speaks – and you became mine. I bathed you in water, I washed the blood off you, I anointed you with oil. I gave you embroidered dresses, fine leather shoes, a linen headband and a cloak of silk. I loaded you with jewels, gave you bracelets for your wrists and a necklace for your throat. I gave you nose-ring and earrings; I put a beautiful diadem on your head. You were loaded with gold and silver, and dressed in fine linen and embroidered silks. Your food was the finest flour, honey and oil. You grew more and more beautiful; and you rose to be queen. The fame of your beauty spread through the nations, since it was perfect, because I had clothed you with my own splendour – it is the Lord who speaks.

"You have become infatuated with your own beauty; you have used your fame to make yourself a prostitute; you have offered your services to all comers. But I will remember the covenant that I made with you when you were a girl, and I will conclude a covenant with you that shall last for ever. So remember and be covered with shame, and in your confusion be reduced to silence, when I have pardoned you for all that you have done – it is the Lord who speaks." '

This is the word of the Lord.

Alternative First Reading

A reading from the prophet Ezekiel 16:59-63

I will remember the covenant that I made with you, and you will be covered with shame.

'The Lord says this: "Jerusalem, I will treat you as you deserve, you who have despised your oath even to the extent of breaking a covenant, but I will remember the covenant that I made with you when you were a girl, and I will conclude a covenant with you that shall last for ever. And you for your part will remember your past behaviour and be covered with shame when I take your elder and younger sisters and make them your daughters, although this was not included in this covenant. I am going to renew my covenant with you; and you will learn that I am the Lord, and so remember and be covered with shame, and in your confusion be reduced to silence, when I have pardoned you for all that you have done – it is the Lord who speaks." '

This is the word of the Lord.

Responsorial Psalm   Is 12:2-6. ℟ v.1

℟ **Your anger has passed, O Lord,
and you give me comfort.**

1. Truly, God is my salvation,
I trust, I shall not fear.
For the Lord is my strength, my song,
he became my saviour. ℟

2. With joy you will draw water
from the wells of salvation.
Give thanks to the Lord, give praise to his name!
Make his mighty deeds known to the peoples! ℟

3. Declare the greatness of his name,
sing a psalm to the Lord!
For he has done glorious deeds,
make them known to all the earth!
People of Zion, sing and shout for joy
for great in your midst is the Holy One of Israel. ℟

Gospel Acclamation   Ps 110:7. 8

Alleluia, alleluia!
Your precepts, O Lord, are all of them sure;
they stand firm for ever and ever.
Alleluia!

or   cf. 1 Thess 2:13

Alleluia, alleluia!
Accept God's message for what it really is:
God's message, and not some human thinking.
Alleluia!

GOSPEL

A reading from the holy Gospel according to Matthew   19:3-12

You were so unteachable that Moses allowed you to divorce your wives; it was not like this from the beginning.

Some Pharisees approached Jesus, and to test him they said, 'Is it against the Law for a man to divorce his wife on any pretext whatever?' He answered, 'Have you not read that the creator from the beginning made them male and female and that he said: This is why a man must leave father and mother, and cling to his wife, and the two become one body? They are no longer two, therefore, but one body. So then, what God has united, man must not divide.'

They said to him, 'Then why did Moses command that a writ of dismissal should be given in cases of divorce?' 'It was because you were so unteachable' he said 'that Moses allowed you to divorce your wives, but it was not like this from the beginning. Now I say this to you: the man who divorces his wife – I am not speaking of fornication – and marries another, is guilty of adultery.'

The disciples said to him, 'If that is how things are between husband and wife, it is not advisable to marry.' But he replied, 'It is not everyone who can accept what I have said, but only those to whom it is granted. There are eunuchs born that way from their mother's womb, there are eunuchs made so by men and there are eunuchs who have made themselves that way for the sake of the kingdom of heaven. Let anyone accept this who can.'

This is the Gospel of the Lord.

SATURDAY

FIRST READING

A reading from the prophet Ezekiel   18:1-10. 13. 30-32

I mean to judge each of you by what he does.

The word of the Lord was addressed to me as follows, 'Why do you keep repeating this proverb in the land of Israel:

    The fathers have eaten unripe grapes;
    and the children's teeth are set on edge?

'As I live – it is the Lord who speaks – there will no longer be any reason to repeat this proverb in Israel. See now: all life belongs to me; the father's life and the son's life, both alike belong to me. The man who has sinned, he is the one who shall die.

'The upright man is law-abiding and honest; he does not eat on the mountains or raise his eyes to the idols of the House of Israel, does not seduce his neighbour's wife or sleep with a woman during her periods. He oppresses no one, returns pledges, never steals, gives his own bread to the hungry, his clothes to the naked. He never charges usury on loans, takes no interest, abstains from evil, gives honest judgement between man and man, keeps my laws and sincerely respects my observances – such a man is truly upright. It is the Lord who speaks.

'But if anyone has a son prone to violence and bloodshed,

who commits one of these misdeeds, then this son shall certainly not live; having committed all these appalling crimes he will have to die, and his blood be on his own head.

'House of Israel, in future I mean to judge each of you by what he does – it is the Lord who speaks. Repent, renounce all your sins, avoid all occasions of sin! Shake off all the sins you have committed against me, and make yourselves a new heart and a new spirit! Why are you so anxious to die, House of Israel? I take no pleasure in the death of anyone – it is the Lord who speaks. Repent and live!'

This is the word of the Lord.

Responsional Psalm   Ps 50:12-15. 18-19. R̸ v.12
R̸ **A pure heart create for me, O God.**

1. A pure heart create for me, O God,
   put a steadfast spirit within me.
   Do not cast me away from your presence,
   nor deprive me of your holy spirit.   R̸

2. Give me again the joy of your help;
   with a spirit of fervour sustain me,
   that I may teach transgressors your ways
   and sinners may return to you.   R̸

3. For in sacrifice you take no delight,
   burnt offering from me you would refuse,
   my sacrifice, a contrite spirit.
   A humbled, contrite heart you will not spurn.   R̸

Gospel Acclamation   Col 3:16. 17
Alleluia, alleluia!
Let the message of Christ, in all its richness,
find a home with you;
through him give thanks to God the Father.
Alleluia!

or   cf. Mt 11:25

Alleluia, alleluia!
Blessed are you, Father,
Lord of heaven and earth,
for revealing the mysteries of the kingdom
to mere children.
Alleluia!

Twentieth Week in Ordinary Time, Year II: Monday

GOSPEL

A reading from the holy Gospel according to Matthew   19:13-15

Do not stop the little children coming to me: for it is to such as these that the kingdom of heaven belongs.

People brought little children to Jesus, for him to lay his hands on them and say a prayer. The disciples turned them away, but Jesus said, 'Let the little children alone, and do not stop them coming to me; for it is to such as these that the kingdom of heaven belongs.' Then he laid his hands on them and went on his way.

This is the Gospel of the Lord.

TWENTIETH WEEK IN ORDINARY TIME
Year II

MONDAY
FIRST READING

A reading from the prophet Ezekiel   24:15-24

Ezekiel is to be a sign for you. You are to do just as he has done.

The word of the Lord was addressed to me as follows, 'Son of man, I am about to deprive you suddenly of the delight of your eyes. But you are not to lament, not to weep, not to let your tears run down. Groan in silence, do not go into mourning for the dead, knot your turban round your head, put your sandals on your feet, do not cover your beard, do not eat common bread.' I told this to the people in the morning, and my wife died in the evening, and the next morning I did as I had been ordered. The people then said to me, 'Are you not going to explain what meaning these actions have for us?' I replied, 'The word of the Lord has been addressed to me as follows, "Say to the House of Israel: The Lord says this. I am about to profane my sanctuary, the pride of your strength, the delight of your eyes, the passion of your souls. Those of your sons and daughters whom you have left behind will fall by the sword. And you are to do as I have done; you must not cover your beards or eat common bread; you must keep your turbans on your heads and your sandals on your feet; you must not lament or weep. You shall waste away owing to your sins and groan among yourselves. Ezekiel is to be a sign for you. You are to do just as he has done. And when this happens, you will learn that I am the Lord." '

This is the word of the Lord.

Responsorial Psalm   Deut 32:18–21. R cf.v.18

   ℟ You forget the God who fathered you

1 You forget the Rock who begot you,
   unmindful now of the God who fathered you.
   The Lord has seen this, and in his anger
   cast off his sons and his daugthers. ℟

2 'I shall hide my face from them,' he says
   and see what becomes of them.
   For they are a deceitful blood,
   children with no loyalty in them. ℟

3 They have roused me to jealousy with what is no god,
   they have angered me with their beings of nothing:
   I, then, will rouse them to jealousy with what is no people,
   I will anger them with an empty-headed nation.' ℟

Gospel Acclamation   Ps 118:34

   Alleluia, alleluia!
   Train me, Lord, to observe your law
   to keep it with my heart.
   Alleluia!

or   Mt 5:3

   Alleluia, alleluia!
   How happy are the poor in spirit;
   theirs is the kingdom of heaven.
   Alleluia!

GOSPEL

A reading from the holy Gospel according to Matthew   19:16–22

If you wish to be perfect, sell what you own and you will have treasure in heaven.

There was a man who came to Jesus and asked, 'Master, what good deed must I do to possess eternal life.' Jesus said to him, 'Why do you ask me about what is good? There is one alone who is good. But if you wish to enter into life, keep the commandments.' He said, 'Which?' 'These,' Jesus replied. 'You must not kill. You must not commit adultery. You must not steal. You must not bring false witness. Honour your father and mother, and: you must love your neighbour as yourself.' The young man said to him, 'I have kept all these. What more do I need to do?' Jesus said, 'If you wish to be perfect, go and sell what you own and give the money to the poor, and you will have treasure in heaven; then come, follow me.' But when the young man heard these words he went away sad, for he was a man of great wealth.

This is the Gospel of the Lord.

TUESDAY

FIRST READING

A reading from the prophet Ezekiel 28:1–10

Though you are a man and not a god, you consider yourself the equal of God.

The word of the Lord was addressed to me as follows, 'Son of man, tell the ruler of Tyre, "The Lord says this:

Being swollen with pride,
you have said: I am a god;
I am sitting on the throne of God,
surrounded by the seas.
Though you are a man and not a god
you consider yourself the equal of God.
You are wiser now than Daniel;
there is no sage as wise as you.
By your wisdom and your intelligence
you have amassed great wealth;
you have piles of gold and silver
inside your treasure-houses.
Such is your skill in trading,
your wealth has continued to increase,
and with this your heart has grown more arrogant.
And so, the Lord says this:
Since you consider yourself the equal of God
very well, I am going to bring foreigners against you,
the most barbarous of the nations.
They will draw sword against your fine wisdom,
they will defile your glory;
they will throw you down into the pit
and you will die a violent death
surrounded by the seas.
Are you still going to say: I am a god,
when your muderers confront you?

No, you are a man and not a god
in the clutches of your murderers!
You will die like the uncircumcised
at the hand of foreigners.
For I have spoken – it is the Lord who speaks." '

This is the word of the Lord.

Responsorial Psalm   Deut 32:26-28. 30. 35-36. ℟ v.39

℟ **It is the Lord who deals death and life.**

1 I should crush them to dust, said the Lord.
   I should wipe out their memory among men,
   did I not fear the boasting of the enemy.
   But let not their foes be mistaken! ℟

2 Let them not say: Our own power wins the victory,
   the Lord plays no part in this.
   What a nation of short sight it is;
   in them there is no understanding. ℟

3 How else could one man rout a thousand,
   how could two put ten thousand to flight,
   were it not that their Rock has sold them,
   that the Lord has delivered them up? ℟

4 For it is close, the day of their ruin;
   their doom comes at speed.
   For the Lord will see his people righted,
   he will take pity on his servants. ℟

Gospel Acclamation   Ps 24:4. 5
Alleluia, alleluia!
Teach me your paths, my God,
make me walk in your truth.
Alleluia!

or   2 Cor 8:9

Alleluia, alleluia!
Jesus Christ was rich,
but he became poor for your sake,
to make you rich out of his poverty.
Alleluia!

GOSPEL

A reading from the holy Gospel according to Mattthew   19:23-30

It is easier for a camel to pass through the eye of a needle than for a rich man to enter the kingdom of heaven.

Jesus said to his disciples, 'I tell you solemnly, it will be hard for a rich man to enter the kingdom of heaven. Yes, I tell you again, it is easier for a camel to pass through the eye of a needle than for a rich man to enter the kingdom of heaven.' When the disciples heard this they were astonished. 'Who can be saved, then?' they said. Jesus gazed at them. 'For men' he told them 'this is impossible; for God everything is possible.'

Then Peter spoke. 'What about us?' he said to him. 'We have left everything and followed you. What are we to have, then?' Jesus said to him, 'I tell you solemnly, when all is made new and the Son of Man sits on his throne of glory, you will yourselves sit on twelve thrones to judge the twelve tribes of Israel. And everyone who has left houses, brothers, sisters, father, mother, children or land for the sake of my name will be repaid a hundred times over, and also inherit eternal life.

'Many who are first will be last, and the last, first.'

This is the Gospel of the Lord.

WEDNESDAY

FIRST READING

A reading from the prophet Ezekiel   34:1-11

I am going to take my flock back from them and I shall not allow them to feed it.

The word of the Lord was addressed to me as follows: 'Son of man, prophesy against the shepherds of Israel; prophesy and say to them, "Shepherds, the Lord says this: Trouble for the shepherds of Israel who feed themselves! Shepherds ought to feed their flock, yet you have fed on milk, you have dressed yourselves in wool, you have sacrificed the fattest sheep, but failed to feed the flock. You have failed to make weak sheep strong, or to care for the sick ones, or bandage the wounded ones. You have failed to bring back strays or look for the lost. On the contrary, you have ruled them cruelly and violently. For lack of a shepherd they have scattered, to become the prey of any wild animal; they have scattered far. My flock is straying this way and that, on mountains and on high hills; my flock has been scattered all over the country; no one bothers about them and no one looks for them.

"Well then, shepherds, hear the word of the Lord. As I live, I swear it – it is the Lord who speaks – since my flock has been looted and for lack of a shepherd is now the prey of any wild animal, since my shepherds have stopped bothering about my flock, since my shepherds feed themselves rather than my flock, in view of all this, shepherds, hear the word of the Lord. The Lord says this: I am going to call the shepherds to account. I am going to take my flock back from them and I shall not allow them to feed my flock. In this way the shepherds will stop feeding themselves. I shall rescue my sheep from their mouths; they will not prey on them any more."'

'For the Lord says this: "I am going to look after my flock myself and keep all of it in view."'

This is the word of the Lord.

Responsorial Psalm

Ps 22. ℟ v.1

℟ **The Lord is my shepherd;
there is nothing I shall want.**

1 The Lord is my shepherd;
there is nothing I shall want.
Fresh and green are the pastures
where he gives me repose.
Near restful waters he leads me,
to revive my drooping spirit. ℟

2 He guides me along the right path;
he is true to his name.
If I should walk in the valley of darkness
no evil would I fear.
You are there with your crook and your staff;
with these you give me comfort. ℟

3 You have prepared a banquet for me
in the sight of my foes.
My head you have anointed with oil;
my cup is overflowing. ℟

4 Surely goodness and kindness shall follow me
all the days of my life.
In the Lord's own house shall I dwell
for ever and ever. ℟

Gospel Acclamation Ps 118:135
  Alleluia! alleluia!
  Let your face shine on your servant,
  and teach me your decrees.
  Alleluia!

or Heb 4:12

  Alleluia, alleluia!
  The word of God is something alive and active;
  it can judge secret emotions and thoughts.
  Alleluia!

GOSPEL

A reading from the holy Gospel according to Matthew 20:1-16
Why be envious because I am generous.

Jesus said to his disciples: 'The kingdom of heaven is like a landowner going out at daybreak to hire workers for his vineyard. He made an agreement with the workers for one denarius a day, and sent them to his vineyard. Going out at about the third hour he saw others standing idle in the market place and said to them, "You go to my vineyard too and I will give you a fair wage." So they went. At about the sixth hour and again at about the ninth hour, he went out and did the same. Then at about the eleventh hour he went out and found more men standing round, and he said to them, "Why have you been standing here idle all day?" "Because no one has hired us" they answered. He said to them, "You go into my vineyard too." In the evening, the owner of the vineyard said to his bailiff, "Call the workers and pay them their wages, starting with the last arrivals and ending with the first." So those who were hired at about the eleventh hour came forward and received one denarius each. When the first came, they expected to get more, but they too received one denarius each. They took it, but grumbled at the landowner. "The men who came last" they said "have done only one hour, and you have treated them the same as us, though we have done a heavy day's work in all the heat." He answered one of them and said, "My friend, I am not being unjust to you; did we not agree on one denarius? Take your earnings and go. I choose to pay the last-comer as much as I pay you. Have I no right to do what I like with my own? Why be envious because I am generous?" Thus the last will be first, and the first, last.'

This is the Gospel of the Lord.

THURSDAY

FIRST READING

A reading from the prophet Ezekiel 36:23-28

I shall give you a new heart, and put a new spirit in you.

The word of the Lord was addressed to me as follows: I mean to display the holiness of my great name, which has been profaned among the nations, which you have profaned among them. And the nations will learn that I am the Lord – it is the Lord who speaks – when I display my holiness for your sake before their eyes. Then I am going to take you from among the nations and gather you together from all the foreign countries, and bring you home to your own land. I shall pour clean water over you and you will be cleansed; I shall cleanse you of all your defilement and all your idols. I shall give you a new heart, and put a new spirit in you; I shall remove the heart of stone from your bodies and give you a heart of flesh instead. I shall put my spirit in you, and make you keep my laws and sincerely respect my observances. You will live in the land which I gave your ancestors. You shall be my people and I will be your God.

This is the word of the Lord.

Responsorial Psalm   Ps 50:12-15. 18-19. ℟ Ez 36:25

  ℟ **I shall pour clean water over you
and all your sins will be washed away.**

1. A pure heart create for me, O God,
   put a steadfast spirit within me.
   Do not cast me away from your presence,
   nor deprive me of your holy spirit. ℟

2. Give me again the joy of your help;
   with a spirit of fervour sustain me,
   that I may teach transgressors your ways
   and sinners may return to you. ℟

3. For in sacrifice you take no delight,
   burnt offering from me you would refuse,
   my sacrifice, a contrite spirit.
   A humbled, contrite heart you will not spurn. ℟

Twentieth Week in Ordinary Time, Year II: Thursday

Gospel Acclamation   Ps 118:27

Alleluia, alleluia!
Make me grasp the way of your precepts,
and I will muse on your wonders.
Alleluia!

or   cf. Ps 94:8

Alleluia, alleluia!
Harden not your heart today,
but listen to the voice of the Lord.
Alleluia!

GOSPEL

A reading from the holy Gospel according to Matthew   22:1-14
Invite everyone you can find to the wedding.

Jesus began to speak to the chief priests and the elders of the people in parables, 'The kingdom of heaven may be compared to a king who gave a feast for his son's wedding. He sent his servants to call those who had been invited, but they would not come. Next he sent some more servants. "Tell those who have been invited" he said "that I have my banquet all prepared, my oxen and fattened cattle have been slaughtered, everything is ready. Come to the wedding." But they were not interested: one went off to his farm, another to his business and the rest seized his servants, maltreated them and killed them. The king was furious. He despatched his troops, destroyed those murderers and burnt their town. Then he said to his servants, "The wedding is ready; but as those who were invited proved to be unworthy, go to the crossroads in the town and invite everyone you can find to the wedding." So these servants went out on to the roads and collected together everyone they could find, bad and good alike; and the wedding hall was filled with guests. When the king came in to look at the guests he noticed one man who was not wearing a wedding garment, and said to him, "How did you get in here, my friend, without a wedding garment?" And the man was silent. Then the king said to the attendants, "Bind him hand and foot and throw him out into the dark, where there will be weeping and grinding of teeth." For many are called, but few are chosen.'

This is the Gospel of the Lord.

FRIDAY

FIRST READING

A reading from the prophet Ezekiel   37:1-4

Dry bones, hear the word of the Lord. I mean to raise you from your graves, House of Israel.

The hand of the Lord was laid on me, and he carried me away by the spirit of the Lord and set me down in the middle of a valley, a valley full of bones. He made me walk up and down among them. There were vast quantities of these bones on the ground the whole length of the valley; and they were quite dried up. He said to me, 'Son of man, can these bones live?' I said, 'You know, Lord.' He said, 'Prophesy over these bones. Say, "Dry bones, hear the word of the Lord. The Lord says this to these bones: I am now going to make the breath enter you, and you will live. I shall put sinews on you, I shall make flesh grow on you. I shall cover you with skin and give you breath, and you will live; and you will learn that I am the Lord."' I prophesied as I had been ordered. While I was prophesying, there was a noise, a sound of clattering; and the bones joined together. I looked, and saw that they were covered with sinews; flesh was growing on them and skin was covering them, but there was no breath in them. He said to me, 'Prophesy to the breath; prophesy, son of man. Say to the breath, "The Lord says this: Come from the four winds, breath; breathe on these dead; let them live!"' I prophesied as he had ordered me, and the breath entered them; they came to life again and stood up on their feet, a great, an immense army.

Then he said, 'Son of man, these bones are the whole House of Israel. They keep saying, "Our bones are dried up, our hope has gone; we are as good as dead." So prophesy. Say to them, "The Lord says this: I am now going to open your graves; I mean to raise you from your graves, my people, and lead you back to the soil of Israel. And you will know that I am the Lord, when I open your graves and raise you from your graves, my people. And I shall put my spirit in you, and you will live, and I shall resettle you on your own soil; and you will know that I, the Lord, have said and done this – it is the Lord who speaks."'

This is the word of the Lord.

Twentieth Week in Ordinary Time, Year II: Friday

Responsorial Psalm Ps 106:2-9. ℟ v.1

 ℟ **O give thanks to the Lord, for he is good;
 for his love has no end.**

or

 ℟ **Alleluia!**

1 Let them say this, the Lord's redeemed,
 whom he redeemed from the hand of the foe
 and gathered from far-off lands,
 from east and west, north and south. ℟

2 Some wandered in the desert, in the wilderness,
 finding no way to a city they could dwell in.
 Hungry they were and thirsty;
 their soul was fainting within them. ℟

3 Then they cried to the Lord in their need
 and he rescued them from their distress
 and he led them along the right way,
 to reach a city they could dwell in. ℟

4 Let them thank the Lord for his love,
 for the wonders he does for men.
 For he satisfies the thirsty soul;
 he fills the hungry with good things. ℟

Gospel Acclamation Ps 118:18
Alleluia, alleluia!
Open my eyes, O Lord, that I may consider
the wonders of your law.
Alleluia!

or Ps 24:4. 5

Alleluia, alleluia!
Teach me your paths, my God,
make me walk in your truth.
Alleluia!

GOSPEL

A reading from the holy Gospel according to Matthew 22:34-40
You must love the Lord your God, and your neighbour as yourself.

When the Pharisees heard that Jesus had silenced the Sadducees they got together and, to disconcert him, one of them put a question, 'Master, which is the greatest commandment of the

Law?' Jesus said, 'You must love the Lord your God with all your heart, with all your soul, and with all your mind. This is the greatest and the first commandment. The second resembles it: You must love your neighbour as yourself. On these two commandments hang the whole Law, and the Prophets also.'

This is the Gospel of the Lord.

SATURDAY

FIRST READING

A reading from the prophet Ezekiel   43:1-7
The glory of the Lord arrived at the Temple.

The angel took me to the gate, the one facing east. I saw the glory of the God of Israel approaching from the east. A sound came with it, like the sound of the ocean, and the earth shone with his glory. This vision was like the one I had seen when I had come for the destruction of the city, and like the one I had seen on the bank of the river Chebar. Then I prostrated myself.

The glory of the Lord arrived at the Temple by the east gate. The spirit lifted me up and brought me into the inner court; I saw the glory of the Lord fill the Temple. And I heard someone speaking to me from the Temple while the man stood beside me. The voice said, 'Son of man, this is the dais of my throne, the step on which I rest my feet. I shall live here among the sons of Israel for ever.'

This is the word of the Lord.

Responsorial Psalm   Ps 84:9-14. ℟ cf. v.10

℟ **The glory of the Lord will dwell in our land.**

1. I will hear what the Lord God has to say,
   a voice that speaks of peace,
   peace for his people and his friends.
   His help is near for those who fear him
   and his glory will dwell in our land. ℟

2. Mercy and faithfulness have met;
   justice and peace have embraced.
   Faithfulness shall spring from the earth
   and justice look down from heaven. ℟

3. The Lord will make us prosper
and our earth shall yield its fruit.
Justice shall march before him
and peace shall follow his steps. ℟

Gospel Acclamation   Ps 118:29. 35
Alleluia, alleluia!
Bend my heart to your will, O Lord,
and teach me your law.
Alleluia!

or   Mt 23:9. 10

Alleluia, alleluia!
You have only one Father,
and he is in heaven;
you have only one Teacher,
the Christ.
Alleluia!

GOSPEL

A reading from the holy Gospel according to Matthew   23:1-12

They do not practise what they preach.

Addressing the people and his disciples Jesus said, 'The scribes and the Pharisees occupy the chair of Moses. You must therefore do what they tell you and listen to what they say; but do not be guided by what they do: since they do not practise what they preach. They tie up heavy burdens and lay them on men's shoulders, but will they lift a finger to move them? Not they! Everything they do is done to attract attention, like wearing broader phylacteries and longer tassels, like wanting to take the place of honour at banquets and the front seats in the synagogues, being greeted obsequiously in the market squares and having people call them Rabbi.

'You, however, must not allow yourselves to be called Rabbi, since you have only one Master, and you are all brothers. You must call no one on earth your father, since you have only one Father, and he is in heaven. Nor must you allow yourselves to be called teachers, for you have only one Teacher, the Christ. The greatest among you must be your servant. Anyone who exalts himself will be humbled, and anyone who humbles himself will be exalted.'

This is the Gospel of the Lord.

TWENTY-FIRST WEEK IN ORDINARY TIME
Year II

MONDAY

FIRST READING

A reading from the second letter of St Paul to the Thessalonians   1:1-5. 11-12

The name of the Lord will be glorified in you and you in him.

From Paul, Silvanus and Timothy, to the Church in Thessalonika which is in God our Father and the Lord Jesus Christ; wishing you grace and peace from God the Father and the Lord Jesus Christ.

We feel we must be continually thanking God for you, brothers; quite rightly, because your faith is growing so wonderfully and the love that you have for one another never stops increasing; and among the churches of God we can take special pride in you for your constancy and faith under all the persecutions and troubles you have to bear. It all shows that God's judgement is just, and the purpose of it is that you may be found worthy of the kingdom of God; it is for the sake of this that you are suffering now. We pray continually that our God will, by his power, fulfil all your desires for goodness and complete all that you have been doing through faith; because in this way the name of our Lord Jesus Christ will be glorified in you and you in him, by the grace of our God and the Lord Jesus Christ.

This is the word of the Lord.

Responsorial Psalm   Ps 95:1-5. ℟ v.3

℟ **Proclaim the wonders of the Lord among all the peoples.**

1. O sing a new song to the Lord,
   sing to the Lord all the earth.
   O sing to the Lord, bless his name. ℟

2. Proclaim his help day by day,
   tell among the nations his glory
   and his wonders among all the peoples. ℟

3. The Lord is great and worthy of praise,
   to be feared above all gods;
   the gods of the heathens are naught. ℟

Gospel Acclamation cf. Jn 17:17

> Alleluia, alleluia!
> Your word is truth, O Lord,
> consecrate us in the truth.
> Alleluia!

or Jn 10:27

> Alleluia, alleluia!
> The sheep that belong to me listen to my voice,
> says the Lord,
> I know them and they follow me.
> Alleluia!

GOSPEL

A reading from the holy Gospel according to Matthew 23:13-22

Alas for you, blind guides!

Jesus said: 'Alas for you, scribes and Pharisees, you hypocrites! You who shut up the kingdom of heaven in men's faces, neither going in yourselves nor allowing others to go in who want to.

'Alas for you, scribes and Pharisees, you hypocrites! You who travel over sea and land to make a single proselyte, and when you have him you make him twice as fit for hell as you are.

'Alas for you, blind guides! You who say, "If a man swears by the Temple, it has no force; but if a man swears by the gold of the Temple, he is bound." Fools and blind! For which is of greater worth, the gold or the Temple that makes the gold sacred? Or else, "If a man swears by the altar it has no force; but if a man swears by the offering that is on the altar, he is bound." You blind men! For which is of greater worth, the offering or the altar that makes the offering sacred? Therefore, when a man swears by the altar he is swearing by that and by everything on it. And when a man swears by the Temple he is swearing by that and by the One who dwells in it. And when a man swears by heaven he is swearing by the throne of God and by the One who is seated there.'

This is the Gospel of the Lord.

TUESDAY

FIRST READING

A reading from the second letter of St Paul to the Thessalonians   2:1-3. 14-17

Keep the traditions that we taught you.

To turn, brothers, to the coming of our Lord Jesus Christ and how we shall all be gathered round him: please do not get excited too soon or alarmed by any prediction or rumour or any letter claiming to come from us, implying that the Day of the Lord has already arrived. Never let anyone deceive you in this way.

Through the Good News that we brought God called you so that you should share the glory of our Lord Jesus Christ. Stand firm, then, brothers, and keep the traditions that we taught you, whether by word of mouth or by letter. May our Lord Jesus Christ himself, and God our Father who has given us his love and, through his grace, such inexhaustible comfort and such sure hope, comfort you and strengthen you in everything good that you do or say.

This is the word of the Lord.

Responsorial Psalm   Ps 95:10-13. ℟ v.13

℟ **The Lord comes to rule the earth.**

1. Proclaim to the nations: 'God is king.'
   The world he made firm in its place;
   he will judge the peoples in fairness.   ℟

2. Let the heavens rejoice and earth be glad,
   let the sea and all within it thunder praise,
   let the land and all it bears rejoice,
   all the trees of the wood shout for joy
   at the presence of the Lord for he comes,
   he comes to rule the earth.   ℟

3. With justice he will rule the world,
   he will judge the peoples with his truth.   ℟

Gospel Acclamation   cf. Acts 16:14

Alleluia, alleluia!
Open our heart, O Lord.
to accept the words of your Son.
Alleluia!

or Heb 4:12

Alleluia, alleluia!
The word of God is something alive and active;
it can judge secret emotions and thoughts.
Alleluia!

GOSPEL

A reading from the holy Gospel according to Matthew 23:23-26

You should have practised these matters of the Law, without neglecting the others.

Jesus said, 'Alas for you, scribes and Pharisees, you hypocrites! You who pay your tithe of mint and dill and cummin and have neglected the weightier matters of the Law – justice, mercy, good faith! These you should have practised, without neglecting the others. You blind guides! Straining out gnats and swallowing camels!

'Alas for you, scribes and Pharisees, you hypocrites. You who clean the outside of cup and dish and leave the inside full of extortion and intemperance. Blind Pharisee! Clean the inside of cup and dish first so that the outside may become clean as well.'

This is the Gospel of the Lord.

WEDNESDAY

FIRST READING

A reading from the second letter of St Paul 3:6-10. 16-18
to the Thessalonians

Let no one have any food if he refuses to do any work.

In the name of the Lord Jesus Christ, we urge you, brothers, to keep away from any of the brothers who refuses to work or to live according to the tradition we passed on to you.

You know how you are supposed to imitate us: now we were not idle when we were with you, nor did we ever have our meals at anyone's table without paying for them; no, we worked night and day, slaving and straining, so as not to be a burden on any of you. This was not because we had no right to be, but in order to make ourselves an example for you to follow.

We gave you a rule when we were with you: not to let anyone have any food if he refused to do any work.

May the Lord of peace himself give you peace all the time and in every way. The Lord be with you all.

From me, PAUL, these greetings in my own handwriting, which is the mark of genuineness in every letter; this is my own writing. May the grace of our Lord Jesus Christ be with you all.

This is the word of the Lord.

Responsorial Psalm   Ps 127:1-2. 4-5. ℟ cf. v.1

℟ **O blessed are those who fear the Lord.**

1. O blessed are those who fear the Lord
   and walk in his ways!
   By the labour of your hands you shall eat.
   You will be happy and prosper.   ℟

2. Indeed thus shall be blessed
   the man who fears the Lord.
   May the Lord bless you from Zion
   all the days of your life!   ℟

Gospel Acclamation   Mt 4:4

Alleluia, alleluia!
Man does not live on bread alone,
but on every word that comes from the mouth of God.
Alleluia!

or   1 Jn 2:5

Alleluia, alleluia!
When anyone obeys what Christ has said,
God's love comes to perfection in him.
Alleluia!

GOSPEL

A reading from the holy Gospel according to Matthew   23:27-32
You are the sons of those who murdered the prophets.

Jesus said, 'Alas for you, scribes and Pharisees, you hypocrites! You who are like whitewashed tombs that look handsome on the outside, but inside are full of dead men's bones and every kind of corruption. In the same way you appear to people from the outside like good honest men, but inside you are full of hypocrisy and lawlessness.

'Alas for you, scribes and Pharisees, you hypocrites! You who build the sepulchres of the prophets and decorate the tombs of holy men, saying, "We would never have joined in shedding the blood of the prophets, had we lived in our fathers' day." So! Your own evidence tells against you! You are the sons of those who murdered the prophets! Very well then, finish off the work that your fathers began.'

This is the Gospel of the Lord.

THURSDAY

FIRST READING

A reading from the first letter from St Paul to the Corinthians 1:1-9

You have been enriched in so many ways in Christ.

I, Paul, appointed by God to be an apostle, together with brother Sosthenes, send greetings to the church of God in Corinth, to the holy people of Jesus Christ, who are called to take their place among all the saints everywhere who pray to our Lord Jesus Christ; for he is their Lord no less than ours. May God our Father and the Lord Jesus Christ send you grace and peace.

I never stop thanking God for all the graces you have received through Jesus Christ. I thank him that you have been enriched in so many ways, especially in your teachers and preachers; the witness to Christ has indeed been strong among you so that you will not be without any of the gifts of the Spirit while you are waiting for our Lord Jesus Christ to be revealed; and he will keep you steady and without blame until the last day, the day of our Lord Jesus Christ, because God by calling you has joined you to his Son, Jesus Christ; and God is faithful.

This is the word of the Lord.

Responsorial Psalm Ps 144:2-7. R̷ cf. v.1

R̷ **I will bless your name for ever, O Lord.**

1 I will bless you day after day
  and praise your name for ever.
  The Lord is great, highly to be praised,
  his greatness cannot be measured. R̷

2 Age to age shall proclaim your works,
  shall declare your mighty deeds,
  shall speak of your splendour and glory,
  tell the tale of your wonderful works. R̷

(continued)

3   They will speak of your terrible deeds,
    recount your greatness and might.
    They will recall your abundant goodness;
    age to age shall ring out your justice.

    ℟. **I will bless your name for ever, O Lord.**

Gospel Acclamation   Jn 15:15
    Alleluia, alleluia!
    I call you friends, says the Lord,
    because I have made known to you
    everything I have learnt from my Father.
    Alleluia!
or   Mt 24:42. 44
    Alleluia, alleluia!
    Stay awake and stand ready,
    because you do not know the hour
    when the Son of Man is coming.
    Alleluia!

GOSPEL

A reading from the holy Gospel according to Matthew   24:42-51
Stand ready.

Jesus said to his disciples: 'Stay awake, because you do not know the day when your master is coming. You may be quite sure of this, that if the householder had known at what time of the night the burglar would come, he would have stayed awake and would not have allowed anyone to break the wall of his house. Therefore, you too must stand ready because the Son of Man is coming at an hour you do not expect.

'What sort of servant, then, is faithful and wise enough for the master to place him over his household to give them their food at the proper time? Happy that servant if his master's arrival finds him at this employment. I tell you solemnly, he will place him over everything he owns. But as for the dishonest servant who says to himself, "My master is taking his time," and sets about beating his fellow servants and eating and drinking with drunkards, his master will come on a day he does not expect and at an hour he does not know. The master will cut him off and send him to the same fate as the hypocrites, where there will be weeping and grinding of teeth.'

This is the Gospel of the Lord.

FRIDAY

FIRST READING

A reading from the first letter of St Paul to the Corinthians   1:17-25

We are preaching a crucified Christ, an obstacle to men, but to those who have been called, the wisdom of God.

Christ did not send me to baptise, but to preach the Good News, and not to preach that in the terms of philosopy in which the crucifixion of Christ cannot be expressed. The language of the cross may be illogical to those who are not on the way to salvation, but those of us who are on the way see it as God's power to save. As scripture says: I shall destroy the wisdom of the wise and bring to nothing all the learning of the learned. Where are the philosophers now? Where are the scribes? Where are any of our thinkers today? Do you see now how God has shown up the foolishness of human wisdom? If it was God's wisdom that human wisdom should not know God, it was because God wanted to save those who have faith through the foolishness of the message that we preach. And so, while the Jews demand miracles and the Greeks look for wisdom, here are we preaching a crucified Christ; to the Jews an obstacle that they cannot get over, to the pagans madness, but to those who have been called, whether they are Jews or Greeks, a Christ who is the power and the wisdom of God. For God's foolishness is wiser than human wisdom, and God's weakness is stronger than human strength.

This is the word of the Lord.

Responsional Psalm   Ps 32:1-2. 4-5. 10-11. ℟ v.5

℟ **The Lord fills the earth with his love.**

1 Ring out your joy to the Lord, O you just;
   for praise is fitting for loyal hearts.
   Give thanks to the Lord upon the harp,
   with a ten-stringed lute sing him songs.   ℟

2 For the word of the Lord is faithful
   and all his works to be trusted.
   The Lord loves justice and right
   and fills the earth with his love.   ℟

(continued)

3   He frustrates the designs of the nations,
    he defeats the plans of the peoples.
    His own designs shall stand for ever,
    the plans of his heart from age to age.

    ℟   **The Lord fills the earth with his love.**

Gospel Acclamation Ps 129:5
   Alleluia, alleluia!
   My soul is waiting for the Lord,
   I count on his word.
   Alleluia!

or Lk 21:36

   Alleluia, alleluia!
   Stay awake, praying at all times
   for the strength to stand with confidence
   before the Son of Man.
   Alleluia!

GOSPEL

A reading from the holy Gospel according to Matthew   25:1-13
The bridegroom is here! Go out and meet him.

Jesus said to his disciples: 'The kingdom of heaven will be like this: Ten bridesmaids took their lamps and went to meet the bridegroom. Five of them were foolish and five were sensible: the foolish ones did take their lamps, but they brought no oil, whereas the sensible ones took flasks of oil as well as their lamps. The bridegroom was late, and they all grew drowsy and fell asleep. But at midnight there was a cry, "The bridegroom is here! Go out and meet him." At this, all those bridesmaids woke up and trimmed their lamps, and the foolish ones said to the sensible ones, "Give us some of your oil: our lamps are going out." But they replied, "There may not be enough for us and for you; you had better go to those who sell it and buy some for yourselves." They had gone off to buy it when the bridegroom arrived. Those who were ready went in with him to the wedding hall and the door was closed. The other bridesmaids arrived later. "Lord, Lord," they said, "open the door for us." But he replied, "I tell you solemnly, I do not know you." So stay awake, because you do not know either the day or the hour.'

This is the Gospel of the Lord.

SATURDAY

FIRST READING

A reading from the first letter of St Paul to the Corinthians 1:26-31

God chose what is weak by human reckoning.

Take yourselves, brothers, at the time when you were called: how many of you were wise in the ordinary sense of the word, how many were influential people, or came from noble families? No, it was to shame the wise that God chose what is foolish by human reckoning, and to shame what is strong that he chose what is weak by human reckoning; those whom the world thinks common and contemptible are the ones that God has chosen – those who are nothing at all to show up those who are everything. The human race has nothing to boast about to God, but you, God has made members of Christ Jesus and by God's doing he has become our wisdom, and our virtue, and our holiness, and our freedom. As scripture says: if anyone wants to boast, let him boast about the Lord.

This is the word of the Lord.

Responsorial Psalm Ps 32:12-13. 18-21. ℟ cf. v.12

℟ **Happy the people the Lord has chosen as his own.**

1. They are happy, whose God is the Lord,
 the people he has chosen as his own.
 From the heavens the Lord looks forth,
 he sees all the children of men. ℟

2. The Lord looks on those who revere him,
 on those who hope in his love,
 to rescue their souls from death,
 to keep them alive in famine. ℟

3. Our soul is waiting for the Lord.
 The Lord is our help and our shield.
 In him do our hearts find joy.
 We trust in his holy name. ℟

Gospel Acclamation Phil 2:15-16
 Alleluia, alleluia!
 You will shine in the world like bright stars
 because you are offering it the word of life.
 Alleluia!

or   Jn 13:34

Alleluia, alleluia!
I give you a new commandment:
love one another just as I have loved you,
says the Lord.
Alleluia!

GOSPEL

A reading from the holy Gospel according to Matthew   25:14-30

You have shown you can be faithful in small things, come and join in your master's happiness.

Jesus told his disciples this parable: 'A man on his way abroad summoned his servants and entrusted his property to them. To one he gave five talents, to another two, to a third one; each in proportion to his ability. Then he set out. The man who had received the five talents promptly went and traded with them and made five more. The man who had received two made two more in the same way. But the man who had received one went off and dug a hole in the ground and hid his master's money. Now a long time after, the master of those servants came back and went through his accounts with them. The man who had received the five talents came forward bringing five more. "Sir," he said "you entrusted me with five talents; here are five more that I have made." His master said to him, "Well done, good and faithful servant; you have shown you can be faithful in small things, I will trust you with greater; come and join in your master's happiness." Next the man with the two talents came forward. "Sir," he said "you entrusted me with two talents; here are two more that I have made." His master said to him, "Well done, good and faithful servant; you have shown you can be faithful in small things, I will trust you with greater; come and join in your master's happiness." Last came forward the man who had the one talent. "Sir," said he "I have heard you were a hard man, reaping where you have not sown and gathering where you have not scattered; so I was afraid, and I went off and hid your talent in the ground. Here it is; it was yours, you have it back." But his master answered him, "You wicked and lazy servant! So you knew that I reap where I have not sown and gather where I have not scattered? Well then, you should have deposited my money with the bankers, and on my return I would have recovered my capital with interest. So now, take the talent from him and give it to the man who has the five talents. For to everyone who has will be given more, and he will have more than enough; but from the man who has not, even what he has will be taken away. As for this good-for-nothing servant, throw him out into the dark, where there will be weeping and grinding of teeth."'

This is the Gospel of the Lord.

TWENTY-SECOND WEEK IN ORDINARY TIME
Year II

MONDAY

FIRST READING

A reading from the first letter of St Paul to the Corinthians   2:1-5

I claimed knowledge about the crucified Christ.

Brothers, when I came to you, it was not with any show of oratory or philosophy, but simply to tell you what God had guaranteed. During my stay with you, the only knowledge I claimed to have was about Jesus, and only about him as the crucified Christ. Far from relying on any power of my own, I came among you in great 'fear and trembling' and in my speeches and the sermons that I gave, there were none of the arguments that belong to philosophy; only a demonstration of the power of the Spirit. And I did this so that your faith should not depend on human philosophy but on the power of God.

This is the word of the Lord.

Responsorial Psalm   Ps 118:97-102. ℟ v.97

℟ **Lord, how I love your law!**

1 Lord, how I love your law!
It is ever in my mind.
Your command makes me wiser than my foes;
for it is mine for ever. ℟

2 I have more insight than all who teach me
for I ponder your will.
I have more understanding than the old
for I keep your precepts. ℟

(continued)

3 I turn my feet from evil paths
to obey your word.
I have not turned away from your decrees;
you yourself have taught me.

℟ **Lord, how I love your law!**

Gospel Acclamation   Jn 8:12
Alleluia, alleluia!
I am the light of the world, says the Lord,
anyone who follows me
will have the light of life.
Alleluia!

or   Lk 4:18

Alleluia, alleluia!
The Lord has sent me to bring the good news to the poor,
to proclaim liberty to captives.
Alleluia!

GOSPEL

A reading from the holy Gospel according to Luke   4:16-30

He has sent me to bring the good news to the poor. No prophet is accepted in his own country.

Jesus came to Nazara, where he had been brought up, and went into the synagogue on the sabbath day as he usually did. He stood up to read, and they handed him the scroll of the prophet Isaiah. Unrolling the scroll he found the place where it is written:

The spirit of the Lord has been given to me,
for he has anointed me.
He has sent me to bring the good news to the poor,
to proclaim liberty to captives
and to the blind new sight,
to set the downtrodden free,
to proclaim the Lord's year of favour.

He then rolled up the scroll, gave it back to the assistant and sat down. And all eyes in the synagogue were fixed on him. Then he began to speak to them, 'This text is being fulfilled today even as you listen.' And he won the approval of all, and they were astonished by the gracious words that came from his lips.

They said, 'This is Joseph's son, surely?' But he replied, 'No doubt you will quote me the saying, "Physician, heal yourself" and tell me, "We have heard all that happened in Capernaum, do the same here in your own countryside." ' And he went on, 'I tell you solemnly, no prophet is ever accepted in his own country.

'There were many widows in Israel, I can assure you, in Elijah's day, when heaven remained shut for three years and six months and a great famine raged throughout the land, but Elijah was not sent to any one of these: he was sent to a widow at Zarephath, a Sidonian town. And in the prophet Elisha's time there were many lepers in Israel, but none of these was cured, except the Syrian, Naaman.'

When they heard this everyone in the synagogue was enraged. They sprang to their feet and hustled him out of the town; and they took him up to the brow of the hill their town was built on, intending to throw him down the cliff, but he slipped through the crowd and walked away.

This is the Gospel of the Lord.

TUESDAY

FIRST READING

A reading from the first letter of St Paul to the Corinthians   2:10-16

An unspiritual person does not accept anything of the Spirit of God. A spiritual man, on the other hand, is able to judge the value of everything.

The Spirit reaches the depths of everything, even the depths of God. After all, the depths of a man can only be known by his own spirit, not by any other man, and in the same way the depths of God can only be known by the Spirit of God. Now instead of the spirit of the world, we have received the Spirit that comes from God, to teach us to understand the gifts that he has given us. Therefore we teach, not in the way in which philosopy is taught, but in the way that the Spirit teaches us: we teach spiritual things spiritually. An unspiritual person is one who does not accept anything of the Spirit of God: he sees it all as nonsense; it is beyond his understanding because it can only be understood by means of the Spirit. A spiritual man, on the other hand, is able to judge the value of everything, and his own value is not to be judged by other men. As scripture says: Who can know the mind of the Lord, so who can teach him? But we are those who have the mind of Christ.

This is the word of the Lord.

Responsorial Psalm
Ps 144:8-14. R̷ v.17

R̷ **The Lord is just in all his ways.**

1 The Lord is kind and full of compassion,
 slow to anger, abounding in love.
 How good is the Lord to all,
 compassionate to all his creatures. R̷

2 All your creaures shall thank you, O Lord,
 and your friends shall repeat their blessing.
 They shall speak of the glory of your reign
 and declare your might, O God,
 to make known to men your mighty deeds
 and the glorious splendour of your reign. R̷

3 Yours is an everlasting kingdom;
 your rule lasts from age to age.
 The Lord is faithful in all his words
 and loving in all his deeds.
 The Lord supports all who fall
 and raises all who are bowed down. R̷

Gospel Acclamation
Heb 4:12

Alleluia, alleluia!
The word of God is something alive and active;
it can judge secret emotions and thoughts.
Alleluia!

or
Lk 7:16

Alleluia, alleluia!
A great prophet has appeared among us;
God has visited his people.
Alleluia!

GOSPEL

A reading from the holy Gospel according to Luke 4:31-37
I know who you are: the Holy One of God.

Jesus went down to Capernaum, a town in Galilee, and taught them on the sabbath. And his teaching made a deep impression on them because he spoke with authority.

In the synagogue there was a man who was possessed by the spirit of an unclean devil, and it shouted at the top of its voice,

'Ha! What do you want with us, Jesus of Nazareth? Have you come to destroy us? I know who you are: the Holy One of God.' But Jesus said sharply, 'Be quiet! Come out of him!' And the devil, throwing the man down in front of everyone, went out of him without hurting him at all. Astonishment seized them and they were all saying to one another, 'What teaching! He gives orders to unclean spirits with authority and power and they come out.' And reports of him went all through the surrounding countryside.

This is the Gospel of the Lord.

WEDNESDAY

FIRST READING

A reading from the first letter of St Paul to the Corinthians 3:1-9
We are fellow workers with God; you are God's farm, God's building.

Brothers, I myself was unable to speak to you as people of the Spirit: I treated you as sensual men, still infants in Christ. What I fed you with was milk, not solid food, for you were not ready for it; and indeed, you are still not ready for it since you are still un-spiritual. Isn't that obvious from all the jealousy and wrangling that there is among you, from the way that you go on behaving like ordinary people? What could be more unspiritual than your slogans, 'I am for Paul' and 'I am for Apollos'?

After all, what is Apollos and what is Paul? They are servants who brought the faith to you. Even the different ways in which they brought it were assigned to them by the Lord. I did the planting, Apollos did the watering, but God made things grow. Neither the planter nor the waterer matters: only God, who makes things grow. It is all one who does the planting and who does the watering, and each will duly be paid according to his share in the work. We are fellow workers with God; you are God's farm, God's building.

This is the word of the Lord.

Responsorial Psalm   Ps 32:12-15. 20-21. ℟ v.12

℟ **Happy the people the Lord has chosen as his own.**

1. They are happy, whose God is the Lord,
   the people he has chosen as his own.
   From the heavens the Lord looks forth,
   he sees all the children of men. ℟

2. From the place where he dwells he gazes
   on all the dwellers on the earth,
   he who shapes the hearts of them all
   and considers all their deeds. ℟

3. Our soul is waiting for the Lord.
   The Lord is our help and our shield.
   In him do our hearts find joy.
   We trust in his holy name. ℟

Gospel Acclamation   1 Peter 1:25

Alleluia, alleluia!
The word of the Lord remains for ever:
What is this word?
It is the Good News that has been brought to you.
Alleluia!

or   Lk 4:18

Alleluia, alleluia!
The Lord has sent me to bring the good news to the poor,
to proclaim liberty to captives.
Alleluia!

GOSPEL

A reading from the holy Gospel according to Luke   4:38-44
I must proclaim the Good News to the other towns too, because that is what I was sent to do.

Leaving the synagogue Jesus went to Simon's house. Now Simon's mother-in-law was suffering from a high fever and they asked him to do something for her. Leaning over her he rebuked the fever and it left her. And she immediately got up and began to wait on them.

At sunset all those who had friends suffering from diseases of one kind or another brought them to him, and laying his hands on each he cured them. Devils too came out of many people, howling, 'You are the Son of God.' But he rebuked them and would not allow them to speak because they knew that he was the Christ.

When daylight came he left the house and made his way to a lonely place. The crowds went to look for him, and when they had caught up with him they wanted to prevent him leaving them, but he answered, 'I must proclaim the Good News of the kingdom of God to the other towns too, because that is what I was sent to do.' And he continued his preaching in the synagogues of Judaea.

This is the Gospel of the Lord.

THURSDAY

FIRST READING

A reading from the first letter of St Paul to the Corinthians 3:18-23

All things are your servants; but you belong to Christ and Christ belongs to God.

Make no mistake about it: if any one of you thinks of himself as wise, in the ordinary sense of the word, then he must learn to be a fool before he really can be wise. Why? Because the wisdom of this world is foolishness to God. As scripture says: The Lord knows wise men's thoughts: he knows how useless they are: or again: God is not convinced by the arguments of the wise. So there is nothing to boast about in anything human: Paul, Apollos, Cephas, the world, life and death, the present and the future, are all your servants; but you belong to Christ and Christ belongs to God.

This is the word of the Lord.

Responsorial Psalm Ps 23:1-6. ℟ v.1

℟ **The Lord's is the earth and its fullness.**

1 The Lord's is the earth and its fullness,
  the world and all its peoples.
  It is he who set it on the seas;
  on the waters he made it firm. ℟

2 Who shall climb the mountain of the Lord?
  Who shall stand in his holy place?
  The man with clean hands and pure heart,
  who desires not worthless things. ℟

(continued)

3   He shall receive blessings from the Lord
    and reward from the God who saves him.
    Such are the men who seek him,
    seek the face of the God of Jacob.

    ℟ **The Lord's is the earth and its fullness.**

Gospel Acclamation   cf. 2 Thess 2:14
  Alleluia, alleluia!
  Through the Good News God called us
  to share the glory of our Lord Jesus Christ.
  Alleluia!

or   Mt 4:19

  Alleluia, alleluia!
  Follow me, says the Lord,
  and I will make you fishers of men.
  Alleluia!

GOSPEL

A reading from the holy Gospel according to Luke   5:1-11
They left everything and followed him.

Jesus was standing one day by the Lake of Gennesaret, with the crowd pressing round him listening to the word of God, when he caught sight of two boats close to the bank. The fishermen had gone out of them and were washing their nets. He got into one of the boats – it was Simon's – and asked him to put out a little from the shore. Then he sat down and taught the crowds from the boat.

When he had finished speaking he said to Simon, 'Put out into deep water and pay out your nets for a catch.' 'Master,' Simon replied 'we worked hard all night long and caught nothing but if you say so, I will pay out the nets.' And when they had done this they netted such a huge number of fish that their nets began to tear, so they signalled to their companions in the other boat to come and help them; when these came, they filled the two boats to sinking point.

When Simon Peter saw this he fell at the knees of Jesus saying, 'Leave me, Lord; I am a sinful man.' For he and all his companions were completely overcome by the catch they had made; so also were James and John, sons of Zebedee, who were Simon's partners. But Jesus said to Simon, 'Do not be afraid; from now on it is men you will catch.' Then, bringing their boats back to land, they left everything and followed him.

This is the Gospel of the Lord.

FRIDAY

FIRST READING

A reading from the first letter of St Paul 4:1-5
to the Corinthians
The Lord will reveal the intentions of men's hearts.

People must think of us as Christ's servants, stewards entrusted with the mysteries of God. What is expected of stewards is that each one should be found worthy of his trust. Not that it makes the slightest difference to me whether you, or indeed any human tribunal, find me worthy or not. I will not even pass judgement on myself. True, my conscience does not reproach me at all, but that does not prove that I am acquitted: the Lord alone is my judge. There must be no passing of premature judgement. Leave that until the Lord comes: he will light up all that is hidden in the dark and reveal the secret intentions of men's hearts. Then will be the time for each one to have whatever praise he deserves, from God.

This is the word of the Lord.

Responsorial Psalm   Ps 36:3-6. 27-28. 39-40. ℟ v.39

℟ **The salvation of the just comes from the Lord.**

1 If you trust in the Lord and do good,
 then you will live in the land and be secure.
 If you find your delight in the Lord,
 he will grant your heart's desire. ℟

2 Commit your life to the Lord,
 trust in him and he will act,
 so that your justice breaks forth like the light,
 your cause like the noon-day sun. ℟

3 Then turn away from evil and do good
 and you shall have a home for ever;
 for the Lord loves justice
 and will never forsake his friends. ℟

(continued)

4. The salvation of the just comes from the Lord,
   their stronghold in time of distress.
   The Lord helps them and delivers them
   and saves them: for their refuge is in him.

℟ **The salvation of the just comes from the Lord.**

Gospel Acclamation cf. Ps 18:9
Alleluia, alleluia!
Your words gladden the heart, O Lord,
they give light to the eyes.
Alleluia!

or Jn 8:12

Alleluia, alleluia!
I am the light of the world, says the Lord,
anyone who follows me
will have the light of life.
Alleluia!

GOSPEL

A reading from the holy Gospel according to Luke 5:33-39
When the bridegroom is taken away from them, then they will fast.

The Pharisees and the scribes said to Jesus, 'John's disciples are always fasting and saying prayers, and the disciples of the Pharisees too, but yours go on eating and drinking.' Jesus replied, 'Surely you cannot make the bridegrooms' attendants fast while the bridegroom is still with them? But the time will come, the time for the bridegroom to be taken away from them; that will be the time when they will fast.'

He also told them this parable, 'No one tears a piece from a new cloak to put it on an old cloak; if he does, not only will he have torn the new one, but the piece taken from the new will not match the old.

'And nobody puts new wine into old skins; if he does, the new wine will burst the skins and then run out, and the skins will be lost. No; new wine must be put into fresh skins. And nobody who has been drinking old wine wants new. "The old is good" he says.'

This is the Gospel of the Lord.

SATURDAY

FIRST READING

A reading from the first letter of St Paul 4:6-15
to the Corinthians
We go without food and drink and clothes.

Take Apollos and myself as an example and remember the maxim, 'Keep to what is written'; it is not for you, so full of your own importance, to go taking sides for one man against another. In any case, brother, has anybody given you some special right? What do you have that was not given to you? And if it was given, how can you boast as though it were not? Is it that you have everything that you want – that you are rich already, in possession of your kingdom, with us left outside? Indeed I wish you were really kings, and we could be kings with you! But instead, it seems to me, God has put us apostles at the end of his parade, with the men sentenced to death; it is true – we have been put on show in front of the whole universe, angels as well as men. Here we are, fools for the sake of Christ, while you are the learned men in Christ; we have no power, but you are influential; you are celebrities, we are nobodies. To this day, we go without food and drink and clothes; we are beaten and have no homes; we work for our living with our own hands. When we are cursed, we answer with a blessing; when we are hounded, we put up with it; we are insulted and we answer politely. We are treated as the offal of the world, still to this day, the scum of the earth.

I am saying all this not just to make you ashamed but to bring you, as my dearest children, to your senses. You might have thousands of guardians in Christ, but no more than one father and it was I who begot you in Christ Jesus by preaching the Good News.

This is the word of the Lord.

Responsorial Psalm Ps 144:17-21. ℟ v.18

℟ **The Lord is close to all who call him.**

1 The Lord is just in all his ways
 and loving in all his deeds.
 He is close to all who call him,
 who call on him from their hearts. ℟

2 He grants the desires of those who fear him,
 he hears their cry and he saves them.

The Lord protects all who love him;
but the wicked he will utterly destroy.

℟ **The Lord is close to all who call him.**

3 Let me speak the praise of the Lord,
let all mankind bless his holy name
for ever, for ages unending. ℟

Gospel Acclamation cf. Ps 26:11
Alleluia, alleluia!
Instruct me, Lord, in your way;
on an even path lead me.
Alleluia!

or Jn 14:6

Alleluia, alleluia!
I am the Way, the Truth and the Life, says the Lord;
no one can come to the Father except through me.
Alleluia!

GOSPEL

A reading from the holy Gospel according to Luke 6:1-5
Why are you doing something that is forbidden on the sabbath?

One sabbath Jesus happened to be taking a walk through the cornfields, and his disciples were picking ears of corn, rubbing them in their hands and eating them. Some of the Pharisees said, 'Why are you doing something that is forbidden on the sabbath day?' Jesus answered them, 'So you have not read what David did when he and his followers were hungry – how he went into the House of God, took the loaves of offering and ate them and gave them to his followers, loaves which only the priests are allowed to eat?' And he said to them, 'The Son of Man is master of the sabbath.'

This is the Gospel of the Lord.

TWENTY-THIRD WEEK IN ORDINARY TIME
Year II

MONDAY

FIRST READING

A reading from the first letter of St Paul to the Corinthians   5:1-8

Get rid of the old yeast, Christ our passover has been sacrificed.

I have been told as an undoubted fact that one of you is living with his father's wife. This is a case of sexual immorality among you that must be unparalleled even among pagans. How can you be so proud of yourselves? You should be in mourning. A man who does a thing like that ought to have been expelled from the community. Though I am far away in body, I am with you in spirit, and have already condemned the man who did this thing as if I were actually present. When you are assembled together in the name of the Lord Jesus, and I am spiritually present with you, then with the power of our Lord Jesus he is to be handed over to Satan so that his sensual body may be destroyed and his spirit saved on the day of the Lord.

The pride that you take in yourselves is hardly to your credit. You must know how even a small amount of yeast is enough to leaven all the dough, so get rid of all the old yeast, and make yourselves into a completely new batch of bread, unleavened as you are meant to be. Christ, our passover, has been sacrificed; let us celebrate the feast, then, by getting rid of all the old yeast of evil and wickedness, having only the unleavened bread of sincerity and truth.

This is the word of the Lord.

Responsorial Psalm   Ps 5:5-7. 12. ℟ v.9

℟ **Lead me, Lord, in your justice.**

1 You are no God who loves evil;
   no sinner is your guest.
   The boastful shall not stand their ground
   before your face.   ℟

2 You hate all who do evil:
   you destroy all who lie.
   The deceitful and bloodthirsty man
   the Lord detests.   ℟

(continued)

3 All those you protect shall be glad
and ring out their joy.
You shelter them; in you they rejoice,
those who love your name.

℟ **Lead me, Lord, in your justice.**

Gospel Acclamation Ps 118:105
Alleluia, alleluia!
Your word is a lamp for my steps
and a light for my path.
Alleluia!

or Jn 10:27

Alleluia, alleluia!
The sheep that belong to me listen to my voice,
says the Lord,
I know them and they follow me.
Alleluia!

GOSPEL

A reading from the holy Gospel according to Luke 6:6-11
They were watching Jesus to see if he would cure a man on the sabbath.

On the sabbath Jesus went into the synagogue and began to teach, and a man was there whose right hand was withered. The scribes and the Pharisees were watching him to see if he would cure a man on the sabbath, hoping to find something to use against him. But he knew their thoughts; and he said to the man with the withered hand, 'Stand up! Come out into the middle.' And he came out and stood there. Then Jesus said to them, 'I put it to you: is it against the law on the sabbath to do good, or to do evil; to save life, or to destroy it?' Then he looked round at them all and said to the man, 'Stretch out your hand.' He did so, and his hand was better. But they were furious, and began to discuss the best way of dealing with Jesus.

This is the Gospel of the Lord.

TUESDAY

FIRST READING

A reading from the first letter of St Paul 6:1-11
to the Corinthians
There are differences between brothers in front of unbelievers.

How dare one of your members take up a complaint against another in the lawcourts of the unjust instead of before the saints? As you know, it is the saints who are to 'judge the world'; and if the world is to be judged by you, how can you be unfit to judge trifling cases? Since we are also to judge angels, it follows that we can judge matters of everyday life; but when you have had cases of that kind, the people you appointed to try them were not even respected in the Church. You should be ashamed: is there really not one reliable man among you to settle differences between brothers and so one brother brings a court case against another in front of unbelievers? It is bad enough for you to have lawsuits at all against one another: oughtn't you to let yourselves be wronged, and let yourselves be cheated? But you are doing the wronging and the cheating, and to your own brothers.

You know perfectly well that people who do wrong will not inherit the kingdom of God: people of immoral lives, idolaters, adulterers, catamites, sodomites, thieves, usurers, drunkards, slanderers and swindlers will never inherit the kingdom of God. These are the sort of people some of you were once, but now you have been washed clean, and sanctified, and justified through the name of the Lord Jesus Christ and through the Spirit of our God.

This is the word of the Lord.

Responsorial Psalm Ps 149:1-6. 9. ℟ v.4

℟ **The Lord takes delight in his people.**

or

℟ **Alleluia!**

1 Sing a new song to the Lord,
his praise in the assembly of the faithful.
Let Israel rejoice in its Maker,
let Zion's sons exult in their king. ℟

2 Let them praise his name with dancing
and make music with timbrel and harp.

For the Lord takes delight in his people.
He crowns the poor with salvation.

℟ **The Lord takes delight in his people.**

or

℟ **Alleluia!**

3. Let the faithful rejoice in their glory,
   shout for joy and take their rest.
   Let the praise of God be on their lips:
   this honour is for all his faithful. ℟

Gospel Acclamation   Phil 2:15-17

Alleluia, alleluia!
You will shine in the world like bright stars
because you are offering it the word of life.
Alleluia!

or   cf. Jn 15:16

Alleluia, alleluia!
I chose you from the world
to go out and to bear fruit,
fruit that will last.
Alleluia!

GOSPEL

A reading from the holy Gospel according to Luke   6:12-19

Jesus spent the whole night in prayer and he picked twelve whom he called 'apostles.'

Jesus went out into the hills to pray; and he spent the whole night in prayer to God. When day came he summoned his disciples and picked out twelve of them; he called them 'apostles': Simon whom he called Peter, and his brother Andrew; James, John, Philip, Bartholomew, Matthew, Thomas, James son of Alphaeus, Simon called the Zealot, Judas son of James, and Judas Iscariot who became a traitor.

He then came down with them and stopped at a piece of level ground where there was a large gathering of his disciples with a great crowd of people from all parts of Judaea and from Jerusalem and from the coastal region of Tyre and Sidon who had come to hear him and to be cured of their diseases. People tormented by unclean spirits were also cured, and everyone in the crowd was trying to touch him because power came out of him that cured them all.

This is the Gospel of the Lord.

WEDNESDAY

FIRST READING

A reading from the first letter of St Paul 7:25-31
to the Corinthians

If you are tied to a wife, do not look for freedom; if you are free of a wife, then do not look for one.

About remaining celibate, I have no directions from the Lord but give my own opinion as one who, by the Lord's mercy, has stayed faithful. Well then, I believe that in these present times of stress this is right: that it is good for a man to stay as he is. If you are tied to a wife, do not look for freedom; if you are free of a wife, then do not look for one. But if you marry, it is no sin, and it is not a sin for a young girl to get married. They will have their troubles, though, in their married life, and I should like to spare you that.

Brothers, this is what I mean: our time is growing short. Those who have wives should live as though they had none, and those who mourn should live as though they had nothing to mourn for; those who are enjoying life should live as though there were nothing to laugh about; those whose life is buying things should live as though they had nothing of their own; and those who have to deal with the world should not become engrossed in it. I say this because the world as we know it is passing away.

This is the word of the Lord.

Responsorial Psalm   Ps 44:11-12. 14-17. ℟ v.11

   ℟ **Listen, O daughter, give ear to my words.**

1   Listen, O daughter, give ear to my words:
    forget your own people and your father's house.
    So will the king desire your beauty:
    He is your lord, pay homage to him.   ℟

2   The daughter of the king is clothed with splendour,
    her robes embroidered with pearls set in gold.
    She is led to the king with her maiden companions.   ℟

3   They are escorted amid gladness and joy;
    they pass within the palace of the king.
    Sons shall be yours in place of your fathers;
    you will make them princes over all the earth.   ℟

Gospel Acclamation 1 Jn 2:5

Alleluia, alleluia!
When anyone obeys what Christ has said,
God's love comes to perfection in him.
Alleluia!

or Lk 6:23

Alleluia, alleluia!
Rejoice and be glad:
your reward will be great in heaven.
Alleluia!

GOSPEL

A reading from the holy Gospel according to Luke 6:20-26
How happy are you who are poor. But alas for you who are rich.

Fixing his eyes on his disciples Jesus said:

'How happy are you who are poor: yours is the kingdom of God.
Happy you who are hungry now: you shall be satisfied.
Happy you who weep now: you shall laugh.

'Happy are you when people hate you, drive you out, abuse you, denounce your name as criminal, on account of the Son of Man. Rejoice when that day comes and dance for joy, for then your reward will be great in heaven. This was the way their ancestors treated the prophets.

'But alas for you who are rich: you are having your consolation now.
Alas for you who have your fill now: you shall go hungry.
Alas for you who laugh now: you shall mourn and weep.

'Alas for you when the world speaks well of you! This was the way their ancestors treated the false prophets.'

This is the Gospel of the Lord.

THURSDAY

FIRST READING

A reading from the first letter of St Paul to the Corinthians   8:1-7. 11-13

By injuring the weak consciences of your brothers you sin against Christ.

'We all have knowledge'; yes, that is so, but knowledge gives self-importance – it is love that makes the building grow. A man may imagine he understands something, but still not understand anything in the way that he ought to. But any man who loves God is known by him. Well then, about eating food sacrificed to idols: we know that idols do not really exist in the world and that there is no god but the One. And even if there were things called gods, either in the sky or on earth – where there certainly seem to be 'gods' and 'lords' in plenty – still for us there is one God, the Father, from whom all things come and for whom we exist; and there is one Lord, Jesus Christ, through whom all things come and through whom we exist.

Some people, however, do not have this knowledge. There are some who have been so long used to idols that they eat this food as though it really had been sacrificed to the idol, and their conscience, being weak, is defiled by it. In this way your knowledge could become the ruin of someone weak, of a brother for whom Christ died. By sinning in this way against your brothers, and injuring their weak consciences, it would be Christ against whom you sinned. That is why, since food can be the occasion of my brother's downfall, I shall never eat meat again in case I am the cause of a brother's downfall.

This is the word of the Lord.

Responsorial Psalm   Ps 138:1-3. 13-14. 23-24. ℟ v.24

℟   **Lead me, O Lord, in the path of life eternal.**

1   O Lord, you search me and you know me,
     you know my resting and my rising,
     you discern my purpose from afar.
     You mark when I walk or lie down,
     all my ways lie open to you.   ℟

2   For it was you who created my being,
     knit me together in my mother's womb.
     I thank you for the wonder of my being,
     for the wonders of all your creation.   ℟   (continued)

3   O search me, God, and know my heart.
    O test me and know my thoughts.
    See that I follow not the wrong path
    and lead me in the path of life eternal.

    ℟ **Lead me, O Lord, in the path of life eternal.**

Gospel Acclamation James 1:21

Alleluia, alleluia!
Accept and submit to the word
which has been planted in you
and can save your souls.
Alleluia!

or 1 Jn 4:12

Alleluia, alleluia!
As long as we love one another
God will live in us,
and his love will be complete in us.
Alleluia!

GOSPEL

A reading from the holy Gospel according to Luke 6:27-38
Be compassionate as your Father is compassionate.

Jesus said to his disciples: 'I say this to you who are listening: Love your enemies, do good to those who hate you, bless those who curse you, pray for those who treat you badly. To the man who slaps you on one cheek, present the other cheek too; to the man who takes your cloak from you, do not refuse your tunic. Give to everyone who asks you, and do not ask for your property back from the man who robs you. Treat others as you would like them to treat you. If you love those who love you, what thanks can you expect? Even sinners love those who love them. And if you do good to those who do good to you, what thanks can you expect? For even sinners do that much. And if you lend to those from whom you hope to receive, what thanks can you expect? Even sinners lend to sinners to get back the same amount. Instead, love your enemies and do good, and lend without any hope of return. You will have a great reward, and you will be sons of the Most High, for he himself is kind to the ungrateful and the wicked.

'Be compassionate as your Father is compassionate. Do not

Twenty-third Week in Ordinary Time, Year II: Friday 1145

judge, and you will not be judged yourselves; do not condemn, and you will not be condemned yourselves; grant pardon, and you will be pardoned. Give, and there will be gifts for you: a full measure, pressed down, shaken together, and running over, will be poured into your lap; because the amount you measure out is the amount you will be given back.'

This is the Gospel of the Lord.

FRIDAY

FIRST READING

A reading from the first letter of St Paul to the Corinthians 9:16-19. 22-27

I made myself all things to all men in order to save some at any cost.

I do not boast of preaching the gospel, since it is a duty which has been laid on me; I should be punished if I did not preach it! If I had chosen this work myself, I might have been paid for it, but as I have not, it is a responsibility which has been put into my hands. Do you know what my reward is? It is this: in my preaching, to be able to offer the Good News free, and not insist on the rights which the gospel gives me.

So though I am not a slave of any man I have made myself the slave of everyone so as to win as many as I could. I made myself all things to all men in order to save some at any cost; and I still do this, for the sake of the gospel, to have a share in its blessing.

All the runners at the stadium are trying to win, but only one of them gets the prize. You must run in the same way, meaning to win. All the fighters at the games go into strict training; they do this just to win a wreath that will wither away, but we do it for a wreath that will never wither. That is how I run, intent on winning; that is how I fight, not beating the air. I treat my body hard and make it obey me, for, having been an announcer myself, I should not want to be disqualified.

This is the word of the Lord.

Responsorial Psalm Ps 83:3-6. 12. ℟ v.2

℟ **How lovely is your dwelling place, Lord, God of hosts.**

1 My soul is longing and yearning,
is yearning for the courts of the Lord.
My heart and my soul ring out their joy

to God, the living God.

℟ **How lovely is your dwelling place,
Lord, God of hosts.**

2 The sparrow herself finds a home
and the swallow a nest for her brood;
she lays her young by your altars,
Lord of hosts, my king and my God. ℟

3 They are happy, who dwell in your house,
for ever singing your praise.
They are happy, whose strength is in you,
in whose hearts are the roads to Zion. ℟

4 For the Lord God is a rampart, a shield;
he will give us his favour and glory.
The Lord will not refuse any good
to those who walk without blame. ℟

Gospel Acclamation Ps 147:12. 15
Alleluia, alleluia!
O praise the Lord, Jerusalem!
He sends out his word to the earth.
Alleluia!

or cf. Jn 17:17
Alleluia, alleluia!
Your word is truth, O Lord,
consecrate us in the truth.
Alleluia!

GOSPEL

A reading from the holy Gospel according to Luke 6:39-42
Can one blind man guide another?

Jesus told a parable to the disciples, 'Can one blind man guide another? Surely both will fall into a pit? The disciple is not superior to his teacher; the fully trained disciple will always be like his teacher. Why do you observe the splinter in your brother's eye and never notice the plank in your own? How can you say to your brother, "Brother, let me take out the splinter that is in your eye," when you cannot see the plank in your own? Hypocrite! Take the plank out of your own eye first, and then you will see clearly enough to take out the splinter that is in your brother's eye.'

This is the Gospel of the Lord.

SATURDAY

FIRST READING

A reading from the first letter of St Paul to the Corinthians   10:14-22

Though there are many of us, we form a single body because we all share in one loaf.

My dear brothers, you must keep clear of idolatry. I say to you as sensible people: judge for yourselves what I am saying. The blessing-cup that we bless is a communion with the blood of Christ, and the bread that we break is a communion with the body of Christ. The fact that there is only one loaf means that, though there are many of us, we form a single body because we all have a share in this one loaf. Look at the other Israel, the race, where those who eat the sacrifices are in communion with the altar. Does this mean that the food sacrificed to idols has a real value, or that the idol itself is real? Not at all. It simply means that the sacrifices that they offer they sacrifice to demons who are not God. I have no desire to see you in communion with demons. You cannot drink the cup of the Lord and the cup of demons. You cannot take your share at the table of the Lord and at the table of demons. Do we want to make the Lord angry; are we stronger than he is?

This is the word of the Lord.

Responsorial Psalm   Ps 115:12-13. 17-18. ℟ v.17

℟ **A thanksgiving sacrifice I make to you, O Lord.**

1. How can I repay the Lord
 for his goodness to me?
 The cup of salvation I will raise;
 I will call on the Lord's name. ℟

2. A thanksgiving sacrifice I make:
 I will call on the Lord's name.
 My vows to the Lord I will fulfil
 before all his people. ℟

Gospel Acclamation   Jn 14:6

Alleluia, alleluia!
I am the Way, the Truth and the Life, says the Lord;
no one can come to the Father except through me.
Alleluia!

or   Jn 14:23
Alleluia, alleluia!
If anyone loves me he will keep my word,
and my Father will love him,
and we shall come to him.
Alleluia!

GOSPEL

A reading from the holy Gospel according to Luke   6:43-49
Why do you call me, 'Lord, Lord' and not do what I say?

Jesus said to his disciples: 'There is no sound tree that produces rotten fruit, nor again a rotten tree that produces sound fruit. For every tree can be told by its own fruit: people do not pick figs from thorns, nor gather grapes from brambles. A good man draws what is good from the store of goodness in his heart; a bad man draws what is bad from the store of badness. For a man's words flow out of what fills his heart.

'Why do you call me, "Lord, Lord" and not do what I say?

'Everyone who comes to me and listens to my words and acts on them – I will show you what he is like. He is like the man who when he built his house dug, and dug deep, and laid the foundations on rock; when the river was in flood it bore down on that house but could not shake it, it was so well built. But the one who listens and does nothing is like the man who built his house on soil, with no foundations: as soon as the river bore down on it, it collapsed; and what a ruin that house became!'

This is the Gospel of the Lord.

TWENTY-FOURTH WEEK IN ORDINARY TIME
Year II

MONDAY

FIRST READING

A reading from the first letter of St Paul   11:17-26. 33
to the Corinthians
If there are separate factions among you, it is not the Lord's Supper that you are eating.

On the subject of instructions, I cannot say that you have done well in holding meetings that do you more harm than good. In the first place, I hear that when you all come together as a community, there are separate factions among you, and I half believe it – since there must no doubt be separate groups among you, to distinguish those who are to be trusted. The point is, when you hold these meetings, it is not the Lord's Supper that you are eating, since when the time comes to eat, everyone is in such a hurry to start his own supper that one person goes hungry while another is getting drunk. Surely you have homes for eating and drinking in? Surely you have enough respect for the community of God not to make poor people embarrassed? What am I to say to you? Congratulate you? I cannot congratulate you on this.

For this is what I received from the Lord, and in turn passed on to you: that on the same night that he was betrayed, the Lord Jesus took some bread, and thanked God for it and broke it, and he said, 'This is my body, which is for you; do this as a memorial of me.' In the same way he took the cup after supper, and said, 'This cup is the new covenant in my blood. Whenever you drink it, do this as a memorial of me.' Until the Lord comes, therefore, every time you eat this bread and drink this cup, you are proclaiming his death.

So to sum up, my dear brothers, when you meet for the Meal, wait for one another.

This is the word of the Lord.

Responsorial Psalm   Ps 39:7-10. 17. ℟ 1 Cor 11:26

   ℟ **Proclaim the death of the Lord,**
      until he comes.

1   You do not ask for sacrifice and offerings,
    but an open ear.
    You do not ask for holocaust and victim.
    Instead, here am I.   ℟

2   In the scroll of the book it stands written
    that I should do your will.
    My God, I delight in your law
    in the depth of my heart.   ℟

3   Your justice I have proclaimed
    in the great assembly.
    My lips I have not sealed;
    you know it, O Lord.   ℟

(continued)

4 O let there be rejoicing and gladness
   for all who seek you.
   Let them ever say: 'The Lord is great,'
   who love your saving help.

   ℟ **Proclaim the death of the Lord,
   until he comes.**

Gospel Acclamation   Ps 118:27
Alleluia, alleluia!
Make me grasp the way of your precepts,
and I will muse on your wonders.
Alleluia!

or   Jn 3:16

Alleluia, alleluia!
God loved the world so much that he gave his only Son;
everyone who believes in him has eternal life.
Alleluia!

GOSPEL

A reading from the holy Gospel according to Luke   7:1-10
Not even in Israel have I found faith like this.

When Jesus had come to the end of all he wanted the people to hear, he went into Capernaum. A centurion there had a servant, a favourite of his, who was sick and near death. Having heard about Jesus he sent some Jewish elders to him to ask him to come and heal his servant. When they came to Jesus they pleaded earnestly with him. 'He deserves this of you' they said 'because he is friendly towards our people; in fact, he is the one who built the synagogue.' So Jesus went with them, and was not very far from the house when the centurion sent word to him by some friends: 'Sir,' he said 'do not put yourself to trouble; because I am not worthy to have you under my roof; and for this same reason I did not presume to come to you myself; but give the word and let my servant be cured. For I am under authority myself, and have soldiers under me; and I say to one man: Go, and he goes; to another: Come here, and he comes; to my servant: Do this, and he does it.' When Jesus heard these words he was astonished at him and, turning round, said to the crowd following him, 'I tell you, not even in Israel have I found faith like this.' And when the messengers got back to the house they found the servant in perfect health.

This is the Gospel of the Lord.

TUESDAY

FIRST READING

A reading from the first letter of St Paul to the Corinthians 12:12-14. 27-31

You together are Christ's body; but each of you is a different part of it.

Just as a human body, though it is made up of many parts, is a single unit because all these parts, though many, make one body, so it is with Christ. In the one Spirit we were all baptised, Jews as well as Greeks, slaves as well as citizens, and one Spirit was given to us all to drink.

Nor is the body to be identified with any one of its many parts. Now you together are Christ's body; but each of you is a different part of it. In the Church, God has given the first place to apostles, the second to prophets, the third to teachers; after them, miracles, and after them the gift of healing; helpers, good leaders, those with many languages. Are all of them apostles, or all of them prophets, or all of them teachers? Do they all have the gift of miracles, or all have the gift of healing? Do all speak strange languages, and all interpret them? Be ambitious for the higher gifts.

This is the word of the Lord.

Responsorial Psalm
Ps 99. R/ v.3

R/ **We are his people,
the sheep of his flock.**

1. Cry out with joy to the Lord, all the earth.
 Serve the Lord with gladness.
 Come before him, singing for joy. R/

2. Know that he, the Lord, is God.
 He made us, we belong to him,
 we are his people, the sheep of his flock. R/

3. Go within his gates, giving thanks.
 Enter his courts with songs of praise.
 Give thanks to him and bless his name. R/

4. Indeed, how good is the Lord,
 eternal his merciful love.
 He is faithful from age to age. R/

Gospel Acclamation cf. 2 Tim 1:10
Alleluia, alleluia!
Our Saviour Christ Jesus abolished death,
and he has proclaimed life through the Good News.
Alleluia!

or Lk 7:16

Alleluia, alleluia!
A great prophet has appeared among us;
God has visited his people.
Alleluia!

GOSPEL

A reading from the holy Gospel according to Luke 7:11-17
Young man, I tell you to get up.

Jesus went to a town called Nain, accompanied by his disciples and a great number of people. When he was near the gate of the town it happened that a dead man was being carried out for burial, the only son of his mother, and she was a widow. And a considerable number of the townspeople were with her. When the Lord saw her he felt sorry for her. 'Do not cry' he said. Then he went up and put his hand on the bier and the bearers stood still, and he said, 'Young man, I tell you to get up.' And the dead man sat up and began to talk, and Jesus gave him to his mother. Everyone was filled with awe and praised God saying, 'A great prophet has appeared among us; God has visited his people.' And this opinion of him spread throughout Judaea and all over the countryside.

This is the Gospel of the Lord.

WEDNESDAY

FIRST READING

A reading from the first letter of St Paul 12:31 – 13: 13
to the Corinthians
There are three things that last: faith, hope and love, and the greatest of these is love.

Be ambitious for the higher gifts. And I am going to show you a way that is better than any of them.
 If I have all the eloquence of men or of angels, but speak without love, I am simply a gong booming or a cymbal clashing.

Twenty-fourth Week in Ordinary Time, Year II: Wednesday 1153

If I have the gift of prophecy, understanding all the mysteries there are, and knowing everything, and if I have faith in all its fullness, to move mountains, but without love, then I am nothing at all. If I give away all that I possess, piece by piece, and if I even let them take my body to burn it, but am without love, it will do me no good whatever.

Love is always patient and kind; it is never jealous; love is never boastful or conceited; it is never rude or selfish; it does not take offence, and is not resentful. Love takes no pleasure in other people's sins but delights in the truth; it is always ready to excuse, to trust, to hope, and to endure whatever comes.

Love does not come to an end. But if there are gifts of prophecy, the time will come when they must fail; or the gift of languages, it will not continue for ever; and knowledge – for this, too, the time will come when it must fail. For our knowledge is imperfect and our prophesying is imperfect; but once perfection comes, all imperfect things will disappear. When I was a child, I used to talk like a child, and think like a child, and argue like a child, but now I am a man, all childish ways are put behind me. Now we are seeing a dim reflection in a mirror; but then we shall be seeing face to face. The knowledge that I have now is imperfect; but then I shall know as fully as I am known.

In short, there are three things that last: faith, hope and love; and the greatest of these is love.

This is the word of the Lord.

Responsorial Psalm Ps 32:2-5. 12. 22. ℟ v.12

℟ **Happy the people the Lord has chosen as his own.**

1 Give thanks to the Lord upon the harp,
  with a ten-stringed lute sing him songs.
  O sing him a song that is new,
  play loudly, with all your skill.   ℟

2 For the word of the Lord is faithful
  and all his works to be trusted.
  The Lord loves justice and right
  and fills the earth with his love.   ℟

3 They are happy, whose God is the Lord,
  the people he has chosen as his own.
  May your love be upon us, O Lord,
  as we place all our hope in you.   ℟

Gospel Acclamation cf. 1 Thess 2:13
Alleluia, alleluia!
Accept God's message for what it really is:
God's message, and not some human thinking.
Alleluia!

or cf. Jn 6:63. 68

Alleluia, alleluia!
Your words are spirit, Lord,
and they are life:
you have the message of eternal life.
Alleluia!

GOSPEL

A reading from the holy Gospel according to Luke 7:31-35
We played the pipes for you, and you wouldn't dance; we sang dirges, and you wouldn't cry.

Jesus said to the people: 'What description can I find for the men of this generation? What are they like? They are like children shouting to one another while they sit in the market place:

"We played the pipes for you,
and you wouldn't dance;
we sang dirges,
and you wouldn't cry."

'For John the Baptist comes, not eating bread, not drinking wine, and you say, "He is possessed." The Son of Man comes, eating and drinking, and you say, "Look, a glutton and a drunkard, a friend of tax collectors and sinners." Yet Wisdom has been proved right by all her children.'

This is the Gospel of the Lord.

THURSDAY

FIRST READING

A reading from the first letter of St Paul 15:1-11
to the Corinthians
I preached and you believed.

Brothers, I want to remind you of the gospel I preached to you, the gospel that you received and in which you are firmly established; because the gospel will save you only if you keep believing exactly what I preached to you – believing anything else will not lead to anything.

Well then, in the first place, I taught you what I had been taught myself, namely that Christ died for our sins, in accordance with the scriptures; that he was buried; and that he was raised to life on the third day, in accordance with the scriptures; that he appeared first to Cephas and secondly to the Twelve. Next he appeared to more than five hundred of the brothers at the same time, most of whom are still alive, though some have died; then he appeared to James, and then to all the apostles; and last of all he appeared to me too; it was as though I was born when no one expected it.

I am the least of the apostles; in fact, since I persecuted the Church of God, I hardly deserve the name apostle; but by God's grace that is what I am, and the grace that he gave me has not been fruitless. On the contrary, I, or rather the grace of God that is with me, have worked harder than any of the others; but what matters is that I preach what they preach, and this is what you all believed.

This is the word of the Lord.

Responsorial Psalm Ps 117:1-2. 15-17. 28. ℟ v.1

℟ **Give thanks to the Lord
for he is good.**

or

℟ **Alleluia!**

1 Give thanks to the Lord for he is good,
for his love has no end.
Let the sons of Israel say:
'His love has no end.' ℟

2 The Lord's right hand has triumphed;
his right hand raised me up.
I shall not die, I shall live
and recount his deeds. ℟

3 You are my God, I thank you.
My God, I praise you.
I will thank you for you have given answer
and you are my saviour. ℟

Gospel Acclamation 2 Cor 5:19

Alleluia, alleluia!
God in Christ was reconciling the world to himself,
and he has entrusted to us the news that they are reconciled.
Alleluia!

or   Mt 11:28

Alleluia, alleluia!
Come to me, all you who labour and are overburdened,
and I will give you rest, says the Lord.
Alleluia!

GOSPEL

A reading from the holy Gospel according to Luke 7:36-50

Her many sins must have been forgiven her, or she would not have shown such great love.

One of the Pharisees invited Jesus to a meal. When he arrived at the Pharisee's house and took his place at table, a woman came in, who had a bad name in the town. She had heard he was dining with the Pharisee and had brought with her an alabaster jar of ointment. She waited behind him at his feet, weeping, and her tears fell on his feet, and she wiped them away with her hair; then she covered his feet with kisses and anointed them with the ointment.

When the Pharisee who had invited him saw this, he said to himself, 'If this man were a prophet, he would know who this woman is that is touching him and what a bad name she has.' Then Jesus took him up and said, 'Simon, I have something to say to you.' 'Speak, Master' was the reply. 'There was once a creditor who had two men in his debt; one owed him five hundred denarii, the other fifty. They were unable to pay, so he pardoned them both. Which of them will love him more?' 'The one who was pardoned more, I suppose' answered Simon. Jesus said, 'You are right.'

Then he turned to the woman. 'Simon,' he said 'you see this woman? I came into your house, and you poured no water over my feet, but she has poured out her tears over my feet and wiped them away with her hair. You gave me no kiss, but she has been covering my feet with kisses ever since I came in. You did not anoint my head with oil, but she has anointed my feet with ointment. For this reason I tell you that her sins, her many sins, must have been forgiven her, or she would not have shown such great love. It is the man who is forgiven little who shows little love.' Then he said to her, 'Your sins are forgiven.' Those who were with him at the table began to say to themselves, 'Who is this man, that he even forgives sins?' But he said to the woman, 'Your faith has saved you; go in peace.'

This is the Gospel of the Lord.

FRIDAY

FIRST READING

A reading from the first letter of St Paul to the Corinthians 15:12-20

If Christ has not been raised then your faith is useless.

If Christ raised from the dead is what has been preached, how can some of you be saying that there is no resurrection of the dead? If there is no resurrection of the dead, Christ himself cannot have been raised and if Christ has not been raised then our preaching is useless and your believing it is useless; indeed, we are shown up as witnesses who have committed perjury before God, because we swore in evidence before God that he had raised Christ to life. For if the dead are not raised, Christ has not been raised, and if Christ has not been raised, you are still in your sins. And what is more serious, all who have died in Christ have perished. If our hope in Christ has been for this life only, we are the most unfortunate of all people.

But Christ has in fact been raised from the dead, the first-fruits of all who have fallen asleep.

This is the word of the Lord.

Responsorial Psalm Ps 16:1. 6-8. 15. ℟ v.15

℟ **I shall be filled, when I awake,
with the sight of your glory, O Lord.**

1 Lord, hear a cause that is just,
   pay heed to my cry.
   Turn your ear to my prayer:
   no deceit is on my lips.   ℟

2 I am here and I call, you will hear me, O God.
   Turn your ear to me; hear my words.
   Display your great love, you whose right hand saves
   your friends from those who rebel against them.   ℟

(continued)

3 Hide me in the shadow of your wings.
   As for me, in my justice I shall see your face
   and be filled, when I awake,
   with the sight of your glory.

   ℟ **I shall be filled, when I awake,
   with the sight of your glory, O Lord.**

Gospel Acclamation cf. Ps 94:8
   Alleluia, alleluia!
   Harden not your hearts today,
   but listen to the voice of the Lord.
   Alleluia!
or cf. Mt 11:25
   Alleluia, alleluia!
   Blessed are you, Father,
   Lord of heaven and earth,
   for revealing the mysteries of the kingdom
   to mere chilren.
   Alleluia!

GOSPEL

A reading from the holy Gospel according to Luke 8:1-3
With Jesus went several women who provided for him out of their own resources.

Jesus made his way through towns and villages preaching, and proclaiming the Good News of the kingdom of God. With him went the Twelve, as well as certain women, who had been cured of evil spirits and ailments: Mary surnamed the Magdalene, from whom seven demons had gone out, Joanna the wife of Herod's steward Chuza, Susanna, and several others who provided for them out of their own resources.

This is the Gospel of the Lord.

SATURDAY

FIRST READING

A reading from the first letter of St Paul 15:35-37. 42-49
to the Corinthians
The thing that is sown is perishable but what is raised is imperishable.

Someone may ask, 'How are dead people raised, and what sort of body do they have when they come back?' They are stupid questions. Whatever you sow in the ground has to die before it is given new life and the thing that you sow is not what is going to come; you sow a bare grain, say of wheat or something like that. It is the same with the resurrection of the dead: the thing that is sown is perishable but what is raised is imperishable; the thing that is sown is contemptible but what is raised is glorious; the thing that is sown is weak but what is raised is powerful; when it is sown it embodies the soul, when it is raised it embodies the spirit.

If the soul has its own embodiment, so does the spirit have its own embodiment. The first man, Adam, as scripture says, became a living soul; but the last Adam has become a life-giving spirit. That is, first the one with the soul, not the spirit, and after that, the one with the spirit. The first man, being from the earth, is earthly by nature; the second man is from heaven. As this earthly man was, so are we on earth; and as the heavenly man is, so are we in heaven. And we, who have been modelled on the earthly man, will be modelled on the heavenly man.

This is the word of the Lord.

Responsorial Psalm
Ps 55:10-14. ℟ cf. v.14

℟ **I shall walk in the presence of God in the light of the living.**

1 My foes will be put to flight
on the day that I call to you.
This I know, that God is on my side. ℟

2 In God, whose word I praise,
in the Lord, whose word I praise,
in God I trust; I shall not fear:
what can mortal man do to me? ℟

3 I am bound by the vows I have made you.
O God, I will offer you praise
for you rescued my soul from death,
you kept my feet from stumbling
that I may walk in the presence of God
in the light of the living. ℟

Gospel Acclamation
Ps 118:18

Alleluia, alleluia!
Open my eyes, O Lord, that I may consider

the wonders of your law.
Alleluia!

or   cf. Lk 8:15

Alleluia, alleluia!
Blessed are those who,
with a noble and generous heart,
take the word of God to themselves
and yield a harvest through their perseverance.
Alleluia!

GOSPEL

A reading from the holy Gospel according to Luke   8:4-15

The part in the rich soil is people who take the word themselves and yield a harvest through their perseverance.

With a large crowd gathering and people from every town finding their way to him, Jesus used this parable:

'A sower went out to sow his seed. As he sowed, some fell on the edge of the path and was trampled on; and the birds of the air ate it up. Some seed fell on rock, and when it came up it withered away, having no moisture. Some seed fell amongst thorns and the thorns grew with it and choked it. And some seed fell into rich soil and grew and produced its crop a hundredfold.' Saying this he cried, 'Listen, anyone who has ears to hear!'

The disciples asked him what this parable might mean, and he said, 'The mysteries of the kingdom of God are revealed to you; for the rest there are only parables, so that

they may see but not perceive,
listen but not understand.

'This, then, is what the parable means: the seed is the word of God. Those on the edge of the path are people who have heard it, and then the devil comes and carries away the word from their hearts in case they should believe and be saved. Those on the rock are people who, when they first hear it, welcome the word with joy. But these have no root; they believe for a while, and in time of trial they give up. As for the part that fell into thorns, this is people who have heard, but as they go on their way they are choked by the worries and riches and pleasures of life and do not reach maturity. As for the part in the rich soil, this is people with a noble and generous heart who have heard the word and take it to themselves and yield a harvest through their perseverance.'

This is the Gospel of the Lord.

TWENTY-FIFTH WEEK IN ORDINARY TIME
Year II

MONDAY

FIRST READING

A reading from the book of Proverbs 3:27-34
The wilful wrong-doer is abhorrent to the Lord.

My son,
do not refuse a kindness to anyone who begs it,
if it is in your power to perform it.
Do not say to your neighbour, 'Go away! Come another time!
I will give it you tomorrow,' if you can do it now.
Do not plot harm against your neighbour
as he lives unsuspecting next door.
Do not pick a groundless quarrel with a man
who has done you no harm.
Do not emulate the man of violence,
never model your conduct on his;
for the wilful wrong-doer is abhorrent to the Lord,
who confides only in honest men.
The Lord's curse lies on the house of the wicked,
but he blesses the home of the virtuous.
He mocks those who mock,
but accords his favour to the humble.

This is the word of the Lord.

Responsorial Psalm Ps 14:2-5. ℟ v.1

℟ **The just will live in the presence of the Lord.**

1. Lord, who shall dwell on your holy mountain?
He who walks without fault;
he who acts with justice
and speaks the truth from his heart;
he who does not slander with his tongue. ℟

2. He who does no wrong to his brother,
who casts no slur on his neighbour,
who holds the godless in disdain,
but honours those who fear the Lord. ℟

3. He who keeps his pledge, come what may;
who takes no interest on a loan

and accepts no bribes against the innocent.
Such a man will stand firm for ever.

℟ **The just will live in the presence of the Lord.**

Gospel Acclamation James 1:18
Alleluia, alleluia!
By his own choice the Father made us his children
by the message of the truth,
so that we should be a sort of first-fruits
of all that he created.
Alleluia!

or Mt 5:16

Alleluia, alleluia!
Your light must shine in the sight of men,
so that, seeing your good works,
they may give the praise to your Father in heaven.
Alleluia!

GOSPEL

A reading from the holy Gospel according to Luke 8:16-18
A lamp is put on a lamp-stand so that people may see the light when they come in.

Jesus said to his disciples: 'No one lights a lamp to cover it with a bowl or to put it under a bed. No, he puts it on a lamp-stand so that people may see the light when they come in. For nothing is hidden but it will be made clear, nothing secret but it will be known and brought to light. So take care how you hear; for anyone who has will be given more; from anyone who has not, even what he thinks he has will be taken away.'

This is the Gospel of the Lord.

TUESDAY

FIRST READING

A reading from the book of Proverbs 21:1-6. 10-13
Various proverbs.

Like flowing water is the heart of the king in the hand of the
    Lord,
who turns it where he pleases.

Twenty-fifth Week in Ordinary Time, Year II: Tuesday 1163

A man's conduct may strike him as upright,
the Lord, however, weighs the heart.

To act virtuously and with justice
is more pleasing to the Lord than sacrifice.

Haughty eye, proud heart,
lamp of the wicked, nothing but sin.

The hardworking man is thoughtful, and all is gain;
too much haste, and all that comes of it is want.

To make a fortune with the help of a lying tongue,
such the idle fantasy of those who look for death.

The wicked man's soul is intent on evil,
he looks on his neighbour with dislike.

When a mocker is punished, the ignorant man grows wiser,
when a wise man is instructed he acquires more knowledge.
The Just One watches the house of the wicked:
he hurls the wicked to destruction.

He who shuts his ear to the poor man's cry
shall himself plead and not be heard.

    This is the word of the Lord.

Responsorial Psalm   Ps 118:1. 27. 30. 34-35. 44. ℟ v.35
  ℟ **Guide me, Lord,
in the path of your commands.**

1 They are happy whose life is blameless,
who follow God's law!
Make me grasp the way of your precepts
and I will muse on your wonders.   ℟

2 I have chosen the way of truth
with your decrees before me.
Train me to observe your law,
to keep it with my heart.   ℟

3 Guide me in the path of your commands;
for there is my delight.
I shall always keep your law
for ever and ever.   ℟

Gospel Acclamation   Ps 129:5

Alleluia, alleluia!
My soul is waiting for the Lord,
I count on his word.
Alleluia!

or   Lk 11:28

Alleluia, alleluia!
Happy are those who hear the word of God
and keep it!
Alleluia!

GOSPEL

A reading from the holy Gospel according to Luke   8:19-21

My mother and my brothers are those who hear the word of God and put it into practice.

The mother and brothers of Jesus came looking for him, but they could not get to him because of the crowd. He was told, 'Your mother and brothers are standing outside and want to see you.' But he said in answer, 'My mother and my brothers are those who hear the word of God and put it into practice.'

This is the Gospel of the Lord.

WEDNESDAY

FIRST READING

A reading from the book of Proverbs   30:5-9

Give me neither poverty nor riches, grant me only my share of bread to eat.

Every word of God is unalloyed,
he is the shield of those who take refuge in him.
To his words make no addition,
lest he reprove you and know you for a fraud.

Two things I beg of you,
do not grudge me them before I die:
keep falsehood and lies far from me,
give me neither poverty nor riches,
grant me only my share of bread to eat,
for fear that surrounded by plenty, I should fall away

and say, 'The Lord – who is the Lord?'
or else, in destitution, take to stealing
and profane the name of my God.

This is the word of the Lord.

Responsorial Psalm Ps 118:29. 72. 89. 101. 104. 163. ℟ v.105
℟ **Your word is a lamp for my steps, O Lord.**

1 Keep me, Lord, from the way of error
   and teach me your law.
   The law from your mouth means more to me
   than silver and gold.   ℟

2 Your word, O Lord, for ever
   stands firm in the heavens.
   I turn my feet from evil paths
   to obey your word.   ℟

3 I gain understanding from your precepts
   and so I hate false ways.
   Lies I hate and detest
   but your law is my love.   ℟

Gospel Acclamation   Col 3:16. 17
Alleluia, alleluia!
Let the message of Christ, in all its richness,
find a home with you;
through him give thanks to God the Father.
Alleluia!

or   Mk 1:15

Alleluia, alleluia!
The kingdom of God is close at hand,
repent and believe the Good News.
Alleluia!

GOSPEL

A reading from the holy Gospel according to Luke   9:1-6
Jesus sent them out to proclaim the kingdom of God and to heal.

Jesus called the Twelve together and gave them power and authority over all devils and to cure diseases, and he sent them out to proclaim the kingdom of God and to heal. He said to them, 'Take nothing for the journey: neither staff, nor haversack, nor bread, nor money, and let none of you take a spare tunic. Whatever house you enter, stay there; and when you leave, let it be from there. As for those who do not welcome you, when you leave their town shake the dust from your feet as a sign to them.' So they set out and went from village to village proclaiming the Good News and healing everywhere.

This is the Gospel of the Lord.

THURSDAY

FIRST READING

A reading from the book of Ecclesiastes 1:2-11
There is nothing new under the sun.

Vanity of vanities, the Preacher says. Vanity of vanities. All is vanity! For all his toil, his toil under the sun, what does man gain by it?

A generation goes, a generation comes, yet the earth stands firm for ever. The sun rises, the sun sets; then to its place it speeds and there it rises. Southward goes the wind, then turns to the north; it turns and turns again; back then to its circling goes the wind. Into the sea all the rivers go, and yet the sea is never filled, and still to their goal the rivers go. All things are wearisome. No man can say that eyes have not had enough of seeing, ears their fill of hearing. What was will be again; what has been done will be done again; and there is nothing new under the sun. Take anything of which it may be said, 'Look now, this is new.' Already, long before our time, it existed. Only no memory remains of earlier times, just as in times to come next year itself will not be remembered.

This is the word of the Lord.

Responsorial Psalm Ps 89:3-6. 12-14.17. ℟ v.1

℟ **O Lord, you have been our refuge
from one generation to the next.**

1 You turn men back into dust
and say: 'Go back, sons of men.'
To your eyes a thousand years
are like yesterday, come and gone,
no more than a watch in the night. ℟

Twenty-fifth Week in Ordinary Time, Year II: Thursday 1167

2   You sweep men away like a dream,
    like grass which springs up in the morning.
    In the morning it springs up and flowers:
    by evening it withers and fades. ℟

3   Make us know the shortness of our life
    that we may gain wisdom of heart.
    Lord, relent! Is your anger for ever?
    Show pity to your servants. ℟

4   In the morning, fill us with your love;
    we shall exult and rejoice all our days.
    Let the favour of the Lord be upon us:
    give success to the work of our hands. ℟

Gospel Acclamation Ps 118:18
   Alleluia, alleluia!
   Open my eyes, O Lord, that I may consider
   the wonders of your law.
   Alleluia!

or Jn 14:6

   Alleluia, alleluia!
   I am the Way, the Truth and the Life, says the Lord;
   no one can come to the Father except through me.
   Alleluia!

GOSPEL

A reading from the holy Gospel according to Luke 9:7-9
I beheaded John, so who is this I hear such reports about?

Herod the tetrarch had heard about all that was being done by Jesus; and he was puzzled, because some people were saying that John had risen from the dead, others that Elijah had reappeared, still others that one of the ancient prophets had come back to life. But Herod said, 'John? I beheaded him. So who is this I hear such reports about?' And he was anxious to see Jesus.

This is the Gospel of the Lord.

FRIDAY

FIRST READING

A reading from the book of Ecclesiastes 3:1-11

There is a time for every occupation under heaven.

There is a season for everything, a time for every occupation under heaven:

A time for giving birth, a time for dying;
a time for planting, a time for uprooting what has been planted.
A time for killing, a time for healing;
a time for knocking down, a time for building.
A time for tears, a time for laughter;
a time for mourning, a time for dancing.
A time for throwing stones away, a time for gathering them up;
a time for embracing, a time to refrain from embracing.
A time for searching, a time for losing;
a time for keeping, a time for throwing away.
A time for tearing, a time for sewing;
a time for keeping silent, a time for speaking.
A time for loving, a time for hating;
a time for war, a time for peace.

What does a man gain for the efforts that he makes? I contemplate the task that God gives mankind to labour at. All that he does is apt for its time; but though he has permitted man to consider time in its wholeness, man cannot comprehend the work of God from beginning to end.

This is the word of the Lord.

Responsorial Psalm Ps 143:1-4. ℟ v.1

℟ **Blessed be the Lord, my rock.**

1 Blessed be the Lord, my rock.
He is my love, my fortress;
he is my stronghold, my saviour,
my shield, my place of refuge. ℟

2 Lord, what is man that you care for him,
mortal man, that you keep him in mind;
man, who is merely a breath
whose life fades like a passing shadow? ℟

Twenty-fifth Week in Ordinary Time, Year II: Saturday

Gospel Acclamation cf. Eph 1:17. 18
Alleluia, alleluia!
May the Father of our Lord Jesus Christ
enlighten the eyes of our mind,
so that we can see what hope his call holds for us.
Alleluia!

or Mk 10:45

Alleluia, alleluia!
The Son of Man came to serve,
and to give his life as a ransom for many.
Alleluia!

GOSPEL

A reading from the holy Gospel according to Luke 9:18-22
You are the Christ of God. The Son of Man is destined to suffer grievously.

One day when Jesus was praying alone in the presence of his disciples he put this question to them, 'Who do the crowds say I am?' And they answered, 'John the Baptist; others Elijah; and others say one of the ancient prophets come back to life.' 'But you,' he said 'who do you say I am?' It was Peter who spoke up. 'The Christ of God' he said. But he gave them strict orders not to tell anyone anything about this.

'The Son of Man' he said 'is destined to suffer grievously, to be rejected by the elders and chief priests and scribes and to be put to death, and to be raised up on the third day.'

This is the Gospel of the Lord.

SATURDAY

FIRST READING

A reading from the book of Ecclesiastes 11:9 – 12:8
Remember your creator in the days of your youth, before the dust returns to the earth, and the breath of God.

Rejoice in your youth, you who are young;
let your heart give you joy in your young days.
Follow the promptings of your heart
and the desires of your eyes.

But this you must know: for all these things God will bring you to judgement.

Cast worry from your heart,
shield your flesh from pain.

Yet youth, the age of dark hair, is vanity. And remember your creator in the days of your youth, before evil days come and the years approach when you say, 'These give me no pleasure', before sun and light and moon and stars grow dark, and the clouds return after the rain;

the day when those who keep the house tremble
and strong men are bowed;
when the women grind no longer at the mill,
because day is darkening at the windows
and the street doors are shut;
when the sound of the mill is faint,
when the voice of the bird is silenced,
and song notes are stilled,
when to go uphill is an ordeal
and a walk is something to dread.

Yet the almond tree is in flower,
the grasshopper is heavy with food
and the caper bush bears its fruit,

while man goes to his everlasting home. And the mourners are already walking to and fro in the street

before the silver cord has snapped,
or the golden lamp been broken,
or the pitcher shattered at the spring,
or the pulley cracked at the well,

or before the dust returns to the earth as it once came from it, and the breath of God who gave it.

Vanity of vanities, the Preacher says. All is vanity.

This is the word of the Lord.

Responsorial Psalm   Ps 89:3-6. 12-14. 17. R/ v.1

R/ **O Lord, you have been our refuge
from one generation to the next.**

1 You turn men back into dust
and say: 'Go back, sons of men.'

Twenty-fifth Week in Ordinary Time, Year II: Saturday

> To your eyes a thousand years
> are like yesterday, come and gone,
> no more than a watch in the night. ℟

2. You sweep men away like a dream,
   like grass which springs up in the morning.
   In the morning it springs up and flowers:
   by evening it withers and fades. ℟

3. Make us know the shortness of our life
   that we may gain wisdom of heart.
   Lord, relent! Is your anger for ever?
   Show pity to your servants. ℟

4. In the morning, fill us with your love;
   we shall exult and rejoice all our days.
   Let the favour of the Lord be upon us:
   give success to the work of our hands. ℟

Gospel Acclamation   cf. Acts 16:14
> Alleluia, alleluia!
> Open our heart, O Lord,
> to accept the words of your Son.
> Alleluia!

or   cf. 2 Tim 1:10

> Alleluia, alleluia!
> Our Saviour Christ Jesus abolished death,
> and he has proclaimed life through the Good News.
> Alleluia!

GOSPEL

A reading from the holy Gospel according to Luke   9:43-45

The Son of Man is going to be handed over. They were afraid to ask him about what he had said.

At a time when everyone was full of admiration for all he did, Jesus said to his disciples, 'For your part, you must have these words constantly in your mind: The Son of Man is going to be handed over into the power of men.' But they did not understand him when he said this; it was hidden from them so that they should not see the meaning of it, and they were afraid to ask him about what he had just said.

This is the Gospel of the Lord.

TWENTY-SIXTH WEEK IN ORDINARY TIME
Year II

MONDAY

FIRST READING

A reading from the book of Job 1:6-22

The Lord gave, the Lord has taken back. Blessed be the name of the Lord!

One day the Sons of God came to attend on the Lord, and among them was Satan. So the Lord said to Satan, 'Where have you been?' 'Round the earth,' he answered 'roaming about.' So the Lord asked him, 'Did you notice my servant Job? There is no one like him on the earth: a sound and honest man who fears God and shuns evil.' 'Yes,' Satan said 'but Job is not God-fearing for nothing, is he? Have you not put a wall round him and his house and all his domain? You have blessed all he undertakes, and his flocks throng the countryside. But stretch out your hand and lay a finger on his possessions: I warrant you, he will curse you to your face.' 'Very well,' the Lord said to Satan 'all he has is in your power. But keep your hands off his person.' So Satan left the presence of the Lord.

On the day when Job's sons and daughters were at their meal and drinking wine at their eldest brother's house, a messenger came to Job. 'Your oxen' he said 'were at the plough, with the donkeys grazing at their side, when the Sabaeans swept down on them and carried them off. Your servants they put to the sword: I alone escaped to tell you.' He had not finished speaking when another messenger arrived. 'The fire of God' he said 'has fallen from the heavens and burnt up all your sheep, and your shepherds too: I alone escaped to tell you.' He had not finished speaking when another messenger arrived. 'The Chaldaeans', he said 'three bands of them, have raided your camels and made off with them. Your servants they put to the sword: I alone escaped to tell you.' He had not finished speaking when another messenger arrived. 'Your sons and daughters' he said 'were at their meals and drinking wine at their eldest brother's house, when suddenly from the wilderness a gale sprang up, and it battered all four corners of the house which fell in on the young people. They are dead: I alone escaped to tell you.'

Job rose and tore his gown and shaved his head. Then falling to the ground he worshipped and said:

'Naked I came from my mother's womb,
naked I shall return.
The Lord gave, the Lord has taken back.
Blessed be the name of the Lord!'

In all this misfortune Job committed no sin nor offered any insult to God.

This is the word of the Lord.

Responsorial Psalm   Ps 16:1-3. 6-7. ℟ v.6

℟ **Turn your ear to me, O Lord; hear my words.**

1 Lord, hear a cause that is just,
   pay heed to my cry.
   Turn your ear to my prayer:
   no deceit is on my lips. ℟

2 From you may my judgement come forth:
   Your eyes discern the truth.
   You search my heart, you visit me by night.
   You test me and you find in me no wrong. ℟

3 I am here and I call, you will hear me, O God.
   Turn your ear to me; hear my words.
   Display your great love, you whose right hand saves
   your friends from those who rebel against them. ℟

Gospel Acclamation   Jn 14:23
Alleluia, alleluia
If anyone loves me he will keep my word,
and my Father will love him,
and we shall come to him.
Alleluia!

or   Mk 10:45

Alleluia, alleluia!
The Son of Man came to serve,
and to give his life as a ransom for many.

GOSPEL

A reading from the holy Gospel according to Luke   9:46-50
The least among you all, that is the one who is great

An argument started between the disciples about which of them was the greatest. Jesus knew what thoughts were going through their minds, and he took a little child and set him by his side and then said to them, 'Anyone who welcomes this little child in my name welcomes me; and anyone who welcomes me welcomes the one who sent me. For the least among you all, that is the one who is great.'

John spoke up. 'Master,' he said 'we saw a man casting out devils in your name, and because he is not with us we tried to stop him.' But Jesus said to him, 'You must not stop him: anyone who is not against you is for you.'

This is the Gospel of the Lord.

TUESDAY

FIRST READING

A reading from the book of Job   3:1-3. 11-17. 20-23
Why give light to a man of grief?

Job broke the silence and cursed the day of his birth. This is what he said:

> May the day perish when I was born,
> and the night that told of a boy conceived.
> Why did I not die new-born,
> not perish as I left the womb?
> Why were there two knees to receive me,
> two breasts for me to suck?
> Had there not been, I should now be lying in peace,
> wrapped in a restful slumber,
> with the kings and high viziers of earth
> who build themselves vast vaults,
> or with princes who have gold and to spare
> and houses crammed with silver.
>
> Or put away like a still-born child that never came to be,
> like unborn babes that never see the light.
> Down there, bad men bustle no more,
> there the weary rest.
> Why give light to a man of grief?
> Why give life to those bitter of heart,
> who long for a death that never comes,
> and hunt for it more than for a buried treasure?

They would be glad to see the grave-mound
and shout with joy if they reached the tomb.
Why make this gift of light to a man who does not see his way,
whom God baulks on every side?

This is the word of the Lord.

Responsorial Psalm   Ps 87:2-8. ℟ v.3

℟ **Let my prayer come into your presence, O Lord.**

1. I call to you, Lord, all the day long;
to you I stretch out my hands.
Will you work your wonders for the dead?
Will the shades stand and praise you? ℟

2. Will your love be told in the grave
or your faithfulness among the dead?
Will your wonders be known in the dark
or your justice in the land of oblivion? ℟

3. As for me, Lord, I call to you for help:
in the morning my prayer comes before you.
Lord, why do you reject me?
Why do you hide your face? ℟

Gospel Acclamation   Ps 118:36. 29
Alleluia, alleluia!
Bend my heart to your will, O Lord,
and teach me your law.
Alleluia!

or   Mk 10:45

Alleluia, alleluia!
The Son of Man came to serve,
and to give his life as a ransom for many.
Alleluia!

GOSPEL

A reading from the holy Gospel according to Luke   9:51-56
Jesus resolutely took the road for Jerusalem.

As the time drew near for him to be taken up to heaven, Jesus resolutely took the road for Jerusalem and sent messengers ahead of him. These set out, and they went into a Samaritan village to make preparations for him, but the people would not receive him because he was making for Jerusalem. Seeing this, the disciples

James and John said, 'Lord, do you want us to call down fire from heaven to burn them up?' But he turned and rebuked them, and they went off to another village.

This is the Gospel of the Lord.

WEDNESDAY

FIRST READING

A reading from the book of Job 9:1-13. 14-16
How can man be in the right against God?

Job spoke to his friends.

> Indeed, I know it is as you say:
> how can man be in the right against God?
> If any were so rash as to challenge him for reasons,
> one in a thousand would be more than they could answer.
> His heart is wise, and his strength is great:
> who then can successfully defy him?
> He moves the mountains, though they do not know it;
> he throws them down when he is angry.
> He shakes the earth, and moves it from its place,
> making all its pillars tremble.
> The sun, at his command, forbears to rise,
> and on the stars he sets a seal.
> He and no other stretched out the skies,
> and trampled the Sea's tall waves.
> The Bear, Orion too, are of his making,
> the Pleiades and the Mansions of the South.
> His works are great, beyond all reckoning,
> his marvels, past all counting.
> Were he to pass me, I should not see him,
> nor detect his stealthy movement.
> Were he to snatch a prize, who could prevent him,
> or dare to say, 'What are you doing?'
> How dare I plead my cause, then,
> or choose arguments against him?
> Suppose I am in the right, what use is my defence?
> For he whom I must sue is judge as well.
> If he deigned to answer my citation,
> could I be sure that he would listen to my voice?

This is the word of the Lord.

Responsorial Psalm Ps 87:10-15. ℟ v.3

℟ **Let my prayer come into your presence, O Lord.**

1 I call to you, Lord, all the day long;
 to you I stretch out my hands.
 Will you work your wonders for the dead?
 Will the shades stand and praise you? ℟

2 Will your love be told in the grave
 or your faithfulness among the dead?
 Will your wonders be known in the dark
 or your justice in the land of oblivion? ℟

3 As for me, Lord, I call to you for help:
 in the morning my prayer comes before you.
 Lord, why do you reject me?
 Why do you hide your face? ℟

Gospel Acclamation Ps 118:105

Alleluia, alleluia!
Your word is a lamp for my steps
and a light for my path.
Alleluia!

or Phil 3:8-9

Alleluia, alleluia!
I have accepted the loss of everything
and I look on everything as so much rubbish
if only I can have Christ
and be given a place in him.
Alleluia!

GOSPEL

A reading from the holy Gospel according to Luke 9:57-62
I will follow you wherever you go.

As Jesus and his disciples travelled along they met a man on the road who said to him, 'I will follow you wherever you go.' Jesus answered, 'Foxes have holes and the birds of the air have nests, but the Son of Man has nowhere to lay his head.'

Another to whom he said, 'Follow me' replied, 'Let me go and bury my father first.' But he answered, 'Leave the dead to bury their dead; your duty is to go and spread the news of the kingdom of God.'

Another said, 'I will follow you, sir, but first let me go and say good-bye to my people at home.' Jesus said to him, 'Once the hand is laid on the plough, no one who looks back is fit for the kingdom of God.'

This is the Gospel of the Lord.

THURSDAY

FIRST READING

A reading from the book of Job 19:21-27
I know that my Avenger lives.

Job said:

Pity me, pity me, you, my friends,
for the hand of God has struck me.
Why do you hound me down like God,
will you never have enough of my flesh?
Ah, would that these words of mine were written down,
inscribed on some monument
with iron chisel and engraving tool,
cut into the rock for ever.
This I know: that my Avenger lives,
and he, the Last, will take his stand on earth.
After my awaking, he will set me close to him,
and from my flesh I shall look on God.
He whom I shall see will take my part:
these eyes will gaze on him and find him not aloof.

This is the word of the Lord.

Responsorial Psalm Ps 26:7-9. 13-14. R̸ v.13

R̸ **I am sure I shall see the Lord's goodness
in the land of the living.**

1 O Lord, hear my voice when I call;
have mercy and answer.
Of you my heart has spoken:
'Seek his face.' R̸

2 It is your face, O Lord, that I seek;
hide not your face.
Dismiss not your servant in anger;
you have been my help. R̸

3 I am sure I shall see the Lord's goodness
   in the land of the living.
   Hope in him, hold firm and take heart.
   Hope in the Lord!   ℟

Gospel Acclamation   Mt 4:4
   Alleluia, alleluia!
   Man does not live on bread alone,
   but on every word that comes from the mouth of God.
   Alleluia!

or   Mk 1:15

   Alleluia, alleluia!
   The kingdom of God is close at hand,
   repent and believe the Good News.
   Alleluia!

GOSPEL

A reading from the holy Gospel according to Luke   10:1-12
Your peace will rest on him.

The Lord appointed seventy-two others and sent them out ahead of him, in pairs, to all the towns and places he himself was to visit. He said to them, 'The harvest is rich but the labourers are few, so ask the Lord of the harvest to send labourers to his harvest. Start off now, but remember, I am sending you out like lambs among wolves. Carry no purse, no haversack, no sandals. Salute no one on the road. Whatever house you go into, let your first words be, "Peace to this house!" And if a man of peace lives there, your peace will go and rest on him; if not, it will come back to you. Stay in the same house, taking what food and drink they have to offer, for the labourer deserves his wages; do not move from house to house. Whenever you go into a town where they make you welcome, eat what is set before you. Cure those in it who are sick, and say, "The kingdom of God is very near to you." But whenever you enter a town and they do not make you welcome, go out into its streets and say, "We wipe off the very dust of your town that clings to our feet, and leave it with you. Yet be sure of this: the kingdom of God is very near." I tell you, on that day it will not go as hard with Sodom as with that town.'

This is the Gospel of the Lord.

FRIDAY

FIRST READING

A reading from the book of Job   38:1. 12-21; 40:3-5
Have you given orders to the morning, or journeyed all the way to the sources of the sea?

From the heart of the tempest the Lord gave Job his answer. He said:

> Have you ever in your life given orders to the morning
> or sent the dawn to its post,
> telling it to grasp the earth by its edges
> and shake the wicked out of it,
> when it changes the earth to sealing clay
> and dyes it as a man dyes clothes;
> stealing the light from wicked men
> and breaking the arm raised to strike?
> Have you journeyed all the way to the sources of the sea,
> or walked where the Abyss is deepest?
> Have you been shown the gates of Death
> or met the janitors of Shadowland?
> Have you an inkling of the extent of the earth?
> Tell me all about it if you have!
> Which is the way to the home of the light,
> and where does darkness live?
> You could then show them the way to their proper places,
> or put them on the path to where they live!
> If you know all this, you must have been born with them,
> you must be very old by now!

Job replied to the Lord:

> My words have been frivolous: what can I reply?
> I had better lay my finger on my lips.
> I have spoken once . . . I will not speak again;
> more than once . . . I will add nothing.

This is the word of the Lord.

Responsorial Psalm   Ps 138:1-3. 7-10. 13-14. R/ v.24

℟ **Lead me, O Lord, in the path of life eternal.**

1 O Lord, you search me and you know me,
   you know my resting and my rising,
   you discern my purpose from afar.

You mark when I walk or lie down,
all my ways lie open to you. ℟

2 O where can I go from your spirit,
   or where can I flee from your face?
   If I climb the heavens, you are there.
   If I lie in the grave, you are there. ℟

3 If I take the wings of the dawn
   and dwell at the sea's furthest end,
   even there your hand would lead me,
   your right hand would hold me fast. ℟

4 For it was you who created my being,
   knit me together in my mother's womb.
   I thank you for the wonders of my being,
   for the wonders of all your creation. ℟

Gospel Acclamation   Ps 144:13
   Alleluia, alleluia!
   The Lord is faithful in all his words
   and loving in all his deeds.
   Alleluia!
or   cf. Ps 94:8
   Alleluia, alleluia!
   Harden not your hearts today,
   but listen to the voice of the Lord.
   Alleluia!

GOSPEL

A reading from the holy Gospel according to Luke   10:13-16
Anyone who rejects me rejects the one who sent me.

Jesus said to his disciples: 'Alas for you, Chorazin! Alas for you, Bethsaida! For if the miracles done in you had been done in Tyre and Sidon, they would have repented long ago, sitting in sackcloth and ashes. And still, it will not go as hard with Tyre and Sidon at the Judgement as with you. And as for you, Capernaum, did you want to be exalted high as heaven? You shall be thrown down to hell.

   'Anyone who listens to you listens to me; anyone who rejects you rejects me, and those who reject me reject the one who sent me.'

   This is the Gospel of the Lord.

SATURDAY

FIRST READING

A reading from the book of Job   42:1-3. 5-6. 12-17
Having seen you with my own eyes, I retract all I have said.

This was the answer Job gave to the Lord:

> I know that you are all-powerful:
> what you conceive, you can perform.
> I am the man who obscured your designs
> with my empty-headed words.
> I have been holding forth on matters I cannot understand,
> on marvels beyond me and my knowledge.
> I knew you then only by hearsay;
> but now, having seen you with my own eyes,
> I retract all I have said,
> and in dust and ashes I repent.

The Lord blessed Job's new fortune even more than his first one. He came to own fourteen thousand sheep, six thousand camels, a thousand yoke of oxen and a thousand she-donkeys. He had seven sons and three daughters; his first daughter he called 'Turtledove', the second 'Cassia' and the third 'Mascara'. Throughout the land there were no women as beautiful as the daughters of Job. And their father gave them inheritance rights like their brothers.

After his trials, Job lived on until he was a hundred and forty years old, and saw his children and his children's children up to the fourth generation. Then Job died, an old man and full of days.

This is the word of the Lord.

Responsorial Psalm   Ps 118:66. 71. 75. 91. 125. 130. ℟ v.135

℟ **Let your face shine on your servant, O Lord.**

1. Teach me discernment and knowledge
   for I trust in your commands.
   It was good for me to be afflicted,
   to learn your statutes. ℟

2. Lord, I know that your decrees are right,
   that you afflicted me justly.
   By your decree the earth endures to this day;
   for all things serve you. ℟

3 I am your servant, make me understand;
then I shall know your will.
The unfolding of your word gives light
and teaches the simple. ℟

Gospel Acclamation cf. Mt 11:25
Alleluia, alleluia!
Blessed are you, Father, Lord of heaven and earth,
for revealing the mysteries of the kingdom to mere children.
Alleluia!

GOSPEL

A reading from the holy Gospel according to Luke 10:17-24
Rejoice that your names are written in heaven.

The seventy-two came back rejoicing. 'Lord,' they said 'even the devils submit to us when we use your name.' Jesus said to them, 'I watched Satan fall like lighting from heaven. Yes, I have given you power to tread underfoot serpents and scorpions and the whole strength of the enemy; nothing shall ever hurt you. Yet do not rejoice that the spirits submit to you; rejoice rather that your names are written in heaven.'

It was then that, filled with joy by the Holy Spirit, he said, 'I bless you, Father, Lord of heaven and of earth, for hiding these things from the learned and the clever and revealing them to mere children. Yes, Father, for that is what it pleased you to do. Everything has been entrusted to me by my Father; and no one knows who the Son is except the Father, and who the Father is except the Son and those to whom the Son chooses to reveal him.'

Then turning to his disciples he spoke to them in private, 'Happy the eyes that see what you see, for I tell you that many prophets and kings wanted to see what you see, and never saw it; to hear what you hear, and never heard it.'

This is the Gospel of the Lord.

A MAN went down from Jerusalem to Jericho. On the way, he was ATTACKED · BEATEN left HALF-DEAD

A priest saw him and hurried past; a levite saw him & went on his way

BUT A SAMARITAN SAW HIM PITIED & CARED

WHO IS MY NEIGHBOUR

and wine on them. He then lifted him on to his own mount, carried him to the inn and looked after him. Next day, he took out two denarii and handed them to the innkeeper. "Look after him," he said "and on my way back I will make good any extra expense you have." Which of these three, do you think, proved himself a neighbour to the man who fell into the brigands' hands?' 'The one who took pity on him' he replied. Jesus said to him, 'Go, and do the same yourself.'

This is the Gospel of the Lord.

TUESDAY

FIRST READING

A reading from the letter of St Paul to the Galatians   1:13-24

God revealed his Son in me, so that I might preach the Good News about him to the pagans.

You must have heard of my career as a practising Jew, how merciless I was in persecuting the Church of God, how much damage I did to it, how I stood out among other Jews of my generation, and how enthusiastic I was for the traditions of my ancestors.

Then God, who had specially chosen me while I was still in my mother's womb, called me through his grace and chose to reveal his Son in me, so that I might preach the Good News about him to the pagans. I did not stop to discuss this with any human being, nor did I go up to Jerusalem to see those who were already apostles before me, but I went off to Arabia at once and later went straight back from there to Damascus. Even when after three years I went up to Jerusalem to visit Cephas and stayed with him for fifteen days, I did not see any of the other apostles; I only saw James, the brother of the Lord, and I swear before God that what I have just written is the literal truth. After that I went to Syria and Cilicia, and was still not known by sight to the churches of Christ in Judaea, who had heard nothing except that their one-time persecutor was now preaching the faith he had previously tried to destroy; and they gave glory to God for me.

This is the word of the Lord.

Responsorial Psalm
Ps 138:1-3. 13-15. ℟ v.24

℟ **Lead me, O Lord, in the path of life eternal.**

1 O Lord, you search me and you know me,
   you know my resting and my rising,
   you discern my purpose from afar.
   You mark when I walk or lie down,
   all my ways lie open to you.   ℟

2 For it was you who created my being,
   knit me together in my mother's womb.
   I thank you for the wonder of my being,
   for the wonders of all your creation.   ℟

3 Already you knew my soul,
   my body held no secret from you,
   when I was being fashioned in secret
   and moulded in the depths of the earth.   ℟

Gospel Acclamation
Jn 15:15

Alleluia, alleluia!
I call you friends, says the Lord,
because I have made known to you
everything I have learnt from my Father.
Alleluia!

or
Lk 11:28

Alleluia, alleluia!
Happy are those who hear the word of God
and keep it!
Alleluia!

GOSPEL

A reading from the holy Gospel according to Luke   10:38-42

Martha welcomed Jesus into her house. It is Mary who has chosen the better part.

Jesus came to a village, and a woman named Martha welcomed him into her house. She had a sister called Mary, who sat down at the Lord's feet and listened to him speaking. Now Martha who was distracted with all the serving said, 'Lord, do you not care that my sister is leaving me to do the serving all by myself? Please tell her to help me.' But the Lord answered: 'Martha, Martha,' he said 'you worry and fret about so many things, and yet few are needed, indeed only one. It is Mary who has chosen the better part; it is not to be taken from her.'

This is the Gospel of the Lord.

WEDNESDAY

FIRST READING

A reading from the letter of St Paul to the Galatians   2:1-2. 7-14
They recognised the grace God had given to me.

It was not till fourteen years had passed that I went up to Jerusalem again. I went with Barnabas and took Titus with me. I went there as the result of a revelation, and privately I laid before the leading men the Good News as I proclaim it among the pagans; I did so for fear the course I was adopting or had already adopted would not be allowed. On the contrary, they recognised that I had been commissioned to preach the Good News to the uncircumcised just as Peter had been commissioned to preach it to the circumcised. The same person whose action had made Peter the apostle of the circumcised had given me a similar mission to the pagans. So, James, Cephas and John, these leaders, these pillars, shook hands with Barnabas and me as a sign of partnership: we were to go to the pagans and they to the circumcised. The only thing they insisted on was that we should remember to help the poor, as indeed I was anxious to do.

When Cephas came to Antioch, however, I opposed him to his face, since he was manifestly in the wrong. His custom had been to eat with the pagans, but after certain friends of James arrived he stopped doing this and kept away from them altogether for fear of the group that insisted on circumcision. The other Jews joined him in this pretence, and even Barnabas felt himself obliged to copy their behaviour.

When I saw they were not respecting the true meaning of the Good News, I said to Cephas in front of everyone, 'In spite of being a Jew, you live like the pagans and not like the Jews, so you have no right to make the pagans copy Jewish ways.'

This is the word of the Lord.

Responsorial Psalm   Ps 116. ℟ Mk 16:15

℟ **Go out to the whole world;
proclaim the Good News.**

or

℟ **Alleluia!**

1. O praise the Lord, all you nations,
acclaim him all you peoples! ℟

2. Strong is his love for us;
he is faithful for ever. ℟

Gospel Acclamation   Ps 118:34
Alleluia, alleluia!
Train me, Lord, to observe your law,
to keep it with my heart.
Alleluia!

or   Rom 8:15

Alleluia, alleluia!
The spirit you received is the spirit of sons,
and it makes us cry out, 'Abba, Father!'
Alleluia!

GOSPEL

A reading from the holy Gospel according to Luke   11:1-4

Lord, teach us to pray.

Once Jesus was in a certain place praying, and when he had finished, one of his disciples said, 'Lord, teach us to pray, just as John taught his disciples.' He said to them, 'Say this when you pray:

"Father, may your name be held holy,
your kingdom come;
give us each day our daily bread,
and forgive us our sins,
for we ourselves forgive each one who is in debt to us.
And do not put us to the test." '

This is the Gospel of the Lord.

THURSDAY

FIRST READING

A reading from the letter of St Paul to the Galatians 3:1-5

Was it because you practised the Law that you received the Spirit, or because you believed what was preached to you?

Are you people in Galatia mad? Has someone put a spell on you, in spite of the plain explanation you have had of the crucifixion of Jesus Christ? Let me ask you one question: was it because you practised the Law that you received the Spirit, or because you believed what was preached to you? Are you foolish enough to end in outward observances what you began in the Spirit? Have all the favours you received been wasted? And if this were so, they would most certainly have been wasted. Does God give you the Spirit so freely and work miracles among you because you practise the Law, or because you believed what was preached to you?

This is the word of the Lord.

Responsorial Psalm
Lk 1:69-75. ℟ cf. v.68

℟ **Blessed be the Lord, the God of Israel!**
He has visited his people.

1. God has raised up for us a mighty saviour
   in the house of David his servant,
   as he promised by the lips of holy men,
   those who were his prophets from of old. ℟

2. A saviour who would free us from our foes,
   from the hands of all who hate us.
   So his love for our fathers is fulfilled
   and his holy covenant remembered. ℟

3. He swore to Abraham our father
   to grant us, that free from fear,
   and saved from the hands of our foes,
   we might serve him in holiness and justice
   all the days of our life in his presence. ℟

Gospel Acclamation
Jn 14:6

Alleluia, alleluia!
I am the Way, the Truth and the Life, says the Lord;
no one can come to the Father except through me.
Alleluia!

or cf. Acts 16:14

Alleluia, alleluia!
Open our heart, O Lord,
to accept the words of your Son.
Alleluia!

GOSPEL

A reading from the holy Gospel according to Luke 11:5-13
Ask, and it will be given to you.

Jesus said to his disciples: 'Suppose one of you has a friend and goes to him in the middle of the night to say, "My friend, lend me three loaves, because a friend of mine on his travels has just arrived at my house and I have nothing to offer him"; and the man answers from inside the house, "Do not bother me. The door is bolted now, and my children and I are in bed; I cannot get up to give it you." I tell you, if the man does not get up and give it him for friendship's sake, persistence will be enough to make him get up and give his friend all he wants.

'So I say to you: Ask, and it will be given to you; search, and you will find; knock, and the door will be opened to you. For the one who asks always receives; the one who searches always finds; the one who knocks will always have the door opened to him. What father among you would hand his son a stone when he asked for bread? Or hand him a snake instead of a fish? Or hand him a scorpion if he asked for an egg? If you then, who are evil, know how to give your children what is good, how much more will the heavenly Father give the Holy Spirit to those who ask him!'

This is the Gospel of the Lord.

FRIDAY

FIRST READING

A reading from the letter of St Paul to the Galatians 3:7-14
Those who rely on faith receive the same blessing as Abraham, the man of faith.

Don't you see that it is those who rely on faith who are the sons of Abraham? Scripture foresaw that God was going to use faith to justify the pagans, and proclaimed the Good News long ago when Abraham was told: In you all the pagans will be blessed. Those therefore who rely on faith receive the same blessing as Abraham, the man of faith.

On the other hand, those who rely on the keeping of the Law are under a curse, since scripture says: Cursed be everyone who does not persevere in observing everything prescribed in the book of the Law. The Law will not justify anyone in the sight of God, because we are told: the righteous man finds life through faith. The Law is not even based on faith, since we are told: The man who practises these precepts finds life through practising them. Christ redeemed us from the curse of the Law by being cursed for our sake, since scripture says: Cursed be everyone who is hanged on a tree. This was done so that in Christ Jesus the blessing of Abraham might include the pagans, and so that through faith we might receive the promised Spirit.

This is the word of the Lord.

Responsorial Psalm

Ps 110:1-6. R︎ v.5

R︎ **The Lord keeps his covenant ever in mind.**

or

R︎ **Alleluia!**

1 I will thank the Lord with all my heart
in the meeting of the just and their assembly.
Great are the works of the Lord;
to be pondered by all who love them. R︎

2 Majestic and glorious his work,
his justice stands firm for ever.
He makes us remember his wonders.
The Lord is compassion and love. R︎

3 He gives food to those who fear him;
keeps his covenant ever in mind.
He has shown his might to his people
by giving them the lands of the nations. R︎

Gospel Acclamation

Jn 10:27

Alleluia, alleluia!
The sheep that belong to me listen to my voice,
says the Lord,
I know them and they follow me.
Alleluia!

or Jn 12:31-32

Alleluia, alleluia!
Now the prince of this world is to be overthrown,
says the Lord;
and when I am lifted up from the earth
I shall draw all men to myself.
Alleluia!

GOSPEL

A reading from the Gospel according to Luke 11:15-26

If it is through the finger of God that I cast out devils, then know that the kingdom of God has overtaken you.

When Jesus had cast out a devil, some of the people said, 'It is through Beelzebul, the prince of devils, that he casts out devils.' Others asked Jesus, as a test, for a sign from heaven; but knowing what they were thinking, he said to them, 'Every kingdom divided against itself is heading for ruin, and a household divided against itself collapses. So too with Satan: if he is divided against himself, how can his kingdom stand? – since you assert that it is through Beelzebul that I cast out devils. Now if it is through Beelzebul that I cast out devils through whom do your own experts cast them out? Let them be your judges, then. But if it is through the finger of God that I cast out devils, then know that the kingdom of God has overtaken you. So long as a strong man fully armed guards his own palace, his goods are undisturbed; but when someone stronger than he is attacks and defeats him, the stronger man takes away all the weapons he relied on and shares out his spoil.

'He who is not with me is against me; and he who does not gather with me scatters.

'When an unclean spirit goes out of a man it wanders through waterless country looking for a place to rest, and not finding one it says, "I will go back to the home I came from." But on arrival, finding it swept and tidied, it then goes off and brings seven other spirits more wicked than itself, and they go in and set up house there, so that the man ends up by being worse than he was before.'

This is the Gospel of the Lord.

SATURDAY

FIRST READING

A reading from the letter of St Paul to the Galatians 3:22-29
You are all sons of God through faith.

Scripture makes no exceptions when it says that sin is master everywhere. In this way the promise can only be given through faith in Jesus Christ and can only be given to those who have this faith.

Before faith came, we were allowed no freedom by the Law; we were being looked after till faith was revealed. The Law was to be our guardian until the Christ came and we could be justified by faith. Now that that time has come we are no longer under that guardian, and you are, all of you, sons of God through faith in Christ Jesus. All baptised in Christ, you have all clothed yourselves in Christ, and there are no more distinctions between Jew and Greek, slave and free, male and female, but all of you are one in Christ Jesus. Merely by belonging to Christ you are the posterity of Abraham, the heirs he was promised.

This is the word of the Lord.

Responsorial Psalm Ps 104:2-7. ℟ v.8

℟ **The Lord remembers his covenant for ever.**

or

℟ **Alleluia!**

1 O sing to the Lord, sing his praise;
 tell all his wonderful works!
 Be proud of his holy name,
 let the hearts that seek the Lord rejoice. ℟

2 Consider the Lord and his strength;
 constantly seek his face.
 Remember the wonders he has done,
 his miracles, the judgements he spoke. ℟

3 O children of Abraham, his servant,
 O sons of the Jacob he chose.
 He, the Lord, is our God:
 his judgements prevail in all the earth. ℟

Gospel Acclamation   Jn 14:23

Alleluia, alleluia!
If anyone loves me he will keep my word,
and my Father will love him,
and we shall come to him.
Alleluia!

or   Lk 11:28

Alleluia, alleluia!
Happy are those who hear the word of God
and keep it!
Alleluia!

GOSPEL

A reading from the holy Gospel according to Luke   11:27-28

Happy the womb that bore you! Still happier those who hear the word of God.

As Jesus was speaking, a woman in the crowd raised her voice and said, 'Happy the womb that bore you and the breasts you sucked!' But he replied, 'Still happier those who hear the word of God and keep it!'

This is the Gospel of the Lord.

TWENTY-EIGHTH WEEK IN ORDINARY TIME
Year II

MONDAY

FIRST READING

A reading from the letter of St Paul   4:22-24. 26-27. 31 – 5:1
to the Galatians

We are the children, not of the slave-girl, but of the free-born wife.

The Law says, if you remember, that Abraham had two sons, one by the slave-girl, and one by his free-born wife. The child of the slave-girl was born in the ordinary way; the child of the free woman was born as the result of a promise. This can be regarded as an allegory: the women stand for the two covenants. The first who comes from Mount Sinai, and whose children are slaves, is Hagar. The Jerusalem above, however, is free and is our mother, since scripture says: Shout for joy, you barren women who bore no children! Break into shouts of joy and gladness, you who were never in labour. For there are more sons of the forsaken one than sons of the wedded wife. So, my brothers, we are the children, not of the slave-girl, but of the free-born wife.

When Christ freed us, he meant us to remain free. Stand firm, therefore, and do not submit again to the yoke of slavery.

This is the word of the Lord.

Responsorial Psalm   Ps 112:1-7. ℟ v.2

    ℟ **May the name of the Lord be blessed for evermore!**

or

    ℟ **Alleluia!**

1. Praise, O servants of the Lord,
   praise the name of the Lord!
   May the name of the Lord be blessed
   both now and for evermore! ℟

2. From the rising of the sun to its setting
   praised be the name of the Lord!
   High above all nations is the Lord,
   above the heavens his glory. ℟

3. Who is like the Lord, our God,
   who stoops from the heights to look down,
   to look down upon heaven and earth?
   From the dust he lifts up the lowly,
   from the dungheap he raises the poor. ℟

Gospel Acclamation   Ps 118:88

    Alleluia, alleluia!
    Because of your love give me life,
    and I will do your will.
    Alleluia!

or   cf. Ps 94:8

    Alleluia, alleluia!
    Harden not your hearts today,
    but listen to the voice of the Lord.
    Alleluia!

GOSPEL

A reading from the holy Gospel according to Luke   11:29-32

The only sign which will be given to this wicked generation is the sign of Jonah.

The crowds got even bigger and Jesus addressed them, 'This is a wicked generation; it is asking for a sign. The only sign it will be given is the sign of Jonah. For just as Jonah became a sign to the Ninevites, so will the Son of Man be to this generation. On Judgement day the Queen of the South will rise up with the men of this generation and condemn them, because she came from the ends of the earth to hear the wisdom of Solomon; and there is something greater than Solomon here. On Judgement day the men of Nineveh will stand up with this generation and condemn it, because when Jonah preached they repented; and there is something greater than Jonah here.'

    This is the Gospel of the Lord.

TUESDAY

FIRST READING

A reading from the letter of St Paul to the Galatians   5:1-6

Whether you are circumcised or not makes no difference – what matters is faith that makes its power felt through love.

When Christ freed us, he meant us to remain free. Stand firm, therefore, and do not submit again to the yoke of slavery. It is I, Paul, who tell you this: if you allow yourselves to be circumcised, Christ will be of no benefit to you at all. With all solemnity I repeat my warning: Everyone who accepts circumcision is obliged to keep the whole Law. But if you do look to the Law to make you justified, then you have separated yourselves from Christ, and have fallen from grace. Christians are told by the Spirit to look to faith for those rewards that righteousness hopes for, since in Christ Jesus whether you are circumcised or not makes no difference – what matters is faith that makes its power felt through love.

    This is the word of the Lord.

Responsional Psalm   Ps 118:41. 43-45. 47-48. ℟ v.41

℟ **Lord, let your love come upon me.**

1. Lord, let your love come upon me,
    the saving help of your promise.
    Do not take the word of truth from my mouth
    for I trust in your decrees. ℟

2. I shall always keep your law
    for ever and ever.
    I shall walk in the path of freedom
    for I see your precepts. ℟

3. Your commands have been my delight;
    these I have loved.
    I will worship your commands and love them
    and ponder your statutes. ℟

Gospel Acclamation   Ps 118:135

Alleluia! alleluia!
Let your face shine on your servant,
and teach me your decrees.
Alleluia!

or   Heb 4:12

Alleluia, alleluia!
The word of God is something alive and active;
it can judge secret emotions and thoughts.
Alleluia!

GOSPEL

A reading from the holy Gospel according to Luke   11:37-41

Give alms and then indeed everything will be clean for you.

Jesus had just finished speaking when a Pharisee invited him to dine at his house. He went in and sat down at the table. The Pharisee saw this and was surprised that he had not first washed before the meal. But the Lord said to him, 'Oh, you Pharisees! You clean the outside of cup and plate, while inside yourselves you are filled with extortion and wickedness. Fools! Did not he who made the outside make the inside too? Instead, give alms from what you have and then indeed everything will be clean for you.'

This is the Gospel of the Lord.

WEDNESDAY

FIRST READING

A reading from the letter of St Paul to the Galatians 5:18-25
You cannot belong to Christ unless you crucify all self-indulgent passions and desires.

If you are led by the Spirit, no law can touch you. When self-indulgence is at work the results are obvious: fornication, gross indecency and sexual irresponsibility; idolatry and sorcery; feuds and wrangling, jealousy, bad temper and quarrels; disagreements, factions, envy; drunkenness, orgies and similar things. I warn you now, as I warned you before: those who behave like this will not inherit the kingdom of God. What the Spirit brings is very different: love, joy, peace, patience, kindness, goodness, trustfulness, gentleness and self-control. There can be no law against things like that, of course. You cannot belong to Christ Jesus unless you crucify all self-indulgent passions and desires.

Since the Spirit is our life, let us be directed by the Spirit.

This is the word of the Lord.

Responsorial Psalm

Ps 1:1-4. 6. ℟ cf. Jn 8:12

℟ **Anyone who follows you, O Lord,
will have the light of life.**

1 Happy indeed is the man,
   who follows not the counsel of the wicked;
   nor lingers in the way of sinners
   nor sits in the company of scorners,
   but whose delight is the law of the Lord
   and who ponders his law day and night. ℟

2 He is like a tree that is planted
   beside the flowing waters,
   that yields its fruit in due season
   and whose leaves shall never fade;
   and all that he does shall prosper. ℟

3 Not so are the wicked, not so!
   For they like winnowed chaff
   shall be driven away by the wind.
   For the Lord guards the way of the just
   but the way of the wicked leads to doom. ℟

Twenty-eighth Week in Ordinary Time, Year II: Thursday

Gospel Acclamation   cf. Ps 26:11
>Alleluia, alleluia!
>Instruct me, Lord, in your way;
>on an even path lead me.
>Alleluia!

or   Jn 10:27

>Alleluia, alleluia!
>The sheep that belong to me listen to my voice,
>says the Lord,
>I know them and they follow me.
>Alleluia!

GOSPEL

A reading from the holy Gospel according to Luke   11:42-46
Alas for you Pharisees! And alas for you lawyers also!

The Lord said to the Pharisees: 'Alas for you Pharisees! You who pay your tithe of mint and rue and all sorts of garden herbs and overlook justice and the love of God! These you should have practised, without leaving the others undone. Alas for you Pharisees who like taking the seats of honour in the synagogues and being greeted obsequiously in the market squares! Alas for you, because you are like the unmarked tombs that men walk on without knowing it!'

A lawyer then spoke up. 'Master,' he said 'when you speak like this you insult us too.' 'Alas for you lawyers also,' he replied 'because you load on men burdens that are unendurable, burdens that you yourselves do not move a finger to lift.'

This is the Gospel of the Lord.

THURSDAY

FIRST READING

A reading from the letter of St Paul to the Ephesians   1:1-10
Before the world was made, he chose us in Christ

From Paul, appointed by God to be an apostle of Christ Jesus, to the saints who are faithful to Christ Jesus: Grace and peace to you from God our Father and from the Lord Jesus Christ.

Blessed be God the Father of our Lord Jesus Christ,

who has blessed us with all the spiritual blessings of heaven in
   Christ.
Before the world was made, he chose us, chose us in Christ,
to be holy and spotless, and to live through love in his presence,
determining that we should become his adopted sons, through
   Jesus Christ
for his own kind purposes,
to make us praise the glory of his grace,
his free gift to us in the Beloved,
in whom, through his blood, we gain our freedom, the
   forgiveness of our sins.
Such is the richness of the grace
which he has showered on us
in all wisdom and insight.
He has let us know the mystery of his purpose,
the hidden plan he so kindly made in Christ from the beginning
to act upon when the times had run their course to the end:
that he would bring everything together under Christ, as head,
everything in the heavens and everything on earth.

    This is the word of the Lord.

Responsorial Psalm   Ps 97:1-6. ℟ v.2
  ℟ **The Lord has shown his salvation.**

1. Sing a new song to the Lord
   for he has worked wonders.
   His right hand and his holy arm
   have brought salvation.   ℟

2. The Lord has made known his salvation;
   has shown his justice to the nations.
   He has remembered his truth and love
   for the house of Israel.   ℟

3. All the ends of the earth have seen
   the salvation of our God.
   Shout to the Lord all the earth,
   ring out your joy.   ℟

4. Sing psalms to the Lord with the harp
   with the sound of music.
   With trumpets and the sound of the horn
   acclaim the King, the Lord.   ℟

Gospel Acclamation

Ps 110:7. 8

Alleluia, alleluia!
Your precepts, O Lord, are all of them sure;
they stand firm for ever and ever.
Alleluia!

or

Jn 14:6

Alleluia, alleluia!
I am the Way, the Truth and the Life, says the Lord;
no one can come to the Father except through me.
Alleluia!

GOSPEL

A reading from the holy Gospel according to Luke 11:47-54

This generation will have to answer for every prophet's blood, from the blood of Abel to the blood of Zechariah.

Jesus said: 'Alas for you who build the tombs of the prophets, the men your ancestors killed! In this way you both witness what your ancestors did and approve it; they did the killing, you do the building.

'And that is why the Wisdom of God said, "I will send them prophets and apostles; some they will slaughter and persecute, so that this generation will have to answer for every prophet's blood that has been shed since the foundation of the world, from the blood of Abel to the blood of Zechariah, who was murdered between the altar and the sanctuary." Yes, I tell you, this generation will have to answer for it all.

'Alas for you lawyers who have taken away the key of knowledge! You have not gone in yourselves, and have prevented others going in who wanted to.'

When he left the house, the scribes and the Pharisees began a furious attack on him and tried to force answers from him on innumerable questions, setting traps to catch him out in something he might say.

This is the Gospel of the Lord.

FRIDAY

FIRST READING

A reading from the letter of St Paul to the Ephesians   1:11-14

We put our hopes in Christ before he came. You too have been stamped with the seal of the Holy Spirit.

It is in Christ that we were claimed as God's own,
chosen from the beginning,
under the predetermined plan of the one who guides all things
as he decides by his own will;
chosen to be,
for his greater glory,
the people who would put their hopes in Christ before he came.
Now you too, in him,
have heard the message of the truth and the good news of your salvation,
and have believed it;
and you too have been stamped with the seal of the Holy Spirit of the Promise,
the pledge of our inheritance
which brings freedom for those whom God has taken for his own,
to make his glory praised.

    This is the word of the Lord.

Responsorial Psalm   Ps 32:1-2. 4-5. 12-13. ℟ v.12

   ℟ **Happy the people the Lord has chosen as his own.**

1   Ring out your joy to the Lord, O you just;
    for praise is fitting for loyal hearts.
    Give thanks to the Lord upon the harp,
    with a ten-stringed lute sing him songs.   ℟

2   For the word of the Lord is faithful
    and all his works to be trusted.
    The Lord loves justice and right
    and fills the earth with his love.   ℟

3   They are happy, whose God is the Lord,
    the people he has chosen as his own.
    From the heavens the Lord looks forth,
    he sees all the children of men.   ℟

Gospel Acclamation
cf. Ps 18:9

Alleluia, alleluia!
Your words gladden the heart, O Lord,
they give light to the eyes.
Alleluia!

or
Ps 32:22

Alleluia, alleluia!
May your love be upon us, O Lord,
as we place all our hope in you.
Alleluia!

GOSPEL

A reading from the holy Gospel according to Luke 12:1-7
Every hair on your head has been counted.

The people had gathered in their thousands so that they were treading on one another. And Jesus began to speak, first of all to his disciples. 'Be on your guard against the yeast of the Pharisees – that is, their hypocrisy. Everything that is now covered will be uncovered, and everything now hidden will be made clear. For this reason, whatever you have said in the dark will be heard in the daylight, and what you have whispered in hidden places will be proclaimed on the housetops.

'To you my friends I say: Do not be afraid of those who kill the body and after that can do no more. I will tell you whom to fear: fear him who, after he has killed, has the power to cast into hell. Yes, I tell you, fear him. Can you not buy five sparrows for two pennies? And yet not one is forgotten in God's sight. Why, every hair on your head has been counted. There is no need to be afraid: you are worth more than hundreds of sparrows.'

This is the Gospel of the Lord.

SATURDAY

FIRST READING

A reading from the letter of St Paul to the Ephesians 1:15-23
God has made Christ the head of the Church, which is his body.

I, having once heard about your faith in the Lord Jesus, and the love that you show towards all the saints, have never failed to remember you in my prayers and to thank God for you. May the God of our Lord Jesus Christ, the Father of glory, give you a spirit of wisdom and perception of what is revealed, to bring you to full knowledge of him. May he enlighten the eyes of your mind so that you can see what hope his call holds for you, what rich glories he has promised the saints will inherit and how infinitely great is the power that he has exercised for us believers. This you can tell from the strength of his power at work in Christ, when he used it to raise him from the dead and to make him sit at his right hand, in heaven, far above every Sovereignty, Authority, Power or Domination, or any other name that can be named, not only in this age but also in the age to come. He has put all things under his feet, and made him, as the ruler of everything, the head of the Church; which is his body, the fullness of him who fills the whole creation.

This is the word of the Lord.

Responsorial Psalm   Ps 8:2-7. ℟ cf. v.7

℟ **You gave your Son power over the works of your hand.**

1. How great is your name, O Lord our God,
through all the earth!
Your majesty is praised above the heavens;
on the lips of children and of babes
you have found praise to foil your enemy. ℟

2. When I see the heavens, the works of your hands,
the moon and the stars which you arranged,
what is man that you should keep him in mind,
mortal man that you care for him? ℟

3. Yet you have made him little less than a god;
with glory and honour you crowned him,
gave him power over the works of your hand,
put all things under his feet. ℟

Gospel Acclamation   1 Sam 3:9; Jn 6:68

Alleluia, alleluia!
Speak, Lord, your servant is listening:
you have the message of eternal life.
Alleluia!

or Jn 15:26. 27

Alleluia, alleluia!
The Spirit of truth will be my witness,
and you too will be witnesses,
says the Lord.
Alleluia!

GOSPEL

A reading from the holy Gospel according to Luke 12:8-12

When the time comes, the Holy Spirit will teach you what you must say.

Jesus said to his disciples, 'I tell you, if anyone openly declares himself for me in the presence of men, the Son of Man will declare himself for him in the presence of God's angels. But the man who disowns me in the presence of men will be disowned in the presence of God's angels.

'Everyone who says a word against the Son of Man will be forgiven, but he who blasphemes against the Holy Spirit will not be forgiven.

'When they take you before synagogues and magistrates and authorities, do not worry about how to defend yourselves or what to say, because when the time comes, the Holy Spirit will teach you what you must say.'

This is the Gospel of the Lord.

TWENTY-NINTH WEEK IN ORDINARY TIME
Year II

MONDAY

FIRST READING

A reading from the letter of St Paul to the Ephesians 2:1-10

God brought us to life with Christ and gave us a place with him in heaven.

You were dead, through the crimes and the sins in which you used to live when you were following the way of this world, obeying the ruler who governs the air, the spirit who is at work in the rebellious. We all were among them too in the past, living sensual lives, ruled entirely by our own physical desires and our own ideas; so that by nature we were as much under God's anger as the rest of the world. But God loved us with so much love that he was generous with his mercy: when we were dead through our sins, he brought us to life with Christ – it is through grace that you have been saved – and raised us up with him and gave us a place with him in heaven, in Christ Jesus.

This was to show for all ages to come, through his goodness towards us in Christ Jesus, how infinitely rich he is in grace. Because it is by grace that you have been saved through faith; not by anything of your own, but by a gift from God; not by anything that you have done, so that nobody can claim the credit. We are God's work of art, created in Christ Jesus to live the good life as from the beginning he had meant us to live it.

This is the word of the Lord.

Responsorial Psalm

Ps 99. ℟ v.3

℟ **He made us, we belong to him.**

1 Cry out with joy to the Lord, all the earth.
  Serve the Lord with gladness.
  Come before him, singing for joy. ℟

2 Know that he, the Lord, is God.
  He made us, we belong to him,
  we are his people, the sheep of his flock. ℟

3 Go within his gates, giving thanks.
  Enter his courts with songs of praise.
  Give thanks to him and bless his name. ℟

4 Indeed, how good is the Lord,
  eternal his merciful love.
  He is faithful from age to age. ℟

Gospel Acclamation

Ps 24:4. 5

Alleluia, alleluia!
Teach me your paths, my God,
make me walk in your truth.
Alleluia!

or

Mt 5:3

Alleluia, alleluia!
How happy are the poor in spirit;
theirs is the kingdom of heaven.
Alleluia!

GOSPEL

A reading from the holy Gospel according to Luke 12:13-21

This hoard of yours, whose will it be?

A man in the crowd said to Jesus, 'Master, tell my brother to give me a share of our inheritance.' 'My friend,' he replied 'who appointed me your judge, or the arbitrator of your claims?' Then he said to them, 'Watch, and be on your guard against avarice of any kind, for a man's life is not made secure by what he owns, even when he has more than he needs.'

Then he told them a parable: 'There was once a rich man who, having had a good harvest from his land, thought to himself, "What am I to do? I have not enough room to store my crops." Then he said, "This is what I will do: I will pull down my barns and build bigger ones, and store all my grain and my goods in them, and I will say to my soul: My soul, you have plenty of good things laid by for many years to come; take things easy, eat, drink, have a good time." But God said to him, "Fool! This very night the demand will be made for your soul; and this hoard of yours, whose will it be then?" So it is when a man stores up treasure for himself in place of making himself rich in the sight of God.'

This is the Gospel of the Lord.

TUESDAY

FIRST READING

A reading from the letter of St Paul to the Ephesians 2:12-22

Christ is the peace between us and has made the two into one.

Do not forget that you had no Christ and were excluded from membership of Israel, aliens with no part in the covenants with their Promise; you were immersed in this world, without hope and without God. But now in Christ Jesus, you that used to be so far apart from us have been brought very close, by the blood of Christ. For he is the peace between us, and has made the two into one and broken down the barrier which used to keep them apart, actually destroying in his own person the hostility caused by the rules and decrees of the Law. This was to create one single New Man in himself out of the two of them and by restoring peace through the cross, to unite them both in a single Body and reconcile them with God. In his own person he killed the hostility. Later he came to bring the good news of peace, peace to you who were far away and peace to those who were near at hand. Through him, both of us have in the one Spirit our way to come to the Father.

So you are no longer aliens or foreign visitors: you are citizens like all the saints, and part of God's household. You are part of a building that has the apostles and prophets for its foundations, and Christ Jesus himself for its main corner stone. As every structure is aligned on him, all grow into one holy temple in the Lord; and you too, in him, are being built into a house where God lives, in the Spirit.

This is the word of the Lord.

Responsorial Psalm   Ps 84:9-14. ℟ cf. v.9

℟ **The Lord speaks peace to his people.**

1 I will hear what the Lord God has to say,
   a voice that speaks of peace.
   His help is near for those who fear him
   and his glory will dwell in our land. ℟

2 Mercy and faithfulness have met;
   justice and peace have embraced.
   Faithfulness shall spring from the earth
   and justice look down from heaven. ℟

3 The Lord will make us prosper
   and our earth shall yield its fruit.
   Justice shall march before him
   and peace shall follow his steps. ℟

Gospel Acclamation   cf. Lk 8:15

Alleluia, alleluia!
Blessed are those who,
with a noble and generous heart,
take the word of God to themselves
and yield a harvest through their perseverance.
Alleluia!

or   Lk 21:36

Alleluia, alleluia!
Stay awake, praying at all times
for the strength to stand with confidence
before the Son of Man.
Alleluia!

Twenty-ninth Week in Ordinary Time, Year II: Wednesday

GOSPEL

A reading from the holy Gospel according to Luke   12:35-38
Happy those servants whom the master finds awake when he comes.

Jesus said to his disciples: 'See that you are dressed for action and have your lamps lit. Be like men waiting for their master to return from the wedding feast, ready to open the door as soon as he comes and knocks. Happy those servants whom the master finds awake when he comes. I tell you solemnly, he will put on an apron, sit them down at table and wait on them. It may be in the second watch he comes, or in the third, but happy those servants if he finds them ready.'

This is the Gospel of the Lord.

WEDNESDAY

FIRST READING

A reading from the letter of St Paul to the Ephesians   3:2-12
The mystery of Christ has now been revealed and the same promise has been made to the pagans.

You have probably heard how I have been entrusted by God with the grace he meant for you, and that it was by a revelation that I was given the knowledge of the mystery, as I have just described it very shortly. If you read my words, you will have some idea of the depths that I see in the mystery of Christ. This mystery that has now been revealed through the Spirit to his holy apostles and prophets was unknown to any men in past generations; it means that pagans now share the same inheritance, that they are parts of the same body, and that the same promise has been made to them, in Christ Jesus, through the gospel. I have been made the servant of that gospel by a gift of grace from God who gave it to me by his own power. I, who am less than the least of all the saints, have been entrusted with this special grace, not only of proclaiming to the pagans the infinite treasure of Christ but also of explaining how the mystery is to be dispensed. Through all the ages, this has been kept hidden in God, the creator of everything. Why? So that the Sovereignties and Powers should learn only now, through the Church, how comprehensive God's wisdom really is, exactly according to the plan which he had had from all eternity in Christ Jesus our Lord. This is why we are bold enough to approach God in complete confidence, through our faith in him.

This is the word of the Lord.

Responsorial Psalm   Is 12:2-6. ℟ cf. v.3
   ℟ **With joy you will draw water
from the wells of salvation.**

1. Truly, God is my salvation,
I trust, I shall not fear.
For the Lord is my strength, my song,
he became my saviour.
With joy you will draw water
from the wells of salvation. ℟

2. Give thanks to the Lord, give praise to his name!
make his mighty deeds known to the peoples!
Declare the greatness of his name,
sing a psalm to the Lord! ℟

3. For he has done glorious deeds,
made them known to all the earth!
People of Zion, sing and shout for joy
for great in your midst is the Holy One of Israel. ℟

Gospel Acclamation   Jn 10:27
   Alleluia, alleluia!
The sheep that belong to me listen to my voice,
says the Lord,
I know them and they follow me.
Alleluia!

or   Mt 24:42. 44
   Alleluia, alleluia!
Stay awake and stand ready,
because you do not know the hour
when the Son of Man is coming.
Alleluia!

GOSPEL

A reading from the holy Gospel according to Luke   12:39-48
When a man has had a great deal given him, a great deal will be demanded of him.

Jesus said to his disciples: 'You may be quite sure of this, that if the householder had known at what hour the burglar would come, he would not have let anyone break through the wall of his house. You too must stand ready, because the Son of Man is coming at an hour you do not expect.'

Peter said, 'Lord, do you mean this parable for us, or for everyone?' The Lord replied, 'What sort of steward, then, is faithful and wise enough for the master to place him over his household to give them their allowance of food at the proper time? Happy that servant if his master's arrival finds him at this employment. I tell you truly, he will place him over everything he owns. But as for the servant who says to himself, "My master is taking his time coming," and sets about beating the menservants and the maids, and eating and drinking and getting drunk, his master will come on a day he does not expect and at an hour he does not know. The master will cut him off and send him to the same fate as the unfaithful.

'The servant who knows what his master wants, but has not even started to carry out those wishes, will receive very many strokes of the lash. The one who did not know, but deserves to be beaten for what he has done, will receive fewer strokes. When a man has had a great deal given him, a great deal will be demanded of him; when a man has had a great deal given him on trust, even more will be expected of him.'

This is the Gospel of the Lord.

THURSDAY

FIRST READING

A reading from the letter of St Paul to the Ephesians 3:14-21

Planted in love and built on love, you are filled with the utter fullness of God.

This is what I pray, kneeling before the Father, from whom every family, whether spiritual or natural, takes its name:

Out of his infinite glory, may he give you the power through his Spirit for your hidden self to grow strong, so that Christ may live in your hearts through faith, and then, planted in love and built on love, you will with all the saints have strength to grasp the breadth and the length, the height and the depth; until, knowing the love of Christ, which is beyond all knowledge, you are filled with the utter fullness of God.

Glory be to him whose power, working in us, can do infinitely more than we can ask or imagine; glory be to him from generation to generation in the Church and in Christ Jesus for ever and ever. Amen.

This is the word of the Lord.

Responsorial Psalm   Ps 32:1-2. 4-5. 11-12. 18-19. ℟ v.5

  ℟ **The Lord fills the earth with his love.**

1. Ring out your joy to the Lord, O you just;
for praise is fitting for loyal hearts.
Give thanks to the Lord upon the harp,
with a ten-stringed lute sing him songs. ℟

2. For the word of the Lord is faithful
and all his works to be trusted.
The Lord loves justice and right
and fills the earth with his love. ℟

3. His own designs shall stand for ever,
the plans of his heart from age to age.
They are happy, whose God is the Lord,
the people he has chosen as his own. ℟

4. The Lord looks on those who revere him,
on those who hope in his love,
to rescue their souls from death,
to keep them alive in famine. ℟

Gospel Acclamation   Jn 8:12

Alleluia, alleluia!
I am the light of the world, says the Lord,
anyone who follows me
will have the light of life.
Alleluia!

or   Phil 3:8-9

Alleluia, alleluia!
I have accepted the loss of everything
and I look on everything as so much rubbish
if only I can have Christ
and be given a place in him.
Alleluia!

Twenty-ninth Week in Ordinary Time, Year II: Friday

GOSPEL

A reading from the holy Gospel according to Luke 12:49-53
I am here not to bring peace but division.

Jesus said to his disciples: 'I have come to bring fire to the earth, and how I wish it were blazing already! There is a baptism I must still receive, and how great is my distress till it is over!

'Do you suppose that I am here to bring peace on earth? No, I tell you, but rather division. For from now on a household of five will be divided: three against two and two against three; the father divided against the son, son against father, mother against daughter, daughter against mother, mother-in-law against daughter-in-law, daughter-in-law against mother-in-law.'

This is the Gospel of the Lord.

FRIDAY

FIRST READING

A reading from the letter of St Paul to the Ephesians 4:1-6
One Body, one Lord, one faith, one baptism.

I, the prisoner in the Lord, implore you to lead a life worthy of your vocation. Bear with one another charitably, in complete selflessness, gentleness and patience. Do all you can to preserve the unity of the Spirit by the peace that binds you together. There is one Body, one Spirit, just as you were all called into one and the same hope when you were called. There is one Lord, one faith, one baptism, and one God who is Father of all, over all, through all and within all.

This is the word of the Lord.

Responsorial Psalm Ps 23:1-6. ℟ cf. v.6

℟ **Such are the men who seek your face, O Lord.**

1 The Lord's is the earth and its fullness,
  the world and all its people.
  It is he who set it on the seas;
  on the waters he made it firm. ℟

2 Who shall climb the mountain of the Lord?
  Who shall stand in his holy place?
  The man with clean hands and pure heart,
  who desires not worthless things. ℟

(continued)

3   He shall receive blessings from the Lord
    and reward from the God who saves him.
    Such are the men who seek him,
    seek the face of the God of Jacob.

    ℟ **Such are the men who seek your face, O Lord.**

Gospel Acclamation   cf. Ps 94:8
Alleluia, alleluia!
Harden not your hearts today,
but listen to the voice of the Lord.
Alleluia!

or   cf. Mt 11:25

Alleluia, alleluia!
Blessed are you, Father,
Lord of heaven and earth,
for revealing the mysteries of the kingdom
to mere children.
Alleluia!

GOSPEL

A reading from the holy Gospel according to Luke   12:54-59

You know how to interpret the face of the earth and the sky. How is it you do not know how to interpret these times?

Jesus said to the crowds, 'When you see a cloud looming up in the west you say at once that rain is coming, and so it does. And when the wind is from the south you say it will be hot, and it is. Hypocrites! You know how to interpret the face of the earth and the sky. How is it you do not know how to interpret these times?

'Why not judge for yourselves what is right? For example: when you go to court with your opponent, try to settle with him on the way, or he may drag you before the judge and the judge hand you over to the bailiff and the bailiff have you thrown into prison. I tell you, you will not get out till you have paid the very last penny.'

This is the Gospel of the Lord.

SATURDAY

FIRST READING

A reading from the letter of St Paul to the Ephesians 4:7-16
Christ is the head by whom the whole body grows.

Each one of us has been given his own share of grace, given as Christ allotted it. It was said that he would:

> When he ascended to the height, he captured prisoners,
> he gave gifts to men.

When it says, 'he ascended', what can it mean if not that he descended right down to the lower regions of the earth? The one who rose higher than all the heavens to fill all things is none other than the one who descended. And to some, his gift was that they should be apostles; to some, prophets; to some, evangelists; to some, pastors and teachers; so that the saints together make a unity in the work of service, building up the body of Christ. In this way we are all to come to unity in our faith and in our knowledge of the Son of God, until we become the perfect Man, fully mature with the fullness of Christ himself.

Then we shall not be children any longer, or tossed one way and another and carried along by every wind of doctrine, at the mercy of all the tricks men play and their cleverness in practising deceit. If we live by the truth and in love, we shall grow in all ways into Christ, who is the head by whom the whole body is fitted and joined together, every joint adding its own strength, for each separate part to work according to its function. So the body grows until it has built itself up, in love.

This is the word of the Lord.

Responsorial Psalm Ps 121:1-5. ℟ v.1

℟ **I rejoiced when I heard them say:**
'Let us go to God's house.'

1 I rejoiced when I heard them say:
   'Let us go to God's house.'
   And now our feet are standing
   within your gates, O Jerusalem. ℟

2 Jerusalem is built as a city
   strongly compact.
   It is there that the tribes go up,
   the tribes of the Lord. ℟

(continued)

3. For Israel's law it is,
   there to praise the Lord's name.
   There were set the thrones of judgement
   of the house of David.

   ℞ **I rejoiced when I heard them say:
   'Let us go to God's house.'**

Gospel Acclamation   Ps 144:13
Alleluia, alleluia!
The Lord is faithful in all his words
and loving in all his deeds.
Alleluia!

or   Ez 33:11

Alleluia, alleluia!
I take pleasure, not in the death of a wicked man,
says the Lord,
but in the turning back of a wicked man
who changes his ways to win life.
Alleluia!

GOSPEL

A reading from the holy Gospel according to Luke   13:1-9
Unless you repent you will all perish as they did.

Some people arrived and told Jesus about the Galileans whose blood Pilate had mingled with that of their sacrifices. At this he said to them, 'Do you suppose these Galileans who suffered like that were greater sinners than any other Galileans? They were not, I tell you. No; but unless you repent you will all perish as they did. Or those eighteen on whom the tower at Siloam fell and killed them? Do you suppose that they were more guilty than all the other people living in Jerusalem? They were not, I tell you. No; but unless you repent you will all perish as they did.'

He told this parable: 'A man had a fig tree planted in his vineyard, and he came looking for fruit on it but found none. He said to the man who looked after the vineyard, "Look here, for three years now I have been coming to look for fruit on this fig tree and finding none. Cut it down: why should it be taking up the ground?" "Sir," the man replied "leave it one more year and give me time to dig round it and manure it: it may bear fruit next year; if not, then you can cut it down." '

This is the Gospel of the Lord.

THIRTIETH WEEK IN ORDINARY TIME
Year II

MONDAY

FIRST READING

A reading from the letter of St Paul to the Ephesians 4:32 – 5:8
Follow Christ by loving as he loved you.

Be friends with one another, and kind, forgiving each other as readily as God forgave you in Christ.

Try, then, to imitate God, as children of his that he loves, and follow Christ by loving as he loved you, giving himself up in our place as a fragrant offering and a sacrifice to God. Among you there must be not even a mention of fornication or impurity in any of its forms, or promiscuity: this would hardly become the saints! There must be no coarseness, or salacious talk and jokes – all this is wrong for you: raise your voices in thanksgiving instead. For you can be quite certain that nobody who actually indulges in fornication or impurity or promiscuity – which is worshipping a false god – can inherit anything of the kingdom of God. Do not let anyone deceive you with empty arguments: it is for this loose living that God's anger comes down on those who rebel against him. Make sure that you are not included with them. You were darkness once, but now you are light in the Lord; be like children of light.

This is the word of the Lord.

Responsorial Psalm Ps 1:1-4. 6. ℟ cf. Eph 5:1

℟ **Try to imitate God, as children of his that he loves.**

1 Happy indeed is the man
 who follows not the counsel of the wicked;
 nor lingers in the way of sinners
 nor sits in the company of scorners,
 but whose delight is the law of the Lord
 and who ponders his law day and night. ℟

2 He is like a tree that is planted
 beside the flowing waters,
 that yields its fruit in due season
 and whose leaves shall never fade;
 and all that he does shall prosper. ℟

(continued)

3 Not so are the wicked, not so!
   For they like winnowed chaff
   shall be driven away by the wind.
   For the Lord guards the way of the just
   but the way of the wicked leads to doom.

   ℟ **Try to imitate God, as children of his that he loves.**

Gospel Acclamation cf. Jn 17:17
Alleluia, alleluia!
Your word is truth, O Lord,
consecrate us in the truth.
Alleluia!

GOSPEL

A reading from the holy Gospel according to Luke 13:10-17
This woman, a daughter of Abraham – was it not right to untie her bonds on the sabbath day?

One sabbath day Jesus was teaching in one of the synagogues, and a woman was there who for eighteen years had been possessed by a spirit that left her enfeebled; she was bent double and quite unable to stand upright. When Jesus saw her he called her over and said, 'Woman, you are rid of your infirmity' and he laid his hands on her. And at once she straightened up, and she glorified God.

But the synagogue official was indignant because Jesus had healed on the sabbath, and he addressed the people present. 'There are six days' he said 'when work is to be done. Come and be healed on one of those days and not on the sabbath.' But the Lord answered him. 'Hypocrites!' he said 'Is there one of you who does not untie his ox or his donkey from the manger on the sabbath and take it out for watering? And this woman, a daughter of Abraham whom Satan has held bound these eighteen years – was it not right to untie her bonds on the sabbath day?' When he said this, all his adversaries were covered with confusion, and all the people were overjoyed at all the wonders he worked.

This is the Gospel of the Lord.

TUESDAY

FIRST READING

A reading from the letter of St Paul to the Ephesians 5:21-33
This mystery has many implications for Christ and the Church.

Give way to one another in obedience to Christ. Wives should regard their husbands as they regard the Lord, since as Christ is head of the Church and saves the whole body, so is a husband the head of his wife; and as the Church submits to Christ, so should wives to their husbands, in everything. Husbands should love their wives just as Christ loved the Church and sacrificed himself for her to make her holy. He made her clean by washing her in water with a form of words, so that when he took her to himself she would be glorious, with no speck or wrinkle or anything like that, but holy and faultless. In the same way, husbands must love their wives as they love their own bodies; for a man to love his wife is for him to love himself. A man never hates his own body, but he feeds it and looks after it; and that is the way Christ treats the Church, because it is the body – and we are its living parts. For this reason, a man must leave his father and mother and be joined to his wife, and the two will become one body. This mystery has many implications; but I am saying it applies to Christ and the Church. To sum up; you too, each one of you, must love his wife as he loves himself; and let every wife respect her husband.

This is the word of the Lord.

Responsorial Psalm

Ps 127:1-5. ℟ cf. v.1

℟ **O blessed are those who fear the Lord!**

1 O blessed are those who fear the Lord
  and walk in his ways!
  By the labour of your hands you shall eat.
  You will be happy and prosper. ℟

2 Your wife like a fruitful vine
  in the heart of your house;
  your children like shoots of the olive
  around your table. ℟

3 Indeed thus shall be blessed
  the man who fears the Lord.
  May the Lord bless you from Zion
  all the days of your life! ℟

Gospel Acclamation   Jn 15:15

Alleluia, alleluia!
I call you friends, says the Lord,
because I have made known to you
everything I have learnt from my Father.
Alleluia!

or   cf. Mt 11:25

Alleluia, alleluia!
Blessed are you, Father,
Lord of heaven and earth,
for revealing the mysteries of the kingdom
to mere children.
Alleluia!

GOSPEL

A reading from the holy Gospel according to Luke   13:18-21
The seed grew and became a tree.

Jesus said, 'What is the kingdom of God like? What shall I compare it with? It is like a mustard seed which a man took and threw into his garden: it grew and became a tree, and the birds of the air sheltered in its branches.'

Another thing he said, 'What shall I compare the kingdom of God with? It is like the yeast a woman took and mixed in with three measures of flour till it was leavened all through.'

This is the Gospel of the Lord.

WEDNESDAY

FIRST READING

A reading from the letter of St Paul to the Ephesians   6:1-9
Not as if only to please men, but because you are slaves of Christ.

Children, be obedient to your parents in the Lord – that is your duty. The first commandment that has a promise attached to it is: Honour your father and mother; and the promise is: and you will prosper and have a long life in the land. And parents, never drive your children to resentment but in bringing them up correct them and guide them as the Lord does.

Thirtieth Week in Ordinary Time, Year II: Wednesday   1223

Slaves, be obedient to the men who are called your masters in this world, with deep respect and sincere loyalty, as you are obedient to Christ: not only when you are under their eye, as if you had only to please men, but because you are slaves of Christ and wholeheartedly do the will of God. Work hard and willingly, but do it for the sake of the Lord and not for the sake of men. You can be sure that everyone, whether a slave or a free man, will be properly rewarded by the Lord for whatever work he has done well. And those of you who are employers, treat your slaves in the same spirit; do without threats, remembering that they and you have the same Master in heaven and he is not impressed by one person more than by another.

This is the word of the Lord.

Responsorial Psalm   Ps 144:10-14. ℟ v. 13

℟ **The Lord is faithful in all his words.**

1 All your creatures shall thank you, O Lord,
   and your friends shall repeat their blessing.
   They shall speak of the glory of your reign
   and declare your might, O God,
   to make known to men your mighty deeds
   and the glorious splendour of your reign. ℟

2 Yours is an everlasting kingdom;
   your rule lasts from age to age. ℟

3 The Lord is faithful in all his words
   and loving in all his deeds.
   The Lord supports all who fall
   and raises all who are bowed down. ℟

Gospel Acclamation   Jn 14:6

Alleluia, alleluia!
I am the Way, the Truth and the Life, says the Lord;
no one can come to the Father except through me.
Alleluia!

or   cf. 2 Thess 2:14

Alleluia, alleluia!
Through the Good News God called us
to share the glory of our Lord Jesus Christ.
Alleluia!

GOSPEL

A reading from the holy Gospel according to Luke 13:22-30

Men from east and west will come to take their places in the kingdom of God.

Through towns and villages Jesus went teaching, making his way to Jerusalem. Someone said to him, 'Sir, will there be only a few saved?' He said to them, 'Try your best to enter by the narrow door, because, I tell you, many will try to enter and will not succeed.

'Once the master of the house has got up and locked the door, you may find yourself knocking on the door, saying, "Lord, open to us" but he will answer, "I do not know where you come from." Then you will find yourself saying, "We once ate and drank in your company; you taught in our streets" but he will reply, "I do not know where you come from. Away from me, all you wicked men!"

'Then there will be weeping and grinding of teeth, when you see Abraham and Isaac and Jacob and all the prophets in the kingdom of God, and yourselves turned outside. And men from east and west, from north and south, will come to take their places at the feast in the kingdom of God.

'Yes, there are those now last who will be first, and those now first who will be last.'

This is the Gospel of the Lord.

THURSDAY

FIRST READING

A reading from the letter of St Paul to the Ephesians 6:10-20

Rely on God's armour to hold your ground.

Grow strong in the Lord, with the strength of his power. Put God's armour on so as to be able to resist the devil's tactics. For it is not against human enemies that we have to struggle, but against the Sovereignties and the Powers who originate the darkness of this world, the spiritual army of evil in the heavens. That is why you must rely on God's armour, or you will not be able to put up any resistance when the worst happens, or have enough resources to hold your ground.

So stand your ground, with truth buckled round your waist, and integrity for a breastplate, wearing for shoes on your feet the eagerness to spread the gospel of peace and always carrying the shield of faith so that you can use it to put out the burning arrows of the evil one. And then you must accept salvation from God to be your helmet and receive the word of God from the Spirit to use as a sword.

Pray all the time, asking for what you need, praying in the Spirit on every possible occasion. Never get tired of staying awake to pray for all the saints; and pray for me to be given an opportunity to open my mouth and speak without fear and give out the mystery of the gospel of which I am an ambassador in chains; pray that in proclaiming it I may speak as boldly as I ought to.

This is the word of the Lord.

Responsorial Psalm
Ps 143:1-2. 9-10. ℟ v.1

℟ **Blessed be the Lord, my rock.**

1 Blessed be the Lord, my rock
 who trains my arms for battle,
 who prepares my hands for war. ℟

2 He is my love, my fortress;
 he is my stronghold, my saviour,
 my shield, my place of refuge.
 He brings peoples under my rule. ℟

3 To you, O God, will I sing a new song;
 I will play on the ten-stringed lute
 to you who give kings their victory,
 who set David your servant free. ℟

Gospel Acclamation
Ps 147:12. 15

Alleluia, alleluia!
O praise the Lord, Jerusalem!
He sends out his word to the earth.
Alleluia!

or
cf. Lk 19:38; 2:14

Alleluia, alleluia!
Blessings on the King who comes,
in the name of the Lord!
Peace in heaven
and glory in the highest heavens!
Alleluia!

GOSPEL

A reading from the holy Gospel according to Luke 13:31-35
It would not be right for a prophet to die outside Jerusalem.

Some Pharisees came up to Jesus. 'Go away' they said 'Leave this place, because Herod means to kill you.' He replied, 'You may go and give that fox this message: Learn that today and tomorrow I cast out devils and on the third day attain my end. But for today and tomorrow and the next day I must go out, since it would not be right for a prophet to die outside Jerusalem.

'Jerusalem, Jerusalem, you that kill the prophets and stone those who are sent to you! How often have I longed to gather your children, as a hen gathers her brood under her wings, and you refused! So be it! Your house will be left to you. Yes, I promise you, you shall not see me till the time comes when you say:

Blessings on him who comes in the name of the Lord!'

This is the Gospel of the Lord.

FRIDAY

FIRST READING

A reading from the letter of St Paul to the Philippians 1:1-11
The One who began this good work in you will see that it is finished when the Day of Christ Jesus comes.

From Paul and Timothy, servants of Christ Jesus, to all the saints in Christ Jesus, together with their presiding elders and deacons. We wish you the grace and peace of God our Father and of the Lord Jesus Christ.

I thank my God whenever I think of you; and every time I pray for all of you, I pray with joy, remembering how you have helped to spread the Good News from the day you first heard it right up to the present. I am quite certain that the One who began this good work in you will see that it is finished when the Day of Christ Jesus comes. It is only natural that I should feel like this towards you all, since you have shared the privileges which have been mine: both my chains and my work defending and establishing the gospel. You have a permanent place in my heart, and God knows how much I miss you all, loving you as Christ Jesus loves you. My prayer is that your love for each other may increase more and more and never stop improving your knowledge and deepening your perception so that you can always recognise what is best. This will help you to become pure and blameless, and prepare you for the Day of Christ, when you will reach the perfect goodness which Christ Jesus produces in us for the glory and praise of God.

This is the word of the Lord.

Responsorial Psalm Ps 110:1-6. R̸ v.2

  R̸ **Great are the works of the Lord.**

or

  R̸ **Alleluia!**

1 I will thank the Lord with all my heart
  in the meeting of the just and their assembly.
  Great are the works of the Lord;
  to be pondered by all who love them. R̸

2 Majestic and glorious his work,
  his justice stands firm for ever.
  He makes us remember his wonders.
  The Lord is compassion and love. R̸

3 He gives food to those who fear him;
  keeps his covenant ever in mind.
  He has shown his might to his people
  by giving them the lands of the nations. R̸

Gospel Acclamation cf. 1 Thess 2:13
  Alleluia, alleluia!
  Accept God's message for what it really is:
  God's message, and not some human thinking.
  Alleluia!

or Jn 10:27

  Alleluia, alleluia!
  The sheep that belong to me listen to my voice,
  says the Lord,
  I know them and they follow me.
  Alleluia!

GOSPEL

A reading from the holy Gospel according to Luke   14:1-6

Which of you here, if his son falls into a well, or his ox, will not pull him out on a sabbath day?

On a sabbath day Jesus had gone for a meal to the house of one of the leading Pharisees; and they watched him closely. There in front of him was a man with dropsy, and Jesus addressed the lawyers and Pharisees, 'Is it against the law' he asked 'to cure a man on the sabbath, or not?' But they remained silent, so he took the man and cured him and sent him away. Then he said to them, 'Which of you here, if his son falls into a well, or his ox, will not pull him out on a sabbath day without hesitation?' And to this they could find no answer.

This is the Gospel of the Lord.

SATURDAY

FIRST READING

A reading from the letter of St Paul   1:18-26
to the Philippians

Life to me is Christ, but death would bring me something more.

Christ is proclaimed; and that makes me happy; and I shall continue being happy, because I know this will help to save me, thanks to your prayers and to the help which will be given to me by the Spirit of Jesus. My one hope and trust is that I shall never have to admit defeat, but that now as always I shall have the courage for Christ to be glorified in my body, whether by my life or by my death. Life to me, of course, is Christ, but then death would bring me something more; but then again, if living in this body means doing work which is having good results – I do not know what I should choose. I am caught in this dilemma: I want to be gone and be with Christ, which would be very much the better, but for me to stay alive in this body is a more urgent need for your sake. This weighs with me so much that I feel sure I shall survive and stay with you all, and help you to progress in the faith and even increase your joy in it; and so you will have another reason to give praise to Christ Jesus on my account when I am with you again.

This is the word of the Lord.

Thirtieth Week in Ordinary Time, Year II: Saturday

Responsorial Psalm   Ps 41:2-3. 5. ℟ v.3

  ℟ **My soul is thirsting for God,
the God of my life.**

1. Like the deer that yearns
for running streams,
so my soul is yearning
for you, my God. ℟

2. My soul is thirsting for God,
the God of my life;
when can I enter and see
the face of God? ℟

3. I would lead the rejoicing crowd
into the house of God,
amid cries of gladness and thanksgiving. ℟

Gospel Acclamation   cf. Col 3:16.17

Alleluia, alleluia!
Let the message of Christ, in all its richness,
find a home with you;
through him give thanks to God the Father.
Alleluia!

or   Mt 11:29

Alleluia, alleluia!
Shoulder my yoke and learn from me, says the Lord,
for I am gentle and humble in heart.
Alleluia!

GOSPEL

A reading from the holy Gospel according to Luke   14:1. 7-11
Everyone who exalts himself will be humbled, and the man who humbles himself will be exalted.

Now on a sabbath day Jesus had gone for a meal to the house of one of the leading Pharisees; and they watched him closely.

He then told the guests a parable, because he had noticed how they picked the places of honour. He said this, 'When someone invites you to a wedding feast, do not take your seat in the place of honour. A more distinguished person than you may have been invited, and the person who invited you both may come and say, "Give up your place to this man." And then, to your embarrassment, you would have to go and take the lowest place. No; when you are a guest, make your way to the lowest place and sit there, so that, when your host comes, he may say, "My friend, move up higher." In that way, everyone with you at the table will see you honoured. For everyone who exalts himself will be humbled, and the man who humbles himself will be exalted.'

This is the Gospel of the Lord.

THIRTY-FIRST WEEK IN ORDINARY TIME
Year II

MONDAY

FIRST READING

A reading from the letter of St Paul 2:1-4
to the Philippians
Be united in a common mind – that is the one thing which would make me completely happy.

If our life in Christ means anything to you, if love can persuade at all, or the Spirit that we have in common, or any tenderness and sympathy, then be united in your convictions and united in your love, with a common purpose and a common mind. That is the one thing which would make me completely happy. There must be no competition among you, no conceit; but everybody is to be self-effacing. Always consider the other person to be better than yourself, so that nobody thinks of his own interests first but everybody thinks of other people's interests instead.

This is the word of the Lord.

Responsorial Psalm Ps 130
℟ **Keep my soul in peace before you, O Lord.**

1 O Lord, my heart is not proud
  nor haughty my eyes.
  I have not gone after things too great
  nor marvels beyond me. ℟

2 Truly I have set my soul
  in silence and peace.
  A weaned child on its mother's breast,
  even so is my soul. ℟

3 O Israel, hope in the Lord,
  both now and for ever. ℟

Gospel Acclamation Ps 118:18

> Alleluia, alleluia!
> Open my eyes, O Lord, that I may consider
> the wonders of your law.
> Alleluia!

or Jn 8:31-32

> Alleluia, alleluia!
> If you make my word your home
> you will indeed be my disciples,
> and you will learn the truth, says the Lord.
> Alleluia!

GOSPEL

A reading from the holy Gospel according to Luke 14:12-14

Do not invite your friends; invite the poor and the crippled.

Jesus said to his host, one of the leading Pharisees, 'When you give a lunch or a dinner, do not ask your friends, brothers, relations or rich neighbours, for fear they repay your courtesy by inviting you in return. No; when you have a party, invite the poor, the crippled, the lame, the blind; that they cannot pay you back means that you are fortunate, because repayment will be made to you when the virtuous rise again.'

This is the Gospel of the Lord.

TUESDAY

FIRST READING

A reading from the letter of St Paul to the Philippians 2:5-11

Christ humbled himself, but God raised him high.

In your minds you must be the same as Christ Jesus:

> His state was divine,
> yet he did not cling
> to his equality with God
> but emptied himself
> to assume the condition of a slave,
> and became as men are;
> and being as all men are,

he was humbler yet,
even to accepting death,
death on a cross.
But God raised him high
and gave him the name
which is above all other names
so that all beings
in the heavens, on earth and in the underworld,
should bend the knee at the name of Jesus
and that every tongue should acclaim
Jesus Christ as Lord,
to the glory of God the Father.

This is the word of the Lord.

Responsorial Psalm
Ps 21:26-32. ℟ v.26

℟ **You are my praise, O Lord, in the great assembly.**

1 My vows I will pay before those who fear the Lord.
   The poor shall eat and shall have their fill.
   They shall praise the Lord, those who seek him.
   May their hearts live for ever and ever! ℟

2 All the earth shall remember and return to the Lord,
   all families of the nations worship before him
   for the kingdom is the Lord's; he is ruler of the nations.
   They shall worship him, all the mighty of the earth. ℟

3 And my soul shall live for him, my children serve him.
   They shall tell of the Lord to generations yet to come,
   declare his faithfulness to peoples yet unborn:
   'These things the Lord has done.' ℟

Gospel Acclamation
cf. Eph 1:17. 18

Alleluia, alleluia!
May the Father of our Lord Jesus Christ
enlighten the eyes of our mind,
so that we can see what hope his call holds for us.
Alleluia!

or
Mt 11:28

Alleluia, alleluia!
Come to me, all you who labour and are overburdened.
and I will give you rest, says the Lord.
Alleluia!

GOSPEL

A reading from the holy Gospel according to Luke   14:15-24

Go to the open roads and the hedgerows and force people to come in to make sure my house is full.

One of those gathered round the table said to Jesus, 'Happy the man who will be at the feast in the kingdom of God!' But he said to him, 'There was a man who gave a great banquet, and he invited a large number of people. When the time for the banquet came, he sent his servant to say to those who had been invited, "Come along: everything is ready now." But all alike started to make excuses. The first said, "I have bought a piece of land and must go and see it. Please accept my apologies." Another said, "I have bought five yoke of oxen and am on my way to try them out. Please accept my apologies." Yet another said, "I have just got married and so am unable to come."

    'The servant returned and reported this to his master. Then the householder, in a rage, said to his servant, "Go out quickly into the streets and alleys of the town and bring in here the poor, the crippled, the blind and the lame." "Sir," said the servant "your orders have been carried out and there is still room." Then the master said to his servant, "Go to the open roads and the hedgerows and force people to come in to make sure my house is full; because, I tell you, not one of those who were invited shall have a taste of my banquet." '

    This is the Gospel of the Lord.

WEDNESDAY

FIRST READING

A reading from the letter of St Paul to the Philippians   2:12-18

Work for your salvation. It is God who puts both the will and the action into you.

My dear friends, continue to do as I tell you, as you always have; not only as you did when I was there with you, but even more now that I am no longer there; and work for your salvation 'in fear and trembling.' It is God, for his own loving purpose, who puts both the will and the action into you. Do all that has to be done without complaining or arguing and then you will be innocent and genuine, perfect children of God among a deceitful and underhand brood, and you will shine in the world like bright stars because you are offering it the word of life. This would give me something to be proud of for the Day of Christ, and would mean that I had not run in the race and exhausted myself for nothing. And then, if my blood has to be shed as part of your own sacrifice and offering – which is your faith – I shall still be happy and rejoice with all of you, and you must be just as happy and rejoice with me.

This is the word of the Lord.

Responsorial Psalm Ps 26:1. 4. 13-14. R/ v.1

R/ **The Lord is my light and my help.**

1 The Lord is my light and my help;
   whom shall I fear?
   The Lord is the stronghold of my life;
   before whom shall I shrink? R/

2 There is one thing I ask of the Lord,
   for this I long,
   to live in the house of the Lord,
   all the days of my life,
   to savour the sweetness of the Lord,
   to behold his temple. R/

3 I am sure I shall see the Lord's goodness
   in the land of the living.
   Hope in him, hold firm and take heart.
   Hope in the Lord! R/

Gospel Acclamation Ps 118:88
Alleluia, alleluia!
Because of your love give me life,
and I will do your will.
Alleluia!

or 1 Peter 4:14

Alleluia, alleluia!
It is a blessing for you,
when they insult you
for bearing the name of Christ,
for the Spirit of God rests on you.
Alleluia!

Thirty-first Week in Ordinary Time, Year II: Thursday 1235

GOSPEL

A reading from the holy Gospel according to Luke 14:25-33
None of you can be my disciple unless he gives up all his possessions.

Great crowds accompanied Jesus on his way and he turned and spoke to them. 'If any man comes to me without hating his father, mother, wife, children, brothers, sisters, yes and his own life too, he cannot be my disciple. Anyone who does not carry his cross and come after me cannot be my disciple.

'And indeed, which of you here, intending to build a tower, would not first sit down and work out the cost to see if he had enough to complete it? Otherwise, if he laid the foundation and then found himself unable to finish the work, the onlookers would all start making fun of him and saying, "Here is a man who started to build and was unable to finish." Or again, what king marching to war against another king would not first sit down and consider whether with ten thousand men he could stand up to the other who advanced against him with twenty thousand? If not, then while the other king was still a long way off, he would send envoys to sue for peace. So in the same way, none of you can be my disciple unless he gives up all his possessions.'

This is the Gospel of the Lord.

THURSDAY

FIRST READING

A reading from the letter of St Paul to the Philippians 3:3-8
Because of Christ, I have come to consider all the advantages that I had as disadvantages.

We are the real people of the circumcision, we who worship in accordance with the Spirit of God; we have our own glory from Christ Jesus without having to rely on a physical operation. If it came to relying on physical evidence, I should be fully qualified myself. Take any man who thinks he can rely on what is physical: I am even better qualified. I was born of the race of Israel and of the tribe of Benjamin, a Hebrew born of Hebrew parents, and I was circumcised when I was eight days old. As for the Law, I was a Pharisee; as for working for religion, I was a persecutor of the Church; as far as the Law can make you perfect, I was faultless. But because of Christ, I have come to consider all the advantages that I had as disadvantages. Not only that, but I believe nothing can happen that will outweigh the supreme advantage of knowing Christ Jesus my Lord.

This is the word of the Lord.

Responsorial Psalm   Ps 104:2-7. ℟ v.3

℟ **Let the hearts that seek the Lord rejoice.**

or

℟ **Alleluia!**

1. O sing to the Lord, sing his praise;
   tell all his wonderful works!
   Be proud of his holy name,
   let the hearts that seek the Lord rejoice. ℟

2. Consider the Lord and his strength;
   constantly seek his face.
   Remember the wonders he has done,
   his miracles, the judgements he spoke. ℟

3. O children of Abraham, his servant,
   O sons of the Jacob he chose.
   He, the Lord, is our God:
   his judgements prevail in all the earth. ℟

Gospel Acclamation   Ps 129:5

Alleluia, alleluia!
My soul is waiting for the Lord,
I count on his word.
Alleluia!

or   Mt 11:28

Alleluia, alleluia!
Come to me, all you who labour and are overburdened,
and I will give you rest, says the Lord.
Alleluia!

GOSPEL

A reading from the holy Gospel according to Luke   15:1-10
There will be rejoicing in heaven over one repentant sinner.

The tax collectors and the sinners were all seeking the company of Jesus to hear what he had to say, and the Pharisees and the scribes complained. 'This man' they said 'welcomes sinners and eats with them.' So he spoke this parable to them:

'What man among you with a hundred sheep, losing one, would not leave the ninety-nine in the wilderness and go after the missing one till he found it? And when he found it, would he not joyfully take it on his shoulders and then, when he got home, call together his friends and neighbours? "Rejoice with me," he would say "I have found my sheep that was lost." In the same way, I tell you, there will be more rejoicing in heaven over one repentant sinner than over ninety-nine virtuous men who have no need of repentance.

'Or again, what woman with ten drachmas would not, if she lost one, light a lamp and sweep out the house and search thoroughly till she found it? And then, when she had found it, call together her friends and neighbours? "Rejoice with me," she would say "I have found the drachma I lost." In the same way, I tell you, there is rejoicing among the angels of God over one repentant sinner.'

This is the Gospel of the Lord.

FRIDAY

FIRST READING

A reading from the letter of St Paul to the Philippians 3:17 – 4:1

We are waiting for the saviour who will transfigure these wretched bodies of ours into copies of his glorious body.

My brothers, be united in following my rule of life. Take as your models everybody who is already doing this and study them as you used to study us. I have told you often, and I repeat it today with tears, there are many who are behaving as the enemies of the cross of Christ. They are destined to be lost. They make foods into their god and they are proudest of something they ought to think shameful; the things they think important are earthly things. For us, our homeland is in heaven, and from heaven comes the saviour we are waiting for, the Lord Jesus Christ, and he will transfigure these wretched bodies of ours into copies of his glorious body. He will do that by the same power with which he can subdue the whole universe.

So then, my brothers and dear friends, do not give way but remain faithful in the Lord. I miss you very much, dear friends; you are my joy and my crown.

This is the word of the Lord.

Responsorial Psalm
Ps 121:1-5. ℟ v.1

℟ **I rejoiced when I heard them say:
'Let us go to God's house.'**

1 I rejoiced when I heard them say:
'Let us go to God's house.'
And now our feet are standing
within your gates, O Jerusalem. ℟

2 Jerusalem is built as a city
strongly compact.
It is there that the tribes go up,
the tribes of the Lord. ℟

3 For Israel's law it is,
there to praise the Lord's name.
There were set the thrones of judgement
of the house of David. ℟

Gospel Acclamation
2 Cor 5:19

Alleluia, alleluia!
God in Christ was reconciling the world to himself,
and he has entrusted to us the news that they are reconciled.
Alleluia!

or
1 Jn 2:5

Alleluia, alleluia!
When anyone obeys what Christ has said,
God's love comes to perfection in him,
Alleluia!

GOSPEL

A reading from the holy Gospel according to Luke
16:1-8

The children of this world are more astute in dealing with their own kind than are the children of light.

Jesus said to his disciples, 'There was a rich man and he had a steward who was denounced to him for being wasteful with his property. He called for the man and said, "What is this I hear about you? Draw me up an account of your stewardship because you are not to be my steward any longer." Then the steward said to himself, "Now that my master is taking the stewardship from me, what am I to do? Dig? I am not strong enough. Go begging? I should be too ashamed. Ah, I know what I will do to make sure that when I am dismissed from office there will be some to welcome me into their homes."

'Then he called his master's debtors one by one. To the first he said, "How much do you owe my master?" "One hundred measures of oil" was the reply. The steward said, "Here, take your bond; sit down straight away and write fifty." To another he said, "And you, sir, how much do you owe?" "One hundred measures of wheat" was the reply. The steward said, "Here, take your bond and write eighty."

'The master praised the dishonest steward for his astuteness. For the children of this world are more astute in dealing with their own kind than are the children of light.'

This is the Gospel of the Lord.

SATURDAY

FIRST READING

A reading from the letter of St Paul to the Philippians   4:10-19

There is nothing I cannot master with the help of the One who gives me strength.

It is a great joy to me, in the Lord, that at last you have shown some concern for me again; though of course you were concerned before, and only lacked an opportunity. I am not talking about shortage of money: I have learnt to manage on whatever I have, I know how to be poor and I know how to be rich too. I have been through my initiation and now I am ready for anything anywhere: full stomach or empty stomach, poverty or plenty. There is nothing I cannot master with the help of the One who gives me strength. All the same, it was good of you to share with me in my hardships. In the early days of the Good News, as you people of Philippi well know, when I left Macedonia, no other church helped me with gifts of money. You were the only ones; and twice since my stay in Thessalonika you have sent me what I needed. It is not your gift that I value; what is valuable to me is the interest that is mounting up in your account. Now for the time being I have everything that I need and more: I am fully provided now that I have received from Epaphroditus the offering that you sent, a sweet fragrance – the sacrifice that God accepts and finds pleasing. In return my God will fulfil all your needs, in Christ Jesus, as lavishly as only God can.

This is the word of the Lord.

Responsorial Psalm   Ps 111:1-2. 5-6. 8. 9. R̥ v.1
    R̥ **Happy the man who fears the Lord.**

or

    R̥ **Alleluia!**

1 Happy the man who fears the Lord,
    who takes delight in all his commands.
    His sons will be powerful on earth;
    the children of the upright are blessed.   R̥

2 The good man takes pity and lends,
    he conducts his affairs with honour.
    The just man will never waver:
    he will be remembered for ever.   R̥

3 With a steadfast heart he will not fear.
    Open-handed, he gives to the poor;
    his justice stands firm for ever.
    His head will be raised in glory.   R̥

Gospel Acclamation   cf. Acts 16:14
    Alleluia, alleluia!
    Open our heart, O Lord,
    to accept the words of your Son.
    Alleluia!

or   2 Cor 8:9

    Alleluia, alleluia!
    Jesus Christ was rich,
    but he became poor for your sake,
    to make you rich out of his poverty.
    Alleluia!

GOSPEL

A reading from the holy Gospel according to Luke   16:9-15

If you cannot be trusted with money, that tainted thing, who will trust you with genuine riches?

Jesus said to his disciples, 'I tell you this: use money, tainted as it is, to win you friends, and thus make sure that when it fails you, they will welcome you into the tents of eternity. The man who can be trusted in little things can be trusted in great; the man who is dishonest in little things will be dishonest in great. If then you cannot be trusted with money, that tainted thing, who will trust you with genuine riches? And if you cannot be trusted with what is not yours, who will give you what is your very own?

'No servant can be the slave of two masters: he will either hate the first and love the second, or treat the first with respect and the second with scorn. You cannot be the slave both of God and of money.'

The Pharisees, who loved money, heard all this and laughed at him. He said to them, 'You are the very ones who pass yourselves off as virtuous in people's sight, but God knows your hearts. For what is thought highly of by men is loathsome in the sight of God.'

This is the Gospel of the Lord.

THIRTY-SECOND WEEK IN ORDINARY TIME
Year II

MONDAY

FIRST READING

A reading from the letter of St Paul to Titus 1:1-9
Appoint elders in the way that I told you.

From Paul, servant of God, an apostle of Jesus Christ to bring those whom God has chosen to faith and to the knowledge of the truth that leads to true religion; and to give them the hope of the eternal life that was promised so long ago by God. He does not lie and so, at the appointed time, he revealed his decision, and, by the command of God our saviour, I have been commissioned to proclaim it. To Titus, true child of mine in the faith that we share, wishing you grace and peace from God the Father and from Christ Jesus our saviour.

The reason I left you behind in Crete was for you to get everything organised there and appoint elders in every town, in the way that I told you: that is, each of them must be a man of irreproachable character: he must not have been married more than once, and his children must be believers and not uncontrollable or liable to be charged with disorderly conduct. Since, as president, he will be God's representative, he must be irreproachable: never an arrogant or hot-tempered man, nor a heavy drinker or violent, nor out to make money; but a man who is hospitable and a friend of all that is good; sensible, moral, devout and self-controlled; and he must have a firm grasp of the unchanging message of the tradition, so that he can be counted on for both expounding the sound doctrine and refuting those who argue against it.

This is the word of the Lord.

Responsorial Psalm   Ps 23:1-6. ℟ cf. v.6

℟ **Such are the men who seek your face, O Lord.**

1 The Lord's is the earth and its fullness,
the world and all its peoples.
It is he who set it on the seas;
on the waters he made it firm. ℟

2 Who shall climb the mountain of the Lord?
Who shall stand in his holy place?
The man with clean hands and pure heart,
who desires not worthless things. ℟

3 He shall receive blessings from the Lord
and reward from the God who saves him.
Such are the men who seek him,
seek the face of the God of Jacob. ℟

Gospel Acclamation   Phil 2:15-16
Alleluia, alleluia!
You will shine in the world like bright stars
because you are offering it the word of life.
Alleluia!

GOSPEL

A reading from the holy Gospel according to Luke   17:1-6

If your brother comes back to you seven times a day and says, 'I am sorry,' you must forgive him.

Jesus said to his disciples, 'Obstacles are sure to come, but alas for the one who provides them! It would be better for him to be thrown into the sea with a millstone put round his neck than that he should lead astray a single one of these little ones. Watch yourselves!

'If your brother does something wrong, reprove him and, if he is sorry, forgive him. And if he wrongs you seven times a day and seven times comes back to you and says, "I am sorry," you must forgive him.'

Thirty-second Week in Ordinary Time, Year II: Tuesday

The apostles said to the Lord, 'Increase our faith.' The Lord replied, 'Were your faith the size of a mustard seed you could say to this mulberry tree, "Be uprooted and planted in the sea," and it would obey you.'

This is the Gospel of the Lord.

TUESDAY

FIRST READING

A reading from the letter of St Paul to Titus   2:1-8. 11-14

We must live religious lives while we are waiting in hope for the blessing which will come with the Appearing of our God and saviour Christ Jesus.

It is for you to preach the behaviour which goes with healthy doctrine. The older men should be reserved, dignified, moderate, sound in faith and love and constancy. Similarly, the older women should behave as though they were religious, with no scandal-mongering and no habitual wine-drinking – they are to be the teachers of the right behaviour and show the younger women how they should love their husbands and love their children, how they are to be sensible and chaste, and how to work in their homes, and be gentle, and do as their husbands tell them, so that the message of God is never disgraced. In the same way, you have got to persuade the younger men to be moderate and in everything you do make yourself an example to them of working for good: when you are teaching, be an example to them in your sincerity and earnestness and in keeping all that you say so wholesome that nobody can make objections to it; and then any opponent will be at a loss, with no accusation to make against us.

You see, God's grace has been revealed, and it has made salvation possible for the whole human race and taught us that what we have to do is to give up everything that does not lead to God, and all our worldly ambitions; we must be self-restrained and live good and religious lives here in this present world, while we are waiting in hope for the blessing which will come with the Appearing of the glory of our great God and saviour Christ Jesus. He sacrificed himself for us in order to set us free from all wickedness and to purify a people so that it could be his very own and would have no ambition except to do good.

This is the word of the Lord.

Responsorial Psalm Ps 36:3-4. 18. 23. 27. 29. ℟ v.39

℟ **The salvation of the just comes from the Lord.**

1 If you trust in the Lord and do good,
   then you will live in the land and be secure.
   If you find your delight in the Lord,
   he will grant your heart's desire. ℟

2 He protects the lives of the upright,
   their heritage will last for ever.
   The Lord guides the steps of a man
   and makes safe the path of one he loves. ℟

3 Then turn away from evil and do good
   and you shall have a home for ever.
   The just shall inherit the land;
   there they shall live for ever. ℟

Gospel Acclamation Mt 4:4
   Alleluia, alleluia!
   Man does not live on bread alone,
   but on every word that comes from the mouth of God.
   Alleluia!

or Jn 14:23
   Alleluia, alleluia!
   If anyone loves me he will keep my word,
   and my Father will love him,
   and we shall come to him.
   Alleluia!

GOSPEL

A reading from the holy Gospel according to Luke 17:7-10
We are merely servants: we have done no more than our duty.

Jesus said to his disciples: 'Which of you, with a servant ploughing or minding sheep, would say to him when he returned from the fields, "Come and have your meal immediately?" Would he not be more likely to say, "Get my supper laid; make yourself tidy and wait on me while I eat and drink. You can eat and drink yourself afterwards?" Must he be grateful to the servant for doing what he was told? So with you: when you have done all you have been told to do, say, "We are merely servants: we have done no more than our duty."'

This is the Gospel of the Lord.

WEDNESDAY

FIRST READING

A reading from the letter of St Paul to Titus 3:1-7
We were misled, but because of his compassion God saved us.

Remind your people that it is their duty to be obedient to the officials and representatives of the government; to be ready to do good at every opportunity; not to go slandering other people or picking quarrels, but to be courteous and always polite to all kinds of people. Remember, there was a time when we too were ignorant, disobedient and misled and enslaved by different passions and luxuries; we lived then in wickedness and ill-will, hating each other and hateful ourselves.

But when the kindness and love of God our saviour for mankind were revealed, it was not because he was concerned with any righteous actions we might have done ourselves; it was for no reason except his own compassion that he saved us, by means of the cleansing water of rebirth and by renewing us with the Holy Spirit which he so generously poured over us through Jesus Christ our saviour. He did this so that we should be justified by his grace, to become heirs looking forward to inheriting eternal life.

This is the word of the Lord.

Responsorial Psalm

Ps 22. ℟ v.1

℟ **The Lord is my shepherd;
there is nothing I shall want.**

1 The Lord is my shepherd;
there is nothing I shall want.
Fresh and green are the pastures
where he gives me repose.
Near restful waters he leads me,
to revive my drooping spirit. ℟

2 He guides me along the right path;
he is true to his name.
If I should walk in the valley of darkness
no evil would I fear.
You are there with your crook and your staff;
with these you give me comfort. ℟

(continued)

3 You have prepared a banquet for me
   in the sight of my foes.
   My head you have anointed with oil;
   my cup is overflowing.

   ℟ **The Lord is my shepherd;
   there is nothing I shall want.**

4 Surely goodness and kindness shall follow me
   all the days of my life.
   In the Lord's own house shall I dwell
   for ever and ever. ℟

Gospel Acclamation cf. 2 Thess 2:14
Alleluia, alleluia!
Through the Good News God called us
to share the glory of our Lord Jesus Christ.
Alleluia!

or 1 Thess 5:18

Alleluia, alleluia!
For all things give thanks,
because this is what God expects you to do in Christ Jesus.
Alleluia!

GOSPEL

A reading from the holy Gospel according to Luke 17:11-19
No one has come back to give praise to God, except this foreigner.

On the way to Jerusalem Jesus travelled along the border between Samaria and Galilee. As he entered one of the villages, ten lepers came to meet him. They stood some way off and called to him, 'Jesus! Master! Take pity on us.' When he saw them he said, 'Go and show yourselves to the priests.' Now as they were going away they were cleansed. Finding himself cured, one of them turned back praising God at the top of his voice and threw himself at the feet of Jesus and thanked him. The man was a Samaritan. This made Jesus say, 'Were not all ten made clean? The other nine, where are they? It seems that no one has come back to give praise to God, except this foreigner.' And he said to the man, 'Stand up and go on your way. Your faith has saved you.'

This is the Gospel of the Lord.

THURSDAY

FIRST READING

A reading from the letter of St Paul to Philemon 7-20

Have him back, not as a slave any more, but as a dear brother.

I am so delighted, and comforted, to know of your love; they tell me, brother, how you have put new heart into the saints.

Now, although in Christ I can have no diffidence about telling you to do whatever is your duty, I am appealing to your love instead, reminding you that this is Paul writing, an old man now and, what is more, still a prisoner of Christ Jesus. I am appealing to you for a child of mine, whose father I became while wearing these chains: I mean Onesimus. He was of no use to you before, but he will be useful to you now, as he has been to me. I am sending him back to you, and with him – I could say – a part of my own self. I should have liked to keep him with me; he could have been a substitute for you, to help me while I am in the chains that the Good News has brought me. However, I did not want to do anything without your consent; it would have been forcing your act of kindness, which should be spontaneous. I know you have been deprived of Onesimus for a time, but it was only so that you could have him back for ever, not as a slave any more, but something better than a slave, a dear brother; especially dear to me, but how much more to you, as a blood-brother as well as a brother in the Lord. So if all that we have in common means anything to you, welcome him as you would me; but if he has wronged you in any way or owes you anything, then let me pay for it. I am writing this in my own handwriting: I, Paul, shall pay it back – I will not add any mention of your debt to me, which is yourself. Well then, brother, I am counting on you, in the Lord; put new heart into me, in Christ.

This is the word of the Lord.

Responsorial Psalm Ps 145:7-10. ℟ v.5

℟ **He is happy who is helped by Jacob's God.**

or

℟ **Alleluia!**

1 It is the Lord who keeps faith for ever,
  who is just to those who are oppressed.
  It is he who gives bread to the hungry,
  the Lord, who sets prisoners free. ℟

2 It is the Lord who gives sight to the blind,
   who raises up those who are bowed down.
   It is the Lord who loves the just,
   the Lord, who protects the stranger.

   ℟ **He is happy who is helped by Jacob's God.**

or
   ℟ **Alleluia!**

3 The Lord upholds the widow and orphan,
   but thwarts the path of the wicked.
   The Lord will reign for ever,
   Zion's God from age to age.   ℟

Gospel Acclamation   1 Peter 1:25
   Alleluia, alleluia!
   The word of the Lord remains for ever:
   What is the word?
   It is the Good News that has been brought to you.
   Alleluia!

or   Jn 15:5
   Alleluia, alleluia!
   I am the vine,
   you are the branches.
   Whoever remains in me, with me in him,
   bears fruit in plenty, says the Lord.
   Alleluia!

GOSPEL

A reading from the holy Gospel according to Luke   17:20-25
The kingdom of God is among you.

Asked by the Pharisees when the kingdom of God was to come, Jesus gave them this answer, 'The coming of the kingdom of God does not admit of observation and there will be no one to say, "Look here! Look there!" For, you must know, the kingdom of God is among you.'

  He said to the disciples, 'A time will come when you will long to see one of the days of the Son of Man and will not see it. They will say to you, "Look there!" or, "Look here!" Make no move; do not set off in pursuit; for as the lightning flashing from one part of heaven lights up the other, so will be the Son of Man when his day comes. But first he must suffer grievously and be rejected by this generation.'

  This is the Gospel of the Lord.

FRIDAY

FIRST READING

A reading from the second letter of St John   4-9

Only those who keep to what he taught can have the Father and Son with them.

It has given me great joy to find that your children have been living the life of truth as we were commanded by the Father. I am writing now, dear lady, not to give you any new commandment, but the one which we were given at the beginning, and to plead: let us love one another.

To love is to live according to his commandments: this is the commandment which you have heard since the beginning, to live a life of love.

There are many deceivers about in the world, refusing to admit that Jesus Christ has come in the flesh. They are the Deceiver; they are the Antichrist. Watch yourselves, or all our work will be lost and not get the reward it deserves. If anybody does not keep within the teaching of Christ but goes beyond it, he cannot have God with him: only those who keep to what he taught can have the Father and the Son with them.

This is the word of the Lord.

Responsorial Psalm   Ps 118:1-2. 10-11. 17-18. ℟ v.1

  ℟ **They are happy who follow God's law.**

1. They are happy whose life is blameless,
   who follow God's law!
   They are happy who do his will,
   seeking him with all their hearts. ℟

2. I have sought you with all my heart:
   let me not stray from your commands.
   I treasure your promise in my heart
   lest I sin against you. ℟

3. Bless your servant and I shall live
   and obey your word.
   Open my eyes that I may see
   the wonders of your law. ℟

Gospel Acclamation   Heb 4:12

Alleluia, alleluia!
The word of God is something alive and active;
it can judge secret emotions and thoughts.
Alleluia!

or   Lk 21:28

Alleluia, alleluia!
Stand erect, hold your heads high,
because your liberation is near at hand.
Alleluia!

GOSPEL

A reading from the holy Gospel according to Luke   17:26-37

When the day comes for the Son of Man to be revealed.

Jesus said to the disciples: 'As it was in Noah's day, so will it also be in the days of the Son of Man. People were eating and drinking, marrying wives and husbands, right up to the day Noah went into the ark, and the Flood came and destroyed them all. It will be the same as it was in Lot's day: people were eating and drinking, buying and selling, planting and building, but the day Lot left Sodom, God rained fire and brimstone from heaven and it destroyed them all. It will be the same when the day comes for the Son of Man to be revealed.

'When that day comes, anyone on the housetop, with his possessions in the house, must not come down to collect them, nor must anyone in the fields turn back either. Remember Lot's wife. Anyone who tries to preserve his life will lose it; and anyone who loses it will keep it safe. I tell you, on that night two will be in one bed: one will be taken, the other left; two women will be grinding corn together: one will be taken, the other left.' The disciples interrupted. 'Where Lord?' they asked. He said, 'Where the body is, there too will the vultures gather.'

This is the Gospel of the Lord.

SATURDAY

FIRST READING

A reading from the third letter of St John   5-8

It is our duty to welcome men of this sort and contribute our share to their work for the truth.

My friend, you have done faithful work in looking after these brothers, even though they were complete strangers to you. They are a proof to the whole Church of your charity and it would be a very good thing if you could help them on their journey in a way that God would approve. It was entirely for the sake of the name that they set out, without depending on the pagans for anything; it is our duty to welcome men of this sort and contribute our share to their work for the truth.

    This is the word of the Lord.

Responsorial Psalm   Ps 111:1-6. R v.1

  R **Happy the man who fears the Lord.**

or

  R **Alleluia!**

1 Happy the man who fears the Lord,
  who takes delight in all his commands.
  His sons will be powerful on earth;
  the children of the upright are blessed.   R

2 Riches and wealth are in his house;
  his justice stands firm for ever.
  He is a light in the darkness for the upright:
  he is generous, merciful and just.   R

3 The good man takes pity and lends,
  he conducts his affairs with honour.
  The just man will never waver:
  he will be remembered for ever.   R

Gospel Acclamation   James 1:21
  Alleluia, alleluia!
  Accept and submit to the word
  which has been planted in you
  and can save your souls.
  Alleluia!

or cf. 2 Thess 2:14

Alleluia, alleluia!
Through the Good news God called us
to share the glory of our Lord Jesus Christ.
Alleluia!

GOSPEL

A reading from the holy Gospel according to Luke 18:1-8
God will see justice done to his chosen who cry to him.

Jesus told his disciples a parable about the need to pray continually and never lose heart. 'There was a judge in a certain town' he said 'who had neither fear of God nor respect for men. In the same town there was a widow who kept on coming to him and saying, "I want justice from you against my enemy!" For a long time he refused, but at last he said to himself, "Maybe I have neither fear of God nor respect for man, but since she keeps pestering me I must give this widow her just rights, or she will persist in coming and worry me to death."'

And the Lord said, 'You notice what the unjust judge has to say? Now will not God see justice done to his chosen who cry to him day and night even when he delays to help them? I promise you, he will see justice done to them, and done speedily. But when the Son of Man comes, will he find any faith on earth?'

This is the Gospel of the Lord.

THIRTY-THIRD WEEK IN ORDINARY TIME
Year II

MONDAY

FIRST READING

A reading from the book of the Apocalypse 1:1-4; 2:1-5
Think where you were before you fell, and repent.

This is the revelation given by God to Jesus Christ so that he could tell his servants about the things which are now to take place very soon; he sent his angel to make it known to his servant John, and John has written down everything he saw and swears it is the word of God guaranteed by Jesus Christ. Happy the man who reads this prophecy, and happy those who listen to him, if they treasure all that it says, because the Time is close.

From John, to the seven churches of Asia: grace and peace to you from him who is, who was, and who is to come, from the seven spirits in his presence before his throne.

I heard the Lord saying to me: 'Write to the angel of the church in Ephesus and say, "Here is the message of the one who holds the seven stars in his right hand and who lives surrounded by the seven golden lampstands: I know all about you: how hard you work and how much you put up with. I know you cannot stand wicked men, and how you tested the impostors who called themselves apostles and proved they were liars. I know, too, that you have patience, and have suffered for my name without growing tired. Nevertheless, I have this complaint to make; you have less love now than you used to. Think where you were before you fell; repent, and do as you used to at first."'

This is the word of the Lord.

Responsorial Psalm Ps 1:1-4. 6. ℟ Apoc 2:7

℟ **Those who prove victorious
I will feed from the tree of life.**

1 Happy indeed is the man
  who follows not the counsel of the wicked;
  nor lingers in the way of sinners
  nor sits in the company of scorners,
  but whose delight is the law of the Lord
  and who ponders his law day and night.   ℟

2 He is like a tree that is planted
  beside the flowing waters,
  that yields its fruit in due season
  and whose leaves shall never fade;
  and all that he does shall prosper.   ℟

3 Not so are the wicked, not so!
  For they like winnowed chaff
  shall be driven away by the wind.
  For the Lord guards the way of the just
  but the way of the wicked leads to doom.   ℟

Gospel Acclamation Jn 8:12

Alleluia, alleluia!
I am the light of the world, says the Lord,
anyone who follows me

GOSPEL

A reading from the holy Gospel according to Luke   18:35-43
What do you want me to do for you? – Let me see again.

As Jesus drew near to Jericho there was a blind man sitting at the side of the road begging. When he heard the crowd going past he asked what it was all about, and they told him that Jesus the Nazarene was passing by. So he called out, 'Jesus, Son of David, have pity on me.' The people in front scolded him and told him to keep quiet, but he shouted all the louder, 'Son of David, have pity on me.' Jesus stopped and ordered them to bring the man to him, and when he came up, asked him, 'What do you want me to do for you?' 'Sir,' he replied 'let me see again.' Jesus said to him, 'Receive your sight. Your faith has saved you.' And instantly his sight returned and he followed him praising God, and all the people who saw it gave praise to God for what had happened.

This is the Gospel of the Lord.

TUESDAY

FIRST READING

A reading from the book of the Apocalypse   3:1-6, 14-22
If one of you opens the door, I will come in to share his meal.

I, John, heard the Lord saying to me: 'Write to the angel of the church in Sardis and say, "Here is the message of the one who holds the seven spirits of God and the seven stars: I know all about you: how you are reputed to be alive and yet are dead. Wake up; revive what little you have left: it is dying fast. So far I have failed to notice anything in the way you live that my God could possibly call perfect, and yet do you remember how eager you were when you first heard the message? Hold on to that. Repent. If you do not wake up, I shall come to you like a thief, without telling you at what hour to expect me. There are a few in Sardis, it is true, who have kept their robes from being dirtied, and they are fit to come with me, dressed in white. Those who prove victorious will be dressed, like these, in white robes; I shall not blot their names out of the book of life, but acknowledge their names in the presence of my Father and his angels. If anyone has ears to hear, let him listen to what the Spirit is saying to the churches."

'Write to the angel of the church in Laodicea and say, "Here is the message of the Amen, the faithful, the true witness, the ultimate source of God's creation: I know all about you: how you are neither cold nor hot. I wish you were one or the other, but since you are neither, but only lukewarm, I will spit you out of my mouth. You say to yourself, "I am rich, I have made a fortune, and have everything I want," never realising that you are wretchedly and pitiably poor, and blind and naked too. I warn you, buy from me the gold that has been tested in the fire to make you really rich, and white robes to clothe you and cover your shameful nakedness, and eye ointment to put on your eyes so that you are able to see. I am the one who reproves and disciplines all those he loves: so repent in real earnest. Look, I am standing at the door, knocking. If one of you hears me calling and opens the door, I will come in to share his meal, side by side with him. Those who prove victorious I will allow to share my throne, just as I was victorious myself and took my place with my Father on his throne. If anyone has ears to hear, let him listen to what the Spirit is saying to the churches." '

This is the word of the Lord.

Responsorial Psalm   Ps 14:2-5. ℟ Apoc 3:21

℟ **Those who prove victorious**
 I will allow to share my throne.

1 Lord, who shall be admitted to your tent?
   He who walks without fault;
   he who acts with justice
   and speaks the truth from his heart;
   he who does not slander with his tongue. ℟

2 He who does no wrong to his brother,
   who casts no slur on his neighbour,
   who holds the godless in disdain,
   but honours those who fear the Lord. ℟

3 He who takes no interest on a loan
   and accepts no bribes against the innocent.
   Such a man will stand firm for ever. ℟

Gospel Acclamation   Ps 129:5
    Alleluia, alleluia!
    My soul is waiting for the Lord,
    I count on his word.
    Alleluia!

or   1 Jn 4:10

    Alleluia, alleluia!
    God so loved us that he sent his Son
    to be the sacrifice that takes our sins away.
    Alleluia!

GOSPEL

A reading from the holy Gospel according to Luke   19:1-10
The Son of Man has come to seek out and save what was lost.

Jesus entered Jericho and was going through the town when a man whose name was Zacchaeus made his appearance; he was one of the senior tax collectors and a wealthy man. He was anxious to see what kind of man Jesus was, but he was too short and could not see him for the crowd; so he ran ahead and climbed a sycamore tree to catch a glimpse of Jesus who was to pass that way. When Jesus reached the spot he looked up and spoke to him: 'Zacchaeus, come down. Hurry, because I must stay at your house today.' And he hurried down and welcomed him joyfully. They all complained when they saw what was happening. 'He has gone to stay at a sinner's house' they said. But Zacchaeus stood his ground and said to the Lord, 'Look, sir, I am going to give half my property to the poor, and if I have cheated anybody I will pay him back four times the amount.' And Jesus said to him, 'Today salvation has come to this house, because this man too is a son of Abraham; for the Son of Man has come to seek out and save what was lost.'

    This is the Gospel of the Lord.

WEDNESDAY

FIRST READING

A reading from the book of the Apocalypse   4:1-11
Holy is the Lord God, the Almighty; he was, he is and he is to come.

In my vision, I, John, saw a door open in heaven and heard the same voice speaking to me, the voice like a trumpet, saying, 'Come up here: I will show you what is to come in the future.' With that, the Spirit possessed me and I saw a throne standing in heaven, and the One who was sitting on the throne, and the Person sitting there looked like a diamond and a ruby. There was a rainbow encircling the throne, and this looked like an emerald. Round the throne in a circle were twenty-four thrones, and on them I saw twenty-four elders sitting, dressed in white robes with golden crowns on their heads. Flashes of lightning were coming from the throne, and the sound of peals of thunder, and in front of the throne there were seven flaming lamps burning, the seven Spirits of God. Between the throne and myself was a sea that seemed to be made of glass, like crystal. In the centre, grouped round the throne itself, were four animals with many eyes, in front and behind. The first animal was like a lion, the second like a bull, the third animal had a human face, and the fourth animal was like a flying eagle. Each of the four animals had six wings and had eyes all the way round as well as inside; and day and night they never stopped singing:

> 'Holy, Holy, Holy
> is the Lord God, the Almighty;
> he was, he is and he is to come.'

Every time the animals glorified and honoured and gave thanks to the One sitting on the throne, who lives forever and ever, the twenty-four elders prostrated themelves before him to worship the One who lives for ever and ever, and threw down their crowns in front of the throne, saying, 'You are our Lord and our God, you are worthy of glory and honour and power, because you made all the universe and it was only by your will that everything was made and exists.'

This is the word of the Lord.

Responsorial Psalm
Ps 150. ℟ Apoc 4:8

℟ **Holy, Holy, Holy
is the Lord God, the Almighty.**

or

℟ **Alleluia!**

1 Praise God in his holy place,
   praise him in his mighty heavens.
   Praise him for his powerful deeds,
   praise his surpassing greatness. ℟

2 O praise him with sound of trumpet,
   praise him with lute and harp.
   Praise him with timbrel and dance,
   praise him with strings and pipes. ℟

3 O praise him with resounding cymbals,
   praise him with clashing of cymbals.
   Let everything that lives and that breathes
   give praise to the Lord. ℟

Gospel Acclamation
1 Jn 2:5

Alleluia, alleluia!
When anyone obeys what Christ has said,
God's love comes to perfection in him.
Alleluia!

or

cf. Jn 15:16

Alleluia, alleluia!
I chose you from the world
to go out and to bear fruit,
fruit that will last.
Alleluia!

GOSPEL

A reading from the holy Gospel according to Luke
19:11-28

Why did you not put my money in the bank?

While the people were listening, Jesus went on to tell a parable, because he was near Jerusalem and they imagined that the kingdom of God was going to show itself then and there. Accordingly he said, 'A man of noble birth went to 'a distant country to be appointed king and afterwards return. He summoned ten of his servants and gave them ten pounds. "Do business with these" he told them "until I get back." But his compatriots detested him and sent a delegation to follow him with this message, "We do not want this man to be our king."

'Now on his return, having received his appointment as king, he sent for those servants to whom he had given the money, to find out what profit each had made. The first came in and said, "Sir, your one pound has brought in ten." "Well done, my good servant!" he replied. "Since you have proved yourself faithful in a very small thing, you shall have the government of ten cities." Then came the second and said, "Sir, your one pound has made five." To this one also he said, "And you shall be in charge of five cities." Next came the other and said, "Sir, here is your pound. I put it away safely in a piece of linen because I was afraid of you; for you are an exacting man: you pick what you have not put down and reap what you have not sown." "You wicked servant!" he said "Out of your own mouth I condemn you. So you knew I was an exacting man, picking up what I have not put down and reaping what I have not sown? Then why did you not put my money in the bank? On my return I could have drawn it out with interest." And he said to those standing by, "Take the pound from him and give it to the man who has ten pounds." And they said to him, "But, sir, he has ten pounds . . ." "I tell you, to everyone who has will be given more; but from the man who has not, even what he has will be taken away.

"But as for my enemies who did not want me for their king, bring them here and execute them in my presence."'

When he had said this he went on ahead, going up to Jerusalem.

This is the Gospel of the Lord.

THURSDAY

FIRST READING

A reading from the book of the Apocalypse 5:1–10

The Lamb was sacrificed, and with his blood he bought men of every nation.

I, John, saw that in the right hand of the One sitting on the throne there was a scroll that had writing on back and front and was sealed with seven seals. Then I saw a powerful angel who called with a loud voice, 'Is there anyone worthy to open the scroll and break the seals of it?' But there was no one, in heaven or on the earth or under the earth, who was able to open the scroll and read it. I wept bitterly because there was nobody fit to open the scroll and read it, but one of the elders said to me, 'There is no need to cry: the Lion of the tribe of Judah, the Root of David, has triumphed, and he will open the scroll and the seven seals of it.'

Then I saw, standing between the throne with its four animals and the circle of the elders, a Lamb that seemed to have been sacrificed; it had seven horns, and it had seven eyes, which are the seven Spirits God has sent out all over the world. The Lamb came forward to take the scroll from the right hand of the One sitting on the throne, and when he took it, the four animals prostrated themselves before him and with them the twenty-four elders; each one of them was holding a harp and had a golden bowl full of incense made of the prayers of the saints. They sang a new hymn:

> 'You are worthy to take the scroll
> and break the seals of it,
> because you were sacrificed, and with your blood
> you bought men for God
> of every race, language, people and nation
> and made them a line of kings and priests.
> to serve our God and to rule the world.'

This is the word of the Lord.

Responsorial Psalm   Ps 149: 1-6. 9. ℟ Apoc 5:10

   ℟ **You made us a line of kings and priests to serve our God.**

or

   ℟ **Alleluia!**

1. Sing a new song to the Lord,
   his praise in the assembly of the faithful.
   Let Israel rejoice in its Maker,
   let Zion's sons exult in their king.   ℟

2. Let them praise his name with dancing
   and make music with timbrel and harp.
   For the Lord takes delight in his people.
   He crowns the poor with salvation.   ℟

3. Let the faithful rejoice in their glory,
   shout for joy and take their rest.

Thirty-third Week in Ordinary Time, Year II: Friday 1261

Let the praise of God be on their lips:
this honour is for all his faithful. ℟

Gospel Acclamation Ps 118:135

Alleluia, alleluia!
Let your face shine on your servant,
and teach me your decrees.
Alleluia!

or cf. Ps 94:8

Alleluia, alleluia!
Harden not your hearts today,
but listen to the voice of the Lord.
Alleluia!

GOSPEL

A reading from the holy Gospel according to Luke 19:41-44
If you had only understood the message of peace!

As Jesus drew near Jerusalem and came in sight of the city he shed tears over it and said, 'If you in your turn had only understood on this day the message of peace! But, alas, it is hidden from your eyes! Yes, a time is coming when your enemies will raise fortifications all round you, when they will encircle you and hem you in on every side; they will dash you and the children inside your walls to the ground; they will leave not one stone standing on another within you – and all because you did not recognise your opportunity when God offered it!'

This is the Gospel of the Lord.

FRIDAY

FIRST READING

A reading from the book of the Apocalypse 10:8-11
I took the book and swallowed it.

I, John, heard the voice I had heard from heaven speaking to me again. 'Go', it said 'and take that open scroll out of the hand of the angel standing on sea and land.' I went to the angel and asked him to give me the small scroll, and he said, 'Take it and eat it; it will turn your stomach sour, but in your mouth it will taste as sweet as honey.' So I took it out of the angel's hand, and swallowed it; it was as sweet as honey in my mouth, but when I had eaten it my stomach turned sour. Then I was told, 'You are to prophesy again, this time about many different nations and countries and languages and emperors.'

This is the word of the Lord.

Responsorial Psalm   Ps 118:14. 24. 72. 103. 111. 131. R v.103

℟ **Your promise is sweet to my taste, O Lord**

1. I rejoiced to do your will
   as though all riches were mine.
   Your will is my delight;
   your statutes are my counsellors.   ℟

2. The law from your mouth means more to me
   than silver and gold.
   Your promise is sweeter to my taste
   than honey in the mouth.   ℟

3. Your will is my heritage for ever,
   the joy of my heart.
   I open my mouth and I sigh
   as I yearn for your commands.   ℟

Gospel Acclamation   cf. 2 Tim 1:10
Alleluia, alleluia!
Our Saviour Christ Jesus abolished death,
and he has proclaimed life through the Good News.
Alleluia!

or   Jn 10:27

Alleluia, alleluia!
The sheep that belong to me listen to my voice,
says the Lord,
I know them and the follow me.
Alleluia!

GOSPEL

A reading from the holy Gospel according to Luke   19:45-48

You have turned the house of God into a robbers' den.

Jesus went into the Temple and began driving out those who were selling. 'According to scripture,' he said 'my house will be a house of prayer. But you have turned it into a robbers' den.'

He taught in the Temple every day. The chief priests and the scribes, with the support of the leading citizens, tried to do away with him, but they did not see how they could carry this out because the people as a whole hung on his words.

This is the Gospel of the Lord.

SATURDAY

FIRST READING

A reading from the book of the Apocalypse 11:4-12
These two prophets have been a plague to the people of the world.

I, John, heard a voice saying: 'These, my two witnesses, are the two olive trees and the two lamps that stand before the Lord of the world. Fire can come from their mouths and consume their enemies if anyone tries to harm them; and if anybody does try to harm them he will certainly be killed in this way. They are able to lock up the sky so that it does not rain as long as they are prophesying; they are able to turn water into blood and strike the whole world with any plague as often as they like. When they have completed their witnessing, the beast that comes out of the Abyss is going to make war on them and overcome them and kill them. Their corpses will lie in the main street of the Great City known by the symbolic names Sodom and Egypt, in which their Lord was crucified. Men out of every people, race, language and nation will stare at their corpses, for three-and-a-half days, not letting them be buried, and the people of the world will be glad about it and celebrate the event by giving presents to each other, because these two prophets have been a plague to the people of the world.'

After the three-and-a-half days, God breathed life into their corpses and they stood up, and everybody who saw it happen was terrified; then they heard a loud voice from heaven say to them, 'Come up here', and while their enemies were watching, they went up to heaven in a cloud.

This is the word of the Lord.

Responsorial Psalm   Ps 143:1-2, 9-10. ℟ v.1

℟ **Blessed be the Lord, my rock.**

1. Blessed be the Lord, my rock
who trains my arms for battle,
who prepares my hands for war. ℟

2. He is my love, my fortress;
he is my stronghold, my saviour,
my shield, my place of refuge.
He brings peoples under my rule. ℟

3. To you, O God, will I sing a new song;
I will play on the ten-stringed lute
to you who give kings their victory,
who set David your servant free. ℟

Gospel Acclamation   cf. Lk 8:15

Alleluia, alleluia!
Blessed are those who,
with a noble and generous heart,
take the word of God to themselves
and yield a harvest through their perseverance.
Alleluia!

or   cf. 2 Tim 1:10

Alleluia, alleluia!
Our Saviour Christ Jesus abolished death,
and he has proclaimed life through the Good News.
Alleluia!

GOSPEL

A reading from the holy Gospel according to Luke   20:27-40

He is God, not of the dead, but of the living.

Some Sadducees – those who say that there is no resurrection – approached Jesus and they put this question to him, 'Master, we have it from Moses in writing, that if a man's married brother dies childless, the man must marry the widow to raise up children for his brother. Well then, there were seven brothers. The first, having married a wife, died childless. The second and then the third married the widow. And the same with all seven, they died leaving no children. Finally the woman herself died. Now, at the resurrection, to which of them will she be wife since she had been married to all seven?'

Jesus replied, 'The children of this world take wives and husbands, but those who are judged worthy of a place in the other world and in the resurrection from the dead do not marry because they can no longer die, for they are the same as the angels, and being children of the resurrection they are sons of God. And Moses himself implies that the dead rise again, in the passage about the bush where he calls the Lord the God of Abraham, the God of Isaac and the God of Jacob. Now he is God, not of the dead, but of the living; for to him all men are in fact alive.'

Some scribes then spoke up. 'Well put, Master' they said – because they would not dare to ask him any more questions.

This is the Gospel of the Lord.

LAST WEEK IN ORDINARY TIME
Year II

MONDAY

FIRST READING

A reading from the book of the Apocalypse 14:1-5
The name of Christ and his Father's name written on their foreheads.

In my vision I, John, saw Mount Zion, and standing on it a Lamb who had with him a hundred and forty-four thousand people, all with his name and his Father's name written on their foreheads. I heard a sound coming out of the sky like the sound of the ocean or the roar of thunder; it seemed to be the sound of harpists playing their harps. There in front of the throne they were singing a new hymn in the presence of the four animals and the elders, a hymn that could only be learnt by the hundred and forty-four thousand who had been redeemed from the world; they follow the Lamb wherever he goes; they have been redeemed from amongst men to be the first-fruits for God and for the Lamb. They never allowed a lie to pass their lips and no fault can be found in them.

This is the word of the Lord.

Responsorial Psalm   Ps 23:1-6. ℟ cf. v.6

   ℟   **Such are the men who seek your face, O Lord.**

1. The Lord's is the earth and its fullness,
   the world and all its peoples.
   It is he who set it on the seas;
   on the waters he made it firm.   ℟

2. Who shall climb the mountain of the Lord?
   Who shall stand in his holy place?
   The man with clean hands and pure heart,
   who desires not worthless things.   ℟

3. He shall receive blessings from the Lord
   and reward from the God who saves him.
   Such are the men who seek him,
   seek the face of the God of Jacob.   ℟

Gospel Acclamation   Apoc 2:10

Alleluia, alleluia!
Even if you have to die, says the Lord,
keep faithful, and I will give you
the crown of life.
Alleluia!

or   Mt 24:42. 44

Alleluia, alleluia!
Stay awake and stand ready,
because you do not know the hour
when the Son of Man is coming.
Alleluia!

GOSPEL

A reading from the holy Gospel according to Luke   21:1-4
He noticed a poverty-stricken widow putting in two small coins.

As Jesus looked up he saw rich people putting their offerings into the treasury; then he happened to notice a poverty-stricken widow putting in two small coins, and he said, 'I tell you truly, this poor widow has put in more than any of them; for these have all contributed money they had over, but she from the little she had has put in all she had to live on.'

This is the Gospel of the Lord.

TUESDAY

FIRST READING

A reading from the book of the Apocalypse 14:14-19
Harvest time has come, and the harvest of the earth is ripe.

In my vision I, John, saw a white cloud and, sitting on it, one like a son of man with a gold crown on his head and a sharp sickle in his hand. Then another angel came out of the sanctuary, and shouted aloud to the one sitting on the cloud, 'Put your sickle in and reap: harvest time has come and the harvest of the earth is ripe.' Then the one sitting on the cloud set his sickle to work on the earth, and the earth's harvest was reaped.

Another angel, who also carried a sharp sickle, came out of the temple in heaven, and the angel in charge of the fire left the altar and shouted aloud to the one with the sharp sickle, 'Put your sickle in and cut all the bunches off the vine of the earth; all its grapes are ripe. So the angel set his sickle to work on the earth and harvested the whole vintage of the earth and put it into a huge winepress, the winepress of God's anger.

This is the word of the Lord.

Responsorial Psalm
Ps 95:10-13. ℟ v.13

℟ **The Lord comes to rule the earth.**

1. Proclaim to the nations: 'God is king.'
   The world he made firm in its place;
   he will judge the peoples in fairness.
   Let the heavens rejoice and earth be glad,
   let the sea and all within it thunder praise. ℟

2. Let the land and all it bears rejoice,
   all the trees of the wood shout for joy
   at the presence of the Lord for he comes,
   he comes to rule the earth.
   With justice he will rule the world,
   he will judge the peoples with his truth. ℟

Gospel Acclamation
Lk 21:28

Alleluia, alleluia!
Stand erect, hold your heads high,
because your liberation is near at hand.
Alleluia!

or   Apoc 2:10

> Alleluia, alleluia!
> Even if you have to die, says the Lord,
> keep faithful, and I will give you
> the crown of life.
> Alleluia!

GOSPEL

A reading from the holy Gospel according to Luke   21:5-11
Not a single stone will be left on another.

When some were talking about the Temple, remarking how it was adorned with fine stonework and votive offerings, Jesus said, 'All these things you are staring at now – the time will come when not a single stone will be left on another: everything will be destroyed.' And they put to him this question: 'Master,' they said 'when will this happen, then, and what sign will there be that this is about to take place?'

'Take care not to be deceived,' he said 'because many will come using my name and saying, "I am he" and, "The time is near at hand." Refuse to join them. And when you hear of wars and revolutions, do not be frightened, for this is something that must happen but the end is not so soon.' Then he said to them, 'Nation will fight against nation, and kingdom against kingdom. There will be great earthquakes and plagues and famines here and there; there will be fearful sights and great signs from heaven.'

This is the Gospel of the Lord.

WEDNESDAY

FIRST READING

A reading from the book of the Apocalypse   15:1-4
They were singing the hymn of Moses and of the Lamb.

What I, John, saw in heaven was a great and wonderful sign: seven angels were bringing the seven plagues that are the last of all, because they exhaust the anger of God. I seemed to see a glass lake suffused with fire, and standing by the lake of glass, those who had fought against the beast and won, and against his statue and the number which is his name. They all had harps from God, and they were singing the hymn of Moses, the servant of God, and of the Lamb:

> 'How great and wonderful are all your works,
> Lord God Almighty;
> just and true are all your ways,
> King of nations.
> Who would not revere and praise your name, O Lord?
> You alone are holy,
> and all the pagans will come and adore you
> for the many acts of justice you have shown.'

This is the word of the Lord.

Responsorial Psalm   Ps 97:1-3. 7-9. ℟ Apoc 15:3

℟ **How great and wonderful are all your works,
Lord God almighty.**

1 Sing a new song to the Lord
 for he has worked wonders.
 His right hand and his holy arm
 have brought salvation. ℟

2 The Lord has made known his salvation;
 has shown his justice to the nations.
 He has remembered his truth and love
 for the house of Israel. ℟

3 Let the sea and all within it, thunder;
 the world, and all its peoples.
 Let the rivers clap their hands.
 and the hills ring out their joy
 at the presence of the Lord. ℟

4 For the Lord comes,
 he comes to rule the earth.
 He will rule the world with justice
 and the peoples with fairness. ℟

Gospel Acclamation   Lk 21:36
Alleluia, alleluia!
Stay awake, praying at all times
for the strength to stand with confidence
before the Son of Man.
Alleluia!

or Apoc 2:10

> Alleluia, alleluia!
> Even if you have to die, says the Lord,
> keep faithful, and I will give you
> the crown of life.
> Alleluia!

GOSPEL

A reading from the holy Gospel according to Luke 21:12-19

You will be hated by all men on account of my name, but not a hair of your head will be lost.

Jesus said to his disciples: 'Men will seize you and persecute you; they will hand you over to the synagogues and to imprisonment, and bring you before kings and governors because of my name – and that will be your opportunity to bear witness. Keep this carefully in mind: you are not to prepare your defence, because I myself shall give you an eloquence and a wisdom that none of your opponents will be able to resist or contradict. You will be betrayed even by parents and brothers, relations and friends; and some of you will be put to death. You will be hated by all men on account of my name, but not a hair of your head will be lost. Your endurance will win you your lives.

This is the Gospel of the Lord.

THURSDAY

FIRST READING

A reading from the book of the Apocalypse 18:1-2. 21-23; 19:1-3. 9

Babylon the Great has fallen.

I, John, saw an angel come down from heaven, with great authority given to him; the earth was lit up with his glory. At the top of his voice he shouted, 'Babylon has fallen, Babylon the Great has fallen, and has become the haunt of devils and a lodging for every foul spirit and dirty, loathsome bird.'

Then a powerful angel picked up a boulder like a great millstone, and as he hurled it into the sea, he said, 'That is how the great city of Babylon is going to be hurled down, never to be seen again.

> 'Never again in you, Babylon,
> will be heard the song of harpists and minstrels,
> the music of flute and trumpet;
> never again will craftsmen of every skill be found
> or the sound of the mill be heard;
> never again will shine the light of the lamp,
> never again will be heard
> the voices of bridegroom and bride.
> Your traders were the princes of the earth,
> all the nations were under your spell.'

After this I seemed to hear the great sound of a huge crowd in heaven, singing, 'Alleluia! Victory and glory and power to our God! He judges fairly, he punishes justly, and he has condemned the famous prostitute who corrupted the earth with her fornication; he has avenged his servants that she killed.' They sang again, 'Alleluia! The smoke of her will go up for ever and ever.'

The angel said, 'Write this: Happy are those who are invited to the wedding feast of the Lamb.'

This is the word of the Lord.

Responsorial Psalm   Ps 99:2-5. ℟ Apoc 19:9

> ℟ **Happy are those who are invited
> to the wedding feast of the Lamb.**

1. Cry out with joy to the Lord, all the earth.
Serve the Lord with gladness.
Come before him, singing for joy. ℟

2. Know that he, the Lord, is God.
He made us, we belong to him,
we are his people, the sheep of his flock. ℟

3. Go within his gates, giving thanks.
Enter his courts with songs of praise.
Give thanks to him and bless his name. ℟

4. Indeed, how good is the Lord,
eternal his merciful love.
He is faithful from age to age. ℟

Gospel Acclamation Mt 24:42. 44
  Alleluia, alleluia!
  Stay awake and stand ready,
  because you do not know the hour when the Son of Man is coming.
  Alleluia!

or Lk 21:28

  Alleluia, alleluia!
  Stand erect, hold you heads high,
  because your liberation is near at hand.
  Alleluia!

GOSPEL

A reading from the holy Gospel according to Luke 21:20-28

Jerusalem will be trampled down by the pagans until the age of the pagans is completely over.

Jesus said to his disciples: 'When you see Jerusalem surrounded by armies, you must realise that she will soon be laid desolate. Then those in Judaea must escape to the mountains, those inside the city must leave it, and those in country districts must not take refuge in it. For this is the time of vengeance when all that scripture says must be fulfilled. Alas for those with child, or with babies at the breast, when those days come!

'For great misery will descend on the land and wrath on this people. They will fall by the edge of the sword and be led captive to every pagan country; and Jerusalem will be trampled down by the pagans until the age of the pagans is completely over.

'There will be signs in the sun and moon and stars; on earth nations in agony, bewildered by the clamour of the ocean and its waves; men dying of fear as they await what menaces the world, for the powers of heaven will be shaken. And then they will see the Son of Man coming in a cloud with power and great glory. When these things begin to take place, stand erect, hold your heads high, because your liberation is near at hand.'

This is the Gospel of the Lord.

FRIDAY

FIRST READING

A reading from the book of the Apocalypse   20:1-4. 11 – 21:2
The dead were judged according to what they had done in their lives. I saw the new Jerusalem coming down from heaven.

I, John, saw an angel come down from heaven with the key of the Abyss in his hand and an enormous chain. He overpowered the dragon, the primeval serpent which is the devil and Satan, and chained him up for a thousand years. He threw him into the Abyss, and shut the entrance and sealed it over him, to make sure he would not deceive the nations again until the thousand years had passed. At the end of that time he must be released, but only for a short while.

Then I saw thrones, and I saw those who are given the power to be judges take their seats on them. I saw the souls of all who had been beheaded for having witnessed for Jesus and for having preached God's word, and those who refused to worship the beast or his statue and would not have the brand-mark on their foreheads or hands; they came to life, and reigned with Christ for a thousand years.

Then I saw a great white throne and the One who was sitting on it. In his presence, earth and sky vanished, leaving no trace. I saw the dead, both great and small, standing in front of his throne, while the book of life was opened, and other books opened which were the record of what they had done in their lives, by which the dead were judged.

The sea gave up all the dead who were in it; Death and Hades were emptied of the dead that were in them; and every one was judged according to the way in which he had lived. Then Death and Hades were thrown into the burning lake. This burning lake is the second death; and anybody whose name could not be found written in the book of life was thrown into the burning lake.

Then I saw a new heaven and a new earth; the first heaven and the first earth had disappeared now, and there was no longer any sea. I saw the holy city, and the new Jerusalem, coming down from God out of heaven, as beautiful as a bride all dressed for her husband.

This is the word of the Lord.

Responsorial Psalm

Ps 83:3-6. 8. ℟ Apoc 21:3

℟ **Here God lives among men.**

1 My soul is longing and yearning,
  is yearning for the courts of the Lord.
  My heart and my soul ring out their joy
  to God, the living God. ℟

2 The sparrow herself finds a home
  and the swallow a nest for her brood;
  she lays her young by your altars,
  Lord of hosts, my king and my God. ℟

3 They are happy, who dwell in your house,
  for ever singing your praise.
  They are happy, whose strength is in you.
  They walk with ever growing strength. ℟

Gospel Acclamation

Lk 21:28

Alleluia, alleluia!
Stand erect, hold your heads high,
because your liberation is near at hand.
Alleluia!

GOSPEL

A reading from the holy Gospel according to Luke 21:29-33

When you see these things happen, know that the kingdom of God is near.

Jesus told his disciples a parable, 'Think of the fig tree and indeed every tree. As soon as you see them bud, you know that summer is now near. So with you when you see these things happening: know that the kingdom of God is near. I tell you solemnly, before this generation has passed away all will have taken place. Heaven and earth will pass away, but my words will never pass away.'

This is the Gospel of the Lord.

SATURDAY

FIRST READING

A reading from the book of the Apocalypse 22:1-7
It will never be night again, because the Lord will be shining on them.

The angel showed me, John, the river of life, rising from the throne of God and of the Lamb and flowing crystal-clear down the middle of the city street. On either side of the river were the trees of life, which bear twelve crops of fruit in a year, one in each month, and the leaves of which are the cure for the pagans.

The ban will be lifted. The throne of God and of the Lamb will be in its place in the city; his servants will worship him, they will see him face to face, and his name will be written on their foreheads. It will never be night again and they will not need lamplight or sunlight, because the Lord God will be shining on them. They will reign for ever and ever.

The angel said to me, 'All that you have written is sure and will come true: the Lord God who gives the spirit to the prophets has sent his angel to reveal to his servants what is soon to take place. Very soon now, I shall be with you again.' Happy are those who treasure the prophetic message of this book.

This is the word of the Lord.

Responsorial Psalm   Ps 94:1-7. ℟ 1 Cor 16:22; Apoc 22:20

    ℟ **Marana tha! Come, Lord Jesus!**

1 Come, ring out our joy to the Lord;
   hail the rock who saves us.
   Let us come before him, giving thanks,
   with songs let us hail the Lord.   ℟

2 A mighty God is the Lord,
   a great king above all gods.
   In his hand are the depths of the earth;
   the heights of the mountains are his.
   To him belongs the sea, for he made it
   and the dry land shaped by his hands.   ℟

3 Come in; let us bow and bend low;
   let us kneel before the God who made us
   for he is our God and we
   the people who belong to his pasture,
   the flock that is led by his hand.   ℟

Gospel Acclamation   Mt 24:42. 44

Alleluia, alleluia!
Stay awake and stand ready,
because you do not know the hour when the Son of Man is
   coming.
Alleluia!

or   Lk 21:36

Alleluia, alleluia!
Stay awake, praying at all times
for the strength to stand with confidence
before the Son of Man.
Alleluia!

GOSPEL

A reading from the holy Gospel according to Luke   21:34-36
Stay awake, praying for the strength to survive all that is going to happen.

Jesus said to his disciples: 'Watch yourselves, or your hearts will be coarsened with debauchery and drunkenness and the cares of life, and that day will be sprung on you suddenly, like a trap. For it will come down on every living man on the face of the earth. Stay awake, praying at all times for the strength to survive all that is going to happen, and to stand with confidence before the Son of Man.'

This is the Gospel of the Lord.

GOSPEL ACCLAMATIONS
For use *ad libitum* on the Weekdays of Ordinary Time

1   1 Sam 3:9; Jn 6:68

Alleluia, alleluia!
Speak, Lord, your servant is listening:
you have the message of eternal life.
Alleluia!

2   cf. Ps 18:9

Alleluia, alleluia!
Your words gladden the heart, O Lord,
they give light to the eyes.
Alleluia!

3   Ps 24:4. 5

Alleluia, alleluia!
Teach me your paths, my God,
make me walk in your truth.
Alleluia!

4   cf. Ps 26:11

Alleluia, alleluia!
Instruct me, Lord, in your way;
on an even path lead me.
Alleluia!

5   cf. Ps 94:8

Alleluia, alleluia!
Harden not your hearts today,
but listen to the voice of the Lord.
Alleluia!

6   Ps 110:7. 8

Alleluia, alleluia!
Your precepts, O Lord, are all of them sure;
they stand firm for ever and ever.
Alleluia!

Gospel Acclamations for Weekdays in Ordinary Time

7 Ps 118:18

Alleluia, alleluia!
Open my eyes, O Lord, that I may consider
the wonders of your law.
Alleluia!

8 Ps 118:27

Alleluia, alleluia!
Make me grasp the way of your precepts,
and I will muse on your wonders.
Alleluia!

9 Ps 118:34

Alleluia, alleluia!
Train me, Lord, to observe your law,
to keep it with my heart.
Alleluia!

10 Ps 118:36. 29

Alleluia, alleluia!
Bend my heart to your will, O Lord,
and teach me your law.
Alleluia!

11 Ps 118:88

Alleluia, alleluia!
Because of your love give me life,
and I will do your will.
Alleluia!

12 Ps 118:105

Alleluia, alleluia!
Your word is a lamp for my steps
and a light for my path.
Alleluia!

13 Ps 118:135

Alleluia! alleluia!
Let your face shine on your servant,
and teach me your decrees.
Alleluia!

Gospel Acclamations for Weekdays in Ordinary Time   1279

14   cf. Ps 129:5

Alleluia, alleluia!
My soul is waiting for the Lord,
I count on his word.
Alleluia!

15   Ps 144:13

Alleluia, alleluia!
The Lord is faithful in all his words
and loving in all his deeds.
Alleluia!

16   Ps 147:12. 15

Alleluia, alleluia!
O praise the Lord, Jerusalem!
He sends out his word to the earth.
Alleluia!

17   Mt 4:4

Alleluia, alleluia!
Man does not live on bread alone,
but on every word that comes from the mouth of God.
Alleluia!

18   cf. Mt 11:25

Alleluia, alleluia!
Blessed are you, Father,
Lord of heaven and earth,
for revealing the mysteries of the kingdom
to mere children.
Alleluia!

19   cf. Lk 8:15

Alleluia, alleluia!
Blessed are those who,
with a noble and generous heart,
take the word of God to themselves
and yield a harvest through their perseverance.
Alleluia!

20   cf. Jn 6:63. 68

Alleluia, alleluia!
Your words are spirit, Lord,
and they are life:
you have the message of eternal life.
Alleluia!

21   Jn 8:12

Alleluia, alleluia!
I am the light of the world, says the Lord,
anyone who follows me
will have the light of life.
Alleluia!

22   Jn 10:27

Alleluia, alleluia!
The sheep that belong to me listen to my voice,
says the Lord,
I know them and they follow me.
Alleluia!

23   Jn 14:6

Alleluia, alleluia!
I am the Way, the Truth and the Life, says the Lord;
no one can come to the Father except through me.
Alleluia!

24   Jn 14:23

Alleluia, alleluia!
If anyone loves me he will keep my word,
and my Father will love him,
and we shall come to him.
Alleluia!

25   Jn 15:15

Alleluia, alleluia!
I call you friends, says the Lord,
because I have made known to you
everything I have learnt from my Father.
Alleluia!

Gospel Acclamations for Weekdays in Ordinary Time   1281

26   cf. Jn 17:17

Alleluia, alleluia!
Your word is truth, O Lord,
consecrate us in the truth.
Alleluia!

27   cf. Acts 16:14

Alleluia, alleluia!
Open our heart, O Lord,
to accept the words of your Son.
Alleluia!

28   2 Cor 5:19

Alleluia, alleluia!
God in Christ was reconciling the world to himself,
and he has entrusted to us the news that they are reconciled.
Alleluia!

29   cf. Eph 1:17. 18

Alleluia, alleluia!
May the Father of our Lord Jesus Christ
enlighten the eyes of our mind,
so that we can see what hope his call holds for us.
Alleluia!

30   Phil 2:15-16

Alleluia, alleluia!
You will shine in the world like bright stars
because you are offering it the word of life.
Alleluia!

31   cf. Col 3:16. 17

Alleluia, alleluia!
Let the message of Christ, in all its richness,
find a home with you;
through him give thanks to God the Father.
Alleluia!

32   cf. 1 Thess 2:13

Alleluia, alleluia!
Accept God's message for what is really is:
God's message, and not some human thinking.
Alleluia!

33   cf. 2 Thess 2:14

Alleluia, alleluia!
Through the Good News God called us
to share the glory of our Lord Jesus Christ.
Alleluia!

34   cf. 2 Tim 1:10

Alleluia, alleluia!
Our Saviour Christ Jesus abolished death,
and he has proclaimed life through the Good News.
Alleluia!

35   Heb 4:12

Alleluia, alleluia!
The word of God is something alive and active;
it can judge secret emotions and thoughts.
Alleluia!

36   James 1:18

Alleluia, alleluia!
By his own choice the Father made us his children
by the message of the truth,
so that we should be a sort of first-fruits
of all that he created.
Alleluia!

37   James 1:21

Alleluia, alleluia!
Accept and submit to the word
which has been planted in you
and can save your souls.
Alleluia!

Gospel Acclamations for Weekdays in Ordinary Time 1283

38 1 Peter 1:25

Alleluia, alleluia!
The word of the Lord remains for ever:
What is this word?
It is the Good News that has been brought to you.
Alleluia!

39 1 Jn 2:5

Alleluia, alleluia!
When anyone obeys what Christ has said,
God's love comes to perfection in him,
Alleluia!

For the last Week in Ordinary Time

1 Mt 24:42. 44

Alleluia, alleluia!
Stay awake and stand ready,
because you do not know the hour
when the Son of Man is coming.
Alleluia!

2 Lk 21:28

Alleluia, alleluia!
Stand erect, hold your heads high,
because your liberation is near at hand.
Alleluia!

3 Lk 21:36

Alleluia, alleluia!
Stay awake, praying at all times
for the strength to stand with confidence
before the Son of Man.
Alleluia!

4 Apoc 2:10

Alleluia, alleluia!
Even if you have to die, says the Lord,
keep faithful, and I will give you
the crown of life.
Alleluia!

BLESSED & BROKEN

HE GAVE **LOAVES** TO THE ASSEMBLY

FISH ALSO

TAKE·EAT BREAD FOR TODAY FATHER'S GIFT

PRAYERS
PREPARATION FOR MASS

I am the living bread which has come down from heaven.
Anyone who eats this bread will live forever;
and that bread that I shall give
is my flesh, for the life of the world. *John 6:51*

This is what I received from the Lord and passed on to you: that on the same night he was betrayed, the Lord Jesus took some bread, and thanked God for it and broke it, and he said, 'This is my body, which is for you; do this as a memorial of me.' In the same way he took the cup after supper, and said, 'This cup is the new covenant in my blood. Whenever you drink it, do this as a memorial of me.' Until the Lord comes, therefore, every time you eat this bread and drink this cup you are proclaiming his death. Everyone is to recollect himself before eating this bread and drinking this cup. *1 Corinthians 11:23-26. 28*

The cup that we bless is a communion with the blood of Christ, and the bread that we break is a communion with the body of Christ. *1 Corinthians 10:1*

Worship God in a way that is worthy of thinking beings, by offering your living bodies as a holy sacrifice, truly pleasing to God. *Romans 12:1*

Prayer of St Thomas Aquinas before Holy Communion
Almighty, everlasting God,
I draw near to the sacrament of your only-begotten Son,
our Lord Jesus Christ.
I who am sick approach the physician of life.
I who am unclean come to the fountain of mercy;
blind, to the light of eternal brightness;
poor and needy, to the Lord of heaven and earth.
Therefore, I implore you, in your boundless mercy,
to heal my sickness, cleanse my defilement,
enlighten my blindness, enrich my poverty,
and clothe my nakedness.
Then shall I dare to receive the bread of angels,
the King of kings and Lord of lords,
with reverence and humility,
contrition and love,

purity and faith.
with the purpose and intention necessary
for the good of my soul.
Grant, I beseech you, that I may receive
not only the Body and Blood of the Lord,
but also the grace and power of the sacrament.
Most merciful God,
enable me so to receive the Body of your only-begotten Son,
our Lord Jesus Christ, which he took from the Virgin Mary,
that I may be found worthy to be incorporated
into his mystical Body, and counted among his members.
Most loving Father,
grant that I may one day see face to face
your beloved Son, whom I now intend to receive
under the veil of the sacrament,
and who with you and the Holy Spirit,
lives and reigns for ever,
one God, world without end. Amen.

Tr. *Stanbrook*

Invocation to the Holy Spirit
Lord Almighty,
send down upon this sacrifice your Holy Spirit.
May he declare this bread that we shall eat
to be the body of Christ,
and this cup that we shall drink
to be the blood of Christ.
May he strengthen and sanctify us
who eat this bread and drink this cup,
grant forgiveness of our sins
and deliver us from the wiles of the devil.
May he fill us with his presence
to make us worthy of Christ, your Son,
and obtain for us eternal life.

Adapted from *The Apostolic Constitutions* 4th century

Prayer of St Ambrose
Lord Jesus Christ,
I approach your banquet table
in fear and trembling,
for I am a sinner,
and dare not rely on my own worth
but only on your goodness and mercy.

Prayers: Preparation for Mass

I am defiled by many sins in body and soul,
and by my unguarded thoughts and words.
Gracious God of majesty and awe,
I seek your protection,
I look for your healing.
Poor troubled sinner that I am,
I appeal to you, the fountain of all mercy.
I cannot bear your judgement,
but I trust in your salvation.
Lord, I show my wounds to you
and uncover my shame before you.
I known my sins are many and great,
and they fill me with fear,
but I hope in your mercies,
for they cannot be numbered.
Lord Jesus Christ, eternal king, God and man,
crucified for mankind,
look upon me with mercy and hear my prayer,
for I trust in you.
Have mercy on me,
full of sorrow and sin,
for the depth of your compassion never ends.
Praise to you, saving sacrifice,
offered on the wood of the cross for me and for all mankind.
Praise to the noble and precious blood,
flowing from the wounds of my crucified Lord Jesus Christ
and washing away the sins of the whole world.
Remember, Lord, your creature,
whom you have redeemed with your blood.
I repent my sins,
and I long to put right what I have done.
Merciful Father, take away all my offences and sins;
purify me in body and soul,
and make me worthy to taste the holy of holies.
May your body and blood,
which I intend to receive, although I am unworthy,
be for me the remission of my sins,
the washing away of my guilt,
the end of my evil thoughts,
and the rebirth of my better instincts.
May it incite me to do the works pleasing to you
and profitable to my health in body and soul,
and be a firm defence
against the wiles of my enemies. Amen.

Tr. *ICEL*

THE ORDER OF MASS

THE INTRODUCTORY RITES

The Mass begins with the Entrance Song. Then the celebrant greets the people. The Penitential Rite, the Gloria, and the Opening Prayer follow. The purpose of these preliminary rites is to help the people, gathered for the celebration of Mass, to join with each other as a worshipping community, and to prepare them to listen to the Word of God and to celebrate the eucharist.

Entrance Song
The celebrant and ministers go to the altar.

> **Entrance Song:** turn to the Proper of the Mass of the Day *or* a hymn is sung

Greeting
The celebrant greets all present. His greeting proclaims the presence of the Lord with the community gathered here. All make the sign of the cross.

Celebrant In the name of the Father, and of the Son, ✠ and of the Holy Spirit.

People **Amen.**

C The grace of our Lord Jesus Christ and the love of God and the fellowship of the Holy Spirit be with you all.
P **And also with you.**

or 2
C The grace and peace of God our Father and the Lord Jesus Christ be with you.
P **Blessed be God, the Father of our Lord Jesus Christ.**
or **And also with you.**

or 3
C The Lord be with you.
P **And also with you.**

The celebrant may briefly introduce the Mass of the day.

The Introductory Rites

1289

C. In the name of the Father, and of the Son, and of the Holy Spirit.

P. Amen.

1

C. The grace of our Lord Jesus Christ and the love of God and the fellowship of the Holy Spirit be with you all.

P. And also with you.

or 2

C. The grace and peace of God our Father and the Lord Jesus Christ be with you.

P. Blessed be God, the Father of our Lord Jesus Christ.

or

P. And also with you.

or 3

C. The Lord be with you.

[Bishop] Peace be with you.

P. And also with you.

Rite of Blessing and Sprinkling Holy Water

This rite may be used instead of the penitential rite at the beginning of Mass. If it is used, the Kyrie is not said.
The priest greets the people. A vessel containing the water to be blessed is placed before him.

Dear friends,
this water will be used
to remind us of our baptism.
Let us ask God to bless it
and to keep us faithful
to the Spirit he has given us.

1: God our Father,
your gift of water
brings life and freshness to the earth;
it washes away our sins
and brings us eternal life.

We ask you now
to bless ✠ this water,
and to give us your protection on this day
which you have made your own.
Renew the living spring of your life within us
and protect us in spirit and body,
that we may be free from sin
and come into your presence
to receive your gift of salvation.

or 2: Lord God almighty,
creator of all life,
of body and soul,
we ask you to bless ✠ this water:
as we use it in faith
forgive our sins
and save us from all illness
and the power of evil.

Lord,
in your mercy
give us living water,
always springing up as a fountain of salvation:
free us, body and soul, from every danger,
and admit us to your presence
in purity of heart.

Blessing and Sprinkling Holy Water

or 3: During the Easter season
Lord God almighty,
hear the prayers of your people:
we celebrate our creation and redemption.
Hear our prayers and bless ✠ this water
which gives fruitfulness to the fields,
and refreshment and cleansing to man.
You chose water to show your goodness
when you led your people to freedom
through the Red Sea
and satisfied their thirst in the desert
with water from the rock.
Water was the symbol used by the prophets
to foretell your new covenant with man.
You made the water of baptism holy
by Christ's baptism in the Jordan:
by it you give us a new birth
and renew us in holiness.
May this water remind us of our baptism
and let us share the joy
of all who have been baptised at Easter.

Where it is customary, salt may be mixed with the holy water.
The priest blesses the salt, saying:
Almighty God,
we ask you to bless ✠ this salt
as once you blessed the salt scattered over the water
by the prophet Elisha.
Wherever this salt and water are sprinkled,
drive away the power of evil,
and protect us always
by the presence of your Holy Spirit.

The priest sprinkles himself, his ministers, and the people. Meanwhile an appropriate song is sung.
When he returns to his place, the priest says:
May almighty God cleanse us of our sins,
and through the eucharist we celebrate
make us worthy to sit at his table
in his heavenly kingdom.   ℟ **Amen.**
When it is prescribed, the *Gloria* is then sung or said, and the Mass continues. Turn to p. 1297.

Penitential Rite

The celebrant invites the people to call their sins to mind, and to repent of them. He may use the following, or similar words:

C My brothers and sisters*,
to prepare ourselves to celebrate the sacred mysteries,
let us call to mind our sins.

or

As we prepare to celebrate the mystery of Christ's love,
let us acknowledge our failures
and ask the Lord for pardon and strength.

or

Coming together as God's family,
with confidence let us ask the Father's forgiveness,
for he is full of gentleness and compassion.

A pause for silent reflection follows. After the silence, one of the following three forms of the penitential rite is chosen:

A

All **I confess to almighty God,
and to you, my brothers and sisters,
that I have sinned through my own fault**
(All strike their breast)
**in my thoughts and in my words,
in what I have done,
and in what I have failed to do;
and I ask blessed Mary, ever virgin,
all the angels and saints,
and you, my brothers and sisters,
to pray for me to the Lord our God.**

C May almighty God have mercy on us,
forgive us our sins,
and bring us to everlasting life.

P **Amen.**

---

*Other words such as 'my dear people, friends, dearly beloved, brethren,' may be used here and in similar places in the liturgy.

The Penitential Rite

C. My brothers and sisters,* to prepare ourselves to celebrate the sacred mysteries, let us call to mind our sins.

A

I confess to almighty God . . .

C. May almighty God have mercy on us, forgive us our sins, and bring us to everlasting life. *P.* Amen.

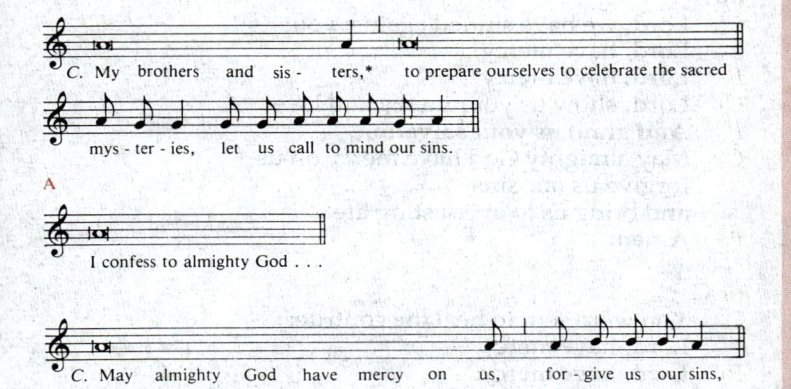

or B
C   Lord, we have sinned against you:
     Lord, have mercy.
P   **Lord, have mercy.**
C   Lord, show us your mercy and love.
P   **And grant us your salvation.**
C   May almighty God have mercy on us,
     forgive us our sins,
     and bring us to everlasting life.
P   **Amen.**

or C
C   You were sent to heal the contrite:
     Lord, have mercy.
P   **Lord, have mercy.**
C   You came to call sinners:
     Christ, have mercy.
P   **Christ, have mercy.**
C   You plead for us at the right hand of the Father:
     Lord, have mercy.
P   **Lord, have mercy.**

C   May almighty God have mercy on us,
     forgive us our sins,
     and bring us to everlasting life.
P   **Amen.**

The Kyrie

A plea for mercy. It is not said here if it has already been incorporated in the penitential rite.

C   Lord, have mercy.
P   **Lord, have mercy.**
C   Christ, have mercy.
P   **Christ, have mercy.**
C   Lord, have mercy.
P   **Lord, have mercy.**

The Kyrie

or B

Lord, we have sinned against you: Lord, have mercy. *P.* Lord, have mercy.

Lord, show us your mercy and love. *P.* And grant us your salvation.

C. May almighty God have mercy on us, forgive us our sins, and bring us to everlasting life. *P.* Amen.

or C

C. You were sent to heal the contrite: Lord, have mercy.
P. Lord, have mercy.
You came to call sinners: Christ, have mercy.
P. Christ, have mercy.
You plead for us at the right hand of the Father: Lord, have mercy.
P. Lord, have mercy.

C. May almighty God have mercy on us, forgive us our sins, and bring us to everlasting life. *P.* Amen.

REBORN IN THE SPIRIT
FATHER WE CELEBRATE
OUR ONENESS IN CHRIST
THE OFFERING OF YOUR CHURCH
THE SACRAMENT OF SALVATION

The Gloria
A hymn of praise. It may be said or sung.
The Gloria is not used on the Sundays of Advent or Lent.
All **Glory to God in the highest,**
  and peace to his people on earth.

Lord God, heavenly King,
almighty God and Father,
  we worship you, we give you thanks,
  we praise you for your glory.

Lord Jesus Christ, only Son of the Father,
Lord God, Lamb of God,
you take away the sin of the world:
  have mercy on us;
you are seated at the right hand of the Father:
  receive our prayer.

For you alone are the Holy One,
you alone are the Lord,
you alone are the Most High,
  Jesus Christ,
  with the Holy Spirit,
  in the glory of God the Father. Amen.

Opening Prayer
C Let us pray.
Celebrant and people pray silently for a while.
Then the celebrant says the opening prayer, which expresses the theme of the day's celebration.

Opening Prayer:
turn to the Proper of the Mass of the Day

At the end of the prayer, the people make it their own by responding:
P **Amen.**

THE LITURGY OF THE WORD

The Liturgy of the Word consists of *readings* from the scriptures; a *homily*, in which the minister explains the readings; the *Profession of Faith*, the creed of God's people; and the *General Intercessions*, or Prayer of the Faithful, in which the people intercede for all mankind.

> **Readings, Responsorial Psalm, Gospel Acclamation:**
> turn to the Proper of the Mass of the Day

First Reading
This is taken from the Old Testament or, during Eastertide, from the Acts of the Apostles. At the end of the reading:
Reader This is the Word of the Lord. *All* **Thanks be to God.**

Responsorial Psalm
The Psalm is a reflection on the First Reading. The Cantor sings or recites the psalm, and the people respond.

Second Reading
The New Testament Reading is generally from the letters of the apostles. It may be taken from the Acts of the Apostles, or from the book of Revelation. At the end:
Reader This is the Word of the Lord. *All* **Thanks be to God.**

Gospel Acclamation and Gospel Reading
To acknowledge Christ, present in his word, all stand. A verse of welcome is sung or said. After the Gospel:
Reader This is the gospel of the Lord.
All **Praise to you, Lord Jesus Christ.**

Homily
Through the readings, God has spoken to his people of redemption and salvation, and nourished their spirit with his word. The homily helps those present understand and reflect upon what they have heard.

The Liturgy of the Word   1299

First and Second Reading
At the end of each reading:

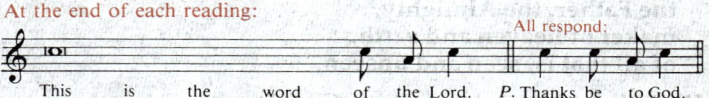

This is the word of the Lord.   *All respond:* P. *Thanks be to God.*

The Gospel

C. *The Lord be with you.* P. *And also with you.*

C. *A reading from the holy gospel according to N.*

P. *Glory to you, Lord.*

C. *This is the gospel of the Lord.* P. *Praise to you, Lord Jesus Christ.*

Profession of Faith (Creed)

We believe in one God,
  the Father, the Almighty,
  maker of heaven and earth,
  of all that is, seen and unseen.

We believe in one Lord, Jesus Christ,
  the only Son of God,
  eternally begotten of the Father,
  God from God, Light from Light,
  true God from true God,
  begotten, not made,
  of one Being with the Father.
  Through him all things were made.
  For us men and for our salvation
    he came down from heaven: All bow
  by the power of the Holy Spirit
he became incarnate from the Virgin Mary, and was made man.

For our sake he was crucified under Pontius Pilate;
  he suffered death and was buried.
  On the third day he rose again
    in accordance with the Scriptures;
  he ascended into heaven
    and is seated at the right hand of the Father.
He will come again in glory to judge the living and the dead,
  and his kingdom will have no end.

We believe in the Holy Spirit, the Lord, the giver of life,
  who proceeds from the Father and the Son.
  With the Father and the Son he is worshipped and glorified.
  He has spoken through the Prophets.
  We believe in one holy catholic and apostolic Church.
  We acknowledge one baptism for the forgiveness of sins.
  We look for the resurrection of the dead,
    and the life of the world to come.   Amen.

The General Intercessions
The celebrant invites the people to pray for the needs of all mankind. The people respond to each of the petitions according to custom.
  The celebrant says the concluding prayer.   *P*   **Amen.**

THE LITURGY OF THE EUCHARIST

The Preparation of the Altar and Gifts
At the beginning of the liturgy of the eucharist, the gifts which will become the Lord's body and blood are brought to the altar. The offerings of the people may also be brought to the altar. During the procession of gifts, an offertory song may be sung.
If no song is sung, then the people may make the responses to the prayer of offering given here.

C   Blessed are you, Lord, God of all creation.
    Through your goodness we have this bread to offer,
    which earth has given and human hands have made.
    It will become for us the bread of life.
P   **Blessed be God for ever.**

C (quietly)   By the mystery of this water and wine
    may we come to share in the divinity of Christ,
    who humbled himself to share in our humanity.

    Blessed are you, Lord, God of all creation.
    Through your goodness we have this wine to offer,
    fruit of the vine and work of human hands.
    It will become our spiritual drink.
P   **Blessed be God for ever.**

C (quietly)   Lord God, we ask you to receive us
    and be pleased with the sacrifice we offer you
    with humble and contrite hearts.

The celebrant washes his hands, saying:
C   Lord, wash away my iniquity; cleanse me from my
    sin.

Invitation to Prayer

Pray, brethren, that our sacrifice*
may be acceptable to God, the almighty Father.
P **May the Lord accept the sacrifice at your hands
for the praise and glory of his name,
for our good, and the good of all his Church.**

> **Prayer over the Gifts**
> turn to the Proper of the Mass of the Day

People **Amen.**

THE EUCHARISTIC PRAYER

The whole congregation joins Christ in acknowledging the works of God, and in offering the sacrifice.

C The Lord be with you.
P **And also with you.**
C Lift up your hearts.
P **We lift them up to the Lord.**
C Let us give thanks to the Lord our God.
P **It is right to give him thanks and praise.**

The celebrant continues alone.

> **Preface:** turn to pp.1338ff.

At the end of the Preface all sing or say:

All **Holy, holy, holy Lord, God of power and might,
heaven and earth are full of your glory.
Hosanna in the highest.**

**Blessed is he who comes in the name of the Lord.
Hosanna in the highest.**

The Eucharistic Prayer follows, pp.1304ff.

---

*In England and Wales: 'my sacrifice and yours'

The Eucharistic Prayer 1303

C. The Lord be with you. *P.* And also with you.

C. Lift up your hearts. *P.* We lift them up to the Lord.

C. Let us give thanks to the Lord our God.

P. It is right to give him thanks and praise.

Holy, holy, holy Lord, God of power and might, heaven and earth are full of your glory, Hosanna in the highest. Blessed is he who comes in the name of the Lord. Hosanna in the highest.

Eucharistic Prayer I

The passages within the brackets may be omitted if the celebrant wishes.

We come to you, Father,
with praise and thanksgiving,
through Jesus Christ your Son.
Through him we ask you to accept and bless
these gifts we offer you in sacrifice.

We pray for the Church
We offer them for your holy catholic Church,
watch over it, Lord, and guide it;
grant it peace and unity throughout the world.
We offer them for N. our Pope,
for N. our bishop,
and for all who hold and teach the catholic faith
that comes to us from the apostles.

For the living
Remember, Lord, your people,
especially those for whom we now pray, N. and N.
Remember all of us gathered here before you.
You know how firmly we believe in you
and dedicate ourselves to you.
We offer you this sacrifice of praise
for ourselves and those who are dear to us.
We pray to you, our living and true God,
for our well-being and redemption.

To honour the saints
In union with the whole Church
we honour Mary,
*the ever-virgin mother of Jesus Christ our Lord and God.
We honour Joseph, her husband,
the apostles and martyrs

Eucharistic Prayer I

Special form of In union with the whole Church
Christmas and during the octave
In union with the whole Church
we celebrate that day [night]
when Mary without loss of her virginity
gave the world its Saviour.
We honour her,*

Epiphany
In union with the whole Church
we celebrate that day
when your only Son,
sharing your eternal glory,
showed himself in a human body.
We honour Mary,*

Holy Thursday
In union with the whole Church
we celebrate that day
when Jesus Christ, our Lord,
was betrayed for us.
We honour Mary,*

From the Easter Vigil to the Second Sunday of Easter inclusive
In union with the whole Church
we celebrate that day [night]
when Jesus Christ, our Lord,
rose from the dead in his human body.
We honour Mary,*

Ascension
In union with the whole Church
we celebrate that day
when your only Son, our Lord,
took his place with you
and raised our frail human nature to glory.
We honour Mary,*

Pentecost
In union with the whole Church
we celebrate the day of Pentecost
when the Holy Spirit appeared to the apostles
in the form of countless tongues.
We honour Mary,*

LORD
Accept our sacrifice as a holy exchange of gifts

Eucharistic Prayer I

Peter and Paul, Andrew,
(James, John, Thomas,
James, Philip,
Bartholomew, Matthew, Simon and Jude;
we honour Linus, Cletus, Clement, Sixtus,
Cornelius, Cyprian, Lawrence, Chrysogonus,
John and Paul, Cosmas and Damian)
and all the saints.
May their merits and prayers
gain us your constant help and protection.
(Through Christ our Lord. Amen.)

For acceptance of this offering*
Father, accept this offering
from your whole family.
Grant us your peace in this life,
save us from final damnation,
and count us among those you have chosen.
(Through Christ our Lord. Amen.)

*From the Easter Vigil to the Second Sunday of Easter
Father, accept this offering
from your whole family
and from those born into the new life
of water and the Holy Spirit,
with all their sins forgiven.
Grant us your peace in this life,
save us from final damnation,
and count us among those you have chosen.
(Through Christ our Lord. Amen.)

Bless and approve our offering;
make it acceptable to you,
an offering in spirit and in truth.
Let it become for us
the body and blood of Jesus Christ,
your only Son, our Lord.
(Through Christ our Lord. Amen.)

The Lord's supper: the consecration
The day before he suffered
he took bread in his sacred hands
and looking up to heaven,
to you, his almighty Father,
he gave you thanks and praise.
He broke the bread,
gave it to his disciples, and said:
Take this, all of you, and eat it:
this is my body which will be given up for you.

When supper was ended,
he took the cup.
Again he gave you thanks and praise,
gave the cup to his disciples, and said:
Take this, all of you, and drink from it:
this is the cup of my blood,
the blood of the new and everlasting covenant.
It will be shed for you and for all men
so that sins may be forgiven.
Do this in memory of me.

Let us proclaim the mystery of faith:

Memorial acclamation of the people

1 **Christ has died,
 Christ is risen,
 Christ will come again.**

2 **Dying you destroyed our death,
 rising you restored our life.
 Lord Jesus, come in glory.**

3 **When we eat this bread and drink this cup,
 we proclaim your death, Lord Jesus,
 until you come in glory.**

4 **Lord, by your cross and resurrection
 you have set us free.
 You are the Saviour of the world.**

Eucharistic Prayer I

C. Let us proclaim the mystery of faith:

1. P. Christ has died, Christ is risen, Christ will come again.

2. P. Dying you destroyed our death, rising you restored our life. Lord Jesus, come in glory.

3. P. When we eat this bread and drink this cup, we proclaim your death, Lord Jesus, until you come in glory.

4. P. Lord, by your cross and resurrection you have set us free. You are the Saviour of the world.

1310 The Order of Mass

Memorial of the paschal mystery and offering
Father, we celebrate the memory of Christ, your Son.
We, your people and your ministers,
recall his passion,
his resurrection from the dead,
and his ascension into glory;
and from the many gifts you have given us
we offer to you, God of glory and majesty,
this holy and perfect sacrifice:
the bread of life
and the cup of eternal salvation.

Look with favour on these offerings
and accept them as once you accepted
the gifts of your servant Abel,
the sacrifice of Abraham, our father in faith,
and the bread and wine offered by your priest
    Melchisedech.
Almighty God,
we pray that your angel may take this sacrifice
to your altar in heaven.
Then, as we receive from this altar
the sacred body and blood of your Son,
let us be filled with every grace and blessing.
(Through Christ our Lord. Amen.)

For the dead
Remember, Lord, those who have died
and have gone before us marked with the sign of faith,
especially those for whom we now pray, N. and N.
May these, and all who sleep in Christ,
find in your presence
light, happiness, and peace.
(Through Christ our Lord. Amen.)

For us sinners
For ourselves, too, we ask
some share in the fellowship of your apostles and martyrs,
with John the Baptist, Stephen, Matthias, Barnabas,

Eucharistic Prayer I   1311

(Ignatius, Alexander, Marcellinus, Peter,
Felicity, Perpetua, Agatha, Lucy,
Agnes, Cecilia, Anastasia)
and all the saints.
Though we are sinners,
we trust in your mercy and love.
Do not consider what we truly deserve,
but grant us your forgiveness.

Through Christ our Lord
you give us all these gifts.
You fill them with life and goodness,
you bless them and make them holy.

Final doxology: in praise of God
Through him,
with him,
in him,
in the unity of the Holy Spirit,
all glory and honour is yours,
almighty Father,
for ever and ever.
P **Amen.**

C. Through him, with him, in him, in the u-ni-ty of the Ho-ly Spir-it, all glo-ry and hon-our is yours, al-might-y Fa-ther, for ev-er and ev-er. *P* A-men.

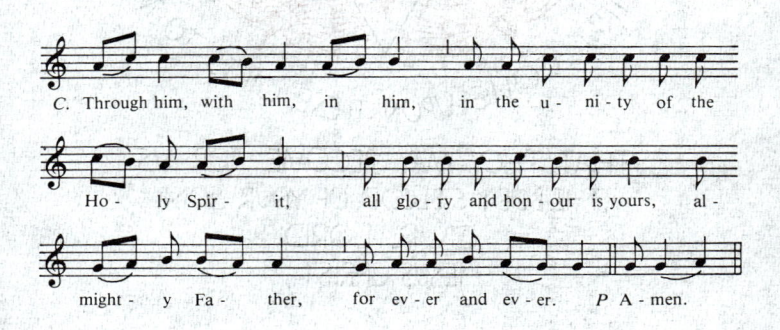

Turn to p.1328.

FATHER YOU ARE HOLY • FOUNT OF HOLINESS
LET YOUR SPIRIT COME UPON THESE GIFTS TO MAKE THEM HOLY

THAT THEY MAY BECOME FOR US
THE BODY & BLOOD OF YOUR SON
OUR LORD
JESUS CHRIST

Eucharistic Prayer II

Preface
This may be replaced by another preface.
Father, it is our duty and our salvation,
always and everywhere
to give you thanks
through your beloved Son, Jesus Christ.

He is the Word through whom you made the universe,
the Saviour you sent to redeem us.
By the power of the Holy Spirit
he took flesh and was born of the Virgin Mary.

For our sake he opened his arms on the cross;
he put an end to death
and revealed the resurrection.
In this he fulfilled your will
and won for you a holy people.

And so we join the angels and the saints
in proclaiming your glory
as we sing (say):
**Holy, holy, holy Lord, God of power and might,
heaven and earth are full of your glory.**
> **Hosanna in the highest.**

Blessed is he who comes in the name of the Lord.
> **Hosanna in the highest.**

Invocation of the Holy Spirit
Lord, you are holy indeed,
the fountain of all holiness.
Let your Spirit come upon these gifts to make them holy,
so that they may become for us
the body and blood of our Lord, Jesus Christ.

The Lord's Supper
Before he was given up to death,
a death he freely accepted,
he took bread and gave you thanks.
He broke the bread,
gave it to his disciples, and said:

Take this, all of you, and eat it:
this is my body which will be given up for you.

When supper was ended, he took the cup.
Again he gave you thanks and praise,
gave the cup to his disciples, and said:
Take this, all of you, and drink from it:
this is the cup of my blood,
the blood of the new and everlasting covenant.
It will be shed for you and for all men
so that sins may be forgiven.
Do this in memory of me.
Let us proclaim the mystery of faith:

Memorial acclamation of the people
1 **Christ has died,
 Christ is risen,
 Christ will come again.**

2 **Dying you destroyed our death,
 rising you restored our life.
 Lord Jesus, come in glory.**

3 **When we eat this bread and drink this cup,
 we proclaim your death, Lord Jesus,
 until you come in glory.**

4 **Lord, by your cross and resurrection
 you have set us free.
 You are the Saviour of the world.**

The memorial prayer
In memory of his death and resurrection,
we offer you, Father, this life-giving bread,
this saving cup.
We thank you for counting us worthy
to stand in your presence and serve you.
May all of us who share in the body and blood of Christ
be brought together in unity by the Holy Spirit.

Intercessions for the Church
Lord, remember your Church throughout the world;

Eucharistic Prayer II

C. Let us proclaim the mystery of faith:

1. P. Christ has died, Christ is risen, Christ will come again.

2. P. Dying you destroyed our death, rising you restored our life.
Lord Jesus, come in glory.

3. P. When we eat this bread and drink this cup, we proclaim your death,
Lord Jesus, until you come in glory.

4. P. Lord, by your cross and resurrection you have set us free.
You are the Saviour of the world.

make us grow in love,
together with N. our Pope,
N. our bishop, and all the clergy.

(In Masses for the Dead the following may be added:
Remember N., whom you have called from this life.
In baptism he [she] died with Christ:
may he [she] also share his resurrection.)
Remember our brothers and sisters
who have gone to their rest
in the hope of rising again;
bring them and all the departed
into the light of your presence.

In communion with the saints

Have mercy on us all;
make us worthy to share eternal life
with Mary, the virgin mother of God,
with the apostles, and with all the saints
who have done your will throughout the ages.
May we praise you in union with them,
and give you glory
through your Son, Jesus Christ.

Final doxology: in praise of God

Through him,
with him,
in him,
in the unity of the Holy Spirit,
all glory and honour is yours,
almighty Father,
for ever and ever.   P **Amen.**   Turn to p.1328.

C. Through him, with him, in him, in the u-ni-ty of the Ho-ly Spir-it, all glo-ry and hon-our is yours, al-might-y Fa-ther, for ev-er and ev-er. P A-men.

Eucharistic Prayer III

Praise to the Father
Father, you are holy indeed,
and all creation rightly gives you praise.
All life, all holiness comes from you
through your Son, Jesus Christ our Lord,
by the working of the Holy Spirit.
From age to age you gather a people to yourself,
so that from east to west
a perfect offering may be made
to the glory of your name.

Invocation of the Holy Spirit
And so, Father, we bring you these gifts.
We ask you to make them holy by the power of your Spirit,
that they may become the body and blood
of your Son, our Lord Jesus Christ,
at whose command we celebrate this eucharist.

The Lord's Supper
On the night he was betrayed,
he took bread and gave you thanks and praise.
He broke the bread, gave it to his disciples, and said:
Take this, all of you, and eat it:
this is my body which will be given up for you.

When supper was ended, he took the cup.
Again he gave you thanks and praise,
gave the cup to his disciples, and said:
Take this, all of you, and drink from it:
this is the cup of my blood,
the blood of the new and everlasting covenant.
It will be shed for you and for all men
so that sins may be forgiven.
Do this in memory of me.

Let us proclaim the mystery of faith:
Memorial acclamation of the people
1 **Christ has died,
   Christ is risen,
   Christ will come again.**

2 **Dying you destroyed our death,
   rising you restored our life.
   Lord Jesus, come in glory.**

3 **When we eat this bread and drink this cup,
   we proclaim your death, Lord Jesus,
   until you come in glory.**

4 **Lord, by your cross and resurrection
   you have set us free.
   You are the Saviour of the world.**

The memorial prayer
Father, calling to mind the death your Son endured for our salvation,
his glorious resurrection and ascension into heaven,
and ready to greet him when he comes again,
we offer you in thanksgiving this holy and living sacrifice.

Look with favour on your Church's offering,
and see the Victim whose death has reconciled us to yourself.
Grant that we, who are nourished by his body and blood,
may be filled with his Holy Spirit,
and become one body, one spirit in Christ.

May he make us an everlasting gift to you
and enable us to share in the inheritance of your saints,
with Mary, the virgin Mother of God;
with the apostles, the martyrs,
(Saint N. – the saint of the day or patron saint) and all your saints,
on whose constant intercession we rely for help.

Lord, may this sacrifice,
which has made our peace with you,
advance the peace and salvation of all the world.

Eucharistic Prayer III

C. Let us proclaim the mystery of faith:

1. P. Christ has died, Christ is risen, Christ will come again.

2. P. Dying you destroyed our death, rising you restored our life. Lord Jesus, come in glory.

3. P. When we eat this bread and drink this cup, we proclaim your death, Lord Jesus, until you come in glory.

4. P. Lord, by your cross and resurrection you have set us free. You are the Saviour of the world.

Strengthen in faith and love your pilgrim Church on earth;
your servant, Pope N., our bishop N.,
and all the bishops,
with the clergy and the entire people your Son has gained
 for you.
Father, hear the prayers of the family you have gathered
 here before you.
In mercy and love unite all your children wherever they
 may be.*
Welcome into your kingdom our departed brothers and
 sisters,
and all who have left this world in your friendship.
We hope to enjoy for ever the vision of your glory,
through Christ our Lord, from whom all good things
 come.

---

*In Masses for the dead, the following may be said:
Remember N.
In baptism he (she) died with Christ:
may he (she) also share his resurrection,
when Christ will raise our mortal bodies
and make them like his own in glory.
Welcome into your kingdom our departed brothers and
 sisters,
and all who have left this world in your friendship.
There we hope to share in your glory
when every tear will be wiped away.
On that day we shall see you, our God, as you are.
We shall become like you
and praise you for ever through Christ our Lord,
from whom all good things come.

Final doxology: in praise of God
Through him,
with him,
in him,
in the unity of the Holy Spirit,
all glory and honour is yours,
almighty Father,
for ever and ever.   *P*   **Amen.**   Turn to p.1328.

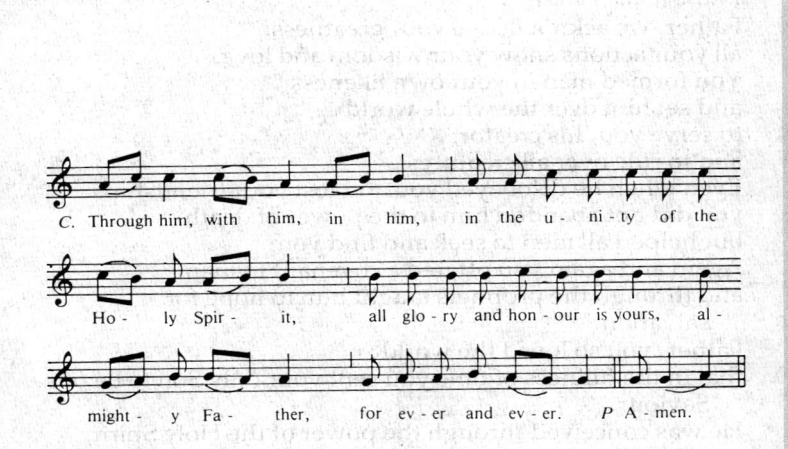

Eucharistic Prayer III

C. Through him, with him, in him, in the u-ni-ty of the Ho-ly Spir-it, all glo-ry and hon-our is yours, al-might-y Fa-ther, for ev-er and ev-er. P A-men.

Eucharistic Prayer IV

Preface
Father in heaven,
it is right that we should give you thanks and glory:
you alone are God, living and true.
Through all eternity you live in unapproachable light.
Source of life and goodness, you have created all things,
to fill your creatures with every blessing
and lead all men to the joyful vision of your light.
Countless hosts of angels stand before you to do your will;
they look upon your splendour
and praise you, night and day.
United with them,
and in the name of every creature under heaven,
we too praise your glory as we say:
Holy, holy, holy Lord, God of power and might,
heaven and earth are full of your glory.
   Hosanna in the highest.
Blessed is he who comes in the name of the Lord.
   Hosanna in the highest.

Praise to the Father
Father, we acknowledge your greatness:
all your actions show your wisdom and love.
You formed man in your own likeness
and set him over the whole world
to serve you, his creator,
and to rule over all creatures.
Even when he disobeyed you and lost your friendship
you did not abandon him to the power of death,
but helped all men to seek and find you.
Again and again you offered a covenant to man,
and through the prophets taught him to hope for
   salvation.
Father, you so loved the world
that in the fullness of time you sent your only Son to be our
   Saviour.
He was conceived through the power of the Holy Spirit,

Eucharistic Prayer IV

and born of the Virgin Mary,
a man like us in all things but sin.
To the poor he proclaimed the good news of salvation,
to prisoners, freedom,
and to those in sorrow, joy.
In fulfilment of your will
he gave himself up to death;
but by rising from the dead,
he destroyed death and restored life.
And that we might live no longer for ourselves but for him,
he sent the Holy Spirit from you, Father,
as his first gift to those who believe,
to complete his work on earth
and bring us the fullness of grace.

Invocation of the Holy Spirit
Father, may this Holy Spirit sanctify these offerings.
Let them become the body and blood of Jesus Christ our
    Lord
as we celebrate the great mystery
which he left us as an everlasting covenant.

The Lord's Supper
He always loved those who were his own in the world.
When the time came for him to be glorified by you, his
    heavenly Father,
he showed the depth of his love.

While they were at supper,
he took bread, said the blessing, broke the bread,
and gave it to his disciples, saying:
Take this, all of you, and eat it:
this is my body which will be given up for you.

In the same way, he took the cup, filled with wine.
He gave you thanks, and giving the cup to his disciples,
   said:
Take this, all of you, and drink from it:
this is the cup of my blood,
the blood of the new and everlasting covenant.
It will be shed for you and for all men
so that sins may be forgiven.
Do this in memory of me.

Let us proclaim the mystery of faith:

Memorial acclamation of the people

1 **Christ has died,
   Christ is risen,
   Christ will come again.**

2 **Dying you destroyed our death,
   rising you restored our life.
   Lord Jesus, come in glory.**

3 **When we eat this bread and drink this cup,
   we proclaim your death, Lord Jesus,
   until you come in glory.**

4 **Lord, by your cross and resurrection
   you have set us free.
   You are the Saviour of the world.**

Eucharistic Prayer IV

C. Let us proclaim the mystery of faith:

1
P. Christ has died, Christ is risen, Christ will come again.

2
P. Dying you destroyed our death, rising you restored our life.
Lord Jesus, come in glory.

3
P. When we eat this bread and drink this cup, we proclaim your death,
Lord Jesus, until you come in glory.

4
P. Lord, by your cross and resurrection you have set us free.
You are the Saviour of the world.

The memorial prayer

Father, we now celebrate this memorial of our redemption.
We recall Christ's death, his descent among the dead,
his resurrection, and his ascension to your right hand;
and, looking forward to his coming in glory,
we offer you his body and blood,
the acceptable sacrifice
which brings salvation to the whole world.

Intercessions: for the Church

Lord, look upon this sacrifice which you have given to your Church;
and by your Holy Spirit, gather all who share[*] this one bread and one cup
into the one body of Christ, a living sacrifice of praise.

Lord, remember those for whom we offer this sacrifice,
especially N. our Pope,
N. our bishop, and bishops and clergy everywhere.
Remember those who take part in this offering,
those here present and all your people,
and all who seek you with a sincere heart.

For the dead

Remember those who have died in the peace of Christ
and all the dead whose faith is known to you alone.

In communion with the saints

Father, in your mercy grant also to us, your children,
to enter into our heavenly inheritance
in the company of the Virgin Mary, the Mother of God,
and your apostles and saints.
Then, in your kingdom, freed from the corruption of sin and death,
we shall sing your glory with every creature through Christ our Lord,
through whom you give us everything that is good.

---

[*] ICEL translation: 'who share this bread and wine'.

Eucharistic Prayer IV

Final doxology: in praise of God

Through him,
with him,
in him,
in the unity of the Holy Spirit,
all glory and honour is yours,
almighty Father,
for ever and ever.
P **Amen.**

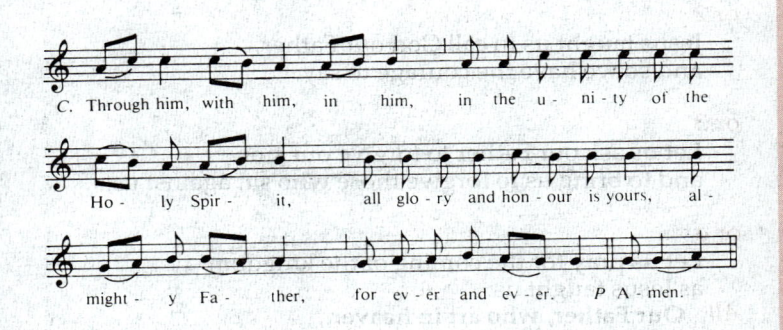

RITE OF COMMUNION

In accordance with the Lord's command, the faithful receive his body and blood as their spiritual food.

In the Our Father, all pray for daily food, and for forgiveness.

C Let us pray with confidence to the Father
in the words our Saviour gave us:

or 2
Jesus taught us to call God our Father,
and so we have the courage to say:

or 3
Let us ask our Father to forgive our sins
and to bring us to forgive those who sin against us:

or 4
Let us pray for the coming of the kingdom
as Jesus taught us:

All **Our Father, who art in heaven,
hallowed be thy name;
Thy kingdom come;
Thy will be done on earth as it is in heaven.
Give us this day our daily bread;
and forgive us our trespasses
as we forgive those who trespass against us;
and lead us not into temptation,
but deliver us from evil.**

C Deliver us, Lord, from every evil,
and grant us peace in our day.
In your mercy keep us free from sin
and protect us from all anxiety
as we wait in joyful hope
for the coming of our Saviour, Jesus Christ.

All **For the kingdom, the power, and the glory are yours,
now and forever.**

The Rite of Communion

C. Let us pray with confidence to the Father in the words our Saviour gave us: *All.* Our Father, who art in heaven, hallowed be thy name. Thy kingdom come. Thy will be done on earth as it is in heaven. Give us this day our daily bread, and forgive us our trespasses, as we forgive those who trespass against us, and lead us not into temptation, but deliver us from evil.

C. Deliver us, Lord, from every evil, and grant us peace in our day. In your mercy keep us free from sin and protect us from all anxiety as we wait in joyful hope for the coming of our Saviour, Jesus Christ. *P.* For the kingdom, the power, and the glory are yours, now and for ever.

1330 *The Order of Mass*

Before they share in the same bread, the people express their love for one another, and pray for peace and unity.
C   Lord Jesus Christ, you said to your apostles:
    I leave you peace, my peace I give you.
    Look not on our sins, but on the faith of your Church,
    and grant us the peace and unity of your kingdom
    where you live for ever and ever.
P   **Amen.**
C   The peace of the Lord be with you always.
P   **And also with you.**

Then the deacon, or the celebrant, may add:
C   Let us offer each other the sign of peace.
All make a sign of peace according to local custom.

All **Lamb of God, you take away the sins of the world:
    have mercy on us.
    Lamb of God, you take away the sins of the world:
    have mercy on us.
    Lamb of God, you take away the sins of the world:
    grant us peace.**

The breaking of bread
While this is sung or said, the celebrant takes the host and breaks it over the paten, saying quietly:
C   May this mingling of the body and blood of our Lord
        Jesus Christ.
    bring eternal life to us who receive it.

Celebrant's private preparation
The celebrant quietly says one of the following prayers.
C   Lord Jesus Christ, Son of the living God,
    by the will of the Father and the work of the Holy
        Spirit
    your death brought life to the world.
    By your holy body and blood
    free me from all my sins and from every evil.
    Keep me faithful to your teaching,
    and never let me be parted from you.

The Rite of Communion

C. Lord Jesus Christ, you said to your apostles: I leave you peace, my peace I give you. Look not on our sins, but on the faith of your Church, and grant us the peace and unity of your kingdom where you live for ever and ever. *P.* Amen.

C. The peace of the Lord be with you always. *P.* And also with you. Let us offer each other the sign of peace.

Let us pray, as Jesus taught us:

Abba Father, who art in heaven, hallowed be thy name, thy kingdom come, thy will be done on earth as it is in heaven. Give us today our daily bread, and forgive us our trespasses as we forgive those who trespass against us, and lead us not into temptation but deliver us from evil. For thine is the kingdom, the power and the glory, world without end. Amen.

or
> Lord Jesus Christ,
> with faith in your love and mercy
> I eat your body and drink your blood.
> Let it not bring me condemnation,
> but health in mind and body.

Holy Communion
C   This is the Lamb of God
    who takes away the sins of the world.
    Happy are those who are called to his supper.
All **Lord, I am not worthy to receive you,
but only say the word and I shall be healed.**

While the celebrant is receiving the body of Christ, the communion song is begun.

> **Communion Song:**
> turn to the Proper of the Mass of the Day
> *or* a hymn is sung

The People's Communion
The communicant is offered the host:
C   The body of Christ.   *P* **Amen.**

When the communicant is offered the chalice:
C   The blood of Christ.   *P* **Amen.**

After the communion of the people, a period of silence, a psalm or song may follow. Then:
C   Let us pray.
Celebrant and people pray in silence for a while, unless the silence has already been observed. Then the celebrant sings or says the prayer after communion.

> **Prayer after Communion:** turn to the Proper of
> the Mass of the Day

The people respond: *P* **Amen.**

CONCLUDING RITE
(Omitted if a liturgical ceremony follows the Mass.)

If there are any brief announcements, they are made at this time.

C The Lord be with you.
P **And also with you.**

Blessing
1 Simple Form
C May almighty God bless you,
 the Father, and the Son, ✠ and the Holy Spirit.
P **Amen.**

or 2 Solemn Blessing
On certain days, a more solemn form of blessing, or prayer over the people, may be used. It always ends with the blessing as above, 1.

> **Solemn Blessing:** turn to the Proper of the Mass of the Day

or 3 Prayer over the People
The celebrant may say a special prayer over the people. It always ends with this blessing:

C May almighty God bless you,
 the Father, and the Son, ✠ and the Holy Spirit.
P **Amen.**

> **Prayer over the People:** turn to the Proper of the Mass of the Day

Concluding Rite 1335

1 Simple Form

Tone 1

C. The Lord be with you. *P.* And al-so with you.

2 Solemn Blessing

Tone 1

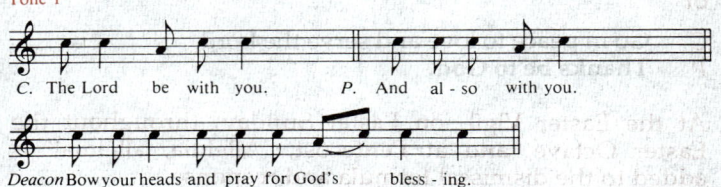

C. The Lord be with you. *P.* And al-so with you.

Deacon Bow your heads and pray for God's bless-ing.

After each blessing or prayer the people respond:

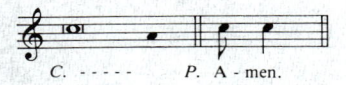

C. - - - - - *P.* A-men.

Tone II

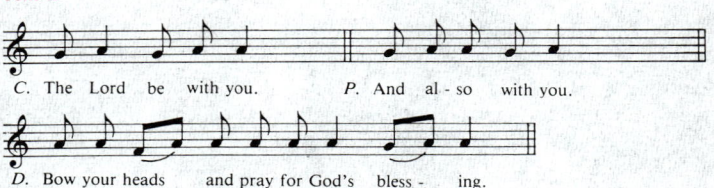

C. The Lord be with you. *P.* And al-so with you.

D. Bow your heads and pray for God's bless-ing.

After each blessing or prayer the people respond:

C. - - - - - - - - - - - - *P.* A-men.

Dismissal

All are sent out into the world, to do good works, blessing and praising the Lord.

C   Go in the peace of Christ.

or

C   The Mass is ended, go in peace.

or

C   Go in peace to love and serve the Lord.
P   **Thanks be to God.**

At the Easter Vigil, on Easter Sunday, throughout the Easter Octave, and at Pentecost, 'Alleluia, alleluia!' is added to the dismissal formula and response.

Dismissal

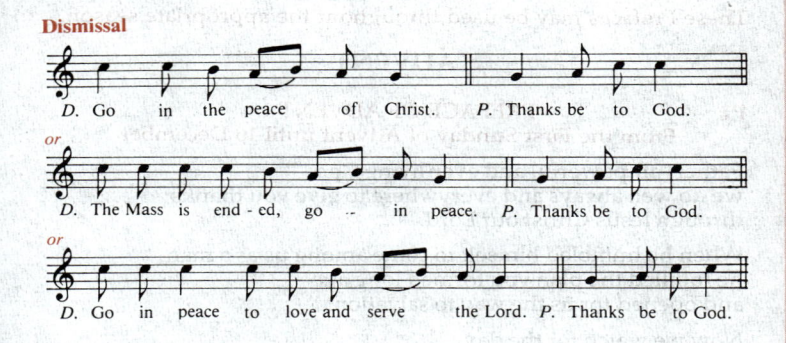

D. Go in the peace of Christ. P. Thanks be to God.

or

D. The Mass is end-ed, go in peace. P. Thanks be to God.

or

D. Go in peace to love and serve the Lord. P. Thanks be to God.

At the Easter Vigil, on Easter Sunday, during the Octave, and at Pentecost

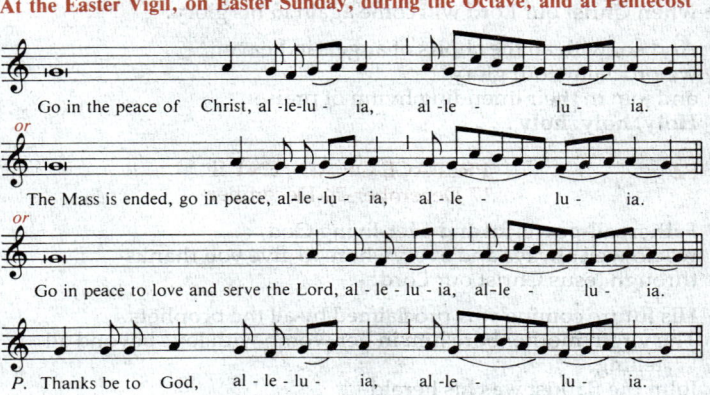

Go in the peace of Christ, al-le-lu-ia, al-le-lu-ia.

or

The Mass is ended, go in peace, al-le-lu-ia, al-le-lu-ia.

or

Go in peace to love and serve the Lord, al-le-lu-ia, al-le-lu-ia.

P. Thanks be to God, al-le-lu-ia, al-le-lu-ia.

PREFACES
These Prefaces may be used throughout the appropriate season.

ADVENT

P1   PREFACE OF ADVENT 1
From the First Sunday of Advent until 16 December

Father, all-powerful and ever-living God,
we do well always and everywhere to give you thanks
through Jesus Christ our Lord.

When he humbled himself to come among us as a man,
he fulfilled the plan you formed long ago
and opened for us the way to salvation.

Now we watch for the day,
hoping that the salvation promised us will be ours
when Christ our Lord will come again in his glory.

And so, with all the choirs of angels in heaven
we proclaim your glory
and join in their unending hymn of praise:
Holy, holy, holy . . .

P2   PREFACE OF ADVENT II
17 December–24 December

Father, all-powerful and ever-living God,
we do well always and everywhere to give you thanks
through Jesus Christ our Lord.

His future coming was proclaimed by all the prophets.
The virgin mother bore him in her womb with love beyond all telling.
John the Baptist was his herald
and made him known when at last he came.

In his love Christ has filled us with joy
as we prepare to celebrate his birth,
so that when he comes he may find us watching in prayer,
our hearts filled with wonder and praise.

And so, with all the choirs of angels in heaven
we proclaim your glory
and join in their unending hymn of praise: **Holy, holy, holy . . .**

CHRISTMAS

The three Prefaces of Christmas may be used in the Masses of Christmas and its Octave, and on the weekdays of the Christmas Season.

P3   PREFACE OF CHRISTMAS I

Father, all-powerful and ever-living God,
we do well always and everywhere to give you thanks
through Jesus Christ our Lord.

In the wonder of the incarnation
your eternal Word has brought to the eyes of faith
a new and radiant vision of your glory.
In him we see our God made visible
and so are caught up in love of the God we cannot see.

And so, with all the choirs of angels in heaven
we proclaim your glory
and join in their unending hymn of praise: **Holy, holy, holy . . .**

P4   PREFACE OF CHRISTMAS II

Father, all-powerful and ever-living God,
we do well always and everywhere to give you thanks
through Jesus Christ our Lord.

Today you fill our hearts with joy
as we recognise in Christ the revelation of your love.
No eye can see his glory as our God,
yet now he is seen as one like us.

Christ is your Son before all ages,
yet now he is born in time.
He has come to lift up all things to himself,
to restore unity to creation,
and to lead mankind from exile into your heavenly kingdom.

With all the angels of heaven
we sing our joyful hymn of praise: **Holy, holy, holy . . .**

P5   PREFACE OF CHRISTMAS III

Father, all-powerful and ever-living God,
we do well always and everywhere to give you thanks
through Jesus Christ our Lord.

Today in him a new light has dawned upon the world:
God has become one with man,
and man has become one again with God.

Your eternal Word has taken upon himself our human weakness,
giving our mortal nature immortal value.
So marvellous is this oneness between God and man
that in Christ man restores to man the gift of everlasting life.

In our joy we sing to your glory
with all the choirs of angels: **Holy, holy, holy . . .**

P6   PREFACE OF EPIPHANY

This is said in Masses on Epiphany, and may be used on the days between Epiphany and the Baptism of the Lord, as may the Christmas prefaces.

Father, all-powerful and ever-living God,
we do well always and everywhere to give you thanks.

Today you revealed in Christ your eternal plan of salvation
and showed him as the light of all peoples.
Now that his glory has shone among us
you have renewed humanity in his immortal image.

Now, with angels and archangels,
and the whole company of heaven,
we sing the unending hymn of your praise: **Holy, holy, holy . . .**

LENT

The Prefaces of Lent I-IV are said in the Masses of Lent. Prefaces of Lent III-IV are also said on fast days.

P8   PREFACE OF LENT 1

Father, all-powerful and ever-living God,
we do well always and everywhere to give you thanks
through Jesus Christ our Lord.

Each year you give us this joyful season
when we prepare to celebrate the paschal mystery
with mind and heart renewed.
You give us a spirit of loving reverence for you, our Father,
and of willing service to our neighbour.

Prefaces

As we recall the great events that gave us a new life in Christ,
you bring the image of your Son to perfection within us.

Now, with angels and archangels,
and the whole company of heaven,
we sing the unending hymn of your praise: **Holy, holy, holy . . .**

P9 — PREFACE OF LENT II

Father, all-powerful and ever-living God,
we do well always and everywhere to give you thanks.

This great season of grace is your gift to your family
to renew us in spirit.
You give us strength to purify our hearts,
to control our desires,
and so to serve you in freedom.
You teach us how to live in this passing world
with our heart set on the world that will never end.

Now, with all the saints and angels,
we praise you for ever: **Holy, holy, holy . . .**

P10 — PREFACE OF LENT III

Father, all-powerful and ever-living God,
we do well always and everywhere to give you thanks.

You ask us to express our thanks by self-denial.
We are to master our sinfulness and conquer our pride.
We are to show to those in need your goodness to ourselves.

Now, with all the saints and angels,
we praise you for ever: **Holy, holy, holy . . .**

P11 — PREFACE OF LENT IV

Father, all-powerful and ever-living God,
we do well always and everywhere to give you thanks.

Through our observance of Lent
you correct our faults and raise our minds to you,
you help us grow in holiness,
and offer us the reward of everlasting life
through Jesus Christ our Lord.

Through him the angels and all the choirs of heaven
worship in awe before your presence.
May our voices be one with theirs
as they sing with joy the hymn of your glory: **Holy, holy, holy**

P17 PREFACE OF THE PASSION OF THE LORD I

This preface is said during the fifth week of Lent, and in Masses of the mysteries of the cross and the passion of the Lord.

Father, all-powerful and ever-living God,
we do well always and everywhere to give you thanks.

The suffering and death of your Son
brought life to the whole world,
moving our hearts to praise your glory.
The power of the cross reveals your judgement on this world
and the kingship of Christ crucified.

We praise you, Lord,
with all the angels and saints in their song of joy:
Holy, holy, holy . . .

P18 PREFACE OF THE PASSION OF THE LORD II

This preface is said on Monday, Tuesday and Wednesday of Holy Week.

Father, all-powerful and ever-living God,
we do well always and everywhere to give you thanks
through Jesus Christ our Lord.

The days of his life-giving death and glorious resurrection are
  approaching.
This is the hour when he triumphed over Satan's pride,
the time when we celebrate the great event of our redemption.

Through Christ
the angels of heaven offer their prayer of adoration
as they rejoice in your presence for ever.
May our voices be one with theirs
in their triumphant hymn of praise:
Holy, holy, holy . . .

P20 PREFACE OF PRIESTHOOD (CHRISM MASS)

Father, all-powerful and ever-living God,
we do well always and everywhere to give you thanks.

By your Holy Spirit
you anointed your only Son
High Priest of the new and eternal covenant.
With wisdom and love you have planned
that this one priesthood should continue in the Church.

Christ gives the dignity of a royal priesthood
to the people he has made his own.
From these, with a brother's love,
he chooses men to share his sacred ministry
by the laying on of hands.

He appoints them to renew in his name
the sacrifice of our redemption
as they set before your family his paschal meal.
He calls them to lead your holy people in love,
nourish them by your word,
and strengthen them through the sacraments.

Father, they are to give their lives in your service
and for the salvation of your people
as they strive to grow in the likeness of Christ
and honour you by their courageous witness of faith and love.

We praise you, Lord, with all the angels and saints
in their song of joy: **Holy, holy, holy . . .**

EASTER

P21 PREFACE OF EASTER I

This Preface is said in the Masses of the Easter Vigil and Easter Sunday and during the octave.

Father, all-powerful and ever-living God,
we do well always and everywhere to give you thanks
through Jesus Christ our Lord.

We praise you with greater joy than ever
on this Easter night [day],
when Christ became our paschal sacrifice.

He is the true Lamb who took away the sins of the world.
By dying he destroyed our death;
by rising he restored our life.

And so, with all the choirs of angels in heaven
we proclaim your glory
and join in their unending hymn of praise:
Holy, holy, holy . . .

P22   PREFACE OF EASTER II

Father, all-powerful and ever-living God,
we do well always and everywhere to give you thanks
through Jesus Christ our Lord.

We praise you with greater joy than ever in this Easter season,
when Christ became our paschal sacrifice.

He has made us children of the light,
rising to new and everlasting life.
He has opened the gates of heaven
to receive his faithful people.
His death is our ransom from death;
his resurrection is our rising to life.

The joy of the resurrection renews the whole world,
while the choirs of heaven sing for ever to your glory:
Holy, holy, holy . . .

P23   PREFACE OF EASTER III

Father, all-powerful and ever-living God,
we do well always and everywhere to give you thanks
through Jesus Christ our Lord.

We praise you with greater joy than ever in this Easter season,
when Christ became our paschal sacrifice.

He is still our priest,
our advocate who always pleads our cause.
Christ is the victim who dies no more,
the Lamb, once slain, who lives for ever.

The joy of the resurrection renews the whole world,
while the choirs of heaven sing for ever to your glory:
Holy, holy, holy . . .

P24   PREFACE OF EASTER IV

Father, all-powerful and ever-living God,
we do well always and everywhere to give you thanks
through Jesus Christ our Lord.

We praise you with greater joy than ever in this Easter season,
when Christ became our paschal sacrifice.

In him a new age has dawned,
the long reign of sin is ended,
a broken world has been renewed,
and man is once again made whole.

The joy of the resurrection renews the whole world,
while the choirs of heaven sing for ever to your glory:
Holy, holy, holy . . .

P25   PREFACE OF EASTER V

Father, all-powerful and ever-living God,
we do well always and everywhere to give you thanks
through Jesus Christ our Lord.

We praise you with greater joy than ever in this Easter season,
when Christ became our paschal sacrifice.

As he offered his body on the cross,
his perfect sacrifice fulfilled all others.
As he gave himself into your hands for our salvation,
he showed himself to be the priest, the altar, and the lamb of
    sacrifice.

The joy of the resurrection renews the whole world,
while the choirs of heaven sing for ever to your glory:
Holy, holy, holy . . .

P26   PREFACE OF THE ASCENSION I

The Prefaces of the Ascension are said on the Ascension, and in all Masses which have no Preface of their own from the Ascension to the Saturday before Pentecost inclusive.

Father, all-powerful and ever-living God,
we do well always and everywhere to give you thanks.

(Today) the Lord Jesus, the king of glory,
the conqueror of sin and death,
ascended to heaven while the angels sang his praises.

Christ, the mediator between God and man,
judge of the world and Lord of all,
has passed beyond our sight,
not to abandon us but to be our hope.
Christ is the beginning, the head of the Church;
where he has gone, we hope to follow.

The joy of the resurrection and ascension renews the whole world.
while the choirs of heaven sing for ever to your glory:
Holy, holy, holy . . .

P27   PREFACE OF THE ASCENSION II

Father, all-powerful and ever-living God,
we do well always and everywhere to give you thanks
through Jesus Christ our Lord.

In his risen body he plainly showed himself to his disciples
and was taken up to heaven in their sight
to claim for us a share in his divine life.

And so, with all the choirs of angels in heaven
we proclaim your glory
and join in their unending hymn of praise: **Holy, holy, holy . . .**

WEEKDAYS IN ORDINARY TIME

The Weekday Prefaces are said in Masses which have no preface of their own, unless they call for a seasonal Preface.

P37   WEEKDAY PREFACE I

Father, all-powerful and ever-living God,
we do well always and everywhere to give you thanks
through Jesus Christ our Lord.

In him you have renewed all things
and you have given us all a share in his riches.

Though his nature was divine,
he stripped himself of glory
and by shedding his blood on the cross

Prefaces

he brought his peace to the world.

Therefore he was exalted above all creation
and became the source of eternal life
to all who serve him.

And so, with all the choirs of angels in heaven
we proclaim your glory
and join in their unending hymn of praise:
Holy, holy, holy . . .

P38   WEEKDAY PREFACE II

Father, all-powerful and ever-living God,
we do well always and everywhere to give you thanks.

In love you created man,
in justice you condemned him,
but in mercy you redeemed him,
through Jesus Christ our Lord.

Through him the angels and all the choirs of heaven
worship in awe before your presence.
May our voices be one with theirs
as they sing with joy
the hymn of your glory: **Holy, holy, holy . . .**

P39   WEEKDAY PREFACE III

Father, all-powerful and ever-living God,
we do well always and everywhere to give you thanks.

Through your beloved Son
you created our human family.
Through him you restored us to your likeness.

Therefore it is your right
to receive the obedience of all creation,
the praise of the Church on earth,
the thanksgiving of your saints in heaven.

We too rejoice with the angels
as we proclaim your glory for ever: **Holy, holy, holy . . .**

P40 WEEKDAY PREFACE IV

Father, all-powerful and ever-living God,
we do well always and everywhere to give you thanks.

You have no need of our praise,
yet our desire to thank you is itself your gift.
Our prayer of thanksgiving adds nothing to your greatness,
but makes us grow in your grace,
through Jesus Christ our Lord.

In our joy we sing to your glory
with all the choirs of angels: **Holy, holy, holy . . .**

P41 WEEKDAY PREFACE V

Father, all-powerful and ever-living God,
we do well always and everywhere to give you thanks
through Jesus Christ our Lord.

With love we celebrate his death.
With living faith we proclaim his resurrection.
With unwavering hope we await his return in glory.

Now, with the saints and all the angels
we praise you for ever: **Holy, holy, holy . . .**

P42 WEEKDAY PREFACE VI

Father, it is our duty and our salvation,
always and everywhere
to give you thanks
through your beloved Son, Jesus Christ.

He is the Word through whom you made the universe,
the Saviour you sent to redeem us.
By the power of the Holy Spirit
he took flesh and was born of the Virgin Mary.

For our sake he opened his arms on the cross;
he put an end to death
and revealed the resurrection.
In this he fulfilled your will
and won for you a holy people.

And so we join the angels and the saints
in proclaiming your glory: **Holy, holy, holy . . .**

P43 PREFACE OF THE HOLY TRINITY

Father, all-powerful and ever-living God,
we do well always and everywhere to give you thanks.

We joyfully proclaim our faith
in the mystery of your Godhead.
You have revealed your glory
as the glory also of your Son
and of the Holy Spirit:
three Persons equal in majesty,
undivided in splendour,
yet one Lord, one God,
ever to be adored in your everlasting glory.

And so, with all the choirs of angels in heaven
we proclaim your glory
and join in their unending hymn of praise:
Holy, holy, holy . . .

P44 PREFACE OF THE ANNUNCIATION
25 March

Father, all-powerful and ever-living God,
we do well always and everywhere to give you thanks
through Jesus Christ our Lord.

He came to save mankind by becoming a man himself.
The Virgin Mary, receiving the angel's message in faith,
conceived by the power of the Spirit
and bore your Son in purest love.

In Christ, the eternal truth,
your promise to Israel came true.
In Christ, the hope of all peoples,
man's hope was realised beyond all expectation.

Through Christ the angels of heaven
offer their prayer of adoration
as they rejoice in your presence for ever.
May our voices be one with theirs
in their triumphant hymn of praise: **Holy, holy, holy . . .**

P45 PREFACE OF THE SACRED HEART

Father, all-powerful and ever-living God,
we do well always and everywhere to give you thanks
through Jesus Christ our Lord.

Lifted high on the cross,
Christ gave his life for us,
so much did he love us.
From his wounded side flowed blood and water,
the fountain of sacramental life in the Church.
To his open heart the Saviour invites all men,
to draw water in joy from the springs of salvation.

Now, with all the saints and angels,
we praise you for ever:
Holy, holy, holy . . .

P46 PREFACE OF THE TRIUMPH OF THE CROSS

Father, all-powerful and ever-living God,
we do well always and everywhere to give you thanks.

You decreed that man should be saved through the wood of the cross.
The tree of man's defeat became his tree of victory;
where life was lost, there life has been restored
through Christ our Lord.

Through him the choirs of angels
and all the powers of heaven
praise and worship your glory.
May our voices blend with theirs
as we join in their unending hymn:
Holy, holy, holy . . .

P47 PREFACE OF THE HOLY EUCHARIST I

This Preface is said in the Mass of the Lord's Supper on Holy Thursday. It may be said on Corpus Christi and in votive Masses of the Holy Eucharist.

Father, all-powerful and ever-living God,
we do well always and everywhere to give you thanks
through Jesus Christ our Lord.

Prefaces 1351

He is the true and eternal priest
who established this unending sacrifice.
He offered himself as a victim for our deliverance
and taught us to make this offering in his memory.
As we eat his body which he gave for us,
we grow in strength.
As we drink his blood which he poured out for us,
we are washed clean.

Now, with angels and archangels,
and the whole company of heaven,
we sing the unending hymn of your praise:
Holy, holy, holy . . .

P48 PREFACE OF THE HOLY EUCHARIST II

This Preface is said on Corpus Christi and in votive Masses of the Holy Eucharist.

Father, all-powerful and ever-living God,
we do well always and everywhere to give you thanks
through Jesus Christ our Lord.

At the last supper,
as he sat at table with his apostles,
he offered himself to you as the spotless lamb,
the acceptable gift that gives you perfect praise.
Christ has given us this memorial of his passion
to bring us its saving power until the end of time.

In this great sacrament you feed your people
and strengthen them in holiness,
so that the family of mankind
may come to walk in the light of one faith,
in one communion of love.
We come then to this wonderful sacrament
to be fed at your table
and grow into the likeness of the risen Christ.

Earth unites with heaven
to sing the new song of creation
as we adore and praise you for ever:
Holy, holy, holy . . .

P49 PREFACE OF THE PRESENTATION OF THE LORD
2 February

Father, all-powerful and ever-living God,
we do well always and everywhere to give you thanks
through Jesus Christ our Lord.

Today your Son,
who shares your eternal splendour,
was presented in the temple,
and revealed by the Spirit
as the glory of Israel
and the light of all peoples.

Our hearts are joyful,
for we have seen your salvation,
and now with the angels and saints
we praise you for ever: **Holy, holy, holy . . .**

P50 PREFACE OF THE TRANSFIGURATION
6 August

Father, all-powerful and ever-living God,
we do well always and everywhere to give you thanks
through Jesus Christ our Lord.

He revealed his glory to the disciples
to strengthen them for the scandal of the cross.
His glory shone from a body like our own,
to show that the Church,
which is the body of Christ,
would one day share his glory.

In our unending joy we echo on earth
the song of the angels in heaven
as they praise your glory for ever: **Holy, holy, holy . . .**

P52 THE DEDICATION OF A CHURCH I
In the dedicated church

Father, all-powerful and ever-living God,
we do well always and everywhere to give you thanks.

We thank you now for this house of prayer
in which you bless your family
as we come to you on pilgrimage.

Here you reveal your presence
by sacramental signs,
and make us one with you
through the unseen bond of grace.
Here you build your temple of living stones,
and bring the Church to its full stature
as the body of Christ throughout the world,
to reach its perfection at last
in the heavenly city of Jerusalem,
which is the vision of your peace.

In communion with all the angels and saints
we bless and praise your greatness
in the temple of your glory: **Holy, holy, holy . . .**

P53 THE DEDICATION OF A CHURCH II
Outside the dedicated church

Father, all-powerful and ever-living God,
we do well always and everywhere to give you thanks.

Your house is a house of prayer,
and your presence makes it a place of blessing.
You give us grace upon grace
to build the temple of your Spirit,
creating its beauty from the holiness of our lives.

Your house of prayer
is also the promise of the Church in heaven.
Here your love is always at work,
preparing the Church on earth
for its heavenly glory
as the sinless bride of Christ,
the joyful mother of a great company of saints.

Now, with the saints and all the angels
we praise you for ever: **Holy, holy, holy . . .**

P54 PREFACE OF HOLY SPIRIT I

Father, all-powerful and ever-living God,
we do well always and everywhere to give you thanks
through Jesus Christ our Lord.

He ascended above all the heavens,
and from his throne at your right hand

poured into the hearts of your adopted children
the Holy Spirit of your promise.

With steadfast love
we sing your unending praise;
we join with the hosts of heaven
in their triumphant song: **Holy, holy, holy . . .**

P55 PREFACE OF HOLY SPIRIT II

Father, all-powerful and ever-living God,
we do well always and everywhere to give you thanks.

You give your gifts of grace
for every time and season
as you guide the Church
in the marvellous ways of your providence.

You give us your Holy Spirit
to help us always by his power,
so that with loving trust
we may turn to you in all our troubles,
and give you thanks in all our joys,
through Jesus Christ our Lord.

In our joy we sing to your glory
with all the choirs of angels: **Holy, holy, holy . . .**

P56 PREFACE OF THE BLESSED VIRGIN MARY I
Motherhood of Mary

Father, all-powerful and ever-living God,
we do well always and everywhere to give you thanks
as we celebrate the motherhood of the Blessed Virgin Mary.

Through the power of the Holy Spirit,
she became the virgin mother of your only Son,
our Lord Jesus Christ,
who is for ever the light of the world.

Through him the choirs of angels
and all the powers of heaven
praise and worship your glory.
May our voices blend with theirs
as we join in their unending hymn:
Holy, holy, holy . . .

P57   PREFACE OF THE BLESSED VIRGIN MARY II

Father, all-powerful and ever-living God,
we do well always and everywhere to give you thanks,
and to praise you for your gifts
as we contemplate your saints in glory.

In celebrating the memory of the Blessed Virgin Mary,
it is our special joy to echo her song of thanksgiving.
What wonders you have worked throughout the world.
All generations have shared the greatness of your love.
When you looked on Mary your lowly servant,
you raised her to be the mother of Jesus Christ, your Son, our Lord,
the saviour of all mankind.

Through him the angels of heaven
offer their prayer of adoration
as they rejoice in your presence for ever.
May our voices be one with theirs
in their triumphant hymn of praise:
Holy, holy, holy . . .

P58   PREFACE OF THE IMMACULATE CONCEPTION
8 December

Father, all-powerful and ever-living God,
we do well always and everywhere to give you thanks.

You allowed no stain of Adam's sin
to touch the Virgin Mary.
Full of grace, she was to be a worthy mother of your Son,
your sign of favour to the Church at its beginning,
and the promise of its perfection as the bride of Christ, radiant in beauty.

Purest of virgins, she was to bring forth your Son,
the innocent lamb who takes away our sins.
You chose her from all women to be our advocate with you
and our pattern of holiness.

In our joy we sing to your glory
with all the choirs of angels: **Holy, holy, holy . . .**

P59 PREFACE OF THE ASSUMPTION
15 August

Father, all-powerful and ever-living God,
we do well always and everywhere to give you thanks
through Jesus Christ our Lord.

Today the virgin Mother of God was taken up into heaven
to be the beginning and the pattern of the Church in its
  perfection,
and a sign of hope and comfort for your people on their pilgrim
  way.
You would not allow decay to touch her body,
for she had given birth to your Son, the Lord of all life,
in the glory of the incarnation.

In our joy we sing to your glory
with all the choirs of angels:
Holy, holy, holy . . .

P60 PREFACE OF ANGELS

Father, all-powerful and ever-living God,
we do well always and everywhere to give you thanks.

In praising your faithful angels and archangels,
we also praise your glory,
for in honouring them, we honour you, their creator.
Their splendour shows us your greatness,
which surpasses in goodness the whole of creation.

Through Christ our Lord
the great army of angels rejoices in your glory.
In adoration and joy
we make their hymn of praise our own:
Holy, holy, holy . . .

P61 PREFACE OF SAINT JOHN THE BAPTIST

Father, all-powerful and ever-living God,
we do well always and everywhere to give you thanks
through Jesus Christ our Lord.

We praise your greatness
as we honour the prophet
who prepared the way before your Son.

You set John the Baptist apart from other men,
marking him out with special favour.
His birth brought great rejoicing:
even in the womb he leapt for joy,
so near was man's salvation.

You chose John the Baptist from all the prophets
to show the world its redeemer,
the lamb of sacrifice.
He baptised Christ, the giver of baptism,
in waters made holy by the one who was baptised.
You found John worthy of a martyr's death,
his last and greatest act of witness to your Son.

In our unending joy we echo on earth
the song of the angels in heaven
as they praise your glory for ever: **Holy, holy, holy . . .**

P62 PREFACE OF SAINT JOSEPH, HUSBAND OF MARY

Father, all-powerful and ever-living God,
we do well always and everywhere to give you thanks
as we honour Saint Joseph.

He is that just man,
that wise and loyal servant,
whom you placed at the head of your family.
With a husband's love he cherished Mary,
the virgin Mother of God.
With fatherly care he watched over Jesus Christ your Son,
conceived by the power of the Holy Spirit.

Through Christ the choirs of angels
and all the powers of heaven
praise and worship your glory.
May our voices blend with theirs
as we join in their unending hymn: **Holy, holy, holy . . .**

P63 PREFACE OF SAINTS PETER AND PAUL, APOSTLES

Father, all-powerful and ever-living God,
we do well always and everywhere to give you thanks.

You fill our hearts with joy
as we honour your great apostles:

Peter, our leader in the faith,
and Paul, its fearless preacher.

Peter raised up the Church
from the faithful flock of Israel.
Paul brought your call to the nations,
and became the teacher of the world.
Each in his chosen way gathered into unity
the one family of Christ.
Both shared a martyr's death
and are praised throughout the world.

Now, with the apostles and all the angels and saints,
we praise you for ever: **Holy, holy, holy . . .**

P64 PREFACE OF APOSTLES I

Father, all-powerful and ever-living God,
we do well always and everywhere to give you thanks.

You are the eternal Shepherd
who never leaves his flock untended.
Through the apostles
you watch over us and protect us always.
You made them shepherds of the flock
to share in the work of your Son,
and from their place in heaven they guide us still.

And so, with all the choirs of angels in heaven
we proclaim your glory
and join in their unending hymn of praise: **Holy, holy, holy . . .**

P65 PREFACE OF APOSTLES II

Father, all powerful and ever-living God,
we do well always and everywhere to give you thanks.

You founded your Church on the apostles
to stand firm for ever
as the sign on earth of your infinite holiness
and as the living gospel for all men to hear.

With steadfast love
we sing your unending praise:
we join with the hosts of heaven
in their triumphant song: **Holy, holy, holy . . .**

P66 PREFACE OF MARTYRS

Father, all powerful and ever-living God,
we do well always and everywhere to give you thanks.

Your holy martyr N. followed the example of Christ,
and gave his (her) life for the glory of your name.
His (her) death reveals your power
shining through our human weakness.

You choose the weak and make them strong
in bearing witness to you,
through Jesus Christ our Lord.

In our unending joy we echo on earth
the song of the angels in heaven
as they praise your glory for ever: **Holy, holy, holy . . .**

P67 PREFACE OF PASTORS

Father, all powerful and ever-living God,
we do well always and everywhere to give you thanks.

You give the Church this feast in honour of Saint N.;
you inspire us by his holy life,
instruct us by his preaching,
and give us your protection in answer to his prayers.

We join the angels and the saints
as they sing their unending hymn of praise: **Holy, holy, holy . . .**

P68 PREFACE OF VIRGINS AND RELIGIOUS

Father, all powerful and ever-living God,
we do well always and everywhere to give you thanks.

Today we honour your saints
who consecrated their lives to Christ
for the sake of the kingdom of heaven.
What love you show us
as you recall mankind to its first innocence,
and invite us to taste on earth
the gifts of the world to come!

Now, with the saints and all the angels
we praise you for ever: **Holy, holy, holy . . .**

P69 PREFACE OF HOLY MEN AND WOMEN I

Father, all-powerful and ever-living God,
we do well always and everywhere to give you thanks.

You are glorified in your saints,
for their glory is the crowning of your gifts.
In their lives on earth
you give us an example.
In our communion with them
you give us their friendship.
In their prayer for the Church
you give us strength and protection.
This great company of witnesses spurs us on to victory,
to share their prize of everlasting glory,
through Jesus Christ our Lord.

With angels and archangels
and the whole company of saints
we sing our unending hymn of praise: **Holy, holy, holy ...**

P70 PREFACE OF HOLY MEN AND WOMEN II

Father, all-powerful and ever-living God,
we do well always and everywhere to give you thanks.

You renew the Church in every age
by raising up men and women outstanding in holiness,
living witnesses of your unchanging love.
They inspire us by their heroic lives,
and help us by their constant prayers
to be the living sign of your saving power.

We praise you, Lord, with all the angels and saints
in their song of joy: **Holy, holy, holy ...**

P71 PREFACE OF ALL SAINTS
1 November

Father, all-powerful and ever-living God,
we do well always and everywhere to give you thanks.

Today we keep the festival of your holy city,
the heavenly Jerusalem, our mother.
Around your throne
the saints, our brothers and sisters,
sing your praise for ever.

Their glory fills us with joy,
and their communion with us in your Church
gives us inspiration and strength
as we hasten on our pilgrimage of faith,
eager to meet them.

With their great company and all the angels
we praise your glory
as we cry out with one voice: **Holy, holy, holy . . .**

P72 PREFACE OF MARRIAGE I

Father, all-powerful and ever-living God,
we do well always and everywhere to give you thanks.

By this sacrament your grace unites man and woman
in an unbreakable bond of love and peace.

You have designed the chaste love of husband and wife
for the increase both of the human family
and of your own family born in baptism.

You are the loving Father of the world of nature;
you are the loving Father of the new creation of grace.
In Christian marriage you bring together the two orders of creation:
nature's gift of children enriches the world
and your grace enriches also your Church.

Through Christ the choirs of angels
and all the saints
praise and worship your glory.
May our voices blend with theirs
as we join in their unending hymn: **Holy, holy, holy . . .**

P73 PREFACE OF MARRIAGE II

Father, all-powerful and ever-living God,
we do well always and everywhere to give you thanks
through Jesus Christ our Lord.

Through him you entered into a new covenant with your people.
You restored man to grace in the saving mystery of redemption.
You gave him a share in the divine life
through his union with Christ.
You made him an heir of Christ's eternal glory.

This outpouring of love in the new covenant of grace
is symbolized in the marriage covenant
that seals the love of husband and wife
and reflects your divine plan of love.

And so, with the angels and all the saints in heaven
we proclaim your glory
and join in their unending hymn of praise: **Holy, holy, holy . . .**

P74 PREFACE OF MARRIAGE III

Father, all-powerful and ever-living God,
we do well always and everywhere to give you thanks.

You created man in love to share your divine life.
We see his high destiny in the love of husband and wife,
which bears the imprint of your own divine love.

Love is man's origin,
love is his constant calling,
love is his fulfilment in heaven.

The love of man and woman
is made holy in the sacrament of marriage,
and becomes the mirror of your everlasting love.

Through Christ the choirs of angels
and all the saints
praise and worship your glory.
May our voices blend with theirs
as we join in their unending hymn: **Holy, holy, holy . . .**

P76 PREFACE OF CHRISTIAN UNITY

Father, all-powerful and ever-living God,
we do well always and everywhere to give you thanks
through Jesus Christ our Lord.

Through Christ you bring us to the knowledge of your truth,
that we may be united by one faith and one baptism
to become his body.
Through Christ you have given the Holy Spirit to all peoples.
How wonderful are the works of the Spirit,
revealed in so many gifts!
Yet how marvellous is the unity
the Spirit creates from their diversity,
as he dwells in the hearts of your children,

Prefaces

filling the whole Church with his presence
and guiding it with his wisdom!

In our joy we sing to your glory
with all the choirs of angels: **Holy, holy, holy . . .**

P77 PREFACE OF CHRISTIAN DEATH I

Father, all-powerful and ever-living God,
we do well always and everywhere to give you thanks
through Jesus Christ our Lord.

In him, who rose from the dead,
our hope of resurrection dawned.
The sadness of death gives way
to the bright promise of immortality.

Lord, for your faithful people life is changed, not ended.
When the body of our earthly dwelling lies in death
we gain an everlasting dwelling place in heaven.

And so, with all the choirs of angels in heaven
we proclaim your glory
and join in their unending hymn of praise: **Holy, holy, holy . . .**

P78 PREFACE OF CHRISTIAN DEATH II

Father, all-powerful and ever-living God,
we do well always and everywhere to give you thanks
through Jesus Christ our Lord.

He chose to die
that he might free all men from dying.
He gave his life
that we might live to you alone for ever.

In our joy we sing to your glory
with all the choirs of angels: **Holy, holy, holy . . .**

P79 PREFACE OF CHRISTIAN DEATH III

Father, all-powerful and ever-living God,
we do well always and everywhere to give you thanks
through Jesus Christ our Lord.

In him the world is saved,
man is reborn,
and the dead rise again to life.

Through Christ the angels of heaven
offer their prayer of adoration
as they rejoice in your presence for ever.
May our voices be one with theirs
in their triumphant hymn of praise: **Holy, holy, holy . . .**

P80 PREFACE OF CHRISTIAN DEATH IV

Father, all-powerful and ever-living God,
we do well always and everywhere to give you thanks.

By your power you bring us to birth.
By your providence you rule our lives.
By your command you free us at last from sin
as we return to the dust from which we came.
Through the saving death of your Son
we rise at your word to the glory of the resurrection.

Now we join the angels and the saints
as they sing their unending hymn of praise: **Holy, holy, holy . . .**

P81 PREFACE OF CHRISTIAN DEATH V

Father, all-powerful and ever-living God,
we do well always and everywhere to give you thanks
through Jesus Christ our Lord.

Death is the just reward for our sins,
yet, when at last we die,
your loving kindness calls us back to life
in company with Christ,
whose victory is our redemption.

Our hearts are joyful,
for we have seen your salvation,
and now with the angels and saints
we praise you for ever: **Holy, holy, holy . . .**

PRAYERS
THANKSGIVING AFTER MASS

With gratitude in your hearts sing psalms and hymns and inspired songs to God. *Colossians 3:16*

Go on singing and chanting to the Lord in your hearts, so that always and everywhere you are giving thanks to God who is our Father in the name of our Lord Jesus Christ. *Ephesians 5:19-20*

Pray constantly, and for all things give thanks to God, because this is what God expects you to do in Christ Jesus.
1 Thessalonians 5:18

From the Didache
As regards the Eucharist, give thanks first, for the cup:
We thank you, Father,
for the holy vine of David, your servant,
which you have made known to us
through your servant, Jesus.
To you be glory for ever!

And for the broken bread:
We thank you, Father,
for the life and knowledge
which you have made known to us
through your servant, Jesus.
To you be glory for ever!

In the same way that this bread which is now broken
was scattered upon the mountains,
was gathered up again, to become one,
so may your Church be gathered together
from the ends of the earth into your kingdom,
for yours is the glory and the power
through Jesus Christ for ever.

And, after you are filled, give thanks in this manner:
We thank you, Holy Father, for your holy name,
which you have made to dwell in our hearts,
and for the knowledge, faith and immortality
which you have made known to us
through your servant, Jesus.
To you be glory for ever! *1st or 2nd century*

Prayer of St Thomas Aquinas

I give you thanks,
Lord, holy Father, everlasting God.
In your great mercy,
and not because of my own merits,
you have fed me, a sinner and your unworthy servant,
with the precious Body and Blood of your Son,
our Lord Jesus Christ.
I pray that this holy communion
may not serve as my judgement and condemnation,
but as my forgiveness and salvation.
May it be my armour of faith
and shield of good purpose.
May it root out in me all vice and evil desires,
increase my love and patience,
humility and obedience, and every virtue.
Make it a firm defence
against all the wiles of all my enemies, seen and unseen,
while restraining all evil impulses of flesh and spirit.
May it help me to cleave to you, the one true God,
and bring me a blessed death when you call.
I beseech you to bring me, a sinner,
to that great feast where,
with your Son and the Holy Spirit,
you are the true light of your holy ones,
their flawless blessedness,
everlasting joy, and perfect happiness.
Through Christ our Lord.   Amen.

Anima Christi

Soul of Christ, sanctify me,
Body of Christ, save me,
Blood of Christ, inebriate me,
Water from the side of Christ, wash me,
Passion of Christ, strengthen me.
O good Jesus, hear me.
Within your wounds hide me.
Let me not be separated from you,
From the malicious enemy defend me,
In the hour of my death call me
And bid me come to you,
That with your saints I may praise you
For ever and ever.   Amen.

O Sacrum Convivium

At this sacred banquet in which Christ is received,
the memory of his passion is renewed,
our lives are filled with grace
and a promise of future glory given to us.

Adoro Te

Godhead here in hiding, whom I do adore
Masked by these bare shadows, shape and nothing more,
See, Lord, at thy service low lies here a heart
Lost, all lost in wonder at the God thou art.

Seeing, touching, tasting are in thee deceived;
How says trusty hearing? That shall be believed;
What God's Son has told me, take for truth I do;
Truth himself speaks truly or there's nothing true.

On the cross thy godhead made no sign to men;
Here thy very manhood steals from human ken:
Both are my confession, both are my belief,
And I pray the prayer of the dying thief.

O thou our reminder of Christ crucified,
Living Bread, the life of us for whom he died,
Lend this life to me then: feed and feast my mind,
There be thou the sweetness man was meant to find.

Jesus whom I look at shrouded here below,
I beseech thee send me what I thirst for so,
Some day to gaze on thee face to face in light
And be blest for ever with thy glory's sight.

Tr Gerard Manley Hopkins

Ave Verum

Hail to thee! true Body sprung
From the Virgin Mary's womb!
The same that on the cross was hung
And bore for man the bitter doom.

Thou whose side was pierc'd, and flowed
Both with water and with blood,
Suffer us to taste of thee
In our life's last agony.

O kind, O Loving One,
O sweet Jesu, Mary's Son!

Tr Manual of Prayers

THE PROPER OF SAINTS
General Roman Calendar, January – December

The rank of the celebrations – solemnity, feast, memorial or optional memorial – is indicated. For memorials proper texts given on certain days should always be used. Prayers and antiphons for Common Masses will be found on pp.1855ff. Where there is reference to a particular common, appropriate texts should be chosen according to the principles at the beginning of the commons. If the reference is to more than one common, one or the other may be used, according to pastoral need.

Choice of readings

'The arrangement of weekday readings provides texts for every day of the week throughout the year. In most cases, therefore, these readings are to be used on their assigned days, unless a solemnity, feast, or memorial with proper readings occurs.

The one using the Order of Readings for weekdays must check to see whether one reading or another from the same biblical book will have to be omitted because of some celebration occurring during the week. With the plan of readings for the entire week in mind, the priest in that case arranges to omit the less significant selections or suitably combines them with other readings, if they contribute to an integral view of a particular theme.' (Introduction to the Lectionary, 82)

'When they exist proper readings are given for celebrations of the saints, that is, biblical passages about the saint or the event in the saint's life that the Mass is celebrating. Even in the case of a memorial these readings must take the place of the weekday readings for the same day. . . . In some cases there are accommodated readings, those, namely, that bring out some particular aspect of a saint's spiritual life or apostolate. Use of such readings does not seem binding, except for compelling pastoral reasons . . . The first concern of a priest celebrating with a congregation is the spiritual benefit of the faithful and he will be careful not to impose his personal preference on them. Above all he will make sure not to omit too often or needlessly the readings assigned for each day in the weekday Lectionary: the Church's desire is to provide the faithful with a richer share at the table of God's word.' (*Introduction to the Lectionary*, 83)

See also General Instruction on the Roman Missal, 319.

In the pages which follow, the proper readings for solemnities, feasts and optional memorials (where they exist) are given, and accommodated readings for other celebrations in the calendar of saints, as suggested in the 1981 edition of the Lectionary. Readings for the Commons are not given – these may be found in the Lectionary, volume II.

JANUARY

1 January: Octave of Christmas
SOLEMNITY OF MARY, MOTHER OF GOD

See *The Sunday Missal*.

2 January
Ss Basil the Great and Gregory Nazianzen, bishops and doctors of the Church — Memorial

Saint Basil and Saint Gregory were life-long friends.

Basil was born in Caesarea in Cappadocia about 330 AD. His family was Christian. He was a brilliant student, but for some years followed a monastic way of life. In 370 he was appointed Bishop of Caesarea. His monastic rules are still followed today by monks of the Eastern Church. He actively fought against the Arian heresy; he defended the poor, and did much to help them. He died 1 January 379.

Gregory was born near Nazianzus, also in Cappadocia, and also about 330 AD. He, too, followed the monastic way of life for some years. He was ordained priest, and became bishop of Constantinople in 379, when the Arian controversy was at its height. He was forced to retire to Nazianzus, where he died on 25 January 389, or 390. His learning and his powers of oratory were remarkable, and he was called The Theologian.

Common of pastors: bishops, pp.1878ff. or of doctors of the Church, pp.1887ff.

Proper of Saints, 2 January 1371

Opening Prayer

God our Father,
you inspired the Church
with the example and teaching of your saints Basil and Gregory.
In humility may we come to know your truth
and put it into action with faith and love.

FIRST READING

A reading from the letter of St Paul
to the Ephesians

4:1-7. 11-13

In the work of service, building up the body of Christ.

I, the prisoner in the Lord, implore you to lead a life worthy of your vocation. Bear with one another charitably, in complete selflessness, gentleness and patience. Do all you can to preserve the unity of the Spirit by the peace that binds you together. There is one Body, one Spirit, just as you were all called into one and the same hope when you were called. There is one Lord, one faith, one baptism, and one God who is Father of all, over all, through all and within all.

Each one of us, however, has been given his own share of grace, given as Christ allotted it. To some his gift was that they should be apostles; to some, prophets; to some, evangelists; to some, pastors and teachers; so that the saints together make a unity in the work of service, building up the body of Christ. In this way we are all to come to unity in our faith and in our knowledge of the Son of God, until we become the perfect man, fully mature with the fullness of Christ himself.

This is the word of the Lord.

Responsorial Psalm   Ps 22. ℟ v.1

℟ **The Lord is my shepherd;
there is nothing I shall want.**

1   The Lord is my shepherd;
    there is nothing I shall want.
    Fresh and green are the pastures
    where he gives me repose.
    Near restful waters he leads me,
    to revive my drooping spirit. ℟

2   He guides me along the right path;
    he is true to his name.

If I should walk in the valley of darkness
no evil would I fear.
You are there with your crook and your staff;
with these you give me comfort.

℟ **The Lord is my shepherd;
there is nothing I shall want.**

3 You have prepared a banquet for me
in the sight of my foes.
My head you have anointed with oil;
my cup is overflowing. ℟

4 Surely goodness and kindness shall follow me
all the days of my life.
In the Lord's own house shall I dwell
for ever and ever. ℟

Gospel Acclamation

Mt 23:9-10

Alleluia, alleluia!
You have only one Father,
and he is in heaven;
you have only one Teacher,
the Christ.
Alleluia!

GOSPEL

A reading from the holy Gospel according to Matthew 23:8-12
The greatest among you must be your servant.

Jesus said to his disciples: 'You must not allow yourselves to be called Rabbi, since you have only one master, and you are all brothers. You must call no one on earth your father, since you have only one Father, and he is in heaven. Nor must you allow yourselves to be called teachers, for you have only one Teacher, the Christ. The greatest among you must be your servant. Anyone who exalts himself will be humbled, and anyone who humbles himself will be exalted.'

This is the Gospel of the Lord.

7 January

St Raymond of Penyafort, priest
Optional memorial

Born at Penyafort, near Barcelona, about 1175. He was ordained, and became a professor of philosophy and law. He entered the Dominican Order in 1222, shortly after the death of St Dominic. He became Master General of the Order. He was a master of moral theology and of canon law; at Gregory IX's request, he edited the Book of Decretals. His Summary of Cases gave rules for the administration of the sacrament of penance. He died on 6 January 1275.

Common of pastors, pp.1876ff.

Opening Prayer
Lord,
you gave Saint Raymond the gift of compassion
in his ministry to sinners.
May his prayers free us from the slavery of sin
and help us to love and serve you in liberty.

FIRST READING

A reading from the second letter of St Paul to the Corinthians 5:14-20
He gave us the work of handing on this reconciliation.

The love of Christ overwhelms us when we reflect that if one man has died for all, then all men should be dead; and the reason he died for all was so that living men should live no longer for themselves, but for him who died and was raised to life for them.

From now onwards, therefore, we do not judge anyone by the standards of the flesh. Even if we did once know Christ in the flesh, that is not how we know him now. And for anyone who is in Christ, there is a new creation; the old creation has gone, and now the new one is here. It is all God's work. It was God who reconciled us to himself through Christ and gave us the work of handing on this reconciliation. In other words, God in Christ was reconciling the world to himself, not holding men's faults against them, and he has entrusted to us the news that they are reconciled. So we are ambassadors for Christ; it is as though God were appealing through us, and the appeal that we make in Christ's name is: be reconciled to God.

This is the word of the Lord.

Responsorial Psalm Ps 102: 1-4. 8-9. 13-14. 17-18. ℟ v.1

℟ **My soul, give thanks to the Lord.**

1 My soul, give thanks to the Lord,
   all my being, bless his holy name.
   My soul, give thanks to the Lord
   and never forget all his blessings. ℟

2 It is he who forgives all your guilt,
   who heals every one of your ills,
   who redeems your life from the grave,
   who crowns you with love and compassion. ℟

3 The Lord is compassion and love,
   slow to anger and rich in mercy.
   His wrath will come to an end;
   he will not be angry for ever. ℟

4 As a father has compassion on his sons,
   the Lord has pity on those who fear him;
   for he knows of what we are made,
   he remembers that we are dust. ℟

5 But the love of the Lord is everlasting
   upon those who hold him in fear;
   his justice reaches out to children's children
   when they keep his covenant in truth. ℟

Gospel Acclamation Lk 21:36

Alleluia, alleluia!
Stay awake, praying at all times
for the strength to stand with confidence
before the Son of Man.
Alleluia!

GOSPEL

A reading from the holy Gospel according to Luke 12:35-40
Stand ready.

Jesus said to his disciples: 'See that you are dressed for action and have your lamps lit. Be like men waiting for their master to return from the wedding feast, ready to open the door as soon as he comes and knocks. Happy those servants whom the master finds awake when he comes. I tell you solemnly, he will put on an apron, sit them down at table and wait on them. It may be in the second watch he comes, or in the third, but happy those servants if he finds them ready. You may be quite sure of this, that if the householder had known at what hour the burglar would come, he would not have let anyone break through the wall of his house. You too must stand ready, because the Son of Man is coming at an hour you do not expect.'

This is the Gospel of the Lord.

13 January

St Hilary, bishop and doctor of the Church
Optional memorial

Born at Poitiers, at the beginning of the fourth century, and became bishop of that city in 350. He was a very active opponent of the Arian heresy, and was exiled for four years by Emperor Constantine for this reason. During his exile he wrote his Treatise on the Trinity, *and many other works.*

Common of pastors: bishops, pp.1878ff., or of doctors of the church, pp.1887.

Opening Prayer
All-powerful God,
as Saint Hilary defended the divinity of Christ your Son,
give us a deeper understanding of this mystery
and help us to profess it in all truth.

FIRST READING

A reading from the first letter of St John 2:18-25
To acknowledge the Son is to have the Father as well.

Children, these are the last days;
you were told that an Antichrist must come,
and now several antichrists have already appeared;
we know from this that these are the last days.
Those rivals of Christ came out of your own number,
 but they had never really belonged;
if they had belonged, they would have stayed with us;
but they left us, to prove that not one of them
ever belonged to us.
But you have been anointed by the Holy One,

and have all received the knowledge.
It is not because you do not know the truth that I am writing to
    you
but rather because you know it already
and know that no lie can come from the truth.
The man who denies that Jesus is the Christ –
he is the liar,
he is Antichrist;
and he is denying the Father as well as the Son,
because no one who has the Father can deny the Son,
and to acknowledge the Son is to have the Father as well
Keep alive in yourselves what you were taught in the beginning:
as long as what you were taught in the beginning is alive in you,
you will live in the Son
and in the Father;
and what is promised to you by his own promise
is eternal life.

   This is the word of the Lord.

Responsional Psalm   Ps 109: 1-4. ℟ v.4

   ℟ **You are a priest for ever,
       a priest like Melchizedek of old.**

1 The Lord's revelation to my Master:
   'Sit on my right:
   I will put your foes beneath your feet.'   ℟

2 The Lord will send from Zion
   your sceptre of power:
   rule in the midst of all your foes.   ℟

3 A prince from the day of your birth
   on the holy mountains;
   from the womb before the daybreak I begot you.   ℟

4 The Lord has sworn an oath he will not change.
   'You are a priest for ever,
   a priest like Melchizedek of old.'   ℟

Gospel Acclamation   Mt 5:16

   Alleluia, alleluia!
   Your light must shine in the sight of men,
   so that, seeing your good works,
   they may give the praise to your Father in heaven.
   Alleluia!

Proper of Saints, 17 January

GOSPEL

A reading from the holy Gospel according to Matthew 5:13-19
You are the light of the world.

Jesus said to his disciples: 'You are the salt of the earth. But if salt becomes tasteless, what can make it salty again? It is good for nothing, and can only be thrown out to be trampled underfoot by men.

'You are the light of the world. A city built on a hill-top cannot be hidden. No one lights a lamp to put it under a tub; they put it on the lamp-stand where it shines for everyone in the house. In the same way your light must shine in the sight of men, so that, seeing your good works, they may give the praise to your Father in heaven.

'Do not imagine that I have come to abolish the Law or the Prophets. I have come not to abolish but to complete them. I tell you solemnly, till heaven and earth disappear, not one dot, not one little stroke, shall disappear from the Law until its purpose is achieved. Therefore, the man who infringes even one of the least of these commandments and teaches others to do the same will be considered the least in the kingdom of heaven; but the man who keeps them and teaches them will be considered great in the kingdom of heaven.'

This is the Gospel of the Lord.

17 January

St Anthony, abbot *Memorial*

Born in Egypt, about 260 AD. When his parents died, he gave his inheritance to the poor, and went into the desert, where he lived a life of penance. Many came to follow him, and he is known as the father of monks. He supported those who suffered for the faith under the persecutions of Diocletian, and helped Saint Athanasius in his fight against the Arians. He died in 356.

Common of holy men and women: religious, pp.1898ff.

Entrance Antiphon: The just man will flourish like the palm tree. Planted in the courts of God's house, he will grow great like the cedars of Lebanon.

Opening Prayer

Father,
you called Saint Anthony
to renounce the world
and serve you in the solitude of the desert.
By his prayers and example,
may we learn to deny ourselves
and to love you above all things.

FIRST READING

A reading from the letter of St Paul to the Ephesians 6:10-13. 18
Rely on God's armour.

Grow strong in the Lord, with the strength of his power. Put God's armour on so as to be able to resist the devil's tactics. For it is not against human enemies that we have to struggle, but against the Sovereignties and the Powers who originate the darkness in this world, the spiritual army of evil in the heavens. That is why you must rely on God's armour, or you will not be able to put up any resistance when the worst happens, or have enough resources to hold your ground.

Pray all the time, asking for what you need, praying in the Spirit on every possible occasion. Never get tired of staying awake to pray for all the saints.

This is the word of the Lord.

Responsorial Psalm   Ps 15: 1-2. 5. 7-8. 11. ℟ cf. v.5

℟ **You are my inheritance, O Lord.**

1 Preserve me, God, I take refuge in you.
   I say to the Lord: 'You are my God.'
   O Lord, it is you who are my portion and cup;
   it is you yourself who are my prize. ℟

2 I will bless the Lord who gives me counsel,
   who even at night directs my heart.
   I keep the Lord ever in my sight:
   since he is at my right hand, I shall stand firm. ℟

3 You will show me the path of life,
   the fullness of joy in your presence,
   at your right hand happiness for ever. ℟

Proper of Saints, 17 January

Gospel Acclamation   Jn 8:31–32

Alleluia, alleluia!
If you make my word your home
you will indeed by my disciples,
and you will learn the truth, says the Lord.
Alleluia!

GOSPEL

A reading from the holy Gospel according to Matthew   19:16–26
If you wish to be perfect, go and sell what you own.

There was a man who came to Jesus and asked, 'Master, what good deed must I do to possess eternal life?' Jesus said to him, 'Why do you ask me about what is good? There is one alone who is good. But if you wish to enter into life, keep the commandments.' He said, 'Which?' 'These:' Jesus replied. 'You must not kill. You must not commit adultery. You must not steal. You must not bring false witness. Honour your father and mother and: You must love your neighbour as yourself.' The young man said to him, 'I have kept all these. What more do I need to do?' Jesus said, 'If you wish to be perfect, go and sell what you own and give the money to the poor, and you will have treasure in heaven; then come, follow me'.

But when the young man heard these words he went away sad, for he was a man of great wealth.

Then Jesus said to his disciples, 'I tell you solemnly, it will be hard for a rich man to enter the kingdom of heaven. Yes, I tell you again, it is easier for a camel to pass through the eye of a needle than for a rich man to enter the kingdom of heaven.' When the disciples heard this they were astonished. 'Who can be saved, then?' they said, Jesus gazed at them. 'For men' he hold them 'this is impossible; for God everything is possible.'

This is the Gospel of the Lord.

Prayer over the Gifts

Lord,
accept the sacrifice we offer at your altar
in commemoration of Saint Anthony.
May no earthly attraction keep us from loving you.

Communion Antiphon: If you wish to be perfect, go, sell what you own, give it all to the poor, then come, follow me.

Prayer after Communion

Lord,
you helped Saint Anthony conquer the powers of darkness.
May your sacrament strengthen us
in our struggle with evil.

20 January

St Fabian, pope and martyr   Optional Memorial

Bishop of Rome from 236-250, when he was martyred at the beginning of the persecution of Decius.

Common of martyrs, pp.1865ff., or of pastors: popes, pp.1876ff.

Opening Prayer

God our Father, glory of your priests,
may the prayers of your martyr Fabian
help us to share his faith
and offer you loving service.

FIRST READING

A reading from the first letter of St Peter   5:1-4
Be the shepherds of the flock of God that is entrusted to you.

I have something to tell your elders: I am an elder myself, and a witness to the sufferings of Christ and with you I have a share in the glory that is to be revealed. Be the shepherds of the flock of God that is entrusted to you; watch over it, not simply as a duty but gladly, because God wants it; not for sordid money, but because you are eager to do it. Never be a dictator over any group that is put in your charge, but be an example that the whole flock can follow. When the chief shepherd appears, you will be given the crown of unfading glory.

This is the word of the Lord.

Responsional Psalm   Ps 39:2. 4. 7-10. ℟ cf. vv. 8-9

℟ **Here I am, Lord!**
 I come to do your will.

1 I waited, I waited for the Lord
 and he stooped down to me;

he heard my cry.
He put a new song into my mouth,
praise of our God. ℟

2 You do not ask for sacrifice and offerings,
but an open ear.
You do not ask for holocaust and victim.
Instead, here am I. ℟

3 In the scroll of the book it stands written
that I should do your will.
My God, I delight in your law
in the depth of my heart. ℟

4 Your justice I have proclaimed
in the great assembly.
My lips I have not sealed;
you know it, O Lord. ℟

Gospel Acclamation

Jn 10:14

Alleluia, alleluia!
I am the good shepherd, says the Lord;
I know my own sheep
and my own know me.
Alleluia!

GOSPEL

A reading from the holy Gospel according to John 21:15-17
Feed my lambs, feed my sheep.

Jesus showed himself to his disciples, and after they had eaten he said to Simon Peter, 'Simon son of John, do you love me more than these others do?' He answered, 'Yes Lord, you know I love you.' Jesus said to him, 'Feed my lambs.' A second time he said to him, 'Simon son of John, do you love me?' He replied, 'Yes, Lord, you know I love you.' Jesus said to him, 'Look after my sheep.' Then he said to him a third time, 'Simon son of John, do you love me?' Peter was upset that he asked him the third time, 'Do you love me?' and said, 'Lord, you know everything; you know I love you.' Jesus said to him, 'Feed my sheep.'

This is the Gospel of the Lord.

also 20 January

St Sebastian, martyr — Optional Memorial

Sebastian was martyred at Rome, at the beginning of the persecution of Diocletian. His tomb is in the Catacomb on the Via Appia.

Common of martyrs, pp.1865ff.

Opening Prayer

Lord,
fill us with that spirit of courage
which gave your martyr Sebastian
strength to offer his life in faithful witness.
Help us to learn from him to cherish your law
and to obey you rather than men.

FIRST READING

A reading from the first letter of St Peter   3:14-17
There is no need to be afraid or to worry about them.

If you have to suffer for being good, you will count it a blessing. There is no need to be afraid or to worry about persecutors. Simply reverence the Lord Christ in your hearts, and always have your answer ready for people who ask you the reason for the hope that you all have. But give it with courtesy and respect and with a clear conscience, so that those who slander you when you are living a good life in Christ may be proved wrong in the accusations that they bring. And if it is the will of God that you should suffer, it is better to suffer for doing right than for doing wrong.

This is the word of the Lord.

Responsorial Psalm   Ps 33:2-9. ℟ v.5

℟ **From all my terrors the Lord set me free.**

1. I will bless the Lord at all times,
   his praise always on my lips;
   in the Lord my soul shall make its boast.
   The humble shall hear and be glad. ℟

2. Glorify the Lord with me.
   Together let us praise his name.

I sought the Lord and he answered me;
from all my terrors he set me free. ℟

3 Look towards him and be radiant;
let your faces not be abashed.
This poor man called; the Lord heard him
and rescued him from all his distress. ℟

4 The angel of the Lord is encamped
around those who revere him, to rescue them.
Taste and see that the Lord is good.
He is happy who seeks refuge in him. ℟

Gospel Acclamation   James 1:12

Alleluia, alleluia!
Happy the man who stands firm when trials come.
He has proved himself,
and will win the prize of life.
Alleluia!

GOSPEL

A reading from the holy Gospel according to Matthew   10:28-33
Do not be afraid of those who kill the body.

Jesus said to his apostles: 'Do not be afraid of those who kill the body but cannot kill the soul; fear him rather who can destroy both body and soul in hell. Can you not buy two sparrows for a penny? And yet not one falls to the ground without your Father knowing. Why, every hair on your head has been counted. So there is no need to be afraid; you are worth more than hundreds of sparrows.

'So if anyone declares himelf for me in the presence of men, I will declare myself for him in the presence of my Father in heaven. But the one who disowns me in the presence of men, I will disown in the presence of my Father in heaven.'

This is the Gospel of the Lord.

21 January

St Agnes, virgin and martyr   Memorial

Put to death at the end of the persecution of Diocletian, probably in the early years of the fourth century, Agnes was perhaps twelve or fifteen.

Common of martyrs, pp.1865ff., or of virgins, pp.1889ff.

Opening Prayer

Almighty, eternal God,
you choose what the world considers weak
to put the worldly power to shame.
May we who celebrate the birth of Saint Agnes into eternal joy
be loyal to the faith she professed.

FIRST READING

A reading from the first letter of St Paul
to the Corinthians   1:26-31
God chose what is foolish by human reckoning.

Take yourselves, brothers, at the time when you were called: how many of you were wise in the ordinary sense of the word, how many were influential people, or came from noble families? No, it was to shame the wise that God chose what is foolish by human reckoning, and to shame what is strong that he chose what is weak by human reckoning; those whom the world think common and contemptible are the ones that God has chosen – those who are nothing at all to show up those who are everything. The human race has nothing to boast about to God, but you, God has made members of Christ Jesus and by God's doing he has become our wisdom, and our virtue, and our holiness, and our freedom. As scripture says: if anyone wants to boast, let him boast about the Lord.

This is the word of the Lord.

Responsorial Psalm   Ps 22. ℟ v.1

℟ **The Lord is my shepherd;
there is nothing I shall want.**

1 The Lord is my shepherd;
there is nothing I shall want.
Fresh and green are the pastures
where he gives me repose.
Near restful waters he leads me,
to revive my drooping spirit. ℟

2 He guides me along the right path;
he is true to his name.
If I should walk in the valley of darkness

no evil would I fear.
You are there with your crook and your staff;
with these you give me comfort. ℟

3 You have prepared a banquet for me
in the sight of my foes.
My head you have anointed with oil;
my cup is overflowing. ℟

4 Surely goodness and kindness shall follow me
all the days of my life.
In the Lord's own house shall I dwell
for ever and ever. ℟

Gospel Acclamation Jn 15:9.5

Alleluia, alleluia!
Remain in my love, says the Lord;
whoever remains in me, with me in him,
bears fruit in plenty.
Alleluia!

GOSPEL

A reading from the holy Gospel according to Matthew 13:44-46
He sells everything he owns and buys the field.

Jesus said to the crowds: 'The kingdom of heaven is like treasure hidden in a field which someone has found; he hides it again, goes off happy, sells everything he owns and buys the field.

'Again, the kingdom of heaven is like a merchant looking for fine pearls; when he finds one of great value he goes and sells everything he owns and buys it.'

This is the Gospel of the Lord.

22 January

St Vincent, deacon and martyr
Optional Memorial

Vincent was a deacon of the Church at Saragossa. He was put to death at Valencia, in Spain, during the persecution of Diocletian, in about 304.

Common of Martyrs, pp.1865ff.

Opening Prayer
Eternal Father,

you gave Saint Vincent
the courage to endure torture and death for the gospel:
fill us with your Spirit
and strengthen us in your love.

FIRST READING

A reading from the second letter of St Paul 4:7-15
to the Corinthians
We carry with us in our body the death of Jesus.

We are only the earthenware jars that hold this treasure, to make it clear that such an overwhelming power comes from God and not from us. We are in difficulties on all sides, but never cornered; we see no answer to our problems, but never despair; we have been persecuted, but never deserted; knocked down, but never killed; always, wherever we may be, we carry with us in our body the death of Jesus, so that the life of Jesus, too, may always be seen in our body. Indeed, while we are still alive, we are consigned to our death every day, for the sake of Jesus, so that in our mortal flesh the life of Jesus, too, may be openly shown. So death is at work in us, but life in you.

But as we have the same spirit of faith that is mentioned in scripture – I believed, and therefore I spoke – we too believe and therefore we too speak, knowing that he who raised the Lord Jesus to life will raise us with Jesus in our turn, and put us by his side and you with us. You see, all this is for your benefit, so that the more grace is multiplied among people, the more thanksgiving there will be, to the glory of God.

This is the word of the Lord.

Responsorial Psalm

Ps 33:2-9. R̷ v.5

R̷ **From all my terrors the Lord set me free.**

1 I will bless the Lord at all times,
   his praise always on my lips;
   in the Lord my soul shall make its boast.
   The humble shall hear and be glad. R̷

2 Glorify the Lord with me.
   Together let us praise his name.
   I sought the Lord and he answered me;
   from all my terrors he set me free. R̷

3. Look towards him and be radiant;
let your faces not be abashed.
This poor man called; the Lord heard him
and rescued him from all his distress. ℟

4. The angel of the Lord is encamped
around those who revere him, to rescue them.
Taste and see that the Lord is good.
He is happy who seeks refuge in him. ℟

Gospel Acclamation Mt 5:10
Alleluia, alleluia!
Happy those who are persecuted in the cause of right:
theirs is the kingdom of heaven.
Alleluia!

GOSPEL

A reading from the holy Gospel according to Matthew 10:17-22

You will be dragged before governors and kings for my sake, to bear witness before them and the pagans.

Jesus said to his apostles: 'Beware of men: they will hand you over to sanhedrins and scourge you in their synagogues. You will be dragged before governors and kings for my sake, to bear witness before them and the pagans. But when they hand you over, do not worry about how to speak or what to say; what you are to say will be given to you when the time comes; because it is not you who will be speaking; the Spirit of your Father will be speaking in you.

'Brother will betray brother to death, and the father his child; children will rise against their parents and have them put to death. You will be hated by all men on account of my name; but the man who stands firm to the end will be saved.'

This is the Gospel of the Lord.

24 January
St Francis de Sales, bishop and doctor of the Church Memorial

Bishop of Geneva at the time of Calvin, he strove for the renewal of the faith. His Introduction to the Devout Life was a classic of spiritual direction, and is still read. He died on 28 December 1622, at the age of 55.

Proper of Saints, 24 January

Common of pastors: bishops, pp.1878ff., or of doctors of the church, pp.1887ff.

Opening Prayer
Father,
you gave Francis de Sales the spirit of compassion
to befriend all men on the way to salvation.
By his example, lead us to show your gentle love
in the service of our fellow men.

FIRST READING

A reading from the letter of St Paul to the Ephesians 3:8-12
Proclaiming to the pagans the infinite treasure of Christ.

I, who am less than the least of all the saints, have been entrusted with this special grace, not only of proclaiming to the pagans the infinite treasure of Christ but also of explaining how the mystery is to be dispersed. Through all the ages, this has been kept hidden in God, the creator of everything. Why? So that the Sovereignties and Powers should learn only now, through the Church, how comprehensive God's wisdom really is, exactly according to the plan which he had from all eternity in Christ Jesus our Lord. This is why we are bold enough to approach God in complete confidence, through our faith in him.

This is the word of the Lord.

Responsorial Psalm Ps 36:3-6. 30-31. ℟ v.30
 ℟ **The just man's mouth utters wisdom.**

1 If you trust in the Lord and do good,
 then you will live in the land and be secure.
 If you find your delight in the Lord,
 he will grant your heart's desire. ℟

2 Commit your life to the Lord,
 trust in him and he will act,
 so that your justice breaks forth like the light,
 your cause like the noon-day sun. ℟

3 The just man's mouth utters wisdom
 and his lips speak what is right;
 the law of his God is in his heart,
 his steps shall be saved from stumbling. ℟

Gospel Acclamation Jn 13:34

Alleluia, alleluia!
I give you a new commandment:
love one another just as I have loved you,
says the Lord.
Alleluia!

GOSPEL

A reading from the holy Gospel according to John 15:9-17
You are my friends if you do what I command you.

Jesus said to his disciples:

'As the Father has loved me,
so I have loved you.
Remain in my love.
If you keep my commandments
you will remain in my love,
just as I have kept my Father's commandments
and remain in his love.
I have told you this
so that my own joy may be in you
and your joy be complete.
This is my commandment:
love one another,
as I have loved you.
A man can have no greater love
than to lay down his life for his friends.
You are my friends,
if you do what I command you.
I shall not call you servants any more,
because a servant does not know
his master's business;
I call you friends,
because I have made known to you
everything I have learnt from my Father.
You did not choose me,
no, I chose you;
and I commissioned you
to go out and to bear fruit,
fruit that will last;
and then the Father will give you
anything you ask him in my name.

What I command you
is to love one another.'

This is the Gospel of the Lord.

Prayer over the Gifts
Lord,
by this offering
may the divine fire of your Holy Spirit,
which burned in the gentle heart of Francis de Sales,
inspire us with compassion and love.

Prayer after Communion
Merciful Father,
may the sacrament we have received
help us to imitate Francis de Sales in love and service;
bring us to share with him the glory of heaven.

25 January
THE CONVERSION OF ST PAUL, APOSTLE Feast

Entrance Antiphon: I know whom I have believed. I am sure that he, the just judge, will guard my pledge until the day of judgement.

Opening Prayer
God our Father,
you taught the gospel to all the world
through the preaching of Paul your apostle.
May we who celebrate his conversion to the faith
follow him in bearing witness to your truth.

FIRST READING

A reading from the Acts of the Apostles 22:3-16

It is time you were baptised and had your sins washed away while invoking the name of Jesus.

Paul said to the people, 'I am a Jew and was born at Tarsus in Cilicia. I was brought up here in this city. I studied under Gamaliel and was taught the exact observance of the Law of our ancestors. In fact, I was as full of duty towards God as you are today. I even persecuted this Way to the death, and sent women as well as men to prison in chains as the high priest and the whole council of elders can testify, since they even sent me with letters to their brothers in Damascus. When I set off it was with the intention of bringing prisoners back from there to Jerusalem for punishment.

'I was on that journey and nearly at Damascus when about midday a bright light from heaven suddenly shone round me. I fell to the ground and heard a voice saying, "Saul, Saul, why are you persecuting me?" I answered: Who are you, Lord? and he said to me, "I am Jesus the Nazarene, and you are persecuting me." The people with me saw the light but did not hear his voice as he spoke to me. I said: What am I to do, Lord? The Lord answered, "Stand up and go into Damascus, and there you will be told what you have been appointed to do." The light had been so dazzling that I was blind and my companions had to take me by the hand; and so I came to Damascus.

'Someone called Ananias, a devout follower of the Law and highly thought of by all the Jews living there, came to see me; he stood beside me and said, "Brother Saul, receive your sight." Instantly my sight came back and I was able to see him. Then he said, "The God of our ancestors has chosen you to know his will, to see the Just One and hear his own voice speaking, because you are to be his witness before all mankind, testifying to what you have seen and heard. And now why delay? It is time you were baptised and had your sins washed away while invoking his name."'

This is the word of the Lord.

Alternative First Reading

A reading from the Acts of the Apostles 9:1-22
Lord, what will you have me do?

Saul was still breathing threats to slaughter the Lord's disciples. He had gone to the high priest and asked for letters addressed to the synagogues in Damascus, that would authorise him to arrest and take to Jerusalem any followers of the Way, men or women, that he could find.

Suddenly, while he was travelling to Damascus and just before he reached the city, there came a light from heaven all round him. He fell to the ground, and then he heard a voice saying, 'Saul, Saul, why are you persecuting me?' 'Who are you, Lord?' he asked, and the voice answered, 'I am Jesus, and you are persecuting me. Get up now and go into the city, and you will be told what you have to do.' The men travelling with Saul stood there speechless, for though they heard the voice they could see no one. Saul got up from the ground, but even with his eyes wide open he could see nothing at all, and they had to lead him into Damascus by the hand. For three days he was without his sight, and took neither food nor drink.

A disciple called Ananias who lived in Damascus had a vision in which he heard the Lord say to him, 'Ananias!' When he replied, 'Here I am, Lord,' the Lord said, 'You must go to Straight Street and ask at the house of Judas for someone called Saul, who comes from Tarsus. At this moment he is praying, having had a vision of man called Ananias coming in and laying hands on him to give him back his sight.'

When he heard that, Ananias said, 'Lord, several people have told me about this man and all the harm he has been doing to your saints in Jerusalem. He has only come here because he holds a warrant from the chief priests to arrest everybody who invokes your name.' The Lord replied, 'You must go all the same, because this man is my chosen instrument to bring my name before pagans and pagan kings and before the people of Israel; I myself will show him how much he himself must suffer for my name.' Then Ananias went. He entered the house, and at once laid his hands on Saul and said, 'Brother Saul, I have been sent by the Lord Jesus who appeared to you on your way here so that you may recover your sight and be filled with the Holy Spirit.' Immediately it was as though scales fell away from Saul's eyes and he could see again. So he was baptised there and then, and after taking some food he regained his strength.

After he had spent only a few days with the disciples in Damascus, he began preaching in the synagogues, 'Jesus is the Son of God.' All his hearers were amazed. 'Surely' they said 'this is the man who organised the attack in Jerusalem against the people who invoke this name, and who came here for the sole purpose of arresting them to have them tried by the chief priests?' Saul's power increased steadily, and he was able to throw the Jewish colony at Damascus into complete confusion by the way he demonstrated that Jesus was the Christ.

This is the word of the Lord.

Responsorial Psalm Ps 116:1-2. ℟ Mk 16:15
℟ **Go out to the whole world;
proclaim the Good News.**

or

℟ **Alleluia!**

1 Praise the Lord, all you nations,
  acclaim him all you people. ℟

2 Strong is his love for us;
  he is faithful for ever. ℟

Gospel Acclamation cf. Jn 15:16
Alleluia, alleluia!
I chose you from the world,
to go out and to bear fruit,
fruit that will last says the Lord.
Alleluia!

GOSPEL

A reading from the holy Gospel according to Mark 16:15-18

Go out to the whole world; proclaim the Good News.

Jesus showed himself to the Eleven and said to them, 'Go out to the whole world; proclaim the Good News to all creation. He who believes and is baptised will be saved; he who does not believe will be condemned. These are the signs that will be associated with believers: in my name they will cast out devils; they will have the gift of tongues; they will pick up snakes in their hands, and be unharmed should they drink deadly poison; they will lay their hands on the sick, who will recover.'

This is the Gospel of the Lord.

These readings are used in a Votive Mass of St Paul.

Prayer over the Gifts
Lord,
may your Spirit who helped Paul the apostle
to preach your power and glory
fill us with the light of faith
as we celebrate this holy eucharist.

Preface of the Apostles I or II, P64 or P65.

Communion Antiphon: I live by faith in the Son of God, who loved me and sacrificed himself for me.

Prayer after Communion
Lord God,
you filled Paul the apostle
with love for all the churches:
may the sacrament we have received
foster in us this love for your people.

26 January
Ss Timothy and Titus, bishops — Memorial

Disciples and co-workers of Saint Paul. Timothy accompanied Paul on his travels. He was put in charge of the Church at Ephesus. Titus was Paul's messenger to various Christian communities where disputes arose, and he was in charge of the Church at Crete. To these two Paul wrote his pastoral epistles.

Common of pastors: bishops, pp.1878ff.

Opening Prayer
God our Father,
you gave your saints Timothy and Titus
the courage and wisdom of the apostles:
may their prayers help us to live holy lives
and lead us to heaven, our true home.

The first reading is proper to this Memorial.

FIRST READING
A reading from the second letter of St Paul to Timothy 1:1-8

I am reminded of the sincere faith which you have.

From Paul, appointed by God to be an apostle of Christ Jesus in his design to promise life in Christ Jesus; to Timothy, dear child of mine, wishing you grace, mercy and peace from God the Father and from Christ Jesus our Lord.

Night and day I thank God, keeping my conscience clear and remembering my duty to him as my ancestors did, and always I remember you in my prayers; I remember your tears and long to see you again to complete my happiness. Then I am reminded of the sincere faith which you have; it came first to live in your grandmother Lois, and you mother Eunice, and I have no doubt that it is the same faith in you as well.

That is why I am reminding you now to fan into a flame the gift that God gave you when I laid my hands on you. God's gift was not a spirit of timidity, but the Spirit of power, and love, and self-control. So you are never to be ashamed of witnessing to the Lord, or ashamed of me for being his prisoner; but with me, bear the hardships for the sake of the Good News, relying on the power of God who has saved us and called us to be holy.

This is the word of the Lord.

Alternative First Reading

A reading from the letter of St Paul to Titus   1:1-5
To Titus, true child of mine in the faith that we share.

From Paul, servant of God, an apostle of Jesus Christ to bring those whom God has chosen to faith and to the knowledge of the truth that leads to true religion; and to give them the hope of the eternal life that was promised so long ago by God. He does not lie and so, at the appointed time, he revealed his decision, and, by the command of God our saviour, I have been commissioned to proclaim it. To Titus, true child of mine in the faith that we share, wishing you grace and peace from God the Father and from Christ Jesus our saviour.

The reason I left you behind in Crete was for you to get everything organised there and appoint elders in every town, in the way that I told you.

This is the word of the Lord.

Responsorial Psalm   Ps 95: 1-3. 7-8. 10. ℟ v. 3

   ℟ **Proclaim the wonders of the Lord among all the peoples.**

1 O sing a new song to the Lord,
   sing to the Lord all the earth.
   O sing to the Lord, bless his name.   ℟

2 Proclaim his help day by day,
   tell among the nations his glory
   and his wonders among all the peoples.   ℟   (continued)

3 Give the Lord, you families of peoples,
   give the Lord glory and power,
   give the Lord the glory of his name.

   ℟ **Proclaim the wonders of the Lord
   among all the peoples.**

4 Proclaim to the nations: 'God is king.'
   The world he made firm in its place;
   he will judge the peoples in fairness. ℟

Gospel Acclamation cf. Lk 4:18
Alleluia, alleluia!
The Lord has sent me to bring the good news to the poor,
to proclaim liberty to captives.
Alleluia!

GOSPEL

A reading from the holy Gospel according to Luke 10:1-9
The harvest is rich but the labourers are few.

The Lord appointed seventy-two others and sent them out ahead of him, in pairs, to all the towns and places he himself was to visit. He said to them, 'The harvest is rich but the labourers are few, so ask the Lord of the harvest to send labourers to his harvest. Start off now, but remember, I am sending you out like lambs among wolves. Carry no purse, no haversack, no sandals. Salute no one on the road. Whatever house you go into, let your first words be, 'Peace to this house!' And if a man of peace lives there, your peace will go and rest on him; if not, it will come back to you. Stay in the same house, taking what food and drink they have to offer, for the labourer deserves his wages; do not move from house to house. Whenever you go into a town where they make you welcome, eat what is set before you. Cure those in it who are sick, and say, "The kingdom of God is very near to you" '.

This is the Gospel of the Lord.

27 January

St Angela Merici, virgin
Optional Memorial

Born at Desenzano, near Brescia, about 1470. Angela saw her task as the formation of Christian women: in 1535 she founded the institute of the Ursulines, who were devoted to the education of poor girls as Christians, and to the missions. She died in 1540.

Common of virgins, pp.1889ff., or of holy men and women: teachers, p.1901.

Opening Prayer
Lord,
may Saint Angela commend us to your mercy;
may her charity and wisdom help us
to be faithful to your teaching
and to follow it in our lives.

FIRST READING

A reading from the first letter of St Peter   4:7-11
Each one of you has received a special grace; so put yourselves at the service of others.

Keep a calm and sober mind. Above all, never let your love for each other grow insincere, since love covers over many a sin. Welcome each other into your houses without grumbling. Each one of you has received a special grace, so, like good stewards responsible for all these different graces of God, put yourselves at the service of others. If you are a speaker, speak in words which seem to come from God; if you are a helper, help as though every action was done at God's orders; so that in everything God may receive the glory, through Jesus Christ, since to him belong all glory and power for ever and ever. Amen.

    This is the word of the Lord.

Responsorial Psalm   Ps 148:1-2. 11-14. R/ cf. vv.12.13

   R/ **Young men and women, praise the name of the Lord.**

or

   R/ **Alleluia!**

1   Praise the Lord from the heavens,
    praise him in the heights.

Praise him, all his angels,
praise him, all his host.

℟ **Young men and women, praise the name of the Lord.**

or

℟ **Alleluia!**

2 All earth's kings and peoples,
earth's princes and rulers;
young men and maidens,
old men together with children. ℟

3 Let them praise the name of the Lord
for he alone is exalted.
The splendour of his name
reaches beyond heaven and earth. ℟

4 He exalts the strength of his people.
He is the praise of all his saints,
of the sons of Israel,
of the people to whom he comes close. ℟

Gospel Acclamation   cf. Mt 11:25

Alleluia, alleluia!
Blessed are you, Father,
Lord of heaven and earth,
for revealing the mysteries of the kingdom
to mere children.
Alleluia!

GOSPEL

A reading from the holy Gospel according to Mark   9:34-37
Anyone who welcomes one of these little children, welcomes me.

On the road the disciples had been arguing which of them was the greatest. So Jesus sat down, called the Twelve to him and said, 'If anyone wants to be first, he must make himself last of all and servant of all.' He then took a little child, set him in front of them, put his arms round him, and said to them, 'Anyone who welcomes one of these little children in my name, welcomes me; and anyone who welcomes me welcomes not me but the one who sent me.'

This is the Gospel of the Lord.

28 January

St Thomas Aquinas, priest and doctor of the Church — Memorial

Born about 1225. Entered the Dominican Order in 1244, and continued his studies in Paris and Cologne. His outstanding writings and teachings in theology, philosophy and scripture were founded on a life of prayer and faith. He died in 1274.

Common of doctors of the Church, pp.1887ff., or of pastors, pp.1876ff.

Opening Prayer
God our Father,
you made Thomas Aquinas known for his holiness and learning.
Help us to grow in wisdom by his teaching,
and in holiness by imitating his faith.

FIRST READING

A reading from the book of Wisdom 7:7-10. 15-16
I loved wisdom more than health or beauty.

I prayed, and understanding was given me;
I entreated, and the spirit of Wisdom came to me.
I esteemed her more than sceptres and thrones;
compared with her, I held riches as nothing.
I reckoned no priceless stone to be her peer,
for compared with her, all gold is a pinch of sand,
and beside her silver ranks as mud.
I love her more than health or beauty,
preferred her to the light,
since her radiance never sleeps.
May God grant me to speak as he would wish
and express thoughts worthy of his gifts,
since he himself is the guide of Wisdom,
since he directs the sages.
We are indeed in his hand, we ourselves and our words,
with all our understanding, too, and technical knowledge.

    This is the word of the Lord.

Responsorial Psalm   Ps 118:9-14. ℟ v.12

℟ **Lord, teach me your statutes.**

1. How shall the young remain sinless?
   By obeying your word.
   I have sought you with all my heart:
   let me not stray from your commands. ℟

2. I treasure your promise in my heart
   lest I sin against you.
   Blessed are you, O Lord;
   teach me your statutes. ℟

3. With my tongue I have recounted
   the decrees of your lips.
   I rejoice to do your will
   as though all riches were mine. ℟

Gospel Acclamation   Mt 23:9. 10

Alleluia, alleluia!
You have only one Father,
and he is in heaven;
you have only one Teacher,
the Christ.
Alleluia!

GOSPEL

A reading from the holy Gospel according to Matthew   23:8-12

Nor must you allow yourselves to be called teachers, for you have only one teacher, the Christ.

Jesus said to his disciples: 'You must not allow yourselves to be called Rabbi, since you have only one Master, and you are all brothers. You must call no one on earth your father, since you have only one Father, and he is in heaven. Nor must you allow yourselves to be called teachers, for you have only one Teacher, the Christ. The greatest among you must be your servant. Anyone who exalts himself will be humbled, and anyone who humbles himself will be exalted.'

This is the Gospel of the Lord.

31 January
St John Bosco, priest — Memorial

Born in the diocese of Turin in 1815, and brought up in poverty, John Bosco devoted his life to the education of working youth. He founded religious congregations – the Salesian Order, and The Daughters of Mary Help of Christians – to carry on his ideals.

Common of pastors, pp.1876ff., or of holy men and women: teachers, p.1901.

Opening Prayer
Lord,
you called John Bosco
to be a teacher and father to the young.
Fill us with love like his:
may we give ourselves completely to your service
and to the salvation of mankind.

FIRST READING
A reading from the letter of St Paul to the Philippians 4:4-9
Fill your minds with everything that is pure.

I want you to be happy, always happy in the Lord; I repeat, what I want is your happiness. Let your tolerance be evident to everyone: the Lord is very near. There is no need to worry; but if there is anything you need, pray for it, asking God for it with prayer and thanksgiving, and that peace of God, which is so much greater than we can understand, will guard your hearts and your thoughts, in Christ Jesus. Finally, brothers, fill your minds with everything that is true, everything that is noble, everything that is good and pure, everything that we love and honour, and everything than can be thought virtuous or worthy of praise. Keep doing all the things that you learnt from me and have been taught by me and have heard or seen that I do. Then the God of peace will be with you.

This is the word of the Lord.

Responsorial Psalm
Ps 102:1-4. 8-9. 13-14. 17-18. ℟ v.1
℟ **My soul, give thanks to the Lord.**

1 My soul, give thanks to the Lord,
all my being, bless his holy name.

My soul, give thanks to the Lord.
and never forget all his blessings.

℟ **My soul, give thanks to the Lord.**

2 It is he who forgives all your guilt,
who heals every one of your ills,
who redeems your life from the grave,
who crowns you with love and compassion. ℟

3 The Lord is compassion and love,
slow to anger and rich in mercy.
His wrath will come to an end;
he will not be angry for ever. ℟

4 As a father has compassion on his sons,
the Lord has pity on those who fear him;
for he knows of what we are made,
he remembers that we are dust. ℟

5 But the love of the Lord is everlasting
upon those who hold him in fear;
his justice reaches out to children's children
when they keep his covenant in truth. ℟

Gospel Acclamation Mt 23:11, 12
Alleluia, alleluia!
The greatest among you must be your servant, says the Lord:
the man who humbles himself will be exalted.
Alleluia!

GOSPEL

A reading from the holy Gospel according to Matthew 18:1-5
Unless you become like little children you will never enter the kingdom of heaven.

The disciples came to Jesus and said, 'Who is the greatest in the kingdom of heaven?' So he called a little child to him and set the child in front of them. Then he said, 'I tell you solemnly, unless you change and become like little children you will never enter the kingdom of heaven. And so, the one who makes himself as little as this little child is the greatest in the kingdom of heaven.

'Anyone who welcomes a little child like this in my name welcomes me.'

This is the Gospel of the Lord.

BE STILL AND KNOW I AM GOD

FEBRUARY

2 February
PRESENTATION OF THE LORD
Feast

Today we celebrate the close of the Christmas festival of light. Candles are blessed and we carry them in procession to welcome Christ, the light to enlighten the Gentiles and the glory of his people.

BLESSING OF CANDLES AND PROCESSION

First Form: Procession

The people gather in a chapel or other suitable place outside the church where the Mass will be celebrated. They carry unlighted candles. While the candles are being lighted, this canticle or another hymn is sung:

The Lord will come with mighty power,
and give light to the eyes of all who serve him, alleluia.

The priest greets the people in these or similar words:

Forty days ago we celebrated the joyful feast of the birth of our Lord Jesus Christ. Today we recall the holy day on which he was presented in the temple, fulfilling the law of Moses and at the same time going to meet his faithful people. Led by the Spirit, Simeon and Anna came to the temple, recognised Christ as their Lord, and proclaimed him with joy.

United by the Spirit, may we now go to the house of God to welcome Christ the Lord. There we shall recognise him in the breaking of bread until he comes again in glory.

The priest blesses the candles:
Let us pray.
God our Father, source of all light,
today you revealed to Simeon
your Light of revelation to the nations.
Bless ✠ these candles and make them holy.
May we who carry them to praise your glory
walk in the path of goodness
and come to the light that shines for ever.
or
God our Father, source of eternal light,
fill the hearts of all believers
with the light of faith.
May we who carry these candles in your church
come with joy to the light of glory.

The priest then takes the candle prepared for him, and the procession begins with the acclamation:
Let us go in peace to meet the Lord.

During the procession, the canticle of Simeon, or another hymn, is sung:
Antiphon: Christ is the light of the nations
and the glory of Israel his people.

Now, Lord, you have kept your word:
let your servant go in peace. (*Ant.*)

With my own eyes I have seen the salvation
which you have prepared in the sight of every people. (*Ant.*)

A light to reveal you to the nations
and the glory of your people Israel. (*Ant.*)

As the procession enters the church, the entrance chant of the Mass is sung. The Mass continues as usual.

Second Form: Solemn Entrance

The people, carrying unlighted candles, assemble in the church. The priest, accompanied by his ministers and by a representative group of the faithful, goes to a suitable place where most of the congregation can easily take part.
     The candles are lighted while the antiphon, Christ is the Light (see above) or another hymn is sung.

Proper of Saints, 2 February

After the greeting and introduction, the priest blesses the candles, as above, and goes in procession to the altar, while all are singing. The Mass continues as usual.

THE MASS

Entrance Antiphon: Within your temple, we ponder your loving kindness, O God. As your name, so also your praise reaches to the ends of the earth; your right hand is filled with justice.

Opening Prayer
All-powerful Father,
Christ your Son became man for us
and was presented in the temple.
May he free our hearts from sin
and bring us into your presence.

FIRST READING

A reading from the prophet Malachi   3:1-4
The Lord you are seeking will suddenly enter his Temple.

The Lord God says this: Look, I am going to send my messenger to prepare a way before me. And the Lord you are seeking will suddenly enter his Temple; and the angel of the covenant whom you are longing for, yes, he is coming, says the Lord of hosts. Who will be able to resist the day of his coming? Who will remain standing when he appears? For he is like the refiner's fire and the fullers' alkali. He will take his seat as refiner and purifier; he will purify the sons of Levi and refine them like gold and silver, and then they will make the offering to the Lord as it should be made. The offering of Judah and Jerusalem will then be welcomed by the Lord as in former days, as in the years of old.

This is the word of the Lord.

Responsional Psalm   Ps 23:7-10. ℟ v.10
℟ **Who is the king of glory?
It is the Lord.**

1   O gates, lift up your heads;
    grow higher, ancient doors.
    Let him enter, the king of glory!   ℟

2   Who is the king of glory?

The Lord, the mighty, the valiant,
the Lord, the valiant in war.

℟ **Who is the king of glory?
It is the Lord.**

3 O gates, lift high your heads;
grow higher, ancient doors.
Let him enter, the king of glory! ℟

4 Who is he, the king of glory?
He, the Lord of armies,
he is the king of glory. ℟

SECOND READING

A reading from the letter to the Hebrews 2:14-18

It was essential that he should in this way become completely like his brothers.

Since all the children share the same blood and flesh, Jesus too shared equally in it, so that by his death he could take away all the power of the devil, who had power over death, and set free all those who had been held in slavery all their lives by the fear of death. For it was not the angels that he took to himself; he took to himself descent from Abraham. It was essential that he should in this way become completely like his brothers so that he could be a compassionate and trustworthy high priest of God's religion, able to atone for human sins. That is, because he has himself been through temptation he is able to help others who are tempted.

This is the word of the Lord.

Gospel Acclamation
Lk 2:32

Alleluia, alleluia!
The light to enlighten the Gentiles
and give glory to Israel, your people.
Alleluia!

GOSPEL

A reading from the holy Gospel according to Luke 2:22-40

My eyes have seen your salvation.

*When the day came for them to be purified as laid down by the Law of Moses, the parents of Jesus took him up to Jerusalem to present him to the Lord – observing what stands written in the

Proper of Saints, 2 February

Law of the Lord: Every first-born male must be consecrated to the Lord – and also to offer in sacrifice, in accordance with what is said in the Law of the Lord, a pair of turtle-doves or two young pigeons. Now in Jerusalem there was a man named Simeon. He was an upright and devout man; he looked forward to Israel's comforting and the Holy Spirit rested on him. It had been revealed to him by the Holy Spirit that he would not see death until he had set eyes on the Christ of the Lord. Prompted by the Spirit he came to the Temple; and when the parents brought in the child Jesus to do for him what the Law required, he took him into his arms and blessed God: and he said:

> "Now, Master, you can let your servant go in peace,
> just as you promised;
> because my eyes have seen the salvation
> which you have prepared for all the nations to see,
> a light to enlighten the pagans
> and the glory of your people Israel." *

As the child's father and mother stood there wondering at the things that were being said about him, Simeon blessed them and said to Mary his mother, 'You see this child: he is destined for the fall and for the rising of many in Israel, destined to be a sign that is rejected – and a sword will pierce your own soul too – so that the secret thoughts of many may be laid bare.'

There was a prophetess also, Anna the daughter of Phanuel, of the tribe of Asher. She was well on in years. Her days of girlhood over, she had been married for seven years before becoming a widow. She was now eighty-four years old and never left the Temple, serving God night and day with fasting and prayer. She came by just at that moment and began to praise God; and she spoke of the child to all who looked forward to the deliverance of Jerusalem.

When they had done everything the Law of the Lord required, they went back to Galilee, to their own town of Nazareth. Meanwhile the child grew to maturity, and he was filled with wisdom; and God's favour was with him.

*This is the Gospel of the Lord. *

*Shorter form, Luke 2:22-32. Read between *.

Prayer over the Gifts
Lord,
accept the gifts your Church offers you with joy,

since in fulfilment of your will
your Son offered himself as a lamb without blemish
for the life of the world.

Preface of the Presentation of the Lord, P49.

Communion Antiphon: With my own eyes I have seen the salvation which you have prepared in the sight of all the nations.

Prayer after Communion
Lord,
you fulfilled the hope of Simeon,
who did not die
until he had been privileged to welcome the Messiah.
May this communion perfect your grace in us
and prepare us to meet Christ
when he comes to bring us into everlasting life,
for he is Lord for ever and ever.

3 February

St Blaise, bishop and martyr
Optional Memorial

Bishop of Sivas in Armenia in the fourth century.

Common of martyrs, pp.1865ff., or of pastors: bishops, pp.1878ff.

Opening Prayer
Lord,
hear the prayers of your martyr Blaise.
Give us the joy of your peace in this life
and help us to gain the happiness that will never end.

FIRST READING

A reading from the letter of St Paul to the Romans 5:1-5
We can boast about our sufferings.

Through our Lord Jesus Christ, by faith we are judged righteous and at peace with God, since it is by faith and through Jesus that we have entered this state of grace in which we can boast about looking forward to God's glory. But that is not all we can boast about; we can boast about our sufferings. These sufferings bring patience, as we know, and patience brings perseverance, and perseverance brings hope, and this hope is not deceptive, because the love of God has been poured into our hearts by the Holy Spirit which has been given us.

This is the word of the Lord.

Responsorial Psalm   Ps 116. ℟ Mk 16:15

   ℟ **Go out to the whole world; proclaim the Good News.**

or

   ℟ **Alleluia!**

1 O praise the Lord, all you nations,
acclaim him all you peoples! ℟

2 Strong is his love for us;
he is faithful for ever. ℟

Gospel Acclamation   Mt 28:19. 20
Alleluia, alleluia!
Go, make disciples of all the nations, says the Lord;
I am with you always, yes, to the end of time.
Alleluia!

GOSPEL

A reading from the holy Gospel according to Mark   16:15-20
Go out to the whole world; proclaim the Good News.

Jesus showed himself to the Eleven, and he said to them, 'Go out to the whole world; proclaim the Good News to all creation. He who believes and is baptised will be saved; he who does not believe will be condemned. These are the signs that will be associated with believers: in my name they will cast out devils; they will have the gift of tongues; they will pick up snakes in their hands, and be unharmed should they drink deadly poison; they will lay their hands on the sick, who will recover.'

And so the Lord Jesus, after he had spoken to them, was taken up into heaven: there at the right hand of God he took his place, while they, going out, preached everywhere, the Lord working with them and confirming the word by the signs that accompanied it.

This is the Gospel of the Lord.

also 3 February

St Ansgar, bishop — Optional Memorial

Born in France in 801. He became a monk of the Abbey of Corbie, and in 826 set out to preach the Gospel in Denmark, and then in Sweden. Made bishop of Hamburg and papal legate to Denmark and Sweden by Gregory IV. He died in 865.

Common of pastors: missionaries, pp. 1885ff., or: bishops, pp. 1878ff.

Opening Prayer

Father,
you sent Saint Ansgar
to bring the light of Christ to many nations.
May his prayers help us
to walk in the light of your truth.

FIRST READING

A reading from the prophet Isaiah 52:7-10
All the ends of the earth shall see the salvation of our God.

How beautiful on the mountains,
are the feet of one who brings good news,
who heralds peace, brings happiness,
proclaims salvation,
and tells Zion
'Your God is king!'

Listen! Your watchmen raise their voices,
they shout for joy together,
for they see the Lord face to face,
as he returns to Zion.

Break into shouts of joy together,
you ruins of Jerusalem;
for the Lord is consoling his people,
redeeming Jerusalem.

The Lord bares his holy arm
in the sight of all the nations,
and all the ends of the earth shall see
the salvation of our God.

This is the word of the Lord.

Responsorial Psalm Ps 95:1-3. 7-8. 10. ℟ v. 3

℟ **Proclaim the wonders of the Lord among all the peoples.**

1 O sing a new song to the Lord,
  sing to the Lord all the earth.
  O sing to the Lord, bless his name. ℟

2 Proclaim his help day by day,
  tell among the nations his glory
  and his wonders among all the peoples. ℟

3 Give the Lord, you families of peoples,
  give the Lord glory and power,
  give the Lord the glory of his name. ℟

4 Proclaim to the nations: 'God is king.'
  The world he made firm in its place;
  he will judge the peoples in fairness. ℟

Gospel Acclamation Mk 1:17

Alleluia, alleluia!
Follow me, says the Lord,
and I will make you into fishers of men.
Alleluia!

GOSPEL

A reading from the holy Gospel according to Mark 1:14-20
I will make you into fishers of men.

After John had been arrested, Jesus went into Galilee. There he proclaimed the Good News from God. 'The time has come,' he said, 'and the kingdom of God is close at hand. Repent, and believe the Good News.'

As he was walking along by the Sea of Galilee he saw Simon and his brother Andrew casting a net in the lake – for they were fishermen. And Jesus said to them, 'Follow me and I will make you into fishers of men.' And at once they left their nets and followed him.

Going on a little farther, he saw James son of Zebedee and his brother John; they too were in their boat, mending their nets. He called them at once and, leaving their father Zebedee in the boat with the men he employed, they went after him.

This is the Gospel of the Lord.

5 February

St Agatha, virgin and martyr — Memorial

Martyred at Catania, in Sicily, probably during the persecution of Decius. She is among the saints commemorated in the Roman Canon.

From the Common of Martyrs, pp. 1865ff., or of Virgins, pp. 1889ff.

Opening Prayer

Lord,
let your forgiveness be won for us
by the pleading of Saint Agatha,
who found favour with you by her chastity
and by her courage in suffering death for the gosepl.

FIRST READING

A reading from the first letter of St Paul to the Corinthians 1:26-31
God chose what is foolish by human reckoning.

Take yourselves, brothers, at the time when you were called: how many of you were wise in the ordinary sense of the word, how many were influential people, or came from noble families? No, it was to shame the wise that God chose what is foolish by human reckoning, and to shame what is strong that he chose what is weak by human reckoning; those whom the world thinks common and contemptible are the ones that God has chosen – those who are nothing at all to show up those who are everything. The human race has nothing to boast about to God, but you, God has made members of Christ Jesus and by God's doing he has become our wisdom, and our virtue, and our holiness, and our freedom. As scripture says: if anyone wants to boast, let him boast about the Lord.

This is the word of the Lord.

Responsorial Psalm

Ps 30:3-4. 6. 8. 16. 17. ℟ v. 6

℟ **Into your hands, O Lord,
I commend my spirit.**

1 Be a rock of refuge for me,
a mighty stronghold to save me,
for you are my rock, my stronghold.
For your name's sake, lead me and guide me. ℟

2. Into your hands I commend my spirit.
   It is you who will redeem me, Lord.
   As for me, I trust in the Lord:
   let me be glad and rejoice in your love. ℟

3. My life is in your hands, deliver me
   from the hands of those who hate me.
   Let your face shine on your servant.
   Save me in your love. ℟

Gospel Acclamation 1 Peter 4:14
Alleluia, alleluia!
It is a blessing for you,
when they insult you for bearing the name of Christ,
for the Spirit of God rests on you.
Alleluia!

GOSPEL

A reading from the holy Gospel according to Luke 9:23-26
Anyone who loses his life for my sake, that man will save it.

To all Jesus said, 'If anyone wants to be a follower of mine, let him renounce himself and take up his cross every day and follow me. For anyone who wants to save his life will lose it; but anyone who loses his life for my sake, that man will save it. What gain, then, is it for a man to have won the whole world and to have lost or ruined his very self? For if anyone is ashamed of me and of my words, of him the Son of Man will be ashamed when he comes in his own glory and in the glory of the Father and the holy angels.'

This is the Gospel of the Lord.

6 February

Ss Paul Miki, priest and companions, martyrs — Memorial

Born in Japan about 1565, Paul Miki entered the Society of Jesus and was a successful preacher of the Gospel. With twenty-five companions, he was tortured and crucified at Nagasaki on 5 February 1597.

Common of martyrs, pp.1865ff.

Opening Prayer

God our Father,
source of strength for all your saints,
you led Paul Miki and his companions
through the suffering of the cross
to the joy of eternal life.
May their prayers give us the courage
to be loyal until death in professing our faith.

FIRST READING

A reading from the letter of St Paul to the Galatians 2:19-20
I live now not with my own life but with the life of Christ who lives in me.

Through the Law I am dead to the Law, so that now I can live for God. I have been crucified with Christ, and I live now not with my own life but with the life of Christ who lives in me. The life I now live in this body I live in faith: faith in the Son of God who loved me and who sacrificed himself for my sake.

This is the word of the Lord.

Responsorial Psalm   Ps 125. ℟ v.5

℟ **Those who are sowing in tears
will sing when they reap.**

1 When the Lord delivered Zion from bondage,
   it seemed like a dream.
   Then was our mouth filled with laughter,
   on our lips there were songs. ℟

2 The heathens themselves said: 'What marvels
   the Lord worked for them!'
   What marvels the Lord worked for us!
   Indeed we were glad. ℟

3 Deliver us, O Lord, from our bondage
   as streams in dry land.
   Those who are sowing in tears
   will sing when they reap. ℟

4 They go out, they go out, full of tears,
   carrying seed for the sowing:
   they come back, they come back, full of song,
   carrying their sheaves. ℟

Gospel Acclamation Mt 28:19. 20
Alleluia, alleluia!
Go, make disciples of all the nations, says the Lord;
I am with you always, yes, to the end of time.
Alleluia!

GOSPEL

A reading from the holy Gospel according to Matthew 28:16-20
Go make disciples of all the nations.

The eleven disciples set out for Galilee, to the mountain where Jesus had arranged to meet them. When they saw him they fell down before him, though some hesitated. Jesus came up and spoke to them. He said, 'All authority in heaven and on earth has been given to me. Go, therefore, make disciples of all the nations; baptise them in the name of the Father and of the Son and of the Holy Spirit, and teach them to observe all the commands I gave you. And know that I am with you always; yes, to the end of time.'

This is the Gospel of the Lord.

In celebrations between 8 February and 28 February, if the day falls within Lent, the acclamation used before the Gospel should be one of the Lenten phrases, and 'Alleluia' should be omitted.

---

8 February

St Jerome Emiliani   Optional Memorial

Born in 1486, at Venice, he began life as a soldier, but was converted to Christ, gave all his possessions to the poor, and devoted his life to serving them. He founded the Order of Clerks Regular known as the Somaschi. He died of the plague in 1537.

From the Common of holy men and women: teachers, p.1901.

Opening Prayer
God of mercy,
you chose Jerome Emiliani
to be a father and friend of orphans.
May his prayers keep us faithful

Proper of Saints, 8 February

to the Spirit we have received,
who makes us your children.

FIRST READING

A reading from the book of Tobit 12:6-13
Prayer with fasting and alms is good.

Raphael took Tobit and his son Tobias aside and said, 'Bless God, utter his praise before all the living for all the favours he has given you. Bless and extol his name. Proclaim before all men the deeds of God as they deserve, and never tire of giving him thanks. It is right to keep the secret of a king, yet right to reveal and publish the works of God. Thank him worthily. Do what is good, and no evil can befall you.

'Prayer with fasting and alms with right conduct are better than riches with inquity. Better to practise almsgiving than to hoard up gold. Almsgiving saves from death and purges every kind of sin. Those who give alms have their fill of days; those who commit sin and do evil, bring harm on themselves.

'I am going to tell you the whole truth, hiding nothing from you. I have already told you that it is right to keep the secret of a king, yet right too to reveal in worthy fashion the works of God. So you must know that when you and Sarah were at prayer, it was I who offered your supplications before the glory of the Lord and who read them; so too when you were burying the dead. When you did not hesitate to get up and leave the table to go and bury a dead man, I was sent to test your faith.'

This is the word of the Lord.

Responsorial Psalm Ps 33:2-11. R̷ v.2 Alt. R̷ v.9

R̷ **I will bless the Lord at all times.**

or

R̷ **Taste and see that the Lord is good.**

1 I will bless the Lord at all times,
  his praise always on my lips;
  in the Lord my soul shall make its boast.
  The humble shall hear and be glad.   R̷

2 Glorify the Lord with me.
  Together let us praise his name.
  I sought the Lord and he answered me;
  from all my terrors he set me free.   R̷

3 Look towards him and be radiant;
   let your faces not be abashed.
   This poor man called; the Lord heard him
   and rescued him from all his distress. ℟

4 The angel of the Lord is encamped
   around those who revere him, to rescue them.
   Taste and see that the Lord is good.
   He is happy who seeks refuge in him. ℟

5 Revere the Lord, you his saints.
   They lack nothing, those who revere him.
   Strong lions suffer want and go hungry
   but those who seek the Lord lack no blessing. ℟

Gospel Acclamation Mt 5:3

Alleluia, alleluia!
How happy are the poor in spirit;
theirs is the kingdom of heaven.
Alleluia!

GOSPEL

A reading from the holy Gospel according to Mark 10:17-30
Go and sell everything you own and follow me.

Jesus was setting out on a journey when a man ran up, knelt before him and put this question to him, 'Good master, what must I do to inherit eternal life?' Jesus said to him, 'Why do you call me good? No one is good but God alone. You know the commandments: You must not kill; You must not commit adultery; You must not steal; You must not bring false witness; You must not defraud; Honour your father and mother.' And he said to him, 'Master, I have kept all these from my earliest days.' Jesus looked steadily at him and loved him, and he said, 'There is one thing you lack. Go and sell everything you own and give the money to the poor, and you will have treasure in heaven; then come, follow me.' But his face fell at these words and he went away sad, for he was a man of great wealth.

Jesus looked round and said to his disciples, 'How hard it is for those who have riches to enter the kingdom of God!' The disciples were astounded by these words, but Jesus insisted, 'My children,' he said to them, 'how hard it is to enter the kingdom of God! It is easier for a camel to pass through the eye of a needle than for a rich man to enter the kingdom of God.' They were more astonished than ever. 'In that case,' they said to one another, 'who can be saved?' Jesus gazed at them. 'For men,' he said, 'it is impossible, but not for God: because everything is possible for God.'*

Peter took this up. 'What about us?' he asked him. 'We have left everything and followed you.' Jesus said, 'I tell you solemnly, there is no one who has left house, brothers, sisters, father, children or land for my sake and for the sake of the gospel who will not be repaid a hundred times over, houses, brothers, sisters, mothers, children and land – not without persecutions – now in this present time and, in the world to come, eternal life.'

This is the Gospel of the Lord.

*Shorter form verses 17-27. Read between *.

10 February

St Scholastica, virgin — Memorial

Born at Norcia in Umbria in the late fifth century, the sister of St Benedict. She consecrated herself to God in early childhood, and lived near her brother's monastery at Monte Cassino.

Common of virgins, pp.1889ff., or of holy men and women: religious, pp.1898ff.

Opening Prayer

Lord,
as we recall the memory of Saint Scholastica,
we ask that by her example
we may serve you with love and obtain perfect joy.

FIRST READING

A reading from the Song of Songs   8:6-7
Love is strong as Death.

Set me like a seal on your heart,
like a seal on your arm.
For love is strong as Death,
jealousy relentless as Sheol.
The flash of it is a flash of fire,

Proper of Saints, 10 February 1419

a flame of the Lord himself.
Love no flood can quench,
no torrents drown.

Were a man to offer all the wealth of his house to buy love, contempt is all he would purchase.

This is the word of the Lord.

Responsorial Psalm Ps 148:1-2. 11-14. ℟ cf. vv.12. 13
℟ **Young men and maidens, praise the name of the Lord.**

or

℟ **Alleluia!**

1. Praise the Lord from the heavens,
   praise him in the heights.
   Praise him, all his angels,
   praise him, all his host. ℟

2. All earth's kings and peoples,
   earth's princes and rulers;
   young men and maidens,
   old men together with children. ℟

3. Let them praise the name of the Lord
   for he alone is exalted.
   The splendour of his name
   reaches beyond heaven and earth. ℟

4. He exalts the strength of his people.
   He is the praise of all his saints,
   of the sons of Israel,
   of the people to whom he comes close. ℟

Gospel Acclamation Jn 14:23
Alleluia, alleluia!
If anyone loves me he will keep my word,
and my Father will love him,
and we shall come to him
and make our home with him.
Alleluia!

GOSPEL

A reading from the holy Gospel according to Luke 10:38-42

Martha welcomed him into her house. Mary has chosen the better part.

In the course of their journey Jesus came to a village, and a woman named Martha welcomed him into her house. She had a sister called Mary, who sat down at the Lord's feet and listened to him speaking. Now Martha who was distracted with all the serving said, 'Lord, do you not care that my sister is leaving me to do the serving all by myself? Please tell her to help me.' But the Lord answered: 'Martha, Martha,' he said, 'you worry and fret about so many things, and yet few are needed, indeed only one. It is Mary who has chosen the better part; it is not to be taken from her.'

This is the Gospel of the Lord.

11 February

Our Lady of Lourdes Optional Memorial

The appearance of the Immaculate Virgin Mary to Bernadette Soubirous in 1858 near Lourdes in France was a call to penance and prayer, which has found particular expression in the service of the sick and disabled.

Common of the Blessed Virgin Mary, pp. 1858ff.

Opening Prayer
God of mercy,
we celebrate the feast of Mary,
the sinless mother of God.
May her prayers help us
to rise above our human weakness.

FIRST READING

A reading from the prophet Isaiah 66:10-14

Now towards her I send flowing peace, like a river.

Rejoice, Jerusalem,
be glad for her, all you who love her!
Rejoice, rejoice for her,
all you who mourned her!
That you may be suckled, filled,
from her consoling breast,

that you may savour with delight
her glorious breasts.
For thus says the Lord:
Now towards her I send flowing
peace, like a river,
and like a stream in spate
the glory of the nations.
At her breast will her nurslings be carried
and fondled in her lap.
Like a son comforted by his mother
will I comfort you.
(And by Jerusalem you will be comforted.)
At the sight your heart will rejoice,
and your bones flourish like the grass.
To his servants the Lord will reveal his hand.

This is the word of the Lord.

Responsorial Psalm   Jud 13:18-19. ℟ 15:9

℟ **You are the highest honour of our race!**

1 May you be blessed, my daughter, by God Most High,
beyond all women on earth;
and may the Lord God be blessed,
the Creator of heaven and earth. ℟

2 The trust you have shown
shall not pass from the memories of men,
but shall ever remind them
of the power of God. ℟

Gospel Acclamation   cf. Lk 1:45

Alleluia, alleluia!
Blessed are you, Virgin Mary,
who believed that the promise made you by the Lord
would be fulfilled.
Alleluia!

GOSPEL

A reading from the holy Gospel according to John   2:1-11
The mother of Jesus was there.

There was a wedding at Cana in Galilee. The mother of Jesus was there, and Jesus and his disciples had also been invited. When they ran out of wine, since the wine provided for the wedding was all finished, the mother of Jesus said to him, 'They have no wine.' Jesus said, 'Woman, why turn to me? My hour has not come yet.' His mother said to the servants, 'Do whatever he tells you.' There were six stone water jars standing there, meant for the ablutions that are customary among the Jews: each could hold twenty or thirty gallons. Jesus said to the servants, 'Fill the jars with water,' and they filled them to the brim. 'Draw some out now,' he told them, 'and take it to the steward.' They did this; the steward tasted the water, and it had turned into wine. Having no idea where it came from – only the servants who had drawn the water knew – the steward called the bridegroom and said, 'People generally serve the best wine first, and keep the cheaper sort till the guests have had plenty to drink; but you have kept the best wine till now.'

This was the first of the signs given by Jesus: it was given at Cana in Galilee. He let his glory be seen, and his disciples believed in him.

This is the Gospel of the Lord.

14 February

Ss Cyril, monk, and Methodius, bishop

Memorial

Cyril and Methodius were brothers, born in Salonika about 825 and educated at Constantinople. They translated the Bible, and liturgical texts, into the slavonic language. Cyril died in Rome on 14 February 869. Methodius was made a bishop and spent many years preaching the gospel in Hungary, despite resistance and hostility. He died in 885.

Common of pastors: founders of churches, pp.1876ff., or: missionaries, pp.1885ff.

Opening Prayer
Father,
you brought the light of the gospel to the Slavic nations
through Saint Cyril and his brother Saint Methodius.
Open our hearts to understand your teaching
and help us to become one in faith and praise.

Proper of Saints, 14 February 1423

FIRST READING

A reading from the Acts of the Apostles 13:46-49
We must turn to the pagans.

Paul and Barnabas spoke out boldly to the Jews, 'We had to proclaim the word of God to you first, but since you have rejected it, since you do not think yourselves worthy of eternal life, we must turn to the pagans. For this is what the Lord commanded us to do when he said:

"I have made you a light for the nations,
so that my salvation may reach the ends of the earth."

It made the pagans very happy to hear this and they thanked the Lord for his message; all who were destined for eternal life became believers. Thus the word of the Lord spread through the whole countryside.

This is the word of the Lord.

Responsorial Psalm Ps 116. ℟ Mk 16:15
℟ **Go out to the whole world;
proclaim the Good News.**

or

℟ **Alleluia!**

1 O praise the Lord, all you nations,
acclaim him all you peoples! ℟

2 Strong is his love for us;
he is faithful for ever. ℟

Gospel Acclamation Lk 4:18
Alleluia, alleluia!
The Lord has sent me to bring the good news to the poor,
to proclaim liberty to captives.
Alleluia!

GOSPEL

A reading from the holy Gospel according to Luke 10:1-9
The harvest is rich but the labourers are few.

The Lord appointed seventy-two others and sent them out ahead of him, in pairs, to all the towns and places he himself was to visit. He said to them, 'The harvest is rich but the labourers are few, so ask the Lord of the harvest to send labourers to his harvest. Start off now, but remember, I am sending you out like lambs among wolves. Carry no purse, no haversack, no sandals. Salute no one on the road. Whatever house you go into, let your first words be, "Peace to this house!" And if a man of peace lives there, your peace will go and rest on him; if not, it will come back to you. Stay in the same house, taking what food and drink they have to offer, for the labourer deserves his wages; do not move from house to house. Whenever you go into a town where they make you welcome, eat what is set before you. Cure those in it who are sick and say, "The kingdom of God is very near to you."'

This is the Gospel of the Lord.

17 February

The Seven Founders of the Order of Servites
Optional Memorial

Seven laymen of the city of Florence, in the mid-thirteenth century, renounced the world and lived as hermits on Monte Senario, about 12 miles from Florence. They had a particular devotion to the Blessed Virgin Mary; they spent themselves in the care of others and in preaching throughout Tuscany. The Order of Servites was founded from those who came to follow them, and was recognised by the Holy See in 1304.

Common of holy men and women: religious, pp.1898ff.

Opening Prayer
Lord,
fill us with the love
which inspired the seven holy brothers
to honour the mother of God with special devotion
and to lead your people to you.

FIRST READING

A reading from the letter of St Paul to the Romans 8:26-30
With those he justified, he shared his glory.

The Spirit comes to help us in our weakness. For when we cannot choose words in order to pray properly, the Spirit himself expresses our plea in a way that could never be put into words,

Proper of Saints, 17 February

and God who knows everything in our hearts knows perfectly well what he means, and that the pleas of the saints expressed by the Spirit are according to the mind of God.

We know that by turning everything to their good God co-operates with all those who love him, with all those that he has called according to his purpose. They are the ones he chose specially long ago and intended to become true images of his Son, so that his Son might be the eldest of many brothers. He called those he intended for this; those he called he justified, and with those he justified he shared his glory.

This is the word of the Lord.

Responsorial Psalm Ps 33:2-11. ℟ v.2. Alt. ℟ v.9

   ℟ **I will bless the Lord at all times.**

or

   ℟ **Taste and see that the Lord is good.**

1 I will bless the Lord at all times,
his praise always on my lips;
in the Lord my soul shall make its boast.
The humble shall hear and be glad. ℟

2 Glorify the Lord with me.
Together let us praise his name.
I sought the Lord and he answered me;
from all my terrors he set me free. ℟

3 Look towards him and be radiant;
let your faces not be abashed.
This poor man called; the Lord heard him
and rescued him from all his distress. ℟

4 The angel of the Lord is encamped
around those who revere him, to rescue them.
Taste and see that the Lord is good
He is happy who seeks refuge in him. ℟

5 Revere the Lord, you his saints.
They lack nothing, those who revere him.
Strong lions suffer want and go hungry
but those who seek the Lord lack no blessing. ℟

Gospel Acclamation

Mt 5:3

Alleluia, alleluia!
Happy the poor in spirit;
the kingdom of heaven is theirs!
Alleluia!

GOSPEL

A reading from the holy Gospel according to Matthew 19:27-29

You who have followed me will be repaid a hundred times over.

Peter said to Jesus: 'What about us? We have left everything and followed you. What are we to have, then?' Jesus said to him, 'I tell you solemnly, when all is made new and the Son of Man sits on his throne of glory, you will yourselves sit on twelve thrones to judge the twelve tribes of Israel. And everyone who has left houses, brothers, sisters, father, mother, children or land for the sake of my name will be repaid a hundred times over, and also inherit eternal life.'

This is the Gospel of the Lord.

21 February

St Peter Damian
bishop and doctor of the Church

Optional Memorial

Born at Ravenna in 1007, Peter Damian became a hermit at Fonte Avellana. He strove to remove the abuses, which had overtaken the church in feudal times, by his writings and his personal example of austere living. He was made Cardinal and Bishop of Ostia in 1057, and went as papal legate to France and Germany as well as Italy on the work of reform. He died in 1072.

Common of doctors of the Church, pp.1887ff., or of pastors: bishops, pp.1878ff.

Opening Prayer

All-powerful God,
help us to follow the teachings and example of Peter Damian.
By making Christ and the service of his Church
the first love of our lives,
may we come to the joys of eternal light,
where he lives and reigns with you and the Holy Spirit,
one God, for ever and ever.

FIRST READING

A reading from the second letter of St Paul to Timothy 4:1-5
Make the preaching of the Good News your life's work.

Before God and before Christ Jesus who is to be judge of the living and the dead, I put this duty to you, in the name of his Appearing and of his kingdom: proclaim the message and, welcome or unwelcome, insist on it. Refute falsehood, correct error, call to obedience – but do all with patience and with the intention of teaching. The time is sure to come when, far from being content with sound teaching, people will be avid for the latest novelty and collect themselves a whole series of teachers according to their own tastes; and then, instead of listening to the truth, they will turn to myths. Be careful always to choose the right course; be brave under trials; make the preaching of the Good News your life's work, in thoroughgoing service.

This is the word of the Lord.

Responsorial Psalm Ps 15:1-2. 5. 7-8. 11. ℟ cf. v.5

℟ **You are my inheritance, O Lord.**

1 Preserve me, God, I take refuge in you.
  I say to the Lord: 'You are my God.'
  O Lord, it is you who are my portion and cup;
  it is you yourself who are my prize.   ℟

2 I will bless the Lord who gives me counsel,
  who even at night directs my heart.
  I keep the Lord ever in my sight:
  since he is at my right hand, I shall stand firm.   ℟

3 You will show me the path of life,
  the fullness of joy in your presence,
  at your right hand happiness for ever.   ℟

Gospel Acclamation Jn 15:9.5
  Alleluia, alleluia!
  Remain in my love, says the Lord;
  whoever remains in me, with me in him,
  bears fruit in plenty.
  Alleluia!

GOSPEL

A reading from the holy Gospel according to John 15:1-8

Whoever remains in me, with me in him, bears fruit in plenty.

Jesus said to his disciples:

> 'I am the true vine,
> and my Father is the vinedresser.
> Every branch in me that bears no fruit
> he cuts away,
> and every branch that does bear fruit he prunes
> to make it bear even more.
> You are pruned already,
> by means of the word that I have spoken to you.
> Make your home in me, as I make mine in you.
> As a branch cannot bear fruit all by itself,
> but must remain part of the vine,
> neither can you unless you remain in me.
> I am the vine,
> you are the branches.
> Whoever remains in me, with me in him,
> bears fruit in plenty;
> for cut off from me you can do nothing.
> Anyone who does not remain in me
> is like a branch that has been thrown away
> – he withers;
> these branches are collected and thrown on the fire,
> and they are burnt.
> If you remain in me
> and my words remain in you,
> you may ask what you will
> and you shall get it.
> It is to the glory of my Father that you should bear much fruit,
> and then you will be my disciples.'

This is the Gospel of the Lord.

22 February
THE CHAIR OF ST PETER, APOSTLE   Feast

This feast has been kept at Rome since the fourth century, as a symbol of the unity of the church.

Entrance Antiphon: The Lord said to Simon Peter: I have prayed that your faith may not fail; and you in your turn must strengthen your brothers.

Opening Prayer
All-powerful Father,
you have built your Church
on the rock of Saint Peter's confession of faith.
May nothing divide or weaken
our unity in faith and love.

FIRST READING

A reading from the first letter of St Peter   5:1-4
I am an elder myself and a witness to the sufferings of Christ.

I have something to tell your elders: I am an elder myself, and a witness to the sufferings of Christ, and with you I have a share in the glory that is to be revealed. Be the shepherds of the flock of God that is entrusted to you: watch over it, not simply as a duty but gladly, because God wants it; not for sordid money, but because you are eager to do it. Never be a dictator over any group that is put in your charge, but be an example that the whole flock can follow. When the chief shepherd appears, you will be given the crown of unfading glory.

This is the word of the Lord.

Responsorial Psalm   Ps 22. ℟ v.1
℟ **The Lord is my shepherd;
there is nothing I shall want.**

1 The Lord is my shepherd;
   there is nothing I shall want.
   Fresh and green are the pastures
   where he gives me repose.
   Near restful waters he leads me,
   to revive my drooping spirit. ℟

2. He guides me along the right path;
   he is true to his name.
   If I should walk in the valley of darkness
   no evil would I fear.
   You are there with your crook and your staff;
   with these you give me comfort.

   ℟ **The Lord is my shepherd;
   there is nothing I shall want.**

3. You have prepared a banquet for me
   in the sight of my foes.
   My head you have anointed with oil;
   my cup is overflowing. ℟

4. Surely goodness and kindness shall follow me
   all the days of my life.
   In the Lord's own house shall I dwell
   for ever and ever. ℟

Gospel Acclamation   Mt 16:18

Alleluia, alleluia!
You are Peter, and on this rock
I will build my church.
And the gates of the underworld
can never hold out against it.
Alleluia!

GOSPEL

A reading from the holy Gospel according to Matthew   16:13-19
You are Peter, and I will give you the keys of the kingdom of heaven.

When Jesus came to the region of Caesarea Philippi he put this question to his disciples, 'Who do people say the Son of Man is?' And they said, 'Some say he is John the Baptist, some Elijah, and others Jeremiah or one of the prophets.' 'But you,' he said, 'who do you say I am?' Then Simon Peter spoke up, 'You are the Christ,' he said, 'the Son of the living God.' Jesus replied, 'Simon son of Jonah, you are a happy man! Because it was not flesh and blood that revealed this to you but my Father in heaven. So I now say to you: You are Peter and on this rock I will build my Church. And the gates of the underworld can never hold out against it. I will give you the keys of the kingdom of heaven: whatever you bind on earth shall be considered bound in heaven; whatever you loose on earth shall be considered loosed in heaven.'

These readings are used in a Votive Mass of St Peter.

Prayer over the Gifts
Lord,
accept the prayers and gifts of your Church.
With Saint Peter as our shepherd,
keep us true to the faith he taught
and bring us to your eternal kingdom.

Preface of the Apostles I or II, P64 or P65.

Communion Antiphon: Peter said: You are the Christ, the Son of the living God. Jesus answered: You are Peter, the rock on which I will build my Church.

Prayer after Communion
God our Father,
you have given us the body and blood of Christ
as the food of life.
On this feast of Peter the apostle,
may this communion bring us redemption
and be the sign and source of our unity and peace.

23 February

St Polycarp, bishop and martyr   Memorial

Bishop of Smyrna in the second century, a disciple of the apostle John, Polycarp was martyred in Smyrna in 155 AD.

From the Common of martyrs, pp.1865ff., or of pastors: bishops, pp.1878ff.

Opening Prayer
God of all creation,
you gave your bishop Polycarp
the privilege of being counted among the saints
who gave their lives in faithful witness to the gospel.
May his prayers give us the courage
to share with him the cup of suffering
and to rise to eternal glory.

FIRST READING

A reading from the book of the Apocalypse 2:8-11

I know the trials you have had, and how poor you are.

I, John, heard the Lord say to me: 'Write to the angel of the Church in Smyrna and say, "Here is the message of the First and the Last, who was dead and has come to life again: I know the trials you have had, and how poor you are – though you are rich – and the slanderous accusations that have been made by the people who profess to be Jews but are really members of the synagogue of Satan. Do not be afraid of the sufferings that are coming to you: I tell you, the devil is going to send some of you to prison to test you, and you must face an ordeal for ten days. Even if you have to die, keep faithful, and I will give you the crown of life for your prize. If anyone has ears to hear, let him listen to what the Spirit is saying to the Churches: for those who prove victorious there is nothing to be afraid of in the second death."'

This is the word of the Lord.

Responsorial Psalm   Ps 30:3-4. 6. 8. 16-17. ℟ v.6

℟ **Into your hands, O Lord,**
   I commend my spirit.

1 Be a rock of refuge for me,
   a mighty stronghold to save me,
   for you are my rock, my stronghold.
   For your name's sake, lead me and guide me.   ℟

2 Into your hands I commend my spirit.
   It is you who will redeem me, Lord.
   As for me, I trust in the Lord:
   let me be glad and rejoice in your love.   ℟

3 My life is in your hands, deliver me
   from the hands of those who hate me.
   Let your face shine on your servant.
   Save me in your love.   ℟

Gospel Acclamation
   Alleluia, alleluia!
   We praise you, O God,
   we acknowledge you to be the Lord;
   the noble army of martyrs praise you, O Lord.
   Alleluia!

Proper of Saints, 23 February

GOSPEL

A reading from the holy Gospel according to John 15:18-21

If they persecuted me, they will persecute you too.

Jesus said to his disciples:

'If the world hates you,
remember that it hated me before you.
If you belonged to the world,
the world would love you as its own;
but because you do not belong to the world,
because my choice withdrew you from the world,
therefore the world hates you.
Remember the words I said to you:
A servant is not greater than his master.
If they persecuted me,
they will persecute you too;
if they kept my word,
they will keep yours as well.
But it will be on my account that they will do all this,
because they do not know the one who sent me.'

This is the Gospel of the Lord.

THE HEAVENS ARE TELLING OF GOD'S GLORY
THE SKIES PROCLAIM HIS HANDIWORK

MARCH

4 March
St Casimir — Optional Memorial

Born in Poland in 1458, son of King Casimir IV of Poland. He died in 1484. He was intelligent and generous, involved in public affairs, but first and foremost a man of prayer. His devotion to the Blessed Sacrament and to Our Lady were most marked; he served the poor.

Common of holy men and women, pp.1894ff.

Opening Prayer
All-powerful God,
to serve you is to reign:
by the prayers of Saint Casimir,
help us to serve you in holiness and justice.

FIRST READING

A reading from the letter of St Paul   3:8-14
to the Philippians

I am racing for the finish, for the prize to which God calls us upwards to receive in Christ Jesus.

I believe nothing can happen that will outweigh the supreme advantage of knowing Christ Jesus my Lord. For him I have accepted the loss of everything, and I look on everything as so much rubbish if only I can have Christ and be given a place in him. I am no longer trying for perfection by my own efforts, the perfection that comes from the Law, but I want only the perfection that comes through faith in Christ, and is from God and based on faith. All I want to know is Christ and the power of his resurrection and to share his sufferings by reproducing the pattern of his death. That is the way I can hope to take my place in the resurrection of the dead. Not that I have become perfect yet: I have not won, but I am still running, trying to capture the prize for which Christ Jesus captured me. I can assure you my brothers, I am far from thinking that I have already won. All I can say is that I forget the past and I strain ahead for what is still to come; I am racing for the finish, for the prize to which God calls us upwards to receive in Christ Jesus.

This is the word of the Lord.

Responsorial Psalm
Ps 14:2-5. R v.1

R **The just will live in the presence of the Lord.**

1 Lord, who shall dwell on your holy mountain?
   He who walks without fault;
   he who acts with justice
   and speaks the truth from his heart;
   he who does not slander with his tongue. R

2 He who does no wrong to his brother,
   who casts no slur on his neighbour,
   who holds the godless in disdain,
   but honours those who fear the Lord. R

3 He who takes no interest on a loan
   and accepts no bribes against the innocent,
   such a man will stand firm for ever. R

Gospel Acclamation
Jn 13:34

Praise to you, O Christ, king of eternal glory!
I give you a new commandment:
love one another just as I have loved you,
says the Lord.
Praise to you, O Christ, king of eternal glory!

GOSPEL

A reading from the holy Gospel according to John 15:9-17
You are my friends if you do what I command you.

Jesus said to his disciples:

'As the Father has loved me,
so I have loved you.
Remain in my love.
If you keep my commandments
you will remain in my love,
just as I have kept my Father's commandments
and remain in his love.
I have told you this
so that my own joy may be in you
and your joy be complete.
This is my commandment:
love one another,
as I have loved you.
A man can have no greater love
than to lay down his life for his friends.
You are my friends,
if you do what I command you.
I shall not call you servants any more,
because a servant does not know
his master's business;
I call you friends,
because I have made known to you
everything I have learnt from my Father.
You did not choose me,
no, I chose you;
and I commissioned you
to go out and to bear fruit,
fruit that will last;
and then the Father will give you
anything you ask him in my name.
What I command you
is to love one another.'

This is the Gospel of the Lord.

7 March

Ss Perpetua and Felicity, martyrs — Memorial

Perpetua was 22, of a patrician family; Felicity was a slave: both were martyred in the public stadium at Carthage, in 203, during the persecution of Septimus Severus.

Common of martyrs, pp.1865ff., or of holy men and women, pp.1894ff.

Opening Prayer
Father,
your love gave the saints Perpetua and Felicity
courage to suffer a cruel martyrdom.
By their prayers, help us to grow in love of you.

FIRST READING

A reading from the letter of St Paul to the Romans　　　8:31-39
Neither death nor life can ever come between us and the love of God.

With God on our side who can be against us? Since God did not spare his own Son, but gave him up to benefit us all, we may be certain, after such a gift, that he will not refuse anything he can give. Could anyone accuse those that God has chosen? When God acquits, could anyone condemn? Could Christ Jesus? No! He not only died for us – he rose from the dead, and there at God's right hand he stands and pleads for us.

Nothing therefore can come between us and the love of Christ, even if we are troubled or worried, or being persecuted, or lacking food or clothes or being threatened or even attacked. As scripture promised: For your sake we are being massacred daily, and reckoned as sheep for the slaughter. These are the trials through which we triumph, by the power of him who loved us.

For I am certain of this: neither death nor life, no angel, no prince, nothing that exists, nothing still to come, not any power, or height or depth, nor any created thing, can ever come between us and the love of God made visible in Christ Jesus our Lord.

This is the word of the Lord.

Responsorial Psalm　　　　　　　　　　　　Ps 123:2-5. 7-8. ℟ v.7
　℟　**Our life, like a bird, has escaped
　　　from the snare of the fowler.**

1　If the Lord had not been on our side
　　when men rose against us,
　　then would they have swallowed us alive
　　when their anger was kindled.　℟

2　Then would the waters have engulfed us,
　　the torrent gone over us;
　　over our head would have swept
　　the raging waters.　℟

　　　　　　　　　　　　　　　　　　　　　　　(continued)

3 Indeed the snare has been broken
and we have escaped.
Our help is in the name of the Lord,
who made heaven and earth.

℟ **Our life, like a bird, has escaped
from the snare of the fowler.**

Gospel Acclamation   Mt 5:10

Praise and honour to you, Lord Jesus Christ.
Happy those who are persecuted in the cause of right:
theirs is the kingdom of heaven.
Praise and honour to you, Lord Jesus Christ.

GOSPEL

A reading from the holy Gospel according to Matthew   10:34-39
It is not peace I have come to bring, but a sword.

Jesus said to his apostles: 'Do not suppose that I have come to bring peace to the earth: it is not peace I have come to bring, but a sword. For I have come to set a man against his father, a daughter against her mother, a daughter-in-law against her mother-in-law. A man's enemies will be those of his own household.

'Anyone who prefers father or mother to me is not worthy of me. Anyone who prefers son or daughter to me is not worthy of me. Anyone who does not take his cross and follow in my footsteps is not worthy of me. Anyone who finds his life will lose it; anyone who loses his life for my sake will find it.'

This is the Gospel of the Lord.

8 March

St John of God, religious
Optional Memorial

Born in Portugal in 1495. He spent an adventurous youth as a soldier. A sermon of St John of Avila turned his mind to the sufferings of the poor and sick, and he devoted the rest of his life to their care. He established hospitals for the outcasts of society. Gradually others joined him in this work, and his followers established the Order of Hospitallers of St John of God. He died in 1550.

Common of holy men and women: religious, pp.1898ff., or: who worked for the under-privileged, pp.1900ff.

Proper of Saints, 8 March

Opening Prayer

Father,
you gave John of God
love and compassion for others.
Grant that by doing good for others
we may be counted among the saints in your kingdom.

FIRST READING

A reading from the first letter of St John   3:14-18
We, too, ought to give up our lives for our brothers.

We have passed out of death and into life,
and of this we can be sure
because we love our brothers.
If you refuse to love, you must remain dead;
to hate your brother is to be a murderer,
and murderers, as you know, do not have eternal life in them.
This has taught us love –
that he gave up his life for us;
and we, too, ought to give up our lives for our brothers.
If a man who was rich enough in this world's goods
saw that one of his brothers was in need,
but closed his heart to him,
how could the love of God be living in him?
My children,
our love is not to be just words or mere talk,
but something real and active.

    This is the word of the Lord.

Responsorial Psalm   Ps 111:1-9. ℟ v.1

  ℟ **Happy the man who fears the Lord.**

or

  ℟ **Alleluia!**

1 Happy the man who fears the Lord,
   who takes delight in his commands.
   His sons will be powerful on earth;
   the children of the upright are blessed. ℟

2 Riches and wealth are in his house;
   his justice stands firm for ever.
   He is a light in the darkness for the upright:
   he is generous, merciful and just. ℟   (continued)

3   The good man takes pity and lends,
    he conducts his affairs with honour.
    The just man will never waver:
    he will be remembered for ever.

    ℟   **Happy the man who fears the Lord.**

or

    ℟   **Alleluia!**

4   He has no fear of evil news;
    with a firm heart he trusts in the Lord.
    With a steadfast heart he will not fear;
    he will see the downfall of his foes.   ℟

5   Open-handed, he gives to the poor;
    his justice stands firm for ever.
    His head will be raised in glory.   ℟

Gospel Acclamation   Jn 13:34
Glory and praise to you, O Christ!
I give you a new commandment:
love one another just as I have loved you,
says the Lord.
Glory and praise to you, O Christ!

GOSPEL

A reading from the holy Gospel according to Matthew   25:31-40
In so far as you did this to one of the least of these brothers of mine, you did it to me.

Jesus said to his disciples: 'When the Son of Man comes in his glory, escorted by all the angels, then he will take his seat on his throne of glory. All the nations will be assembled before him and he will separate men one from another as the shepherd separates sheep from goats. He will place the sheep on his right hand and the goats on his left. Then the King will say to those on his right hand, "Come, you whom my Father has blessed, take for your heritage the kingdom prepared for you since the foundation of the world. For I was hungry and you gave me food; I was thirsty and you gave me drink; I was a stranger and you made me welcome; naked and you clothed me, sick and you visited me, in prison and you came to see me." Then the virtuous will say to him in reply, "Lord, when did we see you hungry and feed you; or thirsty and give you a drink? When did we see you a stranger and make you welcome; naked and clothe you; sick or in prison and go to see you?" And the King will answer, "I tell you solemnly, in so far as you did this to one of the least of these brothers of mine, you did it to me." '

This is the Gospel of the Lord.

9 March

St Frances of Rome, religious
Optional Memorial

Born in Rome, 1384. She was married and had three children. Her husband was well-off, the marriage was a happy one, and she devoted herself to the care of the needy. In 1425 she founded a Congregation of Oblates, following the rule of St Benedict. She died in 1440.

Common of holy men and women: religious, pp.1898ff.

Opening Prayer
Merciful Father,
in Frances of Rome
you have given us a unique example of love in marriage
as well as in religious life.
Keep us faithful in your service,
and help us to see and follow you
in all the aspects of life.

FIRST READING

A reading from the book of Proverbs   31:10-13. 19-20. 30-31
The woman who fears the Lord is the one to praise.

A perfect wife – who can find her?
She is far beyond the price of pearls.
Her husband's heart has confidence in her,
from her he will derive no little profit.
Advantage and not hurt she brings him
all the days of her life.
She is always busy with wool and with flax,
she does her work with eager hands.
She sets her hands to the distaff,
her fingers grasp the spindle.
She holds out her hand to the poor,
she opens her arms to the needy.
Charm is deceitful, and beauty empty;

the woman who is wise is the one to praise.
Give her a share in what her hands have worked for,
and let her works tell her praises at the city gates.

This is the word of the Lord.

Responsorial Psalm   Ps 33:2-11. ℟ v.2. Alt. ℟ v.9
    ℟ **I will bless the Lord at all times.**

or

    ℟ **Taste and see that the Lord is good.**

1 I will bless the Lord at all times,
   his praise always on my lips;
   in the Lord my soul shall make its boast.
   The humble shall hear and be glad. ℟

2 Glorify the Lord with me.
   Together let us praise his name.
   I sought the Lord and he answered me;
   from all my terrors he set me free. ℟

3 Look towards him and be radiant;
   let your faces not be abashed.
   This poor man called; the Lord heard him
   and rescued him from all his distress. ℟

4 The angel of the Lord is encamped
   around those who revere him, to rescue them.
   Taste and see that the Lord is good.
   He is happy who seeks refuge in him. ℟

5 Revere the Lord, you his saints.
   They lack nothing, those who revere him.
   Strong lions suffer want and go hungry
   but those who seek the Lord lack no blessing. ℟

Gospel Acclamation   Jn 13:34
   Glory to you, O Christ, you are the Word of God!
   I give you a new commandment:
   love one another just as I have loved you,
   says the Lord.
   Glory to you, O Christ, you are the Word of God!

Proper of Saints, 17 March

GOSPEL

A reading from the holy Gospel according to Matthew 22:35-40
You must love the Lord your God and your neighbour as yourself.

To disconcert Jesus, one of the Pharisees, a lawyer, put a question, 'Master, which is the greatest commandment of the Law?' Jesus said, 'You must love the Lord your God with all your heart, with all your soul, and with all your mind. This is the greatest and the first commandment. The second resembles it: You must love your neighbour as yourself. On these two commandments hang the whole Law, and the Prophets also.'

This is the Gospel of the Lord.

17 March

St Patrick, bishop — Optional Memorial

The apostle of Ireland was born in Great Britain about 385, and taken captive and sold as a slave to Ireland when a young boy. He worked as a herdsman, escaped, decided to become a priest. He was made Bishop of Ireland, and was indefatigable in preaching the faith throughout the country and in organising the Church there. He died in about 461, and was buried at Downpatrick.

Common of pastors: missionaries, pp. 1885ff., or: bishops, pp. 1878ff.

Opening Prayer

Let us pray
    [that like Saint Patrick the missionary
    we will be fearless witnesses
    to the gospel of Jesus Christ]

God our Father,
you sent Saint Patrick
to preach your glory to the people of Ireland.
By the help of his prayers,
may all Christians proclaim your love to all men.

or

Let us pray
    [that, like Saint Patrick,
    we may be loyal to our faith in Christ]

Father in heaven,
you sent the great bishop Patrick
to the people of Ireland to share his faith
and to spend his life in loving service.

May our lives bear witness
to the faith we profess,
and our love bring others
to the peace and joy of your gospel.

Proper readings for use in countries where this celebration is a solemnity will be found below, p.2045.

FIRST READING

A reading from the first letter of St Peter 4:7-11
Each one of you has received a special grace, so put yourselves at the service of others.

Keep a calm and sober mind. Above all, never let your love for each other grow insincere, since love covers over many a sin. Welcome each other into your houses without grumbling. Each one of you has received a special grace, so, like good stewards responsible for all these different graces of God, put yourselves at the service of others. If you are a speaker, speak in words which seem to come from God; if you are a helper, help as though every action was done at God's orders; so that in everything God may receive the glory, through Jesus Christ, since to him alone belong all glory and power for ever and ever. Amen.

This is the word of the Lord.

Responsorial Psalm Ps 95:1-3. 7-8. 10. ℟ v.3

℟ **Proclaim the wonders of the Lord among all the peoples.**

1. O sing a new song to the Lord,
   sing to the Lord all the earth.
   O sing to the Lord, bless his name. ℟

2. Proclaim his help day by day,
   tell among the nations his glory
   and his wonders among all the peoples. ℟

3. Give the Lord, you families of peoples,
   give the Lord glory and power,
   give the Lord the glory of his name. ℟

Proper of Saints, 17 March

4 Proclaim to the nations: 'God is king.'
  The world he made firm in its place;
  he will judge the peoples in fairness. ℟

Gospel Acclamation   Mk 1:17
  Praise to you, O Christ, king of eternal glory!
  Follow me, says the Lord,
  and I will make you into fishers of men.
  Praise to you, O Christ, king of eternal glory!

GOSPEL

A reading from the holy Gospel according to Luke   5:1-11
If you say so, I will pay out the nets.

Jesus was standing one day by the Lake of Gennesaret, with the crowd pressing round him listening to the word of God, when he caught sight of two boats close to the bank. The fishermen had gone out of them and were washing their nets. He got into one of the boats – it was Simon's – and asked him to put out a little from the shore. Then he sat down and taught the crowds from the boat.

When he had finished speaking he said to Simon, 'Put out into deep water and pay out your nets for a catch.' 'Master,' Simon replied, 'we worked hard all night long and caught nothing, but if you say so, I will pay out the nets.' And when they had done this they netted such a huge number of fish that their nets began to tear, so they signalled to their companions in the other boat to come and help them; when these came, they filled the two boats to sinking point.

When Simon Peter saw this he fell at the knees of Jesus saying, 'Leave me, Lord; I am a sinful man.' For he and all his companions were completely overcome by the catch they had made; so also were James and John, sons of Zebedee, who were Simon's partners. But Jesus said to Simon, 'Do not be afraid; from now on it is men you will catch.' Then, bringing their boats back to land, they left everything and followed him.

This is the Gospel of the Lord.

18 March

St Cyril of Jerusalem, bishop and doctor of the Church
Optional Memorial

Cyril, born in 315, became Bishop of Jerusalem in 348; the Arian controversy was at its height, and he was exiled several times. In his Catecheses *he set out the true teaching of Christianity and scripture and the tradition of the Church. He died in 386.*

Common of pastors: bishops, pp.1878ff., or of doctors of the church, pp.1887ff.

Opening Prayer

Father,
through Cyril of Jerusalem
you led your Church to a deeper understanding
of the mysteries of salvation.
Let his prayers help us to know your Son better
and to have eternal life in all its fullness.

FIRST READING

A reading from the first letter of St John　　　　5:1-5
This is the victory over the world – our faith.

Whoever believes that Jesus is the Christ
has been begotten by God;
and whoever loves the Father that begot him
loves the child whom he begets.
We can be sure that we love God's children
if we love God himself and do what he has commanded us;
this is what loving God is –
keeping his commandments;
and his commandments are not difficult,
because anyone who has been begotten by God
has already overcome the world;
this is the victory over the world –
our faith.
Who can overcome the world?
Only the man who believes that Jesus is the Son of God.

This is the word of the Lord.

Proper of Saints, 18 March 1447

Responsorial Psalm Ps 18:8-11. ℟ v.10. Alt. ℟ Jn 6:63
℟ **The decrees of the Lord are truth
and all of them just.**

or

℟ **Your words, are spirit, Lord,
and they are life.**

1 The law of the Lord is perfect,
 it revives the soul.
 The rule of the Lord is to be trusted,
 it gives wisdom to the simple. ℟

2 The precepts of the Lord are right,
 they gladden the heart.
 The command of the Lord is clear,
 it gives light to the eyes. ℟

3 The fear of the Lord is holy,
 abiding for ever.
 The decrees of the Lord are truth
 and all of them just. ℟

4 They are more to be desired than gold,
 than the purest of gold
 and sweeter are they than honey,
 than honey from the comb. ℟

Gospel Acclamation Jn 15:9. 5
Praise and honour to you, Lord Jesus!
Remain in my love, says the Lord;
whoever remains in me, with me in him,
bears fruit in plenty.
Praise and honour to you, Lord Jesus!

GOSPEL

A reading from the holy Gospel according to John 15:1-8
Whoever remains in me, with me in him, bears fruit in plenty.

Jesus said to his disciples:

 'I am the true vine,
 and my Father is the vinedresser.
 Every branch in me that bears no fruit
 he cuts away,

and every branch that does bear fruit he prunes
to make it bear even more.
You are pruned already,
by means of the word that I have spoken to you.
Make your home in me, as I make mine in you.
As a branch cannot bear fruit all by itself,
but must remain part of the vine,
neither can you unless you remain in me.
I am the vine,
you are the branches.
Whoever remains in me, with me in him,
bears fruit in plenty;
for cut off from me you can do nothing.
Anyone who does not remain in me
is like a branch that has been thrown away
– he withers;
these branches are collected and thrown on the fire,
and they are burnt.
If you remain in me
and my words remain in you,
you may ask what you will
and you shall get it.
It is to the glory of my Father that you should bear much fruit,
and then you will be my disciples.'

This is the Gospel of the Lord.

19 March

ST JOSEPH,
HUSBAND OF THE BLESSED VIRGIN MARY

Solemnity

A simple village carpenter, Joseph, the husband of Mary and guardian of the child Jesus, has become the guardian and patron of Christ's universal Church.

Entrance Antiphon: The Lord has put his faithful servant in charge of his household.

Opening Prayer
Let us pray
    [that the Church will continue
    the saving work of Christ]

Father,
you entrusted our Saviour to the care of Saint Joseph.
By the help of his prayers
may your Church continue to serve its Lord, Jesus Christ,
who lives and reigns with you and the Holy Spirit,
one God, for ever and ever.

FIRST READING

A reading from the second book of Samuel 7:4-5. 12-14. 16

The Lord God will give him the throne of his ancestor David.

The word of the Lord came to Nathan:
  'Go and tell my servant David, "Thus the Lord speaks: When your days are ended and you are laid to rest with your ancestors, I will preserve the offspring of your body after you and make his sovereignty secure. (It is he who shall build a house for my name, and I will make his royal throne secure for ever.) I will be a father to him and he a son to me. Your House and your sovereignty will always stand secure before me and your throne be established for ever." '

This is the word of the Lord.

Responsional Psalm Ps 88:2-5. 27. 29. ℟ v.37

℟ **His dynasty shall last for ever.**

1 I will sing for ever of your love, O Lord;
  through all ages my mouth will proclaim your truth.
  Of this I am sure, that your love lasts for ever,
  that your truth is firmly established as the heavens. ℟

2 I have made a covenant with my chosen one;
  I have sworn to David my servant:
  I will establish your dynasty for ever
  and set up your throne through all ages.' ℟

3 He will say to me: 'You are my father,
  my God, the rock who saves me.'
  I will keep my love for him always;
  for him my covenant shall endure. ℟

SECOND READING

A reading from the letter of St Paul to the Romans   4:13. 16-18. 22

Though it seemed Abraham's hope could not be fulfilled, he hoped and he believed.

The promise of inheriting the world was not made to Abraham and his descendants on account of any law but on account of the righteousness which consists in faith. That is why what fulfils the promise depends on faith, so that it may be a free gift and be available to all of Abraham's descendants, not only those who belong to the Law but also to those who belong to the faith of Abraham who is the father of all of us. As scripture says: I have made you the ancestor of many nations – Abraham is our father in the eyes of God, in whom he put his faith, and who brings the dead to life and calls into being what does not exist.

Though it seemed Abraham's hope could not be fulfilled, he hoped and he believed, and through doing so he did become the father of many nations exactly as he had been promised: Your descendants will be as many as the stars. This is the faith that was 'considered as justifying him'.

This is the word of the Lord.

Gospel Acclamation   Ps 83:5
  Glory and praise to you, O Christ!
  They are happy who dwell in your house, O Lord,
  for ever singing your praise.
  Glory and praise to you, O Christ!

GOSPEL

A reading from the holy Gospel according to Matthew
                                                                1:16. 18-21. 24

Joseph did what the angel of the Lord had told him to do.

Jacob was the father of Joseph the husband of Mary; of her was born Jesus who is called Christ.

This is how Jesus Christ came to be born. His mother Mary was betrothed to Joseph; but before they came to live together she was found to be with child through the Holy Spirit. Her husband Joseph, being a man of honour and wanting to spare her publicity, decided to divorce her informally. He had made up his mind to do this when the angel of the Lord appeared to him in a dream and said, 'Joseph son of David, do not be afraid to take Mary home as your wife, because she has conceived what is in

Proper of Saints, 19 March

her by the Holy Spirit. She will give birth to a son and you must name him Jesus, because he is the one who is to save his people from their sins.' When Joseph woke up he did what the angel of the Lord had told him to do.

This is the Gospel of the Lord.

Alternative Gospel

A reading from the holy Gospel according to Luke 2:41-51
See how worried your father and I have been, looking for you.

Every year the parents of Jesus used to go to Jerusalem for the feast of the Passover. When he was twelve years old, they went up for the feast as usual. When they were on their way home after the feast, the boy Jesus stayed behind in Jerusalem without his parents knowing it. They assumed he was with the caravan, and it was only after a day's journey that they went to look for him among their relations and acquaintances. When they failed to find him they went back to Jerusalem looking for him everywhere.

Three days later, they found him in the Temple, sitting among the doctors, listening to them, and asking them questions; and all those who heard him were astounded at his intelligence and his replies. They were overcome when they saw him, and his mother said to him, 'My child, why have you done this to us? See how worried your father and I have been, looking for you.' 'Why were you looking for me?' he replied 'Did you not know that I must be busy with my Father's affairs?' But they did not understand what he meant.

He then went down with them and came to Nazareth and lived under their authority.

This is the Gospel of the Lord.

The Profession of Faith is made.

Prayer over the Gifts
Father,
with unselfish love Saint Joseph cared for your Son,
born of the Virgin Mary.
May we also serve you at your altar with pure hearts.

Preface of Saint Joseph, P62.

Communion Antiphon: Come, good and faithful servant! Share the joy of your Lord!

Prayer after Communion
Lord,
today you nourish us at this altar
as we celebrate the feast of Saint Joseph.
Protect your Church always,
and in your love watch over the gifts you have given us.

23 March

St Turibius of Mongrovejo, bishop
Optional Memorial

Born in Spain about 1538, his ministry was exercised in South America, where he was sent as Bishop of Lima, Peru, in 1581. The oppression of the native population by the European community, and the decadence of the clergy, led him to set about reforming the Church and caring for the oppressed with zeal. He died in 1606, while on one of his journeys through the diocese.

Common of pastors: bishops, pp.1878ff.

Opening Prayer
Lord,
through the apostolic work of Saint Turibius
and his unwavering love of truth,
you helped your Church to grow.
May your chosen people continue to grow
in faith and holiness.

FIRST READING
A reading from the second letter of St Paul to Timothy

1:13-14; 2:1-3

Guard this precious thing with the help of the Holy Spirit.

Keep as your pattern the sound teaching you have heard from me, in the faith and love that are in Christ Jesus. You have been trusted to look after something precious; guard it with the help of the Holy Spirit who lives in us. Accept the strength, my dear son, that comes from the grace of Christ Jesus. You have heard everything that I teach in public; hand it on to reliable people so that they in turn will be able to teach others.

Proper of Saints, 23 March

Put up with your share of difficulties, like a good soldier of Christ Jesus.

This is the word of the Lord.

Responsorial Psalm Ps 95: 1-3. 7-8. 10. ℟ v.3

℟ **Proclaim the wonders of the Lord
among all the peoples.**

1 O sing a new song to the Lord,
   sing to the Lord all the earth.
   O sing to the Lord, bless his name. ℟

2 Proclaim his help day by day,
   tell among the nations his glory
   and his wonders among all the peoples. ℟

3 Give the Lord, you families of peoples,
   give the Lord glory and power,
   give the Lord the glory of his name. ℟

4 Proclaim to the nations: 'God is king.'
   The world he made firm in its place;
   he will judge the peoples in fairness. ℟

Gospel Acclamation Jn 10:14

Glory to you, O Christ, you are the Word of God!
I am the good shepherd, says the Lord;
I know my own sheep
and my own know me.
Glory to you, O Christ, you are the Word of God!

GOSPEL

A reading from the holy Gospel according to Matthew 9:35-37
The harvest is rich but the labourers are few.

Jesus made a tour through all the towns and villages, teaching in their synagogues, proclaiming the Good News of the kingdom and curing all kinds of diseases and sickness.

And when he saw the crowds he felt sorry for them because they were harassed and dejected, like sheep without a shepherd. Then he said to his disciples, 'The harvest is rich but the labourers are few, so ask the Lord of the harvest to send labourers to his harvest.'

This is the Gospel of the Lord.

25 March

THE ANNUNCIATION OF THE LORD
Solemnity

We celebrate that great day of decision: Mary's acceptance of the role that God has chosen for her in his plan of redemption.

Entrance Antiphon: As Christ came into the world, he said: Behold! I have come to do your will, O God.

Opening Prayer
Let us pray
   [that Christ, the Word made flesh,
   will make us more like him.]

God our Father,
your Word became man and was born of the Virgin Mary.
May we become more like Jesus Christ,
whom we acknowledge as our redeemer, God, and man.

or

Let us pray
   [that we may become more like Christ
   who chose to become one of us]

Almighty Father of our Lord Jesus Christ,
you have revealed the beauty of your power
by exalting the lowly virgin of Nazareth
and making her the mother of our Saviour.
May the prayers of this woman
bring Jesus to the waiting world
and fill the void of incompletion
with the presence of her child,
who lives and reigns . . .

FIRST READING

A reading from the prophet Isaiah   7:10-14. 8:10
The maiden is with child.

The Lord spoke to Ahaz and said, 'Ask the Lord your God for a sign for yourself coming either from the depths of Sheol or from the heights above.' 'No,' Ahaz answered, 'I will not put the Lord to the test.'

Then Isaiah said:

Listen now, House of David:
are you not satisfied with trying the patience of men
without trying the patience of my God, too?
The Lord himself, therefore,
will give you a sign.
It is this: the maiden is with child
and will soon give birth to a son
whom she will call Emmanuel,
a name which means, 'God-is-with-us'.

This is the word of the Lord.

Responsorial Psalm   Ps 39:7-11. ℟ vv.8. 9.

   ℟ **Here I am, Lord!**
      I come to do your will.

1. You do not ask for sacrifice and offerings,
but an open ear.
You do not ask for holocaust and victim.
Instead, here am I.   ℟

2. In the scroll of the book it stands written
that I should do your will.
My God, I delight in your law
in the depth of my heart.   ℟

3. Your justice I have proclaimed
in the great assembly.
My lips I have not sealed;
you know it, O Lord.   ℟

4. I have not hidden your justice in my heart
but declared your faithful help.
I have not hidden your love and your truth
from the great assembly.   ℟

SECOND READING

A reading from the letter to the Hebrews   10:4-10
I was commanded in the scroll of the book, 'God, here I am! I am coming to obey your will.'

Bulls' blood and goats' blood are useless for taking away sins, and this is what Christ said, on coming into the world:

You who wanted no sacrifice or oblation,
prepared a body for me.
You took no pleasure in holocausts or sacrifices for sin;
then I said,
just as I was commanded in the scroll of the book,
'God, here I am! I am coming to obey your will.'

Notice that he says first: You did not want what the Law lays down as the things to be offered, that is: the sacrifices, the oblations, the holocausts and the sacrifices for sin, and you took no pleasure in them; and then he says: Here I am! I am coming to obey your will. He is abolishing the first sort to replace it with the second. And this will was for us to be made holy by the offering of his body made once and for all by Jesus Christ.

This is the word of the Lord.

Gospel Acclamation   Jn 1:14
Praise to you, O Christ, king of eternal glory!
The Word was made flesh,
he lived among us,
and we saw his glory.
Praise to you, O Christ, king of eternal glory!

GOSPEL

A reading from the holy Gospel according to Luke   1:26-38
You are to conceive and bear a son.

The angel Gabriel was sent by God to a town in Galilee called Nazareth, to a virgin betrothed to a man named Joseph, of the House of David; and the virgin's name was Mary. He went in and said to her, 'Rejoice, so highly favoured! The Lord is with you.' She was deeply disturbed by these words and asked herself what this greeting could mean, but the angel said to her, 'Mary, do not be afraid; you have won God's favour. Listen! You are to conceive and bear a son, and you must name him Jesus. He will be great and will be called Son of the Most High. The Lord God will give him the throne of his ancestor David; he will rule over the House of Jacob for ever and his reign will have no end.' Mary said to the angel, 'But how can this come about, since I am a virgin?' 'The Holy Spirit will come upon you,' the angel answered, 'and the power of the Most High will cover you with its shadow. And so the child will be holy and will be called Son of God. Know this too: your kinswoman Elizabeth has, in her old age, herself conceived a son, and she whom people called barren is now in her sixth month, for nothing is impossible to God.' 'I am the handmaid of the Lord,' said Mary, 'let what you have said be done to me.' And the angel left her.

This is the Gospel of the Lord.

In the Profession of Faith, all genuflect at the words, *and was made man.*

Prayer over the Gifts
Almighty Father,
as we recall the beginning of the Church
when your Son became man,
may we celebrate with joy today
this sacrament of your love.

Preface of the Annunciation, P44.

Communion Antiphon: The Virgin is with child and shall bear a son, and she will call him Emmanuel.

Prayer after Communion
Lord,
may the sacrament we share
strengthen our faith and hope in Jesus, born of a virgin
and truly God and man.
By the power of his resurrection
may we come to eternal joy.

In celebrations between 27 March and 22 April, if the day falls within Lent, the acclamation used before the Gospel should be one of the Lenten phrases, and 'Alleluia' should be omitted.

PEACE BE WITH YOU

APRIL

2 April
St Francis of Paola, hermit
Optional Memorial

Born 1416, at Paola in Calabria, Francis lived as a hermit. He attracted many followers by his piety and holiness. He founded a congregation of hermits, which became the Order of Minims. He died at Tours in France in 1507.

Common of holy men and women: religious, pp.1898ff.

Opening Prayer
Father of the lowly,
you raised Saint Francis of Paola
to the glory of your saints.
By his example and prayers,
may we come to the rewards
you have promised the humble.

FIRST READING

A reading from the letter of St Paul to the Philippians   3:8-14

I am racing for the finish, for the prize to which God calls us upwards to receive in Christ Jesus.

I believe nothing can happen that will outweigh the supreme advantage of knowing Christ Jesus my Lord. For him I have accepted the loss of everything, and I look on everything as so much rubbish if only I can have Christ and be given a place in him. I am no longer trying for perfection by my own efforts, the perfection that comes from the Law, but I want only the perfection that comes through faith in Christ, and is from God based on faith. All I want is to know Christ and the power of his resurrection and to share his sufferings by reproducing the pattern of his death. That is the way I can hope to take my place in the resurrection of the dead. Not that I have become perfect yet: I have not yet won, but I am still running, trying to capture the prize for which Christ Jesus captured me. I can assure you my brothers, I am far from thinking that I have already won. All I can say is that I forget the past and I strain ahead for what is still to come; I am racing for the finish, for the prize to which God calls us upwards to receive in Christ Jesus.

This is the word of the Lord.

Responsorial Psalm   Ps 15:1-2. 5. 7-8. 11. ℟ cf. v.5
℟ **You are my inheritance, O Lord.**

1 Preserve me, God, I take refuge in you.
  I say to the Lord: 'You are my God.'
  O Lord, it is you who are my portion and cup;
  it is you yourself who are my prize.   ℟

2 I will bless the Lord who gives me counsel,
  who even at night directs my heart.
  I keep the Lord ever in my sight:
  since he is at my right hand, I shall stand firm.   ℟

3 You will show me the path of life,
  the fullness of joy in your presence,
  at your right hand happiness for ever.   ℟

Gospel Acclamation   Mt 5:3
Alleluia, alleluia!
How happy are the poor in spirit;
theirs is the kingdom of heaven.
Alleluia!

GOSPEL

A reading from the holy Gospel according to Luke   12:32-34
It has pleased your Father to give you the kingdom.

Jesus said to his disciples: 'There is no need to be afraid, little flock, for it has pleased your Father to give you the kingdom.

'Sell your possessions and give alms. Get yourselves purses

that do not wear out, treasure that will not fail you, in heaven where no thief can reach it and no moth destroy it. For where your treasure is, there will your heart be also.'

This is the Gospel of the Lord.

4 April

St Isidore, bishop and doctor of the Church
Optional Memorial

Born in Seville, about 560; appointed Bishop of Seville in 601. Isidore convoked various synods, notably the fourth Council of Toledo in 633, for the good government of the Church in Spain. He wrote a great deal, and was very concerned with the education of young people, founding a school which was much ahead of its time. He died in 636.

Common of pastors: bishops, pp.1876ff., or of doctors of the Church, pp.1887ff.

Opening Prayer
Lord,
hear the prayers we offer in commemoration of Saint Isidore.
May your Church learn from his teaching
and benefit from his intercession.

FIRST READING

A reading from the second letter of St Paul to the Corinthians 4:1-2. 5-7
We preach Christ Jesus and ourselves as your servants for Jesus' sake.

Since we have by an act of mercy been entrusted with this work of administration, there is no weakening on our part. On the contrary, we will have none of the reticence of those who are ashamed, no deceitfulness or watering down the word of God; but the way we commend ourselves to every human being with a conscience is by stating the truth openly in the sight of God. For it is not ourselves that we are preaching, but Christ Jesus as the Lord, and ourselves as your servants for Jesus' sake. It is the same God that said, 'Let there be light shining out of darkness', who has shone in our minds to radiate the light of the knowledge of God's glory, the glory on the face of Christ.

We are only the earthenware jars that hold this treasure, to make it clear that such an overwhelming power comes from God and not from us.

This is the word of the Lord.

Responsorial Psalm   Ps 36:3-6. 30-31. ℟ v.30

℟ **The just man's mouth utters wisdom.**

1 If you trust in the Lord and do good,
    then you will live in the land and be secure.
    If you find your delight in the Lord,
    he will grant your heart's desire. ℟

2 Commit your life to the Lord,
    trust in him and he will act,
    so that your justice breaks forth like the light,
    your cause like the noon-day sun. ℟

3 The just man's mouth utters wisdom
    and his lips speak what is right;
    the law of his God is in his heart,
    his steps shall be saved from stumbling. ℟

Gospel Acclamation   Jn 15:5
Alleluia, alleluia!
I am the vine,
you the branches, says the Lord.
Whoever remains in me, with me in him,
bears fruit in plenty.
Alleluia!

GOSPEL

A reading from the holy Gospel according to Luke   6:43-45
A man's words flow out of what fills his heart.

Jesus said to his disciples: 'There is no sound tree that produces rotten fruit, nor again a rotten tree that produces sound fruit. For every tree can be told by its own fruit: people do not pick figs from thorns, nor gather grapes from brambles. A good man draws what is good from the store of goodness in his heart; a bad man draws what is bad from the store of badness. For a man's words flow out of what fills his heart.'

This is the Gospel of the Lord.

5 April

St Vincent Ferrer, priest
Optional Memorial

Born at Valencia in Spain, in 1350. Joined the Dominican Order at the age of seventeen, and taught and preached until he was forty. Then he began to travel extensively, particularly in France, preaching and exhorting people to the faith.

Common of pastors: missionaries, pp. 1885ff.

Opening Prayer
Father,
you called Saint Vincent Ferrer
to preach the gospel of the last judgement.
Through his prayers may we come with joy
to meet your Son in the kingdom of heaven,
where he lives and reigns with you and the Holy Spirit,
one God, for ever and ever.

FIRST READING

A reading from the second letter of St Paul to Timothy 4:1-5
Make the preaching of the Good News your life's work.

Before God and before Christ Jesus who is to be judge of the living and the dead, I put this duty to you, in the name of his Appearing and of his kingdom: proclaim the message and, welcome or unwelcome, insist on it. Refute falsehood, correct error, call to obedience – but do all with patience and with the intention of teaching. The time is sure to come when, far from being content with sound teaching, people will be avid for the latest novelty and collect themselves a whole series of teachers according to their own tastes; and then, instead of listening to the truth, they will turn to myths. Be careful always to choose the right course; be brave under trials; make the preaching of the Good News your life's work, in thorough-going service.

This is the word of the Lord.

Responsorial Psalm Ps 39:2. 4. 7-10. ℟ cf. vv.8-9
 ℟ **Here I am, Lord!**
  I come to do your will.

1 I waited, I waited for the Lord
 and he stooped down to me;

he heard my cry.
He put a new song into my mouth,
praise of our God.   ℟

2 You do not ask for sacrifice and offerings,
   but an open ear.
   You do not ask for holocaust and victim.
   Instead, here am I.   ℟

3 In the scroll of the book it stands written
   that I should do your will.
   My God, I delight in your law
   in the depth of my heart.   ℟

4 Your justice I have proclaimed
   in the great assembly.
   My lips I have not sealed;
   you know it, O Lord.   ℟

Gospel Acclamation   Lk 21:36
Alleluia, alleluia!
Stay awake, praying at all times
for the strength to stand with confidence
before the Son of Man.
Alleluia!

GOSPEL

A reading from the holy Gospel according to Luke   12:35-40
You too must stand ready.

Jesus said to his disciples:
'See that you are dressed for action and have your lamps lit. Be like men waiting for their master to return from the wedding feast, ready to open the door as soon as he comes and knocks. Happy those servants whom the master finds awake when he comes. I tell you solemnly, he will put on an apron, sit them down at table and wait on them. It may be in the second watch he comes, or in the third, but happy those servants if he finds them ready. You may be quite sure of this, that if the householder had known at what hour the burglar would come, he would not have let anyone break through the wall of his house. You too must stand ready, because the Son of Man is coming at an hour you do not expect.'

This is the Gospel of the Lord.

7 April
St John Baptist de la Salle, priest — Memorial

Born at Rheims, France, in 1651; opened his first school for poor children in 1679 in Rheims, and later in Paris and Rouen. He formed a religious congregation to carry out the work of Christian education, insisting on a life of poverty, penance and prayer. He met with much opposition from his companions. He died in 1719, at Rouen.

Common of pastors, pp.1876ff., or of holy men and women: teachers, p.1901.

Opening Prayer
Father,
you chose Saint John Baptist de la Salle
to give young people a Christian education.
Give your Church teachers who will devote themselves
to helping your children grow
as Christian men and women.

FIRST READING
A reading from the second letter of St Paul to Timothy

1:13-14; 2:1-3

Guard this precious thing with the help of the Holy Spirit.

Keep as your pattern the sound teaching you have heard from me, in the faith and love that are in Christ Jesus. You have been trusted to look after something precious; guard it with the help of the Holy Spirit who lives in us. Accept the strength, my dear son, that comes from the grace of Christ Jesus. You have heard everything that I teach in public; hand it on to reliable people so that they in turn will be able to teach others.

Put up with your share of difficulties, like a good soldier of Christ Jesus.

This is the word of the Lord.

Proper of Saints, 7 April 1465

Responsorial Psalm
Ps 1:1-4. 6. ℟ v.2. Alt. ℟ Ps 39:5. Alt. ℟ Ps 91:13-14

℟ **His delight is the law of the Lord.**

or

℟ **Happy the man who has placed his trust in the Lord.**

or

℟ **The just will flourish like the palm-tree
in the courts of our God.**

1 Happy indeed is the man
who follows not the counsel of the wicked;
nor lingers in the way of sinners
nor sits in the company of scorners,
but whose delight is the law of the Lord
and who ponders his law day and night. ℟

2 He is like a tree that is planted
beside the flowing waters,
that yields its fruit in due season
and whose leaves shall never fade;
and all that he does shall prosper. ℟

3 Not so are the wicked, not so!
For they like winnowed chaff
shall be driven away by the wind;
for the Lord guards the way of the just
but the way of the wicked leads to doom. ℟

Gospel Acclamation Mt 23:11. 12
Alleluia, alleluia!
The greatest among you must be your servant, says the Lord;
the man who humbles himself will be exalted.
Alleluia!

GOSPEL

A reading from the holy Gospel according to Matthew 18:1-5
Unless you become like little children you will never enter the kingdom of heaven.

The disciples came to Jesus and said, 'Who is the greatest in the kingdom of heaven?' So he called a little child to him and set the child in front of them. Then he said, 'I tell you solemnly, unless you change and become like little children you will never enter the kingdom of heaven. And so, the one who makes himself as little as this little child is the greatest in the kingdom of heaven.

Anyone who welcomes a little child like this in my name welcomes me.'

This is the Gospel of the Lord.

11 April

St Stanislaus, bishop and martyr Memorial

Born in Poland about 1030, studied in Paris and Liege, became bishop of Cracow in 1071. Stanislaus was a pastoral bishop, concerned with the reform of the clergy and the sanctity of the people; he helped the poor, and made a visitation of the clergy each year. He came into conflict with the king, Boleslav, who had him murdered in 1079.

Common of martyrs, pp.1865ff., or of pastors: bishops, pp.1878ff.

Opening Prayer
Father,
to honour you, Saint Stanislaus faced martyrdom with courage.
Keep us strong and loyal in our faith until death.

FIRST READING

A reading from the book of the Apocalypse 12:10-12
In the face of death they would not cling to life.

I, John, heard a voice shout from heaven, 'Victory and power and empire for ever have been won by our God, and all authority for his Christ, now that the persecutor, who accused our brothers day and night before our God, has been brought down. They have triumphed over him by the blood of the Lamb and by the witness of their martyrdom, because even in the face of death they would not cling to life. Let the heavens rejoice and all who live there.'

This is the word of the Lord.

Responsorial Psalm Ps 33:2-9. ℟ v.5
℟ **From all my terrors the Lord set me free.**

1 I will bless the Lord at all times,
his praise always on my lips;
in the Lord my soul shall make its boast.
The humble shall hear and be glad. ℟

2   Glorify the Lord with me.
    Together let us praise his name.
    I sought the Lord and he answered me;
    from all my terrors he set me free.   ℟

3   Look towards him and be radiant;
    let your faces not be abashed.
    This poor man called; the Lord heard him
    and rescued him from all his distress.   ℟

4   The angel of the Lord is encamped
    around those who revere him, to rescue them.
    Taste and see that the Lord is good.
    He is happy who seeks refuge in him.   ℟

Gospel Acclamation   2 Cor 1:3-4
    Alleluia, alleluia!
    Blessed be God, a gentle Father,
    and the God of all consolation,
    who comforts us in all our sorrows.
    Alleluia!

GOSPEL

A reading from the holy Gospel according to John   17:11-19
The world hated them.

Jesus raised his eyes to heaven and said,

'Holy Father,
keep those you have given me true to your name,
so that they may be one like us.
While I was with them,
I kept those you had given me true to your name.
I have watched over them and not one is lost
except the one who chose to be lost,
and this was to fulfil the scriptures.
But now I am coming to you
and while still in the world I say these things
to share my joy with them to the full.
I passed your word on to them,
and the world hated them,
because they belong to the world
no more than I belong to the world.
I am not asking you to remove them from the world,

but to protect them from the evil one.
They do not belong to the world
any more than I belong to the world.
Consecrate them in the truth;
your word is truth.
As you sent me into the world,
I have sent them into the world,
and for their sake I consecrate myself
so that they too may be consecrated in truth.'

This is the Gospel of the Lord.

13 April
St Martin I, pope and martyr
Optional Memorial

Born at Todi in Umbria. Martin was elected Pope in 649; he immediately called a Council to condemn the Monothelite heresy, which denied the two natures of Christ. This brought him into conflict with Emperor Constant II, who had him exiled first to Constantinople where he was condemned to death and stripped of his honours, and then to the Crimea, where he died in 656.

Common of martyrs, pp.1865ff., or of pastors: popes, pp.1876ff.

Opening Prayer
Merciful God, our Father,
neither hardship, pain, nor the threat of death
could weaken the faith of Saint Martin.
Through our faith, give us courage
to endure whatever sufferings the world may inflict upon us.

FIRST READING
A reading from the second letter of St Paul to Timothy
2:8-13; 3:10-12

Anybody who tries to live in devotion to Christ is certain to be attacked.

Remember the Good News that I carry, 'Jesus Christ risen from the dead, sprung from the race of David'; it is on account of this that I have my own hardships to bear, even to being chained like a criminal – but they cannot chain up God's news. So I bear it all for the sake of those who are chosen, so that in the end they may have the salvation that is in Christ Jesus and the eternal glory that comes with it.

Here is a saying that you can rely on:

Proper of Saints, 13 April

If we have died with him, then we shall live with him.
If we hold firm, then we shall reign with him.
If we disown him, then he will disown us.
We may be unfaithful, but he is always faithful,
for he cannot disown his own self.

You know what I have taught, how I have lived, what I have aimed at; you know my faith, my patience and my love; my constancy and the persecutions and hardships that came to me in places like Antioch, Iconium and Lystra – all the persecutions I have endured; and the Lord has rescued me from every one of them. You are well aware, then, that anybody who tries to live in devotion to Christ is certain to be attacked.

This is the word of the Lord.

Responsorial Psalm   Ps 125. ℟ v.5

℟ **Those who are sowing in tears**
   will sing when they reap.

1 When the Lord delivered Zion from bondage,
   it seemed like a dream.
   Then was our mouth filled with laughter,
   on our lips there were songs.   ℟

2 The heathens themselves said: 'What marvels
   the Lord worked for them!'
   What marvels the Lord worked for us!
   Indeed we were glad.   ℟

3 Deliver us, O Lord, from our bondage
   as streams in dry land.
   Those who are sowing in tears
   will sing when they reap.   ℟

4 They go out, they go out, full of tears,
   carrying seed for the sowing:
   they come back, they come back, full of song,
   carrying their sheaves.   ℟

Gospel Acclamation
Alleluia, alleluia!
We praise you, O God,
we acknowledge you to be the Lord;
the noble army of martyrs praise you, O Lord.
Alleluia!

GOSPEL

A reading from the holy Gospel according to John 15:18-21

If they persecuted me, they will persecute you too.

Jesus said to his disciples:

'If the world hates you,
remember that it hated me before you.
If you belonged to the world,
the world would love you as its own;
but because you do not belong to the world,
because my choice withdrew you from the world,
therefore the world hates you.
Remember the words I said to you:
A servant is not greater than his master.
If they persecuted me,
they will persecute you too;
if they kept my word,
they will keep yours as well.
But it will be on my account that they will do all this,
because they do not know the one who sent me.'

This is the Gospel of the Lord.

21 April

St Anselm, bishop and doctor of the Church
Optional Memorial

Born in Piedmont in 1033, Anselm entered the Benedictine Order at the monastery of Le Bec in France, where he taught theology. He became Archbishop of Canterbury, in England, in 1093, and fought strenuously for the freedom of the Church from the temporal power. He was a man of great holiness, and his writings, particularly in mystical theology, are renowned.

Common of pastors: bishops, pp.1878ff., or of doctors of the church, pp.1887ff.

Opening Prayer

Father,
you called Saint Anselm
to study and teach the sublime truths you have revealed.
Let your gift of faith come to the aid of our understanding
and open our hearts to your truth.

Proper of Saints, 21 April

FIRST READING

A reading from the letter of St Paul to the Ephesians 3:14-19
To know the love of Christ, which is beyond all knowledge.

This is what I pray, kneeling before the Father, from whom every family, whether spiritual or natural, takes its name:

Out of his infinite glory, may he give you the power through his Spirit for your hidden self to grow strong, so that Christ may live in your hearts through faith, and then, planted in love and built on love, you will with all the saints have strength to grasp the breadth and the length, the height and the depth; until, knowing the love of Christ, which is beyond all knowlege, you are filled with the utter fullness of God.

This is the word of the Lord.

Responsional Psalm Ps 33:2-11. ℟ v.2. Alt. ℟ v.9

℟ **I will bless the Lord at all times.**

or

℟ **Taste and see that the Lord is good.**

1 I will bless the Lord at all times,
 his praise always on my lips;
 in the Lord my soul shall make its boast.
 The humble shall hear and be glad. ℟

2 Glorify the Lord with me.
 Together let us praise his name.
 I sought the Lord and he answered me;
 from all my terrors he set me free. ℟

3 Look towards him and be radiant;
 let your faces not be abashed.
 This poor man called; the Lord heard him
 and rescued him from all his distress. ℟

4 The angel of the Lord is encamped
 around those who revere him, to rescue them.
 Taste and see that the Lord is good.
 He is happy who seeks refuge in him. ℟

5 Revere the Lord, you his saints.
 They lack nothing, those who revere him.
 Strong lions suffer want and go hungry
 but those who seek the Lord lack no blessing. ℟

Gospel Acclamation cf. Jn 6:63. 68
Alleluia, alleluia!
Your words are spirit, Lord, and they are life;
you have the message of eternal life.
Alleluia!

GOSPEL

A reading from the holy Gospel according to Matthew 7:21-29

He taught them with authority.

Jesus said to his disciples: 'It is not those who say to me, "Lord, Lord," who will enter the kingdom of heaven, but the person who does the will of my Father in heaven. When the day comes many will say to me, "Lord, Lord, did we not prophesy in your name, cast out demons in your name, work many miracles in your name?" Then I shall tell them to their faces: I have never known you; away from me, you evil men!

'Therefore, everyone who listens to these words of mine and acts on them will be like a sensible man who built his house on rock. Rain came down, floods rose, gales blew and hurled themselves against that house, and it did not fall; it was founded on rock. But everyone who listens to these words of mine and does not act on them will be like a stupid man who built his house on sand. Rain came down, floods rose, gales blew and struck that house, and it fell, and what a fall it had!'

Jesus had now finished what he wanted to say, and his teaching made a deep impression on the people because he taught them with authority, and not like their own scribes.

This is the Gospel of the Lord.

23 April
St George, martyr   Optional Memorial

Since the fourth century Saint George has been venerated in Lydia, in Palestine. Tradition holds that he was a soldier who died for the faith and his cult spread throughout the East and the West. He was adopted as Patron of England during the Crusades.

Common of martyrs, pp.1865ff.

Opening Prayer
Lord,
hear the prayers of those who praise your mighty power.

Proper of Saints, 23 April 1473

As Saint George was ready to follow Christ in suffering and death,
so may he be ready to help us in our weakness.

FIRST READING

A reading from the book of the Apocalypse 21:5-7

It is the rightful inheritance of the one who proves victorious.

The One sitting on the throne spoke: 'Now I am making the whole of creation new', he said. 'Write this: that what I am saying is sure and will come true.' And then he said, 'It is already done. I am the Alpha and the Omega, the Beginning and the End. I will give water from the well of life free to anybody who is thirsty; it is the rightful inheritance of the one who proves victorious; and I will be his God and he a son to me.'

This is the word of the Lord.

Responsorial Psalm Ps 125. ℟ v.5

℟ **Those who are sowing in tears
will sing when they reap.**

1 When the Lord delivered Zion from bondage,
it seemed like a dream.
Then was our mouth filled with laughter,
on our lips there were songs. ℟

2 The heathens themselves said: 'What marvels
the Lord worked for them!'
What marvels the Lord worked for us!
Indeed we are glad. ℟

3 Deliver us, O Lord, from our bondage
as streams in dry land.
Those who are sowing in tears
will sing when they reap. ℟

4 They go out, they go out, full of tears,
carrying seed for the sowing:
they come back, they come back, full of song,
carrying their sheaves. ℟

Gospel Acclamation 1 Peter 4:14
Alleluia, alleluia!
It is a blessing for you

when they insult you for bearing the name of Christ,
because it means that you have the Spirit of God
resting on you.
Alleluia!

GOSPEL

A reading from the holy Gospel according to Luke 9:23-26
Anyone who loses his life for my sake, that man will save it.

To all Jesus said, 'If anyone wants to be a follower of mine, let him renounce himself and take up his cross every day and follow me. For anyone who wants to save his life will lose it, but anyone who loses his life for my sake, that man will save it. What gain, then, is it for a man to have won the whole world and to have lost or ruined his very self? For if anyone is ashamed of me and of my words, of him the Son of Man will be ashamed when he comes in his own glory and in the glory of the Father and the holy angels.'

This is the Gospel of the Lord.

24 April

St Fidelis of Sigmaringen, priest and martyr — Optional Memorial

Born at Sigmaringen in Germany in 1578. He was a lawyer, and then entered the Order of Friars Minor Capuchin at Freiburg in Breisgau. He lived a life of prayer and penance, and gained a great reputation as a preacher. He was sent by the newly-formed Congregation for the Propagation of the Faith to preach to the Protestants in Switzerland, where he was put to death by a group of fanatics in 1622.

Common of martyrs, pp.1865ff., or of pastors, pp.1876.

Opening Prayer
Father,
you filled Saint Fidelis with the fire of your love
and gave him the privilege of dying
that the faith might live.
Let his prayers keep us firmly grounded in your love,
and help us to come to know the power of Christ's resurrection.

Proper of Saints, 24 April

FIRST READING

A reading from the letter of St Paul of the Colossians 1:24-29
I became the servant of the Church.

It makes me happy to suffer for you, as I am suffering now, and in my own body to do what I can to make up all that has still to be undergone by Christ for the sake of his body, the Church. I became the servant of the Church when God made me responsible for delivering God's message to you, the message which was a mystery hidden for generations and centuries and has now been revealed to his saints. It was God's purpose to reveal it to them and to show all the rich glory of this mystery to pagans. The mystery is Christ among you, your hope of glory: this is the Christ we proclaim, this is the wisdom in which we thoroughly train everyone and instruct everyone, to make them all perfect in Christ. It is for this I struggle wearily on, helped only by his power driving me irresistibly.

This is the word of the Lord.

Responsorial Psalm

Ps 33:2-9. ℟ v. 5

℟ **From all my terrors the Lord set me free.**

1 I will bless the Lord at all times,
his praise always on my lips;
in the Lord my soul shall make its boast.
The humble shall hear and be glad. ℟

2 Glorify the Lord with me.
Together let us praise his name.
I sought the Lord and he answered me;
from all my terrors he set me free. ℟

3 Look towards him and be radiant;
let your faces not be abashed.
This poor man called; the Lord heard him
and rescued him from all his distress. ℟

4 The angel of the Lord is encamped
around those who revere him, to rescue them.
Taste and see that the Lord is good.
He is happy who seeks refuge in him. ℟

Gospel Acclamation

Jn 13:34

Alleluia, alleluia!
I give you a new commandment:

Proper of Saints, 24 April

love one another as I have loved you.
says the Lord.
Alleluia!

GOSPEL

A reading from the holy Gospel according to John 17:20-26
I want them to be with me where I am.

Jesus raised his eyes to heaven and said:

'Holy Father,
I pray not only for these,
but for those also
who through their words will believe in me.
May they all be one.
Father, may they be one in us,
as you are in me and I am in you,
so that the world may believe it was you who sent me.
I have given them the glory you gave to me,
that they may be one as we are one.
With me in them and you in me,
may they be so completely one
that the world will realise that it was you who sent me
and that I have loved them as much as you loved me.
Father,
I want those you have given me
to be with me where I am,
so that they may always see the glory
you have given me
because you loved me
before the foundation of the world.
Father, Righteous One,
the world has not known you,
but I have known you,
and these have known
that you have sent me.
I have made your name known to them
and will continue to make it known,
so that the love with which you loved me may be in them,
and so that I may be in them.'

This is the Gospel of the Lord.

25 April
St Mark, evangelist Feast

Mark went with St Paul on his first missionary journey, along with his cousin Barnabas. He made later journeys with Barnabas alone. He was in Rome with Paul, and with St Peter. His Gospel is based on Peter's teaching in Rome: its concise, direct and vivid style tells us something of Mark's personality. Tradition dating from the third century says that he founded the Church in Alexandria.

Entrance Antiphon: Go out to the whole world, and preach the gospel to all creation, alleluia.

Opening Prayer
Father,
you gave Saint Mark
the privilege of proclaiming your gospel.
May we profit by his wisdom
and follow Christ more faithfully.

FIRST READING
A reading from the first letter of St Peter   5:5-14

My son, Mark, sends you greetings.

All wrap yourselves in humility to be servants of each other, because God refuses the proud and will always favour the humble. Bow down, then, before the power of God now, and he will raise you up on the appointed day; unload all your worries on to him, since he is looking after you. Be calm but vigilant, because your enemy the devil is prowling round like a roaring lion, looking for something to eat. Stand up to him, strong in faith and in the knowledge that your brothers all over the world are suffering the same things. You will have to suffer only for a little while: the God of all grace who called you to eternal glory in Christ will see that all is well again: he will confirm, strengthen and support you. His power lasts for ever and ever. Amen.

I write these few words to you through Silvanus, who is a brother I know I can trust, to encourage you never to let go this true grace of God to which I bear witness.

Your sister in Babylon, who is with you among the chosen, sends you greetings; so does my son, Mark.

Greet one another with a kiss of love.

Peace to you all who are in Christ.

This is the word of the Lord.

Responsorial Psalm   Ps 88:2-3. 6-7. 16-17. R/ cf. v.2

   R/ **I will sing for ever of your love, O Lord.**

or

   R/ **Alleluia!**

1 I will sing for ever of your love, O Lord;
 through all ages my mouth will proclaim your truth.
 Of this I am sure, that your love lasts for ever,
 that your truth is firmly established as the heavens.   R/

2 The heavens proclaim your wonders, O Lord;
 the assembly of your holy ones proclaims your truth.
 For who in the skies can compare with the Lord
 or who is like the Lord among the sons of God?   R/

3 Happy the people who acclaim such a king,
 who walk, O Lord, in the light of your face,
 who find their joy every day in your name,
 who make your justice the source of their bliss.   R/

Gospel Acclamation   1 Cor 1:23-24
Alleluia, alleluia!
We are preaching a crucified Christ,
who is the power and the wisdom of God.
Alleluia!

GOSPEL

A reading from the holy Gospel according to Mark   16:15-20
Proclaim the Good News to all creation.

Jesus said to the Eleven, 'Go out to the whole world; proclaim the Good News to all creation. He who believes and is baptised will be saved; he who does not believe will be condemned. These are the signs that will be associated with believers: in my name they will cast out devils; they will have the gift of tongues; they will pick up snakes in their hands, and be unharmed should they drink deadly poison; they will lay their hands on the sick, who will recover.'

And so the Lord Jesus, after he had spoken to them, was taken up into heaven: there at the right hand of God he took his place, while they, going out, preached everywhere, the Lord working with them and confirming the word by the signs that accompanied it.

This is the Gospel of the Lord.

Prayer over the Gifts
Lord,
as we offer the sacrifice of praise
on the feast of Saint Mark,
we pray that your Church may always be faithful
to the preaching of the gospel.

Preface of Apostles I or II, P64 or P65.

Communion Antiphon: I, the Lord, am with you always, until the end of the world, alleluia.

Prayer after Communion
All-powerful God,
may the gifts we have received at this altar
make us holy, and strengthen us
in the faith of the gospel preached by Saint Mark.

28 April
St Peter Chanel, priest and martyr
Optional Memorial

Born in France in 1803, he did pastoral work there for a few years after ordination, and then entered the Marist Society and was sent to Oceania. There was considerable resistance to missionaries at that time, though he did receive a few converts into the faith before he was clubbed to death on the island of Futuna in 1841.

Common of martyrs, pp.1865ff., or of pastors: missionaries, pp.1876ff.

Opening Prayer
Father,
you called Saint Peter Chanel to work for your Church
and gave him the crown of martyrdom.
May our celebration of Christ's death and resurrection
make us faithful witnesses to the new life he brings,
for he lives and reigns with you and the Holy Spirit,
one God, for ever and ever.

FIRST READING

A reading from the first letter of St Paul　　　　　　　　1:18-25
to the Corinthians

God wanted to save those who have faith through the foolishness of the message that we preach.

The language of the cross may be illogical to those who are not on the way to salvation, but those of us who are on the way to see it as God's power to save. As scripture says: I shall destroy the wisdom of the wise and bring to nothing all the learning of the learned. Where are the philosophers now? Where are the scribes? Where are any of our thinkers today? Do you see now how God has shown up the foolishness of human wisdom? If it was God's wisdom that human wisdom should not know God, it was because God wanted to save those who have faith through the foolishness of the message that we preach. And so, while the Jews demand miracles and the Greeks look for wisdom, here are we preaching a crucified Christ; to the Jews an obstacle that they cannot get over, to the pagans madness, but to those who have been called, whether they are Jews or Greeks, a Christ who is the power and the wisdom of God. For God's foolishness is wiser than human wisdom, and God's weakness is stronger than human strength.

This is the word of the Lord.

Responsorial Psalm　　　　　　　　　　　　　　Ps 116. ℟ Mk 16:15

　℟ **Go out to the whole world;
　proclaim the Good News.**

or

　℟ **Alleluia!**

1　O praise the Lord, all you nations,
　acclaim him all you peoples!　℟

2　Strong is his love for us;
　he is faithful for ever.　℟

Gospel Acclamation　　　　　　　　　　　　　　　　Mk 1:17
　Alleluia, alleluia!
　Follow me, says the Lord,
　and I will make you into fishers of men.
　Alleluia!

GOSPEL

A reading from the holy Gospel according to Mark 1:14-20

I will make you into fishers of men.

After John had been arrested, Jesus went into Galilee. There he proclaimed the Good News from God. 'The time has come,' he said, 'and the kingdom of God is close at hand. Repent, and believe the Good News.'

As he was walking along by the Sea of Galilee he saw Simon and his brother Andrew casting a net in the lake – for they were fishermen. And Jesus said to them, 'Follow me and I will make you into fishers of men.' And at once they left their nets and followed him.

Going on a little farther, he saw James son of Zebedee and his brother John; they too were in their boat, mending their nets. He called them at once and, leaving their father Zebedee in the boat with the men he employed, they went after him.

This is the Gospel of the Lord.

29 April

St Catherine of Siena, virgin and doctor of the Church   Memorial

Born at Siena in 1347, she became a member of the Order of St Dominic. She was filled with an active love for God and neighbour: she strove to bring peace to the quarrelling factions and cities of Italy, and to restore the rights of the papacy, at that time in exile in Avignon. She was a contemplative and ascetic, and her many writings are remarkable for their spirituality and theology.

Entrance Antiphon: Here is a wise and faithful virgin who went with lighted lamp to meet her Lord, alleluia.

Opening Prayer
Father,
in meditating on the sufferings of your Son
and in serving your Church,
Saint Catherine was filled with the fervour of your love.
By her prayers,
may we share in the mystery of Christ's death
and rejoice in the revelation of his glory,
for he lives and reigns with you and the Holy Spirit,
one God, for ever and ever.

Proper of Saints, 29 April

FIRST READING

A reading from the first letter of St John   1:5–2:2
The blood of Christ purifies us from all sin.

This is what we have heard from Jesus Christ,
and the message that we are announcing to you:
God is light; there is no darkness in him at all.
If we say that we are in union with God
while we are living in darkness,
we are lying because we are not living the truth.
But if we live our lives in the light, as he is in the light,
we are in union with one another,
and the blood of Jesus, his Son,
purifies us from all sin.
If we say we have no sin in us,
we are deceiving ourselves
and refusing to admit the truth;
but if we acknowledge our sins,
then God who is faithful and just
will forgive our sins and purify us
from everything that is wrong.
To say that we have never sinned is to call God a liar
and to show that his word is not in us.
I am writing this, my children, to stop you sinning;
but if anyone should sin,
we have our advocate with the Father,
Jesus Christ, who is just;
he is the sacrifice that takes our sins away,
and not only ours, but the whole world's.

This is the word of the Lord.

Responsorial Psalm   Ps 102:1-4. 8-9. 13-14. 17-18. ℟ v.1

℟ **My soul, give thanks to the Lord.**

1 My soul, give thanks to the Lord,
   all my being, bless his holy name.
   My soul, give thanks to the Lord
   and never forget all his blessings.   ℟

2 It is he who forgives all your guilt,
   who heals every one of your ills,
   who redeems your life from the grave,
   who crowns you with love and compassion.   ℟

Proper of Saints, 29 April 1483

3 The Lord is compassion and love,
  slow to anger and rich in mercy.
  His wrath will come to an end;
  he will not be angry for ever. ℟

4 As a father has compassion on his sons,
  the Lord has pity on those who fear him;
  for he knows of what we are made,
  he remembers that we are dust. ℟

5 But the love of the Lord is everlasting
  upon those who hold him in fear;
  his justice reaches out to children's children
  when they keep his covenant in truth. ℟

Gospel Acclamation cf. Mt 11:25
Alleluia, alleluia!
Blessed are you, Father,
Lord of heaven and earth,
for revealing the mysteries of the kingdom
to mere children.
Alleluia!

GOSPEL

A reading from the holy Gospel according to Matthew 11:25-30
You have hidden these things from the learned and have revealed them to mere children.

Jesus exclaimed, 'I bless you, Father, Lord of heaven and of earth, for hiding these things from the learned and the clever and revealing them to mere children. Yes, Father, for that is what it pleased you to do. Everything has been entrusted to me by my Father; and no one knows the Son except the Father, just as no one knows the Father except the Son and those to whom the Son chooses to reveal him.

'Come to me, all you who labour and are overburdened, and I will give you rest. Shoulder my yoke and learn from me, for I am gentle and humble in heart, and you will find rest for your souls. Yes, my yoke is easy and my burden light.'

This is the Gospel of the Lord.

Prayer over the Gifts
Lord,

accept this saving sacrifice
we offer on the feast of Saint Catherine.
By following her teaching and example,
may we offer more perfect praise to you.

Communion Antiphon: If we walk in the light, as God is in light, there is fellowship among us, and the blood of his Son, Jesus Christ, will cleanse us from all sin, alleluia.

Prayer after Communion
Lord,
may the eucharist,
which nourished Saint Catherine in this life,
bring us eternal life.

30 April
St Pius V, pope — Optional Memorial

Born near Allesandria in Italy in 1504, entered the Dominican Order, became Pope in 1566. He put into practice the reforming decrees of the Council of Trent, which ended in 1563: in his name the Catechism, the Breviary, and the Missal were promulgated, and these endured until the recent reform in this century. He encouraged the practice of saying the Rosary. He died in 1572.

Common of pastors: popes, pp.1876ff.

Opening Prayer
Father,
you chose Saint Pius V as pope of your Church
to protect the faith and give you more fitting worship.
By his prayers,
help us to celebrate your holy mysteries
with a living faith and an effective love.

FIRST READING

A reading from the first letter of St Paul 4:1-5
to the Corinthians
Christ's servants, stewards entrusted with the mysteries of God.

People must think of us as Christ's servants, stewards entrusted with the mysteries of God. What is expected of stewards is that

Proper of Saints, 30 April 1485

each one should be found worthy of his trust. Not that it makes the slightest difference to me whether you, or indeed any human tribunal, find me worthy or not. I will not even pass judgement on myself. True, my conscience does not reproach me at all, but that does not prove that I am acquitted: the Lord alone is my judge. There must be no passing of premature judgement. Leave that until the Lord comes: he will light up all that is hidden in the dark and reveal the secret intentions of men's hearts. Then will be the time for each one to have whatever praise he deserves, from God.

This is the word of the Lord.

Responsorial Psalm Ps 109:1-4. ℟ v.4

℟ **You are a priest for ever,
a priest like Melchizedek of old.**

1 The Lord's revelation to my Master:
   'Sit on my right:
   I will put your foes beneath your feet.' ℟

2 The Lord will send from Zion
   your sceptre of power:
   rule in the midst of all your foes. ℟

3 A prince from the day of your birth
   on the holy mountains;
   from the womb before the daybreak I begot you. ℟

4 The Lord has sworn an oath he will not change.
   'You are a priest for ever,
   a priest like Melchizedek of old.' ℟

Gospel Acclamation Jn 10:14
   Alleluia, alleluia!
   I am the good shepherd, says the Lord;
   I know my own sheep
   and my own know me.
   Alleluia!

GOSPEL

A reading from the holy Gospel according to John 21:15-17
Feed my lambs, feed my sheep.

Jesus showed himself to his disciples, and after they had eaten he said to Simon Peter, 'Simon son of John, do you love me more than these others do?' He answered, 'Yes Lord, you know I love you.' Jesus said to him, 'Feed my lambs.' A second time he said to him, 'Simon son of John, do you love me?' He replied, 'Yes, Lord, you know I love you.' Jesus said to him, 'Look after my sheep'. Then he said to him a third time, 'Simon son of John, do you love me?' Peter was upset that he asked him the third time, 'Do you love me?' and said, 'Lord, you know everything; you know I love you.' Jesus said to him, 'Feed my sheep.'

This is the Gospel of the Lord.

HAIL MARY
THE LORD IS WITH YOU

MAY

1 May

St Joseph the worker — Memorial

The commemoration of St Joseph the Worker on this day was established by Pius XII in 1955. St Joseph is the patron of all working people.

Entrance Antiphon: Happy are all who fear the Lord and walk in his ways. You shall enjoy the fruits of your labour, you will prosper and be happy, alleluia.

Opening Prayer
God our Father,
creator and ruler of the universe,
in every age you call man
to develop and use his gifts for the good of others.
With Saint Joseph as our example and guide,
help us to do the work you have asked
and come to the rewards you have promised.

The Gospel is proper to this memorial.

FIRST READING

A reading from the book of Genesis 1:26–2:3
Fill the earth and conquer it.

God said, 'Let us make man in our own image, in the likeness of ourselves, and let them be masters of the fish of the sea, the birds of heaven, the cattle, all the wild beasts and all the reptiles that crawl upon the earth.'

God created man in the image of himself,
in the image of God he created him,
male and female he created them.

God blessed them, saying to them, 'Be fruitful, multiply, fill the earth and conquer it. Be masters of the fish of the sea, the birds of heaven and all living animals on the earth.' God said, 'See, I give you all the seed-bearing plants that are upon the whole earth, and all the trees with seed-bearing fruit; this shall be your food. To all wild beasts, all birds of heaven and all living reptiles on the earth I give all the foliage of plants for food.' And so it was. God saw all he had made, and indeed it was very good. Evening came and morning came: the sixth day.

Thus heaven and earth were completed with all their array. On the seventh day God completed the work he had been doing. He rested on the seventh day after all the work he had been doing. God blessed the seventh day and made it holy, because on that day he had rested after all his work of creating.

This is the word of the Lord.

Alternative First Reading

A reading from the letter of St Paul to the Colossians 3:14-15. 17. 23-24

Whatever your work is, put your heart into it as if it were for the Lord and not for men.

Over all these clothes, to keep them together and complete them, put on love. And may the peace of Christ reign in your hearts, because it is for this that you were called together as parts of one body. Always be thankful. Never say or do anything except in the name of the Lord Jesus, giving thanks to God the Father through him. Whatever your work is, put your heart into it as if it were for the Lord and not for men, knowing that the Lord will repay you by making you his heirs. It is Christ the Lord that you are serving.

This is the word of the Lord.

Responsorial Psalm Ps 89:2-4. 12-14. 16. ℟ v.17

℟ **Give success to the work of our hands, O Lord.**

or

℟ **Alleluia!**

Proper of Saints, 1 May 1489

1 Before the mountains were born
   or the earth or the world brought forth,
   you are God, without beginning or end. ℟

2 You turn men back into dust
   and say: 'Go back, sons of men.'
   To your eyes a thousand years
   are like yesterday, come and gone,
   no more than a watch in the night. ℟

3 Make us know the shortness of our life
   that we may gain wisdom of heart.
   Lord, relent! Is your anger for ever?
   Show pity to your servants. ℟

4 In the morning, fill us with your love;
   we shall exult and rejoice all our days.
   Show forth your work to your servants;
   let your glory shine on their children. ℟

Gospel Acclamation Ps 67:20
   Alleluia, alleluia!
   May the Lord be blessed day after day;
   he bears our burdens, God our saviour.
   Alleluia!

GOSPEL

A reading from the holy Gospel according to Matthew   13:54-58
This is the carpenter's son, surely?

Jesus came to his home town and taught the people in their synagogue in such a way that they were astonished and said, 'Where did the man get this wisdom and these miraculous powers? This is the carpenter's son, surely? Is not his mother the woman called Mary, and his brothers James and Joseph and Simon and Jude? His sisters, too, are they not all here with us? So where did the man get it all?' And they would not accept him. But Jesus said to them, 'A prophet is only despised in his own country and in his own house,' and he did not work many miracles there because of their lack of faith.

   This is the Gospel of the Lord.

Prayer over the Gifts
Lord God,

fountain of all mercy,
look upon our gifts on this feast of Saint Joseph.
Let our sacrifice
become the protection of all who call on you.

Preface of Saint Joseph, P62.

Communion Antiphon: Let everything you do or say be in the name of the Lord with thanksgiving to God, alleluia.

Prayer after Communion
Lord,
hear the prayers of those you nourish in this eucharist.
Inspired by the example of Saint Joseph,
may our lives manifest your love;
may we rejoice for ever in your peace.

2 May

St Athanasius, bishop and doctor of the Church   Memorial

Born at Alexandria in 295. He attended the Council of Nicaea, in 325, which had been called to rebut the heresy of Arius, which denied the divinity of Christ. Arius was also an Alexandrian. Athanasius became bishop of Alexandria in 328, and was tireless in combatting the heresy. He was exiled five times for his persistance. He wrote brilliantly, both in defence of doctrine, and on spiritual matters.

Common of pastors: bishops, pp.1878ff., or of doctors of the church, pp.1887ff.

Opening Prayer
Father,
you raised up Saint Athanasius
to be an outstanding defender
of the truth of Christ's divinity.
By his teaching and protection
may we grow in your knowledge and love.

Proper of Saints, 2 May

FIRST READING

A reading from the first letter of St John 5:1-5
This is the victory over the world – our faith.

Whoever believes that Jesus is the Christ
has been begotten by God;
and whoever loves the Father that begot him
loves the child whom he begets.
We can be sure that we love God's children
if we love God himself and do what he has commanded us;
this is what loving God is –
keeping his commandments;
and his commandments are not difficult,
because anyone who has been begotten by God
has already overcome the world;
this is the victory over the world –
our faith.
Who can overcome the world?
Only the man who believes that Jesus is the Son of God.

This is the word of the Lord.

Responsorial Psalm Ps 36:3-6. 30-31. R v.30

℟ **The just man's mouth utters wisdom.**

1. If you trust in the Lord and do good,
   then you will live in the land and be secure.
   If you find your delight in the Lord,
   he will grant your heart's desire. ℟

2. Commit your life to the Lord,
   trust in him and he will act,
   so that your justice breaks forth like the light,
   your cause like the noon-day sun. ℟

3. The just man's mouth utters wisdom
   and his lips speak what is right;
   the law of his God is in his heart,
   his steps shall be saved from stumbling. ℟

Gospel Acclamation Mt 5:10

Alleluia, alleluia!
Happy those who are persecuted in the cause of right:
theirs is the kingdom of heaven.
Alleluia!

GOSPEL

A reading from the holy Gospel according to Matthew 10:22-25

If they persecute you in one city, take refuge in the next.

Jesus said to his disciples: 'You will be hated by all men on account of my name; but the man who stands firm to the end will be saved. If they persecute you in one town, take refuge in the next; and if they persecute you in that, take refuge in another. I tell you solemnly, you will not have gone the round of the towns of Israel before the Son of Man comes.

'The disciple is not superior to his teacher, nor the slave to his master. It is enough for the disciple that he should grow to be like his teacher.'

This is the Gospel of the Lord.

Prayer over the Gifts
Lord,
look upon the gifts we offer
on the feast of Saint Athanasius.
Keep us true to the faith he professed
and let our own witness to your truth
bring us closer to salvation.

Prayer after Communion
All-powerful God,
we join Saint Athanasius in professing our belief
in the true divinity of Christ your Son.
Through this sacrament
may our faith always give us life and protection.

3 May
SS PHILIP AND JAMES, APOSTLES Feast

Philip was born at Bethsaida; he was a disciple of John the Baptist, who followed the call of Christ.

James, the son of Alphaeus, should not be confused with James the brother of John. The Lord appeared to him after the resurrection; he is the writer of one of the Epistles. He belonged to the Church at Jerusalem, and was martyred there in 62 AD.

Entrance Antiphon: The Lord chose these holy men for their unfeigned love, and gave them eternal glory, alleluia.

Opening Prayer

God our Father,
every year you give us joy
on the festival of the apostles Philip and James.
By the help of their prayers
may we share in the suffering, death, and ressurection
of your only Son
and come to the eternal vision of your glory.

FIRST READING

A reading from the first letter of St Paul   15:1-8
to the Corinthians
The Lord appeared to James, and then to all the apostles.

Brothers, I want to remind you of the gospel I preached to you, the gospel that you received and in which you are firmly established; because the gospel will save you only if you keep believing exactly what I preached to you – believing anything else will not lead to anything.

Well then, in the first place, I taught you what I had been taught myself, namely that Christ died for our sins, in accordance with the scriptures; that he was buried; and that he was raised to life on the third day, in accordance with the scriptures; that he appeared first to Cephas and secondly to the Twelve. Next he appeared to more than five hundred of the brothers at the same time, most of whom are still alive, though some have died; then he appeared to James, and then to all the apostles; and last of all he appeared to me too; it was as though I was born when no one expected it.

This is the word of the Lord.

Responsorial Psalm   Ps 18:2-5. ℟ v.5

   ℟ **Their word goes forth through all the earth.**
or
   ℟ **Alleluia!**

1. The heavens proclaim the glory of God
   and the firmament shows forth the work of his hands.
   Day unto day takes up the story
   and night unto night makes known the message.   ℟

2. No speech, no word, no voice is heard
   yet their span extends through all the earth.
   their words to the utmost bounds of the world.   ℟

Gospel Acclamation
Jn 14:6.9

Alleluia, alleluia!
I am the Way, the Truth and the Life, says the Lord.
Philip, to have seen me is to have seen the Father.
Alleluia!

GOSPEL

A reading from the holy Gospel according to John 14:6-14
Have I been with you all this time, and you still do not know me?

Jesus said to Thomas:

'I am the Way, the Truth and the Life.
No one can come to the Father except through me.
If you know me, you know my Father too.
From this moment you know him and have seen him.'

Philip said, 'Lord, let us see the Father and then we shall be satisfied.' 'Have I been with you all this time, Philip,' said Jesus to him 'and you still do not know me?

'To have seen me is to have seen the Father,
so how can you say, "Let us see the Father?"
Do you not believe
that I am in the Father and the Father is in me?
The words I say to you I do not speak as from myself:
it is the Father, living in me, who is doing this work.
You must believe me when I say
that I am in the Father and the Father is in me;
believe it on the evidence of this work, if for no other reason.
I tell you most solemnly, whoever believes in me
will perform the same works as I do myself,
he will perform even greater works,
because I am going to the Father.
Whatever you ask for in my name I will do,
so that the Father may be glorified in the Son.
If you ask for anything in my name, I will do it.'

This is the Gospel of the Lord.

Prayer over the Gifts

Lord,
accept our gifts
at this celebration in honour of the apostles Philip and James.
Make our religion pure and undefiled.

Preface of the Apostles I or II, P64 or P65.

Communion Antiphon: Lord, let us see the Father, and we shall be content. And Jesus said: Philip, he who sees me, sees the Father, alleluia.

Prayer after Communion
Father,
by the holy gifts we have received
free our minds and hearts from sin.
With the apostles Philip and James
may we see you in your Son
and be found worthy to have eternal life.

12 May

Ss Nereus and Achilleus, martyrs
Optional Memorial

Two Roman soldiers at the time of Diocletian, who were put to death probably in 304, for refusing to serve in the army after their conversion to Christianity.

Common of martyrs, pp.1865ff.

Opening Prayer
Father,
we honour Saints Nereus and Achilleus for their courage
in dying to profess their faith in Christ.
May we experience the help of their prayers
at the throne of your mercy.

FIRST READING

A reading from the book of the Apocalypse   7:9-17
These are the people who have been through the great persecution.

I, John, saw a huge number, impossible to count, of people from every nation, race, tribe and language; they were standing in front of the throne and in front of the Lamb, dressed in white robes and holding palms in their hands. They shouted aloud, 'Victory to our God, who sits on the throne, and to the Lamb!' And all the angels who were standing in a circle round the throne, surrounding the elders and the four animals, prostrated themselves before the throne, and touched the ground with their foreheads, worshipping God with these words, 'Amen. Praise and glory and wisdom and thanksgiving and honour and power and strength to our God for ever and ever. Amen.'

One of the elders then spoke, and asked me, 'Do you know who these people are, dressed in white robes, and where they have come from?' I answered him, 'You can tell me, my Lord.' Then he said, 'These are the people who have been through the great persecution, and because they have washed their robes white again in the blood of the Lamb, they now stand in front of God's throne and serve him day and night in his sanctuary; and the One who sits on the throne will spread his tent over them. They will never hunger or thirst again; neither the sun nor scorching wind will ever plague them, because the Lamb who is at the throne will be their shepherd and will lead them to springs of living water; and God will wipe away all tears from their eyes.'

This is the word of the Lord.

Responsional Psalm Ps 123:2-5. 7-8. ℟ v.7

℟ **Our life, like a bird, has escaped from the snare of the fowler.**

1 If the Lord had not been on our side
   when men rose against us,
   then would they have swallowed us alive
   when their anger was kindled. ℟

2 Then would the waters have engulfed us,
   the torrent gone over us;
   over our heads would have swept
   the raging waters. ℟

3 Indeed the snare has been broken
   and we have escaped.
   Our help is in the name of the Lord,
   who made heaven and earth. ℟

Gospel Acclamation Mt 5:10
Alleluia, alleluia!
Happy those who are persecuted in the cause of right:
theirs is the kingdom of heaven.
Alleluia!

GOSPEL

A reading from the holy Gospel according to Matthew 10:17-22

You will be dragged before governors and kings for my sake, to bear witness before them and the pagans.

Jesus said to his apostles: 'Beware of men: they will hand you over to sanhedrins and scourge you in their synagogues. You will be dragged before governors and kings for my sake, to bear witness before them and the pagans. But when they hand you over, do not worry about how to speak or what to say; what you are to say will be given to you when the time comes; because it is not you who will be speaking; the Spirit of your Father will be speaking in you.

'Brother will betray brother to death, and the father his child; children will rise against their parents and have them put to death. You will be hated by all men on account of my name; but the man who stands firm to the end will be saved.'

This is the Gospel of the Lord.

Also 12 May
St Pancras, martyr Optional Memorial

A Roman martyr from the time of the Diocletian persecution.

Common of martyrs, pp.1865ff.

Opening Prayer
God of mercy,
give your Church joy and confidence
through the prayers of Saint Pancras.
Keep us faithful to you
and steadfast in your service.

FIRST READING

A reading from the book of the Apocalypse 19:1. 5-9

Happy are those who are invited to the wedding feast of the Lamb.

I, John, seemed to hear the great sound of a huge crowd in heaven, singing, 'Alleluia! Victory and glory and power to our God!'

Then a voice came from the throne; it said, 'Praise our God, you servants of his and all who, great or small, revere him.' And I seemed to hear the voices of a huge crowd, like the sound of the ocean or the great roar of thunder, answering, 'Alleluia! The reign of the Lord our God Almighty has begun; let us be glad and joyful and give praise to God, because this is the time for the marriage of the Lamb. His bride is ready, and she has been able to dress herself in dazzling white linen, because her linen is made of the good deeds of the saints.' The angel said, 'Write this: Happy are those who are invited to the wedding feast of the Lamb.'

This is the word of the Lord.

Responsorial Psalm Ps 102:1-4. 8-9. 13-14. 17-18. R̷ v.1
R̷ **My soul, give thanks to the Lord.**

1 My soul, give thanks to the Lord.
   all my being, bless his holy name.
   My soul, give thanks to the Lord
   and never forget all his blessings. R̷

2 It is he who forgives all your guilt,
   who heals every one of your ills,
   who redeems your life from the grave,
   who crowns you with love and compassion. R̷

3 The Lord is compassion and love,
   slow to anger and rich in mercy.
   His wrath will come to an end;
   he will not be angry for ever. R̷

4 As a father has compassion on his sons,
   the Lord has pity on those who fear him;
   for he knows of what we are made,
   he remembers that we are dust. R̷

5 But the love of the Lord is everlasting
   upon those who hold him in fear;
   his justice reaches out to children's children
   when they keep his covenant in truth. R̷

Gospel Acclamation cf. Mt 11:25
Alleluia, alleluia!
Blessed are you, Father,
Lord of heaven and earth,
for revealing the mysteries of the kingdom
to mere children.
Alleluia!

GOSPEL

A reading from the holy Gospel according to Matthew 11:25-30
You have hidden these things from the clever, and revealed them to mere children.

Jesus exclaimed, 'I bless you, Father, Lord of heaven and of earth, for hiding these things from the learned and the clever and revealing them to mere children. Yes, Father, for that is what it pleased you to do. Everything has been entrusted to me by my Father; and no one knows the Son except the Father, just as no one knows the Father except the Son and those to whom the Son chooses to reveal him.

'Come to me, all you who labour and are overburdened, and I will give you rest. Shoulder my yoke and learn from me, for I am gentle and humble in heart, and you will find rest for your souls. Yes, my yoke is easy and my burden light.'

This is the Gospel of the Lord.

14 May

ST MATTHIAS, APOSTLE Feast

Acts 1:15-26, the first reading today, tells how Matthias was chosen by lot to replace Judas.

Entrance Antiphon: You have not chosen me; I have chosen you. Go and bear fruit that will last, alleluia.

Opening Prayer
Father,
you called Saint Matthias to share in the mission of the apostles.
By the help of his prayers
may we receive with joy the love you share with us
and be counted among those you have chosen.

FIRST READING

A reading from the Acts of the Apostles 1:15-17. 20-26
The lot fell to Matthias and he was listed as one of the twelve apostles.

One day Peter stood up to speak to the brothers – there were about a hundred and twenty persons in the congregation: 'Brothers, the passage of scripture has to be fulfilled in which the Holy Spirit, speaking through David, foretells the fate of Judas, who offered himself as a guide to the men who arrested Jesus – after having been one of our number and actually sharing this ministry of ours. Now in the Book of Psalms it says:

> Let his camp be reduced to ruin,
> let there be no one to live in it.

And again:

> Let someone else take his office.

'We must therefore choose someone who has been with us the whole time that the Lord Jesus was travelling round with us, someone who was with us right from the time when John was baptising until the day when he was taken up from us – and he can act with us as a witness to his resurrection.'

Having nominated two candidates, Joseph known as Barsabbas, whose surname was Justus, and Matthias, they prayed, 'Lord, you can read everyone's heart; show us therefore which of these two you have chosen to take over this ministry and apostolate, which Judas abandoned to go to his proper place.' They then drew lots for them, and as the lot fell to Matthias, he was listed as one of the twelve apostles.

This is the word of the Lord.

Responsorial Psalm   Ps 112:1-8. ℟ cf. v.8

  ℟ **The Lord sets him in the company of the princes of his people.**

or

  ℟ **Alleluia!**

1. Praise, O servants of the Lord,
   praise the name of the Lord!
   May the name of the Lord be blessed
   both now and for evermore! ℟

2. From the rising of the sun to its setting
   praised be the name of the Lord!
   High above all nations is the Lord,
   above the heavens his glory. ℟

3. Who is like the Lord, our God,
   who has risen on high to his throne
   yet stoops from the heights to look down,
   to look down upon heaven and earth? ℟

4. From the dust he lifts up the lowly,

Proper of Saints, 14 May   1501

from the dungheap he raises the poor
to set him in the company of princes,
yes, with the princes of his people. ℟

Gospel Acclamation   cf. Jn 15:16
  Alleluia, alleluia!
  I chose you from the world
  to go out and to bear fruit,
  fruit that will last, says the Lord.
  Alleluia!

GOSPEL

A reading from the holy Gospel according to John   15:9-17
You did not choose me, no, I chose you.

Jesus said to his disciples:

  'As the Father has loved me.
  so I have loved you.
  Remain in my love.
  If you keep my commandments
  you will remain in my love,
  just as I have kept my Father's commandments
  and remain in his love.
  I have told you this
  so that my own joy may be in you
  and your joy be complete.
  This is my commandment:
  love one another,
  as I have loved you.
  A man can have no greater love
  than to lay down his life for his friends.
  You are my friends,
  if you do what I command you.
  I shall not call you servants any more,
  because a servant does not know
  his master's business;
  I call you friends,
  because I have made known to you
  everything I have learnt from my Father.
  You did not choose me,
  no, I chose you;
  and I commissioned you

to go out and to bear fruit,
fruit that will last;
and then the Father will give you
anything you ask him in my name.
What I command you
is to love one another.'

This is the Gospel of the Lord.

Prayer over the Gifts
Lord,
accept the gifts your Church offers
on the feast of the apostle, Matthias,
and by this eucharist
strengthen your grace within us.

Preface of the Apostles I or II, P64 or P65.

Communion Antiphon: This is my commandment: love one another as I have loved you.

Prayer after Communion
Lord,
you constantly give life to your people
in this holy eucharist.
By the prayers of the apostle Matthias
prepare us to take our place
among your saints in eternal life.

18 May
St John I, pope and martyr
Optional Memorial

Born in Tuscany, elected pope in 523, John was sent to Constantinople by king Theodoric, to persuade the emperor, Justin I, to desist from the persecution of Arians. Constantinople welcomed the pope with great honour; neither he, nor the emperor, obeyed the wishes of the king, and on John's return to Rome he was exiled to Ravenna, where he died in 526.

Common of martyrs, pp.1865ff., or of pastors: popes, pp.1876ff.

Opening Prayer
God our Father,
rewarder of all who believe,
hear our prayers

as we celebrate the martyrdom of Pope John.
Help us to follow him in loyalty to the faith.

FIRST READING

A reading from the book of the Apocalypse 3:14. 20-22

I will come in to share his meal, side by side with him.

Here is the message of the Amen, the faithful, the true witness, the ultimate source of God's creation:

'Look, I am standing at the door, knocking. If one of you hears me calling and opens the door, I will come in to share his meal, side by side with him. Those who prove victorious I will allow to share my throne, just as I was victorious myself and took my place with my Father on his throne. If anyone has ears to hear, let him listen to what the Spirit is saying to the churches.'

This is the word of the Lord.

Responsorial Psalm Ps 22. ℟ v. 1

℟ **The Lord is my shepherd;**
there is nothing I shall want.

1 The Lord is my shepherd;
 there is nothing I shall want.
 Fresh and green are the pastures
 where he gives me repose.
 Near restful waters he leads me,
 to revive my drooping spirit. ℟

2 He guides me along the right path;
 he is true to his name.
 If I should walk in the valley of darkness
 no evil would I fear.
 You are there with your crook and your staff;
 with these you give me comfort. ℟

3 You have prepared a banquet for me
 in the sight of my foes.
 My head you have anointed with oil;
 my cup is overflowing. ℟

4 Surely goodness and kindness shall follow me
 all the days of my life.
 In the Lord's own house shall I dwell
 for ever and ever. ℟

Gospel Acclamation Jn 15:15
Alleluia, alleluia!
I call you friends, says the Lord,
because I have made known to you
everything I have learnt from my Father.
Alleluia!

GOSPEL

A reading from the holy Gospel according to Luke 22:24-30
I confer a kingdom on you, just as my Father conferred one on me.

A dispute arose between the apostles about which should be reckoned the greatest, but Jesus said to them, 'Among pagans it is the kings who lord it over them, and those who have authority over them are given the title Benefactor. This must not happen with you. No; the greatest among you must behave as if he were the youngest, the leader as if he were the one who serves. For who is the greater: the one at table or the one who serves? The one at table, surely? Yet here am I among you as one who serves!

'You are the men who have stood by me faithfully in my trials; and now I confer a kingdom on you, just as my Father conferred one on me; you will eat and drink at my table in my kingdom, and you will sit on thrones to judge the twelve tribes of Israel.'

This is the Gospel of the Lord.

20 May
St Bernardine of Siena, priest
Optional Memorial

Born in 1380, near Siena, Bernardine entered the Friars Minor and was ordained. He journeyed throughout Italy, preaching of God's mercy; he encouraged devotion to the holy name of Jesus. He died in 1444.

Common of pastors: missionaries, pp. 1885ff.

Opening Prayer
Father,
you gave Saint Bernardine a special love
for the holy name of Jesus.
By the help of his prayers,
may we always be alive with the spirit of your love.

Proper of Saints, 20 May 1505

FIRST READING

A reading from the Acts of the Apostles 4:8-12
This is the only name by which we can be saved.

Peter, filled with the Holy Spirit, said, 'Rulers of the people, and elders! If you are questioning us today about an act of kindness to a cripple, and asking us how he was healed, then I am glad to tell you all, and would indeed be glad to tell the whole people of Israel, that it was by the name of Jesus Christ the Nazarene, the one you crucified, whom God raised from the dead, by this name and by no other that this man is able to stand up perfectly healthy, here in your presence, today. This is the stone rejected by you the builders, but which has proved to be the keystone. For of all the names in the world given to men, this is the only one by which we can be saved.'

This is the word of the Lord.

Responsorial Psalm Ps 39:2. 4. 7-10. ℟ cf. vv. 8. 9

℟ **Here I am, Lord!**
I come to do your will.

1 I waited, I waited for the Lord
   and he stooped down to me;
   he heard my cry.
   He put a new song into my mouth,
   praise of our God.   ℟

2 You do not ask for sacrifice and offerings,
   but an open ear.
   You do not ask for holocaust and victim.
   Instead, here am I.   ℟

3 In the scroll of the book it stands written
   that I should do your will.
   My God, I delight in your law
   in the depth of my heart.   ℟

4 Your justice I have proclaimed
   in the great assembly.
   My lips I have not sealed;
   you know it, O Lord.   ℟

Gospel Acclamation Jn 8:12
Alleluia, alleluia!
I am the light of the world, says the Lord;

anyone who follows me will have the light of life.
Alleluia!

GOSPEL

A reading from the holy Gospel according to Luke 9:57-62
I will follow you, wherever you go.

As Jesus and his disciples travelled along they met a man on the road who said to him, 'I will follow you wherever you go'. Jesus answered, 'Foxes have holes and the birds of the air have nests, but the Son of Man has nowhere to lay his head.'

Another to whom he said, 'Follow me,' replied, 'Let me go and bury my father first.' But he answered, 'Leave the dead to bury their dead; your duty is to go and spread the news of the kingdom of God.'

Another said, 'I will follow you, sir, but first let me go and say good-bye to my people at home'. Jesus said to him, 'Once the hand is laid on the plough, no one who looks back is fit for the kingdom of God.'

This is the Gospel of the Lord.

25 May
St Bede the Venerable, priest and doctor of the Church
Optional Memorial

Bede was born in 673, near the monastery of Wearmouth. He entered the monastery, was ordained, and lived a life of study and contemplation. His holiness was renowned in his lifetime; his pupils and comrades loved him; the works he wrote, particularly the Ecclesiastical History of England, *were remarkable in their time and have endured.*

Common of doctors of the church, pp.1887ff., or of holy men and women: religious, pp.1898ff.

Opening Prayer
Lord,
you have enlightened your Church
with the learning of Saint Bede.
In your love
may your people learn from his wisdom
and benefit from his prayers.

Proper of Saints, 25 May

FIRST READING

A reading from the first letter of St Paul to the Corinthians 2:10-16
We are those who have the mind of Christ.

The Spirit reaches the depths of everything, even the depths of God. After all, the depths of a man can only be known by his own spirit, not by any other man, and in the same way the depths of God can only be known by the Spirit of God. Now instead of the spirit of the world, we have received the Spirit that comes from God, to teach us to understand the gifts that he has given us. Therefore we teach, not in the way in which philosophy is taught, but in the way that the Spirit teaches us: we teach spiritual things spiritually. An unspiritual person is one who does not accept anything of the Spirit of God: he sees it all as nonsense; it is beyond his understanding because it can only be understood by means of the Spirit. A spiritual man, on the other hand, is able to judge the value of everything, and his own value is not to be judged by other men. As scripture says: Who can know the mind of the Lord, so who can teach him? But we are those who have the mind of Christ.

This is the word of the Lord.

Responsorial Psalm   Ps 118:9-14. ℟ v. 12

℟ **Lord, teach me your statutes.**

1 How shall the young remain sinless?
   By obeying your word.
   I have sought you with all my heart:
   let me not stray from your commands.   ℟

2 I treasure your promise in my heart
   lest I sin against you.
   Blessed are you, O Lord;
   teach me your statutes.   ℟

3 With my tongue I have recounted
   the decrees of your lips.
   I rejoiced to do your will
   as though all riches were mine.   ℟

Gospel Acclamation   cf. Jn 6:63. 68
   Alleluia, alleluia!
   Your words are spirit, Lord, and they are life;

you have the message of eternal life.
Alleluia!

GOSPEL

A reading from the holy Gospel according to Matthew 7:21-29
Jesus taught them with authority.

Jesus said to his disciples: 'It is not those who say to me, "Lord, Lord," who will enter the kingdom of heaven, but the person who does the will of my Father in heaven. When the day comes many will say to me, "Lord, Lord, did we not prophesy in your name, cast out demons in your name, work many miracles in your name?" Then I shall tell them to their faces: I have never known you; away from me, you evil men!

'Therefore, everyone who listens to these words of mine and acts on them will be like a sensible man who built his house on rock. Rain came down, floods rose, gales blew and hurled themselves against that house, and it did not fall: it was founded on rock. But everyone who listens to these words of mine and does not act on them will be like a stupid man who built his house on sand. Rain came down, floods rose, gales blew and struck that house, and it fell; and what a fall it had!'

Jesus had now finished what he wanted to say, and his teaching made a deep impression on the people because he taught them with authority, and not like their own scribes.

This is the Gospel of the Lord.

Also 25 May

St Gregory VII, pope Optional Memorial

Gregory VII was born in Tuscany about 1028; until his election as pope in 1073, he was known as the monk Hildebrand. The over-riding concern of his life, both as monk and as pope, was the reform of the Church. This brought him into conflict with the emperor, Henry IV, and he was forced to flee to Salerno, where he died in 1085.

Common of pastors: popes, pp.1876ff.

Opening Prayer
Lord,
give your Church
the spirit of courage and love for justice
which distinguished Pope Gregory.

Make us courageous in condemning evil
and free us to pursue justice with love.

FIRST READING

A reading from the Acts of the Apostles 20:17-18. 28-32. 36

Be on your guard for yourselves and for all the flock of which the Holy Spirit has made you the overseers, to feed the Church of God.

From Miletus Paul sent for the elders of the church of Ephesus. When they arrived he addressed these words to them:

'Be on your guard for yourselves and for all the flock of which the Holy Spirit has made you the overseers, to feed the Church of God which he bought with his own blood. I know quite well that when I have gone fierce wolves will invade you and will have no mercy on the flock. Even from your own ranks there will be men coming forward with a travesty of the truth on their lips to induce the disciples to follow them. So be on your guard, remembering how night and day for three years I never failed to keep you right, shedding tears over each one of you. And now I commend you to God, and to the word of his grace that has power to build you up and to give you your inheritance among all the sanctified.'

When he had finished speaking he knelt down with them all and prayed.

This is the word of the Lord.

Responsorial Psalm Ps 109:1-4. R̷ v.4

℞ **You are a priest for ever,**
 a priest like Melchizedek of old.

1. The Lord's revelation to my Master:
'Sit on my right:
I will put your foes beneath your feet.' ℞

2. The Lord will send from Zion
your sceptre of power:
rule in the midst of all your foes. ℞

3. A prince from the day of your birth
on the holy mountains;
from the womb before the daybreak I begot you. ℞

4. The Lord has sworn an oath he will not change.
'You are a priest for ever,
a priest like Melchizedek of old.' ℞

Gospel Acclamation Mk 1:17
Alleluia, alleluia!
Follow me, says the Lord,
and I will make you into fishers of men.
Alleluia!

GOSPEL

A reading from the holy Gospel according to Matthew 16:13-19
You are Peter and on this rock I will build my Church.

When Jesus came to the region of Caesarea Philippi he put this question to his disciples, 'Who do people say the Son of Man is?' And they said, 'Some say he is John the Baptist, some Elijah, and others Jeremiah or one of the prophets.' 'But you,' he said, 'who do you say I am?' Then Simon Peter spoke up, 'You are the Christ,' he said, 'the Son of the living God.' Jesus replied, 'Simon son of Jonah, you are a happy man! Because it was not flesh and blood that revealed this to you but my Father in heaven. So I now say to you: You are Peter and on this rock I will build my Church. And the gates of the underworld can never hold out against it. I will give you the keys of the kingdom of heaven; whatever you bind on earth shall be considered bound in heaven; whatever you loose on earth shall be considered loosed in heaven.'

This is the Gospel of the Lord.

Also 25 May
St Mary Magdalene de Pazzi, virgin
Optional Memorial

Born in Florence in 1566, died in 1607, Mary Magdalene passed most of her life in a non-reformed Carmelite house. She lived in prayer and self-denial, with complete fidelity to her vows. She offered herself for the reform of the Church and its spiritual renewal. Many of her spiritual experiences and visions were written down.

Common of virgins, pp.1889ff., or of holy men and women: religious, pp.1898ff.

Opening Prayer
Father,
you love those who give themselves completely to your service,
and you filled Saint Mary Magdalene de Pazzi

with heavenly gifts and the fire of your love.
As we honour her today
may we follow her example of purity and charity.

FIRST READING

A reading from the first letter of St Paul to the Corinthians 7:25-35

An unmarried woman can devote herself to the Lord's affairs.

About remaining celibate, I have no directions from the Lord but give my own opinion as one who, by the Lord's mercy, has stayed faithful. Well then, I believe that in these present times of stress this is right: that it is good for a man to stay as he is. If you are tied to a wife, do not look for freedom; if you are free of a wife, then do not look for one. But if you marry, it is no sin, and it is not a sin for a young girl to get married. They will have their troubles, though, in their married life, and I should like to spare you that.

Brothers, this is what I mean: our time is growing short. Those who have wives should live as though they had none, and those who mourn should live as though they had nothing to mourn for; those who are enjoying life should live as though there were nothing to laugh about; those whose life is buying things should live as though they had nothing of their own; and those who have to deal with the world should not become engrossed in it. I say this because the world as we know it is passing away.

I would like to see you free from all worry. An unmarried man can devote himself to the Lord's affairs, all he need worry about is pleasing the Lord; but a married man has to bother about the world's affairs and devote himself to pleasing his wife: he is torn two ways. In the same way an unmarried woman, like a young girl, can devote herself to the Lord's affairs; all she need worry about is being holy in body and spirit. The married woman, on the other hand, has to worry about the world's affairs and devote herself to pleasing her husband. I say this only to help you, not to put a halter round your necks, but simply to make sure that everything is as it should be, and that you give your undivided attention to the Lord.

This is the word of the Lord.

Responsorial Psalm Ps 148: 1-2. 11-14. ℟ vv. 12. 13

   ℟ **Young men and maidens, praise the name of the Lord.**

or

   ℟ **Alleluia!**

1 Praise the Lord from the heavens,
  praise him in the heights.
  Praise him, all his angels,
  praise him, all his host. ℟

2 All earth's kings and peoples,
  earth's princes and rulers;
  young men and maidens,
  old men together with children. ℟

3 Let them praise the name of the Lord
  for he alone is exalted.
  The splendour of his name
  reaches beyond heaven and earth. ℟

4 He exalts the strength of his people.
  He is the praise of all his saints,
  of the sons of Israel,
  of the people to whom he comes close. ℟

Gospel Acclamation Jn 8:31-32

Alleluia, alleluia!
If you make my word your home
you will indeed be my disciples,
and you will learn the truth, says the Lord.
Alleluia!

GOSPEL

A reading from the holy Gospel according to Mark 3:31-35

Anyone who does the will of God, that person is my brother and sister and mother.

The mother and brothers of Jesus arrived and, standing outside, sent in a message asking for him. A crowd was sitting round him at the time the message was passed to him, 'Your mother and brothers and sisters are outside asking for you'. He replied, 'Who are my mother and my brothers?' And looking round at those sitting in a circle about him, he said, 'Here are my mother and my brothers. Anyone who does the will of God, that person is my brother and sister and mother.'

This is the Gospel of the Lord.

Proper of Saints, 26 May

26 May
St Philip Neri, priest — Memorial

Born in Florence in 1515, Philip Neri passed most of his life in Rome. He was very much a man of the Renaissance, and yet a true Christian: he spent hours in discussion with the young men of the city; he worked for the sick and poor and for prisoners; he was a man of prayer, and especially devoted to the Blessed Sacrament. In 1551 he was ordained, and formed the Oratory in which services of spiritual reading and singing were held. His Christianity was full of joy and vigour.

Common of pastors, pp.1876ff., or of holy men and women: religious pp.1894ff.

Opening Prayer
Father,
you continually raise up your faithful
to the glory of holiness.
In your love
kindle in us the fire of the Holy Spirit
who so filled the heart of Philip Neri.

FIRST READING

A reading from the letter of St Paul to the Philippians   4:4-9
Fill your minds with everything that is pure.

I want you to be happy, always happy in the Lord, I repeat, what I want is your happiness. Let your tolerance be evident to everyone: the Lord is very near. There is no need to worry; but if there is anything you need, pray for it, asking God for it with prayer and thanksgiving, and that peace of God, which is so much greater than we can understand, will guard your hearts and your thoughts, in Christ Jesus. Finally, brothers, fill your minds with everything that is true, everthing that is noble, everything that is good and pure, everything that we love and honour, and everything that can be thought virtuous or worthy of praise. Keep doing all the things that you learnt from me and have been taught by me and have heard or seen that I do. Then the God of peace will be with you.
    This is the word of the Lord.

Responsorial Psalm
Ps 33:2-11. ℟ v.2. Alt. ℟. v.9

℟ **I will bless the Lord at all times.**

or

℟ **Taste and see that the Lord is good.**

1. I will bless the Lord at all times,
his praise always on my lips;
in the Lord my soul shall make its boast.
The humble shall hear and be glad. ℟

2. Glorify the Lord with me.
Together let us praise his name.
I sought the Lord and he answered me;
from all my terrors he set me free. ℟

3. Look towards him and be radiant;
let your faces not be abashed.
This poor man called; the Lord heard him
and rescued him from all his distress. ℟

4. The angel of the Lord is encamped
around those who revere him, to rescue them.
Taste and see that the Lord is good.
He is happy who seeks refuge in him. ℟

5. Revere the Lord, you his saints.
They lack nothing, those who revere him.
Strong lions suffer want and go hungry
but those who seek the Lord lack no blessing. ℟

Gospel Acclamation
Jn 15:9. 5

Alleluia, alleluia!
Remain in my love, says the Lord;
whoever remains in me, with me in him,
bears fruit in plenty.
Alleluia!

GOSPEL

A reading from the holy Gospel according to John
17:20-26
I want them to be with me where I am.

Jesus raised his eyes to heaven and said:

'Holy Father,
I pray not only for these,

Proper of Saints, 26 May

but for those also
who through their words will believe in me.
May they all be one.
Father, may they be one in us,
as you are in me and I am in you,
so that the world may believe it was you who sent me.
I have given them the glory you gave to me,
that they may be one as we are one.
With me in them and you in me,
may they be so completely one
that the world will realise that it was you who sent me
and that I have loved them as much as you loved me.
Father,
I want those you have given me
to be with me where I am,
so that they may always see the glory
you have given me
because you loved me
before the foundation of the world.
Father, Righteous One,
the world has not known you,
but I have known you,
and these have known
that you have sent me.
I have made your name known to them
and will continue to make it known,
so that the love with which you loved me may be in them,
and so that I may be in them.'

This is the Gospel of the Lord.

Prayer over the Gifts
Lord,
help us who offer you this sacrifice of praise
to follow the example of Saint Philip.
Keep us always cheerful in our work
for the glory of your name and the good of our neighbour.

Prayer after Communion
Lord,
strengthen us with the bread of life.
May we always imitate Saint Philip
by hungering after this sacrament
in which we find new life.

27 May
St Augustine of Canterbury, bishop
Optional Memorial

Entrance Antiphon: Come, all of you who fear God, and hear the great things the Lord has done for me.

Opening Prayer
Father,
by the preaching of Saint Augustine of Canterbury,
you led the people of England to the gospel.
May the fruits of his work continue in your Church.

FIRST READING
A reading from the first letter of St Paul to the Thessalonians 2:2-8
We were eager to hand over not only the Good News but our whole lives as well.

It was our God who gave us the courage to proclaim his Good News to you in the face of great opposition. We have not taken to preaching because we are deluded, or immoral, or trying to deceive anyone; it was God who decided that we were fit to be entrusted with the Good News, and when we are speaking, we are not trying to please men but God, who can read our inmost thoughts. You know very well, and we can swear it before God, that never at any time have our speeches been simply flattery, or a cover for trying to get money; nor have we ever looked for any special honour from men, either from you or anybody else, when we could have imposed ourselves on you with full weight, as apostles of Christ.

Instead, we were unassuming. Like a mother feeding and looking after her own children, we felt so devoted and protective towards you, and had come to love you so much, that we were eager to hand over to you not only the Good News but our whole lives as well.

This is the word of the Lord.

Responsional Psalm
Ps 95: 1-3. 7-8. 10. ℟ v.3

℟ **Proclaim the wonders of the Lord
among all the peoples.**

1 O sing a new song to the Lord,
sing to the Lord all the earth.
O sing to the Lord, bless his name. ℟

2. Proclaim his help day by day,
   tell among the nations his glory
   and his wonders among all the peoples. ℟

3. Give the Lord, you families of peoples,
   give the Lord glory and power,
   give the Lord the glory of his name. ℟

4. Proclaim to the nations: 'God is king.'
   The world he made firm in its place;
   he will judge the peoples in fairness. ℟

Gospel Acclamation
Jn 10:14

Alleluia, alleluia!
I am the good shepherd, says the Lord;
I know my own sheep
and my own know me.
Alleluia!

GOSPEL

A reading from the holy Gospel according to Matthew 9:35-37
The harvest is rich but the labourers are few.

Jesus made a tour through all the towns and villages, teaching in their synagogues, proclaiming the Good News of the kingdom and curing all kinds of diseases and sickness.

And when he saw the crowds he felt sorry for them because they were harassed and dejected, like sheep without a shepherd. Then he said to his disciples, 'The harvest is rich but the labourers are few, so ask the Lord of the harvest to send labourers to his harvest.'

This is the Gospel of the Lord.

31 May

THE VISITATION OF THE BLESSED VIRGIN MARY
Feast

Entrance Antiphon: Come, all of you who fear God, and hear the great things the Lord has done for me.

Opening Prayer
Eternal Father,
you inspired the Virgin Mary, mother of your Son,

to visit Elizabeth and assist her in her need.
Keep us open to the working of your Spirit,
and with Mary may we praise you for ever.

FIRST READING

A reading from the prophet Zephaniah   3:14-18
The Lord, the king of Israel, is in your midst.

Shout for joy, daughter of Zion,
Israel, shout aloud!
Rejoice, exult with all your heart,
daughter of Jerusalem!
The Lord has repealed your sentence;
he has driven your enemies away.
The Lord, the king of Israel, is in your midst;
you have no more evil to fear.
When that day comes, word will come to Jerusalem;
Zion, have no fear,
do not let your hands fall limp.
The Lord your God is in your midst,
a victorious warrior.
He will exult with joy over you,
he will renew you by his love;
he will dance with shouts of joy for you
as on a day of festival.

This is the word of the Lord.

Alternative First Reading

A reading from the letter of St Paul to the Romans   12:9-16
If any of the saints are in need you must share with them; and you should make hospitality your special care.

Do not let your love be a pretence, but sincerely prefer good to evil. Love each other as much as brothers should, and have a profound respect for each other. Work for the Lord with untiring effort and with great earnestness of spirit. If you have hope, this will make you cheerful. Do not give up if trials come; and keep on praying. If any of the saints are in need you must share with them; and you should make hospitality your special care.

Bless those who persecute you: never curse them, bless them. Rejoice with those who rejoice and be sad with those in sorrow. Treat everyone with equal kindness; never be condescending but make real friends with the poor.

This is the word of the Lord.

Responsorial Psalm   Is 12:2-6. R/ v.6
   R/ **Great in your midst is the Holy One of Israel.**

1 Truly, God is my salvation,
   I trust, I shall not fear.
   For the Lord is my strength, my song,
   he became my saviour.
   With joy you will draw water
   from the wells of salvation.   R/

2 Give thanks to the Lord, give praise to his name!
   Make his mighty deeds known to the peoples!
   Declare the greatness of his name.   R/

3 Sing a psalm to the Lord!
   For he has done glorious deeds.
   make them known to all the earth!
   People of Zion, sing and shout for joy
   for great in your midst is the Holy One of Israel.   R/

Gospel Acclamation   cf. Lk 1:45
   Alleluia, alleluia!
   Blessed is the Virgin Mary who believed
   that the promise made her by the Lord would be fulfilled.
   Alleluia!

GOSPEL

A reading from the holy Gospel according to Luke   1:39-56
Why should I be honoured with a visit from the mother of my Lord?

Mary set out and went as quickly as she could to a town in the hill country of Judah. She went into Zechariah's house and greeted Elizabeth. Now as soon as Elizabeth heard Mary's greeting, the child leapt in her womb and Elizabeth was filled with the Holy Spirit. She gave a loud cry and said, 'Of all women you are the most blessed, and blessed is the fruit of your womb. Why should I be honoured with a visit from the mother of my Lord? For the moment your greeting reached my ears, the child in my womb leapt for joy. Yes, blessed is she who believed that the promise

made her by the Lord would be fulfilled.'
And Mary said:

'My soul proclaims the greatness of the Lord
and my spirit exults in God my saviour;
because he has looked upon his lowly handmaid.
Yes, from this day forward all generations will call me blessed,
for the Almighty has done great things to me.
Holy is his name,
and his mercy reaches from age to age for those who fear him.
He has shown the power of his arm,
he has routed the proud of heart.
He has pulled down princes from their thrones and exalted the lowly.
The hungry he has filled with good things, the rich sent empty away.
He has come to the help of Israel his servant, mindful of his mercy
– according to the promise he made to our ancestors –
of his mercy to Abraham and to his descendants for ever.'

Mary stayed with Elizabeth about three months and then went back home.

This is the Gospel of the Lord.

Prayer over the Gifts
Father,
make our sacrifice acceptable and holy
as you accepted the love of Mary,
the mother of your Son, Jesus Christ,
who is Lord for ever and ever.

Preface of the Blessed Virgin Mary I or II, P56 or P57.

Communion Antiphon: All generations will call me blessed, for the Almighty has done great things for me. Holy is his name.

Prayer after Communion
Lord,
let the Church praise you
for the great things you have done for your people.
May we always recognise with joy
the present of Christ in the eucharist we celebrate,
as John the Baptist hailed the presence
of our Saviour in the womb of Mary.

Proper of Saints; Immaculate Heart of Mary

Saturday following the Second Sunday after Pentecost
The Immaculate Heart of Mary
Optional Memorial

Entrance Antiphon: My heart rejoices in your saving power. I will sing to the Lord for his goodness to me.

Opening Prayer
Father,
you prepared the heart of the Virgin Mary
to be a fitting home for your Holy Spirit.
By her prayers
may we become a more worthy temple of your glory.

The Gospel is proper to this memorial.

FIRST READING

A reading from the prophet Isaiah 61:9-11

I exult for joy in the Lord.

Their race will be famous throughout the nations,
their descendants throughout the peoples.
All who see them will admit
that they are a race whom the Lord has blessed.
I exult for joy in the Lord,
my soul rejoices in my God,
for he has clothed me in the garments of salvation,
he has wrapped me in the cloak of integrity,
like a bridegroom wearing his wreath,
like a bride adorned in her jewels.
For as the earth makes fresh things grow,
as a garden makes seeds spring up,
so will the Lord make both integrity and praise
spring up in the sight of the nations.

    This is the word of the Lord.

Responsorial Psalm
1 Sam 2:1. 4-8. R̷ cf. v.1

  R̷ **My heart exults in the Lord my saviour.**

1 My heart exults in the Lord,
   I find my strength in my God;
   my mouth laughs at my enemies
   as I rejoice in your saving help.   R̷

2. The bows of the mighty are broken,
but the weak are clothed with strength.
Those with plenty must labour for bread,
but the hungry need work no more.
The childless wife has children now
but the fruitful wife bears no more.

℟ **My heart exults in the Lord my saviour.**

3. It is the Lord who gives life and death,
he brings men to the grave and back;
it is the Lord who gives poverty and riches.
He brings men low and raises them on high.   ℟

4. He lifts up the lowly from the dust,
from the dungheap he raises the poor
to set them in the company of princes,
to give them a glorious throne.   ℟

Gospel Acclamation   cf. Lk 2:19
Alleluia, alleluia!
Blessed is the Virgin Mary
who treasured the word of God,
and pondered it in her heart.
Alleluia!

GOSPEL

A reading from the holy Gospel according to Luke   2:41-51

Mary stored up all these things in her heart.

Every year the parents of Jesus used to go to Jerusalem for the feast of the Passover. When he was twelve years old, they went up for the feast as usual. When they were on their way home after the feast, the boy Jesus stayed behind in Jerusalem without his parents knowing it. They assumed he was with the caravan, and it was only after a day's journey that they went to look for him among their relations and acquaintances. When they failed to find him they went back to Jerusalem looking for him everywhere.

Three days later, they found him in the Temple, sitting among the doctors, listening to them, and asking them questions; and all those who heard him were astounded at his intelligence and his replies. They were overcome when they saw him, and his mother said to him, 'My child, why have you done this to us? See how worried your father and I have been, looking for you.' 'Why were you looking for me?' he replied 'Did you not know that I must be busy with my Father's affairs?' But they did not understand what he meant.

He then went down with them and came to Nazareth and lived under their authority. His mother stored up all these things in her heart.

This is the Gospel of Lord.

Prayer over the Gifts
Lord,
accept the prayers and gifts we offer
in honour of Mary, the Mother of God.
May they please you
and bring us your help and forgiveness.

Preface of the Blessed Virgin Mary I or II, P56 or P57.

Communion Antiphon: Mary treasured all these words and pondered them in her heart.

Prayer after Communion
Lord,
you have given us the sacrament of eternal redemption.
May we who honour the mother of your Son
rejoice in the abundance of your blessings
and experience the deepening of your life within us.

Walk in the Spirit

JUNE

1 June
St Justin, martyr — Memorial

Born at the beginning of the second century, at Nablus in Samaria. His family was pagan. He was a philosopher, and became a Christian at about the age of thirty. He went first to Ephesus, and then to Rome, where he established a school. He wrote many works in defence of Christianity, of which the two Apologies, and his Dialogue with Trypho survive. He gives us the earliest description of the rite of baptism, and of a Sunday Mass. He was martyred, with six others, five men and a woman, during the time of Marcus Aurelius, about 165.

Entrance Antiphon: The wicked tempted me with their fables against your law, but I proclaimed your decrees before kings without fear or shame.

Opening Prayer
Father,
through the folly of the cross
you taught Saint Justin the sublime wisdom of Jesus Christ.
May we too reject falsehood
and remain loyal to the faith.

Proper of Saints, 1 June 1525

FIRST READING

A reading from the first letter of St Paul 1:18-25
to the Corinthians
God wanted to save those who have faith through the foolishness of the message that we preach.

The language of the cross may be illogical to those who are not on the way to salvation, but those of us who are on the way see it as God's power to save. As scripture says: I shall destroy the wisdom of the wise and bring to nothing all the learning of the learned. Where are the philosophers now? Where are the scribes? Where are any of our thinkers today? Do you see now how God has shown up the foolishness of human wisdom? If it was God's wisdom that human wisdom should not know God, it was because God wanted to save those who have faith through the foolishness of the message that we preach. And so, while the Jews demand miracles and the Greeks look for wisdom, here are we preaching a crucified Christ; to the Jews an obstacle that they cannot get over, to the pagans madness, but to those who have been called, whether they are Jews or Greeks, a Christ who is the power and the wisdom of God. For God's foolishness is wiser than human wisdom, and God's weakness is stronger than human strength.

This is the word of the Lord.

Responsorial Psalm
Ps 33:2-9. ℟ v.5

℟ **From all my terrors the Lord set me free.**

1 I will bless the Lord at all times,
 his praise always on my lips;
 in the Lord my soul shall make its boast.
 The humble shall hear and be glad. ℟

2 Glorify the Lord with me.
 together let us praise his name.
 I sought the Lord and he answered me;
 from all my terrors he set me free. ℟

3 Look towards him and be radiant;
 let your faces not be abashed.
 This poor man called; the Lord heard him
 and rescued him from all his distress. ℟

4 The angel of the Lord is encamped

around those who revere him, to rescue them.
Taste and see that the Lord is good.
He is happy who seeks refuge in him.

℟ **From all my terrors the Lord set me free.**

Gospel Acclamation
Mt 5:16

Alleluia, alleluia!
Your light must shine in the sight of men,
so that, seeing your good works,
they may give the praise to your Father in heaven.
Alleluia!

GOSPEL

A reading from the holy Gospel according to Matthew 5:13-19
You are the light of the world.

Jesus said to his disciples: 'You are the salt of the earth. But if salt becomes tasteless, what can make it salty again? It is good for nothing, and can only be thrown out to be trampled underfoot by men.

'You are the light of the world. A city built on a hill-top cannot be hidden. No one lights a lamp to put it under a tub; they put it on the lamp-stand where it shines for everyone in the house. In the same way your light must shine in the sight of men, so that, seeing your good works, they may give the praise to your Father in heaven.

'Do not imagine that I have come to abolish the Law or the Prophets. I have come not to abolish but to complete them. I tell you solemnly, till heaven and earth disappear, not one dot, not one little stroke, shall disappear from the Law until its purpose is achieved. Therefore, the man who infringes even one of the least of these commandments and teaches others to do the same will be considered the least in the kingdom of heaven; but the man who keeps them and teaches them will be considered great in the kingdom of heaven.'

This is the Gospel of the Lord.

Prayer over the Gifts
Lord,
help us to worship you as we should
when we celebrate these mysteries
which Saint Justin vigorously defended.

Communion Antiphon: I resolved that while I was with you I would think of nothing but Jesus Christ and him crucified.

Prayer after Communion
Lord,
hear the prayer of those you renew with spiritual food.
By following the teaching of Saint Justin
may we offer constant thanks for the gifts we receive.

2 June

Ss Marcellinus and Peter, martyrs
Optional Memorial

Martyrs from the time of the persecution of Diocletian.

Common of martyrs, pp.1865ff.

Opening Prayer
Father,
may we benefit from the example
of your martyrs Marcellinus and Peter,
and be supported by their prayers.

FIRST READING

A reading from the second letter of St Paul 6:4-10
to the Corinthians
Said to be dying, and here we are alive.

We prove we are servants of God by great fortitude in times of suffering: in times of hardship and distress; when we are flogged, or sent to prison, or mobbed; labouring, sleepless, starving. We prove we are God's servants by our purity, knowledge, patience and kindness; by a spirit of holiness, by a love free from affectation; by the word of truth and by the power of God; by being armed with the weapons of righteousness in the right hand and in the left, prepared for honour or disgrace, for blame or praise; taken for impostors while we are genuine; obscure yet famous; said to be dying and here we are alive; rumoured to be executed before we are sentenced; thought most miserable and yet we are always rejoicing; taken for paupers though we make others rich, for people having nothing though we have everything.

This is the word of the Lord.

Responsorial Psalm
Ps 123:2-5. 7-8. ℟ v.7

℟ **Our life, like a bird, has escaped
from the snare of the fowler.**

1 If the Lord had not been on our side
when men rose against us,
then would they have swallowed us alive
when their anger was kindled. ℟

2 Then would the waters have engulfed us,
the torrent gone over us;
over our heads would have swept
the raging waters. ℟

3 Indeed the snare has been broken
and we have escaped.
Our help is in the name of the Lord,
who made heaven and earth. ℟

Gospel Acclamation
2 Cor 1:3-4

Alleluia, alleluia!
Blessed be God, a gentle Father,
and the God of all consolation,
who comforts us in all our sorrows.
Alleluia!

GOSPEL

A reading from the holy Gospel according to John 17:11-19
The world hated them.

Jesus raised his eyes to heaven and said,

'Holy Father,
keep those you have given me true to your name,
so that they may be one like us.
While I was with them,
I kept those you had given me true to your name.
I have watched over them and not one is lost
except the one who chose to be lost,
and this was to fulfil the scriptures.
But now I am coming to you
and while still in the world I say these things
to share my joy with them to the full.
I passed your word on to them,

and the world hated them,
because they belong to the world
no more than I belong to the world.
I am not asking you to remove them from the world,
but to protect them from the evil one.
They do not belong to the world
any more than I belong to the world.
Consecrate them in the truth;
your word is truth.
As you sent me into the world,
I have sent them into the world,
and for their sake I consecrate myself
so that they too may be consecrated in truth.'

This is the Gospel of the Lord.

3 June
Ss Charles Lwanga and companions, martyrs
Memorial

The twenty-two martyrs of Uganda were put to death by the king, Mwanga, whose objection to their Christianity was reinforced by their resistance to his impure demands of them. Some were quite young boys; some were still catechumens, though Charles Lwanga baptised these before their death. Even the youngest of all, Kizito, persevered to the end despite the entreaties of his family.
Common of Martyrs, pp.1865ff.

Opening Prayer
Father,
you have made the blood of the martyrs
the seed of Christians.
May the witness of Saint Charles and his companions
and their loyalty to Christ in the face of torture
inspire countless men and women
to live the Christian faith.

FIRST READING

A reading from the second book of Maccabees   7:1-2. 9-14
We are prepared to die rather than break the laws of our ancestors.

There were seven brothers who were arrested with their mother. The king tried to force them to taste pig's flesh, which the Law forbids, by torturing them with whips and scourges. One of them, acting as spokesman for the others, said, 'What are you trying to find out from us? We are prepared to die rather than break the laws of our ancestors.' With his last breath the second exclaimed, 'Inhuman fiend, you may discharge us from this present life, but the King of the world will raise us up, since it is for his laws that we die, to live again for ever.'

After him, they amused themselves with the third, who on being asked for his tongue promptly thrust it out and boldly held out his hands, with these honourable words, 'It was heaven that gave me these limbs; for the sake of his laws I disdain them; from him I hope to receive them again.' The king and his attendants were astounded at the young man's courage and his utter indifference to suffering.

When this one was dead they subjected the fourth to the same savage torture. When he neared his end he cried, 'Ours is the better choice, to meet death at men's hands, yet relying on God's promise that we shall be raised up by him; whereas for you there can be no resurection, no new life.'

This is the word of the Lord.

Responsorial Psalm
Ps 123:2-5. 7-8. ℟ v.7

℟ **Our life, like a bird, has escaped from the snare of the fowler.**

1 If the Lord had not been on our side
 when men rose against us,
 then would they have swallowed us alive
 when their anger was kindled. ℟

2 Then would the waters have engulfed us,
 the torrent gone over us;
 over our head would have swept
 the raging waters. ℟

3 Indeed the snare has been broken
 and we have escaped.
 Our help is the name of the Lord,
 who made heaven and earth. ℟

Gospel Acclamation
Mt 5:3

Alleluia, alleluia!
How happy are the poor in spirit;
theirs is the kingdom of heaven.
Alleluia!

GOSPEL

A reading from the holy Gospel according to Matthew 5:1-12
Rejoice and be glad, for your reward will be great in heaven.

Seeing the crowds, Jesus went up the hill. There he sat down and was joined by his disciples. Then he began to speak. This is what he taught them:

> 'How happy are the poor in spirit;
> theirs is the kingdom of heaven.
> Happy the gentle:
> they shall have the earth for their heritage.
> Happy those who mourn:
> they shall be comforted.
> Happy those who hunger and thirst for what is right:
> they shall be satisfied.
> Happy the merciful:
> they shall have mercy shown them.
> Happy the pure in heart:
> they shall see God.
> Happy the peacemakers:
> they shall be called sons of God.
> Happy those who are persecuted in the cause of right:
> theirs is the kingdom of heaven.

'Happy are you when people abuse you and persecute you and speak all kinds of calumny against you on my account. Rejoice and be glad, for your reward will be great in heaven.'

This is the Gospel of the Lord.

Prayer over the Gifts

Lord,
accept the gifts we present at your altar.
As you gave your holy martyrs courage to die rather than sin,
help us to give ourselves completely to you.

Prayer after Communion

Lord,
at this celebration of the triumph of your martyrs,
we have received the sacraments
which helped them endure their sufferings.
In the midst of our own hardships
may this eucharist keep us steadfast in faith and love.

5 June

St Boniface, bishop and martyr — Memorial

Born in England about 673, he was called Winifrid until Pope Gregory II gave him the name of Boniface. A monk from Exeter who was the apostle of Germany, consecrated bishop by Gregory during a visit to Rome in 722, Boniface travelled throughout Germany where he established or restored dioceses, and set up monasteries, notably at Fulda, where he is buried. Although he became Bishop of Mainz, he did not give up his itinerant missionary life, and was killed by pagans in Friesland in 754.

Common of martyrs, pp.1865ff., or of pastors: missionaries, pp.1885ff.

Opening Prayer

Lord,
your martyr Boniface
spread the faith by his teaching
and witnessed to it with his blood.
By the help of his prayers
keep us loyal to our faith
and give us the courage to profess it in our lives.

FIRST READING

A reading from the Acts of the Apostles 26:19-23

Christ was to proclaim that light now shone for our people and for the pagans.

Paul said, 'King Agrippa, I could not disobey the heavenly vision. On the contrary I started preaching, first to the people of Damascus, then to those of Jerusalem and all the countryside of Judaea, and also to the pagans, urging them to repent and turn to God, proving their change of heart by their deeds. This was why the Jews laid hands on me in the Temple and tried to do away with me. But I was blessed with God's help, and so I have stood firm to this day, testifying to great and small alike, saying nothing more than what the prophets and Moses himself said would happen: that the Christ was to suffer and that, as the first to rise from the dead, he was to proclaim that light now shone for our people and for the pagans too.'

This is the word of the Lord.

Proper of Saints, 5 June 1533

Responsorial Psalm Ps 116. ℟ Mk 16:15

℟ **Go out to the whole world;
proclaim the Good News.**

or

℟ **Alleluia!**

1. O praise the Lord, all you nations,
   acclaim him all you peoples! ℟

2. Strong is his love for us;
   he is faithful for ever. ℟

Gospel Acclamation Jn 10:14
Alleluia, alleluia!
I am the good shepherd, says the Lord;
I know my own sheep
and my own know me.
Alleluia!

GOSPEL

A reading from the holy Gospel according to John 10:11-16
The good shepherd is one who lays down his life for his sheep.

Jesus said:

'I am the good shepherd:
the good shepherd is one who lays down his life for his sheep.
The hired man, since he is not the shepherd
and the sheep do not belong to him,
abandons the sheep and runs away
as soon as he sees a wolf coming,
and then the wolf attacks and scatters the sheep;
this is because he is only a hired man
and has no concern for the sheep.
I am the good shepherd;
I know my own
and my own know me,
just as the Father knows me
and I know the Father;
and I lay down my life for my sheep.
And there are other sheep I have
that are not of this fold,
and these I have to lead as well.

They too will listen to my voice,
and there will be only one flock,
and one shepherd.'

This is the Gospel of the Lord.

6 June
St Norbert, bishop — Optional Memorial

Born about 1080 in the Rhineland, ordained in 1115. He lived a life of penance and apostolate, and encouraged other clergy to do the same. This aroused hostility, and he left Germany and went to France, where he established a community of Canons who followed the rule of St Augustine – living in community, celebrating the Divine Office and preaching to the people. From this came the Premonstratensian Order. He was elected bishop of Magdeburg in 1126. He died in 1134.

Common of pastors: bishops, pp.1876ff., or of holy men and women: religious pp.1898ff.

Opening Prayer
Father,
you made the bishop Norbert
an outstanding minister of your Church,
renowned for his preaching and pastoral zeal.
Always grant to your Church faithful shepherds
to lead your people to eternal salvation.

FIRST READING
A reading from the prophet Ezekiel   34:11-16

As a shepherd keeps all his flock in view, so shall I keep my sheep in view.

The Lord says this: I am going to look after my flock myself and keep all of it in view. As a shepherd keeps all his flock in view when he stands up in the middle of his scattered sheep, so shall I keep my sheep in view. I shall rescue them from wherever they have been scattered during the mist and darkness. I shall bring them out of the countries where they are; I shall gather them together from foreign countries and bring them back to their own land. I shall pasture them on the mountains of Israel, in the ravines and in every inhabited place in the land. I shall feed them in good pasturage; the high mountains of Israel will be their grazing ground. There they will rest in good grazing ground;

Proper of Saints, 6 June 1535

they will browse in rich pastures on the mountains of Israel. I myself will pasture my sheep, I myself will show them where to rest – it is the Lord who speaks. I shall look for the lost one, bring back the stray, bandage the wounded and make the weak strong. I shall watch over the fat and healthy. I shall be a true shepherd to them.

This is the word of the Lord.

Responsorial Psalm
Ps 22. ℟ v.1

℟ **The Lord is my shepherd;**
there is nothing I shall want.

1 The Lord is my shepherd;
 there is nothing I shall want.
 Fresh and green are the pastures
 where he gives me respose.
 Near restful waters he leads me,
 to revive my drooping spirit. ℟

2 He guides me along the right path;
 he is true to his name.
 If I should walk in the valley of darkness
 no evil would I fear.
 You are there with your crook and your staff;
 with these you give me comfort. ℟

3 You have prepared a banquet for me
 in the sight of my foes.
 My head you have anointed with oil;
 my cup is overflowing. ℟

4 Surely goodness and kindness shall follow me
 all the days of my life.
 In the Lord's own house shall I dwell
 for ever and ever. ℟

Gospel Acclamation
Mt 5:3

Alleluia, alleluia!
Happy are the poor in spirit;
theirs is the kingdom of heaven.
Alleluia!

GOSPEL

A reading from the holy Gospel according to Luke 14:25-33

None of you can be my disciple unless he gives up all his possesions.

Great crowds accompanied Jesus on his way and he turned and spoke to them. 'If any man comes to me without hating his father, mother, wife, children, brothers, sisters, yes and his own life too, he cannot be my disciple. Anyone who does not carry his cross and come after me cannot be my disciple.

'And indeed, which of you here, intending to build a tower, would not first sit down and work out the cost to see if he had enough to complete it? Otherwise, if he laid the foundation and then found himself unable to finish the work, the onlookers would all start making fun of him and saying, 'Here is a man who started to build and was unable to finish.' Or again, what king marching to war against another king would not first sit down and consider whether with ten thousand men he could stand up to the other who advanced against him with twenty thousand? If not, then while the other king was still a long way off, he would send envoys to sue for peace. So in the same way, none of you can be my disciple unless he gives up all his possessions.'

This is the Gospel of the Lord.

9 June

St Ephrem, deacon and doctor of the Church

Optional Memorial

Born about 306 in Nisibis, Turkey, he was ordained deacon and given charge of a school of theology which later moved to Edessa. He lived an ascetic life; he taught, preached, and wrote extensively. His hymns and sermons survive and are still an inspiration.

Common of doctors of the Church, pp.1887ff.

Opening Prayer
Lord,
in your love fill our hearts with the Holy Spirit,
who inspired the deacon Ephrem to sing the praise of your
    mysteries
and gave him strength to serve you alone.

Proper of Saints, 9 June

FIRST READING

A reading from the letter of St Paul to the Colossians 3:12-17
Over all, to keep them together and complete them, put on love.

You are God's chosen race, his saints; he loves you, and you should be clothed in sincere compassion, in kindness and humility, gentleness and patience. Bear with one another; forgive each other as soon as a quarrel begins. The Lord has forgiven you; now you must do the same. Over all these clothes, to keep them together and complete them, put on love. And may the peace of Christ reign in your hearts, because it is for this that you were called together as parts of one body. Always be thankful.

Let the message of Christ, in all its richness, find a home with you. Teach each other, and advise each other, in all wisdom. With gratitude in your hearts sing psalms and hymns and inspired songs to God; and never say or do anything except in the name of the Lord Jesus, giving thanks to God the Father through him.

This is the word of the Lord.

Responsorial Psalm Ps 36: 3-6. 30-31. ℟ v.30

℟ **The just man's mouth utters wisdom.**

1 If you trust in the Lord and do good,
   then you will live in the land and be secure.
   If you find your delight in the Lord,
   he will grant your heart's desire. ℟

2 Commit your life to the Lord,
   trust in him and he will act,
   so that your justice breaks forth like the light,
   your cause like the noon-day sun. ℟

3 The just man's mouth utters wisdom
   and his lips speak what is right;
   the law of his God is in his heart,
   his steps shall be saved from stumbling. ℟

Gospel Acclamation Jn 15:5
Alleluia, alleluia!
I am the vine,
you are the branches says the Lord.
Whoever remains in me, with me in him,
bears fruit in plenty.
Alleluia!

GOSPEL

A reading from the holy Gospel according to Luke 6:43-45
A man's words flow out of what fills his heart.

Jesus said to his disciples:

'There is no sound tree that produces rotten fruit, nor again a rotten tree that produces sound fruit. For every tree can be told by its own fruit: people do not pick figs from thorns, nor gather grapes from brambles. A good man draws what is good from the store of goodness in his heart; a bad man draws what is bad from the store of badness. For a man's words flow out of what fills his heart.'

This is the Gospel of the Lord.

11 June

St Barnabas, apostle — Memorial

Born in Cyprus. One of the first converts in Jerusalem, soon after Pentecost, Barnabas went with St Paul on his first missionary journey, and took part in the Council of Jerusalem. Then he returned to Cyprus to preach the gospel, and died there.

Entrance Antiphon: Blessed are you, Saint Barnabas: you were a man of faith, filled with the Holy Spirit and counted among the apostles.

Opening Prayer
God our Father,
you filled Saint Barnabas with faith and the Holy Spirit
and sent him to convert the nations.
Help us to proclaim the gospel by word and deed.

The First Reading is proper to this Memorial.

FIRST READING

A reading from the Acts of the Apostles 11:21-26; 13:1-3
He was a good man, filled with the Holy Spirit and with faith.

A great number believed and were converted to the Lord.

The church in Jerusalem heard about this and they sent Barnabas to Antioch. There he could see for himself that God had given grace, and this pleased him, and he urged them all to remain faithful to the Lord with heartfelt devotion; for he was a good man, filled with the Holy Spirit and with faith. And a large number of people were won over to the Lord.

Barnabas then left for Tarsus to look for Saul, and when he found him he brought him to Antioch. As things turned out they were to live together in that church a whole year, instructing a large number of people. It was at Antioch that the disciples were first called 'Christians'.

In the church at Antioch the following were prophets and teachers: Barnabas, Simeon called Niger, and Lucius of Cyrene, Manaen, who had been brought up with Herod the tetrarch, and Saul. One day while they were offering worship to the Lord and keeping a fast, the Holy Spirit said, 'I want Barnabas and Saul set apart for the work to which I have called them.' So it was that after fasting and prayer they laid their hands on them and sent them off.

This is the word of the Lord.

Responsorial Psalm

Ps 97:1-6. R℣ v.2

R℣ **The Lord has shown his salvation to the nations.**

1 Sing a new song to the Lord
   for he has worked wonders.
   His right hand and his holy arm
   have brought salvation. R℣

2 The Lord has made known his salvation;
   has shown his justice to the nations.
   He has remembered his truth and love
   for the house of Israel. R℣

3 All the ends of the earth have seen
   the salvation of our God.
   Shout to the Lord all the earth,
   ring out your joy. R℣

4 Sing psalms to the Lord with the harp,
   with the sound of music.
   With trumpets and the sound of the horn
   acclaim the King, the Lord. R℣

Gospel Acclamation

Mt 28:18. 20

Alleluia, alleluia!
Go, make disciples of all the nations,
says the Lord;

I am with you always;
yes, to the end of time.
Alleluia!

GOSPEL

A reading from the holy Gospel according to Matthew 10:7-13

You received without charge, give without charge.

Jesus said to his apostles, 'As you go, proclaim that the kingdom of heaven is close at hand. Cure the sick, raise the dead, cleanse the lepers, cast out devils. You received without charge, give without charge. Provide yourselves with no gold or silver, not even with a few coppers for your purse, with no haversack for the journey or spare tunic or footwear or a staff, for the workman deserves his keep.

'Whatever town or village you go into, ask for someone trustworthy and stay with him until you leave. As you enter his house, salute it, and if the house deserves it, let your peace descend upon it; if it does not, let your peace come back to you.'

This is the Gospel of the Lord.

Prayer over the Gifts
Lord,
bless these gifts we present to you.
May they kindle in us the flame of love
by which Saint Barnabas brought the light of the gospel
to the nations.

Preface of the Apostles I or II, P64 or P65.

Communion Antiphon: No longer shall I call you servants, for a servant knows not what his master does. Now I shall call you friends, for I have revealed to you all that I have heard from my Father.

Prayer after Communion
Lord,
hear the prayers of those who receive the pledge of eternal life
on the feast of Saint Barnabas.
May we come to share the salvation
we celebrate in this sacrament.

13 June
St Anthony of Padua, priest and doctor of the Church
Memorial

Born at Lisbon, Portugal, in 1195; he first entered the Canons Regular of St Augustine, but after ordination, joined the Friars Minor. He had exceptional talent as a preacher, and was sent throughout Italy and France to preach against the Catharist heresy. He was the first theologian of the Franciscan Order. He died in Padua in 1231.

Common of pastors, pp.1876ff., or of doctors of the church, pp.1887ff., or of holy men and women: religious, pp.1898ff.

Opening Prayer
Almighty God,
you have given Saint Anthony to your people
as an outstanding preacher
and a ready helper in time of need.
With his assistance may we follow the gospel of Christ
and know the help of your grace in every difficulty.

FIRST READING

A reading from the prophet Isaiah 61:1-3

The Lord has anointed me and sent me to bring good news to the poor.

The spirit of the Lord has been given to me,
for the Lord has anointed me.
He has sent me to bring good news to the poor,
to bind up hearts that are broken;
to proclaim liberty to captives,
freedom to those in prison;
to proclaim a year of favour from the Lord,
a day of vengeance for our God,
to comfort all those who mourn and to give them
for ashes a garland;
for mourning robe the oil of gladness,
for despondency, praise.

　　This is the word of the Lord.

Responsorial Psalm
Ps 88:2-5. 21-22. 25. 27. ℟ v.2

℟ **I will sing for ever of your love, O Lord.**

1 I will sing for ever of your love, O Lord;
through all ages my mouth will proclaim your truth.
Of this I am sure, that your love lasts for ever,
that your truth is firmly established as the heavens. ℟

2 'I have made a covenant with my chosen one;
I have sworn to David my servant:
I will establish your dynasty for ever
and set up your throne through all ages. ℟

3 'I have found David my servant
and with my holy oil anointed him.
My hand shall always be with him
and my arm shall make him strong. ℟

4 'My truth and my love shall be with him;
by my name his might shall be exalted.
He will say to me: "You are my father,
my God, the rock who saves me." ' ℟

Gospel Acclamation
Lk 4:18

Alleluia, alleluia!
The Lord has sent me to bring the good news to the poor,
to proclaim liberty to captives.
Alleluia!

GOSPEL

A reading from the holy Gospel according to Luke
10:1-9

The harvest is rich but the labourers are few.

The Lord appointed seventy-two others and sent them out ahead of him, in pairs, to all the towns and places he himself was to visit. He said to them, 'The harvest is rich but the labourers are few, so ask the Lord of the harvest to send labourers to his harvest. Start off now, but remember, I am sending you out like lambs among wolves. Carry no purse, no haversack, no sandals. Salute no one on the road. Whatever house you go into, let your first words be, "Peace to this house!" And if a man of peace lives there, your peace will go and rest on him; if not, it will come back to you. Stay in the same house, taking what food and drink they have to offer, for the labourer deserves his wages; do not move from house to house. Whenever you go into a town where they make you welcome, eat what is set before you. Cure those in it who are sick, and say, "The kingdom of God is very near to you." '

This is the Gospel of the Lord.

19 June
St Romuald, abbot   Optional Memorial

Born in Ravenna in the middle of the tenth century, of aristocratic family. He renouced the world and led the life of a hermit, moving from place to place in search of somewhere to live in solitude. He died about 1027.

Common of holy men and women: religious, pp.1898ff.

Opening Prayer
Father,
through Saint Romuald
you renewed the life of solitude and prayer in your Church.
By our self-denial as we follow Christ
bring us the joy of heaven.

FIRST READING

A reading from the letter of St Paul to the Philippians   3:8-14
I am racing for the finish, for the prize to which God calls us upwards to receive in Christ Jesus.

I believe nothing can happen that will outweigh the supreme advantage of knowing Christ Jesus my Lord. For him I have accepted the loss of everything, and I look on everything as so much rubbish if only I can have Christ and be given a place in him. I am no longer trying for perfection by my own efforts, the perfection that comes from the Law, but I want only the perfection that comes through faith in Christ, and is from God and based on faith. All I want is to know Christ and the power of his resurrection and to share his sufferings by reproducing the pattern of his death. That is the way I can hope to take my place in the resurrection of the dead. Not that I have become perfect yet: I have not yet won, but I am still running, trying to capture the prize for which Christ Jesus captured me. I can assure you my brothers, I am far from thinking that I have already won. All I can say is that I forget the past and I strain ahead for what is still to come; I am racing for the finish, for the prize to which God calls us upwards to receive in Christ Jesus.

This is the word of the Lord.

Responsorial Psalm
Ps 130

℟ **Keep my soul in peace before you, O Lord.**

1 O Lord, my heart is not proud
    nor haughty my eyes.
    I have not gone after things too great
    nor marvels beyond me. ℟

2 Truly I have set my soul
    in silence and peace.
    A weaned child on its mother's breast,
    even so is my soul. ℟

3 O Israel, hope in the Lord
    both now and for ever. ℟

Gospel Acclamation
Mt 5:3

Alleluia, alleluia!
How happy are the poor in spirit;
theirs is the kingdom of heaven.
Alleluia!

GOSPEL

A reading from the holy Gospel according to Luke   14:25-33

None of you can be my disciple unless he gives up all his possessions.

Great crowds accompanied Jesus on his way and he turned and spoke to them. 'If any man comes to me without hating his father, mother, wife, children, brothers, sisters, yes and his own life too, he cannot be my disciple. Anyone who does not carry his cross and come after me cannot be my disciple.

'And indeed, which of you here, intending to build a tower, would not first sit down and work out the cost to see if he had enough to complete it? Otherwise, if he laid the foundation and then found himself unable to finish the work, the onlookers would all start making fun of him and saying, "Here is a man who started to build and was unable to finish." Or again, what king marching to war against another king would not first sit down and consider whether with ten thousand men he could stand up to the other who advanced against him with twenty thousand? If not, then while the other king was still a long way off, he would send envoys to sue for peace. So in the same way, none of you can be my disciple unless he gives up all his possessions.'

This is the Gospel of the Lord.

21 June

St Aloysius Gonzaga, religious — Memorial

Born in 1568 near Mantua, son of a high court official; at the age of seventeen entered the Society of Jesus, renouncing his inheritance. He caught the plague while working in a hospital, and died in 1591.

Entrance Antiphon: Who shall climb the mountain of the Lord and stand in his holy place? The innocent man, the pure of heart!

Opening Prayer

Father of love,
giver of all good things,
in Saint Aloysius you combined remarkable innocence
with the spirit of penance.
By the help of his prayers
may we who have not followed his innocence
follow his example of penance.

FIRST READING

A reading from the first letter of St John   5:1-5
This is the victory over the world – our faith.

Whoever believes that Jesus is the Christ
has been begotten by God;
and whoever loves the Father that begot him
loves the child whom he begets.
We can be sure that we love God's children
if we love God himself and do what he has commanded us;
this is what loving God is –
keeping his commandments;
and his commandments are not difficult,
because anyone who has been begotten by God
has already overcome the world;
this is the victory over the world –
our faith.
Who can overcome the world?
Only the man who believes that Jesus is the Son of God.

    This is the word of the Lord.

Responsorial Psalm
Ps 15:1-2. 5. 7-8. 11. ℟ cf. v.5

℟ **You are my inheritance, O Lord.**

1. Preserve me, God, I take refuge in you.
   I say to the Lord: 'You are my God.'
   O Lord, it is you who are my portion and cup;
   it is you yourself who are my prize. ℟

2. I will bless the Lord who gives me counsel,
   who even at night directs my heart.
   I keep the Lord ever in my sight:
   since he is at my right hand, I shall stand firm. ℟

3. You will show me the path of life,
   the fullness of joy in your presence,
   at your right hand happiness for ever. ℟

Gospel Acclamation
Jn 13:34

Alleluia, alleluia!
I give you a new commandment:
love one another just as I have loved you,
says the Lord.
Alleluia!

GOSPEL

A reading from the holy Gospel according to Matthew 22:34-40
Love the Lord your God, and your neighbour as yourself.

A lawyer, to disconcert Jesus, put a question, 'Master which is the greatest commandment of the Law?' Jesus said, 'You must love the Lord your God with all your heart, with all your soul, and with all your mind. This is the greatest and the first commandment. The second resembles it: You must love your neighbour as yourself. On these two commandments hang the whole Law, and the Prophets also.'

This is the Gospel of the Lord.

Prayer over the Gifts
Lord,
help us to follow the example of Saint Aloysius
and always come to the eucharist
with hearts free from sin.
By our sharing in this mystery
make us rich in your blessings.

Commonion Antiphon: God gave them bread from heaven; men ate the bread of angels.

Prayer after Communion
Lord,
you have nourished us with the bread of life.
Help us to serve you without sin.
By following the example of Saint Aloysius
may we continue to spend our lives in thanksgiving.

22 June

St Paulinus of Nola, bishop
Optional Memorial

Born in Bordeaux in 355, of a patrician Roman family, he became consul in 378, married and had a son, who died in infancy. He owned large estates, but renounced these when he was baptised in 389. Both he and his wife retired from the world. Paulinus was elected bishop of Nola, in Campagna, in 409. For twenty-two years he exercised a pastoral ministry at the service of the people. Many of his letters and poems have survived. He died in 431.

Common of pastors: bishops, pp.1878ff.

Opening Prayer
Lord,
you made Saint Paulinus
renowned for his love of poverty.
May we who celebrate his witness to the gospel
imitate his example of love for others.

FIRST READING

A reading from the second letter of St Paul 8:9-15
to the Corinthians

He was rich, but he became poor for your sake, to make you rich out of his poverty.

Remember how generous the Lord Jesus was: he was rich, but he became poor for your sake, to make you rich out of his poverty. As I say, I am only making a suggestion; it is only fair to you, since you were the first, a year ago, not only in taking action but even in deciding to. So now finish the work and let the results be worthy, as far as you can afford it, of the decision you made so promptly. As long as the readiness is there, a man is acceptable with whatever he can afford; never mind what is beyond his means. This does not mean that to give relief to others you ought to make things difficult for yourselves: it is a question of balancing what happens to be your surplus now against their present need, and one day they may have something to spare that will supply your own need. That is how we strike a balance: as scripture says: The man who gathered much had none too much, the man who gathered little did not go short.

This is the word of the Lord.

Responsional Psalm Ps 39:2. 4. 7-10. ℟ vv.8-9
℟ **Here I am, Lord!**
I come to do your will.

1   I waited, I waited for the Lord
    and he stooped down to me;
    he heard my cry.
    He put a new song into my mouth,
    praise of our God.   ℟

2   You do not ask for sacrifice and offerings,
    but an open ear.
    You do not ask for holocaust and victim.
    Instead, here am I.   ℟

3   In the scroll of the book it stands written
    that I should do your will.
    My God, I delight in your law
    in the depth of my heart.   ℟

4   Your justice I have proclaimed
    in the great assembly.
    My lips I have not sealed;
    you know it, O Lord.   ℟

Gospel Acclamation Mt 5:3
Alleluia, alleluia!
How happy are the poor in spirit;
theirs is the kingdom of heaven.
Alleluia!

Proper of Saints, 1549   1549

GOSPEL

A reading from the holy Gospel according to Luke   12:32-34
It has pleased your Father to give you the kingdom.

Jesus said to his disciples: 'There is no need to be afraid, little flock, for it has pleased your Father to give you the kingdom.

'Sell your possessions and give alms. Get yourselves purses that do not wear out, treasure that will not fail you, in heaven where no thief can reach it and no moth destroy it. For where your treasure is, there will your heart be also.'

This is the Gospel of the Lord.

Also 22 June

Ss John Fisher, bishop, and Thomas More, martyrs
Optional Memorial

John Fisher was born in 1469; he studied at Cambridge University, was ordained, became Bishop of Rochester. He was a pastoral bishop, charitable to the poor, a man of prayer, and a persistent opponent of the errors of the Protestant Reformation.

Thomas More was born in 1477, studied at Oxford University, married and had one son and three daughters. He became Chancellor of England. His writings include Utopia, *and many prayers and letters which reveal his spirituality. Both were executed on the orders of King Henry VIII.*

Common of martyrs, pp.1865ff.

Opening Prayer
Father,
you confirm the true faith
with the crown of martyrdom.
May the prayers of Saints John Fisher and Thomas More
give us the courage to proclaim our faith
by the witness of our lives.

FIRST READING

A reading from the first letter of St Peter   4:12-19
If you have some share in the sufferings of Christ, be glad.

My dear people, you must not think it unaccountable that you should be tested by fire. There is nothing extraordinary in what has happened to you. If you can have some share in the sufferings of Christ, be glad, because you will enjoy a much greater gladness when his glory is revealed. It is a blessing for you when they insult you for bearing the name of Christ, because it means that you have the Spirit of glory, the Spirit of God resting on you. None of you should ever deserve to suffer for being a murderer, a thief, a criminal or an informer; but if anyone of you should suffer for being a Christian, then he is not to be ashamed of it; he should thank God that he has been called one. The time has come for the judgement to begin at the household of God; and if what we know now is only the beginning, what will it be when it comes down to those who refuse to believe God's Good News? If it is hard for a good man to be saved, what will happen to the wicked and to sinners? So even those whom God allows to suffer must trust themselves to the constancy of the creator and go on doing good.

This is the word of the Lord.

Responsorial Psalm
Ps 125. ℟ v.5

℟ **Those who are sowing in tears will sing when they reap.**

1 When the Lord delivered Zion from bondage,
   it seemed like a dream.
   Then was our mouth filled with laughter,
   on our lips there were songs.   ℟

2 The heathens themselves said : 'What marvels
   the Lord worked for them!'
   What marvels the Lord worked for us!
   Indeed we were glad.   ℟

3 Deliver us, O Lord, from our bondage
   as streams in dry land.
   Those who are sowing in tears
   will sing when they reap.   ℟

4 They go out, they go out, full of tears,
   carrying seed for the sowing:
   they come back, they come back, full of song,
   carrying their sheaves.   ℟

Proper of Saints, 24 June 1551

Gospel Acclamation
Mt 5:10

Alleluia, alleluia!
Happy those who are persecuted in the cause of right:
theirs is the kingdom of heaven.
Alleluia!

GOSPEL

A reading from the holy Gospel according to Matthew 10:34-39
It is not peace I have come to bring, but a sword.

Jesus said to his apostles: 'Do not suppose that I have come to bring peace to the earth: it is not peace I have come to bring, but a sword. For I have come to set a man against his father, a daughter against her mother, a daughter-in-law against her mother-in-law. A man's enemies will be those of his own household.

'Anyone who prefers father or mother to me is not worthy of me. Anyone who prefers son or daughter to me is not worthy of me. Anyone who does not take his cross and follow in my footsteps is not worthy of me. Anyone who finds his life will lose it; anyone who loses his life for my sake will find it.'

This is the Gospel of the Lord.

24 June

THE BIRTH OF ST JOHN THE BAPTIST
Solemnity

Vigil Mass

Entrance Antiphon: From his mother's womb, he will be filled with the Holy Spirit, he will be great in the sight of the Lord, and many will rejoice at his birth.

The Gloria is sung or said.

Opening Prayer

Let us pray
  [that we will follow the way of salvation]

All-powerful God,
help your people to walk the path to salvation.
By following the teaching of John the Baptist,
may we come to your Son, our Lord Jesus Christ,
who lives and reigns with you and the Holy Spirit,
one God, for ever and ever.

Proper of Saints, 24 June

FIRST READING

A reading from the prophet Jeremiah 1:4-10
Before I formed you in the womb, I knew you.

In the days of Josiah, the word of the Lord was addressed to me, saying,

> 'Before I formed you in the womb I knew you;
> before you came to birth I consecrated you;
> I have appointed you as prophet to the nations.'

I said, 'Ah, Lord; look, I do not know how to speak: I am a child!' But the Lord replied,

> 'Do not say, "I am a child,"
> Go now to those to whom I send you
> and say whatever I command you.
> Do not be afraid of them,
> for I am with you to protect you –
> it is the Lord who speaks!'

Then the Lord put out his hand and touched my mouth and said to me:

> 'There! I am putting my words into your mouth.
> Look, today I am setting you
> over nations and over kingdoms,
> to tear up and to knock down,
> to destroy and to overthrow,
> to build and to plant.'

This is the word of the Lord.

Responsorial Psalm Ps 70:1-6. 15. 17. ℟ v.6

℟ **From my mother's womb you have been my help.**

1. In you, O Lord, I take refuge;
   let me never be put to shame.
   In your justice rescue me, free me:
   pay heed to me and save me. ℟

2. Be a rock where I can take refuge,
   a mighty stronghold to save me;
   for you are my rock, my stronghold.
   Free me from the hand of the wicked. ℟

3. It is you, O Lord, who are my hope,
   my trust, O Lord, since my youth.

On you I have leaned from my birth,
from my mother's womb you have been my help. ℟

4 My lips will tell of your justice
and day by day of your help.
O God, you have taught me from my youth
and I proclaim your wonders still. ℟

SECOND READING

A reading from the first letter of St Peter 1:8-12

It was this salvation that the prophets were looking and searching so hard for.

You did not see Jesus Christ, yet you love him; and still without seeing him, you are already filled with joy so glorious that it cannot be described, because you believe; and you are sure of the end to which your faith looks forward, that is, the salvation of your souls.

It was this salvation that the prophets were looking and searching so hard for; their prophecies were about the grace which was to come to you. The Spirit of Christ which was in them foretold the sufferings of Christ and the glories that would come after them, and they tried to find out at what time and in what circumstances all this was to be expected. It was revealed to them that the news they brought of all the things which have now been announced to you, by those who preached to you the Good News through the Holy Spirit sent from heaven, was for you and not for themselves. Even the angels long to catch a glimpse of these things.

This is the word of the Lord.

Gospel Acclamation cf. Jn 1:7; Lk 1:17
Alleluia, alleluia!
He came as a witness,
as a witness to speak for the light,
preparing for the Lord a people fit for him.
Alleluia!

GOSPEL

A reading from the holy Gospel according to Luke 1:5-17

She is to bear you a son and you must name him John.

In the days of King Herod of Judaea there lived a priest called Zechariah who belonged to the Abijah section of the priesthood, and he had a wife, Elizabeth by name, who was a descendant of Aaron. Both were worthy in the sight of God, and scrupulously observed all the commandments and observances of the Lord. But they were childless: Elizabeth was barren and they were both getting on in years.

Now it was the turn of Zechariah's section to serve, and he was exercising his priestly office before God when it fell to him by lot, as the ritual custom was, to enter the Lord's sanctuary and burn incense there. And at the hour of incense the whole congregation was outside, praying.

Then there appeared to him the angel of the Lord, standing on the right of the altar of incense. The sight disturbed Zechariah and he was overcome with fear. But the angel said to him, 'Zechariah, do not be afraid, your prayer has been heard. Your wife Elizabeth is to bear you a son and you must name him John. He will be your joy and delight and many will rejoice at his birth, for he will be great in the sight of the Lord; he must drink no wine, no strong drink. Even from his mother's womb he will be filled with the Holy Spirit, and he will bring back many of the sons of Israel to the Lord their God. With the spirit and power of Elijah, he will go before him to turn the hearts of fathers towards their children and the disobedient back to the wisdom that the virtuous have, preparing for the Lord a people fit for him.'

This is the Gospel of the Lord.

Prayer over the Gifts
Lord,
look with favour on the gifts we bring
on this feast of John the Baptist.
Help us put into action
the mystery we celebrate in this sacrament.

Preface of John the Baptist, P61.

Communion Antiphon: Blessed be the Lord God of Israel, for he has visited and redeemed his people.

Prayer after Communion
Father,
may the prayers of John the Baptist
lead us to the Lamb of God.
May this eucharist bring us the mercy of Christ,
who is Lord for ever and ever.

Proper of Saints, 24 June 1555

Mass during the Day

We celebrate the birthday of John the Baptist, the man specially chosen by God to be the herald of the Saviour and to prepare the people for his coming.

Entrance Antiphon: There was a man sent from God whose name was John. He came to bear witness to the light, to prepare an upright people for the Lord.

Opening Prayer
Let us pray
   [that God will give us joy and peace]

God our Father,
you raised up John the Baptist
to prepare a perfect people for Christ the Lord.
Give your Church joy in spirit
and guide those who believe in you
into the way of salvation and peace.

or

Let us pray
   [as we honour John the Baptist
   for the faith to recognise Christ in our midst]

God our Father,
the voice of John the Baptist challenges us to repentance
and points the way to Christ the Lord.

Open our ears to his message, and free our hearts
to turn from our sins and receive the life of the gospel.

FIRST READING

A reading from the prophet Isaiah   49:1-6
I will make you the light of the nations so that my salvation may reach to the ends of the earth.

Islands, listen to me,
pay attention, remotest peoples.
the Lord called me before I was born,
from my mother's womb he pronounced my name.

He made my mouth a sharp sword,
and hid me in the shadow of his hand.

He made me into a sharpened arrow,
and concealed me in his quiver.

He said to me, 'You are my servant, Israel,
in whom I shall be glorified';
while I was thinking, 'I have toiled in vain,
I have exhausted myself for nothing';

and all the while my cause was with the Lord,
my reward with my God.
I was honoured in the eyes of the Lord,
my God was my strength.

And now the Lord has spoken,
he who formed me in the womb to be his servant,
to bring Jacob back to him,
to gather Israel to him:

'It is not enough for you to be my servant,
to restore the tribes of Jacob and bring back the survivors of Israel;
I will make you the light of the nations
so that my salvation may reach to the ends of the earth.'

This is the word of the Lord.

Responsorial Psalm   Ps 138:1-3. 13-15. ℟ v.14

℟   **I thank you for the wonder of my being.**

1   O Lord, you search me and you know me,
    you know my resting and my rising,
    you discern my purpose from afar.
    You mark when I walk or lie down,
    all my ways lie open to you.   ℟

2   For it was you who created my being,
    knit me together in my mother's womb.
    I thank you for the wonder of my being,
    for the wonders of all your creation.   ℟

3   Already you knew my soul,
    my body held no secret from you
    when I was being fashioned in secret
    and moulded in the depths of the earth.   ℟

SECOND READING

A reading from the Acts of the Apostles 13:22-26
Jesus, whose coming was heralded by John.

Paul said: 'God made David the king of our ancestors, of whom he approved in these words, "I have elected David son of Jesse, a man after my own heart, who will carry out my whole purpose." To keep his promise, God has raised up for Israel one of David's descendants, Jesus, as Saviour, whose coming was heralded by John when he proclaimed a baptism of repentance for the whole people of Israel. Before John ended his career he said, "I am not the one you imagine me to be; that one is coming after me and I am not fit to undo his sandal."

'My brothers, sons of Abraham's race, and all you who fear God, this message of salvation is meant for you.'

This is the word of the Lord.

Gospel Acclamation cf. Lk 1:76
Alleluia, alleluia!
As for you, little child, you shall be called
a prophet of God, the Most High.
You shall go ahead of the Lord
to prepare his ways before him.
Alleluia!

GOSPEL

A reading from the holy Gospel according to Luke 1:57-66. 80
His name is John.

The time came for Elizabeth to have her child, and she gave birth to a son; and when her neighbours and relations heard that the Lord had shown her so great a kindness, they shared her joy.

Now on the eighth day they came to circumcise the child; they were going to call him Zechariah after his father, but his mother spoke up. 'No,' she said 'he is to be called John.' They said to her, 'But no one in your family has that name', and made signs to his father to find out what he wanted him called. The father asked for a writing tablet and wrote, 'His name is John.' And they were all astonished. At that instant his power of speech returned and he spoke and praised God. All their neighbours were filled with awe and the whole affair was talked about throughout the hill country of Judaea. All those who heard of it treasured it in their hearts. 'What will this child turn out to be?' they wondered. And indeed the hand of the Lord was with him. The child grew up and his spirit matured. And he lived out in the wilderness until the day he appeared openly to Israel.

This is the Gospel of the Lord.

The Profession of Faith is made.

Prayer over the Gifts
Father,
accept the gifts we bring to your altar
to celebrate the birth of John the Baptist,
who foretold the coming of our Saviour
and made him known when he came.

Preface of John the Baptist, P61.

Communion Antiphon: Through the tender compassion of our God, the dawn from on high shall break upon us.

Prayer after Communion
Lord,
you have renewed us with this eucharist,
as we celebrate the feast of John the Baptist,
who foretold the coming of the Lamb of God.
May we welcome your Son as our Saviour,
for he gives us new life,
and is Lord for ever and ever.

27 June

St Cyril of Alexandria, bishop and doctor of the Church
Optional Memorial

Born in 370; he entered a monastery, was ordained, became Bishop of Alexandria in 412. He opposed the heresy of Nestorius, patriarch of Constantinople, at the Council of Ephesus in 431, which led to a split in the Church. He was a vigorous defender of the faith, and has left many writings.

Common of pastors: bishops, pp.1878ff., or of doctors of the church, pp.1887ff.

Proper of Saints, 27 June

Opening Prayer

Father,
the bishop Cyril courageously taught
that Mary was the Mother of God.
May we who cherish this belief
receive salvation through the incarnation of Christ your Son,
who lives and reigns with you and the Holy Spirit,
one God, for ever and ever.

FIRST READING

A reading from the second letter of St Paul to Timothy 4:1-5
Make the preaching of the Good News your life's work.

Before God and before Christ Jesus who is to be judge of the living and the dead, I put this duty to you, in the name of his Appearing and of his kingdom: proclaim the message and, welcome or unwelcome, insist on it. Refute falsehood, correct error, call to obedience – but do all with patience and with the intention of teaching. The time is sure to come when, far from being content with sound teaching, people will be avid for the latest novelty and collect themselves a whole series of teachers according to their own tastes; and then, instead of listening to the truth, they will turn to myths. Be careful always to choose the right course; be brave under trials; make the preaching of the Good News your life's work, in thoroughgoing service.

This is the word of the Lord.

Responsorial Psalm   Ps 88:2-5. 21-22. 25. 27. ℟ cf. v.2

℟ **I will sing for ever of your love, O Lord.**

1 I will sing for ever of your love, O Lord;
   through all ages my mouth will proclaim your truth.
   Of this I am sure, that your love lasts for ever,
   that your truth is firmly established as the heavens. ℟

2 'I have made a covenant with my chosen one;
   I have sworn to David my servant:
   I will establish your dynasty for ever
   and set up your throne through all ages. ℟

3 'I have found David my servant
   and with my holy oil anointed him.
   My hand shall always be with him
   and my arm shall make him strong. ℟   (continued)

4 'My truth and my love shall be with him;
by my name his might shall be exalted.
He will say to me: "You are my father,
my God, the rock who saves me."'

℟ **I will sing for ever of your love, O Lord.**

Gospel Acclamation   Mt 5:16
Alleluia, alleluia!
Your light must shine in the sight of men.
so that, seeing your good works,
they may give the praise to your Father in heaven.
Alleluia!

GOSPEL

A reading from the holy Gospel according to Matthew   5:13-19
You are the light of the world.

Jesus said to his disciples: 'You are the salt of the earth. But if salt becomes tasteless, what can make it salty again. It is good for nothing, and can only be thrown out to be trampled underfoot by men.

'You are the light of the world. A city built on a hill-top cannot be hidden. No one lights a lamp to put it under a tub; they put it on the lamp-stand where it shines for everyone in the house. In the same way your light must shine in the sight of men, so that, seeing your good works, they may give the praise to your Father in heaven.

'Do not imagine that I have come to abolish the Law or the Prophets. I have come not to abolish but to complete them. I tell you solemnly, till heaven and earth disappear, not one dot, not one little stroke, shall disappear from the Law until its purpose is achieved. Therefore, the man who infringes even one of the least of these commandments and teaches others to do the same will be considered the least in the kingdom of heaven; but the man who keeps them and teaches them will be considered great in the kingdom of heaven.

This is the Gospel of the Lord.

Proper of Saints, 28 June

28 June
St Irenaeus, bishop and martyr — Memorial

Born at Smyrna about 130, a disciple of St Polycarp, bishop of Smyrna. He was a priest at Lyons in France at the time of the persecution there, and became bishop of the city when the previous bishop was martyred. He is known as a theologian, a powerful defender of the faith against the heresy of the Gnostics. He is thought to have been martyred about 200.

Common of martyrs, pp. 1865ff., or of pastors: bishops, pp. 1878ff.

Opening Prayer
Father,
you called Saint Irenaeus to uphold your truth
and bring peace to your Church.
By his prayers renew us in faith and love
that we may always be intent
on fostering unity and peace.

FIRST READING

A reading from the second letter of St Paul to Timothy 2:22-26
A servant of the Lord has to be kind to everyone and gentle when he corrects people.

Fasten your attention on holiness, faith, love and peace, in union with all those who call on the Lord with pure minds. Avoid these futile and silly speculations, understanding that they only give rise to quarrels; and a servant of the Lord is not to engage in quarrels, but has to be kind to everyone, a good teacher, and patient. He has to be gentle when he corrects people who dispute what he says, never forgetting that God may give them a change of mind so that they recognise the truth and come to their senses, once out of the trap where the devil caught them and kept them enslaved.

This is the word of the Lord.

Responsional Psalm Ps 36:3-6. 30-31. ℟ v.30
℟ **The just man's mouth utters wisdom.**

1 If you trust in the Lord and do good,
then you will live in the land and be secure.

If you find your delight in the Lord,
he will grant your heart's desire.

℟ **The just man's mouth utters wisdom.**

2 Commit your life to the Lord,
trust in him and he will act,
so that your justice breaks forth like the light,
your cause like the noon-day sun. ℟

3 The just man's mouth utters wisdom
and his lips speak what is right;
the law of his God is in his heart,
his steps shall be saved from stumbling. ℟

Gospel Acclamation   Jn 15:9. 5

Alleluia, alleluia!
Remain in my love, says the Lord;
whoever remains in me, with me in him,
bears fruit in plenty.
Alleluia!

GOSPEL

A reading from the holy Gospel according to John   17:20-26
I want them to be with me where I am.

Jesus raised his eyes to heaven and said:

'Holy Father,
I pray not only for these,
but for those also
who through their words will believe in me.
May they all be one.
Father, may they be one in us,
as you are in me and I am in you,
so that the world may believe it was you who sent me.
I have given them the glory you gave to me,
that they may be one as we are one.
With me in them and you in me,
may they be so completely one
that the world will realise that it was you who sent me
and that I have loved them as much as you loved me.
Father,
I want those you have given me
to be with me where I am,

so that they may always see the glory
you have given me
because you loved me
before the foundation of the world.
Father, Righteous One,
the world has not known you,
but I have known you,
and these have known
that you have sent me.
I have made your name known to them
and will continue to make it known,
so that the love with which you loved me may be in them,
and so that I may be in them.'

This is the Gospel of the Lord.

Prayer over the Gifts
Lord,
as we celebrate the feast of Saint Irenaeus
may this eucharist bring you glory,
increase our love of truth,
and help your Church to remain firm in faith and unity.

Prayer after Communion
Lord,
by these holy mysteries increase our faith.
As the holy bishop Irenaeus reached eternal glory
by being faithful until death,
so may we be saved by living our faith.

29 June

SS PETER AND PAUL, APOSTLES Solemnity
Vigil Mass

Entrance Antiphon: Peter the apostle and Paul the teacher of the Gentiles have brought us to know the law of the Lord.

The Gloria is sung or said.

Opening Prayer
Let us pray
   [that the prayers of the apostles
   will lead us to salvation.]

Lord our God,
encourage us through the prayers of Saints Peter and Paul.
May the apostles who strengthened the faith of the infant Church
help us on our way to salvation.

or

Let us pray
   [to be true to the faith
   which has come to us through the apostles Peter and Paul]

Father in heaven,
the light of your revelation brought Peter and Paul
the gift of faith in Jesus your Son.

Through their prayers
may we always give thanks for your life
given us in Christ Jesus,
and for having been enriched by him
in all knowledge and love.

FIRST READING

A reading from the Acts of the Apostles   3:1-10

I will give you what I have: in the name of Jesus, walk!

Once, when Peter and John were going up to the Temple for the prayers at the ninth hour, it happened that there was a man being carried past. He was a cripple from birth; and they used to put him down every day near the Temple entrance called the Beautiful Gate so that he could beg from the people going in. When this man saw Peter and John on their way into the Temple he begged from them. Both Peter and John looked straight at him and said, 'Look at us.' He turned to them expectantly, hoping to get something from them, but Peter said, 'I have neither silver nor gold, but I will give you what I have: in the name of Jesus Christ the Nazarene, walk!' Peter then took him by the hand and helped him to stand up. Instantly his feet and ankles became firm, he jumped up, stood, and began to walk, and he went with them into the Temple, walking and jumping and praising God. Everyone could see him walking and praising God, and they recognised him as the man who used to sit begging at the Beautiful Gate of the Temple. They were all astonished and unable to explain what had happened to him.

    This is the word of the Lord.

Proper of Saints, 29 June

Responsorial Psalm   Ps 18:2-5. ℟ v.5

   ℟ **Their word goes forth through all the earth.**

1. The heavens proclaim the glory of God
   and the firmament shows forth the work of his hands.
   Day unto day takes up the story
   and night unto night makes known the message. ℟

2. No speech, no word, no voice is heard
   yet their span extends through all the earth,
   their words to the utmost bounds of the world. ℟

SECOND READING

A reading from the letter of St Paul to the Galatians   1:11-20
God specially chose me while I was still in my mother's womb.

The Good News I preached is not a human message that I was given by men, it is something I learnt only through a revelation of Jesus Christ. You must have heard of my career as a practising Jew, how merciless I was in persecuting the Church of God, how much damage I did to it, how I stood out among other Jews of my generation, and how enthusiastic I was for the traditions of my ancestors.

    Then God, who had specially chosen me while I was still in my mother's womb, called me through his grace and chose to reveal his Son to me, so that I might preach the Good News about him to the pagans. I did not stop to discuss this with any human being, nor did I go up to Jerusalem to see those who were already apostles before me, but I went off to Arabia at once and later went straight back from there to Damascus. Even when after three years I went up to Jerusalem to visit Cephas and stayed with him for fifteen days, I did not see any of the other apostles; I only saw James, the brother of the Lord, and I swear before God that what I have just written is the literal truth.

    This is the word of the Lord.

Gospel Acclamation   Jn 21:17
   Alleluia, alleluia!
   Lord, you know everything;
   you know I love you.
   Alleluia!

GOSPEL

A reading from the holy Gospel according to John 21:15-19
Feed my lambs, feed my sheep.

Jesus showed himself to his disciples, and after they had eaten he said to Simon Peter, 'Simon son of John, do you love me more than these others do?' He answered, 'Yes Lord, you know I love you.' Jesus said to him, 'Feed my lambs.' A second time he said to him, 'Simon son of John, do you love me?' He replied, 'Yes, Lord, you know I love you.' Jesus said to him, 'Look after my sheep.' Then he said to him a third time, 'Simon son of John, do you love me?' Peter was upset that he asked him the third time, "Do you love me?" and said, 'Lord, you know everything; you know I love you.' Jesus said to him, 'Feed my sheep.

> 'I tell you most solemnly,
> when you were young
> you put on your own belt
> and walked where you liked;
> but when you grow old
> you will stretch out your hands,
> and somebody else will put a belt round you
> and take you where you would rather not go.'

In these words he indicated the kind of death by which Peter would give glory to God. After this he said, 'Follow me.'

This is the Gospel of the Lord.

The Profession of Faith is made.

Prayer over the Gifts
Lord,
we present these gifts
on this feast of the Apostles Peter and Paul.
Help us to know our own weakness
and to rejoice in your saving power.

Preface of Peter and Paul, P63.

Communion Antiphon: Simon, son of John, do you love me more than these? Lord, you know all things; you know that I love you.

Prayer after Communion
Father,
you give us light by the teaching of your apostles.
In this sacrament we have received
fill us with your strength.

Proper of Saints, 29 June

Mass during the Day

We celebrate the feast of the princes of the apostles, from whom we derive our Christian faith. The Lord stood by them and gave them power, so that through them the whole message might be proclaimed for all the world to hear.

Entrance Antiphon: These men, conquering all human frailty, shed their blood and helped the Church to grow. By sharing the cup of the Lord's suffering, they became the friends of God.

Opening Prayer
Let us pray
    [that we will remain true to the faith of the apostles]

God our Father,
today you give us the joy
of celebrating the feast of the apostles Peter and Paul.
Through them your Church first received the faith.
Keep us true to their teaching.

or

Let us pray
    [one with Peter and Paul in our faith
    in Christ the Son of the living God]

Praise to you, the God and Father of our Lord Jesus Christ,
who in your great mercy
have given us new birth and hope
through the power of Christ's resurrection.

Through the prayers of the apostles Peter and Paul
may we who received this faith through their preaching
share their joy in following the Lord
to the unfading inheritance
reserved for us in heaven.

FIRST READING

A reading from the Acts of the Apostles   12:1-11
Now I know the Lord really did save me from Herod.

King Herod started persecuting certain members of the Church. He beheaded James the brother of John, and when he saw that this pleased the Jews he decided to arrest Peter as well. This was during the days of Unleavened Bread, and he put Peter in prison, assigning four squads of four soldiers each to guard him in turns. Herod meant to try Peter in public after the end of Passover week. All the time Peter was under guard the Church prayed to God for him unremittingly.

On the night before Herod was to try him, Peter was sleeping between two soldiers, fastened with double chains, while guards kept watch at the main entrance to the prison. Then suddenly the angel of the Lord stood there, and the cell was filled with light. He tapped Peter on the side and woke him. 'Get up!' he said 'Hurry!' – and the chains fell from his hands. The angel then said, 'Put on your belt and sandals.' After he had done this, the angel next said, 'Wrap your cloak round you and follow me.' Peter followed him, but had no idea that what the angel did was all happening in reality; he thought he was seeing a vision. They passed through two guard posts one after the other, and reached the iron gate leading to the city. This opened of its own accord; they went through it and had walked the whole length of one street when suddenly the angel left him. It was only then that Peter came to himself. 'Now I know it is all true,' he said. 'The Lord really did send his angel and has saved me from Herod and from all that the Jewish people were so certain would happen to me.'

This is the word of the Lord.

Responsorial Psalm   Ps 33:2-9. ℟ v.5. Alt. ℟ v.8

   ℟ **From all my terrors the Lord set me free.**

or

   ℟ **The angel of the Lord rescues those who revere him.**

1   I will bless the Lord at all times.
    his praise always on my lips;
    in the Lord my soul shall make its boast.
    The humble shall hear and be glad.   ℟

2   Glorify the Lord with me.
    Together let us praise his name.
    I sought the Lord and he answered me;
    from all my terrors he set me free.   ℟

3   Look towards him and be radiant;
    let your faces not be abashed.
    This poor man called; the Lord heard him
    and rescued him from all his distress.   ℟

4. The angel of the Lord is encamped
   around those who revere him, to rescue them.
   Taste and see that the Lord is good.
   He is happy who seeks refuge in him. ℟

SECOND READING

A reading from the second letter of St Paul to Timothy 4:6-8. 17-18
All there is to come now is the crown of righteousness reserved for me.

My life is already being poured away as a libation, and the time has come for me to be gone. I have fought the good fight to the end; I have run the race to the finish; I have kept the faith; all there is to come now is the crown of righteousness reserved for me, which the Lord, the righteous judge, will give to me on that Day; and not only to me but to all those who have longed for his Appearing.

The Lord stood by me and gave me power, so that through me the whole message might be proclaimed for all the pagans to hear; and so I was rescued from the lion's mouth. The Lord will rescue me from all evil attempts on me, and bring me safely to his heavenly kingdom. To him be glory for ever and ever. Amen.

This is the word of the Lord.

Gospel Acclamation Mt 16:18
   Alleluia, alleluia!
   You are Peter and on this rock I will build my Church.
   And the gates of the underworld can never hold out against it.
   Alleluia!

GOSPEL

A reading from the holy Gospel according to Matthew 16:13-19
You are Peter, and I will give you the keys of the kingdom of heaven.

When Jesus came to the region of Caesarea Philippi he put this question to his disciples, 'Who do people say the Son of Man is?' And they said, 'Some say he is John the Baptist, some Elijah, and others Jeremiah or one of the prophets.' 'But you,' he said 'who do you say I am?' Then Simon Peter spoke up, 'You are the Christ,' he said 'the Son of the living God.' Jesus replied, 'Simon son of Jonah, you are a happy man! Because it was not flesh and blood that revealed this to you but my Father in heaven. So I now say to you: You are Peter and on this rock I will build my Church.

And the gates of the underworld can never hold out against it. I will give you the keys of the kingdom of heaven: whatever you bind on earth shall be considered bound in heaven; whatever you loose on earth shall be considered loosed in heaven.'

This is the Gospel of the Lord.

For a Votive Mass of St Peter, the readings are taken from the feast of the Chair of St Peter, apostle, see above, pp.1429ff. For a Votive Mass of St Paul, the readings are taken from the feast of the Conversion of St Paul, apostle, see above pp.1390ff.

Prayer over the Gifts
Lord,
may your apostles join their prayers to our offering
and help us to celebrate this sacrifice in love and unity.

Preface of Peter and Paul, P63.

Communion Antiphon: Peter said: You are the Christ, the Son of the living God. Jesus answered: You are Peter, the rock on which I will build my Church.

Prayer after Communion
Lord,
renew the life of your Church
with the power of this sacrament.
May the breaking of bread
and the teaching of the apostles
keep us united in your love.

Solemn Blessing
Bow your heads and pray for God's blessing.

The Lord has set you firm within his Church,
which he built upon the rock of Peter's faith.
May he bless you with a faith that never falters. ℟ **Amen.**

The Lord has given you knowledge of the faith
through the labours and preaching of Saint Paul.
May his example inspire you to lead others to Christ
by the manner of your life. ℟ **Amen.**

May the keys of Peter, and the words of Paul,
their undying witness and their prayers,

lead you to the joy of that eternal home
which Peter gained by his cross, and Paul by the sword. ℟ **Amen.**

May almighty God bless you,
the Father, and the Son, ✠ and the Holy Spirit. ℟ **Amen.**

30 June
The First Martyrs of the Church of Rome
Optional Memorial

Many Christians were put to death by the Emperor Nero, after the burning of the City of Rome in 64, for which they were held responsible. Their death is recorded by the historian, Tacitus, and also by Pope Clement I in his letter to the Corinthians.

Common of martyrs, pp.1865ff.

Opening Prayer
Father,
you sanctified the Church of Rome
with the blood of its first martyrs.
May we find strength from their courage
and rejoice in their triumph.

FIRST READING
A reading from the letter of St Paul to the Romans 8:31-39
Neither death nor life can ever come between us and the love of God.

With God on our side who can be against us? Since God did not spare his own Son, but gave him up to benefit us all, we may be certain, after such a gift, that he will not refuse anything he can give. Could anyone accuse those that God has chosen? When God acquits, could anyone condemn? Could Christ Jesus? No! He not only died for us – he rose from the dead, and there at God's right hand he stands and pleads for us.

Nothing therefore can come between us and the love of Christ, even if we are troubled or worried, or being persecuted, or lacking food or clothes or being threatened or even attacked. As scripture promised: For your sake we are being massacred daily, and reckoned as sheep for the slaughter. These are the trials through which we triumph, by the power of him who loved us.

For I am certain of this: neither death nor life, no angel, no prince, nothing that exists, nothing still to come, not any power, or height or depth, nor any created thing, can ever come between us and the love of God made visible in Christ Jesus our Lord.

This is the word of the Lord.

Responsional Psalm
Ps 123:2-5. 7-8. ℟ v.7

℟ **Our life, like a bird, has escaped
from the snare of the fowler.**

1. If the Lord had not been on our side
   when men rose against us,
   then would they have swallowed us alive
   when their anger was kindled.   ℟

2. Then would the waters have engulfed us,
   the torrent gone over us;
   over our heads would have swept
   the raging waters.   ℟

3. Indeed the snare has been broken
   and we have escaped.
   Our help is in the name of the Lord,
   who made heaven and earth.   ℟

Gospel Acclamation
Mt 5:10

Alleluia, alleluia!
Happy those who are persecuted in the cause of right:
theirs is the kingdom of heaven.
Alleluia!

GOSPEL

A reading from the holy Gospel according to Matthew   24:4-13
You will be hated by all the nations on account of my name.

Jesus said to his disciples, 'Take care that no one deceives you; because many will come using my name and saying, "I am the Christ", and they will deceive many. You will hear of wars and rumours of wars; do not be alarmed, for this is something that must happen, but the end will not be yet. For nation will fight against nation, and kingdom against kingdom. There will be famines and eathquakes here and there. All this is only the beginning of the birthpangs.

'Then they will hand you over to be tortured and put to death;

and you will be hated by all the nations on account of my name. And then many will fall away; men will betray one another and hate one another. Many false prophets will arise; they will deceive many, and with the increase of lawlessness, love in most men will grow cold; but the man who stands firm to the end will be saved.'

This is the Gospel of the Lord.

… JULY

3 July
ST THOMAS, APOSTLE — Feast

Nothing is known for certain about the life of St Thomas, apart from the Gospel account. Tradition holds that he preached the gospel in India.

Entrance Antiphon: You are my God: I will give you praise, O my God. I will extol you, for you are my saviour.

Opening Prayer
Almighty Father,
as we honour Thomas the apostle,
let us always experience the help of his prayers.
May we have eternal life by believing in Jesus,
whom Thomas acknowledged as Lord.
who lives and reigns . . .

FIRST READING

A reading from the letter of St Paul to the Ephesians 2:19-22
You are part of a building that has the apostles for its foundations.

You are no longer aliens or foreign visitors; you are citizens like all the saints, and part of God's household. You are part of a building that has the apostles and prophets for its foundations, and Christ Jesus himself for its main cornerstone. As every structure is aligned on him, all grow into one holy temple in the Lord; and you too, in him, are being built into a house where God lives, in the Spirit.

This is the word of the Lord.

Proper of Saints, 3 July

Responsorial Psalm   Ps 116. ℟ Mk 16:15
> ℟ **Go out to the whole world;
> proclaim the Good News.**

1. O praise the Lord, all you nations,
acclaim him all you peoples!   ℟

2. Strong is his love for us;
he is faithful for ever.   ℟

Gospel Acclamation   Jn 20:29
Alleluia, alleluia!
You believe, Thomas, because you can see me, says the Lord.
Happy are those who have not seen and yet believe.
Alleluia!

GOSPEL

A reading from the holy Gospel according to John   20:24-29
My Lord and my God.

Thomas, called the Twin, who was one of the Twelve, was not with the disciples when Jesus came. When they said, 'We have seen the Lord', he answered, 'Unless I see the holes that the nails made in his hands and can put my finger into the holes they made, and unless I can put my hand into his side, I refuse to believe.' Eight days later the disciples were in the house again and Thomas was with them. The doors were closed, but Jesus came in and stood among them. 'Peace be with you,' he said. Then he spoke to Thomas, 'Put your finger here; look, here are my hands. Give me your hand; put it into my side. Doubt no longer but believe.' Thomas replied, 'My Lord and my God!' Jesus said to them:

> 'You believe because you can see me.
> Happy are those who have not seen and yet believe.'

This is the Gospel of the Lord.

Prayer over the Gifts
Lord,
we offer you our service and we pray:
protect the gifts you have given us
as we offer this sacrifice of praise
on the feast of your apostle Thomas.

Preface of the Apostles I or II, P64 or P65.

Communion Antiphon: Jesus spoke to Thomas: Put your hands here, and see the place of the nails. Doubt no longer, but believe.

Prayer after Communion
Father,
in this sacrament we have received
the body and blood of Christ.
With Saint Thomas we acknowledge him to be our Lord and God.
May we show by our lives that our faith is real.

4 July
St Elizabeth of Portugal
Optional Memorial

Born in 1271 into the royal family of Aragon. At the age of twelve she was married to the king of Portugal, and had two children. The marriage was unhappy, and led to many disputes between the families. She lived a life of penance, prayer and fasting. After her husband's death she renounced the world and lived in poverty as a member of the Third Order of St Francis. War broke out between her son and grandson, and while attempting to reconcile them, she died in 1336.

Common of holy men and women: those who worked for the underprivileged, p.1900.

Opening Prayer
Father of peace and love,
you gave Saint Elizabeth the gift of reconciling enemies.
By the help of her prayers
give us the courage to work for peace among men,
that we may be called the sons of God.

FIRST READING

A reading from the first letter of St John 3:14-18
We, too, ought to give up our lives for our brothers.

We have passed out of death and into life,
and of this we can be sure
because we love our brothers.
If you refuse to love, you must remain dead;
to hate your brother is to be a murderer,

Proper of Saints, 4 July

and murderers, as you know, do not have eternal life in them.
This has taught us love –
that he gave up his life for us;
and we, too, ought to give up our lives for our brothers.
If a man who was rich enough in this world's goods
saw that one of his brothers was in need,
but closed his heart to him,
how could the love of God be living in him?
My children,
our love is not to be just words or mere talk,
but something real and active.

This is the word of the Lord.

Responsorial Psalm
Ps 111:1-9. ℟ v.1

℟ **Happy the man who fears the Lord.**

1. Happy the man who fears the Lord,
   who takes delight in his commands.
   His sons will be powerful on earth;
   the children of the upright are blessed. ℟

2. Riches and wealth are in his house;
   his justice stands firm for ever.
   He is a light in the darkness for the upright:
   he is generous, merciful and just. ℟

3. The good man takes pity and lends,
   he conducts his affairs with honour.
   The just man will never waver:
   he will be remembered for ever. ℟

4. He has no fear of evil news;
   with a firm heart he trusts in the Lord.
   With a steadfast heart he will not fear;
   he will see the downfall of his foes. ℟

5. Open-handed, he gives to the poor;
   his justice stands firm for ever.
   His head will be raised in glory. ℟

Gospel Acclamation
Jn 13:34

Alleluia, alleluia!
I give you a new commandment:
love one another just as I have loved you.
Alleluia!

GOSPEL

A reading from the holy Gospel according to Matthew 25:31-46
In so far as you did this to one of the least of these brothers of mine, you did it to me.

Jesus said to his disciples: 'When the Son of Man comes in his glory, escorted by all the angels, then he will take his seat on his throne of glory. All the nations will be assembled before him and he will separate men one from another as the shepherd separates sheep from goats. He will place the sheep on his right hand and the goats on his left. Then the King will say to those on his right hand, "Come, you whom my Father has blessed, take for your heritage the kingdom prepared for you since the foundation of the world. For I was hungry and you gave me food; I was thirsty and you gave me drink; I was a stranger and you made me welcome; naked and you clothed me, sick and you visited me, in prison and you came to see me." Then the virtuous will say to him in reply, "Lord, when did we see you hungry and feed you; or thirsty and give you drink? When did we see you a stranger and make you welcome; naked and clothe you; sick or in prison and go to see you?" And the King will answer, "I tell you solemnly, in so far as you did this to one of the least of these brothers of mine, you did it to me."

'Next he will say to those on his left hand, "Go away from me, with your curse upon you, to the eternal fire prepared for the devil and his angels. For I was hungry and you never gave me food; I was thirsty and you never gave me anything to drink; I was a stranger and you never made me welcome, naked and you never clothed me, sick and in prison and you never visited me." Then it will be their turn to ask, "Lord, when did we see you hungry or thirsty, a stranger or naked, sick, or in prison, and did not come to your help?" Then he will answer, "I tell you solemnly, in so far as you neglected to do this to one of the least of these, you neglected to do it to me." And they will go away to eternal punishment, and the virtuous to eternal life.'

This is the Gospel of the Lord.

*Shorter form, verses 31-40. Read between *.

5 July

St Anthony Zaccaria, priest
Optional Memorial

Born in 1502, at Cremona in Lombardy. He practised medicine for a time, and then was ordained. He worked for the reform of the clergy and the evangelisation of the people. He formed the Congregation of Clerics of St Paul, who came to be known as Barnabites, to make it possible for clergy who were not monks or mendicant friars to live by a rule and to take vows.

Common of pastors, pp.1876ff., or of holy men and women: teachers, p.1901, or religious, pp.1898ff.

Opening Prayer
Lord,
enable us to grasp in the spirit of Saint Paul
the sublime wisdom of Jesus Christ,
the wisdom which inspired Saint Anthony Zaccaria
to preach the message of salvation in your Church.

FIRST READING

A reading from the second letter of St Paul to Timothy
1:13-14; 2:1-3

Guard this precious thing with the help of the Holy Spirit.

Keep as your pattern the sound teaching you have heard from me, in the faith and love that are in Christ Jesus. You have been trusted to look after something precious; guard it with the help of the Holy Spirit who lives in us. Accept the strength, my dear son, that comes from the grace of Christ Jesus. You have heard everything that I teach in public; hand it on to reliable people so that they in turn will be able to teach others.

Put up with your share of difficulties, like a good soldier of Christ Jesus.

This is the word of the Lord.

Responsorial Psalm
                    Ps 1:1-4. 6. ℟ v.2. Alt. ℟ Ps 39:5. Alt. ℟ Ps 91:13-14

> ℟ **His delight is the law of the Lord.**

or

> ℟ **Happy the man who has placed his trust in the Lord.**

or

> ℟ **The just will flourish like the palm-tree
> in the courts of our God.**

1 Happy indeed is the man
  who follows not the counsel of the wicked;
  nor lingers in the way of sinners
  nor sits in the company of scorners,
  but whose delight is the law of the Lord
  and who ponders his law day and night. ℟

2 He is like a tree that is planted
  beside the flowing waters,
  that yields its fruit in due season
  and whose leaves shall never fade;
  and all that he does shall prosper. ℟

3 Not so are the wicked, not so!
  For they like winnowed chaff
  shall be driven away by the wind.
  For the Lord guards the way of the just
  but the way of the wicked leads to doom. ℟

Gospel Acclamation cf. Mt 11:25
Alleluia, alleluia!
Blessed are you, Father,
Lord of heaven and earth,
for revealing the mysteries of the kingdom
to mere children.
Alleluia!

GOSPEL

A reading from the holy Gospel according to Mark 10:13-16
Let the little children come to me.

People were bringing little children to Jesus, for him to touch them. The disciples turned them away, but when Jesus saw this he was indignant and said to them, 'Let the little children come to me; do not stop them; for it is to such as these that the kingdom of God belongs. I tell you solemnly, anyone who does not welcome the kingdom of God like a little child will never enter it.' Then he put his arms round them, laid his hands on them and gave them his blessing.

This is the Gospel of the Lord.

6 July

St Maria Goretti, virgin and martyr
Optional Memorial

Born in 1890, at Ancona in Italy, of a poor Italian family. She was stabbed to death by a youth who was attempting to rape her. Before she died, in hospital, she declared: 'I forgive him for the love of Jesus, and I pray that he may come with me to Paradise.' She was canonised in 1950.

Common of martyrs, pp.1865ff., or of virgins, pp.1889ff.

Opening Prayer

Father,
source of innocence and lover of chastity,
you gave Saint Maria Goretti the privilege
of offering her life in witness to Christ.
As you gave her the crown of martyrdom,
let her prayers keep us faithful to your teaching.

FIRST READING

A reading from the first letter of St Paul to the Corinthians 6:13-15. 17-20

Your bodies are members making up the body of Christ.

The body is not meant for fornication; it is for the Lord, and the Lord for the body. God, who raised the Lord from the dead, will by his power raise us up too.

You know, surely, that your bodies are members making up the body of Christ; anyone who is joined to the Lord is one spirit with him.

Keep away from fornication. All the other sins are committed ouside the body; but to fornicate is to sin against your own body. Your body, you know, is the temple of the Holy Spirit, which is in you since you have received him from God. You are not your own property; you have been bought and paid for. That is why you should use your body for the glory of God.

This is the word of the Lord.

Responsorial Psalm
Ps 30:3-4. 6-8. 16-17. ℟ v.6

℟ **Into your hands, O Lord,
I commend my spirit.**

1 Be a rock of refuge for me,
a mighty stronghold to save me,
for you are my rock, my stronghold.
For your name's sake, lead me and guide me. ℟

2 Into your hands I commend my spirit.
It is you who will redeem me, Lord.
As for me, I trust in the Lord:
let me be glad and rejoice in your love. ℟

3 My life is in your hands, deliver me
from the hands of those who hate me.
Let your face shine on your servant.
Save me in your love. ℟

Gospel Acclamation
James 1:12

Alleluia, alleluia!
Happy the man who stands firm when trials come.
He has proved himself,
and will win the prize of life.
Alleluia!

GOSPEL

A reading from the holy Gospel according to John 12:24-26

If a grain of wheat dies it yields a rich harvest.

Jesus said to his disciples:

'I tell you, most solemnly,
unless a wheat grain falls on the ground and dies,
it remains only a single grain;
but if it dies,
it yields a rich harvest.
Anyone who loves his life loses it;
anyone who hates his life in this world
will keep it for the eternal life.
If a man serves me, he must follow me,
wherever I am, my servant will be there too.
If anyone serves me, my Father will honour him.'

This is the Gospel of the Lord.

11 July
St Benedict, abbot   Memorial

Born at Norcia in Umbria about 480. He studied in Rome, and then turned his back on the world and lived in solitude in Subiaco. Disciples came to him, and he went to Monte Cassino, where he founded a monastery. He wrote his Rule, which established the spirituality and way of life of monastic communities ever since. He died in 547.

Common of holy men and women: religious, pp.1898ff.

Opening Prayer
God our Father,
you made Saint Benedict an outstanding guide
to teach men how to live in your service.
Grant that by preferring your love to everything else,
we may walk in the way of your commandments.

FIRST READING

A reading from the book of Proverbs   2:1-9
Apply your heart to truth.

My son, if you take my words to heart,
if you set store by my commandments,
tuning your ear to wisdom,
and applying your heart to truth:
yes, if your plea is for clear perception,
if you cry out for discernment,
if you look for it as if it were silver,
and search for it as for buried treasure,
you will then understand what the fear of the Lord is,
and discover the knowledge of God.
For the Lord himself is giver of wisdom,
from his mouth issue knowledge and discernment.
He keeps his help for honest men,
he is the shield of those whose ways are honourable;
he stands guard over the paths of justice,
he keeps watch on the way of his devoted ones.
Then you will understand what virtue is, justice, and fair dealing,
all paths that lead to happiness.

This is the word of the Lord.

Responsorial Psalm
Ps 33:2-11. ℟ v.2

℟ **I will bless the Lord at all times.**

or

℟ **Taste and see that the Lord is good.**

1. I will bless the Lord at all times,
   his praise always on my lips;
   in the Lord my soul shall make its boast.
   The humble shall hear and be glad. ℟

2. Glorify the Lord with me.
   Together let us praise his name.
   I sought the Lord and he answered me;
   from all my terrors he set me free. ℟

3. Look towards him and be radiant;
   let your faces not be abashed.
   This poor man called; the Lord heard him
   and rescued him from all his distress. ℟

4. The angel of the Lord is encamped
   around those who revere him, to rescue them.
   Taste and see that the Lord is good.
   He is happy who seeks refuge in him. ℟

5. Revere the Lord, you his saints.
   They lack nothing, those who revere him.
   Strong lions suffer want and go hungry
   but those who seek the Lord lack no blessing. ℟

Gospel Acclamation
Mt 5:3

Alleluia, alleluia!
How happy are the poor in spirit;
theirs is the kingdom of heaven.
Alleluia!

GOSPEL

A reading from the holy Gospel according to Matthew   19:27-29

You who have followed me will be repaid a hundred times over.

Peter spoke to Jesus. 'What about us?' he said. 'We have left everything and followed you. What are we to have, then?' Jesus said to him, 'I tell you solemnly, when all is made new and the Son of Man sits on his throne of glory, you will yourselves sit on twelve thrones to judge the twelve tribes of Israel. And everyone who has left houses, brothers, sisters, father, mother, children or land for the sake of my name will be repaid a hundred times over, and also inherit eternal life.'

This is the Gospel of the Lord.

Prayer over the Gifts
Lord,
look kindly on these gifts we present
on the feast of Saint Benedict.
By following his example in seeking you,
may we know unity and peace in your service.

Prayer after Communion
Lord,
hear the prayers of all
who have received this pledge of eternal life.
By following the teaching of Saint Benedict,
may we be faithful in doing your work
and in loving our brothers and sisters in true charity.

13 July

St Henry — Optional Memorial

Born in 973, Henry became Duke of Bavaria on his father's death in 995, and was crowned Holy Roman Emperor in 1014. He was married, but had no children. He was ardent for the reform of the Church, took part in synods, founded monasteries, appointed bishops of integrity. With his wife he lived a semi-monastic life of prayer and discipline.

Common of holy men and women, pp.1894ff.

Opening Prayer
Lord,
you filled Saint Henry with your love
and raised him from the cares of an earthly kingdom
to eternal happiness in heaven.
In the midst of the changes of this world,
may his prayers keep us free from sin
and help us on our way toward you.

FIRST READING

A reading from the prophet Micah 6:6-8
Man, it has been explained to you what the Lord asks of you.

'With what gift shall I come into the Lord's presence
and bow down before God on high?
Shall I come with holocausts,
with calves one year old?
Will he be pleased with rams by the thousand,
with libations of oil in torrents?
Must I give my first-born for what I have done wrong,
the fruit of my body for my own sin.'
– 'What is good has been explained to you, man;
this is what the Lord asks of you:
only this, to act justly,
to love tenderly
and to walk humbly with your God.'

This is the word of the Lord.

Responsorial Psalm
Ps 1:1-4. 6. ℟ v.2. Alt. ℟ Ps 39:5. Alt. ℟ Ps 91:13-14

℟ **His delight is the law of the Lord.**

or

℟ **Happy the man who has placed his trust in the Lord.**

or

℟ **The just will flourish like the palm-tree
in the courts of our God.**

1 Happy indeed is the man
who follows not the counsel of the wicked;
nor lingers in the way of sinners
nor sits in the company of scorners,
but whose delight is the law of the Lord
and who ponders his law day and night. ℟

2 He is like a tree that is planted
beside the flowing waters,
that yields its fruit in due season
and whose leaves shall never fade;
and all that he does shall prosper. ℟

3 Not so are the wicked, not so!
for they like winnowed chaff
shall be driven away by the wind.
For the Lord guards the way of the just
but the way of the wicked leads to doom. ℟

Gospel Acclamation   Jn 14:23
Alleluia, alleluia!
If anyone loves me he will keep my word,
and my Father will love him,
and we shall come to him
and make our home with him.
Alleluia!

GOSPEL

A reading from the holy Gospel according to Matthew   7:21-27
The house built on rock and the house built on sand.

Jesus said to his disciples: 'It is not those who say to me, "Lord, Lord", who will enter the kingdom of heaven, but the person who does the will of my Father in heaven. When the day comes many will say to me, "Lord, Lord, did we not prophesy in your name, cast out demons in your name, work many miracles in your name?" Then I shall tell them to their faces: I have never known you; away from me, you evil men!

'Therefore, everyone who listens to these words of mine and acts on them will be like a sensible man who built his house on rock. Rain came down, floods rose, gales blew and hurled themselves against that house, and it did not fall: it was founded on rock. But everyone who listens to these words of mine and does not act on them will be like a stupid man who built his house on sand. Rain came down, floods rose, gales blew and struck that house, and it fell; and what a fall it had!'

This is the Gospel of the Lord.

14 July
St Camillus de Lellis, priest
Optional Memorial

Born in the kingdom of Naples in 1550, he became a soldier, and led a dissolute life for some years. Horrified by the misery of the sick he saw in a hospital, he devoted his life to their care. He was ordained and founded a religious congregation to establish hospitals and run them. He did not spare himself in this work, and died in 1614.

Common of holy men and women: those who worked for the underprivileged, p.1900.

Opening Prayer
Father,
you gave Saint Camillus a special love for the sick.
Through his prayers inspire us with your grace,
so that by serving you in our brothers and sisters
we may come safely to you at the end of our lives.

FIRST READING

A reading from the first letter of St John   3:14-18

We, too, ought to give up our lives for our brothers.

We have passed out of death and into life,
and of this we can be sure
because we love our brothers.
If you refuse to love, you must remain dead;
to hate your brother is to be a murderer,
and murderers, as you know, do not have eternal life in them.
This has taught us love –
that he gave up his life for us;
and we, too, ought to give up our lives for our brothers.
If a man who was rich enough in this world's goods
saw that one of his brothers was in need,
but closed his heart to him,
how could the love of God be living in him?
My children,
our love is not to be just words or mere talk,
but something real and active.

    This is the word of the Lord.

Responsorial Psalm   Ps 111:1-9. R v.1

    R **Happy the man who fears the Lord.**

or

    R **Alleluia!**

1 Happy the man who fears the Lord,
   who takes delight in his commands.

Proper of Saints, 14 July   1589

His sons will be powerful on earth;
the children of the upright are blessed. ℟

2. Riches and wealth are in his house;
his justice stands firm for ever.
He is a light in the darkness for the upright:
he is generous, merciful and just. ℟

3. The good man takes pity and lends,
he conducts his affairs with honour.
The just man will never waver:
he will be remembered for ever. ℟

4. He has no fear of evil news:
with a firm heart he trusts in the Lord.
With a steadfast heart he will not fear;
he will see the downfall of his foes. ℟

5. Open-handed, he gives to the poor;
his justice stands firm for ever.
His head will be raised in glory. ℟

Gospel Acclamation   Jn 13:34

Alleluia, alleluia!
I give you a new commandment:
love one another as I have loved you.
Alleluia!

GOSPEL

A reading from the holy Gospel according to John   15:9-17
You are my friends if you do what I command you.

Jesus said to his disciples:

'As the Father has loved me,
so I have loved you.
Remain in my love.
If you keep my commandments
you will remain in my love,
just as I have kept my Father's commandments
and remain in his love.
I have told you this
so that my own joy may be in you
and your joy be complete.
This is my commandment:
love one another,

as I have loved you.
A man can have no greater love
than to lay down his life for his friends.
You are my friends,
if you do what I command you.
I shall not call you servants any more,
because a servant does not know
his master's business;
I call you friends,
because I have made known to you
everything I have learnt from my Father.
You did not choose me,
no, I chose you;
and I commissioned you
to go out and to bear fruit,
fruit that will last;
and then the Father will give you
anything you ask him in my name.
What I command you
is to love one another.'

This is the Gospel of the Lord.

15 July
St Bonaventure, bishop and doctor of the Church Memorial

Born in 1218. He studied in Paris and became professor there. He joined the Franciscan Order and eventually became Minister General in 1257. He endeavoured to reconcile the Franciscan spirit with the administrative demands of a world-wide order. His writings reveal a profound spirituality. He was appointed Cardinal Bishop of Albano, and attended the Council of Lyons, which attempted to reconcile the Churches of East and West. He died in 1274.

Common of pastors: bishops, pp.1878ff., or of doctors of the church, pp.1887ff.

Opening Prayer
All-powerful Father,
may we who celebrate the feast of Saint Bonaventure
always benefit from his wisdom
and follow the example of his love.

Proper of Saints, 15 July

FIRST READING

A reading from the letter of St Paul to the Ephesians   3:14-19
To know the love of Christ, which is beyond all knowledge.

This is what I pray, kneeling before the Father, from whom every family, whether spiritual or natural, takes its name:

Out of his infinite glory, may he give you the power through his Spirit for your hidden self to grow strong so that Christ may live in your hearts through faith, and then, planted in love and built on love, you will with all the saints have strength to grasp the breadth and the length, the height and the depth; until, knowing the love of Christ, which is beyond all knowledge, you are filled with the utter fullness of God.

This is the word of the Lord.

Responsorial Psalm   Ps 118:9-14. ℟ v.12

℟ **Lord, teach me your statutes.**

1. How shall the young remain sinless?
   By obeying your word.
   I have sought you with all my heart:
   let me not stray from your commands. ℟

2. I treasure your promise in my heart
   lest I sin against you.
   Blessed are you, O Lord;
   teach me your statutes. ℟

3. With my tongue I have recounted
   the decrees of your lips.
   I rejoiced to do your will
   as though all riches were mine. ℟

Gospel Acclamation   Mt 23:9-10

Alleluia! Alleluia!
You have only one Father,
and he is in heaven;
you have only one Teacher,
the Christ.
Alleluia!

GOSPEL

A reading from the holy Gospel according to Matthew 23:8-12

The greatest among you must be your servant.

Jesus said to his disciples: 'You must not allow yourselves to be called Rabbi, since you have only one Master, and you are all brothers. You must call no one on earth your father, since you have only one Father, and he is in heaven. Nor must you allow yourselves to be called teachers, for you have only one Teacher, the Christ. The greatest among you must be your servant. Anyone who exalts himself will be humbled, and anyone who humbles himself will be exalted.'

This is the Gospel of the Lord.

16 July

Our Lady of Mount Carmel

Optional Memorial

Carmel was the place where the prophet Elijah proclaimed the faith of Israel in the one God, the meeting place of God and his people. During the Crusades, Christian hermits established themselves in caves on the mountain. In the thirteenth century, they joined together in a religious community known as the Carmelites. Mount Carmel overlooks the plains of Galilee, not far from Nazareth, and is particularly under the protection of the Blessed Virgin Mary.

Common of the Blessed Virgin Mary, pp. 1858ff.

Opening Prayer

Father,
may the prayers of the Virgin Mary protect us
and help us to reach Christ her Son
who lives and reigns . . .

FIRST READING

A reading from the prophet Zechariah 2:14-17

Rejoice, daughter of Zion, for I am coming.

Sing, rejoice,
daughter of Zion;
for I am coming
to dwell in the middle of you
– it is the Lord who speaks.
Many nations will join the Lord,

Proper of Saints, 16 July 1593

on that day;
they will become his people.
But he will remain among you,
and you will know that the Lord of hosts has sent me to you.
But the Lord will hold Judah
as his portion in the Holy Land,
and again make Jerusalem his very own.
Let all mankind be silent before the Lord!
For he is awaking and is coming from his holy dwelling.

This is the word of the Lord.

Responsorial Psalm Lk 1:46-55. ℟ v.49

℟ **The Almighty works marvels for me.**
Holy is his name!

or

℟ **Blessed is the Virgin Mary**
who bore the Son of the eternal Father.

1 My soul glorifies the Lord,
my spirit rejoices in God, my saviour. ℟

2 He looks on his servant in her nothingness;
henceforth all ages will call me blessed.
The Almighty works marvels for me.
Holy his name! ℟

3 His mercy is from age to age,
on those who fear him.
He puts forth his arm in strength
and scatters the proud-hearted. ℟

4 He casts the mighty from their thrones
and raises the lowly.
He fills the starving with good things,
sends the rich away empty. ℟

5 He protects Israel, his servant,
remembering his mercy,
the mercy promised to our fathers,
to Abraham and his sons for ever. ℟

Gospel Acclamation Lk 11:28
Alleluia, alleluia!
Happy are those

who hear the word of God,
and keep it.
Alleluia!

GOSPEL

A reading from the holy Gospel according to Matthew 12:46-50

Stretching out his hand toward his disciples he said, 'Here are my mother and my brothers.'

Jesus was speaking to the crowds when his mother and his brothers appeared; they were standing outside and were anxious to have a word with him. But to the man who told him this Jesus replied, 'Who is my mother? Who are my brothers?' And stretching out his hand towards his disciples he said, 'Here are my mother and my brothers. Anyone who does the will of my Father in heaven, he is my brother and sister and mother.'

This is the Gospel of the Lord.

21 July

St Laurence of Brindisi, priest and doctor of the Church

Optional Memorial

Born at Brindisi in 1559. He was a born preacher, and entered the Capuchin Order at Verona in 1575. He was a man of learning, and took an active part in the Catholic reform; he travelled throughout Europe, preaching; he wrote many works to propound Catholic doctrine. He died at Lisbon in 1619, while on a diplomatic mission.

Common of pastors, pp.1876ff., or of doctors of the Church, pp.1887ff.

Opening Prayer
Lord,
for the glory of your name and the salvation of souls
you gave Laurence of Brindisi
courage and right judgement.
By his prayers,
help us to know what we should do
and give us the courage to do it.

FIRST READING

A reading from the second letter of St Paul to the Corinthians 4:1-2. 5-7

We preach Christ Jesus and ourselves as your servants for Jesus' sake.

Since we have by an act of mercy been entrusted with this work of administration, there is no weakening on our part. On the contrary, we will have none of the reticence of those who are ashamed, no deceitfulness or watering down the word of God; but the way we commend ourselves to every human being with a conscience is by stating the truth openly in the sight of God. For it is not ourselves that we are preaching, but Christ Jesus as the Lord, and ourselves as your servants for Jesus' sake. It is the same God that said, 'Let there be light shining out of darkness,' who has shone in our minds to radiate the light of the knowledge of God's glory, the glory on the face of Christ.

We are only the earthenware jars that hold this treasure, to make it clear that such an overwhelming power comes from God and not from us.

This is the word of the Lord.

Responsorial Psalm   Ps 39:2. 4. 7-10. R̷ cf. vv. 8. 9

R̷ **Here I am, Lord!
I come to do your will.**

1. I waited, I waited for the Lord
and he stooped down to me;
he heard my cry.
He put a new song into my mouth,
praise of our God. R̷

2. You do not ask for sacrifice and offerings,
but an open ear.
You do not ask for holocaust and victim.
Instead, here am I. R̷

3. In the scroll of the book it stands written
that I should do your will.
My God, I delight in your law
in the depth of my heart. R̷

4. Your justice I have proclaimed
in the great assembly.
My lips I have not sealed;
you know it, O Lord. R̷

Gospel Acclamation

Alleluia, alleluia!
The seed is the word of God,
Christ the sower;
whoever finds this seed
will remain for ever.
Alleluia!

GOSPEL

A reading from the holy Gospel according to Mark 4:1-10. 13-20
Imagine a sower going out to sow.

Jesus began to teach by the lakeside, but such a huge crowd gathered round him that he got into a boat on the lake and sat there. The people were all along the shore, at the water's edge. He taught them many things in parables, and in the course of his teaching he said to them, 'Listen! Imagine a sower going out to sow. Now it happened that, as he sowed, some of the seed fell on the edge of the path, and the birds came and ate it up. Some seed fell on rocky ground where it found little soil and sprang up straightaway because there was no depth of earth; and when the sun came up it was scorched and, not having any roots, it withered away. Some seed fell into thorns, and the thorns grew up and choked it, and it produced no crop. And some seeds fell into rich soil and, growing tall and strong, produced crop; and yielded thirty, sixty, even a hundredfold.' And he said, 'Listen, anyone who has ears to hear!'

When he was alone, the Twelve, together with the others who formed his company, asked what the parables meant.

He said to them, 'Do you not understand this parable? Then how will you understand any of the parables? What the sower is sowing is the word. Those on the edge of the path where the word is sown are people who have no sooner heard it than Satan comes and carries away the word that was sown in them. Similarly, those who receive the seed on patches of rock are people who, when first they hear the word, welcome it at once with joy. But they have no root in them, they do not last; should some trial come, or some persecution on account of the word, they fall away at once. Then there are others who receive the seed in thorns. These have heard the word, but the worries of this world, the lure of riches and all the other passions come in to choke the word, and so it produces nothing. And there are those who have received the seed in rich soil: they hear the word and accept it and yield a harvest, thirty and sixty and a hundredfold.'

This is the Gospel of the Lord.

22 July
St Mary Magdalen — Memorial

Mark 16:9 tells us that Mary was the first to whom the risen Christ appeared. She was one of his disciples, accompanied him on his journeys through the villages preaching (Luke 8:3), and stood by the cross.

Entrance Antiphon: The Lord said to Mary Magdalene: Go and tell my brothers that I shall ascend to my Father and your Father, to my God and to your God.

Opening Prayer
Father,
your Son first entrusted to Mary Magdalene
the joyful news of his resurrection.
By her prayers and example
may we proclaim Christ as our living Lord
and one day see him in glory,
for he lives . . .

The Gospel is proper to this memorial.

FIRST READING

A reading from the Song of Songs 3:1-4
I found him whom my heart loves.

The bride says this:

> On my bed, at night, I sought him
> whom my heart loves.
> I sought but did not find him.
> So I will rise and go through the City;
> in the streets and the squares
> I will seek him whom my heart loves.
> I sought but did not find him.
> The watchmen came upon me
> on their rounds in the City:
> 'Have you seen him whom my heart loves?'
> Scarcely had I passed them
> than I found him whom my heart loves.

This is the word of the Lord.

Alternative First Reading

A reading from the second letter of St Paul 5:14-17
to the Corinthians
Even if we did once know Christ in the flesh, that is not how we know him now.

The love of Christ overwhelms us when we reflect that if one man has died for all, then all men should be dead; and the reason he died for all was so that living men should live no longer for themselves, but for him who died and was raised to life for them.

From now onwards, therefore, we do not judge anyone by the standards of the flesh. Even if we did once know Christ in the flesh, that is not how we know him now. And for anyone who is in Christ, there is a new creation; the old creation has gone, and now the new one is here.

This is the word of the Lord.

Responsorial Psalm

Ps 62:2-6. 8-9. ℟ v.2

℟ **For you my soul is thirsting,**
O Lord, my God.

1. O God, you are my God, for you I long;
for you my soul is thirsting.
My body pines for you
like a dry, weary land without water. ℟

2. So I gaze on you in the sanctuary
to see your strength and your glory.
For your love is better than life,
my lips will speak your praise. ℟

3. So I will bless you all my life,
in your name I will lift up my hands.
My soul shall be filled as with a banquet,
my mouth shall praise you with joy. ℟

4. For you have been my help;
in the shadow of your wings I rejoice.
My soul clings to you;
your right hand holds me fast. ℟

Gospel Acclamation

Alleluia, alleluia!
Tell us, Mary: say

Proper of Saints, 22 July 1599

what thou didst see upon the way.
The tomb the Living did enclose;
I saw Christ's glory as he rose!
Alleluia!

GOSPEL

A reading from the holy Gospel according to John 20:1-2. 11-18
Woman, why are you weeping? Who are you looking for?

It was very early on the first day of the week and still dark, when Mary of Magdala came to the tomb. She saw that the stone had been moved away from the tomb and came running to Simon Peter and the other disciple, the one Jesus loved. 'They have taken the Lord out of the tomb' she said 'and we don't know where they have put him.'

Mary stayed outside near the tomb, weeping. Then, still weeping, she stooped to look inside, and saw two angels in white sitting where the body of Jesus had been, one at the head, the other at the feet. They said, 'Woman, why are you weeping?' 'They have taken my Lord away' she replied 'and I don't know where they have put him.' As she said this she turned round and saw Jesus standing there, though she did not recognise him. Jesus said, 'Woman why are you weeping? Who are you looking for?' Supposing him to be the gardener, she said, 'Sir, if you have taken him away, tell me where you have put him, and I will go and remove him.' Jesus said, 'Mary!' She knew him then and said to him in Hebrew, 'Rabbuni!' – which means Master. Jesus said to her, 'Do not cling to me, because I have not yet ascended to my Father. But go and find the brothers, and tell them: I am ascending to my Father and your Father, to my God and your God.' So Mary of Madgala went and told the disciples that she had seen the Lord and that he had said these things to her.

This is the Gospel of the Lord.

Prayer over the Gifts
Lord,
accept the gifts we present in memory of Saint Mary Magdalene;
her loving worship was accepted by your Son,
who is Lord for ever and ever.

Communion Antiphon: The love of Christ compels us to live not for ourselves but for him who died and rose for us.

Prayer after Communion
Father,
may the sacrament we have received
fill us with the same faithful love
that kept Mary Magdalene close to Christ,
who is Lord for ever and ever.

23 July
St Bridget, religious   Optional Memorial

Born in Sweden in 1303, married in 1316, a member of high Swedish society. She had eight children. She and her husband lived devout lives. After her husband's death in 1344 she lived with even greater asceticism; she received revelations and appealed to the kings of Europe and the Pope for peace and the restoration of the papacy to Rome. She journeyed to Rome for the Holy Year in 1350, and lived there for the rest of her life in poverty. She asked the Pope to approve the foundation of a religious community (now known as the Bridgetines), but this was not approved until after her death, in 1373.

Common of holy men and women, pp.1894ff.

Opening Prayer
Lord our God,
you revealed the secrets of heaven to Saint Bridget
as she meditated on the suffering and death of your Son.
May your people rejoice in the revelation of your glory.

FIRST READING

A reading from the letter of St Paul to the Galatians   2:19-20
I live now not with my own life but with the life of Christ who lives in me.

Through the Law I am dead to the Law, so that now I can live for God. I have been crucified with Christ, and I live now not with my own life but with the life of Christ who lives in me. The life I now live in this body I live in faith: faith in the Son of God who loved me and who sacrificed himself for my sake.

This is the word of the Lord.

Responsorial Psalm

Ps 33:2-11. ℟ v.2. Alt. ℟ v.9

℟ **I will bless the Lord at all times.**

or

℟ **Taste and see that the Lord is good.**

1. I will bless the Lord at all times,
   his praise always on my lips;
   in the Lord my soul shall make its boast.
   The humble shall hear and be glad. ℟

2. Glorify the Lord with me.
   Together let us praise his name.
   I sought the Lord and he answered me;
   from all my terrors he set me free. ℟

3. Look towards him and be radiant;
   let your faces not be abashed.
   This poor man called; the Lord heard him
   and rescued him from all his distress. ℟

4. The angel of the Lord is encamped
   around those who revere him, to rescue them.
   Taste and see that the Lord is good.
   He is happy who seeks refuge in him. ℟

5. Revere the Lord, you his saints.
   They lack nothing, those who revere him.
   Strong lions suffer want and go hungry ℟
   but those who seek the Lord lack no blessing.

Gospel Acclamation

Jn 15:9. 5

Alleluia, alleluia!
Remain in my love, says the Lord;
whoever remains in me, with me in him,
bears fruit in plenty.
Alleluia!

GOSPEL

A reading from the holy Gospel according to John 15:1-8
Whoever remains in me, with me in him, bears fruit in plenty.

Jesus said to his disciples;

'I am the true vine,
and my Father is the vinedresser.

Every branch in me that bears no fruit
he cuts away,
and every branch that does bear fruit he prunes
to make it bear even more.
You are pruned already,
by means of the word that I have spoken to you.
Make your home in me, as I make mine in you.
As a branch cannot bear fruit all by itself,
but must remain part of the vine,
neither can you unless you remain in me.
I am the vine,
you are the branches.
Whoever remains in me, with me in him,
bears fruit in plenty;
for cut off from me you can do nothing.
Anyone who does not remain in me
is like a branch that has been thrown away
– he withers;
these branches are collected and thrown on the fire,
and they are burnt.
If you remain in me
and my words remain in you,
you may ask what you will
and you shall get it.
It is to the glory of my Father that you should bear much fruit,
and then you will be my disciples.'

This is the Gospel of the Lord.

25 July
ST JAMES, APOSTLE   Feast

James was the brother of John the Apostle, son of Zebedee, the fisherman. He was present at the bringing of life of Jairus' daughter, and at the Transfiguration. He was beheaded by Herod Agrippa in about 42 AD.

Entrance Antiphon: **Walking by the Sea of Galilee, Jesus saw James and John, the sons of Zebedee, mending their nets, and called them to follow him.**

Opening Prayer
Almighty Father,
by the martyrdom of Saint James

you blessed the work of the early Church.
May his profession of faith give us courage
and his prayers bring us strength.

FIRST READING

A reading from the second letter of St Paul to the Corinthians

4:7-15

We always carry with us in our body the death of Jesus.

We are only the earthenware jars that hold this treasure, to make it clear that such an overwhelming power comes from God and not from us. We are in difficulties on all sides, but never cornered; we see no answer to our problems, but never despair; we have been persecuted, but never deserted; knocked down, but never killed; always wherever we may be, we carry with us in our body the death of Jesus, so that the life of Jesus, too, may always be seen in our body. Indeed, while we are still alive, we are consigned to our death every day, for the sake of Jesus, so that in our mortal flesh the life of Jesus, too, may be openly shown. So death is at work in us, but life in you.

But as we have the same spirit of faith that is mentioned in scripture – I believed, and therefore I spoke – we too believe and therefore we too speak, knowing that he who raised the Lord Jesus to life will raise us with Jesus in our turn, and put us by his side and you with us. You see, all this is for your benefit, so that the more grace is multiplied among people, the more thanksgiving there will be, to the glory of God.

This is the word of the Lord.

Responsorial Psalm   Ps 125. ℟ v.5

  ℟ **Those who are sowing in tears
will sing when they reap.**

1 When the Lord delivered Zion from bondage,
it seemed like a dream.
Then was our mouth filled with laughter,
on our lips there were songs. ℟

2 The heathens themselves said: 'What marvels
the Lord worked for them!'
What marvels the Lord worked for us!
Indeed we were glad. ℟

(continued)

3 Deliver us, O Lord, from our bondage
as streams in dry land.
Those who are sowing in tears
will sing when they reap.

℟ **Those who are sowing in tears
will sing when they reap.**

4 They go out, they go out, full of tears,
carrying seed for the sowing:
they come back, they come back, full of song,
carrying their sheaves. ℟

Gospel Acclamation cf. Jn 15:16

Alleluia, alleluia!
I chose you from the world
to go out and to bear fruit,
fruit that will last, says the Lord.
Alleluia!

GOSPEL

A reading from the holy Gospel according to Matthew 20:20-28
You shall drink my cup.

The mother of the sons of Zebedee came with them to make a request of him, and bowed low; and he said to her, 'What is it you want?' She said to him, 'Promise that these two sons of mine may sit one at your right hand and the other at your left in your kingdom.' 'You do not know what you are asking' Jesus answered. 'Can you drink the cup that I am going to drink?' They replied, 'We can.' 'Very well,' he said 'you shall drink my cup, but as for seats at my right hand and my left, these are not mine to grant; they belong to those to whom they have been allotted by my Father.'

When the other ten heard this they were indignant with the two brothers. But Jesus called them to him and said, 'You know that among the pagans the rulers lord it over them, and their great men make their authority felt. This is not to happen among you. No; anyone who wants to be great among you must be your servant, and anyone who wants to be first among you must be your slave, just as the Son of Man came not to be served but to serve, and to give his life as a ransom for many.'

This is the Gospel of the Lord.

Prayer over the Gifts
Lord,
as we honour Saint James,
the first apostle to share the cup of suffering and death,
wash away our sins
by the saving passion of your Son,
and make our sacrifice pleasing to you.

Preface of Apostles I or II, P64 or P65.

Communion Antiphon: By sharing the cup of the Lord's suffering they became the friends of God.

Prayer after Communion
Father,
we have received this holy eucharist with joy
as we celebrate the feast of the apostle James.
Hear his prayers
and bring us your help.

26 July
Ss Joachim and Anne
parents of the Blessed Virgin Mary Memorial

These names are given to the mother and father of the Blessed Virgin by a tradition dating back to the second century. As St John Damascene wrote: 'O blessed couple. All creation is in your debt. For through you is presented the noblest of gifts to the creator, namely a spotless mother who alone was worthy for the creator.'

Entrance Antiphon: Praised be Joachim and Ann for the child they bore. The Lord gave them the blessing of all the nations.

Opening Prayer
God of our fathers,
you gave Saints Joachim and Ann
the privilege of being the parents of Mary,
the mother of your incarnate Son.
May their prayers help us to attain
the salvation you have promised to your people.

FIRST READING

A reading from the book of Ecclesiasticus 44:1. 10-15

Their name lives on for all generations.

Let us praise illustrious men,
our ancestors in their successive generations.
Here is a list of generous men
whose good works have not been forgotten.
In their descendants there remains
a rich inheritance born of them.
Their descendants stand by the covenants
and, thanks to them, so do their children's children.
Their offspring will last for ever,
their glory will not fade.
Their bodies have been buried in peace,
and their name lives on for all generations.
The peoples will proclaim their wisdom,
the assembly will celebrate their praises.

This is the word of the Lord.

Responsorial Psalm
Ps 131:11.13-14. 17-18. R/ Lk 1:32

R/ **The Lord God will give him
the throne of his father David.**

1 The Lord swore an oath to David;
he will not go back on his word:
'A son, the fruit of your body,
will I set upon your throne.' R/

2 For the Lord has chosen Zion;
he has desired it for his dwelling:
'This is my resting-place for ever,
here have I chosen to live. R/

3 'There David's stock will flower:
I will prepare a lamp for my anointed.
I will cover his enemies with shame
but on him my crown shall shine.' R/

Gospel Acclamation
cf. Lk 2:25

Alleluia, alleluia!
They looked forward to Israel's comforting
and the Holy Spirit rested on them.
Alleluia!

Proper of Saints, 29 July   1607

GOSPEL

A reading from the holy Gospel according to Matthew   13:16-17
Many prophets and holy men longed to see what you see.

Jesus said to his disciples: 'Happy are your eyes because they see, your ears because they hear! I tell you solemnly, many prophets and holy men longed to see what you see, and never saw it; to hear what you hear, and never heard it.'

    This is the Gospel of the Lord.

Prayer over the Gifts
Lord,
receive these gifts as signs of our love
and give us a share in the blessing you promised
to Abraham and his descendants.

Communion Antiphon: They received a blessing from the Lord, and kindness from God their Saviour.

Prayer after Communion
Father,
your Son was born as a man
so that men could be born again in you.
As you nourish us with the bread of life,
given only to your sons and daughters,
fill us with the Spirit who makes us your children.

29 July
St Martha   Memorial

The sister of Mary and Lazarus; she appears in the Gospel three times – when she receives the Lord into her house and waits on him; at the resurrection of Lazarus, when she proclaims her faith in Jesus, 'son of the living God'; and in John 12:2, at the meal given to Jesus six days before the Passover.

Entrance Antiphon: As Jesus entered a certain village a woman called Martha welcomed him into her house.

Opening Prayer
Father,
your Son honoured Saint Martha
by coming to her home as a guest.

By her prayers
may we serve Christ in our brothers and sisters
and be welcomed by you into heaven, our true home.

The Gospel is proper to this memorial.

FIRST READING

A reading from the first letter of St John   4:7-16
As long as we love one another God will live in us.

My dear people,
let us love one another
since love comes from God
and everyone who loves is begotten by God and knows God.
Anyone who fails to love can never have known God,
because God is love.
God's love for us was revealed
when God sent into the world his only Son
so that we could have life through him:
this is the love I mean:
not our love for God,
but God's love for us when he sent his Son
to be the sacrifice that takes our sins away.
My dear people,
since God has loved us so much,
we too should love one another
No one has ever seen God;
but as long as we love one another.
God will live in us
and his love will be complete in us.
We can know that we are living in him
and he is living in us
because he lets us share his Spirit.
We ourselves saw and we testify
that the Father sent his Son
as saviour of the world.
If anyone acknowledges that Jesus is the Son of God,
God lives in him, and he in God.
We ourselves have known and put our faith in
God's love towards ourselves.
God is love
and anyone who lives in love lives in God,
and God lives in him.

    This is the word of the Lord.

Proper of Saints, 29 July

Responsorial Psalm   Ps 33:2-11. ℟ v.9
    ℟ **I will bless the Lord at all times.**

or

    ℟ **Taste and see that the Lord is good.**

1. I will bless the Lord at all times,
   his praise always on my lips;
   in the Lord my soul shall make its boast.
   The humble shall hear and be glad. ℟

2. Glorify the Lord with me.
   Together let us praise his name.
   I sought the Lord and he answered me;
   from all my terrors he set me free. ℟

3. Look towards him and be radiant;
   let your faces not be abashed.
   This poor man called; the Lord heard him
   and rescued him from all his distress. ℟

4. The angel of the Lord is encamped
   around those who revere him, to rescue them.
   Taste and see that the Lord is good.
   He is happy who seeks refuge in him. ℟

5. Revere the Lord, you his saints.
   They lack nothing, those who revere him.
   Strong lions suffer want and go hungry
   but those who seek the Lord lack no blessing. ℟

Gospel Acclamation   Jn 8:12
Alleluia, alleluia!
I am the light of the world, says the Lord;
anyone who follows me will have the light of life.
Alleluia!

GOSPEL

A reading from the holy Gospel according to John   11:19-27
I believe that you are the Christ, the Son of the living God.

Many Jews had come to Martha and Mary to sympathise with them over their brother. When Martha heard that Jesus had come she went to meet him. Mary remained sitting in the house. Martha said to Jesus, 'If you had been here, my brother would not have died, but I know that, even now, whatever you ask of

God, he will grant you.' 'Your brother' said Jesus to her 'will rise again.' Martha said, 'I know he will rise again at the resurrection on the last day.' Jesus said:

'I am the resurrection and the life.
If anyone believes in me, even though he dies he will live,
and whoever lives and believes in me
will never die.
Do you believe this?'

'Yes, Lord,' she said 'I believe that you are the Christ, the Son of God, the one who has to come into this world.'

This is the Gospel of the Lord.

Alternative Gospel

A reading from the holy Gospel according to Luke 10:38-42
Martha, Martha, you worry and fret about so many things.

Jesus came to a village, and a woman named Martha welcomed him into her house. She had a sister called Mary, who sat down at the Lord's feet and listened to him speaking. Now Martha who was distracted with all the serving said, 'Lord, do you not care that my sister is leaving me to do the serving all by myself? Please tell her to help me.' But the Lord answered: 'Martha, Martha' he said 'you worry and fret about so many things, and yet few are needed, indeed only one. It is Mary who has chosen the better part; it is not to be taken from her.'

This is the Gospel of the Lord.

Prayer over the Gifts
Father,
we praise you for your glory
on the feast of Saint Martha.
Accept this service of our worship
as you accepted her love.

Communion Antiphon: Martha said to Jesus: You are the Christ, the Son of God, who was to come into this world.

Prayer after Communion
Lord,

you have given us the body and blood of your Son
to free us from undue attachment to this passing life.
By following the example of Saint Martha,
may we grow in love for you on earth
and rejoice for ever in the vision of your glory in heaven.

30 July

St Peter Chrysologus, bishop and doctor of the Church
Optional Memorial

Born about 400, bishop of Ravenna. His preaching was famous, and more than 180 sermons, mainly on scripture and the liturgical year, have survived. He died about 450.

Common of pastors: bishops, pp.1878ff., or of doctors of the church, pp.1887ff.

Opening Prayer
Father,
you made Peter Chrysologus
an outstanding preacher of your incarnate Word.
May the prayers of Saint Peter help us to cherish
the mystery of our salvation
and make its meaning clear in our love for others.

FIRST READING

A reading from the letter of St Paul to the Ephesians 3:8-12
Proclaiming to the pagans the infinite treasure of Christ.

I, who am less than the least of all the saints, have been entrusted with this special grace, not only of proclaiming to the pagans the infinite treasure of Christ but also of explaining how the mystery is to be dispensed. Through all the ages, this has been kept hidden in God, the creator of everything. Why? So that the Sovereignties and Powers should learn only now, through the Church, how comprehensive God's wisdom really is, exactly according to the plan which he had had from all eternity in Christ Jesus our Lord. This is why we are bold enough to approach God in complete confidence, through our faith in him.

This is the word of the Lord.

Responsorial Psalm   Ps 118:9-14. R̷ v.12

  R̷ **Lord, teach me your statutes.**

1 How shall the young remain sinless?
  By obeying your word.
  I have sought you with all my heart:
  let me not stray from your commands.   R̷

2 I treasure your promise in my heart
  lest I sin against you.
  Blessed are you, O Lord;
  teach me your statutes.   R̷

3 With my tongue I have recounted
  the decrees of your lips.
  I rejoiced to do your will
  as though all riches were mine.   R̷

Gospel Acclamation   Jn 15:5
Alleluia, alleluia!
I am the vine,
you are the branches.
Whoever remains in me, with me in him,
bears fruit in plenty, says the Lord.
Alleluia!

GOSPEL

A reading from the holy Gospel according to Luke   6:43-45

A man's words flow out of what fills his heart.

Jesus said to his disciples: 'There is no sound tree that produces rotten fruit, nor again a rotten tree that produces sound fruit. For every tree can be told by its own fruit: people do not pick figs from thorns, nor gather grapes from brambles. A good man draws what is good from the store of goodness in his heart; a bad man draws what is bad from the store of badness. For a man's words flow out of what fills his heart.'

This is the Gospel of the Lord.

Proper of Saints, 31 July

31 July
St Ignatius of Loyola, priest — Memorial

Born in 1491 at Loyola in the north of Spain, of a courtly family, he became a soldier, but during convalescence from a wound was converted to a deep love of Christ and a missionary sense. He studied theology in Paris. With companions, he formed the Society of Jesus, to resist the Protestant Reformation, to reform the Church from within, and to educate the young in religion. He died in 1556, at Rome.

Common of pastors, pp.1876ff., or of holy men and women: religious, pp.1898ff.

Entrance Antiphon: At the name of Jesus every knee must bend, in heaven, on earth, and under the earth; every tongue should proclaim to the glory of God the Father: Jesus Christ is Lord.

Opening Prayer
Father,
you gave Saint Ignatius of Loyola to your Church
to bring greater glory to your name.
May we follow his example on earth
and share the crown of life in heaven.

FIRST READING

A reading from the first letter of St Paul
to the Corinthians 10:31 – 11:1
Whatever you do at all, do it for the glory of God.

Whatever you eat, whatever you drink, whatever you do at all, do it for the glory of God. Never do anything offensive to anyone – to Jews or Greeks or to the Church of God; just as I try to be helpful to everyone at all times, not anxious for my own advantage but for the advantage of everybody else, so that they may be saved.

Take me for your model, as I take Christ.

This is the word of the Lord.

Responsorial Psalm
Ps 33:2-11. ℟ v.2. Alt. ℟ v.9

℟ **I will bless the Lord at all times.**

or

℟ **Taste and see that the Lord is good.**

1. I will bless the Lord at all times,
   his praise always on my lips;
   in the Lord my soul shall make its boast.
   the humble shall hear and be glad. ℟

2. Glorify the Lord with me.
   Together let us praise his name.
   I sought the Lord and he answered me;
   from all my terrors he set me free. ℟

3. Look towards him and be radiant;
   let your faces not be abashed.
   This poor man called; the Lord heard him
   and rescued him from all his distress. ℟

4. The angel of the Lord is encamped
   around those who revere him, to rescue them.
   Taste and see that the Lord is good.
   He is happy who seeks refuge in him. ℟

5. Revere the Lord, you his saints.
   They lack nothing, those who revere him.
   Strong lions suffer want and go hungry
   but those who seek the Lord lack no blessing. ℟

Gospel Acclamation
Mt 5:3

Alleluia, alleluia!
How happy are the poor in spirit;
theirs is the kingdom of heaven.
Alleluia!

GOSPEL

A reading from the holy Gospel according to Luke 14:25-33

None of you can be my disciple unless he gives up all his possessions.

Great crowds accompanied Jesus on his way and he turned and spoke to them. 'If any man comes to me without hating his father, mother, wife, children, brothers, sisters, yes and his own life too, he cannot be my disciple. Anyone who does not carry his cross and come after me cannot be my disciple.

'And indeed, which of you here, intending to build a tower, would not first sit down and work out the cost to see if he had enough to complete it? Otherwise, if he laid the foundation and then found himself unable to finish the work, the onlookers would all start making fun of him and saying, "Here is a man who started to build and was unable to finish." Or again, what king marching to war against another king would not first sit down and consider whether with ten thousand men he could stand up to the other who advanced against him with twenty thousand? If not, then while the other king was still a long way off, he would send envoys to sue for peace. So in the same way, none of you can be my disciple unless he gives up all his possessions.'

This is the Gospel of the Lord.

Prayer over the Gifts
Lord God,
be pleased with the gifts we present to you
at this celebration in honour of Saint Ignatius.
Make us truly holy by this eucharist
which you give us as the source of all holiness.

Communion Antiphon: I have come to bring fire to the earth. How I wish it were already blazing!

Prayer after Communion
Lord,
may the sacrifice of thanksgiving which we have offered
on the feast of Saint Ignatius
lead us to the eternal praise of your glory.

PRAISE TO YOU O CHRIST

AUGUST

1 August

**St Alphonsus Liguori,
bishop and doctor of the Church** Memorial

Born 1696 in Naples. A lawyer who became a priest, Alphonsus founded the Congregation of the Most Holy Redeemer (the Redemptorists). He was a fervent preacher, and a moral theologian of eminence, who opposed the rigours of Jansenism. He was much in demand as a confessor, seeking to win back the sinful by gentle and direct appeal to the Gospel. He wrote many works of devotion which became very popular. He was made bishop of Sant' Agata dei Gotti, but after thirteen years returned to his Congregation. He died in 1787.

Common of pastors: bishops, pp.1878ff., or of doctors of the Church, pp.1887ff.

Opening Prayer
Father,
you constantly build up your Church
by the lives of your saints.
Give us grace to follow Saint Alphonsus
in his loving concern for the salvation of men,
and so come to share his reward in heaven.

FIRST READING

A reading from the letter of St Paul to the Romans   8:1-4
The law of the spirit of life in Christ Jesus has set me free from the law of sin and death.

The reason why those who are in Christ Jesus are not condemned, is that the law of the spirit of life in Christ Jesus has set you free from the law of sin and death. God has done what the law, because of our unspiritual nature, was unable to do. God dealt with sin by sending his own Son in a body as physical as any sinful body, and in that body God condemned sin. He did this in order that the Law's just demands might be satisfied in us, who behave not as our unspiritual nature but as the spirit dictates.

This is the word of the Lord.

Responsorial Psalm   Ps 118:9-14. R/ v.12

R/ **Lord, teach me your statutes.**

1 How shall the young remain sinless?
 By obeying your word.
 I have sought you with all my heart:
 let me not stray from your commands. R/

2 I treasure your promise in my heart
 lest I sin against you.
 Blessed are you, O Lord;
 teach me your statutes. R/

3 With my tongue I have recounted
 the decrees of your lips.
 I rejoiced to do your will
 as though all riches were mine. R/

Gospel Acclamation   Mt 5:16
Alleluia, alleluia!
Your light must shine in the sight of men,
so that, seeing your good works,
they may give the praise to your Father in heaven.
Alleluia!

GOSPEL

A reading from the holy Gospel according to Matthew   5:13-19
You are the light of the world.

Jesus said to his disciples: 'You are the salt of the earth. But if salt becomes tasteless, what can make it salty again? It is good for nothing, and can only be thrown out to be trampled underfoot by men.

'You are the light of the world. A city built on a hill-top cannot be hidden. No one lights a lamp to put it under a tub; they put it on the lamp-stand where it shines for everyone in the house. In the same way your light must shine in the sight of men, so that, seeing your good works, they may give the praise to your Father in heaven.

'Do not imagine that I have come to abolish the Law or the Prophets. I have come not to abolish but to complete them. I tell you solemnly, till heaven and earth disappear, not one dot, not one little stroke, shall disappear from the Law until its purpose is achieved. Therefore, the man who infringes even one of the least of these commandments and teaches others to do the same will be considered the least in the kingdom of heaven; but the man who keeps them and teaches them will be considered great in the kingdom of heaven.'

This is the Gospel of the Lord.

Prayer over the Gifts
Father,
inflame our hearts with the Spirit of your love
as we present these gifts on the feast of Saint Alphonsus,
who dedicated his life to you in the eucharist.

Prayer after Communion
Lord,
you made Saint Alphonsus
a faithful minister and preacher of this holy eucharist.
May all who believe in you receive it often
and give you never-ending praise.

2 August
St Eusebius of Vercelli, bishop
Optional Memorial

Born about 300, he became bishop of Vercelli in 345. The Arian heresy was prevalent at that time, and he worked unceasingly to maintain the true doctrine of the divinity of Christ. Emperor Constantius exiled him in 355, and he travelled to visit Christian communities in the Holy Land, Cappadocia and Egypt. He returned to Vercelli when a new emperor came to power in 361; he established monasticism in the diocese, and gave his clergy a rule of life which was semi-monastic.

Common of pastors: bishops, pp.1878ff.

Opening Prayer
Lord God,
Saint Eusebius affirmed the divinity of your Son.
By keeping the faith he taught,
may we come to share the eternal life of Christ,
who lives and reigns . . .

FIRST READING

A reading from the first letter of St John   5:1-5
This is the victory over the world – our faith.

Whoever believes that Jesus is the Christ
has been begotten by God;
and whoever loves the Father that begot him
loves the child whom he begets.
We can be sure that we love God's children
if we love God himself and do what he has commanded us;
this is what loving God is –
keeping his commandments;
and his commandments are not difficult,
because anyone who has been begotten by God
has already overcome the world;
this is the victory over the world –
our faith.
Who can overcome the world?
Only the man who believes that Jesus is the Son of God.

    This is the word of the Lord.

Responsorial Psalm
Ps 88:2-5. 21-22. 25. 27. ℟ cf. v.2

℟ **I will sing for ever of your love, O Lord.**

1. I will sing for ever of your love, O Lord;
through all ages my mouth will proclaim your truth.
Of this I am sure, that your love lasts for ever,
that your truth is firmly established as the heavens. ℟

2. 'I have made a covenant with my chosen one;
I have sworn to David my servant:
I will establish your dynasty for ever
and set up your throne through all ages. ℟

3. 'I have found David my servant
and with my holy oil anointed him.
My hand shall always be with him
and my arm shall make him strong. ℟

4. 'My truth and my love shall be with him;
by my name his might shall be exalted.
He will say to me: "You are my father,
my God, the rock who saves me."' ℟

Gospel Acclamation
Mt 5:3

Alleluia, alleluia!
How happy are the poor in spirit;
theirs is the kingdom of heaven.
Alleluia!

GOSPEL

A reading from the holy Gospel according to Matthew 5:1-12
Rejoice and be glad, for your reward will be great in heaven.

Seeing the crowds, Jesus went up the hill. There he sat down and was joined by his disciples. Then he began to speak. This is what he taught them:

'How happy are the poor in spirit;
theirs is the kingdom of heaven.
Happy the gentle:
they shall have the earth for their heritage.
Happy those who mourn:
they shall be comforted.
Happy those who hunger and thirst for what is right:
they shall be satisfied.

Happy the merciful:
they shall have mercy shown them.
Happy the pure in heart:
they shall see God.
Happy the peacemakers:
they shall be called sons of God.
Happy those who are persecuted in the cause of right:
theirs is the kingdom of heaven.

'Happy are you when people abuse you and persecute you and speak all kinds of calumny against you on my account. Rejoice and be glad, for your reward will be great in heaven.'

This is the Gospel of the Lord.

4 August

St John Vianney, priest — Memorial

Born in 1786, near Lyons in France; he was not quick at study and had great difficulty in being accepted for ordination. He was sent to the parish of Ars, which he transformed by his preaching, his personal mortification, his life of prayer and charity for all, and particularly by his fame as a confessor – people came to him for spiritual help from all over the world. He died in 1859.

Common of pastors, pp.1876ff.

Opening Prayer

Father of mercy,
you made Saint John Vianney outstanding
in his priestly zeal and concern for your people.
By his example and prayers,
enable us to win our brothers and sisters
to the love of Christ
and come with them to eternal glory.

FIRST READING

A reading from the prophet Ezekiel 3:16-21

I have appointed you as sentry to the House of Israel.

The word of the Lord was addressed to me as follows, 'Son of man, I have appointed you as sentry to the House of Israel. Whenever you hear a word from me, warn them in my Name. If I say to a wicked man: You are to die, and you do not warn him; if you do not speak and warn him to renounce his evil ways and so live, then he shall die for his sin, but I will hold you responsible for his death. If, however, you do warn a wicked man and he does not renounce his wickedness and his evil ways, then he shall die for his sin, but you yourself will have saved your life. When the upright man renounces his integrity to do evil and I set a trap for him, he too shall die; since you failed to warn him, he shall die for his sin and the integrity he practised will no longer be remembered; but I will hold you responsible for his death. If, however, you warn the upright man not to sin and he abstains from sinning, he shall live, thanks to your warning, and you too will have saved your life.'

This is the word of the Lord.

Responsorial Psalm   Ps 116. ℟ Mk 16:15

  ℟ **Go out to the whole world; proclaim the Good News.**

or

  ℟ **Alleluia!**

1 O praise the Lord, all you nations,
   acclaim him all you peoples!   ℟

2 Strong his love for us;
   he is faithful for ever.   ℟

Gospel Acclamation   Lk 4:18
  Alleluia, alleluia!
  The Lord has sent me to bring the good news to the poor,
  to proclaim liberty to captives.
  Alleluia!

GOSPEL

A reading from the holy Gospel according to Matthew   9:35—10:1
When he saw the crowds he felt sorry for them.

Jesus made a tour through all the towns and villages, teaching in their synagogues, proclaiming the Good News of the kingdom and curing all kinds of diseases and sickness.

And when he saw the crowds he felt sorry for them because they were harassed and dejected, like sheep without a shepherd. Then he said to his disciples, 'The harvest is rich but the labourers are few, so ask the Lord of the harvest to send labourers to his harvest.'

He summoned his twelve disciples, and gave them authority over unclean spirits with power to cast them out and to cure all kinds of diseases and sickness.

This is the Gospel of the Lord.

5 August
The Dedication of the Basilica of St Mary Major
Optional Memorial

When the doctrine of Mary, Mother of God, was proclaimed at the Council of Ephesus in 431, the pope, Sixtus III, had erected in Rome a basilica in her honour. This is the oldest church in the West to be dedicated to Mary, and is called St Mary Major.
Common of the Blessed Virgin Mary, pp.1858ff.

Opening Prayer
Lord,
pardon the sins of your people.
May the prayers of Mary, the mother of your Son,
help to save us,
for by ourselves we cannot please you.

FIRST READING

A reading from the book of the Apocalypse 21:1-5

I saw the new Jerusalem, as beautiful as a bride all dressed for her husband.

I, John, saw a new heaven and a new earth; the first heaven and the first earth had disappeared now, and there was no longer any sea. I saw the holy city, and the new Jerusalem, coming down from God out of heaven, as beautiful as a bride all dressed for her husband. Then I heard a loud voice call from the throne, 'You see this city? Here God lives among men. He will make his home among them; they shall be his people, and he will be their God; his name is God-with-them. He will wipe away all tears from their eyes; there will be no more death, and no more mourning or sadness. The world of the past has gone.'

Then the One sitting on the throne spoke: 'Now I am making the whole of creation new.'

This is the word of the Lord.

Responsional Psalm Judith 13:18-19. ℟ 15:9
℟ **You are the highest honour of our race!**

1. May you be blessed, my daughter, by God Most High,
   beyond all women on earth;
   and may the Lord God be blessed,
   the Creator of heaven and earth. ℟

2. The trust you have shown
   shall not pass from the memories of men,
   but shall ever remind them
   of the power of God. ℟

Gospel Acclamation Lk 11:28
Alleluia, alleluia!
Happy are those
who hear the word of God,
and keep it.
Alleluia!

GOSPEL

A reading from the holy Gospel according to Luke 11:27-28
Happy the womb that bore you!

As Jesus was speaking, a woman in the crowd raised her voice and said, 'Happy the womb that bore you and the breasts you sucked!' But he replied, 'Still happier those who hear the word of God and keep it!'

This is the Gospel of the Lord.

6 August
THE TRANSFIGURATION OF THE LORD Feast

It is wonderful for us to be here today as we celebrate the transfigured Christ, the Christ of prophecy, in whom we have believed.

Entrance Antiphon: In the shining cloud the Spirit is seen; from it the voice of the Father is heard: This is my Son, my beloved, in whom is all my delight. Listen to him.

Opening Prayer
Let us pray
  [that we may hear the Lord Jesus
  and share his everlasting life]

Proper of Saints, 6 August

God our Father,
in the transfigured glory of Christ your Son,
you strengthen our faith
by confirming the witness of your prophets,
and show us the splendour of your beloved sons and daughters.
As we listen to the voice of your Son,
help us to become heirs to eternal life with him
who lives and reigns with you and the Holy Spirit,
one God, for ever and ever.

FIRST READING

A reading from the book of Daniel   7:9-10. 13-14

His robe as white as snow.

As I watched:
Thrones were set in place
and one of great age took his seat.
His robe was white as snow,
the hair of his head as pure as wool.
His throne was a blaze of flames,
its wheels were a burning fire.
A stream of fire poured out,
issuing from his presence.
A thousand thousand waited on him,
ten thousand times ten thousand stood before him.
A court was held and the books were opened.
I gazed into the visions of the night.
And I saw, coming on the clouds of heaven,
one like a son of man.
He came to the one of great age
and was led into his presence.
On him was conferred sovereignty,
glory and kingship,
and men of all peoples, nations and languages became his
    servants.
His sovereignty is an eternal sovereignty
which shall never pass away,
nor will his empire ever be destroyed.

    This is the word of the Lord.

Responsorial Psalm   Ps 96:1-2. 5-6. 9. ℟ vv.1. 9
   ℟ **The Lord is king, most high above all the earth.**

1. The Lord is king, let earth rejoice,
   let all the coastlands be glad.
   Cloud and darkness are his raiment;
   his throne, justice and right.   ℟

2. The mountains melt like wax
   before the Lord of all the earth.
   the skies proclaim his justice;
   all peoples see his glory.   ℟

3. For you indeed are the Lord
   most high above all the earth
   exalted far above all spirits.   ℟

SECOND READING

A reading from the second letter of St Peter   1:16-19
We heard this ourselves, spoken from heaven.

It was not any cleverly invented myths that we were repeating when we brought you the knowledge of the power and the coming of our Lord Jesus Christ; we had seen his majesty for ourselves. He was honoured and glorified by God the Father, when the Sublime Glory itself spoke to him and said, 'This is my Son, the Beloved; he enjoys my favour.' We heard this ourselves, spoken from heaven, when we were with him on the holy mountain.

    So we have confirmation of what was said in prophecies; and you will be right to depend on prophecy and take it as a lamp for lighting a way through the dark until the dawn comes and the morning star rises in your minds.

    This is the word of the Lord.

Gospel Acclamation   Mt 17:5
   Alleluia, alleluia!
   This is my Son, the Beloved,
   he enjoys my favour;
   listen to him.
   Alleluia!

GOSPEL

Year A

A reading from the holy Gospel according to Matthew 17:1-9
His face shone like the sun.

Jesus took with him Peter and James and his brother John and led them up a high mountain where they could be alone. There in their presence he was transfigured: his face shone like the sun and his clothes became as white as the light. Suddenly Moses and Elijah appeared to them; they were talking with him. Then Peter spoke to Jesus. 'Lord,' he said 'it is wonderful for us to be here; if you wish, I will make three tents here, one for you, one for Moses and one for Elijah.' He was still speaking when suddenly a bright cloud covered them with shadow, and from the cloud there came a voice which said, 'This is my Son, the Beloved; he enjoys my favour. Listen to him.' When they heard this, the disciples fell on their faces, overcome with fear. But Jesus came up and touched them. 'Stand up,' he said 'do not be afraid.' And when they raised their eyes they saw no one but only Jesus.

As they came down from the mountain Jesus gave them this order, 'Tell no one about the vision until the Son of Man has risen from the dead.'

This is the Gospel of the Lord.

Year B

A reading from the holy Gospel according to Mark 9:2-10
This is my Son, the Beloved.

Jesus took with him Peter and James and John and led them up a high mountain where they could be alone by themselves. There in their presence he was transfigured; his clothes became dazzlingly white, whiter than any earthly bleacher could make them. Elijah appeared to them with Moses; and they were talking with Jesus. Then Peter spoke to Jesus: 'Rabbi,' he said 'it is wonderful for us to be here; so let us make three tents, one for you, one for Moses and one for Elijah.' He did not know what to say; they were so frightened. And a cloud came, covering them in shadow; and there came a voice from the cloud, 'This is my Son, the Beloved. Listen to him.' Then suddenly, when they looked round, they saw no one with them any more but only Jesus.

As they came down from the mountain he warned them to tell

no one what they had seen, until after the Son of Man had risen from the dead. They observed the warning faithfully, though among themselves they discussed what 'rising from the dead' could mean.

This is the Gospel of the Lord.

Year C

A reading from the holy Gospel according to Luke 9:28-36
As he prayed the aspect of his face was changed.

Jesus took with him Peter and John and James and went up the mountain to pray. As he prayed, the aspect of his face was changed and his clothing became brilliant as lightning. Suddenly there were two men there talking to him; they were Moses and Elijah appearing in glory, and they were speaking of his passing which he was to accomplish in Jerusalem. Peter and his companions were heavy with sleep, but they kept awake and saw his glory and the two men standing with him. As these were leaving him, Peter said to Jesus, 'Master, it is wonderful for us to be here; so let us make three tents, one for you, one for Moses and one for Elijah.' – He did not know what he was saying. As he spoke, a cloud came and covered them with shadow; and when they went into the cloud the disciples were afraid. And a voice came from the cloud, saying, 'This is my Son, the Chosen One. Listen to him.' And after the voice had spoken, Jesus was found alone. The disciples kept silence and, at that time, told no one what they had seen.

This is the Gospel of the Lord.

Prayer over the Gifts
Lord,
by the transfiguration of your Son
make our gifts holy,
and by his radiant glory free us from our sins.
We ask this in the name of Jesus the Lord.

Preface of the Transfiguration, P50.

Communion Antiphon: When Christ is revealed we shall be like him, for we shall see him as he is.

Prayer after Communion
Lord,

you revealed the true radiance of Christ
in the glory of his transfiguration.
May the food we receive from heaven
change us into his image.

7 August

Ss Sixtus II, pope and martyr, and companions, martyrs

Optional Memorial

Sixtus became Bishop of Rome in 257. On 6 August 258 he was arrested while saying Mass in the catacombs of Saint Callistus, and with four deacons, put to death immediately. This was at the height of the persecution of Valerian.

Common of martyrs, pp.1865ff.

Opening Prayer
Father,
by the power of the Holy Spirit
you enabled Saint Sixtus and his companions to lay down their lives
for your word in witness to Jesus.
Give us the grace to believe in you
and the courage to profess our faith.

FIRST READING

A reading from the book of Wisdom   3:1-9
He accepted them as a holocaust.

The souls of the virtuous are in the hands of God,
no torment shall ever touch them.
In the eyes of the unwise, they did appear to die,
their going looked like a disaster,
their leaving us, like annihilation;
but they are in peace.
If they experienced punishment as men see it,
their hope was rich with immortality;
slight was their affliction, great will their blessings be.
God has put them to the test
and proved them worthy to be with him;
he has tested them like gold in a furnace,
and accepted them as a holocaust.

When the time comes for his visitation they will shine out;
as sparks run through the stubble, so will they.
They shall judge nations, rule over peoples,
and the Lord will be their king for ever.
They who trust in him will understand the truth,
those who are faithful will live with him in love;
for grace and mercy await those he has chosen.

    This is the word of the Lord.

Responsorial Psalm   Ps 125. ℟ v.5

    ℟ **Those who are sowing in tears
will sing when they reap.**

1. When the Lord delivered Zion from bondage,
it seemed like a dream.
Then was our mouth filled with laughter,
on our lips there were songs. ℟

2. The heathens themselves said: 'What marvels
the Lord worked for them!'
What marvels the Lord worked for us!
Indeed we were glad. ℟

3. Deliver us, O Lord, from our bondage
as streams in dry land.
Those who are sowing in tears
will sing when they reap. ℟

4. They go out, they go out, full of tears,
carrying seed for the sowing:
they come back, they come back, full of song,
carrying their sheaves. ℟

Gospel Acclamation   James 1:12

    Alleluia, alleluia!
Happy the man who stands firm when trials come.
He has proved himself,
and will win the prize of life.
Alleluia!

GOSPEL

A reading from the holy Gospel according to Matthew   10:28-33
Do not be afraid of those who kill the body.

Jesus said to his apostles: 'Do not be afraid of those who kill the body but cannot kill the soul; fear him rather who can destroy both body and soul in hell. Can you not buy two sparrows for a penny? And yet not one falls to the ground without your Father knowing. Why, every hair on your head has been counted. So there is no need to be afraid; you are worth more than hundreds of sparrows.

'So if anyone declares himself for me in the presence of men, I will declare myself for him in the presence of my Father in heaven. But the one who disowns me in the presence of men, I will disown in the presence of my Father in heaven.'

This is the Gospel of the Lord.

Also 7 August

St Cajetan, priest   Optional Memorial

Born at Vicenza in 1480. Became a prelate in the Roman curia, and devoted himself to prayer and service of his neighbour, particularly the sick. He founded a congregation of Clerks, which came to be called the Theatines, particularly devoted to the work of preaching and liturgical renewal. For the congregation, of which he became superior in 1527, he travelled throughout Italy. He died at Naples in 1547.

Common of pastors, pp.1876ff., or of holy men and women: religious, pp.1898ff.

Opening Prayer
Lord,
you helped Saint Cajetan
to imitate the apostolic way of life.
By his example and prayers
may we trust in you always
and be faithful in seeking your kingdom.

FIRST READING

A reading from the book of Ecclesiasticus   2:7-13
You who fear the Lord, trust, hope and love.

You who fear the Lord, wait for his mercy;
do not turn aside in case you fall.
You who fear the Lord, trust him,
and you will not be baulked of your reward.
You who fear the Lord, hope for good things,

for everlasting happiness and mercy.
Look at the generations of old and see:
who ever trusted in the Lord and was put to shame?

Or who ever feared him steadfastly and was left forsaken?
Or who ever called out to him, and was ignored?
For the Lord is compassionate and merciful,
he forgives sins, and saves in days of distress.

   This is the word of the Lord.

Responsorial Psalm   Ps 111:1-9. ℟ v.1
   ℟   **Happy the man who fears the Lord.**

or

   ℟   **Alleluia!**

1 Happy the man who fears the Lord,
   who takes delight in his commands.
   His sons will be powerful on earth;
   the children of the upright are blessed.   ℟

2 Riches and wealth are in his house;
   his justice stands firm for ever.
   He is a light in the darkness for the upright:
   he is generous, merciful and just.   ℟

3 The good man takes pity and lends,
   he conducts his affairs with honour.
   The just man will never waver:
   he will be remembered for ever.   ℟

4 He has no fear of evil news;
   with a firm heart he trusts in the Lord.
   With a steadfast heart he will not fear;
   he will see the downfall of his foes.   ℟

5 Open-handed, he gives to the poor;
   his justice stands firm for ever.
   His head will be raised in glory.   ℟

Gospel Acclamation   Mt 5:3
   Alleluia, alleluia!
   How happy are the poor in spirit;
   theirs is the kingdom of heaven.
   Alleluia!

Proper of Saints, 8 August

GOSPEL

A reading from the holy Gospel according to Luke 12:32-34
It has pleased your Father to give you the kingdom.

Jesus said to his disciples: 'There is no need to be afraid, little flock, for it has pleased your Father to give you the kingdom.

'Sell your possessions and give alms. Get yourselves purses that do not wear out, treasure that will not fail you, in heaven where no thief can reach it and no moth destroy it. For where your treasure is, there will your heart be also.'

This is the Gospel of the Lord.

8 August

St Dominic, priest — Memorial

Born at Calaruega, Spain, in 1170. He wanted to go to Russia as a missionary, but the Pope sent him to Toulouse, where the Albigensian heresy was particularly strong. He lived by the Gospel, and preached the Gospel. Men came to join him, to follow his way of preaching and poverty, and from these grew the Order of Preachers (Dominicans). Sisters also joined this new order, supporting its work by their prayers from the enclosures where they lived. Dominic died in 1221.

Common of pastors, pp.1876ff., or of holy men and women; religious, pp.1894ff.

Opening Prayer
Lord,
let the holiness and teaching of Saint Dominic
come to the aid of your Church.
May he help us now with his prayers
as he once inspired people by his preaching.

FIRST READING

A reading from the first letter of St Paul 2:1-10
to the Corinthians
We teach the hidden wisdom of God in our mysteries.

When I came to you, brothers, it was not with any show of oratory or philosophy, but simply to tell you what God had guaranteed. During my stay with you, the only knowledge I claimed to have was about Jesus and only about him as the crucified Christ. Far from relying on any power of my own, I came among you in great 'fear and trembling' and in my speeches and the sermons that I gave, there were none of the arguments that belong to philosophy; only a demonstration of the power of the Spirit. And I did this so that your faith should not depend on human philosophy but on the power of God.

But still we have a wisdom to offer those who have reached maturity, not a philosophy of our age, it is true, still less of the masters of our age, which are coming to their end. The hidden wisdom of God which we teach in our mysteries is the wisdom that God predestined to be for our glory before the ages began. It is a wisdom that none of the masters of this age have ever known, or they would not have crucified the Lord of Glory; we teach what scripture calls; the things that no eye has seen and no ear has heard, things beyond the mind of man, all that God has prepared for those who love him.

These are the very things that God has revealed to us through the Spirit.

This is the word of the Lord.

Responsorial Psalm   Ps 95:1-3. 7-8. 10. ℟ v.3

℟ **Proclaim the wonders of the Lord among all the peoples.**

1 O sing a new song to the Lord,
   sing to the Lord all the earth.
   O sing to the Lord, bless his name.   ℟

2 Proclaim his help day by day,
   tell among the nations his glory
   and his wonders among all the peoples.   ℟

3 Give the Lord, you families of peoples,
   give the Lord glory and power,
   give the Lord the glory of his name.   ℟

4 Proclaim to the nations: 'God is king.'
   The world he made firm in its place;
   he will judge the peoples in fairness.   ℟

Gospel Acclamation   Jn 8:12
Alleluia, alleluia!
I am the light of the world, says the Lord;
anyone who follows me will have the light of life.
Alleluia!

GOSPEL

A reading from the holy Gospel according to Luke 9:57-62
I will follow you wherever you go.

As Jesus and his disciples travelled along they met a man on the road who said to him, 'I will follow you wherever you go.' Jesus answered, 'Foxes have holes and the birds of the air have nests, but the Son of Man has nowhere to lay his head.'

Another to whom he said, 'Follow me,' replied, 'Let me go and bury my father first.' But he answered, 'Leave the dead to bury their dead; your duty is to go and spread the news of the kingdom of God.'

Another said, 'I will follow you, sir, but first let me go and say good-bye to my people at home.' Jesus said to him, 'Once the hand is laid on the plough, no one who looks back is fit for the kingdom of God.'

This is the Gospel of the Lord.

Prayer over the Gifts
Lord of mercy,
at the intercession of Saint Dominic
hear our prayers,
and by the power of this sacrifice
give us the grace to preach and defend our faith.

Prayer after Communion
Lord,
may your Church share with a living faith
the power of the sacrament we have received.
As the preaching of Saint Dominic helped your Church to grow,
may his prayers help us to live for you.

10 August
ST LAWRENCE, DEACON AND MARTYR Feast

A deacon of the Church of Rome, who died four days after Pope Sixtus and his four companion deacons.

Entrance Antiphon: Today let us honour Saint Lawrence, who spent himself for the poor of the Church. Thus he merited to suffer martyrdom and to ascend in joy to Jesus Christ the Lord.

Opening Prayer

Father,
you called Saint Lawrence to serve you by love
and crowned his life with glorious martyrdom.
Help us to be like him
in loving you and doing your work.

FIRST READING

A reading from the second letter of St Paul 9:6-10
to the Corinthians
God loves a cheerful giver.

Thin sowing means thin reaping; the more you sow, the more you reap. Each one should give what he has decided in his own mind, not grudgingly or because he is made to, for God loves a cheerful giver. And there is no limit to the blessings which God can send you – he will make sure that you will always have all you need for yourselves in every possible circumstance, and still have something to spare for all sorts of good works. As scripture says: He was free in almsgiving, and gave to the poor: his good deeds will never be forgotten.

The one who provides seed for the sower and bread for food will provide you with all the seed you want and make the harvest of your good deeds a larger one.

This is the word of the Lord.

Responsorial Psalm   Ps 111:1-2. 5-9. ℟ v.5

℟ **Happy the man who takes pity and lends.**

1   Happy the man who fears the Lord,
    who takes delight in his commands.
    His sons will be powerful on earth;
    the children of the upright are blessed.   ℟

2   The good man takes pity and lends,
    he conducts his affairs with honour.
    The just man will never waver:
    he will be remembered for ever.   ℟

3   He has no fear of evil news;
    with a firm heart he trusts in the Lord.
    With a steadfast heart he will not fear;
    he will see the downfall of his foes.   ℟

Proper of Saints, 10 August

4 Open-handed, he gives to the poor;
his justice stands firm for ever.
His head will be raised in glory. ℟

Gospel Acclamation   Jn 8:12
Alleluia, alleluia!
Anyone who follows me will not be walking in the dark, says the Lord,
he will have the light of life.
Alleluia!

GOSPEL

A reading from the holy Gospel according to John   12:24-26
If anyone serves me, my Father will honour him.

Jesus said to his disciples:

'I tell you, most solemnly,
unless a wheat grain falls on the ground and dies,
it remains only a single grain;
but if it dies,
it yields a rich harvest.
Anyone who loves his life loses it;
anyone who hates his life in this world
will keep it for the eternal life.
If a man serves me, he must follow me,
wherever I am, my servant will be there too.
If anyone serves me, my Father will honour him.'

This is the Gospel of the Lord.

Prayer over the Gifts
Lord,
at this celebration in honour of Saint Lawrence,
accept the gifts we offer
and let them become a help to our salvation.

Communion Antiphon: He who serves me, follows me, says the Lord; and where I am, my servant will also be.

Prayer after Communion
Lord,
we have received your gifts
on this feast of Saint Lawrence.

As we offer you our worship in this eucharist,
may we experience the increase of your saving grace.

11 August

St Clare, virgin — Memorial

Born in Assisi in 1193, Clare followed Saint Francis of Assisi in his life of poverty. She founded the order of Poor Clares. Her life was austere and prayerful.

Common of virgins, pp.1889ff., or of holy men and women: religious, pp.1898ff.

Opening Prayer

God of mercy,
you inspired Saint Clare with the love of poverty.
By the help of her prayers
may we follow Christ in poverty of spirit
and come to the joyful vision of your glory
in the kingdom of heaven.

FIRST READING

A reading from the letter of St Paul to the Philippians 3:8-14

I am racing for the finish, for the prize to which God calls us upwards to receive in Christ Jesus.

I believe nothing can happen that will outweigh the supreme advantage of knowing Christ Jesus my Lord. For him I have accepted the loss of everything, and I look on everything as so much rubbish if only I can have Christ and be given a place in him. I am no longer trying for perfection by my own efforts, the perfection that comes from the Law, but I want only the perfection that comes through faith in Christ, and is from God and based on faith. All I want is to know Christ and the power of his resurrection and to share his sufferings by reproducing the pattern of his death. That is the way I can hope to take my place in the resurrection of the dead. Not that I have become perfect yet: I have not yet won, but I am still running, trying to capture the prize for which Christ Jesus captured me. I can assure you, my brothers, I am far from thinking that I have already won. All I can say is that I forget the past and I strain ahead for what is still to come; I am racing for the finish, for the prize to which God calls us upwards to receive in Christ Jesus.

This is the word of the Lord.

Proper of Saints, 13 August

Responsorial Psalm Ps 15:1-2. 5. 7-8. 11. ℟ cf. v.5

℟   **You are my inheritance, O Lord.**

1 Preserve me, God, I take refuge in you.
   I say to the Lord: 'You are my God.'
   O Lord, it is you who are my portion and cup;
   it is you yourself who are my prize. ℟

2 I will bless the Lord who gives me counsel,
   who even at night directs my heart.
   I keep the Lord ever in my sight:
   since he is at my right hand, I shall stand firm. ℟

3 You will show me the path of life,
   the fullness of joy in your presence,
   at your right hand happiness for ever. ℟

Gospel Acclamation Mt 5:3
   Alleluia, alleluia!
   How happy are the poor in spirit;
   theirs is the kingdom of heaven.
   Alleluia!

GOSPEL

A reading from the holy Gospel according to Matthew   19:27-29
You who have followed me will be repaid a hundred times over.

Peter spoke to Jesus. 'What about us?' he said, 'We have left everything and followed you. What are we to have, then?' Jesus said to him, 'I tell you solemnly, when all is made new and the Son of Man sits on his throne of glory, you will yourselves sit on twelve thrones to judge the twelve tribes of Israel. And everyone who has left houses, sisters, father, mother, children or land for the sake of my name will be repaid a hundred times over, and also inherit eternal life.'

This is the Gospel of the Lord.

13 August

Ss Pontian, pope
and Hippolytus, priest, martyrs

Optional Memorial

Pontian became bishop of Rome in 231. During the persecution of Emperor Maximinus, he was exiled to Sardinia, along with Hippolytus.

He resigned the papacy, so that the Church might have an active leader. They both died in Sardinia. Hippolytus is buried in the cemetery on the via Tiburtina, and Pontian in the catacombs of Callistus.

Common of martyrs, pp.1865ff., or of pastors, pp.1876ff.

Opening Prayer
Lord,
may the loyal suffering of your saints, Pontian and Hippolytus,
fill us with your love
and make our hearts steadfast in faith.

FIRST READING

A reading from the first letter of St Peter 4:12-19
If you have some share in the sufferings of Christ, be glad.

My dear people, you must not think it unaccountable that you should be tested by fire. There is nothing extraordinary in what has happened to you. If you can have some share in the sufferings of Christ, be glad, because you will enjoy a much greater gladness when his glory is revealed. It is a blessing for you when they insult you for bearing the name of Christ, because it means that you have the Spirit of glory, the Spirit of God resting on you. None of you should ever deserve to suffer for being a murderer, a thief, a criminal or an informer; but if anyone of you should suffer for being a Christian, then he is not to be ashamed of it; he should thank God that he has been called one. The time has come for the judgement to begin at the household of God; and if what we know now is only the beginning, what will it be when it comes down to those who refuse to believe God's Good News? If it is hard for a good man to be saved, what will happen to the wicked and to sinners? So even those whom God allows to suffer must trust themselves to the constancy of the creator and go on doing good.

This is the word of the Lord.

Responsional Psalm
Ps 123:2-5. 7-8. ℟ v.7

℟ **Our life, like a bird, has escaped
from the snare of the fowler.**

1 If the Lord had not been on our side
   when men rose against us,
   then would they have swallowed us alive
   when their anger was kindled. ℟

Proper of Saints, 13 August

2 Then would the waters have engulfed us,
   the torrent gone over us;
   over our head would have swept
   the raging waters. ℟

3 Indeed the snare has been broken
   and we have escaped.
   Our help is in the name of the Lord,
   who made heaven and earth. ℟

Gospel Acclamation
Alleluia, alleluia!
We praise you, O God,
we acknowledge you to be the Lord;
the noble army of martyrs praise you, O Lord.
Alleluia.

GOSPEL

A reading from the holy Gospel according to John 15:18-21
If they have persecuted me, they will persecute you too.

Jesus said to his disciples:

'If the world hates you,
remember that it hated me before you.
If you belonged to the world,
the world would love you as its own;
but because you do not belong to the world,
because my choice withdrew you from the world,
therefore the world hates you.
Remember the words I said to you:
A servant is not greater than his master.
If they persecuted me,
they will persecute you too;
if they kept my word
they will keep yours as well.
But it will be on my account that they will do all this,
because they do not know the one who sent me.'

This is the Gospel of the Lord.

15 August

THE ASSUMPTION OF THE BLESSED VIRGIN MARY   Solemnity

Vigil Mass

Entrance Antiphon: All honour to you, Mary! Today you were raised above the choirs of angels to lasting glory with Christ.

The Gloria is sung or said.

Opening Prayer
Let us pray
  [that the Virgin Mary will help us
  with her prayers]

Almighty God,
you gave a humble virgin
the privilege of being the mother of your Son,
and crowned her with the glory of heaven.
May the prayers of the Virgin Mary
bring us to the salvation of Christ
and raise us up to eternal life.
or
Let us pray
  [with Mary to the Father,
  in whose presence she now dwells]

Almighty Father of our Lord Jesus Christ,
you have revealed the beauty of your power
by exalting the lowly virgin of Nazareth
and making her the mother of our Saviour.
May the prayers of this woman clothed with the sun
bring Jesus to the waiting world
and fill the void of incompletion
with the presence of her child
who lives and reigns . . .

FIRST READING

A reading from the first book of Chronicles   15:3-4. 15-16; 16:1-2
They brought the ark of God in and put it inside the tent that David had pitched for it.

David gathered all Israel together in Jerusalem to bring the ark of

Proper of Saints, 15 August

God up to the place he had prepared for it. David called together the sons of Aaron and the sons of Levi, and the Levites carried the ark of God with the shafts on their shoulders, as Moses had ordered in accordance with the word of the Lord.

David then told the heads of the Levites to assign duties for their kinsmen as cantors, with their various instruments of music, harps and lyres and cymbals, to play joyful tunes.

They brought the ark of God in and put it inside the tent that David had pitched for it; and they offered holocausts before God, and communion sacrifices. And when David had finished offering holocausts and communion sacrifices, he blessed the people in the name of the Lord.

This is the word of the Lord.

Responsorial Psalm Ps 131:6-7. 9-10. 13-14. ℟ v.8

℟ **Go up, Lord, to the place of your rest,
you and the ark of your strength.**

1 At Ephrata we heard of the ark;
we found it in the plains of Yearim.
'Let us go to the place of his dwelling;
let us go to kneel at his footstool.' ℟

2 Your priests shall be clothed with holiness:
your faithful shall ring out their joy.
For the sake of David your servant
do not reject your anointed. ℟

3 For the Lord has chosen Zion;
he has desired it for his dwelling:
'This is my resting-place for ever,
here have I chosen to live.' ℟

SECOND READING

A reading from the first letter of St Paul 15:54-57
to the Corinthians
He gave us the victory through our Lord Jesus Christ.

When this perishable nature has put on imperishability, and when this mortal nature has put on immortality, then the words of scripture will come true: Death is swallowed up in victory. Death, where is your victory? Death, where is your sting? Now the sting of death is sin, and sin gets its power from the Law. So let us thank God for giving us the victory through our Lord Jesus Christ.

This is the word of the Lord.

Gospel Acclamation
Lk 11:28
Alleluia, alleluia!
Happy are those
who hear the word of God, and keep it.
Alleluia!

GOSPEL

A reading from the holy Gospel according to Luke 11:27-28
Happy the womb that bore you!

As Jesus was speaking, a woman in the crowd raised her voice and said, 'Happy the womb that bore you and the breasts you sucked!' But he replied, 'Still happier those who hear the word of God and keep it!'

This is the Gospel of the Lord.

The Profession of Faith is made.

Prayer over the Gifts
Lord,
receive this sacrifice of praise and peace
in honour of the assumption of the Mother of God.
May our offering bring us pardon
and make our lives a thanksgiving to you.

Preface of the Assumption, P59.

Communion Antiphon: Blessed is the womb of the Virgin Mary; she carried the Son of the eternal Father.

Prayer after Communion
God of mercy,
we rejoice because Mary, the mother of our Lord,
was taken into the glory of heaven.
May the holy food we receive at this table
free us from evil.

Proper of Saints, 15 August

Mass during the Day

In Mary's glorious assumption we celebrate the fulfilment of our Christian destiny, and with her we proclaim the greatness of the Lord.

Entrance Antiphon: A great sign appeared in heaven: a woman clothed with the sun, the moon beneath her feet, and a crown of twelve stars on her head.

or

Let us rejoice in the Lord and celebrate this feast in honour of the Virgin Mary, at whose assumption the angels rejoice, giving praise to the Son of God.

Opening Prayer
Let us pray
   [that we will join Mary, the mother of the Lord, in the glory of
      heaven]

All-powerful and ever-living God,
you raised the sinless Virgin Mary, mother of your Son,
body and soul to the glory of heaven.
May we see heaven as our final goal
and come to share her glory.

or

Let us pray
   [that with the help of Mary's prayers
   we too may reach our heavenly home]

Father in heaven,
all creation rightly gives you praise,
for all life and all holiness come from you.

In the plan of your wisdom
she who bore the Christ in her womb
was raised body and soul in glory to be with him in heaven.
May we follow her example in reflecting your holiness
and join in her hymn of endless life and praise.

FIRST READING

A reading from the book of the Apocalypse   11:19; 12:1-6. 10

A woman adorned with the sun, standing on the moon.

The sanctuary of God in heaven opened, and the ark of the covenant could be seen inside it. Now a great sign appeared in heaven: a woman, adorned with the sun, standing on the moon, and with the twelve stars on her head for a crown. She was pregnant, and in labour, crying aloud in the pangs of childbirth. Then a second sign appeared in the sky, a huge red dragon which had seven heads and ten horns, and each of the seven heads crowned with a coronet. Its tail dragged a third of the stars from the sky and dropped them to the earth, and the dragon stopped in front of the woman as she was having the child, so that he could eat it as soon as it was born from its mother. The woman brought a male child into the world, the son who was to rule all the nations with an iron sceptre, and the child was taken straight up to God and to his throne, while the woman escaped into the desert, where God had made a place of safety ready. Then I heard a voice shout from heaven, 'Victory and power and empire for ever have been won by our God, and all authority for his Christ.'

This is the word of the Lord.

Responsorial Psalm   Ps 44:10-12. 16. ℟ v.10

℟ **On your right stands the queen, in garments of gold.**

1. The daughters of kings are among your loved ones.
   On your right stands the queen in gold of Ophir.
   Listen, O daughter, give ear to my words:
   forget your own people and your father's house. ℟

2. So will the king desire your beauty:
   He is your lord, pay homage to him.
   They are escorted amid gladness and joy;
   they pass within the palace of the king. ℟

SECOND READING

A reading from the first letter of St Paul   15:20-26
to the Corinthians

Christ as the first-fruits and then those who belong to him.

Christ has been raised from the dead, the first-fruits of all who have fallen asleep. Death came through one man and in the same way the resurrection of the dead has come through one man. Just as all men die in Adam, so all men will be brought to life in Christ; but all of them in their proper order; Christ as the first-fruits and then, after the coming of Christ, those who belong to him. After that will come the end, when he hands over the kingdom to God the Father, having done away with every sovereignty, authority and power. For he must be king until he has put all his enemies under his feet and the last of the enemies to be destroyed is death, for everything is to be put under his feet.

This is the word of the Lord.

Gospel Acclamation
Alleluia, alleluia!
Mary has been taken up into heaven;
all the choirs of angels are rejoicing.
Alleluia!

GOSPEL

A reading from the holy Gospel according to Luke 1:39-56
The Almighty has done great things for me, he has exalted the lowly.

Mary set out and went as quickly as she could to a town in the hill country of Judah. She went into Zechariah's house and greeted Elizabeth. Now as soon as Elizabeth heard Mary's greeting, the child leapt in her womb and Elizabeth was filled with the Holy Spirit. She gave a loud cry and said, 'Of all women you are the most blessed, and blessed is the fruit of your womb. Why should I be honoured with a visit from the mother of my Lord? For the moment your greeting reached my ears, the child in my womb leapt for joy. Yes, blessed is she who believed that the promise made her by the Lord would be fulfilled.'

And Mary said:

'My soul proclaims the greatness of the Lord
and my spirit exults in God my saviour;
because he has looked upon his lowly handmaid.
Yes, from this day forward all generations will call me blessed,
for the Almighty has done great things for me.
Holy is his name,
and his mercy reaches from age to age for those who fear him.
He has shown the power of his arm,
he has routed the proud of heart.
He has pulled down princes from their thrones and exalted

the lowly.
The hungry he has filled with good things, the rich sent empty away.
He has come to the help of Israel his servant, mindful of his mercy
– according to the promise he made to our ancestors –
of his mercy to Abraham and to his descendants for ever.'

Mary stayed with Elizabeth about three months and then went back home.

This is the Gospel of the Lord.

Prayer over the Gifts
Lord,
receive this offering of our service.
You raised the Virgin Mary to the glory of heaven.
By her prayers, help us to seek you
and to live in your love.

Preface of the Assumption, P59.

Communion Antiphon: All generations will call me blessed, for the Almighty has done great things for me.

Prayer after Communion
Lord,
may we who receive this sacrament of salvation
be led to the glory of heaven
by the prayers of the Virgin Mary.

16 August
St Stephen of Hungary
Optional Memorial

Born about 969, baptised about 985, crowned king of Hungary in 1000, Stephen ruled wisely in the country, and did all he could for the establishment of the Church there. He died in 1038.

Common of holy men and women, pp.1894ff.

Opening Prayer
Almighty Father,
grant that Saint Stephen of Hungary,

Proper of Saints, 16 August 1649

who fostered the growth of your Church on earth,
may continue to be our powerful helper in heaven.

FIRST READING

A reading from the book of Deuteronomy 6:3-9
You shall love the Lord your God with all your heart.

Moses said to the people:

'Listen Israel, keep and observe what will make you prosper and give you great increase, as the Lord, the God of your fathers has promised you, giving you a land where milk and honey flow.

'Listen, Israel: the Lord our God is the one Lord. You shall love the Lord your God with all your heart, with all your soul, with all your strength. Let these words I urge on you today be written on your heart. You shall repeat them to your children and say them over to them whether at rest in your house or walking abroad, at your lying down or at your rising; you shall fasten them on your hand as a sign and on your forehead as a circlet; you shall write them on the doorposts of your house and on your gates.'

This is the word of the Lord.

Responsorial Psalm Ps 111:1-9. ℟ v.1
℟ **Happy the man who fears the Lord.**

or

℟ **Alleluia!**

1 Happy the man who fears the Lord,
who takes delight in his commands.
His sons will be powerful on earth;
the children of the upright are blessed. ℟

2 Riches and wealth are in his house;
his justice stands firm for ever.
He is a light in the darkness for the upright:
he is generous, merciful and just. ℟

3 The good man takes pity and lends,
he conducts his affairs with honour.
The just man will never waver:
he will be remembered for ever. ℟

4 He has no fear of evil news;
with a firm heart he trusts in the Lord.

With a steadfast heart he will not fear;
he will see the downfall of his foes.

℟ **Happy the man who fears the Lord.**

or

℟ **Alleluia!**

5 Open-handed he gives to the poor;
his justice stands firm for ever.
His head will be raised in glory. ℟

Gospel Acclamation Jn 14:23
Alleluia, alleluia!
If anyone loves me he will keep my word,
and my Father will love him
and we shall come to him
and make our home with him.
Alleluia!

GOSPEL

A reading from the holy Gospel according to Matthew 25:14-30
You have shown you can be faithful in small things; come and join in your master's happiness.

Jesus spoke this parable to his disciples: 'A man on his way abroad summoned his servants and entrusted his property to them. To one he gave five talents, to another two, to a third, one; each in proportion to his ability. Then he set out. The man who had received the five talents promptly went and traded with them and made five more. The man who had received two made two more in the same way. But the man who had received one went off and dug a hole in the ground and hid his master's money. Now a long time after, the master of those servants came back and went through his accounts with them. The man who had received the five talents came forward bringing five more. "Sir," he said, "you entrusted me with five talents; here are five more that I have made." His master said to him, "Well done, good and faithful servant; you have shown you can be faithful in small things, I will trust you with greater; come and join in your master's happiness." Next the man with the two talents came forward. "Sir," he said, "you entrusted me with two talents; here are two more that I have made." His master said to him, "Well done, good and faithful servant; you have shown you can be faithful in small things, I will trust you with greater; come and join in your master's happiness."

Last came forward the man who had the one talent. "Sir," said he, "I had heard you were a hard man, reaping where you have not sown and gathering where you have not scattered; so I was afraid, and I went off and hid your talent in the ground. Here it is; it was yours, you have it back." But his master answered him, "You wicked and lazy servant! So you knew that I reap where I have not sown and gather where I have not scattered? Well then, you should have deposited my money with the bankers, and on my return I would have recovered my capital with interest. So now, take the talent from him and give it to the man who has the five talents. For to everyone who has will be given more, and he will have more than enough; but from the man who has not, even what he has will be taken away. As for this good-for-nothing servant, throw him out into the dark, where there will be weeping and grinding of teeth."′

This is the Gospel of the Lord.

*Shorter form, verses 14-23. Read between *.

19 August
St John Eudes, priest Optional Memorial

Born in France in 1601, most of his life was passed in Normandy. He founded the Institute of Our Lady of Charity to help prostitutes, and the Congregation of Jesus and Mary, whose work was the running of seminaries, which he established at Caen, Coutances, Lisieux and Rouen. He left spiritual writings, and promoted devotion to the Sacred Heart of Jesus and of Mary.

Common of pastors, pp.1876ff., or of holy men and women: religious, pp.1898ff.

Opening Prayer
Father,
you chose the priest John Eudes
to preach the infinite riches of Christ.
By his teaching and example
help us to know you better
and live faithfully in the light of the gospel.

FIRST READING

A reading from the letter of St Paul to the Ephesians   3:14-19
To know the love of Christ, which is beyond all knowledge.

This is what I pray, kneeling before the Father, from whom every family, whether spiritual or natural, takes its name:

Out of his infinite glory, may he give you the power through his Spirit for your hidden self to grow strong, so that Christ may live in your hearts through faith, and then, planted in love and built on love, you will with all the saints have strength to grasp the breadth and the length, the height and the depth; until, knowing the love of Christ, which is beyond all knowledge, you are filled with the utter fullness of God.

This is the word of the Lord.

Responsorial Psalm   Ps 130

℟ **Keep my soul in peace before you, O Lord.**

1 O Lord, my heart is not proud
 nor haughty my eyes.
 I have not gone after things too great
 nor marvels beyond me. ℟

2 Truly I have set my soul
 in silence and peace.
 A weaned child on its mother's breast,
 even so is my soul. ℟

3 O Israel, hope in the Lord
 both now and for ever. ℟

Gospel Acclamation   cf. Mt 11:25

Alleluia, alleluia!
Blessed are you, Father,
Lord of heaven and earth,
for revealing the mysteries of the kingdom
to mere children.
Alleluia!

GOSPEL

A reading from the holy Gospel according to Matthew   11:25-30
You have hidden these things from the learned and have revealed them to mere children.

Jesus exclaimed, 'I bless you, Father, Lord of heaven and of earth, for hiding these things from the learned and the clever and revealing them to mere children. Yes, Father, for that is what it pleased you to do. Everything has been entrusted to me by my Father; and no one knows the Son except the Father, just as no one knows the Father except the Son and those to whom the Son chooses to reveal him.

'Come to me, all you who labour and are overburdened, and I will give you rest. Shoulder my yoke and learn from me, for I am gentle and humble in heart, and you will find rest for your souls. Yes, my yoke is easy and my burden light.'

This is the Gospel of the Lord.

20 August

St Bernard, abbot and doctor of the Church — Memorial

Born near Dijon in France in 1090, Bernard entered the Cistercian Order at the age of 22; he became the Abbot of Clairvaux. Despite his longing for the solitary contemplative life, he travelled a great deal in France, Germany and Italy, trying to reconcile the divisions of the Church of the time. He wrote many works on the spiritual life and theology.

Common of doctors of the Church, pp.1887ff., or of holy men and women: religious, pp.1898ff.

Opening Prayer
Heavenly Father,
Saint Bernard was filled with zeal for your house
and was a radiant light in your Church.
By his prayers
may we be filled with this spirit of zeal
and walk always as children of light.

FIRST READING

A reading from the book of Ecclesiasticus 15:1-6
He will fill him with the spirit of wisdom and understanding.

Whoever fears the Lord will act like this,
and whoever grasps the Law will obtain wisdom.
She will come to meet him like a mother,
and receive him like a virgin bride.
She will give him the bread of understanding to eat,

and the water of wisdom to drink.
He will lean on her and will not fall,
he will rely on her and not be put to shame.
She will raise him high above his neighbours,
and in full assembly she will open his mouth.
He will find happiness and a crown of joy,
he will inherit an everlasting name.

This is the word of the Lord.

Responsorial Psalm

Ps 118:9-14. ℟ v.12

℟ **Lord, teach me your statutes.**

1. How shall the young remain sinless?
   By obeying your word.
   I have sought you with all my heart:
   let me not stray from your commands. ℟

2. I treasure your promise in my heart
   lest I sin against you.
   Blessed are you, O Lord;
   teach me your statutes. ℟

3. With my tongue I have recounted
   the decrees of your lips.
   I rejoiced to do your will
   as though all riches were mine. ℟

Gospel Acclamation

Jn 15:9. 5

Alleluia, alleluia!
Remain in my love, says the Lord;
whoever remains in me, with me in him,
bears fruit in plenty.
Alleluia!

GOSPEL

A reading from the holy Gospel according to John   17:20-26

I want them to be with me where I am.

Jesus raised his eyes to heaven and said:

'Holy Father,
I pray not only for these,
but for those also
who through their words will believe in me.

Proper of Saints, 20 August 1655

May they all be one.
Father, may they be one in us,
as you are in me and I am in you,
so that the world may believe it was you who sent me.
I have given them the glory you gave to me,
that they may be one as we are one.
With me in them and you in me,
may they be so completely one
that the world will realise that it was you who sent me
and that I have loved them as much as you loved me.
Father,
I want those you have given me
to be with me where I am,
so that they may always see the glory
you have given me
because you loved me
before the foundation of the world.
Father, Righteous One,
the world has not known you,
but I have known you,
and these have known
that you have sent me.
I have made your name known to them
and will continue to make it known,
so that the love with which you loved me may be in them,
and so that I may be in them.'

This is the Gospel of the Lord.

Prayer over the Gifts
Lord our God,
may the eucharist we offer
be a sign of unity and peace
as we celebrate the memory of Saint Bernard,
who strove in word and deed
to bring harmony to your Church.

Prayer after Communion
Father,
may the holy food we have received
at this celebration of the feast of Saint Bernard
continue your work of salvation in us.
By his example, give us courage,

by his teachings, make us wise,
so that we too may burn with love for your Word, Jesus Christ,
who is Lord for ever and ever.

21 August

St Pius X, pope   Memorial

Joseph Sarto was born in 1835, at Riese in the province of Venice. He became Patriarch of Venice in 1893, and pope in 1903. The aim of his life was to 'restore all things in Christ'. He defended the deposit of faith, exhorted the people to take part in the liturgy, encouraged frequent communion – his motivation was always pastoral. He died in 1914.

From the common of pastors: popes, pp.1876ff.

Opening Prayer
Father,
to defend the Catholic faith
and to make all things new in Christ,
you filled Saint Pius X
with heavenly wisdom and apostolic courage.
May his example and teaching
lead us to the reward of eternal life.

FIRST READING

A reading from the first letter of St Paul   2:2-8
to the Thessalonians
We were eager to hand over to you not only the Good News but our whole lives as well.

It was our God who gave us the courage to proclaim his Good News to you in the face of great opposition. We have not taken to preaching because we are deluded, or immoral, or trying to deceive anyone; it was God who decided that we were fit to be entrusted with the Good News, and when we are speaking, we are not trying to please men but God, who can read our inmost thoughts. You know very well, and we can swear it before God, *that never at any time have our speeches been simply flattery*, or a cover for trying to get money; nor have we ever looked for any special honour from men, either from you or anybody else, when we could have imposed ourselves on you with full weight, as apostles of Christ.

Proper of Saints, 21 August

Instead, we were unassuming. Like a mother feeding and looking after her own children, we felt so devoted and protective towards you, and had come to love you so much, that we were eager to hand over to you not only the Good News but our whole lives as well.

This is the word of the Lord.

Responsorial Psalm   Ps 88:2-5. 21-22. 25. 27. ℟ cf. v.2

  ℟ **I will sing for ever of your love, O Lord.**

1 I will sing for ever of your love, O Lord;
    through all ages my mouth will proclaim your truth.
    Of this I am sure, that your love lasts for ever,
    that your truth is firmly established as the heavens. ℟

2 'I have made a covenant with my chosen one;
    I have sworn to David my servant:
    I will establish your dynasty for ever
    and set up your throne through all ages. ℟

3 'I have found David my servant
    and with my holy oil anointed him.
    My hand shall always be with him
    and my arm shall make him strong. ℟

4 'My truth and my love shall be with him;
    by my name his might shall be exalted.
    He will say to me: "You are my father,
    my God, the rock who saves me."' ℟

Gospel Acclamation   Jn 10:14
  Alleluia, alleluia!
  I am the good shepherd, says the Lord;
  I know my own sheep
  and my own know me.
  Alleluia!

GOSPEL

A reading from the holy Gospel according to John   21:15-17
Feed my lambs, feed my sheep.

Jesus showed himself to his disciples, and after they had eaten he said to Simon Peter, 'Simon son of John, do you love me more than these others do?' He answered, 'Yes Lord, you know I love you.' Jesus said to him, 'Feed my lambs.' A second time he said to him, 'Simon son of John, do you love me?' He replied, 'Yes, Lord, you know I love you.' Jesus said to him, 'Look after my sheep.' Then he said to him a third time, 'Simon son of John, do you love me?' Peter was upset that he asked him the third time, 'Do you love me?' and said, 'Lord, you know everything; you know I love you.' Jesus said to him, 'Feed my sheep.'

This is the Gospel of the Lord.

Prayer over the Gifts
Lord,
be pleased to accept our offerings.
May we follow the teaching of Saint Pius X,
and so come to these mysteries with reverence
and receive them with faith.

Prayer after Communion
Lord our God,
we honour the memory of Saint Pius X
by sharing the bread of heaven.
May it strengthen our faith and unite us in your love.

22 August

The Queenship of Mary — Memorial

Entrance Antiphon: The queen stands at your right hand arrayed in cloth of gold.

Opening Prayer
Father,
you have given us the mother of your Son
to be our queen and mother.
With the support of her prayers
may we come to share the glory of your children
in the kingdom of heaven.

FIRST READING

A reading from the prophet Isaiah 9:1-6
A Son is given to us.

The people that walked in darkness
has seen a great light;
on those who live in a land of deep shadow

Proper of Saints, 22 August

a light has shone.
You have made their gladness greater,
you have made their joy increase;
they rejoice in your presence
as men rejoice at harvest time,
as men are happy when they are dividing the spoils.

For the yoke that was weighing on him,
the bar across his shoulders,
the rod of his oppressor,
these you break as on the day of Midian.

For all the footgear of battle,
every cloak rolled in blood,
is burnt
and consumed by fire.
For there is a child born for us,
a son given to us
and dominion is laid on his shoulders;
and this is the name they give him:
Wonder-Counsellor, Mighty-God,
Eternal-Father, Prince-of-Peace.
Wide is his dominion
in a peace that has no end,
for the throne of David
and for his royal power,
which he establishes and makes secure
in justice and integrity.
From this time onwards and for ever,
the jealous love of the Lord of hosts will do this.

This is the word of the Lord.

Responsorial Psalm   Ps 112:1-8. ℟ v.2

℟ **May the name of the Lord be blessed for evermore!**

or

℟ **Alleluia!**

1 Praise, O servants of the Lord,
   praise the name of the Lord!
   May the name of the Lord be blessed
   both now and for evermore!   ℟

2 From the rising of the sun to its setting
   praised be the name of the Lord!

High above all nations is the Lord,
above the heavens his glory.

℟ **May the name of the Lord be blessed for evermore!**

or

℟ **Alleluia!**

3 Who is like the Lord, our God,
who has risen on high to his throne
yet stoops from the heights to look down,
to look down upon heaven and earth?   ℟

4 From the dust he lifts up the lowly,
from the dungheap he raises the poor
to set him in the company of princes,
yes, with the princes of his people.   ℟

Gospel Acclamation   cf. Lk 1:28
Alleluia, alleluia!
Hail, Mary, full of grace, the Lord is with thee!
Blessed art thou among women.
Alleluia!

GOSPEL

A reading from the holy Gospel according to Luke   1:26-38
You are to conceive and bear a son.

The angel Gabriel was sent by God to a town in Galilee called Nazareth, to a virgin betrothed to a man named Joseph, of the House of David; and the virgin's name was Mary. He went in and said to her, 'Rejoice, so highly favoured! The Lord is with you.' She was deeply disturbed by these words and asked herself what this greeting could mean, but the angel said to her, 'Mary, do not be afraid; you have won God's favour. Listen! You are to conceive and bear a son, and you must name him Jesus. He will be great and will be called Son of the Most High. The Lord God will give him the throne of his ancestor David; he will rule over the House of Jacob for ever and his reign will have no end.' Mary said to the angel, 'But how can this come about, since I am a virgin?' 'The Holy Spirit will come upon you,' the angel answered, 'and the power of the Most High will cover you with its shadow. And so the child will be holy and will be called Son of God. Know this too: your kinswoman Elizabeth has, in her old age, herself conceived a son, and she whom people called barren is now in her sixth month, for nothing is impossible to God.' 'I am the

Proper of Saints, 23 August 1661

handmaid of the Lord,' said Mary, 'let what you have said be done to me.' And the angel left her.

This is the Gospel of the Lord.

Prayer over the Gifts
Lord,
celebrating the feast of the Virgin Mary,
we offer you our gifts and prayers:
may Christ, who offered himself as a perfect sacrifice,
bring mankind the peace and love of your kingdom,
where he lives and reigns for ever and ever.

Preface of the Virgin Mary I or II, P56 or P57.

Communion Antiphon: Blessed are you for your firm believing, that the promises of the Lord would be fulfilled.

Prayer after Communion
Lord,
we have eaten the bread of heaven.
May we who honour the memory of the Virgin Mary
share one day in your banquet of eternal life.

23 August

St Rose of Lima, virgin

Optional Memorial

Born of a Spanish family at Lima in Peru in 1586, Rose entered the Third Order of St Dominic. She lived a life of penance and contemplation, offering herself for the salvation of the Indian people. She died in 1617.

Common of virgins, pp.1889ff., or of holy men and women: religious, pp.1898ff.

Opening Prayer
God our Father,
for love of you
Saint Rose gave up everything
to devote herself to a life of penance.
By the help of her prayers
may we imitate her selfless way of life on earth
and enjoy the fullness of your blessings in heaven.

FIRST READING

A reading from the second letter of St Paul to the Corinthians 10:17–11:2

I arranged for you to marry Christ so that I might give you away as a chaste virgin to this one husband.

If anyone wants to boast, let him boast of the Lord. It is not the man who commends himself that can be accepted, but the man who is commended by the Lord.

I only wish you were able to tolerate a little foolishness from me. But of course: you are tolerant towards me. You see, the jealousy that I feel for you is God's own jealousy: I arranged for you to marry Christ so that I might give you away as a chaste virgin to this one husband.

This is the word of the Lord.

Gospel Acclamation Ps 148:1-2. 11-14. ℟ vv.12. 13

℟ **Young men and maidens, praise the name of the Lord.**

or

℟ **Alleluia!**

1 Praise the Lord from the heavens,
  praise him in the heights.
  Praise him, all his angels,
  praise him, all his host. ℟

2 All earth's kings and peoples,
  earth's princes and rulers;
  young men and maidens,
  old men together with children. ℟

3 Let them praise the name of the Lord
  for he alone is exalted.
  The splendour of his name
  reaches beyond heaven and earth. ℟

4 He exalts the strength of his people.
  He is the praise of all his saints,
  of the sons of Israel,
  of the people to whom he comes close. ℟

Gospel Acclamation Jn 15:9. 5

Alleluia, alleluia!
Remain in my love, says the Lord;

whoever remains in me, with me in him,
bears fruit in plenty.
Alleluia!

GOSPEL

A reading from the holy Gospel according to Matthew 13:44-46
He sells everything he owns and buys the field.

Jesus said to the crowds: 'The kingdom of heaven is like treasure hidden in a field which someone has found; he hides it again, goes off happy, sells everything he owns and buys the field.

'Again, the kingdom of heaven is like a merchant looking for fine pearls; when he finds one of great value he goes and sells everything he owns and buys it.'

This is the Gospel of the Lord.

24 August
ST BARTHOLOMEW, APOSTLE   Feast

Born in Galilee, one of the twelve apostles. He is probably to be identified with Nathanael, whom Philip called to follow Jesus. Tradition says that he preached the gospel in India and was martyred there.

Entrance Antiphon: Day after day proclaim the salvation of the Lord. Proclaim his glory to all nations.

Opening Prayer
Lord,
sustain within us the faith
which made Saint Bartholomew ever loyal to Christ.
Let your Church be the sign of salvation
for all the nations of the world.

FIRST READING

A reading from the book of the Apocalypse 21:9-14
Each of the twelve foundation stones bore the name of one of the twelve apostles of the Lamb.

The angel came to speak to me, and said, 'Come here and I will show you the bride that the Lamb has married.' In the spirit he took me to the top of an enormous high mountain and showed me Jerusalem, the holy city, coming down from God out of heaven. It had all the radiant glory of God and glittered like some precious jewel of crystal-clear diamond. The walls of it were of a great height, and had twelve gates; at each of the twelve gates there was an angel, and over the gates were written the names of the twelve tribes of Israel; on the east there were three gates, on the north three gates, on the south three gates, and on the west three gates. The city walls stood on twelve foundation stones, each one of which bore the name of the one of the twelve apostles of the Lamb.

This is the word of the Lord.

Responsorial Psalm   Ps 144:10-13. 17-18. ℟ cf. v.12

℟ **Your friends, O Lord, make known the glorious splendour of your reign.**

1 All your creatures shall thank you, O Lord,
 and your friends shall repeat their blessing.
 They shall speak of the glory of your reign
 and declare your might, O God. ℟

2 They make known to me your mighty deeds
 and the glorious splendour of your reign.
 Yours is an everlasting kingdom;
 your rule lasts from age to age. ℟

3 The Lord is just in all his ways
 and loving in all his deeds.
 He is close to all who call him,
 who call on him from their hearts. ℟

Gospel Acclamation   Jn 1:49
Alleluia, alleluia!
Rabbi, you are the Son of God,
you are the King of Israel.
Alleluia!

GOSPEL

A reading from the holy Gospel according to John   1:45-51

There is an Israelite who deserves the name, incapable of deceit.

Philip found Nathanael and said to him, 'We have found the one Moses wrote about in the Law, the one about whom the prophets wrote: he is Jesus son of Joseph, from Nazareth,' 'From Nazareth?' said Nathanael. 'Can anything good come from that place?' 'Come and see' replied Philip. When Jesus saw Nathanael coming he said of him, 'There is an Israelite who deserves the name, incapable of deceit.' 'How do you know me?' said Nathanael. 'Before Philip came to call you,' said Jesus 'I saw you under the fig tree.' Nathanael answered, 'Rabbi, you are the Son of God, you are the King of Israel.' Jesus replied, 'You believe that just because I said: I saw you under the fig tree. You will see greater things than that.' And then he added, 'I tell you most solemnly, you will see heaven laid open and, above the Son of Man, the angels of God ascending and descending.'

This is the Gospel of the Lord.

Prayer over the Gifts
Lord,
we offer you this sacrifice of praise
on this feast of Saint Bartholomew.
May his prayers win us your help.

Preface of the Apostles I or II, P64 or P65.

Communion Antiphon: I will give you the kingdom that my Father gave to me, and in that kingdom you will eat and drink at my table.

Prayer after Communion
Lord,
as we celebrate the feast of Saint Bartholomew,
we receive the pledge of eternal salvation.
May it help us in this life
and in the life to come.

25 August
St Louis   Optional Memorial

Born in 1214, became King of France in 1226. Louis belonged to the Third Order of Saint Francis, and his life was governed by penance, prayer, and love and service of the poor. He had 11 children, and was a good father to them; he was a just and considerate ruler. He died while on Crusade to the Holy Land, near Carthage, in 1270.
Common of holy men and women, pp.1894ff.

Opening Prayer
Father,
you raised Saint Louis

from the cares of earthly rule
to the glory of your heavenly kingdom.
By the help of his prayers
may we come to your eternal kingdom
by our work here on earth.

FIRST READING

A reading from the prophet Isaiah 58:6-11
Share your bread with the hungry.

Is not this the sort of fast that pleases me
– it is the Lord who speaks –
to break unjust fetters
and undo the thongs of the yoke,

to let the oppressed go free,
and break every yoke,
to share your bread with the hungry,
and shelter the homeless poor,

to clothe the man you see to be naked
and not turn from your own kin?
Then will your light shine like the dawn
and your wound be quickly healed over.

Your integrity will go before you
and the glory of the Lord behind you.
Cry, and the Lord will answer;
call, and he will say, 'I am here.'

If you do away with the yoke,
the clenched fist, the wicked word,
if you give your bread to the hungry,
and relief to the oppressed,

your light will rise in the darkness,
and your shadows become like noon,
The Lord will always guide you,
giving you relief in desert places.

He will give strength to your bones
and shall be like a watered garden,
like a spring of water
whose waters never run dry.

    This is the word of the Lord.

Responsorial Psalm   Ps 111:1-9. ℟ v.1

   ℟ **Happy the man who fears the Lord.**

or

   ℟ **Alleluia!**

1. Happy the man who fears the Lord,
   who takes delight in his commands.
   His sons will be powerful on earth;
   the children of the upright are blessed. ℟

2. Riches and wealth are in his house;
   his justice stands firm for ever.
   He is a light in the darkness for the upright:
   he is generous, merciful and just. ℟

3. The good man takes pity and lends,
   he conducts his affairs with honour.
   The just man will never waver:
   he will be remembered for ever. ℟

4. He has no fear of evil news;
   with a firm heart he trusts in the Lord.
   With a steadfast heart he will not fear;
   he will see the downfall of his foes. ℟

5. Open-handed, he gives to the poor;
   his justice stands firm for ever.
   His head will be raised in glory. ℟

Gospel Acclamation   Jn 13:34

Alleluia, alleluia!
I give you a new commandment:
love one another just as I have loved you.
Alleluia!

GOSPEL

A reading from the holy Gospel according to Matthew   22:35-40
Love the Lord your God, and your neighbour as yourself.

To disconcert Jesus, one of the Pharisees, a lawyer, put a question, 'Master, which is the greatest commandment of the Law?' Jesus said, 'You must love the Lord your God with all your heart, with all your soul, and with all your mind. This is the greatest and the first commandment. The second resembles it: You must love your neighbour as yourself. On these two commandments hang the whole Law, and the Prophets also.'

   This is the Gospel of the Lord.

Proper of Saints, 25 August

Also 25 August
St Joseph Calasanz, priest
Optional Memorial

Born of a wealthy family in Aragon in 1556; he was ordained when he was in his thirties, and went to Rome in 1592. He gave his life to the education of young people. He founded the first free school there; others came to work with him, and a religious congregation was formed to carry on the work, which spread through Italy and to Germany. As its success grew, jealousy and intrigue made his life very difficult. The Pope suppressed the institute in 1646, but it began again after his death in 1648.

Common of holy men and women: teachers, p.1901, or of pastors, pp.1876ff.

Opening Prayer
Lord,
you blessed Saint Joseph Calasanz
with such charity and patience
that he dedicated himself
to the formation of Christian youth.
As we honour this teacher of wisdom
may we follow his example in working for truth.

FIRST READING

A reading from the first letter of St Paul 12:31–13:13
to the Corinthians
Love never dies.

Be ambitious for the higher gifts. And I am going to show you a way that is better than any of them.

If I have all the eloquence of men or of angels, but speak without love, I am simply a gong booming or a cymbal clashing. If I have the gift of prophecy, understanding all the mysteries there are, and knowing everything, and if I have faith in all its fullness, to move mountains, but without love, then I am nothing at all. If I give away all that I possess, piece by piece, and if I even let them take my body to burn it, but am without love, it will do me no good whatever.

*Love is always patient and kind; it is never jealous; love is never boastful or conceited; it is never rude or selfish; it does not take offence, and is not resentful. Love takes no pleasure in other people's sins but delights in the truth; it is always ready to excuse, to trust, to hope, and to endure whatever comes.

Love does not come to an end. But if there are gifts of prophecy, the time will come when they must fail; or the gift of languages, it will not continue for ever; and knowledge – for this, too, the time will come when it must fail. For our knowledge is imperfect and our prophesying is imperfect; but once perfection comes, all imperfect things will disappear. When I was a child, I used to talk like a child, and think like a child, and argue like a child, but now I am a man, all childish ways are put behind me. Now we are seeing a dim reflection in a mirror; but then we shall be seeing face to face. The knowledge that I have now is imperfect; but then I shall know as fully as I am known.

In short, there are three things that last: faith, hope and love; and the greatest of these is love.

This is the word of the Lord.*

*Shorter form, verses 4-13. Read between *.

Responsorial Psalm Ps 33:2-11. ℟ v.2. Alt ℟ v.9

℟ **I will bless the Lord at all times.**

or

℟ **Taste and see that the Lord is good.**

1 I will bless the Lord at all times,
 his praise always on my lips;
 in the Lord my soul shall make its boast.
 The humble shall hear and be glad. ℟

2 Glorify the Lord with me.
 Together let us praise his name.
 I sought the Lord and he answered me;
 from all my terrors he set me free. ℟

3 Look towards him and be radiant;
 let your faces not be abashed.
 This poor man called; the Lord heard him
 and rescued him from all his distress. ℟

4 The angel of the Lord is encamped
 around those who revere him, to rescue them.
 Taste and see that the Lord is good.
 He is happy who seeks refuge in him. ℟ (continued)

5 Revere the Lord, you his saints.
They lack nothing, those who revere him.
Strong lions suffer want and go hungry
but those who seek the Lord lack no blessing.

℟ **I will bless the Lord at all times.**

or

℟ **Tasteand see that the Lord is good.**

Gospel Acclamation Jn 15:9. 5
Alleluia, alleluia!
Remain in my love, says the Lord;
whoever remains in me, with me in him
bears fruit in plenty.
Alleluia!

GOSPEL

A reading from the Gospel according to Matthew Mt 18:1-5
Unless you become like little children you will never enter the kingdom heaven.

The disciples came to Jesus and said, 'Who is the greatest in the kingdom of heaven?' So he called a little child to him and set the child in front of them. Then he said, 'I tell you solemnly, unless you change and become like little children you will never enter the kingdom of heaven. And so, the one who makes himself as little as this little child is the greatest in the kingdom of heaven. Anyone who welcomes a little child like this in my name welcomes me.'

This is the Gospel of the Lord.

27 August
St Monica
Memorial

Born in 332, in North Africa, of a Christian family, married to a pagan, Patricius, whom she brought to the faith, Monica is best known as the mother of St Augustine of Hippo. She had four children altogether. She prayed and wept for Augustine, and his conversion filled her with joy.

Common of holy men and women, pp.1894ff.

Opening Prayer
God of mercy,

comfort of those in sorrow,
the tears of Saint Monica moved you
to convert her son Saint Augustine to the faith of Christ.
By their prayers, help us to turn from our sins
and to find your loving forgiveness.

FIRST READING

A reading from the book of Ecclesiasticus   26:1-4. 13-16
The beauty of a good wife in a well-kept house is like the rising sun.

Happy the husband of a really good wife;
the number of his days will be doubled.
A perfect wife is the joy of her husband,
he will live out the years of his life in peace.
A good wife is the best of portions,
reserved for those who fear the Lord;
rich or poor, they will be glad of heart,
cheerful of face, whatever the season.
The grace of a wife will charm her husband,
her accomplishment will make him the stronger.
A silent wife is a gift from the Lord,
no price can be put on a well-trained character.
A modest wife is a boon twice over,
a chaste character cannot be weighed on scales.
Like the sun rising over the mountains of the Lord
is the beauty of a good wife in a well-kept house.

This is the word of the Lord.

Responsorial Psalm   Ps 130

℟ **Keep my soul in peace before you, O Lord.**

1 O Lord, my heart is not proud
nor haughty my eyes.
I have not gone after things too great
nor marvels beyond me. ℟

2 Truly I have set my soul
in silence and peace.
A weaned child on its mother's breast,
even so is my soul. ℟

3 O Israel, hope in the Lord
both now and for ever. ℟

Gospel Acclamation Jn 8:12
Alleluia, alleluia!
I am the light of the world, says the Lord;
anyone who follows me will have the light of life.
Alleluia!

GOSPEL

A reading from the holy Gospel according to Luke 7:11-17

She never let me out of her prayers, that you might say to the widow's son: Young man, I tell you to get up (Augustine, Confessions, bk 6, no 2).

Jesus went to a town called Nain, accompanied by his disciples and a great number of people. When he was near the gate of the town it happened that a dead man was being carried out for burial, the only son of his mother, and she was a widow. And a considerable number of the townspeople were with her. When the Lord saw her he felt sorry for her. 'Do not cry' he said. Then he went up and put his hand on the bier and the bearers stood still, and he said, 'Young man, I tell you to get up.' And the dead man sat up and began to talk, and Jesus gave him to his mother. Everyone was filled with awe and praised God saying, 'A great prophet has appeared among us; God has visited his people.' And this opinion of him spread throughout Judaea and all over the countryside.

This is the Gospel of the Lord.

28 August
St Augustine, bishop and doctor of the Church — Memorial

Born at Thagaste in North Africa in 354, Augustine was a brilliant young man whose early life was wild and unsettled. He was converted by the prayers of his mother, and baptised by Saint Ambrose, bishop of Milan, in 387. He returned to Africa, and lived an ascetic life. He became Bishop of Hippo. His many writings present a theology and a spirituality that are exceptional, and have had great influence.

Entrance Antiphon: The Lord opened his mouth in the assembly, and filled him with the spirit of wisdom and understanding, and clothed him in a robe of glory.

Proper of Saints, 28 August 1673

Opening Prayer
Lord,
renew in your Church
the spirit you gave Saint Augustine.
Filled with this spirit,
may we thirst for you alone as the fountain of wisdom
and seek you as the source of eternal love.

FIRST READING

A reading from the first letter of St John 4:7-16
As long as we love one another God will live in us.

My dear people,
let us love one another
since love comes from God
and everyone who loves is begotten by God and knows God.
Anyone who fails to love can never have known God,
because God is love.
God's love for us was revealed
when God sent into the world his only Son
so that we could have life through him;
this is the love I mean:
not our love for God,
but God's love for us when he sent his Son
to be the sacrifice that takes our sins away.
My dear people,
since God has loved us so much,
we too should love one another.
No one has ever seen God;
but as long as we love one another
God will live in us
and his love will be complete in us.
We can know that we are living in him
and he is living in us
because he lets us share his Spirit.
We ourselves saw and we testify
that the Father sent his Son
as saviour of the world.
If anyone acknowledges that Jesus is the Son of God,
God lives in him, and he in God.
We ourselves have known and put our faith in
God's love towards ourselves.
God is love

Proper of Saints, 28 August

and anyone who lives in love lives in God,
and God lives in him.

    This is the word of the Lord.

Responsorial Psalm   Ps 118:9-14. R̸ v.12
    R̸ **Lord, teach me your statutes.**

1 How shall the young remain sinless?
   By obeying your word.
   I have sought you with all my heart:
   let me not stray from your commands.   R̸

2 I treasure your promise in my heart
   lest I sin against you.
   Blessed are you, O Lord;
   teach me your statutes.   R̸

3 With my tongue I have recounted
   the decrees of your lips.
   I rejoiced to do your will
   as though all riches were mine.   R̸

Gospel Acclamation   Mt 23:9. 10
    Alleluia, alleluia!
    You have only one Father,
    and he is in heaven;
    you have only one Teacher,
    the Christ.
    Alleluia!

GOSPEL

A reading from the holy Gospel according to Matthew   23:8-12
The greatest among you must be your servant.

Jesus said to his disciples: 'You must not allow yourselves to be called Rabbi, since you have only one Master, and you are all brothers. You must call no one on earth your father, since you have only one Father, and he is in heaven. Nor must you allow yourselves to be called teachers, for you have only one Teacher, the Christ. The greatest among you must be your servant. Anyone who exalts himself will be humbled, and anyone who humbles himself will be exalted.'

    This is the Gospel of the Lord.

Prayer over the Gifts
Lord,
as we celebrate the memorial of our salvation,
we pray that this sacrament may be for us
a sign of unity and a bond of love.

Communion Antiphon: Christ is your only teacher: and all of you are brothers.

Prayer after Communion
Lord,
make us holy by our sharing at the table of Christ.
As members of his body,
help us to become what we have received.

29 August
The Beheading of John the Baptist

Memorial

Entrance Antiphon: Lord, I shall expound your law before kings and not fear disgrace; I shall ponder your decrees, which I have always loved.

Opening Prayer
God our Father,
you called John the Baptist
to be the herald of your Son's birth and death.
As he gave his life in witness to truth and justice,
so may we strive to profess our faith in your gospel.

The Gospel is proper to this memorial.

FIRST READING
A reading from the prophet Jeremiah   1:17-19
Stand up and tell them all I command you; do not be dismayed at their presence.

The word of the Lord was addressed to me, saying:

'Brace yourself for action.
Stand up and tell them
all I command you.
Do not be dismayed at their presence,

or in their presence I will make you dismayed.
I, for my part, today will make you
into a fortified city,
a pillar of iron,
and a wall of bronze
to confront all this land:
the kings of Judah, its princes,
its priests and the country people.
They will fight against you
but shall not overcome you,
for I am with you to deliver you –
it is the Lord who speaks.'

This is the word of the Lord.

Responsorial Psalm Ps 70:1-6. 15. 17. R̥ v.15
℟ **My lips will tell of your justice, O Lord.**

1 In you, O Lord, I take refuge;
   let me never be put to shame.
   In your justice rescue me, free me:
   pay heed to me and save me. ℟

2 Be a rock where I can take refuge,
   a mighty stronghold to save me;
   for you are my rock, my stronghold.
   Free me from the hand of the wicked. ℟

3 It is you, O Lord, who are my hope,
   my trust, O Lord, since my youth.
   On you I have leaned from my birth,
   from my mother's womb you have been my help. ℟

4 My lips will tell of your justice
   and day by day of your help.
   O God, you have taught me from my youth
   and I proclaim your wonders still. ℟

Gospel Acclamation Mt 5:10
Alleluia, alleluia!
Happy those who are persecuted in the cause of right:
theirs is the kingdom of heaven.
Alleluia!

Proper of Saints, 29 August

GOSPEL

A reading from the holy Gospel according to Mark 6:17-29
I want you to give me John the Baptist's head, here and now, on a dish.

Herod had sent to have John arrested, and had him chained up in prison because of Herodias, his brother Philip's wife whom he had married. For John had told Herod, 'It is against the law for you to have your brother's wife.' As for Herodias, she was furious with him and wanted to kill him; but she was not able to, because Herod was afraid of John, knowing him to be a good and holy man, and gave him his protection. When he had heard him speak he was greatly perplexed, and yet he liked to listen to him.

An opportunity came on Herod's birthday when he gave a banquet for the nobles of his court, for his army officers and for the leading figures in Galilee. When the daughter of this same Herodias came in and danced, she delighted Herod and his guests; so the king said to the girl, 'Ask me anything you like and I will give it you.' And he swore her an oath, 'I will give you anything you ask, even half my kingdom.' She went out and said to her mother, 'What shall I ask for?' She replied, 'The head of John the Baptist.' The girl hurried straight back to the king and made her request, 'I want you to give me John the Baptist's head, here and now, on a dish.' The king was deeply distressed, but thinking of the oaths he had sworn and of his guests, he was reluctant to break his word to her. So the king at once sent one of the bodyguard with orders to bring John's head. The man went off and beheaded him in prison; then he brought the head on a dish and gave it to the girl, and the girl gave it to her mother. When John's disciples heard about this, they came and took his body and laid it in a tomb.

This is the Gospel of the Lord.

Prayer over the Gifts
Lord,
by these gifts we offer,
keep us faithful to your way of life,
which John the Baptist preached in the wilderness,
and to which he courageously witnessed
by shedding his blood.

Preface of John the Baptist, P61.

Communion Antiphon: **John's answer was: He must grow greater and I must grow less.**

Prayer after Communion
Lord,
may we who celebrate the martyrdom of John the Baptist
honour this sacrament of our salvation
and rejoice in the life it brings us.

PEACE
☩ I LEAVE TO YOU

SEPTEMBER

3 September

St Gregory the Great, pope and doctor of the Church — Memorial

Born about 540, Gregory was Prefect of Rome when he renounced the world and entered a monastery about 575. He was ordained deacon, and sent on a papal mission to Constantinople from 580-585. He became pope in 590. It was the time of the barbarian attacks on Rome; he cared for the poor and refugees, made contact with the Barbarians, sent missionaries to England. His writings are extensive, particularly the commentaries on scripture. His liturgies, collected in the Gregorian Sacramentary, have been influential to our own day.

Common of Pastors: popes, pp.1876ff., or of doctors of the church, pp.1887ff.

Opening Prayer
Father,
you guide your people with kindness
and govern us with love.
By the prayers of Saint Gregory
give the spirit of wisdom
to those you have called to lead your Church.
May the growth of your people in holiness
be the eternal joy of our shepherds.

FIRST READING

A reading from the second letter of St Paul to the Corinthians   4:1-2. 5-7

We preach Christ Jesus and ourselves as your servants for Jesus' sake.

Since we have by an act of mercy been entrusted with this work of administration, there is no weakening on our part. On the contrary, we will have none of the reticence of those who are ashamed, no deceitfulness or watering down the word of God; but the way we commend ourselves to every human being with a conscience is by stating the truth openly in the sight of God. For it is not ourselves that we are preaching, but Christ Jesus as the Lord, and ourselves as your servants for Jesus' sake. It is the same God that said, 'Let there be light shining out of darkness', who has shone in our minds to radiate the light of the knowledge of God's glory, the glory on the face of Christ.

We are only the earthenware jars that hold this treasure, to make it clear that such an overwhelming power comes from God and not from us.

This is the word of the Lord.

Responsorial Psalm   Ps 95:1-3. 7-8. 10. ℟ v.3

℟ **Proclaim the wonders of the Lord among all the peoples.**

1 O sing a new song to the Lord,
   sing to the Lord all the earth.
   O sing to the Lord, bless his name. ℟

2 Proclaim his help day by day,
   tell among the nations his glory
   and his wonders among all the peoples. ℟

3 Give the Lord, you families of peoples,
   give the Lord glory and power,
   give the Lord the glory of his name. ℟

4 Proclaim to the nations: 'God is king.'
   The world he made firm in its place;
   he will judge the peoples in fairness. ℟

Gospel Acclamation   Jn 15:15

Alleluia, alleluia!
I call you friends, says the Lord,

Proper of Saints, 8 September

because I have made known to you
everything I have learnt from my Father.
Alleluia!

GOSPEL

A reading from the holy Gospel according to Luke 22:24-30
I confer a kingdom on you, just as my Father conferred one on me.

A dispute arose between the apostles about which should be reckoned the greatest, but Jesus said to them, 'Among pagans it is the kings who lord it over them, and those who have authority over them are given the title Benefactor. This must not happen with you. No; the greatest among you must behave as if he were the youngest, the leader as if he were the one who serves. For who is the greater: the one at table or the one who serves? The one at table, surely? Yet here am I among you as one who serves!

'You are the men who have stood by me faithfully in my trials; and now I confer a kingdom on you, just as my Father conferred one on me: you will eat and drink at my table in my kingdom, and you will sit on thrones to judge the twelve tribes of Israel.'

This is the Gospel of the Lord.

Prayer over the Gifts
Lord,
by this sacrifice you free the world from sin.
As we offer it in memory of Saint Gregory,
may it bring us closer to eternal salvation.

Prayer after Communion
Lord,
at this eucharist you give us Christ to be our living bread.
As we celebrate the feast of Saint Gregory,
may we also come to know your truth
and live it in love for others.

8 September
THE BIRTHDAY OF THE BLESSED VIRGIN MARY
Feast

Entrance Antiphon: Let us celebrate with joyful hearts the birth of the Virgin Mary, of whom was born the sun of justice, Christ our Lord.

Opening Prayer

Father of mercy,
give your people help and strength from heaven.
The birth of the Virgin Mary's Son
was the dawn of our salvation.
May this celebration of her birthday
bring us closer to lasting peace.

FIRST READING

A reading from the prophet Micah   5:1-4

The time will come when she who is to give birth will give birth.

The Lord says this:

'You, Bethlehem Ephrathah, the least of the clans of Judah,
out of you will be born for me
the one who is to rule over Israel;
his origin goes back to the distant past,
to the days of old.
The Lord is therefore going to abandon them
till the time when she who is to give birth gives birth.
Then the remnant of his brothers will come back
to the sons of Israel.
He will stand and feed his flock
with the power of the Lord,
with the majesty of the name of his God.
They will live secure, for from then on he will extend his power
to the ends of the land.
He himself will be peace.'

This is the word of the Lord.

Alternative First Reading

A reading from the letter of St Paul to the Romans   8:28-30

Those whom God foreknew he also predestined.

We know that by turning everything to their good God co-operates with all those who love him, with all those that he has called according to his purpose. They are the ones he chose specially long ago and intended to become true images of his Son, so that his Son might be the eldest of many brothers. He called those he intended for this; those he called he justified, and with those he justified he shared his glory.

This is the word of the Lord.

Responsorial Psalm
Ps 12:6-7. ℟ Is 61:10

℟ **I exult for joy in the Lord.**

1. Lord, I trust in your merciful love.
   Let my heart rejoice in your saving help. ℟

2. Let me sing to the Lord for his goodness to me,
   singing psalms to the name of the Lord, the Most High. ℟

Gospel Acclamation
Alleluia, alleluia!
Blessed are you, holy Virgin Mary,
and most worthy of all praise,
for the sun of justice, Christ our God,
was born of you.
Alleluia!

GOSPEL

A reading from the holy Gospel according to Matthew
1:1-16. 18-23

Mary has conceived what is in her by the Holy Spirit.

A genealogy of Jesus Christ, son of David, son of Abraham:

Abraham was the father of Isaac,
Isaac the father of Jacob,
Jacob the father of Judah and his brothers,
Judah was the father of Perez and Zerah, Tamar being their mother,
Perez was the father of Hezron,
Hezron the father of Ram,
Ram was the father of Amminadab,
Amminadab the father of Nahshon,
Nahshon the father of Salmon,
Salmon was the father of Boaz, Rahab being his mother,
Boaz was the father of Obed, Ruth being his mother,
Obed was the father of Jesse;
and Jesse was the father of King David.

David was the father of Solomon, whose mother had been
   Uriah's wife,
Solomon was the father of Rehoboam,
Rehoboam the father of Abijah,
Abijah the father of Asa,
Asa was the father of Jehoshaphat,
Jehoshaphat the father of Joram,
Joram the father of Azariah,
Azariah was the father of Jotham,
Jotham the father of Ahaz,
Ahaz the father of Hezekiah,
Hezekiah was the father of Manasseh,
Manasseh the father of Amon,
Amon the father of Josiah;
and Josiah was the father of Jechoniah and his brothers.
Then the deportation to Babylon took place.
After the deportation to Babylon:
Jechoniah was the father of Shealtiel,
Shealtiel the father of Zerubbabel,
Zerubbabel the father of Abiud,
Abiud the father of Eliakim,
Eliakim the father of Azor,
Azor was the father of Zadok,
Zadok the father of Achim,
Achim the father of Eliud,
Eliud was the father of Eleazar,
Eleazar the father of Matthan,
Matthan the father of Jacob;
and Jacob was the father of Joseph the husband of Mary; of her was born Jesus who is called Christ.

*This is how Jesus Christ came to be born. His mother Mary was betrothed to Joseph; but before they came to live together she was found to be with child through the Holy Spirit. Her husband Joseph, being a man of honour and wanting to spare her publicity, decided to divorce her informally. He had made up his mind to do this when the angel of the Lord appeared to him in a dream and said, 'Joseph son of David, do not be afraid to take Mary home as your wife, because she has conceived what is in her by the Holy Spirit. She will give birth to a son and you must name him Jesus, because he is the one who is to save his people from their sins.' Now all this took place to fufil the words spoken by the Lord through the prophet:

> The virgin will conceive and give birth to a son
> and they will call him Emmanuel,

a name which means 'God-is-with-us.'

> This is the Gospel of the Lord. *

*Shorter form, verses 18-23. Read between *.

Prayer over the Gifts
Father,
the birth of Christ your Son
increased the virgin mother's love for you.
May his sharing in our human nature
give us courage in our weakness,
free us from our sins,
and make our offering acceptable.

Preface of the Blessed Virgin Mary I or II, P56 or P57.

Communion Antiphon: The Virgin shall bear a son, who will save his people from their sins.

Prayer after Communion
Lord,
may your Church, renewed in this holy eucharist,
be filled with joy at the birth of the Virgin Mary,
who brought the dawn of hope and salvation to the world.

13 September
St John Chrysostom, bishop and doctor of the Church — Memorial

Born at Antioch about 349, where he was ordained and exercised his pastoral ministry for many years. His preaching bore great fruit, and his writings revealed the brilliance of his intellect and his strength of faith. He lived an austere life, striving to reform the morals of clergy and people. In 397 he became Bishop of Constantinople; he was exiled by the emperor, who took exception to his work, and died in 404 in Turkey.

Common of pastors: bishops, pp.1876ff., or of doctors of the church, pp.1887ff.

Opening Prayer
Father,
the strength of all who trust in you,
you made John Chrysostom
renowned for his eloquence
and heroic in his sufferings.
May we learn from his teaching
and gain courage from his patient endurance.

FIRST READING

A reading from the letter of St Paul 4:1-7. 11-13
to the Ephesians
In the work of service, building up the body of Christ.

I, the prisoner in the Lord, implore you to lead a life worthy of your vocation. Bear with one another charitably, in complete selflessness, gentleness and patience. Do all you can to preserve the unity of the Spirit by the peace that binds you together. There is one Body, one Spirit, just as you were all called into one and the same hope when you were called. There is one Lord, one faith, one baptism, and one God who is Father of all, over all, through all and within all.

Each one of us, however, has been given his own share of grace, given as Christ allotted it. To some his gift was that they should be apostles; to some, prophets; to some, evangelists; to some, pastors and teachers; so that the saints together make a unity in the work of service, building up the body of Christ. In this way we are all to come to unity in our faith and in our knowledge of the Son of God, until we become the perfect Man, fully mature with the fullness of Christ himself.

This is the word of the Lord.

Responsorial Psalm
Ps 39:2. 4. 7-10. ℟ cf. vv.8. 9.

℟ **Here I am, Lord!**
   I come to do your will.

1 I waited, I waited for the Lord
   and he stooped down to me;
   he heard my cry.
   He put a new song into my mouth,
   praise of our God. ℟

2 You do not ask for sacrifice and offerings,

> but an open ear.
> You do not ask for holocaust and victim.
> Instead, here am I. ℟

3 In the scroll of the book it stands written
> that I should do your will.
> My God, I delight in your law
> in the depth of my heart. ℟

4 Your justice I have proclaimed
> in the great assembly.
> My lips I have not sealed;
> you know it, O Lord. ℟

Gospel Acclamation
> Alleluia, alleluia!
> The seed is the word of God,
> Christ the sower;
> whoever finds this seed
> will remain for ever.
> Alleluia!

GOSPEL

A reading from the holy Gospel according to Mark 4:1-10. 13-20
Imagine a sower going out to sow.

Jesus began to teach by the lakeside, but such a huge crowd gathered round him that he got into a boat on the lake and sat there. The people were all along the shore, at the water's edge. He taught them many things in parables, and in the course of his teaching he said to them, 'Listen! Imagine a sower going out to sow. Now it happened that, as he sowed, some of the seed fell on the edge of the path, and the birds came and ate it up. Some seed fell on rocky ground where it found little soil and sprang up straightaway, because there was no depth of earth; and when the sun came up it was scorched and, not having any roots, it withered away. Some seed fell into thorns, and the thorns grew up and choked it, and it produced no crop. And some seeds fell into rich soil, and growing tall and strong, produced crop; and yielded thirty, sixty, even a hundredfold. And he said, 'Listen, anyone who has ears to hear!'

When he was alone, the Twelve, together with the others who formed his company, asked what the parables meant.

He said to them, 'Do you not understand this parable? Then how will you understand any of the parables? What the sower is sowing is the word. Those on the edge of the path where the word is sown are people who have no sooner heard it than Satan comes and carries away the word that was sown in them. Similarly, those who receive the seed on patches of rock are people who, when first they hear the word, welcome it at once with joy. But they have no root in them, they do not last; should some trial come, or some persecution on account of the word, they fall away at once. Then there are others who receive the seed in thorns. These have heard the word, but the worries of this world, the lure of riches and all the other passions come in to choke the word, and so it produces nothing. And there are those who have received the seed in rich soil: they hear the word and accept it and yield a harvest, thirty and sixty and a hundredfold.'

*This is the Gospel of the Lord. *

*Shorter form, verses 1-9. Read between *.

Prayer over the Gifts
Lord,
be pleased with this sacrifice we present
in honour of John Chrysostom,
for we gather to praise you as he taught us.

Prayer after Communion
God of mercy,
may the sacrament we receive
in memory of John Chrysostom
make us strong in your love
and faithful in our witness to your truth.

14 September
THE TRIUMPH OF THE CROSS   Feast

The cross on which Jesus, the Son of Man, was lifted up has become the symbol of his victory over the power of evil. He made the instrument of humiliation, torture and death the instrument of our redemption.

Entrance Antiphon: We should glory in the cross of our Lord Jesus Christ, for he is our salvation, our life and our resurrection; through him we are saved and made free.

Proper of Saints, 14 September   1689

Opening Prayer
Let us pray
> [that the death of Christ on the cross
> will bring us to the glory of the resurrection]

God our Father,
in obedience to you
your only Son accepted death on the cross
for the salvation of mankind.
We acknowledge the mystery of the cross on earth.
May we receive the gift of redemption in heaven.

FIRST READING

A reading from the book of Numbers   21:4-9
If anyone was bitten by a serpent, he looked at the bronze serpent and lived.

On the way through the wilderness the people lost patience. They spoke against God and against Moses, 'Why did you bring us out of Egypt to die in this wilderness? For there is neither bread nor water here: we are sick of this unsatisfying food.'

At this God sent fiery serpents among the people; their bite brought death to many in Israel. The people came and said to Moses, 'We have sinned by speaking against the Lord and against you. Intercede for us with the Lord to save us from these serpents.' Moses interceded for the people, and the Lord answered him, 'Make a fiery serpent and put it on a standard. If anyone is bitten and looks at it, he shall live.' So Moses fashioned a bronze serpent which he put on a standard, and if anyone was bitten by a serpent, he looked at the bronze serpent and lived.

This is the word of the Lord.

Responsorial Psalm   Ps 77:1-2. 34-38. ℞ v.7
    ℞ **Never forget the deeds of the Lord.**

1 Give heed, my people, to my teaching;
turn your ear to the words of my mouth.
I will open my mouth in a parable
and reveal hidden lessons of the past. ℞

2 When he slew them then they would seek him,
return and seek him in earnest.
They would remember that God was their rock,
God the Most High their redeemer.   (continued)

3   But the words they spoke were mere flattery;
    they lied to him with their lips.
    For their hearts were not truly with him;
    they were not faithful to his covenant.

    ℟ **Never forget the deeds of the Lord.**

4   Yet he who is full of compassion
    forgave their sin and spared them.
    So often he held back his anger
    when he might have stirred up his rage.   ℟

SECOND READING

A reading from the letter of St Paul to the Philippians   2:6-11
He humbled himself, therefore God raised him high.

The state of Jesus Christ was divine,
yet he did not cling
to his equality with God
but emptied himself
to assume the condition of a slave,
and became as men are:
and being as all men are,
he was humbler yet,
even to accepting death,
death on a cross.
But God raised him high
and gave him the name
which is above all other names
so that all beings
in the heavens, on earth and in the underworld,
should bend the knee at the name of Jesus
and that every tongue should acclaim
Jesus Christ as Lord,
to the glory of God the Father.

   This is the word of the Lord.

Gospel Acclamation
   Alleluia, alleluia!
   We adore you, O Christ,
   and we bless you;
   because by your cross

Proper of Saints, 14 September   1691

you have redeemed the world.
Alleluia!

GOSPEL

A reading from the holy Gospel according to John   3:13-17
The Son of Man must be lifted up.

Jesus said to Nicodemus:

> 'No one has gone up to heaven
> except the one who came down from heaven,
> the Son of Man who is in heaven;
> and the Son of Man must be lifted up
> as Moses lifted up the serpent in the desert,
> so that everyone who believes may have eternal life in him.
> Yes, God loved the world so much
> that he gave his only Son,
> so that everyone who believes in him may not be lost
> but may have eternal life.
> For God sent his Son into the world
> not to condemn the world,
> but so that through him the world might be saved.'

This is the Gospel of the Lord.

Prayer over the Gifts
Lord,
may this sacrifice once offered on the cross
to take away the sins of the world
now free us from our sins.

Preface of the Triumph of the Cross, P46, or of the Passion of the Lord I, P17.

Communion Antiphon: When I am lifted up from the earth, I will draw all men to myself, says the Lord.

Prayer after Communion
Lord Jesus Christ,
you are the holy bread of life.
Bring to the glory of the resurrection
the people you have redeemed by the wood of the cross.

Solemn Blessing

Bow your heads and pray for God's blessing.

May almighty God keep you from all harm
and bless you with every good gift. ℟ **Amen.**

May he set his Word in your heart
and fill you with lasting joy. ℟ **Amen.**

May you walk in his ways,
always knowing what is right and good,
until you enter your heavenly inheritance. ℟ **Amen.**

May almighty God bless you,
the Father, and the Son, ✠ and the Holy Spirit. ℟ **Amen.**

15 September

Our Lady of Sorrows — Memorial

Entrance Antiphon: Simeon said to Mary: This child is destined to be a sign which men will reject; he is set for the fall and the rising of many in Israel; and your own soul a sword shall pierce.

Opening Prayer

Father,
as your Son was raised on the cross,
his mother Mary stood by him, sharing his sufferings.
May your Church be united with Christ
in his suffering and death
and so come to share in his rising to new life,
where he lives and reigns . . .

The Gospel is proper to this memorial.

FIRST READING

A reading from the letter to the Hebrews 5:7-9
He learnt to obey and he became the source of eternal salvation.

During his life on earth, Christ offered up prayer and entreaty, aloud and in silent tears, to the one who had the power to save him out of death, and he submitted so humbly that his prayer was heard. Although he was Son, he learnt to obey through suffering; but having been made perfect, he became for all who obey him the source of eternal salvation.

This is the word of the Lord.

Proper of Saints, 15 September

Responsorial Psalm Ps 30:2-6. 15-16. 20. ℟ v.17

℟ **Save me, O Lord, in your love.**

1 In you, O Lord, I take refuge.
   Let me never be put to shame.
   In your justice, set me free,
   hear me and speedily rescue me. ℟

2 Be a rock of refuge for me,
   a mighty stronghold to save me,
   for you are my rock, my stronghold,
   For your name's sake, lead me and guide me. ℟

3 Release me from the snares they have hidden
   for you are my refuge, Lord.
   Into your hands I commend my spirit.
   It is you who will redeem me, Lord. ℟

4 As for me, I trust in you, Lord,
   I say: 'You are my God.
   My life is in your hands, deliver me
   from the hands of those who hate me.' ℟

5 How great is the goodness, Lord,
   that you keep for those who fear you,
   that you show to those who trust you
   in the sight of men. ℟

SEQUENCE

The sequence may be said or sung.

At the cross her station keeping
stood the mournful Mother weeping,
close to Jesus to the last;

through her heart, his sorrow sharing,
all his bitter anguish bearing,
now at length the sword had passed.

Oh, how sad and sore distressed
was that Mother highly blessed
of the sole-begotten One.

Christ above in torments hangs;
she beneath beholds the pangs
of her dying glorious Son.

Is there one who would not weep,

whelmed in miseries so deep,
Christ's dear Mother to behold?

Can the human heart refrain
from partaking in her pain,
in that Mother's pain untold?

Bruised, derided, cursed, defiled
she beheld her tender child
all with bloody scourges rent;

for the sins of his own nation
saw him hang in desolation,
till his spirit forth he sent.

O you Mother, fount of love!
Touch my spirit from above,
make my heart with yours accord:

make me feel as you have felt;
make my soul to glow and melt
with the love of Christ our Lord.

Holy Mother, pierce me through;
in my heart each wound renew
of my Saviour crucified:

let me share with you his pain
who for all my sins was slain,
who for me in torments died.

Let me mingle tears with you,
mourning him who mourned for me
all the days that I may live:

by the cross with you to stay,
there with you to weep and pray,
is all I ask of you to give.

Virgin of all virgins best,
listen to my fond request:
let me share your grief divine;

let me, to my latest breath,
in my body bear the death
of that dying Son of yours.

Wounded with his every wound,

steep my soul till it has swooned
in his very blood away;

be to me, O Virgin, nigh,
lest in flames I burn and die
in his awful judgement day.

Christ, when you shall call me hence,
be your Mother my defence,
be your cross my victory.

While my body here decays,
may my soul your goodness praise,
safe in paradise with you.

Gospel Acclamation
Alleluia, alleluia!
Happy is the blessed Virgin Mary
who, without dying,
won the palm of martyrdom
beneath the cross of the Lord.
Alleluia!

GOSPEL

A reading from the holy Gospel according to John 19:25-27
Christ above in torments hangs; she beneath beholds the pangs of her dying glorious Son.

Near the cross of Jesus stood his mother and his mother's sister, Mary the wife of Clopas, and Mary of Magdala. Seeing his mother and the disciple he loved standing near her, Jesus said to his mother, 'Woman, this is your son.' Then to the disciple he said, 'This is your mother.' And from that moment the disciple made a place for her in his home.

This is the Gospel of the Lord.

Alternative Gospel

A reading from the holy Gospel according to Luke 2:33-35
A sword will pierce your own soul.

As the father and mother of Jesus stood wondering at the things that were being said about him, Simeon blessed them and said to Mary his mother, 'You see this child: he is destined for the fall and for the rising of many in Israel, destined to be a sign that is rejected – and a sword will pierce your own soul too – so that the secret thoughts of many may be laid bare.'

This is the Gospel of the Lord.

Prayer over the Gifts
God of mercy,
receive the prayers and gifts we offer
in praise of your name
on this feast of the Virgin Mary.
While she stood beside the cross of Jesus
you gave her to us as our loving mother.

Preface of the Blessed Virgin Mary I or II, P56 or P57.

Communion Antiphon: Be glad to share in the sufferings of Christ! When he comes in glory, you will be filled with joy.

Prayer after Communion
Lord,
hear the prayers
of those who receive the sacraments of eternal salvation.
As we honour the compassionate love of the Virgin Mary,
may we make up in our own lives
whatever is lacking in the sufferings of Christ
for the good of the Church.

16 September

Ss Cornelius, pope, and Cyprian, bishop, martyrs — Memorial

Cyprian was born in Carthage in 210, and became its bishop in 249. At a time of fierce persecution, he encouraged his people, and by word and example led them to understand and witness to the faith. He was martyred in 258. Cornelius became Bishop of Rome in 251, was exiled by Emperor Gallus, and died in exile in 253.

Common of martyrs, pp.1865ff, or of pastors: bishops pp.1876ff.

Opening Prayer

God our Father,
in Saints Cornelius and Cyprian
you have given your people an inspiring example
of dedication to the pastoral ministry
and constant witness to Christ in their suffering.
May their prayers and faith give us courage
to work for the unity of your Church.

FIRST READING

A reading from the second letter of St Paul to the Corinthians 4:7-15

We carry with us in our body the death of Jesus.

We are only the earthenware jars that hold this treasure, to make it clear that such an overwhelming power comes from God and not from us. We are in difficulties on all sides, but never cornered; we see no answer to our problems, but never despair; we have been persecuted, but never deserted; knocked down, but never killed; always, wherever we may be, we carry with us *in our body the death of Jesus*, so that the life of Jesus, too, may always be seen in our body. Indeed, while we are still alive, we are consigned to our death every day, for the sake of Jesus, so that in our mortal flesh the life of Jesus, too, may be openly shown. So death is at work in us, but life in you.

But as we have the same spirit of faith that is mentioned in scripture – I believed, and therefore I spoke – we too believe and therefore we too speak, knowing that he who raised the Lord Jesus to life will raise us with Jesus in our turn, and put us by his side and you with us. You see, all this is for your benefit, so that the more grace is multiplied among people, the more thanksgiving there will be, to the glory of God.

This is the word of the Lord.

Responsorial Psalm
Ps 125. ℟ v.5

℟ **Those who are sowing in tears
will sing when they reap.**

1. When the Lord delivered Zion from bondage,
   it seemed like a dream.
   Then was our mouth filled with laughter,
   on our lips there were songs. ℟

2. The heathens themselves said: 'What marvels
   the Lord worked for them!'
   What marvels the Lord worked for us!
   Indeed we were glad. ℟

3. Deliver us, O Lord, from our bondage
   as streams in dry land.
   Those who are sowing in tears
   will sing when they reap. ℟

4. They go out, they go out, full of tears,
   carrying seed for the sowing:
   they come back, they come back, full of song,
   carrying their sheaves. ℟

Gospel Acclamation
2 Cor 1:3-4

Alleluia, alleluia!
Blessed be God, a gentle Father,
and the God of all consolation,
who comforts us in all our sorrows.
Alleluia!

GOSPEL

A reading from the holy Gospel according to John   17:11-19
The world hated them.

Jesus raised his eyes to heaven and said,

'Holy Father,
keep those you have given me true to your name,
so that they may be one like us.
While I was with them,

I kept those you had given me true to your name.
I have watched over them and not one is lost
except the one who chose to be lost,
and this was to fulfil the scriptures.
But now I am coming to you
and while still in the world I say these things
to share my joy with them to the full.
I passed your word on to them,
and the world hated them,
because they belong to the world
no more than I belong to the world.
I am not asking you to remove them from the world,
but to protect them from the evil one.
They do not belong to the world
any more than I belong to the world.
Consecrate them in the truth;
your word is truth.
As you sent me into the world,
I have sent them into the world,
and for their sake I consecrate myself
so that they too may be consecrated in truth.'

This is the Gospel of the Lord.

Prayer over the Gifts
Lord,
accept the gifts of your people
as we honour the suffering and death
of Saints Cornelius and Cyprian.
The eucharist gave them courage
to offer their lives for Christ.
May it keep us faithful in all our trials.

Prayer after Communion
Lord,
by the example of your martyrs Cornelius and Cyprian
and by the sacrament we have received,
make us strong in the Spirit
so that we may offer faithful witness
to the truth of your gospel.

17 September
St Robert Bellarmine, bishop and doctor of the Church

Optional Memorial

Born in Tuscany in 1542, became a Jesuit and was ordained priest. He was a vigorous defender of the faith at the time of the Reformation. He was made a Cardinal in 1599, but after a disagreement with the Pope was sent as bishop to Capua in 1602. He was a very pastoral bishop, visiting, preaching and teaching, and giving the example of a truly Christian life. He returned to Rome in 1605, and died in 1621.

Common of pastors: bishops, pp.1878ff., or of doctors of the church, pp.1887ff.

Opening Prayer
God our Father,
you gave Robert Bellarmine wisdom and goodness
to defend the faith of your Church.
By his prayers
may we always rejoice in the profession of our faith.

FIRST READING

A reading from the book of Wisdom 7:7-10. 15-16

I loved wisdom more than health or beauty.

I prayed, and understanding was given me;
I entreated, and the spirit of Wisdom came to me.
I esteemed her more than sceptres and thrones;
compared with her, I held riches as nothing.
I reckoned no priceless stone to be her peer,
for compared with her, all gold is a pinch of sand,
and beside her silver ranks as mud.
I loved her more than health or beauty,
preferred her to the light,
since her radiance never sleeps.
May God grant me to speak as he would wish
and express thoughts worthy of his gifts,
since he himself is the guide of Wisdom,
since he directs the sages.
We are indeed in his hand, we ourselves and our words,
with all our understanding, too, and technical knowledge.

This is the word of the Lord.

Proper of Saints, 17 September 1701

Responsorial Psalm Ps 18:8-11. ℟ v.10. Alt. ℟ Jn 6:63

℟ **The decrees of the Lord are truth
and all of them just.**

or

℟ **Your words are spirit, Lord,
and they are life.**

1 The law of the Lord is perfect,
it revives the soul.
The rule of the Lord is to be trusted,
it gives wisdom to the simple. ℟

2 The precepts of the Lord are right,
they gladden the heart.
The command of the Lord is clear,
it gives light to the eyes. ℟

3 The fear of the Lord is holy,
abiding for ever.
The decrees of the Lord are truth
and all of them just. ℟

4 They are more to be desired than gold,
than the purest of gold
and sweeter are they than honey,
than honey from the comb. ℟

Gospel Acclamation cf. Jn 6:63. 68
Alleluia, alleluia!
Your words are spirit, Lord, and they are life;
you have the message of eternal life.
Alleluia!

GOSPEL

A reading from the holy Gospel according to Matthew 7:21-29
He taught them with authority.

Jesus said to his disciples: 'It is not those who say to me, "Lord, Lord," who will enter the kingdom of heaven, but the person who does the will of my Father in heaven. When the day comes many will say to me, "Lord, Lord, did we not prophesy in your name, cast out demons in your name, work many miracles in your name?" Then I shall tell them to their faces: I have never known you; away from me, you evil men!

'Therefore, everyone who listens to these words of mine and acts on them will be like a sensible man who built his house on rock. Rain came down, floods rose, gales blew and hurled themselves against that house, and it did not fall: it was founded on rock. But everyone who listens to these words of mine and does not act on them will be like a stupid man who built his house on sand. Rain came down, floods rose, gales blew and struck that house, and it fell; and what a fall it had!'

Jesus had now finished what he wanted to say, and his teaching made a deep impression on the people because he taught them with authority, and not like their own scribes.

This is the Gospel of the Lord.

19 September

St Januarius, bishop and martyr
Optional Memorial

Bishop of Benevento, martyred in 305, with six other Christians, during the persecution of Diocletian, at Naples.

Common of martyrs, pp.1865ff., or of pastors: bishops, pp.1878ff.

Opening Prayer
God our Father,
enable us who honour the memory of Saint Januarius
to share with him the joy of eternal life.

FIRST READING

A reading from the letter to the Hebrews 10:32-36
Remember all the sufferings that you had to meet.

Remember all the sufferings that you had to meet after you received the light, in earlier days; sometimes by being yourselves publicly exposed to insults and violence, and sometimes as associates of others who were treated in the same way. For you not only shared in the sufferings of those who were in prison, but you happily accepted being stripped of your belongings, knowing that you owned something that was better and lasting. Be as confident now, then, since the reward is so great. You will need endurance to do God's will and gain what he has promised.

This is the word of the Lord.

Responsorial Psalm
Ps 125. ℟ v.5

℟ **Those who are sowing in tears
will sing when they reap.**

1. When the Lord delivered Zion from bondage,
   it seemed like a dream.
   Then was our mouth filled with laughter,
   on our lips there were songs. ℟

2. The heathens themselves said: 'What marvels
   the Lord worked for them!'
   What marvels the Lord worked for us!
   Indeed we were glad. ℟

3. Deliver us, O Lord, from our bondage
   as streams in dry land.
   Those who are sowing in tears
   will sing when they reap. ℟

4. They go out, they go out, full of tears,
   carrying seed for the sowing:
   they come back, they come back, full of song,
   carrying their sheaves. ℟

Gospel Acclamation
James 1:12

Alleluia, alleluia!
Happy the man who stands firm when trials come.
He has proved himself,
and will win the crown of life.
Alleluia!

GOSPEL

A reading from the holy Gospel according to John   12:24-26
If a grain of wheat dies, it yields a rich harvest.

Jesus said to his disciples:

'I tell you, most solemnly,
unless a wheat grain falls on the ground and dies,
it remains only a single grain;
but if it dies,
it yields a rich harvest.
Anyone who loves his life loses it;
anyone who hates his life in this world
will keep it for the eternal life.

If a man serves me, he must follow me,
wherever I am, my servant will be there too.
If anyone serves me, my Father will honour him.'

This is the Gospel of the Lord.

21 September
ST MATTHEW, APOSTLE AND EVANGELIST

Feast

Matthew was a tax gatherer, born at Capernaum, called by Jesus, for whom he left everything and turned to a new life. His Gospel was written in Hebrew. Tradition tells that he preached in the East.

Entrance Antiphon: Go and preach to all nations: baptise them and teach them to observe all that I have commanded you, says the Lord.

Opening Prayer
God of mercy,
you chose a tax collector, Saint Matthew,
to share the dignity of the apostles.
By his example and prayers
help us to follow Christ
and remain faithful in your service.

FIRST READING

A reading from the letter of St Paul 4:1-7. 11-13
to the Ephesians

To some, his gift was that they should be apostles; to some evangelists.

I, the prisoner in the Lord, implore you to lead a life worthy of your vocation. Bear with one another charitably, in complete selflessness, gentleness and patience. Do all you can to preserve the unity of the Spirit by the peace that binds you together. There is one Body, one Spirit, just as you were all called into one and the same hope when you were called. There is one Lord, one faith, one baptism, and one God who is Father of all, over all, through all and within all.

Each one of us, however, has been given his own share of grace, given as Christ allotted it. And to some, his gift was that they should be apostles; to some, prophets; to some, evangelists; to some, pastors and teachers; so that the saints together make a unity in the work of service, building up the body of Christ. In this way we are all to come to unity in our faith and in our knowledge of the Son of God, until we become the perfect Man, fully mature with the fullness of Christ himself.

This is the word of the Lord.

Responsorial Psalm
Ps 18:2-5. ℟ v.5

℟ **Their word goes forth through all the earth.**

1. The heavens proclaim the glory of God
and the firmament shows forth the work of his hands.
Day unto day takes up the story
and night unto night makes known the message. ℟

2. No speech, no word, no voice is heard
yet their span extends through all the earth,
their words to the utmost bounds of the world. ℟

Gospel Acclamation
Alleluia, alleluia!
We praise you, O God,
we acknowledge you to be the Lord.
The glorious company of the apostles
praise you, O Lord.
Alleluia!

GOSPEL

A reading from the holy Gospel according to Matthew 9:9-13
Follow me. And he got up and followed him.

As Jesus was walking on he saw a man named Matthew sitting by the customs house, and he said to him, 'Follow me.' And he got up and followed him.

While he was at dinner in the house it happened that a number of tax collectors and sinners came to sit at the table with Jesus and his disciples. When the Pharisees saw this, they said to his disciples, 'Why does your master eat with tax collectors and sinners?' When he heard this he replied, 'It is not the healthy who need the doctor, but the sick. Go and learn the meaning of the words: What I want is mercy, not sacrifice. And indeed I did not come to call the virtuous, but sinners.'

This is the Gospel of the Lord.

Prayer over the Gifts
Lord,
accept the prayers and gifts we present
on this feast of Saint Matthew.
Continue to guide us in your love
as you nourished the faith of your Church
by the preaching of the apostles.

Preface of the Apostles I or II, P64 or P65.

Communion Antiphon: I did not come to call the virtuous, but sinners, says the Lord.

Prayer after Communion
Father,
in this eucharist we have shared the joy of salvation
which Saint Matthew knew when he welcomed your Son.

May this food renew us in Christ,
who came to call not the just
but sinners to salvation in his kingdom
where he is Lord for ever and ever.

26 September
Ss Cosmas and Damian, martyrs
Optional Memorial

Nothing but the names, and the fact that their cult was established in the fifth century, is known of these two, who are listed among the saints in the Roman canon.

Common of martyrs, pp.1865ff.

Opening Prayer
Lord,
we honour the memory of Saints Cosmas and Damian.
Accept our grateful praise
for raising them to eternal glory
and for giving us your fatherly care.

FIRST READING

A reading from the book of Wisdom 3:1-9
He accepted them as a holocaust.

The souls of the virtuous are in the hands of God,

Proper of Saints, 26 September

no torment shall ever touch them.
In the eyes of the unwise, they did appear to die,
their going looked like a disaster,
their leaving us, like annihilation;
but they are in peace.
If they experienced punishment as men see it,
their hope was rich with immortality;
slight was their affliction, great will their blessings be.
God has put them to the test
and proved them worthy to be with him;
he has tested them like gold in a furnace,
and accepted them as a holocaust.
When the time comes for his visitation they will shine out;
as sparks run through the stubble, so will they.
They shall judge nations, rule over peoples,
and the Lord will be their king for ever.
They who trust in him will understand the truth,
those who are faithful will live with him in love;
for grace and mercy await those he has chosen.

This is the word of the Lord.

Responsorial Psalm
Ps 125. ℟ v.5

℟ **Those who are sowing in tears
will sing when they reap.**

1 When the Lord delivered Zion from bondage,
it seemed like a dream.
Then was our mouth filled with laughter,
on our lips there were songs. ℟

2 The heathens themselves said: 'What marvels
the Lord worked for them!'
What marvels the Lord worked for us!
Indeed we were glad. ℟

3 Deliver us, O Lord, from our bondage
as streams in dry land.
Those who are sowing in tears
will sing when they reap. ℟

4 They go out, they go out, full of tears,
carrying seed for the sowing:
they come back, they come back, full of song,
carrying their sheaves. ℟

Gospel Acclamation
James 1:12
Alleluia, alleluia!
Happy the man who stands firm,
for he has proved himself,
and will win the prize of life.
Alleluia!

GOSPEL

A reading from the holy Gospel according to Matthew 10:28-33
Do not be afraid of those who kill the body.

Jesus said to his apostles: 'Do not be afraid of those who kill the body but cannot kill the soul; fear him rather who can destroy both body and soul in hell. Can you not buy two sparrows for a penny? And yet not one falls to the ground without your Father knowing. Why, every hair on your head has been counted. So there is no need to be afraid; you are worth more than hundreds of sparrows.

'So if anyone declares himself for me in the presence of men, I will declare myself for him in the presence of my Father in heaven. But the one who disowns me in the presence of men, I will disown in the presence of my Father in heaven.'

This is the Gospel of the Lord.

Prayer over the Gifts
Lord,
we who celebrate the death of your holy martyrs
offer you the sacrifice
which gives all martyrdom its meaning.
Be pleased with our praise.

Prayer after Communion
Lord,
keep your gift ever strong within us.
May the eucharist we receive
in memory of Saints Cosmas and Damian
bring us salvation and peace.

27 September
St Vincent de Paul, priest   Memorial

Born about 1580, of a peasant family in SW France, he was ordained in 1600. He resolved to devote his life to works of charity. He did much to relieve the sufferings of prisoners held on the galleys. He founded confraternities of charity for men and women, working with Pierre de Berulle, and with Louise de Marillac. The Congregation of the Mission was founded to preach missions especially in the countryside, and to help form the clergy; the Sisters of Charity, whose work was with the sick and poor, was the first congregation of woman without enclosure.

Entrance Antiphon: The Spirit of God is upon me; he has anointed me. He sent me to bring good news to the poor, and to heal the broken-hearted.

Opening Prayer
God our Father,
you gave Vincent de Paul
the courage and holiness of an apostle
for the well-being of the poor
and the formation of the clergy.
Help us to be zealous in continuing his work.

FIRST READING

A reading from the first letter of St Paul to the Corinthians   1:26-31
God chose what is foolish by human reckoning.

Take yourselves, brothers, at the time when you were called: how many of you were wise in the ordinary sense of the word, how many were influential people, or came from noble families? No, it was to shame the wise that God chose what is foolish by human reckoning, and to shame what is strong that he chose what is weak by human reckoning; those whom the world thinks common and contemptible are the ones that God has chosen – those who are nothing at all to show up those who are everything. The human race has nothing to boast about to God, but you, God has made members of Christ Jesus and by God's doing he has become our wisdom, and our virtue, and our holiness, and our freedom. As scripture says: if anyone wants to boast let him boast about the Lord.

    This is the word of the Lord.

Responsorial Psalm   Ps 111:1-9. ℟ v.1

    ℟   **Happy the man who fears the Lord.**

or

    ℟   **Alleluia!**

1. Happy the man who fears the Lord,
    who takes delight in his commands.
    His sons will be powerful on earth;
    the children of the upright are blessed. ℟

2. Riches and wealth are in his house;
    his justice stands firm for ever.
    He is a light in the darkness for the upright:
    he is generous, merciful and just. ℟

3. The good man takes pity and lends,
    he conducts his affairs with honour.
    The just man will never waver:
    he will be remembered for ever. ℟

4. He has no fear of evil news;
    with a firm heart he trusts in the Lord.
    With a steadfast heart he will not fear;
    he will see the downfall of his foes. ℟

5. Open-handed, he gives to the poor;
    his justice stands firm for ever.
    His head will be raised in glory. ℟

Gospel Acclamation   Jn 10:14
Alleluia, alleluia!
I am the good shepherd, says the Lord;
I know my own sheep
and my own know me.
Alleluia!

GOSPEL

A reading from the holy Gospel according to Matthew   9:35-37
The harvest is rich but the labourers are few.

Jesus made a tour through all the towns and villages, teaching in their synagogues, proclaiming the Good News of the kingdom and curing all kinds of diseases and sickness.

    And when he saw the crowds he felt sorry for them because they were harassed and dejected, like sheep without a shepherd.

Then he said to his disciples, 'The harvest is rich but the labourers are few, so ask the Lord of the harvest to send labourers to his harvest'.

This is the Gospel of the Lord.

Prayer over the Gifts
Lord,
you helped Saint Vincent
to imitate the love he celebrated in these mysteries.
By the power of this sacrifice
may we also become an acceptable gift to you.

Communion Antiphon: Give praise to the Lord for his kindness, for his wonderful deeds toward men. He has filled the hungry with good things, he has satisfied the thirsty.

Prayer after Communion
Lord,
hear the prayers
of those you have renewed with your sacraments from heaven.
May the example and prayers of Saint Vincent
help us to imitate your Son
in preaching the good news to the poor.

28 September
St Wenceslaus, martyr Optional Memorial

Born in Bohemia about 905, he was brought up as a Christian, and became Duke in about 922. He was a man of great piety, and worked for the religious and social benefit of his people. He was murdered by his brother in 929, perhaps at the instigation of non-Christians, and was venerated as a martyr.

Common of martyrs, pp.1865ff.

Opening Prayer
Lord,
you taught your martyr Wenceslaus
to prefer the kingdom of heaven
to all that the earth has to offer.
May his prayers free us from our self-seeking
and help us to serve you with all our hearts.

Proper of Saints, 28 September

FIRST READING

A reading from the first letter of St Peter 3:14-17
There is no need to be afraid or to worry about them.

If you have to suffer for being good, you will count it a blessing. There is no need to be afraid or to worry about persecutors. Simply reverence the Lord Christ in your hearts, and always have your answer ready for people who ask you the reason for the hope that you all have. But give it with courtesy and respect and with a clear conscience, so that those who slander you when you are living a good life in Christ may be proved wrong in the accusations that they bring. And if it is the will of God that you should suffer, it is better to suffer for doing right than for doing wrong.

This is the word of the Lord.

Responsorial Psalm

Ps 125. R v.5

R **Those who are sowing in tears will sing when they reap.**

1. When the Lord delivered Zion from bondage,
it seemed like a dream.
Then was our mouth filled with laughter,
on our lips there were songs. R

2. The heathens themselves said: 'What marvels
the Lord worked for them!'
What marvels the Lord worked for us!
Indeed we were glad. R

3. Deliver us, O Lord, from our bondage
as streams in dry land.
Those who are sowing in tears
will sing when they reap. R

4. They go out, they go out, full of tears,
carrying seed for the sowing:
they come back, they come back, full of song,
carrying their sheaves. R

Gospel Acclamation

Mt 5:10

Alleluia, alleluia!
Happy those who are persecuted in the cause of right:
theirs is the kingdom of heaven.
Alleluia!

GOSPEL

A reading from the holy Gospel according to Matthew 10:34-39
It is not peace I have come to bring, but a sword.

Jesus said to his apostles: 'Do not suppose that I have come to bring peace to the earth: it is not peace I have come to bring, but a sword. For I have come to set a man against his father, a daughter against her mother, a daughter-in-law against her mother-in-law. A man's enemies will be those of his own household.

'Anyone who prefers father or mother to me is not worthy of me. Anyone who prefers son or daughter to me is not worthy of me. Anyone who does not take his cross and follow in my footsteps is not worthy of me. Anyone who finds his life will lose it; anyone who loses his life for my sake will find it.'

This is the Gospel of the Lord.

29 September
SS MICHAEL, GABRIEL AND RAPHAEL, ARCHANGELS   Feast

Entrance Antiphon: Bless the Lord, all you his angels, mighty in power, you obey his word and heed the sound of his voice.

Opening Prayer
God our Father,
in a wonderful way you guide the work of angels and men.
May those who serve you constantly in heaven
keep our lives safe from all harm on earth.

FIRST READING

A reading from the prophet Daniel 7:9-10. 13-14
A thousand thousand waited on him.

As I watched:
'Thrones were set in place
and one of great age took his seat.
His robe was white as snow,
the hair of his head as pure as wool.
His throne was a blaze of flames,
its wheels were a burning fire.
A stream of fire poured out,
issuing from his presence.

A thousand thousand waited on him,
ten thousand times ten thousand stood before him.
A court was held
and the books were opened.
I gazed into the visions of the night.
And I saw, coming on the clouds of heaven,
one like a son of man.
He came to the one of great age
and was led into his presence.
On him was conferred sovereignty,
glory and kingship,
and men of all peoples, nations and languages became his servants.
His sovereignty is an eternal sovereignty
which shall never pass away,
nor will his empire ever be destroyed.'

This is the word of the Lord.

Alternative First Reading

A reading from the book of the Apocalypse 12:7-12
Michael with his angels attacked the dragon.

Now war broke out in heaven, when Michael with his angels attacked the dragon. The dragon fought back with his angels, but they were defeated and driven out of heaven. The great dragon, the primeval serpent, known as the devil of Satan, who had deceived all the world, was hurled down to the earth and his angels were hurled down with him. Then I heard a voice shout from heaven, 'Victory and power and empire for ever have been won by our God, and all authority for his Christ, now that the persecutor, who accused our brothers day and night before our God, has been brought down. They have triumphed over him by the blood of the Lamb and by the witness of their martyrdom, because even in the face of death they would not cling to life. Let the heavens rejoice and all who live there.'

This is the word of the Lord.

Proper of Saints, 29 September

Responsorial Psalm
Ps 137:1-5. ℟ v.1

℟ **In the presence of the angels I will bless you, O Lord.**

1 I thank you, Lord, with all my heart,
   you have heard the words of my mouth,
   in the presence of the angels I will bless you.
   I will adore before your holy temple. ℟

2 I thank you for your faithfulness and love
   which excel all we ever knew of you.
   On the day I called, you answered;
   you increased the strength of my soul. ℟

3 All the earth's kings shall thank you
   when they hear the words of your mouth.
   They shall sing of the Lord's ways:
   'How great is the glory of the Lord!' ℟

Gospel Acclamation
Ps 102:21

Alleluia, alleluia!
Give thanks to the Lord, all his hosts,
his servants who do his will.
Alleluia!

GOSPEL

A reading from the holy Gospel according to John 1:47-51
You will see the angels of God ascending and descending above the Son of Man.

When Jesus saw Nathanael coming he said of him, 'There is an Israelite who deserves the name, incapable of deceit.' 'How do you know me?' said Nathanael. 'Before Philip came to call you,' said Jesus 'I saw you under the fig tree.' Nathanael answered, 'Rabbi, you are the Son of God, you are the King of Israel.' Jesus replied, 'You believe that just because I said: I saw you under the fig tree. You will see greater things than that.' And then he added, 'I tell you most solemnly, you will see heaven laid open and, above the Son of Man, the angels of God ascending and descending.'

This is the Gospel of the Lord.

Prayer over the Gifts
Lord,
by the ministry of your angels

let our sacrifice of praise come before you.
May it be pleasing to you and helpful to our own salvation.

Preface of the Angels, P60.

Communion Antiphon: In the sight of the angels I will sing your praise, my God.

Prayer after Communion
Lord,
hear the prayers of those you renew with the bread of life.
Made strong by the courage it gives,
and under the watchful care of the angels,
may we advance along the way of salvation.

30 September
St Jerome, priest and doctor of the Church
Memorial

Born about 342, he studied in Rome, where he was baptised. He lived for some years as a hermit in the Syrian desert, then returned to Antioch and was ordained priest by Paulinus. He lived in Constantinople and then in Rome, preaching asceticism, and studying. Eventually he settled in Bethlehem, where he was head of the monastery and devoted himself to study. His scholarship was unparalleled in the early Church. He translated the Bible from its original tongues into Latin (the Vulgate), wrote biblical commentaries, and other works. He fought against the heresies of Arianism, Pelagianism and Origenism.

Entrance Antiphon: The book of the law must be ever on your lips; reflect on it night and day. Observe and do all that it commands: then you will direct your life with understanding.

Opening Prayer
Father,
you gave Saint Jerome delight
in his study of holy scripture.
May your people find in your word
the food of salvation and the fountain of life.

Proper of Saints, 30 September 1717

FIRST READING

A reading from the second letter of St Paul to Timothy 3:14-17
All scripture is inspired by God and can profitably be used for teaching.

You must keep to what you have been taught and know to be true; remember who your teachers were, and how, ever since you were a child, you have known the holy scriptures – from these you can learn the wisdom that leads to salvation through faith in Christ Jesus. All scripture is inspired by God and can profitably be used for teaching, for refuting error, for guiding people's lives and teaching them to be holy. This is how the man who is dedicated to God becomes fully equipped and ready for any good work.

This is the word of the Lord.

Responsorial Psalm
Ps 118:9-14. ℟ v.12

℟ **Lord, teach me your statutes.**

1 How shall the young remain sinless?
 By obeying your word.
 I have sought you with all my heart:
 let me not stray from your commands. ℟

2 I treasure your promise in my heart
 lest I sin against you.
 Blessed are you, O Lord;
 teach me your statutes. ℟

3 With my tongue I have recounted
 the decrees of your lips.
 I rejoiced to do your will
 as though all riches were mine. ℟

Gospel Acclamation
cf. Acts 16:14

Alleluia, alleluia!
Open our heart, O Lord,
to accept the words of your Son.
Alleluia!

GOSPEL

A reading from the holy Gospel according to Matthew 13:47-52

They collect the good ones in a basket and throw away those that are no use.

Jesus said to the crowds: 'The kingdom of heaven is like a dragnet cast into the sea that brings in a haul of all kinds. When it is full, the fishermen haul it ashore; then, sitting down, they collect the good ones in a basket and throw away those that are no use. This is how it will be at the end of time; the angels will appear and separate the wicked from the just to throw them into the blazing furnace where there will be weeping and grinding of teeth.

'Have you understood all this?' They said, 'Yes.' And he said to them, 'Well then, every scribe who becomes a disciple of the kingdom of heaven is like a householder who brings out from his storeroom things both new and old.'

This is the Gospel of the Lord.

Prayer over the Gifts
Lord,
help us to follow the example of Saint Jerome.
In reflecting on your word
may we better prepare ourselves
to offer you this sacrifice of salvation.

Communion Antiphon: When I discovered your teaching, I devoured it. Your words brought me joy and gladness; you have called me your own, O Lord my God.

Prayer after Communion
Lord,
let this holy eucharist we receive
on the feast of Saint Jerome
stir up the hearts of all who believe in you.
By studying your sacred teachings,
may we understand the gospel we follow
and come to eternal life.

GLORY TO YOU O CHRIST

OCTOBER

1 October

St Teresa of the child Jesus, virgin   Memorial

Born in 1873, she entered Carmel at the age of 15. She achieved perfection through the daily renunciation of little things, and through prayer and meditation on the life of Christ. She wanted to be a missionary, and as her health made this impossible, offered her daily life within the convent for the mission of the Church. She died in 1897.

Common of virgins, pp.1889ff., or of holy men and women: religious, pp.1898.

Entrance Antiphon: The Lord nurtured and taught her; he guarded her as the apple of his eye. As the eagle spreads its wings to carry its young, he bore her on his shoulders. The Lord alone was her leader.

Opening Prayer
God our Father,
you have promised your kingdom
to those who are willing to become like little children.
Help us to follow the way of Saint Theresa with confidence
so that by her prayers
we may come to know your eternal glory.

FIRST READING

A reading from the prophet Isaiah 66:10-14
Now towards her I send flowing peace, like a river.

Rejoice, Jerusalem,
be glad for her, all you who love her!

Rejoice, rejoice for her,
all you who mourned her!
That you may be suckled, filled,
from her consoling breast,
that you may savour with delight
her glorious breasts.
For thus says the Lord:
Now towards her I send flowing
peace, like a river,
and like a stream in spate
the glory of the nations.
At her breast will her nurslings be carried
and fondled in her lap.
Like a son comforted by his mother
will I comfort you.
(And by Jerusalem you will be comforted.)
At the sight your heart will rejoice,
and your bones flourish like the grass.
To his servants the Lord will reveal his hand.

This is the word of the Lord.

Responsorial Psalm   Ps 130

℟ **Keep my soul in peace before you, O Lord.**

1 O Lord, my heart is not proud
   nor haughty my eyes.
   I have not gone after things too great
   nor marvels beyond me.   ℟

2 Truly I have set my soul
   in silence and peace.
   A weaned child on its mother's breast,
   even so is my soul.   ℟

3 O Israel, hope in the Lord
   both now and for ever.   ℟

Gospel Acclamation   cf. Mt 11:25

Alleluia, alleluia!
Blessed are you, Father,
Lord of heaven and earth,
for revealing the mysteries of the kingdom
to mere children.
Alleluia!

GOSPEL

A reading from the holy Gospel according to Matthew 18:1-5

Unless you become like little children you will never enter the kingdom of heaven.

The disciples came to Jesus and said, 'Who is the greatest in the kingdom of heaven?' So he called a little child to him and set the child in front of them. Then he said, 'I tell you solemnly, unless you change and become like little children you will never enter the kingdom of heaven. And so, the one who makes himself as little as this little child is the greatest in the kingdom of heaven. Anyone who welcomes a little child like this in my name welcomes me.'

This is the Gospel of the Lord.

Prayer over the Gifts
Lord,
we praise the wonder of your grace in Saint Teresa.
As you were pleased with the witness she offered,
be pleased also to accept this service of ours.

Communion Antiphon: Unless you change and become like little children, says the Lord, you shall not enter the kingdom of heaven.

Prayer after Communion
Lord,
by the power of your love
Saint Teresa offered herself completely to you
and prayed for the salvation of all mankind.
May the sacraments we have received fill us with love
and bring us forgiveness.

2 October
The Guardian Angels — Memorial

Entrance Antiphon: Bless the Lord, all you angels of the Lord. Sing his glory and praise for ever.

Opening Prayer
God our Father,
in your loving providence

you send your holy angels to watch over us.
Hear our prayers,
defend us always by their protection
and let us share your life with them for ever.

The Gospel is proper to this memorial.

FIRST READING

A reading from the book of Exodus 23:20-23
My angel will go before you.

The Lord says this: 'I myself will send an angel before you to guard you as you go and to bring you to the place that I have prepared. Give him reverence and listen to all that he says. Offer him no defiance; he would not pardon such a fault, for my name is in him. If you listen carefully to his voice and do all that I say, I shall be enemy to your enemies, foe to your foes. My angel will go before you.'

This is the word of the Lord.

Responsorial Psalm Ps 90:1-6. 10-11. ℟ v.11

℟ **The Lord has commanded his angels
to keep you in all your ways.**

1 He who dwells in the shelter of the Most High
   and abides in the shade of the Almighty
   says to the Lord: 'My refuge,
   my stronghold, my God in whom I trust!' ℟

2 It is he who will free you from the snare
   of the fowler who seeks to destroy you;
   he will conceal you with his pinions
   and under his wings you will find refuge. ℟

3 You will not fear the terror of the night
   nor the arrow that flies by day,
   nor the plague that prowls in the darkness
   nor the scourge that lays waste at noon. ℟

4 Upon you no evil shall fall,
   no plague approach where you dwell.
   For you has he commanded his angels,
   to keep you in all your ways. ℟

Proper of Saints, 2 October

Gospel Acclamation   Ps 102:21
   Alleluia, alleluia!
   Give thanks to the Lord, all his hosts,
   his servants who do his will.
   Alleluia!

GOSPEL

A reading from the holy Gospel according to Matthew   18:1-5. 10
Their angels in heaven are continually in the presence of my Father in heaven.

The disciples came to Jesus and said, 'Who is the greatest in the kingdom of heaven?' So he called a little child to him and set the child in front of them. Then he said, 'I tell you solemnly, unless you change and become like little children you will never enter the kingdom of heaven. And so, the one who makes himself as little as this little child is the greatest in the kingdom of heaven.

   'Anyone who welcomes a little child like this in my name welcomes me.

   'See that you never despise any of these little ones, for I tell you that their angels in heaven are continually in the presence of my Father in heaven.'

   This is the Gospel of the Lord.

Prayer over the Gifts
Father,
accept the gifts we bring you
in honour of your holy angels.
Under their constant care,
keep us free from danger in this life
and bring us to the joy of eternal life,
where Jesus is Lord for ever and ever.

Preface of the Angels, P60.

Communion Antiphon: In the sight of the angels I will sing your praises, my God.

Prayer after Communion
Lord,
you nourish us with the sacraments of eternal life.
By the ministry of your angels
lead us into the way of salvation and peace.

4 October
St Francis of Assisi   Memorial

Born in 1181, the son of a wealthy merchant, Francis gave up everything to obey the words of the Lord: 'Leave all, and follow me.' He lived in complete poverty, preaching the gospel. Others came to join him, and they lived by a simple rule based on the Gospel. From them grew the Franciscan Order, which spread rapidly during his own lifetime, though he ceased to be its leader and left its administration to others. His life was a putting into practice of the beatitudes, and was marked by faith, joy, service of others, prayer, and love of all created things. He died in 1226.

Common of holy men and women: religious, pp.1898ff.

Entrance Antiphon: Francis, a man of God, left his home and gave away his wealth to become poor and in need. But the Lord cared for him.

Opening Prayer
Father,
you helped Saint Francis to reflect the image of Christ
through a life of poverty and humility.
May we follow your Son
by walking in the footsteps of Francis of Assisi,
and by imitating his joyful love.

FIRST READING

A reading from the letter of St Paul to the Galatians   6:14-18
Through Christ the world is crucified to me, and I to the world.

As for me, the only thing I can boast about is the cross of our Lord Jesus Christ, through whom the world is crucified to me, and I to the world. It does not matter if a person is circumcised or not; what matters is for him to become an altogether new creature. Peace and mercy to all who follow this rule, who form the Israel of God.

    I want no more trouble from anybody after this; the marks on my body are those of Jesus. The grace of our Lord Jesus Christ be with your spirit, my brothers. Amen.

    This is the word of the Lord.

Responsorial Psalm Ps 15:1-2. 5. 7-8. 11. ℟ cf. v.5
   ℟ **You are my inheritance, O Lord.**

1 Preserve me, God, I take refuge in you.
   I say to the Lord, 'You are my God.'
   O Lord, it is you who are my portion and cup;
   it is you yourself who are my prize.   ℟

2 I will bless the Lord who gives me counsel,
   who even at night directs my heart.
   I keep the Lord ever in my sight:
   since he is at my right hand, I shall stand firm.   ℟

3 You will show me the path of life,
   the fullness of joy in your presence,
   at your right hand happiness for ever.   ℟

Gospel Acclamation   cf. Mt 11:25
   Alleluia, alleluia!
   Blessed are you, Father,
   Lord of heaven and earth,
   for revealing the mysteries of the kingdom
   to mere children.
   Alleluia!

GOSPEL

A reading from the holy Gospel according to Matthew   11:25-30
You have hidden these things from the clever, and have revealed them to mere children.

Jesus exclaimed, 'I bless you, Father, Lord of heaven and of earth, for hiding these things from the learned and the clever and revealing them to mere children. Yes, Father, for that is what it pleased you to do. Everything has been entrusted to me by my Father; and no one knows the Son except the Father, just as no one knows the Father except the Son and those to whom the Son chooses to reveal him.

'Come to me, all you who labour and are overburdened, and I will give you rest. Shoulder my yoke and learn from me, for I am gentle and humble in heart, and you will find rest for your souls. Yes, my yoke is easy and my burden light.'

This is the Gospel of the Lord.

Prayer over the Gifts
Lord,

as we bring you our gifts,
prepare us to celebrate the mystery of the cross,
to which Saint Francis adhered with such burning love.

Communion Antiphon: Blessed are the poor in spirit; the kingdom of heaven is theirs!

Prayer after Communion
Lord,
by the holy eucharist we have celebrated,
help us to imitate
the apostolic love and zeal of Saint Francis.
May we who receive your love
share it for the salvation of all mankind.

6 October

St Bruno, priest — Optional Memorial

Born at Cologne about 1030, Bruno was ordained and for many years ran the Cathedral school of Rheims. He felt called to a life of asceticism and solitude, and retired to the mountains near Grenoble with a few companions. From their community grew the Carthusian Order. He died in 1101.

Common of pastors, pp.1876ff., or of holy men and women: religious, pp.1898ff.

Opening Prayer
Father,
you called Saint Bruno to serve you in solitude.
In answer to his prayers
help us to remain faithful to you
amid the changes of this world.

FIRST READING

A reading from the letter of St Paul to the Philippians   3:8-14
I am racing for the finish, for the prize to which God calls us upwards to receive in Christ Jesus.

I believe nothing can happen that will outweigh the supreme advantage of knowing Christ Jesus my Lord. For him I have accepted the loss of everything, and I look on everything as so much rubbish if only I can have Christ and be given a place in him. I am no longer trying for perfection by my own efforts, the perfection that comes from the Law, but I want only the perfection that comes through faith in Christ, and is from God and based on faith. All I want is to know Christ and the power of his resurrection and to share his sufferings by reproducing the pattern of his death. That is the way I can hope to take my place in the resurrection of the dead. Not that I have become perfect yet: I have not yet won, but I am still running, trying to capture the prize for which Christ Jesus captured me. I can assure you, my brothers, I am far from thinking that I have already won. All I can say is that I forget the past and I strain ahead for what is still to come; I am racing for the finish, for the prize to which God calls us upwards to receive in Christ Jesus.

This is the word of the Lord.

Responsorial Psalm
Ps 1:1-4. 6. ℟ v.2. Alt. ℟ Ps 39:5. Alt. ℟ Ps 91:13-14

℟ **His delight is the law of the Lord.**

or

℟ **Happy the man who has placed his trust in the Lord.**

or

℟ **The just will flourish like the palm-tree in the courts of our God.**

1 Happy indeed is the man
who follows not the counsel of the wicked;
nor lingers in the way of sinners
nor sits in the company of scorners,
but whose delight is the law of the Lord
and who ponders his law day and night. ℟

2 He is like a tree that is planted
beside the flowing waters,
that yields its fruit in due season
and whose leaves shall never fade;
and all that he does shall prosper. ℟

3 Not so are the wicked, not so!
For they like winnowed chaff
shall be driven away by the wind.
For the Lord guards the way of the just
but the way of the wicked leads to doom. ℟

Gospel Acclamation Jn 8:12
Alleluia, alleluia!
I am the light of the world, says the Lord,
anyone who follows me will have the light of life.
Alleluia!

GOSPEL

A reading from the holy Gospel according to Luke 9:57-62
I will follow you wherever you go.

As Jesus and his disciples travelled along they met a man on the road who said to him, 'I will follow you wherever you go.' Jesus answered, 'Foxes have holes and the birds of the air have nests, but the Son of Man has nowhere to lay his head.'

Another to whom he said, 'Follow me,' replied, 'Let me go and bury my father first.' But he answered, 'Leave the dead to bury their dead; your duty is to go and spread the news of the kingdom of God.'

Another said, 'I will follow you, sir, but first let me go and say good-bye to my people at home.' Jesus said to him, 'Once the hand is laid on the plough, no one who looks back is fit for the kingdom of God.'

This is the Gospel of the Lord.

7 October

Our Lady of the Rosary — Memorial

This feast has been celebrated since the Christian victory over the Turks at the Battle of Lepanto in 1571.

Entrance Antiphon: Hail, Mary, full of grace, the Lord is with you; blessed are you among women and blessed is the fruit of your womb.

Opening Prayer
Lord,
fill our hearts with your love,
and as you revealed to us by an angel
the coming of your Son as man,
so lead us through his suffering and death
to the glory of his resurrection,
who lives and reigns . . .

FIRST READING

A reading from the Acts of the Apostles 1:12-14
They joined in continuous prayer with Mary, the mother of Jesus.

After Jesus had ascended into heaven, the apostles went back to Jerusalem, a short distance away, no more than a sabbath walk; and when they reached the city they went to the upper room where they were staying; there were Peter and John, James and Andrew, Philip and Thomas, Bartholomew and Matthew, James son of Alphaeus and Simon the Zealot, and Jude son of James. All these joined in continuous prayer, together with several women, including Mary the mother of Jesus, and with his brothers.

This is the word of the Lord.

Responsorial Psalm Lk 1:46-55. ℟ v.49

℟ **The Almighty works marvels for me.**
Holy is his name!

or

℟ **Blessed is the Virgin Mary**
who bore the son of the eternal Father.

1. My soul glorifies the Lord,
my spirit rejoices in God, my saviour. ℟

2. He looks on his servant in her nothingness;
henceforth all ages will call me blessed.
The Almighty works marvels for me.
Holy his name! ℟

3. His mercy is from age to age,
on those who fear him.
He puts forth his arm in strength
and scatters the proud-hearted. ℟

4. He casts the mighty from their thrones
and raises the lowly.
He fills the starving with good things,
sends the rich away empty. ℟

5. He protects Israel, his servant,
remembering his mercy,
the mercy promised to our fathers,
to Abraham and his sons for ever. ℟

Proper of Saints, 7 October

Gospel Acclamation cf. Lk 1:28
Alleluia, alleluia!
Hail Mary, full of grace; the Lord is with thee.
Blessed art thou among women.
Alleluia!

GOSPEL

A reading from the holy Gospel according to Luke 1:26-38
You are to conceive and bear a son.

The angel Gabriel was sent by God to a town in Galilee called Nazareth, to a virgin betrothed to a man named Joseph, of the House of David; and the virgin's name was Mary. He went in and said to her, 'Rejoice, so highly favoured! The Lord is with you.' She was deeply disturbed by these words and asked herself what this greeting could mean, but the angel said to her, 'Mary, do not be afraid; you have won God's favour. Listen! You are to conceive and bear a son, and you must name him Jesus. He will be great and will be called Son of the Most High. The Lord God will give him the throne of his ancestor David; he will rule over the House of Jacob for ever and his reign will have no end.' Mary said to the angel, 'But how can this come about, since I am a virgin?' 'The Holy Spirit will come upon you,' the angel answered, 'and the power of the Most High will cover you with its shadow. And so the child will be holy and will be called Son of God. Know this too: your kinswoman Elizabeth has, in her old age, herself conceived a son, and she whom people called barren is now in her sixth month, for nothing is impossible to God.' 'I am the handmaid of the Lord,' said Mary, 'Let what you have said be done to me.' And the angel left her.

This is the Gospel of the Lord.

Prayer over the Gifts
Lord,
may these gifts we offer in sacrifice transform our lives.
By celebrating the mysteries of your Son,
may we become worthy of the eternal life he promises,
for he is Lord for ever and ever.

Preface of the Blessed Virgin Mary I or II, P56 or P57.

Communion Antiphon: You shall conceive and bear a Son, and you shall call his name Jesus.

Prayer after Communion

Lord our God,
in this eucharist we have proclaimed
the death and resurrection of Christ.
Make us partners in his suffering
and lead us to share his happiness
and the glory of eternal life,
where he is Lord for ever and ever.

9 October

St Denis, bishop and martyr, and companions, martyrs

Optional Memorial

Lived in the third century. Was one of seven bishops sent to convert Gaul, became bishop of Paris and was martyred, perhaps in 251.

Common of martyrs, pp.1865ff.

Opening Prayer

Father,
you sent Saint Denis and his companions
to preach your glory to the nations,
and you gave them the strength
to be steadfast in their sufferings for Christ.
Grant that we may learn from their example
to reject the power and wealth of this world
and to brave all earthly trials.

FIRST READING

A reading from the second letter of St Paul 6:4-10
to the Corinthians

Said to be dying, and here are we alive.

We prove we are servants of God by great fortitude in times of suffering: in times of hardship and distress; when we are flogged, or sent to prison, or mobbed; labouring, sleepless, starving. We prove we are God's servants by our purity, knowledge, patience and kindness; by a spirit of holiness, by a love free from affectation; by the word of truth and by the power of God; by being armed with the weapons of righteousness in the right hand and in the left, prepared for honour or disgrace, for blame or praise; taken for impostors while we are genuine; obscure yet famous; said to be dying and here we are alive; rumoured to be executed before we are sentenced; thought most miserable and yet we are always rejoicing; taken for paupers though we make others rich, for people having nothing though we have everything.

This is the word of the Lord.

Responsorial Psalm Ps 125. ℟v.5
℟ **Those who are sowing in tears
will sing when they reap.**

1 When the Lord delivered Zion from bondage,
 it seemed like a dream.
 Then was our mouth filled with laughter,
 on our lips there were songs. ℟

2 The heathens themselves said: 'What marvels
 the Lord worked for them!'
 What marvels the Lord worked for us!
 Indeed we were glad. ℟

3 Deliver us, O Lord, from our bondage
 as streams in dry land.
 Those who are sowing in tears
 will sing when they reap. ℟

4 They go out, they go out, full of tears,
 carrying seed for the sowing:
 they come back, they come back, full of song,
 carrying their sheaves. ℟

Gospel Acclamation Jn 8:12
Alleluia alleluia!
I am the light of the world, says the Lord,
anyone who follows me
will have the light of life.
Alleluia!

GOSPEL

A reading from the holy Gospel according to Matthew 5:13-16
You are the light of the world.

Jesus said to his disciples: 'You are the salt of the earth. But if salt becomes tasteless, what can make it salty again? It is good for nothing, and can only be thrown out to be trampled underfoot by men.

'You are the light of the world. A city built on a hill-top cannot be hidden. No one lights a lamp to put it under a tub; they put it on the lamp-stand where it shines for everyone in the house. In the same way your light must shine in the sight of men, so that, seeing your good works, they may give the praise to your Father in heaven.'

This is the Gospel of the Lord.

Also 9 October
St John Leonardi, priest
Optional Memorial

Born in Tuscany about 1541. He was ordained priest, and founded a community to teach the young and to instruct adults against the Protestant Reformers. He went to Rome and worked with Philip Neri for a time. In preparing priests for mission work, he laid the foundations of the Congregation for the Propagation of the Faith. He died in 1609.

Common of pastors: missionaries, pp.1885ff., or of holy men and women: those who worked for the underprivileged, p.1900.

Opening Prayer
Father,
giver of all good things,
you proclaimed the good news to countless people
through the ministry of Saint John Leonardi.
By the help of his prayers
may the true faith continue to grow.

FIRST READING

A reading from the second letter of St Paul to the Corinthians
4:1-2. 5-7

We preach Christ Jesus and ourselves as your servants for Jesus' sake.

Since we have by an act of mercy been entrusted with this work of administration, there is no weakening on our part. On the contrary, we will have none of the reticence of those who are ashamed, no deceitfulness or watering down the word of God; but the way we commend ourselves to every human being with a conscience is by stating the truth openly in the sight of God. For it is not ourselves that we are preaching, but Christ Jesus as the Lord, and ourselves as your servants for Jesus' sake. It is the same God that said, 'Let there be light shining out of darkness,' who has shone in our minds to radiate the light of the knowledge of God's glory, the glory on the face of Christ.

We are only the earthenware jars that hold this treasure, to make it clear that such an overwhelming power comes from God and not from us.

This is the word of the Lord.

Responsorial Psalm
Ps 95:1-3. 7-8. 10. ℟ v.3

℟ **Proclaim the wonders of the Lord among all the peoples.**

1. O sing a new song to the Lord,
   sing to the Lord all the earth.
   O sing to the Lord, bless his name.   ℟

2. Proclaim his help day by day,
   tell among the nations his glory
   and his wonders among all the peoples.   ℟

3. Give the Lord, you families of peoples,
   give the Lord glory and power,
   give the Lord the glory of his name.   ℟

4. Proclaim to the nations: 'God is king,'
   The world he made firm in its place;
   he will judge the peoples in fairness.   ℟

Gospel Acclamation
Mk 1:17

Alleluia, alleluia!
Follow me, says the Lord,
and I will make you into fishers of men.
Alleluia!

GOSPEL

A reading from the holy Gospel according to Luke   5:1-11
If you say so, I will pay out the nets.

Jesus was standing one day by the Lake of Gennesaret, with the crowd pressing round him listening to the word of God, when he caught sight of two boats close to the bank. The fishermen had gone out of them and were washing their nets. He got into one of the boats – it was Simon's – and asked him to put out a little from the shore. Then he sat down and taught the crowds from the boat.

When he had finished speaking he said to Simon, 'Put out into deep water and pay out your nets for a catch.' 'Master,' Simon replied, 'we worked hard all night long and caught nothing, but if you say so, I will pay out the nets.' And when they had done this they netted such a huge number of fish that their nets began to tear, so they signalled to their companions in the other boat to come and help them; when these came, they filled the two boats to sinking point.

When Simon Peter saw this he fell at the knees of Jesus saying, 'Leave me, Lord; I am a sinful man.' For he and all his companions were completely overcome by the catch they had made; so also were James and John, sons of Zebedee, who were Simon's partners. But Jesus said to Simon, 'Do not be afraid; from now on it is men you will catch.' Then, bringing their boats back to land, they left everything and followed him.

This is the Gospel of the Lord.

14 October

St Callistus I, pope and martyr

Optional Memorial

Became pope in 217. His papacy was marked by controversy, particularly with Hippolytus. He was martyred in 222.
Common of martyrs, pp.1865ff., or of pastors: popes, pp.1876ff.

Opening Prayer
God of mercy,
hear the prayers of your people
that we may be helped by Saint Callistus,
whose martyrdom we celebrate with joy.

FIRST READING

A reading from the first letter of St Peter 5:1-4
Be the shepherds of the flock of God that is entrusted to you.

I have something to tell your elders: I am an elder myself, and a witness to the sufferings of Christ, and with you I have a share in the glory that is to be revealed. Be the shepherds of the flock of God that is entrusted to you: watch over it, not simply as a duty but gladly, because God wants it; not for sordid money, but because you are eager to do it. Never be a dictator over any group that is put in your charge, but be an example that the whole flock can follow. When the chief shepherd appears, you will be given the crown of unfading glory.

This is the word of the Lord.

Responsorial Psalm   Ps 39:2. 4. 7-10. ℟ cf. vv.8. 9
    ℟ **Here I am, Lord!**
        I come to do your will.

1   I waited, I waited for the Lord
     and he stooped down to me;
     he heard my cry.
     He put a new song into my mouth,
     praise of our God.   ℟

2   You do not ask for sacrifice and offerings,
     but an open ear.
     You do not ask for holocaust and victim.
     Instead, here am I.   ℟

3   In the scroll of the book it stands written
     that I should do your will.
     My God, I delight in your law
     in the depth of my heart.   ℟

4   Your justice I have proclaimed
     in the great assembly.
     My lips I have not sealed;
     you know it, O Lord.   ℟

Gospel Acclamation   Jn 15:15
     Alleluia, alleluia!
     I call you friends, says the Lord,
     because I have made known to you
     everything I have learnt from my Father.
     Alleluia!

GOSPEL

A reading from the holy Gospel according to Luke   22:24-30
I confer a kingdom on you, just as my Father conferred one on me.

A dispute arose between the apostles about which should be

reckoned the greatest, but Jesus said to them, 'Among pagans it is the kings who lord it over them, and those who have authority over them are given the title Benefactor. This must not happen with you. No; the greatest among you must behave as if he were the youngest, the leader as if he were the one who serves. For who is the greater: the one at table or the one who serves? The one at table, surely? Yet here am I among you as one who serves!

'You are the men who have stood by me faithfully in my trials; and now I confer a kingdom on you, just as my Father conferred one on me; you will eat and drink at my table in my kingdom, and you will sit on thrones to judge the twelve tribes of Israel.'

This is the Gospel of the Lord.

15 October
St Teresa of Avila, virgin and doctor of the Church — Memorial

Born at Avila in Spain in 1515, entered Carmel in 1533. For some time she did not lead a very rigorous life, but in 1555 committed herself to the way of perfection. She decided to found a religious house that lived by the primitive rule (the Discalced Carmelites), and eventually succeeded despite much opposition. She persevered in prayer, enjoying many mystical experiences, and her spiritual writings are still influential. She uniquely combined mystic experience with the strenuous work of a reformer and administrator.

Entrance Antiphon: Like a deer that longs for running streams, my soul longs for you, my God. My soul is thirsting for the living God.

Opeing Prayer
Father,
by your Spirit you raised up Saint Teresa of Avila
to show your Church the way of perfection.
May her inspired teaching
awaken in us a longing for true holiness.

FIRST READING
A reading from the letter of St Paul to the Romans   8:22-27
The Spirit expresses our plea in a way that could never be put into words.

From the beginning till now the entire creation, as we know, has been groaning in one great act of giving birth; and not only creation, but all of us who possess the first-fruits of the Spirit, we too groan inwardly as we wait for our bodies to be set free. For we must be content to hope that we shall be saved – our salvation is not in sight, we should not have to be hoping for it if it were – but, as I say, we must hope to be saved since we are not saved yet – it is something we must wait for with patience.

The Spirit too comes to help us in our weakness. For when we cannot choose words in order to pray properly, the Spirit himself expresses our plea in a way that could never be put into words, and God who knows everything in our hearts knows perfectly well what he means, and that the pleas of the saints expressed by the Spirit are according to the mind of God.

This is the word of the Lord.

Responsorial Psalm   Ps 18:8-11. ℟ v.10. Alt. ℟ Jn 6:63

  ℟ **The decrees of the Lord are truth
and all of them just.**

or

  ℟ **Your words are spirit, Lord,
and they are life.**

1. The law of the Lord is perfect,
it revives the soul.
The rule of the Lord is to be trusted,
it gives wisdom to the simple.   ℟

2. The precepts of the Lord are right,
they gladden the heart.
The command of the Lord is clear,
it gives light to the eyes.   ℟

3. The fear of the Lord is holy,
abiding for ever.
The decrees of the Lord are truth
and all of them just.   ℟

4. They are more to be desired than gold,
than the purest of gold
and sweeter are they than honey,
than honey from the comb.   ℟

Gospel Acclamation   Jn 15:9. 5
Alleluia, alleluia!

Remain in my love, says the Lord;
whoever remains in me, with me in him,
bears fruit in plenty.
Alleluia!

GOSPEL

A reading from the holy Gospel according to John 15:1-8
Whoever remains in me, with me in him, bears fruit in plenty.

Jesus said to his disciples:

'I am the true vine,
and my Father is the vinedresser.
Every branch in me that bears no fruit
he cuts away,
and every branch that does bear fruit he prunes
to make it bear even more.
You are pruned already,
by means of the word that I have spoken to you.
Make your home in me, as I make mine in you.
As a branch cannot bear fruit all by itself,
but must remain part of the vine,
neither can you unless you remain in me.
I am the vine,
you are the branches.
Whoever remains in me, with me in him,
bears fruit in plenty;
for cut off from me you can do nothing.
Anyone who does not remain in me
is like a branch that has been thrown away
– he withers;
these branches are collected and thrown on the fire,
and they are burnt.
If you remain in me
and my words remain in you,
you may ask what you will
and you shall get it.
It is to the glory of my Father that you should bear much fruit,
and then you will be my disciples.'

This is the Gospel of the Lord.

Prayer over the Gifts
King of heaven,

accept the gifts we bring in your praise,
as you were pleased with Saint Teresa's offering
of her life in your service.

Communion Antiphon: For ever I will sing the goodness of the Lord; I will proclaim your faithfulness to all generations.

Prayer after Communion
Lord our God,
watch over the family you nourish
with the bread from heaven.
Help us to follow Saint Teresa's example
and sing your merciful love for ever.

16 October
St Hedwig, religious Optional Memorial

Born in Bavaria about 1174, married at the age of twelve to Henry, duke of Silesia and Poland, mother of seven children. The family lived a very religious life, marked by penance, fasting, and charity. She took under her protection the poor and founded a hospital for them. After the death of her husband she lived in the convent of which her surviving daughter was Abbess. She died in 1243.

Common of holy men and women: religious, pp.1898ff.

Opening Prayer
All-powerful God,
may the prayers of Saint Hedwig bring us your help
and may her life of remarkable humility
be an example to us all.

FIRST READING

A reading from the book of Ecclesiasticus   26:1-4. 13-16
The beauty of a good wife in a well-kept house is like the rising sun.

Happy the husband of a really good wife;
the number of his days will be doubled.
A perfect wife is the joy of her husband,
he will live out the years of his life in peace.
A good wife is the best of portions,
reserved for those who fear the Lord;

Proper of Saints, 16 October

rich or poor, they will be glad of heart,
cheerful of face, whatever the reason.
The grace of a wife will charm her husband,
her accomplishments will make him the stronger.
A silent wife is a gift from the Lord,
no price can be put on a well-trained character.
A modest wife is a boon twice over,
a chaste character cannot be weighed on scales.
Like the sun rising over the mountains of the Lord
is the beauty of a good wife in a well-kept house.

This is the word of the Lord.

Responsorial Psalm Ps 127:1-5. ℟ v.1
℟ **O blessed are those who fear the Lord.**

1 O blessed are those who fear the Lord
   and walk in his ways!
   By the labour of your hands you shall eat.
   you will be happy and prosper.   ℟

2 Your wife will be like a fruitful vine
   in the heart of your house;
   your children like shoots of the olive,
   around your table.   ℟

3 Indeed thus shall be blessed
   the man who fears the Lord.
   May the Lord bless you from Zion
   all the days of your life!   ℟

Gospel Acclamation Jn 8:31-32
Alleluia, alleluia!
If you make my word your home
you will indeed be my disciples,
and you will learn the truth, says the Lord.
Alleluia!

GOSPEL

A reading from the holy Gospel according to Mark 3:31-35
Anyone who does the will of God, that person is my brother and sister and mother.

The mother and brothers of Jesus arrived and, standing outside, sent in a message asking for him. A crowd was sitting round him at the time the message was passed to him, 'Your mother and brothers and sisters are outside asking for you.' He replied, 'Who are my mother and my brothers?' And looking round at those sitting in a circle about him, he said, 'Here are my mother and my brothers. Anyone who does the will of God, that person is my brother and sister and mother.'

This is the Gospel of the Lord.

Also 16 October
St Margaret Mary Alacoque, virgin
Optional Memorial

Born in 1647, her childhood was unhappy, and she entered the Visitation Convent of Paray-le-Moniale in France in 1671. She received visions of the Sacred Heart of Jesus, and in her visions was told to encourage devotion to the Sacred Heart, and to have a feast in his honour established. She met a great deal of opposition and scorn, particularly at first, but gradually overcame this with the help of the Blessed Claude de la Colombiere, her confessor at the time.

Common of virgins, pp.1889ff., or of holy men and women: religious, pp.1898ff.

Opening Prayer
Lord,
pour out on us the riches of the Spirit
which you bestowed on Saint Margaret Mary.
May we come to know the love of Christ,
which surpasses all human understanding,
and be filled with the fullness of God.

FIRST READING
A reading from the letter of St Paul to the Ephesians   3:14-19
To know the love of Christ, which is beyond all knowledge.

This is what I pray, kneeling before the Father, from whom every family, whether spiritual or natural, takes its name:

Out of his infinite glory, may he give you the power through his Spirit for your hidden self to grow strong, so that Christ may live in your hearts through faith, and then, planted in love and built on love, you will with all the saints have strength to grasp the breadth and the length, the height and the depth; until, knowing the love of Christ, which is beyond all knowledge, you are filled with the utter fullness of God.

This is the word of the Lord.

Responsorial Psalm
Ps 22. ℟ v.1

℟ **The Lord is my shepherd;
there is nothing I shall want.**

1 The Lord is my shepherd;
   there is nothing I shall want.
   Fresh and green are the pastures
   where he gives me repose.
   Near restful waters he leads me,
   to revive my drooping spirit. ℟

2 He guides me along the right path;
   he is true to his name.
   If I should walk in the valley of darkness
   no evil would I fear.
   You are there with your crook and your staff;
   with these you give me comfort. ℟

3 You have prepared a banquet for me
   in the sight of my foes.
   My head you have anointed with oil;
   my cup is overflowing. ℟

4 Surely goodness and kindness shall follow me
   all the days of my life.
   In the Lord's own house shall I dwell
   for ever and ever. ℟

Gospel Acclamation
cf. Mt 11:25

Alleluia, alleluia!
Blessed are you, Father,
Lord of heaven and earth,
for revealing the mysteries of the kingdom
to mere children.
Alleluia!

GOSPEL

A reading from the holy Gospel according to Matthew 11:25-30

You have hidden these things from the learned and have revealed them to mere children.

Jesus exclaimed, 'I bless you, Father, Lord of heaven and of earth, for hiding these things from the learned and the clever and revealing them to mere children. Yes, Father, for that is what it pleased you to do. Everything has been entrusted to me by my Father; and no one knows the Son except the Father, just as no one knows the Father except the Son and those to whom the Son chooses to reveal him.

'Come to me, all you who labour and are overburdened, and I will give you rest. Shoulder my yoke and learn from me, for I am gentle and humble in heart, and you will find rest for your souls. Yes, my yoke is easy and my burden light.'

This is the Gospel of the Lord.

17 October

St Ignatius of Antioch, bishop and martyr

Memorial

Bishop of Antioch in the first century. Little is known of Ignatius' life, except that it ended in martyrdom in Rome, about 107. On his journey to Rome as a prisoner, he met Polycarp in Smyrna, and many other Christians from the neighbouring communities. He wrote a number of epistles to the Christian communities at Ephesus, Philadelphia, Smyrna etc., which show his passionate commitment to Christ, his longing for martyrdom, his faith and true understanding of doctrine.

Entrance Antiphon: With Christ I am nailed to the cross. I live now not with my own life, but Christ lives within me. I live by faith in the Son of God, who loved me and sacrificed himself for me.

Opening Prayer

All-powerful and ever-living God,
you ennoble your Church
with the heroic witness of all
who give their lives for Christ.
Grant that the victory of Saint Ignatius of Antioch
may bring us your constant help
as it brought him eternal glory.

FIRST READING

A reading from the letter of St Paul to the Philippians 3:17–4:1
Our homeland is in heaven.

My brothers, be united in following my rule of life. Take as your models everybody who is already doing this and study them as you used to study us. I have told you often, and I repeat it today with tears, there are many who are behaving as the enemies of the cross of Christ. They are destined to be lost. They make foods into their god and they are proudest of something they ought to think shameful; the things they think important are earthly things. For us, our homeland is in heaven, and from heaven comes the saviour we are waiting for, the Lord Jesus Christ, and he will transfigure these wretched bodies of ours into copies of his glorious body. He will do that by the same power with which he can subdue the whole universe.

So then, my brothers and dear friends, do not give way but remain faithful to the Lord. I miss you very much, dear friends; you are my joy and my crown.

This is the word of the Lord.

Responsional Psalm
Ps 33:2-9. ℟ v.5

℟ **From all my terrors the Lord set me free.**

1 I will bless the Lord at all times,
   his praise always on my lips;
   in the Lord my soul shall make its boast.
   The humble shall hear and be glad.   ℟

2 Glorify the Lord with me.
   Together let us praise his name.
   I sought the Lord and he answered me;
   from all my terrors he set me free.   ℟

3 Look towards him and be radiant;
   let your faces not be abashed.
   This poor man called; the Lord heard him
   and rescued him from all his distress.   ℟

4 The angel of the Lord is encamped
   around those who revere him, to rescue them.
   Taste and see that the Lord is good.
   He is happy who seeks refuge in him.   ℟

Gospel Acclamation
James 1:12

Alleluia, alleluia!
Happy the man who stands firm when trials come,
for he has proved himself,
and will win the crown of life.
Alleluia!

GOSPEL

A reading from the holy Gospel according to John 12:24-26
If a grain of wheat dies it yields a rich harvest.

Jesus said to his disciples:

'I tell you, most solemnly,
unless a wheat grain falls on the ground and dies,
it remains only a single grain;
but if it dies,
it yields a rich harvest.
Anyone who loves his life loses it;
anyone who hates his life in this world
will keep it for the eternal life.
If a man serves me, he must follow me,
wherever I am, my servant will be there too.
If anyone serves me, my Father will honour him.'

This is the Gospel of the Lord.

Prayer over the Gifts
Lord,
receive our offering
as you accepted Saint Ignatius
when he offered himself to you as the wheat of Christ,
formed into pure bread by his death for Christ,
who lives and reigns for ever and ever.

Communion Antiphon: I am the wheat of Christ, ground by the teeth of beasts to become pure bread.

Prayer after Communion
Lord,
renew us by the bread of heaven
which we have received on the feast of Saint Ignatius.
May it transform us into loyal and true Christians.

18 October
ST LUKE, EVANGELIST   Feast

Author of the Gospel according to Luke, and the Acts of the Apostles. From Acts we learn that he was a gentile convert to Christianity, a doctor, who accompanied Paul on his second and third missionary

Proper of Saints, 18 October

journeys, and stayed in Rome with him while he was in captivity.

Entrance Antiphon: How beautiful on the mountains are the feet of the man who brings tidings of peace, joy and salvation.

Opening Prayer

Father,
you chose Luke the evangelist to reveal
by preaching and writing
the mystery of your love for the poor.
Unite in one heart and spirit
all who glory in your name,
and let all nations come to see your salvation.

FIRST READING

A reading from the second letter of St Paul to Timothy 4:10-17
Only Luke is with me.

Demas has deserted me for love of this life and gone to Thessalonika, Crescens has gone to Galatia and Titus to Dalmatia; only Luke is with me. Get Mark to come and bring him with you; I find him a useful helper in my work. I have sent Tychicus to Ephesus. When you come, bring the cloak I left with Carpus in Troas, and the scrolls, especially the parchment ones. Alexander the coppersmith has done me a lot of harm; the Lord will repay him for what he has done. Be on your guard against him yourself, because he has been bitterly contesting everything that we say.

The first time I had to present my defence, there was not a single witness to support me. Everyone of them deserted me – may they not be held accountable for it. But the Lord stood by me and gave me power, so that through me the whole message might be proclaimed for all the pagans to hear.

This is the word of the Lord.

Responsorial Psalm Ps 144:10-13. 17-18. ℟ v.12

℟ **Your friends, O Lord, shall make known
the glorious splendour of your reign.**

1 All your creatures shall thank you, O Lord,
and your friends shall repeat their blessing.
They shall speak of the glory of your reign
and declare your might, O God. ℟

2   They make known to men your mighty deeds
and the glorious splendour of your reign.
Yours is an everlasting kingdom;
your rule lasts from age to age.

℟ **Your friends, O Lord, shall make known
the glorious splendour of your reign.**

3   The Lord is just in all his ways
and loving in all his deeds.
He is close to all who call him,
who call on him from their hearts.   ℟

Gospel Acclamation cf. Jn 15:16
Alleluia, alleluia!
I chose you from the world
to go out and to bear fruit,
fruit that will last, says the Lord.
Alleluia!

GOSPEL

A reading from the holy Gospel according to Luke 10:1-9
The harvest is rich but the labourers are few.

The Lord appointed seventy-two others and sent them out ahead of him, in pairs, to all the towns and places he himself was to visit. He said to them, 'The harvest is rich but the labourers are few, so ask the Lord of the harvest to send labourers to his harvest. Start off now, but remember, I am sending you out like lambs among wolves. Carry no purse, no haversack, no sandals. Salute no one on the road. Whatever house you go into, let your first words be, "Peace to this house!" And if a man of peace lives there, your peace will go and rest on him; if not, it will come back to you. Stay in the same house, taking what food and drink they have to offer, for the labourer deserves his wages; do not move from house to house. Whenever you go into a town where they make you welcome, eat what is set before you. Cure those in it who are sick, and say, "The kingdom of God is very near to you." '

This is the Gospel of the Lord.

Prayer over the Gifts
Father,
may your gifts from heaven free our hearts to serve you.

May the sacrifice we offer on the feast of Saint Luke
bring us healing and lead us to eternal glory,
where Jesus is Lord for ever and ever.

Preface of the Apostles II, P65.

Communion Antiphon: The Lord sent disciples to proclaim to all the towns: the kingdom of God is very near to you.

Prayer after Communion
All-powerful God,
may the eucharist we have received at your altar
make us holy
and strengthen us in the faith of the gospel
preached by Saint Luke.

19 October

Ss John de Brébeuf and Isaac Jogues, priests and martyrs, and companions, martyrs

Optional Memorial

These eight men were Jesuit missionaries in North America in the 17th century, put to death by the Indians. John de Brébeuf was a man of deep spirituality, noted for his life of prayer and penance.

Common of martyrs, pp. 1865ff., or of pastors: missionaries, pp. 1885ff.

Opening Prayer
Father,
you consecrated the first beginnings
of the faith in North America
by the preaching and martyrdom
of Saints John and Isaac and their companions.
By the help of their prayers
may the Christian faith continue to grow
throughout the world.

FIRST READING

A reading from the second letter of St Paul to the Corinthians
4:7-15

We carry with us in our body the death of Jesus.

We are only the earthenware jars that hold this treasure, to make it clear that such an overwhelming power comes from God and not from us. We are in difficulties on all sides, but never cornered; we see no answer to our problems, but never despair; we have been persecuted, but never deserted; knocked down, but never killed; always, wherever we may be, we carry with us in our body the death of Jesus, so that the life of Jesus, too, may always be seen in our body. Indeed, while we are still alive, we are consigned to our death every day, for the sake of Jesus, so that in our mortal flesh the life of Jesus, too, may be openly shown. So death is at work in us, but life in you.

But as we have the same spirit of faith that is mentioned in scripture – I believed, and therefore I spoke – we too believe and therefore we too speak, knowing that he who raised the Lord Jesus to life will raise us with Jesus in our turn, and put us by his side and you with us. You see, all this is for your benefit, so that the more grace is multiplied among people, the more thanksgiving there will be, to the glory of God.

This is the word of the Lord.

Responsorial Psalm

Ps 125. ℟ v.5

℟ **Those who are sowing in tears
will sing when they reap.**

1 When the Lord delivered Zion from bondage,
it seemed like a dream.
Then was our mouth filled with laughter,
on our lips there were songs. ℟

2 The heathens themselves said : 'What marvels
the Lord worked for them!'
What marvels the Lord worked for us!
Indeed we were glad. ℟

3 Deliver us, O Lord, from our bondage
as streams in dry land.
Those who are sowing in tears
will sing when they reap. ℟

4. They go out, they go out, full of tears,
carrying seed for the sowing:
they come back, they come back, full of song,
carrying their sheaves. ℟

Gospel Acclamation Mt 28:19. 20
Alleluia, alleluia!
Go, make disciples of all the nations;
I am with you always; yes, to the end of time.
Alleluia!

GOSPEL

A reading from the holy Gospel according to Matthew 28:16-20
Go, make disciples of all the nations.

The eleven disciples set out for Galilee, to the mountain where Jesus had arranged to meet them. When they saw him they fell down before him, though some hesitated. Jesus came up and spoke to them. He said, 'All authority in heaven and on earth has been given to me. Go, therefore, make disciples of all the nations; baptise them in the name of the Father and of the Son and of the Holy Spirit, and teach them to observe all the commands I gave you. And know that I am with you always; yes, to the end of time.'

This is the Gospel of the Lord.

Also 19 October
St Paul of the Cross, priest
Optional Memorial

Born 1693, of a noble family, he led a life of prayer and asceticism in the world until in 1721 he was inspired by a vision to found a religious order in honour of the Passion of Christ. He was ordained priest in 1726. He travelled throughout Italy, preaching, particularly on the Passion, living with great austerity, calling all to penance. His rule was approved in 1741. He set up 'Retreats', as the house of his Order were known, and a women's Order also began. He died in 1775.

Entrance Antiphon: I resolved that while I was with you I would think of nothing but Jesus Christ and him crucified.

Opening Prayer
Father,
you gave your priest Saint Paul
a special love for the cross of Christ.
May his example inspire us
to embrace our own cross with courage.

FIRST READING

A reading from the first letter of St Paul to the Corinthians 1:18-25
God wanted to save those who have faith through the foolishness of the message that we preach.

The language of the cross may be illogical to those who are not on the way to salvation, but those of us who are on the way see it as God's power to save. As scripture says: I shall destroy the wisdom of the wise and bring to nothing all the learning of the learned. Where are the philosophers now? Where are the scribes? Where are any of our thinkers today? Do you see now how God has shown up the foolishness of human wisdom? If it was God's wisdom that human wisdom should not know God, it was because God wanted to save those who have faith through the foolishness of the message that we preach. And so, while the Jews demand miracles and the Greeks look for wisdom, here are we preaching a crucified Christ; to the Jews an obstacle that they cannot get over, to the pagans madness, but to those who have been called, whether they are Jews or Greeks, a Christ who is the power and the wisdom of God. For God's foolishness is wiser than human wisdom, and God's weakness is stronger than human strength.

This is the word of the Lord.

Responsorial Psalm Ps 116. ℟ Mk 16:15

℟ **Go out to the whole world;
proclaim the Good News.**

or

℟ **Alleluia!**

1 O praise the Lord, all you nations,
acclaim him all you peoples! ℟

2 Strong is his love for us;
he is faithful for ever. ℟

Proper of Saints, 19 October

Gospel Acclamation   Mt 5:6
>Alleluia, alleluia!
>Happy those who hunger and thirst for what is right:
>they shall be satisfied.
>Alleluia!

GOSPEL

A reading from the holy Gospel according to Matthew   16:24-27

Anyone who loses his life for my sake will find it.

Jesus said to his disciples, 'If anyone wants to be a follower of mine, let him renounce himself and take up his cross and follow me. For anyone who wants to save his life will lose it; but anyone who loses his life for my sake will find it. What, then, will a man gain if he wins the whole world and ruins his life? Or what has a man to offer in exchange for his life?

'For the Son of Man is going to come in the glory of his Father with his angels, and, when he does, he will reward each one according to his behaviour.'

This is the Gospel of the Lord.

Prayer over the Gifts
All-powerful God,
receive the gifts we offer
in memory of Saint Paul of the Cross.
May we who celebrate the mystery
of the Lord's suffering and death
put into effect the self-sacrificing love
we proclaim in this eucharist.

Communion Antiphon: We preach a Christ who was crucified; he is the power and the wisdom of God.

Prayer after Communion
Lord,
in the life of Saint Paul
you helped us to understand the mystery of the cross.
May the sacrifice we have offered strengthen us,
keep us faithful to Christ,
and help us to work in the Church
for the salvation of all mankind.

23 October

St John of Capistrano, priest
Optional Memorial

Born in 1386, he had a vision while a prisoner of war that made him long to enter religion. In 1416 he joined the Franciscan Order, was ordained in 1420, and began to preach throughout Italy. He was several times vicar general of the Order. He preached in various countries of Eastern Europe against the Hussite heresy, with great success, until the Turks captured Constantinople in 1453. He raised an army to fight the Turks in Hungary, and defeated them in 1456. He died that year, of the plague.

Common of pastors: missionaries, pp.1885ff.

Opening Prayer
Lord,
you raised up Saint John of Capistrano
to give your people comfort in their trials.
May your Church enjoy unending peace
and be secure in your protection.

FIRST READING

A reading from the second letter of St Paul to the Corinthians   5:14-20

He gave us the work of handing on this reconciliation.

The love of Christ overwhelms us when we reflect that if one man has died for all, then all men should be dead; and the reason he died for all was so that living men should live no longer for themselves, but for him who died and was raised to life for them.

From now onwards, therefore, we do not judge anyone by the standards of the flesh. Even if we did once know Christ in the flesh, that is not how we know him now. And for anyone who is in Christ, there is a new creation; the old creation has gone, and now the new one is here. It is all God's work. It was God who reconciled us to himself through Christ and gave us the work of handing on this reconciliation. In other words, God in Christ was reconciling the world to himself, not holding men's faults against them, and he has entrusted to us the news that they are reconciled. So we are ambassadors for Christ; it is as though God were appealing through us, and the appeal that we make in Christ's name is: be reconciled to God.

This is the word of the Lord.

Responsional Psalm Ps 15:1-2. 5. 7-8. 11. ℟ v.5
℟ **You are my inheritance, O Lord.**

1 Preserve me, God, I take refuge in you.
I say to the Lord: 'You are my God.'
O Lord it is you who are my portion and cup;
it is you yourself who are my prize. ℟

2 I will bless the Lord who gives me counsel,
who even at night directs my heart.
I keep the Lord ever in my sight:
since he is at my right hand, I shall stand firm. ℟

3 You will show me the path of life,
the fullness of joy in your presence,
at your right hand happiness for ever. ℟

Gospel Acclamation Jn 8:12
Alleluia, alleluia!
I am the light of the world, says the Lord;
anyone who follows me will have the light of life.
Alleluia!

GOSPEL

A reading from the holy Gospel according to Luke 9:57-62
I will follow you wherever you go.

As Jesus and his disciples travelled along they met a man on the road who said to him, 'I will follow you wherever you go'. Jesus answered, 'Foxes have holes and the birds of the air have nests, but the Son of Man has nowhere to lay his head'.

Another to whom he said, 'Follow me', replied, 'Let me go and bury my father first'. But he answered, 'Leave the dead to bury their dead; your duty is to go and spread the news of the kingdom of God'.

Another said, 'I will follow you, sir, but first let me go and say good-bye to my people at home'. Jesus said to him, 'Once the hand is laid on the plough, no one who looks back is fit for the kingdom of God.'

This is the Gospel of the Lord.

24 October

St Anthony Claret, bishop
Optional Memorial

Born in Spain in 1807, ordained priest in 1835, became a popular preacher. His uncompromising preaching raised hostility against him. In 1849 he founded a missionary institute of priests. He was appointed bishop of Santiago in Cuba in 1850 and spent six years of arduous pastoral work there. He antagonised the slave owners, and attempts were made on his life. In 1857 he was appointed confessor to Queen Isabella of Spain. In 1868, revolution caused him to go into exile in France, where he died in 1870.

Common of pastors: missionaries, pp. 1885ff., or bishops, pp. 1878ff.

Opening Prayer

Father,
you endowed Anthony Claret
with the strength of love and patience
to preach the gospel to many nations.
By the help of his prayers
may we work generously for your kingdom
and gain our brothers and sisters for Christ,
who lives and reigns . . .

FIRST READING

A reading from the prophet Isaiah 52:7-10
All the ends of the earth shall see the salvation of our God.

How beautiful on the mountains,
are the feet of one who brings good news,
who heralds peace, brings happiness,
proclaims salvation,
and tells Zion,
'Your God is king!'

Listen! Your watchmen raise their voices,
they shout for joy together,
for they see the Lord face to face,
as he returns to Zion.
Break into shouts of joy together,
you ruins of Jerusalem;

Proper of Saints, 24 October

for the Lord is consoling his people,
redeeming Jerusalem.

The Lord bares his holy arm
in the sight of all the nations,
and all the ends of the earth shall see
the salvation of our God.

This is the word of the Lord.

Responsorial Psalm   Ps 95:1-3. 7-8. 10. ℟ v.3

℟ **Proclaim the wonders of the Lord among all the peoples**

1 O sing a new song to the Lord,
 sing to the Lord all the earth.
 O sing to the Lord, bless his name. ℟

2 Proclaim his help day by day,
 tell among the nations his glory
 and his wonders among all the peoples. ℟

3 Give the Lord, you families of peoples,
 give the Lord glory and power,
 give the Lord the glory of his name. ℟

4 Proclaim to the nations: 'God is king.'
 The world he made firm in its place;
 he will judge the peoples in fairness. ℟

Gospel Acclamation   Mk 1:17
Alleluia, alleluia!
Follow me, says the Lord,
and I will make you into fishers of men.
Alleluia!

GOSPEL

A reading from the holy Gospel according to Mark   1:14-20
I will make you into fishers of men.

After John had been arrested, Jesus went into Galilee. There he proclaimed the Good News from God. 'The time has come,' he said, 'and the kingdom of God is close at hand. Repent, and believe the Good News.'

As he was walking along by the Sea of Galilee he saw Simon and his brother Andrew casting a net in the lake – for they were fishermen. And Jesus said to them, 'Follow me and I will make you into fishers of men.' And at once they left their nets and followed him.

Going on a little farther, he saw James son of Zebedee and his brother John; they too were in their boat, mending their nets. He called them at once and, leaving their father Zebedee in the boat with the men he employed, they went after him.

This is the Gospel of the Lord.

28 October
SS SIMON AND JUDE, APOSTLES   Feast

Little is known of these two apostles, whose names are always linked in the Gospel accounts. Simon is called the Zealot, and Jude 'son of James'.

Entrance Antiphon: The Lord chose these holy men for their unfeigned love, and gave them eternal glory.

Opening Prayer
Father,
you revealed yourself to us
through the preaching of your apostles Simon and Jude.
By their prayers,
give your Church continued growth
and increase the number of those who believe in you.

FIRST READING

A reading from the letter of St Paul to the Ephesians   2:19-22
You are part of a building that has the apostles for its foundations.

You are no longer aliens or foreign visitors: you are citizens like all the saints, and part of God's household. You are part of a building that has the apostles and prophets for its foundations, and Christ Jesus himself for its main cornerstone. As every structure is aligned on him, all grow into one holy temple in the Lord; and you too, in him, are being built into a house where God lives, in the spirit.

This is the word of the Lord.

Proper of Saints, 28 October 1759

Responsorial Psalm Ps 18:2-5. ℞ v.5
℞ **Their word goes forth through all the earth.**

1 The heavens proclaim the glory of God
and the firmament shows forth the work of his hands.
Day unto day takes up the story
and night unto night makes known the message. ℞

2 No speech, no word, no voice is heard
yet their span goes forth through all the earth,
their words to the utmost bounds of the world. ℞

Gospel Acclamation
Alleluia, alleluia!
We praise you, O God, we acknowledge you to be the Lord.
The glorious company of the apostles praise you, O Lord.
Alleluia!

GOSPEL

A reading from the holy Gospel according to Luke 6:12-19
Jesus picked out twelve of his disciples and called them 'apostles'.

Jesus went out into the hills to pray; and he spent the whole night in prayer to God. When day came he summoned his disciples and picked out twelve of them; he called them 'apostles': Simon whom he called Peter, and his brother Andrew; James, John, Philip, Bartholomew, Matthew, Thomas, James son of Alphaeus, Simon called the Zealot, Judas son of James, and Judas Iscariot who became a traitor.

He then came down with them and stopped at a piece of level ground where there was a large gathering of his disciples with a great crowd of people from all parts of Judaea and from Jerusalem and from the coastal region of Tyre and Sidon who had come to hear him and to be cured of their diseases. People tormented by unclean spirits were also cured, and everyone in the crowd was trying to touch him because power came out of him that cured them all.

This is the Gospel of the Lord.

These readings are used in Votive Masses of the apostles, or of one apostle.

Prayer over the Gifts
Lord,
each year we recall the glory

of your apostles Simon and Jude.
Accept our gifts
and prepare us to celebrate these holy mysteries.

Communion Antiphon: If anyone loves me, he will hold to my words, and my Father will love him, and we will come to him, and make our home with him.

Prayer after Communion
Father,
in your Spirit we pray:
may the sacrament we receive today
keep us in your loving care
as we honour the death of Saints Simon and Jude.

PRAY WITHOUT CEASING

NOVEMBER

1 November

ALL SAINTS
Solemnity

Today we offer the Lamb and celebrate the victory of our God in the company of all the redeemed in the heavenly kingdom.

Entrance Antiphon: Let us all rejoice in the Lord and keep a festival in honour of all the saints. Let us join with the angels in joyful praise to the Son of God.

Opening Prayer
Let us pray
  [that the prayers of all the saints
  will bring us forgiveness for our sins]

Father, all-powerful and ever-living God,
today we rejoice in the holy men and women of every time and
    place.
May their prayers bring us your forgiveness and love.

or

Let us pray
  [as we rejoice and keep festival
  in honour of all the saints]

God our Father,
source of all holiness,
the work of your hands is manifest in your saints,
the beauty of your truth is reflected in their faith.

May we who aspire to have part in their joy
be filled with the Spirit that blessed their lives,
so that having shared their faith on earth
we may also know their peace in your kingdom.

FIRST READING

A reading from the book of the Apocalypse   7:2-4. 9-14

I saw a huge number, impossible to count, of people from every nation, race, tribe and language.

I, John, saw another angel rising where the sun rises, carrying the seal of the living God; he called in a powerful voice to the four angels whose duty was to devastate land and sea, 'Wait before you do any damage on land or at sea or to the trees, until we have put the seal on the foreheads of the servants of our God.' Then I heard how many were sealed: a hundred and forty-four thousand, out of all the tribes of Israel.

After that I saw a huge number, impossible to count, of people from every nation, race, tribe and language; they were standing in front of the throne and in front of the Lamb, dressed in white robes and holding palms in their hands. They shouted aloud, 'Victory to our God, who sits on the throne, and to the Lamb!' And all the angels who were standing in a circle round the throne, surrounding the elders and the four animals, prostrated themselves before the throne, and touched the ground with their foreheads, worshipping God with these words, 'Amen. Praise and glory and wisdom and thanksgiving and honour and power and strength to our God for ever and ever. Amen.'

One of the elders then spoke, and asked me, 'Do you know who these people are, dressed in white robes, and where they have come from?' I answered him, 'You can tell me, my lord.' Then he said, These are the people who have been through the great persecution, and they have washed their robes white again in the blood of the Lamb.'

This is the word of the Lord.

Responsorial Psalm   Ps 23:1-6. ℟ cf. v.6

℟ **Such are the men who seek your face, O Lord.**

1. The Lord's is the earth and its fullness,
   the world and all its peoples.
   It is he who set it on the seas;
   on the waters he made it firm. ℟

2. Who shall climb the mountain of the Lord?
   Who shall stand in his holy place?
   The man with clean hands and pure heart,
   who desires not worthless things. ℟

3 He shall receive blessings from the Lord
and reward from the God who saves him.
Such are the men who seek him,
seek the face of the God of Jacob. ℟

SECOND READING

A reading from the first letter of St John 3:1-3
We shall see God as he really is.

Think of the love that the Father has lavished on us,
by letting us be called God's children;
and that is what we are.
Because the world refused to acknowledge him,
therefore it does not acknowledge us.
My dear people, we are already the children of God
but what we are to be in the future has not yet been revealed;
all we know is, that when it is revealed
we shall be like him
because we shall see him as he really is.
Surely everyone who entertains this hope
must purify himself, must try to be as pure as Christ.

This is the word of the Lord.

Gospel Acclamation Mt 11:28
Alleluia, alleluia!
Come to me, all you who labour and are overburdened,
and I will give you rest, says the Lord.
Alleluia!

GOSPEL

A reading from the holy Gospel according to Matthew 5:1-12
Rejoice and be glad for your reward will be great in heaven.

Seeing the crowds, Jesus went up the hill. There he sat down and was joined by his disciples. Then he began to speak. This is what he taught them:

'How happy are the poor in spirit;
theirs is the kingdom of heaven.
Happy the gentle:
they shall have the earth for their heritage.
Happy those who mourn:
they shall be comforted.

> Happy those who hunger and thirst for what is right:
> they shall be satisfied.
> Happy the merciful:
> they shall have mercy shown them.
> Happy the pure in heart:
> they shall see God.
> Happy the peacemakers:
> they shall be called sons of God.
> Happy those who are persecuted in the cause of right:
> theirs is the kingdom of heaven.

'Happy are you when people abuse you and persecute you and speak all kinds of calumny against you on my account. Rejoice and be glad, for your reward will be great in heaven.'

This is the Gospel of the Lord.

The Profession of Faith is made.

Prayer over the Gifts

Lord,
receive our gifts in honour of the holy men and women
who live with you in glory.
May we always be aware
of their concern to help and save us.

Preface of All Saints, P71.

Communion Antiphon: Happy are the pure of heart for they shall see God. Happy the peacemakers; they shall be called sons of God. Happy are they who suffer persecution for justice' sake; the kingdom of heaven is theirs.

Prayer after Communion

Father, holy one,
we praise your glory reflected in the saints.
May we who share at this table
be filled with your love
and prepared for the joy of your kingdom,
where Jesus is Lord for ever and ever.

Solemn Blessing

Bow your heads and pray for God's blessing.

God is the glory and joy of all his saints,
whose memory we celebrate today.
May his blessing be with you always. ℟ **Amen.**

May the prayers of the saints deliver you from present evil;
may their example of holy living
turn your thoughts to the service of God and
   neighbour. ℟ **Amen.**

God's holy Church rejoices that her children
are one with the saints in lasting peace.
May you come to share with them
in all the joys of our Father's house ℟ **Amen.**

May almighty God bless you,
the Father, and the Son, ✠ and the Holy Spirit. ℟ **Amen.**

2 November
THE COMMEMORATION OF ALL THE FAITHFUL DEPARTED

Three Masses are given here for All Souls. Readings are included in the first Mass. Other readings may be used as in the Masses for the Dead, see below pp.1982ff.

First Mass

Entrance Antiphon: Just as Jesus died and rose again, so will the Father bring with him those who have died in Jesus. Just as in Adam all men die, so in Christ all will be made alive.

Opening Prayer
Let us pray
   [for all our departed brothers and sisters]

Merciful Father,
hear our prayers and console us.
As we renew our faith in your Son,
whom you raised from the dead,
strengthen our hope that all our departed brothers and sisters
will share in his resurrection,
who lives and reigns . . .

Proper of Saints, 2 November

FIRST READING

A reading from the prophet Isaiah 25:6-9

The Lord will destroy Death for ever.

On this mountain,
the Lord of hosts will prepare for all peoples
a banquet of rich food.
On this mountain he will remove
the mourning veil covering all peoples,
and the shroud enwrapping all nations,
he will destroy Death for ever.
The Lord will wipe away
the tears from every cheek;
he will take away his people's shame
everywhere on earth,
for the Lord has said so.
That day, it will be said: See, this is our God
in whom we hoped for salvation;
the Lord is the one in whom we hoped.
We exult and we rejoice
that he has saved us.

This is the word of the Lord.

Responsorial Psalm Ps 26:1. 4. 7-9. 13-14. ℟ v.1. Alt. ℟ v.13

℟ **The Lord is my light and my help.**

or

℟ **I believe that I shall see the Lord's goodness in the land of the living.**

1. The Lord is my light and my help;
   whom shall I fear?
   The Lord is the stronghold of my life;
   before whom shall I shrink? ℟

2. There is one thing I ask of the Lord,
   for this I long,
   to live in the house of the Lord,
   all the days of my life,
   to savour the sweetness of the Lord,
   to behold his temple. ℟

3. O Lord, hear my voice when I call;
   have mercy and answer.

It is your face, O Lord, that I seek;
hide not your face. ℟

4 I am sure I shall see the Lord's goodness
in the land of the living.
Hope in him, hold firm and take heart.
Hope in the Lord! ℟

SECOND READING

A reading from the letter of St Paul to the Romans 5:5-11

Having died to make us righteous, is it likely that he would now fail to save us from God's anger?

Hope is not deceptive, because the love of God has been poured into our hearts by the Holy Spirit which has been given us. We were still helpless when at his appointed moment Christ died for sinful men. It is not easy to die even for a good man – though of course for someone really worthy, a man might be prepared to die – but what proves that God loves us is that Christ died for us while we were still sinners. Having died to make us righteous, is it likely that he would now fail to save us from God's anger? When we were reconciled to God by the death of his Son, we were still enemies; now that we have been reconciled, surely we may count on being saved by the life of his Son? Not merely because we have been reconciled but because we are filled with joyful trust in God, through our Lord Jesus Christ, through whom we have already gained our reconciliation.

This is the word of the Lord.

Gospel Acclamation
Jn 6:39

Alleluia, alleluia!
It is my Father's will, says the Lord,
that I should lose nothing
of all that he has given me,
and that I should raise it up on the last day.
Alleluia!

GOSPEL
Year A

A reading from the holy Gospel according to Matthew 11:25-30

You have hidden these things from the learned and have revealed them to mere children.

Jesus exclaimed, 'I bless you, Father, Lord of heaven and of earth, for hiding these things from the learned and the clever and revealing them to mere children. Yes, Father, for that is what it pleased you to do. Everything has been entrusted to me by my Father; and no one knows the Son except the Father, just as no one knows the Father except the Son and those to whom the Son chooses to reveal him.

'Come to me, all you who labour and are overburdened, and I will give you rest. Shoulder my yoke and learn from me, for I am gentle and humble in heart, and you will find rest for your souls. Yes, my yoke is easy and my burden light.'

This is the Gospel of the Lord.

Year B

A reading from the holy Gospel according to Mark 15:33-39; 16:1-6

Jesus gave a loud cry and breathed his last.

When the sixth hour came there was darkness over the whole land until the ninth hour. And at the ninth hour Jesus cried out in a loud voice, 'Eloi, Eloi, lama sabachthani?' which means, 'My God, my God, why have you deserted me?' When some of those who stood by heard this, they said, 'Listen, he is calling on Elijah'. Someone ran and soaked a sponge in vinegar and, putting it on a reed, gave it him to drink saying, 'Wait and see if Elijah will come to take him down'. But Jesus gave a loud cry and breathed his last. And the veil of the Temple was torn in two from top to bottom. The centurion, who was standing in front of him, had seen how he had died, and he said, 'In truth this man was a son of God'.

When the sabbath was over, Mary of Magdala, Mary the mother of James, and Salome, bought spices with which to go and anoint him. And very early in the morning on the first day of the week they went to the tomb, just as the sun was rising.

They had been saying to one another, 'Who will roll away the stone for us from the entrance to the tomb?' But when they looked they could see that the stone – which was very big – had already been rolled back. On entering the tomb they saw a young man in a white robe seated on the right-hand side, and they were struck with amazement. But he said to them, 'There is no need for alarm. You are looking for Jesus of Nazareth, who was crucified: he has risen, he is not here. See, here is the place where they laid him.'

This is the Gospel of the Lord.

Year C

A reading from the holy Gospel according to Luke 7:11-17
Young man, I tell you to get up.

Jesus went to a town called Nain, accompanied by his disciples and a great number of people. When he was near the gate of the town it happened that a dead man was being carried out for burial, the only son of his mother, and she was a widow. And a considerable number of the townspeople were with her. When the Lord saw her he felt sorry for her. 'Do not cry,' he said. Then he went up and put his hand on the bier and the bearers stood still, and he said, 'Young man, I tell you to get up'. And the dead man sat up and began to talk, and Jesus gave him to his mother. Everyone was filled with awe and praised God saying, 'A great prophet has appeared among us; God has visited his people'. And this opinion of him spread throughout Judaea and all over the countryside.

This is the Gospel of the Lord.

Prayer over the Gifts
Lord,
we are united in this sacrament
by the love of Jesus Christ.
Accept these gifts
and receive our brothers and sisters
into the glory of your Son,
who is Lord for ever and ever.

Preface of Christian Death I-V, P77-P81.

Communion Antiphon: I am the resurrection and the life, says the Lord. If anyone believes in me, even though he dies, he will live. Anyone who lives and believes in me, will not die for ever.

Prayer after Communion
Lord God,
may the death and resurrection of Christ
which we celebrate in this eucharist
bring the departed faithful to the peace of your eternal home.
We ask this in the name of Jesus the Lord.

Solemn Blessing
Bow your heads and pray for God's blessing.

In his great love,
that God of all consolation gave man the gift of life.
May he bless you with faith
in the resurrection of his Son,
and with the hope of rising to new life. ℟ **Amen.**

To us who are alive
may he grant forgiveness,
and to all who have died
a place of light and peace. ℟ **Amen.**

As you believe that Jesus rose from the dead,
so may you live with him for ever in joy. ℟ **Amen.**

May almighty God bless you,
the Father, and the Son, ✠ and the Holy Spirit. ℟ **Amen.**

Second Mass

Entrance Antiphon: Give them eternal rest, O Lord, and may your light shine on them for ever.

Opening Prayer
Let us pray
   [for all our departed brothers and sisters]

Lord God,
you are the glory of believers
and the life of the just.
Your Son redeemed us
by dying and rising to life again.
Since our departed brothers and sisters believed in the mystery of our resurrection,
let them share the joys and blessings of the life to come.

Prayer over the Gifts
All-powerful Father,
may this sacrifice wash away
the sins of our departed brothers and sisters in the blood of
    Christ.
You cleansed them in the waters of baptism.
In your loving mercy grant them pardon and peace.

Preface of Christian Death I-V, P77-P81.

Communion Antiphon: May eternal light shine on them, O Lord, with all your saints for ever, for you are rich in mercy. Give them eternal rest, O Lord, and may perpetual light shine on them for ever, for you are rich in mercy.

Prayer after Communion
Lord,
in this sacrament you give us your crucified and risen Son.
Bring to the glory of the resurrection our departed brothers and
    sisters
who have been purified by this holy mystery.

Solemn Blessing: as in First Mass, see above p.1770.

Third Mass

Entrance Antiphon: God, who raised Jesus from the dead, will give new life to our own mortal bodies through his Spirit living in us.

Opening Prayer
Let us pray
    [for all our departed brothers and sisters]

God, our creator and redeemer,
by your power Christ conquered death
and returned to you in glory.
May all your people who have gone before us in faith
share his victory
and enjoy the vision of your glory for ever.

Prayer over the Gifts
Lord,
in your kindness accept these gifts for our departed brothers and
    sisters

and for all who sleep in Christ.
May his perfect sacrifice
free them from the power of death
and give them eternal life.

Preface of Christian Death I-V, P77-P81.

Communion Antiphon: We are waiting for our Saviour, the Lord Jesus Christ; he will transfigure our lowly bodies into copies of his own glorious body.

Prayer after Communion
Lord,
may our sacrifice bring peace and forgiveness
to our brothers and sisters who have died.
Bring the new life given to them in baptism
to the fullness of eternal joy.

Solemn Blessing: as in First Mass, see above, p.1770.

3 November
St Martin de Porres, religious
Optional Memorial

Born at Lima in Peru in 1579 of a native mother and Spanish father, Martin entered the Dominican Order in Lima, where he continued his profession as medical assistant. He lived a life of fasting and prayer and died in 1639.

Common of holy men and women: religious, pp.1898ff.

Opening Prayer
Lord,
you led Martin de Porres by a life of humility
to eternal glory.
May we follow his example
and be exalted with him in the kingdom of heaven.

FIRST READING

A reading from the letter of St Paul to the Philippians   4:4-9
Fill your minds with everything that is pure.

I want you to be happy, always happy in the Lord; I repeat, what

Proper of Saints, 3 November 1773

I want is your happiness. Let your tolerance be evident to everyone: the Lord is very near. There is no need to worry; but if there is anything you need, pray for it, asking God for it with prayer and thanksgiving, and that peace of God, which is so much greater than we can understand, will guard your hearts and your thoughts, in Christ Jesus. Finally, brothers, fill your minds with everything that is true, everything that is noble, everything that is good and pure, everything that we love and honour, and everything that can be thought virtuous or worthy of praise. Keep doing all the things that you learnt from me and have been taught by me and have heard or seen that I do. Then the God of peace will be with you.

This is the word of the Lord.

Responsorial Psalm Ps 130

℟ **Keep my soul in peace before you, O Lord.**

1 O Lord, my heart is not proud
 nor haughty my eyes.
 I have not gone after things too great
 nor marvels beyond me. ℟

2 Truly I have set my soul
 in silence and peace.
 A weaned child on its mother's breast,
 even so is my soul. ℟

3 O Israel, hope in the Lord
 both now and for ever. ℟

Gospel Acclamation Jn 13:34

Alleluia, alleluia!
I give you a new commandment:
love one another just as I have loved you,
says the Lord.
Alleluia!

GOSPEL

A reading from the holy Gospel according to Matthew 22:34-40
You must love the Lord your God and your neighbour as yourself.

When the Pharisees heard that Jesus had silenced the Sadducees they got together and, to disconcert him, one of them put a question, 'Master, which is the greatest commandment of the

Law?' Jesus said, 'You must love the Lord your God with all your heart, with all your soul, and with all your mind. This is the greatest and the first commandment. The second resembles it: You must love your neighbour as yourself. On these two commandments hang the whole Law, and the Prophets also.'

This is the Gospel of the Lord.

4 November

St Charles Borromeo, bishop — Memorial

Born in Italy in 1538, Charles Borromeo became a prominent defender of the faith at the time of the Counter-Reformation. He was ordained young, studied canon and civil law, was made a cardinal and Archbishop of Milan by his uncle, Pope Pius IV in 1559. He played a leading part in the last sessions of the Council of Trent, and drafted the Catechism. He was a reforming archbishop, concerned with administration and with the moral life of the clery. He established seminaries, organisations for the religious education of children, and in the plague of 1576 was active in the care of the sick. He died in 1584.

Common of pastors: bishops, pp.1878ff.

Opening Prayer

Father,
keep in your people the spirit
which filled Charles Borromeo.
Let your Church be continually renewed
and show the image of Christ to the world
by being conformed to his likeness,
who lives and reigns . . .

FIRST READING

A reading from the letter of St Paul to the Romans   12:3-13
Our gifts differ according to the grace given to us.

In the light of the grace I have received I want to urge each one among you not to exaggerate his real importance. Each of you must judge himself soberly by the standards of the faith God has given him. Just as each of our bodies has several parts and each part has a separate function, so all of us, in union with Christ, form one body, and as parts of it we belong to each other. Our gifts differ according to the grace given us. If your gift is prophecy, then use it as your faith suggests; if administration, then use it for administration; if teaching, then use it for teaching. Let the preachers deliver sermons, the almsgivers give freely, the officials be diligent and those who do works of mercy do them cheerfully.

Do not let your love be a pretence, but sincerely prefer good to evil. Love each other as much as brothers should, and have a profound respect for each other. Work for the Lord with untiring effort and with great earnestness of spirit. If you have hope, this will make you cheerful. Do not give up if trials come; and keep on praying. If any of the saints are in need you must share with them; and you should make hospitality your special care.

This is the word of the Lord.

Responsorial Psalm   Ps 88:2-5. 21-22. 25. 27. ℟ cf. v.2

℟ **I will sing for ever of your love, O Lord;**

1 I will sing for ever of your love, O Lord;
through all ages my mouth will proclaim your truth.
Of this I am sure, that your love lasts for ever,
that your truth is firmly established as the heavens. ℟

2 'I have made a covenant with my chosen one;
I have sworn to David my servant:
I will establish your dynasty for ever
and set up your throne through all ages. ℟

3 'I have found David my servant
and with my holy oil anointed him.
My hand shall always be with him
and my arm shall make him strong. ℟

4 'My truth and my love shall be with him;
by my name his might shall be exalted.
He will say to me: "You are my father,
my God, the rock who saves me." ' ℟

Gospel Acclamation   Jn 10:14
Alleluia, alleluia!
I am the good shepherd, says the Lord;
I know my own sheep and my own know me.
Alleluia!

Proper of Saints, 4 November

GOSPEL

A reading from the holy Gospel according to John 10:11-16
The good shepherd is one who lays down his life for his sheep.

Jesus said:
'I am the good shepherd:
the good shepherd is one who lays down his life for his sheep.
The hired man, since he is not the shepherd
and the sheep do not belong to him,
abandons the sheep and runs away
as soon as he sees a wolf coming,
and then the wolf attacks and scatters the sheep;
this is because he is only a hired man
and has no concern for the sheep.
I am the good shepherd;
I know my own
and my own know me
just as the Father knows me
and I know the Father;
and I lay down my life for my sheep.
And there are other sheep I have
that are not of this fold,
and these I have to lead as well.
They too will listen to my voice,
and there will be only one flock,
and one shepherd.'

This is the Gospel of the Lord.

Prayer over the Gifts
Lord,
look with kindness on the gifts we bring to your altar
on this feast of Saint Charles.
You made him an example of virtue
and concern for the pastoral ministry.
Through the power of this sacrifice
may we abound in good works.

Prayer after Communion
Lord,
may the holy mysteries we have received
give us that courage and strength
which made Saint Charles faithful in his ministry
and constant in his love.

Proper of Saints, 9 November

9 November
THE DEDICATION OF THE LATERAN BASILICA
Feast

Prayers and antiphons from Common of the dedication of a Church, Anniversary, pp.1855ff.

FIRST READING

A reading from the prophet Ezekiel 47:1-2. 8-9. 12

I saw a stream of water coming from the Temple, bringing life to all wherever it flowed.

The angel brought me to the entrance of the Temple, where a stream came out from under the Temple threshold and flowed eastwards, since the Temple faced east. The water flowed from under the right side of the Temple, south of the altar. He took me out by the north gate and led me right round outside as far as the outer east gate where the water flowed out on the right-hand side. He said, 'This water flows east down to the Arabah and to the sea; and flowing into the sea it makes its waters wholesome. Wherever the river flows, all living creatures teeming in it will live. Fish will be very plentiful, for wherever the water goes it brings health, and life teems wherever the river flows. Along the river, on either bank, will grow every kind of fruit tree with leaves that never wither and fruit that never fails; they will bear new fruit every month, because this water comes from the sanctuary. And their fruit will be good to eat and the leaves medicinal.'

This is the word of the Lord.

Responsorial Psalm Ps 45:2-3. 5-6. 8-9. ℟ v.5

℟ **The waters of a river give joy to God's city, the holy place where the Most High dwells.**

1 God is for us a refuge and strength,
a helper close at hand, in time of distress:
so we shall not fear though the earth should rock,
though the mountains fall into the depths of the sea. ℟

2 The waters of a river give joy to God's city,
the holy place where the Most High dwells.
God is within, it cannot be shaken;
God will help it at the dawning of the day. ℟ (continued)

3 The Lord of hosts is with us:
   the God of Jacob is our stronghold.
   Come, consider the works of the Lord,
   the redoubtable deeds he has done on the earth.

   ℟ **The waters of a river give joy to God's city,
   the holy place where the Most High dwells.**

SECOND READING

A reading from the first letter of St Paul   3:9-11. 16-17
to the Corinthians
You are the temple of God.

You are God's building. By the grace God gave me, I succeeded as an architect and laid the foundations, on which someone else is doing the building. Everyone doing the building must work carefully. For the foundation, nobody can lay any other than the one which has already been laid, that is Jesus Christ.

Didn't you realise that you were God's temple and that the Spirit of God was living among you? If anybody should destroy the temple of God, God will destroy him, because the temple of God is sacred; and you are that temple.

This is the word of the Lord.

Gospel Acclamation   2 Chron 7:16
   Alleluia, alleluia!
   I have chosen and consecrated this house, says the Lord,
   for my name to be there for ever.
   Alleluia!

GOSPEL

A reading from the holy Gospel according to John   2:13-22
He was speaking of the sanctuary that was his body.

Just before the Jewish Passover Jesus went up to Jerusalem, and in the Temple he found people selling cattle and sheep and pigeons, and the money changers sitting at their counters there. Making a whip out of some cord, he drove them all out of the Temple, cattle and sheep as well, scattered the money changers' coins, knocked their tables over and said to the pigeon-sellers, 'Take all this out of here and stop turning my Father's house into a market'. Then his disciples remembered the words of scripture: Zeal for your house will devour me. The Jews intervened and said, 'What sign can you show us to justify what you have done?' Jesus answered, 'Destroy this sanctuary, and in three days I will raise it up'. The Jews replied, 'It has taken forty-six years to build this sanctuary: are you going to raise it up in three days?' But he was speaking of the sanctuary that was his body, and when Jesus rose from the dead, his disciples remembered that he had said this, and they believed the scripture and the words he had said.

This is the Gospel of the Lord.

10 November

St Leo the Great, pope and doctor of the Church — Memorial

Elected pope in 440, Leo consolidated the organisation of the Church and its government from Rome at a time of civil and doctrinal disorder: Attila's invasion was threatening, and the monophysite heresy was abroad. He persuaded the Huns to withdraw beyond the Danube, and negotiated with the Vandals when they seized Rome in 455. The Council of Chalcedon in 451 restated the doctrine of the incarnation, and the primacy of Peter. Many of his sermons and letters survive, and reveal him as a man of clear and forceful intellect and faith. He died about 461.

Common of pastors: popes, pp.1876ff., or of doctors of the Church, pp.1887ff.

Opening Prayer
God our Father,
you will never allow the power of hell
to prevail against your Church,
founded on the rock of the apostle Peter.
Let the prayers of Pope Leo the Great
keep us faithful to your truth
and secure in your peace.

FIRST READING

A reading from the book of Ecclesiasticus 39:6-10
He will be filled with the spirit of understanding.

If it is the will of the great Lord,
the scholar will be filled with the spirit of understanding,
he will shower forth words of wisdom,
and in prayer give thanks to the Lord.

He will grow upright in purpose and learning,
he will ponder the Lord's hidden mysteries.
He will display the instruction he has received,
taking his pride in the Law of the Lord's covenant.
Many will praise his understanding,
and it will never be forgotten.
His memory will not disappear,
generation after generation his name will live.
Nations will proclaim his wisdom,
the assembly will celebrate his praises.

This is the word of the Lord.

Responsorial Psalm Ps 36:3-6. 30-31. ℟ v.30
℟ **The just man's mouth utters wisdom.**

1 If you trust in the Lord and do good,
   then you will live in the land and be secure.
   If you find your delight in the Lord,
   he will grant your heart's desire. ℟

2 Commit your life to the Lord,
   trust in him and he will act,
   so that your justice breaks forth like the light,
   your cause like the noon-day sun. ℟

3 The just man's mouth utters wisdom
   and his lips speak what is right;
   the law of his God is in his heart,
   his steps shall be saved from stumbling. ℟

Gospel Acclamation Mk 1:17
Alleluia, alleluia!
Follow me, says the Lord,
and I will make you into fishers of men.
Alleluia!

GOSPEL

A reading from the holy Gospel according to Matthew 16:13-19
You are Peter and on this rock I will build my Church.

When Jesus came to the region of Caesarea Philippi he put this question to his disciples, 'Who do people say the Son of Man is?' And they said, 'Some say he is John the Baptist, some Elijah, and others Jeremiah or one of the prophets'. 'But you,' he said,' who do you say I am?' Then Simon Peter spoke up, 'You are the Christ,' he said, 'the Son of the living God'. Jesus replied, 'Simon son of Jonah, you are a happy man! Because it was not flesh and blood that revealed this to you but my Father in heaven. So I now say to you: You are Peter and on this rock I will build my Church. And the gates of the underworld can never hold out against it. I will give you the keys of the kingdom of heaven: whatever you bind on earth shall be considered bound in heaven; whatever you loose on earth shall be considered loosed in heaven.'

This is the Gospel of the Lord.

Prayer over the Gifts
Lord,
by these gifts we bring,
fill your people with your light.
May your Church continue to grow everywhere under your guidance
and under the leadership of shepherds pleasing to you.

Prayer after Communion
Lord,
as you nourish your Church with this holy banquet,
govern it always with your love.
Under your powerful guidance
may it grow in freedom
and continue in loyalty to the faith.

11 November
St Martin of Tours, bishop — Memorial

Born about 335, in a pagan family, Martin was a soldier in the Roman army until his conversion and baptism. In 360 he joined St Hilary at Poitiers and founded the first monastery in Gaul, at Liguge. He was made Bishop of Tours in 372, and did much to spread monasticism in Gaul.

Entrance Antiphon: I will raise up for myself a faithful priest; he will do what is in my heart and in my mind, says the Lord.

Opening Prayer
Father,
by his life and death
Martin of Tours offered you worship and praise.

Renew in our hearts the power of your love,
so that neither death nor life may separate us from you.

FIRST READING

A reading from the prophet Isaiah 61:1-3

The Lord God has anointed me and sent me to bring good news to the poor.

The spirit of the Lord has been given to me,
for the Lord has anointed me.
He has sent me to bring good news to the poor,
to bind up hearts that are broken;

to proclaim liberty to captives,
freedom to those in prison;
to proclaim a year of favour from the Lord,
a day of vengeance for our God,
to comfort all those who mourn and to give them
for ashes a garland;
for mourning robe the oil of gladness,
for despondency, praise.

This is the word of the Lord.

Responsorial Psalm Ps 88: 2-5. 21-22. 25. 27. ℟ cf. v.2

℟ **I will sing for ever of your love, O Lord.**

1 I will sing for ever of your love, O Lord;
 through all ages my mouth will proclaim your truth.
 Of this I am sure, that your love lasts for ever,
 that your truth is firmly established as the heavens. ℟

2 'I have made a covenant with my chosen one;
 I have sworn to David my servant:
 I will establish your dynasty for ever
 and set up your throne through all ages. ℟

3 'I have found David my servant
 and with my holy oil anointed him.
 My hand shall always be with him
 and my arm shall make him strong. ℟

4 'My truth and my love shall be with him;
 by my name his might shall be exalted.
 He will say to me: "You are my father,
 my God, the rock who saves me." ' ℟

Gospel Acclamation
Jn 13:34
Alleluia, alleluia!
I give you a new commandment:
love one another, just as I have loved you,
says the Lord.
Alleluia!

GOSPEL

A reading from the holy Gospel according to Matthew 25:31-40
In so far as you did this to one of the least of these brothers of mine, you did it to me.

Jesus said to his disciples: 'When the Son of Man comes in his glory, escorted by all the angels, then he will take his seat on his throne of glory. All the nations will be assembled before him and he will separate men one from another as the shepherd separates sheep from goats. He will place the sheep on his right hand and the goats on his left. Then the King will say to those on his right hand, "Come, you whom my Father has blessed, take for your heritage the kingdom prepared for you since the foundation of the world. For I was hungry and you gave me food; I was thirsty and you gave me drink; I was a stranger and you made me welcome; naked and you clothed me, sick and you visited me, in prison and you came to see me." Then the virtuous will say to him in reply, "Lord, when did we see you hungry and feed you; or thirsty and give you drink? When did we see you a stranger and make you welcome; naked and clothe you; sick or in prison and go to see you?" And the King will answer, "I tell you solemnly, in so far as you did this to one of the least of these brothers of mine, you did it to me." '

This is the Gospel of the Lord.

Prayer over the Gifts
Lord God,
bless these gifts we present
on this feast of Saint Martin.
May this eucharist help us
in joy and sorrow.

Communion Antiphon: I tell you, anything you did for the least of my brothers, you did for me, says the Lord.

Prayer after Communion

Lord,
you have renewed us with the sacrament of unity:
help us to follow your will in all that we do.
As Saint Martin gave himself completely to your service,
may we rejoice in belonging to you.

12 November

St Josaphat, bishop and martyr   Memorial

Born in the Ukraine about 1580, ordained about 1604, became a monk. He was a noted theologian and preacher, and loyal to Rome. He was made bishop of Polotz in 1617, and embarked on a thorough-going pastoral reform, visiting his clergy, seeing that the people were instructed and taking an interest in the liturgy. His reforms aroused hostility, and he was murdered at Vitebsk, during a pastoral visit, in 1623.

Common of martyrs, pp. 1865ff., or of pastors: bishops, pp. 1878ff.

Opening Prayer

Lord,
fill your Church with the Spirit
that gave Saint Josaphat courage
to lay down his life for his people.
By his prayers
may your Spirit make us strong
and willing to offer our lives
for our brothers and sisters.

FIRST READING

A reading from the letter of St Paul to the Ephesians   4:1-7. 11-13

The work of service, building up the body of Christ.

I, the prisoner in the Lord, implore you to lead a life worthy of your vocation. Bear with one another charitably, in complete selflessness, gentleness and patience. Do all you can to preserve the unity of the Spirit by the peace that binds you together. There is one Body, one Spirit, just as you were all called into one and the same hope when you were called. There is one Lord, one faith, one baptism, and one God who is Father of all, over all, through all and within all.

Each one of us, however, has been given his own share of grace, given as Christ allotted it. And to some, his gift was that they should be apostles, to some, prophets; to some, evangelists; to some, pastors and teachers so that the saints together make a unity in the work of service, building up the body of Christ. In this way we are all to come to unity in our faith and in our knowledge of the Son of God, until we become the perfect Man, fully mature with the fullness of Christ himself.

This is the word of the Lord.

Responsorial Psalm
Ps 1:1-4. 6. ℟ v.2. Alt ℟ Ps 39:5. Alt. ℟ Ps 91:13-14

℟ **His delight is the law of the Lord.**

or

℟ **Happy the man who has placed his trust in the Lord.**

or

℟ **The just will flourish like the palm-tree in the courts of our God.**

1 Happy indeed is the man
who follows not the counsel of the wicked;
nor lingers in the way of sinners
nor sits in the company of scorners,
but whose delight is the law of the Lord
and who ponders his law day and night.   ℟

2 He is like a tree that is planted
beside the flowing waters,
that yields its fruit in due season
and whose leaves shall never fade;
and all that he does shall prosper.   ℟

3 Not so are the wicked, not so!
For they like winnowed chaff
shall be driven away by the wind;
for the Lord guards the way of the just
but the way of the wicked leads to doom.   ℟

Gospel Acclamation
Jn 15:9. 5
Alleluia, alleluia!
Remain in my love, says the Lord;

whoever remains in me, with me in him,
bears fruit in plenty.
Alleluia!

GOSPEL

A reading from the holy Gospel according to John 17:20-26

I want them to be with me where I am.

Jesus raised his eyes to heaven and said:

'Holy Father,
I pray not only for these,
but for those also
who through their words will believe in me.
May they all be one.
Father, may they be one in us,
as you are in me and I am in you,
so that the world may believe it was you who sent me.
I have given them the glory you gave to me,
that they may be one as we are one.
With me in them and you in me,
may they be so completely one
that the world will realise that it was you who sent me
and that I have loved them as much as you loved me.
Father,
I want those you have given me
to be with me where I am,
so that they may always see the glory
you have given me
because you loved me
before the foundation of the world.
Father, Righteous One,
the world has not known you,
but I have known you,
and these have known
that you have sent me.
I have made your name known to them
and will continue to make it known,
so that the love with which you loved me may be in them,
and so that I may be in them.'

This is the Gospel of the Lord.

Proper of Saints, 15 November

Prayer over the Gifts
God of mercy,
pour out your blessing upon these gifts,
and make us strong in the faith
which Saint Josaphat professed by shedding his blood.

Prayer after Communion
Lord,
may this eucharist we have shared
fill us with your Spirit of courage and peace.
Let the example of Saint Josaphat
inspire us to spend our lives
working for the honour and unity of your Church.

15 November

St Albert the Great, bishop and doctor of the Church

Optional Memorial

Born about 1200. He was a member of the Order of Preachers, and a teacher of Thomas Aquinas. He was for a short period Bishop of Ratisbon, but resigned in order to return to the study and writing which was his real metier. His many works of theology and philosophy foreshadow those of his more famous pupil. He was interested in all the fields of study of his time. He died in 1280.

Common of pastors: bishops, pp.1878ff., or of doctors of the Church, pp.1887ff.

Opening Prayer
God our Father,
you endowed Saint Albert with the talent
of combining human wisdom with divine faith.
Keep us true to his teachings
that the advance of human knowledge
may deepen our knowledge and love of you.

FIRST READING

A reading from the book of Ecclesiasticus 15:1-6
He will fill him with the spirit of wisdom and understanding.

Whoever fears the Lord will act like this,

and whoever grasps the Law will obtain wisdom.
She will come to meet him like a mother,
and receive him like a virgin bride.
She will give him the bread of understanding to eat,
and the water of wisdom to drink.
He will lean on her and will not fall,
he will rely on her and not be put to shame.
She will raise him high above his neighbours,
and in full assembly she will open his mouth.
He will find happiness and a crown of joy,
he will inherit an everlasting name.

This is the word of the Lord.

Responsorial Psalm Ps 118:9-14. ℟ v.12

℟ **Lord, teach me your statutes.**

1 How shall the young remain sinless?
   By obeying your word.
   I have sought you with all my heart:
   let me not stray from your commands.   ℟

2 I treasure your promise in my heart
   lest I sin against you.
   Blessed are you, O Lord;
   teach me your statutes.   ℟

3 With my tongue I have recounted
   the decrees of your lips.
   I rejoiced to do your will
   as though all riches were mine.   ℟

Gospel Acclamation cf. Acts 16:14
Alleluia, alleluia!
Open our heart, O Lord,
to accept the words of your Son.
Alleluia!

GOSPEL

A reading from the holy Gospel according to Matthew   13:47-52
They collect the good ones in a basket and throw away those that are no use.

Jesus said to the crowds: 'The kingdom of heaven is like a dragnet cast out into the sea that brings in a haul of all kinds. When it is full, the fishermen haul it ashore; then, sitting down, they collect the good ones in a basket and throw away those that are no use. This is how it will be at the end of time; the angels will appear and separate the wicked from the just to throw them into the blazing furnace where there will be weeping and grinding of teeth.

'Have you understood all this?' They said, 'Yes.' And he said to them 'Well then, every scribe who becomes a disciple of the kingdom of heaven is like a householder who brings out from his storeroom things both new and old.'

This is the Gospel of the Lord.

16 November

St Margaret of Scotland

Optional Memorial

Born, perhaps in Hungary, in 1045, Margaret took refuge in the court of Malcolm III of Scotland after the Battle of Hastings. She married him in 1070. She lived with great piety, spending her time in prayer and fasting, caring for the poor. She used her position to reform the abuses of the time, and had synods held to this end. The Church of the Holy Trinity at Dunfermline was founded at her benefaction.

Common of holy men and women: those who worked for the underprivileged, p.1900.

Opening Prayer
Lord,
you gave Saint Margaret of Scotland
a special love for the poor.
Let her example and prayers
help us to become a living sign of your goodness.

FIRST READING

A reading from the prophet Isaiah 58:6-11
Share your bread with the hungry.

Is not this the sort of fast that pleases me
– it is the Lord who speaks –
to break unjust fetters
and undo the thongs of the yoke,

to let the oppressed go free,
and break every yoke,
to share your bread with the hungry,

and shelter the homeless poor,

to clothe the man you see to be naked
and not turn from your own kin?
Then will your light shine like the dawn
and your wound be quickly healed over.

Your integrity will go before you
and the glory of the Lord behind you.
Cry, and the Lord will answer;
call, and he will say, 'I am here.'

If you do away with the yoke,
the clenched fist, the wicked word,
if you give your bread to the hungry,
and relief to the oppressed,

your light will rise in the darkness,
and your shadows become like noon.
The Lord will always guide you,
giving you relief in desert places.

He will give strength to your bones
and you shall be like a watered garden,
like a spring of water
whose waters never run dry.

This is the word of the Lord.

Responsorial Psalm Ps 111:1-9. ℟ v.1

℟ **Happy the man who fears the Lord.**

or

℟ **Alleluia!**

1 Happy the man who fears the Lord,
 who takes delight in his commands.
 His sons will be powerful on earth;
 the children of the upright are blessed. ℟

2 Riches and wealth are in his house;
 his justice stands firm for ever.
 He is a light in the darkness for the upright:
 he is generous, merciful and just. ℟

3 The good man takes pity and lends,
 he conducts his affairs with honour.

Proper of Saints, 16 November 1791

The just man will never waver:
he will be remembered for ever. ℟

4 He has no fear of evil news;
with a firm heart he trusts in the Lord.
With a steadfast heart he will not fear;
he will see the downfall of his foes. ℟

5 Open-handed, he gives to the poor;
his justice stands firm for ever.
His head will be raised in glory. ℟

Gospel Acclamation Jn 13:34
Alleluia, alleluia!
I give you a new commandment:
love one another, just as I have loved you,
says the Lord.
Alleluia!

GOSPEL

A reading from the holy Gospel according to John 15:9-17
You are my friends if you do what I command you.

Jesus said to his disciples,

'As the Father has loved me,
so I have loved you.
Remain in my love.
If you keep my commandments
you will remain in my love,
just as I have kept my Father's commandments
and remain in his love.
I have told you this
so that my own joy may be in you
and your joy be complete.
This is my commandment:
love one another,
as I have loved you.
A man can have no greater love
than to lay down his life for his friends.
You are my friends,
if you do what I command you.
I shall not call you servants any more,
because a servant does not know

his master's business;
I call you friends,
because I have made known to you
everything I have learnt from my Father.
You did not choose me,
no, I chose you;
and I commissioned you
to go out and to bear fruit,
fruit that will last;
and then the Father will give you
anything you ask him in my name.
What I command you
is to love one another.'

This is the Gospel of the Lord.

Also 16 November

St Gertrude, virgin Optional Memorial

Born in 1256, given into a convent at the age of five, she received a broad education particularly in Latin, music and painting. When she was about 25, she underwent a conversion, and from then on devoted herself to a life of contemplation, based on the liturgy. She wrote books concerned with the mystical life, and a collection of prayers, called Spiritual Exercises. She was devoted to the Sacred Heart, and writes about her visions of the Sacred Heart with beauty and simplicity.

Common of virgins, pp.1889ff., or of holy men and women: religious, pp.1898ff.

Opening Prayer
Father,
you filled the heart of Saint Gertrude
with the presence of your love.
Bring light into our darkness
and let us experience the joy of your presence
and the power of your grace.

FIRST READING

A reading from the letter of St Paul to the Ephesians 3:14-19
To know the love of Christ, which is beyond all knowledge.

This is what I pray, kneeling before the Father, from whom every family, whether spiritual or natural, takes its name:

Out of his infinite glory, may he give you the power through his Spirit for your hidden self to grow strong, so that Christ may live in your hearts through faith, and then, planted in love and built on love, you will with all the saints have strength to grasp the breadth and the length, the height and the depth, until, knowing the love of Christ which is beyond all knowledge, you are filled with the utter fullness of God.

This is the word of the Lord.

Responsorial Psalm   Ps 22. ℟ v.1

℟ **The Lord is my shepherd
there is nothing I shall want.**

1 The Lord is my shepherd;
there is nothing I shall want.
Fresh and green are the pastures
where he gives me repose.
Near restful waters he leads me,
to revive my drooping spirit. ℟

2 He guides me along the right path;
he is true to his name.
If I should walk in the valley of darkness
no evil would I fear.
You are there with your crook and your staff;
with these you give me comfort. ℟

3 You have prepared a banquet for me
in the sight of my foes.
My head you have anointed with oil;
my cup is overflowing. ℟

4 Surely goodness and kindness shall follow me
all the days of my life.
In the Lord's own house shall I dwell
for ever and ever. ℟

Gospel Acclamation   Jn 15:9. 5

Alleluia, alleluia!
Remain in my love, says the Lord;
whoever remains in me, with me in him,
bears fruit in plenty.
Alleluia!

Proper of Saints, 16 November

GOSPEL

A reading from the holy Gospel according to John 15:1-8
Whoever remains in me, with me in him, bears fruit in plenty.

Jesus said to his disciples:

'I am the true vine,
and my Father is the vinedresser.
Every branch in me that bears no fruit
he cuts away,
and every branch that does bear fruit he prunes
to make it bear even more.
You are pruned already,
by means of the word that I have spoken to you.
Make your home in me, as I make mine in you.
As a branch cannot bear fruit all by itself,
but must remain part of the vine,
neither can you unless you remain in me.
I am the vine,
you are the branches.
Whoever remains in me, with me in him,
bears fruit in plenty;
for cut off from me you can do nothing.
Anyone who does not remain in me
is like a branch that has been thrown away
– he withers;
these branches are collected and thrown on the fire,
and they are burnt.
If you remain in me
and my words remain in you,
you may ask what you will
and you shall get it.
It is the glory of my Father that you should bear much fruit,
and then you will be my disciples.'

This is the Gospel of the Lord.

17 November
St Elizabeth of Hungary, religious — Memorial

Born in 1207, daughter of the King of Hungary, married in 1221 Louis the Landgrave of Thuringia. She turned naturally to the ascetic life, and was influenced by Franciscans she met in Germany. After her husband's death on the Crusade in 1227, she lived with complete austerity, visiting the poor and caring for the sick. She died in 1231.

Common of holy men and women: those who worked for the underprivileged, p.1900.

Opening Prayer
Father,
you helped Elizabeth of Hungary
to recognise and honour Christ
in the poor of this world.
Let her prayers help us to serve our brothers and sisters
in time of trouble and need.

FIRST READING
A reading from the first letter of St John 3:14-18
We, too, ought to give up our lives for our brothers.

We have passed out of death and into life,
and of this we can be sure
because we love our brothers.
If you refuse to love, you must remain dead;
to hate your brother is to be a murderer,
and murderers, as you know, do not have eternal life in them.
This has taught us love –
that he gave up his life for us;
and we, too, ought to give up our lives for our brothers.
If a man who was rich enough in this world's goods
saw that one of his brothers was in need,
but closed his heart to him,
how could the love of God be living in him?
My children,
our love is not to be just words or mere talk,
but something real and active.

This is the word of the Lord.

Responsorial Psalm
Ps 33:2-11. ℟ v.2

℟ **I will bless the Lord at all times.**

or

℟ **Taste and see that the Lord is good.**

1. I will bless the Lord at all times,
   his praise always on my lips;
   in the Lord my soul shall make its boast.
   The humble shall hear and be glad. ℟

2. Glorify the Lord with me.
   Together let us praise his name.
   I sought the Lord and he answered me;
   from all my terrors he set me free. ℟

3. Look towards him and be radiant;
   let your faces not be abashed.
   This poor man called; the Lord heard him
   and rescued him from all his distress. ℟

4. The angel of the Lord is encamped
   around those who revere him, to rescue them.
   Taste and see that the Lord is good.
   He is happy who seeks refuge in him. ℟

5. Revere the Lord, you his saints.
   They lack nothing, those who revere him.
   Strong lions suffer want and go hungry
   but those who seek the Lord lack no blessing. ℟

Gospel Acclamation
Jn 13:34

Alleluia, alleluia!
I give you a new commandment:
love one another just as I have loved you,
says the Lord.
Alleluia!

GOSPEL

A reading from the holy Gospel according to Luke
6:27-38

Be compassionate as your Father is compassionate.

Jesus said to his disciples: 'I say this to you who are listening: Love your enemies, do good to those who hate you, bless those who curse you, pray for those who treat you badly. To the man who slaps you on one cheek, present the other cheek too; to the man who takes your cloak from you, do not refuse your tunic. Give to everyone who asks you, and do not ask for your property back from the man who robs you. Treat others as you would like them to treat you. If you love those who love you, what thanks can you expect? Even sinners love those who love them. And if you do good to those who do good to you, what thanks can you expect? For even sinners do that much. And if you lend to those from whom you hope to receive, what thanks can you expect? Even sinners lend to sinners to get back the same amount. Instead, love your enemies and do good, and lend without any hope of return. You will have a great reward, and you will be sons of the Most High, for he himself is kind to the ungrateful and the wicked.

'Be compassionate as your Father is compassionate. Do not judge, and you will not be judged yourselves; do not condemn, and you will not be condemned yourselves; grant pardon, and you will be pardoned. Give, and there will be gifts for you: a full measure, pressed down, shaken together, and running over, will be poured into your lap; because the amount you measure out is the amount you will be given back.'

This is the Gospel of the Lord.

18 November

The Dedication of the Basilicas of Ss Peter and Paul, Apostles

Optional Memorial

The tomb of St Peter in the Vatican was the site for the great basilica of St Peter built by the Emperor Constantine about 330. The basilica of St Paul was built about the end of the fourth century. These two sites have always been centres of Christian pilgrimage.

Entrance Antiphon: You have made them princes over all the earth; they declared your fame to all generations; for ever will the nations declare your praise.

Opening Prayer

Lord,
give your Church the protection of the apostles.
From them it first received the faith of Christ.
May they help your Church to grow in your grace
until the end of time.

FIRST READING

A reading from the Acts of the Apostles 28:11-16. 30-31
So we came to Rome.

At the end of three months we set sail in a ship that had wintered in the island; she came from Alexandria and her figurehead was the Twins. We put in at Syracuse and spent three days there; from there we followed the coast up to Rhegium. After one day there a south wind sprang up and on the second day we made Puteoli, where we found some brothers and were much rewarded by staying a week with them. And so we came to Rome.

When the brothers there heard of our arrival they came to meet us, as far as the Forum of Appius and the Three Taverns. When Paul saw them he thanked God and took courage. On our arrival in Rome Paul was allowed to stay in lodgings of his own with the soldier who guarded him.

Paul spent the whole of the two years in his own rented lodging. He welcomed all who came to visit him, proclaiming the kingdom of God and teaching the truth about the Lord Jesus Christ with complete freedom and without hindrance from anyone.

This is the word of the Lord.

Responsorial Psalm

Ps 97:1-6. ℟ v.2

℟ **The Lord has shown his salvation to the nations.**

1. Sing a new song to the Lord
   for he has worked wonders.
   His right hand and his holy arm
   have brought salvation. ℟

2. The Lord has made known his salvation;
   has shown his justice to the nations.
   He has remembered his truth and love
   for the house of Israel. ℟

3. All the ends of the earth have seen
   the salvation of our God.
   Shout to the Lord all the earth,
   ring out your joy. ℟

4. Sing psalms to the Lord with the harp
   with the sound of music.

With trumpets and the sound of the horn
acclaim the King, the Lord. ℟

Gospel Acclamation
Alleluia, alleluia!
We praise you, O God, we acknowledge you to be the Lord.
The glorious company of the apostles praise you.
Alleluia!

GOSPEL

A reading from the holy Gospel according to Matthew 14:22-33
Tell me to come to you across the water.

After the crowds had eaten as much as they wanted, Jesus made the disciples get into the boat and go on ahead to the other side while he would send the crowds away. After sending the crowds away he went up into the hills by himself to pray. When evening came, he was there alone, while the boat, by now far out on the lake, was battling with a heavy sea for there was a head-wind. In the fourth watch of the night he went towards them, walking on the lake, and when the disciples saw him walking on the lake they were terrified. 'It is a ghost' they said, and cried out in fear. But at once Jesus called out to them saying, 'Courage! It is I! Do not be afraid.' It was Peter who answered. 'Lord,' he said 'if it is you, tell me to come to you across the water.' 'Come' said Jesus. Then Peter got out of the boat and started walking towards Jesus across the water, but as soon as he felt the force of the wind, he took fright and began to sink. 'Lord! Save me!' he cried. Jesus put out his hand at once and held him. 'Man of little faith,' he said, 'why did you doubt?' And as they got into the boat the wind dropped. The men in the boat bowed down before him and said, 'Truly, you are the Son of God.'

This is the Gospel of the Lord.

Prayer over the Gifts
Lord,
accept the gift of our worship
and hear our prayers for mercy.
Keep alive in our hearts the truth you gave us
through the ministry of your apostles Peter and Paul.

Preface of the Apostles I or II, P64 or P65.

Communion Antiphon: Lord, you have the words of everlasting life, and we believe that you are God's Holy One.

Prayer after Communion
Lord,
you have given us bread from heaven.
May this celebration
in memory of your apostles Peter and Paul
bring us the joy of their constant protection.

21 November

The Presentation of the Blessed Virgin Mary
Memorial

This celebration commemorates the presentation of the child Mary, in the Temple at Jerusalem, when she was three. The feast was firt kept in the eighth century. It symbolises the consecration of her life to the Lord.

Common of the Blessed Virgin Mary, pp.1858ff.

Opening Prayer
Eternal Father,
we honour the holiness and glory of the Virgin Mary.
May her prayers bring us
the fullness of your life and love.

FIRST READING

A reading from the prophet Zechariah 2:14-17
Rejoice, daughter of Zion, for I am coming.

Sing, rejoice,
daughter of Zion;
for I am coming
to dwell in the middle of you
– it is the Lord who speaks.
Many nations will join the Lord,
on that day;
they will become his people.
But he will remain among you,
and you will know that the Lord of hosts has sent me to you.
But the Lord will hold Judah
as his portion in the Holy Land,

Proper of Saints, 21 November

and again make Jerusalem his very own.
Let all mankind be silent before the Lord!
For he is awakening and is coming from his holy dwelling.

This is the word of the Lord.

Responsorial Psalm   Lk 1:46-55. ℟ v.49

℟ **The Almighty works marvels for me.**
Holy is his name!

or

℟ **Blessed is the Virgin Mary**
who bore the Son of the eternal Father.

1 My soul glorifies the Lord,
my spirit rejoices in God, my saviour. ℟

2 He looks on his servant in her nothingness;
henceforth all ages will call me blessed.
The Almighty works marvels for me.
Holy his name! ℟

3 His mercy is from age to age,
on those who fear him.
He puts forth his arm in strength
and scatters the proud-hearted. ℟

4 He casts the mighty from their thrones
and raises the lowly.
He fills the starving with good things,
sends the rich away empty. ℟

5 He protects Israel, his servant,
remembering his mercy,
the mercy promised to our fathers,
to Abraham and his sons for ever. ℟

Gospel Acclamation   Lk 11:28
Alleluia, alleluia!
Happy are those
who hear the word of God,
and keep it.
Alleluia!

GOSPEL

A reading from the holy Gospel according to Matthew 12:46-50

Stretching out his hand towards his disciples he said, 'Here are my mother and brothers.'

Jesus was speaking to the crowds when his mother and his brothers appeared; they were standing outside and were anxious to have a word with him. But to the man who told him this Jesus replied, 'Who is my mother? Who are my brothers?' And stretching out his hand towards his disciples he said, 'Here are my mother and my brothers. Anyone who does the will of my Father in heaven, he is my brother and sister and mother.'

This is the Gospel of the Lord.

22 November

St Cecilia, virgin and martyr — Memorial

A martyr of the second or third century. She is thought to have converted her husband and his brother to Christianity, and they were martyred before her. She is the patron saint of musicians.

Common of martyrs, pp.1865ff., or of virgins, pp.1889ff.

Opening Prayer
Lord of mercy,
be close to those who call upon you.
With Saint Cecilia to help us
hear and answer our prayers.

FIRST READING

A reading from the prophet Hosea 2:16-17. 21-22

I will betroth you to myself for ever.

The Lord says this:

> I am going to lead her out into the wilderness
> and speak to her heart.
> There she will respond to me as she did when she was young,
> as she did when she came out of the land of Egypt.
> I will betroth you to myself for ever,
> betroth you with integrity and justice,
> with tenderness and love;

Proper of Saints, 22 November

I will betroth you to myself with faithfulness,
and you will come to know the Lord.

This is the word of the Lord.

Responsorial Psalm Ps 44:11-12. 14-17. ℟ v.11. Alt. ℟ Mt 25:6
  ℟ **Listen, O daughter, give ear to my words.**

or

  ℟ **The bridegroom is here!
  Go out and meet Christ the Lord.**

1 Listen, O daughter, give ear to my words:
   forget your own people and your father's house.
   So will the king desire your beauty:
   He is your lord, pay homage to him. ℟

2 The daughter of the king is clothed with splendour,
   her robes embroidered with pearls set in gold.
   She is led to the king with her maiden companions. ℟

3 They are escorted amid gladness and joy;
   they pass within the palace of the king.
   Sons shall be yours in place of your fathers:
   you will make them princes over all the earth. ℟

Gospel Acclamation
  Alleluia, alleluia!
  This is a wise virgin whom the Lord found watching;
  she went in to the wedding feast with him when he came.
  Alleluia!

GOSPEL

A reading from the holy Gospel according to Matthew 25:1-13
The bridegroom is here, go out and meet him.

Jesus spoke this parable to his disciples:
  'The kingdom of heaven will be like this: Ten bridesmaids took their lamps and went to meet the bridegroom. Five of them were foolish and five were sensible: the foolish ones did take their lamps, but they brought no oil, whereas the sensible ones took flasks of oil as well as their lamps. The bridegroom was late, and they all grew drowsy and fell asleep. But at midnight there was a cry, "The bridegroom is here! Go out and meet him." At this, all those bridesmaids woke up and trimmed their lamps, and the

foolish ones said to the sensible ones, "Give us some of your oil: our lamps are going out". But they replied, "There may not be enough for us and for you; you had better go to those who sell it and buy some for yourselves". They had gone off to buy it when the bridegroom arrived. Those who were ready went in with him to the wedding hall and the door was closed. The other bridesmaids arrived later, "Lord, Lord," they said, "open the door for us." But he replied, "I tell you solemnly, I do not know you". So stay awake, because you do not know either the day or the hour.'

This is the Gospel of the Lord.

23 November

St Clement I, pope and martyr
Optional Memorial

Clement probably followed Peter as Bishop of Rome; he may be the Clement mentioned in Phil 3:4. His Epistle to the Corinthians was written about 96 AD, and calls on the Church there to repent and restore peace, after some internal dissension. It suggests that he himself knew Peter and Paul, and reveals a man of strong faith and prayer.

Common of martyrs, pp.1865ff., or of pastors: popes, pp.1876ff.

Opening Prayer
All-powerful and ever-living God,
we praise your power and glory
revealed to us in the lives of all your saints.
Give us joy on this feast of Saint Clement,
the priest and martyr
who bore witness with his blood to the love he proclaimed
and the gospel he preached.

FIRST READING

A reading from the first letter of St Peter 5:1-4
Be the shepherds of the flock of God that is entrusted to you.

I have something to tell your elders: I am an elder myself, and a witness to the sufferings of Christ, and with you I have a share in the glory that is to be revealed. Be the shepherds of the flock of God that is entrusted to you: watch over it, not simply as a duty but gladly, because God wants it; not for sordid money, but because you are eager to do it. Never be a dictator over any group that is put in your charge, but be an example that the whole flock can follow. When the chief shepherd appears, you will be given the crown of unfading glory.

This is the word of the Lord.

Responsorial Psalm Ps 88:2-5. 21-22. 25. 27. ℟ cf. v.2

℟ **I will sing for ever of your love, O Lord.**

1 I will sing for ever of your love, O Lord;
through all ages my mouth will proclaim your truth.
Of this I am sure, that your love lasts for ever,
that your truth is firmly established as the heavens. ℟

2 'I have made a covenant with my chosen one;
I have sworn to David my servant:
I will establish your dynasty for ever
and set up your throne through all ages. ℟

3 'I have found David my servant
and with my holy oil anointed him.
My hand shall always be with him
and my arm shall make him strong. ℟

4 'My truth and my love shall be with him;
by my name his might shall be exalted.
He will say to me: "You are my father,
my God, the rock who saves me." ' ℟

Gospel Acclamation Mk 1:17
Alleluia, alleluia!
Follow me, says the Lord,
and I will make you into fishers of men.
Alleluia!

GOSPEL

A reading from the holy Gospel according to Matthew 16:13-19
You are Peter and on this rock I will build my Church.

When Jesus came to the region of Caesarea Philippi he put this question to his disciples, 'Who do people say the Son of Man is?' And they said, 'Some say he is John the Baptist, some Elijah, and others Jeremiah or one of the prophets'. 'But you,' he said, 'who do you say I am?' Then Simon Peter spoke up, 'You are the

Christ,' he said, 'the Son of the living God'. Jesus replied, 'Simon son of Jonah, you are a happy man! Because it was not flesh and blood that revealed this to you but my Father in heaven. So I now say to you: You are Peter and on this rock I will build my Church. And the gates of the underworld can never hold out against it. I will give you the keys of the kingdom of heaven: whatever you bind on earth shall be considered bound in heaven; whatever you loose on earth shall be considered loosed in heaven.'

This is the Gospel of the Lord.

Also 23 November

St Columban, abbot Optional Memorial

Born in Ireland in the middle of the sixth century, Columban went with a group of monks to Gaul, where he established monasteries whose rule was particularly austere. Many were attracted to this way of life, but conflict with the local Church in Gaul arose, and he had to leave there, eventually settling in Northern Italy at Bobbio, where the house he established became a centre of learning. He died there in 615.

Common of pastors: missionaries, pp.1885ff., or of holy men and women: religious, pp.1898ff.

Opening Prayer
Lord,
you called Saint Columban to live the monastic life
and to preach the gospel with zeal.
May his prayers and example
help us to seek you above all things
and to work with all our hearts
for the spread of the faith.

FIRST READING

A reading from the prophet Isaiah   52:7-10
All the ends of the earth shall see the salvation of our God.

How beautiful on the mountains,
are the feet of one who brings good news,
who heralds peace, brings happiness,
proclaims salvation,
and tells Zion,
'Your God is king!'

Proper of Saints, 23 November

Listen! Your watchmen raise their voices,
they shout for joy together,
for they see the Lord face to face,
as he returns to Zion.
Break into shouts of joy together,
you ruins of Jerusalem;
for the Lord is consoling his people,
redeeming Jerusalem.

The Lord bares his holy arm
in the sight of all the nations,
and all the ends of the earth shall see
the salvation of our God.

This is the word of the Lord.

Responsorial Psalm   Ps 95:1-3. 7-8. 10. ℟ v.3
  ℟ **Proclaim the wonders of the Lord
      among all the peoples.**

1 O sing a new song to the Lord,
   sing to the Lord all the earth.
   O sing to the Lord, bless his name.   ℟

2 Proclaim his help day by day,
   tell among the nations his glory
   and his wonders among all the peoples.   ℟

3 Give the Lord, you families of peoples,
   give the Lord glory and power,
   give the Lord the glory of his name.   ℟

4 Proclaim to the nations: 'God is king.'
   The world he made firm in its place;
   he will judge the peoples in fairness.   ℟

Gospel Acclamation   Jn 8:12
   Alleluia, alleluia!
   I am the light of the world, says the Lord;
   anyone who follows me will have the light of life.
   Alleluia!

GOSPEL

A reading from the holy Gospel according to Luke   9:57-62
I will follow you wherever you go.

As Jesus and his disciples travelled along they met a man on the road who said to him, 'I will follow you wherever you go'. Jesus answered, 'Foxes have holes and the birds of the air have nests, but the Son of Man has nowhere to lay his head'.

Another to whom he said, 'Follow me', replied, 'Let me go and bury my father first'. But he answered, 'Leave the dead to bury their dead; your duty is to go and spread the news of the kingdom of God'.

Another said, 'I will follow you, sir, but first let me go and say good-bye to my people at home'. Jesus said to him, 'Once the hand is laid on the plough, no one who looks back is fit for the kingdom of God'.

This is the Gospel of the Lord.

30 November
ST ANDREW, APOSTLE Feast

The brother of St Peter, born in Bethsaida, disciple of John the Baptist until, with Peter, he answered the call of Christ. He is mentioned several times in the gospels: he brought the Gentiles to Jesus, and pointed out the boy with the loaves and the fishes. He is thought to have preached in Scythia, and to have been martyred at Patras in Achaia.

Entrance Antiphon: By the Sea of Galilee the Lord saw two brothers, Peter and Andrew. He called them: come and follow me, and I will make you fishers of men.

Opening Prayer
Lord,
in your kindness hear our petitions.
You called Andrew the apostle
to preach the gospel and guide your Church in faith.
May he always be our friend in your presence
to help us with his prayers.

FIRST READING
A reading from the letter of St Paul to the Romans 10:9-18

Faith comes from what is preached, and what is preached comes from the word of Christ.

If your lips confess that Jesus is Lord and if you believe in your heart that God raised him from the dead, then you will be saved. By believing from the heart you are made righteous; by confessing with your lips you are saved. When scripture says: those who believe in him will have no cause for shame, it makes no distinction between Jew and Greek: all belong to the same Lord who is rich enough however many ask his help, for everyone who calls on the name of the Lord will be saved.

But they will not ask his help unless they believe in him, and they will not believe in him unless they have heard of him, and they will not hear of him unless they get a preacher, and they will never have a preacher unless one is sent, but as scripture says: The footsteps of those who bring good news are a welcome sound. Not everyone, of course, listens to the Good News. As Isaiah says: Lord, how many believed what we proclaimed? So faith comes from what is preached, and what is preached comes from the word of Christ.

Let me put the question: is it possible that they did not hear? Indeed they did; in the words of the psalm, their voice has gone out through all the earth, and their message to the ends of the world.

This is the word of the Lord.

Responsorial Psalm

Ps 18:2-5. ℟ v.5

℟ **Their word goes forth through all the earth.**

1 The heavens proclaim the glory of God
and the firmament shows forth the work of his hands.
Day unto day takes up the story
and night unto night makes known the message. ℟

2 No speech, no word, no voice is heard
yet their span goes forth through all the earth,
their words to the utmost bounds of the world. ℟

Gospel Acclamation

Mt 4:19

Alleluia, alleluia!
Follow me, says the Lord,
and I will make you into fishers of men.
Alleluia!

GOSPEL

A reading from the holy Gospel according to Matthew 4:18-22
And they left their nets at once and followed him.

As Jesus was walking by the Sea of Galilee he saw two brothers,

Simon, who was called Peter, and his brother Andrew; they were making a cast in the lake with their net, for they were fishermen. And he said to them, 'Follow me and I will make you fishers of men.' And they left their nets at once and followed him.

Going on from there he saw another pair of brothers, James son of Zebedee and his brother John; they were in their boat with their father Zebedee, mending their nets, and he called them. At once, leaving the boat and their father, they followed him.

This is the Gospel of the Lord.

Prayer over the Gifts
All-powerful God,
may these gifts we bring on the feast of Saint Andrew
be pleasing to you
and give life to all who receive them.

Preface of the Apostles I or II, P64 or P65.

Communion Antiphon: Andrew told his brother Simon: We have found the Messiah, the Christ; and he brought him to Jesus.

Prayer after Communion
Lord,
may the sacrament we have received give us courage
to follow the example of Andrew the apostle.
By sharing in Christ's suffering
may we live with him for ever in glory,
for he is Lord for ever and ever.

DECEMBER

3 December
St Francis Xavier, priest Memorial

Born in 1506, in Spain, he was an original member of the Society of Jesus with St Ignatius – he took vows of poverty and chastity, and committed himself to evangelise the pagans. He is one of the greatest of all Christian missionaries, preaching in Goa, South East Asia, Japan – where he landed in 1549. He learned Japanese, and formed a Church that endured long drawn-out persecution. He died while on his way from Goa to China, in 1552. Not only was his preaching effective in drawing people to Christ, but he was able to organise the communities so that they could survive when he left them.
Common of pastors: missionaries, pp.1885ff.

Opening Prayer
God our Father,
by the preaching of Francis Xavier
you brought many nations to yourself.
Give his zeal for the faith to all who believe in you,
that your Church may rejoice in continued growth
throughout the world.

FIRST READING

A reading from the first letter of St Paul 9:16-19. 22-23
to the Corinthians
I should be punished if I did not preach the gospel.

I do not boast of preaching the gospel, since it is a duty which has been laid on me; I should be punished if I did not preach it! If I had chosen this work myself, I might have been paid for it, but as I have not, it is a responsibility which has been put into my hands. Do you know what my reward is? It is this: in my preaching, to be able to offer the Good News free, and not insist on the rights which the Gospel gives me.

So though I am not a slave of any man I have made myself the slave of everyone so as to win as many as I could. For the weak I made myself weak. I made myself all things to all men in order to save some at any cost; and I still do this, for the sake of the Gospel, to have a share in its blessings.

This is the word of the Lord.

Responsorial Psalm Ps 116:1.2. ℟ Mk 16:15

℟ **Go out to the whole world; proclaim the Good News.**

or

℟ **Alleluia!**

1 O praise the Lord, all you nations,
acclaim him all you peoples! ℟

2 Strong is his love for us;
he is faithful for ever. ℟

Gospel Acclamation Mt 28:19. 20
Alleluia, alleluia!
Go, make disciples of all the nations, says the Lord;
I am with you always; yes, to the end of time.
Alleluia!

GOSPEL

A reading from the holy Gospel according to Mark 16:15-20
Go out to the whole world; proclaim the Good News.

Jesus showed himself to the Eleven, and he said to them, 'Go out to the whole world; proclaim the Good News to all creation. He who believes and is baptised will be saved; he who does not believe will be condemned. These are the signs that will be associated with believers: in my name they will cast out devils; they will have the gift of tongues; they will pick up snakes in their hands, and be unharmed should they drink deadly poison; they will lay their hands on the sick, who will recover.'

And so the Lord Jesus, after he had spoken to them, was taken up into heaven: there at the right hand of God he took his place, while they, going out, preached everywhere, the Lord working with them and confirming the word by the signs that accompanied it.

This is the Gospel of the Lord.

Prayer over the Gifts
Lord,
receive the gifts we bring on the feast of Francis Xavier.
As his zeal for the salvation of mankind
led him to the ends of the earth,
may we be effective witnesses to the gospel
and come with our brothers and sisters
to be with you in the joy of our kingdom.

Prayer after Communion
Lord God,
may this eucharist fill us with the same love
that inspired Francis Xavier
to work for the salvation of all.
Help us to live in a manner more worthy of our Christian calling
and so inherit the promise of eternal life.

4 December

St John Damascene, priest and doctor of the Church

Optional Memorial

Born in Damascus about 675. After holding public office for a time, he withdrew to the monastery of Sabas near Jerusalem. He wrote The Fount of Wisdom, *in which he presented a comprehensive teaching on Christian doctrine, which had great influence on later theology. He died about 750.*

Common of pastors, pp.1876ff., or of doctors of the Church, pp.1887ff.

Opening Prayer
Lord,
may the prayers of Saint John Damascene help us,
and may the true faith he taught so well
always be our light and our strength.

FIRST READING

A reading from the second letter of St Paul to Timothy   1:13-14; 2:1-3

Guard this precious thing with the help of the Holy Spirit.

Keep as your pattern the sound teaching you have heard from me, in the faith and love that are in Christ Jesus. You have been trusted to look after something precious; guard it with the help of the Holy Spirit who lives in us. Accept the strength, my dear son, that comes from the grace of Christ Jesus. You have heard everything that I teach in public; hand it on to reliable people so that they in turn will be able to teach others.

Put up with your share of difficulties, like a good soldier of Christ Jesus.

This is the word of the Lord.

Responsorial Psalm   Ps 18:8-11. ℟ v.10. Alt. ℟ Jn 6:63

℟ **The decrees of the Lord are truth
and all of them just.**

or

℟ **Your words are spirit, Lord,
and they are life.**

1 The law of the Lord is perfect,
   it revives the soul.
   The rule of the Lord is to be trusted,
   it gives wisdom to the simple. ℟

2 The precepts of the Lord are right,
   they gladden the heart.
   The command of the Lord is clear,
   it gives light to the eyes. ℟

3 The fear of the Lord is holy,
   abiding for ever.
   The decrees of the Lord are truth
   and all of them just. ℟

4   They are more to be desired than gold,
    than the purest of gold
    and sweeter are they than honey,
    than honey from the comb. ℟

Gospel Acclamation   Jn 14:23
  Alleluia, alleluia!
  If anyone loves me he will keep my word,
  and my Father will love him,
  and we shall come to him,
  and make our home with him.
  Alleluia!

GOSPEL

A reading from the holy Gospel according to Matthew   25:14-30
You have shown you can be faithful in small things; come and join in your master's happiness.

Jesus spoke this parable to his disciples: 'A man on his way abroad summoned his servants and entrusted his property to them. To one he gave five talents, to another two, to a third, one; each in proportion to his ability. Then he set out. The man who had received the five talents promptly went and traded with them and made five more. The man who had received two made two more in the same way. But the man who had received one went off and dug a hole in the ground and hid his master's money. Now a long time after, the master of those servants came back and went through his accounts with them. The man who had received the five talents came forward bringing five more. 'Sir,' he said, 'you entrusted me with five talents; here are five more that I have made.' His master said to him, 'Well done, good and faithful servant; you have shown you can be faithful in small things, I will trust you with greater; come and join in your master's happiness.' Next the man with the two talents came forward. 'Sir,' he said, 'you entrusted me with two talents; here are two more that I have made.' His master said to him, 'Well done, good and faithful servant; you have shown you can be faithful in small things, I will trust you with greater; come and join in your master's happiness.'

'Last came forward the man who had the one talent. "Sir," said he, "I had heard you were a hard man, reaping where you have not sown and gathering where you have not scattered; so I was afraid, and I went off and hid your talent in the ground. Here it is; it was yours, you have it back." But his master answered him, "You wicked and lazy servant! So you knew I reap where I have not sown and gather where I have not scattered? Well then, you should have deposited my money with the bankers, and on my return I would have recovered my capital with interest. So now, take the talent from him and give it to the man who has the five talents. For to everyone who has will be given more, and he will have more than enough; but from the man who has not, even what he has will be taken away. As for this good-for-nothing servant, throw him out into the dark, where there will be weeping and grinding of teeth." '

This is the Gospel of the Lord.

6 December

St Nicholas, bishop — Optional Memorial

Bishop of Myra in Lycia in the third century. Practically nothing is known of his life, though there has been popular devotion to him from early times.

Common of pastors: bishops, pp.1878ff.

Opening Prayer

Father,
hear our prayers for mercy,
and by the help of Saint Nicholas
keep us safe from all danger,
and guide us on the way of salvation.

FIRST READING

A reading from the prophet Isaiah 6:1-8
Whom shall I send? Who will be our messenger?

In the year of King Uzziah's death I saw the Lord seated on a high throne; his train filled the sanctuary; above him stood seraphs, each one with six wings:two to cover its face, two to cover its feet and two for flying.

And they cried out one to another in this way,

'Holy, holy, holy is the Lord of hosts.
His glory fills the whole earth.'

The foundations of the threshold shook with the voice of the one who cried out, and the Temple was filled with smoke. I said:

'What a wretched state I am in! I am lost,
for I am a man of unclean lips
and I live among a people of unclean lips.
and my eyes have looked at the King, the Lord of hosts.'

Then one of the seraphs flew to me, holding in his hand a live coal which he had taken from the altar with a pair of tongs. With this he touched my mouth and said:

'See now, this has touched your lips,
your sin is taken away,
your iniquity is purged.'

Then I heard the voice of the Lord saying: 'Whom shall I send? Who will be our messenger?' I answered, 'Here I am, send me.'

This is the word of the Lord.

Responsorial Psalm   Ps 39:2. 4. 7-10. ℟ cf. vv. 8.9
> ℟ **Here I am, Lord!
> I come to do your will.**

1. I waited, I waited for the Lord
and he stooped down to me;
he heard my cry.
He put a new song into my mouth,
praise of our God. ℟

2. You do not ask for sacrifice and offerings,
but an open ear.
You do not ask for holocaust and victim.
Instead, here am I. ℟

3. In the scroll of the book it stands written
that I should do your will.
My God, I delight in your law
in the depth of my heart. ℟

4. Your justice I have proclaimed
in the great assembly.
My lips I have not sealed;
you know it, O Lord. ℟

Gospel Acclamation   Lk 4:18
> Alleluia, alleluia!
> The Lord has sent me to bring the good news to the poor,
> to proclaim liberty to captives.
> Alleluia!

GOSPEL

A reading from the holy Gospel according to Luke   10:1-9

The harvest is rich but the labourers are few.

The Lord appointed seventy-two others and sent them out ahead of him, in pairs, to all the towns and places he himself was to visit. He said to them, 'The harvest is rich but the labourers are few, so ask the Lord of the harvest to send labourers to his harvest. Start off now, but remember, I am sending you out like lambs among wolves. Carry no purse, no haversack, no sandals. Salute no one on the road. Whatever house you go into, let your first words be, "Peace to this house!" And if a man of peace lives there, your peace will go and rest on him; if not, it will come back to you. Stay in the same house, taking what food and drink they have to offer, for the labourer deserves his wages; do not move from house to house. Whenever you go into a town where they make you welcome, eat what is set before you. Cure those in it who are sick, and say, 'The kingdom of God is very near to you."'

This is the Gospel of the Lord.

7 December

St Ambrose,
bishop and doctor of the Church   Memorial

Born about 339, at Trier, practised in the Roman law-courts, and was appointed to office in Milan. While still a catechumen, he was elected Bishop of Milan by the laity – he hesitated to accept, but was baptised and ordained, studied theology, and became famous as a preacher and defender of the faith. He received St Augustine into the Church. He fought paganism, protected the Church against the political power; his writings on ethics and ascetics, his letters and sermons, his instruction to catechumens – all reveal a Christian bishop of great faith and energy.

Common of pastors: bishops, pp.1878ff., or of doctors of the Church, pp.1887ff.

Opening Prayer
Lord,
you made Saint Ambrose
an outstanding teacher of the Catholic faith
and gave him the courage of an apostle.
Raise up in your Church more leaders after your own heart,
to guide us with courage and wisdom.

FIRST READING

A reading from the letter of St Paul to the Ephesians 3:8-12
Proclaiming to the pagans the infinite treasure of Christ.

I, who am less than the least of all the saints, have been entrusted with this special grace, not only of proclaiming to the pagans the infinite treasure of Christ but also of explaining how the mystery is to be dispensed. Through all the ages, this has been kept hidden in God, the creator of everything. Why? So that the Sovereignties and Powers should learn only now, through the Church, how comprehensive God's wisdom really is, exactly according to the plan which he had had from all eternity in Christ Jesus our Lord. This is why we are bold enough to approach God in complete confidence, through our faith in him.

This is the word of the Lord.

Responsorial Psalm Ps 88:2-5. 21-22. 25. 27. ℟ cf. v.2
 ℟ **I will sing for ever of your love, O Lord.**

1 I will sing for ever of your love, O Lord;
    through all ages my mouth will proclaim your truth.
    Of this I am sure, that your love lasts for ever,
    that your truth is firmly established as the heavens. ℟

2 'I have made a covenant with my chosen one;
    I have sworn to David my servant:
    I will establish your dynasty for ever
    and set up your throne through all ages. ℟

3 'I have found David my servant
    and with my holy oil anointed him.
    My hand shall always be with him
    and my arm shall make him strong. ℟

4 'My truth and my love shall be with him;
    by my name his might shall be exalted.
    He will say to me: "You are my father,
    my God, the rock who saves me." ' ℟

Proper of Saints, 7 December

Gospel Acclamation
Jn 10:14

Alleluia, alleluia!
I am the good shepherd, says the Lord,
I know my own sheep and my own know me.
Alleluia!

GOSPEL

A reading from the holy Gospel according to John   10:11-16
The good shepherd is one who lays down his life for his sheep.

Jesus said:

'I am the good shepherd:
the good shepherd is one who lays down his life for his sheep.
The hired man, since he is not the shepherd
and the sheep do not belong to him,
abandons the sheep and runs away
as soon as he sees a wolf coming,
and then the wolf attacks and scatters the sheep;
this is because he is only a hired man
and has no concern for the sheep.
I am the good shepherd;
I know my own
and my own know me,
just as the Father knows me
and I know the Father;
and I lay down my life for my sheep.
And there are other sheep I have
that are not of this fold,
and these I have to lead as well.
They too will listen to my voice,
and there will be only one flock,
and one shepherd.'

This is the Gospel of the Lord.

Prayer over the Gifts
Lord,
as we celebrate these holy rites,
send your Spirit to give us the light of faith
which guided Saint Ambrose to make your glory known.

Prayer after Communion
Father,

you have renewed us by the power of this sacrament.
Through the teachings of Saint Ambrose,
may we follow your way with courage
and prepare ourselves for the feast of eternal life.

8 December
THE IMMACULATE CONCEPTION OF THE BLESSED VIRGIN MARY — Solemnity

Entrance Antiphon: I exult for joy in the Lord, my soul rejoices in my God; for he has clothed me in the garment of salvation and robed me in the cloak of justice, like a bride adorned with her jewels.

Opening Prayer
Let us pray
   [that through the prayers of the sinless Virgin Mary,
   God will free us from our sins]

Father,
you prepared the Virgin Mary
to be the worthy mother of your Son.
You let her share beforehand
in the salvation Christ would bring by his death,
and kept her sinless from the first moment of her conception.
Help us by her prayers
to live in your presence without sin.

or

Let us pray
   [on this feast of Mary
   who experienced the perfection of God's saving power]

Father,
the image of the Virgin is found in the Church.
Mary had a faith that your Spirit prepared
and a love that never knew sin,
for you kept her sinless from the first moment of her conception.

Trace in our actions the lines of her love,
in our hearts her readiness of faith.
Prepare once again a world for your Son
who lives and reigns . . .

Proper of Saints, 8 December

FIRST READING

A reading from the book of Genesis 3:9-15. 20

I will make enemies of your offspring and the offspring of the woman.

After Adam had eaten of the tree the Lord God called to him, 'Where are you?' he asked. 'I heard the sound of you in the garden.' he replied. 'I was afraid because I was naked, so I hid.' 'Who told you that you were naked?' he asked. 'Have you been eating of the tree I forbade you to eat?' The man replied, 'It was the woman you put with me; she gave me the fruit, and I ate it.' Then the Lord God asked the woman, 'What is this you have done?' The woman replied, 'The serpent tempted me and I ate.'

Then the Lord God said to the serpent, 'Because you have done this,

> 'Be accursed beyond all cattle,
> all wild beasts.
> You shall crawl on your belly and eat dust
> every day of your life.
> I will make you enemies of each other:
> you and the woman,
> your offspring and her offspring.
> It will crush your head
> and you will strike its heel.'

The man named his wife 'Eve' because she was the mother of all those who live.

This is the word of the Lord.

Responsorial Psalm Ps 97:1-4. ℟ v.1

℟ **Sing a new song to the Lord
for he has worked wonders.**

1. Sing a new song to the Lord
for he has worked wonders.
His right hand and his holy arm
have brought salvation.   ℟

2. The Lord has made known his salvation;
has shown his justice to the nations.
He has remembered his truth and love
for the house of Israel.   ℟

3. All the ends of the earth have seen
the salvation of our God.

Shout to the Lord all the earth,
ring out your joy. ℟

SECOND READING

A reading from the letter of St Paul to the Ephesians   1:3-6. 11-12

Before the world was made, God chose us in Christ.

Blessed be God the Father of our Lord Jesus Christ,
who has blessed us with all the spiritual blessings of heaven in Christ.
Before the world was made, he chose us, chose us in Christ,
to be holy and spotless, and to live through love in his presence,
determining that we should become his adopted sons, through Jesus Christ
for his own kind purposes,
to make us praise the glory of his grace,
his free gift to us in the Beloved.
And it is in him that we were claimed as God's own,
chosen from the beginning,
under the predetermined plan of the one who guides all things
as he decides by his own will;
chosen to be,
for his greater glory,
the people who would put their hopes in Christ before he came.

This is the word of the Lord.

Gospel Acclamation   cf. Lk 1:28
Alleluia, alleluia!
Hail, Mary, full of grace; the Lord is with thee!
Blessed art thou among women.
Alleluia!

GOSPEL

A reading from the holy Gospel according to Luke   1:26-38

Rejoice, so highly favoured! The Lord is with you.

The angel Gabriel was sent by God to a town in Galilee called Nazareth, to a virgin betrothed to a man named Joseph, of the House of David; and the virgin's name was Mary. He went in and said to her, 'Rejoice, so highly favoured! The Lord is with you.' She was deeply disturbed by these words and asked herself what this greeting could mean, but the angel said to her, 'Mary, do not be afraid; you have won God's favour. Listen! You are to conceive and bear a son, and you must name him Jesus. He will be great and will be called Son of the Most High. The Lord God will give him the throne of his ancestor David; he will rule over the House of Jacob for ever and his reign will have no end.' Mary said to the angel, 'But how can this come about, since I am a virgin?' 'The Holy Spirit will come upon you' the angel answered 'and the power of the Most High will cover you with its shadow. And so the child will be holy and will be called Son of God. Know this too: your kinswoman Elizabeth has, in her old age, herself conceived a son, and she whom people called barren is now in her sixth month, for nothing is impossible to God.' 'I am the handmaid of the Lord,' said Mary 'let what you have said be done to me.' And the angel left her.

This is the Gospel of the Lord.

The Profession of Faith is made.

Prayer over the Gifts
Lord,
accept this sacrifice
on the feast of the sinless Virgin Mary.
You kept her free from sin
from the first moment of her life.
Help us by her prayers,
and free us from our sins.

Preface of the Immaculate Conception, P58, p.1060.

Communion Antiphon: All honour to you, Mary! From you arose the sun of justice, Christ our God.

Prayer after Communion
Lord our God,
in your love, you chose the Virgin Mary
and kept her free from sin.
May this sacrament of your love
free us from our sins.

Solemn Blessing
Bow your heads and pray for God's blessing.

Born of the Blessed Virgin Mary,
the Son of God redeemed mankind.

Proper of Saints, 11 December 1825

May he enrich you with his blessings. ℟ **Amen.**

You received the author of life through Mary.
May you always rejoice in her loving care. ℟ **Amen.**

You have come to rejoice at Mary's feast.
May you be filled with the joys of the Spirit
and the gifts of your eternal home. ℟ **Amen.**

May almighty God bless you,
the Father, and the Son, ✠ and the Holy Spirit. ℟ **Amen.**

11 December
St Damasus I, pope Optional Memorial

Born about 305, he was elected pope by the clergy and people of Rome in 366. He summoned synods to suppress various heresies rife at the time, particularly Arianism and Donatism. He commissioned St Jerome to undertake his translation of the scriptures. He embellished and conserved the tombs of the martyrs. He died in 384.

Common of pastors: popes, pp.1876ff.

Opening Prayer
Father,
as Saint Damasus loved and honoured your martyrs,
so may we continue to celebrate their witness for Christ,
who lives and reigns . . .

FIRST READING

A reading from the Acts of the Apostles 20:17-18. 28-32. 36

Be on your guard for yourselves and for all the flock of which the Holy Spirit has made you the overseers, to feed the Church of God.

From Miletus Paul sent for the elders of the church of Ephesus. When they arrived he addressed these words to them:

'Be on your guard for yourselves and for all the flock of which the Holy Spirit has made you the overseers, to feed the Church of God which he bought with his own blood. I know quite well that when I have gone fierce wolves will invade you and will have no mercy on the flock. Even from your own ranks there will be men coming forward with a travesty of the truth on their lips to induce the disciples to follow them. So be on your guard, remembering how night and day for three years I never failed to keep you right, shedding tears over each one of you. And now I commend you to God, and to the word of his grace that has power to build you up and to give you your inheritance among all the sanctified.'

When he had finished speaking he knelt down with them all and prayed.

This is the word of the Lord.

Responsorial Psalm   Ps 109:1-4. ℟ v.4

℟ **You are a priest for ever,**
a priest like Melchizedek of old.

1. The Lord's revelation to my Master:
   'Sit on my right:
   I will put your foes beneath your feet.'   ℟

2. The Lord will send from Zion
   your sceptre of power:
   rule in the midst of all your foes.   ℟

3. A prince from the day of your birth
   on the holy mountains;
   from the womb before the daybreak I begot you.   ℟

4. The Lord has sworn an oath he will not change.
   'You are a priest for ever,
   a priest like Melchizedek of old.'   ℟

Gospel Acclamation   Jn 15:15
Alleluia, alleluia!
I call you friends, says the Lord,
because I have made known to you
everything I have learnt from my Father.
Alleluia!

GOSPEL

A reading from the holy Gospel according to John   15:9-17
I shall not call you servants any more, I call you friends.

Jesus said to his disciples:

'As the Father has loved me,
so I have loved you.
Remain in my love.
If you keep my commandments
you will remain in my love,

just as I have kept my Father's commandments
and remain in his love.
I have told you this
so that my own joy may be in you
and your joy be complete.
This is my commandment:
love one another
as I have loved you.
A man can have no greater love
than to lay down his life for his friends.
You are my friends,
if you do what I command you.
I shall not call you servants any more,
because a servant does not know
his master's business;
I call you friends,
because I have made known to you
everything I have learnt from my Father.
You did not choose me,
no, I chose you;
and I commissioned you
to go out and to bear fruit,
fruit that will last;
and then the Father will give you
anything you ask him in my name.
What I command you
is to love one another.'

This is the Gospel of the Lord.

12 December
St Jane Frances de Chantal, religious
Optional Memorial

Born at Dijon, France in 1572, she married and had six children. After her husband's death, Francis de Sales became her spiritual director. She founded the Congregation of the Visitation for women who wished to live a religious life but could not endure the austerities of existing orders. She spent her life in the care of the sick and poor, and died in 1641.
Common of holy men and women: religious, pp.1898ff.

Opening Prayer
Lord,

you chose Saint Jane Frances to serve you
both in marriage and in religious life.
By her prayers
help us to be faithful in our vocation
and always to be the light of the world.

FIRST READING

A reading from the book of Proverbs 31:10-13. 19-20. 30-31

The woman who fears the Lord is the one to praise.

A perfect wife – who can find her?
She is far beyond the price of pearls.

Her husband's heart has confidence in her,
from her he will derive no little profit.

Advantage and not hurt she brings him
all the days of her life.

She is always busy with wool and with flax,
she does her work with eager hands.

She sets her hands to the distaff,
her fingers grasp the spindle.

She holds out her hand to the poor,
she opens her arms to the needy.

Charm is deceitful, and beauty empty;
the woman who is wise is the one to praise.

Give her a share in what her hands have worked for,
and let her works tell her praises at the city gates.

This is the word of the Lord.

Responsorial Psalm Ps 130

℟ **Keep my soul in peace before you, O Lord.**

1 O Lord my heart is not proud
  nor haughty my eyes.
  I have not gone after things too great
  nor marvels beyond me. ℟

2 Truly I have set my soul
  in silence and peace.
  A weaned child on its mother's breast,
  even so is my soul. ℟

Proper of Saints, 13 December

3   O Israel, hope in the Lord
    both now and for ever. ℟

Gospel Acclamation　　　　　　　　　　　　　　　　　　Jn 8:31-32
　　Alleluia, alleluia!
　　If you make my word your home
　　you will indeed be my disciples,
　　and you will learn the truth, says the Lord.
　　Alleluia!

GOSPEL

A reading from the holy Gospel according to Mark　　　3:31-35

Anyone who does the will of God, that person is my brother and sister and mother.

The mother and brothers of Jesus arrived and, standing outside, sent in a message asking for him. A crowd was sitting round him at the time the message was passed to him, 'Your mother and brothers and sisters are outside asking for you.' He replied, 'Who are my mother and my brothers?' And looking round at those sitting in a circle about him, he said, 'Here are my mother and my brothers. Anyone who does the will of God, that person is my brother and sister and mother.'

　　This is the Gospel of the Lord.

13 December
St Lucy, virgin and martyr　　　Memorial

Born in Syracus, she lived her Christianity without concealment, and was martyred during the persecution of Diocletian.

Common of martyrs, pp.1865ff., or of virgins, pp.1889ff.

Opening Prayer
Lord,
give us courage through the prayers of Saint Lucy.
As we celebrate her entrance into eternal glory,
we ask to share her happiness in the life to come.

FIRST READING

A reading from the second letter of St Paul to the Corinthians   10:17 — 11:2

I arranged for you to marry Christ so that I might give you away as a chaste virgin to this one husband.

If anyone wants to boast, let him boast of the Lord. It is not the man who commends himself that can be accepted, but the man who is commended by the Lord.

I only wish you were able to tolerate a little foolishness from me. But of course: you are tolerant towards me. You see, the jealousy that I feel for you is God's own jealousy: I arranged for you to marry Christ so that I might give you away as a chaste virgin to this one husband.

This is the word of the Lord.

Responsorial Psalm
Ps 30:3-4. 6-8. 16-17. ℟ v.6

℟ **Into your hands, O Lord,
I commend my spirit.**

1. Be a rock of refuge for me,
   a mighty stronghold to save me,
   for you are my rock, my stronghold.
   For your name's sake, lead me and guide me. ℟

2. Into your hands I commend my spirit.
   It is you who will redeem me, Lord.
   As for me, I trust in the Lord:
   let me be glad and rejoice in your love. ℟

3. My life is in your hands, deliver me
   from the hands of those who hate me.
   Let your face shine on your servant.
   Save me in your love. ℟

Gospel Acclamation
Alleluia, alleluia!
This is a wise virgin whom the Lord found watching;
she went in to the wedding feast with him when he came.
Alleluia!

Proper of Saints, 14 December

GOSPEL

A reading from the holy Gospel according to Matthew 25:1-13

The bridegroom is here, go out and meet him.

Jesus spoke this parable to his disciples:

'The kingdom of heaven will be like this: Ten bridesmaids took their lamps and went to meet the bridegroom. Five of them were foolish and five were sensible: the foolish ones did take their lamps, but they brought no oil, whereas the sensible ones took flasks of oil as well as their lamps. The bridegroom was late, and they all grew drowsy and fell asleep. But at midnight there was a cry, "The bridegroom is here! Go out and meet him." At this, all those bridesmaids woke up and trimmed their lamps, and the foolish ones said to the sensible ones, "Give us some of your oil: our lamps are going out". But they replied, "There may not be enough for us and for you; you had better go to those who sell it and buy some for yourselves". They had gone off to buy it when the bridegroom arrived. Those who were ready went in with him to the wedding hall and the door was closed. The other bridesmaids arrived later. "Lord, Lord," they said, "open the door for us." But he replied, "I tell you solemnly, I do not know you". So stay awake, because you do not know either the day or the hour.'

This is the Gospel of the Lord.

14 December

St John of the Cross, priest and doctor of the Church Memorial

Born in Spain in 1542, became a Carmelite, was ordained priest in 1567. St Teresa of Avila encouraged him to undertake the reform of his Order. He was strenuously opposed and suffered many trials and setbacks. He led a life of prayer which bore fruit in a number of writings that are classics of the mystical life. The Ascent of Mount Carmel, The Dark Night of the Soul, The Spiritual Canticle, The Living Flame of Love. *His outstanding holiness, austerity of life, poetic genius and charity remain a living example.*

Entrance Antiphon: I should boast of nothing but the cross of our Lord Jesus Christ; through him the world is crucified to me, and I to the world.

Proper of Saints, 14 December

Opening Prayer
Father,
you endowed John of the Cross with a spirit of self-denial
and a love of the cross.
By following his example,
may we come to the eternal vision of your glory.

FIRST READING

A reading from the first letter of St Paul 2:1-10
to the Corinthians

We teach the hidden wisdom of God in our mysteries.

When I came to you, brothers, it was not with any show of oratory or philosophy, but simply to tell you what God had guaranteed. During my stay with you, the only knowledge I claimed to have was about Jesus, and only about him as the crucified Christ. Far from relying on any power of my own, I came among you in great 'fear and trembling' and in my speeches and the sermons that I gave, there were none of the arguments that belong to philosophy; only a demonsration of the power of the Spirit. And I did this so that your faith should not depend on human philosophy but on the power of God.

But still we have a wisdom to offer those who have reached maturity: not a philosophy of our age, it is true, still less of the masters of our age, which are coming to their end. The hidden wisdom of God which we teach in our mysteries is the wisdom that God predestined to be for our glory before the ages began. It is a wisdom that none of the masters of this age have ever known, or they would not have crucified the Lord of Glory; we teach what scripture calls: the things that no eye has seen and no ear has heard, things beyond the mind of man, all that God has prepared for those who love him.

These are the very things that God has revealed to us through the Spirit.

This is the word of the Lord.

Responsorial Psalm Ps 36:3-6. 30-31. ℟ v.30

℟ **The just man's mouth utters wisdom.**

1 If you trust in the Lord and do good,
then you will live in the land and be secure.
If you find your delight in the Lord,
he will grant your heart's desire. ℟

Proper of Saints, 14 December   1833

2 Commit your life to the Lord,
 trust in him and he will act,
 so that your justice breaks forth like the light,
 your cause like the noon-day sun. ℞

3 The just man's mouth utters wisdom
 and his lips speak what is right;
 the law of his God is in his heart,
 his steps shall be saved from stumbling. ℞

Gospel Acclamation   Mt 5:3
 Alleluia, alleluia!
 How happy are the poor in spirit;
 theirs is the kingdom of heaven.
 Alleluia!

GOSPEL

A reading from the holy Gospel according to Luke   14:25-33
None of you can be my disciple unless he gives up all his possessions.

Great crowds accompanied Jesus on his way and he turned and spoke to them. 'If any man comes to me without hating his father, mother, wife, children, brothers, sisters, yes and his own life too, he cannot be my disciple. Anyone who does not carry his cross and come after me cannot be my disciple.

'And indeed, which of you here, intending to build a tower, would not first sit down and work out the cost to see if he had enough to complete it? Otherwise, if he laid the foundation and then found himself unable to finish the work, the onlookers would all start making fun of him and saying, "Here is a man who started to build and was unable to finish." Or again, what king marching to war against another king would not first sit down and consider whether with ten thousand men he could stand up to the other who advanced against him with twenty thousand? If not, then while the other king was still a long way off, he would send envoys to sue for peace. So in the same way, none of you can be my disciple unless he gives up all his possessions.'

This is the Gospel of the Lord.

Prayer over the Gifts
Almighty Lord,
look upon the gifts we offer

in memory of Saint John of the Cross.
May we imitate the love we proclaim
as we celebrate the mystery
of the suffering and death of Christ,
who is Lord for ever and ever.

Communion Antiphon: If anyone wishes to come after me, he must renounce himself, take up his cross, and follow me, says the Lord.

Prayer after Communion
God our Father,
you have shown us the mystery of the cross
in the life of Saint John.
May this sacrifice make us strong,
keep us faithful to Christ
and help us to work in the Church
for the salvation of all mankind.

21 December

St Peter Canisius, priest and doctor of the Church

Optional Memorial

Born in 1521, at Nijmegen in Holland, he entered the Society of Jesus, was ordained in 1546, and went to Cologne, where he founded a Jesuit house. He was a vigorous defender of Catholicism, and published a catechism which was very influential in the Counter-Reformation. He died in 1597.

Common of pastors, pp.1876ff., or of doctors of the Church, pp.1887ff.

Opening Prayer
Lord,
you gave Saint Peter Canisius
wisdom and courage to defend the Catholic faith.
By the help of his prayers
may all who seek the truth rejoice in finding you,
and may all who believe in you
be loyal in professing their faith.

FIRST READING

A reading from the second letter of St Paul to Timothy 4:1-5
Make the preaching of the Good News your life's work.

Before God and before Christ Jesus who is to be judge of the living and the dead, I put this duty to you, in the name of his Appearing and of his kingdom: proclaim the message and, welcome or unwelcome, insist on it. Refute falsehood, correct error, call to obedience – but do all with patience and with the intention of teaching. The time is sure to come when, far from being content with sound teaching, people will be avid for the latest novelty and collect themselves a whole series of teachers according to their own tastes; and then, instead of listening to the truth, they will turn to myths. Be careful always to choose the right course; be brave under trials; make the preaching of the Good News your life's work, in thoroughgoing service.

This is the word of the Lord.

Responsorial Psalm Ps 39:2. 4. 7-10. ℟ vv.8. 9

℟ **Here I am, Lord!**
 I come to do your will.

1 I waited, I waited for the Lord
 and he stooped down to me;
 he heard my cry.
 He put a new song into my mouth,
 praise of our God. ℟

2 You do not ask for sacrifice and offerings,
 but an open ear.
 You do not ask for holocaust and victim.
 Instead, here am I. ℟

3 In the scroll of the book it stands written
 that I should do your will.
 My God, I delight in your law
 in the depth of my heart. ℟

4 Your justice I have proclaimed
 in the great assembly.
 My lips I have not sealed;
 you know it, O Lord. ℟

Gospel Acclamation   Mt 5:16

Alleluia, alleluia!
Your light must shine in the sight of men,
so that, seeing your good works,
they may give the praise to your Father in heaven.
Alleluia!

GOSPEL

A reading from the holy Gospel according to Matthew   5:13-19
You are the light of the world.

Jesus said to his disciples: 'You are the salt of the earth. But if salt becomes tasteless, what can make it salty again? It is good for nothing, and can only be thrown out to be trampled underfoot by men.

'You are the light of the world. A city built on a hill-top cannot be hidden. No one lights a lamp to put it under a tub; they put it on the lamp-stand where it shines for everyone in the house. In the same way your light must shine in the sight of men, so that, seeing your good works, they may give the praise to your Father in heaven.

'Do not imagine that I have come to abolish the Law or the Prophets. I have come not to abolish but to complete them. I tell you solemnly, till heaven and earth disappear, not one dot, not one little stroke, shall disappear from the Law until its purpose is achieved. Therefore, the man who infringes even one of the least of these commandments and teaches others to do the same will be considered the least in the kingdom of heaven; but the man who keeps them and teaches them will be considered great in the kingdom of heaven.'

This is the Gospel of the Lord.

23 December

St John of Kanty, priest

Optional Memorial

Born in Kanty, Poland, in 1390, he was ordained and taught at the University of Cracow for some years before becoming parish priest at Olkuscz. He was an outstanding teacher of the faith, and his holiness and charity to all were noted. He died in 1473.

Common of pastors, pp.1876ff., or of holy men and women: those who worked for the underprivileged, p.1900.

Opening Prayer

Almighty Father,
through the example of John of Kanty
may we grow in the wisdom of the saints.
As we show understanding and kindness to others,
may we receive your forgiveness.

FIRST READING

A reading from the letter of St James 2:14-17
Faith is quite dead if good works do not go with it.

Take the case, my brothers, of someone who has never done a single good act but claims that he has faith. Will that faith save him? If one of the brothers or one of the sisters is in need of clothes and has not enough food to live on, and one of you says to them, 'I wish you well; keep yourself warm and eat plenty', without giving them these bare necessities of life, then what good is that? Faith is like that: if good works do not go with it, it is quite dead.

This is the word of the Lord.

Responsorial Psalm Ps 111:1-9. ℟ v.1

℟ **Happy the man who fears the Lord.**

or

℟ **Alleluia!**

1 Alleluia!
   Happy the man who fears the Lord,
   who takes delight in his commands.
   His sons will be powerful on earth;
   the children of the upright are blessed. ℟

2 Riches and wealth are in his house;
   his justice stands firm for ever.
   He is a light in the darkness for the upright:
   he is generous, merciful and just. ℟

3 The good man takes pity and lends,
   he conducts his affairs with honour.
   The just man will never waver:
   he will be remembered for ever. ℟

4 He has no fear of evil news;
   with a firm heart he trusts in the Lord.

(continued)

With a steadfast heart he will not fear;
he will see the downfall of his foes.

℟ **Happy the man who fears the Lord,
who takes delight in his commands.**

5 Open-handed, he gives to the poor;
his justice stands firm for ever.
His head will be raised in glory. ℟

Gospel Acclamation   Jn 13:34
Alleluia, alleluia!
I give you a new commandment:
love one another just as I have loved you,
says the Lord.
Alleluia!

GOSPEL

A reading from the holy Gospel according to Luke   6:27-38
Be compassionate as your Father is compassionate.

Jesus said to his disciples: 'I say this to you who are listening: Love your enemies, do good to those who hate you, bless those who curse you, pray for those who treat you badly. To the man who slaps you on one cheek, present the other cheek too; to the man who takes your cloak from you, do not refuse your tunic. Give to everyone who asks you, and do not ask for your property back from the man who robs you. Treat others as you would like them to treat you. If you love those who love you, what thanks can you expect? Even sinners love those who love them. And if you do good to those who do good to you, what thanks can you expect? For even sinners do that much. And if you lend to those from whom you hope to receive, what thanks can you expect? Even sinners lend to get back the same amount. Instead, love your enemies and do good, and lend without any hope of return. You will have a great reward, and you will be sons of the Most High, for he himself is kind to the ungrateful and the wicked.

'Be compassionate as your Father is compassionate. Do not judge, and you will not be judged yourselves; do not condemn, and you will not be condemned yourselves; grant pardon, and you will be pardoned. Give, and there will be gifts for you: a full measure, pressed down, shaken together, and running over, will be poured into your lap; because the amount you measure out is the amount you will be given back.'

This is the Gospel of the Lord.

26 December
ST STEPHEN, FIRST MARTYR — Feast

Entrance Antiphon: The gates of heaven opened for Stephen, the first of the martyrs; in heaven he wears the crown of victory.

Opening Prayer
Lord,
today we celebrate the entrance of Saint Stephen
into eternal glory.
He died praying for those who killed him.
Help us to imitate his goodness
and to love our enemies.

FIRST READING

A reading from the Acts of the Apostles 6:8-10; 7:54-59
I can see heaven thrown open.

Stephen was filled with grace and power and began to work miracles and great signs among the people. But then certain people came forward to debate with Stephen, some from Cyrene and Alexandria who were members of the synagogue called the Synagogue of Freedmen, and others from Cilicia and Asia. They found they could not get the better of him because of his wisdom, and because it was the Spirit that prompted what he said. They were infuriated when they heard what he said, and ground their teeth at him.

But Stephen, filled with the Holy Spirit, gazed into heaven and saw the glory of God, and Jesus standing at God's right hand. 'I can see heaven thrown open' he said 'and the Son of Man standing at the right hand of God.' At this all the members of the council shouted out and stopped their ears with their hands; then they all rushed at him, sent him out of the city and stoned him. The witnesses put down their clothes at the feet of a young man called Saul. As they were stoning him, Stephen said in invocation, 'Lord Jesus, receive my spirit.' Then he knelt down and said aloud, 'Lord, do not hold this sin against them'; and with these words he fell asleep. Saul entirely approved of the killing.

This is the word of the Lord.

Responsorial Psalm
Ps 30:3-4. 6. 8. 16-17. ℟ v.6

℟ **Into your hands, O Lord, I commend my spirit.**

1 Be a rock of refuge for me,
   a mighty stronghold to save me,
   for you are my rock, my stronghold.
   For your name's sake, lead me and guide me.   ℟

2 Into your hands I commend my spirit.
   It is you who will redeem me, Lord.
   As for me, I trust in the Lord:
   let me be glad and rejoice in your love.   ℟

3 My life is in your hands, deliver me
   from the hands of those who hate me.
   Let your face shine on your servant.
   Save me in your love.   ℟

Gospel Acclamation
Ps 117:26. 27

Alleluia, alleluia!
Blessed is he who comes in the name of the Lord;
the Lord God is our light.
Alleluia!

GOSPEL

A reading from the holy Gospel according to Matthew   10:17-22

You will be dragged before governors and kings for my sake, to bear witness before them and the pagans.

Jesus said to his apostles: 'Beware of men: they will hand you over to sanhedrins and scourge you in their synagogues. You will be dragged before governors and kings for my sake, to bear witness before them and the pagans. But when they hand you over, do not worry about how to speak or what to say; what you are to say will be given to you when the time comes; because it is not you who will be speaking; the Spirit of your Father will be speaking in you.

'Brother will betray brother to death, and the father his child; children will rise against their parents and have them put to death. You will be hated by all men on account of my name; but the man who stands firm to the end will be saved.'

This is the Gospel of the Lord.

Proper of Saints, 27 December 1841

Prayer over the Gifts
Father,
be pleased with the gifts we bring in your honour
as we celebrate the memory of Saint Stephen.

Preface of Christmas I-III, P3-P5.

Communion Antiphon: As they stoned him, Stephen prayed aloud:
Lord Jesus, receive my spirit.

Prayer after Communion
Lord,
we thank you for the many signs of your love for us.
Save us by the birth of your Son
and give us joy in honouring Saint Stephen the martyr.

27 December

ST JOHN, APOSTLE AND EVANGELIST   Feast

The author of the Fourth Gospel, the Apocalypse, and three Epistles, John was son of Zebedee, and one of the three (with Peter and James) who were closest to the Lord, present at the Transfiguration, the Agony in the Garden, the raising of the daughter of Jairus. He is the 'beloved disciple' referred to in the gospels.

Entrance Antiphon: The Lord opened his mouth in the assembly, and filled him with the spirit of wisdom and understanding, and clothed him in a robe of glory.

or

At the last supper, John reclined close to the Lord. Blessed apostle, to you were revealed the heavenly secrets! Your lifegiving words have spread over all the earth!

Opening Prayer
God our Father,
you have revealed the mysteries of your Word
through John the apostle.
By prayer and reflection
may we come to understand the wisdom he taught.

FIRST READING

A reading from the first letter of St John 1:1-4
What we have seen and heard we are telling you.

Something which has existed since the beginning,
that we have heard,
and we have seen with our own eyes;
that we have watched
and touched with our hands:
the Word, who is life –
this is our subject.
That life was made visible:
we saw it and we are giving our testimony,
telling you of the eternal life
which was with the Father and has been made visible to us.
What we have seen and heard
we are telling you
so that you too may be in union with us,
as we are in union
with the Father
and with his Son Jesus Christ.
We are writing this to you to make our own joy complete.

This is the word of the Lord.

Responsional Psalm Ps 96:1-2. 5-6. 11-12. ℟ v.12

℟ **Rejoice, you just, in the Lord.**

1 The Lord is king, let earth rejoice,
   the many coastlands be glad.
   Cloud and darkness are his raiment;
   his throne, justice and right.   ℟

2 The mountains melt like wax
   before the Lord of all the earth.
   The skies proclaim his justice;
   all peoples see his glory.   ℟

3 Light shines forth for the just
   and joy for the upright of heart.
   Rejoice, you just, in the Lord;
   give glory to his holy name.   ℟

Gospel Acclamation
Alleluia, alleluia!
We praise you, O God, we acknowledge you to be the Lord.
The glorious company of the apostles praise you, O Lord.
Alleluia!

GOSPEL

A reading from the holy Gospel according to John   20:2-8
The other disciple, running faster than Peter, reached the tomb first.

On the first day of the week Mary of Magdala came running to Simon Peter and the other disciple, the one Jesus loved. 'They have taken the Lord out of the tomb' she said 'and we don't know where they have put him.'

So Peter set out with the other disciple to go to the tomb. They ran together, but the other disciple, running faster than Peter, reached the tomb first; he bent down and saw the linen cloths lying on the ground, but did not go in. Simon Peter who was following now came up, went right into the tomb, saw the linen cloths on the ground, and also the cloth that had been over his head; this was not with the linen cloths but rolled up in a place by itself. Then the other disciple who had reached the tomb first also went in; he saw and he believed.

This is the Gospel of the Lord.

Prayer over the Gifts
Lord,
bless these gifts we present to you.
With Saint John may we share
in the hidden wisdom of your eternal Word
which you reveal at this eucharistic table.

Preface of Christmas I-III, P3-P5.

Communion Antiphon: The Word of God became man, and lived among us. Of his riches we have all received.

Prayer after Communion
Almighty God,
Saint John proclaimed that your Word became flesh for our
   salvation.
Through this eucharist may your Son always live in us,
for he is Lord for ever and ever.

28 December
THE HOLY INNOCENTS, MARTYRS — Feast

Children under the age of two in Bethlehem were massacred by Herod the Great in an attempt to kill the child Jesus.

Entrance Antiphon: These innocent children were slain for Christ. They follow the spotless Lamb, and proclaim for ever: Glory to you, Lord.

Opening Prayer
Father,
the Holy Innocents offered you praise
by the death they suffered for Christ.
May our lives bear witness
to the faith we profess with our lips.

FIRST READING

A reading from the first letter of St John   1:5 – 2:2
The blood of Jesus Christ purifies us from all sin.

This is what we have heard from Jesus Christ,
and the message that we are announcing to you:
God is light; there is no darkness in him at all.
If we say that we are in union with God
while we are living in darkness,
we are lying because we are not living the truth.
But if we live our lives in the light,
as he is in the light,
we are in union with one another,
and the blood of Jesus, his Son,
purifies us from all sin.
If we say we have no sin in us,
we are deceiving ourselves
and refusing to admit the truth;
but if we acknowledge our sins,
then God who is faithful and just
will forgive our sins and purify us
from everything that is wrong.
To say that we have never sinned
is to call God a liar
and to show that his word is not in us.

I am writing this, my children,
to stop you sinning;
but if anyone should sin,
we have our advocate with the Father,
Jesus Christ, who is just;
he is the sacrifice that takes our sins away,
and not only ours,
but the whole world's.

This is the word of the Lord.

Responsorial Psalm
Ps 123:2-5. 7-8. ℟ v.7

℟ **Our life, like a bird, has escaped
from the snare of the fowler.**

1   If the Lord had not been on our side
    when men rose against us,
    then would they have swallowed us alive
    when their anger was kindled.   ℟

2   Then would the waters have engulfed us,
    the torrent gone over us;
    over our head would have swept
    the raging waters.   ℟

3   Indeed the snare has been broken
    and we have escaped.
    Our help is in the name of the Lord,
    who made heaven and earth.   ℟

Gospel Acclamation
Alleluia, alleluia!
We praise you, O God, we acknowledge you to be the Lord.
The noble army of martyrs praise you, O Lord.
Alleluia!

GOSPEL

A reading from the holy Gospel according to Matthew   2:13-18
In Bethlehem Herod had all the male children killed.

After the wise men had left, the angel of the Lord appeared to Joseph in a dream and said, 'Get up, take the child and his mother with you, and escape into Egypt, and stay there until I tell you, because Herod intends to search for the child and do away with him.' So Joseph got up and, taking the child and his mother with him, left that night for Egypt, where he stayed until Herod was dead. This was to fulfil what the Lord had spoken through the prophet:

I called my son out of Egypt.

Herod was furious when he realised that he had been outwitted by the wise men and in Bethlehem and its surrounding district he had all the male children killed who were two years old or under, reckoning by the date he had been careful to ask the wise men. It was then that the words spoken through the prophet Jeremiah were fulfilled:

A voice was heard in Ramah,
sobbing and loudly lamenting:
it was Rachel weeping for her children,
refusing to be comforted
because they were no more.

This is the Gospel of the Lord.

Prayer over the Gifts
Lord,
you give us your life even before we understand.
Receive the offerings we bring in love,
and free us from sin.

Preface of Christmas I-III, P3-P5, pp.1042-3.

Communion Antiphon: These have been ransomed for God and the Lamb as the first-fruits of mankind; they follow the Lamb wherever he goes.

Prayer after Communion
Lord,
by a wordless profession of faith in your Son,
the innocents were crowned with life at his birth.
May all people who receive your holy gifts today
come to share in the fullness of salvation.

29 December
St Thomas à Becket, bishop and martyr
Optional Memorial

Born in London, about 1118, studied in Paris, became a deacon in the church at Canterbury, Chancellor of England under King Henry II. He was a friend and companion of the King on various expeditions. In 1162 he was appointed Archbishop of Canterbury, and from then on, lived with austerity and defended the rights of the Church against the King. He was exiled to France for six years, and murdered on the King's orders on his return, in 1170.

Common of martyrs, pp. 1865ff., or of pastors: bishops, pp. 1878ff.

Opening Prayer
Almighty God,
you granted the martyr Thomas
the grace to give his life for the cause of justice.
By his prayers
make us willing to renounce for Christ
our life in this world
so that we may find it in heaven.

FIRST READING

A reading from the second letter of St Paul to Timothy
2:8-13; 3:10-12
Anybody who tries to live in devotion to Christ is certain to be attacked.

Remember the Good News that I carry, 'Jesus Christ risen from the dead, sprung from the race of David'; it is on account of this that I have my own hardships to bear, even to being chained like a criminal – but they cannot chain up God's news. So I bear it all for the sake of those who are chosen, so that in the end they may have the salvation that is in Christ Jesus and the eternal glory that comes with it.

Here is a saying that you can rely on:

If we have died with him, then we shall live with him.
If we hold firm, then we shall reign with him.
If we disown him, then he will disown us.
We may be unfaithful, but he is always faithful,
for he cannot disown his own self.

You know what I have taught, how I have lived, what I have aimed at; you know my faith, my patience and my love; my constancy and the persecutions and hardships that came to me in places like Antioch, Iconium and Lystra – all the persecutions I have endured; and the Lord has rescued me from every one of them. You are well aware, then, that anybody who tries to live in devotion to Christ is certain to be attacked.

This is the word of the Lord.

Responsorial Psalm
Ps 33:2-9. R v.5

℟ **From all my terrors the Lord set me free.**

1   I will bless the Lord at all times,
    his praise always on my lips;
    in the Lord my soul shall make its boast.
    The humble shall hear and be glad.   ℟

2   Glorify the Lord with me.
    Together let us praise his name.
    I sought the Lord and he answered me;
    from all my terrors he set me free.   ℟

3   Look towards him and be radiant;
    let your faces not be abashed.
    This poor man called; the Lord heard him
    and rescued him from all his distress.   ℟

4   The angel of the Lord is encamped
    around those who revere him, to rescue them.
    Taste and see that the Lord is good.
    He is happy who seeks refuge in him.   ℟

Gospel Acclamation
Mt 5:6

Alleluia, alleluia!
Happy those who hunger and thirst for what is right:
they shall be satisfied.
Alleluia!

GOSPEL

A reading from the holy Gospel according to Matthew   16:24-27
Anyone who loses his life for my sake, will save it.

Jesus said to his disciples, 'If anyone wants to be a follower of mine, let him renounce himself and take up his cross and follow me. For anyone who wants to save his life will lose it; but anyone who loses his life for my sake will find it. What, then, will a man gain if he wins the whole world and ruins his life? Or what has a man to offer in exchange for his life?

'For the Son of Man is going to come in the glory of his Father with his angels, and, when he does, he will reward each one according to his behaviour.'

This is the Gospel of the Lord.

31 December

St Sylvester I, pope   Optional Memorial

He became Bishop of Rome in 314, at the time of Emperor Constantine, whom he may have baptised. This was the time of the Donatist schism and the Arian heresy, against which he defended the Church. He died in 335.

Common of pastors: popes, pp.1876ff.

Opening Prayer
Lord,
help and sustain your people
by the prayers of Pope Sylvester.
Guide us always in this present life
and bring us to the joy that never ends.

FIRST READING

A reading from the prophet Ezekiel   34:11-16
I myself will pasture my sheep, I myself will show them where to rest.

The Lord says this: I am going to look after my flock myself and keep all of it in view. As a shepherd keeps all his flock in view when he stands up in the middle of his scattered sheep, so shall I keep my sheep in view. I shall rescue them from wherever they have been scattered during the mist and darkness. I shall bring them out of the countries where they are; I shall gather them together from foreign countries and bring them back to their own land. I shall pasture them on the mountains of Israel, in the ravines and in every inhabited place in the land. I shall feed them in good pasturage; the high mountains of Israel will be their grazing ground. There they will rest in good grazing ground; they will browse in rich pastures on the mountains of Israel. I myself will pasture my sheep, I myself will show them where to rest – it is the Lord who speaks. I shall look for the lost one, bring back the stray, bandage the wounded and make the weak strong. I shall watch over the fat and healthy. I shall be a true shepherd to them.

This is the word of the Lord.

Responsorial Psalm
Ps 22. ℟ v.1

℟ **The Lord is my shepherd;**
  there is nothing I shall want.

1 The Lord is my shepherd;
  there is nothing I shall want.
  Fresh and green are the pastures
  where he gives me repose.
  Near restful waters he leads me,
  to revive my drooping spirit. ℟

2 He guides me along the right path;
  he is true to his name.
  If I should walk in the valley of darkness
  no evil would I fear.
  You are there with your crook and your staff;
  with these you give me comfort. ℟

3 You have prepared a banquet for me
  in the sight of my foes.
  My head you have anointed with oil;
  my cup is overflowing. ℟

4 Surely goodness and kindness shall follow me
  all the days of my life.
  In the Lord's own house shall I dwell
  for ever and ever. ℟

Gospel Acclamation
Mk 1:17

Alleluia, alleluia!
Follow me, says the Lord,
and I will make you into fishers of men.
Alleluia!

GOSPEL

A reading from the holy Gospel according to Matthew 16:13-19
You are Peter and on this rock I will build my Church.

When Jesus came to the region of Caesarea Philippi he put this question to his disciples, 'Who do people say the Son of Man is?' And they said, 'Some say he is John the Baptist, some Elijah, and others Jeremiah or one of the prophets'. 'But you,' he said, 'who do you say I am?' Then Simon Peter spoke up, 'You are the Christ,' he said, 'the Son of the living God'. Jesus replied, 'Simon son of Jonah, you are a happy man! Because it was not flesh and blood that revealed this to you but my Father in heaven. So I now say to you: You are Peter and on this rock I will build my Church. And the gates of the underworld can never hold out against it. I will give you the keys of the kingdom of heaven: whatever you bind on earth shall be considered bound in heaven; whatever you loose on earth shall be considered loosed in heaven.'

This is the Gospel of the Lord.

1853

COMMON MASSES

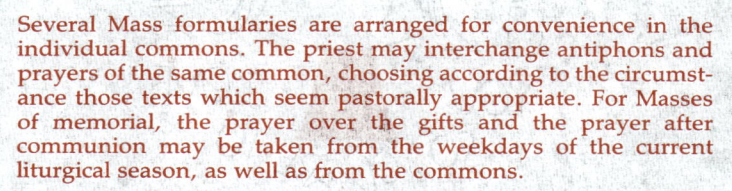

Several Mass formularies are arranged for convenience in the individual commons. The priest may interchange antiphons and prayers of the same common, choosing according to the circumstance those texts which seem pastorally appropriate. For Masses of memorial, the prayer over the gifts and the prayer after communion may be taken from the weekdays of the current liturgical season, as well as from the commons.

Certain Masses which are given for specific seasons and circumstances should be used for those seasons and circumstances. During the Easter season, an *alleluia* should be added at the end of the entrance and communion antiphons.

The Lectionary offers a variety of readings of each Common. However, as specific readings are proposed for each celebration in the Proper of Saints, these are not reproduced in this volume.

A NEW COMMANDMENT I GIVE YOU LOVE EACH OTHER AS I LOVED YOU SO YOU ARE TO LOVE ONE ANOTHER

COMMON OF THE DEDICATION OF A CHURCH

I. On the Day of Dedication

Entrance Antiphon: This is a place of awe; this is God's house, the gate of heaven, and it shall be called the royal court of God.

Opening Prayer
All-powerful and ever-living God,
fill this church with your love
and give your help to all who call on you in faith.
May the power of your word and sacraments in this place
bring strength to the people gathered here.

Prayer over the Gifts
Lord,
accept the gifts of your Church
which we offer with joy.
May all your people gathered in this holy place
come to eternal salvation by these mysteries.

Preface of the Dedication of a Church I, P52.

Communion Antiphon: My house shall be called a house of prayer, says the Lord; ask here and you shall receive, seek and you shall find, knock and the door will open.

Prayer after Communion
Lord,
may your truth grow in our hearts
by the holy gifts we receive.
May we worship you always in your holy temple
and come to rejoice with all the saints in your presence.

2. Anniversary of Dedication

A. In the Dedicated Church

Entrance Antiphon: Greatly to be feared is God in his sanctuary; he, the God of Israel, gives power and strength to his people. Blessed be God!

1856 *Common of the Dedication of a Church*

Opening Prayer
Father,
each year we recall the dedication of this church to your service.
Let our worship always be sincere
and help us to find your saving love in this church.

Prayer over the Gifts
Lord,
as we recall the day you filled this church
with your glory and holiness,
may our lives also become an acceptable offering to you.

Preface of the Dedication of a Church I, P52.

Communion Antiphon: You are the temple of God, and God's spirit dwells in you. The temple of God is holy; you are that temple.

Prayer after Communion
Lord,
we know the joy and power of your blessing in our lives.
As we celebrate the dedication of this church,
may we give ourselves once more to your service.

B. Outside the Dedicated Church

Entrance Antiphon: I saw the holy city, new Jerusalem, coming down from God out of heaven, like a bride adorned in readiness for her husband.

Opening Prayer
God our Father,
from living stones, your chosen people,
you built an eternal temple to your glory.
Increase the spiritual gifts you have given to your Church,
so that your faithful people may continue to grow
into the new and eternal Jerusalem.

or

Father,
you called your people to be your Church.
As we gather together in your name,
may we love, honour, and follow you
to eternal life in the kingdom you promise.

Prayer over the Gifts
Lord,
receive our gifts.
May we who share this sacrament
experience the life and power it promises,
and hear the answer to our prayers.

Preface of the Dedication of a Church II, P53.

Communion Antiphon: Like living stones let yourselves be built on Christ as a spiritual house, a holy priesthood.

Prayer after Communion
Father,
you make your Church on earth
a sign of the new and eternal Jerusalem.
By sharing in this sacrament
may we become the temple of your presence
and the home of your glory.

COMMON OF THE BLESSED VIRGIN MARY

These Masses are also used for the Saturday celebrations of the Blessed Virgin Mary, and for Votive Masses of the Blessed Virgin Mary.

I

Entrance Antiphon: Hail, holy Mother! The child to whom you gave birth is the King of heaven and earth for ever.

Opening Prayer
Lord God,
give to your people the joy
of continual health in mind and body.
With the prayers of the Virgin Mary to help us,
guide us through the sorrows of this life
to eternal happiness in the life to come.

or

Lord,
take away the sins of your people.
May the prayers of Mary the mother of your Son help us,
for alone and unaided we cannot hope to please you.

Prayer over the Gifts
Father,
the birth of Christ your Son
deepened the virgin mother's love for you,
and increased her holiness.
May the humanity of Christ
give us courage in our weakness;
may it free us from our sins,
and make our offering acceptable.

Preface of the Blessed Virgin Mary I, P56 (feasts and memorials), or II, P57 (Votive Masses).

Communion Antiphon: Blessed is the womb of the Virgin Mary; she carried the Son of the eternal Father.

Prayer after Communion
Lord,
we rejoice in your sacraments and ask your mercy
as we honour the memory of the Virgin Mary.
May her faith and love
inspire us to serve you more faithfully
in the work of salvation.

2

Entrance Antiphon: Blessed are you, Virgin Mary, who carried the creator of all things in your womb; you gave birth to your maker, and remain for ever a virgin.

Opening Prayer
God of mercy,
give us strength.
May we who honour the memory of the Mother of God
rise above our sins and failings with the help of her prayers.

or

Lord,
may the prayers of the Virgin Mary
bring us protection from danger
and freedom from sin
that we may come to the joy of your peace.

Prayer over the Gifts
Lord,
we honour the memory of the mother of your Son.
May the sacrifice we share
make of us an everlasting gift to you.

Preface of the Blessed Virgin Mary I, P56 (feasts and memorials), or II, P57 (Votive Masses).

Communion Antiphon: The Almighty has done great things for me. Holy is his name.

Prayer after Communion
Lord,
you give us the sacraments of eternal redemption.
May we who honour the memory of the mother of your Son

rejoice in the abundance of your grace
and experience your unfailing help.

3

Entrance Antiphon: You have been blessed, O Virgin Mary, above all other women on earth by the Lord the most high God; he has so exalted your name that your praises shall never fade from the mouths of men.

Opening Prayer
Lord,
as we honour the glorious memory of the Virgin Mary,
we ask that by the help of her prayers
we too may come to share the fullness of your grace.

or

Lord Jesus Christ,
you chose the Virgin Mary to be your mother,
a worthy home in which to dwell.
By her prayers keep us from danger
and bring us to the joy of heaven,
where you live . . .

Prayer over the Gifts
Lord,
we bring you our sacrifice of praise
at this celebration in honour of Mary,
    the mother of your Son.
May this holy exchange of gifts
help us on our way to eternal salvation.

Preface of the Blessed Virgin Mary I, P56 (feasts and memorials), or II, P57 (Votive Masses).

Communion Antiphon: All generations will call me blessed, because God has looked upon his lowly handmaid.

Prayer after Communion
Lord,
we eat the bread of heaven.
May we who honour the memory of the Virgin Mary
come one day to your banquet of eternal life.

4. Advent Season

Entrance Antiphon: Let the clouds rain down the Just One, and the earth bring forth a Saviour.

or

The angel said to Mary: You have won God's favour. You will conceive and bear a Son, and he will be called Son of the Most High.

Opening Prayer
Father,
in your plan for our salvation
your Word became man,
announced by an angel and born of the Virgin Mary.
May we who believe that she is the Mother of God
receive the help of her prayers.

Prayer over the Gifts
Lord,
may the power of your Spirit,
which sanctified Mary the mother of your Son,
make holy the gifts we place upon this altar.

Preface of the Blessed Virgin Mary I, P56 (feasts and memorials), or II, P57 (Votive Masses), or Preface of Advent II, P2.

Communion Antiphon: The Virgin is with child and shall bear a son, and she will call him Emmanuel.

Prayer after Communion
Lord our God,
may the sacraments we receive
show us your forgiveness and love.
May we who honour the mother of your Son
be saved by his coming among us as man,
for he is Lord for ever and ever.

Common of the Blessed Virgin Mary

5. Christmas Season

Entrance Antiphon: Giving birth to the King whose reign is unending, Mary knows the joys of motherhood together with a virgin's honour; none like her before, and there shall be none hereafter.

or

O virgin Mother of God, the universe cannot hold him, and yet, becoming man, he confined himself in your womb.

Opening Prayer
Father,
you gave the human race eternal salvation
through the motherhood of the Virgin Mary.
May we experience the help of her prayers in our lives,
for through her we received the very source of life,
your Son, our Lord Jesus Christ,
who lives and reigns . . .

Prayer over the Gifts
Lord,
accept our gifts and prayers
and fill our hearts with the light of your Holy Spirit.
Help us to follow the example of the Virgin Mary:
to seek you in all things
and to do your will with gladness.

Preface of the Blessed Virgin Mary I, P56 (feasts or memorials), or II, P57 (Votive Masses).

Communion Antiphon: The Word of God became man, and lived among us, full of grace and truth.

Prayer after Communion
Lord,
as we celebrate this feast of the Blessed Virgin Mary,
you renew us with the body and blood of Christ your Son.
May this sacrament give us a share in his life,
for he is Lord for ever and ever.

6. Easter Season

Entrance Antiphon: The disciples were constantly at prayer together, with Mary the mother of Jesus, alleluia.

Opening Prayer
God our Father,
you give joy to the world
by the resurrection of your Son, our Lord Jesus Christ.
Through the prayers of his mother, the Virgin Mary,
bring us to the happiness of eternal life.

or

God our Father,
you gave the Holy Spirit to your apostles
as they joined in prayer with Mary, the mother of Jesus.
By the help of her prayers
keep us faithful in your service
and let our words and actions be so inspired
as to bring glory to your name.

Prayer over the Gifts
Father,
as we celebrate the memory of the Virgin Mary,
we offer you our gifts and prayers.
Sustain us by the love of Christ,
who offered himself as a perfect sacrifice on the cross,
and is Lord for ever and ever.

Preface of the Blessed Virgin Mary I, P56 (feasts or memorials), or II, P57 (Votive Masses).

Communion Antiphon: Rejoice, virgin mother, for Christ has arisen from his grave, alleluia.

Prayer after Communion
Lord,
may this sacrament strengthen the faith in our hearts.
May Mary's Son, Jesus Christ,
whom we proclaim to be God and man,
bring us to eternal life
by the saving power of his resurrection,
for he is Lord for ever and ever.

Common of the Blessed Virgin Mary

Other Prayers for Masses of the Blessed Virgin Mary

Opening Prayer
All-powerful God,
we rejoice in the protection of the holy Virgin Mary.
May her prayers help to free us from all evils here on earth
and lead us to eternal joy in heaven.

Prayer over the Gifts
Lord,
accept the prayers and gifts we present today
as we honour Mary, the Mother of God.
May they please you
and bring us your forgiveness and help.

Prayer after Communion
Lord,
we are renewed with the sacraments of salvation.
May we who celebrate the memory of the Mother of God
come to realise the eternal redemption you promise.

COMMON OF MARTYRS

1. For Several Martyrs, outside the Easter Season

Entrance Antiphon: The saints are happy in heaven because they followed Christ. They rejoice with him for ever because they shed their blood for love of him.

Opening Prayer
Father,
we celebrate the memory of Saints N. and N.
who died for their faithful witnessing to Christ.
Give us the strength to follow their example,
loyal and faithful to the end.

Prayer over the Gifts
Father,
receive the gifts we bring
in memory of your holy martyrs.
Keep us strong in our faith
and in our witness to you.

Communion Antiphon: You are the men who have stood by me faithfully in my trials, and now I confer a kingdom on you, says the Lord. You will eat and drink at my table in my kingdom.

Prayer after Communion
God our Father,
in your holy martyrs you show us the glory of the cross.
Through this sacrifice, strengthen our resolution
to follow Christ faithfully
and to work in your Church for the salvation of all.

2. For Several Martyrs, outside the Easter Season

Entrance Antiphon: Many are the sufferings of the just, and from them all the Lord has delivered them; the Lord preserves all their bones, not one of them shall be broken.

Opening Prayer
All-powerful, ever-living God,
turn our weakness into strength.
As you gave your martyrs N. and N.

the courage to suffer death for Christ,
give us the courage to live in faithful witness to you.

Prayer over the Gifts
Lord,
accept the gifts we bring
to celebrate the feast of your martyrs.
May this sacrifice free us from sin
and make our service pleasing to you.

Communion Antiphon: No one has greater love, says the Lord, than the man who lays down his life for his friends.

Prayer after Communion
Lord,
we eat the bread from heaven
and become one body in Christ.
Never let us be separated from his love
and help us to follow your martyrs N. and N.
by having the courage to overcome all things through Christ,
who loved us all,
and lives and reigns with you for ever and ever.

3. For Several Martyrs, outside the Easter Season

Entrance Antiphon: The salvation of the just comes from the Lord.
He is their strength in time of need.

Opening Prayer
Lord,
may the victory of your martyrs give us joy.
May their example strengthen our faith,
and their prayers give us renewed courage.

or

Lord,
hear the prayers of the martyrs N. and N.
and give us courage to bear witness to your truth.

Prayer over the Gifts
Lord,
accept the gifts of your people

Common of Martyrs 1867

as we honour the suffering and death
of your martyrs N. and N.
As the eucharist gave them strength in persecution
may it keep us faithful in every difficulty.

Communion Antiphon: Whoever loses his life for my sake and the gospel, says the Lord, will save it.

Prayer after Communion
Lord,
keep this eucharist effective within us.
May the gift we receive
on this feast of the martyrs N. and N.
bring us salvation and peace.

4. For Several Martyrs, outside the Easter Season

Entrance Antiphon: The Lord will hear the just when they cry out, from all their afflictions he will deliver them.

Opening Prayer
God our Father,
every year you give us the joy
of celebrating this feast of Saints N. and N.
May we who recall their birth to eternal life
imitate their courage in suffering for you.

or

God our Father,
your generous gift of love
brought Saints N. and N. to unending glory.
Through the prayers of your martyrs
forgive our sins and free us from every danger.

Prayer over the Gifts
Lord,
you gave Saints N. and N. the fulfilment of their faith
in the vision of your glory.
May the gifts we bring to honour their memory
gain us your pardon and peace.

Communion Antiphon: We are given over to death for Jesus, that the life of Jesus may be revealed in our dying flesh.

Prayer after Communion
Lord,
may this food of heaven
bring us a share in the grace you gave the martyrs N. and N.
From their bitter sufferings may we learn to become strong
and by patient endurance earn the victory of rejoicing in your holiness.

5. For Several Martyrs, outside the Easter Season

Entrance Antiphon: The holy martyrs shed their blood on earth for Christ; therefore they have received an everlasting reward.

Opening Prayer
Lord,
we honour your martyrs N. and N.
who were faithful to Christ
even to the point of shedding their blood for him.
Increase our own faith and free us from our sins,
and help us to follow their example of love.

Prayer over the Gifts
Lord,
be pleased with the gifts we bring.
May we who celebrate the mystery of the passion of your Son
make this mystery part of our lives
by the inspiration of the martyrs N. and N.

or

Lord,
may these gifts which we bring you in sacrifice
to celebrate the victory of Saints N. and N.
fill our hearts with your love
and prepare us for the reward you promise
to those who are faithful.

Communion Antiphon: Neither death nor life nor anything in all creation can come between us and Christ's love for us.

Prayer after Communion
Lord,
you give us the body and blood of Christ your only Son
on this feast of your martyrs N. and N.

By being faithful to your love
may we live in you,
receive life from you,
and always be true to your inspiration.

6. For One Martyr, outside the Easter Season

Entrance Antiphon: This holy man fought to the death for the law of his God, never cowed by the threats of the wicked; his house was built on solid rock.

Opening Prayer
God of power and mercy,
you gave N., your martyr, victory over pain and suffering.
Strengthen us who celebrate this day of his triumph
and help us to be victorious over the evils that threaten us.

Prayer over the Gifts
Lord,
bless our offerings and make them holy.
May these gifts fill our hearts
with the love which gave Saint N. victory
over all his suffering.

or

Lord,
accept the gifts we offer in memory of the martyr N.
May they be pleasing to you
as was the shedding of his blood for the faith.

Communion Antiphon: If anyone wishes to come after me, he must renounce himself, take up his cross, and follow me, says the Lord.

Prayer after Communion
Lord,
may the mysteries we receive
give us the spiritual courage which made your martyr N.
faithful in your service and victorious in his suffering.

7. For One Martyr, outside the Easter Season

Entrance Antiphon: Here is a true martyr who shed his blood for Christ; his judges could not shake him by their menaces, and so he won through to the kingdom of heaven.

Opening Prayer
All-powerful, ever-living God,
you gave Saint N. the courage to witness to the gospel of Christ
even to the point of giving his life for it.
By his prayers help us to endure all suffering for love of you
and to seek you with all our hearts,
for you alone are the source of life.

Prayer over the Gifts
God of love,
pour out your blessing on our gifts
and make our faith strong,
the faith which Saint N. professed by shedding his blood.

or

Lord,
accept these gifts we present in memory of Saint N.,
for no temptation could turn him away from you.

Communion Antiphon: I am the vine and you are the branches, says the Lord; he who lives in me, and I in him, will bear much fruit.

Prayer after Communion
Lord,
we are renewed by the mystery of the eucharist.
By imitating the fidelity of Saint N. and by your patience
may we come to share the eternal life you have promised.

8. For Several Martyrs, in the Easter Season

Entrance Antiphon: Come, you whom my Father has blessed; inherit the kingdom prepared for you since the foundation of the world, alleluia.

Opening Prayer
Father,
you gave your martyrs N. and N.
the courage to die in witness to Christ and the gospel.
By the power of your Holy Spirit,
give us the humility to believe
and the courage to profess
the faith for which they gave their lives.

or

God our all-powerful Father,
you strengthen our faith
and take away our weakness.
Let the prayers and example of your martyrs N. and N. help us
to share in the passion and resurrection of Christ
and bring us to eternal joy with all your saints.

Prayer over the Gifts
Lord,
we celebrate the death of your holy martyrs.
May we offer the sacrifice which gives all martyrdom its meaning.

Communion Antiphon: Those who are victorious I will feed from the tree of life, which grows in the paradise of my God, alleluia.

Prayer after Communion
Lord,
at this holy meal
we celebrate the heavenly victory of your martyrs N. and N.
May this bread of life
give us the courage to conquer evil,
so that we may come to share the fruit of the tree of life in
    paradise.

Common of Martyrs

9. For Several Martyrs, in the Easter Season

Entrance Antiphon: These are the saints who were victorious in the blood of the Lamb, and in the face of death they did not cling to life; therefore they are reigning with Christ for ever, alleluia.

Opening Prayer
Lord,
you gave your martyrs N. and N.
the privilege of shedding their blood
in boldly proclaiming the death and resurrection of your Son.
May this celebration of their victory give them honour among
  your people.

Prayer over the Gifts
Lord,
fill these gifts with the blessing of your Holy Spirit
and fill our hearts with the love
which gave victory to Saints N. and N.
in dying for the faith.

Communion Antiphon: If we die with Christ, we shall live with him, and if we are faithful to the end, we shall reign with him, alleluia.

Prayer after Communion
Lord,
we are renewed by the breaking of one bread
in honour of the martyrs N. and N.
Keep us in your love
and help us to live the new life Christ won for us.

10. For One Martyr, in the Easter Season

Entrance Antiphon: Light for ever will shine on your saints, O Lord, alleluia.

Opening Prayer
God our Father,
you have honoured the Church with the victorious witness of
    Saint N.,
who died for his faith.
As he imitated the sufferings and death of the Lord,
may we follow in his footsteps and come to eternal joy.

Prayer over the Gifts
Lord,
accept this offering of praise and peace
in memory of your martyr N.
May it bring us your forgiveness
and inspire us to give you thanks now and for ever.

Communion Antiphon: I tell you solemnly: Unless a grain of wheat falls on the ground and dies, it remains a single grain; but if it dies, it yields a rich harvest, alleluia.

Prayer after Communion
Lord,
we receive your gifts from heaven
at this joyful feast.
May we who proclaim at this holy table
the death and resurrection of your Son
come to share his glory with all your holy martyrs.

Common of Martyrs

Other Prayers for Martyrs
For Missionary Martyrs

Opening Prayer
God of mercy and love,
through the preaching of your martyrs N. and N.
you brought the good news of Christ
to people who had not known him.
May the prayers of Saints N. and N.
make our own faith grow stronger.

Prayer over the Gifts
Lord,
at this celebration of the eucharist
we honour the suffering and death of your martyrs N. and N.
In offering this sacrifice
may we proclaim the death of your Son
who gave these martyrs courage not only by his words
but also by the example of his own passion,
for he is Lord for ever and ever.

Prayer after Communion
Lord,
may we who eat at your holy table
be inspired by the example of Saints N. and N.
May we keep before us the loving sacrifice of your Son,
and come to the unending peace of your kingdom.

For a Virgin Martyr

Opening Prayer
God our Father,
you give us joy each year
in honouring the memory of Saint N.
May her prayers be a source of help for us,
and may her example of courage and chastity be our inspiration.

Prayer over the Gifts
Lord,
receive our gifts
as you accepted the suffering and death of Saint N.
in whose honour we celebrate this eucharist.

Common of Martyrs 1875

Prayer after Communion
Lord God,
you gave Saint N. the crown of eternal joy
because she gave her life
rather than renounce the virginity she had promised
in witness to Christ.
With the courage this eucharist brings
help us to rise out of the bondage of our earthly desires
and attain to the glory of your kingdom.

For a Holy Woman Martyr

Opening Prayer
Father,
in our weakness your power reaches perfection.
You gave Saint N. the strength
to defeat the power of sin and evil.
May we who celebrate her glory share in her triumph.

Prayer over the Gifts
Lord,
today we offer this sacrifice in joy
as we recall the victory of Saint N.
May we proclaim to others the great things
you have done for us
and rejoice in the constant help of your martyr's prayers.

Prayer after Communion
Lord,
by this sacrament you give us eternal joys
as we recall the memory of Saint N.
May we always embrace the gift of life
we celebrate at this eucharist.

COMMON OF PASTORS

1. For Popes or Bishops

Entrance Antiphon: The Lord chose him to be his high priest; he opened his treasures and made him rich in all goodness.

Opening Prayer (for popes)
All-powerful and ever-living God,
you called Saint N. to guide your people
by his word and example.
With him we pray to you:
watch over the pastors of your Church
with the people entrusted to their care,
and lead them to salvation.

or (for bishops)
Father,
you gave Saint N. to your Church
as an example of a good shepherd.
May his prayers
help us on our way to eternal life.

Prayer over the Gifts
Lord,
we offer you this sacrifice of praise
in memory of your saints.
May their prayers keep us from evil
now and in the future.

Communion Antiphon: The good shepherd gives his life for his sheep.

Prayer after Communion
Lord God,
Saint N. loved you
and gave himself completely in the service of your Church.
May the eucharist awaken in us that same love.

Common of Pastors

2. For Popes or Bishops

Entrance Antiphon: The Lord sealed a covenant of peace with him and made him a prince, bestowing the priestly dignity upon him for ever.

Opening Prayer (for popes)
Father,
you made Saint N. shepherd of the whole Church
and gave to us the witness of his virtue and teaching.
Today as we honour this outstanding bishop,
we ask that our light may shine before men
and that our love for you may be sincere.

or (for bishops)

All-powerful God,
you made Saint N. a bishop and leader of the Church
to inspire your people with his teaching and example.
May we give fitting honour to his memory
and always have the assistance of his prayers.

Prayer over the Gifts
Lord,
may the sacrifice which wipes away the sins of all the world
bring us your forgiveness.
Help us as we offer it
on this yearly feast in honour of Saint N.

Communion Antiphon: Lord, you know all things: you know that I love you.

Prayer after Communion
Lord God,
let the power of the gifts we receive
on this feast of Saint N.
take full effect within us.
May this eucharist bring us your help in this life
and lead us to happiness in the unending life to come.

3. For Bishops

Entrance Antiphon: I will look after my sheep, says the Lord, and I will raise up one shepherd who will pasture them. I, the Lord, will be their God.

Opening Prayer
All-powerful, ever-living God,
you made Saint N. bishop and leader of your people.
May his prayers help to bring us your forgiveness and love.

Prayer over the Gifts
Lord,
accept the gifts we bring to your holy altar
on this feast of Saint N.
May our offering bring honour to your name
and pardon to your people.

Communion Antiphon: You have not chosen me; I have chosen you. Go and bear fruit that will last.

Prayer after Communion
Lord,
may we who receive this sacrament
be inspired by the example of Saint N.
May we learn to proclaim what he believed
and put his teaching into action.

4. For Bishops

Entrance Antiphon: I will raise up for myself a faithful priest; he will do what is in my heart and in my mind, says the Lord.

Opening Prayer
Lord God,
you counted Saint N. among your holy pastors,
renowned for faith and love which conquered evil in this world.
By the help of his prayers
keep us strong in faith and love
and let us come to share his glory.

Common of Pastors 1879

Prayer over the Gifts
Lord,
accept the gifts your people offer you
on this feast of Saint N.
May these gifts bring us
your help for which we long.

Communion Antiphon: I came that men may have life, and have it to the full, says the Lord.

Prayer after Communion
Lord our God,
you give us the holy body and blood
of your Son.
May the salvation we celebrate
be our undying hope.

5. For Pastors

Entrance Antiphon: The Spirit of God is upon me; he has anointed me. He sent me to bring good news to the poor, and to heal the broken-hearted.

Opening Prayer
God our Father,
in Saint (bishop) N. you gave
a light to your faithful people.
You made him a pastor of the Church
to feed your sheep with his word
and to teach them by his example.
Help us by his prayers to keep the faith he taught
and follow the way of life he showed us.

Prayer over the Gifts
Father of mercy,
we have these gifts to offer in honour of your saints
who bore witness to your mighty power.
May the power of the eucharist
bring us your salvation.

Communion Antiphon: I, the Lord, am with you always, until the end of the world.

Prayer after Communion
Lord,
may the mysteries we receive
prepare us for the eternal joys
Saint N. won by his faithful ministry.

or

All-powerful God,
by our love and worship
may we who share this holy meal
always follow the example of Saint N.

6. For Pastors

Entrance Antiphon: I will give you shepherds after my own heart, and they shall feed you on knowledge and sound teaching.

or

Priests of God, bless the Lord; praise God, all you that are holy and humble of heart.

Opening Prayer
Lord God,
you gave your Saints (bishops) N. and N.
the spirit of truth and love
to shepherd your people.
May we who honour them on this feast
learn from their example
and be helped by their prayers.

Prayer over the Gifts
Lord,
accept these gifts from your people.
May the eucharist we offer to your glory
in honour of Saints N. and N.
help us on our way to salvation.

Communion Antiphon: The Son of Man did not come to be served, but to serve, and to give his life as a ransom for many.

Prayer after Communion
Lord,
we receive the bread of heaven
as we honour the memory of your Saints N. and N.
May the eucharist we now celebrate
lead us to eternal joys.

7. For Pastors

Entrance Antiphon: Lord, may your priests be clothed in justice, and your holy ones leap for joy.

Opening Prayer
All-powerful God,
hear the prayers of Saints N. and N.
Increase your gifts within us
and give us peace in our days.

Prayer over the Gifts
Lord,
accept the gifts we bring to your altar
in memory of your Saints N. and N.
As you led them to glory through these mysteries,
grant us also your pardon and love.

Communion Antiphon: Blessed is the servant whom the Lord finds watching when he comes; truly I tell you, he will set him over all his possessions.

or

The Lord has put his faithful servant in charge of his household, to give them their share of bread at the proper time.

Prayer after Communion
All-powerful God,
by the eucharist we share at your holy table
on this feast of Saints N. and N.
increase our strength of character and love for you.
May we guard from every danger the faith you have given us
and walk always in the way that leads to salvation.

8. For Founders of Churches

Entrance Antiphon: My words that I have put in your mouth, says the Lord, will never be absent from your lips, and your gifts will be accepted on my altar.

Opening Prayer
God of mercy,
you gave our fathers the light of faith
through the preaching of Saint N.
May we who glory in the Christian name
show in our lives the faith we profess.

or

Lord,
look upon the family whom your Saint (bishop) N. brought to life
with the word of truth
and nourished with the sacrament of life.
By his ministry you gave us the faith;
by his prayers help us grow in love.

Prayer over the Gifts
Lord,
may the gifts your people bring
in memory of Saint N.
bring us your gifts from heaven.

Communion Antiphon: The Son of Man came to give his life as a ransom for many.

Prayer after Communion
Lord,
may this pledge of our eternal salvation
which we receive on this feast of Saint N.
be our help now and always.

9. For Founders of Churches

Entrance Antiphon: The Lord chose these holy men for their unfeigned love, and gave them eternal glory. The Church has light by their teaching.

Opening Prayer
Lord,
look with love on the church of N.
Through the apostolic zeal of Saints N. and N.
you gave us the beginnings of our faith:
through their prayers keep alive our Christian love.

or

Lord,
you called our fathers to the light of the gospel
by the preaching of your bishop N.
By his prayers help us to grow in the love and knowledge
of your Son, our Lord Jesus Christ,
who lives and reigns . . .

Prayer over the Gifts
Lord,
accept the gifts your people bring
on this feast of Saints N. and N.
Give us purity of heart
and make us pleasing to you.

Communion Antiphon: No longer shall I call you servants, for a servant knows not what his master does. Now I shall call you friends, for I have revealed to you all that I have heard from my Father.

Prayer after Communion
Lord,
as we share in your gifts,
we celebrate this feast of Saints N. and N.
We honour the beginnings of our faith
and proclaim your glory in the saints.
May the salvation we receive from your altar
be our unending joy.

1884   *Common of Pastors*

10. For Missionaries

Entrance Antiphon: These are holy men who became God's friends and glorious heralds of his truth.

Opening Prayer
Father,
through your Saint (bishop) N.
you brought those who had no faith
out of darkness into the light of truth.
By the help of his prayers,
keep us strong in our faith
and firm in the hope of the gospel he preached.

or

All-powerful and ever-living God,
you made this day holy
by welcoming Saint N. into the glory of your kingdom.
Keep us true to the faith he professed with untiring zeal,
and help us to bring it to perfection by acting in love.

Prayer over the Gifts
All-powerful God,
look upon the gifts we bring on this feast
in honour of Saint N.
May we who celebrate the mystery of the death of the Lord
imitate the love we celebrate.

Communion Antiphon: I will feed my sheep, says the Lord, and give them repose.

Prayer after Communion
Lord,
Saint N. worked tirelessly for the faith,
spending his life in its service.
With the power this eucharist gives
make your people strong in the same true faith
and help us to proclaim it everywhere
by all we say and do.

11. For Missionaries

Entrance Antiphon: How beautiful on the mountains are the feet of the man who brings tidings of peace, joy and salvation.

Opening Prayer
Father,
you made your Church grow
through the Christian zeal and apostolic work of Saint N.
By the help of his prayers
give your Church continued growth in holiness and faith.

Prayer over the Gifts
Lord,
be pleased with our prayers
and free us from all guilt.
In your love, wash away our sins
that we may celebrate the mysteries which set us free.

Communion Antiphon: Go out to all the world, and tell the good news: I am with you always, says the Lord.

or

Live in me and let me live in you, says the Lord; he who lives in me, and I in him, will bear much fruit.

Prayer after Communion
Lord our God,
by these mysteries help our faith grow to maturity
in the faith the apostles preached and taught,
and the faith which Saint N. watched over with such care.

12. For Missionaries

Entrance Antiphon: Proclaim his glory among the nations, his marvellous deeds to all the peoples; great is the Lord and worthy of all praise.

Opening Prayer
God of mercy,
you gave us Saint N. to proclaim the riches of Christ.
By the help of his prayers
may we grow in knowledge of you,
be eager to do good,
and learn to walk before you
by living the truth of the gospel.

or (for martyrs)

All-powerful God,
help us to imitate with steadfast love
the faith of Saints N. and N.
who won the crown of martyrdom
by giving their lives in the service of the gospel.

Prayer over the Gifts
Lord,
we who honour the memory of Saint N.
ask you to send your blessing on these gifts.
By receiving them may we be freed from all guilt
and share in the food from the heavenly table.

Communion Antiphon: The Lord sent disciples to proclaim to all the towns: the kingdom of God is very near to you.

Prayer after Communion
Lord,
let the holy gifts we receive fill us with life
so that we who rejoice in honouring the memory of Saint N.
may also benefit from his example of apostolic zeal.

COMMON OF DOCTORS OF THE CHURCH

1

Entrance Antiphon: The Lord opened his mouth in the assembly, and filled him with the spirit of wisdom and understanding, and clothed him in a robe of glory.

or

The mouth of the just man utters wisdom, and his tongue speaks what is right; the law of his God is in his heart.

Opening Prayer
God our Father,
you made your Saint (bishop) N. a teacher in your Church.
By the power of the Holy Spirit
establish his teaching in our hearts.
As you give him to us as a patron,
may we have the protection of his prayers.

Prayer over the Gifts
Lord,
accept our sacrifice on this feast of Saint N.,
and following his example
may we give you our praise
and offer you all we have.

Communion Antiphon: The Lord has put his faithful servant in charge of his household, to give them their share of bread at the proper time.

Prayer after Communion
God our Father,
Christ the living bread renews us.
Let Christ our teacher instruct us
that on this feast of Saint N.
we may learn your truth
and practise it in love.

2

Entrance Antiphon: The learned will shine like the brilliance of the firmament, and those who train many in the ways of justice will sparkle like the stars for all eternity.

or

Let the peoples declare the wisdom of the saints and the Church proclaim their praises; their names shall live for ever.

Opening Prayer

Lord God,
you filled Saint N. with heavenly wisdom.
By his help may we remain true to his teaching
and put it into practice.

Prayer over the Gifts

Lord,
by this celebration,
may your Spirit fill us with the same light of faith
that shines in the teaching of Saint N.

Communion Antiphon: We preach a Christ who was crucified; he is the power and the wisdom of God.

Prayer after Communion

Lord,
you renew us with the food of heaven.
May Saint N. remain our teacher and example
and keep us thankful for all we have received.

COMMON OF VIRGINS

1

Entrance Antiphon: Here is a wise and faithful virgin who went with lighted lamp to meet her Lord.

Opening Prayer
God our Saviour,
as we celebrate with joy the memory of the virgin N.,
may we learn from her example of faithfulness and love.

Prayer over the Gifts
Lord,
we see the wonder of your love
in the life of the virgin N.
and her witness to Christ.
Accept our gifts of praise
and make our offering pleasing to you.

Communion Antiphon: The bridegroom is here; let us go out to meet Christ the Lord.

Prayer after Communion
Lord God,
may this eucharist renew our courage and strength.
May we remain close to you, like Saint N.,
by accepting in our lives
a share in the suffering of Jesus Christ,
who lives and reigns with you for ever and ever.

2

Entrance Antiphon: Let us rejoice and shout for joy, because the Lord of all things has favoured this holy and glorious virgin with his love.

Opening Prayer
Lord God,
you endowed the virgin N. with gifts from heaven.
By imitating her goodness here on earth
may we come to share her joy in eternal life.

or (for a virgin foundress)

Lord our God,
may the witness of your faithful bride the virgin N.
awaken the fire of divine love in our hearts.
May it inspire other young women to give their lives
to the service of Christ and his Church.

Prayer over the Gifts
Lord,
may the gifts we bring you
help us follow the example of Saint N.
Cleanse us from our earthly way of life,
and teach us to live the new life of your kingdom.

Communion Antiphon: The five sensible virgins took flasks of oil as well as their lamps. At midnight a cry was heard: the bridegroom is here; let us go out to meet Christ the Lord.

Prayer after Communion
Lord,
may our reception of the body and blood of your Son
keep us from harmful things.
Help us by the example of Saint N.
to grow in your love on earth
that we may rejoice for ever in heaven.

Common of Virgins

3

Entrance Antiphon: Come, bride of Christ, and receive the crown, which the Lord has prepared for you for ever.

Opening Prayer
Lord,
you have told us that you live for ever
in the hearts of the chaste.
By the prayers of the virgin N.,
help us to live by your grace
and remain a temple of your Spirit.

or

Lord,
hear the prayers of those who recall the devoted life of the virgin
 N.
Guide us on our way and help us to grow
in love and devotion as long as we live.

Prayer over the Gifts
Lord,
receive our worship in memory of N. the virgin.
By this perfect sacrifice
make us grow in unselfish love for you
and for our brothers.

Communion Antiphon: The wise virgin chose the better part for herself, and it shall not be taken away from her.

Prayer after Communion
God of mercy,
we rejoice that on this feast of Saint N.
you give us the bread of heaven.
May it bring us pardon for our sins,
health of body,
your grace in this life,
and glory in heaven.

4

Entrance Antiphon: Let virgins praise the name of the Lord, for his name alone is supreme; its majesty outshines both earth and heaven.

Opening Prayer
Lord,
increase in us your gifts of mercy and forgiveness.
May we who rejoice at this celebration
in honour of the virgins N. and N.
receive the joy of sharing eternal life with them.

Prayer over the Gifts
Lord,
we bring you our gifts and prayers.
We praise your glory on this feast of the virgins N. and N.,
whose witness to Christ was pleasing to you.
Be pleased also with the eucharist we now offer.

Communion Antiphon: The bridegroom has come, and the virgins who were ready have gone in with him to the wedding.

or

Whoever loves me will be loved by my Father. We shall come to him and make our home with him.

Prayer after Communion
Lord,
may the mysteries we receive
on this feast of the virgins N. and N.
keep us alert and ready to welcome your Son at his return,
that he may welcome us to the feast of eternal life.

HAPPY ARE THEY WHO HEAR THE WORD OF GOD & KEEP IT

COMMON OF HOLY MEN AND WOMEN

If no specific indication is given, the following Masses may be used for saints of any rank.

1

Entrance Antiphon: May all your works praise you, Lord, and your saints bless you; they will tell of the glory of your kingdom and proclaim your power.

Opening Prayer
Ever-living God,
the signs of your love are manifest
in the honour you give your saints.
May their prayers and their example encourage us
to follow your Son more faithfully.

Prayer over the Gifts
Lord,
in your kindness hear our prayers
and the prayers which the saints offer on our behalf.
Watch over us that we may offer fitting service at your altar.

Communion Antiphon: May the just rejoice as they feast in God's presence, and delight in gladness of heart.

or

Blessed are those servants whom the Lord finds watching when he comes; truly I tell you, he will seat them at his table and wait on them.

Prayer after Communion
Father, our comfort and peace,
we have gathered as your family
to praise your name and honour your saints.
Let the sacrament we have received
be the sign and pledge of our salvation.

2

Entrance Antiphon: The just man will rejoice in the Lord and hope in him, and all the upright of heart will be praised.

Common of Holy Men and Women 1895

Opening Prayer
God our Father,
you alone are holy;
without you nothing is good.
Trusting in the prayers of Saint N.
we ask you to help us
to become the holy people you call us to be.
Never let us be found undeserving
of the glory you have prepared for us.

Prayer over the Gifts
All-powerful God,
may the gifts we present
bring honour to your saints,
and free us from sin in mind and body.

Communion Antiphon: He who serves me, follows me, says the Lord; and where I am, my servant will also be.

Prayer after Communion
Lord,
your sacramental gifts renew us
at this celebration of the birth of your saints to glory.
May the good things you give us
lead us to the joy of your kingdom.

3

Entrance Antiphon: Lord, your strength gives joy to the just; they greatly delight in your saving help. You have granted them their heart's desire.

Opening Prayer
Father,
your saints guide us when in our weakness we tend to stray.
Help us who celebrate the birth of Saint N. to glory
grow closer to you by following his (her) example.

Prayer over the Gifts
Lord,
let the sacrifice we offer
in memory of Saint N.
bring to your people the gifts of unity and peace.

Communion Antiphon: If anyone wishes to come after me, he must renounce himself, take up his cross, and follow me, says the Lord.

Prayer after Communion
Lord,
may the sacraments we receive
on this feast in honour of N.
give us holiness of mind and body
and bring us into your divine life.

4

Entrance Antiphon: The teaching of truth was in his mouth, and no wrong was found on his lips; he walked with me in peace and justice, and turned many away from wickedness.

Opening Prayer
Merciful Father,
we fail because of our weakness.
Restore us to your love
through the example of your saints.

Prayer over the Gifts
Lord,
may this sacrifice we share
on the feast of Saint N.
give you praise
and help us on our way to salvation.

Communion Antiphon: Happy are the pure of heart for they shall see God. Happy the peacemakers; they shall be called sons of God. Happy are they who suffer persecution for justice' sake; the kingdom of heaven is theirs.

Prayer after Communion
Lord,
our hunger is satisfied by your holy gift.
May we who have celebrated this eucharist
experience in our lives the salvation which it brings.

Common of Holy Men and Women 1897

5

Entrance Antiphon: The just man will flourish like the palm tree. Planted in the courts of God's house, he will grow great like the cedars of Lebanon.

Opening Prayer
Lord,
may the prayers of the saints
bring help to your people.
Give to us who celebrate the memory of your saints
a share in their eternal joy.

Prayer over the Gifts
Lord,
give to us who offer these gifts at your altar
the same spirit of love that filled Saint N.
By celebrating this sacred eucharist with pure minds and loving hearts
may we offer a sacrifice that pleases you,
and brings salvation to us.

Communion Antiphon: Come to me, all you that labour and are burdened, and I will give you rest, says the Lord.

Prayer after Communion
Lord,
may the sacrament of holy communion which we receive
bring us health and strengthen us
in the light of your truth.

6

Entrance Antiphon: Blessed is the man who puts his trust in the Lord; he will be like a tree planted by the waters, sinking its roots into the moist earth; he will have nothing to fear in time of drought.

Opening Prayer
All-powerful God,
help us who celebrate the memory of Saint N.
to imitate his (her) way of life.
May the example of your saints
be our challenge to live holier lives.

Prayer over the Gifts
Lord,
we bring our gifts to your holy altar
on this feast of your saints.
In your mercy let this eucharist
give you glory
and bring us to the fullness of your love.

Communion Antiphon: As the Father has loved me, so have I loved you; remain in my love.

Prayer after Communion
Lord our God,
may the divine mysteries we celebrate
in memory of your saint
fill us with eternal peace and salvation.

7. For Religious

Entrance Antiphon: The Lord is my inheritance and my cup; he alone will give me my reward. The measuring line has marked a lovely place for me; my inheritance is my great delight.

Opening Prayer
Lord God,
you kept Saint N. faithful to Christ's pattern of poverty and
   humility.
May his (her) prayers help us to live in fidelity to our calling
and bring us to the perfection you have shown us in your Son,
who lives and reigns . . .

or

Lord,
in your abbot N.
you give an example of the gospel lived to perfection.
Help us to follow him
by keeping before us the things of heaven
amid all the changes of this world.

Prayer over the Gifts
God of all mercy,
you transformed Saint N.
and made him (her) a new creature in your image.

Common of Holy Men and Women

Renew us in the same way
by making our gifts of peace acceptable to you.

Communion Antiphon: I solemnly tell you: those who have left everything and followed me will be repaid a hundredfold and will gain eternal life.

Prayer after Communion
All-powerful God,
may we who are strengthened by the power of this sacrament
learn from the example of Saint N.
to seek you above all things
and to live in this world as your new creation.

8. For Religious

Entrance Antiphon: These are the saints who received blessings from the Lord, a prize from God their Saviour. They are the people that long to see his face.

Opening Prayer
God our Father,
you called Saint N. to seek your kingdom in this world
by striving to live in perfect charity.
With his (her) prayers to give us courage,
help us to move forward with joyful hearts in the way of love.

Prayer over the Gifts
Lord,
may the gifts we bring to your altar
in memory of Saint N.
be acceptable to you.
Free us from the things that keep us from you
and teach us to seek you as our only good.

Communion Antiphon: Taste and see the goodness of the Lord; blessed is he who hopes in God.

Prayer after Communion
Lord,
by the power of this sacrament and the example of Saint N.
guide us always in your love.
May the good work you have begun in us

reach perfection in the day of Christ Jesus
who is Lord for ever and ever.

9. For Those who Worked for the Underprivileged

Entrance Antiphon: Come, you whom my Father has blessed, says the Lord: I was ill and you comforted me. I tell you, anything you did for one of my brothers, you did for me.

Opening Prayer

Lord God,
you teach us that the commandments of heaven
are summarised in love of you and love of our neighbour.
By following the example of Saint N.
in practising works of charity
may we be counted among the blessed in your kingdom.

Prayer over the Gifts

Lord,
accept the gifts of your people.
May we who celebrate the love of your Son
also follow the example of your saints
and grow in love for you and for one another.

Communion Antiphon: No one has greater love, says the Lord, than the man who lays down his life for his friends.

or

By the love you have for one another, says the Lord, everyone will know that you are my disciples.

Prayer after Communion

Lord,
may we who are renewed by these mysteries
follow the example of Saint N.
who worshipped you with love
and served your people with generosity.

or

Lord,
we who receive the sacrament of salvation ask your mercy.
Help us to imitate the love of Saint N.
and give to us a share in his (her) glory.

10. For Teachers

Entrance Antiphon: Let the children come to me, and do not stop them, says the Lord; to such belongs the kingdom of God.

or

The man that keeps these commandments and teaches them, he is the one who will be called great in the kingdom of heaven, says the Lord.

Opening Prayer
Lord God,
you called Saint N. to serve you in the Church
by teaching his (her) fellow man the way of salvation.
Inspire us by his (her) example:
help us to follow Christ our teacher,
and lead us to our brothers and sisters in heaven.

Prayer over the Gifts
Lord,
accept the gifts your people bring
in memory of your saints.
May our sharing in this mystery
help us to live the example of love you give us.

Communion Antiphon: Unless you change, and become like little children, says the Lord, you shall not enter the kingdom of heaven.

or

I am the light of the world, says the Lord; the man who follows me will have the light of life.

Prayer after Communion
All-powerful God,
may this holy meal help us
to follow the example of your saints
by showing in our lives
the light of truth and love for our brothers.

11: For Holy Women

Entrance Antiphon: Honour the woman who fears the Lord. Her sons will bless her, and her husband praise her.

Opening Prayer
God our Father,
every year you give us joy on this feast of Saint N.
As we honour her memory by this celebration,
may we follow the example of her holy life.

or (for several)

All-powerful God,
may the prayers of Saints N. and N. bring us help from heaven
as their lives have already given us
an example of holiness.

Prayer over the Gifts
Lord,
may the gifts we present in memory of Saint N.
bring us your forgiveness and salvation.

Communion Antiphon: The kingdom of heaven is like a merchant in search of fine pearls; on finding one rare pearl he sells everything he has and buys it.

Prayer after Communion
All-powerful God,
fill us with your light and love
by the sacrament we receive on the feast of Saint N.
May we burn with love for your kingdom
and let our light shine before men.

12. For Holy Women

Entrance Antiphon: Praise to the holy woman whose home is built on faithful love and whose pathway leads to God.

Opening Prayer
Father,
rewarder of the humble,
you blessed Saint N. with charity and patience.
May her prayers help us, and her example inspire us
to carry our cross and to love you always.

or

Lord,
pour upon us the spirit of wisdom and love
with which you filled your servant Saint N.
By serving you as she did,
may we please you with our faith and our actions.

Prayer over the Gifts
Lord,
receive the gifts your people bring to you
in honour of your saints.
By the eucharist we celebrate
may we progress toward salvation.

Communion Antiphon: Whoever does the will of my Father in heaven is my brother and sister and mother, says the Lord.

Prayer after Communion
Lord,
we receive your gifts
at this celebration in honour of Saint N.
May they free us from sin
and strengthen us by your grace.

MASSES FOR VARIOUS OCCASIONS

The Roman Missal proposes a variety of Masses for various occasions and needs. A selection of these is given in the pages that follow.

The readings are arranged as follows:
Old Testament readings are presented in 'pairings' with a responsorial psalm. Any other suitable pairing of psalm and Old Testament reading may be chosen.
New Testament readings, when used as a first reading, may be followed by any responsorial psalm chosen from those given.
Gospel readings are presented in 'pairings' with a Gospel Acclamation. Any other suitable pairing may be chosen.

I THE VINE
YOU THE BRANCHES
HE WHO LIVES IN ME & I IN HIM BEARS FRUIT

1907

FOR UNITY OF CHRISTIANS

(Lectionary 10) (Roman Missal 13)

A

Entrance Antiphon: I am the Good Shepherd. I know my sheep, and mine know me, says the Lord, just as the Father knows me and I know the Father. I give my life for my sheep.

Opening Prayer
Almighty and eternal God,
you keep together those you have united.
Look kindly on all who follow Jesus your Son.
We are all consecrated to you by our common baptism;
make us one in the fullness of faith
and keep us one in the fellowship of love.

or

Lord,
lover of mankind,
fill us with the love your Spirit gives.
May we live in a manner worthy of our calling;
make us witnesses of your truth to all men
and help us work to bring all believers together
in the unity of faith and the fellowship of peace.

Readings: see below, pp.1910ff.

Prayer over the Gifts
Lord,
by one perfect sacrifice
you gained us as your people.
Bless us and all your Church
with gifts of unity and peace.

Preface of Christian Unity, P76.

Communion Antiphon: Because there is one bread, we, though many, are one body, for we all share in the one loaf and in the one cup.

Prayer after Communion
Lord,

may this holy communion,
the sign and promise of our unity in you,
make that unity a reality in your Church.

B

Entrance Antiphon: Save us, Lord our God, and gather us together from the nations, that we may proclaim your holy name and glory in your praise.

Opening Prayer
God our Father,
you bring many nations together
to unite in praising your name.
Make us able and willing to do what you ask.
May the people you call to your kingdom
be one in faith and love.

or

Lord,
hear the prayers of your people
and bring the hearts of believers together in your praise
and in common sorrow for their sins.
Heal all divisions among Christians
that we may rejoice in the perfect unity of your Church
and move together as one
to eternal life in your kingdom.

Readings: see below, p.1910ff.

Prayer over the Gifts
Lord,
hear our prayer for your mercy
as we celebrate this memorial of our salvation.
May this sacrament of your love
be our sign of unity and our bond of charity.

Preface of Christian Unity, P76.

Communion Antiphon: To crown all things there must be love, to bind them together and bring them to completion; and may the peace of Christ rule in your hearts, that peace to which all of you are called as one body.

For Unity of Christians 1909

Prayer after Communion
Lord,
fill us with the Spirit of love;
by the power of this sacrifice
bring together in love and peace
all who believe in you.

C

Entrance Antiphon: **There is one body and one spirit as there is one hope held out to you by your call; there is one Lord, one faith, one baptism; one God, the Father of all, and through all; he lives in all of us.**

Opening Prayer
Father,
look with love on your people
and pour out upon them the gifts of your Spirit.
May they constantly grow in the love of truth.
May they study and work together
for perfect unity among Christians.

or

Lord,
pour out upon us the fullness of your mercy
and by the power of your Spirit
remove divisions among Christians.
Let your Church rise more clearly as a sign for all the nations
that the world may be filled with the light of your Spirit,
and believe in Jesus Christ whom you have sent,
who lives and reigns . . .

Readings: see below, pp.1910ff.

Prayer over the Gifts
Father,
may the sacrifice we offer you
free us from our sins
and bring together all who are joined by one baptism
to share this mystery of the eucharist.

Preface of Christian Unity, P76.

Communion Antiphon: May all be one as you are, Father, in me, and I in you; may they be one in us: I in them and you in me, may they be completely one.

Prayer after Communion
Lord,
we who share in the sacraments of Christ
ask you to renew the gift of holiness in your Church.
May all who glory in the name of Christian
come to serve you in the unity of faith.

OLD TESTAMENT READING

1

A reading from the book of Deuteronomy   30:1-4
He will gather you once again out of all the peoples where he has scattered you.

Moses said to the people: 'When all these words come true for you, the blessing and the curse I have set before you, if you meditate on them in your heart wherever among the nations the Lord your God drives you, if you return to the Lord your God, if you obey his voice with all your heart and soul in everything I enjoin on you today, you and your children, then the Lord your God will bring back your captives, he will have pity on you and gather you once again out of all the peoples where the Lord your God has scattered you. Had you wandered to the ends of the heavens, the Lord your God would gather you even from there, would come there to reclaim you.'

This is the word of the Lord.

Responsorial Psalm   Jer 31:10-14. ℟ cf. v.10
   ℟ **Gather your scattered people, O Lord.**
       and guard them like a shepherd guarding his flock.

1 O nations, hear the word of the Lord,
   proclaim it to the far-off coasts.
   Say: 'He who scattered Israel will gather him
   and guard him as a shepherd guards his flock.'   ℟

2 For the Lord has ransomed Jacob,
has saved him from an overpowering hand.
They will come and shout for joy on Mount Zion,
they will stream to the blessings of the Lord. ℟

3 Then the young girls will rejoice and will dance,
the men, young and old, will be glad.
I will turn their mourning into joy,
I will console them, give gladness for grief.
The priests I will again feed with plenty,
and my people shall be filled with my blessings. ℟

2

A reading from the prophet Ezekiel 36:24-28

I am going to gather you from all the foreign countries; and I shall give you a new heart.

The Lord God says this:
I am going to take you from among the nations and gather you together from all the foreign countries, and bring you home to your own land. I shall pour clean water over you and you will be cleansed; I shall cleanse you of all your defilement and all your idols. I shall give you a new heart, and put a new spirit in you; I shall remove the heart of stone from your bodies and give you a heart of flesh instead. I shall put my spirit in you, and make you keep my laws and sincerely respect my observances. You will live in the land which I gave your ancestors. You shall be my people and I will be your God.

This is the word of the Lord.

Responsional Psalm Ps 22. ℟ v.1

℟ **The Lord is my shepherd;
there is nothing I shall want.**

1 The Lord is my shepherd;
there is nothing I shall want.
Fresh and green are the pastures
where he gives me repose.
Near restful waters he leads me,
to revive my drooping spirit. ℟

2 He guides me along the right path;
he is true to his name.

If I should walk in the valley of darkness
no evil would I fear.
You are there with your crook and your staff;
with these you give me comfort.

℟ **The Lord is my shepherd;
there is nothing I shall want.**

3 You have prepared a banquet for me
in the sight of my foes.
My head you have anointed with oil;
my cup is overflowing. ℟

4 Surely goodness and kindness shall follow me
all the days of my life.
In the Lord's own house shall I dwell
for ever and ever. ℟

3

A reading from the prophet Ezekiel 37:15-19. 21-22. 26-28
They will no longer form two nations.

The word of the Lord was addressed to me as follows, 'Son of man, take a stick and write on it, "Judah and those Israelites loyal to him." Take another stick and write on it, "Joseph, the wood of Ephraim, and all the House of Israel loyal to him."

'Join one to the other to make a single piece of wood, a single stick in your hand. And when the members of your nation say, "Tell us what you mean," say, "The Lord says this: I am taking the stick of Joseph, now in the hand of Ephraim, and those tribes of Israel loyal to him, and I am going to put the stick of Judah with them. I shall make one stick out of the two, and I shall hold them as one.

' "I am going to take the sons of Israel from the nations where they have gone. I shall gather them together from everywhere and bring them home to their own soil. I shall make them into one nation in my own land and on the mountains of Israel, and one king is to be king of them all; they will no longer form two nations, nor be two separate kingdoms. I shall make a covenant of peace with them, an eternal covenant with them. I shall resettle them and increase them; I shall settle my sanctuary among them for ever. I shall make my home above them; I will be their God, they shall be my people. And the nations will learn

For Unity of Christians, Readings 1913

that I am the Lord the sanctifier of Israel, when my sanctuary is with them for ever" '.

This is the word of the Lord.

Responsorial Psalm   Ps 117:22-23. 25-26. 28. ℟ v.22

   ℟ **The stone which the builders rejected
has become the corner stone.**

or

   ℟ **Alleluia!**

1   The stone which the builders rejected
has become the corner stone.
This is the work of the Lord,
a marvel in our eyes.   ℟

2   O Lord, grant us salvation;
O Lord, grant success.
Blessed in the name of the Lord
is he who comes.
We bless you from the house of the Lord.   ℟

3   You are my God, I thank you.
My God, I praise you.   ℟

4

A reading from the prophet Zephaniah   3:16-20
When the time comes, I will gather you in.

Zion, have no fear,
do not let your hands fall limp.
The Lord your God is in your midst,
a victorious warrior.
He will exult with joy over you,
he will renew you by his love;
he will dance with shouts of joy for you
as on a day of festival.
I have taken away your misfortune,
no longer need you bear the disgrace of it.
I am taking action here and now
against your oppressors.
When that time comes I will rescue the lame,
and gather the strays,
and I will win them praise and renown

when I restore their fortunes.
When that times comes, I will be your guide,
when that time comes, I will gather you in;
I will give you praise and renown
among all the peoples of the earth
when I restore your fortunes under your own eyes,
says the Lord.

    This is the word of the Lord.

Responsorial Psalm   Ps 99:2-5. ℟ v.3. Alt. ℟ v.2

    ℟ **We are his people: the sheep of his flock.**

or

    ℟ **Come before the Lord, singing for joy.**

1   Cry out with joy to the Lord, all the earth.
    Serve the Lord with gladness.
    Come before him, singing for joy.   ℟

2   Know that he, the Lord, is God.
    He made us, we belong to him,
    we are his people, the sheep of his flock.   ℟

3   Go within his gates, giving thanks.
    Enter his courts with songs of praise.
    Give thanks to him and bless his name.   ℟

4   Indeed, how good is the Lord,
    eternal his merciful love.
    He is faithful from age to age.   ℟

NEW TESTAMENT READING

1

A reading from the first letter of St Paul   1:10-13
to the Corinthians
Make up the differences between you. Has Christ been parcelled out?

I appeal to you, brothers, for the sake of our Lord Jesus Christ, to make up the differences between you, and instead of disagreeing among yourselves, to be united again in your belief and practice. From what Chloe's people have been telling me, my dear brothers, it is clear that there are serious differences among you.

What I mean are all these slogans that you have, like: 'I am for Paul', 'I am for Apollos,' 'I am for Cephas,' 'I am for Christ.' Has Christ been parcelled out? Was it Paul that was crucified for you? Were you baptised in the name of Paul?

This is the word of the Lord.

2

A reading from the letter of St Paul to the Ephesians   2:19-22
You are part of a building that has the apostles for its foundations, and Christ Jesus himself for its main cornerstone.

You are no longer aliens or foreign visitors: you are citizens like all the saints, and part of God's household. You are part of a building that has the apostles and prophets for its foundations, and Christ Jesus himself for its main cornerstone. As every structure is aligned on him, all grow into one holy temple in the Lord; and you too, in him, are being built into a house where God lives, in the Spirit.

This is the word of the Lord.

3

A reading from the letter of St Paul to the Ephesians   4:1-6
Do all you can to preserve the unity of the Spirit by the peace that binds you together.

I, the prisoner in the Lord, implore you to lead a life worthy of your vocation. Bear with one another charitably, in complete selflessness, gentleness and patience. Do all you can to preserve the unity of the Spirit by the peace that binds you together. There is one Body, one Spirit, just as you were called into one and the same hope when you were called. There is one Lord, one faith, one baptism, and one God who is Father of all, over all, through all and within all.

This is the word of the Lord.

4

A reading from the letter of St Paul to the Ephesians   4:30 – 5:2
Forgive each other as readily as God forgave you in Christ.

Do not grieve the Holy Spirit of God who has marked you with his seal for you to be set free when the day comes. Never have grudges against others, or lose your temper, or raise your voice to anybody, or call each other names, or allow any sort of spitefulness. Be friends with one another, and kind, forgiving each other as readily as God forgave you in Christ.

    Try, then, to imitate God, as children of his that he loves, and follow Christ by loving as he loved you, giving himself up in our place as a fragrant offering and a sacrifice to God.

    This is the word of the Lord.

5

A reading from the letter of St Paul to the Philippians   2:1-13
Be united with a common purpose.

If our life in Christ means anything to you, if love can persuade at all, or the Spirit that we have in common, or any tenderness and sympathy, then be united in your convictions and united in your love, with a common purpose and a common mind. That is the one thing which would make me completely happy. There must be no competition among you, no conceit; but everybody is to be self-effacing. Always consider the other person to be better than yourself, so that nobody thinks of his own interests first but everybody thinks of other people's interests instead. In your minds you must be the same as Christ Jesus:

> His state was divine,
> yet he did not cling
> to his equality with God
> but emptied himself
> to assume the condition of a slave,
> and became as men are;
> and being as all men are,
> he was humbler yet,
> even to accepting death,
> death on a cross.
> But God raised him high
> and gave him the name
> which is above all other names

so that all beings
in the heavens, on earth and in the underworld,
should bend the knee at the name of Jesus
and that every tongue should acclaim
Jesus Christ as Lord,
to the glory of God the Father.

So then, my dear friends, continue to do as I tell you, as you always have; not only as you did when I was there with you, but even more now that I am no longer there; and work for your salvation 'in fear and trembling'. It is God, for his own loving purpose, who puts both the will and the action into you.

This is the word of the Lord.

6

A reading from the letter of St Paul to the Colossians　　3:9-17
You were called together as parts of one body.

You have stripped off your old behaviour with your old self, and you have put on a new self which will progress towards true knowledge the more it is renewed in the image of its creator; and in that image there is no room for distinction between Greek and Jew, between the circumcised or the uncircumcised, or between barbarian and Scythian, slave and free man. There is only Christ: he is everything and he is in everything.

You are God's chosen race, his saints; he loves you, and you should be clothed in sincere compassion, in kindness and humility, gentleness and patience. Bear with one another; forgive each other as soon as a quarrel begins. The Lord has forgiven you; now you must do the same. Over all these clothes, to keep them together and complete them, put on love. And may the peace of Christ reign in your hearts, because it is for this that you were called together as parts of one body. Always be thankful.

Let the message of Christ, in all its richness, find a home with you. Teach each other, and advise each other, in all wisdom. With gratitude in your hearts sing psalms and hymns and inspired songs to God; and never say or do anything except in the name of the Lord Jesus, giving thanks to God the Father through him.

This is the word of the Lord.

7

A reading from the first letter of St Paul to Timothy   2:5-8
There is only one mediator between God and mankind, himself a man, Christ Jesus.

There is only one God, and there is only one mediator between God and mankind, himself a man, Christ Jesus, who sacrificed himself as a ransom for them all. He is the evidence of this, sent at the appointed time, and I have been named a herald and apostle of it and – I am telling the truth and no lie – a teacher of the faith and the truth to the pagans.

In every place, then, I want the men to lift their hands up reverently in prayer, with no anger or argument.

This is the word of the Lord.

8

A reading from the first letter of St John   4:9-15
Since God has loved us so much, we too should love one another.

God's love for us was revealed
when God sent into the world his only Son
so that we could have life through him;
this is the love I mean;
not our love for God,
but God's love for us when he sent his Son
to be the sacrifice that takes our sins away.
My dear people,
since God has loved us so much,
we too should love one another.
No one has ever seen God;
but as long as we love one another
God will live in us
and his love will be complete in us.
We can know that we are living in him
and he is living in us
because he lets us share his Spirit.
We ourselves saw and we testify
that the Father sent his Son
as saviour of the world.
If anyone acknowledges that Jesus is the Son of God,
God lives in him, and he in God.

This is the word of the Lord.

For Unity of Christians, Readings

GOSPEL

1

Gospel Acclamation
Alleluia, alleluia!
The Church of the Lord is a single beacon light
which shines over the whole world.
It remains forever one.
Alleluia!

A reading from the holy Gospel according to Matthew 18:19-22
Where two or three meet in my name, I shall be there with them.

Jesus said to his disciples:
'I tell you solemnly, if two of you on earth agree to ask anything at all, it will be granted to you by my Father in heaven. For where two or three meet in my name, I shall be there with them.'

Then Peter went up to him and said, 'Lord, how often must I forgive my brother if he wrongs me? As often as seven times?' Jesus answered, 'Not seven, I tell you, but seventy-seven times.'

This is the Gospel of the Lord.

2

Gospel Acclamation Col 3:15
Alleluia, alleluia!
May the peace of Christ reign in your hearts,
because it is for this that you were called together
as parts of one body.
Alleluia!

A reading from the holy Gospel according to Luke 9:49-56
Anyone who is not against you is for you.

John said to Jesus: 'Master, we saw a man casting out devils in your name, and because he is not with us we tried to stop him.' But Jesus said to him, 'You must not stop him: anyone who is not against you is for you.'

Now as the time drew near for him to be taken up to heaven, he resolutely took the road for Jerusalem and sent messengers ahead of him. These set out, and they went into a Samaritan village to make preparations for him, but the people would not receive him because he was making for Jerusalem. Seeing this, the disciples James and John said, 'Lord, do you want us to call down fire from heaven to burn them up?' But he turned and rebuked them, saying, 'You do not know what spirit you are made of. The Son of Man came not to destroy souls but to save them.'

This is the Gospel of the Lord.

3

Gospel Acclamation Eph 4:5
Alleluia, alleluia!
There is one Lord, one faith, one baptism,
and one God who is Father of all.
Alleluia!

A reading from the holy Gospel according to John 10:11-16
There will be one flock, and one shepherd.

Jesus said:

'I am the good shepherd:
the good shepherd is one who lays down his life for his sheep.
The hired man, since he is not the shepherd
and the sheep do not belong to him,
abandons the sheep and runs away
as soon as he sees a wolf coming,
and then the wolf attacks and scatters the sheep;
this is because he is only a hired man
and has no concern for the sheep.
I am the good shepherd;
I know my own
and my own know me
just as the Father knows me
and I know the Father;
and I lay down my life for my sheep.
And there are other sheep I have
that are not of this fold,
and these I have to lead as well.
They too will listen to my voice,
and there will be only one flock,
and one shepherd.'

This is the Gospel of the Lord.

4

Gospel Acclamation
Alleluia, alleluia!
Gather your Church together, Lord,
from the ends of the earth into your kingdom,
for glory and power are yours
through Jesus Christ for ever.
Alleluia!

A reading from the holy Gospel according to John 11:45-52
To gather together in unity the scattered children of God.

Many of the Jews who had come to visit Mary and Martha and had seen what Jesus did believed in him, but some of them went to tell the Pharisees what Jesus had done. Then the chief priests and Pharisees called a meeting. 'Here is this man working all these signs,' they said, 'and what action are we taking? If we let him go on in this way everybody will believe in him, and the Romans will come and destroy the Holy Place and our nation.' One of them, Caiaphas, the high priest that year, said, 'You don't seem to have grasped the situation at all; you fail to see that it is better for one man to die for the people, than for the whole nation to be destroyed.' He did not speak in his own person, it was as high priest that he made this prophecy that Jesus was to die for the nation – and not for the nation only, but to gather together in unity the scattered children of God.

This is the Gospel of the Lord.

5

Gospel Acclamation
Alleluia, alleluia!
Gather your church together, Lord,
from the ends of the earth into your kingdom,
for glory and power are yours
through Jesus Christ for ever.
Alleluia!

A reading from the holy Gospel according to John 13:1-5
I have given you an example that you may copy what I have done to you.

It was before the festival of the Passover, and Jesus knew that the hour had come for him to pass from this world to the Father. He had always loved those who were his in the world, but now he showed how perfect his love was.

They were at supper, and the devil had already put it into the mind of Judas Iscariot son of Simon, to betray him. Jesus knew that the Father had put everything into his hands, and that he had come from God and was returning to God, and he got up from table, removed his outer garment and, taking a towel, wrapped it round his waist; he then poured water into a basin and began to wash the disciples' feet and to wipe them with the towel he was wearing.

He came to Simon Peter, who said to him, 'Lord, are you going to wash my feet?' Jesus answered, 'At the moment you do not know what I am doing but later you will understand'. 'Never!' said Peter. 'You shall never wash my feet.' Jesus replied, 'If I do not wash you, you can have nothing in common with me.' 'Then, Lord,' said Simon Peter, 'not only my feet, but my hands and my head as well!' Jesus said, 'No one who has taken a bath needs washing, he is clean all over. You too are clean, though not all of you are.' He knew who was going to betray him, that was why he said, 'though not all of you are'.

When he had washed their feet and put on his clothes again he went back to the table. 'Do you understand,' he said, 'what I have done to you? You call me Master and Lord, and rightly; so I am. If I, then, the Lord and Master, have washed your feet, you should wash each other's feet. I have given you an example so that you may copy what I have done to you.'

This is the Gospel of the Lord.

6

Gospel Acclamation Eph 4:5
Alleluia, alleluia!
There is one Lord, one faith, one baptism,
and one God who is Father of all.
Alleluia!

A reading from the holy Gospel according to John 17:1-11
They were yours and you gave them to me, and they have kept your word.

Jesus raised his eyes to heaven and said:

'Father, the hour has come:

glorify your Son
so that your Son may glorify you;
and through the power over all mankind that you have given him,
let him give eternal life to all those you have entrusted to him.
And eternal life is this:
to know you,
the only true God,
and Jesus Christ whom you have sent.
I have glorified you on earth
and finished the work
that you gave me to do.
Now, Father, it is time for you to glorify me
with that glory I had with you
before ever the world was.
I have made your name known
to the men you took from the world to give me.
They were yours and you gave them to me,
and they have kept your word.
Now at last they know
that all you have given me comes indeed from you;
for I have given them
the teaching you gave to me,
and they have truly accepted this, that I came from you,
and have believed that it was you who sent me.
I pray for them;
I am not praying for the world
but for those you have given me,
because they belong to you:
all I have is yours
and all you have is mine,
and in them I am glorified.
I am not in the world any longer,
but they are in the world,
and I am coming to you.'

This is the Gospel of the Lord.

7

Gospel Acclamation   Jn 17:21
Alleluia, alleluia!
May they all be one,

For Unity of Christians, Readings

> Father, may they be one in us,
> as you are in me and I am in you,
> so that the world may believe it was you who sent me,
> says the Lord.
> Alleluia!

A reading from the holy Gospel according to John   17:11-19
That they may be one like us.

Jesus raised his eyes to heaven and prayed:

> 'Holy Father,
> keep those you have given me true to your name,
> so that they may be one like us.
> While I was with them,
> I kept those you had given me true to your name.
> I have watched over them and not one is lost
> except the one who chose to be lost,
> and this was to fulfill the scriptures.
> But now I am coming to you
> and while still in the world I say these things
> to share my joy with them to the full.
> I passed your word on to them,
> and the world hated them,
> because they belong to the world
> no more than I belong to the world.
> I am not asking you to remove them from the world,
> but to protect them from the evil one.
> They do not belong to the world
> any more than I belong to the world.
> Consecrate them in the truth;
> your word is truth.
> As you sent me into the world,
> I have sent them into the world,
> and for their sake I consecrate myself
> so that they too may be consecrated in truth.'

This is the Gospel of the Lord.

8

Gospel Acclamation   Jn 17:21
Alleluia, alleluia!
May they all be one.

For Unity of Christians, Readings

Father, may they be one in us,
as you are in me and I am in you,
so that the world may believe it was you who sent me,
says the Lord.
Alleluia!

A reading from the holy Gospel according to John 17:20-26
May they be so completely one.

Jesus raised his eyes to heaven and said:

'Holy Father,
I pray not only for these,
but for those also
who through their words will believe in me.
May they all be one.
Father, may they be one in us,
as you are in me and I am in you
so that the world may believe it was you who sent me.
I have given them the glory you gave to me,
that they may be one as we are one.
With me in them and you in me,
may they be so completely one
that the world will realise that it was you who sent me
and that I have loved them as much as you loved me.
Father,
I want those you have given me
to be with me where I am,
so that they may always see the glory
you have given me
because you loved me
before the foundation of the world.
Father, Righteous One,
the world has not known you,
but I have known you,
and these have known
that you have sent me.
I have made your name known to them
and will continue to make it known,
so that the love with which you loved me may be in them,
and so that I may be in them.'

This is the Gospel of the Lord.

FOR PEACE AND JUSTICE

(Lectionary 14) (Roman Missal 22)

Entrance Antiphon: Give peace, Lord, to those who wait for you; listen to the prayers of your servants, and guide us in the way of justice.

Opening Prayer
God our Father,
you reveal that those who work for peace
will be called your sons.
Help us to work without ceasing
for that justice
which brings true and lasting peace.

or

Lord,
you guide all creation with fatherly care.
As you have given all men one common origin,
bring them together peacefully into one family
and keep them united in brotherly love.

Readings: see below, pp.1927ff.

Prayer over the Gifts
Lord,
may the saving sacrifice of your Son, our King and peacemaker,
which we offer through these sacramental signs of unity and peace,
bring harmony and concord to all your children.

Communion Antiphon: Happy the peacemakers; they shall be called sons of God.

or

Peace I leave with you, my own peace I give you, says the Lord.

Prayer after Communion
Lord,
you give us the body and blood of your Son
and renew our strength.
Fill us with the spirit of love
that we may work effectively to establish among men
Christ's farewell gift of peace.

OLD TESTAMENT READING

1

A reading from the prophet Isaiah 9:1-6

Wide is his dominion in a peace that has no end.

The people that walked in darkness
has seen a great light;
on those who live in a land of deep shadow
a light has shone.
You have made their gladness greater,
you have made their joy increase;
they rejoice in your presence
as men rejoice at harvest time,
as men are happy when they are dividing the spoils.
For the yoke that was weighing on him,
the bar across his shoulders,
the rod of his oppressor,
these you break as on the day of Midian.
For all the footgear of battle,
every cloak rolled in blood,
is burnt,
and consumed by fire.
For there is a child born for us,
a son given to us
and dominion is laid on his shoulders;
and this is the name they give him:
Wonder-Counsellor, Mighty-God,
Eternal-Father, Prince-of-Peace.
Wide is his dominion
in a peace that has no end,
for the throne of David
and for his royal power,
which he establishes and makes secure
in justice and integrity.
From this time onwards and for ever,
the jealous love of the Lord of Hosts will do this.

This is the word of the Lord.

1928   *For Peace and Justice, Readings*

Responsorial Psalm   Ps 71:2-4. 7-8. 12-13. 17. ℟ v.7

  ℟ **In his days justice shall flourish
and peace till the moon fails.**

1. O God, give your judgement to the King,
to a king's son your justice,
that he may judge your people in justice
and your poor in right judgement. ℟

2. May the mountains bring forth peace for the people
and the hills, justice.
May he defend the poor of the people
and save the children of the needy. ℟

3. In his days justice shall flourish
and peace till the moon fails.
He shall rule from sea to sea,
from the Great River to earth's bounds. ℟

4. For he shall save the poor when they cry
and the needy who are helpless.
He will have pity on the weak
and save the lives of the poor. ℟

5. May his name be blessed for ever
and endure like the sun.
Every tribe shall be blessed in him,
all nations bless his name. ℟

2

A reading from the prophet Isaiah   32:15-18

Integrity will bring peace.

There will be poured on us
the spirit from above;
then shall the wilderness be fertile land
and fertile land become forest.

In the wilderness justice will come to live
and integrity in the fertile land;
integrity will bring peace,
justice give lasting security.
My people will live in a peaceful home,
in safe houses,
in quiet dwellings.

    This is the word of the Lord.

Responsorial Psalm   Ps 84:9-14. ℟ cf. v. 9

   ℟ **The Lord speaks peace to his people.**

1. I will hear what the Lord God has to say,
   a voice that speaks of peace.
   His help is near for those who fear him
   and his glory will dwell in our land. ℟

2. Mercy and faithfulness have met;
   justice and peace have embraced.
   Faithfulness shall spring from the earth
   and justice look down from heaven. ℟

3. The Lord will make us prosper
   and our earth shall yield its fruit.
   Justice shall march before him
   and peace shall follow his steps. ℟

3

A reading from the prophet Isaiah   57:15-19
Peace to far and near.

Thus speaks the Most High,
whose home is in eternity,
whose name is holy:
   'I live in a high and holy place,
   but I am also with the contrite and humbled spirit,
   to give the humbled spirit new life,
   to revive contrite hearts.

'For I will not quarrel for ever
nor be always angry,
for then the spirit would give way before me,
the very souls I have made.
Angered by his wicked brutality,
I hid my face and struck him in anger.
Like a rebel he went the way of his choice;
but I have seen the way he went.

'But I will heal him, and console him,
I will comfort him to the full,
both him and his afflicted fellows,
bringing praise to their lips.
Peace, peace to far and near.
I will indeed heal him' says the Lord.

This is the word of the Lord.

For Peace and Justice, Readings

Responsorial Psalm   Ps 121. ℟ cf. Ecclus 36:18

℟ **Give peace, O Lord,
to those who wait for you.**

1. I rejoiced when I heard them say:
'Let us go to God's house.'
And now our feet are standing
within your gates, O Jerusalem. ℟

2. Jerusalem is built as a city
strongly compact.
It is there that the tribes go up,
the tribes of the Lord. ℟

3. For Israel's law it is,
there to praise the Lord's name.
There were set the thrones of judgement
of the house of David. ℟

4. For the peace of Jerusalem pray:
'Peace be to your homes!
May peace reign in your walls,
in your palaces, peace!' ℟

5. For love of my brethren and friends
I say: 'Peace upon you!'
For love of the house of the Lord
I will ask for your good. ℟

NEW TESTAMENT READING
1

A reading from the letter of St Paul to the Philippians   4:6-9

May the peace of God guard your hearts and your thoughts.

There is no need to worry; but if there is anything you need, pray for it, asking God for it with prayer and thanksgiving, and that peace of God, which is so much greater than we can understand, will guard your hearts and your thoughts, in Christ Jesus. Finally, brothers, fill your minds with everything that is true, everything that is noble, everything that is good and pure, everything that we love and honour, and everything that can be thought virtuous or worthy of praise. Keep doing all the things that you learnt from me and have been taught by me and have heard or seen that I do. Then the God of peace will be with you.

This is the word of the Lord.

2

A reading from the letter of St Paul to the Colossians 3:12-15
May the peace of Christ reign in your hearts.

You are God's chosen race, his saints; he loves you, and you should be clothed in sincere compassion, in kindness and humility, gentleness and patience. Bear with one another; forgive each other as soon as a quarrel begins. The Lord has forgiven you; now you must do the same. Over all these clothes, to keep them together and complete them, put on love. And may the peace of Christ reign in your hearts, because it is for this that you were called together as parts of one body. Always be thankful.

This is the word of the Lord.

3

A reading from the letter of St James 3:13-18
Peacemakers, when they work for peace, sow the seeds which will bear fruit in holiness.

If there are any wise or learned men among you, let them show it by their good lives, with humility and wisdom in their actions. But if at heart you have the bitterness of jealousy, or a self-seeking ambition, never make any claims for yourself or cover up the truth with lies – principles of this kind are not the wisdom that comes down from above: they are only earthly, animal and devilish. Wherever you find jealousy and ambition, you find disharmony, and wicked things of every kind being done; whereas the wisdom that comes down from above is essentially something pure; it also makes for peace, and is kindly and considerate; it is full of compassion and shows itself by doing good; nor is there any trace of partiality or hypocrisy in it. Peacemakers, when they work for peace, sow the seeds which will bear fruit in holiness.

This is the word of the Lord.

GOSPEL

1

Gospel Acclamation   Mt 5:9
> Alleluia, alleluia!
> Happy the peacemakers:
> they shall be called sons of God.
> Alleluia!

A reading from the holy Gospel according to Matthew   5:1-12
Happy the peacemakers: they shall be called sons of God.

Seeing the crowds, Jesus went up the hill. There he sat down and was joined by his disciples. Then he began to speak. This is what he taught them:

> 'How happy are the poor in spirit;
> theirs is the kingdom of heaven.
> Happy the gentle;
> they shall have the earth for their heritage.
> Happy those who mourn:
> they shall be comforted.
> Happy those who hunger and thirst for what is right:
> they shall be satisfied.
> Happy the merciful:
> they shall have mercy shown them.
> Happy the pure in heart:
> they shall see God.
> Happy the peacemakers:
> they shall be called sons of God.
> Happy those who are persecuted in the cause of right:
> theirs is the kingdom of heaven.

'Happy are you when people abuse you and persecute you and speak all kinds of calumny against you on my account. Rejoice and be glad, for your reward will be great in heaven.'

    This is the Gospel of the Lord.

2

Gospel Acclamation   Mt 5:9
Alleluia, alleluia!
Happy the peacemakers:
they shall be called sons of God.
Alleluia!

A reading from the holy Gospel according to Matthew   5:38-48
I say this to you: offer the wicked man no resistance.

Jesus said to his disciples: 'You have learnt how it was said: Eye for eye and tooth for tooth. But I say this to you: offer the wicked man no resistance. On the contrary, if anyone hits you on the right cheek, offer him the other as well; if a man takes you to law and would have your tunic, let him have your cloak as well. And if anyone orders you to go one mile, go two miles with him. Give to anyone who asks, and if anyone wants to borrow, do not turn away.

'You have learnt how it was said: You must love your neighbour and hate your enemy. But I say this to you: love your enemies and pray for those who persecute you; in this way you will be sons of your Father in heaven, for he causes his sun to rise on bad men as well as good, and his rain to fall on honest and dishonest men alike. For if you love those who love you, what right have you to claim any credit? Even the tax collectors do as much, do they not? And if you save your greetings for your brothers, are you doing anything exceptional? Even the pagans do as much, do they not? You must therefore be perfect just as your heavenly Father is perfect.'

This is the Gospel of the Lord.

3

Gospel Acclamation Jn 14:27

> Alleluia, alleluia!
> Peace I bequeath to you,
> says the Lord,
> my own peace I give you.
> Alleluia!

A reading from the holy Gospel according to John 14:23-29

Peace I bequeath to you.

Jesus said to his disciples:

> 'If anyone loves me he will keep my word,
> and my Father will love him,
> and we shall come to him
> and make our home with him.
> Those who do not love me do not keep my words.
> And my word is not my own:
> it is the word of the one who sent me.
> I have said these things to you
> while still with you;
> but the Advocate, the Holy Spirit,
> whom the Father will send in my name,
> will teach you everything
> and remind you of all I have said to you.
> Peace I bequeath to you,
> my own peace I give you,
> a peace the world cannot give, this is my gift to you.
> Do not let your hearts be troubled or afraid.
> You heard me say:
> I am going away, and shall return.
> If you loved me you would have been glad to know that I am going to the Father,
> for the Father is greater than I.
> I have told you this now before it happens,
> so that when it does happen you may believe.'

This is the Gospel of the Lord.

4

Gospel Acclamation   Jn 14:27

    Alleluia, alleluia!
    Peace I bequeath to you,
    says the Lord,
    my own peace I give you.
    Alleluia!

A reading from the holy Gospel according to John   20:19-23
Peace be with you.

In the evening of the first day of the week, the doors were closed in the room where the disciples were, for fear of the Jews. Jesus came and stood among them. He said to them, 'Peace be with you,' and showed them his hands and his side. The disciples were filled with joy when they saw the Lord, and he said to them again, 'Peace be with you.

    'As the Father sent me,
    so am I sending you.'

After saying this he breathed on them and said:

    'Receive the Holy Spirit.
    For those whose sins you forgive,
    they are forgiven;
    for those whose sins you retain,
    they are retained.'

This is the Gospel of the Lord.

AFTER THE HARVEST

(Lectionary 20)   (Roman Missal, 27)

Entrance Antiphon: The earth has yielded its fruit, the Lord our God has blessed us.

Opening Prayer
Father, God of goodness,
you give man the land to provide him with food.
May the produce we harvest sustain our lives,
and may we always use it for your glory and the good of all.

or

Lord,
we thank you for the harvest earth has produced
for the good of man.
These gifts witness to your infinite love;
may the seeds of charity and justice also bear fruit in our hearts.

Readings: see below, pp.1937ff.

Prayer over the Gifts
Lord,
make holy the gifts we offer with gratitude
from the produce of the earth.
As you have made our land bear a rich harvest,
make our hearts fruitful with your life and love.

Communion Antiphon: Lord, the earth is filled with your gift from heaven; man grows bread from earth, and wine to cheer his heart.

Prayer after Communion
Lord,
we thank you for the fruits of the earth.
May the power of this saving mystery
bring us even greater gifts.

After the Harvest, Readings 1937

OLD TESTAMENT READING

1

A reading from the book of Deuteronomy 8:7-18
Remember the Lord your God: it was he who gave you this strength.

Moses said to the people: 'The Lord your God is bringing you into a prosperous land, a land of streams and springs, of waters that well up from the deep in valleys and hills, a land of wheat and barley, of vines, of figs, of pomegranates, a land of olives, of oil, of honey, a land where you will eat bread without stint, where you will want nothing, a land where the stones are of iron, where the hills may be quarried for copper. You will eat and have all you want and you will bless the Lord your God in the rich land he has given you.

'Take care you do not forget the Lord your God, neglecting his commandments and customs and laws which I lay on you today. When you have eaten and had all you want, when you have built fine houses to live in, when you have seen your flocks and herds increase, your silver and gold abound and all your possessions grow great, do not become proud of heart. Do not then forget the Lord your God who brought you out of the land of Egypt, out of the house of slavery: who guided you through this vast and dreadful wilderness, a land of fiery serpents, scorpions, thirst; who in this waterless place brought you water from the hardest rock; who in this wilderness fed you with manna that your fathers had not known, to humble you and test you and so make your future the happier. Beware of saying in your heart, "My own strength and the might of my own hand won this power for me". Remember the Lord your God: it was he who gave you this strength and won you this power, thus keeping the covenant then, as today, that he swore to your fathers.'

This is the word of the Lord.

Responsorial Psalm Ps 125:2-6. ℟ v.3
  ℟ **What marvels the Lord worked for us!**

1 The heathens themselves said: 'What marvels
  the Lord worked for them!'
  What marvels the Lord worked for us!
  Indeed we were glad. ℟

2 Deliver us, O Lord, from our bondage
   as streams in dry land.
   Those who are sowing in tears
   will sing when they reap.

   ℟ **What marvels the Lord worked for us!**

3 They go out, they go out, full of tears,
   carrying seed for the sowing;
   they come back, they come back, full of song,
   carrying their sheaves.   ℟

2

A reading from the book of Joel   2:21-24. 26-27
The threshing floors will be full of grain.

O soil, do not be afraid;
be glad, rejoice,
for the Lord has done great things.

Beasts of the field, do not be afraid;
the pastures on the heath are green again,
the trees bear fruit,
vine and fig tree yield abundantly.

Sons of Zion, be glad,
rejoice in the Lord your God;
for he has given you
the autumn rain, since he is just,
and has poured the rains down for you,
the autumn and spring rain as before.
The threshing-floors will be full of grain,
the vats overflow with wine and oil.

You will eat to your heart's content, will eat your fill,
and praise the name of the Lord your God
who has treated you so wonderfully.
(My people will not be disappointed any more.)
And you will know that I am in the midst of Israel,
that I am the Lord your God, with none to equal me.
My people will not be disappointed any more.

   This is the word of the Lord.

After the Harvest, Readings 1939

Responsorial Psalm   Ps 66:2-3. 5. 7-8. ℟ v.7. Alt. ℟ v.4

℟ **The earth has yielded its fruit
for God, our God, has blessed us.**

or

℟ **Let the peoples praise you, O God;
let all the peoples praise you.**

1 O God, be gracious and bless us
   and let your face shed its light upon us.
   So will your ways be known upon earth
   and all nations learn your saving help.   ℟

2 Let the nations be glad and exult
   for you rule the world with justice.
   With fairness you rule the peoples,
   you guide the nations on earth.   ℟

3 The earth has yielded its fruit
   for God, our God, has blessed us.
   May God still give us his blessing
   till the ends of the earth revere him.   ℟

NEW TESTAMENT READING

1

A reading from the first letter of St Paul to the Corinthians   3:6-10
God makes things grow.

I did the planting, Apollos did the watering, but God made things grow. Neither the planter nor the waterer matters: only God, who makes things grow. It is all one who does the planting and who does the watering, and each will be duly paid according to his share in the work. We are fellow workers with God; you are God's farm, God's building.

By the grace God gave me, I succeeded as an architect and laid the foundations, on which someone else is doing the building. Everyone doing the building must work carefully.

This is the word of the Lord.

2

A reading from the first letter of St Paul to Timothy 6:6-11. 17-19
Warn those who are rich not to set their hopes on money.

Religion brings large profits, but only to those who are content with what they have. We brought nothing into the world, and we can take nothing out of it; but as long as we have food and clothing, let us be content with that. People who long to be rich are a prey to temptation; they get trapped into all sorts of foolish and dangerous ambitions which eventually plunge them into ruin and destruction. 'The love of money is the root of all evils' and there are some who, pursuing it, have wandered away from the faith, and so given their souls any number of fatal wounds. But, as a man dedicated to God, you must avoid all that. You must aim to be saintly and religious, filled with faith and love, patient and gentle.

Warn those who are rich in this world's goods that they are not to look down on other people; and not to set their hopes on money, which is untrustworthy, but on God who, out of his riches, gives us all that we need for our happiness. Tell them that they are to do good, and be rich in good works, to be generous and willing to share – this is the way they can save up a good capital sum for the future if they want to make sure of the only life that is real.

This is the word of the Lord.

GOSPEL

1

Gospel Acclamation Ps 125:5

Alleluia, alleluia!
Those who are sowing in tears
will sing when they reap.
Alleluia!

A reading from the holy Gospel according to Luke 12:15-21
A man's life is not made secure by what he owns.

Jesus said to the crowd: 'Watch, and be on your guard against avarice of any kind, for a man's life is not made secure by what he owns, even when he has more than he needs'.

Then he told them a parable: 'There was once a rich man who, having had a good harvest from his land, thought to himself,

"What am I to do? I have not enough room to store my crops." Then he said, "This is what I will do: I will pull down my barns and build bigger ones, and store all my grain and my goods in them, and I will say to my soul: My soul, you have plenty of good things laid by for many years to come; take things easy, eat, drink, have a good time". But God said to him, "Fool! This very night the demand will be made for your soul; and this hoard of yours, whose will it be then?" So it is when a man stores up treasure for himself in place of making himself rich in the sight of God.'

This is the Gospel of the Lord.

2

Gospel Acclamation   Ps 125:5
Alleluia, alleluia!
Those who are sowing in tears
will sing when they reap.
Alleluia!

A reading from the holy Gospel according to Luke   17:11-19

He threw himself at the feet of Jesus and thanked him.

On the way to Jerusalem Jesus travelled along the border between Samaria and Galilee. As he entered one of the villages, ten lepers came to meet him. They stood some way off and called to him, 'Jesus! Master! Take pity on us.' When he saw them he said, 'Go and show yourselves to the priests.' Now as they were going away they were cleansed. Finding himself cured, one of them turned back praising God at the top of his voice and threw himself at the feet of Jesus and thanked him. The man was a Samaritan. This made Jesus say, 'Were not all ten made clean? The other nine, where are they? It seems that no one has come back to give praise to God, except this foreigner.' And he said to the man, 'Stand up and go on your way. Your faith has saved you.'

This is the Gospel of the Lord.

Readings may also be chosen from those In Thanksgiving, see below, pp.1964ff.

IN TIME OF FAMINE
OR
FOR THOSE WHO WORK TO ALLEVIATE FAMINE

(Lectionary 21) (Roman Missal, 28)

Entrance Antiphon: Lord, be true to your covenant, forget not the life of your poor ones for ever.

Opening Prayer
All-powerful Father,
God of goodness,
you provide for all your creation.
Give us an effective love for our brothers and sisters
who suffer from lack of food.
Help us do all we can to relieve their hunger,
that they may serve you with carefree hearts.

Readings: see below, pp.1943ff.

Prayer over the Gifts
Lord,
look upon this offering which we make to you
from the many good things you have given us.
This eucharist is the sign of your abundant life
and the unity of all men in your love.
May it keep us aware of our Christian duty
to give our brothers a just share in what is ours.

Communion Antiphon: Come to me, all you that labour and are burdened, and I will give you rest, says the Lord.

Prayer after Communion
God, all-powerful Father,
may the living bread from heaven
give us the courage and strength
to go to the aid of our hungry brothers and sisters.

In Time of Famine, Readings 1943

FIRST READING

1

A reading from the book of Deuteronomy 24:17-22
Let anything left be for the stranger, the orphan and the widow.

Moses said to the people:

'You must not pervert justice in dealing with a stranger or an orphan, nor take a widow's garment in pledge. Remember that you were a slave in Egypt and that the Lord your God redeemed you from there. That is why I lay this charge on you.

'When reaping the harvest in your field, if you have overlooked a sheaf in that field, do not go back for it. Leave it for the stranger, the orphan and the widow, so that the Lord your God may bless you in all your undertakings.

'When you beat your olive trees you must not go over the branches twice. Let anything left be for the stranger, the orphan and the widow.

'When you harvest your vineyard you must not pick it over a second time. Let anything left be for the stranger, the orphan and the widow.

'Remember that you were a slave in the land of Egypt. That is why I lay this charge on you.'

This is the word of the Lord.

Responsorial Psalm Ps 21:23-24. 26-28. 31-32. ℟ v.27

℟ **The poor shall eat and have their fill.**

1 I will tell of your name to my brethren
 and praise you where they are assembled.
 'You who fear the Lord give him praise;
 all sons of Jacob, give him glory.
 Revere him, Israel's sons.' ℟

2 You are my praise in the great assembly.
 My vows I will pay before those who fear him.
 The poor shall eat and shall have their fill.
 They shall praise the Lord, those who seek him.
 May their hearts live for ever and ever! ℟

3 All the earth shall remember and return to the Lord,
 all families of the nations worship before him.
 My soul shall live for him, my children serve him.

They shall tell of the Lord to generations yet to come,
declare his faithfulness to peoples yet unborn:
'These things the Lord has done.'

℟ **The poor shall eat and have their fill.**

2

A reading from the book of Job 31:16-20. 24-25. 31-32

Have I taken my share of bread alone, not giving a share to the orphan?

Have I been insensible to poor men's needs,
or let a widow's eyes grow dim?
Or taken my share of bread alone,
not giving a share to the orphan?
I, whom God has fostered father-like, from childhood,
and guided since I left my mother's womb.
Have I ever seen a wretch in need of clothing,
or a beggar going naked,
without his having cause to bless me from his heart,
as he felt the warmth of the fleece from my lambs?
Have I put all my trust in gold,
from finest gold sought my security?
Have I ever gloated over my great wealth,
or the riches that my hands have won?
The people of my tent, did they not say,
'Is there a man he has not filled with meat?'
No stranger ever had to sleep outside,
my door was always open to the traveller.

This is the word of the Lord.

Responsorial Psalm Ps 111:1-9. ℟ cf. vv.1. 9
℟ **Happy the man who gives to the poor.**

or

℟ **Alleluia!**

1 Happy the man who fears the Lord,
  who takes delight in his commands.
  His sons will be powerful on earth;
  the children of the upright are blessed. ℟

2 Riches and wealth are in his house;
  his justice stands firm for ever.

In Time of Famine, Readings

> He is light in the darkness for the upright:
> he is generous, merciful and just. ℟

3 The good man takes pity and lends,
> he conducts his affairs with honour.
> The just man will never waver:
> he will be remembered for ever. ℟

4 He has no fear of evil news;
> with a firm heart he trusts in the Lord.
> With a steadfast heart he will not fear;
> he will see the downfall of his foes. ℟

5 Open-handed, he gives to the poor;
> his justice stands firm for ever.
> His head will be raised in glory. ℟

3

A reading from the prophet Isaiah 58:6-11
Share your bread with the hungry.

Is not this the sort of fast that pleases me
– it is the Lord who speaks –
to break unjust fetters
and undo the thongs of the yoke,

to let the oppressed go free,
and break every yoke,
to share your bread with the hungry,
and shelter the homeless poor,

to clothe the man you see to be naked
and not turn from your own kin?
Then will your light shine like the dawn
and your wound be quickly healed over.

Your integrity will go before you
and the glory of the Lord behind you.
Cry, and the Lord will answer;
call, and he will say, 'I am here'.

If you do away with the yoke,
the clenched fist, the wicked word,
if you give your bread to the hungry,
and relief to the oppressed,

your light will rise in the darkness.

and your shadows become like noon.
The Lord will always guide you,
giving you relief in desert places.

He will give strength to your bones
and you shall be like a watered garden,
like a spring of water
whose waters never run dry.

This is the word of the Lord.

Responsorial Psalm Ps 111:1-9. ℟ cf. vv. 1. 9

℟ **Happy the man who gives to the poor.**

or

℟ **Alleluia!**

1 Happy the man who fears the Lord,
  who takes delight in his commands.
  His sons will be powerful on earth;
  the children of the upright are blessed. ℟

2 Riches and wealth are in his house;
  his justice stands firm for ever.
  He is a light in the darkness for the upright:
  he is generous, merciful and just. ℟

3 The good man takes pity and lends,
  he conducts his affairs with honour.
  The just man will never waver:
  he will be remembered for ever. ℟

4 He has no fear of evil news;
  with a firm heart he trusts in the Lord.
  With a steadfast heart he will not fear;
  he will see the downfall of his foes. ℟

5 Open-handed, he gives to the poor;
  his justice stands firm for ever.
  His head will be raised in glory. ℟

4

A reading from the Acts of the Apostles 11:27-30

The disciples decided to send relief, each to contribute what he could afford, to the brothers living in Judaea.

While Saul and Barnabas were in Antioch, some prophets came down from Jerusalem, and one of them whose name was Agabus, seized by the Spirit, stood up and predicted that a famine would spread over the whole empire. This in fact happened before the reign of Claudius came to an end. The disciples decided to send relief, each to contribute what he could afford, to the brothers living in Judaea. They did this and delivered their contributions to the elders in the care of Barnabas and Saul.

This is the word of the Lord.

Responsorial Psalm Ps 106:2-9. R̷ v.1

R̷ **Give thanks to the Lord
for his love has no end.**

or

R̷ **Alleluia!**

1 Let them say this, the Lord's redeemed,
whom he redeemed from the hand of the foe
and gathered from far-off lands,
from east and west, north and south. R̷

2 Some wandered in the desert, in the wilderness,
finding no way to a city they could dwell in.
Hungry they were and thirsty;
their soul was fainting within them. R̷

3 Then they cried to the Lord in their need
and he rescued them from their distress
and he led them along the right way,
to reach a city they could dwell in. R̷

4 Let them thank the Lord for his love,
for the wonders he does for men.
For he satisfies the thirsty soul;
he fills the hungry with good things. R̷

SECOND READING

1

A reading from the second letter of St Paul to the Corinthians   8:1-5. 9-15

It is a question of balancing what happens to be your surplus now against their present need.

Here is the news of the grace of God which was given in the churches in Macedonia; and of how, throughout great trials by suffering, their constant cheerfulness and their intense poverty have overflowed in a wealth of generosity. I can swear that they gave not only as much as they could afford, but far more, and quite spontaneously, begging and begging us for the favour of sharing in this service to the saints and, what was quite unexpected, they offered their own selves first to God and, under God, to us.

Remember how generous the Lord Jesus was: he was rich, but he became poor for your sake, to make you rich out of his poverty. As I say, I am only making a suggestion; it is only fair to you, since you were the first, a year ago, not only in taking action but even in deciding to. So now finish the work and let the results be worthy, so far as you can afford it, of the decision you made so promptly. As long as the readiness is there, a man is acceptable with whatever he can afford; never mind what is beyond his means. This does not mean that to give relief to others you ought to make things difficult for yourselves: it is a question of balancing what happens to be your surplus now against their present need, and one day they may have something to spare that will supply your own need. That is how we strike a balance: as scripture says: The man who gathered much had none too much, the man who gathered little did not go short.

This is the word of the Lord.

2

A reading from the second letter of St Paul to the Corinthians   9:6-15

Each one should give what he has decided to in his own mind, not grudgingly or because he is made to.

Thin sowing means thin reaping; the more you sow, the more you reap. Each one should give what he has decided in his own mind, not grudgingly or because he is made to, for God loves a cheerful giver. And there is no limit to the blessings which God can send you – he will make sure that you will always have all you need for yourselves in every possible circumstance, and still have something to spare for all sorts of good works. As scripture says: He was free in almsgiving, and gave to the poor: his good deeds will never be forgotten.

The one who provides seed for the sower and bread for food will provide you with all the seed you want and make the harvest of your good deeds a larger one, and, made richer in every way, you will be able to do all the generous things which, through us, are the cause of thanksgiving to God. For doing this holy service is not only supplying all the needs of the saints, but it is also increasing the amount of thanksgiving that God receives. By offering this service, you show them what you are, and that makes them give glory to God for the way you accept and profess the gospel of Christ, and for your sympathetic generosity to them and to all. And their prayers for you, too, show how they are drawn to you on account of all the grace that God has given you. Thanks be to God for his inexpressible gift!

This is the word of the Lord.

GOSPEL

1

Gospel Acclamation Mt 25:34

Alleluia, alleluia!
Come, you whom my Father has blessed,
says the Lord;
take for your heritage the kingdom prepared for you
since the foundation of the world.
Alleluia!

A reading from the holy Gospel according to Matthew 25:31-46
I was hungry and you gave me food.

Jesus said to his disciples: 'When the Son of Man comes in his glory, escorted by all the angels, then he will take his seat on his throne of glory. All the nations will be assembled before him and he will separate men one from another as the shepherd separates sheep from goats. He will place the sheep on his right hand and the goats on his left. Then the King will say to those on his right hand, "Come, you whom my Father has blessed, take for your heritage the kingdom prepared for you since the foundation of the world. For I was hungry and you gave me food; I was thirsty and you gave me drink; I was a stranger and you made me welcome; naked and you clothed me, sick and you visited me, in prison and you came to see me." Then the virtuous will say to him in reply, "Lord, when did we see you hungry and feed you; or thirsty and give you drink? When did we see you a stranger and make you welcome; naked and clothe you; sick or in prison and go to see you?" And the King will answer, "I tell you solemnly, in so far as you did this to one of the least of these brothers of mine, you did it to me". Next he will say to those on his left hand, "Go away from me, with your curse upon you, to the eternal fire prepared for the devil and his angels. For I was hungry and you never gave me food; I was thirsty and you never gave me anything to drink; I was a stranger and you never made me welcome, naked and you never clothed me, sick and in prison and you never visited me." Then it will be their turn to ask, "Lord, when did we see you hungry or thirsty, a stranger or naked, sick or in prison, and did not come to your help?" Then he will answer, "I tell you solemnly, in so far as you neglected to do this to one of the least of these, you neglected to do it to me." And they will go away to eternal punishment, and the virtuous to eternal life.'

This is the Gospel of the Lord.

2

Gospel Acclamation   2 Cor 8:9
    Alleluia, alleluia!
    Jesus Christ was rich,
    but he became poor for your sake,
·   to make you rich out of his poverty.
    Alleluia!

A reading from the holy Gospel according to Mark   6:34-44
Give them something to eat yourselves.

As Jesus stepped ashore he saw a large crowd; and he took pity on them because they were like sheep without a shepherd, and he set himself to teach them at some length. By now it was getting very late, and his disciples came up to him and said, 'This is a lonely place and it is getting very late, so send them away, and they can go to the farms and villages round about, to buy themselves something to eat.' He replied, 'Give them something to eat yourselves.' They answered, 'Are we to go and spend two hundred denarii on bread for them to eat?' 'How many loaves have you?' he asked. 'Go and see.' And when they had found out they said, 'Five, and two fish.' Then he ordered them to get all the people together in groups on the green grass, and they sat down on the ground in squares of hundreds and fifties. Then he took the five loaves and the two fish, raised his eyes to heaven and said the blessing; then he broke the loaves and handed them to his disciples to distribute among the people. He also shared out the two fish among them all. They all ate as much as they wanted. They collected twelve basketfuls of scraps of bread and pieces of fish. Those who had eaten the loaves numbered five thousand men.

This is the Gospel of the Lord.

3

Gospel Acclamation   2 Cor 8:9
    Alleluia, alleluia!
    Jesus Christ was rich,
    but he became poor for your sake,
    to make you rich out of his poverty.
    Alleluia!

A reading from the holy Gospel according to Luke   14:12-14
When you have a party, invite the poor.

Jesus said to his host, one of the leading Pharisees, 'When you give a lunch or a dinner, do not ask your friends, brothers, relations, or rich neighbours, for fear they repay your courtesy by inviting you in return. No; when you have a party, invite the poor, the crippled, the lame, the blind; that they cannot pay you back means that you are fortunate, because repayment will be made to you when the virtuous rise again.'

This is the Gospel of the Lord.

4

Gospel Acclamation   Mt 25:34
Alleluia, alleluia!
Come, you whom my Father has blessed,
says the Lord;
take for your heritage the kingdom prepared for you
since the foundation of the world.
Alleluia!

A reading from the holy Gospel according to Luke   16:19-31
There was a poor man called Lazarus.

Jesus said to the Pharisees: 'There was a rich man who used to dress in purple and fine linen and feast magnificently every day. And at his gate there lay a poor man called Lazarus, covered with sores, who longed to fill himself with the scraps that fell from the rich man's table. Dogs even came and licked his sores. Now the poor man died and was carried away by the angels to the bosom of Abraham. The rich man also died and was buried.

'In his torment in Hades he looked up and saw Abraham a long way off with Lazarus in his bosom. So he cried out, "Father Abraham, pity me and send Lazarus to dip the tip of his finger in water and cool my tongue, for I am in agony in these flames." "My son," Abraham replied "remember that during your life good things came your way, just as bad things came the way of Lazarus. Now he is being comforted here while you are in agony. But that is not all: between us and you a great gulf has been fixed, to stop anyone, if he wanted to, crossing from our side to yours, and to stop any crossing from your side to ours."

'The rich man replied, "Father, I beg you then to send Lazarus to my father's house, since I have five brothers, to give them warning so that they do not come to this place of torment too." "They have Moses and the prophets", said Abraham "let them listen to them." "Ah no, father Abraham", said the rich man "but if someone comes to them from the dead, they will repent." Then Abraham said to him, "If they will not listen either to Moses or to the prophets, they will not be convinced even if someone should rise from the dead." '

This is the Gospel of the Lord.

FOR THE SICK

(Lectionary 24) (Roman Missal 32)

Entrance Antiphon: Have mercy on me, God, for I am sick; heal me, Lord, my bones are racked with pain.

or

The Lord has truly borne our sufferings; he has carried all our sorrows.

Opening Prayer
Father,
your Son accepted our sufferings
to teach us the virtue of patience in human illness.
Hear the prayers we offer for our sick brothers and sisters.
May all who suffer pain, illness or disease
realise that they are chosen to be saints,
and know that they are joined to Christ
in his suffering for the salvation of the world,
who lives and reigns . . .

or

All-powerful and ever-living God,
the lasting health of all who believe in you,
hear us as we ask your loving help for the sick;
restore their health,
that they may again offer joyful thanks in your Church.

Readings: see below, pp.1955ff.

Prayer over the Gifts
God our Father,
your love guides every moment of our lives.
Accept the prayers and gifts we offer
for our sick brothers and sisters;
restore them to health
and turn our anxiety for them into joy.

Communion Antiphon: I will make up in my own body what is lacking in the suffering of Christ, for the sake of his body, the Church.

Prayer after Communion
God our Father,
our help in human weakness,
show our sick brothers and sisters
the power of your loving care.
In your kindness make them well
and restore them to your Church.

FOR THE DYING

The Mass for the Sick is celebrated, with the following prayers:

Opening Prayer
God of power and mercy,
you have made death itself
the gateway to eternal life.
Look with love on our dying brother (sister),
and make him (her) one with your Son in his suffering and death,
that, sealed with the blood of Christ,
he (she) may come before you free from sin.

Prayer over the Gifts
Father,
accept this sacrifice we offer
for our dying brother (sister),
and by it free him (her) from all his (her) sins.
As he (she) accepted the sufferings you asked him (her) to bear in this life,
may he (she) enjoy happiness and peace for ever in the life to come.

Prayer after Communion
Lord,
by the power of this sacrament
keep your servant safe in your love.
Do not let evil conquer him (her) at the hour of death,
but let him (her) go in the company of your angels
to the joy of eternal life.

FIRST READING

1

A reading from the second book of Kings 20:1-6

I have seen your tears, I will cure you.

King Hezekiah fell ill and was at the point of death. The prophet Isaiah son of Amoz came and said to him, 'The Lord says this, "Put your affairs in order, for you are going to die, you will not live" '. Hezekiah turned his face to the wall and addressed this prayer to the Lord, 'Ah, Lord, remember I beg you how I have behaved faithfully and with sincerity of heart in your presence and done what is right in your eyes'. And Hezekiah shed many tears.

Isaiah had not left the middle court, before the word of the Lord came to him, 'Go back and say to Hezekiah, prince of my people, "The Lord, the God of David your ancestor, says this: I have heard your prayer and seen your tears. I will cure you: in three days' time you shall go up to the Temple of the Lord. I will add fifteen years to your life. I will save you and this city from the hands of the king of Assyria, I will protect this city for my own sake and the sake of my servant David." '

This is the word of the Lord.

Responsorial Psalm Ps 101:2-3. 24-25. 19-21. ℟ v.2

℟ **O Lord, listen to my prayer**
 and let my cry for help reach you.

1 O Lord, listen to my prayer
   and let my cry for help reach you.
   Do not hide your face from me
   in the day of my distress.
   Turn your ear towards me
   and answer me quickly when I call. ℟

2 He has broken my strength in mid-course;
   he has shortened the days of my life.
   I say to God: 'Do not take me away
   before my days are complete,
   you, whose days last from age to age.' ℟

3 Let this be written for ages to come
   that a people yet unborn may praise the Lord;

for the Lord leaned down from his sanctuary on high.
He looked down from heaven to the earth
that he might hear the groans of the prisoners
and free those condemned to die.

℟ **O Lord, listen to my prayer
and let my cry for help reach you.**

2

A reading from the prophet Isaiah 53:1-5. 10-11
Ours were the sufferings he bore.

'Who could believe what we have heard,
and to whom has the power of the Lord been revealed?'

Like a sapling he grew up in front of us,
like a root in arid ground.
Without beauty, without majesty (we saw him),
no looks to attract our eyes;
a thing despised and rejected by men,
a man of sorrows and familiar with suffering,
a man to make people screen their faces;
he was despised and we took no account of him.

And yet ours were the sufferings he bore,
ours the sorrows he carried.
But we, we thought of him as someone punished,
struck by God, and brought low.
Yet he was pierced through for our faults,
crushed for our sins.
On him lies a punishment that brings us peace,
and through his wounds we are healed.

The Lord has been pleased to crush him with suffering.
If he offers his life in atonement,
he shall see his heirs, he shall have a long life
and through him what the Lord wishes will be done.

His soul's anguish over
he shall see the light and be content.
By his sufferings shall my servant justify many,
taking their faults on himself.

This is the word of the Lord.

For the Sick and Dying, Readings

Responsorial Psalm   Is 38:10-12. 16. ℟ cf. v.17

℟ **You have held back my life
from the pit of doom, O Lord.**

1. I said, 'I must go away,
my life half spent,
assigned to the world below
for the rest of my years.' ℟

2. I said, 'No more shall I see the Lord
in the land of the living,
no more shall I look upon men
within this world. ℟

3. 'My home is pulled up and removed
like a shepherd's tent.
Like a weaver you have rolled up my life,
you cut it from the loom.' ℟

4. For you, Lord, my heart will live,
you gave me back my spirit;
you cured me, kept me alive,
changed my sickness into health. ℟

3

A reading from the Acts of the Apostles   28:7-10
The sick people on the island came to Paul and were cured.

In the neighbourhood where we were there were estates belonging to the prefect of the island, whose name was Publius. He received us and entertained us hospitably for three days. It so happened that Publius' father was in bed, suffering from feverish attacks and dysentery. Paul went in to see him, and after a prayer he laid his hands on the man and healed him. When this happened, the other sick people on the island came as well and were cured; they honoured us with many marks of respect, and when we sailed they put on board the provisions we needed.

This is the word of the Lord.

Responsorial Psalm Ps 101:2-3. 24-25. 19-21. R̂ v.2

R̂ **O Lord, listen to my prayer
and let my cry for help reach you.**

1 O Lord, listen to my prayer
and let my cry for help reach you.
Do not hide your face from me
in the day of my distress.
Turn your ear towards me
and answer me quickly when I call. R̂

2 He has broken my strength in mid-course;
he has shortened the days of my life.
I say to God: 'Do not take me away
before my days are complete,
you, whose days last from age to age.' R̂

3 Let this be written for ages to come
that a people yet unborn may praise the Lord;
for the Lord leaned down from his sanctuary on high.
He looked down from heaven to the earth
that he might hear the groans of the prisoners
and free those condemned to die. R̂

SECOND READING

1

A reading from the second letter of St Paul 4:10-18
to the Corinthians
We are consigned to our death for the sake of Jesus.

Always, wherever we may be, we carry with us in our body the death of Jesus, so that the life of Jesus, too, may always be seen in our body. Indeed, while we are still alive, we are consigned to our death every day, for the sake of Jesus, so that in our mortal flesh the life of Jesus, too, may be openly shown. So death is at work in us, but life in you.

But as we have the same spirit of faith that is mentioned in scripture – I believed, and therefore I spoke – we too believe and therefore we too speak, knowing that he who raised the Lord Jesus to life will raise us with Jesus in our turn, and put us by his side and you with us. You see, all this is for your benefit, so that the more grace is multiplied among people, the more thanksgiving there will be, to the glory of God.

That is why there is no weakening on our part, and instead, though this outer man of ours may be falling into decay, the inner man is renewed day by day. Yes, the troubles which are soon over, though they weigh little, train us for the carrying of a weight of eternal glory which is out of all proportion to them. And so we have no eyes for things that are visible, but only for things that are invisible; for visible things last only for a time, and the invisible things are eternal.

This is the word of the Lord.

2

A reading from the second letter of St Paul 12:7-10
to the Corinthians
My grace is enough for you: my power is at its best in weakness.

I was given a thorn in the flesh, an angel of Satan to beat me and stop me from getting too proud! About this thing, I have pleaded with the Lord three times for it to leave me, but he has said, 'My grace is enough for you: my power is at its best in weakness.' So I shall be very happy to make my weaknesses my special boast so that the power of Christ may stay over me, and that is why I am quite content with my weaknesses, and with insults, hardships, persecutions, and the agonies I go through for Christ's sake. For it is when I am weak that I am strong.

This is the word of the Lord.

3

A reading from the letter of St James 5:13-16
The prayer of faith shall save the sick man.

If any one of you is in trouble, he should pray; if anyone is feeling happy, he should sing a psalm. If one of you is ill, he should send for the elders of the church, and they must anoint him with oil in the name of the Lord and pray over him. The prayer of faith will save the sick man and the Lord will raise him up again; and if he has committed any sins, he will be forgiven. So confess your sins to one another, and pray for one another, and this will cure you; the heartfelt prayer of a good man works very powerfully.

This is the word of the Lord.

For the Sick and Dying, Readings

GOSPEL

1

Gospel Acclamation Mt 8:17

Alleluia, alleluia!
He took our sicknesses away,
and carried our diseases for us.
Alleluia!

A reading from the holy Gospel according to Matthew 8:14-17
He took our sicknesses away.

Going into Peter's house Jesus found Peter's mother-in-law in bed with fever. He touched her hand and the fever left her, and she got up and began to wait on him.

That evening they brought him many who were possessed by devils. He cast out the spirits with a word and cured all who were sick. This was to fulfil the prophecy of Isaiah:

He took our sicknesses away
and carried our diseases for us.

This is the Gospel of the Lord.

2

Gospel Acclamation 2 Cor 1:3-4

Alleluia, alleluia!
Blessed be God, a gentle Father
and the God of all consolation,
who comforts us in all our sorrows.
Alleluia!

A reading from the holy Gospel according to Mark 16:15-20
They will lay their hands on the sick, who will recover.

Jesus showed himself to the Eleven, and said to them, 'Go out to the whole world; proclaim the Good News to all creation. He who believes and is baptised will be saved; he who does not believe will be condemned. These are the signs that will be associated with believers: in my name they will cast out devils; they will have the gift of tongues; they will pick up snakes in their hands,

For the Sick and Dying, Readings 1961

and be unharmed should they drink deadly poison; they will lay their hands on the sick, who will recover.'

And so the Lord Jesus, after he had spoken to them, was taken up into heaven: there at the right hand of God he took his place, while they, going out, preached everywhere, the Lord working with them and confirming the word by the signs that accompanied it.

This is the Gospel of the Lord.

3

Gospel Acclamation Mt 8:17
Alleluia, alleluia!
He took our sicknesses away,
and carried out diseases for us.
Alleluia!

A reading from the holy Gospel according to Luke 22:39-43

Father, let your will be done, not mine.

Jesus made his way as usual to the Mount of Olives, with the disciples following. When they reached the place he said to them, 'Pray not to be put to the test.'

Then he withdrew from them, about a stone's throw away, and knelt down and prayed. 'Father,' he said 'if you are willing, take this cup away from me. Nevertheless, let your will be done, not mine.' Then an angel appeared to him, coming from heaven to give him strength.

This is the Gospel of the Lord.

4

Gospel Acclamation Col 1:24
Alleluia, alleluia!
In my own body I do what I can
to make up all that has still to be undergone by Christ,
for the sake of his body, the Church.
Alleluia!

For the Sick and Dying, Readings

A reading from the holy Gospel according to John 15:1-8

Every branch that does bear fruit he prunes to make it bear even more.

Jesus said to his disciples:

'I am the true vine,
and my Father is the vinedresser.
Every branch in me that bears no fruit
he cuts away,
and every branch that does bear fruit he prunes
to make it bear even more.
You are pruned already,
by means of the word that I have spoken to you.
Make your home in me, as I make mine in you.
As a branch cannot bear fruit all by itself,
but must remain part of the vine,
neither can you unless you remain in me.
I am the vine,
you are the branches.
Whoever remains in me, with me in him,
bears fruit in plenty;
for cut off from me you can do nothing.
Anyone who does not remain in me
is like a branch that has been thrown away
– he withers;
these branches are collected and thrown on the fire,
and they are burnt.
If you remain in me
and my words remain in you,
you may ask what you will
and you shall get it.
It is to the glory of my Father that you should bear much fruit,
and then you will be my disciples.'

This is the Gospel of the Lord.

IN THANKSGIVING

(Lectionary 26)   (Roman Missal, 39)

Entrance Antiphon: Sing and play music in your hearts to the Lord, always giving thanks for everything to God the Father in the name of our Lord Jesus Christ.

Opening Prayer

Father of mercy,
you always answer your people in their sufferings.
We thank you for your kindness
and ask you to free us from all evil,
that we may serve you in happiness all our days.

Readings: see below p.1964.

Prayer over the Gifts

Lord,
you gave us your only Son
to free us from death and from every evil.
Mercifully accept this sacrifice
in gratitude for saving us from our distress.

Preface of Weekdays IV, P40.

Communion Antiphon: I will give thanks to you with all my heart O Lord, for you have answered me.

or

What return can I make to the Lord for all that he gives to me? I will take the cup of salvation, and call on the name of the Lord.

Prayer after Communion

All-powerful God,
by this bread of life
you free your people from the power of sin
and in your love renew their strength.
Help us grow constantly in the hope of eternal glory.

Other prayers may be used.

OLD TESTAMENT READING

1

A reading from the first book of Kings 8:55-61
Blessed be the Lord who has granted rest to this people.

King Solomon stood erect, and in a loud voice he blessed the whole assembly of Israel. 'Blessed be the Lord' he said 'who has granted rest to his people of Israel, keeping all his promises; of all the promises of good that he made through Moses his servant, not one has failed. May the Lord our God be with us, as he was with our ancestors; may he never desert us or cast us off. May he turn our hearts towards him so that we may follow all his ways and keep the commandments, and laws, and ordinances he gave to our ancestors. May these words of mine, of my entreaty before the Lord, be present with the Lord our God day and night, that he may uphold the cause of his servant and the cause of Israel his people, as each day requires, so that all the people of the earth may come to know that the Lord is God indeed, and that there is no other. May your hearts be wholly with the Lord our God, following his laws and keeping his commandments as at this present day.'

This is the word of the Lord.

Responsorial Psalm 1 Chron 29:10-12. ℟ v.13

℟ **We praise your glorious name, O Lord.**

1 Blessed are you, O Lord,
 the God of Israel our father,
 for ever, for ages unending. ℟

2 Yours, Lord, are greatness and power,
 and splendour, triumph and glory.
 All is yours, in heaven and on earth. ℟

3 Yours, O Lord, is the kingdom,
 you are supreme over all.
 Both honour and riches come from you. ℟

4 You are the ruler of all,
 from your hand come strength and power,
 from your hand come greatness and might. ℟

In Thanksgiving, Readings 1965

2

A reading from the book of Ecclesiasticus 50:24-26
God has done great deeds everywhere.

Bless the God of all things,
the doer of great deeds everywhere,
who has exalted our days from the womb
and acted towards us in his mercy.
May he grant us cheerful hearts
and bring peace in our time,
in Israel for ages on ages.
May his mercy be faithfully with us,
may he redeem us in our time.

This is the word of the Lord.

Responsorial Psalm Ps 137:1-5. ℟ v.2
℟ **I thank you, Lord, for your faithfulness and love.**

1 I thank you, Lord, with all my heart,
 you have heard the words of my mouth.
 Before the angels I will bless you.
 I will adore before your holy temple. ℟

2 I thank you for your faithfulness and love
 which excel all we ever knew of you.
 On the day I called, you answered;
 you increased the strength of my soul. ℟

3 All earth's kings shall thank you
 when they hear the words of your mouth.
 They shall sing of the Lord's ways:
 'How great is the glory of the Lord!' ℟

3

A reading from the prophet Isaiah 63:7-9
Let me sing the Lord's praises in return for his boundless goodness.

Let me sing the praises of the Lord's goodness,
and of his marvellous deeds,
in return for all that he has done for us
and for the great kindness
he has shown us in his mercy
and in his boundless goodness.

He said, 'Truly they are my people,
sons and no rogues.'
He proved himself their saviour
in all their troubles.
It was neither messenger nor angel
but his Presence that saved them.
In his love and pity
he redeemed them himself,
he lifted them up, carried them,
throughout the days of old.

    This is the word of the Lord.

Responsorial Psalm
Ps 144:2-11. ℟ v.1

  ℟ **I will bless your name for ever, O Lord.**

1. I will bless you day after day
and praise your name for ever.
The Lord is great, highly to be praised,
his greatness cannot be measured. ℟

2. Age to age shall proclaim your works,
shall declare your mighty deeds,
shall speak of your splendour and glory,
tell the tale of your wonderful works. ℟

3. They will speak of your terrible deeds,
recount your greatness and might.
They will recall your abundant goodness;
age to age shall ring out your justice. ℟

4. The Lord is kind and full of compassion,
slow to anger, abounding in love.
How good is the Lord to all,
compassionate to all his creatures. ℟

5. All your creatures shall thank you, O Lord,
and your friends shall repeat their blessing.
They shall speak of the glory of your reign
and declare your might, O God. ℟

4

A reading from the prophet Zephaniah 3:14-15

The Lord, the King of Israel, is in your midst.

Shout for joy, daughter of Zion,
Israel, shout aloud!
Rejoice, exult with all your heart,
daughter of Jerusalem!
The Lord has repealed your sentence;
he has driven your enemies away.
The Lord, the king of Israel, is in your midst;
you have no more evil to fear.

This is the word of the Lord.

Responsorial Psalm Ps 112:1-8. R̷ v.2

R̷ **May the name of the Lord be blessed for evermore!**

or

R̷ **Alleluia!**

1 Praise, O servants of the Lord,
 praise the name of the Lord!
 May the name of the Lord be blessed
 both now and for evermore! R̷

2 From the rising of the sun to its setting
 praised be the name of the Lord!
 High above all nations is the Lord,
 above the heavens his glory. R̷

3 Who is like the Lord, our God,
 who has risen on high to his throne
 yet stoops from the heights to look down,
 to look down upon heaven and earth? R̷

4 From the dust he lifts up the lowly,
 from the dungheap he raises the poor
 to set him in the company of princes,
 yes, with the princes of his people. R̷

NEW TESTAMENT READING

1

A reading from the first letter of St Paul to the Corinthians 1:3-9

I never stop thanking God for all the graces you have received.

May God our Father and the Lord Jesus Christ send you grace and peace.

I never stop thanking God for all the graces you have received through Jesus Christ. I thank him that you have been enriched in so many ways, especially in your teachers and preachers; the witness to Christ has indeed been strong among you so that you will not be without any of the gifts of the Spirit while you are waiting for our Lord Jesus Christ to be revealed; and he will keep you steady and without blame until the last day, the day of our Lord Jesus Christ, because God by calling you has joined you to his Son, Jesus Christ; and God is faithful.

This is the word of the Lord.

2

A reading from the letter of St Paul to the Ephesians 1:3-14

To make us praise the glory of his grace.

Blessed be God the Father of our Lord Jesus Christ,
who has blessed us with all the spiritual blessings of heaven in Christ.
Before the world was made, he chose us, chose us in Christ,
to be holy and spotless, and to live through love in his presence,
determining that we should become his adopted sons, through Jesus Christ
for his own kind purposes,
to make us praise the glory of his grace,
his free gift to us in the Beloved,
in whom, through his blood, we gain our freedom, the forgiveness of our sins.
Such is the richness of the grace
which he has showered on us
in all wisdom and insight.
He has let us know the mystery of his purpose,
the hidden plan he so kindly made in Christ from the beginning,

to act upon when the times had run their course to the end:
that he would bring everything together under Christ, as head,
everything in the heavens and everything on earth.
And it is in him that we were claimed as God's own, chosen from
  the beginning,
under the predetermined plan of the one who guides all things
as he decides by his own will;
chosen to be,
for his greater glory,
the people who would put their hopes in Christ before he came.
Now you too, in him,
have heard the message of the truth and the good news of your
  salvation,
and have believed it;
and you too have been stamped with the seal of the Holy Spirit of
  the Promise,
the pledge of our inheritance
which brings freedom for those whom God has taken for his
  own,
to make his glory praised.

   This is the word of the Lord.

3

A reading from the letter of St Paul to the Colossians   3:12-17
Giving thanks to God the Father through Christ.

You are God's chosen race, his saints; he loves you, and you should be clothed in sincere compassion, in kindness and humility, gentleness and patience. Bear with one another; forgive each other as soon as a quarrel begins. The Lord has forgiven you; now you must do the same. Over all these clothes, to keep them together and complete them, put on love. And may the peace of Christ reign in your hearts, because it is for this that you were called together as parts of one body. Always be thankful.

Let the message of Christ, in all its richness, find a home with you. Teach each other, and advise each other, in all wisdom. With gratitude in your hearts sing psalms and hymns and inspired songs to God; and never say or do anything except in the name of the Lord Jesus, giving thanks to God the Father through him.

   This is the word of the Lord.

GOSPEL

1

Gospel Acclamation   Ps 137:1
Alleluia, alleluia!
I thank you, Lord, with all my heart,
for you have heard my prayer.
Alleluia!

A reading from the holy Gospel according to Matthew   7:7-11
The one who asks always receives.

Jesus said to his disciples: 'Ask, and it will be given to you; search, and you will find; knock, and the door will be opened to you. For the one who asks always receives; the one who searches always finds; the one who knocks will always have the door opened to him. Is there a man among you who would hand his son a stone when he asked for bread? Or would hand him a snake when he asked for a fish? If you, then, who are evil, know how to give your children what is good, how much more will your Father in heaven give good things to those who ask him!'

This is the Gospel of the Lord.

2

Gospel Acclamation   cf. Mt 11:25
Alleluia, alleluia!
Blessed are you, Father,
Lord of heaven and earth,
for revealing the mysteries of the kingdom
to children.
Alleluia!

A reading from the holy Gospel according to Matthew   11:25-30
You have hidden these things from the learned and revealed them to mere children.

Jesus exclaimed, 'I bless you, Father, Lord of heaven and of earth, for hiding these things from the learned and the clever and revealing them to mere children. Yes, Father, for that is what it pleased you to do. Everything has been entrusted to me by my

Father; and no one knows the Son except the Father, just as no one knows the Father except the Son and those to whom the Son chooses to reveal him.

'Come to me, all you who labour and are overburdened, and I will give you rest. Shoulder my yoke and learn from me, for I am gentle and humble in heart, and you will find rest for your souls. Yes, my yoke is easy and my burden light.'

This is the Gospel of the Lord.

3

Gospel Acclamation Ps 65:16
Alleluia, alleluia!
Come and hear, all who fear God.
I will tell what he did for my soul.
Alleluia!

A reading from the holy Gospel according to Mark 5:18-20
Tell your people all that the Lord has done for you.

As Jesus was getting into a boat, the man who had been possessed begged to be allowed to stay with him. Jesus would not let him but said to him, 'Go home to your people and tell them all that the Lord in his mercy has done for you'. So the man went off and proceeded to spread throughout the Decapolis all that Jesus had done for him. And everyone was amazed.

This is the Gospel of the Lord.

4

Gospel Acclamation Lk 1:49
Alleluia, alleluia!
The Almighty works marvels for me.
Holy is his name!
Alleluia!

A reading from the holy Gospel according to Luke 1:39-55
My soul proclaims the greatness of the Lord.

Mary set out and went as quickly as she could to a town in the hill country of Judah. She went into Zechariah's house and greeted Elizabeth. Now as soon as Elizabeth heard Mary's greeting, the child leapt in her womb and Elizabeth was filled with the Holy Spirit. She gave a loud cry and said, 'Of all women you are the most blessed, and blessed is the fruit of your womb. Why should I be honoured with a visit from the mother of my Lord? For the moment your greeting reached my ears, the child in my womb leapt for joy. Yes, blessed is she who believed that the promise made her by the Lord would be fulfilled.'

And Mary said:

'My soul proclaims the greatness of the Lord
and my spirit exults in God my saviour;
because he has looked upon his lowly handmaid.
Yes, from this day forward all generations will call me blessed,
for the Almighty has done great things for me.
Holy is his name,
and his mercy reaches from age to age for those who fear him.
He has shown the power of his arm,
he has routed the proud of heart.
He has pulled down princes from their thrones and exalted the lowly.
The hungry he has filled with good things, the rich sent empty away.
He has come to the help of Israel his servant, mindful of his mercy
– according to the promise he made to our ancestors –
of his mercy to Abraham and to his descendants for ever.'

This is the Gospel of the Lord.

5

Gospel Acclamation Eph 1:3
Alleluia, alleluia!
Blessed be God, the Father of our Lord Jesus Christ,
who has blessed us with all the spiritual blessings of heaven in Christ.
Alleluia!

A reading from the holy Gospel according to Luke 10:17-24
Rejoice that your names are written in heaven.

The seventy-two came back rejoicing. 'Lord,' they said 'even the devils submit to us when we use your name.' Jesus said to them, 'I watched Satan fall like lightning from heaven. Yes, I have given you power to tread underfoot serpents and scorpions and the whole strength of the enemy; nothing shall ever hurt you. Yet do not rejoice that the spirits submit to you; rejoice rather that your names are written in heaven.'

It was then that, filled with joy by the Holy Spirit, he said, 'I bless you, Father, Lord of heaven and of earth, for hiding these things from the learned and the clever and revealing them to mere children. Yes, Father, for that is what it pleased you to do. Everything has been entrusted to me by my Father; and no one knows who the Son is except the Father, and who the Father is except the Son and those to whom the Son chooses to reveal him.'

Then turning to his disciples he spoke to them in private, 'Happy the eyes that see what you see, for I tell you that many prophets and kings wanted to see what you see, and never saw it; to hear what you hear, and never heard it.'

This is the Gospel of the Lord.

6

Gospel Acclamation 1 Thess 5:18
Alleluia, alleluia!
For all things give thanks,
because this is what God expects you to do in Christ Jesus.
Alleluia!

A reading from the holy Gospel according to Luke 17:11-19
He threw himself at the feet of Jesus and thanked him.

On the way to Jerusalem Jesus travelled along the border between Samaria and Galilee. As he entered one of the villages, ten lepers came to meet him. They stood some way off and called to him, 'Jesus! Master! Take pity on us.' When he saw them he said, 'Go and show yourselves to the priests.' Now as they were going away they were cleansed. Finding himself cured, one of them turned back praising God at the top of his voice and threw himself at the feet of Jesus and thanked him. The man was a Samaritan. This made Jesus say, 'Were not all ten made clean? The other nine, where are they? It seems that no one has come back to give praise to God, except this foreigner.' And he said to the man, 'Stand up and go on your way. Your faith has saved you.'

This is the Gospel of the Lord.

7

Gospel Acclamation   Jn 15:11
    Alleluia, alleluia!
    I have told you this, says the Lord,
    so that my own joy may be in you
    and your joy may be complete.
    Alleluia!

A reading from the holy Gospel according to John   15:9-17
What I command you is to love one another.

Jesus said to his disciples:

    'As the Father has loved me,
    so I have loved you.
    Remain in my love.
    If you keep my commandments
    you will remain in my love,
    just as I have kept my Father's commandments
    and remain in his love.
    I have told you this
    so that my own joy may be in you
    and your joy be complete.
    This is my commandment:
    Love one another,
    as I have loved you.
    A man can have no greater love
    than to lay down his life for his friends.
    You are my friends,
    if you do what I command you.
    I shall not call you servants any more,
    because a servant does not know
    his master's business;
    I call you friends,
    because I have made known to you
    everything I have learnt from my Father.
    You did not choose me,
    no, I chose you;
    and I commissioned you
    to go out and to bear fruit,
    fruit that will last;
    and then the Father will give you
    anything you ask him in my name.

What I command you
is to love one another.'

This is the Gospel of the Lord.

8

Gospel Acclamation
Alleluia, alleluia!
We praise you, O God,
we acknowledge you to be the Lord.
The holy Church throughout the world acknowledges you.
Alleluia!

A reading from the holy Gospel according to John 16:20-22
No one shall take your joy away from you.

Jesus said to his disciples:

'I tell you most solemnly,
you will be weeping and wailing
while the world will rejoice;
you will be sorrowful,
but your sorrow will turn to joy.
A woman in childbirth suffers,
because her time has come;
but when she has given birth to the child she forgets the
    suffering
in her joy that a man has been born into the world.
So it is with you: you are sad now,
but I shall see you again, and your hearts will be full of joy,
and that joy no one shall take from you.'

This is the Gospel of the Lord.

MASS FOR THE DEAD

Three Masses for Christian Death, to be used at the Funeral, and two to be used on the Anniversary of Death, are given here. The Roman Missal contains many other Masses for the Dead.

FUNERAL MASS

Outside the Easter Season I

Entrance Antiphon: Give them eternal rest, O Lord, and may perpetual light shine on them for ever.

Opening Prayer
Almighty God, our Father,
we firmly believe that your Son died and rose to life.
We pray for our brother (sister) N.,
who has died in Christ.
Raise him (her) at the last day
to share the glory of the risen Christ,
who lives and reigns . . .

or

God,
you have called your son (daughter) N. from this life.
Father of all mercy,
fulfil his (her) faith and hope in you,
and lead him (her) safely home to heaven,
to be happy with you for ever.

Readings: see below, pp.1982ff.

Prayer over the Gifts
Lord,
receive the gifts we offer
for the salvation of N.
May Christ be merciful in judging our brother (sister) N.
for he (she) believed in Christ
as his (her) Lord and Saviour.

Preface of Christian Death I-V, P77-P81.

Communion Antiphon: May eternal light shine on them, O Lord, with all your saints for ever, for you are rich in mercy. Give them eternal rest, O Lord, and may perpetual light shine on them for ever, for you are rich in mercy.

Prayer after Communion
Lord God,
your Son Jesus Christ gave us
the sacrament of his body and blood
to guide us on our pilgrim way to your kingdom.
May our brother (sister) N., who shared in the eucharist,
come to the banquet of life Christ has prepared for us.

Outside the Easter Season II

Entrance Antiphon: The Lord will open to them the gate of paradise, and they will return to that homeland where there is no death, but only lasting joy.

Opening Prayer
God of mercy,
you are the hope of sinners
and the joy of saints.
We pray for our brother (sister) N.,
whose body we honour with Christian burial.
Give him (her) happiness with your saints,
and raise up his (her) body in glory at the last day
to be in your presence for ever.

Readings: see below, pp.1982ff.

Prayer over the Gifts
Lord,
accept this sacrifice we offer for our brother (sister) N.
on the day of his (her) burial.
May your love cleanse him (her)
from his (her) human weakness
and forgive any sins he (she) may have committed.

Preface of Christian Death I-V, P77-P81.

Communion Antiphon: We are waiting for our Saviour, the Lord Jesus Christ; he will transfigure our lowly bodies into copies of his own glorious body.

Prayer after Communion
Father, all-powerful God,
we pray for our brother (sister) N.

whom you have called (today) from this world.
May this eucharist cleanse him (her),
forgive his (her) sins,
and raise him (her) up to eternal joy in your presence.

In the Easter Season

Entrance Antiphon: Just as Jesus died and rose again, so will the Father bring with him those who have died in Jesus. Just as in Adam all men die, so in Christ all will be made alive, alleluia.

Opening Prayer
Lord, hear our prayers.
By raising your Son from the dead, you have given us faith.
Strengthen our hope that N., our brother (sister),
will share in his resurrection.

Readings: see below, pp.1982ff.

Prayer over the Gifts
Lord,
we are united in this sacrament
by the love of Jesus Christ.
Accept these gifts
and receive our brother (sister) N.
into the glory of your Son,
who is Lord for ever and ever.

Preface of Christian Death P77-P81.

Communion Antiphon: I am the resurrection and the life, says the Lord. If anyone believes in me, even though he dies, he will live. Anyone who lives and believes in me, will not die, alleluia.

Prayer after Communion
Lord God,
may the death and resurrection of Christ
which we celebrate in this eucharist
bring our brother (sister) N. the peace of your eternal home.

Mass for the Dead

ANNIVERSARY MASS

Outside the Easter Season

Entrance Antiphon: God will wipe every tear from their eyes; there will be no more death, no more weeping or pain, for the old order has passed away.

Opening Prayer
Lord God,
you are the glory of believers
and the life of the just.
Your Son redeemed us
by dying and rising to life again.
Our brother (sister) N. was faithful
and believed in our own resurrection.
Give to him (her) the joys and blessings
of the life to come.

Readings: see below, pp.1982ff.

Prayer over the Gifts
Lord,
accept these gifts we offer
for N. our brother (sister).
May they free him (her) from sin
and bring him (her) to the happiness of life in your presence.

Preface of Christian Death I-V, P77-P81.

Communion Antiphon: I am the resurrection and the life, says the Lord. Anyone who believes in me will have eternal life; he will not be condemned but pass from death to life.

Prayer after Communion
Lord,
you renew our lives by this holy eucharist;
free N. our brother (sister) from sin
and raise him (her) to eternal life.

Mass for the Dead 1981

During the Easter Season

Entrance Antiphon: God, who raised Jesus from the dead, will give new life to our own mortal bodies through his Spirit living in us, alleluia.

Opening Prayer
Almighty and merciful God,
may our brother (sister) N. share the victory of Christ
who loved us so much that he died and rose again
to bring us new life.

Readings: see below, pp.1982ff.

Prayer over the Gifts
God of love,
by this sacrifice
wash away the sins of our brother (sister) N.
in the blood of Jesus Christ.
In your love complete what you began
in the waters of baptism.

Preface of Christian Death I-V, P77-P81.

Communion Antiphon: I am the living bread from heaven, says the Lord. If anyone eats this bread he will live for ever; the bread I shall give is my flesh for the life of the world, alleluia.

Prayer after Communion
Lord,
we celebrate your Son's death for us
and his rising to eternal glory.
May these Easter mysteries free our brother (sister) N.
and bring him (her) to share in the joyful resurrection to come.

FIRST READING FROM THE OLD TESTAMENT
Outside the Easter Season

1

A reading from the book of Job   19:1. 23-27
This I know: that my Avenger lives.

Job said:

'Ah, would that these words of mine were written down,
inscribed on some monument
with iron chisel and engraving tool,
cut into the rock for ever.
This I know: that my Avenger lives,
and he, the Last, will take his stand on earth.
After my awaking, he will set me close to him,
and from my flesh I shall look on God.
He whom I shall see will take my part:
these eyes will gaze on him and find him not aloof.'

This is the word of the Lord.

Responsorial Psalm   Ps 26:1. 4. 7-9. 13-14. ℟ v.1. Alt. ℟ v.13

  ℟ **The Lord is my light and my help.**

or

    ℟ **I am sure I shall see the Lord's goodness
    in the land of the living.**

1 The Lord is my light and my help;
   whom shall I fear?
   The Lord is the stronghold of my life;
   before whom shall I shrink? ℟

2 There is one thing I ask of the Lord,
   for this I long,
   to live in the house of the Lord,
   all the days of my life,
   to savour the sweetness of the Lord,
   to behold his temple. ℟

3 O Lord, hear my voice when I call;
   have mercy and answer.
   It is your face, O Lord, that I seek;
   hide not your face. ℟

4 I am sure I shall see the Lord's goodness
   in the land of the living.
   Hope in him, hold firm and take heart.
   Hope in the Lord! ℟

2

A reading from the book of Wisdom 3:1-9
He accepted them as a holocaust.

*The souls of the virtuous are in the hands of God,
no torment shall ever touch them.
In the eyes of the unwise, they did appear to die,
their going looked like a disaster,
their leaving us, like annihilation;
but they are in peace.
If they experienced punishment as men see it,
their hope was rich with immortality;
slight was their affliction, great will their blessings be.
God has put them to the test
and proved them worthy to be with him;
he has tested them like gold in a furnace,
and accepted them as a holocaust.*
When the time comes for his visitation they will shine out;
as sparks run through the stubble, so will they.
They shall judge nations, rule over peoples,
and the Lord will be their king for ever.
*They who trust in him will understand the truth,
those who are faithful will live with him in love;
for grace and mercy await those he has chosen.

This is the word of the Lord.*

*Shorter Form, verses 1-6. 9. Read between *.

Responsorial Psalm   Pss 114:5-6; 115:10-11. 15-16. ℟ Ps 114:9
   ℟ **I will walk in the presence of the Lord
      in the land of the living.**

or

   ℟ **Alleluia!**

1 How gracious is the Lord, and just;
   our God has compassion.
   The Lord protects the simple hearts;
   I was helpless so he saved me. ℟

2 I trusted, even when I said:
'I am sorely afflicted,'
and when I said in my alarm:
'No man can be trusted'.

℟ **I will walk in the presence of the Lord
in the land of the living.**

or

℟ **Alleluia!**

3 O precious in the eyes of the Lord
is the death of his faithful.
Your servant, Lord, your servant am I;
you have loosened my bonds. ℟

3

A reading from the book of Wisdom 4:7-15
Untarnished life, this is ripe old age.

The virtuous man, though he die before his time, will find rest.
Length of days is not what makes age honourable,
nor number of years the true measure of life;
understanding, this is man's grey hairs,
untarnished life, this is ripe old age.
He has sought to please God, so God has loved him;
as he was living among sinners, he has been taken up.
He has been carried off so that evil may not warp his
    understanding
or treachery seduce his soul;
for the fascination of evil throws good things into the shade,
and the whirlwind of desire corrupts a simple heart.
Coming to perfection in so short a while, he achieved long life;
his soul being pleasing to the Lord,
he has taken him quickly from the wickedness around him.
Yet people look on, uncomprehending;
it does not enter their heads
that grace and mercy await the chosen of the Lord,
and protection, his holy ones.

This is the word of the Lord.

Mass for the Dead, Readings

Responsorial Psalm   Ps 22. ℟ v.4

   ℟   **If I should walk in the valley of darkness
no evil would I fear,
for you are there with me.**

1. The Lord is my shepherd;
there is nothing I shall want
Fresh and green are the pastures
where he gives me repose.
Near restful waters he leads me,
to revive my drooping spirit. ℟

2. He guides me along the right path;
he is true to his name.
If I should walk in the valley of darkness
no evil would I fear.
You are there with your crook and your staff;
with these you give me comfort. ℟

3. You have prepared a banquet for me
in the sight of my foes.
My head you have anointed with oil;
my cup is overflowing. ℟

4. Surely goodness and kindness shall follow me
all the days of my life.
In the Lord's own house shall I dwell
for ever and ever. ℟

4

A reading from the prophet Isaiah   25:6-9

The Lord will destroy Death for ever.

On this mountain,
the Lord of hosts will prepare for all peoples
a banquet of rich food.
On this mountain he will remove
the mourning veil covering all peoples,
and the shroud enwrapping all nations,
he will destroy Death for ever.
The Lord will wipe away
the tears from every cheek;

he will take away his people's shame
everywhere on earth,
for the Lord has said so.
That day, it will be said: See, this is our God
in whom we hoped for salvation;
the Lord is the one in whom we hoped.
We exult and we rejoice
that he has saved us.

    This is the word of the Lord.

Responsorial Psalm Ps 22. R̸ v.1
  R̸ **The Lord is my shepherd;**
    there is nothing I shall want.

1 The Lord is my shepherd;
    there is nothing I shall want.
    Fresh and green are the pastures
    where he gives me repose.
    Near restful waters he leads me,
    to revive my drooping spirit. R̸

2 He guides me along the right path;
    he is true to his name.
    If I should walk in the valley of darkness
    no evil would I fear.
    You are there with your crook and your staff;
    with these you give me comfort. R̸

3 You have prepared a banquet for me
    in the sight of my foes.
    My head you have anointed with oil;
    my cup is overflowing. R̸

4 Surely goodness and kindness shall follow me
    all the days of my life.
    In the Lord's own house shall I dwell
    for ever and ever. R̸

5

A reading from the book of Lamentations   3:17-26
It is good to wait in silence for the Lord to save.

My soul is shut out from peace;
I have forgotten happiness.

And now I say, 'My strength is gone,
that hope which came from the Lord'.
Brooding on my anguish and affliction
is gall and wormwood.
My spirit ponders it continually
and sinks within me.
This is what I shall tell my heart,
and so recover hope:
the favours of the Lord are not all past,
his kindnesses are not exhausted;
every morning they are renewed;
great is his faithfulness.
'My portion is the Lord' says my soul
'and so I will hope in him.'
The Lord is good to those who trust him,
to the soul that searches for him.
It is good to wait in silence
for the Lord to save.

    This is the word of the Lord.

Responsorial Psalm   Ps 24:6-7. 17-18. 20-21. ℟ v.1. Alt ℟ v.3

  ℟ **To you, O Lord, I lift up my soul.**

or

  ℟ **Those who hope in you, O Lord,
shall not be disappointed.**

1. Remember your mercy, Lord,
   and the love you have shown from of old.
   In your love remember me,
   because of your goodness, O Lord. ℟

2. Relieve the anguish of my heart
   and set me free from my distress.
   See my affliction and my toil
   and take all my sins away. ℟

3. Preserve my life and rescue me.
   Do not disappoint me, you are my refuge.
   May innocence and uprightness protect me:
   for my hope is in you, O Lord. ℟

6

A reading from the prophet Daniel 12:1-3

Those who lie sleeping in the dust will awake.

I, Daniel, was doing penance when I received this message from the Lord:

'At that time Michael will stand up, the great prince who mounts guard over your people. There is going to be a time of great distress, unparalleled since nations first came into existence. When that time comes, your own people will be spared, all those whose names are found written in the Book. Of those who lie sleeping in the dust of the earth many will awake, some to everlasting life, some to shame and everlasting disgrace. The learned will shine as brightly as the vault of heaven, and those who have instructed many in virtue, as bright as stars for all eternity.'

This is the word of the Lord.

Responsorial Psalm Ps 41:2. 3. 5. ℟ v.3

℟ **My soul is thirsting for God,
the God of my life.**

1 Like the deer that yearns
for running streams,
so my soul is yearning
for you, my God. ℟

2 My soul is thirsting for God,
the God of my life;
when can I enter and see
the face of God? ℟

3 These things will I remember
as I pour out my soul:
how I would lead the rejoicing crowd
into the house of God,
amid cries of gladness and thanksgiving,
the throng wild with joy. ℟

7

A reading from the second book of Maccabees 12:43-45
A fine and noble action, in which he took account of the resurrection.

Judas, the leader of the Jews, took a collection from the people individually, amounting to nearly two thousand drachmae, and sent it to Jerusalem to have a sacrifice for sin offered, an altogether fine and noble action, in which he took full account of the resurrection. For if he had not expected the fallen to rise again it would have been superfluous and foolish to pray for the dead, whereas if he had in view the splendid recompense reserved for those who make a pious end, the thought was holy and devout. This was why he had this atonement sacrifice offered for the dead, so that they might be released from their sin.

This is the word of the Lord.

Responsorial Psalm Ps 102:8. 10. 13-18. ℟ v.8. Alt ℟ Ps 36:39
  ℟ **The Lord is compassion and love.**

or

  ℟ **The salvation of the just
    comes from the Lord.**

1 The Lord is compassion and love,
   slow to anger and rich in mercy.
   He does not treat us according to our sins
   nor repay us according to our faults. ℟

2 As a father has compassion on his sons,
   the Lord has pity on those who fear him;
   for he knows of what we are made,
   he remembers that we are dust. ℟

3 As for man, his days are like grass;
   he flowers like the flower of the field;
   the wind blows and he is gone
   and his place never sees him again. ℟

4 But the love of the Lord is everlasting
   upon those who hold him in fear;
   his justice reaches out to children's children
   when they keep his covenant in truth. ℟

FIRST READING FROM THE NEW TESTAMENT

In the Easter Season

1

A reading from the Acts of the Apostles 10:34-43

God has appointed him to judge everyone, alive or dead.

*Peter addressed Cornelius and his household:

'The truth I have now come to realise,' he said, 'is that God does not have favourites, but that anybody of any nationality who fears God and does what is right is acceptable to him.

'It is true, God sent his word to the people of Israel, and it was to them that the good news of peace was brought by Jesus Christ – but Jesus Christ is Lord of all men.* You must have heard about the recent happenings in Judaea; about Jesus of Nazareth and how he began in Galilee, after John had been preaching baptism. God had anointed him with the Holy Spirit and with power, and because God was with him, Jesus went about doing good and curing all who had fallen into the power of the devil. Now I, and those with me, can witness to everything he did throughout the countryside of Judaea and in Jerusalem itself: and also to the fact that they killed him by hanging him on a tree, yet three days afterwards God raised him to life and allowed him to be seen, not by the whole people but only by certain witnesses God had chosen beforehand. Now we are those witnesses – we have eaten and drunk with him after his resurrection from the dead – *and he has ordered us to proclaim this to his people and to tell them that God has appointed him to judge everyone alive or dead. It is to him that all the prophets bear this witness: that all who believe in Jesus will have their sins forgiven through his name.'

This is the word of the Lord.*

*Shorter Form, verses 34-36. 42-43. Read between *.

Responsorial Psalm Ps 62:2-6. 8-9. ℟ v.2

℟ **For you my soul is thirsting,**
O Lord, my God.

1 O God, you are my God, for you I long;
for you my soul is thirsting.
My body pines for you
like a dry, weary land without water. ℟

Mass for the Dead, Readings

2. So I gaze on you in the sanctuary
   to see your strength and your glory.
   For your love is better than life,
   my lips will speak your praise. ℟

3. So I will bless you all my life,
   in your name I will lift up my hands.
   My soul shall be filled as with a banquet,
   my mouth shall praise you with joy. ℟

4. You have been my help;
   in the shadow of your wings I rejoice.
   My soul clings to you;
   your right hand holds me fast. ℟

2

A reading from the book of the Apocalypse   14:13
Happy are those who die in the Lord!

I, John, heard a voice from heaven say to me, 'Write down: Happy are those who die in the Lord! Happy indeed, the Spirit says; now they can rest for ever after their work, since their good deeds go with them.'

This is the word of the Lord.

Responsorial Psalm   Ps 129. ℟ v.1. Alt. ℟ cf. v.5

℟ **Out of the depths, I cry to you, O Lord.**

or

℟ **I wait for the Lord,
I count on his word.**

1. Out of the depths I cry to you, O Lord,
   Lord, hear my voice!
   O let your ears be attentive
   to the voice of my pleading. ℟

2. If you, O Lord, should mark our guilt,
   Lord, who would survive?
   But with you is found forgiveness:
   for this we revere you. ℟

3. My soul is waiting for the Lord,
   I count on his word.

My soul is longing for the Lord
more than watchman for daybreak.

℟ **Out of the depths I cry to you, O Lord.**

or

℟ **I wait for the Lord,
I count on his word.**

4 Because with the Lord there is mercy
and fullness of redemption,
Israel indeed he will redeem
from all its iniquity.   ℟

3

A reading from the book of the Apocalypse   20:11 – 21:1
The dead were judged according to what they had done in their lives.

I, John, saw a great white throne and the One who was sitting on it. In his presence, earth and sky vanished, leaving no trace. I saw the dead, both great and small, standing in front of his throne, while the book of life was opened, and other books opened which were the record of what they had done in their lives, by which the dead were judged.

The sea gave up all the dead who were in it; Death and Hades were emptied of the dead that were in them; and every one was judged according to the way in which he had lived. Then Death and Hades were thrown into the burning lake. This burning lake is the second death; and anybody whose name could not be found written in the book of life was thrown into the burning lake.

Then I saw a new heaven and a new earth; the first heaven and the first earth had disappeared now, and there was no longer any sea.

This is the word of the Lord.

Responsorial Psalm   Ps 142:1-2. 5-8. 10. ℟ v.1
   ℟ **Lord, listen to my prayer.**

1 Lord, listen to my prayer:
turn your ear to my appeal.
You are faithful, you are just; give answer.
Do not call your servant to judgement
for no one is just in your sight.   ℟

2 I remember the days that are past:
I ponder all your works.
I muse on what your hand has wrought
and to you I stretch out my hands.
Like a parched land my soul thirsts for you.   ℟

3 Lord, make haste and give me answer:
for my spirit fails within me.
In the morning let me know your love
for I put my trust in you.   ℟

4 Teach me to do your will
for you, O Lord, are my God.
Let your good spirit guide me
in ways that are level and smooth.   ℟

4

A reading from the book of the Apocalypse   21:1-7
There will be no more death.

I, John, saw a new heaven and a new earth; the first heaven and the first earth had disappeared now, and there was no longer any sea. I saw the holy city, and the new Jerusalem, coming down from God out of heaven, as beautiful as a bride all dressed for her husband. Then I heard a loud voice call from the throne, 'You see this city? Here God lives among men. He will make his home among them; they shall be his people, and he will be their God; his name is God-with-them. He will wipe away all tears from their eyes; there will be no more death, and no more mourning or sadness. The world of the past has gone.'

Then the One sitting on the throne spoke: 'Now I am making the whole of creation new,' he said. 'I will give water from the well of life free to anybody who is thirsty; it is the rightful inheritance of the one who proves victorious; and I will be his God and he a son to me.'

This is the word of the Lord.

Mass for the Dead, Readings

Responsorial Psalm Ps 121. ℟ v.1. Alt. ℟ cf. v.1

> ℟ **I rejoiced when I heard them say:
> 'Let us go to God's house.'**

or

> ℟ **Let us go to God's house, rejoicing.**

1. I rejoiced when I heard them say:
   'Let us go to God's house.'
   And now our feet are standing
   within your gates, O Jerusalem. ℟

2. Jerusalem is built as a city
   strongly compact.
   It is there that the tribes go up,
   the tribes of the Lord. ℟

3. For Israel's law it is,
   there to praise the Lord's name.
   There were set the thrones of judgement
   of the house of David. ℟

4. For the peace of Jerusalem pray:
   'Peace be to your homes!
   May peace reign in your walls,
   in your palaces, peace!' ℟

5. For love of my brethren and friends
   I say: 'Peace upon you!'
   For love of the house of the Lord
   I will ask for your good. ℟

SECOND READING FROM THE NEW TESTAMENT

1

A reading from the letter of St Paul to the Romans 5:5-11

Having died to make us righteous, is it likely that he would now fail to save us from God's anger?

Hope is not deceptive, because the love of God has been poured into our hearts by the Holy Spirit which has been given us. We were still helpless when at his appointed moment Christ died for sinful men. It is not easy to die even for a good man – though of course for someone really worthy, a man might be prepared to die – but what proves that God loves us is that Christ died for us while we were still sinners. Having died to make us righteous, is it likely that he would now fail to save us from God's anger? When we were reconciled to God by the death of his Son, we were still enemies; now that we have been reconciled, surely we may count on being saved by the life of his Son? Not merely because we have been reconciled but because we are filled with joyful trust in God, through our Lord Jesus Christ, through whom we have already gained our reconciliation.

This is the word of the Lord.

2

A reading from the letter of St Paul to the Romans   5:17-21
However great the number of sins committed, grace was even greater.

If it is certain that death reigned over everyone as the consequence of one man's fall, it is even more certain that one man, Jesus Christ, will cause everyone to reign in life who receives the free gift that he does not deserve, of being made righteous. Again, as one man's fall brought condemnation on everyone, so the good act of one man brings everyone life and makes them justified. As by one man's disobedience many were made sinners, so by one man's obedience many will be made righteous. When law came, it was to multiply the opportunities of falling, but however great the number of sins committed, grace was even greater; and so, just as sin reigned wherever there was death, so grace will reign to bring eternal life thanks to the righteousness that comes through Jesus Christ our Lord.

This is the word of the Lord.

3

A reading from the letter of St Paul to the Romans   6:3-9
Let us live a new life.

When we were baptised in Christ Jesus we were baptised in his death; in other words, when we were baptised we went into the tomb with him and joined him in death, so that as Christ was raised from the dead by the Father's glory, we too might live a new life.

If in union with Christ we have imitated his death, we shall also imitate him in his resurrection. We must realise that our former selves have been crucified with him to destroy this sinful body and to free us from the slavery of sin. When a man dies, of course, he has finished with sin.

*But we believe that having died with Christ we shall return to life with him: Christ, as we know, having been raised from the dead will never die again. Death has no power over him any more.

This is the word of the Lord.*

*Shorter Form, verses 3-4. 8-9. Read between *.

4

A reading from the letter of St Paul to the Romans   8:14-23
We wait for our bodies to be set free.

Everyone moved by the Spirit is a son of God. The spirit you received is not the spirit of slaves bringing fear into your lives again; it is the spirit of sons, and it makes us cry out, 'Abba, Father!' The Spirit himself and our spirit bear united witness that we are children of God. And if we are children we are heirs as well: heirs of God and coheirs with Christ, sharing his sufferings so as to share his glory.

I think that what we suffer in this life can never be compared to the glory, as yet unrevealed, which is waiting for us. The whole creation is eagerly waiting for God to reveal his sons. It was not for any fault on the part of creation that it was made unable to attain its purpose, it was made so by God; but creation still retains the hope of being freed, like us, from its slavery to decadence, to enjoy the same freedom and glory as the children of God. From the beginning till now the entire creation, as we know, has been groaning in one great act of giving birth; and not only creation, but all of us who possess the first-fruits of the Spirit, we too groan inwardly as we wait for our bodies to be set free.

This is the word of the Lord.

5

A reading from the letter of St Paul to the Romans   8:31-35. 37-39
Nothing can come between us and the love of Christ.

With God on our side who can be against us? Since God did not spare his own Son, but gave him up to benefit us all, we may be certain, after such a gift, that he will not refuse anything he can give. Could anyone accuse those that God has chosen? When God acquits, could anyone condemn? Could Christ Jesus? No! He not only died for us – he rose from the dead, and there at God's right hand he stands and pleads for us.

Nothing therefore can come between us and the love of Christ, even if we are troubled or worried, or being persecuted, or lacking food or clothes, or being threatened or even attacked. These are the trials through which we triumph, by the power of him who loved us.

For I am certain of this: neither death nor life, no angel, no prince, nothing that exists, nothing still to come, not any power, or height or depth, nor any created thing, can ever come between us and the love of God made visible in Christ Jesus our Lord.

This is the word of the Lord.

6

A reading from the letter of St Paul to the Romans   14:7-12
Alive or dead, we belong to the Lord.

The life and death of each of us has its influence on others; if we live, we live for the Lord; and if we die, we die for the Lord, so that alive or dead we belong to the Lord. This explains why Christ both died and came to life, it was so that he might be Lord both of the dead and of the living. We shall all have to stand before the judgement seat of God; as scripture says: By my life – it is the Lord who speaks – every knee shall bend before me, and every tongue shall praise God. It is to God, therefore, that each of us must give an account of himself.

This is the word of the Lord.

7

A reading from the first letter of St Paul 15:20-28
to the Corinthians
All men will be brought to life in Christ.

Christ has been raised from the dead, the first-fruits of all who have fallen asleep. Death came through one man and in the same way the resurrection of the dead has come through one man. Just as all men die in Adam, so all men will be brought to life in Christ; but all of them in their proper order; Christ as the first-fruits and then, after the coming of Christ, those who belong to him. After that will come the end, when he hands over the kingdom to God the Father. For he must be king until he has put all his enemies under his feet and the last of the enemies to be destroyed is death, for everything is to be put under his feet. – Though when it is said that everything is subjected, this clearly cannot include the One who subjected everything to him. And when everything is subjected to him, then the Son himself will be subject in his turn to the One who subjected all things to him, so that God may be all in all.

This is the word of the Lord.

*Shorter Form, verses 20-23. Read between *.

8

A reading from the first letter of St Paul 15:51-57
to the Corinthians
Death is swallowed up in victory.

I will tell you something that has been secret: that we are not all going to die, but we shall all be changed. This will be instantaneous, in the twinkling of an eye, when the last trumpet sounds. It will sound, and the dead will be raised, imperishable, and we shall be changed as well, because our present perishable nature must put on imperishability and this mortal nature must put on immortality.

When this perishable nature has put on imperishability, and when this mortal nature has put on immortality, then the words of scripture will come true: Death is swallowed up in victory. Death, where is your victory? Death, where is your sting? Now the sting of death is sin, and sin gets its power from the Law. So

Mass for the Dead, Readings 1999

let us thank God for giving us the victory through our Lord Jesus Christ.

This is the word of the Lord.

9

A reading from the second letter of St Paul 4:14 – 5:1
to the Corinthians
Visible things last only for a time, but the invisible are eternal.

We know that he who raised the Lord Jesus to life will raise us with Jesus in our turn, and put us by his side and you with us. You see, all this is for your benefit, so that the more grace is multiplied among people, the more thanksgiving there will be, to the glory of God.

That is why there is no weakening on our part, and instead, though this outer man of ours may be falling into decay, the inner man is renewed day by day. Yes the troubles which are soon over, though they weigh little, train us for the carrying of a weight of eternal glory which is out of all proportion to them. And so we have no eyes for things that are visible, but only for things that are invisible; for visible things last only for a time, and the invisible things are eternal.

For we know that when the tent that we live in on earth is folded up, there is a house built by God for us, an everlasting home not made by human hands, in the heavens.

This is the word of the Lord.

10

A reading from the second letter of St Paul 5:1. 6-10
to the Corinthians
We have an everlasting home in heavens.

We know that when the tent that we live in on earth is folded up, there is a house built by God for us, an everlasting home not made by human hands, in the heavens.

We are always full of confidence, then, when we remember that to live in the body means to be exiled from the Lord, going as we do by faith and not by sight – we are full of confidence, I say, and actually want to be exiled from the body and make our home with the Lord. Whether we are living in the body or exiled from it, we are intent on pleasing him. For all the truth about us will be brought out in the law court of Christ, and each of us will get what he deserves for the things he did in the body, good or bad.

This is the word of the Lord.

11

A reading from the letter of St Paul to the Philippians   3:20-21
He will transfigure these wretched bodies of ours into copies of his glorious body.

For us, our homeland is in heaven, and from heaven comes the saviour we are waiting for, the Lord Jesus Christ, and he will transfigure these wretched bodies of ours into copies of his glorious body. He will do that by the same power with which he can subdue the whole universe.

This is the word of the Lord.

12

A reading from the first letter of St Paul   4:13-18
to the Thessalonians
We shall stay with the Lord for ever.

We want you to be quite certain, brothers, about those who have died, to make sure that you do not grieve about them, like the other people who have no hope. We believe that Jesus died and rose again, and that it will be the same for those who have died in Jesus: God will bring them with him. We can tell you this from the Lord's own teaching, that any of us who are left alive until the Lord's coming will not have any advantage over those who have died. At the trumpet of God, the voice of the archangel will call out the command and the Lord himself will come down from heaven; those who have died in Christ will be the first to rise, and then those of us who are still alive will be taken up in the clouds, together with them, to meet the Lord in the air. So we shall stay with the Lord for ever. With such thoughts as these you should comfort one another.

This is the word of the Lord.

Mass for the Dead, Readings

13

A reading from the second letter of St Paul to Timothy 2:8-13
If we die with him, then we shall live with him.

Remember the Good News that I carry, 'Jesus Christ risen from the dead, sprung from the race of David'; it is on account of this that I have my own hardships to bear, even to being chained like a criminal – but they cannot chain up God's news. So I bear it all for the sake of those who are chosen so that in the end they may have the salvation that is in Christ Jesus and the eternal glory that comes with it.

Here is a saying that you can rely on:

If we have died with him, then we shall live with him.
If we hold firm, then we shall reign with him.
If we disown him, then he will disown us.
We may be unfaithful, but he is always faithful,
for he cannot disown his own self.

This is the word of the Lord.

14

A reading from the first letter of St John 3:1-2
We shall see him as he really is.

Think of the love that the Father has lavished on us,
by letting us be called God's children;
and that is what we are.
Because the world refused to acknowledge him,
therefore it does not acknowledge us.
My dear people, we are already the children of God
but what we are to be in the future has not yet been revealed;
all we know is, that when it is revealed
we shall be like him
because we shall see him as he really is.

This is the word of the Lord.

15

A reading from the first letter of St John 3:14-16
We have passed out of death and into life because we love our brothers.

We have passed out of death and into life,

and of this we can be sure
because we love our brothers.
If you refuse to love, you must remain dead;
to hate your brother is to be a murderer,
and murderers, as you know, do not have eternal life in them.
This has taught us love –
that he gave up his life for us;
and we, too, ought to give up our lives for our brothers.

This is the word of the Lord.

GOSPEL

1

Gospel Acclamation Mt 25:34
Alleluia, alleluia!
Come, you whom my Father has blessed,
says the Lord;
take for your heritage the kingdom prepared for you
since the foundation of the world.
Alleluia!

A reading from the holy Gospel according to Matthew 5:1-12
Rejoice and be glad, for your reward will be great in heaven.

Seeing the crowds, Jesus went up the hill. There he sat down and was joined by his disciples. Then he began to speak. This is what he taught them:

'How happy are the poor in spirit;
theirs is the kingdom of heaven.
Happy the gentle:
they shall have the earth for their heritage.
Happy those who mourn:
they shall be comforted.
Happy those who hunger and thirst for what is right:
they shall be satisfied.
Happy the merciful:
they shall have mercy shown them.
Happy the pure in heart:
they shall see God.
Happy the peacemakers:

they shall be called sons of God.
Happy those who are persecuted in the cause of right:
theirs is the kingdom of heaven.

'Happy are you when people abuse you and persecute you and speak all kinds of calumny against you on my account. Rejoice and be glad, for your reward will be great in heaven.'

This is the Gospel of the Lord.

2

Gospel Acclamation cf. Mt 11:25
Alleluia, alleluia!
Blessed are you, Father,
Lord of heaven and earth;
for revealing the mysteries of the kingdom
to mere children.
Alleluia!

A reading from the holy Gospel according to Matthew 11:25-30
Come to me, and I will give you rest.

Jesus exclaimed, 'I bless you, Father, Lord of heaven and of earth, for hiding these things from the learned and the clever and revealing them to mere children. Yes, Father, for that is what it pleased you to do. Everything has been entrusted to me by my Father; and no one knows the Son except the Father, just as no one knows the Father except the Son and those to whom the Son chooses to reveal him.

'Come to me, all you who labour and are overburdened, and I will give you rest. Shoulder my yoke and learn from me, for I am gentle and humble in heart, and you will find rest for your souls. Yes, my yoke is easy and my burden light.'

This is the Gospel of the Lord.

3

Gospel Acclamation cf. Phil 3:20
Alleluia, alleluia!
Our homeland is in heaven,
and from heaven comes the Saviour we are waiting for,

the Lord Jesus Christ.
Alleluia!

A reading from the holy Gospel according to Matthew 25:1-13
The bridegroom is here! Go out and meet him.

Jesus spoke this parable to his disciples:
   'The kingdom of heaven will be like this: Ten bridesmaids took their lamps and went to meet the bridegroom. Five of them were foolish and five were sensible: the foolish ones did take their lamps, but they brought no oil, whereas the sensible ones took flasks of oil as well as their lamps. The bridegroom was late and they all grew drowsy and fell asleep. But at midnight there was a cry. "The bridegroom is here! Go out and meet him." At this, all those bridesmaids woke up and trimmed their lamps, and the foolish ones said to the sensible ones, "Give us some of your oil: our lamps are going out". But they replied, "There may not be enough for us and for you; you had better go to those who sell it and buy some for yourselves". They had gone off to buy it when the bridegroom arrived. Those who were ready went in with him to the wedding hall and the door was closed. The other bridesmaids arrived later. "Lord, Lord," they said, "open the door for us." But he replied, "I tell you solemnly, I do not know you". So stay awake, because you do not know either the day or the hour.'
   This is the Gospel of the Lord.

4

Gospel Acclamation Mt 25:34
   Alleluia, alleluia!
   Come, you whom my Father has blessed,
   says the Lord;
   take for your heritage the kingdom prepared for you
   since the foundation of the world.
   Alleluia!

A reading from the holy Gospel according to Matthew 25:31-46
Come, you whom my Father has blessed.

Jesus said to his disciples: 'When the Son of Man comes in his glory, escorted by all the angels, then he will take his seat on his throne of glory. All the nations will be assembled before him and he will separate men one from another as the shepherd separates sheep from goats. He will place the sheep on his right hand and the goats on his left. Then the King will say to those on his right hand, "Come, you whom my Father has blessed, take for your heritage the kingdom prepared for you since the foundation of the world. For I was hungry and you gave me food; I was thirsty and you gave me drink; I was a stranger and you made me welcome; naked and you clothed me, sick and you visited me, in prison and you came to see me." Then the virtuous will say to him in reply, "Lord, when did we see you hungry and feed you; or thirsty and give you drink? When did we see you a stranger and make you welcome; naked and clothe you; sick or in prison and go to see you?" And the King will answer, "I tell you solemnly, in so far as you did this to one of the least of these brothers of mine, you did it to me." Next he will say to those on his left hand, "Go away from me, with your curse upon you, to the eternal fire prepared for the devil and his angels. For I was hungry and you never gave me food; I was thirsty and you never gave me anything to drink; I was a stranger and you never made me welcome, naked and you never clothed me, sick and in prison and you never visited me." Then it will be their turn to ask, "Lord when did we see you hungry or thirsty, a stranger or naked, sick or in prison, and did not come to your help?" Then he will answer, "I tell you solemnly, in so far as you neglected to do this to one of the least of these, you neglected to do it to me." And they will go away to eternal punishment, and the virtuous to eternal life.'

This is the Gospel of the Lord.

5

Gospel Acclamation 2 Tim 2:11-12
Alleluia, alleluia!
If we have died with Christ, then we shall live with him;
if we hold firm, then we shall reign with him.
Alleluia!

A reading from the holy Gospel according to Mark 15:33-39;16:1-6
Jesus gave a loud cry and breathed his last.

*When the sixth hour came there was darkness over the whole land until the ninth hour. And at the ninth hour Jesus cried out in a loud voice, 'Eloi, Eloi, lama sabachthani?' which means, 'My

God, my God, why have you deserted me?' When some of those who stood by heard this, they said, 'Listen, he is calling on Elijah.' Someone ran and soaked a sponge in vinegar and, putting it on a reed, gave it him to drink saying, 'Wait and see if Elijah will come to take him down.' But Jesus gave a loud cry and breathed his last. And the veil of the Temple was torn in two from top to bottom. The centurion, who was standing in front of him, had seen how he had died and he said, 'In truth this man was a son of God.'*

When the sabbath was over, Mary of Magdala, Mary the mother of James, and Salome, bought spices with which to go and anoint him. And very early in the morning on the first day of the week they went to the tomb, just as the sun was rising.

They had been saying to one another, 'Who will roll away the stone for us from the entrance to the tomb?' But when they looked they could see that the stone – which was very big – had already been rolled back. On entering the tomb they saw a young man in a white robe seated on the right-hand side, and they were struck with amazement. But he said to them, 'There is no need for alarm. You are looking for Jesus of Nazareth, who was crucified: he has risen, he is not here. See, here is the place where they laid him.'

This is the Gospel of the Lord.

*Shorter Form, verses 33-39. Read between *.

6

Gospel Acclamation   Jn 11:25-26
    Alleluia, alleluia!
    I am the resurrection and the life,
    says the Lord:
    whoever believes in me will never die.
    Alleluia!

A reading from the holy Gospel according to Luke   7:11-17
Young man, I tell you to get up.

Jesus went to a town called Nain, accompanied by his disciples and a great number of people. When he was near the gate of the town it happened that a dead man was being carried out for burial, the only son of his mother, and she was a widow. And a considerable number of the townspeople were with her. When the Lord saw her he felt sorry for her. 'Do not cry,' he said. Then he went up and put his hand on the bier and the bearers stood still, and he said, 'Young man, I tell you to get up'. And the dead man sat up and began to talk, and Jesus gave him to his mother. Everyone was filled with awe and praised God saying, 'A great prophet has appeared among us; God has visited his people'. And this opinion of him spread throughout Judaea and all over the countryside.

This is the Gospel of the Lord.

7

Gospel Acclamation Phil 3:20
Alleluia, alleluia!
Our homeland is in heaven,
and from heaven comes the Saviour we are waiting for,
the Lord Jesus Christ.
Alleluia!

A reading from the holy Gospel according to Luke 12:35-40
Stand ready.

Jesus said to his disciples: 'See that you are dressed for action and have your lamps lit. Be like men waiting for their master to return from the wedding feast, ready to open the door as soon as he comes and knocks. Happy those servants whom the master finds awake when he comes. I tell you solemnly, he will put on an apron, sit them down at table and wait on them. It may be in the second watch he comes, or in the third, but happy those servants if he finds them ready. You may be quite sure of this, that if the householder had known at what hour the burglar would come, he would not have let anyone break through the wall of his house. You too must stand ready, because the Son of Man is coming at an hour you do not expect.'

This is the Gospel of the Lord.

8

Gospel Acclamation Apoc 14:13
Alleluia, alleluia!
Happy are those who die in the Lord!
Now they can rest for ever after their work,
since their good deeds go with them.
Alleluia!

A reading from the holy Gospel according to Luke   23:33. 39-43
Today you will be with me in paradise.

When the soldiers reached the place called The Skull, they crucified Jesus there and the two criminals also, one on the right, the other on the left.

One of the criminals hanging there abused him. 'Are you not the Christ?' he said. 'Save yourself and us as well.' But the other spoke up and rebuked him. 'Have you no fear of God at all?' he said. 'You got the same sentence as he did, but in our case we deserved it: we are paying for what we did. But this man has done nothing wrong. Jesus,' he said, 'remember me when you come into your kingdom.' 'Indeed, I promise you,' he replied, 'today you will be with me in paradise.'

This is the Gospel of the Lord.

9

Gospel Acclamation Apoc 1:5-6
Alleluia, alleluia!
Jesus Christ is the First-born from the dead;
to him be glory and power for ever and ever. Amen.
Alleluia!

A reading from the holy Gospel   23:44-46. 50. 52-53. 24:1-6
according to Luke
Father, into your hands I commend my spirit.

* It was about the sixth hour and, with the sun eclipsed, a darkness came over the whole land until the ninth hour. The veil of the Temple was torn right down the middle; and when Jesus had cried out in a loud voice, he said, 'Father, into your hands I commit my spirit'. With these words he breathed his last.

Then a member of the council arrived, an upright and

virtuous man named Joseph. This man went to Pilate and asked for the body of Jesus. He then took it down, wrapped it in a shroud and put him in a tomb which was hewn in stone in which no one had yet been laid.*

On the first day of the week, at the first sign of dawn, the women went to the tomb with the spices they had prepared. They found that the stone had been rolled away from the tomb, but on entering discovered that the body of the Lord Jesus was not there. As they stood there not knowing what to think, two men in brilliant clothes suddenly appeared at their side. Terrified, the women lowered their eyes. But the two men said to them, 'Why look among the dead for someone who is alive? He is not here; he has risen.'

This is the Gospel of the Lord.

*Shorter Form, verses 44-46. 50. 52-53. Read between *.

10

Gospel Acclamation   Jn 3:16
Alleluia, alleluia!
God loved the world so much
that he gave his only Son;
everyone who believes in him has eternal life.
Alleluia!

A reading from the holy Gospel according to Luke   24:13-35
Was it not ordained that the Christ should suffer and enter into his glory?

On the first day of the week, two of the disciples were on their way to a village called Emmaus, seven miles from Jerusalem, and they were talking together about all that had happened. Now as they talked this over, Jesus himself came up and walked by their side; but something prevented them from recognising him. He said to them, 'What matters are you discussing as you walk along?' They stopped short, their faces downcast.

Then one of them, called Cleopas, answered him, 'You must be the only person staying in Jerusalem who does not know the things that have been happening there these last few days.' 'What things?'' he asked. 'All about Jesus of Nazareth,' they answered, 'who proved he was a great prophet by the things he said and did in the sight of God and of the whole people; and how our chief priests and our leaders handed him over to be sentenced to death, and had him crucified. Our own hope had been that he would be the one to set Israel free. And this is not all: two whole days have gone by since it all happened: and some women from our group have astounded us; they went to the tomb in the early morning, and when they did not find the body, they came back to tell us they had seen a vision of angels who declared he was alive. Some of our friends went to the tomb and found everything exactly as the women had reported, but of him they saw nothing.'

Then he said to them, 'You foolish men! So slow to believe the full message of the prophets! Was it not ordained that the Christ should suffer and so enter into his glory?' Then, starting with Moses and going through all the prophets, he explained to them the passages throughout the scriptures that were about himself.

*When they drew near to the village to which they were going, he made as if to go on; but they pressed him to stay with them. 'It is nearly evening,' they said, 'and the day is almost over.' So he went in to stay with them. Now while he was with them at table, he took the bread and said the blessing; then he broke it and handed it to them. And their eyes were opened and they recognised him; but he had vanished from their sight. Then they said to each other, 'Did not our hearts burn within us as he talked to us on the road and explained the scriptures to us?'

They set out that instant and returned to Jerusalem. There they found the Eleven assembled together with their companions, who said to them, 'Yes, it is true. The Lord has risen and has appeared to Simon.' Then they told their story of what had happened on the road and how they had recognised him at the breaking of bread.

This is the Gospel of the Lord.*

*Shorter Form, verses 13-16. 28-35. Read between *.

11

Gospel Acclamation   Mt 25:34
>Alleluia, alleluia!
>Come, you whom my Father has blessed,
>says the Lord;
>take for your heritage the kingdom prepared for you
>since the foundation of the world.
>Alleluia!

A reading from the holy Gospel according to John   5:24-29
Whoever listens to my words and believes has passed from death to life.

Jesus said to the Jews:

>I tell you most solemnly,
>whoever listens to my words,
>and believes in the one who sent me,
>has eternal life;
>without being brought to judgement
>he has passed from death to life.
>I tell you most solemnly,
>the hour will come – in fact it is here already –
>when the dead will hear the voice of the Son of God,
>and all who hear it will live.
>For the Father, who is the source of life,
>has made the Son the source of life;
>and, because he is the Son of Man,
>has appointed him supreme judge.
>Do not be suprised at this,
>for the hour is coming
>when the dead will leave their graves
>at the sound of his voice;
>those who did good
>will rise again to life;
>and those who did evil, to condemnation.
>I can do nothing by myself;
>I can only judge as I am told to judge,
>and my judging is just,
>because my aim is to do not my own will,
>but the will of him who sent me.'

This is the Gospel of the Lord.

12

Gospel Acclamation   Jn 6:39
Alleluia, alleluia!
It is my Father's will, says the Lord,
that I should lose nothing
of all that he has given to me,
and that I should raise it up on the last day.
Alleluia!

A reading from the holy Gospel according to John   6:37-40
Whoever believes in the Son has eternal life, and I shall raise him up on the last day.

Jesus said to the crowd:

'All that the Father gives me will come to me,
and whoever comes to me
I shall not turn him away;
because I have come from heaven,
not to do my own will,
but to do the will of the one who sent me.
Now the will of him who sent me
is that I should lose nothing
of all that he has given to me,
and that I should raise it up on the last day.
Yes, it is my Father's will
that whoever sees the Son and believes in him
shall have eternal life,
and that I shall raise him up on the last day.'

This is the Gospel of the Lord.

13

Gospel Acclamation   Jn 6:51-52
Alleluia, alleluia!
I am the living bread
which has come down from heaven,
says the Lord.
Anyone who eats this bread
will live for ever.
Alleluia!

A reading from the holy Gospel according to John 6:51-58

Anyone who eats this bread has eternal life, and I shall raise him up on the last day.

Jesus said to the crowd:

'I am the living bread which has come down from heaven.
Anyone who eats this bread will live for ever;
and the bread that I shall give
is my flesh, for the life of the world.'

Then the Jews started arguing with one another: 'How can this man give us his flesh to eat?' they said. Jesus replied:

'I tell you most solemnly,
if you do not eat the flesh of the Son of Man
and drink his blood,
you will not have life in you.
Anyone who does eat my flesh and drink my blood
has eternal life,
and I shall raise him up on the last day.
For my flesh is real food
and my blood is real drink.
He who eats my flesh and drinks my blood
lives in me
and I live in him.
As I, who am sent by the living Father,
myself draw life from the Father,
so whoever eats me will draw life from me.
This is the bread come down from heaven;
not like the bread our ancestors ate:
they are dead,
but anyone who eats this bread will live for ever.'

This is the Gospel of the Lord.

14

Gospel Acclamation Jn 11:25. 26
Alleluia, alleluia!
I am the resurrection and the life,
says the Lord,
whoever believes in me will never die.
Alleluia!

A reading from the holy Gospel according to John 11:17-21
I am the resurrection and the life.

On arriving at Bethany, Jesus found that Lazarus had been in the tomb for four days already. Bethany is only about two miles from Jerusalem, and many Jews had come to Martha and Mary to sympathise with them over their brother. When Martha heard that Jesus had come she went to meet him. Mary remained sitting in the house. *Martha said to Jesus, 'If you had been here, my brother would not have died, but I know that, even now, whatever you ask of God, he will grant you'. 'Your brother,' said Jesus to her, 'will rise again.' Martha said, 'I know he will rise again at the resurrection on the last day'. Jesus said:

'I am the resurrection and the life.
If anyone believes in me, even though he dies he will live,
and whoever lives and believes in me
will never die.
Do you believe this?'

'Yes, Lord,' she said, 'I believe that you are the Christ, the Son of God, the one who was to come into this world.'

This is the Gospel of the Lord.*

*Shorter Form, verses 21-27. Read between *.

15

Gospel Acclamation Jn 3:16
Alleluia, alleluia!
God loved the world so much
that he gave his only Son;
everyone who believes in him has eternal life.
Alleluia!

A reading from the holy Gospel according to John 11:32-45
Lazarus, come out.

Mary the sister of Lazarus went to Jesus, and as soon as she saw him she threw herself at his feet, saying, 'Lord, if you had been here, my brother would not have died.' At the sight of her tears, and those of the Jews who followed her, Jesus said in great distress, with a sigh that came straight from the heart, 'Where have you put him?' They said, 'Lord, come and see'. Jesus wept;

and the Jews said, 'See how much he loved him!' But there were some who remarked, 'He opened the eyes of the blind man, could he not have prevented this man's death?' Still sighing, Jesus reached the tomb: it was a cave with a stone to close the opening. Jesus said, 'Take the stone away.' Martha said to him, 'Lord, by now he will smell; this is the fourth day.' Jesus replied, 'Have I not told you that if you believe you will see the glory of God?' So they took away the stone. Then Jesus lifted up his eyes and said:

> 'Father, I thank you for hearing my prayer.
> I knew indeed that you always hear me,
> but I speak
> for the sake of all these who stand round me,
> so that they may believe it was you who sent me.'

When he had said this, he cried in a loud voice, 'Lazarus, here! Come out!' The dead man came out, his feet and hands bound with bands of stuff and a cloth round his face. Jesus said to them, 'Unbind him, let him go free.'

Many of the Jews who had come to visit Mary and had seen what he did believed in him.

This is the Gospel of the Lord.

16

Gospel Acclamation Apoc. 14:13
Alleluia, alleluia!
Happy are those who die in the Lord!
Now they can rest for ever after their work,
since their good deeds go with them.
Alleluia!

A reading from the holy Gospel according to John 12:23-28
If a wheat grain dies, it yields a rich harvest.

*Jesus said to his disciples:

> 'Now the hour has come
> for the Son of Man to be glorified.
> I tell you, most solemnly,
> unless a wheat grain falls on the ground and dies,
> it remains only a single grain;
> but if it dies,
> it yields a rich harvest.

Anyone who loves his life loses it;
anyone who hates his life in this world
will keep it for the eternal life.
If a man serves me, he must follow me,
wherever I am my servant will be there too.
If anyone serves me, my Father will honour him.*
Now my soul is troubled.
What shall I say:
Father, save me from this hour?
But it is for this very reason that I have come to this hour.
Father, glorify your name!'

A voice came from heaven, 'I have glorified it, and I will glorify it again.'

This is the Gospel of the Lord.

*Shorter Form, verses 23-26. Read between *.

17

Gospel Acclamation   Jn 6:40
Alleluia, alleluia!
It is my Father's will, says the Lord,
that whoever believes in the Son
shall have eternal life,
and that I shall raise him up on the last day.
Alleluia!

A reading from the holy Gospel according to John   14:1-6
There are many rooms in my Father's house.

Jesus said to his disciples:

'Do not let your hearts be troubled
Trust in God still, and trust in me.
There are many rooms in my Father's house;
if there were not, I should have told you.
I am going now to prepare a place for you,
and after I have gone and prepared you a place,
I shall return to take you with me;
so that where I am
you may be too.
You know the way to the place where I am going.'

Thomas said, 'Lord, we do not know where you are going, so how can we know the way?' Jesus said:

'I am the Way, the Truth and the Life.
No one can come to the Father except through me.'

This is the Gospel of the Lord.

18

Gospel Acclamation   Jn 6:39
Alleluia, alleluia!
It is my Father's will, says the Lord,
that I should lose nothing
of all that he has given to me,
and that I should raise it up on the last day.
Alleluia!

A reading from the holy Gospel according to John   17:24-26
I want them to be with me where I am.

Jesus raised his eyes to heaven and said:

'Father,
I want those you have given me
to be with me where I am,
so that they may always see the glory
you have given me
because you loved me
before the foundation of the world.
Father, Righteous One,
the world has not known you,
but I have known you,
and these have known
that you have sent me.
I have made your name known to them
and will continue to make it known
so that the love with which you loved me may be in them,
and so that I may be in them.'

This is the Gospel of the Lord.

19

Gospel Acclamation   Jn 11:25. 26
    Alleluia, alleluia!
    I am the resurrection and the life,
    says the Lord,
    whoever believes in me will never die.
    Alleluia!

A reading from the holy Gospel   19:17-18. 25-30
according to John

Bowing his head he gave up his spirit.

Carrying his own cross, Jesus went out of the city to the place of the skull or, as it was called in Hebrew, Golgotha, where they crucified him with two others, one on either side with Jesus in the middle.

Near the cross of Jesus stood his mother and his mother's sister, Mary the wife of Clopas, and Mary of Magdala. Seeing his mother and the disciple he loved standing near her, Jesus said to his mother, 'Woman, this is your son'. Then to the disciple he said, 'This is your mother'.

After this, Jesus knew that everything had now been completed, and to fulfil the scripture perfectly he said:

'I am thirsty'.

A jar full of vinegar stood there, so putting a sponge soaked in the vinegar on a hyssop stick they held it up to his mouth. After Jesus had taken the vinegar he said, 'It is accomplished'; and bowing his head he gave up his spirit.

It was Preparation Day, and to prevent the bodies remaining on the cross during sabbath – since that sabbath was a day of special solemnity – the Jews asked Pilate to have the legs broken and the bodies taken away. Consequently the soldiers came and broke the legs of the first man who had been crucified with him and then of the other. When they came to Jesus, they found he was already dead, and so instead of breaking his legs one of the soldiers pierced his side with a lance; and immediately there came out blood and water. This is the evidence of one who saw it – trustworthy evidence, and he knows he speaks the truth – and he gives it so that you may believe as well. Because all this happened to fulfil the words of scripture:

Not one bone of his will be broken;

and again, in another place scripture says:

They will look on the one whom they have pierced.

After this, Joseph of Arimathaea, who was a disciple of Jesus – though a secret one because he was afraid of the Jews – asked Pilate to let him remove the body of Jesus. Pilate gave permission, so they came and took it away. Nicodemus came as well – the same one who had first come to Jesus at night-time – and he brought a mixture of myrrh and aloes weighing about a hundred pounds.

This is the Gospel of the Lord.

FOR THE BURIAL OF CHILDREN

a Burial of Baptised Children

FIRST READING FROM THE OLD TESTAMENT
Outside the Easter Season

1

A reading from the prophet Isaiah 25:6. 7-9
The Lord will destroy Death for ever.

On this mountain,
the Lord of hosts will prepare for all peoples
a banquet of rich food.
On this mountain he will remove
the mourning veil covering all peoples,
and the shroud enwrapping all nations,
he will destroy Death for ever.
The Lord will wipe away
the tears from every cheek;
he will take away his people's shame
everywhere on earth,
for the Lord has said so.
That day, it will be said: See, this is our God
in whom we hoped for salvation;
the Lord is the one in whom we hoped.
We exult and we rejoice

Responsorial Psalm   Ps 22:1 ℟ v.1
℟ **The Lord is my shepherd;
there is nothing I shall want.**

1 The Lord is my shepherd;
there is nothing I shall want.
Fresh and green are the pastures
where he gives me repose.
Near restful waters he leads me
to revive my drooping spirit.   ℟

2 He guides me along the right path;
he is true to his name.
If I should walk in the valley of darkness
no evil would I fear.
You are there with your crook and your staff;
with these you give me comfort.   ℟

3 You have prepared a banquet for me
in the sight of my foes.
My head you have anointed with oil;
my cup is overflowing.   ℟

4 Surely goodness and kindness shall follow me
all the days of my life.
In the Lord's own house shall I dwell
for ever and ever.   ℟

2

A reading from the book of Lamentations   3:22-26
It is good to wait in silence for the Lord to save.

The favours of the Lord are not all past,
his kindnesses are not exhausted;
every morning they are renewed;
great is his faithfulness.
'My portion is the Lord' says my soul
'and so I will hope in him.'
The Lord is good to those who trust him,
to the soul that searches for him.

It is good to wait in silence
for the Lord to save.

> This the word of the Lord.

Responsorial Psalm   Ps 24:4-7. 20-21. ℟ v.1

    ℟ **To you, O Lord, I lift up my soul.**

1 Lord, make me know your ways.
   Lord, teach me your paths.
   Make me walk in your truth, and teach me:
   for you are God my saviour. ℟

2 Remember your mercy, Lord,
   and the love you have shown from of old.
   In your love remember me,
   because of your goodness, O Lord. ℟

3 Preserve my life and rescue me.
   Do not disappoint me, you are my refuge.
   May innocence and uprightness protect me:
   for my hope is in you, O Lord. ℟

FIRST READING FROM THE NEW TESTAMENT

In the Easter Season

1

A reading from the book of the Apocalypse   7:9-10. 15-17

God will wipe away all tears from their eyes.

I, John, saw a huge number, impossible to count, of people from every nation, race, tribe and language; they were standing in front of the throne and in front of the Lamb, dressed in white robes and holding palms in their hands. They shouted aloud, 'Victory to our God, who sits on the throne, and to the Lamb!' They now stand in front of God's throne and serve him day and night in his sanctuary; and the One who sits on the throne will spread his tent over them. They will never hunger or thirst again; neither the sun nor scorching wind will ever plague them, because the Lamb who is at the throne will be their shepherd and will lead them to springs of living water; and God will wipe away all tears from their eyes.

> This is the word of the Lord.

Responsorial Psalm   Ps 148:1-2. 11-14. ℟ v.13

  ℟ **Praise the name of the Lord.**

or

  ℟ **Alleluia!**

1. Praise the Lord from the heavens,
   praise him in the heights.
   Praise him, all his angels,
   praise him, all his host.   ℟

2. All earth's kings and peoples,
   earth's princes and rulers;
   young men and maidens,
   old men together with children.   ℟

3. Let them praise the name of the Lord
   for he alone is exalted.
   The splendour of his name
   reaches beyond heaven and earth.   ℟

4. He exalts the strength of his people.
   He is the praise of all his saints,
   of the sons of Israel,
   of the people to whom he comes close.   ℟

2

A reading from the book of the Apocalypse   21:1. 3-5

There will be no more death.

I, John, saw a new heaven and a new earth. Then I heard a loud voice call from the throne, 'You see this city? Here God lives among men. He will make his home among them; they shall be his people, and he will be their God; his name is God-with-them. He will wipe away all tears from their eyes; there will be no more death, and no more mourning or sadness. The world of the past has gone.'

Then the One sitting on the throne spoke: 'Now I am making the whole of creation new'.

This is the word of the Lord.

Responsorial Psalm   Ps 41:2-3. 5. 42:3-5. ℟ Ps 41:3

℟ **My soul is thirsting for God,
the God of my life.**

1. Like the deer that yearns
for running streams,
so my soul is yearning
for you, my God. ℟

2. My soul is thirsting for God,
the God of my life;
when can I enter and see
the face of God? ℟

3. These things will I remember
as I pour out my soul:
how I would lead the rejoicing crowd
into the house of God,
amid cries of gladness and thanksgiving,
the throng wild with joy. ℟

4. O send forth your light and your truth;
let these be my guide.
Let them bring me to your holy mountain
to the place where you dwell. ℟

5. And I will come to the altar of God,
the God of my joy.
My redeemer, I will thank you on the harp,
O God, my God. ℟

6. Why are you cast down, my soul,
why groan within me?
Hope in God; I will praise him still,
my saviour and my God. ℟

SECOND READING FROM THE NEW TESTAMENT

1

A reading from the letter of St Paul to the Romans 6:3-4. 8-9
We believe that we shall return to life with Christ.

You have been taught that when we were baptised in Christ Jesus we were baptised in his death; in other words, when we were baptised we went into the tomb with him and joined him in death, so that as Christ was raised from the dead by the Father's glory, we too might live a new life.

We believe that having died with Christ we shall return to life with him: Christ, as we know, having been raised from the dead will never die again. Death has no power over him any more.

This is the word of the Lord.

2

A reading from the letter of St Paul to the Romans 14:7-9
Alive or dead, we belong to the Lord.

The life and death of each of us has its influence on others; if we live, we live for the Lord; and if we die, we die for the Lord, so that alive or dead we belong to the Lord. This explains why Christ both died and came to life, it was so that he might be Lord both of the dead and of the living.

This is the word of the Lord.

3

A reading from the first letter of St Paul 15:20-23
to the Corinthians
All men will be brought to life in Christ.

Christ has been raised from the dead, the first-fruits of all who have fallen asleep. Death came through one man and in the same way the resurrection of the dead has come through one man. Just as all men die in Adam, so all men will be brought to life in Christ; but all of them in their proper order; Christ as the first-fruits and and after the coming of Christ, those who belong to him.

This is the word of the Lord.

4

A reading from the first letter of St Paul to the Ephesians   1:3-5
Before the world was made God chose us in Christ.

Blessed be God the Father of our Lord Jesus Christ,
who has blessed us with all the spiritual blessings of heaven in Christ.
Before the world was made, he chose us, chose us in Christ,
to be holy and spotless, and to live through love in his presence,
determining that we should become his adopted sons, through Jesus Christ
for his own kind purposes.

    This is the word of the Lord.

5

A reading from the first letter of St Paul   4:13-14. 18
to the Thessalonians
We shall stay with the Lord for ever.

We want you to be quite certain, brothers, about those who have died, to make sure that you do not grieve about them, like the other people who have no hope. We believe that Jesus died and rose again, and that it will be the same for those who have died in Jesus: God will bring them with him. With such thoughts as these you should comfort one another.

    This is the word of the Lord.

GOSPEL

1

Gospel Acclamation   cf. Mt 11:25
    Alleluia, alleluia!
    Blessed are you, Father,
    Lord of heaven and of earth,
    for revealing the mysteries of the kingdom
    to children.
    Alleluia!

A reading from the holy Gospel according to Matthew 11:25-30

You have hidden these things from the clever, and have revealed them to mere children.

Jesus exclaimed, 'I bless you, Father, Lord of heaven and of earth, for hiding these things from the learned and the clever and revealing them to mere children. Yes, Father, for that is what it pleased you to do. Everything has been entrusted to me by my Father; and no one knows the Son except the Father, just as no one knows the Father except the Son and those to whom the Son chooses to reveal him.

'Come to me, all you who labour and are overburdened, and I will give you rest. Shoulder my yoke and learn from me, for I am gentle and humble in heart, and you will find rest for your souls. Yes, my yoke is easy and my burden light.'

This is the Gospel of the Lord.

2

Gospel Acclamation Jn 6:39
> Alleluia, alleluia!
> The will of my Father, says the Lord,
> is that I should lose nothing
> of all that he has given to me,
> and that I should raise it up on the last day.
> Alleluia!

A reading from the holy Gospel according to John 6:37-40

It is my Father's will that I should lose nothing of all that he has given to me.

*Jesus said to the crowd:

> 'All that the Father gives me will come to me,
> and whoever comes to me
> I shall not turn him away;
> because I have come from heaven,
> not to do my own will,
> but to do the will of the one who sent me.
> Now the will of him who sent me
> is that I should lose nothing
> of all that he has given to me,
> and that I should raise it up on the last day. *
> Yes, it is my Father's will

Burial of Children, Readings 2027

that whoever sees the Son and believes in him
shall have eternal life,
and that I shall raise him up on the last day.'

* This is the Gospel of the Lord.*

*Shorter Form, verses 37-39. Read between *.

3

For a child who has received the eucharist

Gospel Acclamation Jn 6:39
Alleluia, alleluia!
The will of my Father, says the Lord,
is that I should lose nothing
of all that he has given to me,
and that I should raise it up on the last day.
Alleluia!

A reading from the holy Gospel according to John 6:51-58
Anyone who eats this bread has eternal life, and I shall raise him up on the last day.

Jesus said to the crowd:

'I am the living bread which has come down from heaven.
Anyone who eats this bread will live for ever;
and the bread that I shall give
is my flesh, for the life of the world.'

Then the Jews started arguing with one another: 'How can this man give us his flesh to eat?' they said. Jesus replied:

'I tell you most solemnly,
if you do not eat the flesh of the Son of Man
and drink his blood,
you will not have life in you.
Anyone who does eat my flesh and drink my blood
has eternal life,
and I shall raise him up on the last day.
For my flesh is real food
and my blood is real drink.
He who eats my flesh and drinks my blood
lives in me
and I live in him.
As I, who am sent by the living Father,

myself draw life from the Father,
so whoever eats me will draw life from me.
This is the bread come down from heaven;
not like the bread our ancestors ate:
they are dead,
but anyone who eats this bread will live for ever.'

This is the Gospel of the Lord.

4

Gospel Acclamation   2 Cor 1:3-4
Alleluia, alleluia!
Blessed be God, a gentle Father
and the God of all consolation,
who comforts us in all our sorrows.
Alleluia!

A reading from the holy Gospel according to John   11:32-38. 40
If you believe, you will see the glory of God.

Mary, the sister of Lazarus, went to Jesus, and as soon as she saw him she threw herself at his feet, saying, 'Lord, if you had been here, my brother would not have died'. At the sight of her tears, and those of the Jews who followed her, Jesus said in great distress, with a sigh that came straight from the heart, 'Where have you put him?' They said, 'Lord, come and see'. Jesus wept; and the Jews said, 'See how much he loved him!' But there were some who remarked, 'He opened the eyes of the blind man, could he not have prevented this man's death?' Still sighing, Jesus reached the tomb: it was a cave with a stone to close the opening. Jesus said, 'Have I not told you that if you believe you will see the glory of God?'

This is the Gospel of the Lord.

5

Gospel Acclamation   2 Cor 1:3-4
Alleluia, alleluia!
Blessed be God, a gentle Father
and the God of all consolation,
who comforts us in all our sorrows.
Alleluia!

A reading from the holy Gospel according to John   19:25-30
This is your mother.

Near the cross of Jesus stood his mother and his mother's sister, Mary the wife of Clopas, and Mary of Magdala. Seeing his mother and the disciple he loved standing near her, Jesus said to his mother, 'Woman, this is your son'. Then to the disciple he said, 'This is your mother'. And from that moment the disciple made a place for her in his home.

After this, Jesus knew that everything had now been completed, and to fulfil the scripture perfectly he said:

'I am thirsty.'

A jar full of vinegar stood there, so putting a sponge soaked in vinegar on a hyssop stick they held it up to his mouth. After Jesus had taken the vinegar he said, 'It is accomplished'; and bowing his head he gave up his spirit.

This is the Gospel of the Lord.

b Burial of Non-baptised Children

FIRST READING FROM THE OLD TESTAMENT

1

A reading from the prophet Isaiah   25:6-8
The Lord will destroy Death for ever.

On this mountain,
the Lord of hosts will prepare for all peoples
a banquet of rich food.
On this mountain he will remove
the mourning veil covering all peoples,
and the shroud enwrapping all nations,
he will destroy Death for ever.
The Lord will wipe away
the tears from every cheek.

This is the word of the Lord.

Responsorial Psalm Ps 24:4-7. 17. 20. ℟ v.1. Alt ℟ v.3

℟ **To you, O Lord, I lift up my soul.**

or

℟ **Those who hope in you, O Lord,
shall not be disappointed.**

1 Lord, make me know your ways.
Lord, teach me your paths.
Make me walk in your truth, and teach me:
for you are God my saviour. ℟

2 Remember your mercy, Lord,
and the love you have shown from of old.
In your love remember me
because of your goodness, O Lord. ℟

3 Relieve the anguish of my heart
and set me free from my distress.
Preserve my life and rescue me.
Do not disappoint me, you are my refuge. ℟

2

A reading from the book of Lamentations 3:22-26
It is good to wait in silence for the Lord to save.

The favours of the Lord are not all past,
his kindnesses are not exhausted;
every morning they are renewed;
great is his faithfulness.
'My portion is the Lord' says my soul
'and so I will hope in him.'
The Lord is good to those who trust him,
to the soul that searches for him.
It is good to wait in silence
for the Lord to save.

This is the word of the Lord.

Burial of Children, Readings

Responsorial Psalm Ps 24:4-7. 7. 20. ℟ v.1. Alt ℟ v.3
  ℟ **To you, O Lord, I lift up my soul.**

or

  ℟ **Those who hope in you, O Lord,
shall not be disappointed.**

1. Lord, make me know your ways.
Lord, teach me your paths.
Make me walk in your truth, and teach me:
for you are God my saviour. ℟

2. Remember your mercy, Lord,
and the love you have shown from of old.
In your love remember me
because of your goodness, O Lord. ℟

3. Relieve the anguish of my heart
and set me free from my distress.
Preserve my life and rescue me.
Do not disappoint me, you are my refuge. ℟

GOSPEL

1

Gospel Acclamation Apoc 1:5-6
Alleluia, alleluia!
Jesus Christ is the First-born from the dead;
to him be glory and power for ever and ever. Amen.
Alleluia!

A reading from the holy Gospel according to Matthew 11:25-30
You have hidden these things from the clever, revealed them to mere children.

Jesus exclaimed, 'I bless you, Father, Lord of heaven and of earth, for hiding these things from the learned and the clever and revealing them to mere children. Yes, Father, for that is what it pleased you to do. Everything has been entrusted to me by my Father; and no one knows the Son except the Father, just as no one knows the Father except the Son and those to whom the Son chooses to reveal him.

  'Come to me, all you who labour and are overburdened, and I

will give you rest. Shoulder my yoke and learn from me, for I am gentle and humble in heart, and you will find rest for your souls. Yes, my yoke is easy and my burden light.'

This is the Gospel of the Lord.

2

Gospel Acclamation 2 Cor 1:3-4
Alleluia, alleluia!
Blessed be God, a gentle Father
and the God of all consolation,
who comforts us in all our sorrows.
Alleluia!

A reading from the holy Gospel according to Mark 15:33-46
Jesus gave a loud cry and breathed his last.

When the sixth hour came there was darkness over the whole land until the ninth hour. And at the ninth hour Jesus cried out in a loud voice, 'Eloi, Eloi, lama sabachthani?' which means, 'My God, my God, why have you deserted me?' When some of those who stood by heard this, they said, 'Listen, he is calling on Elijah'. Someone ran and soaked a sponge in vinegar and, putting it on a reed, gave it him to drink saying, 'Wait and see if Elijah will come to take him down'. But Jesus gave a loud cry and breathed his last. And the veil of the Temple was torn in two from top to bottom. The centurion, who was standing in front of him, had seen how he had died, and he said, 'In truth this man was a son of God.'

There were some women watching from a distance. Among them were Mary of Magdala, Mary who was the mother of James the younger and Joset, and Salome. These used to follow him and look after him when he was in Galilee. And there were many other women there who had come up to Jerusalem with him.

It was now evening, and since it was Preparation Day (that is, the vigil of the sabbath), there came Joseph of Arimathaea, a prominent member of the Council, who himself lived in the hope of seeing the kingdom of God, and he boldly went to Pilate and asked for the body of Jesus. Pilate, astonished that he should have died so soon, summoned the centurion and enquired if he was already dead. Having been assured of this by the centurion, he granted the corpse to Joseph who bought a shroud, took Jesus down from the cross, wrapped him in the shroud and laid him in a tomb which had been hewn out of rock. He then rolled a stone against the entrance to the tomb.

This is the Gospel of the Lord.

3

Gospel Acclamation 2 Cor 1:3-4
Alleluia, alleluia!
Blessed be God, a gentle Father
and the God of all consolation,
who comforts us in all our sorrows.
Alleluia!

A reading from the holy Gospel according to John 19:25-30
This is your mother.

Near the cross of Jesus stood his mother and his mother's sister, Mary the wife of Clopas, and Mary of Magdala. Seeing his mother and the disciple he loved standing near her, Jesus said to his mother, "Woman, this is your son.' Then to the disciple he said, 'This is your mother.' And from that moment the disciple made a place for her in his home.

After this, Jesus knew that everything had now been completed, and to fulfil the scripture perfectly he said:

'I am thirsty.'

A jar full of vinegar stood there, so putting a sponge soaked in vinegar on a hyssop stick they held it up to his mouth. After Jesus had taken the vinegar he said, 'It is accomplished'; and bowing his head he gave up his spirit.

This is the Gospel of the Lord.

THE PROPER OF SAINTS

NATIONAL CALENDAR FOR ENGLAND

Approved by the Sacred Congregation for Divine Worship on 21 November 1971 (Prot. Num: 25/71)

March	1	ST DAVID, BISHOP, PATRON OF WALES	Feast
	17	ST PATRICK, BISHOP, PATRON OF IRELAND	Feast
April	21	St Anselm, bishop and doctor of the Church	Memorial
	23	ST GEORGE, MARTYR, PATRON OF ENGLAND	Feast
May	4	THE BEATIFIED MARTYRS OF ENGLAND AND WALES	Feast
	25	St Bede the Venerable, priest and doctor of the Church	Memorial
	27	ST AUGUSTINE OF CANTERBURY, BISHOP, APOSTLE OF ENGLAND	Feast
June	20	St Alban, protomartyr of England	Memorial
	22	SS JOHN FISHER, BISHOP, AND THOMAS MORE, MARTYRS	Feast
August	26	Bl Dominic of the Mother of God, priest*	
September	3	ST GREGORY THE GREAT, POPE AND DOCTOR OF THE CHURCH, APOSTLE OF THE ENGLISH	Feast
	24	Our Lady of Ransom	Memorial
October	13	St Edward the Confessor, king	Memorial
	25	THE FORTY MARTYRS OF ENGLAND AND WALES	Feast
December	29	ST THOMAS À BECKET, BISHOP AND MARTYR, PATRON OF THE PASTORAL CLERGY OF ENGLAND	Feast

*When no rank is given, it is an optional memorial.

NATIONAL CALENDAR FOR WALES

February	9	St Teilo, bishop	
March	1	ST DAVID, BISHOP, PATRON OF WALES	Solemnity
	17	ST PATRICK, BISHOP, PATRON OF IRELAND	Feast
April	20	St Beuno, abbot	
	23	ST GEORGE, MARTYR, PATRON OF ENGLAND	Feast
May	4	The Beatified Martyrs of England and Wales	
	5	St Asaph, bishop	
June	20	Ss Alban, Julius and Aaron, protomartyrs of Britain	Memorial
	22	Ss John Fisher, bishop, and Thomas More, martyrs	Memorial
July	12	St John Jones, priest and martyr	
	23	Ss Philip Evans and John Lloyd, priests and martyrs	
August	3	St Germanus of Auxerre, bishop	
	26	St David Lewis, priest and martyr	
September	11	St Deiniol, bishop	
October	16	St Richard Gwyn, schoolmaster, martyr	
	25	THE SIX WELSH MARTYRS AND COMPANIONS, MARTYRS	Feast
November	3	St Winefride, virgin	
	6	St Illtud, abbot	
	8	ALL SAINTS OF WALES	Feast
	14	St Dyfrig, bishop	
December	10	St John Roberts, priest and martyr	

NATIONAL CALENDAR FOR IRELAND

Approved by the Sacred Congregation for Divine Worship on 6 November 1972 (Prot. Num. 203/72)

February	1	ST BRIGID, VIRGIN	Feast
March	17	ST PATRICK, BISHOP, PATRON OF IRELAND	Solemnity
June	9	ST COLUMBA (COLUM CILLE), ABBOT	Feast
July	1	ST OLIVER PLUNKETT, BISHOP AND MARTYR	Feast
November	6	ALL SAINTS OF IRELAND	Feast
	23	ST COLUMBAN, ABBOT	Feast

NATIONAL CALENDAR FOR SCOTLAND

Approved by the Sacred Congregation for Divine Worship on 14 March 1972 (Prot. Num: 2222/70)

January	13	St Kentigern, bishop	Memorial
March	10	ST JOHN OGILVIE, PRIEST AND MARTYR	Feast
	17	ST PATRICK, BISHOP	Feast
June	9	St Columba, abbot	Memorial
August	26	St Ninian, bishop	Memorial
November	16	ST MARGARET, SECONDARY PATRON OF SCOTLAND	Feast
	30	ST ANDREW, APOSTLE, PRINCIPAL PATRON OF SCOTLAND	Solemnity

THE PROPER OF SAINTS
National Calendars for England, Wales, Ireland, Scotland

13 January
St Kentigern, bishop
In Scotland: Memorial

Common of pastors: bishops, pp.1876ff.

Opening Prayer
Lord our God,
you chose Saint Kentigern as bishop
to spread the light of faith
by the preaching of your Word:
grant our prayer
that we who celebrate his memory
may be always true to his teaching
and so grow daily in faith and holiness.

1 February
ST BRIGID, VIRGIN
In Ireland: Feast

Common of virgins, pp.1889ff., or holy men and women: religious, pp.1898ff.

Opening Prayer
Lord,
you inspired in Saint Brigid such whole-hearted dedication to your work
that she is known as Mary of the Gael;
through her intercession bless our country:
may we follow the example of her life
and be united with her and the Virgin Mary in your presence.

FIRST READING

A reading from the letter of St Paul to the Romans 12:3-13
Our gifts differ according to the grace given us.

In the light of the grace I have received I want to urge each one among you not to exaggerate his real importance. Each of you must judge himself soberly by the standard of the faith God has given him. Just as each of our bodies has several parts and each part has a separate function, so all of us, in union with Christ, form one body, and as parts of it we belong to each other. Our gifts differ according to the grace given us. If your gift is prophecy, then use it as your faith suggests; if administration, then use it for administration; if teaching, then use it for teaching. Let the preachers deliver sermons, the almsgivers give freely, the officials be diligent, and those who do works of mercy do them cheerfully.

Do not let your love be a pretence, but sincerely prefer good to evil. Love each other as much as brothers should, and have a profound respect for each other. Work for the Lord with untiring effort and with great earnestness of spirit. If you have hope, this will make you cheerful. Do not give up if trials come; and keep on praying. If any of the saints are in need you must share with them; and you should make hospitality your special care.

This is the word of the Lord.

Responsorial Psalm   Ps 148:1-2. 11-14

℟ **Praise the name of the Lord.**

1   Praise the Lord from the heavens,
    praise him in the heights.
    praise him, all his angels,
    praise him, all his host.   ℟

2   All earth's kings and peoples,
    earth's princes and rulers;
    young men and maidens,
    old men together with children.   ℟

3   Let them praise the name of the Lord
    for he alone is exalted.
    The splendour of his name
    reaches beyond heaven and earth.   ℟

4   He exalts the strength of his people.
    He is the praise of all his saints,
    of the sons of Israel,
    of the people to whom he comes close.   ℟

Gospel Acclamation   Mt 5:8
Alleluia, alleluia!
Happy the pure in heart:
they shall see God.
Alleluia!

GOSPEL

A reading from the holy Gospel according to Mark   3:31-35
Anyone who does the will of God, that person is my brother and sister and mother.

The mother and brothers of Jesus arrived and, standing outside, sent in a message asking for him. A crowd was sitting round him at the time the message was passed to him, 'Your mother and brothers and sisters are outside asking for you', He replied, 'Who are my mother and my brothers?' And looking round at those sitting in a circle about him, he said, 'Here are my mother and my brothers. Anyone who does the will of God, that person is my brother and sister and mother.'

This is the Gospel of the Lord.

Alternative Gospel

A reading from the holy Gospel according to Luke   11:27-28
Happy the womb that bore you!

As Jesus was speaking, a woman in the crowd raised her voice and said, 'Happy the womb that bore you and the breasts you sucked!' But he replied, 'Still happier those who hear the word of God and keep it!'

This is the Gospel of the Lord.

---

1 March

ST DAVID, BISHOP
Patron of Wales
In Wales: Solemnity
In England: Feast

Entrance Antiphon: My teaching, which I have put in your mouth, will never fail, says the Lord; the gifts which you offered on my altar will be accepted.

or

You, Lord, are my portion and cup, you restore my inheritance to me; the way of life you marked out for me has made my heritage glorious.

or

Common of pastors: bishops, pp.1878ff., or of holy men and women: religious, pp.1898ff.

Opening Prayer
God our Father,
you gave the bishop David to the Welsh Church
to uphold the faith
and to be an example of Christian perfection.
In this changing world
may he help us to hold fast to the values
which bring eternal life.

FIRST READING

A reading from the letter of St Paul to the Philippians 3:8-14

I am racing for the finish, for the prize to which God calls us upwards to receive in Christ Jesus.

I believe nothing can happen that will outweigh the supreme advantage of knowing Christ Jesus my Lord. For him I have accepted the loss of everything, and I look on everything as so much rubbish if only I can have Christ and be given a place in him. I am no longer trying for perfection by my own efforts, the perfec- tion that comes from the Law, but I want only the perfection that comes through faith in Christ, and is from God and based on faith. All I want is to know Christ and the power of his resurrection and to share his sufferings by reproducing the pattern of his death. That is the way I can hope to take my place in the resurrection of the dead. Not that I have become perfect yet: I have not yet won, but I am still running, trying to capture the prize for which Christ Jesus captured me. I can assure you my brothers, I am far from thinking that I have already won. All I can say is that I forget the past and I strain ahead for what is still to come; I am racing for the finish, for the prize to which God calls us upwards to receive in Christ Jesus.

This is the word of the Lord.

Responsorial Psalm Ps 1. ℟ Ps 39:5

℟ **Happy the man who has placed his trust in the Lord.**

1 Happy indeed is the man
who follows not the counsel of the wicked;
nor lingers in the way of sinners
nor sits in the company of scorners,
but whose delight is the law of the Lord
and who ponders his law day and night. ℟

2 He is like a tree that is planted
beside the flowing waters,
that yields its fruit in due season
and whose leaves shall never fade;
and all that he does shall prosper. ℟

3 Not so are the wicked, not so!
For they like winnowed chaff
shall be driven away by the wind;
for the Lord guards the way of the just
but the way of the wicked leads to doom. ℟

Gospel Acclamation Jn 8:31-32
Alleluia, alleluia!
If you make my word your home
you will indeed be my disciples,
and you will learn the truth, says the Lord.
Alleluia!

GOSPEL

A reading from the holy Gospel according to Matthew 5:13-16
You are the light of the world.

Jesus said to his disciples: 'You are the salt of the earth. But if salt becomes tasteless, what can make it salty again? It is good for nothing, and can only be thrown out to be trampled underfoot by men.

'You are the light of the world. A city built on a hill-top cannot be hidden. No one lights a lamp to put it under a tub; they put it on the lamp-stand where it shines for everyone in the house. In the same way your light must shine in the sight of men, so that, seeing your good works, they may give the praise to your Father in heaven.'

This is the Gospel of the Lord.

Prayer over the Gifts
Lord, accept the gifts we bring
on the feast of Saint David.
We offer them to win your forgiveness
and to give honour to your name.

Preface of Holy Men and Women I or II, P69 or P70.

Communion Antiphon: The Son of Man came to give his life as a ransom for all.

or

I assure you who left all and followed me: you will receive a hundredfold in return and inherit eternal life.

or

Common of pastors: bishops, pp.1878ff., or of holy men and women: religious, pp.1898ff.

Prayer after Communion
All-powerful God,
you have strengthened us with this sacrament.
May we learn from Saint David's example
to seek you above all things,
and to live always as new men in Christ,
who lives and reigns for ever and ever.

10 March
ST JOHN OGILVIE, PRIEST AND MARTYR

In Scotland: Feast

Common of martyrs, pp.1865ff, or of pastors: missionaries, pp.1885.

Opening Prayer
Almighty and eternal God,
you gave to blessed John
wisdom in defending the Catholic faith
and courage in facing a martyr's death:
listen to our prayers,
and send us an ever greater harvest
of faith, hope and love.

FIRST READING

A reading from the prophet Isaiah 50:5-9
I offered my back to those who struck me.

The Lord has opened my ear.
For my part, I made no resistance,
neither did I turn away.
I offered my back to those who struck me,
my cheeks to those who tore at my beard;
I did not cover my face
against insult and spittle.

The Lord comes to my help,
so that I am untouched by the insults.
So, too, I set my face like flint;
I know I shall not be shamed.
My vindicator is here at hand. Does anyone start proceedings against me?
Then let us go to court together.
Who thinks he has a case against me?
Let him approach me.

The Lord is coming to my help,
who dare condemn me?

This is the word of the Lord.

Responsorial Psalm Ps 76:12-16. 21. ℟ v.12

℟ **I remember the deeds of the Lord.**

1. I remember the deeds of the Lord,
   I remember your wonders of old,
   I muse on all your works
   and ponder your mighty deeds. ℟

2. Your ways, O God, are holy.
   What god is great as our God?
   You are the God who works wonders.
   You showed your power among the peoples. ℟

3. Your strong arm redeemed your people,
   the sons of Jacob and Joseph.
   You guided your people like a flock
   by the hand of Moses and Aaron. ℟

SECOND READING

A reading from the second letter of St Paul to the Corinthians 1:3-7
God comforts us, so that we can offer others consolation in their sorrows.

Blessed be the God and Father of our Lord Jesus Christ, a gentle Father and the God of all consolation, who comforts us in all our sorrows, so that we can offer others, in their sorrows, the consolation that we have received from God ourselves. Indeed, as the sufferings of Christ overflow to us, so, through Christ, does our consolation overflow. When we are made to suffer, it is for your consolation and salvation. When, instead, we are comforted, this should be a consolation to you, supporting you in patiently bearing the same sufferings as we bear. And our hope for you is confident, since we know that, sharing our sufferings, you will also share our consolations.

This is the word of the Lord.

Gospel Acclamation   Jn 12:26

Alleluia, alleluia!
If a man serves me, says the Lord, he must follow me,
wherever I am, my servant will be there too.
Alleluia!

GOSPEL

A reading from the holy Gospel according to John   12:24-26
If a grain of wheat dies, it yields a rich harvest.

Jesus said to his disciples:

'I tell you, most solemnly,
unless a wheat grain falls on the ground and dies,
it remains only a single grain;
but if it dies,
it yields a rich harvest.
Anyone who loves his life loses it;
anyone who hates his life in this world
will keep it for the eternal life.
If a man serves me, he must follow me,
wherever I am, my servant will be there too.
If anyone serves me, my Father will honour him.'

This is the Gospel of the Lord.

17 March
ST PATRICK, BISHOP
Patron of Ireland
In Ireland and Australia: Solemnity
In England, Wales and Scotland: Feast

Entrance Antiphon: Go from your country and your kindred and your father's house to the land that I will show you; and I will make you the father of a great people.

Opening Prayer
Let us pray
    [that like Saint Patrick the missionary
    we will be fearless witnesses
    to the gospel of Jesus Christ]

God our Father,
you sent Saint Patrick
to preach your glory to the people of Ireland.
By the help of his prayers,
may all Christians proclaim your love to all men.

or

Let us pray
    [that, like Saint Patrick,
    we may be loyal to our faith in Christ]

Father in heaven,
you sent the great bishop Patrick
to the people of Ireland to share his faith
and to spend his life in loving service.

May our lives bear witness
to the faith we profess,
and our love bring others
to the peace and joy of your gospel.

FIRST READING

A reading from the prophet Jeremiah   1:4-9
Go now to those to whom I send you.

The word of the Lord was addressed to me, saying,

    'Before I formed you in the womb I knew you;

before you came to birth I consecrated you;
I have appointed you as prophet to the nations.'

I said, 'Ah, Lord; look, I do not know how to speak: I am a child!'
But the Lord replied,

'Do not say, "I am a child".
Go now to those to whom I send you
and say whatever I command you.
Do not be afraid of them,
for I am with you to protect you –
it is the Lord who speaks!'

Then the Lord put out his hand and touched my mouth and said to me:

'There! I am putting my words into your mouth.'

This is the word of the Lord.

Responsorial Psalm   Ps 116. ℟ Mk 16:15

℟ **Go out to all the world,
and tell the Good News.**

or (outside Lent only)

℟ **Alleluia!**

1 O praise the Lord, all you nations,
  acclaim him all you peoples!   ℟

2 Strong is his love for us;
  he is faithful for ever.   ℟

SECOND READING

A reading from the Acts of the Apostles   13:46-49
We must turn to the pagans.

Paul and Barnabas spoke out boldly to the Jews, 'We had to proclaim the word of God to you first, but since you have rejected it, since you do not think yourselves worthy of eternal life, we must turn to the pagans. For this is what the Lord commanded us to do when he said:

'I have made you a light for the nations,
so that my salvation may reach the ends of the earth.'

It made the pagans very happy to hear this and they thanked

the Lord for his message; all who were destined for eternal life became believers. Thus the word of the Lord spread through the whole countryside.

This is the word of the Lord.

Gospel Acclamation   Lk 4:18

Outside Lent

Alleluia, alleluia!
The Lord sent me to bring Good News to the poor,
and freedom to prisoners.
Alleluia!

In Lent

Praise and honour to you, Lord Jesus!
The Lord sent me to bring Good News to the poor,
and freedom to prisoners.
Praise and honour to you, Lord Jesus!

GOSPEL

A reading from the holy Gospel according to Luke   10:1-12. 17-20
Your peace will rest on that man.

The Lord appointed seventy-two others and sent them out ahead of him, in pairs, to all the towns and places he himself was to visit. He said to them, 'The harvest is rich but the labourers are few, so ask the Lord of the harvest to send labourers to his harvest. Start off now, but remember, I am sending you out like lambs among wolves. Carry no purse, no haversack, no sandals. Salute no one on the road. Whatever house you go into, let your first words be, "Peace to this house!" And if a man of peace lives there, your peace will go and rest on him; if not, it will come back *to you*. Stay in the same house, taking what food and drink they have to offer, for the labourer deserves his wages; do not move from house to house. Whenever you go into a town where they make you welcome, eat what is set before you. Cure those in it who are sick, and say, "The kingdom of God is very near to you." But whenever you enter a town and they do not make you welcome, go out into its streets and say, "We wipe off the very dust of your town that clings to our feet, and leave it with you. Yet be sure of this: the kingdom of God is very near." I tell you, on that day it will not go as hard with Sodom as with that town.'

The seventy-two came back rejoicing. 'Lord,' they said 'even the devils submit to us when we use your name.' He said to them, 'I watched Satan fall like lightning from heaven. Yes, I have given you power to tread underfoot serpents and scorpions and the whole strength of the enemy; nothing shall ever hurt you. Yet do not rejoice that the spirits submit to you; rejoice rather that your names are written in heaven.'

This is the Gospel of the Lord.

Prayer over the Gifts
Lord our God,
by the power of this sacrament
deepen our love
and strengthen our faith:
as we celebrate the feast of Saint Patrick
bind us more and more to each other
in unity and peace.

Preface of Holy Men and Women I or II, P69 or P79.

Communion Antiphon: The Lord sent disciples to proclaim to the people: the Kingdom of God is very near to you.

Prayer after Communion
Lord,
by the power of this sacrament
strengthen our faith;
may all we do or say
proclaim your truth
in imitation of Saint Patrick,
who did not spare himself
but gave his whole life
to the preaching of your Word.

21 April

St Anselm, bishop and doctor of the Church

In England: Memorial

Common of pastors: bishops, pp.1878ff., or of doctors of the Church, pp.1887ff.

Opening Prayer

Father,
you called Saint Anselm
to study and teach the sublime truths you have revealed.
Let your gift of faith come to the aid of our understanding
and open our hearts to your truth.

23 April

ST GEORGE, MARTYR

Patron of England

In England and Wales: Feast

Entrance Antiphon: Light for ever will shine on your saints, O Lord, alleluia.

Opening Prayer

Lord, hear the prayers of those who praise your mighty power.
As Saint George was ready to follow Christ in suffering and death,
so may he be ready to help us in our weakness.

FIRST READING

A reading from the book of the Apocalypse   12:10-12
In the face of death they would not cling to life.

I, John, heard a voice shout from heaven, 'Victory and power and empire for ever have been won by our God, and all authority for his Christ, now that the persecutor, who accused our brothers day and night before our God, has been brought down. They have triumphed over him by the blood of the Lamb and by the witness of their martyrdom, because even in the face of death they would not cling to life. Let the heavens rejoice and all who live there.'

This is the word of the Lord.

Responsorial Psalm
Ps 125. ℟ v.5

℟ **Those who are sowing in tears
will sing when they reap.**

1. When the Lord delivered Zion from bondage,
   it seemed like a dream.
   Then was our mouth filled with laughter,
   on our lips there were songs. ℟

2. The heathens themselves said: 'What marvels
   the Lord worked for them!'
   What marvels the Lord worked for us!
   Indeed we were glad. ℟

3. Deliver us, O Lord, from our bondage
   as streams in dry land.
   Those who are sowing in tears
   will sing when they reap. ℟

4. They go out, they go out, full of tears,
   carrying seed for the sowing;
   they come back, they come back, full of song,
   carrying their sheaves. ℟

Gospel Acclamation
James 1:12

Alleluia, alleluia!
Happy the man who stands firm.
for he has proved himself,
and will win the crown of life.
Alleluia!

GOSPEL

A reading from the holy Gospel according to John 15:18-21
If they persecuted me, they will persecute you too.

Jesus said to his disciples:

'If the world hates you,
remember that it hated me before you.
If you belonged to the world,
the world would love you as its own;
but because you do not belong to the world,
because my choice withdrew you from the world,
therefore the world hates you.
Remember the words I said to you:

A servant is not greater than his master.
If they persecuted me,
they will persecute you too;
if they kept my word,
they will keep yours as well.
But it will be on my account that they will do this,
because they do not know the one who sent me.'

This is the Gospel of the Lord.

Alternative Gospel

A reading from the holy Gospel according to John   15:1-8
Whoever remains in me, with me in him, bears fruit in plenty.

Jesus said to his disciples:

'I am the true vine,
and my Father is the vinedresser.
Every branch in me that bears no fruit
he cuts away,
and every branch that does bear fruit he prunes
to make it bear even more.
You are pruned already,
by means of the word that I have spoken to you.
Make your home in me, as I make mine in you.
As a branch cannot bear fruit all by itself,
but must remain part of the vine,
neither can you unless you remain in me.
I am the vine,
you are the branches.
Whoever remains in me, with me in him,
bears fruit in plenty;
for cut off from me you can do nothing.
Anyone who does not remain in me
is like a branch that has been thrown away
– he withers;
these branches are collected and thrown on the fire,
and they are burnt.
If you remain in me
and my words remain in you,
you may ask what you will
and you shall get it.
It is to the glory of my Father that you should bear much fruit,

and then you will be my disciples.'
This is the Gospel of the Lord.

Prayer over the Gifts
Lord, bless our offerings and make them holy.
May these gifts fill our hearts
with the love which gave Saint George victory
over all his suffering.

Preface of Martyrs, P66.

Communion Antiphon: I tell you solemnly: Unless a grain of wheat falls on the ground and dies, it remains a single grain; but if it dies, it yields a rich harvest, alleluia.

Prayer after Communion
Lord,
we receive your gifts from heaven
at this joyful feast.
May we who proclaim at this holy table
the death and resurrection of your Son
come to share his glory with Saint George
and all your holy martyrs.

4 May

THE BEATIFIED MARTYRS OF ENGLAND AND WALES

In England: Feast
In Wales: Memorial

Entrance Antiphon: Come, you whom my Father has blessed; inherit the kingdom prepared for you since the foundation of the world, alleluia.

Opening Prayer
God, all-powerful Father,
you strengthen our faith
and take away our weakness.
Let the prayers and example of the blessed martyrs of England and Wales
help us to share in the passion and resurrection of Christ
and bring us to eternal joy with all your saints.

FIRST READING

A reading from the Acts of the Apostles 7:55-60
Lord Jesus, receive my spirit.

Stephen, filled with the Holy Spirit, gazed into heaven and saw the glory of God, and Jesus standing at God's right hand. 'I can see heaven thrown open', he said, 'and the Son of Man standing at the right hand of God.' At this all the members of the council shouted out and stopped their ears with their hands; then they all rushed at him, sent him out of the city and stoned him. The witnesses put down their clothes at the feet of a young man called Saul. As they were stoning him, Stephen said in invocation, 'Lord Jesus, receive my spirit'. Then he knelt down and said aloud, 'Lord, do not hold this sin against them'; and with these words he fell asleep.

This is the word of the Lord.

Responsorial Psalm Ps 30:3-4. 6. 8. 17. 21. ℟ v.6

℟ **Into your hands, O Lord, I commend my spirit.**

1 Be a rock of refuge for me,
a mighty stronghold to save me,
for you are my rock, my stronghold.
For your name's sake, lead me and guide me. ℟

2 Into your hands I commend my spirit.
It is you who will redeem me, Lord.
As for me, I trust in the Lord:
let me be glad and rejoice in your love. ℟

3 Let your face shine on your servant.
Save me in your love.
You hide them in the shelter of your presence
from the plotting of men. ℟

Gospel Acclamation
Alleluia, alleluia!
We praise you, O God,
we acknowledge you to be the Lord;
the noble army of martyrs praise you, O Lord.
Alleluia!

GOSPEL

A reading from the holy Gospel according to Matthew 10:17-20

You will be dragged before governors and kings for my sake, to bear witness before them and the pagans.

Jesus said to his apostles: 'Beware of men: they will hand you over to sanhedrins and scourge you in their synagogues. You will be dragged before governors and kings for my sake, to bear witness before them and the pagans. But when they hand you over, do not worry about how to speak or what to say; what you are to say will be given to you when the time comes; because it is not you who will be speaking; the Spirit of your Father will be speaking in you.

'Brother will betray brother to death, and the father his child; children will rise against their parents and have them put to death. You will be hated by all men on account of my name; but the man who stands firm to the end will be saved.'

This is the Gospel of the Lord.

Prayer over the Gifts

Lord,
we celebrate the death of your holy martyrs.
May we offer the sacrifice which gives all martyrdom its meaning.

Preface of Martyrs, P66.

Communion Antiphon: If we died with Christ, we shall live with him, and if we are faithful to the end, we shall reign with him, alleluia.

Prayer after Communion

Lord,
we are renewed by the breaking of bread
in honour of the blessed martyrs of England and Wales.
Keep us in your love
and help us live the new life Christ won for us.

25 May
St Bede the Venerable, priest and doctor of the Church
In England: Memorial

Common of doctors of the Church, pp.1887ff., or of holy men and women: religious, pp.1898ff.

or

Entrance Antiphon: The learned will shine as bright as the heavens, and those who have taught many to be virtuous will be like the stars for ever.

Opening Prayer
God our Father,
you gave Saint Bede his learning
for the glory of your Church.
May we benefit by his wisdom
and share his love of prayer.

FIRST READING

A reading from the book of Ecclesiasticus 39:6-10
He will be filled with the spirit of understanding.

If it is the will of the great Lord,
the scholar will be filled with the spirit of understanding,
he will shower forth words of wisdom,
and in prayer give thanks to the Lord.
He will grow upright in purpose and learning,
he will ponder the Lord's hidden mysteries.
He will display the instruction he has received,
taking his pride in the Law of the Lord's covenant.
Many will praise his understanding,
and it will never be forgotten.
His memory will not disappear,
generation after generation his name will live.
Nations will proclaim his wisdom,
the assembly will celebrate his praises.

This is the word of the Lord.

Responsorial Psalm   Ps 36:3-6. 20-21. ℟ v.30

   ℟ **The just man's mouth utters wisdom.**

1 If you trust in the Lord and do good,
then you will live in the land and be secure.
If you find your delight in the Lord,
he will grant your heart's desire. ℟

2 Commit your life to the Lord,
trust in him and he will act,
so that your justice breaks forth like the light,
your cause like the noon-day sun. ℟

3 The just man's mouth utters wisdom
and his lips speak what is right;
the law of his God is in his heart,
his steps shall be saved from stumbling. ℟

Gospel Acclamation   Mt 5:16
Alleluia, alleluia!
Your light must shine in the sight of men,
so that, seeing your good works,
they may give the praise to your Father in heaven.
Alleluia!

GOSPEL

A reading from the holy Gospel according to Matthew   5:13-16
You are the light of the world.

Jesus said to his disciples: 'You are the salt of the earth. But if salt becomes tasteless, what can make it salty again? It is good for nothing, and can only be thrown out to be trampled underfoot by men.

'You are the light of the world. A city built on a hill-top cannot be hidden. No one lights a lamp to put it under a tub, they put it on the lamp-stand where it shines for everyone in the house. In the same way your light must shine in the sight of men, so that, seeing your good works, they may give the praise to your Father in heaven.'

   This is the Gospel of the Lord.

Prayer over the Gifts
Lord,
the venerable Bede sought always to know you better

and to share his knowledge with others.
May our offerings be supported by his prayers
and help us to serve you with the same dedication.

Communion Antiphon: We preach to you Christ crucified; Christ the power and the wisdom of God.

Prayer after Communion
Lord,
we have received Christ our King
under the forms of bread and wine.
May it strengthen in us a longing like Saint Bede's
to see him face to face in glory.

27 May

ST AUGUSTINE OF CANTERBURY, BISHOP
In England : Feast

Entrance Antiphon: How beautiful on the mountains are the feet of the man who brings tidings of peace, joy and salvation.

Opening Prayer
Father,
you sent Saint Augustine
to be the first apostle to the people of England.
May the work he began
be renewed in this land
and continue to prosper.

FIRST READING

A reading from the first letter of St Paul to the Thessalonians 2:2-8
We were eager to hand over not only the Good News but our whole lives as well.

It was our God who gave us the courage to proclaim his Good News to you in the face of great opposition. We have not taken to preaching because we are deluded, or immoral, or trying to deceive anyone; it was God who decided that we were fit to be entrusted with the Good News, and when we are speaking, we are not trying to please men but God, who can read our inmost thoughts. You know very well, and we can swear it before God, that never at any time have our speeches been simply flattery, or a cover for trying to get money; nor have we ever looked for any special honour from men, either from you or anybody else, when we could have imposed ourselves on you with full weight, as apostles of Christ.

Instead, we were unassuming. Like a mother feeding and looking after her own children we felt so devoted and protective towards you, and had come to love you so much, that we were eager to hand over to you not only the Good News but our whole lives as well.

This is the word of the Lord.

Responsorial Psalm   Ps 116. ℟ Mk 6:15

℟ **Go out to the whole world;
proclaim the Good News.**

or

℟ **Alleluia!**

1. O praise the Lord, all you nations,
   acclaim him all you peoples! ℟

2. Strong is his love for us;
   he is faithful for ever. ℟

Gospel Acclamation   Lk 4:18

Alleluia, alleluia!
The Lord has sent me to bring the good news to the poor,
to proclaim liberty to captives.
Alleluia!

GOSPEL

A reading from the holy Gospel according to Luke   10:1-9
The harvest is rich but the labourers are few.

The Lord appointed seventy-two others and sent them out ahead of him, in pairs, to all the towns and places he himself was to visit. He said to them, 'The harvest is rich but the labourers are few, so ask the Lord of the harvest to send labourers to his harvest. Start off now, but remember, I am sending you out like lambs among wolves. Carry no purse, no haversack, no sandals. Salute no one on the road. Whatever house you go into, let your first words be, "Peace to this house!" And if a man of peace lives there, your peace will go and rest on him; if not, it will come back to you. Stay in the same house, taking what food and drink they have to offer, for the labourer deserves his wages; do not move from house to house. Whenever you go into a town where they make you welcome, eat what is set before you. Cure those in it who are sick, and say, "The kingdom of God is very near to you".'

This is the Gospel of the Lord.

Prayer over the Gifts
Lord,
accept the gifts we present to you
in honour of Saint Augustine,
whose life of innocence and simplicity
converted many people to you.

Preface of Pastors, P67.

Communion Antiphon: The Lord sent disciples to proclaim to all the towns: the kingdom of God is very near to you.

Prayer after Communion
Lord,
strengthen us by the sacrament we have received.
Just as Saint Augustine persevered to the end
in the fulfilment of his mission,
so may we not falter
in our work for Christian unity.

9 June
ST COLUMBA (COLUM CILLE), ABBOT

In Ireland: Feast
In Scotland: Memorial

Entrance Antiphon: If I take the wings of the dawn and dwell at the sea's farthest end, even there your hand would lead me, your right hand would hold me fast.

Opening Prayer
Lord,
warm our hearts
with zeal for your kingdom
and a longing for its fulfilment:

make our lives rich in good works
and so bring us to share in the glory of Saint Columba
when we see you face to face
and are one with you always.

FIRST READING

A reading from the letter of St Paul to the Colossians 1:24-29
I became the servant of the Church.

It makes me happy to suffer for you, as I am suffering now, and in my own body to do what I can to make up all that has still to be undergone by Christ for the sake of his body, the Church. I became the servant of the Church when God made me responsible for delivering God's message to you, the message which was a mystery hidden for generations and centuries and has now been revealed to his saints. It was God's purpose to reveal it to them and to show all the rich glory of this mystery to pagans. The mystery is Christ among you, your hope of glory: this is the Christ we proclaim, this is the wisdom in which we thoroughly train everyone and instruct everyone, to make them all perfect in Christ. It is for this I struggle wearily on, helped only by his power driving me irresistibly.

This is the word of the Lord.

Responsorial Psalm Ps 15:1-2. 5. 7-8. 11. ℟ cf. v.5
 ℟ **You are my inheritance, O Lord.**

1 Preserve me, God, I take refuge in you.
 I say to the Lord: 'You are my God.'
 O Lord, it is you who are my portion and cup;
 it is you yourself who are my prize. ℟

2 I will bless the Lord who gives me counsel,
 who even at night directs my heart.
 I keep the Lord ever in my sight:
 since he is at my right hand, I shall stand firm. ℟

3 You will show me the path of life,
 the fullness of joy in your presence,
 at your right hand happiness for ever. ℟

Gospel Acclamation Mt 28:19-20
 Alleluia, alleluia!
 Go, make disciples of all the nations, says the Lord;

I am with you always, yes, to the end of time.
Alleluia!

GOSPEL

A reading from the holy Gospel according to Mark 10:17-30
Go and sell everything you own and follow me.

Jesus was setting out on a journey when a man ran up, knelt before him and put this question to him, 'Good master, what must I do to inherit eternal life?' Jesus said to him, 'Why do you call me good? No one is good but God alone. You know the commandments: You must not kill; You must not commit adultery; You must not steal; You must not bring false witness; You must not defraud; Honour your father and mother.' And he said to him, 'Master, I have kept all these from my earliest days'. Jesus looked steadily at him and loved him, and he said, 'There is one thing you lack. Go and sell everything you own and give the money to the poor, and you will have treasure in heaven; then come, follow me.' But his face fell at these words and he went away sad, for he was a man of great wealth.

Jesus looked round and said to his disciples, 'How hard it is for those who have riches to enter the kingdom of God!' The disciples were astounded by these words, but Jesus insisted, 'My children,' he said to them, 'how hard it is to enter the kingdom of God! It is easier for a camel to pass through the eye of a needle than for a rich man to enter the kingdom of God.' They were more astonished than ever. 'In that case,' they said to one another, 'who can be saved?' Jesus gazed at them. 'For men,' he said, 'it is impossible, but not for God: because everything is possible for God.'

Peter took this up. 'What about us?' he asked him. 'We have left everything and followed you.' Jesus said, 'I tell you solemnly, there is no one who has left house, brothers, sisters, father, children or land for my sake and for the sake of the gospel who will not be repaid a hundred times over, houses, brothers, sisters, mothers, children and land – not without persecutions – now in this present time and, in the world to come, eternal life.'

This is the Gospel of the Lord.

In the Easter Season

Alternative Gospel

A reading from the holy Gospel according to John 15:9-17
You are my friends if you do what I command you.

Jesus said to his disciples:

'As the Father has loved me,
so I have loved you.
Remain in my love.
If you keep my commandments
you will remain in my love,
just as I have kept my Father's commandments
and remain in his love.
I have told you this
so that my own joy may be in you
and your joy be complete.
This is my commandment:
love one another,
as I have loved you.
A man can have no greater love
than to lay down his life for his friends.
You are my friends,
if you do what I command you.
I shall not call you servants any more,
because a servant does not know his master's business:
I call you friends,
because I have made known to you
everything I have learnt from my Father.
You did not choose me,
no, I chose you;
and I commissioned you
to go out and to bear fruit,
fruit that will last;
and then the Father will give you
anything you ask him in my name.
What I command you
is to love one another.'

This is the Gospel of the Lord.

Prayer over the Gifts
God of mercy,
you freed Saint Columba from the power of sin
and restored in him the likeness of your Son:
in your goodness renew us also,
and make us worthy to offer this sacrifice,
which gains for us your peace.

Communion Antiphon: He ate and drank, and in the strength of that food he walked to the mountain of God.

Prayer after Communion
Lord,
you have given us here on earth
your body and blood to be our food and drink:
on this feast of Saint Columba
we pray that we may enjoy in heaven
the vision of your glory
as you live and reign for ever and ever.

20 June

St Alban,
protomartyr of Britain
In England: Memorial

Ss Alban, Julius
and Aaron, protomartyrs
In Wales: Memorial

Entrance Antiphon: This holy man fought to the death for the law of his God, never cowed by threats of the wicked; his house was built on solid rock.

or

For the name of Christ he shed his blood and did not fear the threats of false judges. He gave a true witness and gained a heavenly reward.

Opening Prayer
Father,
by your grace Saint Alban gave himself up for his friend
and was the first in this land to shed his blood for Christ.
May we who celebrate his feast be helped continually by his
   prayers.

National Calendars, 20 June

FIRST READING

A reading from the second letter of St Paul to Timothy 2:8-13; 3:10-12

Anyody who tries to live in devotion to Christ is certain to be attacked.

Remember the Good News that I carry, 'Jesus Christ risen from the dead, sprung from the race of David'; it is on account of this that I have my own hardships to bear, even to being chained like a criminal – but they cannot chain up God's news. So I bear it all for the sake of those who are chosen, so that in the end they may have the salvation that is in Christ Jesus and the eternal glory that comes with it.

Here is a saying that you can rely on:

If we have died with him, then we shall live with him.
If we hold firm, then we shall reign with him.
If we disown him, then he will disown us.
We may be unfaithful, but he is always faithful,
for he cannot disown his own self.

You know, though, what I have taught, how I have lived, what I have aimed at; you know my faith, my patience and my love; my constancy and the persecutions and hardships that came to me in places like Antioch, Iconium and Lystra – all the persecutions I have endured; and the Lord has rescued me from every one of them. You are all aware, then, that anybody who tries to live in devotion to Christ is certain to be attacked.

This is the word of the Lord.

Responsorial Psalm Ps 123:2-5. 7-8. ℟ v.7

℟ **Our life, like a bird, has escaped
from the snare of the fowler.**

1 If the Lord had not been on our side
 when men rose against us
 then would they have swallowed us alive
 when their anger was kindled. ℟

2 Then would the waters have engulfed us,
 the torrent gone over us;
 over our head would have swept
 the raging waters. ℟

3 Indeed the snare has been broken
 and we have escaped.

Our help is in the name of the Lord,
who made heaven and earth. ℟

Gospel Acclamation 2 Cor 1:3-4
Alleluia, alleluia!
Blessed be God, a gentle Father,
and the God of all consolation,
who comforts us in all our sorrows.
Alleluia!

GOSPEL

A reading from the holy Gospel according to John 12:24-26
If a grain of wheat dies, it yields a rich harvest.

Jesus said to his disciples:

'I tell you, most solemnly,
unless a wheat grain falls on the ground and dies,
it remains only a single grain;
but if it dies,
it yields a rich harvest.
Anyone who loves his life loses it;
anyone who hates his life in this world
will keep it for the eternal life.
If a man serves me, he must follow me,
wherever I am, my servant will be there too.
If anyone serves me, my Father will honour him.'

This is the Gospel of the Lord.

Prayer over the Gifts
God of love,
pour out your blessing on our gifts
and make our faith strong,
the faith which Saint Alban professed by shedding his blood.

Preface of Martyrs, P66.

Communion Antiphon: The Lord said: If anyone wishes to be my disciple, let him deny himself and take up his cross and follow in my footsteps.

or

I am the true vine, you are the branches, says the Lord. He who abides in me, and I in him, he it is who bears much fruit.

Prayer after Communion
Lord,
we are renewed by the mystery of the eucharist.
By imitating the fidelity of Saint Alban, and by your patience,
may we come to share the eternal life you have promised.

22 June
SS JOHN FISHER, BISHOP
AND ST THOMAS MORE, MARTYRS

In England: Feast
In Wales: Memorial

Entrance Antiphon: These are the brave who resisted the king's command, saying: in this matter it is our duty to disobey.

or

These holy men fought to the death for the law of their God, never cowed by the threats of the wicked; their house was built on solid rock.

Opening Prayer
Father,
you made the martyrs John and Thomas
the foremost champions of the Church in our land.
Through their prayers
make us obedient to your law
and manifestly one in Christ,
who lives and reigns . . .

FIRST READING
A reading from the second book of Maccabees   6:18. 21. 24-31

I am glad to suffer because the awe which he inspires in me.

Eleazar, one of the foremost teachers of the Law, a man already advanced in years and of most noble appearance, was being forced to open his mouth wide to swallow pig's flesh. Those in charge of the impious banquet, because of their long-standing friendship with him, took him aside and privately urged him to have meat brought of a kind he could properly use, prepared by himself, and only pretend to eat the portions of sacrificial meat as prescribed by the king. 'Such pretence', he said, 'does not square with our time of life; many young people would suppose that Eleazar at the age of ninety had conformed to the foreigners' way of life, and because I had played this part for the sake of a paltry brief spell of life might themselves be led astray on my account; I should only bring defilement and disgrace on my old age. Even though for the moment I avoid execution by man, I can never, living or dead, elude the grasp of the Almighty. Therefore if I am man enough to quit this life here and now I shall prove myself worthy of my old age, and I shall have left the young a noble example of how to make a good death eagerly and generously, for the venerable and holy laws.'

With these words he went straight to the block. His escorts, so recently well disposed towards him, turned against him after this declaration, which they regarded as sheer madness. Just before he died under the blows, he groaned aloud and said, 'The Lord whose knowledge is holy sees clearly that, though I might have escaped death, whatever agonies of body I now endure under this bludgeoning, in my soul I am glad to suffer, because of the awe which he inspires in me'.

This was how he died, leaving his death as an example of nobility and a record of virtue not only for the young but for the great majority of the nation.

This is the word of the Lord.

Responsorial Psalm   Ps 30:2. 6. 8-9. 15-17. 25. ℟ Lk 23:46

    ℟ **Father, into your hands I commend my spirit.**

1   In you, O Lord, I take refuge,
Let me never be put to shame.
In your justice, set me free.
Into your hands I commend my spirit.
It is you who will redeem me, Lord.   ℟

2   You who have seen my affliction
and taken heed of my soul's distress,
have not handed me over to the enemy,
but set my feet at large.   ℟

3   But as for me, I trust in you, Lord,
I say: 'You are my God.
My life is in your hands, deliver me
from the hands of those who hate me.   ℟   (continued)

4 'Let your face shine on your servant.
   Save me in your love.'
   Be strong, let your heart take courage,
   all who hope in the Lord.

   ℟ **Father, into your hands I commend my spirit.**

Gospel Acclamation
James 1:12

Alleluia, alleluia!
Happy the man who stands firm when trials come.
He has proved himself,
and will win the crown of life.
Alleluia!

GOSPEL

A reading from the holy Gospel according to Matthew 24:4-13
You will be hated by all the nations on account of my name.

Jesus said to his disciples, 'Take care that no one deceives you; because many will come using my name and saying, "I am the Christ", and they will deceive many. You will hear of wars and rumours of wars; do not be alarmed, for this is something that must happen, but the end will not be yet. For nation will fight against nation, and kingdom against kingdom. There will be famines and earthquakes here and there. All this is only the beginning of the birthpangs.

'Then they will hand you over to be tortured and put to death; and you will be hated by all the nations on account of my name. And then many will fall away; men will betray one another and hate one another. Many false prophets will arise; they will deceive many, and with the increase of lawlessness, love in most men will grow cold; but the man who stands firm to the end will be saved.'

This is the Gospel of the Lord.

Prayer over the Gifts
Lord,
look with favour on our gifts,
and through the prayers of the martyrs John and Thomas
increase our love for you.

Preface of Martyrs, P66.

Communion Antiphon: Eternal life is this: to know you, the one, true God, and Jesus Christ whom you have sent.

or

We are given over to death for Jesus, that the life of Jesus may be revealed in our dying flesh.

Prayer after Communion
Lord,
renew us with this food from heaven
and strengthen us by the example of your martyrs John and
 Thomas,
so that we may always follow conscience
and be the king's good servant, but God's first.

1 July
ST OLIVER PLUNKETT, BISHOP AND MARTYR
In Ireland: Feast

Common of martyrs, pp.1865ff., or pastors, pp.1876ff.

or

Entrance Antiphon: Here is a true martyr who shed his blood for Christ; his judges could not shake him by their menaces, and so he won through to the kingdom of heaven.

Opening Prayer
God our Father,
you filled Saint Oliver with your Spirit of fortitude
enabling him to feed your flock with his word
and lay down his life for your sheep.
Help us by his prayers to keep the faith he taught
and follow the way of reconciliation which he showed by his
 example.

FIRST READING

A reading from the prophet Ezekiel 34:11-16
As a shepherd keeps all his flock in view, so shall I keep my sheep in view.

The Lord says this: I am going to look after my flock myself and keep all of it in view. As a shepherd keeps all his flock in view when he stands up in the middle of his scattered sheep, so shall I keep my sheep in view. I shall rescue them from wherever they have been scattered during the mist and darkness. I shall bring them out of the countries where they are; I shall gather them together from foreign countries and bring them back to their own land. I shall pasture them on the mountains of Israel, in the ravines and in every inhabited place in the land. I shall feed them in good pasturage; the high mountains of Israel will be their grazing ground. There they will rest in good grazing ground; they will browse in rich pastures on the mountains of Israel. I myself will pasture my sheep, I myself will show them where to rest – it is the Lord who speaks. I shall look for the lost one, bring back the stray, bandage the wounded and make the weak strong. I shall watch over the fat and healthy. I shall be a true shepherd to them.

This is the word of the Lord.

Alternative First Reading

A reading from the first letter of St Peter   3:8-18
He must never yield to evil but must practise good; he must seek peace and pursue it.

You should all agree among yourselves and be sympathetic; love the brothers, have compassion and be self-effacing. Never pay back one wrong with another, or an angry word with another one; instead, pay back with a blessing. That is what you are called to do, so that you inherit a blessing yourself. Remember: Anyone who wants to have a happy life and to enjoy prosperity must banish malice from his tongue, deceitful conversation from his lips; he must never yield to evil but must practise good; he must seek peace and pursue it. Because the face of the Lord frowns on evil men, but the eyes of the Lord are turned towards the virtuous.

No one can hurt you if you are determined to do only what is right; if you do have to suffer for being good, you will count it a blessing. There is no need to be afraid or to worry about them. Simply reverence the Lord Christ in your hearts, and always have your answer ready for people who ask you the reason for the hope that you all have. But give it with courtesy and respect and with a clear conscience, so that those who slander you when you are living a good life in Christ may be proved wrong in the accusations that they bring. And if it is the will of God that you should suffer, it is better to suffer for doing right than for doing wrong.

Why, Christ himself, innocent though he was, had died once for sins, died for the guilty, to lead us to God. In the body he was put to death, in the spirit he was raised to life.

This is the word of the Lord.

Responsorial Psalm Ps 30:3-4. 6. 8. 17. 21. ℟ v.6

℟ **Into your hands, O Lord,
I commend my spirit.**

1 Be a rock of refuge for me,
a mighty stronghold to save me,
for you are my rock, my stronghold.
For your name's sake, lead me and guide me. ℟

2 Into your hands I commend my spirit.
It is you who will redeem me, Lord.
As for me, I trust in the Lord:
let me be glad and rejoice in your love. ℟

3 Let your face shine on your servant.
Save me in your love.
You hide them in the shelter of your presence
from the plotting of men. ℟

Gospel Acclamation James 1:12
Alleluia, alleluia!
Happy the man who stands firm when trials come.
He has proved himself,
and will win the crown of life.
Alleluia!

GOSPEL

A reading from the holy Gospel according to John 10:11-16
The good shepherd is one who lays down his life for his sheep.

Jesus said:

'I am the good shepherd:
the good shepherd is one who lays down his life for his sheep.
The hired man, since he is not the shepherd

and the sheep do not belong to him,
abandons the sheep and runs away
as soon as he sees a wolf coming,
and then the wolf attacks and scatters the sheep;
this is because he is only a hired man
and has no concern for the sheep
I am the good shepherd;
I know my own
and my own know me,
just as the Father knows me
and I know the Father;
and I lay down my life for my sheep.
And there are other sheep I have
that are not of this fold,
and these I have to lead as well.
They too will listen to my voice,
and there will be only one flock,
and one shepherd.'

This is the Gospel of the Lord.

Prayer over the Gifts
All-powerful God,
look upon the gifts we bring on this feast
in honour of Saint Oliver.
May we who celebrate the mystery of the death of the Lord
imitate the love we celebrate.

Communion Antiphon: I tell you solemnly: unless a grain of wheat falls on the ground and dies, it remains a single grain; but if it dies, it yields a rich harvest, alleluia.

Prayer after Communion
Lord,
Saint Oliver worked tirelessly for the faith,
spending his life in its service.
With the power this eucharist gives,
make your people strong in the same true faith
and help us to proclaim it everywhere
by all we say and do.

26 August
St Ninian, Bishop

In Scotland: Memorial

Common of pastors: bishops, pp.1878ff.

Opening Prayer
Lord our God,
you brought the Picts and Britons
to a knowledge of the faith
through the teaching of Saint Ninian, the bishop:
in your goodness listen to our prayers:
grant that we who have received from him
the light of your truth
may remain strong in faith
and active in works of charity.

Also 26 August
Blessed Dominic of the Mother of God, priest

In England: Optional Memorial

Common of pastors: missionaries, pp.1885ff.

or

Entrance Antiphon: How beautiful on the mountains are the feet of him who brings good tidings of peace, joy and salvation.

Opening Prayer
Father,
you chose Dominic as a minister of your love
so that his teaching and example helped many to find
pardon and peace in the unity of your Church.
Grant that we may follow in the same way of love
and so gain an eternal reward.

or

Holy and gracious God
whom we call Father,
unrelenting is your love for men,
untiring your concern for our good.

In every age you raise up men like Dominic
who reveal your goodness in their own lives,

and through whose simple faith and love
you win great minds and hearts
for your Church.

Help us to serve you as he did,
sharing the joy of your love
with those who come into our lives.

FIRST READING

A reading from the first letter of St Paul to the Corinthians 1:18-25

God wanted to save those who have faith through the foolishness of the message that we preach.

The language of the cross may be illogical to those who are not on the way to salvation, but those of us who are on the way see it as God's power to save. As scripture says: I shall destroy the wisdom of the wise and bring to nothing all the learning of the learned. Where are the philosophers now? Where are the scribes? Where are any of our thinkers today? Do you see how God has shown up the foolishness of human wisdom? If it was God's wisdom that human wisdom should not know God, it was because God wanted to save those who have faith through the foolishness of the message that we preach. And so, while the Jews demand miracles and the Greeks look for wisdom, here are we preaching a crucified Christ; to the Jews an obstacle that they cannot get over, to the pagans madness, but to those who have been called, whether they are Jews or Greeks, a Christ who is the power and the wisdom of God. For God's foolishness is wiser than human wisdom, and God's weakness is stronger than human strength.

This is the word of the Lord.

Responsorial Psalm Ps 116. ℟ Mk 6:15

℟ **Go out to the whole world;
proclaim the Good News.**

or

℟ **Alleluia!**

1 O praise the Lord, all you nations,
acclaim him all you peoples! ℟

2 Strong is his love for us;
he is faithful for ever. ℟

Gospel Acclamation
2 Cor 5:19

Alleluia, alleluia!
God in Christ was reconciling the world to himself,
and he has entrusted to us
the news that they are reconciled.
Alleluia!

GOSPEL

A reading from the holy Gospel according to Mark 1:14-20

I will make you into fishers of men.

After John had been arrested, Jesus went into Galilee. There he proclaimed the Good News from God. 'The time has come,' he said, 'and the kingdom of God is close at hand. Repent, and believe the Good News.'

As he was walking along by the Sea of Galilee he saw Simon and his brother Andrew casting a net in the lake – for they were fishermen. And Jesus said to them, 'Follow me and I will make you into fishers of men.' And at once they left their nets and followed him.

Going on a little farther, he saw James son of Zebedee and his brother John; they too were in their boat, mending their nets. He called them at once and, leaving their father Zebedee in the boat with the men he employed, they went after him.

This is the Gospel of the Lord.

Prayer over the Gifts
Grant to all of us, Lord,
a fullness of charity as lived by your priest Dominic.
So may this sacrifice we offer
fully effect our reconciliation.

Communion Antiphon: Make your home in me, as I will in you, says the Lord: he who lives in me, and I in him, will bear much fruit.

Prayer after Communion
Our strength is renewed at your table, Lord,
so we ask you,
through the merits and prayers of blessed Dominic,
to bring all wanderers into the one fold of Christ,
who lives and reigns for ever and ever.

3 September
ST GREGORY THE GREAT, POPE AND DOCTOR OF THE CHURCH
Apostle of the English

In England: Feast

Common of pastors: popes, pp.1876ff., or of doctors of the Church, pp.1887ff.

Opening Prayer

Father,
you guide your people with kindness
and govern us with love.
By the prayers of Saint Gregory
give the spirit of wisdom
to those you have called to lead your Church.
May the growth of your people in holiness
be the eternal joy of our shepherds.

FIRST READING

A reading from the first letter of St Paul to the Thessalonians   2:2-8

We were eager to hand over not only the Good News but our whole lives as well.

It was our God who gave us the courage to proclaim his Good News to you in the face of great opposition. We have not taken to preaching because we are deluded, or immoral, or trying to deceive anyone; it was God who decided that we were fit to be entrusted with the Good News, and when we are speaking, we are not trying to please men but God, who can read our inmost thoughts. You know very well, and we can swear it before God, that never at any time have our speeches been simply flattery, or a cover for trying to get money; nor have we ever looked for any special honour from men, either from you or anybody else, when we could have imposed ourselves on you with full weight, as apostles of Christ.

Instead, we were unassuming. Like a mother feeding and looking after her own children, we felt so devoted and protective towards you, and had come to love you so much, that we were eager to hand over to you not only the Good News but our whole lives as well.

This is the word of the Lord.

Responsorial Psalm
Ps 95:1-3. 7-8. 10. ℟ v.3

℟ **Proclaim the wonders of the Lord among all the peoples.**

1 O sing a new song to the Lord,
 sing to the Lord all the earth.
 O sing to the Lord, bless his name.   ℟

2 Proclaim his help day by day,
 tell among the nations his glory
 and his wonders among all the peoples.   ℟

3 Give the Lord, you families of peoples,
 give the Lord glory and power,
 give the Lord the glory of his name.   ℟

4 Proclaim to the nations: 'God is king.'
 The world he made firm in its place;
 he will judge the peoples in fairness.   ℟

Gospel Acclamation
Lk 4:18

Alleluia, alleluia!
The Lord has sent me to bring the good news to the poor,
to proclaim liberty to captives.
Alleluia!

GOSPEL

A reading from the holy Gospel according to Matthew   16:13-19

You are Peter and on this rock I will build my Church.

When Jesus came to the region of Caesarea Philippi he put this question to his disciples, 'Who do people say the Son of Man is?' And they said, 'Some say he is John the Baptist, some Elijah, and others Jeremiah or one of the prophets'. 'But you,' he said, 'who do you say I am?' Then Simon Peter spoke up, 'You are the Christ,' he said, 'the Son of the living God'. Jesus replied, 'Simon son of Jonah, you are a happy man! Because it was not flesh and blood that revealed this to you but my Father in heaven. So I now say to you: You are Peter and on this rock I will build my Church. And the gates of the underworld can never hold out against it. I will give you the keys of the kingdom of heaven; whatever you bind on earth shall be considered bound in heaven; whatever you loose on earth shall be considered loosed in heaven.'

This is the Gospel of the Lord.

Prayer over the Gifts
Lord,
by this sacrifice you free the world from sin.
As we offer it in memory of Saint Gregory,
may it bring us closer to eternal salvation.

Prayer after Communion
Lord,
at this eucharist you give us Christ to be our living bread.
As we celebrate the feast of Saint Gregory,
may we also come to know your truth
and live it in love for others.

Alternative Mass proper

Entrance Antiphon: The Lord chose him to be his high priest; from his treasures he made him rich in goodness.

Opening Prayer
Lord,
when the Gospel came from Rome to Kent,
brought by monks at Pope Saint Gregory's command,
he wished us here to be one with all the Church
in praising you
and sharing the life your Son had won for us.

Give us again leaders like him
that, with a renewed spirit of faith,
we may celebrate your glory, mighty God,
Father, Son and Holy Spirit, who live and reign
for ever and ever.

Readings as above.

Prayer over the Gifts
Lord,
by this sacrifice you free the world from its sin.
As we honour Saint Gregory
may this offering bring us your saving grace.

Preface of Pastors, P67.

Communion Antiphon: The good shepherd has given his life for his flock.

Prayer after Communion
The bread of angels has refreshed us, Lord.
Make us fit to inherit the kingdom with them
as Saint Gregory desired
from his first sight of English slaves.

---

24 September

Our Lady of Ransom
In England: Memorial

Common of the Blessed Virgin Mary, pp. 1858ff.

or

Entrance Antiphon: The disciples were constantly at prayer together, with Mary the mother of Jesus.

Opening Prayer
Lord,
we have long been the dowry of Mary
and subject of Peter, prince of the apostles.
Let us hold to the Catholic faith
and remain devoted to the Blessed Virgin
and obedient to Peter.

or

Times and seasons change,
centuries and ages pass;
you seem above them, Lord,
untouched, unmoved.

But
your Son entered in,
born of a woman,
crushed and crucified,
to ransom us.

Will you be deaf to our cries?
Can you ignore the appeals
of the creatures your Son embraced?
Can you refuse the prayer
of Mary, his Mother?

Let us know the freedom of your kingdom
where you live with your Son

and with the Holy Spirit,
one infinite Freedom
for ever and ever.

FIRST READING

A reading from the letter of St Paul to the Galatians   4:4-7

God sent his Son, born of a woman.

When the appointed time came, God sent his Son, born of a woman, born a subject of the Law, to redeem the subjects of the Law and to enable us to be adopted as sons. The proof that you are sons is that God has sent the Spirit of his Son into our hearts: the Spirit that cries, 'Abba, Father', and it is this that makes you a son, you are not a slave any more; and if God has made you son, then he has made you heir.

This is the word of the Lord.

Responsorial Psalm   Lk 1:46-55. ℟ v.49

  ℟ **The Almighty works marvels for me.**
     Holy is his name!

or

  ℟ **Blessed is the Virgin Mary**
     who bore the Son of the eternal Father.

1. My soul glorifies the Lord,
my spirit rejoices in God, my saviour. ℟

2. He looks on his servant in her nothingness;
henceforth all ages will call me blessed.
The Almighty works marvels for me.
Holy his name! ℟

3. His mercy is from age to age,
on those who fear him.
He puts forth his arm in strength
and scatters the proud-hearted. ℟

4. He casts the mighty from their thrones
and raises the lowly.
He fills the starving with good things,
sends the rich away empty. ℟

   He protects Israel, his servant,
   remembering his mercy,

the mercy promised to our fathers,
to Abraham and his sons for ever. ℟

Gospel Acclamation   Lk 2:19
Alleluia, alleluia!
Blessed is the Virgin Mary
who treasured the word of God,
and pondered it in her heart.
Alleluia!

GOSPEL

A reading from the holy Gospel according to John   19:25-27
This is your son. This is your mother.

Near the cross of Jesus stood his mother and his mother's sister, Mary the wife of Clopas, and Mary of Magdala. Seeing his mother and the disciple he loved standing near her, Jesus said to his mother, 'Woman, this is your son'. Then to the disciple he said, 'This is your mother'. And from that moment the disciple made a place for her in his home.

This is the Gospel of the Lord.

Prayer over the Gifts
Lord,
accept our gifts
so that by the help of Mary's prayers
we may continue in this faith
which bears fruit in charity.

Preface of the Blessed Virgin Mary I, P56.

Communion Antiphon: All generations will call me blessed, because God has looked upon his servant in her lowliness.

Prayer after Communion
Lord,
grant that this sacrament may strengthen us
in love for Mary our mother
and in obedience to Peter.

13 October
St Edward the Confessor, king
In England: Memorial

Common of holy men and women, pp.1894ff.
or
Entrance Antiphon: The just man will rejoice in the Lord and hope in him, and all the upright of heart will be praised.

Opening Prayer
Lord,
you raised Saint Edward, king and confessor,
to excel in good government and faithful service.
May these ideals survive and flourish among us
through his prayers.

FIRST READING

A reading from the letter of St Paul to the Romans   8:26-30
With those he justified, he shared his glory.

The Spirit comes to help us in our weakness. For when we cannot choose words in order to pray properly, the Spirit himself expresses our plea in a way that could never be put into words, and God who knows everything in our hearts knows perfectly well what he means, and that the pleas of the saints expressed by the Spirit are according to the mind of God.

We know that by turning everything to their good God co-operates with all those who love him, with all those that he has called according to his purpose. They are the ones he chose specially long ago and intended to become true images of his Son, so that his Son might be the eldest of many brothers. He called those he intended for this; those he called he justified, and with those he justified he shared his glory.

This is the word of the Lord.

Responsorial Psalm   Ps 130
℟ **Keep my soul in peace before you, O Lord.**

1 O Lord, my heart is not proud
   nor haughty my eyes.
   I have not gone after things too great
   nor marvels beyond me.   ℟

2 Truly I have set my soul
in silence and peace.
A weaned child on its mother's breast,
even so is my soul.

℟ **Keep my soul in peace before you, O Lord.**

3 O Israel, hope in the Lord
both now and for ever. ℟

Gospel Acclamation
Mt 5:3
Alleluia, alleluia!
How happy are the poor in spirit;
theirs is the kingdom of heaven.
Alleluia!

GOSPEL

A reading from the holy Gospel according to Matthew 5:1-12
Rejoice and be glad, for your reward will be great in heaven.

Seeing the crowds, Jesus went up the hill. There he sat down and was joined by his disciples. Then he began to speak. This is what he taught them:

'How happy are the poor in spirit;
theirs is the kingdom of heaven.
Happy the gentle:
they shall have the earth for their heritage.
Happy those who mourn:
they shall be comforted.
Happy those who hunger and thirst for what is right:
they shall be satisfied.
Happy the merciful:
they shall have mercy shown them.
Happy the pure in heart:
they shall see God.
Happy the peacemakers:
they shall be called sons of God.
Happy those who are persecuted in the cause of right:
theirs is the kingdom of heaven.

'Happy are you when people abuse you and persecute you and speak all kinds of calumny against you on my account. Rejoice and be glad, for your reward will be great in heaven.'

This is the Gospel of the Lord.

Prayer over the Gifts
Lord,
accept the gifts of your people.
May we who celebrate the love of your Son
also follow the example of Saint Edward
and grow in love for you and for one another.

Communion Antiphon: He who serves me, follows me, says the Lord; and where I am, my servant will also be.

Prayer after Communion
Lord,
our hunger is satisfied by your holy gift
as we honour the memory of Saint Edward.
May we who have celebrated this eucharist
experience in our lives the salvation which it brings.

25 October

THE FORTY MARTYRS OF ENGLAND AND WALES In England: Feast

THE SIX WELSH MARTYRS AND COMPANIONS, MARTYRS In Wales: Feast

Entrance Antiphon: The saints are happy in heaven because they followed Christ. They rejoice with him for ever because they shed their blood for love of him.

Opening Prayer
God our Father,
you raised up martyrs – saints among our countrymen
from every walk of life.
They vindicated the authority of your Church
in teaching and worship.
Through their prayers
may our whole nation be gathered once again
to celebrate the same sacraments
under one Shepherd, Jesus Christ, your Son,
who lives and reigns . . .

FIRST READING

A reading from the letter to the Hebrews 11:33-40

Through faith they conquered kingdoms. God will make provision for us to have something better.

Gideon, Barak, Samson, Jephthah, David, Samuel and the prophets – these were men who through faith conquered kingdoms, did what is right and earned the promises. They could keep a lion's mouth shut, put out blazing fires and emerge unscathed from battle. They were weak people who were given strength, to be brave in war and drive back foreign invaders. Some came back to their wives from the dead, by resurrection; and others submitted to torture, refusing release so that they would rise again to a better life. Some had to bear being pilloried and flogged, or even chained up in prison. They were stoned or sawn in half, or beheaded; they were homeless, and dressed in the skins of sheep and goats; they were penniless and were given nothing but ill-treatment. They were too good for the world and they went out to live in deserts and mountains and in caves and ravines. These are all heroes of faith, but they did not receive what was promised, since God had made provision for us to have something better, and they were not to reach perfection except with us.

This is the word of the Lord.

Responsorial Psalm Ps 15:1-2. 5. 7. 8-11 ℟ v.5

℟ **You are my inheritance, O Lord.**

1 Preserve me, God, I take refuge in you.
 I say to the Lord: 'You are my God.'
 O Lord, it is you who are my portion and cup;
 it is you yourself who are my prize. ℟

2 I will bless the Lord who gives me counsel,
 who even at night directs my heart.
 I keep the Lord ever in my sight:
 since he is at my right hand, I shall stand firm. ℟

3 You will show me the path of life,
 the fullness of joy in your presence,
 at your right hand happiness for ever. ℟

Gospel Acclamation

Alleluia, alleluia!
We praise you, O God,
we acknowledge you to be the Lord;
the noble army of martyrs praise you, O Lord.
Alleluia!

GOSPEL

A reading from the holy Gospel according to John 12:24-26

If a grain of wheat dies, it yields a rich harvest.

Jesus said to his disciples:

'I tell you, most solemnly,
unless a wheat grain falls on the ground and dies,
it remains only a single grain;
but if it dies,
it yields a rich harvest.
Anyone who loves his life loses it;
anyone who hates his life in this world
will keep it for the eternal life.
If a man serves me, he must follow me,
wherever I am, my servant will be there too.
If anyone serves me, my Father will honour him.'

This is the Gospel of the Lord.

Alternative Gospel 1

A reading from the holy Gospel according to John 15:18-21

If they persecuted me, they will persecute you too.

Jesus said to his disciples:

'If the world hates you,
remember that it hated me before you.
If you belonged to the world,
the world would love you as its own;
but because you do not belong to the world,
because my choice withdrew you from the world,
therefore the world hates you.
Remember the words I said to you:
A servant is not greater than his master.
If they persecuted me,
they will persecute you too;

if they kept my word,
they will keep yours as well.
But it will be on my account that they will do all this,
because they do not know the one who sent me.'

This is the Gospel of the Lord.

Alternative Gospel 2

A reading from the holy Gospel according to John 17:11-19
The world hated them.

Jesus raised his eyes to heaven and said,

'Holy Father,
keep those you have given me true to your name,
so that they may be one like us.
While I was with them,
I kept those you had given me true to your name.
I have watched over them and not one is lost
except the one who chose to be lost,
and this was to fulfil the scriptures.
But now I am coming to you
and while still in the world I say these things
to share my joy with them to the full.
I passed your word on to them,
and the world hated them,
because they belong to the world
no more than I belong to the world.
I am not asking you to remove them from the world,
but to protect them from the evil one.
They do not belong to the world
any more than I belong to the world.
Consecrate them in the truth;
your word is truth.
As you sent me into the world,
I have sent them into the world,
and for their sake I consecrate myself
so that they too may be consecrated in truth.'

This is the Gospel of the Lord.

Prayer over the Gifts

Lord,
accept the gifts of your people
who honour the suffering and death
of these forty martyrs.
As the eucharist gave them strength in persecution
may it keep us faithful in every difficulty.

Preface of Martyrs, P66.

Communion Antiphon: Neither death nor life nor anything in all creation can come between us and Christ's love for us.

Prayer after Communion

Lord,
we eat the bread from heaven
and become one body in Christ.
Never let us be separated from his love
and, through the example of your martyrs,
may all who glory in the name of Christian
come to serve you in the unity of faith.

6 November
ALL SAINTS OF IRELAND In Ireland: Feast

Entrance Antiphon: Let the peoples proclaim the wisdom of the saints: let the assembly announce their praises: their name shall be remembered for ever.

Opening Prayer

Lord,
grant us your grace more abundantly
as we keep the feast of all the saints of our land:
we rejoice to be their countrymen on earth,
may we merit to be their fellow-citizens in heaven.

FIRST READING

A reading from the book of Ecclesiasticus 44:1-15
Their name lives on for all generations.

Let us praise illustrious men,
our ancestors in their successive generations.

The Lord has created an abundance of glory,
and displayed his greatness from earliest times.
Some wielded authority as kings
and were renowned for their strength;
others were intelligent advisers
and uttered prophetic oracles.
Others directed the people by their advice,
by their understanding of the popular mind,
and by the wise words of their teaching;
others composed musical melodies,
and set down ballads;
others were rich and powerful,
living peacefully in their homes.
All these were honoured by their contemporaries,
and were the glory of their day.
Some of them left a name behind them,
so that their praises are still sung.
While others have left no memory,
and disappeared as though they had not existed,
they are now as though they had never been,
and so too, their children after them.

Here is a list of generous men
whose good works have not been forgotten.
In their descendants there remains
a rich inheritance born of them.
Their descendants stand by the covenants
and, thanks to them, so do their children's children.
Their offspring will last for ever,
their glory will not fade.
Their bodies have been buried in peace,
and their name lives on for all generations.
The peoples will proclaim their wisdom,
the assembly will celebrate their praises.

    This is the word of the Lord.

Responsorial Psalm   Ps 14:2-5. ℟ Ps 39:5

   ℟ **Happy the man who has placed his trust in the Lord.**

1   Lord, who shall dwell on your holy mountain?
    He who walks without fault;
    he who acts with justice

and speaks the truth from his heart;
he who does not slander with his tongue.

℟ **Happy the man who has placed his trust in the Lord.**

2 He who does no wrong to his brother,
who casts no slur on his neighbour,
who holds the godless in disdain,
but honours those who fear the Lord. ℟

3 He who takes no interest on a loan
and accepts no bribes against the innocent.
Such a man will stand firm for ever. ℟

Gospel Acclamation   Mt 11:28
Alleluia, alleluia!
Come to me, all you who labour and are overburdened,
and I will give you rest.
Alleluia!

GOSPEL
A reading from the holy Gospel according to Luke   6:17-23
How happy are you who are poor. Alas for you who are rich.

Jesus came down with the Twelve and stopped at a piece of level ground where there was a large gathering of his disciples with a great crowd of people from all parts of Judaea and from Jerusalem and from the coastal region of Tyre and Sidon who had come to hear him and to be cured of their diseases. People tormented by unclean spirits were also cured, and everyone in the crowd was trying to touch him because power came out of him that cured them all.

Then fixing his eyes on his disciples he said:

'How happy are you who are poor: yours is the kingdom of
  God.
Happy you who are hungry now: you shall be satisfied.
Happy you who weep now: you shall laugh.

'Happy are you when people hate you, drive you out, abuse you, denounce your name as criminal, on account of the Son of Man. Rejoice when that day comes and dance for joy, for then your reward will be great in heaven.'

This is the Gospel of the Lord.

Prayer over the Gifts
Lord,
we pray you, accept the gifts we offer:
and through the prayers of all the saints of our land
keep us true to the faith of our fathers.

Preface of All Saints, P71.

Communion Antiphon: Happy the pure in heart: they shall see God. Happy the peacemakers: they shall be called sons of God. Happy those who are persecuted in the cause of right: theirs is the kingdom of heaven.

Prayer after Communion
Lord,
may this communion cleanse us of sin,
and through the intercession of all the saints of our land
let it bring us a share in healing from heaven.

16 November
ST MARGARET
Secondary patron of Scotland
In Scotland: Feast

Common of holy men and women: those who worked for the underprivileged p.1900ff.

Opening Prayer
Lord,
you gave Saint Margaret of Scotland
a special love for the poor.
Let her example and prayers
help us to become a living sign of your goodness.

FIRST READING

A reading from the book of Proverbs   31:10-13. 19-20. 30-31
A perfect wife – who can find her?

A perfect wife – who can find her?
She is far beyond the price of pearls.

Her husband's heart has confidence in her,
from her he will derive no little profit.

Advantage and not hurt she brings him
all the days of her life.

She is always busy with wool and with flax,
she does her work with eager hands.

She sets her hands to the distaff,
her fingers grasp the spindle.

She holds out her hand to the poor,
she opens her arms to the needy.

Charm is deceitful, and beauty empty;
the woman who is wise is the one to praise.

Give her a share in what her hands have worked for,
and let her works tell her praises at the city gates.

This is the word of the Lord.

Responsorial Psalm Ps 127:1-5. R̷ v.1

R̷ **O blessed are those who fear the Lord.**

1 O blessed are those who fear the Lord
 and walk in his ways!
 By the labour of your hands you shall eat.
 You will be happy and prosper. R̷

2 Your wife like a fruitful vine
 in the heart of your house;
 your children like shoots of the olive,
 around your table. R̷

3 Indeed thus shall be blessed
 the man who fears the Lord.
 May the Lord bless you from Zion
 in a happy Jerusalem
 all the days of your life. R̷

SECOND READING

A reading from the first letter of St Paul 12:31–13:13
to the Corinthians

Love does not come to an end.

Be ambitious for the higher gifts. And I am going to show you a way that is better than any of them.

 If I have all the eloquence of men or of angels, but speak

without love, I am simply a gong booming or a cymbal clashing. If I have the gift of prophecy, understanding all the mysteries there are, and knowing everything, and if I have faith in all its fullness, to move mountains, but without love, then I am nothing at all. If I give away all that I possess, piece by piece, and if I even let them take my body to burn it, but am without love, it will do me no good whatever.

Love is always patient and kind; it is never jealous; love is never boastful or conceited; it is never rude or selfish; it does not take offence, and is not resentful. Love takes no pleasure in other people's sins but delights in the truth; it is always ready to excuse, to trust, to hope, and to endure whatever comes.

Love does not come to an end. But if there are gifts of prophecy, the time will come when they must fail; or the gift of languages, it will not continue for ever; and knowledge – for this, too, the time will come when it must fail. For our knowledge is imperfect and our prophesying is imperfect; but once perfection comes, all imperfect things will disappear. When I was a child, I used to talk like a child, and think like a child, and argued like a child, but now I am a man, all childish ways are put behind me. Now we are seeing a dim reflection in a mirror; but then we shall be seeing face to face. The knowledge that I have now is imperfect; but then I shall know as fully as I am known.

In short, there are three things that last: faith, hope and love; and the greatest of these is love.

This is the word of the Lord.

Gospel Acclamation   Mt 25:34
Alleluia, alleluia!
Come, you whom my Father has blessed,
says the Lord,
take for your heritage the kingdom prepared for you
since the foundation of the world.
Alleluia!

GOSPEL

A reading from the holy Gospel according to Matthew   25:31-46
In so far as you did this to one of the least of these brothers of mine, you did it to me.

Jesus said to his disciples: 'When the Son of Man comes in his glory, escorted by all the angels, then he will take his seat on his throne of glory. All the nations will be assembled before him and he will separate men one from another as the shepherd separates sheep from goats. He will place the sheep on his right hand and the goats on his left. Then the King will say to those on his right hand, "Come, you whom my Father has blessed, take for your heritage the kingdom prepared for you since the foundation of the world. For I was hungry and you gave me food; I was thirsty and you gave me drink; I was a stranger and you made me welcome; naked and you clothed me, sick and you visited me, in prison and you came to see me." Then the virtuous will say to him in reply, "Lord, when did we see you hungry and feed you; or thirsty and give you drink? When did we see you a stranger and make you welcome; naked and clothe you; sick or in prison and go to see you?" And the King will answer, "I tell you solemnly, in so far as you did this to one of the least of these brothers of mine, you did it to me". Next he will say to those on his left hand, "Go away from me, with your curse upon you, to the eternal fire prepared for the devil and his angels. For I was hungry and you never gave me food; I was thirsty and you never gave me anything to drink; I was a stranger and you never made me welcome, naked and you never clothed me, sick and in prison and you never visited me." Then it will be their turn to ask, "Lord, when did we see you hungry or thirsty, a stranger or naked, sick or in prison, and did not come to your help?" Then he will answer, "I tell you solemnly, in so far as you neglected to do this to one of the least of these, you neglected to do it to me". And they will go away to eternal punishment, and the virtuous to eternal life.'

This is the Gospel of the Lord.

23 November

ST COLUMBAN, ABBOT In Ireland: Feast

As in the Proper of Saints, General Calendar pp. 1806ff.

30 November
ST ANDREW, APOSTLE
Principal patron of Scotland
In Scotland: Solemnity

Prayers and Antiphons as in Proper of Saints, General Calendar, pp. 1808ff.

FIRST READING

A reading from the book of Wisdom   3:1-9
He accepted them as a holocaust.

The souls of the virtuous are in the hands of God,
no torment shall ever touch them.
In the eyes of the unwise, they did appear to die,
their going looked like a disaster,
their leaving us, like annihilation;
but they are in peace.
If they experienced punishment as men see it,
their hope was rich with immortality;
slight was their affliction, great will their blessings be.
God has put them to the test
and proved them worthy to be with him;
he has tested them like gold in a furnace,
and accepted them as a holocaust.
When the time comes for his visitation they will shine out;
as sparks run through the stubble, so will they.
They shall judge nations, rule over peoples,
and the Lord will be their king for ever.
They who trust in him will understand the truth,
those who are faithful will live with him in love;
for grace and mercy await those he has chosen.

    This is the word of the Lord.

Responsorial Psalm   Ps 30:3-4. 6. 8. 17. 21. ℟ v.6

    ℟ **Into your hands, O Lord,**
       I commend my spirit.

1   Be a rock of refuge for me,
    a mighty stronghold to save me,
    for you are my rock, my stronghold.
    For your name's sake, lead me and guide me. ℟

2. Into your hands I commend my spirit.
It is you who will redeem me, Lord.
As for me, I trust in the Lord:
let me be glad and rejoice in your love.

℟ **Into your hands, O Lord,
I commend my spirit.**

3. Let your face shine on your servant.
Save me in your love.
You hide them in the shelter of your presence
from the plotting of men. ℟

SECOND READING

A reading from the letter of St Paul to the Romans 10:9-18
Faith comes from what is preached, and what is preached comes from the word of Christ.

If your lips confess that Jesus is Lord and if you believe in your heart that God raised him from the dead, then you will be saved. By believing from the heart you are made righteous; by confessing with your lips you are saved. When scripture says: those who believe in him will have no cause for shame, it makes no distinction between Jew and Greek: all belong to the same Lord who is rich enough, however many ask his help, for everyone who calls on the name of the Lord will be saved.

But they will not ask his help unless they believe in him, and they will not believe in him unless they have heard of him, and they will not hear of him unless they get a preacher, and they will never have a preacher unless one is sent, but as scripture says: The footsteps of those who bring good news are a welcome sound. Not everyone, of course, listens to the Good News. As Isaiah says: Lord, how many believed what we proclaimed? So faith comes from what is preached, and what is preached comes from the word of Christ.

Let me put the question: is it possible that they did not hear? Indeed they did; in the words of the psalm, their voice has gone out through all the earth, and their message to the ends of the world.

This is the word of the Lord.

Gospel Acclamation Mt 4:19
Alleluia, alleluia!
Follow me, says the Lord,
and I will make you into fishers of men.
Alleluia!

GOSPEL

A reading from the holy Gospel according to Matthew 4:18-22
And they left their nets at once and followed him.

As Jesus was walking by the Sea of Galilee he saw two brothers, Simon, who was called Peter, and his brother Andrew; they were making a cast in the lake with their net, for they were fishermen. And he said to them, 'Follow me and I will make you fishers of men.' And they left their nets at once and followed him.

Going on from there he saw another pair of brothers, James son of Zebedee and his brother John; they were in their boat with their father Zebedee, mending their nets, and he called them. At once, leaving the boat and their father, they followed him.

This is the Gospel of the Lord.

29 December

ST THOMAS OF CANTERBURY, BISHOP AND MARTYR

In England: Feast

Entrance Antiphon: I will raise up for myself a faithful priest; he will do what is in my heart and in my mind, says the Lord.

Opening Prayer
Almighty God,
you granted your martyr, Thomas of Canterbury,
the grace to give his life willingly
for the freedom of your Church.
By his prayers
make us willing to renounce our life in this world for Christ
so that we may find it in heaven.

FIRST READING

A reading from the letter of St Paul to the Colossians 1:24-29
I became the servant of the Church.

It makes me happy to suffer for you, as I am suffering now, and in my own body to do what I can to make up all that has still to be undergone by Christ for the sake of his body, the Church. I became the servant of the Church when God made me responsible for delivering God's message to you, the message which was a mystery hidden for generations and centuries and has now been revealed to his saints. It was God's purpose to reveal it to them and to show all the rich glory of this mystery to pagans. The mystery is Christ among you, your hope of glory: this is the Christ we proclaim, this is the wisdom in which we thoroughly train everyone and instruct everyone, to make them all perfect in Christ. It is for this I struggle wearily on, helped only by his power driving me irresistibly.

This is the word of the Lord.

Responsorial Psalm

Ps 22. ℟ v.1

℟ **The Lord is my shepherd;**
there is nothing I shall want.

1 The Lord is my shepherd;
there is nothing I shall want.
Fresh and green are the pastures
where he gives me repose.
Near restful waters he leads me,
to revive my drooping spirit. ℟

2 He guides me along the right path;
he is true to his name.
If I should walk in the valley of darkness
no evil would I fear.
You are there with your crook and your staff;
with these you give me comfort. ℟

3 You have prepared a banquet for me
in the sight of my foes.
My head you have anointed with oil;
my cup is overflowing. ℟

4 Surely goodness and kindness shall follow me
all the days of my life.
In the Lord's own house shall I dwell
for ever and ever. ℟

Gospel Acclamation Jn 10:14
  Alleluia, alleluia!
  I am the good shepherd, says the Lord;
  I know my own sheep
  and my own know me.
  Alleluia!

or Mt 5:10

  Alleluia, alleluia!
  Happy those who are persecuted in the cause of right:
  theirs is the kingdom of heaven.
  Alleluia!

GOSPEL

A reading from the holy Gospel according to Luke 22:24-30
I confer a kingdom on you, just as my Father conferred one on me.

A dispute arose between the apostles about which should be reckoned the greatest, but Jesus said to them, 'Among the pagans it is the kings who lord it over them, and those who have authority over them are given the title Benefactor. This must not happen with you. No; the greatest among you must behave as if he were the youngest, the leader as if he were the one who serves. For who is the greater: the one at table or the one who serves? The one at table, surely? Yet here am I among you as one who serves!

  'You are the men who have stood by me faithfully in my trials; and now I confer a kingdom on you, just as my Father conferred one on me: you will eat and drink at my table in my kingdom, and you will sit on thrones to judge the twelve tribes of Israel.'

  This is the Gospel of the Lord.

Alternative Gospel

A reading from the holy Gospel according to Matthew 10:28-33
Do not be afraid of those who kill the body.

Jesus said to his apostles: 'Do not be afraid of those who kill the body but cannot kill the soul; fear him rather who can destroy both body and soul in hell. Can you not buy two sparrows for a penny? And yet not one falls to the ground without your Father knowing. Why, every hair on your head has been counted. So there is no need to be afraid; you are worth more than hundreds of sparrows.

'So if anyone declares himself for me in the presence of men, I will declare myself for him in the presence of my Father in heaven. But the one who disowns me in the presence of men, I will disown in the presence of my Father in heaven.'

This is the Gospel of the Lord.

Prayer over the Gifts
God of all mercy,
you transformed Saint Thomas
and made him a new creature in your image.
Renew us in the same way
by making our gifts of peace acceptable to you.

Preface of Martyrs, P66.

Communion Antiphon: You have not chosen me; I have chosen you. Go and bear fruit that will last.

Prayer after Communion
All-powerful God,
may we who share this holy meal
follow the example of Saint Thomas
in faithfully serving you
and caring for all in need.

INDEX OF CELEBRATIONS
GENERAL ROMAN CALENDAR

Our Lord Jesus Christ
   Annunciation, 25 March   1454
   Presentation, 2 February   1403
   Transfiguration 6 August   1624
   Triumph of the Cross,
     14 September   1688

The Blessed Virgin Mary
   Assumption, 15 August   1642
   Birthday, 8 September   1681
   Immaculate Conception,
     8 December   1821
   Immaculate Heart of
     Mary   1521
   Mary, Mother of God,
     1 January   1360
   Our Lady of Lourdes,
     11 February   1420
   Our Lady of Mount Carmel,
     16 July   1592
   Our Lady of Sorrows,
     15 September   1692
   Our Lady of the Rosary,
     7 October   1728
   Presentation,
     21 November   1800
   Queenship, 22 August   1658
   Visitation, 31 May   1517

Achilleus, 12 May   1495
Agatha, 5 February   1412
Agnes, 21 January   1384
Albert the Great,
   15 November   1787
All Saints, 1 November   1761
All the Faithful Departed,
   2 November   1765
Aloysius Gonzaga, 21 June   1545
Alphonsus Liguori,
   1 August   1616
Ambrose, 7 December   1818
Andrew, 30 November   1808
Angela Merici, 27 January   1397
Anne, 26 July   1605

Anselm, 21 April   1470
Ansgar, 3 February   1410
Anthony, abbot, 17 January   1377
Anthony Claret, 24 October   1756
Anthony of Padua, 13 June   1541
Anthony Zaccaria, 5 July   1579
Athanasius, 2 May   1490
Augustine,
   bishop, 28 August   1672
Augustine of Canterbury,
   27 May   1516

Barnabas, 11 June   1538
Bartholomew, 24 August   1663
Basil, 2 January   1370
Bede the Venerable, 25 May   1506
Benedict, 11 July   1583
Bernard, 20 August   1653
Bernardine of Siena,
   20 May   1504
Blaise, 3 February   1408
Bonaventure, 15 July   1590
Boniface, 5 June   1532
Bridget, 23 July   1600
Bruno, 6 October   1726

Cajetan, 7 August   1631
Callistus I, 14 October   1735
Camillus de Lellis, 14 July   1587
Casimir, 4 March   1434
Catherine of Siena, 29 April   1481
Cecilia, 22 November   1802
Charles Borromeo,
   4 November   1774
Charles Lwanga and companions,
   3 June   1529
Clare, 11 August   1638
Clement I, 23 November   1804
Columban, 23 November   1806
Cornelius, 16 September   1697
Cosmas, 26 September   1706
Cyprian, 16 September   1697
Cyril, monk, 14 February   1422
Cyril of Alexandria, 27 June   1558

Index of Celebrations

Cyril of Jerusalem, 8 March   1446

Damasus I, 11 December   1825
Damian, 26 September   1706
Dedication of the Basilica of
   St Mary Major,
      5 August   1623
   Ss Peter and Paul,
      18 November   1797
   the Lateran, 9 November   1777
Denis, 9 October   1731
Dominic, 8 August   1633

Elizabeth of Hungary,
   17 November   1795
Elizabeth of Portugal,
   4 July   1576
Ephrem, 9 June   1536
Eusebius of Vercelli,
   2 August   1619

Fabian, 20 January   1380
Felicity, 7 March   1436
Fidelis of Sigmaringen,
   24 April   1474
First Martyrs of the Church of
   Rome, 30 June   1571
Frances of Rome, 9 March   1441
Frances of Paola, 2 April   1458
Francis de Sales, 24 January   1377
Francis of Assisi, 4 October   1724
Francis Xavier, 3 December   1811

Gabriel, 29 September   1713
George, 23 April   1472
Gertrude, 16 November   1892
Gregory VII, 25 May   1508
Gregory Nazianzen,
   2 January   1370
Gregory the Great,
   3 September   1679
Guardian Angels,
   2 October   1721

Hedwig, 16 October   1740
Henry, 13 July   1585
Hilary, 13 January   1375
Hippolytus, 13 August   1639
Holy Innocents,
   28 December   1844

Ignatius of Antioch,
   17 October   1744
Ignatius of Loyola, 31 July   1613
Irenaeus, 28 June   1561
Isaac Jogues, 19 October   1749
Isidore, 4 April   1460

James, 3 May   1492
James, apostle, 25 July   1603
Jane Frances de Chantal,
   12 December   1827
Januarius, 19 September   1702
Jerome, 30 September   1716
Jerome Emiliani,
   8 February   1415
Joachim, 26 July   1605
John, apostle and evangelist,
   27 December   1841
John I, 18 May   1502
John Baptist de la Salle,
   7 April   1464
John Bosco, 31 January   1401
John Chrysostom,
   13 September   1685
John Damascene,
   4 December   1813
John de Brébeuf,
   10 October   1749
John Eudes, 19 August   1651
John Fisher, 22 June   1549
John Leonardi, 9 October   1733
John of Capistrano,
   23 October   1754
John of God, 8 March   1438
John of Kanty,
   23 December   1836
John of the Cross,
   4 December   1831
John the Baptist,
   Beheading of, 29 August   1675
   Birth of, 24 June   1551
John Vianney, 4 August   1621
Josaphat, 12 November   1784
Joseph,
   husband of the Blessed Virgin,
      19 March   1448
   the worker, 1 May   1487
Joseph Calasanz, 25 August   1668

Index of Celebrations

Jude, 28 October   1758
Justin, 1 June   1524

Laurence, deacon,
  10 August   1636
Laurence of Brindisi,
  21 July   1595
Leo the Great, 10 November   1779
Louis, 25 August   1666
Lucy, 13 December   1829
Luke, 18 October   1746

Marcellinus, 2 June   1527
Margaret Mary Alacoque,
  16 October   1742
Margaret of Scotland,
  16 November   1789
Maria Goretti, 6 July   1581
Mark, 25 April   1477
Martha, 29 July   1607
Martin I, 13 April   1468
Martin de Porres,
  3 November   1772
Martin of Tours,
  11 November   1781
Mary Magdalen, 22 July   1597
Mary Magdalene de Pazzi,
  25 May   1510
Matthew, 21 September   1704
Matthias, 14 May   1499
Methodius, 14 February   1422
Michael, 29 September   1713
Monica, 27 August   1670

Nereus, 12 May   1495
Nicholas, 6 December   1816
Norbert, 6 June   1534

Pancras, 12 May   1497
Patrick, 17 March   1443
Paul, apostle, 29 June   1563
  Conversion of,
    25 January   1390
Paul Miki and companions,
  6 February   1413
Paul of the Cross,
  19 October   1751
Paulinus of Nola, 22 June   1547
Perpetua, 7 March   1436

Peter, apostle, 29 June   1563
  Chair of, 22 February   1429
Peter, martyr, 2 June   1527
Peter Canisius,
  21 December   1835
Peter Chanel, 28 April   1479
Peter Chrysologus, 30 July   1611
Peter Damian, 21 February   1426
Philip, apostle, 3 May   1492
Philip Neri, 26 May   1513
Pius V, 30 April   1484
Pius X, 21 August   1656
Polycarp, 23 February   1431
Pontian, 13 August   1639

Raphael, 29 September   1713
Raymond of Penyafort,
  7 January   1373
Robert Bellarmine,
  17 September   1700
Romuald, 19 June   1543
Rose of Lima, 23 August   1661

Scholastica, 10 February   1418
Sebastian, 20 January   1382
Servites, Founders of,
  17 February   1424
Simon, 28 October   1758
Sixtus II, 7 August   1629
Stanislaus, 11 April   1466
Stephen, first martyr,
  26 December   1839
Stephen of Hungary,
  16 August   1648
Sylvester, 31 December   1849

Teresa of Avila, 15 October   1737
Teresa of the Child Jesus,
  1 October   1719
Thomas, apostle, 3 July   1847
Thomas à Becket,
  29 December   1574
Thomas Aquinas,
  28 January   1399
Thomas More, 22 June   1549
Timothy, 26 January   1394
Titus, 26 January   1394
Turibius of Mongrovejo,
  23 March   1452

Vincent, deacon, 22 January   1385
Vincent de Paul,
  27 September   1709
Vincent Ferrer, 5 April   1462
Wenceslaus, 28 September   1711

INDEX OF CELEBRATIONS
NATIONAL CALENDARS

For England, Wales, Ireland, Scotland

Our Lady of Ransom, (E)
  24 September   2079
Aaron (W), 20 June   2063
Alban (E, W), 20 June   2063
All Saints of Ireland (I),
  6 November   2088
Andrew (S), 30 November   2095
Anselm (E), 21 April   2049
Augustine of Canterbury (E),
  27 May   2057

Beatified Martyrs of England
  and Wales (E, W), 4 May   2052
Bede the Venerable (E),
  25 May   2055
Brigid (I), 1 February   2037

Columba (Colum Cille) (I, S),
  9 June   2059
Columban (I), 23 November   2094

David (E, W), 1 March   2039
Dominic of the Mother of God (E),
  26 August   2073

Edward the Confessor (E),
  13 October   2082

Forty Martyrs of England and
  Wales (E, W), 25 October   2084

George (E), 23 April   2049
Gregory the Great (E),
  3 September   2076

John Fisher (E, W), 22 June   2066
John Ogilvie (S), 10 March   2042
Julius (W), 20 June   2063

Kentigern (S), 13 January   2037

Margaret (S), 16 November   2091

Ninian (S), 16 November   2073

Oliver Plunkett (I), 1 July   2069

Patrick (E, I, S, W), 17
  March   2045

Six Welsh Martyrs and
  companions,
  25 October   2084

Thomas of Canterbury (E, W)
  29 December   2097
Thomas More (E, W), 22
  June   2066

(E) England; (I) Ireland; (S) Scotland; (W) Wales